CIVIL
AIRCRAFT
MARKINGS
1997

Alan J. Wright

D1393098

IAN ALLAN

Publishing

Contents

This forty-eighth edition published 1997

ISBN 0 7110 2498 7

Published by Ian Allan Publishing

an imprint of Ian Allan Ltd,
Terminal House, Station Approach,
Shepperton, Surrey TW17 8AS.
Printed by Ian Allan Printing Ltd at its works at Coombelands in Runnymede, England.

Code: 9703/Q

Front cover: 4X-AXB, Boeing 747-258B of El Al. *Austin J. Brown/APL*

Back cover: D-ABAE, Boeing 767-46J of Air Berlin.
All photographs by Alan J. Wright unless otherwise indicated.

Introduction

The 'G' prefixed four letter registration system was adopted in 1919 after a short-lived spell of about three months with serial numbers beginning at K-100. Until July 1928 the UK allocations were in the G-Exxx range, but as a result of further International agreements, this series was ended at G-EBZZ, the replacement being G-Axxx. From this point the registrations were issued in a reasonably orderly manner through to G-AZZZ, reached in July 1972. There were two exceptions. To avoid possible confusion with signal codes, the G-AQxx sequence was omitted, while G-AUxx were reserved for Australian use originally. In recent years however, an individual request for a mark in the latter range has been granted by the Authorities.

Although the next logical sequence was started at G-Bxxx, it was not long before the strictly applied rules relating to aircraft registration began to be relaxed. Permission was readily given for personalised marks to be issued incorporating virtually any four letter combination, while re-registration has also become a common feature, a practice almost unheard of in the past. In this book, where this has taken place at some time, all previous UK civil identities appear in parenthesis after the owner's/operator's name. An example of this is BAe 146-200 G-MANS which originally carried G-CHSR.

Some aircraft have also been allowed to wear military markings without displaying their civil identity. In this case the serial number actually carried is shown in parenthesis after the type's name. For example EE Canberra TT.18 G-BURM flies as in RAF colours as WJ680. As an aid to the identification of these machines, a military conversion list is provided.

Other factors caused a sudden acceleration in the number of registrations allocated by the Civil Aviation Authority in the early 1980s. The first surge came with the discovery that it was possible to register plastic bags and other items even less likely to fly, on payment of the standard fee. This erosion of the main register was checked in early 1982 by the issue of a special sequence for such devices commencing at G-FYAA. Powered hang-gliders provided the second glut of allocations as a result of the decision that these types should be officially registered. Although a few of the early examples penetrated the normal in-sequence register, the vast majority were given marks in other special ranges, this time G-MBxx, G-MGxx, G-MJxx, G-MMxx, G-MNxx, G-MTxx, G-MVxx, G-MWxx, G-MYxx and G-MZxx. At first it was common practice for microlights to ignore the requirement to carry their official identity. However the vast majority now display their registration somewhere on the structure, the size and position depending on the dimensions of the component to which it is applied.

Throughout the UK section of this book, there are many instances where the probable base of the aircraft has been included. This is positioned at the end of the owner/operator details preceded by an oblique stroke. It must of course be borne in mind that changes do take place and that no attempt has been made to record the residents at the many private strips. The base of airline equipment has been given as the company's headquarter's airport, although frequently aircraft are outstationed for long periods.

Non-airworthy and preserved aircraft are shown with a star after the type.

The three-letter codes used by airlines to prefix flight numbers are included for those carriers appearing in the book. Radio frequencies for the larger airfields/airports are also listed.

The air transport scene has changed considerably through the years with many airlines now leasing aircraft as required. It has therefore become increasingly difficult to record all of the frequent changes, especially since the companies often do not finalise their plans for the coming summer season until the early months of the year. However, every effort is made to produce an accurate source of reference, but it must be borne in mind that it is inevitable that discrepancies will occur.

Acknowledgments
Once again thanks are extended to the Registration Department of the Civil Aviation Authority for its assistance and allowing access to its files. The comments and amendments flowing from the indefatigable Wal Gandy have as always proved of considerable value, while Richard Cawsey, Bob Elliot, Kenneth Nimbley and Ian Wikberg also contributed useful facts. The help given by numerous airlines or their information agencies has been much appreciated. Both A. S. Wright and C. P. Wright provided valuable assistance during the update of this edition which enabled the multitude of facts to be assembled to meet the press deadline.   **AJW**

International Civil Aircraft Markings

A2-	Botswana	P-	Korea (North)
A3-	Tonga	P2-	Papua New Guinea
A4O-	Oman	P4-	Aruba
A5-	Bhutan	PH-	Netherlands
A6-	United Arab Emirates	PJ-	Netherlands Antilles
A7-	Qatar	PK-	Indonesia and West Irian
A9C-	Bahrain	PP-, PT-	Brazil
AP-	Pakistan	PZ-	Surinam
B-	China/Taiwan	RA-	Russia
C-F, C-G	Canada	RDPL-	Laos
C2-	Nauru	RP-	Philippines
C3	Andora	S2-	Bangladesh
C5-	Gambia	S5-	Slovenia
C6-	Bahamas	S7-	Seychelles
C9-	Mozambique	S9-	São Tomé
CC-	Chile	SE-	Sweden
CN-	Morocco	SP-	Poland
CP-	Bolivia	ST-	Sudan
CS-	Portugal	SU-	Egypt
CU-	Cuba	SX-	Greece
CX-	Uruguay	T2-	Tuvalu
D-	Germany	T3-	Kiribati
D2-	Angola	T7-	San Marino
D4-	Cape Verde Islands	T9-	Bosnia-Herzegovina
D6-	Comores Islands	TC-	Turkey
DQ-	Fiji	TF-	Iceland
E3-	Eritrea	TG-	Guatemala
EC-	Spain	TI-	Costa Rica
EI-	Republic of Ireland	TJ-	United Republic of Cameroon
EK-	Armenia	TL-	Central African Republic
EL-	Liberia	TN-	Republic of Congo (Brazzaville)
EP-	Iran	TR-	Gabon
ER-	Moldova	TS-	Tunisia
ES-	Estonia	TT-	Tchad
ET-	Ethiopia	TU-	Ivory Coast
EW-	Belarus	TY-	Benin
EX-	Kyrgyzstan	TZ-	Mali
EY-	Tajikistan	UK-	Uzbekistan
EZ-	Turkmenistan	UN-	Kazakhstan
F-	France, Colonies and Protectorates	UR-	Ukraine
G-	United Kingdom	V2-	Antigua
H4-	Solomon Islands	V3-	Belize
HA-	Hungary	V4	St Kitts & Nevis
HB-	Switzerland and Liechtenstein	V5-	Namibia
HC-	Ecuador	V6	Micronesia
HH-	Haiti	V7-	Marshall Islands
HI-	Dominican Republic	V8-	Brunei
HK-	Colombia	VH-	Australia
HL-	Korea (South)	VN-	Vietnam
HP-	Panama	VP-F	Falkland Islands
HR-	Honduras	VP-LA	Anguilla
HS-	Thailand	VP-LM	Montserrat
HV-	The Vatican	VP-LV	Virgin Islands
HZ-	Saudi Arabia	VQ-T	Turks & Caicos Islands
I-	Italy	VR-B	Bermuda
J2-	Djibouti	VR-C	Cayman Islands
J3-	Grenada	VR-G	Gibraltar
J5-	Guinea Bissau	VR-H	Hong Kong
J6-	St Lucia	VT-	India
J7-	Dominica	XA-, XB-, XC-	Mexico
J8-	St Vincent	XT-	Burkina Faso
JA-	Japan	XU-	Cambodia
JY-	Jordan	XY-	Myanmar
LN-	Norway	YA-	Afghanistan
LV-	Argentina	YI-	Iraq
LX-	Luxembourg	YJ-	Vanuatu
LY-	Lithuania	YK-	Syria
LZ-	Bulgaria	YL-	Latvia
MT-	Mongolia	YN-	Nicaragua
N-	United States of America	YR-	Romania
OB-	Peru	YS-	El Salvador
OD-	Lebanon	YU-	Yugoslavia
OE-	Austria	YV-	Venezuela
OH-	Finland	Z-	Zimbabwe
OK-	Czechia	Z3-	Macedonia
OM-	Slovakia	ZA-	Albania
OO-	Belgium	ZK-	New Zealand
OY-	Denmark	ZP-	Paraguay

ZS-	South Africa	6V-	Senegal
3A-	Monaco	6Y-	Jamaica
3B-	Mauritius	7O-	Yemen
3C-	Equatorial Guinea	7P-	Lesotho
3D-	Swaziland	7Q-	Malawi
3X-	Guinea	7T-	Algeria
4K-	Azerbaijan	8P-	Barbados
4L-	Georgia	8Q-	Maldives
4R-	Sri Lanka	8R-	Guyana
4X-	Israel	9A-	Croatia
5A-	Libya	9G-	Ghana
5B-	Cyprus	9H-	Malta
5H-	Tanzania	9J-	Zambia
5N-	Nigeria	9K-	Kuwait
5R-	Malagasy Republic (Madagascar)	9L-	Sierra Leone
5T-	Mauritania	9M-	Malaysia
5U-	Niger	9N-	Nepal
5V-	Togo	9Q-	Zaïre
5W-	Western Samoa (Polynesia)	9U-	Burundi
5X-	Uganda	9V-	Singapore
5Y-	Kenya	9XR-	Rwanda
6O-	Somalia	9Y-	Trinidad and Tobago

Aircraft Type Designations & Abbreviations

(eg PA-28 Piper Type 28)

A.	Beagle, Auster, Airbus	HP.	Handley Page
AA-	American Aviation, Grumman American	HR.	Robin
AB	Agusta-Bell	H.S.	Hawker Siddeley
AG	American General	IHM	International Helicopter Museum
AS	Aérospatiale	IL	Ilyushin
A.S.	Airspeed	IMCO	Intermountain Manufacturing Co
A.W.	Armstrong Whitworth	J.	Auster
B.	Blackburn, Bristol, Boeing, Beagle	L.	Lockheed
BA	British Airways	L.A.	Luton, Lake
BAC	British Aircraft Corporation	M.	Miles, Mooney
BAe	British Aerospace	MBB	Messerschmitt-Bölkow-Blohm
BAPC	British Aviation Preservation Council	McD	McDonnell Douglas
BAT	British Aerial Transport	MH	Max Holste
B.K.	British Klemm	MJ	Jurca
BN	Britten-Norman	M.S.	Morane-Saulnier
Bo	Bolkow	NA	North American
Bu	Bucker	NE	North East
CAARP	Co-operative des Ateliers Aer de la Région Parisienne	P.	Hunting (formerly Percival), Piaggio
		PA-	Piper
CAC	Commonwealth Aircraft Corporation	PC.	Pilatus
CAF	Canadian Air Force	QAC	Quickie Aircraft Co
C.A.S.A.	Construcciones Aeronautics SA	R.	Rockwell
CCF	Canadian Car & Foundry Co	RAAF	Royal Australian Air Force
C.H.	Chrislea	RAFGSA	Royal Air Force Gliding & Soaring Association
CHABA	Cambridge Hot-Air Ballooning Association		
CLA	Comper	RCAF	Royal Canadian Air Force
CP.	Piel	R.N.	Royal Navy
CUAS	Cambridge University Air Squadron	S.	Short, Sikorsky
Cycl	Cyclone	SA, SE, SO	Sud-Aviation, Aérospatiale, Scottish Aviation
D.	Druine		
DC-	Douglas Commercial	SAAB	Svenska Aeroplan Aktieboleg
D.H.	de Havilland	SC	Short
D.H.A	de Havilland Australia	SCD	Side Cargo Door
D.H.C.	de Havilland Canada	SNCAN	Societe Nationale de Constructions Aeronautiques du Nord
DR.	Jodel (Robin-built)		
EE	English Electric	SOCATA	Societe de Construction d'Avions de Tourisme et d'Affaires
EMB	Embraer		
EoN	Elliotts of Newbury	Soc	Society
EP	Edgar Percival	S.R.	Saunders-Roe, Stinson
F.	Fairchild, Fokker	SS	Special Shape
F.A.A.	Fleet Air Arm	ST	SOCATA
FFA	Flug und Fahrzeugwerke AG	SW	Solar Wings
FH	Fairchild-Hiller	T.	Tipsy
FrAF	French Air Force	TB	SOCATA
FRED	Flying Runabout Experimental Design	Tu	Tupolev
Fw	Focke-Wulf	UH.	United Helicopters (Hiller)
G.	Grumman	UK	United Kingdom
GA	Gulfstream American	USAF	United States Air Force
G.A.L.	General Aircraft	USAAC	United States Army Air Corps
G.C.	Globe	USN	United States Navy
GY	Gardan	V.	Vickers-Armstrongs
H	Helio	V.S.	Vickers-Supermarine
HM.	Henri Mignet	WAR	War Aircraft Replicas
		W.S.	Westland
		Z.	Zlin

British Civil Aircraft Registrations

Reg.	Type (†False registration)	Owner or Operator	Notes
G-EAGA	Sopwith Dove (replica)	Governor & Co of the Bank of Scotland	
G-EAOU	Vickers Vimy (replica)(NX71MY)	Greenco (UK) Ltd	
G-EASD	Avro 504L	AJD Engineering Ltd	
G-EASQ†	Bristol Babe (replica) (BAPC87) ★	*(stored)* Bristol Aero Collection	
G-EAVX	Sopwith Pup (B1807)	K. A. M. Baker	
G-EBHX	D.H.53 Humming Bird	The Shuttleworth Collection/O. Warden	
G-EBIA	RAF SE-5A (F904)	The Shuttleworth Collection/O. Warden	
G-EBIB	RAF SE-5A ★	Science Museum/S. Kensington	
G-EBIC	RAF SE-5A (F938) ★	RAF Museum	
G-EBIR	D.H.51	The Shuttleworth Collection/O. Warden	
G-EBJE	Avro 504K (E449) ★	RAF Museum	
G-EBJG	Parnall Pixie III ★	Midland Aircraft Preservation Soc	
G-EBJO	ANEC II ★	The Shuttleworth Collection/O. Warden	
G-EBKY	Sopwith Pup (N6181)	The Shuttleworth Collection/O. Warden	
G-EBLV	D.H.60 Cirrus Moth	British Aerospace PLC/Woodford	
G-EBMB	Hawker Cygnet I ★	RAF Museum	
G-EBNV	English Electric Wren	The Shuttleworth Collection/O. Warden	
G-EBQP	D.H.53 Humming Bird (J7326) ★	Russavia Collection	
G-EBWD	D.H.60X Hermes Moth	The Shuttleworth Collection/O. Warden	
G-EBXU	D.H.60X Moth Seaplane	D. E. Cooper-Maguire	
G-EBZM	Avro 594 Avian IIIA ★	Manchester Museum of Science & Industry	
G-EBZN	D.H.60X Moth	J. Hodgkinson (G-UAAP)	
G-AAAH†	D.H.60G Moth (replica) (BAPC 168) ★	Hilton Hotel/Gatwick Science Museum/S. Kensington	
G-AACA†	Avro 504K (BAPC 177)	Brooklands Museum of Aviation/ Weybridge	
G-AACN	H.P.39 Gugnunc ★	Science Museum/Wroughton	
G-AADR	D.H.60GM Moth	H. F. Moffatt	
G-AAEG	D.H.60G Moth	J. Dixon	
G-AAHI	D.H.60G Moth	N. J. W. Reid	
G-AAHY	D.H.60M Moth	D. J. Elliott	
G-AAIN	Parnall Elf II	The Shuttleworth Collection/O. Warden	
G-AAMX	D.H.60GM Moth ★	RAF Museum	
G-AAMY	D.H.60GMW Moth	Totalsure Ltd	
G-AAMZ	D.H.60G Moth	C. C. & J. M. Lovell	
G-AANG	Blériot XI	The Shuttleworth Collection/O. Warden	
G-AANH	Deperdussin Monoplane	The Shuttleworth Collection/O. Warden	
G-AANI	Blackburn Monoplane	The Shuttleworth Collection/O. Warden	
G-AANJ	L.V.G.-C VI (7198/18)	The Shuttleworth Collection/O. Warden	
G-AANL	D.H.60M Moth	P. L. Allwork	
G-AANM	Bristol 96A F.2B (D7889)	Aero Vintage Ltd	
G-AANO	D.H.60GMW Moth	A. W. & M. E. Jenkins	
G-AANV	D.H.60G Moth	R. I. Souch	
G-AAOK	Curtiss Wright Travel Air 12Q	Shipping & Airlines Ltd/Biggin Hill	
G-AAOR	D.H.60G Moth (EM-01)	J. A. Pothecary/Shoreham	
G-AAPZ	Desoutter I (mod.)	The Shuttleworth Collection/O. Warden	
G-AAUP	Klemm L.25-1A	J. I. Cooper	
G-AAWO	D.H.60G Moth	N. J. W. Reid & L. A. Fenwick	
G-AAXK	Klemm L.25-1A ★	C. C. Russell-Vick *(stored)*	
G-AAYX	Southern Martlet	The Shuttleworth Collection/O. Warden	
G-AAZP	D.H.80A Puss Moth	R. P. Williams	
G-ABAA	Avro 504K ★	Manchester Museum of Science & Industry	
G-ABAG	D.H.60G Moth	The Shuttleworth Collection/O. Warden	
G-ABDA	D.H.60G-III Moth Major	I. M. Castle	
G-ABDW	D.H.80A Puss Moth (VH-UQB) ★	Museum of Flight/E. Fortune	
G-ABDX	D.H.60G Moth	M. D. Souch	
G-ABEV	D.H.60G Moth	Wessex Aviation & Transport Ltd	
G-ABLM	Cierva C.24 ★	Mosquito Aircraft Museum	
G-ABLS	D.H.80A Puss Moth	R. C. F. Bailey	
G-ABMR	Hart 2 (J9941) ★	RAF Museum	
G-ABNT	Civilian C.A.C.1 Coupe	Shipping & Airlines Ltd/Biggin Hill	
G-ABNX	Redwing 2	J. A. Pothecary *(stored)*	
G-ABOI	Wheeler Slymph ★	Midland Air Museum	
G-ABOX	Sopwith Pup (N5195)	C. M. D. & A. P. St. Cyrien/Middle Wallop	

Notes	Reg.	Type	Owner or Operator
	G-ABSD	D.H. A60G Moth	M. E. Vaisey
	G-ABTC	CLA.7 Swift	P. Channon *(stored)*
	G-ABUL†	D.H.82A Tiger Moth ★	F.A.A. Museum (G-AOXG)/Yeovilton
	G-ABUS	CLA.7 Swift	R. C. F. Bailey
	G-ABUU	CLA.7 Swift	H. F. Moffatt
	G-ABVE	Arrow Active 2	J. D. Penrose
	G-ABWP	Spartan Arrow	R. E. Blain/Barton
	G-ABXL	Granger Archaeopteryx ★	The Shuttleworth Collection/O. Warden
	G-ABYN	Spartan Three Seater II	J. D. Souch
	G-ABZB	D.H.60G-III Moth Major	R. E. & B. A. Ogden
	G-ACAA	Bristol 96A F.2B (D8084†)	Patina Ltd/Duxford
	G-ACBH	Blackburn B.2 ★	–/West Hanningfield, Essex
	G-ACCB	D.H.83 Fox Moth	E. A. Gautrey
	G-ACDA	D.H.82A Tiger Moth	R. J. Biddle
	G-ACDC	D.H.82A Tiger Moth	Tiger Club Ltd/Headcorn
	G-ACDI	D.H.82A Tiger Moth	J. A. Pothecary/Shoreham
	G-ACDJ	D.H.82A Tiger Moth	P. Henley & J. K. Moorhouse
	G-ACEJ	D.H.83 Fox Moth	Newbury Aeroplane Co
	G-ACET	D.H.84 Dragon	M. D. Souch
	G-ACGT	Avro 594 Avian IIIA ★	Yorkshire Light Aircraft Ltd/Leeds
	G-ACIT	D.H.84 Dragon ★	Science Museum/Wroughton
	G-ACLL	D.H.85 Leopard Moth	D. C. M. & V. M. Stiles
	G-ACMA	D.H.85 Leopard Moth	S. J. Filhol/Sherburn
	G-ACMD	D.H.82A Tiger Moth	M. J. Bonnick
	G-ACMN	D.H.85 Leopard Moth	H. D. Labouchere
	G-ACOJ	D.H.85 Leopard Moth	M. Gibbs
	G-ACOL	D.H.85 Leopard Moth	M. J. Abbott
	G-ACSP	D.H.88 Comet ★	K. Fern
	G-ACSS	D.H.88 Comet ★	The Shuttleworth Collection *Grosvenor House*/O. Warden
	G-ACTF	CLA.7 Swift ★	The Shuttleworth Collection/O. Warden
	G-ACUS	D.H.85 Leopard Moth	T. P. A. Norman
	G-ACUU	Cierva C.30A (HM580) ★	G. S. Baker/Duxford
	G-ACUX	S.16 Scion (VH-UUP) ★	Ulster Folk & Transport Museum
	G-ACVA	Kay Gyroplane ★	Glasgow Museum of Transport
	G-ACWM	Cierva C.30A (AP506) ★	IHM/Weston-s-Mare
	G-ACWP	Cierva C.30A (AP507) ★	Science Museum/S. Kensington
	G-ACXB	D.H.60G-III Moth Major	D. F. Hodgkinson
	G-ACXE	B.K.L-25C Swallow	J. C. Wakeford
	G-ACYK	Spartan Cruiser III ★	Museum of Flight *(front fuselage)*/E. Fortune
	G-ACZE	D.H.89A Dragon Rapide	Wessex Aviation & Transport Ltd (G-AJGS)/Henstridge
	G-ADAH	D.H.89A Dragon Rapide ★	Manchester Museum of Science & Industry *Pioneer*
	G-ADEV	Avro 504K (H5199)	The Shuttleworth Collection (G-ACNB)/O. Warden
	G-ADFV	Blackburn B-2 ★	Lincolnshire Aviation Heritage Centre/E. Kirkby
	G-ADGP	M.2L Hawk Speed Six	R. I. Souch
	G-ADGT	D.H.82A Tiger Moth	D. R. & Mrs M. Wood
	G-ADGV	D.H.82A Tiger Moth	K. J. Whitehead
	G-ADHD	D.H.60G-III Moth Major	M. E. Vaisey
	G-ADIA	D.H.82A Tiger Moth	F. A. de Munck
	G-ADJJ	D.H.82A Tiger Moth	J. M. Preston
	G-ADKC	D.H.87B Hornet Moth	A. J. Davy/Carlisle
	G-ADKK	D.H.87B Hornet Moth	C. P. B. Horsley & R. G. Anniss
	G-ADKL	D.H.87B Hornet Moth	A. de Cadenet
	G-ADKM	D.H.87B Hornet Moth	L. V. Mayhead
	G-ADLY	D.H.87B Hornet Moth	Totalsure Ltd
	G-ADMT	D.H.87B Hornet Moth	P. A. de Courcy Swaffer
	G-ADMW	M.2H Hawk Major (DG590) ★	Museum of Army Flying/Middle Wallop
	G-ADND	D.H.87B Hornet Moth (W9385)	The Shuttleworth Collection/O. Warden
	G-ADNE	D.H.87B Hornet Moth	G-ADNE Ltd
	G-ADNL	M.5 Sparrowhawk	K. D. Dunkerley
	G-ADNZ	D.H.82A Tiger Moth (DE673)	D. C. Wall
	G-ADOT	D.H.87B Hornet Moth ★	Mosquito Aircraft Museum
	G-ADPC	D.H.82A Tiger Moth	N. J. Baker & J. Beattie
	G-ADPJ	B.A.C. Drone ★	N. H. Ponsford/Breighton
	G-ADPS	B.A. Swallow 2	J. F. Hopkins
	G-ADRA	Pietenpol Air Camper	A. J. Mason

Reg.	Type	Owner or Operator	Notes
G-ADRG†	Mignet HM.14 (replica) (BAPC77) ★	Stratford Aircraft Collection	
G-ADRR	Aeronca C.3	S. J. Rudkin	
G-ADRY†	Mignet HM.14 (replica) (BAPC29) ★	Brooklands Museum of Aviation/ Weybridge	
G-ADSK	D.H.87B Hornet Moth	R. G. Grocott	
G-ADUR	D.H.87B Hornet Moth	Wessex Aviation & Transport Ltd	
G-ADVU	Mignet HM.14 (BAPC211) ★	N.E. Aircraft Museum/Usworth	
G-ADWJ	D.H.82A Tiger Moth	C. R. Hardiman	
G-ADWO	D.H.82A Tiger Moth (BB807) ★	Southampton Hall of Aviation	
G-ADXS	Mignet HM.14 ★	Thameside Aviation Museum/Shoreham	
G-ADXT	D.H. 82A Tiger Moth	R. G. Hanauer/Goodwood	
G-ADYS	Aeronca C.3	B. C. Cooper	
G-AEBB	Mignet HM.14 ★	The Shuttleworth Collection/O. Warden	
G-AEBJ	Blackburn B-2	British Aerospace (Operations) Ltd/Brough	
G-AEDB	B.A.C. Drone 2	M. C. Russell & P. L. Kirk	
G-AEDU	D.H.90 Dragonfly	T. P. A. Norman	
G-AEEG	M.3A Falcon	Skysport Engineering Ltd	
G-AEEH	Mignet HM.14 ★	Aerospace Museum/Cosford	
G-AEFG	Mignet HM.14 (BAPC75) ★	N. H. Ponsford/Breighton	
G-AEFT	Aeronca C.3	N. S. Chittenden	
G-AEGV	Mignet HM.14 ★	Midland Air Museum/Coventry	
G-AEHM	Mignet HM.14 ★	Science Museum/Wroughton	
G-AEJZ	Mignet HM.14 (BAPC120) ★	Bomber County Museum/Hemswell	
G-AEKR	Mignet HM.14 (BAPC121) ★	S. Yorks Aviation Soc/Breighton	
G-AEKV	Kronfeld Drone ★	Brooklands Museum of Aviation/ Weybridge	
G-AELO	D.H.87B Hornet Moth	D. E. Wells	
G-AEML	D.H.89 Dragon Rapide	Amanda Investments Ltd	
G-AENP	Hawker Hind (K5414) (BAPC78)	The Shuttleworth Collection/O. Warden	
G-AEOA	D.H.80A Puss Moth	P. & A. Wood/O. Warden	
G-AEOF†	Mignet HM.14 (BAPC22) ★	Aviodome/Schiphol, Holland	
G-AEOF	Rearwin 8500	Shipping & Airlines Ltd/Biggin Hill	
G-AEOH	Mignet HM.14 ★	Midland Air Museum	
G-AEPH	Bristol F.2B (D8096)	The Shuttleworth Collection/O. Warden	
G-AERV	M.11A Whitney Straight ★	Ulster Folk & Transport Museum	
G-AESB	Aeronca C.3	D. S. & I. M. Morgan	
G-AESE	D.H.87B Hornet Moth	J. G. Green/Redhill	
G-AESZ	Chilton D.W.1	R. E. Nerou	
G-AETA	Caudron G.3 (3066) ★	RAF Museum/Hendon	
G-AEUJ	M.11A Whitney Straight	R. E. Mitchell	
G-AEVS	Aeronca 100	A. M. Lindsay & N. H. Ponsford/Breighton	
G-AEVZ	B. A. Swallow 2	J. R. H. Ealand/Riseley	
G-AEXD	Aeronca 100	Mrs M. A. & R. W. Mills	
G-AEXF	P.6 Mew Gull	J. D. Penrose/Old Warden	
G-AEXT	Dart Kitten II	A. J. Hartfield	
G-AEXZ	Piper J-2 Cub	Mrs M. & J. R. Dowson/Leicester	
G-AEYY	Martin Monoplane ★	Martin Monoplane Syndicate (G-AAJK)	
G-AEZF	S.16 Scion 2 ★	Acebell Aviation/Redhill	
G-AEZJ	P.10 Vega Gull	R. A. J. Spurrell/White Waltham	
G-AEZX	Bucker Bu133C Jungmeister (LG+03)	A. J. E. Ditheridge	
G-AFAP†	C.A.S.A. C.352L ★	Aerospace Museum/Cosford	
G-AFAX	B. A. Eagle 2	J. G. Green	
G-AFBS	M.14A Hawk Trainer 3 ★	G. D. Durbridge-Freeman (G-AKKU)/ Duxford	
G-AFCL	B. A. Swallow 2	A. M. Dowson/O. Warden	
G-AFDO	Piper J-3F-60 Cub	R. Wald	
G-AFDX	Hanriot HD.1 (75) ★	RAF Museum/Hendon	
G-AFEL	Monocoupe 90A	M. Rieser	
G-AFFD	Percival Q-6 ★	B. D. Greenwood	
G-AFFH	Piper J-2 Cub	M. J. Honeychurch	
G-AFFI	Mignet HM.14 (replica) (BAPC76) ★	Yorkshire Air Museum/Elvington	
G-AFGC	B. A. Swallow 2	G. E. Arden	
G-AFGD	B. A. Swallow 2	A. T. Williams & ptnrs/Shobdon	
G-AFGE	B. A. Swallow 2	G. R. French	
G-AFGH	Chilton D.W.1.	M. L. & G. L. Joseph	
G-AFGI	Chilton D.W.1.	J. E. McDonald	
G-AFGM	Piper J-4A Cub Coupé	A. J. P. Marshall/Carlisle	
G-AFGZ	D.H.82A Tiger Moth	M. R. Paul & P. A. Shaw (G-AMHI)	

Notes	Reg.	Type	Owner or Operator
	G-AFHA	Mosscraft M.A.1. ★	C. V. Butler
	G-AFIN	Chrislea Airguard ★	Aeroplane Collection Ltd
	G-AFIR	Luton LA-4 Minor	A. J. Mason
	G-AFIU	Parker C.A.4 Parasol (LA-3 Minor) ★	Aeroplane Collection Ltd
	G-AFJA	Watkinson Dingbat ★	K. Woolley
	G-AFJB	Foster-Wikner G.M.1. Wicko (DR613) ★	K. Woolley
	G-AFJR	Tipsy Trainer 1	M. E. Vaisey (stored)
	G-AFJU	M.17 Monarch ★	Museum of Flight/E. Fortune
	G-AFJV	Mosscraft MA.2	C. V. Butler
	G-AFLW	M.17 Monarch	N. I. Dalziel/Biggin Hill
	G-AFNG	D.H.94 Moth Minor	The Gullwing Trust
	G-AFNI	D.H.94 Moth Minor	B. N. C. & C. M. Mogg
	G-AFOB	D.H.94 Moth Minor	Wessex Aviation & Transport Ltd
	G-AFOJ	D.H.94 Moth Minor	Mosquito Aircraft Museum
	G-AFPN	D.H.94 Moth Minor	J. W. & A. R. Davy/Carlisle
	G-AFPR	D.H.94 Moth Minor	M. D. Souch
	G-AFRZ	M.17 Monarch	R. E. Mitchell (G-AIDE)
	G-AFSC	Tipsy Trainer 1	G. A. Cull
	G-AFSV	Chilton D.W.1A	R. E. Nerou
	G-AFSW	Chilton D.W.2 ★	R. I. Souch
	G-AFTA	Hawker Tomtit (K1786)	The Shuttleworth Collection/O. Warden
	G-AFTN	Taylorcraft Plus C2	Leicestershire County Council Museums
	G-AFUP	Luscombe 8A Silvaire	P. C. J. Stone
	G-AFVE	D.H.82A Tiger Moth (T7230)	P. A. Shaw & M. R. Paul
	G-AFVN	Tipsy Trainer 1	D. F. Lingard
	G-AFWH	Piper J-4A Cub Coupé	J. R. Edwards & D. D. Smith
	G-AFWI	D.H.82A Tiger Moth	E. Newbigin
	G-AFWT	Tipsy Trainer 1	C. C. & J. M. Lovell
	G-AFYD	Luscombe 8F Silvaire	J. D. Iliffe
	G-AFYO	Stinson H.W.75	R. N. Wright
	G-AFZA	Piper J-4A Cub Coupe	M. L. Ryan
	G-AFZK	Luscombe 8A Silvaire	M. G. Byrnes
	G-AFZL	Porterfield CP.50	P. G. Lucas & S. H. Sharpe/ White Waltham
	G-AFZN	Luscombe 8A Silvaire	A. L. Young/Henstridge
	G-AGAT	Piper J-3F-50 Cub	G. S. Williams
	G-AGBN	G.A.L.42 Cygnet 2 ★	Museum of Flight/E. Fortune
	G-AGEG	D.H.82A Tiger Moth	T. P. A. Norman/Rendcomb
	G-AGFT	Avia FL.3 (W7)	P. A. Smith/Leicester
	G-AGHY	D.H.82A Tiger Moth	P. Groves
	G-AGIV	Piper J-3C-65 Cub	P. C. & F. M. Gill
	G-AGJG	D.H.89A Dragon Rapide	M. J. & D. J. T. Miller/Duxford
	G-AGLK	Auster 5D	Goldhawk Print Services Ltd/Biggin Hill
	G-AGMI	Luscombe 8A Silvaire	P. R. Bush
	G-AGNJ	D.H.82A Tiger Moth	B. P. Borsberry & Ptnrs
	G-AGNV	Avro 685 York 1 (TS798) ★	Aerospace Museum/Cosford
	G-AGOH	J/1 Autocrat ★	Newark Air Museum
	G-AGOS	R.S.4 Desford Trainer (VZ728)	Museum of Flight/E. Fortune
	G-AGOY	M.48 Messenger 3 (U-0247)	P. A. Brook
	G-AGPG	Avro 19 Srs 2 ★	Brenzett Aviation Museum
	G-AGPK	D.H.82A Tiger Moth	P. D. Castle
	G-AGRU	V.498 Viking 1A ★	Brooklands Museum of Aviation/Weybridge
	G-AGSH	D.H.89A Dragon Rapide 6	Venom Jet Promotions Ltd/Bournemouth
	G-AGTM	D.H.89A Dragon Rapide 6	Aviation Heritage Ltd
	G-AGTO	J/1 Autocrat	M. J. Barnett & D. J. T. Miller/Duxford
	G-AGTT	J/1 Autocrat	R. Farrer
	G-AGVG	J/1 Autocrat	S. J. Riddington/Leicester
	G-AGVN	J/1 Autocrat	G. H. Farrar
	G-AGVV	Piper J-3C-65 Cub	M. Molina-Ruano/Spain
	G-AGXN	J/1N Alpha	R. J. Fray & J. Evans
	G-AGXT	J/1N Alpha ★	Nene Valley Aircraft Museum
	G-AGXU	J/1N Alpha	G. T. Fisher/Sibson
	G-AGXV	J/1 Autocrat	B. S. Dowsett
	G-AGYD	J/1N Alpha	P. D. Hodson
	G-AGYH	J/1N Alpha	W. R. V. Marklew
	G-AGYK	J/1 Autocrat	Autocrat Syndicate
	G-AGYL	J/1N Alpha ★	Military Vehicle Conservation Group
	G-AGYT	J/1N Alpha	P. J. Barrett
	G-AGYU	DH.82A Tiger Moth (DE208)	A. Grimshaw
	G-AGYY	Ryan ST.3KR (27)	G-AGYY Group/Sandown

Reg.	Type	Owner or Operator	Notes
G-AGZZ	D.H.82A Tiger Moth	G. C. P. Shea-Simonds/Netheravon	
G-AHAL	J/1N Alpha	Wickenby Flying Club Ltd	
G-AHAM	J/1 Autocrat	A. J. Twemlow	
G-AHAN	D.H.82A Tiger Moth	Tiger Associates Ltd	
G-AHAP	J/1 Autocrat	V. H. Bellamy	
G-AHAU	J/1 Autocrat	A. C. Webber & ptnrs	
G-AHAV	J/1 Autocrat	C. J. Freeman/Headcorn	
G-AHBL	D.H.87B Hornet Moth	Dr Ursula H. Hamilton	
G-AHBM	D.H.87B Hornet Moth	P. A. & E. P. Gliddon	
G-AHCK	J/1N Alpha	Skegness Air Taxi Service Ltd	
G-AHCL	J/1N Alpha	Electronic Precision Ltd (G-OJVC)	
G-AHCR	Gould-Taylorcraft Plus D Special	D. E. H. Balmford & D. R. Shepherd/ Dunkeswell	
G-AHEC	Luscombe 8A Silvaire	S. P. Parsons/Rush Green	
G-AHED	D.H.89A Dragon Rapide (RL962) ★	RAF Museum Storage & Restoration Centre/Cardington	
G-AHGD	D.H.89A Dragon Rapide	R. Jones	
G-AHGW	Taylorcraft Plus D (LB375)	C. V. Butler/Coventry	
G-AHGZ	Taylorcraft Plus D	M. Pocock	
G-AHHH	J/1 Autocrat	H. A. Jones/Norwich	
G-AHHP	J/1N Alpha	D. J. Hutcheson (G-SIME)	
G-AHHT	J/1N Alpha	A. C. Barber & N. J. Hudson	
G-AHHU	J/1N Alpha ★	L. A. Groves & I. R. F. Hammond	
G-AHIP	Piper J-3C-65 Cub	R. T. & D. H. Tanner	
G-AHIZ	D.H.82A Tiger Moth	C.F.G. Flying Ltd/Cambridge	
G-AHKX	Avro 19 Srs 2	British Aerospace PLC/Woodford	
G-AHKY	Miles M.18 Series 2 ★	Museum of Flight/E. Fortune	
G-AHLI	Auster 3	G. A. Leathers	
G-AHLK	Auster 3	E. T. Brackenbury/Leicester	
G-AHLT	D.H.82A Tiger Moth	R. C. F. Bailey	
G-AHMJ	Cierva C.30A (K4235)	The Shuttleworth Collection/O. Warden	
G-AHMN	D.H.82A Tiger Moth (N6985)	Museum of Army Flying/Middle Wallop	
G-AHNR	Taylorcraft BC-12D	P. E. Hinkley/Redhill	
G-AHOO	D.H.82A Tiger Moth	G. W. Bisshopp	
G-AHRI	D.H.104 Dove 1 ★	Newark Air Museum	
G-AHRO	Cessna 140	R. H. Screen/Kidlington	
G-AHSA	Avro 621 Tutor (K3215)	The Shuttleworth Collection/O. Warden	
G-AHSD	Taylorcraft Plus D	A. Tucker	
G-AHSO	J/1N Alpha	W. P. Miller	
G-AHSP	J/1 Autocrat	N. J. Hudson & A. C. Barber	
G-AHSS	J/1N Alpha	Felthorpe Auster Group	
G-AHST	J/1N Alpha	M. J. Bonnick	
G-AHTE	P.44 Proctor V	D. K. Tregilgas	
G-AHTW	A.S.40 Oxford (V3388) ★	Skyfame Collection/Duxford	
G-AHUF	D.H.82A Tiger Moth (T7997)	L. D. Chapman	
G-AHUG	Taylorcraft Plus D	D. Nieman	
G-AHUI	M.38 Messenger 2A ★	Museum of Berkshire Aviation/Woodley	
G-AHUJ	M.14A Hawk Trainer 3 (R1914)	—/Breighton	
G-AHUN	Globe GC-1B Swift	R. J. Hamlett	
G-AHUV	D.H.82A Tiger Moth	W. G. Gordon	
G-AHVU	D.H.82A Tiger Moth (T6313)	Foley Farm Flying Group	
G-AHVV	D.H.82A Tiger Moth	R. Jones	
G-AHWJ	Taylorcraft Plus D (LB294)	M. D. Pitcher	
G-AHXE	Taylorcraft Plus D (HH982)	J. M. C. Pothecary/Shoreham	
G-AIBE	Fulmar II (N1854) ★	F.A.A. Museum/Yeovilton	
G-AIBH	J/1N Alpha	M. J. Bonnick	
G-AIBM	J/1 Autocrat	D. G. Greatrex	
G-AIBR	J/1 Autocrat	C. T. Murphy	
G-AIBW	J/1N Alpha	W. E. Bateson/Blackpool	
G-AIBX	J/1 Autocrat	Wasp Flying Group	
G-AIBY	J/1 Autocrat	D. Morris/Sherburn	
G-AICX	Luscombe 8A Silvaire	R. V. Smith/Henstridge	
G-AIDL	D.H.89A Dragon Rapide 6	Atlantic Air Transport Ltd/Caernarfon	
G-AIDS	D.H.82A Tiger Moth	K. D. Pogmore & T. Dann	
G-AIEK	M.38 Messenger 2A (RG333)	J. Buckingham	
G-AIFZ	J/1N Alpha	M. D. Ansley & P. V. Flack	
G-AIGD	J/1 Autocrat	C. J. Harrison	
G-AIGF	J/1N Alpha	A. R. C. Mathie	
G-AIGT	J/1N Alpha	P. R. & J. S. Johnson	
G-AIGU	J/1N Alpha	N. K. Geddes	
G-AIIH	Piper J-3C-65 Cub	J. A. de Salis	

Notes	Reg.	Type	Owner or Operator
	G-AIJI	J/1N Alpha ★	C. J. Baker
	G-AIJM	Auster J/4	N. Huxtable
	G-AIJR	Auster J/4	R. J. Bentley
	G-AIJS	Auster J/4 ★	stored
	G-AIJT	Auster J/4 Srs 100	Aberdeen Auster Flying Group
	G-AIJZ	J/1 Autocrat	stored
	G-AIKE	Auster 5	C. J. Baker
	G-AIPR	Auster J/4	MPM Flying Group/Booker
	G-AIPV	J/1 Autocrat	W. P. Miller
	G-AIRC	J/1 Autocrat	R. C. Tebbett/Shobdon
	G-AIRI	D.H.82A Tiger Moth	E. R. Goodwin (stored)
	G-AIRK	D.H.82A Tiger Moth	R. C. Teverson & ptnrs
	G-AISA	Tipsy B Srs 1	G. A. Cull
	G-AISC	Tipsy B Srs 1	Wagtail Flying Group
	G-AISS	Piper J-3C-65 Cub	K. W. Wood & F. Watson
	G-AIST	V.S.300 Spitfire 1A (AR213)	Sheringham Aviation UK Ltd
	G-AISX	Piper J-3C-65 Cub	V. Luck
	G-AISY	D.H.82A Tiger Moth	R. H. & J. A. Cooper
	G-AITB	A.S.10 Oxford (MP425) ★	RAF Museum Store/Cardington
	G-AIUA	M.14A Hawk Trainer 3	P. A. Brook
	G-AIUL	D.H.89A Dragon Rapide 6	I. Jones/Chirk
	G-AIXA	Taylorcraft Plus D	A. A. & M. J. Copse
	G-AIXJ	D.H.82A Tiger Moth	D. Green/Goodwood
	G-AIXN	Benes-Mraz M.1C Sokol	M. Howells
	G-AIYG	SNCAN Stampe SV-4B	L. Casteleyn/Belgium
	G-AIYR	D.H.89A Dragon Rapide	Clacton Aero Club (1988) Ltd/Duxford
	G-AIYS	D.H.85 Leopard Moth	Wessex Aviation & Transport Ltd
	G-AIZE	F.24W Argus 2 ★	RAF Museum/Henlow
	G-AIZF	D.H.82A Tiger Moth ★	stored
	G-AIZG	V.S. Walrus 1 (L2301) ★	F.A.A. Museum/Yeovilton
	G-AIZU	J/1 Autocrat	C. J. & J. G. B. Morley
	G-AJAC	J/1N Alpha	N. J. Mortimore & H. A. Bridgman
	G-AJAD	Piper J-3C-65 Cub	R. A. D. Wilson & D. J. Morris
	G-AJAE	J/1N Alpha	M. G. Stops
	G-AJAJ	J/1N Alpha	R. B. Lawrence
	G-AJAM	J/2 Arrow	D. A. Porter
	G-AJAO	Piper J-3C-65 Cub	G. M. Perfect & M. Stow
	G-AJAP	Luscombe 8A Silvaire	R. J. Thomas
	G-AJAS	J/1N Alpha	C. J. Baker
	G-AJCP	D.31 Turbulent	B. R. Pearson
	G-AJDW	J/1 Autocrat	D. R. Hunt
	G-AJDY	J/1 Autocrat	Truck Panels Ltd
	G-AJEB	J/1N Alpha ★	Manchester Museum of Science & Industry
	G-AJEE	J/1 Autocrat	A. R. C. De Albanoz/Bournemouth
	G-AJEH	J/1N Alpha	J. T. Powell-Tuck
	G-AJEI	J/1N Alpha	W. P. Miller
	G-AJEM	J/1 Autocrat	K. A. Jones
	G-AJES	Piper J-3C-65 Cub (330485)	P. A. Crawford
	G-AJGJ	Auster 5 (RT486)	British Classic Aircraft Restoration Flying Group
	G-AJHJ	Auster 5	stored
	G-AJHS	D.H.82A Tiger Moth	J. M. Voeten & H. van der Paauw/Holland
	G-AJHU	D.H.82A Tiger Moth (T7471)	G. Valentini
	G-AJIH	J/1 Autocrat	A. H. Diver
	G-AJIS	J/1N Alpha	Husthwaite Auster Group
	G-AJIT	J/1 Kingsland Autocrat	A. J. Kay
	G-AJIU	J/1 Autocrat	M. D. Greenhalgh/Netherthorpe
	G-AJIW	J/1N Alpha	Millair Services Ltd
	G-AJJP	Jet Gyrodyne (XJ389) ★	Museum of Berkshire Aviation/Woodley
	G-AJJS	Cessna 120	Robhurst Flying Group
	G-AJJT	Cessna 120	J. S. Robson
	G-AJJU	Luscombe 8E Silvaire	L. C. Moon
	G-AJKB	Luscombe 8E Silvaire	A. F. Hall & P. S. Hatwell/Ipswich
	G-AJOA	D.H.82A Tiger Moth (T5424)	F. P. Le Coyte
	G-AJOC	M.38 Messenger 2A ★	Ulster Folk & Transport Museum
	G-AJOE	M.38 Messenger 2A	Cotswold Aircraft Restoration Group
	G-AJON	Aeronca 7AC Champion	A. Biggs & J. L. Broad/Booker
	G-AJOV†	Sikorsky S-51 ★	Aerospace Museum/Cosford
	G-AJOZ	F.24W Argus 2 ★	Thorpe Camp Preservation Group
	G-AJPI	F.24R-41a Argus 3 (314887)	T. H. Bishop
	G-AJPZ	J/1 Autocrat ★	Wessex Aviation Soc
	G-AJRB	J/1 Autocrat	N. Ravine/Sywell

Reg.	Type	Owner or Operator	Notes
G-AJRC	J/1 Autocrat	A. Foster	
G-AJRE	J/1 Autocrat (Lycoming)	C. W. & A. A. M. Huke	
G-AJRH	J/1N Alpha	Leicestershire Museum of Science & Industry/Coalville	
G-AJRS	M.14A Hawk Trainer 3 (P6382)	The Shuttleworth Collection/O. Warden	
G-AJTW	D.H.82A Tiger Moth (N6965)	J. A. Barker/Tibenham	
G-AJUD	J/1 Autocrat	C. L. Sawyer	
G-AJUE	J/1 Autocrat	P. H. B. Cole	
G-AJUL	J/1N Alpha	M. J. Crees	
G-AJVE	D.H.82A Tiger Moth	P. A. Layzell	
G-AJWB	M.38 Messenger 2A	G. E. J. Spooner	
G-AJXC	Auster 5	J. E. Graves	
G-AJXV	Auster 4 (NJ695)	B. A. Farries/Leicester	
G-AJXY	Auster 4	P. D. Lowdon	
G-AJYB	J/1N Alpha	P. J. Shotbolt	
G-AKAT	M.14A Hawk Trainer 3 (T9738)	G. Beda/France	
G-AKAZ	Piper J-3C-65 Cub (57-H)	AKAZ Group	
G-AKBM	M.38 Messenger 2A ★	Bristol Plane Preservation Unit	
G-AKBO	M.38 Messenger 2A	B. du Cros	
G-AKDN	D.H.C. 1A Chipmunk 10	D. S. Backhouse	
G-AKDW	D.H.89A Dragon Rapide	De Havilland Aircraft Museum Trust Ltd	
G-AKEL	M.65 Gemini 1A ★	Ulster Folk & Transport Museum	
G-AKER	M.65 Gemini 1A ★	Berkshire Aviation Group	
G-AKEZ	M.38 Messenger 2A (RG333)	P. G. Lee	
G-AKGD	M.65 Gemini 1A ★	Berkshire Aviation Group/Woodley	
G-AKGE	M.65 Gemini 3C ★	Ulster Folk & Transport Museum	
G-AKHP	M.65 Gemini 1A	P. G. Lee	
G-AKHZ	M.65 Gemini 7 ★	Museum of Berkshire Aviation/Woodley	
G-AKIB	Piper J-3C-90 Cub (480015)	M. C. Bennett	
G-AKIF	D.H.89A Dragon Rapide	Airborne Taxi Services Ltd/Booker	
G-AKIN	M.38 Messenger 2A	R. Spiller & Sons/Sywell	
G-AKIU	P.44 Proctor V	G. Reddish	
G-AKKB	M.65 Gemini 1A	J. Buckingham	
G-AKKH	M.65 Gemini 1A	M. C. Russell	
G-AKKR	M.14A Magister (T9707) ★	Manchester Museum of Science & Industry	
G-AKKY	M.14A Hawk Trainer 3 (L6906) (BAPC44) ★	Museum of Berkshire Aviation/Woodley	
G-AKLW	SA.6 Sealand 1 ★	Ulster Folk & Transport Museum	
G-AKOE	D.H.89A Dragon Rapide 4	J. E. Pierce/Chirk	
G-AKOT	Auster 5 H	C. J. Baker	
G-AKOW	Auster 5 (TJ569) ★	Museum of Army Flying/Middle Wallop	
G-AKPF	M.14A Hawk Trainer 3 (V1075)	P. A. Brook/Sandown	
G-AKPI	Auster 5 (NJ703)	B. H. Hargrave/Doncaster	
G-AKRA	Piper J-3C-65 Cub	W. R. Savin	
G-AKRP	D.H.89A Dragon Rapide ★	Fordaire Ltd/Sywell	
G-AKSY	Auster 5	Aerofab Flying Group	
G-AKSZ	Auster 5	A. R. C. Mathie	
G-AKTH	Piper J-3C-65 Cub	A. L. Wickens	
G-AKTI	Luscombe 8A Silvaire	N. C. W. N. Lester	
G-AKTK	Aeronca 11AC Chief	R. W. Marshall & ptnrs	
G-AKTM	Luscombe 8F Silvaire	B. Bayley	
G-AKTN	Luscombe 8A Silvaire	M. G. Rummey	
G-AKTO	Aeronca 7BCM Champion	D. C. Murray	
G-AKTP	PA-17 Vagabond	L. A. Maynard	
G-AKTR	Aeronca 7AC Champion	C. Fielder/Dunkeswell	
G-AKTS	Cessna 120	J. J. Boon/Popham	
G-AKTT	Luscombe 8A Silvaire	S. J. Charters	
G-AKUE	D.H.82A Tiger Moth	D. F. Hodgkinson	
G-AKUF	Luscombe 8F Silvaire	A. G. Palmer	
G-AKUG	Luscombe 8A Silvaire	P. & L. A. Groves	
G-AKUH	Luscombe 8E Silvaire	I. M. Bower	
G-AKUI	Luscombe 8E Silvaire	J. A. Pothecary/Shoreham	
G-AKUJ	Luscombe 8E Silvaire	P. R. Edwards	
G-AKUK	Luscombe 8A Silvaire	Leckhampstead Flying Group	
G-AKUL	Luscombe 8A Silvaire	E. A. Taylor	
G-AKUM	Luscombe 8F Silvaire	M. J. Willies	
G-AKUN	Piper J-3F-65 Cub	W. R. Savin	
G-AKUO	Aeronca 11AC Chief	KUO Flying Group/White Waltham	
G-AKUP	Luscombe 8E Silvaire	R. J. Willies	
G-AKUR	Cessna 140	J. Greenaway & C. A. Davies/Popham	
G-AKUW	C.H.3 Super Ace	D. R. Bean	
G-AKVF	C.H.3 Super Ace	T. Pate	

Notes	Reg.	Type	Owner or Operator
	G-AKVM	Cessna 120	N. Wise & S. Walker
	G-AKVN	Aeronca 11AC Chief	Breckland Aeronca Group
	G-AKVO	Taylorcraft BC-12D	Albion Flyers
	G-AKVP	Luscombe 8A Silvaire	J. M. Edis
	G-AKVZ	M.38 Messenger 4B	Shipping & Airlines Ltd/Biggin Hill
	G-AKWS	Auster 5A-160	J. E. Homewood
	G-AKWT	Auster 5 ★	Loughborough & Leicester Aircraft Preservation Soc
	G-AKXP	Auster 5	M. Pocock
	G-AKXS	D.H.82A Tiger Moth	P. A. Colman
	G-AKZN	P.34A Proctor 3 (Z7197) ★	RAF Museum/Hendon
	G-ALAH	M.38 Messenger 4A (RH377) ★	RAF Museum/Henlow
	G-ALAX	D.H.89A Dragon Rapide ★	Durney Aeronautical Collection/Andover
	G-ALBJ	Auster 5	P. N. Elkington
	G-ALBK	Auster 5	S. J. Wright & Co (Farmers) Ltd
	G-ALBN	Bristol 173 (XF785) ★	RAF Museum Storage & Restoration Centre/Cardington
	G-ALCK	P.34A Proctor 3 (LZ766) ★	Skyfame Collection/Duxford
	G-ALCS	M.65 Gemini 3C ★	stored
	G-ALCU	D.H.104 Dove 2 ★	Midland Air Museum/Coventry
	G-ALDG	HP.81 Hermes 4 ★	Duxford Aviation Soc (fuselage only)
	G-ALEH	PA-17 Vagabond	A. D. Pearce/White Waltham
	G-ALFA	Auster 5	Golf Alpha Auster Group
	G-ALFT	D.H.104 Dove 6 ★	Caernarfon Air World
	G-ALFU	D.H.104 Dove 6 ★	Duxford Aviation Soc
	G-ALGA	PA-15 Vagabond	D. A. Lord
	G-ALIJ	PA-17 Vagabond	Popham Flying Group/Popham
	G-ALIW	D.H.82A Tiger Moth	D. I. M. Geddes & F. Curry/Booker
	G-ALJF	P.34A Proctor 3	J. F. Moore/Biggin Hill
	G-ALJL	D.H.82A Tiger Moth	C. G. Clarke
	G-ALLF	Slingsby T.30A Prefect (ARK)	J. F. Hopkins & K. M. Fresson
	G-ALNA	D.H.82A Tiger Moth	R. J. Doughton
	G-ALND	D.H.82A Tiger Moth (N9191)	J. T. Powell-Tuck
	G-ALNV	Auster 5 ★	C. J. Baker (stored)
	G-ALOD	Cessna 140	J. R. Stainer
	G-ALRH	EoN Type 8 Baby	P. D. Moran/Chipping
	G-ALRI	D.H.82A Tiger Moth (T5672)	Wessex Aviation & Transport Ltd
	G-ALSP	Bristol 171 Sycamore (WV783) ★	R.N. Fleetlands Museum
	G-ALSS	Bristol 171 Sycamore (WA576) ★	Dumfries & Galloway Aviation Museum
	G-ALST	Bristol 171 Sycamore (WA577) ★	N.E. Aircraft Museum/Usworth
	G-ALSW	Bristol 171 Sycamore (WT933) ★	Newark Air Museum
	G-ALSX	Bristol 171 Sycamore (G-48-1) ★	IHM/Weston-s-Mare
	G-ALTO	Cessna 140	J. P. Bell
	G-ALTW	D.H.82A Tiger Moth ★	A. Mangham
	G-ALUC	D.H.82A Tiger Moth	D. R. & M. Wood
	G-ALVP	D.H.82A Tiger Moth ★	V. & R. Wheele (stored)
	G-ALWB	D.H.C.1 Chipmunk 22A	M. L. & J. M. Soper/Perth
	G-ALWF	V.701 Viscount ★	Viscount Preservation Trust RMA Sir John Franklin/Duxford
	G-ALWS	D.H.82A Tiger Moth	A. P. Benyon
	G-ALWW	D.H.82A Tiger Moth	D. E. Findon
	G-ALXT	D.H.89A Dragon Rapide ★	Science Museum/Wroughton
	G-ALXZ	Auster 5-150	M. F. Cuming
	G-ALYB	Auster 5 (RT520) ★	S. Yorks Aircraft Preservation Soc
	G-ALYG	Auster 5D	A. L. Young/Henstridge
	G-ALYW	D.H.106 Comet 1 ★	RAF Exhibition Flight (fuselage converted to Nimrod)
	G-ALZE	BN-1F ★	M. R. Short/Southampton Hall of Aviation
	G-ALZO	A.S.57 Ambassador ★	Duxford Aviation Soc
	G-AMAI	D.H.89A Dragon Rapide	The Island Aeroplane Co/Sandown
	G-AMAW	Luton L.A-4 Minor	R. H. Coates
	G-AMBB	D.H.82A Tiger Moth	J. Eagles
	G-AMCA	Douglas C-47B	Air Atlantique Ltd/Coventry
	G-AMCK	D.H.82A Tiger Moth	D. L. Frankel
	G-AMCM	D.H.82A Tiger Moth	B. C. Cooper & ptnrs
	G-AMDA	Avro 652A Anson 1 (N4877) ★	Skyfame Collection/Duxford
	G-AMEN	PA-18 Super Cub 95	A. Lovejoy & W. Cook
	G-AMHF	D.H.82A Tiger Moth	Wavendon Social Housing Ltd
	G-AMHJ	Douglas C-47A	Air Atlantique Ltd/Coventry
	G-AMIU	D.H.82A Tiger Moth	R. & Mrs J. L. Jones
	G-AMKU	J/1B Aiglet	P. G. Lipman

Reg.	Type	Owner or Operator	Notes
G-AMLZ	P.50 Prince 6E ★	Caernarfon Air World Museum	
G-AMMS	J/5K Aiglet Trainer	A. J. Large	
G-AMNN	D.H.82A Tiger Moth	M. Thrower/Shoreham	
G-AMOG	V.701 Viscount ★	Aerospace Museum/Cosford	
G-AMPG	PA-12 Super Cruiser	R. Simpson	
G-AMPI	SNCAN Stampe SV-4C	M-A. Newman	
G-AMPO	Douglas C-47B	Air Atlantique Ltd/Coventry	
G-AMPY	Douglas C-47B	Air Atlantique Ltd/Coventry	
G-AMPZ	Douglas C-47B	Air Atlantique Ltd/Coventry	
G-AMRA	Douglas C-47B	Air Atlantique Ltd/Coventry	
G-AMRF	J/5F Aiglet Trainer	A. I. Topps/E. Midlands	
G-AMRK	G.37 Gladiator I (N2308)	The Shuttleworth Collection/O. Warden	
G-AMSG	SIPA 903	S. W. Markham	
G-AMSN	Douglas C-47B ★	Aces High Ltd/North Weald	
G-AMSV	Douglas C-47B	Air Atlantique Ltd/Coventry	
G-AMTA	J/5F Aiglet Trainer	N. H. T. Cottrell	
G-AMTD	J/5F Aiglet Trainer	Leicestershire Aero Club Ltd	
G-AMTF	D.H.82A Tiger Moth (T7842)	M. W. Zipfell/Marham	
G-AMTK	D.H.82A Tiger Moth	S. W. McKay & M. E. Vaisey	
G-AMTM	J/1 Autocrat	R. J. Stobo & D. Clewley (G-AJUJ)	
G-AMTV	D.H.82A Tiger Moth	Medalbest Ltd	
G-AMUF	D.H.C.1 Chipmunk 21	Redhill Tailwheel Flying Club Ltd	
G-AMUI	J/5F Aiglet Trainer	M. J. & A. A. Copse	
G-AMVD	Auster 5	R. F. Tolhurst	
G-AMVP	Tipsy Junior	A. R. Wershat	
G-AMVS	D.H.82A Tiger Moth	J. T. Powell-Tuck	
G-AMXA	D.H.106 Comet 2 (nose only) ★	Spectators' Terrace/Gatwick	
G-AMXT	D.H.104 Sea Devon C.20	W. Gentle & P. C. Gill	
G-AMYA	Zlin Z.381	D. M. Fenton	
G-AMYD	J/5L Aiglet Trainer	G. H. Maskell	
G-AMYJ	Douglas C-47B	Air Atlantique Ltd/Coventry	
G-AMYL	PA-17 Vagabond	P. J. Penn-Sayers/Shoreham	
G-AMZI	J/5F Aiglet Trainer	J. F. Moore/Biggin Hill	
G-AMZT	J/5F Aiglet Trainer	D. Hyde & J. W. Saull/Cranfield	
G-AMZU	J/5F Aiglet Trainer	J. A. Longworth & ptnrs	
G-ANAF	Douglas C-47B	Air Atlantique Ltd/Coventry	
G-ANAP	D.H.104 Dove 6 ★	Brunel Technical College/Lulsgate	
G-ANCF	B.175 Britannia 308 ★	(stored) Bristol Aero Collection/Kemble	
G-ANCS	D.H.82A Tiger Moth	M. A. B. Mitchell	
G-ANCX	D.H.82A Tiger Moth	D. R. Wood/Biggin Hill	
G-ANDE	D.H.82A Tiger Moth	Montrose Aviation Ltd/Duxford	
G-ANDM	D.H.82A Tiger Moth	J. G. Green	
G-ANDP	D.H.82A Tiger Moth	A. H. Diver	
G-ANDX	D.H.104 Devon C.2 (XG496) ★	L. Richards (stored)	
G-ANEC	D.H.82A Tiger Moth ★	(stored)	
G-ANEH	D.H.82A Tiger Moth (N6797)	G. J. Wells/Goodwood	
G-ANEL	D.H.82A Tiger Moth	Chauffair Ltd	
G-ANEM	D.H.82A Tiger Moth	P. J. Benest	
G-ANEN	D.H.82A Tiger Moth	R. J. Jackson	
G-ANEW	D.H.82A Tiger Moth	A. L. Young	
G-ANEZ	D.H.82A Tiger Moth	C. D. J. Bland & T. S. Warren/Sandown	
G-ANFC	D.H.82A Tiger Moth	H. J. Jauncey/Rochester	
G-ANFH	Westland S-55 ★	IHM/Weston-s-Mare	
G-ANFI	D.H.82A Tiger Moth (DE623)	G. P. Graham	
G-ANFL	D.H.82A Tiger Moth	R. P. Whitby & ptnrs	
G-ANFM	D.H.82A Tiger Moth	S. A. Brook & ptnrs/Booker	
G-ANFP	D.H.82A Tiger Moth ★	Mosquito Aircraft Museum	
G-ANFU	Auster 5 (NJ719) ★	N.E. Aircraft Museum/Usworth	
G-ANFV	D.H.82A Tiger Moth (DF155)	R. A. L. Falconer	
G-ANFW	D.H.82A Tiger Moth	G. M. Fraser/Denham	
G-ANGK	Cessna 140A	D. W. Munday	
G-ANHK	D.H.82A Tiger Moth	J. D. Iliffe	
G-ANHR	Auster 5	C. G. Winch	
G-ANHS	Auster 4	Tango Uniform Group	
G-ANHU	Auster 4	D. J. Baker (stored)	
G-ANHX	Auster 5D	D. J. Baker	
G-ANIE	Auster 5 (TW467)	S. J. Partridge	
G-ANIJ	Auster 5D (TJ672)	M. Pocock & R. Eastmann	
G-ANIS	Auster 5	J. Clarke-Cockburn	
G-ANIX	D.H.82 Tiger Moth	The Island Aeroplane Co/Sandown	
G-ANJA	D.H.82A Tiger Moth (N9389)	P. Auckland	
G-ANJD	D.H.82A Tiger Moth	H. J. Jauncey (stored)/Rochester	

Notes	Reg.	Type	Owner or Operator
	G-ANJV	W.S.55 Whirlwind 3 (VR-BET) ★	IHM/Weston-s-Mare
	G-ANKK	D.H.82A Tiger Moth (T5854)	Halfpenny Green Tiger Group
	G-ANKL	D.H.82A Tiger Moth	M. D. Souch
	G-ANKT	D.H.82A Tiger Moth (T6818)	The Shuttleworth Collection/O. Warden
	G-ANKV	D.H.82A Tiger Moth (T7793)	Westmead Business Group/Croydon
	G-ANKZ	D.H.82A Tiger Moth (N6466)	D. W. Graham
	G-ANLD	D.H.82A Tiger Moth	K. Peters
	G-ANLH	D.H.82A Tiger Moth	Wessex Aviation & Transport Ltd
	G-ANLS	D.H.82A Tiger Moth	P. A. Gliddon
	G-ANLU	Auster 5	B. H. Hargrave
	G-ANLW	W.B.1. Widgeon (MD497) ★	Sloane Helicopters Ltd (stored)
	G-ANLX	D.H.82A Tiger Moth	B. J. Borsberry & ptnrs
	G-ANMO	D.H.82A Tiger Moth	E. & K. M. Lay
	G-ANMV	D.H.82A Tiger Moth (T7404)	J. W. Davy/Cardiff
	G-ANMY	D.H.82A Tiger Moth (DE470)	R. Earl & B. Morris
	G-ANNB	D.H.82A Tiger Moth	Cormack (Aircraft Services) Ltd
	G-ANNE	D.H.82A Tiger Moth	C. R. Hardiman
	G-ANNG	D.H.82A Tiger Moth	P. F. Walter
	G-ANNI	D.H.82A Tiger Moth	A. R. Brett
	G-ANNK	D.H.82A Tiger Moth	P. J. Wilcox/Cranfield
	G-ANNN	D.H.82A Tiger Moth	H. C. Cox
	G-ANOA	Hiller UH-12A ★	Redhill Technical College
	G-ANOD	D.H.82A Tiger Moth	P. G. Grafton
	G-ANOH	D.H.82A Tiger Moth	N. Parkhouse/White Waltham,
	G-ANOK	SAAB S.91C Safir ★	A. F. Galt & Co (stored)
	G-ANOM	D.H.82A Tiger Moth	P. R. & A. L. Williams
	G-ANON	D.H.82A Tiger Moth (T7909)	A. C. Mercer/Sherburn
	G-ANOO	D.H.82A Tiger Moth	R. K. Packman/Shoreham
	G-ANOR	D.H.82A Tiger Moth (T6991)	Ghyllside Ltd
	G-ANOV	D.H.104 Dove 6 ★	Museum of Flight/E. Fortune
	G-ANPE	D.H.82A Tiger Moth	I. E. S. Huddleston (G-IESH)
	G-ANPK	D.H.82A Tiger Moth	The D. & P. Group
	G-ANPP	P.34A Proctor 3	C. P. A. & J. Jeffrey
	G-ANRF	D.H.82A Tiger Moth	C. D. Cyster
	G-ANRM	D.H.82A Tiger Moth	Clacton Aero Club (1988) Ltd & A. B. Cutting
	G-ANRN	D.H.82A Tiger Moth	J. J. V. Elwes/Rush Green
	G-ANRP	Auster 5 (TW439)	A. Brier
	G-ANRX	D.H.82A Tiger Moth ★	Mosquito Aircraft Museum
	G-ANSM	D.H.82A Tiger Moth	J. L. Bond
	G-ANTE	D.H.82A Tiger Moth	T. I. Sutton & B. J. Champion/Chester
	G-ANTK	Avro 685 York ★	Duxford Aviation Soc
	G-ANTS	D.H.82A Tiger Moth (N6532)	J. G. Green
	G-ANUO	D.H.114 Heron 2D (G-AOXL) ★	Westmead Business Group/Croydon
	G-ANUW	D.H.104 Dove 6 ★	Aces High Ltd/North Weald
	G-ANWB	D.H.C.1 Chipmunk 21	G. Briggs/Blackpool
	G-ANWO	M.14A Hawk Trainer 3 ★	A. G. Dunkerley
	G-ANXB	D.H.114 Heron 1B ★	Newark Air Museum
	G-ANXC	J/5R Alpine	C. J. Repek & ptnrs
	G-ANXR	P.31C Proctor 4 (RM221)	L. H. Oakins/Biggin Hill
	G-ANYP	P.31C Proctor 4 (NP184)	R. A. Anderson
	G-ANZJ	P.31C Proctor 4 (NP303) ★	A. Hillyard
	G-ANZT	Thruxton Jackaroo	D. J. Neville & P. A. Dear
	G-ANZU	D.H.82A Tiger Moth	P. A. Jackson
	G-ANZZ	D.H.82A Tiger Moth	D. L. Frankel
	G-AOAA	D.H.82A Tiger Moth	R. C. P. Brookhouse
	G-AOAR	P.31C Proctor 4 (NP181) ★	Historic Aircraft Preservation Soc
	G-AOBG	Somers-Kendall SK.1 ★	(stored)/Breighton
	G-AOBH	D.H.82A Tiger Moth (NL750)	P. Nutley/Thruxton
	G-AOBJ	D.H.82A Tiger Moth (DE970)	D. H. R. Jenkins
	G-AOBO	D.H.82A Tiger Moth	P. A. Brook
	G-AOBU	P.84 Jet Provost T.1	T. J. Manna/Cranfield
	G-AOBV	J/5P Autocar	P. E. Champney (stored)
	G-AOBX	D.H.82A Tiger Moth	D. G. Ross
	G-AOCP	Auster 5 ★	C. J. Baker (stored)
	G-AOCR	Auster 5D	D. J. Russell-Fenwick
	G-AOCU	Auster 5	S. J. Ball/Leicester
	G-AODA	Westland S-55 Srs 3 ★	IHM/Weston-s-Mare
	G-AODT	D.H.82A Tiger Moth (R5250)	R. A. Harrowven
	G-AOEH	Aeronca 7AC Champion	R. A & S. P. Smith
	G-AOEI	D.H.82A Tiger Moth	C.F.G. Flying Ltd/Cambridge
	G-AOEL	D.H.82A Tiger Moth ★	Museum of Flight/E. Fortune

Reg.	Type	Owner or Operator	Notes
G-AOES	D.H.82A Tiger Moth	A. Twemlow & G. A. Cordery	
G-AOET	D.H.82A Tiger Moth	Venom Jet Promotions Ltd/Bournemouth	
G-AOEX	Thrujxton Jackaroo	A. T. Christian	
G-AOFE	D.H.C.1 Chipmunk 22A (WB702)	E. J. F. McEntee	
G-AOFM	J/5P Autocar	N. P. Beaumont	
G-AOFS	J/5L Aiglet Trainer	P. N. A. Whitehead	
G-AOGA	M.75 Aries ★	Irish Aviation Museum (stored)	
G-AOGE	P.34A Proctor 3	N. I. Dalziel/Biggin Hill	
G-AOGI	D.H.82A Tiger Moth	W. J. Taylor	
G-AOGR	D.H.82A Tiger Moth (T6099)	M. I. Edwards	
G-AOGV	J/5R Alpine	R. E. Heading	
G-AOHL	V.802 Viscount ★	(Cabin Trainer)/Southend	
G-AOHM	V.802 Viscount	British World Airlines Ltd Viscount Sir George Edwards/Southend	
G-AOHY	D.H.82A Tiger Moth	Historic Aircraft Flight/Middle Wallop	
G-AOHZ	J/5P Autocar	A. D. Hodgkinson	
G-AOIL	D.H.82A Tiger Moth	T. C. Lawless	
G-AOIM	D.H.82A Tiger Moth	C. R. Hardiman/Shobdon	
G-AOIR	Thruxton Jackaroo	L. H. Smith & I. M. Oliver	
G-AOIS	D.H.82A Tiger Moth	J. K. Ellwood	
G-AOIY	J/5G Autocar	J. B. Nicholson	
G-AOJH	D.H.83C Fox Moth	R. M. Brooks	
G-AOJJ	D.H.82A Tiger Moth (DF128)	E. & K. M. Lay	
G-AOJK	D.H.82A Tiger Moth	P. A. de Courcy Swoffer	
G-AOJT	D.H.106 Comet 1 (fuselage only) (F-BGNX) ★	Mosquito Aircraft Museum	
G-AOJZ	D.H.C.1 Chipmunk 22 ★	–	
G-AOKH	P.40 Prentice 1	J. F. Moore/Biggin Hill	
G-AOKL	P.40 Prentice 1 (VS610)	G-AOKL Flying Group	
G-AOKO	P.40 Prentice 1 ★	J. F. Coggins/Coventry	
G-AOKZ	P.40 Prentice 1 (VS623) ★	Midland Air Museum	
G-AOLK	P.40 Prentice 1	Hilton Aviation Ltd/Southend	
G-AOLU	P.40 Prentice 1 (VS356)	N. J. Butler	
G-AORB	Cessna 170B	Eaglescott Parachute Centre	
G-AORG	D.H.114 Heron 2	Duchess of Brittany (Jersey) Ltd	
G-AORW	D.H.C.1 Chipmunk 22A	R. C. McCarthy	
G-AOSF	D.H.C.1 Chipmunk 22 (WB571)	D. Mercer	
G-AOSK	D.H.C.1 Chipmunk 22	E. J. Leigh	
G-AOSO	D.H.C.1 Chipmunk 22	Earl of Suffolk & Berkshire & J. Hoerner	
G-AOSU	D.H.C.1 Chipmunk 22 (Lycoming)	RAFGSA/Kinloss	
G-AOSY	D.H.C.1 Chipmunk 22 (WB585)	Franbrave Ltd	
G-AOTD	D.H.C.1 Chipmunk 22 (WB588)	S. Piech	
G-AOTF	D.H.C.1 Chipmunk 23 (Lycoming)	RAFGSA/Dishforth	
G-AOTI	D.H.114 Heron 2D ★	Mosquito Aircraft Museum	
G-AOTK	D.53 Turbi	The T. K. Flying Group	
G-AOTR	D.H.C.1 Chipmunk 22	M. R. Woodgate	
G-AOTY	D.H.C.1 Chipmunk 22A (WG472)	T. E. W. Terrell/Leicester	
G-AOUJ	Fairey Ultra-Light ★	IHM/Weston-s-Mare	
G-AOUO	D.H.C.1 Chipmunk 22 (Lycoming)	RAFGSA/Bicester	
G-AOUP	D.H.C.1 Chipmunk 22	A. R. Harding	
G-AOUR	D.H.82A Tiger Moth ★	Ulster Folk & Transport Museum	
G-AOVF	B.175 Britannia 312F ★	Aerospace Museum/Cosford	
G-AOVT	B.175 Britannia 312F ★	Duxford Aviation Soc	
G-AOVW	Auster 5	B. Marriott/Cranwell	
G-AOXL	See G-ANUO		
G-AOXN	D.H.82A Tiger Moth	S. L. G. Darch	
G-AOZH	D.H.82A Tiger Moth (K2572)	R. G. & G. J. Wheele/Shoreham	
G-AOZL	J/5Q Alpine	E. A. Taylor/Southend	
G-AOZP	D.H.C.1 Chipmunk 22	H. Darlington	
G-AOZU	D.H.C.1 Chipmunk 22A	R. H. Cooper & R. I. Vaughan	
G-APAA	J/5R Alpine ★	L. A. Groves (stored)	
G-APAF	Auster 5 (TW511)	J. E. Allen (G-CMAL)	
G-APAH	Auster 5	Cumbernauld Cubbers	
G-APAL	D.H.82A Tiger Moth (N6847)	P. S. & R. A. Chapman	
G-APAM	D.H.82A Tiger Moth	R. P. Williams	
G-APAO	D.H.82A Tiger Moth	Clacton Aero Club (1988) Ltd	
G-APAP	D.H.82A Tiger Moth	J. Romain/Duxford	
G-APAS	D.H.106 Comet 1XB ★	Aerospace Museum/Cosford	
G-APBE	Auster 5	J. McCullough	
G-APBI	D.H.82A Tiger Moth (EM903)	R. Devaney & ptnrs/Audley End	
G-APBO	D.53 Turbi	R. C. Hibberd	
G-APBW	Auster 5	N. Huxtable	

Notes	Reg.	Type	Owner or Operator
	G-APCB	J/5Q Alpine	A. A. Beswick & I. A. Freeman
	G-APCC	D.H.82A Tiger Moth	L. J. Rice/Henstridge
	G-APDB	D.H.106 Comet 4 ★	Duxford Aviation Soc
	G-APEG	V.953C Merchantman ★	Airport Fire Service/E. Midlands
	G-APEP	V.953C Merchantman ★	Brooklands Museum of Aviation/Weybridge
	G-APES	V.953C Merchantman ★	–/E. Midlands
	G-APEY	V.806 Viscount	British World Airlines Ltd/Southend
	G-APFA	D.54 Turbi	A. Eastelow & F. J. Keitch/Dunkeswell
	G-APFG	Boeing 707-436 ★	Cabin water spray tests/Cardington
	G-APFJ	Boeing 707-436 ★	Aerospace Museum/Cosford
	G-APFU	D.H.82A Tiger Moth	Mithril Racing Ltd/Goodwood
	G-APGL	D.H.82A Tiger Moth	K. A. Broomfield
	G-APHV	Avro 19 Srs 2 (VM360) ★	Museum of Flight/E. Fortune
	G-APIE	Tipsy Belfair B	D. Beale
	G-APIH	D.H.82A Tiger Moth	K. Stewering
	G-APIK	J/1N Alpha	N. D. Voce
	G-APIM	V.806 Viscount ★	Brooklands Museum of Aviation/Weybridge
	G-APIT	P.40 Prentice 1 (VR192) ★	WWII Aircraft Preservation Soc/Lasham
	G-APIU	P.40 Prentice 1 ★	J. F. Coggins/Coventry
	G-APIY	P.40 Prentice 1 (VR249) ★	Newark Air Museum
	G-APIZ	D.31 Turbulent	M. J. Whatley/White Waltham
	G-APJB	P.40 Prentice 1 (VR259)	Atlantic Air Transport Ltd/Coventry
	G-APJJ	Fairey Ultra-light ★	Midland Aircraft Preservation Soc
	G-APJO	D.H.82A Tiger Moth	D. R. & M. Wood
	G-APJZ	J/1N Alpha	P. G. Lipman
	G-APKH	D.H.85 Leopard Moth	R. G. Grocott (G-ACGS)
	G-APKM	J/1N Alpha	D. E. A. Huggins (stored)
	G-APKN	J/1N Alpha	P. R. Hodson Ltd
	G-APKY	Hiller UH-12B	D. A. George (stored)
	G-APLG	J/5L Aiglet Trainer	G. R. W. Brown
	G-APLO	D.H.C.1 Chipmunk 22A (WD379)	Lindholme Aircraft Ltd/Jersey
	G-APLU	D.H.82A Tiger Moth	R. A. Bishop & M. E. Vaisey
	G-APMB	D.H.106 Comet 4B ★	Gatwick Handling Ltd (ground trainer)
	G-APMH	J/1U Workmaster	J. L. Thorogood
	G-APML	Douglas C-47B	Air Atlantique Ltd/Coventry
	G-APMX	D.H.82A Tiger Moth	G. A. Broughton
	G-APMY	PA-23 Apache 160 ★	NE Wales Institute of Higher Education *(instructional airframe)*/Clwyd
	G-APNJ	Cessna 310 ★	Chelsea College/Shoreham
	G-APNS	Garland-Bianchi Linnet	Paul Penn-Sayers Model Services Ltd
	G-APNT	Currie Wot	J. W. Salter
	G-APNZ	D.31 Turbulent	J. Knight
	G-APOD	Tipsy Belfair	L. F. Potts
	G-APOI	Saro Skeeter Srs 8 ★	–
	G-APOL	D.31 Turbulent	A. Gregori & S. Tinker
	G-APPA	D.H.C.1 ChipMmunk 22	I. R. Young/Glasgow
	G-APPL	P.40 Prentice 1	S. J. Saggers/Biggin Hill
	G-APPM	D.H.C.1 Chipmunk 22	Freston Aviation Ltd
	G-APPN	D.H.82A Tiger Moth	E. C. Waite-Roberts
	G-APRF	Auster 5	J. T. & J. R. Sime
	G-APRJ	Avro 694 Lincoln B.2 ★	Aces High Ltd/North Weald
	G-APRL	AW.650 Argosy 101 ★	Midland Air Museum/Coventry
	G-APRR	Super Aero 45	R. H. Jowett
	G-APRS	SA. Twin Pioneer 3	Bravo Aviation Ltd (G-BCWF)
	G-APRT	Taylor JT.1 Monoplane	M. J. Snelling
	G-APSA	Douglas DC-6A	Instone Air Line Ltd/Coventry
	G-APSO	D.H.104 Dove 5	C. R. Hardiman/Shobdon
	G-APSR	J/1U Workmaster	D. & K. Aero Services Ltd/Shobdon
	G-APTP	PA-22 Tri-Pacer 150 (tailwheel)	Contest (Ralph & Susan Chesters) Ltd
	G-APTR	J/1N Alpha	C. J. & D. J. Baker
	G-APTU	Auster 5	G-APTU Flying Group
	G-APTW	W.B.1 Widgeon ★	N.E. Aircraft Museum/Usworth
	G-APTY	Beech G.35 Bonanza	G. E. Brennand & ptnrs
	G-APTZ	D.31 Turbulent	The Tiger Club (1990) Ltd/Headcorn
	G-APUD	Bensen B.7M (modified) ★	Manchester Museum of Science & Industry
	G-APUE	L.40 Meta Sokol	S. E. & M. J. Aherne
	G-APUP	Sopwith Pup (replica) (N5182) ★	RAF Museum/Hendon
	G-APUR	PA-22 Tri-Pacer 160	P. J. Hewitt
	G-APUW	J/5V-160 Autocar	Anglia Auster Syndicate
	G-APUY	D.31 Turbulent	C. Jones/Barton
	G-APUZ	PA-24 Comanche 250	D. Bottomley/Sandown
	G-APVF	Putzer Elster B (97+04)	A. J. Robinson
	G-APVG	J/5L Aiglet Trainer	C. M. Daggett/Cranfield

Reg.	Type	Owner or Operator	Notes
G-APVN	D.31 Turbulent	R. Sherwin/Shoreham	
G-APVS	Cessna 170B	N. Simpson	
G-APVU	L.40 Meta Sokol	S. E. & M. J. Aherne	
G-APVZ	D.31 Turbulent	M. J. A. Trudgill	
G-APWA	HPR-7 Herald 101 ★	Museum of Berkshire Aviation/Woodley	
G-APWJ	HPR-7 Herald 201 ★	Duxford Aviation Soc	
G-APWL	EoN 460 Srs 1A	A. J. Langdon & R. A. Munday	
G-APWN	WS-55 Whirlwind 3 ★	Midland Air Museum	
G-APWY	Piaggio P.166 ★	Science Museum/Wroughton	
G-APWZ	EP.9 Prospector	Prospector Flying Group	
G-APXJ	PA-24 Comanche 250	T. Wildsmith/Netherthorpe	
G-APXR	PA-22 Tri-Pacer 160	A. Troughton	
G-APXT	PA-22 Tri-Pacer 150 (modified)	J. W. & I. Daniels	
G-APXU	PA-22 Tri-Pacer 125	K. Hassall	
G-APXW	EP.9 Prospector (XM819) ★	Museum of Army Flying/Middle Wallop	
G-APXX	D.H.A.3 Drover 2 (VH-FDT) ★	WWII Aircraft Preservation Soc/Lasham	
G-APXY	Cessna 150	Merlin Flying Club Ltd/Hucknall	
G-APYB	Tipsy T.66 Nipper 3	B. O. Smith	
G-APYD	D.H.106 Comet 4B ★	Science Museum/Wroughton	
G-APYG	D.H.C.1 Chipmunk 22	E. J. I. Musty & P. A. Colman	
G-APYI	PA-22 Tri-Pacer 135	B. T. & J. Cullen	
G-APYN	PA-22 Tri-Pacer 160	S. J. Raw	
G-APYT	Champion 7FC Tri-Traveller	B. J. Anning	
G-APZJ	PA-18 Super Cub 150	Southern Sailplanes/Membury	
G-APZL	PA-22 Tri-Pacer 160	R. T. Evans	
G-APZR	Cessna 150 ★	*Engine test-bed*/Biggin Hill	
G-APZS	Cessna 175A	G. A. Nash/Booker	
G-APZX	PA-22 Tri-Pacer 150	Applied Signs Ltd	
G-ARAD	Luton LA-5A Major	D. J. Bone & P. L. Jobes	
G-ARAI	PA-22 Tri-Pacer 160	T. Richards & G. C. Winters	
G-ARAM	PA-18 Super Cub 150	Clacton Aero Club (1988) Ltd	
G-ARAN	PA-18 Super Cub 150	A. P. Docherty/Redhill	
G-ARAO	PA-18 Super Cub 95 (607327)	R. G. Manton	
G-ARAS	Champion 7FC Tri-Traveller	Clipgate Flying Group	
G-ARAT	Cessna 180C	S. Peck	
G-ARAW	Cessna 182C Skylane	P. Channon	
G-ARAX	PA-22 Tri-Pacer 150	P. J. Fahie	
G-ARAZ	D.H.82A Tiger Moth	S. G. North	
G-ARBE	D.H.104 Dove 8	M. Whale & M. W. A. Lunn/Old Sarum	
G-ARBG	Tipsy T.66 Nipper 2	J. Horovitz & J. McLeod	
G-ARBM	J/1B Aiglet	B. V. Nabbs & C. Chaddock	
G-ARBO	PA-24 Comanche 250	D. M. Harbottle & I. S. Graham/Goodwood	
G-ARBP	Tipsy T.66 Nipper 2	F. W. Kirk	
G-ARBS	PA-22 Tri-Pacer 160 (tailwheel)	S. D. Rowell	
G-ARBV	PA-22 Tri-Pacer 160	The Oaksey Pacers	
G-ARBZ	D.31 Turbulent	J. Mickleburgh	
G-ARCC	PA-22 Tri-Pacer 150	Popham Flying Group/Popham	
G-ARCF	PA-22 Tri-Pacer 150	B. Southerland	
G-ARCS	Auster D6/180	E. A. Matty/Shobdon	
G-ARCT	PA-18 Super Cub 95	K. A. Kirk & C. M. Goodwin	
G-ARCV	Cessna 175A	R. Francis & C. Campbell	
G-ARCW	PA-23 Apache 160	D. R. C. Reeves	
G-ARCX	A.W. Meteor 14 ★	Museum of Flight/E. Fortune	
G-ARDB	PA-24 Comanche 250	Delta Bravo Aircraft Associates/Booker	
G-ARDD	CP.301C1 Emeraude	R. M. Shipp	
G-ARDE	D.H.104 Dove 6	A. J. Corr & T. E. Evans	
G-ARDG	EP.9 Prospector ★	Museum of Army Flying/Middle Wallop	
G-ARDJ	Auster D.6/180	RN Aviation (Leicester Airport) Ltd	
G-ARDO	Jodel D.112	W. R. Prescott	
G-ARDP	PA-22 Tri-Pacer 150	G. M. Jones	
G-ARDS	PA-22 Caribbean 150	A. C. Donaldson & C. I. Lavery	
G-ARDT	PA-22 Tri-Pacer 160	M. Henderson	
G-ARDV	PA-22 Tri-Pacer 160	G. L. Brown	
G-ARDY	Tipsy T.66 Nipper 2	I. D. Daniels	
G-ARDZ	Jodel D.140A	M. J. Wright	
G-AREA	D.H.104 Dove 8 ★	Mosquito Aircraft Museum	
G-AREB	Cessna 175B Skylark	R. J. Postlethwaite & ptnrs/Wellesbourne	
G-AREF	PA-23 Aztec 250 ★	Southall College of Technology	
G-AREH	D.H.82A Tiger Moth	N. K. Geddes	
G-AREI	Auster 3 (MT438)	P. J. Stock	
G-AREL	PA-22 Caribbean 150	H. H. Cousins/Fenland	
G-AREO	PA-18 Super Cub 150	DRA (Farnborough) Gliding Club Ltd	

Notes	Reg.	Type	Owner or Operator
	G-ARET	PA-22 Tri-Pacer 160	I. S. Runnalls
	G-AREV	PA-22 Tri-Pacer 160	Spatrek Ltd/Barton
	G-AREX	Aeronca 15AC Sedan	R. J. Middleton-Turnbull & P. Lowndes
	G-AREZ	D.31 Turbulent	J. St. Clair-Quentin/Shobdon
	G-ARFB	PA-22 Caribbean 150	C. T. Woodward & ptnrs
	G-ARFD	PA-22 Tri-Pacer 160	J. R. Dunnett
	G-ARFG	Cessna 175A Skylark	Foxtrot Golf Group
	G-ARFH	PA-24 Comanche 250	L. M. Walton
	G-ARFI	Cessna 150A	J. H. Fisher
	G-ARFL	Cessna 175B Skylark	D. J. Mason
	G-ARFN	Cessna 150A ★	*Instructional airframe*/Perth
	G-ARFO	Cessna 150A	Tindon Ltd/Little Snoring
	G-ARFT	Jodel DR. 1050	R. Shaw
	G-ARFV	Tipsy T.66 Nipper 2	C. G. Stone/Biggin Hill
	G-ARGB	Auster 6A ★	C. J. Baker *(stored)*
	G-ARGG	D.H.C.1 Chipmunk 22 (WD305)	B. Hook
	G-ARGO	PA-22 Colt 108	B. E. Goodman/Liverpool
	G-ARGV	PA-18 Super Cub 180	Deeside Gliding Club (Aberdeenshire) Ltd/ Aboyne
	G-ARGY	PA-22 Tri-Pacer 160	G. K. Hare (G-JEST)
	G-ARGZ	D.31 Turbulent	J. C. Mansell
	G-ARHB	Forney F-1A Aircoupe	A. V. Rash & D. R. Wickes
	G-ARHC	Forney F-1A Aircoupe	A. P. Gardner/Elstree
	G-ARHI	PA-24 Comanche 180	D. D. Smith
	G-ARHL	PA-23 Aztec 250	C. J. Freeman/Headcorn
	G-ARHM	Auster 6A	D. Hollowell & ptnrs/Finmere
	G-ARHN	PA-22 Caribbean 150	D. B. Furniss & A. Munro/Doncaster
	G-ARHP	PA-22 Tri-Pacer 160	R. N. Morgan
	G-ARHR	PA-22 Caribbean 150	C. C. Wagner
	G-ARHT	PA-22 Caribbean 150 ★	Moston Technical College
	G-ARHU	PA-22 Tri-Pacer 160	B. L. Newbold & H. Streets
	G-ARHW	D.H.104 Dove 8	Pacelink Ltd
	G-ARHX	D.H.104 Dove 8 ★	N.E. Aircraft Museum/Usworth
	G-ARHZ	D.62 Condor	T. J. Goodwin/Andrewsfield
	G-ARID	Cessna 172B	L. M. Edwards
	G-ARIE	PA-24 Comanche 250	The Com Group
	G-ARIF	Ord-Hume O-H.7 Minor Coupé	N. H. Ponsford *(stored)*
	G-ARIH	Auster 6A (TW591)	India Hotel Group
	G-ARIK	PA-22 Caribbean 150	C. J. Berry
	G-ARIL	PA-22 Caribbean 150	K. Knight
	G-ARIM	D.31 Turbulent	A. Gregori
	G-ARJB	D.H.104 Dove 8	Cormack (Aircraft Services) Ltd
	G-ARJC	PA-22 Colt 108	F. W. H. Dulles
	G-ARJE	PA-22 Colt 108	Touchdown Aviation Ltd
	G-ARJF	PA-22 Colt 108	M. J. Collins
	G-ARJH	PA-22 Colt 108	A. Vine
	G-ARJR	PA-23 Apache 160G ★	*Instructional airframe*/Kidlington
	G-ARJS	PA-23 Apache 160G	Bencray Ltd/Blackpool
	G-ARJT'	PA-23 Apache 160G	Hiveland Ltd
	G-ARJU	PA-23 Apache 160G	G. R. Manley
	G-ARJV	PA-23 Apache 160G	Economic Insulations Ltd
	G-ARJW	PA-23 Apache 160G	*stored*/Bristol
	G-ARJZ	D.31 Turbulent	C. J. Tilson
	G-ARKG	J/5G Autocar	C. M. Milborrow
	G-ARKJ	Beech N35 Bonanza	T. Cust
	G-ARKK	PA-22 Colt 108	Rochford Hundred Flying Group/Southend
	G-ARKM	PA-22 Colt 108	B. V. & E. A. Howes/Earls Colne
	G-ARKN	PA-22 Colt 108	R. A. & N. L. E. Dupee
	G-ARKP	PA-22 Colt 108	C. J. & J. Freeman/Headcorn
	G-ARKR	PA-22 Colt 108	B. J. M. Montegut
	G-ARKS	PA-22 Colt 108	R. A. Nesbitt-Dufort
	G-ARLG	Auster D.4/108	Auster D4 Group
	G-ARLK	PA-24 Comanche 250	Gibad Aviation Ltd
	G-ARLO	A.61 Terrier 1 ★	*stored*
	G-ARLP	A.61 Terrier 1	Gemini Flying Group
	G-ARLR	A.61 Terrier 2	M. J. Breeze
	G-ARLU	Cessna 172B Skyhawk ★	*Instructional airframe*/Irish AC
	G-ARLW	Cessna 172B Skyhawk ★	*(spares' source)*/Barton
	G-ARLX	Jodel D.140B	Shipping & Airlines Ltd/Biggin Hill
	G-ARLZ	D.31A Turbulent	Turb Group
	G-ARMA	PA-23 Apache 160G ★	*Instructional airframe*/Kidlington
	G-ARMB	D.H.C.1 Chipmunk 22A (WB660)	P. A. Layzell
	G-ARMC	D.H.C.1 Chipmunk 22A (WB703)	John Henderson Children's Trust

Reg.	Type	Owner or Operator	Notes
G-ARMD	D.H.C.1 Chipmunk 22A ★	K. & L. Aero Services (stored)	
G-ARMF	D.H.C.1 Chipmunk 22A (WZ868)	Chipmunk G-BCIW Syndicate	
G-ARMG	D.H.C.1 Chipmunk 22A	MG Group/Wellesbourne	
G-ARML	Cessna 175B Skylark	R. W. Boote	
G-ARMN	Cessna 175B Skylark	G. A. Nash	
G-ARMO	Cessna 172B Skyhawk	G. M. Jones	
G-ARMR	Cessna 172B Skyhawk	Sunsaver Ltd/Barton	
G-ARMZ	D.31 Turbulent	J. Mickleburgh & D. Clark	
G-ARNB	J/5G Autocar	R. F. Tolhurst	
G-ARND	PA-22 Colt 108	E. J. Clarke	
G-ARNE	PA-22 Colt 108	T. D. L. Bowden/Shipdham	
G-ARNG	PA-22 Colt 108	S. S. Delwarte/Shoreham	
G-ARNH	PA-22 Colt 108 ★	Fenland Aircraft Preservation Soc	
G-ARNI	PA-22 Colt 108	B. A. Drury	
G-ARNJ	PA-22 Colt 108	M. A. Vincent	
G-ARNK	PA-22 Colt 108 (tailwheel)	N. G. & A-L. N. M. McDonald	
G-ARNL	PA-22 Colt 108	J. A. Dodsworth/White Waltham	
G-ARNO	A.61 Terrier 1 ★	–/Sywell	
G-ARNP	A.109 Airedale	S. W. & M. Isbister	
G-ARNY	Jodel D.117	D. P. Jenkins	
G-ARNZ	D.31 Turbulent	The Tiger Club (1990) Ltd/Headcorn	
G-AROA	Cessna 172B Skyhawk	D. E. Partridge	
G-AROE	Aero 145	K. Plaza	
G-AROF	L.40 Meta-Sokol	G. D. H. Crawford	
G-AROJ	A.109 Airedale ★	D. J. Shaw (stored)	
G-ARON	PA-22 Colt 108	K. N. Stephens	
G-AROO	Forney F-1A Aircoupe	W. J. McMeekan/Newtownards	
G-AROW	Jodel D.140B	Cubair Ltd/Redhill	
G-AROY	Boeing Stearman A.75N.1	W. A. Jordan	
G-ARPH	H.S.121 Trident 1C ★	Aerospace Museum/Cosford	
G-ARPK	H.S.121 Trident 1C ★	Manchester Airport Authority	
G-ARPL	H.S.121 Trident 1C ★	BAA Airport Fire Service/Edinburgh	
G-ARPO	H.S.121 Trident 1C ★	CAA Fire School/Teesside	
G-ARPP	H.S.121 Trident 1C ★	BAA Airport Fire Service/Glasgow	
G-ARPX	H.S.121 Trident 1C ★	Air Service Training Ltd/Perth	
G-ARPZ	H.S.121 Trident 1C ★	RFD Ltd/Dunsfold	
G-ARRD	Jodel DR.1050	C. M. Fitton	
G-ARRE	Jodel DR.1050	A. Luty & M. P. Edwards/Barton	
G-ARRF	Cessna 150A	Electrical Engineering Services	
G-ARRL	J/1N Alpha	G. N. Smith & C. Webb	
G-ARRM	Beagle B.206-X ★	(stored) Bristol Aero Collection	
G-ARRS	CP.301A Emeraude	M. J. A. Trudgill	
G-ARRT	Wallis WA-116-1	K. H. Wallis	
G-ARRU	D.31 Turbulent	N. A. Morgan & J. Paget	
G-ARRX	Auster 6A (VF512)	J. E. D. Mackie	
G-ARRY	Jodel D.140B	Fictionview Ltd	
G-ARRZ	D.31 Turbulent	C. I. Jefferson	
G-ARSG	Roe Triplane Type IV (replica)	The Shuttleworth Collection/O. Warden	
G-ARSJ	CP.301-C2 Emeraude	R. J. Lewis	
G-ARSL	A.61 Terrier 1	D. J. Colclough	
G-ARSU	PA-22 Colt 108	D. P. Owen	
G-ARSW	PA-22 Colt 108	M. J. Kirk	
G-ARSX	PA-22 Tri-Pacer 160	S. Hutchinson	
G-ARTD	PA-23 Apache 160	D. A. Jones/Caernarfon	
G-ARTH	PA-12 Super Cruiser	R. I. Souch & B. J. Dunford	
G-ARTJ	Bensen B.8M ★	Museum of Flight/E. Fortune	
G-ARTL	D.H.82A Tiger Moth (T7281)	F. G. Clacherty	
G-ARTT	M.S.880B Rallye Club	R. N. Scott	
G-ARTZ	McCandless M.4 gyroplane		
G-ARUG	J/5G Autocar	D. P. H. Hulme/Biggin Hill	
G-ARUH	Jodel DR.1050	PFA Group/Denham	
G-ARUI	A.61 Terrier	A. C. Ladd	
G-ARUL	LeVier Cosmic Wind	P. G. Kynsey/Headcorn	
G-ARUO	PA-24 Comanche 180	Uniform Oscar Group	
G-ARUV	CP.301A Emeraude	J. F. Sully & ptnrs	
G-ARUY	J/1N Alpha	Gullwing Aviation Ltd/Headcorn	
G-ARUZ	Cessna 175C	Cardiff Skylark Group	
G-ARVM	V.1101 VC10 ★	Aerospace Museum/Cosford	
G-ARVO	PA-18 Super Cub 95	Deltair Ltd	
G-ARVS	PA-28 Cherokee 160	M. & K. Harper	
G-ARVT	PA-28 Cherokee 160	Red Rose Aviation Ltd/Liverpool	
G-ARVU	PA-28 Cherokee 160	G-ARVU Flying Group	
G-ARVV	PA-28 Cherokee 160	G. E. Hopkins/Shobdon	

Notes	Reg.	Type	Owner or Operator
	G-ARVZ	D.62B Condor	J. D. Jewitt
	G-ARWB	D.H.C.1 Chipmunk 22 (WK611)	Thruxton Chipmunk Flying Club
	G-ARWH	Cessna 172C ★	*stored*
	G-ARWO	Cessna 172C	J. P. Stafford
	G-ARWR	Cessna 172C	Devanha Flying Group
	G-ARWS	Cessna 175C	E. N. Skinner & P. F. N. Burrow
	G-ARXD	A.109 Airedale	D. Howden
	G-ARXG	PA-24 Comanche 250	P. & H. Robinson
	G-ARXH	Bell 47G	A. B. Searle
	G-ARXP	Luton LA-4 Minor	E. Evans
	G-ARXT	Jodel DR.1050	CJM Flying Group
	G-ARXU	Auster AOP.6A (VF526)	E. C. Tait & M. Pocock
	G-ARXW	M.S.885 Super Rallye	A. F. Danton & A. Kennedy
	G-ARYB	H.S.125 Srs 1 ★	Midland Air Museum/Coventry
	G-ARYC	H.S.125 Srs 1 ★	The Mosquito Aircraft Museum
	G-ARYD	Auster AOP.6 ★	Museum of Army Flying/Middle Wallop
	G-ARYF	PA-23 Aztec 250B	I. J. T. Branson/Biggin Hill
	G-ARYH	PA-22 Tri-Pacer 160	C. Watt
	G-ARYI	Cessna 172C	J. Rhodes
	G-ARYK	Cessna 172C	Thermodata Components
	G-ARYR	PA-28 Cherokee 180	G-ARYR Flying Group
	G-ARYS	Cessna 172C	Squires Gear & Engineering Ltd
	G-ARYV	PA-24 Comanche 250	Ilford Business Machines Ltd
	G-ARYZ	A.109 Airedale	Rutland Aviation
	G-ARZB	Wallis WA-116 Srs 1	K. H. Wallis
	G-ARZE	Cessna 172C ★	*Parachute jump trainer*/Cockerham
	G-ARZM	D.31 Turbulent ★	The Tiger Club (1990) Ltd/Headcorn
	G-ARZN	Beech N35 Bonanza	D. W. Micleburgh/Leicester
	G-ARZW	Currie Wot	B. R. Pearson/Eaglescott
	G-ARZX	Cessna 150B	Gate Flyers/Manston
	G-ASAA	Luton LA-4 Minor	J. W. Cudby
	G-ASAI	A.109 Airedale	K. R. Howden & ptnrs
	G-ASAJ	A.61 Terrier 2 (WE569)	G-ASAJ Flying Group
	G-ASAK	A.61 Terrier 2	J. H. Oakins/Biggin Hill
	G-ASAL	SA Bulldog Srs 120/124	Pioneer Flying Co. Ltd/Prestwick
	G-ASAM	D.31 Turbulent ★	The Tiger Club (1990) Ltd/Headcorn
	G-ASAN	A.61 Terrier 2	R. J. Bentley
	G-ASAT	M.S.880B Rallye Club	M. Cutovic
	G-ASAU	M.S.880B Rallye Club	T. C. & R. Edwards
	G-ASAX	A.61 Terrier 2	P. G. & F. M. Morris
	G-ASAZ	Hiller UH-12E4 (XS165)	Pan-Air Ltd/North Weald
	G-ASBA	Currie Wot	M. A. Kaye
	G-ASBB	Beech 23 Musketeer	Five Musketeers Flying Group/Bourn
	G-ASBH	A.109 Airedale	D. T. Smollett
	G-ASBY	A.109 Airedale	M. R. H. Wheatley & R. K. Wilson
	G-ASCC	Beagle E3 Mk 11 (XP254)	K. R. Harris
	G-ASCD	A.61 Terrier 2 (TJ704) ★	Yorkshire Air Museum/Elvington
	G-ASCM	Isaacs Fury II (K2050)	M. M. Ward
	G-ASCU	PA-18A Super Cub 150	Farm Aviation Services Ltd
	G-ASCZ	CP.301A Emeraude	I. Denham-Brown
	G-ASDF	Edwards Gyrocopter ★	B. King
	G-ASDK	A.61 Terrier 2	M. L. Rose
	G-ASDL	A.61 Terrier 2	C. E. Mason
	G-ASDO	Beech 95-A55 Baron ★	No 2498 Sqn ATC/Jersey
	G-ASDY	Wallis WA-116/F	K. H. Wallis
	G-ASEA	Luton LA-4A Minor	J. Bradstock
	G-ASEB	Luton LA-4A Minor	S. R. P. Harper
	G-ASEG	A.61 Terrier (VF548)	M. J. Kirk
	G-ASEO	PA-24 Comanche 250	Planetalk Ltd
	G-ASEP	PA-23 Apache 235	Arrowstate Ltd/Denham
	G-ASEU	D.62A Condor	W. M. Grant
	G-ASFA	Cessna 172D	D. Halfpenny
	G-ASFD	L-200A Morava	M. Emery/Bournemouth
	G-ASFK	J/5G Autocar	A. I. Milne/Swanton Morley
	G-ASFL	PA-28 Cherokee 180	P. Stoyle
	G-ASFR	Bo 208A1 Junior	S. T. Dauncey
	G-ASFX	D.31 Turbulent	E. F. Clapham & W. B. S. Dobie
	G-ASGC	V.1151 Super VC10 ★	Duxford Aviation Soc
	G-ASHD	Brantly B-2A ★	IHM/Weston-s-Mare
	G-ASHS	SNCAN Stampe SV-4C	Three Point Flying Ltd
	G-ASHT	D.31 Turbulent	C. W. N. Huke
	G-ASHU	PA-15 Vagabond	G. J. Romanes & T. J. Ventham/ Henstridge

Reg.	Type	Owner or Operator	Notes
G-ASHV	PA-23 Aztec 250B	R. J. Ashley & G. O'Gorman	
G-ASHX	PA-28 Cherokee 180	Powertheme Ltd/Barton	
G-ASIB	Cessna F.172D	G-ASIB Flying Group	
G-ASII	PA-28 Cherokee 180	T. R. Hart & Natocars Ltd	
G-ASIJ	PA-28 Cherokee 180	Precision Products Ltd & A. K. Hulme	
G-ASIL	PA-28 Cherokee 180	J. Dickenson & C. D. Powell	
G-ASIT	Cessna 180	A. & P. A. Wood	
G-ASIY	PA-25 Pawnee 235	RAFGSA/Bicester	
G-ASJL	Beech H.35 Bonanza	C. B. Ranald	
G-ASJM	PA-30 Twin Comanche 160 ★	Via Nova Ltd (stored)	
G-ASJO	Beech B.23 Musketeer	S. Boon/Sandown	
G-ASJV	V.S.361 Spitfire IX (MH434)	Nalfire Aviation Ltd/Duxford	
G-ASJY	GY-80 Horizon 160	A. H. Wooffindin	
G-ASJZ	Jodel D.117A	P. J. & M. Edwards	
G-ASKC	D.H.98 Mosquito 35 (TA719) ★	Skyfame Collection/Duxford	
G-ASKJ	A.61 Terrier 1 (VX926)	C. C. Irvine	
G-ASKK	HPR-7 Herald 211 ★	Norwich Aviation Museum	
G-ASKL	Jodel 150	J. M. Graty	
G-ASKP	D.H.82A Tiger Moth	Tiger Club (1990) Ltd/Headcorn	
G-ASKT	PA-28 Cherokee 180	A. A. Mattacks	
G-ASKV	PA-25 Pawnee 235	Southdown Gliding Club Ltd	
G-ASLH	Cessna 182F	J. M. Powell & J. A. Horton	
G-ASLK	PA-25 Pawnee 235	Bristol Gliding Club (Pty) Ltd/Nympsfield	
G-ASLL	Cessna 336 ★	(stored)/Bournemouth	
G-ASLR	Agusta-Bell 47J-2	N. M. G. Pearson	
G-ASLV	PA-28 Cherokee 235	Sackville Flying Group/Riseley	
G-ASLX	CP.301A Emeraude	D. Wallace	
G-ASMA	PA-30 Twin Comanche 160 C/R	B. D. Glynn/Redhill	
G-ASME	Bensen B.8M	R. M. Harris & R. T. Bennett	
G-ASMF	Beech D.95A Travel Air	M. J. A. Hornblower	
G-ASMJ	Cessna F.172E	A. J. G. Crawshaw	
G-ASML	Luton LA-4A Minor	Fenland Strut Flying Group	
G-ASMM	D.31 Tubulent	G. E. Arthur	
G-ASMO	PA-23 Apache 160G ★	Aviation Enterprises/Fairoaks	
G-ASMS	Cessna 150A	A. K. Jones	
G-ASMT	Fairtravel Linnet 2	A. F. Cashin	
G-ASMV	CP.1310-C3 Super Emeraude	P. F. D. Waltham/Leicester	
G-ASMW	Cessna 150D	Yorkshire Light Aircraft Ltd/Leeds	
G-ASMY	PA-23 Apache 160H	R. D. & E. Forster	
G-ASMZ	A.61 Terrier 2 (VF516)	R. C. Burden	
G-ASNB	Auster 6A (VX118)	M. J. Miller & G. Hengeveld	
G-ASNC	Beagle D.5/180 Husky	Peterborough & Spalding Gliding Club/ Boston	
G-ASND	PA-23 Aztec 250	M. Gardner	
G-ASNF	Ercoupe 415CD	C. R. Weldon	
G-ASNH	PA-23 Aztec 250B	J. Hoerner & The Earl of Suffolk & Berkshire	
G-ASNI	CP.1310-C3 Super Emeraude	D. Chapman	
G-ASNK	Cessna 205	Justgold Ltd	
G-ASNN	Cessna 182F ★	(Parachute jump trainer)/Tilstock	
G-ASNW	Cessna F.172E	G-ASNW Group	
G-ASOC	Auster 6A	D. J. Moore	
G-ASOH	Beech 95-B55A Baron	GMD Group	
G-ASOI	A.61 Terrier 2	N. K. & C. M. Geddes	
G-ASOK	Cessna F.172E	Okay Flying Group/Denham	
G-ASOM	A.61 Terrier 2	S. J. Tootell (G-JETS)	
G-ASOX	Cessna 205A	A. Turnbull	
G-ASPF	Jodel D.120	T. J. Bates	
G-ASPI	Cessna F.172E	Icarus Flying Group/Rochester	
G-ASPK	PA-28 Cherokee 140	Westward Airways (Lands End) Ltd/St Just	
G-ASPP	Bristol Boxkite (replica)	The Shuttleworth Collection/O. Warden	
G-ASPS	Piper J-3C-90 Cub	A. J. Chalkley/Blackbushe	
G-ASPU	D.31 Turbulent	C. R. Steer	
G-ASPV	D.H.82A Tiger Moth	B. S. Charters/Shipdham	
G-ASRB	D.62B Condor	T. J. McRae & H. C. Palmer/Shoreham	
G-ASRC	D.62C Condor	O. R. Pluck	
G-ASRH	PA-30 Twin Comanche 160	Island Aviation & Travel Ltd	
G-ASRI	PA-23 Aztec 250B ★	Graham Collins Associates Ltd	
G-ASRK	A.109 Airedale	R. K. Wilson & M. R. H. Wheatley	
G-ASRO	PA-30 Twin Comanche 160	D. W. Blake	
G-ASRR	Cessna 182G	J. A. Rees	
G-ASRT	Jodel 150	P. Turton	
G-ASRW	PA-28 Cherokee 180	R. J. Keyte	

Notes	Reg.	Type	Owner or Operator
	G-ASSE	PA-22 Colt 108	S. J. Gane
	G-ASSF	Cessna 182G Skylane	B. W. Wells
	G-ASSM	H.S.125 Srs 1/522 ★	Science Museum/S. Kensington
	G-ASSP	PA-30 Twin Comanche 160	P. H. Tavener
	G-ASSS	Cessna 172E	D. H. N. Squires & P. R. March/Bristol
	G-ASST	Cessna 150D	F. R. H. Parker
	G-ASSU	CP.301A Emeraude	R. W. Millward (stored)/Redhill
	G-ASSV	Kensinger KF	C. I. Jefferson
	G-ASSW	PA-28 Cherokee 140	W. G. R. Wunderlich/Biggin Hill
	G-ASTA	D.31 Turbulent	P. A. Cooke
	G-ASTH	Mooney M.20C ★	E. L. Martin (stored)/Guernsey
	G-ASTI	Auster 6A	Islanders Gliding Club Ltd
	G-ASTL	Fairey Firefly I (DK431) ★	Skyfame Collection/Duxford
	G-ASTP	Hiller UH-12C ★	IHM/Weston-s-Mare
	G-ASTV	Cessna 150D (tailwheel) ★	stored
	G-ASUB	Mooney M.20E Super 21	S. C. Coulbeck
	G-ASUD	PA-28 Cherokee 180	S. J. Rogers & M. N. Petchey
	G-ASUE	Cessna 150D	D. Huckle/Panshanger
	G-ASUG	Beech E18S ★	Museum of Flight/E. Fortune
	G-ASUI	A.61 Terrier 2	K. W. Chigwell & D. R. Lee
	G-ASUL	Cessna 182G Skylane	Blackpool & Fylde Aero Club Ltd
	G-ASUP	Cessna F.172E	GASUP Air/Cardiff
	G-ASUR	Dornier Do 28A-1	Sheffair Ltd
	G-ASUS	Jurca MJ.2B Tempete	D. G. Jones/Coventry
	G-ASVG	CP.301B Emeraude	K. R. Jackson
	G-ASVM	Cessna F.172E	GATRL Flying Group
	G-ASVN	Cessna U.206 Super Skywagon	L. Rawson
	G-ASVO	HPR-7 Herald 214	Channel Express (Air Services) Ltd/ Bournemouth
	G-ASVP	PA-25 Pawnee 235	Aquila Gliding Club Ltd
	G-ASVZ	PA-28 Cherokee 140	J. H. Mitchell & A. W. Parker
	G-ASWB	A.109 Airedale	A. E. F. Bryant
	G-ASWH	Luton LA-5A Major	J. T. Powell-Tuck
	G-ASWJ	Beagle 206 Srs 1 (8449M) ★	Brunel Technical College/Bristol
	G-ASWL	Cessna F.172F	Bagby Aviation Flying Group
	G-ASWN	Bensen B.8M	D. R. Shepherd
	G-ASWP	Beech A.23 Musketeer	J. Holdon & G. Benet
	G-ASWW	PA-30 Twin Comanche 160	R. J. Motors
	G-ASWX	PA-28 Cherokee 180	A. F. Dadds
	G-ASXC	SIPA 901	M. K. Dartford & M. Cookson
	G-ASXD	Brantly B.2B	Lousada PLC
	G-ASXI	Tipsy T.66 Nipper 3	K. D. Pearce
	G-ASXJ	Luton LA-4A Minor	M. R. Sallows
	G-ASXR	Cessna 210	A. Schofield
	G-ASXS	Jodel DR.1050	R. A. Hunter
	G-ASXU	Jodel D.120A	The Jodel Group Defford
	G-ASXX	Avro 683 Lancaster 7 (NX611) ★	Lincolnshire Aviation Heritage Centre/ E. Kirkby
	G-ASXY	Jodel D.117A	P. A. Davies & ptnrs/Cardiff
	G-ASXZ	Cessna 182G Skylane	P. M. Robertson/Perth
	G-ASYD	BAC One-Eleven 475 ★	Brooklands Museum of Aviation/ Weybridge
	G-ASYG	A.61 Terrier 2	G. Rea
	G-ASYJ	Beech D.95A Travel Air	Crosby Aviation (Jersey) Ltd
	G-ASYP	Cessna 150E	Henlow Flying Group
	G-ASYW	Bell 47G-2	Helisport Ltd/Biggin Hill
	G-ASYZ	Victa Airtourer 100	N. C. Grayson
	G-ASZB	Cessna 150E	W. A. Smale/Exeter
	G-ASZD	Bo 208A2 Junior	A. J. Watson & M. J. Ayers
	G-ASZE	A.61 Terrier 2	P. J. Moore
	G-ASZJ	S.C.7 Skyvan 3A-100	GEC Marconi Ltd/Luton
	G-ASZR	Fairtravel Linnet 2	Shoreham Linnet Group
	G-ASZS	GY.80 Horizon 160	ZS Group
	G-ASZU	Cessna 150E	T. H. Milburn
	G-ASZV	Tipsy T.66 Nipper 2	R. L. Mitcham/Elstree
	G-ASZX	A.61 Terrier 1	C. A. Bailey
	G-ATAF	Cessna F.172F	N. C. R. Jackson & M. D. Lenney
	G-ATAG	Jodel DR. 1050	T. M. Dawes-Gamble
	G-ATAS	PA-28 Cherokee 180	E. J. Titterrell
	G-ATAT	Cessna 150E	The Derek Pointon Group (stored)
	G-ATAU	D.62B Condor	M. A. Peare/Redhill
	G-ATAV	D.62C Condor	R. W. H. Watson

Reg.	Type	Owner or Operator	Notes
G-ATBG	Nord 1002 (NJ+C11)	L. M. Walton/Duxford	
G-ATBH	Aero 145	P. D. Aberbach	
G-ATBI	Beech A.23 Musketeer	R. F. G. Dent/Staverton	
G-ATBJ	Sikorsky S-61N	Brintel Helicopters	
G-ATBL	D.H.60G Moth	J. M. Greenland	
G-ATBP	Fournier RF-3	D. McNicholl	
G-ATBS	D.31 Turbulent	D. R. Keene & J. A. Lear	
G-ATBU	A.61 Terrier 2	P. R. Anderson	
G-ATBW	Tipsy T.66 Nipper 2	Stapleford Nipper Group	
G-ATBX	PA-20 Pacer 135	G. D. & P. M. Thomson	
G-ATBZ	W.S.58 Wessex 60 ★	IHM/Weston-s-Mare	
G-ATCC	A.109 Airedale	J. R. Bowden	
G-ATCD	Beagle D.5/180 Husky	Oxford Flying & Gliding Group/Enstone	
G-ATCE	Cessna U.206	J. Fletcher & D. Hickling/Langar	
G-ATCJ	Luton LA-4A Minor	D. P. Copse	
G-ATCL	Victa Airtourer 100	A. D. Goodall	
G-ATCN	Luton LA-4A Minor	J. C. Gates & C. Neilson	
G-ATCR	Cessna 310 ★	ITD Aviation Ltd/Denham	
G-ATCU	Cessna 337	University of Cambridge	
G-ATCX	Cessna 182H Skylane	K. J. Fisher/Bodmin	
G-ATDA	PA-28 Cherokee 160	S. A. Vale/Basle	
G-ATDB	Nord 1101 Noralpha	J. W. Hardie	
G-ATDN	A.61 Terrier 2 (TW641)	S. J. Saggers/Biggin Hill	
G-ATDO	Bo 208C1 Junior	H. Swift	
G-ATEF	Cessna 150E	Swans Aviation	
G-ATEM	PA-28 Cherokee 180	Chiltern Valley Aviation Ltd	
G-ATEP	EAA Biplane ★	E. L. Martin (stored)/Guernsey	
G-ATES	PA-32 Cherokee Six 260 ★	Parachute jump trainer/Stirling	
G-ATET	PA-30 Twin Comanche 160	R. Marsden & P. E. T. Price/Shobdon	
G-ATEV	Jodel DR. 1050	R. A. Smith	
G-ATEW	PA-30 Twin Comanche 160	Air Northumbria Group/Newcastle	
G-ATEX	Victa Airtourer 100	Medway Victa Group	
G-ATEZ	PA-28 Cherokee 140	J. A. Burton/E. Midlands	
G-ATFD	Jodel DR. 1050	V. Usher	
G-ATFF	PA-23 Aztec 250C	Neatspin Ltd	
G-ATFG	Brantly B.2B ★	Museum of Flight/E. Fortune	
G-ATFK	PA-30 Twin Comanche 160	D. J. Crinnon/White Waltham	
G-ATFM	Sikorsky S-61N	Brintel Helicopters	
G-ATFR	PA-25 Pawnee 150	Borders (Milfield) Gliding Club Ltd	
G-ATFU	D.H.85 Leopard Moth	A. de Cadenet	
G-ATFV	Agusta-Bell 47J-2A ★	Caernarfon Air World	
G-ATFW	Luton LA-4A Minor	P. C. Bird	
G-ATFY	Cessna F.172G	H. Cowan	
G-ATGE	Jodel DR.1050	J. R. Roberts	
G-ATGH	Brantly B.2B	Helihire Ltd	
G-ATGN	Thorn Coal Gas balloon	British Balloon Museum	
G-ATGO	Cessna F.172G	P. J. Spedding & M. Johnston	
G-ATGP	Jodel DR.1050	Madley Flying Group/Shobdon	
G-ATGY	GY.80 Horizon	P. W. Gibberson/Birmingham	
G-ATGZ	Griffiths GH-4 Gyroplane	R. W. J. Cripps	
G-ATHA	PA-23 Apache 235 ★	Brunel Technical College/Bristol	
G-ATHD	D.H.C.1 Chipmunk 22 (WP971)	Spartan Flying Group Ltd/Denham	
G-ATHF	Cessna 150F ★	Lincolnshire Aviation Heritage Centre/ E. Kirkby	
G-ATHK	Aeronca 7AC Champion	N. S. Chittenden	
G-ATHM	Wallis WA-116 Srs 1	Wallis Autogyros Ltd	
G-ATHN	Nord 1101 Noralpha ★	E. L. Martin (stored)/Guernsey	
G-ATHR	PA-28 Cherokee 180	Britannia Airways Ltd/Luton	
G-ATHT	Victa Airtourer 115	D. A. Breeze	
G-ATHU	A.61 Terrier 1	J. A. L. Irwin	
G-ATHV	Cessna 150F	D. Hutchinson	
G-ATHX	Jodel DR. 100A	Mourne Flying Club	
G-ATHZ	Cessna 150F	E. & R. D. Forster	
G-ATIA	PA-24 Comanche 260	L. A. Brown	
G-ATIC	Jodel DR.1050	R. J. Major	
G-ATID	Cessna 337	Harlow Investment Ltd/Portugal	
G-ATIE	Cessna 150F ★	Parachute jump trainer/Chetwynd	
G-ATIN	Jodel D.117	G. G. Simpson	
G-ATIR	AIA Stampe SV-4C	N. M. Bloom	
G-ATIS	PA-28 Cherokee 160	R. M. Jenner & J. H. Peploe	
G-ATIZ	Jodel D.117	D. K. Shipton/Leicester	
G-ATJA	Jodel DR.1050	Bicester Flying Group	
G-ATJC	Victa Airtourer 100	Aviation West Ltd/Cumbernauld	

Notes	Reg.	Type	Owner or Operator
	G-ATJG	PA-28 Cherokee 140	H. M. Wittman
	G-ATJL	PA-24 Comanche 260	M. J. Berry & T. R. Quinn/Blackbushe
	G-ATJM	Fokker Dr.1 (replica) (152/17)	R. Lamplough/Duxford
	G-ATJN	Jodel D.119	R. F. Bradshaw
	G-ATJT	GY.80 Horizon 160	N. Huxtable
	G-ATJV	PA-32 Cherokee Six 260	SMK Engineers Ltd
	G-ATKF	Cessna 150F	C. J. Freeman/Headcorn
	G-ATKH	Luton LA-4A Minor	H. E. Jenner
	G-ATKI	Piper J-3C-65 Cub	J. H. Allistone/Booker
	G-ATKT	Cessna F.172G	P. J. Megson
	G-ATKU	Cessna F.172G	Holdcroft Aviation Services Ltd
	G-ATKX	Jodel D.140C	A. J. White & G. A. Piper/Biggin Hill
	G-ATKZ	Tipsy T.66 Nipper 2	M. W. Knights
	G-ATLA	Cessna 182J Skylane	Shefford Transport Engineers Ltd/Luton
	G-ATLB	Jodel DR.1050/M1	La Petite Oiseau Syndicate/Breighton
	G-ATLC	PA-23 Aztec 250C ★	Alderney Air Charter Ltd *(stored)*
	G-ATLG	Hiller UH-12B	Bristow Helicopters Ltd
	G-ATLM	Cessna F.172G	Air Fotos Aviation Ltd/Newcastle
	G-ATLP	Bensen B.8M	C. D. Julian
	G-ATLT	Cessna U-206A	Activity Aviation Ltd/Perth
	G-ATLV	Jodel D.120	L. S. Thorne
	G-ATLW	PA-28 Cherokee 180	R. D. Masters
	G-ATMC	Cessna F.150F	C. J. & E. J. Leigh
	G-ATMG	M.S.893 Rallye Commodore 180	D. R. Wilkinson & T. Coldwell
	G-ATMH	Beagle D.5/180 Husky	Dorset Gliding Club Ltd
	G-ATMI	H.S.748 Srs 2A	Emerald Airways Ltd *Old Ben*/Liverpool
	G-ATMJ	H.S.748 Srs 2A	Emerald Airways Ltd/Liverpool
	G-ATML	Cessna F.150F	B. A. Pickers
	G-ATMM	Cessna F.150F	C. H. Mitchell & P. Bloomfield
	G-ATMT	PA-30 Twin Comanche 160	Montagu-Smith & Co Ltd
	G-ATMU	PA-23 Apache 160G	P. K. Martin & R. W. Harris
	G-ATMW	PA-28 Cherokee 140	Bencray Ltd/Blackpool
	G-ATMX	Cessna F.150F	N. E. Binner
	G-ATMY	Cessna 150F	C. F. Read
	G-ATNB	PA-28 Cherokee 180	G. Taylor
	G-ATNE	Cessna F.150F	J. & S. Brew
	G-ATNJ	Cessna F.150F ★	*Instructional airframe*/Perth
	G-ATNK	Cessna F.150F	Pegasus Aviation Ltd
	G-ATNL	Cessna F.150F	G-ATNL Flying Group/Blackbushe
	G-ATNV	PA-24 Comanche 260	B. S. Reynolds & P. R. Fortescue/Bourn
	G-ATOA	PA-23 Apache 160G	K. A. Passmore
	G-ATOD	Cessna F.150F	E. Watson & ptnrs/St Just
	G-ATOE	Cessna F.150F	Kesh Flyers Group
	G-ATOF	Cessna F.150F ★	*Instructional airframe*/Perth
	G-ATOG	Cessna F.150F ★	*Instructional airframe*/Perth
	G-ATOH	D.62B Condor	Three Spires Flying Group
	G-ATOI	PA-28 Cherokee 140	R. W. Nash
	G-ATOJ	PA-28 Cherokee 140	A Flight Aviation Ltd
	G-ATOK	PA-28 Cherokee 140	ILC Flying Group
	G-ATOL	PA-28 Cherokee 140	L. J. Nation & G. Alford
	G-ATOM	PA-28 Cherokee 140	A. Flight Aviation Ltd
	G-ATON	PA-28 Cherokee 140	R. G. Walters/Shobdon
	G-ATOO	PA-28 Cherokee 140	I. Wilson
	G-ATOP	PA-28 Cherokee 140	P. R. Coombs/Blackbushe
	G-ATOR	PA-28 Cherokee 140	D. Palmer & V. G. Whitehead/Shobdon
	G-ATOS	PA-28 Cherokee 140	E. Alexander
	G-ATOT	PA-28 Cherokee 180	Totair Ltd
	G-ATOU	Mooney M.20E Super 21	M20 Flying Group
	G-ATOY	PA-24 Comanche 260 ★	Museum of Flight/E. Fortune
	G-ATOZ	Bensen B.8M	A. H. Brent
	G-ATPD	H.S.125 Srs 1B	Wessex Air (Holdings) Ltd
	G-ATPN	PA-28 Cherokee 140	M. F. Hatt & ptnrs/Southend
	G-ATPT	Cessna 182J Skylane	G. B. Scholes
	G-ATPV	JB.01 Minicab	C. F. O'Neill
	G-ATRA	LET L.13 Blanik	Blanik Syndicate/Husbands Bosworth
	G-ATRB	LET L.13 Blanik (BXW)	Avon Soaring Centre/Bickmarsh
	G-ATRC	Beech B.95A Travel Air	Multi-Air/Biggin Hill
	G-ATRG	PA-18 Super Cub 150	Lasham Gliding Soc Ltd
	G-ATRI	Bo 208C1 Junior	Chertwood Ltd
	G-ATRK	Cessna F.150F	R. J. MacKenzie & W. A. Barclay
	G-ATRL	Cessna F.150F	A. A. W. Stevens
	G-ATRM	Cessna F.150F	E. T. Wicks
	G-ATRO	PA-28 Cherokee 140	390th Flying Group

Reg.	Type	Owner or Operator	Notes
G-ATRR	PA-28 Cherokee 140	Marnham Investments Ltd	
G-ATRW	PA-32 Cherokee Six 260	Pringle Brandon Architects	
G-ATRX	PA-32 Cherokee Six 260	J. W. Stow	
G-ATSI	Bo 208C1 Junior	M. R. Reynolds & B. A. Riseborough	
G-ATSL	Cessna F.172G	L. McMullin	
G-ATSM	Cessna 337A	Landscape & Ground Maintenance	
G-ATSR	Beech M.35 Bonanza	Bonanza International Ltd	
G-ATSX	Bo 208C1 Junior	R. J. C. Campbell & M. H. Goley	
G-ATSY	Wassmer WA41 Super Baladou IV	Baladou Flying Group	
G-ATSZ	PA-30 Twin Comanche 160B	P. A. Brook	
G-ATTB	Wallis WA-116-1 (XR944)	D. A. Wallis	
G-ATTD	Cessna 182J Skylane	K. M. Brennan & ptnrs	
G-ATTF	PA-28 Cherokee 140	D. H. Fear	
G-ATTG	PA-28 Cherokee 140	D. E. Spells	
G-ATTI	PA-28 Cherokee 140	Avon Flying Group	
G-ATTK	PA-28 Cherokee 140	G-ATTK Flying Group/Southend	
G-ATTM	Jodel DR.250-160	R. W. Tomkinson	
G-ATTN	Piccard balloon ★	Science Museum/S. Kensington	
G-ATTR	Bo 208C1 Junior	S. Luck	
G-ATTV	PA-28 Cherokee 140	D. B. & M. E. Meeks	
G-ATTX	PA-28 Cherokee 180	IPAC Aviation Ltd	
G-ATUB	PA-28 Cherokee 140	R. H. Partington & M. J. Porter	
G-ATUD	PA-28 Cherokee 140	Midair Aviation Ltd/Bournemouth	
G-ATUF	Cessna F.150F	D. P. Williams	
G-ATUG	D.62B Condor	J. R. Rowell & J. E. Hobbs/Sandown	
G-ATUH	Tipsy T.66 Nipper 1	D. G. Spruce	
G-ATUI	Bo 208C1 Junior	A. W. Wakefield	
G-ATUL	PA-28 Cherokee 180	Kirkland Ltd	
G-ATVF	D.H.C.1 Chipmunk 22 (Lycoming)	RAFGSA/Syerston	
G-ATVK	PA-28 Cherokee 140	JRB Aviation Ltd/Southend	
G-ATVL	PA-28 Cherokee 140	White Waltham Airfield Ltd	
G-ATVO	PA-28 Cherokee 140	L. A. Mills	
G-ATVP	F.B.5 Gunbus (2345) ★	RAF Museum/Hendon	
G-ATVS	PA-28 Cherokee 180	Markel Aviation	
G-ATVW	D.62B Condor	J. P. Coulter & J. Chidley/Panshanger	
G-ATVX	Bo 208C1 Junior	G. & G. E. F. Warren	
G-ATWA	Jodel DR.1050	Jodel Syndicate	
G-ATWB	Jodel D.117	Andrewsfield Whiskey Bravo Group	
G-ATWE	M.S.892A Rallye Commodore	D. I. Murray	
G-ATWJ	Cessna F.172F	C. J. & J. Freeman/Headcorn	
G-ATWR	PA-30 Twin Comanche 160B	Lubair (Transport Services) Ltd/ E. Midlands	
G-ATXA	PA-22 Tri-Pacer 150	R. C. Teverson	
G-ATXD	PA-30 Twin Comanche 160B	Jet Heritage Ltd/Bournemouth	
G-ATXF	GY-80 Horizon 150	C. J. A. Macaulay	
G-ATXJ	H.P.137 Jetstream 300 ★	Museum of Flight/E. Fortune	
G-ATXM	PA-28 Cherokee 180	D. J. Bates	
G-ATXN	Mitchell-Proctor Kittiwake 1	P. A. Dawson	
G-ATXO	SIPA 903	S. A. & D. C. Whitehead	
G-ATXZ	Bo 208C1 Junior	Bradbury & Ptnrs	
G-ATYM	Cessna F.150G	J. F. Perry & Co	
G-ATYN	Cessna F.150G	J. S. Grant	
G-ATYS	PA-28 Cherokee 180	W. J. Waite	
G-ATZA	Bo 208C1 Junior	C. M. Barnes/Popham	
G-ATZG	AFB2 gas balloon	Flt Lt S. Cameron	
G-ATZK	PA-28 Cherokee 180	Austen Associates Partnership	
G-ATZM	Piper J-3C-90 Cub	R. W. Davison	
G-ATZS	Wassmer WA41 Super Baladou IV	G. R. Outwin & D. P. Bennett	
G-ATZY	Cessna F.150G	J. Easson/Edinburgh	
G-AVAK	M.S.893A Rallye Commodore 180	W. K. Anderson *(stored)*/Perth	
G-AVAR	Cessna F.150G	J. A. Rees & F. Doncaster	
G-AVAU	PA-30 Twin Comanche 160B	Enrico Ermano Ltd	
G-AVAW	D.62B Condor	Condor Aircraft Group	
G-AVAX	PA-28 Cherokee 180	J. J. Parkes	
G-AVBG	PA-28 Cherokee 180	G-AVBG Flying Group/White Waltham	
G-AVBH	PA-28 Cherokee 180	T. R. Smith (Agricultural Machinery) Ltd	
G-AVBP	PA-28 Cherokee 140	W. B. Ware	
G-AVBS	PA-28 Cherokee 180	Camborne Insurance Brokers Ltd	
G-AVBT	PA-28 Cherokee 180	J. F. Mitchell	
G-AVBZ	Cessna F.172H	M. Byl/Crosland Moor	
G-AVCE	Cessna F.172H	Leisure Aviation Ltd	
G-AVCM	PA-24 Comanche 260	F. Smith & Sons Ltd/Stapleford	

Notes	Reg.	Type	Owner or Operator
	G-AVCT	Cessna F.150G	K. R. Henville
	G-AVCU	Cessna F.150G	M. Hussein
	G-AVCV	Cessna 182J Skylane	University of Manchester Institute of Science & Technology/Woodford
	G-AVCX	PA-30 Twin Comanche 160B	T. Barge
	G-AVDA	Cessna 182K Skylane	F. W. Ellis & M. C. Burnett
	G-AVDF	Beagle Pup 100 ★	Beagle Owners Club
	G-AVDG	Wallis WA-116 Srs 1	K. H. Wallis
	G-AVDT	Aeronca 7AC Champion	D. Cheney & J. G. Woods
	G-AVDV	PA-22 Tri-Pacer 150 (tailwheel)	S. C. Brooks/Slinfold
	G-AVDW	D.62B Condor	Druine Condor G-AVDW Group
	G-AVDY	Luton LA-4A Minor	P. J. Manifold & M. J. Nairn
	G-AVEC	Cessna F.172H	W. H. Ekin (Engineering) Co Ltd
	G-AVEF	Jodel 150	Tiger Club (1990) Ltd/Headcorn
	G-AVEH	SIAI-Marchetti S.205	EH Aviation
	G-AVEM	Cessna F.150G	G-AVEM Flying Group
	G-AVEN	Cessna F.150G	N. J. Budd/Aberdeen
	G-AVER	Cessna F.150G	E. Altherton
	G-AVEU	Wassmer WA.41 Baladou IV	G. J. Richardson
	G-AVEX	D.62B Condor	R. Marsden/Bicester
	G-AVEY	Currie Super Wot	B. J. Anning
	G-AVEZ	HPR-7 Herald 210 ★	*Rescue trainer*/Norwich
	G-AVFB	H.S.121 Trident 2E ★	Duxford Aviation Soc
	G-AVFE	H.S.121 Trident 2E ★	Belfast Airport Authority
	G-AVFG	H.S.121 Trident 2E ★	*Ground handling trainer*/Heathrow
	G-AVFH	H.S.121 Trident 2E ★	Mosquito Aircraft Museum *(fuselage only)*
	G-AVFK	H.S.121 Trident 2E ★	Metropolitan Police Training Centre/ Hounslow
	G-AVFM	H.S.121 Trident 2E ★	Brunel Technical College/Bristol
	G-AVFP	PA-28 Cherokee 140	R. L. Howells/Barton
	G-AVFR	PA-28 Cherokee 140	VFR Flying Group/Newtownards
	G-AVFS	PA-32 Cherokee Six 300	A. S. Janes
	G-AVFU	PA-32 Cherokee Six 300	Ashley Gardner Flying Club Ltd
	G-AVFX	PA-28 Cherokee 140	Wessex Flyers Group/Thruxton
	G-AVFZ	PA-28 Cherokee 140	G-AVFZ Flying Group
	G-AVGA	PA-24 Comanche 260	Conram Aviation/Biggin Hill
	G-AVGC	PA-28 Cherokee 140	P. A. Hill
	G-AVGD	PA-28 Cherokee 140	S. & G. W. Jacobs
	G-AVGE	PA-28 Cherokee 140	H. H. T. Wolf
	G-AVGI	PA-28 Cherokee 140	D. G. Smith & C. D. Barden
	G-AVGK	PA-28 Cherokee 180	Golf Kilo Flying Group
	G-AVGY	Cessna 182K Skylane	R. M. C. Sears & R. N. Howgego
	G-AVGZ	Jodel DR.1050	D. C. Webb
	G-AVHH	Cessna F.172H	M. J. Mann & J. Hickinbotom
	G-AVHL	Jodel DR.105A	Jodel G-AVHL Flying Group
	G-AVHM	Cessna F.150G	Thornhill Aviation & G. Baldock
	G-AVHT	Auster AOP.9 (WZ711)	M. Somerton-Rayner/Middle Wallop
	G-AVHY	Fournier RF.4D	J. Connelly
	G-AVIA	Cessna F.150G	Cheshire Air Training Services Ltd/ Liverpool
	G-AVIB	Cessna F.150G	S. R. Smith & P. Hemingway
	G-AVIC	Cessna F.172H	Pembrokeshire Air Ltd/Haverfordwest
	G-AVID	Cessna 182J	J. Rolston
	G-AVII	AB-206A JetRanger	Bristow Helicopters Ltd
	G-AVIL	Alon A.2 Aircoupe (VX147)	M. J. Close
	G-AVIN	M.S.880B Rallye Club	W. Fairney
	G-AVIP	Brantly B.2B	N. J. R. Minchin
	G-AVIS	Cessna F.172H	R. T. Jones/Rochester
	G-AVIT	Cessna F.150G	Shropshire Aero Club Ltd/Sleap
	G-AVIZ	Scheibe SF.25A Motorfalke	D. C. Pattison & D. A. Wilson
	G-AVJE	Cessna F.150G	G-AVJE Syndicate
	G-AVJF	Cessna F.172H	J. A. & G. M. Rees
	G-AVJI	Cessna F.172H	G-AVJI Group
	G-AVJJ	PA-30 Twin Comanche 160B	A. H. Manser
	G-AVJK	Jodel DR.1050/M1	M. H. Wylde
	G-AVJO	Fokker E.III (replica) (422-15)	Bianchi Aviation Film Services Ltd/Booker
	G-AVJV	Wallis WA-117 Srs 1	K. H. Wallis (G-ATCV)
	G-AVJW	Wallis WA-118 Srs 2	K. H. Wallis (G-ATPW)
	G-AVKB	MB.50 Pipistrelle	B. H. Pickard
	G-AVKD	Fournier RF-4D	Lasham RF4 Group
	G-AVKE	Gadfly HDW.1 ★	IHM/Weston-s-Mare
	G-AVKG	Cessna F.172H	P. E. P. Sheppard
	G-AVKI	Slingsby T.66 Nipper 3	J. M. Greenway

Reg.	Type	Owner or Operator	Notes
G-AVKJ	Slingsby T.66 Nipper 3	L. B. Clark	
G-AVKK	Slingsby T.66 Nipper 3	C. Watson	
G-AVKL	PA-30 Twin Comanche 160B	Channel Islands Travel Service Ltd	
G-AVKN	Cessna 401	Law Leasing Ltd	
G-AVKP	A.109 Airedale	D. R. Williams	
G-AVKR	Bo 208C1 Junior	C. W. Grant	
G-AVLB	PA-28 Cherokee 140	M. Wilson	
G-AVLC	PA-28 Cherokee 140	G. E. & A. Murray	
G-AVLD	PA-28 Cherokee 140	WLS Flying Group/Blackbushe	
G-AVLE	PA-28 Cherokee 140	Video Security Services/Tollerton	
G-AVLF	PA-28 Cherokee 140	G. H. Hughesdon	
G-AVLG	PA-28 Cherokee 140	R. Friedlander & D. C. Raymond	
G-AVLH	PA-28 Cherokee 140	M. B. Rothschild	
G-AVLI	PA-28 Cherokee 140	J. V. White	
G-AVLJ	PA-28 Cherokee 140	Demeter Aviation Ltd	
G-AVLN	B.121 Pup 2	C. A. Thorpe	
G-AVLO	Bo 208C1 Junior	P. J. Swain	
G-AVLR	PA-28 Cherokee 140	Group 140/Panshanger	
G-AVLT	PA-28 Cherokee 140	D. Jenvey & K. Piper/Southend	
G-AVLU	PA-28 Cherokee 140	London Transport Flying Club Ltd/ Fairoaks	
G-AVLW	Fournier RF-4D	N. M. Groome	
G-AVLY	Jodel D.120A	N. V. de Candole	
G-AVMA	GY-80 Horizon 180	B. R. Hildick	
G-AVMB	D.62B Condor	J. C. Mansell	
G-AVMD	Cessna 150G	Bagby Aviation Flying Group	
G-AVMF	Cessna F. 150G	J. F. Marsh	
G-AVMH	BAC One-Eleven 510ED	European Aircharter Ltd	
G-AVMI	BAC One-Eleven 510ED	European Aircharter Ltd	
G-AVMJ	BAC One-Eleven 510ED ★	European Aviation Ltd (Cabin trainer)	
G-AVMK	BAC One-Eleven 510ED	European Aircharter Ltd	
G-AVML	BAC One-Eleven 510ED	European Aviation Ltd	
G-AVMM	BAC One-Eleven 510ED	European Aviation Ltd	
G-AVMN	BAC One-Eleven 510ED	Air Bristol	
G-AVMO	BAC One-Eleven 510ED ★	Aerospace Museum/Cosford	
G-AVMP	BAC One-Eleven 510ED	European Aircharter Ltd	
G-AVMR	BAC One-Eleven 510ED	European Aviation Ltd	
G-AVMS	BAC One-Eleven 510ED	European Aviation Ltd	
G-AVMT	BAC One-Eleven 510ED	Air Bristol/AB Shannon	
G-AVMU	BAC One-Eleven 510ED ★	Duxford Aviation Soc	
G-AVMV	BAC One-Eleven 510ED	European Aviation Ltd	
G-AVMW	BAC One-Eleven 510ED	Air Bristol/Filton	
G-AVMX	BAC One-Eleven 510ED	European Aviation Ltd	
G-AVMY	BAC One-Eleven 510ED	European Aviation Ltd	
G-AVMZ	BAC One-Eleven 510ED	European Aviation Ltd	
G-AVNC	Cessna F.150G	J. Turner	
G-AVNE	W.S.58 Wessex Mk 60 Srs 1 ★	IHM/Weston-s-Mare	
G-AVNN	PA-28 Cherokee 180	B. Andrews & C. S. Mitchell	
G-AVNO	PA-28 Cherokee 180	Allister Flight Ltd	
G-AVNP	PA-28 Cherokee 180	R. W. Harris & ptnrs	
G-AVNR	PA-28 Cherokee 180	R. R. Livingstone	
G-AVNS	PA-28 Cherokee 180	D. D. Delaney/Earls Colne	
G-AVNU	PA-28 Cherokee 180	D. Durrant	
G-AVNW	PA-28 Cherokee 180	Len Smith's School of Sports Ltd	
G-AVNX	Fournier RF-4D	W. G. Woollard	
G-AVNZ	Fournier RF-4D	V. S. E. Norman	
G-AVOA	Jodel DR.1050	D. A. Willies/Cranwell	
G-AVOH	D.62B Condor	Rankhart Ltd	
G-AVOM	Jodel DR.221	M. A. Mountford/Headcorn	
G-AVOO	PA-18 Super Cub 150	London Gliding Club Ltd/Dunstable	
G-AVOZ	PA-28 Cherokee 180	J. R. Winning/Booker	
G-AVPC	D.31 Turbulent	S. A. Sharp	
G-AVPD	Jodel D.9 Bebe	S. W. McKay (stored)	
G-AVPH	Cessna F.150G	W. Lancashire Aero Club/Woodvale	
G-AVPI	Cessna F.172H	R. W. Cope	
G-AVPJ	D.H.82A Tiger Moth	C. C. Silk	
G-AVPK	M.S.892A Rallye Commodore	B.A.Bridgewater/Halfpenny Green	
G-AVPM	Jodel D.117	J. C. Haynes	
G-AVPN	HPR-7 Herald 213	Channel Express (Air Services) Ltd/ Bournemouth	
G-AVPO	Hindustan HAL-26 Pushpak	J. A. Rimell	
G-AVPR	PA-30 Twin Comanche 160B	J. O. Coundley	
G-AVPS	PA-30 Twin Comanche 160B	J. M. Bisco/Staverton	

Notes	Reg.	Type	Owner or Operator
	G-AVPT	PA-18 Super Cub 150	The Tiger Club (1990) Ltd/Headcorn
	G-AVPV	PA-18 Cherokee 180	S. Moore
	G-AVRK	PA-28 Cherokee 180	J. Gama
	G-AVRP	PA-28 Cherokee 140	T. Hiscox
	G-AVRS	GY-80 Horizon 180	Air Venturas Ltd
	G-AVRT	PA-28 Cherokee 140	Star Aviation Trust Group/Stapleford
	G-AVRU	PA-28 Cherokee 180	G-AVRU Partnership/Clacton
	G-AVRW	GY-20 Minicab	Kestrel Flying Group/Tollerton
	G-AVRY	PA-28 Cherokee 180	Brigfast Ltd/Blackbushe
	G-AVRZ	PA-28 Cherokee 180	Mantavia Group Ltd
	G-AVSA	PA-28 Cherokee 180	G-AVSA Flying Group
	G-AVSB	PA-28 Cherokee 180	T. H. Lloyd
	G-AVSC	PA-28 Cherokee 180	Medidata Ltd
	G-AVSD	PA-28 Cherokee 180	Landmate Ltd
	G-AVSE	PA-28 Cherokee 180	G. Cortrulia
	G-AVSP	PA-28 Cherokee 180	L. J. Jones
	G-AVSR	Beagle D.5/180 Husky	A. L. Young
	G-AVSZ	AB-206B JetRanger	Burman Aviation Ltd/Cranfield
	G-AVTJ	PA-32 Cherokee Six 260	B. L. Morgan
	G-AVTK	PA-32 Cherokee Six 260	Flying Work SRL/Italy
	G-AVTP	Cessna F.172H	Tango Papa Group
	G-AVTT	Ercoupe 415D	Wright's Farm Eggs Ltd/Andrewsfield
	G-AVTV	M.S.893A Rallye Commodore	D. B. & M. E. Meeks
	G-AVUD	PA-30 Twin Comanche 160B	F.M.Aviation/Biggin Hill
	G-AVUG	Cessna F.150H	Skyways Flying Group
	G-AVUH	Cessna F.150H	C. M. Chinn
	G-AVUS	PA-28 Cherokee 140	Arrow Air Centre Ltd/Shipdham
	G-AVUT	PA-28 Cherokee 140	Bencray Ltd/Blackpool
	G-AVUU	PA-28 Cherokee 140	A. Jahanfar & ptnrs/Southend
	G-AVUZ	PA-32 Cherokee Six 300	Ceesix Ltd/Jersey
	G-AVVC	Cessna F.172H	J. S. M. Cattle
	G-AVVE	Cessna F.150H ★	R. Windley (stored)
	G-AVVF	D.H.104 Dove ★	Airport Fire Service/Staverton
	G-AVVI	PA-30 Twin Comanche 160B	H. E. Boulter & D. G. Bligh
	G-AVVJ	M.S.893A Rallye Commodore	Chris Ebbs Aeroservices
	G-AVVL	Cessna F.150H	N. E. Sams/Cra nfield
	G-AVVO	Avro 652A Anson 19 (VL348) ★	Newark Air Museum
	G-AVVX	Cessna F.150H	Franklyns Flying Group
	G-AVWA	PA-28 Cherokee 140	SFG Ltd
	G-AVWD	PA-28 Cherokee 140	M. P. Briggs
	G-AVWI	PA-28 Cherokee 140	L. M. Veitch
	G-AVWJ	PA-28 Cherokee 140	M. J. Steer/Biggin Hill
	G-AVWL	PA-28 Cherokee 140	P. J. Pratt/Dunkeswell
	G-AVWM	PA-28 Cherokee 140	P. E. Preston & ptnrs/Southend
	G-AVWN	PA-28R Cherokee Arrow 180	Vawn Air Ltd/Jersey
	G-AVWO	PA-28R Cherokee Arrow 180	R. G. Tweddle
	G-AVWR	PA-28R Cherokee Arrow 180	S. J. French & ptnrs/Exeter
	G-AVWT	PA-28R Cherokee Arrow 180	Cloudbase Aviation Ltd
	G-AVWU	PA-28R Cherokee Arrow 180	Arrow Flyers Ltd
	G-AVWV	PA-28R Cherokee Arrow 180	Strathtay Flying Group
	G-AVWY	Fournier RF-4D	B. Houghton
	G-AVXA	PA-25 Pawnee 235	S. Wales Gliding Club Ltd
	G-AVXC	Slingsby T.66 Nipper 3	D. S. T. Eggleton
	G-AVXD	Slingsby T.66 Nipper 3	D. A. Davidson
	G-AVXF	PA-28R Cherokee Arrow 180	JDR Arrow Group
	G-AVXI	H.S.748 Srs 2A	Flight Precision Ltd/Bournemouth
	G-AVXJ	H.S.748 Srs 2A	Flight Precision Ltd/Bournemouth
	G-AVXW	D.62B Condor	A. J. Cooper/Rochester
	G-AVXY	Auster AOP.9 (XK417)	Auster Nine Group
	G-AVXZ	PA-28 Cherokee 140 ★	ATC Hayle (instructional airframe)
	G-AVYB	H.S.121 Trident 1E-140 ★	SAS training airframe/Hereford
	G-AVYE	H.S.121 Trident 1E-140 ★	–
	G-AVYK	A.61 Terrier 3	A. R. Wright/Booker
	G-AVYL	PA-28 Cherokee 180	Cherokee G-AVYL Flying Group
	G-AVYM	PA-28 Cherokee 180	Carlisle Aviation (1985) Ltd/Crosby
	G-AVYP	PA-28 Cherokee 140	T. D. Reid (Braids) Ltd/Newtownards
	G-AVYR	PA-28 Cherokee 140	D.R. Flying Club Ltd/Staverton
	G-AVYS	PA-28R Cherokee Arrow 180	A. M. Playford
	G-AVYT	PA-28R Cherokee Arrow 180	E. J. Booth & B. D. Tipler
	G-AVYV	Jodel D.120	A. J. Sephton
	G-AVZB	Aero Z-37 Cmelak ★	Science Museum/Wroughton
	G-AVZI	Bo 208C1 Junior	C. F. Rogers
	G-AVZM	B.121 Pup 1	ARAZ Group/Elstree

Reg.	Type	Owner or Operator	Notes
G-AVZN	B.121 Pup 1	E. M. Lewis & C. A. Homewood	
G-AVZO	B.121 Pup 1 ★	Thamesside Aviation Museum/E. Tilbury	
G-AVZP	B.121 Pup 1	T. A. White	
G-AVZR	PA-28 Cherokee 180	Lincoln Aero Club Ltd/Sturgate	
G-AVZU	Cessna F.150H	R. D. & E. Forster/Swanton Morley	
G-AVZV	Cessna F.172H	E. M. & D. S. Lightbown/Crosland Moor	
G-AVZW	EAA Biplane Model P	R. G. Maidment & G. R. Edmundson/ Goodwood	
G-AVZX	M.S.880B Rallye Club	T. C. Bayes/Shobdon	
G-AWAA	M.S.880B Rallye Club	P. A. Cairns/Dunkeswell	
G-AWAC	GY-80 Horizon 180	Gardan Party Ltd	
G-AWAH	Beech 95-D55 Baron	B. J. S. Grey/Duxford	
G-AWAJ	Beech 95-D55 Baron	Standard Hose Ltd/Leeds	
G-AWAT	D.62B Condor	Tarwood Ltd/Redhill	
G-AWAU	Vickers F.B.27A Vimy (replica) (F8614) ★	Bomber Command Museum/Hendon	
G-AWAW	Cessna F.150F ★	Science Museum/S. Kensington	
G-AWAX	Cessna 150D	H. H. Cousins	
G-AWAZ	PA-28R Cherokee Arrow 180	R. Staniszewski & R. Nevitt	
G-AWBA	PA-28R Cherokee Arrow 180	March Flying Group/Stapleford	
G-AWBB	PA-28R Cherokee Arrow 180	M. D. Parker & J. Lowe	
G-AWBC	PA-28R Cherokee Arrow 180	Anglo Aviation (UK) Ltd	
G-AWBE	PA-28 Cherokee 140	B. E. Boyle	
G-AWBH	PA-28 Cherokee 140	R. C. A. Mackworth	
G-AWBJ	Fournier RF-4D	J. M. Adams	
G-AWBM	D.31 Turbulent	A. D. Pratt	
G-AWBN	PA-30 Twin Comanche 160B	Stourfield Investments Ltd/Jersey	
G-AWBS	PA-28 Cherokee 140	M. A. English & T. M. Brown	
G-AWBT	PA-30 Twin Comanche 160B ★	Instructional airframe/Cranfield	
G-AWBU	Morane-Saulnier N (replica) (MS.824)	Personal Plane Services Ltd/Booker	
G-AWBV	Cessna 182L Skylane	C. W. Norman	
G-AWBW	Cessna F.172H ★	Brunel Technical College/Bristol	
G-AWBX	Cessna F.150H	A. L. Hall-Carpenter	
G-AWCM	Cessna F.150H	Bobbington Air Training School Ltd	
G-AWCN	Cessna FR.172E	Superfast Labels Ltd/Biggin Hill	
G-AWCP	Cessna F.150H (tailwheel)	C. E. Mason/Shobdon	
G-AWDA	Slingsby T.66 Nipper 3	J. A. Cheesebrough	
G-AWDI	PA-23 Aztec 250C	(stored)	
G-AWDO	D.31 Turbulent	R. N. Crosland	
G-AWDP	PA-28 Cherokee 180	B. H. & P. M. Illston/Shipdham	
G-AWDR	Cessna FR.172E	B. A. Wallace	
G-AWDU	Brantly B.2B	G. E. J. Redwood	
G-AWEF	SNCAN Stampe SV-4B	The Tiger Club (1990) Ltd/Headcorn	
G-AWEI	D.62B Condor	M. J. Steer	
G-AWEK	Fournier RF-4D	P. Barrett	
G-AWEL	Fournier RF-4D	A. B. Clymo/Halfpenny Green	
G-AWEM	Fournier RF-4D	B. J. Griffin/Wickenby	
G-AWEP	Barritault JB-01 Minicab	J. A. Stewart & J. Taylor	
G-AWER	PA-23 Aztec 250C	H. McC. Clarke/Ronaldsway	
G-AWET	PA-28 Cherokee 180D	Broadland Flying Group Ltd/ Shipdham	
G-AWEV	PA-28 Cherokee 140	Norflight Ltd	
G-AWEX	PA-28 Cherokee 140	R. Badham	
G-AWEZ	PA-28R Cherokee Arrow 180	T. R. Leighton & ptnrs	
G-AWFB	PA-28R Cherokee Arrow 180	Luke Aviation Ltd/Bristol	
G-AWFC	PA-28R Cherokee Arrow 180	K. A. Goodchild/Southend	
G-AWFD	PA-28R Cherokee Arrow 180	D. J. Hill	
G-AWFF	Cessna F.150H	C. R. & S. A. Hardiman/Shobdon	
G-AWFJ	PA-28R Cherokee Arrow 180	Parplon Ltd	
G-AWFN	D.62B Condor	R. James	
G-AWFO	D.62B Condor	T. A. Major	
G-AWFP	D.62B Condor	Blackbushe Flying Club	
G-AWFR	D.31 Turbulent	J. R. Froud	
G-AWFT	Jodel D.9 Bebe	W. H. Cole	
G-AWFW	Jodel D.117	F. H. Greenwell	
G-AWFZ	Beech A23 Musketeer	R. Sweet & B. D. Corbett	
G-AWGA	A.109 Airedale ★	stored/Sevenoaks	
G-AWGD	Cessna F.172H	D. Whitton & P. Storey	
G-AWGJ	Cessna F.172H	J. & C. J. Freeman/Headcorn	
G-AWGK	Cessna F.150H	L. A. & L. Groves	
G-AWGM	Arkle Kittiwake 2	M. K. Field	
G-AWGN	Fournier RF-4D	R. H. Ashforth/Staverton	

Notes	Reg.	Type	Owner or Operator
	G-AWGR	Cessna F.172H	P. A. Hallam
	G-AWGZ	Taylor JT.1 Monoplane	R. L. Sambell
	G-AWHB	C.A.S.A. 2-111D (6J+PR) ★	Aces High Ltd/North Weald
	G-AWHX	Rollason Beta B.2	S. G. Jones
	G-AWHY	Falconar F.11-3	B. E. Smith (G-BDPB)
	G-AWIF	Brookland Mosquito 2	–/Husbands Bosworth
	G-AWII	V.S.349 Spitfire VC (AR501)	The Shuttleworth Collection/O. Warden
	G-AWIP	Luton LA-4A Minor	J. Houghton
	G-AWIR	Midget Mustang	K. E. Sword/Leicester
	G-AWIT	PA-28 Cherokee 180	Manco Softwares Ltd
	G-AWIV	Airmark TSR.3	D. J. & F. M. Nunn
	G-AWIW	SNCAN Stampe SV-4B	R. E. Mitchell
	G-AWJE	Slingsby T.66 Nipper 3	T. Mosedale
	G-AWJV	D.H.98 Mosquito TT Mk 35 (TA634) ★	Mosquito Aircraft Museum
	G-AWJX	Zlin Z.526 Trener Master	Aerobatics International Ltd
	G-AWJY	Zlin Z.526 Trener Master	M. Gainza
	G-AWKB	M.J.5 Sirocco F2/39	G. D. Claxton
	G-AWKD	PA-17 Vagabond	A. T. & M. R. Dowie/ White Waltham
	G-AWKM	B.121 Pup 1	D. M. G. Jenkins/Swansea
	G-AWKO	B.121 Pup 1	Bustard Flying Club Ltd
	G-AWKP	Jodel DR.253	G-AWKP Group
	G-AWKX	Beech A65 Queen Air ★	(Instructional airframe)/Shoreham
	G-AWLA	Cessna F.150H	J. A. Clegg
	G-AWLF	Cessna F.172H	Gannet Aviation Ltd/Aldergrove
	G-AWLG	SIPA 903	S. W. Markham
	G-AWLI	PA-22 Tri-Pacer 150	J. S. Lewery/Shoreham
	G-AWLO	Boeing Stearman E.75	N. D. Pickard/Shoreham
	G-AWLP	Mooney M.20F	I. C. Lomax
	G-AWLR	Slingsby T.66 Nipper 3	T. D. Reid
	G-AWLS	Slingsby T.66 Nipper 3	G. A. Dunster & B. Gallagher
	G-AWLZ	Fournier RF-4D	Nympsfield RF-4 Group
	G-AWMD	Jodel D.11	G. E. Valler
	G-AWMF	PA-18 Super Cub 150 (modified)	Booker Gliding Club Ltd
	G-AWMI	Glos-Airtourer 115	W. G. Jones
	G-AWMK	AB-206B JetRanger	Bristow Helicopters Ltd
	G-AWMM	M.S.893A Rallye Commodore 180	D. P. & S. White
	G-AWMN	Luton LA-4A Minor	C. F. O'Neill/Newtownards
	G-AWMP	Cessna F.172H	R. J. D. Blois
	G-AWMR	D.31 Turbulent	T. Pearce
	G-AWMT	Cessna F.150H	Oilfield Expertise Ltd/Tilstock
	G-AWMZ	Cessna F.172H ★	Parachute jump trainer/Cark
	G-AWNA	Boeing 747-136	British Airways Colliford Lake
	G-AWNB	Boeing 747-136	British Airways Llangorse Lake
	G-AWNC	Boeing 747-136	British Airways Lake Windermere
	G-AWNE	Boeing 747-136	British Airways Derwent Water
	G-AWNF	Boeing 747-136	British Airways Blagdon Lake
	G-AWNG	Boeing 747-136	British Airways Rutland Water
	G-AWNH	Boeing 747-136	British Airways Devoke Water
	G-AWNJ	Boeing 747-136	British Airways Bassenthwaite Lake
	G-AWNL	Boeing 747-136	British Airways Ennerdale Water
	G-AWNM	Boeing 747-136	British Airways Ullswater
	G-AWNN	Boeing 747-136	British Airways Loweswater
	G-AWNO	Boeing 747-136	British Airways Grafham Water
	G-AWNP	Boeing 747-136	British Airways Hanningfield Water
	G-AWNT	BN-2A Islander	Aerofilms Ltd/Elstree
	G-AWOA	M.S.880B Rallye Club	J. A. Rimmer
	G-AWOE	Aero Commander 680E	J. M. Houlder/Elstree
	G-AWOF	PA-15 Vagabond	C. M. Hicks
	G-AWOH	PA-17 Vagabond	The High Flatts Flying Group
	G-AWOT	Cessna F.150H	J. M. Montgomerie & J. Ferguson
	G-AWOU	Cessna 170B	S. Billington/Denham
	G-AWOX	W.S.58 Wessex 60 ★	IHM/Weston-s-Mare
	G-AWPH	P.56 Provost T.1	J. A. D. Bradshaw
	G-AWPJ	Cessna F.150H	W. J. Greenfield
	G-AWPN	Shield Xyla	M. J. Herlihy
	G-AWPP	Cessna F.150H	K2 Aviation Ltd & R. S. Willcock
	G-AWPS	PA-28 Cherokee 140	D. J. Hewitt/Halfpenny Green
	G-AWPU	Cessna F.150J	LAC (Enterprises) Ltd/Barton
	G-AWPW	PA-12 Super Cruiser	AK Leasing (Jersey) Ltd
	G-AWPY	Bensen B.8M	J. Jordan
	G-AWPZ	Andreasson BA-4B	J. M. Vening
	G-AWRK	Cessna F.150J	Systemroute Ltd/Shoreham

Reg.	Type	Owner or Operator	Notes
G-AWRP	Cierva Rotorcraft ★	IHM/Weston-s-Mare	
G-AWRS	Avro 19 Srs. 2 H	N. E. Aircraft Museum/Usworth	
G-AWRY	P.56 Provost T.1 (XF836)	Slymar Aviation & Services Ltd	
G-AWSA	Avro 652A Anson 19 (VL349) ★	Norfolk & Suffolk Aviation Museum	
G-AWSL	PA-28 Cherokee 180D	Fascia Services Ltd/Southend	
G-AWSM	PA-28 Cherokee 235	S. J. Green	
G-AWSN	D.62B Condor	J. Leader	
G-AWSP	D.62B Condor	R. Q. & A. S. Bond/Wellesbourne	
G-AWSS	D.62A Condor	G. Bruce/Fordoun	
G-AWST	D.62B Condor	P. L. Clements	
G-AWSV	Skeeter 12 (XM553)	Maj. M. Somerton-Rayner/Middle Wallop	
G-AWSW	D.5/180 Husky (XW635)	Windmill Aviation/Spanhoe	
G-AWTJ	Cessna F.150J	D. G. Williams	
G-AWTL	PA-28 Cherokee 180D	E. Alexander	
G-AWTS	Beech A.23 Musketeer	J. Holden & G. Benet	
G-AWTV	Beech A.23 Musketeer	Channel Airways Ltd/Guernsey	
G-AWTX	Cessna F.150J	Norfolk & Norwich Aero Club	
G-AWUB	GY-201 Minicab	H. P. Burrill	
G-AWUE	Jodel DR.1050	S. Bichan	
G-AWUG	Cessna F.150H	J. Easson/Edinburgh	
G-AWUH	Cessna F.150H	H. D. Hounsell	
G-AWUJ	Cessna F.150H	W. Lawton	
G-AWUL	Cessna F.150H	N. P. Chitty & G. F. de Wilde	
G-AWUN	Cessna F.150H	S. Martin	
G-AWUO	Cessna F.150H	SAS Flying Group	
G-AWUT	Cessna F.150J	S. J. Black/Leeds	
G-AWUU	Cessna F.150J	A. L. Grey	
G-AWUX	Cessna F.172H	D. K. Brian & ptrs	
G-AWUZ	Cessna F.172H	G. F. Burling	
G-AWVA	Cessna F.172H	Barton Air Ltd	
G-AWVB	Jodel D.117	H. Davies	
G-AWVC	B.121 Pup 1	J. H. Marshall & J. J. West	
G-AWVE	Jodel DR.1050/M1	E. A. Taylor/Southend	
G-AWVF	P.56 Provost T.1 (XF877)	Hunter Wing Ltd/Bournemouth	
G-AWVG	AESL Airtourer T.2	C. J. Schofield	
G-AWVN	Aeronca 7AC Champion	W. S. & W. A. Bowker/Rush Green	
G-AWVZ	Jodel D.112	D. C. Stokes	
G-AWWE	B.121 Pup 2	J. M. Randle/Coventry	
G-AWWI	Jodel D.117	W. J. Evans	
G-AWWM	GY-201 Minicab	J. S. Brayshaw	
G-AWWN	Jodel DR.1051	T. W. M. Beck & ptnrs	
G-AWWO	Jodel DR.1050	Whiskey Oscar Group/Barton	
G-AWWP	Aerosport Woody Pusher III	M. S. Bird & R. D. Bird	
G-AWWT	D.31 Turbulent	C. R. Isbell	
G-AWWU	Cessna FR.172F	Westward Airways (Lands End) Ltd	
G-AWWW	Cessna 401	Treble Whisky Aviation Ltd	
G-AWXR	PA-28 Cherokee 180D	A. A. O. Pereira/Portugal	
G-AWXS	PA-28 Cherokee 180D	C. R. & S. A. Hardiman/Shobdon	
G-AWXY	M.S.885 Super Rallye	K. Henderson	
G-AWXZ	SNCAN Stampe SV-4C	Personal Plane Services Ltd/Booker	
G-AWYB	Cessna FR.172F	C. W. Larkin/Southend	
G-AWYJ	B.121 Pup 2	H. C. Taylor	
G-AWYL	Jodel DR.253B	I. R. Elms	
G-AWYO	B.121 Pup 1	B. R. C. Wild/Popham	
G-AWYR	BAC One-Eleven 501EX	Maersk Air/British Airways/Birmingham	
G-AWYS	BAC One-Eleven 501EX	Maersk Air/British Airways/Birmingham	
G-AWYV	BAC One-Eleven 501EX	European Aviation Ltd/Maersk Air/ British Airways	
G-AWYX	M.S.880B Rallye Club	J. M. L. Edwards/Exeter	
G-AWYY	T.57 Camel replica (B6401) ★	F.A.A. Museum/Yeovilton	
G-AWZE	H.S.121 Trident 3B ★	*Instructional airframe*/Heathrow	
G-AWZI	H.S.121 Trident 3B ★	Surrey Fire Brigade *(instructional airframe)*/Reigate	
G-AWZJ	H.S.121 Trident 3B ★	British Airports Authority/Prestwick	
G-AWZK	H.S.121 Trident 3B ★	*Ground trainer*/Heathrow	
G-AWZM	H.S.121 Trident 3B ★	Science Museum/Wroughton	
G-AWZN	H.S.121 Trident 3B ★	Cranfield University	
G-AWZO	H.S.121 Trident 3B ★	Mosquito Aircraft Museum/Hatfield	
G-AWZP	H.S.121 Trident 3B ★	Manchester Museum of Science & Industry *(nose only)*	
G-AWZU	H.S.121 Trident 3B ★	BAA Airport Fire Service/Stansted	
G-AWZX	H.S.121 Trident 3B ★	BAA Airport Fire Services/Gatwick	
G-AWZZ	H.S.121 Trident 3B ★	Airport Fire Services/Birmingham	

Notes	Reg.	Type	Owner or Operator
	G-AXAB	PA-28 Cherokee 140	Bencray Ltd/Blackpool
	G-AXAK	M.S.880B Rallye Club	R. L. & C. Stewart
	G-AXAN	D.H.82A Tiger Moth (EM720)	M. E. Carrell
	G-AXAS	Wallis WA-116T	K. H. Wallis (G-AVDH)
	G-AXAT	Jodel D.117A	P. S. Wilkinson
	G-AXAU	PA-30 Twin Comanche 160C	Bartcourt Ltd *(derelict)*/Bournemouth
	G-AXAX	PA-23 Aztec 250D	G-WATS Aviation Ltd/Halfpenny Green
	G-AXBF	Beagle D.5/180 Husky	C. H. Barnes
	G-AXBH	Cessna F.172H	D. F. Ranger
	G-AXBJ	Cessna F.172H	Bravo Juliet Group/Leicester
	G-AXBW	D.H.82A Tiger Moth (T5879)	R. Venning
	G-AXBZ	D.H.82A Tiger Moth	D. H. McWhir
	G-AXCA	PA-28R Cherokee Arrow 200	M. D. & J. E. M. Williams
	G-AXCG	Jodel D.117	Charlie Golf Group/Andrewsfield
	G-AXCI	Bensen B.8M	N. Martin *(stored)*
	G-AXCL	M.S.880B Rallye Club	P. P. Loucas/Andrewsfield
	G-AXCM	M.S.880B Rallye Club	D. C. Manifold
	G-AXCN	M.S.880B Rallye Club	J. E. Compton
	G-AXCX	B.121 Pup 2	L. A. Pink
	G-AXCY	Jodel D.117	C. L. Betts & ptnrs/Shoreham
	G-AXDC	PA-23 Aztec 250D	N. J. Lilley/Bodmin
	G-AXDI	Cessna F.172H	M. F. & J. R. Leusby/Conington
	G-AXDK	Jodel DR.315	Delta Kilo Flying Group/Sywell
	G-AXDM	H.S.125 Srs 400B	GEC Ferranti Defence Systems Ltd/ Edinburgh
	G-AXDN	BAC-Sud Concorde 01 ★	Duxford Aviation Soc
	G-AXDU	B.121 Pup 2	R. G. Hayes/Elstree
	G-AXDV	B.121 Pup 1	T. A. White
	G-AXDW	B.121 Pup 1	Cranfield Delta Whiskey Group
	G-AXDY	Falconar F-11	J. Nunn
	G-AXDZ	Cassutt Racer Srs IIIM	A. Chadwick/Little Staughton
	G-AXEB	Cassutt Racer Srs IIIM	G. E. Horder/Redhill
	G-AXED	PA-25 Pawnee 235	Wolds Gliding Club Ltd/Pocklington
	G-AXEH	B.125 Bulldog 1 ★	Museum of Flight/E. Fortune
	G-AXEI	Ward Gnome ★	Lincolnshire Aviation Museum
	G-AXEO	Scheibe SF.25B Falke	R. Cassidy & W. P. Stephen
	G-AXEV	B.121 Pup 2	D. S. Russell
	G-AXFG	Cessna 337D	Cumbria Constabulary/Carlisle
	G-AXFH	D.H.114 Heron 1B/C	*(stored)*/Southend
	G-AXFN	Jodel D.119	D. G. West
	G-AXGC	M.S.880B Rallye Club	P. A. Crawford & M. C. Bennett
	G-AXGE	M.S.880B Rallye Club	R. P. Loxton
	G-AXGG	Cessna F.150J	CTC Associates/Cranfield
	G-AXGP	Piper J-3C-65 Cub	W. K. Butler
	G-AXGR	Luton LA-4A Minor	B. A. Schlussler
	G-AXGS	D.62B Condor	B. W. Haston
	G-AXGV	D.62B Condor	R. J. Wrixon
	G-AXGZ	D.62B Condor	J. Evans
	G-AXHA	Cessna 337A	G. Evans
	G-AXHC	SNCAN Stampe SV-4C	D. L. Webley
	G-AXHE	BN-2A Islander ★	Airport Fire Service/Cumbernauld
	G-AXHO	B.121 Pup 2	L. W. Grundy/Stapleford
	G-AXHP	Piper J-3C-65 Cub (480636)	P. J. Acreman
	G-AXHR	Piper J-3C-65 Cub (329601)	G-AXHR Cub Group
	G-AXHS	M.S.880B Rallye Club	B. & A. Swales
	G-AXHT	M.S.880B Rallye Club	D. E. Guck
	G-AXHV	Jodel D.117A	Derwent Flying Group/Hucknall
	G-AXIA	B.121 Pup 1	Cranfield University
	G-AXIE	B.121 Pup 2	G. A. Ponsford/Goodwood
	G-AXIF	B.121 Pup 2	P. Nash
	G-AXIG	B.125 Bulldog 104	George House (Holdings) Ltd
	G-AXIO	PA-28 Cherokee 140B	White Waltham Airfield Ltd
	G-AXIR	PA-28 Cherokee 140B	J. E. T. Lock
	G-AXIT	M.S.893A Rallye Commodore 180	T. J. Price
	G-AXIW	Scheibe SF.25B Falke	M. B. Hill
	G-AXIX	Glos-Airtourer 150	J. C. Wood
	G-AXIY	Bird Gyrocopter ★	–
	G-AXJB	Omega 84 balloon	Southern Balloon Group
	G-AXJH	B.121 Pup 2	J. S. Chillingworth
	G-AXJI	B.121 Pup 2	D. M. & J. Glinternick
	G-AXJJ	B.121 Pup 2	Bumpf Group/Crosland Moor
	G-AXJO	B.121 Pup 2	J. A. D. Bradshaw
	G-AXJR	Scheibe SF.25B Falke	D. R. Chatterton

Reg.	Type	Owner or Operator	Notes
G-AXJV	PA-28 Cherokee 140B	N. J. Atherton	
G-AXJX	PA-28 Cherokee 140B★	Patrolwatch Ltd/Sleap	
G-AXJY	Cessna U-206D	Falcon Flying Services/Biggin Hill	
G-AXKH	Luton LA-4A Minor	M. E. Vaisey	
G-AXKI	Jodel D.9 Bebe	M. R. M. Welch	
G-AXKJ	Jodel D.9 Bebe	C. C. Gordon & N. Mowbray	
G-AXKO	Westland-Bell 47G-4A	G. P. Hinkley	
G-AXKS	Westland Bell 47G-4A ★	Museum of Army Flying/Middle Wallop	
G-AXKW	Westland-Bell 47G-4A	Eyre Spier Associates Ltd	
G-AXKX	Westland Bell 47G-4A	Copley Farms Ltd	
G-AXKY	Westland Bell 47G-4A	G. A. Knight & G. M. Vowles	
G-AXLG	Cessna 310K	Smiths (Outdrives) Ltd	
G-AXLI	Slingsby T.66 Nipper 3	R. Bailes-Brown & M. J. D. Probert	
G-AXLL	BAC One-Eleven 523FJ	European Aircharter Ltd	
G-AXLS	Jodel DR.105A	E. Gee/Southampton	
G-AXLZ	PA-18 Super Cub 95	R. J. Quantrell	
G-AXMA	PA-24 Comanche 180	R. E. Leech	
G-AXMD	Omega O-56 balloon ★	British Balloon Museum	
G-AXMN	J/5B Autocar	A. Phillips	
G-AXMP	PA-28 Cherokee 180	T. M. P. Tomsett	
G-AXMT	Bücker B133 Jungmeister	G. L. Carpenter	
G-AXMW	B.121 Pup 1	DJP Engineering (Knebworth) Ltd	
G-AXMX	B.121 Pup 2	Susan A. Jones/Cannes	
G-AXNJ	Wassmer Jodel D.120	Clive Flying Group/Sleap	
G-AXNL	B.121 Pup 1	Northamptonshire School of Flying Ltd/ Sywell	
G-AXNM	B.121 Pup 1	J. & F. E. Green	
G-AXNN	B.121 Pup 2	Gabrielle Aviation Ltd/Shoreham	
G-AXNP	B.121 Pup 2	J. W. Ellis	
G-AXNR	B.121 Pup 2	P. A. Jackson	
G-AXNS	B.121 Pup 2	Derwent Aero Group/Netherthorpe	
G-AXNW	SNCAN Stampe SV-4C	C. S. Grace	
G-AXNX	Cessna 182M	D. B. Harper	
G-AXNZ	Pitts S.1C Special	W. A. Jordan	
G-AXOG	PA-E23 Aztec 250D	R. W. Diggens/Denham	
G-AXOH	M.S.894 Rallye Minerva	Bristol Cars Ltd/White Waltham	
G-AXOJ	B.121 Pup 2	Pup Flying Group	
G-AXOR	PA-28 Cherokee 180D	Oscar Romeo Aviation Ltd	
G-AXOS	M.S.894A Rallye Minerva	P. Mather	
G-AXOT	M.S.893 Rallye Commodore 180	P. Evans & J. C. Graves	
G-AXOZ	B.121 Pup 1	R. J. Ogborn	
G-AXPB	B.121 Pup 1	M. J. K. Seary & R. T. Austin	
G-AXPC	B.121 Pup 2	T. A. White	
G-AXPF	Cessna F.150K	D. R. Marks/Denham	
G-AXPG	Mignet HM-293	W. H. Cole (stored)	
G-AXPM	B.121 Pup 1	R. G. Hayes/Elstree	
G-AXPN	B.121 Pup 2	D. J. Elborn & ptnrs	
G-AXPZ	Campbell Cricket	W. R. Partridge	
G-AXRC	Campbell Cricket	K. W. Hayr	
G-AXRO	PA-30 Twin Comanche 160C	Comanche Hire Ltd/Staverton	
G-AXRP	SNCAN Stampe SV-4C	C. C. Manning (G-BLOL)	
G-AXRR	Auster AOP.9 (XR241)	The Aircraft Restoration Co/Duxford	
G-AXRT	Cessna FA.150K (tailwheel)	J. K. Horne	
G-AXRU	Cessna FA.150K	Arrival Enterprises Ltd	
G-AXSC	B.121 Pup 1	R. J. MacCarthy	
G-AXSD	B.121 Pup 1	A. C. Townend	
G-AXSF	Nash Petrel	Nash Aircraft Ltd/Lasham	
G-AXSG	PA-28 Cherokee 180	J. Montgomery	
G-AXSI	Cessna F.172H	R. I. Chantry & A. J. G. Davis (G-SNIP)	
G-AXSM	Jodel DR.1051	K. D. Doyle	
G-AXSR	Brantly B.2B	S. Lee (G-ROOF)	
G-AXSV	Jodel DR.340	Leonard F. Jollye Ltd	
G-AXSW	Cessna FA.150K	Furness Aviation Ltd/Walney Island	
G-AXSZ	PA-28 Cherokee 140B	The White Wings Flying Group/ White Waltham	
G-AXTA	PA-28 Cherokee 140B	G-AXTA Syndicate	
G-AXTC	PA-28 Cherokee 140B	G-AXTC Group	
G-AXTD	PA-28 Cherokee 140B	K. P. Rossetti	
G-AXTJ	PA-28 Cherokee 140B	A. P. Merrifield/Stapleford	
G-AXTL	PA-28 Cherokee 140B	Pegasus Aviation (Midlands) Ltd	
G-AXTO	PA-24 Comanche 260	J. L. Wright	
G-AXTP	PA-28 Cherokee 180	C. W. R. Moore/Elstree	
G-AXTX	Jodel D.112	T. J. Price	

Notes	Reg.	Type	Owner or Operator
	G-AXTZ	B.121 Pup 1	R. S. & A. D. Kent
	G-AXUA	B.121 Pup 1	F. R. Blennerhassett & ptnrs
	G-AXUB	BN-2A Islander	Headcorn Parachute Club
	G-AXUC	PA-12 Super Cruiser	J. J. Bunton
	G-AXUF	Cessna FA.150K	A. D. McLeod
	G-AXUJ	J/1 Autocrat	J. H. W. Lee & G. L. Brown/Sibson
	G-AXUK	Jodel DR.1050	Ambassadeurs Flying Group
	G-AXUM	H.P.137 Jetstream 1	Cranfield University
	G-AXUW	Cessna FA.150K	Coventry Air Training School
	G-AXVB	Cessna F.172H	J. E. Compton & R. Turner
	G-AXVK	Campbell Cricket	L. W. Harding
	G-AXVM	Campbell Cricket	D. M. Organ
	G-AXVN	McCandless M.4	W. R. Partridge
	G-AXVV	Piper J-3C-65 Cub	J. D. MacCarthy
	G-AXVW	Cessna F.150K	General Aircraft Services
	G-AXWA	Auster AOP.9 (XN437)	M. L. & C. M. Edwards/Biggin Hill
	G-AXWH	BN-2A Islander	Cormack (Aircraft Services) Ltd
	G-AXWT	Jodel D.11	R. C. Owen
	G-AXWV	Jodel DR.253	J. R. D. Bygraves/O. Warden
	G-AXWZ	PA-28R Cherokee Arrow 200	E. J. M. Kroes
	G-AXXV	D.H.82A Tiger Moth (DE992)	C. N. Wookey
	G-AXXW	Jodel D.117	A. Szep/Netherthorpe
	G-AXYK	Taylor JT.1 Monoplane	D. J. Hulks & R. W. Davies
	G-AXYU	Jodel D.9 Bebe	D. J. Laughlin
	G-AXYY	WHE Airbuggy	R. A. A. Chiles
	G-AXYZ	WHE Airbuggy	W. B. Lumb
	G-AXZA	WHE Airbuggy	C. Verlaan/Holland
	G-AXZB	WHE Airbuggy	D. R. C. Pugh
	G-AXZD	PA-28 Cherokee 180E	A. W. Bottoms
	G-AXZF	PA-28 Cherokee 180E	E. P. C. & W. R. Rabson/Southampton
	G-AXZK	BN-2A-26 Islander	Headcorn Parachute Club Ltd
	G-AXZM	Slingsby T.66 Nipper 3	G. R. Harlow
	G-AXZO	Cessna 180	Golf Centres Balloons Ltd
	G-AXZP	PA-E23 Aztec 250D	D. J. Skidmore
	G-AXZT	Jodel D.117	N. Batty
	G-AXZU	Cessna 182N	S. E. Bradney
	G-AYAA	PA-28 Cherokee 180E	Alpha-Alpha Ltd
	G-AYAB	PA-28 Cherokee 180E	Films Ltd
	G-AYAC	PA-28R Cherokee Arrow 200	Fersfield Flying Group
	G-AYAJ	Cameron O-84 balloon	E. T. Hall
	G-AYAL	Omega 56 balloon ★	British Balloon Museum
	G-AYAN	Slingsby Motor Cadet III	N. C. Stone
	G-AYAR	PA-28 Cherokee 180E	D. M. Markscheffel/Stapleford
	G-AYAT	PA-28 Cherokee 180E	AYAT Flying Group
	G-AYAU	PA-28 Cherokee 180E	A. G. & J. Wintle/Elstree
	G-AYAV	PA-28 Cherokee 180E	Tee Tee Aviation Ltd/Biggin Hill
	G-AYAW	PA-28 Cherokee 180E	R. C. Pendle & M. J. Rose
	G-AYBD	Cessna F.150K	Cubair Ltd/Redhill
	G-AYBG	Scheibe SF.25B Falke	D. J. Rickman
	G-AYBO	PA-23 Aztec 250D	Twinguard Aviation Ltd/Elstree
	G-AYBP	Jodel D.112	G. J. Langston
	G-AYBR	Jodel D.112	D. Lamb
	G-AYCC	Campbell Cricket	D. J. M. Charity
	G-AYCE	CP.301C Emeraude	S. D. Glover
	G-AYCF	Cessna FA.150K	E. J. Atkins/Popham
	G-AYCG	SNCAN Stampe SV-4C	N. Bignall/Booker
	G-AYCJ	Cessna TP.206D	G. James
	G-AYCK	AIA Stampe SV-4C	J. F. Graham (G-BUNT)
	G-AYCN	Piper J-3C-65 Cub	W. R. & B. M. Young
	G-AYCO	CEA DR.360	G. T. Birks & T. M. Curry/Booker
	G-AYCP	Jodel D.112	D. J. Nunn
	G-AYCT	Cessna F.172H	Haimoss Ltd & D. C. Scouller
	G-AYDG	M.S.894A Rallye Minerva	Earthline Ltd
	G-AYDI	D.H.82A Tiger Moth	R. B. Woods & ptnrs
	G-AYDR	SNCAN Stampe SV-4C	A. J. McLuskie
	G-AYDV	Coates SA.II-1 Swalesong	J. R. Coates
	G-AYDW	A.61 Terrier 2	A. S. Topen
	G-AYDX	A.61 Terrier 2	D. G. Roberts
	G-AYDY	Luton LA-4A Minor	T. Littlefair & N. Clark
	G-AYDZ	Jodel DR.200	L. J. Cudd & C. A. Bailey
	G-AYEB	Jodel D.112	C. H. G. Baulf
	G-AYEC	CP.301A Emeraude	Redwing Flying Group

Reg.	Type	Owner or Operator	Notes
G-AYED	PA-24 Comanche 260	J. V. Hutchinson	
G-AYEE	PA-28 Cherokee 180E	D. J. Beale	
G-AYEF	PA-28 Cherokee 180E	B. Chalcroft & J. C. Rideout	
G-AYEG	Falconar F-9	T. J. Wilkinson	
G-AYEH	Jodel DR.1050	John Scott Jodel Group	
G-AYEJ	Jodel DR.1050	J. M. Newbold	
G-AYEN	Piper J-3C-65 Cub	P. Warde & C. F. Morris	
G-AYET	M.S.892A Rallye Commodore 150	A. T. R. Bingley	
G-AYEV	Jodel DR.1050	L. G. Evans/Headcorn	
G-AYEW	Jodel DR.1051	Taildragger Group/Halfpenny Green	
G-AYEY	Cessna F.150K	W. J. Moyse	
G-AYFA	SA Twin Pioneer 3 ★	Macclesfield Historical Aviation Soc	
G-AYFC	D.62B Condor	A. D. Pearce	
G-AYFD	D.62B Condor	B. G. Manning	
G-AYFE	D.62C Condor	D. I. H. Johnstone & W. T. Barnard	
G-AYFF	D.62B Condor	A. F. S. Caldecourt	
G-AYFG	D.62C Condor	W. A. Braim	
G-AYFJ	M.S.880B Rallye Club	Rallye FJ Group	
G-AYFP	Jodel D.140	F. L. Rivett	
G-AYFT	PA-39 Twin Comanche 160 C/R	G. A. Barber/Blackbushe	
G-AYFV	Crosby BA-4B	A. R. C. Mathie/Norwich	
G-AYGA	Jodel D.117	R. L. E. Horrell	
G-AYGB	Cessna 310Q ★	*Instructional airframe*/Perth	
G-AYGC	Cessna F.150K	Alpha Aviation Group/Barton	
G-AYGD	Jodel DR.1051	P. J. Pengilly	
G-AYGE	SNCAN Stampe SV-4C	The Hon A. M. J. Rothschild/Booker	
G-AYGG	Jodel D.120	J. M. Dean	
G-AYGK	BN-2A-6 Islander	Pathcircle Ltd/Langar	
G-AYGX	Cessna FR.172G	A. Douglas & J. K. Brockley	
G-AYHA	AA-1 Yankee	G-AYHA Flying Group	
G-AYHI	Campbell Cricket	J. F. MacKay/Inverness	
G-AYHX	Jodel D.117A	L. J. E. Goldfinch	
G-AYHY	Fournier RF-4D	P. M. & S. M. Wells	
G-AYIA	Hughes 369HS ★	G. D. E. Bilton/Sywell	
G-AYIF	PA-28 Cherokee 140C	The Hare Flying Group/Elstree	
G-AYIG	PA-28 Cherokee 140C	Caernarfon Air World	
G-AYII	PA-28R Cherokee Arrow 200	P. W. J. & P. A. S. Gove/Exeter	
G-AYIJ	SNCAN Stampe SV-4B	E. A. Stevenson-Rouse & T. C. Beadle/Headcorn	
G-AYIM	H.S.748 Srs 2A	Emerald Airways Ltd/Liverpool	
G-AYIT	D.H.82A Tiger Moth	Ulster Tiger Group/Newtownards	
G-AYJA	Jodel DR.1050	G. Connell	
G-AYJB	SNCAN Stampe SV-4C	F. J. M. & J. P. Esson/Middle Wallop	
G-AYJD	Alpavia-Fournier RF-3	E. Shouler	
G-AYJP	PA-28 Cherokee 140C	RAF Brize Norton Flying Club Ltd	
G-AYJR	PA-28 Cherokee 140C	RAF Brize Norton Flying Club Ltd	
G-AYJW	Cessna FR.172G	J. D. Kelsall & ptnrs	
G-AYJY	Isaacs Fury II	M. G. Jeffries/Little Gransden	
G-AYKA	Beech 95-B55A Baron	Walsh Bros (Tunnelling) Ltd/Elstree	
G-AYKD	Jodel DR.1050	S. D. Morris	
G-AYKJ	Jodel D.117A	Juliet Group/Shoreham	
G-AYKK	Jodel D.117	D. M. Whitham	
G-AYKL	Cessna F.150L	M. A. Judge	
G-AYKS	Leopoldoff L-7	W. B. Cooper	
G-AYKT	Jodel D.117	G. Wright/Sherburn	
G-AYKW	PA-28 Cherokee 140C	T. A. Hird	
G-AYKX	PA-28 Cherokee 140C	Robin Flying Group	
G-AYKZ	SAI KZ-8	R. E. Mitchell/Coventry	
G-AYLA	Glos-Airtourer 115	D. S. P. Disney	
G-AYLB	PA-39 Twin Comanche 160 C/R	G. N. Snell	
G-AYLF	Jodel DR.1051	Sicile Group	
G-AYLL	Jodel DR.1050	C. Joly	
G-AYLP	AA-1 Yankee	D. Nairn & E. Y. Hawkins	
G-AYLV	Jodel D.120	M. R. Henham	
G-AYLX	Hughes 269C	M. Johnson	
G-AYLZ	SPP Super Aero 45 Srs 04	M. Emery	
G-AYME	Fournier RF-5	R. D. Goodger/Biggin Hill	
G-AYMG	HPR-7 Herald 213	Jet Heritage Ltd/Bournemouth	
G-AYMK	PA-28 Cherokee 140C	The Piper Flying Group	
G-AYMO	PA-23 Aztec 250C	R. A. Hastings	
G-AYMP	Currie Wot Special	H. F. Moffatt	
G-AYMR	Lederlin 380L Ladybug	J. S. Brayshaw	
G-AYMI	Jodel DR.1050	Merlin Flying Club Ltd/Hucknall	

Notes	Reg.	Type	Owner or Operator
	G-AYMU	Jodel D.112	M. R. Baker
	G-AYMV	Western 20 balloon	G. F. Turnbull
	G-AYMW	Bell 206A JetRanger 2	PLM Dollar Group Ltd
	G-AYMZ	PA-28 Cherokee 140C	B. E. Walshe
	G-AYNA	Currie Wot	J. Evans
	G-AYND	Cessna 310Q	Source Ltd/Thruxton
	G-AYNF	PA-28 Cherokee 140C	W. S. Bath
	G-AYNJ	PA-28 Cherokee 140C	Southern Flight Training Ltd
	G-AYNN	Cessna 185B Skywagon	Bencray Ltd/Blackpool
	G-AYNP	W.S.55 Whirlwifind Srs 3 ★	IHM/Weston-s-Mare
	G-AYOM	Sikorsky S-61N Mk 2	British International Helicopters
	G-AYOP	BAC One-Eleven 530FX	European Aircharter Ltd
	G-AYOW	Cessna 182N Skylane	A. T. Jay/Sleap
	G-AYOY	Sikorsky S-61N Mk 2	British International Helicopters
	G-AYOZ	Cessna FA.150L	T. K. Day
	G-AYPD	Beech 95-B55A Baron	F. Sherwood & Sons (Transport) Ltd
	G-AYPE	MBB Bo 209 Monsun	Papa Echo Ltd/Biggin Hill
	G-AYPG	Cessna F.177RG	D. Davies
	G-AYPH	Cessna F.177RG	W. J. D. Tollett
	G-AYPI	Cessna F.177RG	Cardinal Aviation Ltd/Guernsey
	G-AYPJ	PA-28 Cherokee 180	Mona Aviation Ltd
	G-AYPM	PA-18 Super Cub 95	J. M. Campbell & R. Horner
	G-AYPO	PA-18 Super Cub 95	A. W. Knowles
	G-AYPR	PA-18 Super Cub 95	D. G. Holman & J. E. Burrell
	G-AYPS	PA-18 Super Cub 95	Tony Dyer Television
	G-AYPT	PA-18 Super Cub 95	B. L. Proctor & T. F. Lyddon
	G-AYPU	PA-28R Cherokee Arrow 200	Alpine Ltd/Jersey
	G-AYPV	PA-28 Cherokee 140D	Ashley Gardner Flying Club Ltd
	G-AYPZ	Campbell Cricket	A. Melody
	G-AYRF	Cessna F.150L	D. T. A. Rees
	G-AYRG	Cessna F.172K	Comed Aviation Ltd
	G-AYRH	M.S.892A Rallye Commodore 150	J. D. Watt
	G-AYRI	PA-28R Cherokee Arrow 200	E. P. Van Mechelen & Delta Motor Co (Windsor) Sales Ltd/White Waltham
	G-AYRO	Cessna FA.150L Aerobat	Flying Services
	G-AYRS	Jodel D.120A	Claybourns Garage Ltd
	G-AYRT	Cessna F.172K	K. W. J. & A. B. L. Hayward
	G-AYRU	BN-2A-6 Islander	Joint Service Parachute Centre/ Netheravon
	G-AYSA	PA-23 Aztec 250C	N. Parkinson & W. Smith
	G-AYSB	PA-30 Twin Comanche 160C	D. L. Davies
	G-AYSD	Slingsby T.61A Falke	P. W. Hextall
	G-AYSH	Taylor JT.1 Monoplane	C. J. Lodge
	G-AYSJ	Bücker B133C Jungmeister (LG+01)	Patina Ltd/Duxford
	G-AYSK	Luton LA-4A Minor	Luton Minor Group
	G-AYSX	Cessna F.177RG	C. P. Heptonstall
	G-AYSY	Cessna F.177RG	Horizon Flyers Ltd/Denham
	G-AYTA	SOCATA M.S.880B Rallye Club ★	Manchester Musuem of Science & Industry
	G-AYTR	CP.301A Emeraude	G. N. Hopcraft
	G-AYTT	Phoenix PM-3 Duet	H. E. Jenner
	G-AYTV	MJ.2A Tempete	D. Perry
	G-AYUA	Auster AOP.9 (XK416)	De Havilland Aviation Ltd
	G-AYUB	CEA DR.253B	D. J. Brook
	G-AYUH	PA-28 Cherokee 180F	G-AYUH Group
	G-AYUI	PA-28 Cherokee 180	Ansair Aviation Ltd/Andrewsfield
	G-AYUJ	Evans VP-1	T. N. Howard
	G-AYUM	Slingsby T.61A Falke	Hereward Flying Group//Crowland
	G-AYUN	Slingsby T.61A Falke	C. W. Vigar & R. J. Watts
	G-AYUP	Slingsby T.61A Falke	P. R. Williams
	G-AYUR	Slingsby T.61A Falke	R. Hanningan & R. Lingard
	G-AYUS	Taylor JT.1 Monoplane	R. R. McKinnon
	G-AYUT	Jodel DR.1050	R. Norris
	G-AYVO	Wallis WA-120 Srs 1	K. H. Wallis
	G-AYVP	Woody Pusher	J. R. Wraight
	G-AYVT	Brochet MB.84 ★	Dunelm Flying Group (stored)
	G-AYWA	Avro 19 Srs 2 ★	N. K. Geddes
	G-AYWD	Cessna 182N	Chartec Ltd
	G-AYWE	PA-28 Cherokee 140	N. RobersWon
	G-AYWH	Jodel D.117A	D. Kynaston & J. Deakin
	G-AYWM	Glos-Airtourer Super 150	The Star Flying Group/Staverton
	G-AYWT	AIA Stampe SV-4C	B. K. Lecomber/Denham

Reg.	Type	Owner or Operator	Notes
G-AYXP	Jodel D.117A	G. N. Davies	
G-AYXS	SIAI-Marchetti S205-18R	M. D. Friend	
G-AYXT	W.S. 55 Whirlwind Srs 2 (XK940)	G. P. Hinkley	
G-AYXU	Champion 7KCAB Citabria	Norfolk Gliding Club Ltd/Tibenham	
G-AYXW	Evans VP-1	J. S. Penny	
G-AYYG	H.S.748 Srs 2A	Emerald Airways Ltd/Liverpool	
G-AYYK	Slingsby T.61A Falke	Cornish Gliding & Flying Club Ltd/ Perranporth	
G-AYYL	Slingsby T.61A Falke	C. Wood	
G-AYYO	Jodel DR.1050/M1	Bustard Flying Club Ltd	
G-AYYT	Jodel DR.1050/M1	Echo November Flight	
G-AYYU	Beech C23 Musketeer	Sundowner Aviation	
G-AYYW	BN-2A Islander	RN & R. Marines Sport Parachute Association/Dunkeswell	
G-AYYX	M.S.880B Ralle Club	J. G. MacDonald	
G-AYYY	M.S.880B Rallye Club	T. W. Heffer/Elstree	
G-AYZE	PA-39 Twin Comanche 160 C/R	J. E. Palmer/Staverton	
G-AYZH	Taylor JT.2 Titch	P. J. G. Goddard	
G-AYZI	SNCAN Stampe SV-4C	W. H. Smout	
G-AYZJ	W.S.55 Whirlwind Srs 2 (XM685) ★	Newark Air Museum	
G-AYZK	Jodel DR.1050/M1	D. G. Hesketh & R. L. Sambell	
G-AYZS	D.62B Condor	P. E. J. Huntley & M. N. Thrush	
G-AYZU	Slingsby T.61A Falke	The Falcon Gliding Group/Elstree	
G-AYZW	Slingsby T.61A Falke	Portmoak Falke Syndicate	
G-AZAB	PA-30 Twin Comanche 160B	T. W. P. Sheffield/Humberside	
G-AZAD	Jodel DR.1050	Cawdor Flying Group/Inverness	
G-AZAJ	PA-28R Cherokee Arrow 200B	J. McHugh & ptnrs/Stapleford	
G-AZAV	Cessna 337F	Orbit Resource Ltd	
G-AZAW	GY-80 Horizon 160	C. Prosser/Biggin Hill	
G-AZAZ	Bensen B.8M ★	F.A.A. Museum/Yeovilton	
G-AZBA	T.66 Nipper 3	C. R. A. Scrope	
G-AZBB	MBB Bo 209 Monsun 160FV	G. N. Richardson/Staverton	
G-AZBC	PA-39 Twin Comanche 160 C/R	H. G. Orchin	
G-AZBE	Glos-Airtourer Super 150	BE Flying Group/Staverton	
G-AZBI	Jodel 150	F. M. Ward	
G-AZBL	Jodel D.9 Bebe	J. Hill	
G-AZBN	AT-16 Harvard IIB (FT391)	Swaygate Ltd/Shoreham	
G-AZBU	Auster AOP.9 (XR246)	Auster Nine Group	
G-AZBY	W.S.58 Wessex 60 Srs 1★	IHM/Weston-s-Mare	
G-AZBZ	W.S.58 Wessex 60 Srs 1★	IHM/Weston-s-Mare	
G-AZCB	SNCAN Stampe SV-4C	M. L. Martin	
G-AZCK	B.121 Pup 2	D. R. Newell	
G-AZCL	B.121 Pup 2	L. Bax	
G-AZCN	B.121 Pup 2	R. C. Antonini/Biggin Hill	
G-AZCP	B.121 Pup 1	T. J. Watson/Elstree	
G-AZCT	B.121 Pup 1	Northamptonshire School of Flying Ltd/ Sywell	
G-AZCU	B.121 Pup 1	A. A. Harris/Shobdon	
G-AZCV	B.121 Pup 1	N. R. W. Long/Elstree	
G-AZCY	B.121 Pup 2	Europlus Services Ltd	
G-AZCZ	B.121 Pup 2	L. & J. M. Northover	
G-AZDA	B.121 Pup 1	B. D. Deubelbeiss	
G-AZDD	MBB Bo 209 Monsun 150FF	Double Delta Flying Group/Biggin Hill	
G-AZDE	PA-28R Cherokee Arrow 200B	Electro-Motion UK (Export) Ltd	
G-AZDF	Cameron O-84 balloon	K. L. C. M. Busemeyer	
G-AZDG	B.121 Pup 2	D. J. Sage & J. R. Heaps	
G-AZDK	Beech 95-B55 Baron	C. C. Forrester	
G-AZDX	PA-28 Cherokee 180F	M. Cowan	
G-AZDY	D.H.82A Tiger Moth	J. B. Mills	
G-AZEE	M.S.880B Rallye Club	J. Shelton	
G-AZEF	Jodel D.120	J. R. Legge	
G-AZEG	PA-28 Cherokee 140D	Ashley Gardner Flying Club Ltd	
G-AZEU	B.121 Pup 2	P. Tonkin & R. S. Kinman	
G-AZEV	B.121 Pup 2	G. P. Martin	
G-AZEW	B.121 Pup 2	K. Cameron	
G-AZEY	B.121 Pup 2	R. Hodgson	
G-AZFA	B.121 Pup 2	K. F. Plummer	
G-AZFC	PA-28 Cherokee 140D	M. L. Hannah/Blackbushe	
G-AZFF	Jodel D.112	R. Pidcock	
G-AZFI	PA-28R Cherokee Arrow 200B	G-AZFI Ltd/Sherburn	
G-AZFM	PA-28R Cherokee Arrow 200B	T. N. Jenness	
G-AZFP	Cessna F.177RG	R. E. Knapton	

41

Notes	Reg.	Type	Owner or Operator
	G-AZFR	Cessna 401B	Westair Flying Services Ltd/Blackpool
	G-AZGA	Jodel D.120	D. H. Pattison
	G-AZGC	SNCAN Stampe SV-4C (No 120)	V. Lindsay
	G-AZGE	SNCAN Stampe SV-4A	M. R. L. Astor/Booker
	G-AZGF	B.121 Pup 2	K. Singh
	G-AZGI	M.S.880B Rallye Club	B. McIntyre
	G-AZGJ	M.S.880B Rallye Club	P. Rose
	G-AZGL	M.S.894A Rallye Minerva	The Cambridge Aero Club Ltd
	G-AZGY	CP.301B Emeraude	J. R. Riley-Gale
	G-AZGZ	D.H.82A Tiger Moth (NM181)	F. R. Manning
	G-AZHB	Robin HR.100-200	C. & P. P. Scarlett/Sywell
	G-AZHC	Jodel D.112	J. A. Summer & A. Burton/Netherthorpe
	G-AZHD	Slingsby T.61A Falke	J. Sentance
	G-AZHE	Slingsby T.61B Falke	M. R. Shelton/Tatenhill
	G-AZHH	SA 102.5 Cavalier	D. W. Buckle
	G-AZHI	Glos-Airtourer Super 150	H. J. Douglas/Biggin Hill
	G-AZHJ	SA Twin Pioneer Srs 3	Prestwick Pioneer Preservation Soc Ltd
	G-AZHK	Robin HR.100/200B	Hotel Kilo Flying Group (G-ILEG)
	G-AZHR	Piccard Ax6 balloon	C. Fisher
	G-AZHT	Glos-Airtourer T.3	Aviation West Ltd/Glasgow
	G-AZHU	Luton LA-4A Minor	W. Cawrey/Netherthorpe
	G-AZIB	ST-10 Diplomate	Diplomate Group
	G-AZID	Cessna FA.150L	G. C. B. Weir
	G-AZII	Jodel D.117A	J. S. Brayshaw
	G-AZIJ	Jodel DR.360	Rob Airway Ltd/Guernsey
	G-AZIK	PA-34-200 Seneca II	Xaxanaka Aviation Ltd
	G-AZIL	Slingsby T.61A Falke	D. W. Savage/Portmoak
	G-AZIO	SNCAN Stampe SV-4C (Lycoming) ★	—/Booker
	G-AZIP	Cameron O-65 balloon	Dante Balloon Group *Dante*
	G-AZJC	Fournier RF-5	W. St. G. V. Stoney/Italy
	G-AZJE	Ord-Hume JB-01 Minicab	J. B. Evans/Sandown
	G-AZJN	Robin DR.300/140	Wright Farm Eggs Ltd
	G-AZJV	Cessna F.172L	J. A. & A. J. Boyd/Cardiff
	G-AZJY	Cessna FRA.150L	G. Firbank/Manchester
	G-AZKC	M.S.880B Rallye Club	L. J. Martin/Redhill
	G-AZKE	M.S.880B Rallye Club	B. S. Rowden & W. L. Rogers
	G-AZKK	Cameron O-56 balloon	Gemini Balloon Group *Gemini*
	G-AZKO	Cessna F.337F	Crispair Aviation Services Ltd
	G-AZKP	Jodel D.117	J. Lowe
	G-AZKR	PA-24 Comanche 180	S. McGovern
	G-AZKS	AA-1A Trainer	M. D. Henson
	G-AZKW	Cessna F.172L	J. C. C. Wright
	G-AZKZ	Cessna F.172L	R. D. & E. Forster/Swanton Morley
	G-AZLE	Boeing N2S-5 Kaydet	Air Farm Flyers
	G-AZLF	Jodel D.120	M. S. C. Ball
	G-AZLH	Cessna F.150L	P. T. W. Sheffield
	G-AZLJ	BN-2A Mk III-1 Trislander	Hebridean Air Services Ltd (G-OREG/G-OAVW)
	G-AZLL	Cessna FRA.150L	Rankart Ltd
	G-AZLN	PA-28 Cherokee 180F	Liteflite Ltd/Kidlington
	G-AZLO	Cessna F.337F	*stored*/Bourn
	G-AZLV	Cessna 172K	B. L. F. Karthaus
	G-AZLY	Cessna F.150L	Cleveland Flying School Ltd/Teesside
	G-AZLZ	Cessna F.150L	G-AZLZ Group
	G-AZMB	Bell 47G-3B	Helitech (Luton) Ltd
	G-AZMC	Slingsby T.61A Falke	Essex Gliding Club Ltd
	G-AZMD	Slingsby T.61C Falke	R. A. Rice/Wellesbourne
	G-AZMF	BAC One-Eleven 530FX	European Aircharter Ltd
	G-AZMH	Morane-Saulnier M.S.500 (7A+WN)	Old Flying Machine Co/Duxford
	G-AZMJ	AA-5 Traveler	R. T. Love/Bodmin
	G-AZMN	Glos-Airtourer T.5	W. Crozier & I. Young
	G-AZMX	PA-28 Cherokee 140 ★	NE Wales Institute of Higher Education (Instructional airframe)/Clwyd
	G-AZMZ	M.S.893A Rallye Commodore 150	P. J. Wilcox/Cranfield
	G-AZNK	SNCAN Stampe SV-4A	P. D. Jackson
	G-AZNL	PA-28R Cherokee Arrow 200D	B. P. Liversidge
	G-AZNO	Cessna 182P	W. Hay & M. P. Grimshaw
	G-AZOA	MBB Bo 209 Monsun 150FF	M. W. Hurst
	G-AZOB	MBB Bo 209 Monsun 150FF	G. N. Richardson/Staverton
	G-AZOE	Glos-Airtourer 115	G-AZOE 607 Group
	G-AZOF	Glos-Airtourer Super 150	Cirrus Flying Group/Denham

Reg.	Type	Owner or Operator	Notes
G-AZOG	PA-28R Cherokee Arrow 200D	J. G. Collins/Cambridge	
G-AZOL	PA-34-200 Seneca II	St Bridgets Aviation Ltd & ptnrs	
G-AZOR	MBB Bo 105D	Bond Helicopters Ltd/Bourn	
G-AZOS	Jurca MJ.5-F1 Sirocco	M. K. Field	
G-AZOT	PA-34-200 Seneca II	AJ Air Services (Aircraft Leasing) Ltd	
G-AZOU	Jodel DR.1050	Horsham Flying Group/Slinfold	
G-AZOZ	Cessna FRA.150L	Seawing Flying Club Ltd/Southend	
G-AZPA	PA-25 Pawnee 235	Black Mountain Gliding Co Ltd	
G-AZPC	Slingsby T.61C Falke	M. F. Cuming	
G-AZPF	Fournier RF-5	R. Pye/Blackpool	
G-AZPH	Craft-Pitts S-1S Special ★	Science Museum/S. Kensington	
G-AZPV	Luton LA-4A Minor	J. R. Faulkner	
G-AZRA	MBB Bo 209 Monsun 150FF	Alpha Flying Ltd/Denham	
G-AZRD	Cessna 401B	Romeo Delta Group	
G-AZRH	PA-28 Cherokee 140D	Joseph Carter & Sons (Jersey) Ltd	
G-AZRK	Fournier RF-5	P. M. Brocklington & J. F. Rogers	
G-AZRL	PA-18 Super Cub 95	B. J. Stead	
G-AZRM	Fournier RF-5	A. R. Dearden & R. Speer/Shoreham	
G-AZRN	Cameron O-84 balloon	C. A. Butter & J. J. T. Cooke	
G-AZRP	Glos-Airtourer 115	B. F. Strawford/Shobdon	
G-AZRR	Cessna 310Q	Routarrow Ltd/Norwich	
G-AZRS	PA-22 Tri-Pacer 150	Sandpiper Group	
G-AZRV	PA-28R Cherokee Arrow 200B	General Airline Ltd	
G-AZRZ	Cessna U.206F	M. E. Bolton	
G-AZSA	Stampe et Renard SV-4B	J. K. Faulkner/Biggin Hill	
G-AZSC	AT-16 Harvard IIB	Machine Music Ltd	
G-AZSD	Slingsby T.29B Motor Tutor	Essex Aviation	
G-AZSF	PA-28R Cherokee Arrow 200D	Flight Simulation/Coventry	
G-AZSH	PA-28R Cherokee Arrow 180	C. & G. Clarkex	
G-AZSW	B.121 Pup 1	I. T. Dall/Sywell	
G-AZSZ	PA-23 Aztec 250D	International Cladding Systems Ltd	
G-AZTA	MBB Bo 209 Monsun 150FF	A. I. D. Rich/Elstree	
G-AZTD	PA-32 Cherokee Six 300D	Presshouse Publications Ltd/Enstone	
G-AZTF	Cessna F.177RG	Air Tabernacle Ltd/Sandown	
G-AZTK	Cessna F.172F	Vascas Ltd	
G-AZTR	SNCAN Stampe SV-4C	P. G. Palumbo/Booker	
G-AZTS	Cessna F.172L	C. E. Stringer	
G-AZTV	Stolp SA.500 Starlet	G. R. Rowland	
G-AZTW	Cessna F.177RG	R. M. Clarke/Leicester	
G-AZUM	Cessna F.172L	Fowlmere Fliers	
G-AZUP	Cameron O-65 balloon	R. S. Bailey & A. B. Simpson	
G-AZUT	M.S.893A Rallye Commodore 180	J. Palethorpe	
G-AZUV	Cameron O-65 balloon ★	British Balloon Museum	
G-AZUX	Western O-56 balloon	D. M. & K. R. Sandford	
G-AZUY	Cessna E.310L	Euromarine Group Ltd	
G-AZUZ	Cessna FRA.150L	D. J. Parker/Netherthorpe	
G-AZVB	MBB Bo 209 Monsun 150FF	P. C. Logsdon/Dunkeswell	
G-AZVE	AA-5 Traveler	R. Peters/Rochester	
G-AZVF	M.S.894A Rallye Minerva	J. B. Ballagh	
G-AZVG	AA-5 Traveler	Grumair Flying Group	
G-AZVH	M.S.894A Rallye Minerva	P. L. Jubb	
G-AZVI	M.S.892A Rallye Commodore	Shobdon Flying Group	
G-AZVJ	PA-34-200 Seneca II	Skyfotos Ltd/Lydd	
G-AZVL	Jodel D.119	Forest Flying Group/Stapleford	
G-AZVM	Hughes 369HS	Diagnostic Reagents Ltd	
G-AZVP	Cessna F.177RG	Cardinal Flyers Ltd	
G-AZWB	PA-28 Cherokee 140	B. N. Rides & L. Connor	
G-AZWD	PA-28 Cherokee 140	BM Aviation (Winchester)	
G-AZWE	PA-28 Cherokee 140	G-AZWE Flying Group	
G-AZWF	SAN Jodel DR.1050	G-AZWF Jodel Syndicate	
G-AZWS	PA-28R Cherokee Arrow 180	Arrow 88 Flying Group	
G-AZWT	Westland Lysander IIIA (V9441)	Strathallan Aircraft Collection	
G-AZWY	PA-24 Comanche 260	Keymer Son & Co Ltd/Biggin Hill	
G-AZXA	Beech 95-C55 Baron	F.R. Aviation Ltd/Bournemouth	
G-AZXB	Cameron O-65 balloon	R. J. Mitchener & P. F.Smart	
G-AZXC	Cessna F.150L	D. C. Bonsall	
G-AZXD	Cessna F.172L	Birdlake Ltd/Wellesbourne	
G-AZXG	PA-23 Aztec 250D★	*instructional airframe*/Cranfield	
G-AZYA	GY-80 Horizon 160	T. Poole & ptnrs/Sywell	
G-AZYB	Bell 47H-1 ★	IHM/Weston-s-Mare	
G-AZYD	M.S.893A Rallye Commodore	Buckminster Gliding Club Ltd/Saltby	
G-AZYM	Cessna E.310Q	Offshore Marine Consultants Ltd	
G-AZYS	CP.301C-1 Emeraude	F. P. L. Clauson	

Notes	Reg.	Type	Owner or Operator
	G-AZYU	PA-23 Aztec 250E	L. J. Martin/Biggin Hill
	G-AZYV	Burns O-77 balloon	Gioiland SRL/Italy
	G-AZYY	Slingsby T.61A Falke	J. A. Towers
	G-AZYZ	WA.51A Pacific	L. M. Palmer/Biggin Hill
	G-AZZG	Cessna 188 Agwagon	N. C. Kensington
	G-AZZH	Practavia Pilot Sprite 115	A. Moore
	G-AZZO	PA-28 Cherokee 140	R. J. Hind/Elstree
	G-AZZP	Cessna F.172H	Weald Air Services Ltd/Headcorn
	G-AZZR	Cessna F.150L	R. J. Doughton
	G-AZZS	PA-34-200 Seneca II	Robin Cook Aviation/Shoreham
	G-AZZT	PA-28 Cherokee.180 ★	Ground instruction airframe/Cranfield
	G-AZZV	Cessna F.172L	D. J. Hockings
	G-AZZW	Fournier RF-5	R. G. Trute
	G-AZZZ	D.H.82A Tiger Moth	S. W. McKay
	G-BAAD	Evans Super VP-1	R. A. Burn
	G-BAAF	Manning-Flanders MF1 (replica)	Aviation Film Services Ltd/Booker
	G-BAAI	M.S.893A Rallye Commodore	R. D. Taylor/Thruxton
	G-BAAL	Cessna 172A	Rochester Aviation Ltd
	G-BAAU	Enstrom F-28C-UK	M. Upton
	G-BAAW	Jodel D.119	K. J. Cockrill/Ipswich
	G-BAAZ	PA-28R Cherokee Arrow 200D	A. W. Rix/Guernsey
	G-BABB	Cessna F.150L	Seawing Flying Club Ltd/Southend
	G-BABC	Cessna F.150L	Fordaire Aviation Ltd
	G-BABD	Cessna FRA.150L	C. J. Hopewell
	G-BABE	Taylor JT.2 Titch	P. D. G. Grist/Sibson
	G-BABG	PA-28 Cherokee 180	Mendip Flying Group/Bristol
	G-BABH	Cessna F.150L	Skyviews & General Ltd
	G-BABK	PA-34-200 Seneca II	D. F. J. Flashman/Biggin Hill
	G-BABY	Taylor JT.2 Titch	R. E. Finlay
	G-BACB	PA-34-200 Seneca II	London Flight Centre (Stansted) Ltd
	G-BACC	Cessna FRA.150L	C. M. & J. H. Cooper/Cranfield
	G-BACE	Fournier RF-5	R. W. K. Stead/Perranporth
	G-BACJ	Jodel D.120	Wearside Flying Association/Newcastle
	G-BACL	Jodel 150	M. L. Sargeant/Biggin Hill
	G-BACN	Cessna FRA.150L	Air Service Training Ltd/Perth
	G-BACO	Cessna FRA.150L	M. M. Pepper/Sibson
	G-BACP	Cessna FRA.150L	Vectair Aviation 1995 Ltd
	G-BADC	Rollason Beta B.2A	J. C. Mead
	G-BADH	Slingsby T.61A Falke	Falke Flying Group
	G-BADI	PA-23 Aztec 250D	W. London Aero Services Ltd/ White Waltham
	G-BADJ	PA-E23 Aztec 250E	Bell Aviation
	G-BADL	PA-34-200 Seneca II	K. Smith & M. Corbett
	G-BADM	D.62B Condor	M. Harris & J. Taylor
	G-BADO	PA-32 Cherokee Six 300E	M. A. S. Talbot
	G-BADW	Pitts S-2A Special	R. E. Mitchell/Coventry
	G-BADZ	Pitts S-2A Special	A. F. D. Kingdon
	G-BAEB	Robin DR.400/160	P. D. W. King
	G-BAEC	Robin HR.100/210	Robin Travel & Designways (Interior Design) Ltd
	G-BAED	PA-23 Aztec 250C	K. G. Manktelow & N. Brewitt
	G-BAEE	Jodel DR.1050/M1	R. Little
	G-BAEM	Robin DR.400/125	M. A. Webb/Booker
	G-BAEN	Robin DR.400/180	European Soaring Club Ltd
	G-BAEP	Cessna FRA.150L (modified)	A. M. Lynn
	G-BAER	Cosmic Wind	R. S. Voice/Redhill
	G-BAET	Piper J-3C-65 Cub	C. J. Rees
	G-BAEU	Cessna F.150L	Skyviews & General Ltd
	G-BAEV	Cessna FRA.L150L	B. A. Mills
	G-BAEW	Cessna F.172M	Westley Aircraft/Cranfield
	G-BAEY	Cessna F.172M	R. Fursman/Southampton
	G-BAEZ	Cessna FRA.150L	Donair Flying Club Ltd/E. Midlands
	G-BAFA	AA-5 Traveler	C. F. Mackley/Stapleford
	G-BAFD	MBB Bo 105D	Bond Helicopters Ltd/Aberdeen
	G-BAFG	D.H.82A Tiger Moth	J. E. & P. J. Shaw
	G-BAFH	Evans VP-1	C. M. Gibson
	G-BAFI	Cessna F.177RG	Gloucestershire Flying Club
	G-BAFL	Cessna 182P	Farm Aviation Services Ltd
	G-BAFP	Robin DR.400/160	A. S. Langdale & J. Bevis-Lawson
	G-BAFS	PA-18 Super Cub 150	G-BAFS Group/Sandown
	G-BAFT	PA-18 Super Cub 150	T. J. Wilkinson/Riseley
	G-BAFU	PA-28 Cherokee 140	M. Kostiuk

Reg.	Type	Owner or Operator	Notes
G-BAFV	PA-18 Super Cub 95	T. F. & S. J. Thorpe	
G-BAFW	PA-28 Cherokee 140	P. H. Marlow & R. W. Bonner-Davies	
G-BAFX	Robin DR.400/140	K. R. Gough	
G-BAGB	SIAI-Marchetti SF.260	British Midland Airways Ltd/E. Midlands	
G-BAGC	Robin DR.400/140	W. P. Nutt	
G-BAGE	Cessna T.210L ★	Aeroplane Collection Ltd	
G-BAGF	Jodel D.92 Bebe	E. Evans	
G-BAGG	PA-32 Cherokee Six 300E	Guernsey Colour Laboratories Ltd	
G-BAGI	Cameron O-31 balloon	Red Section Balloon Group	
G-BAGL	SA.341G Gazelle Srs 1	Crown Colourprint Ltd	
G-BAGN	Cessna F.177RG	R. W. J. Andrews	
G-BAGO	Cessna 421B	Golden Aviation Ltd	
G-BAGR	Robin DR.400/140	F. C. Aris & J. D. Last/Mona	
G-BAGS	Robin DR.400/180 2+2	Headcorn Flying School Ltd	
G-BAGT	Helio H.295 Courier	B. J. C. Woodall Ltd	
G-BAGV	Cessna U.206F	Scottish Parachute Club/Strathallan	
G-BAGX	PA-28 Cherokee 140	Golf X-Ray Group	
G-BAGY	Cameron O-84 balloon	P. G. Dunnington	
G-BAHD	Cessna 182P Skylane	G. G. Ferriman	
G-BAHE	PA-28 Cherokee 140	A. H. Evans & A. O. Jones	
G-BAHF	PA-28 Cherokee 140	W. E. Jevons	
G-BAHG	PA-24 Comanche 260	E. & M. Green	
G-BAHH	Wallis WA-121	K. H. Wallis	
G-BAHI	Cessna F.150H	A. G. Brindle/Blackpool	
G-BAHJ	PA-24 Comanche 250	K. Cooper	
G-BAHL	Robin DR.400/160	M. A. Newman/Thruxton	
G-BAHO	Beech C.23 Sundowner	P. H. White & J. A. L. Staig	
G-BAHP	Volmer VJ.22 Sportsman	Seaplane Group	
G-BAHS	PA-28R Cherokee Arrow 200-II	Border Reivers Flying Group	
G-BAHX	Cessna 182P	PP Dupost Group	
G-BAIB	Enstrom F-28A	Farmax Helicopters	
G-BAIH	PA-28R Cherokee Arrow 200-II	M. G. West & J. A. Havers	
G-BAII	Cessna FRA.150L	Air Service Training Ltd/Perth	
G-BAIK	Cessna F.150L	Wickenby Aviation Ltd	
G-BAIL	Cessna FR.172J	Gloucestershire Flying Club	
G-BAIM	Cessna 310Q	(Instructional airframe)/Perth	
G-BAIN	Cessna FRA.150L	Air Service Training Ltd/Perth	
G-BAIP	Cessna F.150L	G. & S. A. Jones	
G-BAIS	Cessna F.177RG	Cardinal Syndicate	
G-BAIW	Cessna F.172M	W. J. Greenfield/Humberside	
G-BAIX	Cessna F.172M	R. A. Nichols/Elstree	
G-BAIZ	Slingsby T.61A Falke	Falke Syndicate/Hinton-in-the-Hedges	
G-BAJA	Cessna F.177RG	Don Ward Productions Ltd/Biggin Hill	
G-BAJB	Cessna F.177RG	C. M. Bain	
G-BAJC	Evans VP-1	R. A. Hazelton	
G-BAJE	Cessna 177 Cardinal	N. C. Butcher	
G-BAJN	AA-5 Traveler	Janacrew Flying Group	
G-BAJO	AA-5 Traveler	G-BAJO Group	
G-BAJR	PA-28 Cherokee 180	Chosen Few Flying Group/Newtownards	
G-BAJY	Robin DR.400/180	Rolines Aviation	
G-BAJZ	Robin DR.400/125	Rochester Aviation Ltd	
G-BAKD	PA-34-200 Seneca II	Andrews Professional Colour Laboratories/ Elstree	
G-BAKH	PA-28 Cherokee 140	Marnham Investments Ltd	
G-BAKJ	PA-30 Twin Comanche 160B	M. F. Fisher & W. R. Lawes/Biggin Hill	
G-BAKK	Cessna 172H ★	Parachute jump trainer/Hinton-in-the-Hedges	
G-BAKM	Robin DR.400/140	D. V. Pieri	
G-BAKN	SNCAN Stampe SV-4C	M. Holloway	
G-BAKR	Jodel D.117	A. B. Bailey/White Waltham	
G-BAKS	AB-206B JetRanger 2	Stephenson Marine Co Ltd	
G-BAKV	PA-18 Super Cub 150	Pounds Marine Shipping Ltd/Goodwood	
G-BAKW	B.121 Pup 2	M. N. Mendonca/Portugal	
G-BAKY	Slingsby T.61C Falke	Buckminster Gliding Club Ltd/Saltby	
G-BALF	Robin DR.400/140	N. A. Smith	
G-BALG	Robin DR.400/180	R. Jones	
G-BALH	Robin DR.400/140B	G-BALH Flying Group	
G-BALI	Robin DR.400 2+2	Robin Flying Group	
G-BALJ	Robin DR.400/180	D. A. Bett & D. de Lacey-Rowe	
G-BALK	SNCAN Stampe SV-4C	L. J. Rice	
G-BALN	Cessna T.310Q	O'Brien ÓProperties Ltd/Shoreham	
G-BALX	D.H.82A Tiger Moth (N6848)	S. Cranfield	
G-BALZ	Bell 212	Bristow Helicopters Ltd	

Notes	Reg.	Type	Owner or Operator
	G-BAMB	Slingsby T.61C Falke	G-BAMB Syndicate
	G-BAMC	Cessna F.150L	Barry Aviation Ltd
	G-BAMF	MBB Bo 105D	Bond Helicopters Ltd/Bourn
	G-BAMJ	Cessna 182P	A. E. Kedros
	G-BAMK	Cameron D-96 airship	D. W. Liddiard
	G-BAML	Bell 206B JetRanger 2	Heliscott Ltd
	G-BAMM	PA-28 Cherokee 235	T. A. Astell/Shoreham
	G-BAMR	PA-16 Clipper	H. Royce
	G-BAMS	Robin DR.400/160	G-BAMS Ltd/Headcorn
	G-BAMU	Robin DR.400/160	The Alternative Flying Group
	G-BAMV	Robin DR.400/180	K. Jones & E. A. Anderson/Booker
	G-BAMY	PA-28R Cherokee Arrow 200-II	G-BAMY Group/Birmingham
	G-BANA	Robin DR.221	G. T. Pryor
	G-BANB	Robin DR.400/180	M. J. Cuttell
	G-BANC	GY-201 Minicab	J. T. S. Lewis & J. E. Williams
	G-BAND	Cameron O-84 balloon	Mid-Bucks Farmers Balloon Group
	G-BANE	Cessna FRA.150L	Belfast Flying Club Ltd/Aldergrove
	G-BANG	Cameron O-84 balloon	R. F. Harrower
	G-BANK	PA-34-200 Seneca II	Cleveland Flying School Ltd/Teesside
	G-BANU	Wassmer Jodel D.120	C. E. McKinney
	G-BANV	Phoenix Currie Wot	K. Knight
	G-BANW	CP.1330 Super Emeraude	P. S. Milner
	G-BANX	Cessna F.172M	J. F. Davis/Badminton
	G-BAOB	Cessna F.172M	Rentair Ltd & ptnrs
	G-BAOG	M.S.880B Rallye Club	A. D. Marks
	G-BAOH	M.S.880B Rallye Club	R. D. Andrews
	G-BAOJ	M.S.880B Rallye Club	R. E. Jones
	G-BAOM	M.S.880B Rallye Club	D. H. Tonkin
	G-BAOP	Cessna FRA.150L	C. M. Dixon
	G-BAOS	Cessna F.172M	Wingtask 1995 Ltd
	G-BAOU	AA-5 Traveler	S. A. Westhorp
	G-BAOW	Cameron O-65 balloon	I. Chadwick
	G-BAPA	Fournier RF-5B Sperber	Nuthampstead G-BAPA Group
	G-BAPB	D.H.C.1 Chipmunk 22	G. V. Bunyan
	G-BAPC	Luton LA-4A Minor ★	Midland Aircraft Preservation Soc
	G-BAPI	Cessna FRA.150L	Industrial Supplies (Peterborough) Ltd/ Sibson
	G-BAPJ	Cessna FRA.150L	M. D. Page/Manston
	G-BAPK	Cessna F.150L	Andrewsfield Flying Club Ltd
	G-BAPL	PA-23 Turbo Aztec 250E	Donington Aviation Ltd/E. Midlands
	G-BAPM	Fuji FA.200-160	Oakfleet Ltd
	G-BAPP	Evans VP-1	V. Mitchell
	G-BAPR	Jodel D.11	J. B. Liber & J. F. M. Bartlett
	G-BAPS	Campbell Cougar ★	IHM/Weston-s-Mare
	G-BAPV	Robin DR.400/160	J. D. & M. Millne
	G-BAPW	PA-28R Cherokee Arrow 180	I. W. Lindsey & P. S. Ferren/Elstree
	G-BAPX	Robin DR.400/160	M. A. Musselwhite
	G-BAPY	Robin HR.100/210	Gloria Baby Aviation Ltd
	G-BARC	Cessna FR.172J	Severn Valley Aviation Group
	G-BARD	Cessna 337C	D. W. Horton
	G-BARF	Jodel D.112 Club	J. J. Penney
	G-BARG	Cessna E.310Q	M. S. Harvell
	G-BARH	Beech C.23 Sundowner	J. R. Pybus
	G-BARJ	Bell 212	Autair International Ltd/Panshanger
	G-BARP	Bell 206B JetRanger 2	S.W. Electricity Board/Bristol
	G-BARS	D.H.C.1 Chipmunk 22 (1377)	P. Cawte
	G-BARV	Cessna 310Q	Old England Watches Ltd/Elstree
	G-BARZ	Scheibe SF.28A Tandem Falke	K. Kiely
	G-BASG	AA-5 Traveler	ASG Aviation Group/Glenrothes
	G-BASH	AA-5 Traveler	BASH Flying Group
	G-BASJ	PA-28 Cherokee 180	D. J. Skidmore & E. F. Rowland
	G-BASL	PA-28 Cherokee 140	Air Navigation & Trading Ltd/Blackpool
	G-BASM	PA-34-200 Seneca II	Poplar Aviation Group
	G-BASN	Beech C.23 Sundowner	M. F. Fisher
	G-BASO	Lake LA-4 Amphibian	M. J. Willies
	G-BASP	B.121 Pup 1	B. J. Coutts/Sywell
	G-BASX	PA-34-200 Seneca II	London Executive Aviation Ltd
	G-BATC	MBB Bo 105D	Bond Helicopters Ltd/Swansea
	G-BATJ	Jodel D.119	D. J. & K. S. Thomas
	G-BATN	PA-23 Aztec 250E	Marshall of Cambridge Ltd
	G-BATR	PA-34-200 Seneca II	Falcon Flying Services/Biggin Hill
	G-BATT	Hughes 269C	Victoria Helicopters
	G-BATV	PA-28 Cherokee 180D	J. N. Rudsdale

Reg.	Type	Owner or Operator	Notes
G-BATW	PA-28 Cherokee 140	Tango Whiskey Flying Partnership	
G-BATX	PA-23 Aztec 250E	Tayside Aviation Ltd/Dundee	
G-BAUA	PA-23 Aztec 250D	David Parr & Associates Ltd/Shobdon	
G-BAUC	PA-25 Pawnee 235	Southdown Gliding Club Ltd/Parham Park	
G-BAUE	Cessna 310Q	A. J. Dyer/Elstree	
G-BAUH	Jodel D.112	G. A. & D. Shepherd	
G-BAUJ	PA-23 Aztec 250E	S. J. & C. J. Westley/Cranfield	
G-BAUK	Hughes 269C	Curtis Engineering (Frome) Ltd	
G-BAUN	Bell 206B JetRanger	Bristow Helicopters Ltd	
G-BAUV	Cessna F.150L	Skyviews & General Ltd	
G-BAUW	PA-23 Aztec 250E	R. E. Myson	
G-BAUY	Cessna FRA.150L	Old Buckenham Airfield Ltd	
G-BAUZ	SNCAN NC.854S	W. A. Ashley & D. Horne	
G-BAVB	Cessna F.172M	T. J. Nokes & T. V. Phillips	
G-BAVH	D.H.C.1 Chipmunk 22	Portsmouth Naval Gliding Club/ Lee-on-Solent	
G-BAVL	PA-23 Aztec 250E	S. P. & A. V. Chillott	
G-BAVO	Boeing Stearman N2S (26)	Vallingstone Aviation Ltd	
G-BAVR	AA-5 Traveler	E. R. Pyatt	
G-BAVS	AA-5 Traveler	V. J. Peake/Headcorn	
G-BAVU	Cameron A-105 balloon	J. D. Michaelis	
G-BAVZ	PA-23 Aztec 250E	Ravenair/Manchester	
G-BAWG	PA-28R Cherokee Arrow 200-II	Solent Air Ltd	
G-BAWK	PA-28 Cherokee 140	Newcastle-upon-Tyne Aero Club Ltd	
G-BAWN	PA-30 Twin Comanche 160C	R. A. & J. M. Nunn	
G-BAWR	Robin HR.100/210	T. Taylor	
G-BAWU	PA-30 Twin Comanche 160B	CCH Aviation Ltd	
G-BAXE	Hughes 269A	Reethorpe Engineering Ltd	
G-BAXJ	PA-32 Cherokee Six 300B	UK Parachute Services	
G-BAXK	Thunder Ax7-77 balloon	A. R. Snook	
G-BAXP	PA-23 Aztec 250E	derelict/Shobdon	
G-BAXS	Bell 47G-5	LRC Leisure Ltd	
G-BAXT	PA-28R Cherokee Arrow 200-II	P. R. Phealon/Old Sarum	
G-BAXU	Cessna F.150L	W. Lancs Aero Club Ltd/Woodvale	
G-BAXY	Cessna F.172M	R. J. W. Wood	
G-BAXZ	PA-28 Cherokee 140	H. Martin & D. Norris/Halton	
G-BAYL	SNCAN Nord 1101 Norecrin ★	stored/Chirk	
G-BAYO	Cessna 150L	J. Dixon & Son Ltd	
G-BAYP	Cessna 150L	Popham Pilots Flying Group	
G-BAYR	Robin HR.100/210	L. A. Christie/Stapleford	
G-BAYV	SNCAN 1101 Noralpha (3) ★	Macclesfield Historical Aviation Soc/Barton	
G-BAYZ	Bellanca 7GCBC Citabria	Cambridge University Gliding Trust Ltd/ Gransden Lodge	
G-BAZJ	Robin DR.400/160	Southern Sailplanes	
G-BAZJ	HPR-7 Herald 209 ★	Guernsey Airport Fire Services	
G-BAZM	Jodel D.11	Bingley Flying Group	
G-BAZS	Cessna F.150L	Sherburn Aero Club Ltd	
G-BAZT	Cessna F.172M	M. Fraser/Exeter	
G-BAZU	PA-28R Cherokee Arrow 200	S. C. Simmons/White Waltham	
G-BBAE	L.1011-385 TriStar 100	Caledonian Airways Loch Earn/Gatwick	
G-BBAF	L.1011-385 TriStar 100	Caledonian Airways Loch Fyne/Gatwick	
G-BBAH	L.1011-385 TriStar 100	Caledonian Airways Loch Avon/Gatwick	
G-BBAI	L.1011-385 TriStar 100	Caledonian Airways Loch Inver/Gatwick	
G-BBAJ	L.1011-385 TriStar 100	Caledonian Airways Loch Rannoch/ Gatwick	
G-BBAK	M.S.894A Rallye Minerva	R. B. Hemsworth & C. L. Hill/Exeter	
G-BBAW	Robin HR.100/210	J. R. Williams	
G-BBAX	Robin DR.400/140	G. J. Bissex & P. H. Garbutt	
G-BBAY	Robin DR.400/140	Rothwell Group	
G-BBBC	Cessna F.150L	W. J. Greenfield	
G-BBBI	AA-5 Traveler	D. A. de H. Rowntree	
G-BBBK	PA-28 Cherokee 140	Bencray Ltd/Blackpool	
G-BBBM	Bell 206B JetRanger 2	Express Newspapers PLC	
G-BBBN	PA-28 Cherokee 180	Estuary Aviation Ltd	
G-BBBO	SIPA 903	J. S. Hemmings & C. R. Steer	
G-BBBW	FRED Srs 2	C. Briggs	
G-BBBX	Cessna E310L	Atlantic Air Transport Ltd/Coventry	
G-BBBY	PA-28 Cherokee 140	J. L. Yourell/Luton	
G-BBCA	Bell 206B JetRanger 2	Kelly Trucks Ltd	
G-BBCC	PA-23 Aztec 250D	M. A. S. Talbot	
G-BBCH	Robin DR.400/2+2	Headcorn Flying School Ltd	
G-BBCI	Cessna 150H	L. Jayasekara	

Notes	Reg.	Type	Owner or Operator
	G-BBCN	Robin HR.100/210	K. T. G. Atkins/Teesside
	G-BBCP	Thunder Ax6-56 balloon	J. M. Robinson
	G-BBCS	Robin DR.400/140	C. J. & S. C. Partridge
	G-BBCW	PA-23 Aztec 250E	JDT Holdings Ltd/Sturgate
	G-BBCY	Luton LA-4A Minor	Shoestring Flying Group/Shoreham
	G-BBCZ	AA-5 Traveler	Sky Leisure Aviation Ltd
	G-BBDC	PA-28 Cherokee 140	A. Dunk
	G-BBDD	PA-28 Cherokee 140	Midland Air Training School
	G-BBDE	PA-28R Cherokee Arrow 200-II	R. L. Coleman & A. E. Stevens/ Panshanger
	G-BBDG	Concorde 100 ★	British Aerospace PLC/Filton
	G-BBDH	Cessna F.172M	P. S. C. & B. J. Comina
	G-BBDL	AA-5 Traveler	Delta Lima Flying Group
	G-BBDM	AA-5 Traveler	P. J. Marchant
	G-BBDO	PA-23 Turbo Aztec 250E	Anstee & Ware Ltd/Bristol
	G-BBDP	Robin DR.400/160	Robin Lance Aviation Associates Ltd
	G-BBDT	Cessna 150H	Delta Tango Group
	G-BBDV	SIPA S.903	W. McAndrew
	G-BBEA	Luton LA-4A Minor	G-BBEA Group
	G-BBEB	PA-28R Cherokee Arrow 200-II	R. D. Rippingale/Thruxton
	G-BBEC	PA-28 Cherokee 180	J. B. Conway
	G-BBED	M.S.894A Rallye Minerva 220	Vista Products
	G-BBEF	PA-28 Cherokee 140	Comed Aviation Ltd/Blackpool
	G-BBEI	PA-31 Turbo Navajo	BKS Surveys Ltd/Exeter
	G-BBEL	PA-28R Cherokee Arrow 180	J. Paulson
	G-BBEN	Bellanca 7GCBC Citabria	C. A. G. Schofield
	G-BBEO	Cessna FRA.150L	Moray Flying Club (1990) Ltd/Kinloss
	G-BBEV	PA-28 Cherokee 140	Comed Aviation Ltd/Blackpool
	G-BBEX	Cessna 185A	V. M. McCarthy
	G-BBEY	PA-23 Aztec 250E	M. Hall
	G-BBFC	AA-1B Trainer	I. J. Hiatt
	G-BBFD	PA-28R Cherokee Arrow 200-II	CR Aviation Ltd
	G-BBFL	GY-201 Minicab	D. Silsbury
	G-BBFS	Van Den Bemden gas balloon	A. J. F. Smith
	G-BBFV	PA-32 Cherokee Six 260	Airlaunch/Ipswich
	G-BBGB	PA-E23 Aztec 250E	Ravenair/Manchester
	G-BBGC	M.S.893E Rallye 180GT	Golf Charlie Syndicate
	G-BBGH	AA-5 Traveler	L. W. Mitchell & D. Abbiss
	G-BBGI	Fuji FA.200-160	Sunny Sky Aviation (Jersey) Ltd
	G-BBGL	Baby Great Lakes	F. Ball
	G-BBGR	Cameron O-65 balloon	M. L. & L. P. Willoughby
	G-BBGX	Cessna 182P Skylane	GX Aviation Ltd
	G-BBGZ	CHABA 42 balloon	G. Laslett & ptnrs
	G-BBHF	PA-23 Aztec 250E	Birmingham Aerocentre Ltd
	G-BBHG	Cessna E310Q	G. P. Williams
	G-BBHI	Cessna 177RG	T. G. W. Bunce
	G-BBHJ	Piper J-3C-65 Cub	R. V. Miller & J. Stanbridge
	G-BBHK	AT-16 Harvard IIB (FH153)	Bob Warner Aviation/Exeter
	G-BBHL	Sikorsky S-61N Mk II	Bristow Helicopters Ltd Glamis
	G-BBHM	Sikorsky S-61N	Bristow Helicopters Ltd
	G-BBHY	PA-28 Cherokee 180	Air Operations Ltd/Guernsey
	G-BBIA	PA-28R Cherokee Arrow 200-II	A. G. (Commodities) Ltd/Stapleford
	G-BBIF	PA-23 Aztec 250E	Home Doors (GB) Ltd
	G-BBIH	Enstrom F-28A-UK	Pyramid Precision Engineering Ltd
	G-BBII	Fiat G-46-3B (14)	V. S. E. Norman/Rendcomb
	G-BBIL	PA-28 Cherokee 140	India Lima Flying Group
	G-BBIN	Enstrom F-28A	Southern Air Ltd/Shoreham
	G-BBIO	Robin HR.100/210	R. A. King/Headcorn
	G-BBIT	Hughes 269B	Contract Development & Projects (Leeds) Ltd (stored)
	G-BBIV	Hughes 269C	Biggin Hill Helicopters
	G-BBIX	PA-28 Cherokee 140	Sterling Contract Hire Ltd
	G-BBJB	Thunder Ax7-77 balloon	St Crispin Balloon Group Dick Darby
	G-BBJI	Isaacs Spitfire (RN218)	A. N. R. Houghton & C. R. Williamson
	G-BBJU	Robin DR.400/140	J. C. Lister
	G-BBJV	Cessna F.177RG	Pilot Magazine/Biggin Hill
	G-BBJX	Cessna F.150L	Yorkshire Flying Services Ltd/Leeds
	G-BBJY	Cessna F.172M	J. Lucketti/Barton
	G-BBJZ	Cessna F.172M	Burks, Green & ptnrs
	G-BBKA	Cessna F.150L	R. Hall & L. W. Scattergood
	G-BBKB	Cessna F.150L	Justgold Ltd/Blackpool
	G-BBKE	Cessna F.150L	G. M. Bauer
	G-BBKF	Cessna FRA.150L	Compton Abbas Airfield Ltd

Reg.	Type	Owner or Operator	Notes
G-BBKG	Cessna FR.172J	H. J. Edwards & Son	
G-BBKI	Cessna F.172M	C. W. & S.A . Burman	
G-BBKL	CP.301A Emeraude	P. J. Griggs	
G-BBKR	Scheibe SF.24A Motorspatz	P. I. Morgans	
G-BBKU	Cessna FRA.150L	Penguin Group	
G-BBKX	PA-28 Cherokee 180	DRA Flying Club Ltd/Farnborough	
G-BBKY	Cessna F.150L	Automicro Ltd/Barton	
G-BBKZ	Cessna 172M	KZ Flying Group/Exeter	
G-BBLE	Hiller UH-12E	Agricopters Ltd/Chilbolton	
G-BBLH	Piper J-3C-65 Cub (31145)	M. J. Dunkerley & P. Greenyer/Biggin Hill	
G-BBLL	Cameron O-84 balloon ★	British Balloon Museum	
G-BBLM	SOCATA Rallye 100S	M. J. White & N. S. Porter	
G-BBLP	PA-23 Aztec 250D	Donington Aviation Ltd/E. Midlands	
G-BBLS	AA-5 Traveler	D. A. Reid & G. Graham/Prestwick	
G-BBLU	PA-34-200 Seneca II	Surrey & Kent Flying Club Ltd/Biggin Hill	
G-BBMB	Robin DR.400/180	Regent Flying Group/Biggin Hill	
G-BBMH	EAA. Sports Biplane Model P.1	K. Dawson	
G-BBMJ	PA-23 Aztec 250E	R. & M. International Engineering Ltd	
G-BBMN	D.H.C.1 Chipmunk 22	R. Steiner/Rush Green	
G-BBMO	D.H.C.1 Chipmunk 22	Holland Aerobatics Ltd/Lelystad	
G-BBMR	D.H.C.1 Chipmunk 22 (WB763)	A. J. Parkhouse	
G-BBMT	D.H.C.1 Chipmunk 22	V. F. J. Falconer & W. A. Lee/Dunstable	
G-BBMV	D.H.C.1 Chipmunk 22 (WG348)	P. J. Morgan (Aviation) Ltd	
G-BBMW	D.H.C.1 Chipmunk 22 (WK628)	Mike Whisky Group/Shoreham	
G-BBMX	D.H.C.1 Chipmunk 22	A. L. Brown & P. S. Murchison	
G-BBMZ	D.H.C.1 Chipmunk 22	Wycombe Gliding School Syndicate/ Booker	
G-BBNA	D.H.C.1 Chipmunk 22 (Lycoming)	Coventry Gliding Club Ltd/ Husbands Bosworth	
G-BBNC	D.H.C.1 Chipmunk T.10 (WP790) ★	Mosquito Aircraft Museum	
G-BBND	D.H.C.1 Chipmunk 22 (WD286)	Chipmunk G-BCIW Syndicate 1984	
G-BBNG	Bell 206B JetRanger 2	Helicopter Crop Spraying Ltd	
G-BBNH	PA-34-200 Seneca II	Lawrence Goodwin Machine Tools Ltd/ Coventry	
G-BBNI	PA-34-200 Seneca II	Channel Aviation Holdings Ltd	
G-BBNJ	Cessna F.150L	Sherburn Aero Club Ltd	
G-BBNO	PA-23 Aztec 250E ★	stored/Biggin Hill	
G-BBNV	Fuji FA.200-160	Caseright Ltd	
G-BBNX	Cessna FRA.150L	General Airline Ltd	
G-BBNZ	Cessna F.172M	R. J. Nunn	
G-BBOA	Cessna F.172M	J. W. J. Adkins/Southend	
G-BBOC	Cameron O-77 balloon	J. A. B. Gray	
G-BBOD	Thunder O-45 balloon	B. R. & M. Boyle	
G-BBOE	Robin HR.200/100	T. D. Saveker	
G-BBOH	Pitts S-1S Special	Venom Jet Promotions Ltd/Bournemouth	
G-BBOJ	PA-23 Aztec 250E ★	Instructional airframe/Cranfield	
G-BBOL	PA-18 Super Cub 150	Lakes Gliding Club Ltd/Walney Island	
G-BBOO	Thunder Ax6-56 balloon	K. Meehan Tigerjack	
G-BBOR	Bell 206B JetRanger 2	M. J. Easey	
G-BBOX	Thunder Ax7-77 balloon	R. C. Weyda	
G-BBPK	Evans VP-1	G. D. E. MacDonald	
G-BBPM	Enstrom F-28A	D. Newman & R. Brennan	
G-BBPN	Enstrom F-28A	Jeffers Air Ltd	
G-BBPO	Enstrom F-28A	Southern Air Ltd & Jewelhaven Ltd	
G-BBPS	Jodel D.117	A. Appleby/Redhill	
G-BBPU	Boeing 747-136	British Airways Virginia Water	
G-BBPW	Robin HR.100/210	S. D. Cole	
G-BBPX	PA-34-200 Seneca II	Richel Investments Ltd/Guernsey	
G-BBPY	PA-28 Cherokee 180	Sunsaver Ltd	
G-BBRA	PA-23 Aztec 250D	M. Gardner	
G-BBRB	D.H.82A Tiger Moth (DF198)	R. Barham/Biggin Hill	
G-BBRC	Fuji FA.200-180	BBRC Ltd	
G-BBRH	Bell 47G-5A	Helicopter Supplies & Engineering Ltd	
G-BBRI	Bell 47G-5A	Alan Mann Helicopters Ltd/Fairoaks	
G-BBRJ	PA-23 Aztec 250E	Duellist Enterprises Ltd	
G-BBRN	Procter Kittiwake 1 (XW784)	R. de H. Dobree-Carey	
G-BBRV	D.H.C.1 Chipmunk 22	G-BBRV Group	
G-BBRX	SIAI-Marchetti S.205-18F	R. C. & A. K. West	
G-BBRZ	AA-5 Traveler	C. P. Osbourne	
G-BBSA	AA-5 Traveler	Usworth 84 Flying Associates Ltd	
G-BBSB	Beech C23 Sundowner	Sundowner Group/Manchester	
G-BBSC	Beech B24R Sierra	Beechcombers Flying Group	

Notes	Reg.	Type	Owner or Operator
	G-BBSM	PA-32 Cherokee Six 300E	Paul James Knitware Ltd
	G-BBSS	D.H.C.1A Chipmunk 22	Coventry Gliding Club Ltd/ Husbands Bosworth
	G-BBSW	Pietenpol Air Camper	J. K. S. Wills
	G-BBTB	Cessna FRA.150L	Griffin Marston Ltd/Compton Abbas
	G-BBTG	Cessna F.172M	R. W. & V. P. J. Simpson/Redhill
	G-BBTH	Cessna F.172M	S. Gilmore/Newtownards
	G-BBTJ	PA-23 Aztec 250E	Cooper Aerial Surveys Ltd/Sandtoft
	G-BBTK	Cessna FRA.150L	Air Service Training Ltd/Perth
	G-BBTL	PA-23 Aztec 250C	Air Navigation & Trading Co Ltd/Blackpool
	G-BBTS	Beech V35B Bonanza	Eastern Air
	G-BBTU	ST-10 Diplomate	D. Hayden-Wright
	G-BBTX	Beech C23 Sundowner	K. Harding/Blackbushe
	G-BBTY	Beech C23 Sundowner	A. W. Roderick & W. Price
	G-BBTZ	Cessna F.150L	Marnham Investments Ltd
	G-BBUE	AA-5 Traveler	Hebog (Mon) Cyfyngedig/Mona
	G-BBUF	AA-5 Traveler	W. McLaren
	G-BBUG	PA-16 Clipper	J. Dolan
	G-BBUJ	Cessna 421B	Church Green Aviation Ltd
	G-BBUL	Mitchell-Procter Kittiwake 1	R. C. Bull
	G-BBUT	Western O-65 balloon	G. F. Turnbull
	G-BBUU	Piper J-3C-65 Cub	O. J. J. Rogers
	G-BBUW	SA.102.5 Cavalier ★	Aeroplane Collection Ltd
	G-BBVA	Sikorsky S-61N Mk II	Bristow Helicopters Ltd Vega
	G-BBVF	SA Twin Pioneer Srs III ★	Museum of Flight/E. Fortune
	G-BBVG	PA-23 Aztec 250C ★	(stored)/Little Staughton
	G-BBVI	Enstrom F-28A ★	Ground trainer/Kidlington
	G-BBVJ	Beech B24R Sierra	S. K. T. & C. M. Neofytou
	G-BBVO	Isaacs Fury II (S1579)	C. M. Barnes & D. A. Wirdnam
	G-BBVP	Westland-Bell 47G-3B1	CKS Air Ltd/Southend
	G-BBWZ	AA-1B Trainer	P. A. Ellwat & R. M. Bainbridge
	G-BBXB	Cessna FRA.150L	C. J. Hopewell
	G-BBXH	Cessna FR.172F	D. Ridley
	G-BBXK	PA-34-200 Seneca	Poyston Aviation
	G-BBXO	Enstrom F-28A	Stephenson Marine Ltd
	G-BBXS	Piper J-3C-65 Cub	M. J. Butler (G-ALMA)/Langham
	G-BBXU	Beech B24R Sierra	B. M. Russell/Coventry
	G-BBXY	Bellanca 7GCBC Citabria	R. R. L. Windus
	G-BBXZ	Evans VP-1	R. W. Burrows
	G-BBYB	PA-18 Super Cub 95	Tiger Club (1990) Ltd/Headcorn
	G-BBYH	Cessna 182P	Croftmarsh Ltd
	G-BBYM	H.P.137 Jetstream 200	British Aerospace (Operations) Ltd (G-AYWR)/Warton
	G-BBYP	PA-28 Cherokee 140	Yankee Papa Flying Ltd
	G-BBYS	Cessna 182P Skylane	I. M. Jones
	G-BBZF	PA-28 Cherokee 140	Winchester 95 Associates Ltd
	G-BBZH	PA-28R Cherokee Arrow 200-II	Zulu Hotel Club
	G-BBZI	PA-31-310 Turbo Navajo	Air Care (South West) Ltd
	G-BBZJ	PA-34-200 Seneca II	Eurofly Share Ltd
	G-BBZN	Fuji FA.200-180	J. Westwood & P. D. Wedd
	G-BBZO	Fuji FA.200-160	G-BBZO Group
	G-BBZV	PA-28R Cherokee Arrow 200-II	P. B. Mellor/Kidlington
	G-BCAH	D.H.C.1 Chipmunk 22 (WG316)	Southern Air Ltd/Shoreham
	G-BCAN	Thunder Ax7-77 balloon	D. D. Owen
	G-BCAP	Cameron O-56 balloon	S. R. Seager
	G-BCAR	Thunder Ax7-77 balloon ★	British Balloon Museum/Newbury
	G-BCAZ	PA-12 Super Cruiser	A. D. Williams
	G-BCBH	Fairchild 24R-46A Argus III	Ebork Ltd
	G-BCBJ	PA-25 Pawnee 235	Deeside Gliding Club (Aberdeenshire) Ltd/Aboyne
	G-BCBK	Cessna 421B	Reynard Racing Designs Ltd
	G-BCBL	Fairchild 24R-46A Argus III (HB751)	F. J. Cox
	G-BCBM	PA-23 Aztec 250C	S. Lightbrown & M. Kavanagh
	G-BCBR	AJEP/Wittman W.8 Tailwind	R. J. Willies
	G-BCBX	Cessna F.150L	J. Kelly/Newtownards
	G-BCBY	Cessna F.150L	Scottish Airways Flyers (Prestwick) Ltd
	G-BCBZ	Cessna 337C	J. J. Zwetsloot
	G-BCCB	Robin HR.200/100	M. J. Ellis
	G-BCCC	Cessna F.150L	Fleeting Moments Ltd
	G-BCCD	Cessna F.172M	Austin Aviation Ltd
	G-BCCE	PA-23 Aztec 250E	Falcon Flying Services/Biggin Hill

Reg.	Type	Owner or Operator	Notes
G-BCCF	PA-28 Cherokee 180	Topcat Aviation Ltd	
G-BCCG	Thunder Ax7-65 balloon	N. H. Ponsford	
G-BCCJ	AA-5 Traveler	T. Needham/Manchester	
G-BCCK	AA-5 Traveler	Prospect Air Ltd/Barton	
G-BCCR	CP.301A Emeraude (modified)	J. H. & C. J. Waterman	
G-BCCU	BN-2A Mk.III-1 Trislander	Keenair Cargo/Liverpool	
G-BCCX	D.H.C.1 Chipmunk 22 (Lycoming)	RAFGSA/Dishforth	
G-BCCY	Robin HR.200/100	G. J. Blower & G. Priestley	
G-BCDB	PA-34-200 Seneca II	A. & G. Aviation Ltd/Bournemouth	
G-BCDJ	PA-28 Cherokee 140	C. Wren/Southend	
G-BCDK	Partenavia P.68B	G. Fleck	
G-BCDL	Cameron O-42 balloon	D. P. & Mrs B. O. Turner *Chums*	
G-BCDR	Thunder Ax7-77 balloon	W. G. Johnston & ptnrs	
G-BCDY	Cessna FRA.150L	Ipswich School of Flying Ltd	
G-BCEA	Sikorsky S-61N Mk II	Brintel Helicopters	
G-BCEB	Sikorsky S-61N Mk II	Brintel Helicopters	
G-BCEC	Cessna F.172M	A. R. & S. D. Bamber	
G-BCEE	AA-5 Traveler	Echo Echo Ltd/Bournemouth	
G-BCEF	AA-5 Traveler	MCP Aviation	
G-BCEN	BN-2A-26 Islander	Atlantic Air Transport Ltd/Coventry	
G-BCEO	AA-5 Traveler	Echo Oscar Flying Group	
G-BCEP	AA-5 Traveler	P. Curley & A. J. Radford	
G-BCER	GY-201 Minicab	D. Beaumont/Sherburn	
G-BCEU	Cameron O-42 balloon	Entertainment Services Ltd *Harlequin*	
G-BCEX	PA-23 Aztec 250E	Western Air Training Ltd/Thruxton	
G-BCEY	D.H.C.1 Chipmunk 22	Gopher Flying Group	
G-BCEZ	Cameron O-84 balloon	Balloon Collection	
G-BCFC	Cameron O-65 balloon	B. H. Mead *Candy Twist*	
G-BCFD	West balloon ★	British Balloon Museum *Hellfire*/Newbury	
G-BCFF	Fuji FA-200-160	G. W. Brown & M. R. Gibbons	
G-BCFO	PA-18 Super Cub 150	Portsmouth Naval Gliding Club/ Lee-on-Solent	
G-BCFR	Cessna FRA.150L	Rentair Ltd	
G-BCFW	SAAB 91D Safir	D. R. Williams	
G-BCFY	Luton LA-4A Minor	G. Capes	
G-BCGB	Bensen B.8	A. Melody	
G-BCGC	D.H.C.1 Chipmunk 22 (WP903)	Culdrose Gliding Club	
G-BCGG	Jodel DR.250 Srs 160	C. G. Gray (G-ATZL)	
G-BCGH	SNCAN NC.854S	Nord Flying Group	
G-BCGI	PA-28 Cherokee 140	A. Dodd/Redhill	
G-BCGJ	PA-28 Cherokee 140	BCT Aircraft Leasing Ltd	
G-BCGM	Jodel D.120	D. N. K. & M. A. Symon	
G-BCGN	PA-28 Cherokee 140	Oxford Flyers Ltd/Kidlington	
G-BCGS	PA-28R Cherokee Arrow 200	Arrow Aviation Group	
G-BCGT	PA-28 Cherokee 140	EFS Flying Group/Earls Colne	
G-BCGW	Jodel D.11	G. H. & M. D. Chittenden	
G-BCHK	Cessna F.172H	E. C. & A. K. Shimmin	
G-BCHL	D.H.C.1 Chipmunk 22A (WP788)	Shropshire Soaring Ltd/Sleap	
G-BCHM	SA.341G Gazelle 1	Westland Helicopters Ltd/Yeovil	
G-BCHP	CP.1310-C3 Super Emeraude	G. Hughes & A. G. Just (G-JOSI)	
G-BCHT	Schleicher ASK.16	Dunstable K16 Group	
G-BCHV	D.H.C.1 Chipmunk 22	N. F. Charles/Sywell	
G-BCHX	SF.23A Sperling	*(stored)*/Rufforth	
G-BCID	PA-34-200 Seneca II	C. J. Freeman/Headcorn	
G-BCIE	PA-28-151 Warrior	Scottish Airways Flyers (Prestwick) Ltd	
G-BCIH	D.H.C.1 Chipmunk 22 (WD363)	J. M. Hosey/Stansted	
G-BCIJ	AA-5 Traveler	I. J. Boyd & D. J. McCooke	
G-BCIK	AA-5 Traveler	Trent Aviation Ltd	
G-BCIN	Thunder Ax7-77 balloon	P. G & R. A. Vale	
G-BCIR	PA-28-151 Warrior	P. J. Brennan	
G-BCIT	CIT/A1 Srs 1	Cranfield University	
G-BCJF	Beagle B.206 Srs 1	A. T. Mattacks & G. H. Nolan	
G-BCJH	Mooney M.20F	P. B. Bossard	
G-BCJM	PA-28 Cherokee 140	Top Cat Aviation Ltd	
G-BCJN	PA-28 Cherokee 140	G. D. Connolly	
G-BCJO	PA-28R Cherokee Arrow 200	R. Ross	
G-BCJP	PA-28 Cherokee 140	Omletair Flying Group	
G-BCKN	D.H.C.1A Chipmunk 22	RAFGSA/Cranwell	
G-BCKP	Luton LA-5A Major	D. & W. H. Gough	
G-BCKS	Fuji FA.200-180	J. T. Hicks/Goodwood	
G-BCKT	Fuji FA.200-180	M. A. Petrie	
G-BCKU	Cessna FRA.150L	Cardiff-Wales Flying Club Ltd	
G-BCKV	Cessna FRA.150L	Air Service Training Ltd/Perth	

Notes	Reg.	Type	Owner or Operator
	G-BCLC	Sikorsky S-61N	Bristow Helicopters/HM Coastguard
	G-BCLD	Sikorsky S-61N	Bristow Helicopters Ltd
	G-BCLI	AA-5 Traveler	Hoe (Office Equipment) Ltd
	G-BCLJ	AA-5 Traveler	E. A. A. A. Wiltens
	G-BCLL	PA-28 Cherokee 180	K. J. Scamp
	G-BCLS	Cessna 170B	Teesside Flight Centre Ltd
	G-BCLT	M.S.894A Rallye Minerva 220	S. Clough
	G-BCLU	Jodel D.117	N. A. Wallace
	G-BCLW	AA-1B Trainer	E. J. McMillan
	G-BCMC	Bell 212	Bristow Helicopters Ltd
	G-BCMD	PA-18 Super Cub 95	J. G. Brooks/Dunkeswell
	G-BCMJ	SA.102.5 Cavalier (tailwheel)	R. G. Sykes/Shoreham
	G-BCMT	Isaacs Fury II	M. H. Turner
	G-BCNC	GY-201 Minicab	J. R. Wraight
	G-BCNP	Cameron O-77 balloon	P. Spellward
	G-BCNX	Piper J-3C-65 Cub	K. J. Lord/Ipswich
	G-BCNZ	Fuji FA.200-160	J. Bruton & A. Lincoln/Manchester
	G-BCOB	Piper J-3C-65 Cub (329405)	R. W. & Mrs J. W. Marjoram
	G-BCOG	Jodel D.112	A. J. Craven-Howe & ptnrs
	G-BCOI	D.H.C.1 Chipmunk 22	D. S. McGregor
	G-BCOJ	Cameron O-56 balloon	T. J. Knott & M. J. Webber
	G-BCOL	Cessna F.172M	A. H. Creaser
	G-BCOM	Piper J-3C-65 Cub	Dougal Flying Group/Shoreham
	G-BCOO	D.H.C.1 Chipmunk 22	T. G. Fielding & M. S. Morton/Blackpool
	G-BCOP	PA-28R Cherokee Arrow 200-II	E. A. Saunders/Halfpenny Green
	G-BCOR	SOCATA Rallye 100ST	P. R. W. Goslin & ptnrs
	G-BCOU	D.H.C.1 Chipmunk 22 (WK522)	P. J. Loweth
	G-BCOX	Bede BD-5A	H. J. Cox & B. L. Robinson
	G-BCOY	D.H.C.1 Chipmunk 22 (Lycoming)	Coventry Gliding Club Ltd/Husbands Bosworth
	G-BCPB	Howes radio-controlled model free balloon	R. B. & Mrs C. Howes
	G-BCPD	GY-201 Minicab	A. H. K. Denniss/Halfpenny Green
	G-BCPE	Cessna F.150M	B. W. Jones
	G-BCPG	PA-28R Cherokee Arrow 200-II	Roses Flying Group/Liverpool
	G-BCPH	Piper J-3C-65 Cub (329934)	M. J. Janaway
	G-BCPJ	Piper J-3C-65 Cub	Piper Cub Group
	G-BCPK	Cessna F.172M	Osprey Flying Club/Cranfield
	G-BCPN	AA-5 Traveler	B.W. Agricultural Equipments Ltd
	G-BCPO	Partenavia P.68B	Golden Airways Ltd
	G-BCPU	D.H.C.1 Chipmunk 22	P. Waller/Booker
	G-BCPX	Szep HFC.125	A. Szep/Netherthorpe
	G-BCRB	Cessna F.172M	D. E. Lamb
	G-BCRE	Cameron O-77 balloon	A. R. Langton
	G-BCRH	Alaparma Baldo B.75 ★	A. L. Scadding (stored)
	G-BCRI	Cameron O-65 balloon	V. J. Thorne
	G-BCRJ	Taylor JT.1 Monoplane	J. D. Muldowney & S. A. Cooper
	G-BCRK	SA.102.5 Cavalier	S. B. Churchill
	G-BCRL	PA-28-151 Warrior	F. N. Garland/Biggin Hill
	G-BCRN	Cessna FRA.150L	L. D. Johnston
	G-BCRP	PA-E23 Aztec 250E	County Garage (Cheltenham) Ltd/Staverton
	G-BCRR	AA-5B Tiger	Capulet Flying Group/Elstree
	G-BCRT	Cessna F.150M	Fordaire Aviation Ltd
	G-BCRX	D.H.C.1 Chipmunk 22 (WD292)	Tuplin Ltd/Denham
	G-BCSA	D.H.C.1 Chipmunk 22 (Lycoming)	RAFGSA/Bicester
	G-BCSB	D.H.C.1 Chipmunk 22 (Lycoming)	RAFGSA/Cosford
	G-BCSL	D.H.C.1 Chipmunk 22	Jalawain Ltd/Barton
	G-BCSM	Bellanca 8GCBC Scout	B. T. Spreckley/Southampton
	G-BCST	M.S.893A Rallye Commodore 180	P. J. Wilcox/Cranfield
	G-BCSX	Thunder Ax7-77 balloon	C. Wolstenholm
	G-BCSY	Taylor JT.2 Titch	I. L. Harding
	G-BCTA	PA-28-151 Warrior	TG Aviation Ltd/Manston
	G-BCTF	PA-28-151 Warrior	The St. George Flying Club/Teesside
	G-BCTI	Schleicher ASK.16	Tango India Syndicate/Cranfield
	G-BCTJ	Cessna 310Q	TJ Flying Group
	G-BCTK	Cessna FR.172J	R. T. Love
	G-BCTT	Evans VP-1	B. J. Boughton
	G-BCTU	Cessna FRA.150M	J. H. Fisher & N. D. Hall
	G-BCUB	Piper J-3C-65 Cub	A. L. Brown & G. Attwell/Bourn
	G-BCUF	Cessna F.172M	D. J. Parkinson
	G-BCUH	Cessna F.150M	M. G. Montgomerie
	G-BCUJ	Cessna F.150M	S. Chappell

Reg.	Type	Owner or Operator	Notes
G-BCUL	SOCATA Rallye 100ST	C. A. Ussher & Fountain Estates Ltd	
G-BCUS	SA Bulldog Srs 120/122	S. J. & J. J. Oliver	
G-BCUV	SA Bulldog Srs 120/122	Dolphin Property (Management) Ltd	
G-BCUW	Cessna F.177RG	S. J. Westley	
G-BCUY	Cessna FRA.150M	S. R. Cameron	
G-BCVA	Cameron O-65 balloon	J. C. Bass & ptnrs	
G-BCVB	PA-17 Vagabond	A. T. Nowak/Popham	
G-BCVC	SOCATA Rallye 100ST	C. Smith & P. F. Crosby	
G-BCVE	Evans VP-2	D. Masterson & D. B. Winstanley	
G-BCVF	Practavia Pilot Sprite	D. G. Hammersley	
G-BCVG	Cessna FRA.150L	Surrey Flying Services Ltd	
G-BCVH	Cessna FRA.150L	Yorkshire Light Aircraft Ltd/Leeds	
G-BCVJ	Cessna F.172M	Rothland Ltd	
G-BCVW	GY-80 Horizon 180	P. M. A. Parrett/Dunkeswell	
G-BCVY	PA-34-200T Seneca II	C.S.E. Aviation Ltd/Kidlington	
G-BCWB	Cessna 182P	Skylane Whisky Bravo Ltd	
G-BCWH	Practavia Pilot Sprite	R. Tasker/Blackpool	
G-BCWK	Alpavia Fournier RF-3	T. J. Hartwell & D. R. Wilkinson	
G-BCWL	Westland Lysander III (V9545)	Wessex Aviation & Transport Ltd	
G-BCXB	SOCATA Rallye 100ST	A. Smails	
G-BCXE	Robin DR.400/2+2	C. J. Freeman	
G-BCXJ	Piper L-4J Cub (480752)	Major W. F. Stockdale MBE/Old Sarum	
G-BCXN	D.H.C.1 Chipmunk 22 (WP800)	G. M. Turner/Duxford	
G-BCYH	DAW Privateer Mk. 3	D. B. Limbert	
G-BCYJ	D.H.C.1 Chipmunk 22 (WG307)	R. A. L. Falconer	
G-BCYK	Avro CF.100 Mk 4 Canuck (18393) ★	Imperial War Museum/Duxford	
G-BCYM	D.H.C.1 Chipmunk 22	M. H. Thomson	
G-BCYR	Cessna F.172M	Donne Enterprises	
G-BCZH	D.H.C.1 Chipmunk 22 (WK622)	A. C. Byrne/Norwich	
G-BCZI	Thunder Ax7-77 balloon	R. G. Griffin & R. Blackwell	
G-BCZM	Cessna F.172M	Cornwall Flying Club Ltd/Bodmin	
G-BCZN	Cessna F.150M	Mona Aviation Ltd	
G-BCZO	Cameron O-77 balloon	W. O. T. Holmes *Leo*	
G-BDAD	Taylor JT.1 Monoplane	G-BDAD Group	
G-BDAG	Taylor JT.1 Monoplane	S. Edmunds	
G-BDAH	Evans VP-1	S. B. Robson	
G-BDAI	Cessna FRA.150M	A. Sharma	
G-BDAK	R. Commander 112A	C. Boydon	
G-BDAL	R. 500S Shrike Commander	Quantel Ltd	
G-BDAM	AT-16 Harvard IIB (FE992)	N. A. Lees	
G-BDAO	SIPA S.91	B. F. Arnall	
G-BDAP	AJEP Tailwind	J. Whiting	
G-BDAR	Evans VP-1	R. B. Valler	
G-BDAY	Thunder Ax5-42A balloon	T. M. Donnelly *Meconium*	
G-BDBD	Wittman W.8 Tailwind	Tailwind Taildragger Group	
G-BDBF	FRED Srs 2	I. D. Worthington	
G-BDBH	Bellanca 7GCBC Citabria	R. Dixon	
G-BDBI	Cameron O-77 balloon	C. A. Butter & J. J. Cook	
G-BDBJ	Cessna 182P	H. C. Wilson	
G-BDBP	D.H.C.1 Chipmunk 22 (WP843)	F. A. de Munck	
G-BDBS	Short SD3-30 ★	Ulster Aviation Soc	
G-BDBU	Cessna F.150M	Andrewsfield Flying Club Ltd	
G-BDBV	Jodel D.11A	Seething Jodel Group	
G-BDBZ	W.S.55 Whirlwind Srs 2 ★	*Ground instruction airframe*/Kidlington	
G-BDCC	D.H.C.1 Chipmunk 22 (Lycoming)	Coventry Gliding Club Ltd/ Husbands Bosworth	
G-BDCD	Piper J-3C-85 Cub (480133)	Suzanne C. Brooks/Slinfold	
G-BDCE	Cessna F.172H	W. Henney	
G-BDCI	CP.301A Emeraude	D. L. Sentqance	
G-BDCK	AA-5 Traveler	Northfield Garage Ltd	
G-BDCL	AA-5 Traveler	J. Crowe	
G-BDCO	B.121 Pup 1	Shipdham Aviators Flying Group	
G-BDCS	Cessna 421B	British Aerospace (Operations) Ltd/Warton	
G-BDCU	Cameron O-77 balloon	H. P. Carlton	
G-BDDD	D.H.C.1 Chipmunk 22	DRA Aero Club Ltd/Farnborough	
G-BDDF	Jodel D.120	Sywell Skyriders Flying Group	
G-BDDG	Jodel D.112	Wandering Imp Group	
G-BDDS	PA-25 Pawnee 235	Vale of Neath Gliding Club/Rhigos	
G-BDDT	PA-25 Pawnee 235	Boston Aviation Services	
G-BDDX	Whittaker MW.2B Excalibur ★	Cornwall Aero Park/Helston	
G-BDDZ	CP.301A Emeraude	V. W. Smith & E. C. Mort/Barton	

Notes	Reg.	Type	Owner or Operator
	G-BDEC	SOCATA Rallye 100ST	P. White
	G-BDEF	PA-34-200T Seneca II	Haylock Son & Hunter
	G-BDEH	Jodel D.120A	EH Flying Group
	G-BDEI	Jodel D.9 Bebe	The Noddy Group/Booker
	G-BDET	D.H.C.1 Chipmunk 22 (WP851)	C. Zoeteman/Holland
	G-BDEU	D.H.C.1 Chipmunk 22 (WP808)	A. Taylor
	G-BDEW	Cessna FRA.150M	Griffin Marston Ltd/Compton Abbas
	G-BDEX	Cessna FRA.150M	Griffin Marston Ltd
	G-BDEY	Piper J-3C-65 Cub	Ducksworth Flying Club
	G-BDEZ	Piper J-3C-65 Cub	R. J. M. Turnbull
	G-BDFB	Currie Wot	J. Jennings
	G-BDFC	R. Commander 112A	R. Fletcher
	G-BDFG	Cameron O-65 balloon	N. A. Robertson Golly II
	G-BDFH	Auster AOP.9 (XR240)	R. O. Holden/Booker
	G-BDFJ	Cessna F.150M	C. J. Hopewell
	G-BDFM	Caudron C.270 Luciole	G. V. Gower
	G-BDFR	Fuji FA.200-160	A. G. Brindle & A. Houghton
	G-BDFS	Fuji FA.200-160	B. Sharbati & B. Lawrence
	G-BDFU	Dragonfly MPA Mk 1 ★	Museum of Flight/E. Fortune
	G-BDFW	R. Commander 112A	M. & D. A. Doubleday
	G-BDFX	Auster 5 (TW517)	J. Eagles
	G-BDFY	AA-5 Traveler	Grumman Group
	G-BDFZ	Cessna F.150M	A. T. Wright
	G-BDGA	Bushby-Long Midget Mustang	J. R. Owen
	G-BDGB	GY-20 Minicab	D. G. Burden
	G-BDGH	Thunder Ax7-77 balloon	R. J. Mitchener & P. F. Smart
	G-BDGM	PA-28-151 Warrior	B. Whiting
	G-BDGO	Thunder Ax7-77 balloon	International Distillers & Vintners Ltd
	G-BDGP	Cameron V-65 balloon	A. Mayers & V. Lawton
	G-BDGY	PA-28 Cherokee 140	S. J. Willcox
	G-BDHJ	Pazmany PL.1	C. T. Millner
	G-BDHK	Piper J-3C-65 Cub (329417)	A. Liddiard
	G-BDIE	R. Commander 112A	R. J. Adams
	G-BDIG	Cessna 182P	Air Group 6/Gamston
	G-BDIH	Jodel D.117	N. D. H. Stokes
	G-BDIJ	Sikorsky S-61N	Bristow Helicopters Ltd
	G-BDIM	D.H.C.1 Chipmunk 22	Historic Flying Ltd/Cambridge
	G-BDIX	D.H.106 Comet 4C	Museum of Flight/E. Fortune
	G-BDJB	Taylor JT.1 Monoplane	J. F. Barber
	G-BDJC	AJEP W.8 Tailwind	J. H. Medforth
	G-BDJD	Jodel D.112	R. Everitt
	G-BDJF	Bensen B.8MV	R. P. White
	G-BDJG	Luton LA-4A Minor	A. W. Anderson & A. J. Short
	G-BDJN	Robin HR.200/100	Haimoss Ltd/Old Sarum
	G-BDJP	Piper J-3C-90 Cub	Holdcroft Aviation Services Ltd
	G-BDJR	SNCAN NC.858	R. F. M. Marson & P. M. Harmer
	G-BDKB	SOCATA Rallye 150ST	N. C. Anderson
	G-BDKC	C'essna A185F	Bridge of Tilt Co Ltd
	G-BDKD	Enstrom F-28A	Normans (Burton-on-Trent) Ltd
	G-BDKH	CP.301A Emeraude	P. N. Marshall
	G-BDKJ	K. & S. SA.102.5 Cavalier	B. D. Battman
	G-BDKM	SIPA 903	S. W. Markham
	G-BDKU	Taylor JT.1 Monoplane	C. M. Harding & J. Ball
	G-BDKW	R. Commander 112A	R. W. Denny/Ipswich
	G-BDLO	AA-5A Cheetah	S. & J. Dolan/Denham
	G-BDLR	AA-5B Tiger	MAGEC Aviation Ltd/Luton
	G-BDLS	AA-1B Trainer	Lima Sierra Partnership/Mona
	G-BDLT	R. Commander 112A	D. L. Churchward
	G-BDLY	SA.102.5 Cavalier	P. R. Stevens/Southampton
	G-BDMM	Jodel D.11	P. N. Marshall
	G-BDMS	Piper J-3C-65 Cub (FR886)	A. T. H. Martin
	G-BDMW	Jodel DR.100A	R. O. F. Harper
	G-BDNC	Taylor JT.1 Monoplane	A. W. Wright & P. Gaskell
	G-BDNG	Taylor JT.1 Monoplane	W. Buchan
	G-BDNO	Taylor JT.1 Monoplane	D. A. Healey
	G-BDNP	BN-2A Islander ★	Ground parachute trainer/Headcorn
	G-BDNR	Cessna FRA.150M	Cheshire Air Training School Ltd/Liverpool
	G-BDNT	Jodel D.92	R. F. Morton
	G-BDNU	Cessna F.172M	J. & K. G. McVicar
	G-BDNW	AA-1B Trainer	P. R. Huntley
	G-BDNX	AA-1B Trainer	R. M. North
	G-BDNZ	Cameron O-77 balloon	I. L. McHale
	G-BDOC	Sikorsky S-61N Mk II	Bristow Helicopters Ltd

Reg.	Type	Owner or Operator	Notes
G-BDOD	Cessna F.150M	D. M. Moreau	
G-BDOE	Cessna FR.172J	P. E. Ward & ptnrs	
G-BDOF	Cameron O-56 balloon	The New Holker Estates Co Ltd	
G-BDOG	SA Bulldog Srs 200/2100	D. C. Bonsall/Netherthorpe	
G-BDOL	Piper J-3C-65 Cub	L. R. Balthazor	
G-BDON	Thunder Ax7-77A balloon	J. R. Henderson & ptnrs	
G-BDOT	BN-2A Mk.III-2 Trislander	Hebridean Air Services Ltd	
G-BDOW	Cessna FRA.150M	M. H. Sims & N. A. Stone	
G-BDPA	PA-28-151 Warrior	G-BDPA Flying Group/Staverton	
G-BDPF	Cessna F.172M	J. M. Mothersall	
G-BDPK	Cameron O-56 balloon	Rango Balloon & Kite Co	
G-BDPV	Boeing 747-136	British Airways *Blea Water*	
G-BDRD	Cessna FRA.150M	Air Service Training Ltd/Perth	
G-BDRF	Taylor JT.1 Monoplane	B. R. Ratcliffe	
G-BDRG	Taylor JT.2 Titch	D. R. Gray	
G-BDRJ	D.H.C.1 Chipmunk 22 (WP857)	J. C. Schooling	
G-BDRK	Cameron O-65 balloon	D. L. Smith *Smirk*	
G-BDRL	Stitts SA-3A Playboy	O. C. Bradley	
G-BDSA	FRED Srs 2	W. D. M. Turtle	
G-BDSB	PA-28-181 Archer II	Testair Ltd/Blackbushe	
G-BDSE	Cameron O-77 balloon	British Airways *Concorde*	
G-BDSF	Cameron O-56 balloon	A. R. Greensides & B. H. Osbourne	
G-BDSH	PA-28 Cherokee 140	The Wright Brothers Flying Group	
G-BDSK	Cameron O-65 balloon	Southern Balloon Group *Carousel II*	
G-BDSL	Cessna F.150M	Cleveland Flying School Ltd/Teesside	
G-BDSM	Slingsby T.31B Cadet III	N. F. James	
G-BDTB	Evans VP-1	T. F. Crossman	
G-BDTL	Evans VP-1	A. K. Lang	
G-BDTN	BN-2A Mk III-2 Trislander	Aurigny Air Services Ltd/Guernsey	
G-BDTU	Omega III gas balloon	G. F. Turnbull	
G-BDTV	Mooney M.20F	S. Redfearn	
G-BDTW	Cassutt Racer	B. E. Smith	
G-BDTX	Cessna F.150M	S. L. Lefley & F. W. Ellis	
G-BDUI	Cameron V-56 balloon	D. C. Johnson	
G-BDUL	Evans VP-1	P. M. Beresford	
G-BDUM	Cessna F.150M	SFG Ltd/Shipdham	
G-BDUN	PA-34-200T Seneca II	Air Medical Ltd/Oxford	
G-BDUO	Cessna F.150M	T. E. G. Buckett	
G-BDUX	Slingsby T.31B Cadet III	J. C. Anderson/Cranfield	
G-BDUY	Robin DR.400/140B	J. G. Anderson	
G-BDUZ	Cameron V-56 balloon	Zebedee Balloon Service	
G-BDVA	PA-17 Vagabond	I. M. Callier	
G-BDVB	PA-15 (PA-17) Vagabond	B. P. Gardner	
G-BDVC	PA-17 Vagabond	A. R. Caveen	
G-BDVU	Mooney M.20F	Peakmyth Ltd	
G-BDWA	SOCATA Rallye 150ST	J. Thompson-Wilson/Newtownards	
G-BDWE	Flaglor Scooter	M. Stewart	
G-BDWH	SOCATA Rallye 150ST	M. A. Jones	
G-BDWJ	SE-5A (replica) (F8010)	S. M. Smith/Booker	
G-BDWL	PA-25 Pawnee 235	Peterborough & Spalding Gliding Club	
G-BDWM	Mustang scale replica (FB226)	D. C. Bonsall	
G-BDWO	Howes Ax6 balloon	R. B. & C. Howes	
G-BDWP	PA-32R Cherokee Lance 300	W. M. Brown & B. J. Wood/Birmingham	
G-BDWV	BN-2A Mk III-2 Trislander	Aurigny Air Services Ltd/Guernsey	
G-BDWX	Jodel D.120A	J. P. Lassey	
G-BDWY	PA-28 Cherokee 140	Comed Aviation Ltd/Blackpool	
G-BDXA	Boeing 747-236B	British Airways *City of Peterborough*	
G-BDXB	Boeing 747-236B	British Airways *City of Liverpool*	
G-BDXC	Boeing 747-236B	British Airways *City of Manchester*	
G-BDXD	Boeing 747-236B	British Airways *City of Plymouth*	
G-BDXE	Boeing 747-236B	British Airways *City of Glasgow*	
G-BDXF	Boeing 747-236B	British Airways *City of York*	
G-BDXG	Boeing 747-236B	British Airways *City of Oxford*	
G-BDXH	Boeing 747-236B	British Airways *City of Elgin*	
G-BDXI	Boeing 747-236B	British Airways *City of Cambridge*	
G-BDXJ	Boeing 747-236B	British Airways *City of Birmingham*	
G-BDXK	Boeing 747-236B	British Airways *City of Canterbury*	
G-BDXL	Boeing 747-236B	British Airways *City of Winchester*	
G-BDXM	Boeing 747-236B (SCD)	British Airways *City of Derby*	
G-BDXN	Boeing 747-236B (SCD)	British Airways *City of Stoke-on-Trent*	
G-BDXO	Boeing 747-236B	British Airways *City of Bath*	
G-BDXP	Boeing 747-236B (SCD)	British Airways *City of Salisbury*	
G-BDXX	SNCAN NC.858S	S. A. Chambers	

Notes	Reg.	Type	Owner or Operator
	G-BDYD	R. Commander 114	L. A. & A. A. Buckley
	G-BDYF	Cessna 421C	Hawkair
	G-BDYG	P.56 Provost T.1 (WV493) ★	Museum of Flight/E. Fortune
	G-BDYH	Cameron V-56 balloon	B. J. Godding
	G-BDZA	Scheibe SF.25E Super Falke	Norfolk Gliding Club Ltd/Tibenham
	G-BDZB	Cameron S-31 balloon	Kenning Motor Group Ltd
	G-BDZC	Cessna F.150M	A. M. Lynn/Sibson
	G-BDZD	Cessna F.172M	Northamptonshire School of Flying Ltd
	G-BDZS	Scheibe SF.25E Super Falke	S. Sagar
	G-BDZU	Cessna 421C	Eagle Flying Group
	G-BDZX	PA-28-151 Warrior	Catalina Seaplanes Ltd
	G-BDZY	Luton LA-4A Minor	P. J. Dalby
	G-BEAB	Jodel DR.1051	C. Fitton
	G-BEAC	PA-28 Cherokee 140	Clipwing Flying Group/Humberside
	G-BEAD	WG.13 Lynx ★	Instructional airframe/Middle Wallop
	G-BEAG	PA-34-200T Seneca II	C.S.E. Aviation Ltd/Kidlington
	G-BEAH	J/2 Arrow	W. J. & Mrs M. D. Horler
	G-BEBC	W.S.55 Whirlwind 3 (XP355) ★	Norwich Aviation Museum
	G-BEBE	AA-5A Cheetah	Bills Aviation Ltd
	G-BEBG	WSK-PZL SDZ-45A Ogar	The Ogar Syndicate/Hinton-in-the-Hedges
	G-BEBI	Cessna F.172M	Hatfield Flying Club
	G-BEBL	Douglas DC-10-30	British Airways Forest of Dean/Gatwick
	G-BEBM	Douglas DC-10-30	British Airways Sherwood Forest/Gatwick
	G-BEBN	Cessna 177B	A. J. Franchi
	G-BEBO	Turner TSW-2 Wot	The Turner Special Flying Group
	G-BEBR	GY-201 Minicab	A. S. Jones & D. R. Upton
	G-BEBS	Andreasson BA-4B	N. J. W. Reid
	G-BEBT	Andreasson BA-4B	A. Horsfall
	G-BEBU	R. Commander 112A	R. Hodgkinson
	G-BEBZ	PA-28-151 Warrior	Goodwood Terrena Ltd/Goodwood
	G-BECA	SOCATA Rallye 100ST	Bredon Flying Group
	G-BECB	SOCATA Rallye 100ST	A. J. Trible
	G-BECC	SOCATA Rallye 150ST	D. T. Price
	G-BECF	Scheibe SF.25A Falke	D. A. Wilson & ptnrs
	G-BECG	Boeing 737-204 ADV	Independent Aviation Group/easyJet
	G-BECH	Boeing 737-204 ADV	Independent Aviation Group/easyJet
	G-BECK	Cameron V-56 balloon	H. & D. J. Farrar
	G-BECN	Piper J-3C-65 Cub (480480)	R. C. Partridge & M. Oliver
	G-BECT	C.A.S.A.1.131E Jungmann 2000 (A-57)	Shoreham 131 Group
	G-BECW	C.A.S.A.1.131E Jungmann 2000	N. C. Jensen/Redhill
	G-BECZ	CAARP CAP.10B	Aerobatic Associates Ltd
	G-BEDA	C.A.S.A.1.131E Jungmann 2000	M. G. Kates & D. J. Berry
	G-BEDB	Nord 1203 Norecrin ★	B. F. G. Lister (stored)/Chirk
	G-BEDD	Jodel D.117A	A. T. Croy/Kirkwall
	G-BEDF	Boeing B-17G-105-VE (124485)	B-17 Preservation Ltd/Duxford
	G-BEDG	R. Commander 112A	L. E. Blackburn
	G-BEDI	Sikorsky S-61N	British International Helicopters
	G-BEDJ	Piper J-3C-65 Cub (44-80594)	R. Earl
	G-BEDK	Hiller UH-12E	Agricopters Ltd/Chilbolton
	G-BEDL	Cessna T.337D	T. J. Brammer & D. T. Colley
	G-BEDP	BN-2A Mk.III-2 Trislander	Hebridean Air Services Ltd
	G-BEDV	V.668 Varsity T.1 (WJ945) ★	Duxford Aviation Soc
	G-BEEE	Thunder Ax6-56A balloon	I. R. M. Jacobs Avia
	G-BEEG	BN-2A-26 Islander	North West Parachute Centre Ltd
	G-BEEH	Cameron V-56 balloon	B. & N. V. Moreton
	G-BEEI	Cameron N-77 balloon	P. S. & G. G. Rankin
	G-BEEP	Thunder Ax5-42 balloon	B. C. Faithfull/Holland
	G-BEER	Isaacs Fury II (K2075)	Baycol Aviation
	G-BEEU	PA-28 Cherokee 140F	Touch & Go Ltd
	G-BEEW	Taylor JT.1 Monoplane	P. A. Boyden
	G-BEFA	PA-28-151 Warrior	Firmbeam Ltd/Booker
	G-BEFC	AA-5B Tiger	J. F. Gosling & N. R. J. Mifflin/Shobdon
	G-BEFF	PA-28 Cherokee 140F	C. Haymes
	G-BEFO	BN-2A Mk III-2 Trislander	Keen Leasing Ltd (G-SARN)
	G-BEFV	Evans VP-2	D. A. Cotton
	G-BEGA	Westland-Bell 47G-3B1	Flight 47 Ltd
	G-BEGG	Scheibe SF.25E Super Falke	G-BEGG Flying Group
	G-BEGV	PA-23 Aztec 250F	Widehawk Aviation Ltd/Ipswich
	G-BEHH	PA-32R Cherokee Lance 300	SMK Engineering Ltd/Leeds
	G-BEHS	PA-25 Pawnee 260C	Southern Sailplanes Ltd
	G-BEHU	PA-34-200T Seneca II	ANT Aviation Ltd

Reg.	Type	Owner or Operator	Notes
G-BEHV	Cessna F.172N	J. Easson/Edinburgh	
G-BEHX	Evans VP-2	G. S. Adams	
G-BEIA	Cessna FRA.150M	Rankart Ltd	
G-BEIB	Cessna F.172N	J. Shelton	
G-BEIC	Sikorsky S-61N	Brintel Helicopters	
G-BEIF	Cameron O-65 balloon	C. Vening	
G-BEIG	Cessna F.150M	Herefordshire Aero Club Ltd/Shobdon	
G-BEII	PA-25 Pawnee 235D	Burn Gliding Club Ltd	
G-BEIL	SOCATA Rallye 150T	The Rallye Flying Group	
G-BEIP	PA-28-181 Archer II	C. C. W. Hart	
G-BEIS	Evans VP-1	P. J. Hunt	
G-BEJB	Thunder Ax6-56A balloon	International Distillers & Vinters Ltd	
G-BEJD	Avro 748 Srs 1	Emerald Airways Ltd *John Case*/Liverpool	
G-BEJE	Avro 748 Srs 1	Emerald Airways Ltd/Liverpool	
G-BEJK	Cameron S-31 balloon	Rango Balloon & Kite Co	
G-BEJL	Sikorsky S-61N	Brintel Helicopters	
G-BEJM	BAC One-Eleven 423ET	Ford Motor Co Ltd/Stansted	
G-BEJV	PA-34-200T Seneca II	C.S.E. Aviation Ltd/Kidlington	
G-BEKM	Evans VP-1	G. J. McDill/Glenrothes	
G-BEKN	Cessna FRA.150M ★	RFC (Bourn) Ltd/Sibson	
G-BEKO	Cessna F.182Q	Tyler International	
G-BEKR	Rand KR-2	A. N. Purchase	
G-BELF	BN-2A-26 Islander	Activity Aviation Ltd	
G-BELP	PA-28-151 Warrior	Devon School of Flying/Dunkeswell	
G-BELT	Cessna F.150J	Yorkshire Light Aircraft Ltd (G-AWUV)/Leeds	
G-BELX	Cameron V-56 balloon	V. & A. M. Dyer	
G-BEMB	Cessna F.172M	Stocklaunch Ltd	
G-BEMM	Slingsby T.31B Motor Cadet	M. N. Martin	
G-BEMU	Thunder Ax5-42 balloon	I. J. Liddiard & A. Merritt	
G-BEMW	PA-28-181 Archer II	Southern Air Ltd/Shoreham	
G-BEMY	Cessna FRA.150M	P. A. Dunk	
G-BEND	Cameron V-56 balloon	Dante Balloon Group *Le Billet*	
G-BENJ	R. Commander 112B	E. J. Percival/Blackbushe	
G-BENK	Cessna F.172M	Graham Churchill Plant Ltd	
G-BENN	Cameron V-56 balloon	S. H. Budd	
G-BEOD	Cessna 180 H	Avionics Research Ltd/Cranfield	
G-BEOE	Cessna FRA.150M	W. J. Henderson	
G-BEOH	PA-28R-201T Turbo Arrow III	G-BEOH Group	
G-BEOI	PA-18 Super Cub 150	Southdown Gliding Club Ltd/Parham Park	
G-BEOK	Cessna F.150M	D. C. Bonsall	
G-BEOO	Sikorsky S-61N Mk. II	Brintel Helicopters	
G-BEOX	L-414 Hudson IV (A16-199) ★	RAF Museum/Hendon	
G-BEOY	Cessna FRA.150L	R. W. Denny	
G-BEOZ	A.W.650 Argosy 101 ★	Aeropark/E. Midlands	
G-BEPB	Pereira Osprey II	J. J. & A. J. C. Zwetsloot/Bourn	
G-BEPC	SNCAN Stampe SV-4C	Dawn Patrol Flight Training Ltd	
G-BEPF	SNCAN Stampe SV-4A	L. J. Rice	
G-BEPH	BN-2A Mk III-2 Trislander	Aurigny Air Services Ltd/Guernsey	
G-BEPI	BN-2A Mk III-2 Trislander	Aurigny Air Services Ltd/Guernsey	
G-BEPO	Cameron N-77 balloon	G. Camplin & V. Aitken	
G-BEPS	SC.5 Belfast	HeavyLift Cargo Airlines Ltd/Stansted	
G-BEPV	Fokker S.11-1 Instructor	L. C. MacKnight	
G-BEPY	R. Commander 112B	G-BEPY Group/Blackbushe	
G-BERA	SOCATA Rallye 150ST	Air Touring Services Ltd/Biggin Hill	
G-BERC	SOCATA Rallye 150ST	Severn Valley Aero Group	
G-BERD	Thunder Ax6-56A balloon	P. M. Gaines	
G-BERI	R. Commander 114	K. B. Harper/Blackbushe	
G-BERN	Saffrey S-330 balloon	B. Martin *Beeze*	
G-BERT	Cameron V-56 balloon	Southern Balloon Group *Bert*	
G-BERW	R. Commander 114	Malvern Holdings Ltd	
G-BERY	AA-1D Trainer	H. J. J. Levi	
G-BETD	Robin HR.200/100	R. A. Parsons/Bourn	
G-BETE	Rollason B.2A Beta	T. M. Jones/Tatenhill	
G-BETF	Cameron 'Champion' SS balloon	British Balloon Museum/Newbury	
G-BETG	Cessna 180K Skywagon	T. P. A. Norman	
G-BETI	Pitts S-1D Special	P. Metcalfe/Teesside	
G-BETL	PA-25 Pawnee 235D	Cambridge University Gliding Trust Ltd	
G-BETM	PA-25 Pawnee 235D	Yorkshire Gliding Club (Pty) Ltd	
G-BETP	Cameron O-65 balloon	J. R. Rix & Sons Ltd	
G-BETT	PA-34-200 Seneca II	Andrews Professional Colour Laboratories Ltd/Headcorn	
G-BEUA	PA-18 Super Cub 150	London Gliding Club (Pty) Ltd/Dunstable	

Notes	Reg.	Type	Owner or Operator
	G-BEUD	Robin HR.100/285R	E. A. & L. M. C. Payton/Cranfield
	G-BEUI	Piper J-3C-65 Cub	J. P. Conlan
	G-BEUK	Fuji FA.200-160	BM Aviation
	G-BEUL	Beech 95-58 Baron	Foyle Flyers Ltd/Eglinton
	G-BEUM	Taylor JT.1 Monoplane	J. Riley
	G-BEUN	Cassutt Racer IIIM	R. McNulty
	G-BEUP	Robin DR.400/180	A. V. Pound & Co Ltd
	G-BEUU	PA-18 Super Cub 95	F. Sharples/Sandown
	G-BEUV	Thunder Ax6-56A balloon	Silhouette Balloon Group
	G-BEUX	Cessna F.172N	ABK Aviation Services Ltd
	G-BEUY	Cameron N-31 balloon	A. C. Beaumont
	G-BEVA	SOCATA Rallye 150ST	The Rallye Group
	G-BEVB	SOCATA Rallye 150ST	N. R. Haines
	G-BEVC	SOCATA Rallye 150ST	B. W. Walpole
	G-BEVG	PA-34-200T-2 Seneca	Aranair Ltd/Bournemouth
	G-BEVO	Sportavia-Pützer RF-5	T. Barlow
	G-BEVP	Evans VP-2	G. Moscrop & R. C. Crowley
	G-BEVS	Taylor JT.1 Monoplane	D. Hunter
	G-BEVT	BN-2A Mk III-2 Trislander	Aurigny Air Services Ltd/Guernsey
	G-BEVW	SOCATA Rallye 150ST	P. C. Goodwin
	G-BEWJ	Westland-Bell 47G-3B1	Heli-Highland Ltd
	G-BEWM	Sikorsky S-61N Mk II	Brintel Helicopters
	G-BEWN	D.H.82A Tiger Moth	H. D. Labouchere
	G-BEWO	Zlin Z.326 Trener Master	Nimrod Group Ltd/Staverton
	G-BEWR	Cessna F.172N	Cheshire Air Training Services Ltd/ Liverpool
	G-BEWX	PA-28R-201 Arrow III	A. Vickers
	G-BEWY	Bell 206B JetRanger 3	PLM Dollar Group Ltd (G-CULL)
	G-BEXK	PA-25 Pawnee 235D	Howard Avis (Aviation) Ltd
	G-BEXN	AA-1C Lynx	Lynx Flying Group
	G-BEXO	PA-23 Apache 160	G. R. Moore & A. K. Hulme
	G-BEXR	MuAdry/CAARP CAP-10B	R. P. Lewis
	G-BEXW	PA-28-181 Archer II	Motorman Ltd/Elstree
	G-BEXZ	Cameron N-56 balloon	D. C. Eager & G. C. Clark
	G-BEYA	Enstrom 280C	Hovercam Ltd
	G-BEYB	Fairey Flycatcher (replica) (S1287) ★	F.A.A. Museum/Yeovilton
	G-BEYF	HPR-7 Herald 401	Channel Express (Air Services) Ltd/ Bournemouth
	G-BEYL	PA-28 Cherokee 180	B. G. & G. Airlines Ltd/Jersey
	G-BEYO	PA-28 Cherokee 140	A. Grant
	G-BEYT	PA-28 Cherokee 140	H. Foulds
	G-BEYV	Cessna T.210M	Ausen Aviation
	G-BEYW	Taylor JT.1 Monoplane	R. A. Abrahams/Barton
	G-BEYZ	Jodel DR.1051/M1	M. L. Balding
	G-BEZA	Zlin Z.226T Trener	L. Bezak
	G-BEZC	AA-5 Traveler	P. N. & S. E. Field
	G-BEZE	Rutan Vari-Eze	H. C. Mackinnon
	G-BEZF	AA-5 Traveler	G. A. Randall/Leeds
	G-BEZG	AA-5 Traveler	M. D. R. Harling & T. W. Cubbin
	G-BEZH	AA-5 Traveler	L. & S. M. Sims
	G-BEZI	AA-5 Traveler	BEZI Flying Group/Cranfield
	G-BEZJ	MBB Bo 105D	Bond Helicopters Ltd/Bourn
	G-BEZK	Cessna F.172H	Zulu Kilo Flying Group
	G-BEZO	PA-31-310 Turbo Navajo C	London Flight Centre (Stansted) Ltd
	G-BEZO	Cessna F.172M	Staverton Flying Services Ltd
	G-BEZP	PA-32 Cherokee Six 300D	Falcon Styles Ltd/Booker
	G-BEZR	Cessna F.172M	Kirmington Aviation Ltd
	G-BEZV	Cessna F.172M	Insch Flying Group
	G-BEZY	Rutan Vari-Eze	R. J. Jones/Cranfield
	G-BEZZ	Jodel D.112	G-BEZZ Jodel Group
	G-BFAA	GY-80 Horizon 160	Mary Poppins Ltd
	G-BFAC	Cessna A.177RG	Global Avionicare Ltd
	G-BFAF	Aeronca 7BCM (7797)	D. C. W. Harper/Finmere
	G-BFAH	Phoenix Currie Wot	R. W. Clarke
	G-BFAI	R. Commander 114	D. S. Innes/Guernsey
	G-BFAK	M.S.892A Rallye Commodore 150	P. G. Wells & J. D. Hensby
	G-BFAM	PA-31P Pressurised Navajo	CMH Management Services
	G-BFAO	PA-20 Pacer 135	E. A. M. Austin
	G-BFAP	SIAI-Marchetti S.205-20R	A. O. Broin
	G-BFAS	Evans VP-1	A. I. Sutherland
	G-BFAW	D.H.C.1 Chipmunk 22	R. V. Bowles/Husbands Bosworth

Reg.	Type	Owner or Operator	Notes
G-BFAX	D.H.C.1 Chipmunk 22 (WG422)	A. C. Kerr	
G-BFBA	Jodel DR.100A	W. H. Sherlock	
G-BFBB	PA-23 Aztec 250E	Air Training Sevices Ltd/Booker	
G-BFBE	Robin HR.200/100	Silver Machine Ltd	
G-BFBF	PA-28 Cherokee 140	Marnham Investments Ltd	
G-BFBM	Saffery S.330 balloon	B. Martin *Beeze II*	
G-BFBR	PA-28-161 Warrior II	Lowery Holdings Ltd/Fairoaks	
G-BFBU	Partenavia P.68B	Premair Charter Ltd	
G-BFBY	Piper J-3C-65 Cub	L. W. Usherwood	
G-BFCT	Cessna TU.206F	Cecil Aviation Ltd/Cambridge	
G-BFCZ	Sopwith Camel (B7270) ★	Brooklands Museum Trust Ltd/Weybridge	
G-BFDC	D.H.C.1 Chipmunk 22	N. F. O'Neill/Newtownards	
G-BFDE	Sopwith Tabloid (replica) (168) ★	RAF Museum Storage & Restoration Centre/Cardington	
G-BFDF	SOCATA Rallye 235E	D. K. Lawry	
G-BFDG	PA-28R-201T Turbo-Arrow III	Southern Union Trading Ltd	
G-BFDI	PA-28-181 Archer II	Truman Aviation Ltd/Tollerton	
G-BFDK	PA-28-161 Warrior II	Priory Garage	
G-BFDL	Piper J-3C-65 Cub (454537)	S. Beresford & G. S. Claybourn/Sandtoft	
G-BFDO	PA-28R-201T Turbo Arrow III	A. J. Gow	
G-BFDZ	Taylor JT.1 Monoplane	L. J. Greenhough	
G-BFEB	Jodel 150	S. Russell	
G-BFEE	Beech 95-E55 Baron	Chase Aviation Ltd	
G-BFEF	Agusta-Bell 47G-3B1	R. C. Hields	
G-BFEH	Jodel D.117A	C. V. & S. J. Philpott	
G-BFEK	Cessna F.152	Staverton Flying Services Ltd	
G-BFER	Bell 212	Bristow Helicopters Ltd	
G-BFEV	PA-25 Pawnee 235	Trent Valley Aerotowing Club Ltd	
G-BFEW	PA-25 Pawnee 235	Cornish Gliding & Flying Club Ltd	
G-BFFB	Evans VP-2 ★	*(stored)*/Eaton Bray	
G-BFFC	Cessna F.152-II	Yorkshire Flying Services Ltd/Leeds	
G-BFFE	Cessna F.152-II	J. Easson/Edinburgh	
G-BFFG	Beech 95-B55 Baron	V. Westley	
G-BFFJ	Sikorsky S-61N Mk II	British International Helicopters	
G-BFFK	Sikorsky S-61N Mk II	British International Helicopters	
G-BFFP	PA-18 Super Cub 150 (modified)	Booker Gliding Club Ltd	
G-BFFT	Cameron V-56 balloon	R. I. M. Kerr & D. C. Boxall	
G-BFFW	Cessna F.152	Tayside Aviation Ltd/Dundee	
G-BFFY	Cessna F.150M	G. & S. A. Jones	
G-BFFZ	Cessna FR.172 Hawk XP	Bravo Aviation Ltd/Caernarfon	
G-BFGD	Cessna F.172N-II	J. T. Armstrong	
G-BFGF	Cessna F.177RG	J. E. Searson	
G-BFGG	Cessna FRA.150M	Cornwall Flying Club Ltd/Bodmin	
G-BFGH	Cessna F.337G	T. Perkins/Sherburn	
G-BFGK	Jodel D.117	B. F. J. Hope	
G-BFGL	Cessna FA.152	Yorkshire Flying Services Ltd/Leeds	
G-BFGO	Fuji FA.200-160	Butane Buzzard Aviation Corporation Ltd	
G-BFGS	M.S.893E Rallye 180GT	K. M. & H. Bowen	
G-BFGW	Cessna F.150H	C. E. Stringer	
G-BFGX	Cessna FRA.150M	Air Service Training Ltd/Perth	
G-BFGZ	Cessna FRA.150M	Air Service Training Ltd/Perth	
G-BFHH	D.H.82A Tiger Moth	P. Harrison & M. J. Gambrell/Redhill	
G-BFHI	Piper J-3C-65 Cub	J. McD. Robinson/Bann Foot	
G-BFHP	Champion 7GCAA Citabria	Small World Aviation Ltd	
G-BFHR	Jodel DR.220/2+2	T. W. Greaves	
G-BFHT	Cessna F.152-II	Westward Airways (Lands End) Ltd	
G-BFHU	Cessna F.152-II	Deltair Ltd/Liverpool	
G-BFHV	Cessna F.152-II	Falcon Flying Services/Biggin Hill	
G-BFHX	Evans VP-1	P. Johnson	
G-BFIB	PA-31 Turbo Navajo	Falcon Aviation Ltd	
G-BFID	Taylor JT.2 Titch Mk III	J. C. Lidgard	
G-BFIE	Cessna FRA.150M	B. J. Parker	
G-BFIG	Cessna FR.172K XPII	Tenair Ltd	
G-BFIJ	AA-5A Cheetah	S. W. Jackson	
G-BFIN	AA-5A Cheetah	G-BFIN Group	
G-BFIP	Wallbro Monoplane 1909 replica	K. H. Wallis/Swanton Morley	
G-BFIR	Avro 652A Anson 21 (WD413)	G. M. K. Fraser	
G-BFIT	Thunder Ax6-56Z balloon	J. A. G. Tyson	
G-BFIU	Cessna FR.172K XP	B. M. Jobling	
G-BFIV	Cessna F.177RG	Kingfishair Ltd/Blackbushe	
G-BFIX	Thunder Ax7-77A balloon	R. Owen	
G-BFIY	Cessna F.150M	Yorkshire Aeroplane Club/Leeds/Bradford	
G-BFJJ	Evans VP-1	M. J. Collins	

Notes	Reg.	Type	Owner or Operator
	G-BFJK	PA-23 Aztec 250F	H. G. Keighley
	G-BFJR	Cessna F.337G	Mannix Aviation/E. Midlands
	G-BFJW	AB-206B JetRanger	European Aviation Ltd
	G-BFJZ	Robin DR.400/140B	Rochester Aviation Ltd
	G-BFKB	Cessna F.172N	R. M. Collins
	G-BFKC	Rand KR-2	L. H. S. Stephens & I. S. Hewitt
	G-BFKF	Cessna FA.152	Klingair Ltd/Conington
	G-BFKH	Cessna F.152	TG Aviation Ltd/Manston
	G-BFKL	Cameron N-56 balloon	Merrythought Toys Ltd *Merrythought*
	G-BFKY	PA-34-200 Seneca II	S.L.H. Construction Ltd/Biggin Hill
	G-BFLH	PA-34-200T Seneca II	Air Medical Ltd
	G-BFLI	PA-28R-201T Turbo Arrow III	J. K. Chudzicki
	G-BFLM	Cessna 150M	Cornwall Flying Club Ltd/Bodmin
	G-BFLP	Amethyst Ax6 balloon	K. J. Hendry *Amethyst*
	G-BFLU	Cessna F.152	Bravo Aviation Ltd
	G-BFLX	AA-5A Cheetah	Plane Talking Ltd/Elstree
	G-BFLZ	Beech 95-A55 Baron	Caterite Food Service
	G-BFME	Cameron V-56 balloon	Warwick Balloons
	G-BFMF	Cassutt Racer Mk IIIM	P. H. Lewis
	G-BFMG	PA-28-161 Warrior II	Stardial Ltd
	G-BFMH	Cessna 177B	Span Aviation Ltd/Newcastle
	G-BFMK	Cessna FA.152	RAF Halton Aeroplane Club Ltd
	G-BFMM	PA-28-181 Archer II	Bristol & Wessex Aeroplane Club Ltd
	G-BFMR	PA-20 Pacer 125	J. Knight
	G-BFMX	Cessna F.172N	Broomco (406) Ltd
	G-BFMY	Sikorsky S-61N	Bristow Helicopters Ltd
	G-BFMZ	Payne Ax6 balloon	E. G. Woolnough
	G-BFNG	Jodel D.112	K. M. Moores
	G-BFNI	PA-28-161 Warrior II	P. Elliott/Biggin Hill
	G-BFNJ	PA-28-161 Warrior II	Ebbrise Ltd
	G-BFNK	PA-28-161 Warrior II	C.S.E. Aviation Ltd/Kidlington
	G-BFOD	Cessna F.182Q	G. N. Clarke
	G-BFOE	Cessna F.152	Plane Talking Ltd/Elstree
	G-BFOF	Cessna F.152	Staverton Flying School Ltd
	G-BFOG	Cessna 150M	P. H. Wilmot-Allistone
	G-BFOJ	AA-1 Yankee	A. J. Morton/Bournemouth
	G-BFOP	Jodel D.120	R. J. Wesley & G. D. Western/Ipswich
	G-BFOS	Thunder Ax6-56A balloon	N. T. Petty
	G-BFOU	Taylor JT.1 Monoplane	G. Bee
	G-BFOV	Cessna F.172N	D. J. Walker
	G-BFPA	Scheibe SF.25B Falke	N. Meiklejohn & J. Steel
	G-BFPB	AA-5B Tiger	Guernsey Aero Club
	G-BFPH	Cessna F.172K	Linc-Air Flying Group
	G-BFPL	Fokker D.VII (replica) (4253/18)	F. Actis/Switzerland
	G-BFPM	Cessna F.172M	N. R. Havercroft
	G-BFPO	R. Commander 112B	J. G. Hale Ltd
	G-BFPP	Bell 47J-2	K. Goodyear
	G-BFPS	PA-25 Pawnee 235D	Kent Gliding Club Ltd/Challock
	G-BFPZ	Cessna F.177RG	A. B. van Eeckhoudt/Belgium
	G-BFRA	R. Commander 114	Ischia Investments Ltd
	G-BFRD	Bowers Fly-Baby 1A	F. R. Donaldson
	G-BFRF	Taylor JT.1 Monoplane	E. R. Bailey
	G-BFRI	Sikorsky S-61N	Bristow Helicopters Ltd *Braerich*
	G-BFRL	Cessna F.152	M. K. Barnes & G. N. Olsen
	G-BFRM	Cessna 550 Citation II	Marshall of Cambridge (Engineering) Ltd
	G-BFRO	Cessna F.150M	Skyviews & General Ltd/Carlisle
	G-BFRR	Cessna FRA.150M	J. R. Duller
	G-BFRS	Cessna F.172N	Poplar Toys Ltd
	G-BFRV	Cessna FA.152	Turnhouse Flying Club
	G-BFRY	PA-25 Pawnee 260	Yorkshire Gliding Club (Pty) Ltd/ Sutton Bank
	G-BFSA	Cessna F.182Q	Clark Masts Ltd/Sandown
	G-BFSB	Cessna F.152	Tatenhill Aviation
	G-BFSC	PA-25 Pawnee 235D	Farm Aviation Services Ltd/Enstone
	G-BFSD	PA-25 Pawnee 235D	Deeside Gliding Club (Aberdeenshire) Ltd/ Aboyne
	G-BFSK	PA-23 Apache 160 ★	*Sub-aqua instructional airframe*/Croughton
	G-BFSR	Cessna F.150J	S. Jayyousi
	G-BFSS	Cessna FR.172G	Minerva Services
	G-BFSY	PA-28-181 Archer II	Downland Aviation
	G-BFTC	PA-28R-201T Turbo Arrow III	M. J. Milns
	G-BFTF	AA-5B Tiger	F. C. Burrow Ltd/Leeds
	G-BFTG	AA-5B Tiger	D. Hepburn & G. R. Montgomery

Reg.	Type	Owner or Operator	Notes
G-BFTH	Cessna F.172N	J. Birkett	
G-BFTT	Cessna 421C	P&B Metal Components Ltd/Manston	
G-BFTX	Cessna F.172N	E. Kent Flying Group	
G-BFTY	Cameron V-77 balloon	Regal Motors (Bilston) Ltd	
G-BFUB	PA-32RT-300 Lance II	Jolida Holdings Ltd	
G-BFUD	Scheibe SF.25E Super Falke	S. H. Hart	
G-BFUG	Cameron N-77 balloon	Headland Services Ltd	
G-BFUZ	Cameron V-77 balloon	Skysales Ltd	
G-BFVF	PA-38-112 Tomahawk	Truman Aviation Ltd/Tollerton	
G-BFVG	PA-28-181 Archer II	G-BFVG Flying Group/Blackpool	
G-BFVH	D.H.2 Replica (5894)	Wessex Aviation & Transport Ltd	
G-BFVM	Westland-Bell 47G-3B1	K. R. Dossett	
G-BFVP	PA-23 Aztec 250F	Litton Aviation Services Ltd	
G-BFVS	AA-5B Tiger	S. W. Biroth & T. Chapman/Denham	
G-BFVU	Cessna 150L	Flying Services	
G-BFWB	PA-28-161 Warrior II	Ipswich School of Flying Ltd	
G-BFWD	Currie Wot	F. R. Donaldson	
G-BFWE	PA-23 Aztec 250E	Air Navigation & Trading Co Ltd/Blackpool	
G-BFWK	PA-28-161 Warrior II	Marnham Investments Ltd	
G-BFWL	Cessna F.150L	G-BFWL Flying Group/Barton	
G-BFXD	PA-28-161 Warrior II	C.S.E. Aviation Ltd/Kidlington	
G-BFXE	PA-28-161 Warrior II	C.S.E. Aviation Ltd/Kidlington	
G-BFXF	Andreasson BA.4B	A. Brown/Sherburn	
G-BFXH	Cessna F.152	M. Entwistle	
G-BFXK	PA-28 Cherokee 140	G. S. & M. T. Pritchard/Southend	
G-BFXL	Albatross D.5A (D5397/17)	F.A.A. Museum/Yeovilton	
G-BFXR	Jodel D.112	Jodel Flying Group	
G-BFXS	R. Commander 114	Keats Printing Ltd	
G-BFXW	AA-5B Tiger	Campsol Ltd	
G-BFXX	AA-5B Tiger	M. J. Porter	
G-BFYA	MBB Bo 105DB	Sterling Helicopters Ltd	
G-BFYB	PA-28-161 Warrior II	C.S.E. Aviation Ltd/Kidlington	
G-BFYC	PA-32RT-300 Lance II	A. A. Barnes	
G-BFYE	Robin HR.100/285 ★	stored/Sywell	
G-BFYI	Westland-Bell 47G-3B1	B. Walker & Co (Dursley) Ltd	
G-BFYK	Cameron V-77 balloon	L. E. Jones	
G-BFYL	Evans VP-2	W. C. Brown	
G-BFYM	PA-28-161 Warrior II	C.S.E. Aviation Ltd/Kidlington	
G-BFYO	SPAD XIII (replica) (3398) ★	F.A.A. Museum/Yeovilton	
G-BFZB	Piper J-3C-85 Cub	Zebedee Flying Group/Shoreham	
G-BFZD	Cessna FR.182RG	R. B. Lewis & Co/Sleap	
G-BFZG	PA-28-161 Warrior II	C.S.E. Aviation Ltd/Kidlington	
G-BFZH	PA-28R Cherokee Arrow 200	W. E. Lowe/Shobdon	
G-BFZL	V.836 Viscount	British World Airlines Ltd/Southend	
G-BFZM	R. Commander 112TC	R. J. Lamplough/North Weald	
G-BFZN	Cessna FA.152	Falcon Flying Services/Biggin Hill	
G-BFZO	AA-5A Cheetah	Giles & Partners Ltd/Liverpool	
G-BFZT	Cessna FA.152	Zulu Tango Ltd/Guernsey	
G-BFZU	Cessna FA.152	Plane Talking Ltd/Elstree	
G-BFZV	Cessna F.172M	R. Thomas	
G-BGAA	Cessna 152 II	PJC Leasing Ltd	
G-BGAB	Cessna F.152 II	TG Aviation Ltd/Manston	
G-BGAD	Cessna F.152 II	Marnham Investments Ltd/Newtownards	
G-BGAE	Cessna F.152 II	Klingair Ltd/Conington	
G-BGAF	Cessna FA.152	M. F. Hatt & ptnrs/Southend	
G-BGAG	Cessna F.172N	Aerohire Ltd/Halfpenny Green	
G-BGAJ	Cessna F.182Q II	Ground Airport Services Ltd/Guernsey	
G-BGAK	Cessna F.182Q II	D. R. Joubert	
G-BGAX	PA-28 Cherokee 140	C. D. Brack	
G-BGAY	Cameron O-77 balloon	S. W. C. & P. C. A. Hall	
G-BGAZ	Cameron V-77 balloon	C. J. Madigan & D. H. McGibbon	
G-BGBA	Robin R.2100A	D. Faulkner/Redhill	
G-BGBE	Jodel DR.1050	J. A. & B. Mawby	
G-BGBF	D.31A Turbulent	S. M. Cryer	
G-BGBG	PA-28-181 Archer II	Harlow Printing Ltd/Newcastle	
G-BGBI	Cessna F.150L	Falcon Flying Services/Biggin Hill	
G-BGBK	PA-38-112 Tomahawk	F. Marshall & R. C. Priest/Netherthorpe	
G-BGBN	PA-38-112 Tomahawk	Bonus Aviation Ltd/Cranfield	
G-BGBP	Cessna F.152	Stapleford Flying Club Ltd	
G-BGBR	Cessna F.172N	Falcon Flying Services/Biggin Hill	
G-BGBU	Auster AOP.9 (XN435)	P. Neilson	
G-BGBW	PA-38-112 Tomahawk	Truman Aviation Ltd/Tollerton	

Notes	Reg.	Type	Owner or Operator
	G-BGBY	PA-38-112 Tomahawk	Ravenair/Manchester
	G-BGBZ	R. Commander 114	R. S. Fenwick/Biggin Hill
	G-BGCG	Douglas C-47A	on rebuild
	G-BGCM	AA-5A Cheetah	G. & S. A. Jones
	G-BGCO	PA-44-180 Seminole	J. R. Henderson
	G-BGCX	Taylor JT.1 Monoplane	G. M. R. Walters
	G-BGCY	Taylor JT.1 Monoplane	M. T. Taylor
	G-BGDA	Boeing 737-236	British Airways Manchester Bridgwater
	G-BGDB	Boeing 737-236	British Airways River Tweed
	G-BGDE	Boeing 737-236	British Airways Pride of Manchester
	G-BGDF	Boeing 737-236	British Airways River Thames
	G-BGDG	Boeing 737-236	British Airways Manchester Trough of Bowland
	G-BGDI	Boeing 737-236	British Airways Manchester River Ouse
	G-BGDJ	Boeing 737-236	British Airways Manchester Delamere Forest
	G-BGDK	Boeing 737-236	British Airways Manchester Ribble Valley
	G-BGDL	Boeing 737-236	British Airways Vale of Lune
	G-BGDO	Boeing 737-236	British Airways River Usk
	G-BGDP	Boeing 737-236	British Airways River Taff
	G-BGDR	Boeing 737-236	British Airways River Bann
	G-BGDS	Boeing 737-236	GB Airways Ltd Mons Calpe
	G-BGDT	Boeing 737-236	British Airways Manchester Wirral Peninsula
	G-BGDU	Boeing 737-236	GB Airways Ltd Mons Abyla
	G-BGEA	Cessna F.150M	Agricultural & General Aviation Ltd/ Bournemouth
	G-BGED	Cessna U.206F	Chapman Aviation Ltd
	G-BGEE	Evans VP-1	R. Wheeler & B. E. Holmes
	G-BGEF	Jodel D.112	G. G. Johnson & S. J. Davies
	G-BGEH	Monnett Sonerai II	P. C. Dowbor-Musnicki
	G-BGEI	Baby Great Lakes	I. D. Trask
	G-BGEK	PA-38-112 Tomahawk	Ravenair/Manchester
	G-BGEL	PA-38-112 Tomahawk	Ravenair/Manchester
	G-BGEP	Cameron D-38 balloon	Aeronord SAS/Italy
	G-BGEW	SNCAN NC.854S	Tavair Ltd
	G-BGFC	Evans VP-2	S. W. C. Hollins
	G-BGFF	FRED Srs 2	J. T. Taylor
	G-BGFG	AA-5A Cheetah	Plane Talking Ltd/Elstree
	G-BGFH	Cessna F.182Q	Barmoor Aviation
	G-BGFI	AA-5A Cheetah	I. J. Hay & A. Nayyar/Biggin Hill
	G-BGFJ	Jodel D.9 Bebe	M. D. Mold
	G-BGFK	Evans VP-1	I. N. M. Cameron
	G-BGFT	PA-34-200T Seneca II	C.S.E. Aviation Ltd/Kidlington
	G-BGFX	Cessna F.152	Falcon Flying Services/Biggin Hill
	G-BGGA	Bellanca 7GCBC Citabria	L. A. King
	G-BGGB	Bellanca 7GCBC Citabria	G. H. N. Chamberlain
	G-BGGC	Bellanca 7GCBC Citabria	R. P. Ashfield & J. P. Stone
	G-BGGD	Bellanca 8GCBC Scout	Bristol & Gloucestershire Gliding Club/ Nympsfield
	G-BGGE	PA-38-112 Tomahawk	Truman Aviation Ltd/Tollerton
	G-BGGF	PA-38-112 Tomahawk	Truman Aviation Ltd/Tollerton
	G-BGGG	PA-38-112 Tomahawk	Teesside Flight Centre Ltd
	G-BGGI	PA-38-112 Tomahawk	Truman Aviation Ltd/Tollerton
	G-BGGL	PA-38-112 Tomahawk	Grunwick Processing Laboratories Ltd/ Elstree
	G-BGGM	PA-38-112 Tomahawk	Grunwick Processing Laboratories Ltd/ Elstree
	G-BGGN	PA-38-112 Tomahawk	Domeastral Ltd/Elstree
	G-BGGO	Cessna F.152	E. Midlands Flying School Ltd
	G-BGGP	Cessna F.152	E. Midlands Flying School Ltd
	G-BGGU	Wallis WA-116/RR	K. H. Wallis
	G-BGGW	Wallis WA-112	K. H. Wallis
	G-BGGY	AB-206B Jet Ranger ★	Instructional airframe/Cranfield
	G-BGHE	Convair L-13A	J. M. Davis/Wichita
	G-BGHF	Westland WG.30 ★	IHM/Weston-s-Mare
	G-BGHI	Cessna F.152	Taxon Ltd/Shoreham
	G-BGHM	Robin R.1180T	H. Price
	G-BGHP	Beech 76 Duchess	Magneta Ltd
	G-BGHS	Cameron N-31 balloon	W. R. Teasdale
	G-BGHT	Falconar F-12	C. R. Coates
	G-BGHU	NA T-6G Texan (115042)	C. E. Bellhouse
	G-BGHV	Cameron V-77 balloon	E. Davies

Reg.	Type	Owner or Operator	Notes
G-BGHW	Thunder Ax8-90 balloon	Edinburgh University Balloon Group	
G-BGHY	Taylor JT.1 Monoplane	R. A. Hand	
G-BGHZ	FRED Srs 2	A. Smith	
G-BGIB	Cessna 152 II	Mona Aviation Ltd	
G-BGID	Westland-Bell 47G-3B1	M. J. Cuttell	
G-BGIG	PA-38-112 Tomahawk	Air Claire Ltd	
G-BGII	PA-32 Cherokee Six 300E	West India Flying Group	
G-BGIO	Bensen B.8M	R. M. Savage & F. G. Shepherd	
G-BGIP	Colt 56A balloon	J. G. N. Perfect	
G-BGIU	Cessna F.172H	P. M. Smalley & M. Ruggieri	
G-BGIX	H.295 Super Courier	C. M. Lee	
G-BGIY	Cessna F.172N	Glasgow 172 Group	
G-BGJE	Boeing 737-236	British Airways *River Wear*/Gatwick	
G-BGJF	Boeing 737-236	British Airways *River Axe*/Gatwick	
G-BGJH	Boeing 737-236	British Airways *River Lyne*/Gatwick	
G-BGJI	Boeing 737-236	British Airways *River Wey*/Gatwick	
G-BGJJ	Boeing 737-236	British Airways *River Swale*/Gatwick	
G-BGJU	Cameron V-65 Balloon	J. A Folkes	
G-BGJW	GA-7 Cougar	P. G. Lawrence	
G-BGKC	SOCATA Rallye 110ST	J. H. Cranmer & T. A. Timms	
G-BGKD	SOCATA Rallye 110ST	P. A. Cairns	
G-BGKJ	MBB Bo 105D ★	*Instructional airframe*/Bourn	
G-BGKO	GY-20 Minicab	R. B. Webber	
G-BGKS	PA-28-161 Warrior II	Marnham Investments Ltd	
G-BGKT	Auster AOP.9 (XN441)	Auster Nine Group	
G-BGKU	PA-28R-201 Arrow III	Caplane Ltd	
G-BGKV	PA-28R-201 Arrow III	R. Haverson & R. G. Watson	
G-BGKY	PA-38-112 Tomahawk	Prospect Air Ltd	
G-BGKZ	J/5F Aiglet Trainer	M. J. & A. A. Copse	
G-BGLA	PA-38-112 Tomahawk	Norwich School of Flying	
G-BGLB	Bede BD-5B ★	Science Museum/Wroughton	
G-BGLF	Evans VP-1 Srs 2	R. A. Yates	
G-BGLG	Cessna 152	Skyviews & General Ltd/Bourn	
G-BGLI	Cessna 152	Luton Flying Club *(stored)*	
G-BGLJ	Bell 212	Bristow Helicopters Ltd	
G-BGLK	Monnett Sonerai II	N. M. Smorthit	
G-BGLN	Cessna FA.152	Bournemouth Flying Club	
G-BGLO	Cessna F.172N	A. H. Slaughter/Southend	
G-BGLS	Oldfield Super Baby Lakes	J. F. Dowe	
G-BGLW	PA-34-200 Seneca II	London Executive Aviation Ltd	
G-BGLX	Cameron N-56 balloon	S. L. G. Williams	
G-BGLZ	Stits SA-3A Playboy	C. A. Wills	
G-BGME	SIPA S.903	M. Emery & C. A. Suckling (G-BCML)/ Redhill	
G-BGMJ	GY-201 Minicab	S. L. Wakefield & ptnrs	
G-BGMO	H.S.748 Srs 2	Emerald Airways Ltd/Liverpool	
G-BGMP	Cessna F.172G	R. W. Collings	
G-BGMR	GY-201 Minicab	Mike Romeo Flying Group	
G-BGMS	Taylor JT.2 Titch	M. A. J. Spice	
G-BGMT	MS.894E Rallye 235GT	C. S. Simmons	
G-BGMU	Westland-Bell 47G-3B1	V. L. J. & V. English	
G-BGMV	Scheibe SF.25B Falke	Mendip Falke Flying Group	
G-BGMX	Enstrom 280C-UK	Stephenson Aviation Ltd (G-SHXX)	
G-BGND	Cessna F.172N	A. J. M. Freeman	
G-BGNR	Cessna F.172N	Aviators Flight Centre/Southend	
G-BGNT	Cessna F.152	Klingair Ltd/Conington	
G-BGNV	GA-7 Cougar	G. H. Smith & Son	
G-BGOD	Colt 77A balloon	C. Allen & M. D. Steuer	
G-BGOG	PA-28-161 Warrior II	W. D. Moore	
G-BGOI	Cameron O-56 balloon	S. H. Budd	
G-BGOL	PA-28R-201T Turbo Arrow III	Valley Flying Co Ltd	
G-BGON	GA-7 Cougar	Plane Talking Ltd/Elstree	
G-BGOO	Colt 56 SS balloon	British Gas Corporation	
G-BGOP	Dassault Falcon 20F	Nissan (UK) Ltd/Heathrow	
G-BGOR	AT-6D Harvard III (14863)	M. L. Sargeant	
G-BGPA	Cessna 182Q	Papa Alpha Group	
G-BGPB	CCF T-6J Texan (20385)	J. Romain/Duxford	
G-BGPD	Piper J-3C-65 Cub (479744)	P. D. Whiteman	
G-BGPH	AA-5B Tiger	A. J. Dales	
G-BGPI	Plumb BGP-1	B. G. Plumb	
G-BGPJ	PA-28-161 Warrior II	W. Lancs Warrior Co Ltd	
G-BGPK	AA-5B Tiger	G. A. Platon/Bournemouth	
G-BGPL	PA-28-161 Warrior II	TG Aviation Ltd/Manston	

Notes	Reg.	Type	Owner or Operator
	G-BGPM	Evans VP-2	M. G. Reilly
	G-BGPN	PA-18 Super Cub 150	Clacton Aero Club (1988) Ltd
	G-BGPU	PA-28 Cherokee 140	Air Navigation & Trading Ltd/Blackpool
	G-BGPZ	M.S.890A Rallye Commodore	Popham Flying Group
	G-BGRC	PA-28 Cherokee 140	Arrow Air Centre Ltd/Shipdham
	G-BGRE	Beech A200 Super King Air	Martin-Baker (Engineering) Ltd/Chalgrove
	G-BGRG	Beech 76 Duchess	Motionscope Ltd/Blackpool
	G-BGRH	Robin DR.400/22	Rochester Aviation Ltd
	G-BGRI	Jodel DR.1051	B. Gunn & K. L. Burnett
	G-BGRK	PA-38-112 Tomahawk	Goodwood Terrena Ltd/Goodwood
	G-BGRL	PA-38-112 Tomahawk	Goodwood Terrena Ltd/Goodwood
	G-BGRM	PA-38-112 Tomahawk	Goodwood Terrena Ltd/Goodwood
	G-BGRN	PA-38-112 Tomahawk	Goodwood Terrena Ltd/Goodwood
	G-BGRO	Cessna F.172M	Northfield Garage Ltd/Prestwick
	G-BGRR	PA-38-112 Tomahawk	Prospect Air Ltd
	G-BGRS	Thunder Ax7-77Z balloon	P. M. Gaines & P. B. Fountain
	G-BGRT	Steen Skybolt	J. H. Kimber & O. Meier
	G-BGRX	PA-38-112 Tomahawk	Bonus Aviation Ltd
	G-BGSA	M.S.892E Rallye 150GT	D. H. Tonkin
	G-BGSG	PA-44-180 Seminole	D. J. McSorley
	G-BGSH	PA-38-112 Tomahawk	Scotia Safari Ltd/Prestwick
	G-BGSI	PA-38-112 Tomahawk	Ravenair/Manchester
	G-BGSJ	Piper J-3C-65 Cub	A. J. Higgins
	G-BGST	Thunder Ax7-65 balloon	J. L. Bond
	G-BGSV	Cessna F.172N	Southwell Air Services Ltd
	G-BGSW	Beech F33 Debonair	Marketprior Ltd/Swansea
	G-BGSX	Cessna F.152	Plane Talking Ltd/Elstree
	G-BGSY	GA-7 Cougar	Van Allen Ltd/Guernsey
	G-BGTB	SOCATA TB.10 Tobago ★	D. Pope (stored)
	G-BGTC	Auster AOP.9 (XP282)	P. T. Bolton
	G-BGTF	PA-44-180 Seminole	NG Trustees & Nominees Ltd
	G-BGTG	PA-23 Aztec 250F	Thompson & Morgan (Young Plants) Ltd
	G-BGTI	Piper J-3C-65 Cub	A. P. Broad
	G-BGTJ	PA-28 Cherokee 180	Serendipity Aviation/Staverton
	G-BGTP	Robin HR.100/210	J. C. Parker
	G-BGTT	Cessna 310R	Aviation Beauport Ltd/Jersey
	G-BGTX	Jodel D.117	Madley Flying Group/Shobdon
	G-BGUA	PA-38-112 Tomahawk	Rhodair Maintenance Ltd/Cardiff
	G-BGUB	PA-32 Cherokee Six 300E	A. P. Diplock
	G-BGUY	Cameron V-56 balloon	J. L. Guy
	G-BGVB	Robin DR.315	Victor Bravo Group
	G-BGVE	CP.1310-C3 Super Emeraude	Victor Echo Group
	G-BGVH	Beech 76 Duchess	Velco Marketing
	G-BGVK	PA-28-161 Warrior II	D. S. Wells
	G-BGVN	PA-28RT-201 Arrow IV	H. S. Davies
	G-BGVS	Cessna F.172M	Kirkwall Flying Club
	G-BGVT	Cessna R.182RG	Bain Transport
	G-BGVU	PA-28 Cherokee 180	P. E. Toleman
	G-BGVV	AA-5A Cheetah	A. H. McVicar
	G-BGVW	AA-5A Cheetah	Plane Talking Ltd/Elstree
	G-BGVY	AA-5B Tiger	R. J. C. Neal-Smith
	G-BGVZ	PA-28-181 Archer II	Aerohire Ltd/Halfpenny Green
	G-BGWC	Robin DR.400/180	Shepherd Aviation Ltd/Rochester
	G-BGWH	PA-18 Super Cub 150	Clacton Aero Club (1988) Ltd
	G-BGWI	Cameron V-65 balloon	Army Balloon Club/Germany
	G-BGWJ	Sikorsky S-61N	British Executive Air Services Ltd
	G-BGWK	Sikorsky S-61N	Bristow Helicopters Ltd
	G-BGWM	PA-28-181 Archer II	Thames Valley Flying Club Ltd
	G-BGWN	PA-38-112 Tomahawk	Teesside Flight Centre Ltd
	G-BGWO	Jodel D.112	K. McBride
	G-BGWR	Cessna U.206A	C. M. J. Parton (G-DISC)/Tilstock
	G-BGWS	Enstrom 280C Shark	Stephenson Marine Co. Ltd
	G-BGWU	PA-38-112 Tomahawk	J. S. & L. M. Markey
	G-BGWV	Aeronca 7AC Champion	RFC Flying Group/Popham
	G-BGWW	PA-23 Turbo Aztec 250E	Aerodynamics Ltd
	G-BGWY	Thunder Ax6-56Z balloon	P. J. Eley
	G-BGWZ	Eclipse Super Eagle ★	F.A.A. Museum/Yeovilton
	G-BGXA	Piper J-3C-65 Cub (329471)	K. Nicholls
	G-BGXB	PA-38-112 Tomahawk	Sightest Ltd/Biggin Hill
	G-BGXC	SOCATA TB.10 Tobago	N. N. Tullah/Cranfield
	G-BGXD	SOCATA TB.10 Tobago	C. C. Brown
	G-BGXJ	Partenavia P.68B	Cecil Aviation Ltd/Cambridge
	G-BGXK	Cessna 310R	Edinburgh Flying Club

Reg.	Type	Owner or Operator	Notes
G-BGXL	Bensen B.8MV	B. P. Triefus	
G-BGXN	PA-38-112 Tomahawk	Panshanger School of Flying Ltd	
G-BGXO	PA-38-112 Tomahawk	Goodwood Terrena Ltd	
G-BGXP	Westland-Bell 47G-3B1	Ace Motor Salvage (Norfolk)	
G-BGXR	Robin HR.200/100	E. G. Cleobury	
G-BGXS	PA-28-236 Dakota	Bawtry Road Service Station Ltd	
G-BGXT	SOCATA TB.10 Tobago	D. A. H. Morris	
G-BGYG	PA-28-161 Warrior II	C.S.E. Aviation Ltd/Kidlington	
G-BGYH	PA-28-161 Warrior II	C.S.E. Aviation Ltd/Kidlington	
G-BGYN	PA-18 Super Cub 150	B. J. Dunford	
G-BGYR	H.S.125 Srs 600B	British Aerospace (Operations) Ltd/Warton	
G-BGYT	EMB-110P1 Bandeirante	Air South West Ltd/Exeter	
G-BGZF	PA-38-112 Tomahawk	Aerohire Ltd/Halfpenny Green	
G-BGZJ	PA-38-112 Tomahawk	W. R. C. M. Foyle	
G-BGZK	Westland-Bell 47G-3B1	Pan Air Ltd	
G-BGZL	Eiri PIK-20E	G-BGZL Flying Group/Enstone	
G-BGZN	WMB.2 Windtracker balloon	S. R. Woolfries	
G-BGZO	PA-38-112 Tomahawk	Ravenair/Manchester	
G-BGZY	Jodel D.120	M. Hale	
G-BGZZ	Thunder Ax6-56 balloon	J. M. Robinson	
G-BHAA	Cessna 152 II	Herefordshire Aero Club Ltd/Shobdon	
G-BHAC	Cessna A.152	Herefordshire Aero Club Ltd/Shobdon	
G-BHAD	Cessna A.152	Shropshire Aero Club Ltd/Sleap	
G-BHAF	PA-38-112 Tomahawk	Notelevel Ltd	
G-BHAI	Cessna F.152	J. Easson/Edinburgh	
G-BHAJ	Robin DR.400/160	Rowantask Ltd	
G-BHAL	Rango Saffery S.200 SS	A. M. Lindsay *Anneky Panky*	
G-BHAM	Thunder Ax6-56 balloon	D. Sampson	
G-BHAR	Westland-Bell 47G-3B1	E. A. L. Sturmer	
G-BHAT	Thunder Ax7-77 balloon	C. P. Witter Ltd *Witter*	
G-BHAV	Cessna F.152	Iceni Leasing	
G-BHAW	Cessna F.172N	A. J. Osmond/Biggin Hill	
G-BHAX	Enstrom F-28C-UK-2	PVS (Barnsley) Ltd	
G-BHAY	PA-28RT-201 Arrow IV	Alpha Yankee Ltd	
G-BHBA	Campbell Cricket	S. M. Irwin	
G-BHBB	Colt 77A balloon	S. D. Bellew	
G-BHBE	Westland-Bell 47G-3B1 (Soloy)	T. R. Smith (Agricultural Machinery) Ltd	
G-BHBF	Sikorsky S-76A	Bristow Helicopters Ltd	
G-BHBG	PA-32R Cherokee Lance 300	L. T. Halpin	
G-BHBI	Mooney M.20J	M. Smith	
G-BHBT	Marquart MA.5 Charger	R. G. & C. J. Maidment/Shoreham	
G-BHBZ	Partenavia P.68B	Philip Hamer & Co	
G-BHCC	Cessna 172M	Langtry Flying Group Ltd	
G-BHCE	Jodel D.112	D. M. Parsons	
G-BHCM	Cessna F.172H	The English Connection Ltd/Panshanger	
G-BHCP	Cessna F.152	Sherburn Aero Club Ltd	
G-BHCT	PA-23 Aztec 250F	Falcon Flying Services (G-OLBC)/ Biggin Hill	
G-BHCW	PA-22 Tri-Pacer 150	V. F. Kemp	
G-BHCZ	PA-38-112 Tomahawk	J. E. Abbott	
G-BHDD	V.668 Varsity T.1 (WL626) ★	Aeropark/E. Midlands	
G-BHDE	SOCATA TB.10 Tobago	A. E. Allsop	
G-BHDH	Douglas DC-10-30	British Airways/Gatwick	
G-BHDI	Douglas DC-10-30	British Airways *Forest of Ae*/Gatwick	
G-BHDJ	Douglas DC-10-30	British Airways *Glengap Forest*/Gatwick	
G-BHDK	Boeing B-29A-BN (461748) ★	Imperial War Museum/Duxford	
G-BHDM	Cessna F.152 II	Tayside Aviation Ltd/Dundee	
G-BHDP	Cessna F.182Q II	A. K. Denson	
G-BHDR	Cessna F.152 II	Tayside Aviation Ltd/Dundee	
G-BHDS	Cessna F.152 II	Tayside Aviation Ltd/Dundee	
G-BHDT	SOCATA TB.10 Tobago	R. D. Hill	
G-BHDU	Cessna F.152 II	Falcon Flying Services/Biggin Hill	
G-BHDV	Cameron V-77 balloon	P. Glydon	
G-BHDW	Cessna F.152	Tayside Aviation Ltd/Dundee	
G-BHDX	Cessna F.172N	Skyhawk Group	
G-BHDZ	Cessna F.172N	J. B. Roberts	
G-BHEC	Cessna F.152	Stapleford Flying Club Ltd	
G-BHED	Cessna FA.152	TG Aviation Ltd/Manston	
G-BHEG	Jodel 150	D. M. Griffiths	
G-BHEH	Cessna 310G	F. J. Shevill	
G-BHEK	CP.1315-C3 Super Emeraude	D. B. Winstanley/Barton	
G-BHEL	Jodel D.117	N. Wright & C. M. Kettlewell	

Notes	Reg.	Type	Owner or Operator
	G-BHEM	Bensen B.8M	A. J. Maxwell
	G-BHEN	Cessna FA.152	Leicestershire Aero Club Ltd
	G-BHEO	Cessna FR.182RG	J. G. Hogg
	G-BHER	SOCATA TB.10 Tobago	Vale Aviation Ltd
	G-BHET	SOCATA TB.10 Tobago	Claude Hooper Ltd
	G-BHEU	Thunder Ax7-65 balloon	J. E. R. Govett
	G-BHEV	PA-28R Cherokee Arrow 200	J. L. Marshall
	G-BHEX	Colt 56A balloon	A. S. Dear & ptnrs *Super Wasp*
	G-BHEZ	Jodel 150	B. N. Stevens
	G-BHFC	Cessna F.152	TG Aviation Ltd/Manston
	G-BHFE	PA-44-180 Seminole	Grunwick Ltd/Elstree
	G-BHFF	Jodel D.112	P. A. Dowell
	G-BHFG	SNCAN Stampe SV-4C (45)	Stormswift Ltd
	G-BHFH	PA-34-200T Seneca II	Hendefern Ltd/Goodwood
	G-BHFI	Cessna F.152	BAe (Warton) Flying Group/Blackpool
	G-BHFJ	PA-28RT-201T Turbo Arrow IV	T. L. P. Delaney
	G-BHFK	PA-28-151 Warrior	Ilkeston Car Sales Ltd
	G-BHFM	Murphy S.200 balloon	M. Murphy
	G-BHFR	Eiri PIK-20E-1	J. T. Morgan
	G-BHFS	Robin DR.400/180	D. S. Chandler
	G-BHGA	PA-31-310 Turbo Navajo	Heltor Ltd
	G-BHGC	PA-18 Super Cub 150	M. R. & P. A. Dawson
	G-BHGF	Cameron V-56 balloon	P. Smallward
	G-BHGJ	Jodel D.120	Q. M. B. Oswell
	G-BHGK	Sikorsky S-76A	Bond Helicopters Ltd
	G-BHGM	Beech 76 Duchess	Visual Phantom Ltd
	G-BHGO	PA-32 Cherokee Six 260	DOCS Ltd
	G-BHGP	SOCATA TB.10 Tobago	Inter Textiles Ltd
	G-BHGX	Colt 56B balloon	M. N. Dixon
	G-BHGY	PA-28R Cherokee Arrow 200	V. Humphries/Gamston
	G-BHHB	Cameron V-77 balloon	R. Powell
	G-BHHE	Jodel DR.1051/M1	P. Bridges
	G-BHHG	Cessna F.152 II	TG Aviation Ltd/Manston
	G-BHHH	Thunder Ax7-65 balloon	C. A. Hendley (Essex) Ltd
	G-BHHK	Cameron N-77 balloon	I. S. Bridge
	G-BHHN	Cameron V-77 balloon	Itchen Valley Balloon Group
	G-BHHU	Short SD3-30 Variant 100	BAC Express Ltd
	G-BHHX	Jodel D.112	D. I. Walker
	G-BHHZ	Rotorway Scorpion 133	L. W. & O. Usherwood
	G-BHIB	Cessna F.182Q	J. Blackburn & J. J. Feeney/Elstree
	G-BHIC	Cessna F.182Q	C. W. Makin
	G-BHIG	Colt 31A balloon	P. A. Lindstrand
	G-BHIH	Cessna F.172N	K. L. Burnett
	G-BHII	Cameron V-77 balloon	R. V. Brown
	G-BHIJ	Eiri PIK-20E-1	I. W. Paterson/Portmoak
	G-BHIK	Adam RA-14 Loisirs	L. Lewis
	G-BHIN	Cessna F.152	P. Skinner/Egginton
	G-BHIR	PA-28R Cherokee Arrow 200	Factorcore Ltd/Barton
	G-BHIS	Thunder Ax7-65 balloon	Hedgehoppers Balloon Group
	G-BHIT	SOCATA TB.9 Tampico	J. B. Iles
	G-BHIY	Cessna F.150K	Westfield Flying Group
	G-BHJA	Cessna A.152	Cornwall Flying Club Ltd/Bodmin
	G-BHJB	Cessna A.152	Sky Pro Ltd
	G-BHJF	SOCATA TB.10 Tobago	Flying Fox Group
	G-BHJI	Mooney M.20J	S. F. Lister
	G-BHJK	Maule M5-235C Lunar Rocket	P. M. Breton
	G-BHJN	Fournier RF-4D	RF-4 Flying Group
	G-BHJO	PA-28-161 Warrior II	The Brackla Flying Group/Inverness
	G-BHJS	Partenavia P.68B	Shepherd Aviation Ltd
	G-BHJU	Robin DR.400/2+2	T. J. Harlow
	G-BHKA	Evans VP-1	M. L. Perry
	G-BHKH	Cameron O-65 balloon	D. G. Body
	G-BHKJ	Cessna 421C	Crosslee PLC
	G-BHKR	Colt 12A balloon ★	British Balloon Museum
	G-BHKT	Jodel D.112	The Evans Flying Group
	G-BHKV	AA-5A Cheetah	Alouette Flying Club Ltd/Biggin Hill
	G-BHKY	Cessna 310R II	Air Service Training Ltd/Perth
	G-BHLE	Robin DR.400/180	L. H. Mayall
	G-BHLH	Robin DR.400/180	W. A. Clark
	G-BHLJ	Saffery-Rigg S.200 balloon	I. A. Rigg
	G-BHLT	D.H.82A Tiger Moth	P. J. & A. J. Borsberry
	G-BHLU	Fournier RF-3	M. C. Roper
	G-BHLW	Cessna 120	L. W. Scattergood

Reg.	Type	Owner or Operator	Notes
G-BHLX	AA-5B Tiger	Tiger Aviation (Jersey) Ltd	
G-BHLY	Sikorsky S-76A	Bristow Helicopters Ltd	
G-BHMA	SIPA 903	H. J. Taggart	
G-BHME	WMB.2 Windtracker balloon	I. R. Bell & ptnrs	
G-BHMG	Cessna FA.152	R. D. Smith	
G-BHMI	Cessna F.172N	W. Lancs Aero Club Ltd (G-WADE)/ Woodvale	
G-BHMJ	Avenger T.200-2112 balloon	R. Light *Lord Anthony 1*	
G-BHMK	Avenger T.200-2112 balloon	P. Kinder *Lord Anthony 2*	
G-BHMM	Avenger T.200-2112 balloon	M. Murphy *Lord Anthony 4*	
G-BHMO	PA-20M Cerpa Special (Pacer)	A. B. Holloway & ptnrs	
G-BHMR	Stinson 108-3	D. G. French/Sandown	
G-BHMT	Evans VP-1	P. E. J. Sturgeon	
G-BHNA	Cessna F.152	Sheffield Aero Club Ltd/Netherthorpe	
G-BHNC	Cameron O-65 balloon	D. & C. Bareford	
G-BHND	Cameron N-65 balloon	S. M. Wellband	
G-BHNK	Jodel D.120A	G-BHNK Flying Group	
G-BHNL	Jodel D.112	G. van der Gaag	
G-BHNO	PA-28-181 Archer II	Davison Plant Hire Co/Compton Abbas	
G-BHNP	Eiri PIK-20E-1	D. A. Sutton/Riseley	
G-BHNX	Jodel D.117	R. V. Rendall	
G-BHOA	Robin DR.400/160	M. J. Ferguson	
G-BHOF	Sikorsky S-61N	Bristow Helicopters Ltd	
G-BHOG	Sikorsky S-61N	Bristow Helicopters Ltd	
G-BHOH	Sikorsky S-61N	Bristow Helicopters Ltd	
G-BHOL	Jodel DR.1050	D. G. Hart	
G-BHOM	PA-18 Super Cub 95	C. H. A. Bott	
G-BHOO	Thunder Ax7-65 balloon	D. Livesey & J. M. Purves *Scraps*	
G-BHOR	PA-28-161 Warrior II.	Oscar Romeo Flying Group/Biggin Hill	
G-BHOT	Cameron V-65 balloon	Dante Balloon Group	
G-BHOU	Cameron V-65 balloon	F. W. Barnes	
G-BHOZ	SOCATA TB.9 Tampico	M. Brown	
G-BHPK	Piper J-3C-65 Cub (236800)	L-4 Group	
G-BHPL	C.A.S.A. 1.131E Jungmann 1000	M. G. Jeffries	
G-BHPM	PA-18 Super Cub 95	P. I. Morgans	
G-BHPN	Colt 14A balloon	Lindstrand Balloons Ltd	
G-BHPS	Jodel D.120A	R. A. Morris & R. V. Emerson	
G-BHPT	Piper J-3C-65 Cub	Rolfe Air Services	
G-BHPX	Cessna 152 II	Southern Air Ltd/Shoreham	
G-BHPY	Cessna 152 II	A. T. Hooper & T. E. Evans/Wellesbourne	
G-BHPZ	Cessna 172N	O'Brien Properties Ltd/Redhill	
G-BHRA	R. Commander 114A	P. A. Warner	
G-BHRB	Cessna F.152 II	LAC (Enterprises) Ltd/Barton	
G-BHRC	PA-28-161 Warrior II	Sherwood Flying Club Ltd/Tollerton	
G-BHRD	D.H.C.1 Chipmunk 22 (WP977)	G-BHRD Group/Kidlington	
G-BHRH	Cessna FA.150K	Merlin Flying Club Ltd/Hucknall	
G-BHRI	Saffery S.200 balloon	N. J. & H. L. Dunnington	
G-BHRM	Cessna F.152	Aerohire Ltd/Halfpenny Green	
G-BHRN	Cessna F.152	J. Easson/Edinburgh	
G-BHRO	R. Commander 112A	John Raymond Transport Ltd/Cardiff	
G-BHRP	PA-44-180 Seminole	Merlinrun Ltd/E. Midlands	
G-BHRR	CP.301A Emeraude	T. W. Offen	
G-BHRW	Jodel DR.221	Dauphin Flying Group	
G-BHRY	Colt 56A balloon	A. S. Davidson	
G-BHSA	Cessna 152 II	Skyviews & General Ltd/Sherburn	
G-BHSB	Cessna 172N	Saunders Caravans Ltd	
G-BHSD	Scheibe SF.25E Super Falke	Lasham Gliding Soc Ltd	
G-BHSE	R. Commander 114	604 Sqdn Flying Group Ltd	
G-BHSN	Cameron N-56 balloon	I. Bentley	
G-BHSP	Thunder Ax7-77Z balloon	Out-Of-The-Blue	
G-BHSS	Pitts S-1C Special	Bottoms Up Syndicate	
G-BHSY	Jodel DR.1050	S. R. Orwin & T. R. Allebone	
G-BHTA	PA-28-236 Dakota	Dakota Ltd	
G-BHTC	Jodel DR.1050/M1	G. Clark	
G-BHTD	Cessna T.188C AgHusky	ADS (Aerial) Ltd/Southend	
G-BHTG	Thunder Ax6-56 balloon	F. R. & Mrs S. H. MacDonald	
G-BHTH	NA T-6G Texan (2807)	J. J. Woodhouse	
G-BHTR	Bell 206B JetRanger 3	Huktra (UK) Ltd	
G-BHUB	Douglas C-47A (315509) ★	Imperial War Museum/Duxford	
G-BHUE	Jodel DR.1050	M. J. Harris	
G-BHUG	Cessna 172N	Propwash Investments Ltd/Swansea	
G-BHUI	Cessna 152	Roylair Services Ltd	
G-BHUJ	Cessna 172N	Northamptonshire School of Flying Ltd	

Notes	Reg.	Type	Owner or Operator
	G-BHUM	D.H.82A Tiger Moth	S. G. Towers
	G-BHUO	Evans VP-2	D. A. Wood
	G-BHUR	Thunder Ax3 balloon	B. F. G. Ribbans
	G-BHUU	PA-25 Pawnee 235	Pawnee Aviation/Boston
	G-BHVB	PA-28-161 Warrior II	Castle Electronics
	G-BHVC	Cessna 172RG Cutlass	I. B. Willis/Panshanger
	G-BHVE	Saffery S.330 balloon	P. M. Randles
	G-BHVF	Jodel 150A	J. D. Walton
	G-BHVP	Cessna 182Q	Battleflat Group
	G-BHVR	Cessna 172N	Maxhill Ltd
	G-BHVV	Piper J-3C-65 Cub	P. R. Wright/Barton
	G-BHWA	Cessna F.152	Wickenby Aviation Ltd
	G-BHWB	Cessna F.152	Wickenby Aviation Ltd
	G-BHWG	Mahatma S.200SR balloon	H. W. Gandy *Spectrum*
	G-BHWH	Weedhopper JC-24A	G. A. Clephane
	G-BHWK	M.S.880B Rallye Club	L. L. Gayther
	G-BHWS	Cessna F.152 II	Turnhouse Flying Club
	G-BHWY	PA-28R Cherokee Arrow 200-II	Kilo Foxtrot Flying Group/Sandown
	G-BHWZ	PA-28-181 Archer II	I. R. McCue
	G-BHXA	SA Bulldog Srs 120/1210	D. A. Williams/Liverpool
	G-BHXB	SA Bulldog Srs 120/1210	D. A. Williams/Liverpool
	G-BHXD	Jodel D.120	P. H. C. Hall
	G-BHXK	PA-28 Cherokee 140	GXK Flying Group
	G-BHXL	Evans VP-2	R. S. Wharton
	G-BHXS	Jodel D.120	I. R. Willis
	G-BHXT	Thunder Ax6-56Z balloon	Ocean Traffic Services Ltd
	G-BHXV	AB-206B JetRanger 3	PLM Dollar Group Ltd (G-OWJM)/Denham
	G-BHXY	Piper J-3C-65 Cub (44-79609)	F. W. Rogers/Aldergrove
	G-BHYA	Cessna R.182RG II	B. El Chalabi
	G-BHYC	Cessna 172RG II	Red Rose International Ltd
	G-BHYD	Cessna R.172K XP II	Sylmar Aviation Services Ltd
	G-BHYE	PA-34-200T Seneca II	C.S.E. Aviation Ltd/Kidlington
	G-BHYF	PA-34-200T Seneca II	C.S.E. Aviation Ltd/Kidlington
	G-BHYG	PA-34-200T Seneca II	C.S.E. Aviation Ltd/Kidlington
	G-BHYI	SNCAN Stampe SV-4A	P. A. Irwin
	G-BHYN	Evans VP-2	D. Cromie
	G-BHYP	Cessna F.172M	Avior Ltd/Biggin Hill
	G-BHYR	Cessna F.172M	Alumvale Ltd/Stapleford
	G-BHYV	Evans VP-1	L. Chiappi/Blackpool
	G-BHYX	Cessna 152 II	Stapleford Flying Club Ltd
	G-BHZE	PA-28-181 Archer II	Northfield Garage Ltd
	G-BHZF	Evans VP-2	W. J. Evans
	G-BHZH	Cessna F.152	1013 Ltd/Guernsey
	G-BHZK	AA-5B Tiger	N. K. Margolis/Elstree
	G-BHZO	AA-5A Cheetah	Scotia Safari Ltd/Prestwick
	G-BHZR	SA Bulldog Srs 120/1210	M. A. Elobeid
	G-BHZS	SA Bulldog Srs 120/1210	D. A. Williams/Liverpool
	G-BHZT	SA Bulldog Srs 120/1210	W. M. Bax
	G-BHZU	Piper J-3C-65 Cub	J. K. Tomkinson
	G-BHZV	Jodel D.120A	K. J. Scott
	G-BHZX	Thunder Ax7-65A balloon	R. J. & H. M. Beattie
	G-BIAB	SOCATA TB.9 Tampico	H. W. A. Thirlway
	G-BIAC	SOCATA Rallye 235E	Aerial Group Ltd
	G-BIAH	Jodel D.112	D. Mitchell
	G-BIAI	WMB.2 Windtracker balloon	I. Chadwick
	G-BIAK	SOCATA TB.10 Tobago	Real Life Ltd
	G-BIAL	Rango NA.8 balloon	A. M. Lindsay
	G-BIAO	Evans VP-2	P. J. Hall
	G-BIAP	PA-16 Clipper	P. J. Bish & M. J. Mothershaw
	G-BIAR	Rigg Skyliner II balloon	I. A. Rigg
	G-BIAU	Sopwith Pup (replica) (N6452)	F.A.A. Museum/Yeovilton
	G-BIAX	Taylor JT.2 Titch	J. T. Everest
	G-BIAY	AA-5 Traveler	M. D. Dupay & ptnrs
	G-BIBA	SOCATA TB.9 Tampico	TB Aviation Ltd
	G-BIBB	Mooney M.20C	B. Walker & Sons (Dursley) Ltd
	G-BIBG	Sikorsky S-76A	Bristow Helicopters Ltd
	G-BIBJ	Enstrom 280C-UK-2	Tindon Ltd/Little Snoring
	G-BIBK	Taylor JT.2 Titch	J. G. McTaggart
	G-BIBN	Cessna FA.150K	G. A. Eaton & C. G. Wilson
	G-BIBO	Cameron V-65 balloon	I. Harris
	G-BIBP	AA-5A Cheetah	Scotia Safari Ltd/Prestwick
	G-BIBS	Cameron P-20 balloon	Cameron Balloons Ltd

Reg.	Type	Owner or Operator	Notes
G-BIBT	AA-5B Tiger	Bibit Group	
G-BIBW	Cessna F.172N	Deltair Ltd/Liverpool	
G-BIBX	WMB.2 Windtracker balloon	I. A. Rigg	
G-BIBY	Beech F33A Bonanza	G. T. Grimward	
G-BICD	Auster 5	R. T. Parsons	
G-BICE	AT-6C Harvard IIA (41-33275)	C. M. L. Edwards	
G-BICG	Cessna F.152 II	Falcon Flying Services/Biggin Hill	
G-BICJ	Monnett Sonerai II	D. J. Marks	
G-BICM	Colt 56A balloon	Avon Advertiser Balloon Club	
G-BICN	F.8L Falco	R. J. Barber	
G-BICP	Robin DR.360	Bravo India Flying Group/Woodvale	
G-BICR	Jodel D.120A	Beehive Flying Group/White Waltham	
G-BICS	Robin R.2100A	G-BICS Group/Sibson	
G-BICT	Evans VP-1	A. S. Coombe & D. L. Tribe	
G-BICU	Cameron V-56 balloon	S. D. Bather & D. Scott	
G-BICW	PA-28-161 Warrior II	D. Gellhorn	
G-BICX	Maule M5-235C Lunar Rocket	A. T. Jeans & J. F. Clarkson/Old Sarum	
G-BICY	PA-23 Apache 160	A. M. Lynn/Sibson	
G-BIDD	Evans VP-1	G. J. McDill	
G-BIDF	Cessna F.172P	E. Alexander	
G-BIDG	Jodel 150A	D. R. Gray/Barton	
G-BIDH	Cessna 152 II	Cumbria Aero Club (G-DONA)/Carlisle	
G-BIDI	PA-28R-201 Arrow III	Ambrit Ltd	
G-BIDJ	PA-18A Super Cub 150	AB Plant (Bristol) Ltd	
G-BIDK	PA-18 Super Cub 150	R. G. Warwick	
G-BIDO	CP.301A Emeraude	A. R. Plumb	
G-BIDU	Cameron V-77 balloon	E. Eleazor	
G-BIDV	Colt 14A balloon	International Distillers & Vintners (House Trade) Ltd	
G-BIDW	Sopwith 1 1/2 Strutter (replica) (A8226) ★	RAF Museum/Hendon	
G-BIDX	Jodel D.112	H. N. Nuttall & P. Turton	
G-BIEF	Cameron V-77 balloon	D. S. Bush	
G-BIEJ	Sikorsky S-76A	Bristow Helicopters Ltd	
G-BIEN	Jodel D.120A	R. J. Baker	
G-BIEO	Jodel D.112	Clipgate Flyers	
G-BIES	Maule M5-235C Lunar Rocker	William Proctor Farms	
G-BIET	Cameron O-77 balloon	G. M. Westley	
G-BIEY	PA-28-151 Warrior	Southern Air Ltd/Shoreham	
G-BIFA	Cessna 310R II	Booth Plant & Equipment Ltd	
G-BIFB	PA-28 Cherokee 150C	N. A. Ayub	
G-BIFN	Bensen B.8MR	B. Gunn	
G-BIFO	Evans VP-1	R. Broadhead	
G-BIFP	Colt 56C balloon	J. Philp	
G-BIFY	Cessna F.150L	Jureen Aviation	
G-BIFZ	Partenavia P.68C	Jet Airmotive Ltd	
G-BIGD	Cameron V-77 balloon	D. L. Clark	
G-BIGF	Thunder Ax7-77 balloon	M. D. Stever & C. A. Allen	
G-BIGJ	Cessna F.172M	Clacton Aero Club (1988) Ltd	
G-BIGK	Taylorcraft BC-12D	N. P. St. J. Ramsey	
G-BIGL	Cameron O-65 balloon	P. L. Mossman	
G-BIGM	Avenger T.200-2112 balloon	M. Murphy	
G-BIGP	Bensen B.8M	R. H. S. Cooper	
G-BIGR	Avenger T.200-2112 balloon	R. Light	
G-BIGX	Bensen B.8M	W. C. Turner	
G-BIGY	Cameron V-65 balloon	Dante Balloon Group	
G-BIGZ	Scheibe SF.25B Falke	G-BIGZ Syndicate/Saltby	
G-BIHD	Robin DR.400/160	K. B. Mainstone	
G-BIHE	Cessna FA.152	J. Easson/Edinburgh	
G-BIHF	SE-5A (replica) (F943)	K. J. Garrett/Booker	
G-BIHG	PA-28 Cherokee 140	T. M. Plewman	
G-BIHI	Cessna 172M	R. D. & S. R. Spencer	
G-BIHO	D.H.C.6 Twin Otter 310	Isles of Scilly Skybus Ltd/St. Just	
G-BIHP	Van Den Bemden gas balloon	J. J. Harris	
G-BIHT	PA-17 Vagabond	G. H. Cork	
G-BIHU	Saffrey S.200 balloon	B. L. King	
G-BIHW	Aeronca A65TAC Defender	T. J. Ingrouille	
G-BIHX	Bensen B.8M	P. P. Willmott	
G-BIHY	Isaacs Fury	P. C. Butler	
G-BIIA	Fournier RF-3	T. M. W. Webster	
G-BIIB	Cessna F.172M	Civil Service Flying Club (Biggin Hill) Ltd	
G-BIID	PA-18 Super Cub 95	D. A. Lacey	
G-BIIE	Cessna F.172P	F. A. L. Castleden	

Notes	Reg.	Type	Owner or Operator
	G-BIIG	Thunder Ax6-56Z balloon	Chiltern Flyers Ltd
	G-BIIJ	Cessna F.152 II	Leicestershire Aero Club Ltd
	G-BIIK	M.S.883 Rallye 115	Chiltern Flyers Ltd
	G-BIIL	Thunder Ax6-56 balloon	G. W. Reader
	G-BIIT	PA-28-161 Warrior II	Tayside Aviation Ltd/Dundee
	G-BIIV	PA-28-181 Archer II	Stratton Motor Co Ltd
	G-BIIX	Rango NA.12 balloon	Rango Kite Co
	G-BIIZ	Great Lakes 2T-1A Sport Trainer	J. R. Lindsay
	G-BIJB	PA-18 Super Cub 150	Essex Gliding Club Ltd/North Weald
	G-BIJD	Bo 208C Junior	C. G. Stone
	G-BIJE	Piper J-3C-65 Cub	R. L. Hayward & A. G. Scott
	G-BIJS	Luton LA-4A Minor	I. J. Smith
	G-BIJU	CP-301A Emeraude	Eastern Taildraggers Flying Group (G-BHTX)
	G-BIJV	Cessna F.152 II	Falcon Flying Services/Biggin Hill
	G-BIJW	Cessna F.152 II	Falcon Flying Services/Biggin Hill
	G-BIJX	Cessna F.152 II	Falcon Flying Services/Biggin Hill
	G-BIKA	Boeing 757-236	British Airways *Dover Castle*
	G-BIKB	Boeing 757-236	British Airways *Windsor Castle*
	G-BIKC	Boeing 757-236	British Airways *Edinburgh Castle*
	G-BIKD	Boeing 757-236	British Airways *Caernarfon Castle*
	G-BIKE	PA-28R Cherokee Arrow 200	R. V. Webb Ltd/Elstree
	G-BIKF	Boeing 757-236	British Airways *Carrickfergus Castle*
	G-BIKG	Boeing 757-236	British Airways *Stirling Castle*
	G-BIKH	Boeing 757-236	British Airways *Richmond Castle*
	G-BIKI	Boeing 757-236	British Airways *Tintagel Castle*
	G-BIKJ	Boeing 757-236	British Airways *Conwy Castle*
	G-BIKK	Boeing 757-236	British Airways *Eilean Donan Castle*
	G-BIKL	Boeing 757-236	British Airways *Nottingham Castle*
	G-BIKM	Boeing 757-236	British Airways *Glamis Castle*
	G-BIKN	Boeing 757-236	British Airways *Bodiam Castle*
	G-BIKO	Boeing 757-236	British Airways *Harlech Castle*
	G-BIKP	Boeing 757-236	British Airways *Enniskillen Castle*
	G-BIKR	Boeing 757-236	British Airways *Bamburgh Castle*
	G-BIKS	Boeing 757-236	British Airways *Corfe Castle*
	G-BIKT	Boeing 757-236	British Airways *Carisbrooke Castle*
	G-BIKU	Boeing 757-236	British Airways *Inveraray Castle*
	G-BIKV	Boeing 757-236	British Airways *Raglan Castle*
	G-BIKW	Boeing 757-236	British Airways *Belvoir Castle*
	G-BIKX	Boeing 757-236	British Airways *Warwick Castle*
	G-BIKY	Boeing 757-236	British Airways *Leeds Castle*
	G-BIKZ	Boeing 757-236	British Airways *Kenilworth Castle*
	G-BILA	Daletol DM.165L Viking	R. Lamplough *(stored)*
	G-BILB	WMB.2 Windtracker balloon	B. L. King
	G-BILE	Scruggs BL.2B balloon	P. D. Ridout
	G-BILF	Practavia Sprite 125	G. Harfield
	G-BILG	Scruggs BL.2B balloon	P. D. Ridout
	G-BILI	Piper J-3C-65 Cub (454467)	G-BILI Flying Group
	G-BILJ	Cessna FA.152	Shoreham Flight Simulation Ltd/Bournemouth
	G-BILK	Cessna FA.152	Exeter Flying Club Ltd
	G-BILL	PA-25 Pawnee 235	Pawnee Aviation
	G-BILR	Cessna 152	Skyviews & General Ltd
	G-BILS	Cessna 152	Skyviews & General Ltd
	G-BILU	Cessna 172RG	Full Sutton Flying Centre Ltd
	G-BILZ	Taylor JT.1 Monoplane	A. Petheridge
	G-BIMK	Tiger T.200 Srs 1 balloon	M. K. Baron
	G-BIMM	PA-18 Super Cub 150	Clacton Aero Club (1988) Ltd
	G-BIMN	Steen Skybolt	G. P. Gregg
	G-BIMO	SNCAN Stampe SV-4C	R. A. Roberts
	G-BIMT	Cessna FA.152	Staverton Flying Services Ltd
	G-BIMU	Sikorsky S-61N	Bristow Helicopters Ltd
	G-BIMX	Rutan Vari-Eze	D. G. Crow/Biggin Hill
	G-BIMZ	Beech 76 Duchess	A. J. Nurse
	G-BINF	Saffery S.200 balloon	T. Lewis
	G-BING	Cessna F.172P	Foyle Flyers Ltd
	G-BINI	Scruggs BL.2C balloon	S. R. Woolfries
	G-BINL	Scruggs BL.2B balloon	P. D. Ridout
	G-BINM	Scruggs BL.2B balloon	P. D. Ridout
	G-BINO	Evans VP-1	G. Ravichadran
	G-BINR	Unicorn UE.1A balloon	Unicorn Group
	G-BINS	Unicorn UE.2A balloon	Unicorn Group
	G-BINT	Unicorn UE.1A balloon	Unicorn Group

Reg.	Type	Owner or Operator	Notes
G-BINU	Saffery S.200 balloon	T. Lewis	
G-BINX	Scruggs BL.2B balloon	P. D. Ridout	
G-BINY	Oriental balloon	J. L. Morton	
G-BIOB	Cessna F.172P	Aerofilms Ltd/Elstree	
G-BIOC	Cessna F.150L	Seawing Flying Club/Southend	
G-BIOE	Short SD3-30 Variant 100	Gill Airways Ltd/Newcastle	
G-BIOI	Jodel DR.1051/M	H. F. Hambling	
G-BIOJ	R. Commander 112TCA	A. T. Dalby	
G-BIOK	Cessna F.152	Tayside Aviation Ltd/Dundee	
G-BIOM	Cessna F.152	Falcon Flying Services/Luton	
G-BION	Cameron V-77 balloon	Flying Doctors Balloon Syndicate	
G-BIOR	M.S.880B Rallye Club	R. L. & K. P. McLean	
G-BIOU	Jodel D.117A	Dubious Group/Booker	
G-BIOW	Slingsby T.67A	A. B. Slinger/Sherburn	
G-BIPA	AA-5B Tiger	J. Campbell/Walney Island	
G-BIPH	Scruggs BL.2B balloon	C. M. Dewsnap	
G-BIPI	Everett Blackbird Mk 1	R. Spall	
G-BIPN	Fournier RF-3	J. C. R. Rogers & I. F. Fairhead	
G-BIPO	Mudry/CAARP CAP.20LS-200M.	C. Sandford	
G-BIPS	SflOCATA Rallye 100ST	McAully Flying Group/Little Snoring	
G-BIPT	Jodel D.112	C. R. Davies	
G-BIPV	AA-5B Tiger	J. R. & S. Nuter	
G-BIPW	Avenger T.200-2112 balloon	B. L. King	
G-BIPY	Bensen B.8	D. F. Hughes	
G-BIRD	Pitts S-1C Special	Pitts Artists Flying Group	
G-BIRE	Colt 56 Bottle SS balloon	K. R. Gafney	
G-BIRH	PA-18 Super Cub 135 (R-163)	Marchington Gliding Club Ltd/Tatenhill	
G-BIRI	C.A.S.A. 1.131E Jungmann 1000	M. G. & J. R. Jeffries	
G-BIRK	Avenger T.200-2112 balloon	D. Harland	
G-BIRL	Avenger T.200-2112 balloon	R. Light	
G-BIRM	Avenger T.200-2112 balloon	P. Higgins	
G-BIRP	Arena Mk 17 Skyship balloon	A. S. Viel	
G-BIRS	Cessna 182P	John E. Birks & Associates Ltd (G-BBBS)	
G-BIRT	Robin R.1180TD	W. D'A. Hall/Booker	
G-BIRW	M.S.505 Criquet (F+IS) ★	Museum of Flight/E. Fortune	
G-BIRY	Cameron V-77 balloon	J. J. Winter	
G-BIRZ	Zenair CH.250	T. N. Fox & I. R. Nash	
G-BISG	FRED Srs 3	R. A. Coombe	
G-BISH	Cameron O-42 balloon	Zebedee Balloon Service	
G-BISJ	Cessna 340A	Billair	
G-BISK	R. Commander 112B ★	P. A. Warner	
G-BISL	Scruggs BL.2B balloon	P. D. Ridout	
G-BISM	Scruggs BL.2B balloon	P. D. Ridout	
G-BISS	Scruggs BL.2C balloon	P. D. Ridout	
G-BIST	Scruggs BL.2C balloon	P. D. Ridout	
G-BISV	Cameron O-65 balloon	Hylyne Rabbits Ltd	
G-BISW	Cameron O-65 balloon	Rango Balloon & Kite Co	
G-BISX	Colt 56A balloon	J. R. Gore	
G-BISZ	Sikorsky S-76A	Bristow Helicopters Ltd	
G-BITA	PA-18 Super Cub 150	Intrepid Aviation Co/North Weald	
G-BITE	SOCATA TB.10 Tobago	M. A. Smith & R. J. Bristow/Fairoaks	
G-BITF	Cessna F.152 II	Tayside Aviation Ltd/Dundee	
G-BITH	Cessna F.152 II	Tayside Aviation Ltd/Dundee	
G-BITK	FRED Srs 2	D. J. Wood	
G-BITM	Cessna F.172P	D. G. Crabtree/Barton	
G-BITO	Jodel D.112D	A. Dunbar/Barton	
G-BITR	Sikorsky S-76A	Bristow Helicopters Ltd	
G-BITS	Drayton B-56 balloon	M. J. Betts	
G-BITW	Short SD3-30 Variant 100	Figurepart Trading Ltd (G-EASI)	
G-BITY	FD.31T balloon	A. J. Bell	
G-BIUL	Cameron 60 SS balloon	D. C. Patrick-Brown	
G-BIUM	Cessna F.152	Sheffield Aero Club Ltd/Netherthorpe	
G-BIUP	SNCAN NC.854S	BIUP Flying Group	
G-BIUU	PA-23 Aztec 250D ★	G. Cormack/Glasgow	
G-BIUV	H.S.748 Srs 2A	Emerald Airways Ltd *City of Liverpool* (G-AYYH)/Liverpool	
G-BIUW	PA-28-161 Warrior II	D. R. Staley	
G-BIUY	PA-28-181 Archer II	E. S. Singh	
G-BIVA	Robin R.2112	J. A. Fell	
G-BIVB	Jodel D.112	D. H. Anderson	
G-BIVC	Jodel D.112	M. J. Barmby/Cardiff	
G-BIVK	Bensen B.8M	J. G. Toy	
G-BIVL	Bensen B.8M	R. Gardiner	

Notes	Reg.	Type	Owner or Operator
	G-BIVT	Saffery S.80 balloon	L. F. Guyot
	G-BIVV	AA-5A Cheetah	W. Dass
	G-BIVZ	D.31A Turbulent	The Tiger Club (1990) Ltd/Headcorn
	G-BIWB	Scruggs RS.5000 balloon	P. D. Ridout
	G-BIWC	Scruggs RS.5000 balloon	P. D. Ridout
	G-BIWD	Scruggs RS.5000 balloon	D. Eaves
	G-BIWF	Warren balloon	P. D. Ridout
	G-BIWG	Zelenski Mk 2 balloon	P. D. Ridout
	G-BIWJ	Unicorn UE.1A balloon	B. L. King
	G-BIWK	Cameron V-65 balloon	I. R. Williams & R. G. Bickerdicke
	G-BIWL	PA-32-301 Saratoga	Primark Enterprises Ltd
	G-BIWN	Jodel D.112	C. R. Coates
	G-BIWP	Mooney M.20J	Whiskey Papa Flying Group
	G-BIWR	Mooney M.20F	A. C. Brink
	G-BIWU	Cameron V-65 balloon	D. Stuttard & B. Skuse
	G-BIWW	AA-5 Traveler	B & K Aviation/Cranfield
	G-BIWX	AT-16 Harvard IV (FT239)	D. R. G. Baillie
	G-BIWY	Westland WG.30 ★	instructional airframe/Sherborne
	G-BIXB	SOCATA TB.9 Tampico	Tampico Club
	G-BIXH	Cessna F.152	Cambridge Aero Club Ltd
	G-BIXI	Cessna 172RG Cutlass	J. F. P. Lewis/Sandown
	G-BIXL	P-51D Mustang (472216)	R. Lamplough/North Weald
	G-BIXN	Boeing Stearman A.75N1	R. R. White
	G-BIXR	Cameron A-140 balloon	Skysales Ltd
	G-BIXS	Avenger T.200-2112 balloon	M. Stuart
	G-BIXV	Bell 212	Bristow Helicopters Ltd
	G-BIXW	Colt 56B balloon	N. A. P. Bates
	G-BIXX	Pearson Srs 2 balloon	D. Pearson
	G-BIXZ	Grob G-109	D. L. Nind & I. Allum/Booker
	G-BIYI	Cameron V-65 balloon	Sarnia Balloon Group
	G-BIYJ	PA-18 Super Cub 95	S. Russell
	G-BIYK	Isaacs Fury	R. S. Martin/Dunkeswell
	G-BIYO	PA-31-310 Turbo Navajo	Executive Jet Leasing Ltd
	G-BIYP	PA-20 Pacer 125	R. J. Whitcombe
	G-BIYR	PA-18 Super Cub 150	Delta Foxtrot Flying Group/Dunkeswell
	G-BIYT	Colt 17A balloon	J. M. Francois/France
	G-BIYU	Fokker S.11.1 Instructor (E-15)	C. Briggs & R. Broadhead
	G-BIYW	Jodel D.112	Pollard/Balaam/Bye Flying Group
	G-BIYX	PA-28 Cherokee 140	Comed Aviation Ltd/Blackpool
	G-BIYY	PA-18 Super Cub 95	A. E. & W. J. Taylor/Ingoldmells
	G-BIZF	Cessna F.172P	R. S. Bentley/Bourn
	G-BIZG	Cessna F.152	M. A. Judge
	G-BIZI	Robin DR.400/120	Headcorn Flying School Ltd
	G-BIZK	Nord 3202	A. I. Milne/Swanton Morley
	G-BIZM	Nord 3202	Magnificent Obsessions Ltd
	G-BIZN	Slingsby T.67A	Sport to Business
	G-BIZO	PA-28R Cherokee Arrow 200	A. T. Humphries
	G-BIZR	SOCATA TB.9 Tampico	R. M. Shears (G-BSEC)
	G-BIZT	Bensen B.8M	J. Ferguson
	G-BIZU	Thunder Ax6-56Z balloon	M. J. Loades
	G-BIZV	PA-18 Super Cub 95 (18-2001)	S. J. Pugh & R. L. Wademan
	G-BIZW	Champion 7GCBC Citabria	G. Read & Sons
	G-BIZY	Jodel D.112	Wayland Tunley & Associates/Cranfield
	G-BJAD	FRED Srs 2	C. Allison
	G-BJAE	Lavadoux Starck AS.80	D. J. & S. A. E. Phillips/Coventry
	G-BJAF	Piper J-3C-65 Cub	P. J. Cottle
	G-BJAG	PA-28-181 Archer II	J. F. Clark
	G-BJAJ	AA-5B Tiger	A. H. McVicar/Prestwick
	G-BJAL	C.A.S.A. 1.131E Jungmann 1000	I. C. Underwood & S. B. J. Chandler
	G-BJAN	SA.102-5 Cavalier	J. Powlesland
	G-BJAO	Bensen B.8M	N. J. Hall
	G-BJAP	D.H.82A Tiger Moth (K2587)	K. Knight
	G-BJAR	Unicorn UE.3A balloon	Unicorn Group
	G-BJAS	Rango NA.9 balloon	A. Lindsay
	G-BJAV	GY-80 Horizon 160	A. J. Martlew
	G-BJAW	Cameron V-65 balloon	G. W. McCarthy
	G-BJAX	Pilatus P2-05 (U-108) ★	(stored)
	G-BJAY	Piper J-3C-65 Cub	K. L. Clarke/Ingoldmells
	G-BJBK	PA-18 Super Cub 95	M. S. Bird/Old Sarum
	G-BJBM	Monnett Sonerai II	T. C. Webber/Southend
	G-BJBO	Jodel DR.250/160	Wiltshire Flying Group
	G-BJBW	PA-28-161 Warrior II	J. C. Lucas

Reg.	Type	Owner or Operator	Notes
G-BJBX	PA-28-161 Warrior II	Haimoss Ltd	
G-BJBY	PA-28-161 Warrior II	Haimoss Ltd	
G-BJBZ	Rotorway Executive 133	P. J. D. Kerr	
G-BJCA	PA-28-161 Warrior II	D. M. & J. E. Smith	
G-BJCF	CP.1310-C3 Super Emeraude	K. M. Hodson & C. G. H. Gurney	
G-BJCI	PA-18 Super Cub 150 (modified)	The Borders (Milfield) Aero-Tour Club Ltd	
G-BJCW	PA-32R-301 Saratoga SP	G. R. Patrick & Co Ltd	
G-BJDE	Cessna F.172M	H. P. K. Ferdinand/Denham	
G-BJDF	M.S.880B Rallye 100T	W. R. Savin & ptnrs	
G-BJDI	Cessna FR.182RG	J. M. Henderson & J. J. B. Hamilton	
G-BJDK	European E.14 balloon	Aeroprint Tours	
G-BJDO	AA-5A Cheetah	J. R. & S. Nuter	
G-BJDT	SOCATA TB.9 Tampico	Bignell Surgical Instruments Ltd	
G-BJDW	Cessna F.172M	J. Rae/Ipswich	
G-BJEI	PA-18 Super Cub 95	H. J. Cox	
G-BJEL	SNCAN NC.854	N. F. & S. G. Hunter	
G-BJEN	Scruggs RS.5000 balloon	N. J. Richardson	
G-BJEV	Aeronca 11AC Chief (897)	R. F. Willcox	
G-BJEX	Bo 208C Junior	G. D. H. Crawford/Thruxton	
G-BJFB	Mk 1A balloon	Aeroprint Tours	
G-BJFC	European E.8 balloon	P. D. Ridout	
G-BJFE	PA-18 Super Cub 95	J. H. Allistone	
G-BJFI	Bell 47G-2A1	Helicopter Supplies & Engineering Ltd/ Bournemouth	
G-BJFL	Sikorsky S-76A	Bristow Helicopters Ltd	
G-BJFM	Jodel D.120	J. V. George & P. A. Smith/Popham	
G-BJGD	Mk IV balloon	Windsor Balloon Group	
G-BJGF	Mk 1 balloon	D. & D. Eaves	
G-BJGG	Mk 2 balloon	D. & D. Eaves	
G-BJGK	Cameron V-77 balloon	T. J. Orchard & ptnrs	
G-BJGL	Cremer balloon	G. Lowther	
G-BJGM	Unicorn UE.1A balloon	D. Eaves & P. D. Ridout	
G-BJGO	Cessna 172N	R. M. Hunt	
G-BJGX	Sikorsky S-76A	Bristow Helicopters Ltd	
G-BJGY	Cessna F.172P	Lucca Wines Ltd	
G-BJHA	Cremer balloon	G. Cope	
G-BJHB	Mooney M.20J	Zitair Flying Club Ltd/Redhill	
G-BJHK	EAA Acro Sport	D. M. Cue	
G-BJHP	Osprey 1C balloon	N. J. Richardson	
G-BJHT	Thunder Ax7-65 balloon	A. H. & L. Symonds	
G-BJHV	Voisin Replica ★	Brooklands Museum of Aviation/Weybridge	
G-BJHW	Osprey 1C balloon	N. J. Richardson	
G-BJIA	Allport balloon	D. J. Allport	
G-BJIC	Dodo 1A balloon	P. D. Ridout	
G-BJID	Osprey 1B balloon	P. D. Ridout	
G-BJIF	Bensen B.8M	H. Redwin	
G-BJIG	Slingsby T.67A	Acebell G-BJIG Syndicate/Redhill	
G-BJIR	Cessna 550 Citation II	Gator Aviation Ltd	
G-BJIV	PA-18 Super Cub 180	Yorkshire Gliding Club (Pty) Ltd/ Sutton Bank	
G-BJJE	Dodo Mk 3 balloon	D. Eaves	
G-BJJN	Cessna F.172M	Ospreystar Ltd (stored)/Stapleford	
G-BJKB	SA.365C-3 Dauphin 2	Bond Helicopters Ltd	
G-BJKF	SOCATA TB.9 Tampico	Venue Solutions	
G-BJKW	Wills Aera II	J. K. S. Wills	
G-BJKY	Cessna F.152	Air Charter & Travel Ltd/Ronaldsway	
G-BJLB	SNCAN NC.854S	M. J. Barnaby	
G-BJLC	Monnett Sonerai IIL	P. J. Robins & R. King/Sywell	
G-BJLE	Osprey 1B balloon	I. Chadwick	
G-BJLF	Unicorn UE.1C balloon	I. Chadwick	
G-BJLG	Unicorn UE.1B balloon	I. Chadwick	
G-BJLH	PA-18 Super Cub 95 (44)	D. S. Kirkham	
G-BJLK	Short SD3-30 Variant 100	Figureapart Trading Ltd	
G-BJLO	PA-31-310 Turbo Navajo	Superpower Engineering System	
G-BJLX	Cremer balloon	P. W. May	
G-BJLY	Cremer balloon	P. Cannon	
G-BJMG	European E.26C balloon	D. Eaves & A. P. Chown	
G-BJMI	European E.84 balloon	D. Eaves	
G-BJMJ	Bensen B.8V	J. I. Hewlett	
G-BJML	Cessna 120	D. F. Lawlor/Inverness	
G-BJMO	Taylor JT.1 Monoplane	R. C. Mark	
G-BJMR	Cessna 310R	J. McL. Robinson/Sherburn	
G-BJMW	Thunder Ax8-105 balloon	G. M. Westley	

Notes	Reg.	Type	Owner or Operator
	G-BJMX	Jarre JR.3 balloon	P. D. Ridout
	G-BJMZ	European EA.8A balloon	P. D. Ridout
	G-BJNA	Arena Mk 117P balloon	P. D. Ridout
	G-BJND	Osprey Mk 1E balloon	A. Billington & D. Whitmore
	G-BJNF	Cessna F.152	Exeter Flying Club Ltd
	G-BJNG	Slingsby T.67A	Dophin Property (Management) Ltd
	G-BJNN	PA-38-112 Tomahawk	Scotia Safari Ltd/Prestwick
	G-BJNP	Rango NA.32 balloon	N. H. Ponsford
	G-BJNX	Cameron O-65 balloon	B. J. Petteford
	G-BJNY	Aeronca 11CC Super Chief	P. I. & D. M. Morgans
	G-BJNZ	PA-23 Aztec 250F	Bonus Aviation Ltd (G-FANZ) Cranfield
	G-BJOA	PA-28-181 Archer II	Channel Islands Aero Holdings (Jersey) Ltd
	G-BJOB	Jodel D.140C	T. W. M. Beck & M. J. Smith
	G-BJOE	Jodel D.120A	Forth Flying Group
	G-BJOP	BN-2B-26 Islander	British Regional Airlines/BA Express
	G-BJOT	Jodel D.117	E. Davies
	G-BJOV	Cessna F.150K	W. H. Webb & G. J. Clapp
	G-BJPI	Bede BD-5G	M. D. McQueen
	G-BJPV	Haigh balloon	M. J. Haigh
	G-BJRA	Osprey Mk 4B balloon	E. Osborn
	G-BJRB	European E.254 balloon	D. Eaves
	G-BJRC	European E.84R balloon	D. Eaves
	G-BJRD	European E.84R balloon	D. Eaves
	G-BJRG	Osprey Mk 4B balloon	A. E. de Gruchy
	G-BJRH	Rango NA.36 balloon	N. H. Ponsford
	G-BJRP	Cremer balloon	M. D. Williams
	G-BJRV	Cremer balloon	M. D. Williams
	G-BJRW	Cessna U.206G	A. I. Walgate & Son Ltd
	G-BJRZ	Partenavia P.68C	Ampy Automation Digilog Ltd (G-OAKP)
	G-BJSA	BN-2A-26 Islander	Police Aviation Services Ltd/Staverton
	G-BJSC	Osprey Mk 4D balloon	N. J. Richardson
	G-BJSD	Osprey Mk 4D balloon	N. J. Richardson
	G-BJSF	Osprey Mk 4B balloon	N. J. Richardson
	G-BJSG	V.S.361 Spitfire LF.IXE (ML417)	Patina Ltd/Duxford
	G-BJSI	Osprey Mk 1E balloon	N. J. Richardson
	G-BJSP	Guido 1A Srs 61 balloon	G. A. Newsome
	G-BJSS	Allport balloon	D. J. Allport
	G-BJST	CCFT-6J Harvard IV	G. R. B. Schilling/Germany
	G-BJSU	Bensen B.8M	J. D. Newlyn
	G-BJSV	PA-28-161 Warrior II	Airways Flight Training (Exeter) Ltd
	G-BJSW	Thunder Ax7-65 balloon	Sandicliffe Garage Ltd
	G-BJSX	Unicorn UE-1C balloon	N. J. Richardson
	G-BJSZ	Piper J-3C-65 Cub	H. Gilbert
	G-BJTB	Cessna A.150M	Clacton Aero Club (1988) Ltd
	G-BJTK	Taylor JT.1 Monoplane	E. N. Simmons
	G-BJTO	Piper J-3C-65 Cub	K. R. Nunn
	G-BJTP	PA-18 Super Cub 95 (115302)	J. T. Parkins
	G-BJTW	European E.107 balloon	C. J. Brealey
	G-BJTY	Osprey Mk 4B balloon	A. E. de Gruchy
	G-BJUB	BVS Special 01 balloon	P. G. Wild
	G-BJUC	Robinson R-22	Brian Seedle Helicopters/Blackpool
	G-BJUD	Robin DR.400/180R	Lasham Gliding Soc Ltd
	G-BJUI	Osprey Mk 4B balloon	B. A. de Gruchy
	G-BJUR	PA-38-112 Tomahawk	Truman Aviation Ltd/Tollerton
	G-BJUS	PA-38-112 Tomahawk	Panshanger School of Flying
	G-BJUV	Cameron V-20 balloon	P. Spellward
	G-BJUY	Colt Ax7-77 Golf Ball SS balloon	Lindstrand Balloons Ltd
	G-BJVC	Evans VP-2	J. J. Morrissey
	G-BJVF	Thunder Ax3 balloon	A. G. R. Calder/California
	G-BJVH	Cessna F.182Q	R. J. de Courcy Cuming/ Wellesbourne
	G-BJVJ	Cessna F.152	Cambridge Aero Club Ltd
	G-BJVK	Grob G-109	B. Kimberley/Enstone
	G-BJVM	Cessna 172N	I. C. MacLennan
	G-BJVS	CP.1310-C3 Super Emeraude	A. E. Futter/Norwich
	G-BJVT	Cessna F.152	Cambridge Aero Club Ltd
	G-BJVU	Thunder Ax6-56 Bolt SS balloon	G. V. Beckwith
	G-BJVV	Robin R.1180	Medway Flying Group Ltd/Rochester
	G-BJVX	Sikorsky S-76A	Bristow Helicopters Ltd
	G-BJWC	Saro Skeeter AOP.12 (XK 482) ★	Sloane Helicopters Ltd/Sywell
	G-BJWH	Cessna F.152	Plane Talking Ltd/Elstree
	G-BJWI	Cessna F.172P	Agricultural & General Aviation Ltd/ Bournemouth

Reg.	Type	Owner or Operator	Notes
G-BJWJ	Cameron V-65 balloon	R. G. Turnbull & S. G. Forse	
G-BJWO	BN-2A-26 Islander	Peterborough Parachute Centre Ltd (G-BAXC)/Sibson	
G-BJWT	Wittman W.10 Tailwind	Tailwind Group	
G-BJWV	Colt 17A balloon	D. T. Meyes	
G-BJWW	Cessna F.172N	Air Charter & Travel Ltd/Blackpool	
G-BJWX	PA-18 Super Cub 95	Acebell JWX Syndicate	
G-BJWY	S-55 Whirlwind HAR.21 (WV198) ★	Solway Aviation Museum/Carlisle	
G-BJWZ	PA-18 Super Cub 95	R. A. G. Lucas	
G-BJXA	Slingsby T.67A	Comed Aviation Ltd/Blackpool	
G-BJXB	Slingsby T.67A	A. K. Halvorsen/Barton	
G-BJXK	Fournier RF-5	G-BJXK Syndicate/Cardiff	
G-BJXP	Colt 56B balloon	Rishtons (Chichester) Ltd	
G-BJXR	Auster AOP.9 (XR267)	Cotswold Aircraft Restoration Group	
G-BJXX	PA-23 Aztec 250E	V. Bojovic	
G-BJXZ	Cessna 172N	T. M. Jones	
G-BJYD	Cessna F.152 II	Cleveland Flying School Ltd/Teesside	
G-BJYG	PA-28-161 Warrior II	Browns of Stoke Ltd	
G-BJYK	Jodel D.120A	T. Fox & D. A. Thorpe	
G-BJYN	PA-38-112 Tomahawk	Panshanger School of Flying Ltd (G-BJTE)	
G-BJZA	Cameron N-65 balloon	A. D. Pinner	
G-BJZB	Evans VP-2	J. A. MacLeod	
G-BJZC	Thunder Ax7-65Z balloon	Greenpeace (UK) Ltd/S. Africa	
G-BJZF	D.H.82A Tiger Moth	R. Blast	
G-BJZN	Slingsby T.67A	J. Hartup	
G-BJZR	Colt 42A balloon	Selfish Balloon Group	
G-BJZT	Cessna FA.152	E. Blanche/Biggin Hill	
G-BJZX	Grob G.109	Oxfordshire Sport Flying Ltd/Enstone	
G-BJZY	Bensen B.8MV	P. J. Dockerill	
G-BKAC	Cessna F.150L	Motioncraft Ltd	
G-BKAE	Jodel D.120	M. P. Wakem	
G-BKAF	FRED Srs 2	J. Mc. D. Robinson	
G-BKAM	Slingsby T.67M Firefly	A. J. Daley	
G-BKAO	Jodel D.112	R. Broadhead	
G-BKAR	PA-38-112 Tomahawk	Deltair/Liverpool	
G-BKAS	PA-38-112 Tomahawk	Deltair/Liverpool	
G-BKAY	R. Commander 114	The Rockwell Group	
G-BKAZ	Cessna 152	Skyviews & General Ltd	
G-BKBB	Hawker Fury Mk I (replica)	R. Landuyt/Belgium	
G-BKBD	Thunder Ax3 balloon	G. A. McCarthy	
G-BKBF	M.S.894A Rallye Minerva 220	J. A. Gibbs	
G-BKBN	SOCATA TB.10 Tobago	RFA Flying Club Ltd	
G-BKBO	Colt 17A balloon	J. Armstrong & ptnrs	
G-BKBP	Bellanca 7GCBC Scout	H. G. Jefferies & Son/Little Gransden	
G-BKBR	Cameron Chateau 84 SS balloon	Forbes Europe Ltd/France	
G-BKBS	Bensen B.8MV	Construction & Site Administration Ltd	
G-BKBV	SOCATA TB.10 Tobago	R. M. Messenger	
G-BKBW	SOCATA TB.10 Tobago	Merlin Aviation	
G-BKCB	PA-28R Cherokee Arrow 200	J. D. Rose	
G-BKCC	PA-28 Cherokee 180	Cowie Aviation Ltd/Staverton	
G-BKCE	Cessna F.172P II	Far North Flight Training/Wick	
G-BKCF	Rutan LongEz	I. C. Fallows	
G-BKCH	Thompson Cassutt	S. C. Thompson/Redhill	
G-BKCI	Brügger MB.2 Colibri	E. R. Newall	
G-BKCJ	Oldfield Baby Great Lakes	S. V. Roberts/Sleap	
G-BKCK	CCF Harvard IV (P5865)	E. D. & A. Haig-Thomas/North Weald	
G-BKCL	PA-30 Twin Comanche 160C	Yorkair Ltd/Leeds	
G-BKCN	Currie Wot	N. A. A. Podmore	
G-BKCR	SOCATA TB.9 Tampico	Air Touring Services Ltd/Biggin Hill	
G-BKCT	Cameron V-77 balloon	Quality Products General Engineering (Wickwar) Ltd	
★ G-BKCV	EAA Acro Sport II	T. N. Jinks	
G-BKCW	Jodel D.120A	A. Greene & G. Kerr/Dundee	
G-BKCX	Mudry CAARP CAP.10	Mahon & Associates/Booker	
G-BKCY	PA-38-112 Tomahawk II ★	Pool Aviation Ltd/Welshpool	
G-BKCZ	Jodel D.120A	M. R. Baker/Shoreham	
G-BKDC	Monnett Sonerai II	K. J. Towell	
G-BKDH	Robin DR.400/120	Thornhill Music Ltd	
G-BKDI	Robin DR.400/120	Cotswold Aero Club Ltd/Staverton	
G-BKDJ	Robin DR.400/120	M. D. Joyce & R. R. Wills	
G-BKDK	Thunder Ax7-77SZ balloon	A. J. Byrne	

Notes	Reg.	Type	Owner or Operator
	G-BKDP	FRED Srs 3	M. Whittaker
	G-BKDR	Pitts S.1S Special-	G-BKDR Group
	G-BKDT	SE-5A (replica) (F943) ★	Yorkshire Air Museum/Elvington
	G-BKDX	Jodel DR.1050	J. E. Nurse
	G-BKEK	PA-32 Cherokee Six 300	S. W. Turley
	G-BKEP	Cessna F.172M	R. Green/Glasgow
	G-BKER	SE-5A (replica) (F5447)	N. K. Geddes
	G-BKET	PA-18 Super Cub 95	H. M. MacKenzie
	G-BKEU	Taylor JT.1 Monoplane	R. J. Whybrow & J. M. Springham
	G-BKEV	Cessna F.172M	One Zero One Three Ltd
	G-BKEW	Bell 206B JetRanger 3	N. R. Foster
	G-BKEX	Rich Prototype glider	D. B. Rich
	G-BKEY	FRED Srs 3	G. S. Taylor
	G-BKEZ	PA-18 Super Cub 95	D. G. Marwick
	G-BKFA	Monnett Sonerai IIL	R. F. Bridge
	G-BKFC	Cessna F.152 II	Sulby Aerial Surveys Ltd
	G-BKFG	Thunder Ax3 balloon	P. Ray
	G-BKFI	Evans VP-1	Foxtrot India Flying Group
	G-BKFK	Isaacs Fury II	G. C. Jones
	G-BKFL	Aerosport Scamp	J. Sherwood
	G-BKFM	QAC Quickie	F. Rothers
	G-BKFN	Bell 214ST	Bristow Helicopters Ltd
	G-BKFP	Bell 214ST	Bristow Helicopters Ltd
	G-BKFR	CP.301C Emeraude	C. R. Beard
	G-BKFW	P.56 Provost T.1 (XF597)	Sylmar Aviation & Services Ltd
	G-BKFZ	PA-28R Cherokee Arrow 200	Shacklewell Flying Group
	G-BKGA	M.S.892E Rallye 150GT	BJJ Aviation
	G-BKGB	Jodel D.120	R. W. Greenwood
	G-BKGC	Maule M.6-235	Witham (Specialist) Vehicles Ltd
	G-BKGL	Beech D.18S (1164)	Classic Wings/Duxford
	G-BKGM	Beech D.18S (HB275)	A. E. Hutton/North Weald
	G-BKGR	Cameron O-65 balloon	K. Kidner & L. E. More
	G-BKGT	SOCATA Rallye 110ST	Long Marston Flying Group
	G-BKGW	Cessna F.152-II	Leicestershire Aero Club Ltd
	G-BKHA	W.S.55 Whirlwind HAR.10 (XJ763) ★	C. J. Evans
	G-BKHD	Oldfield Baby Great Lakes	P. J. Tanulak/Sleap
	G-BKHG	Piper J-3C-65 Cub (479766)	K. G. Wakefield
	G-BKHJ	Cessna 182P	Augur Films Ltd
	G-BKHL	Thunder Ax9-140 balloon	R. Carr/France
	G-BKHR	Luton LA-4 Minor	C. B. Buscombe & R. Goldsworthy
	G-BKHT	BAe 146-100	British Aerospace PLC
	G-BKHW	Stoddard-Hamilton Glasair SH.2RG	G. Fleck
	G-BKHY	Taylor JT.1 Monoplane	B. C. J. O'Neill
	G-BKHZ	Cessna F.172P	Warwickshire Flying Training Centre Ltd
	G-BKIA	SOCATA TB.10 Tobago	M. F. McGinn
	G-BKIB	SOCATA TB.9 Tampico	G. A. Vickers
	G-BKIC	Cameron V-77 balloon	C. A. Butler
	G-BKIE	Short SD3-30 Variant 100	BAC Group Ltd (G-SLUG/G-METP/ G-METO)
	G-BKIF	Fournier RF-6B	G. G. Milton
	G-BKII	Cessna F.172M	M. S. Knight/Goodwood
	G-BKIJ	Cessna F.172M	V. Speck
	G-BKIK	Cameron DG-10 airship	Airspace Outdoor Advertising Ltd
	G-BKIM	Unicorn UE.5A balloon	I. Chadwick & K. H. Turner
	G-BKIN	Alon A.2A Aircoupe	P. A. Williams & M. Quinn/Blackbushe
	G-BKIR	Jodel D.117	R. Shaw & D. M. Hardaker/Sherburn
	G-BKIS	SOCATA TB.10 Tobago	I. R. Carver
	G-BKIT	SOCATA TB.9 Tampico	D. N. Garlick & ptnrs
	G-BKIU	Colt 17A balloon	Robert Pooley Ltd
	G-BKIX	Cameron V-31 balloon	G. Stevens (G-BKGJ)
	G-BKIY	Thunder Ax3 balloon	A. Hornak
	G-BKIZ	Cameron V-31 balloon	A. P. S. Cox
	G-BKJB	PA-18 Super Cub 135	Haimoss Ltd/O. Sarum
	G-BKJD	Bell 214ST	Bristow Helicopters Ltd
	G-BKJF	M.S.880B Rallye 100T	Journeyman Aviation Ltd
	G-BKJG	BN-2B-21 Islander	Pilatus BN Ltd/Bembridge
	G-BKJR	Hughes 269C	March Helicopters Ltd/Sywell
	G-BKJS	Jodel D.120A	A. J. Bourner
	G-BKJW	PA-23 Aztec 250E	Alan Williams Entertainments Ltd
	G-BKKN	Cessna 182R	R A. Marven/Elstree
	G-BKKO	Cessna 182R	B. & G. Jebson Ltd/Crosland Moor

Reg.	Type	Owner or Operator	Notes
G-BKKR	Rand KR-2	D. Beale & S. P. Gardner	
G-BKKZ	Pitts S-1D Special	G. C. Masterton	
G-BKLC	Cameron V-56 balloon	M. A. & J. R. H. Ashworth	
G-BKLJ	Westland Scout AH.1 ★	N. R. Windley	
G-BKLO	Cessna F.172M	Stapleford Flying Club Ltd	
G-BKLP	Cessna F.172N	P. A. Dunk	
G-BKMA	Mooney M.20J Srs 201	Foxtrot Whisky Aviation	
G-BKMB	Mooney M.20J Srs 201	W. A. Cook & ptnrs	
G-BKMD	SC.7 Skyvan Srs 3	Army Parachute Association/Netheravon	
G-BKMG	Handley Page O/400 (replica)	Paralyser Group	
G-BKMI	V.S.359 Spitfire HF.VIIIc (MT928)	Aerial Museum (North Weald) Ltd	
G-BKMK	PA-38-112 Tomahawk	D. J. Campbell/Glasgow	
G-BKMR	Thunder Ax3 balloon	B. F. G. Ribbans	
G-BKMT	PA-32R-301 Saratoga SP	Severn Valley Aviation Group	
G-BKMX	Short SD3-60 Variant 100	British Regional Airlines/BA Express	
G-BKNA	Cessna 421	Launchapart Ltd	
G-BKNB	Cameron V-42 balloon	D. N. Close	
G-BKND	Colt 56A balloon	T. A. Hains	
G-BKNI	GY-80 Horizon 160D	A. Hartigan & ptnrs/Fenland	
G-BKNL	Cameron D-96 airship	Sport Promotion SRL/Italy	
G-BKNO	Monnett Sonerai IIL	M. D. Hughes	
G-BKNP	Cameron V-77 balloon	E. K. K. & C. E. Odman	
G-BKNY	Bensen B.8MPV	D. A. C. MacCormack	
G-BKNZ	CP.301A Emeraude	R. N. Crosland & P. R. Teager	
G-BKOA	SOCATA M.S.893E Rallye 180GT	M. & J. Grafton	
G-BKOB	Z.326 Trener Master	W. G. V. Hall	
G-BKOR	Barnes 77 balloon	Robert Pooley Ltd	
G-BKOT	Wassmer WA.81 Piranha	B. N. Rolfe	
G-BKOU	P.84 Jet Provost T.3 (XN637)	A. Haig-Thomas/North Weald	
G-BKOV	Jodel DR.220A	Merlin Flying Club Ltd/Hucknall	
G-BKOW	Colt 77A balloon	Hot Air Balloon Co Ltd	
G-BKPA	Hoffmann H-36 Dimona	A. Mayhew	
G-BKPB	Aerosport Scamp	E. D. Burke	
G-BKPC	Cessna A.185F	Black Knights Parachute Centre	
G-BKPD	Viking Dragonfly	E. P. Browne & G. J. Sargent	
G-BKPE	Jodel DR.250/160	J. S. & J. D. Lewer	
G-BKPK	Everett gyroplane	J. C. McHugh	
G-BKPN	Cameron N-77 balloon	R. H. Sanderson	
G-BKPS	AA-5B Tiger	Earthline Ltd	
G-BKPT	M.H.1521M Broussard (07)	R. H. Reeves/Barton	
G-BKPX	Jodel D.120A	N. H. Martin	
G-BKPY	SAAB 91B/2 Safir (56321) ★	Newark Air Museum Ltd	
G-BKPZ	Pitts S-1T Special	M. A. Frost	
G-BKRA	NA T-6G Texan (51-15227)	Pulsegrove Ltd/Shoreham	
G-BKRB	Cessna 172N	Saunders Caravans Ltd	
G-BKRF	PA-18 Super Cub 95	K. M. Bishop	
G-BKRG	Beechcraft C-45G	Aces High Ltd/North Weald	
G-BKRH	Brügger MB.2 Colibri	M. R. Benwell	
G-BKRI	Cameron V-77 balloon	J. R. Lowe & R. J. Fuller	
G-BKRK	SNCAN Stampe SV-4C	Strathgadie Stampe Group	
G-BKRL	Chichester-Miles Leopard	Chichester-Miles Consultants Ltd	
G-BKRN	Beechcraft D.18S ★	A. S. Topen	
G-BKRS	Cameron V-56 balloon	D. N. & L. J. Close	
G-BKRU	Ensign Crossley Racer	M. Crossley	
G-BKRV	Hovey Beta Bird	A. M. Witt	
G-BKRZ	Dragon G-77 balloon	J. R. Barber	
G-BKSB	Cessna T.310Q II	Flightline Ltd/Southend	
G-BKSC	Saro Skeeter AOP.12 (XN351)	R. A. L. Falconer	
G-BKSD	Colt 56A balloon	M. J. & G. C. Casson	
G-BKSE	QAC Quickie Q.1	M. D. Burns	
G-BKSH	Colt 21A balloon	J. Bartholomew & D. L. Smith	
G-BKSP	Schleicher ASK.14	J. H. Bryson/Bellarena	
G-BKSS	Jodel D.150	D. H. Wilson-Spratt/Ronaldsway	
G-BKST	Rutan Vari-Eze	R. Towle	
G-BKSX	SNCAN Stampe SV-4C	C. A. Bailey & J. A. Carr	
G-BKTA	PA-18 Super Cub 95	V. D. Long	
G-BKTH	CCF Hawker Sea Hurricane IB (Z7015)	The Shuttleworth Collection/Duxford	
G-BKTM	PZL SZD-45A Ogar	Repclif Chemical Services Ltd	
G-BKTR	Cameron V-77 balloon	C. Wilson	
G-BKTV	Cessna F.152	Seawing Flying Club Ltd/Southend	
G-BKTY	SOCATA TB.10 Tobago	B. M. & G. M. McClelland	
G-BKTZ	Slingsby T.67M Firefly	E. Hopper (G-SFTV)	

Notes	Reg.	Type	Owner or Operator
	G-BKUE	SOCATA TB.9 Tampico	W. J. Moore/Kirkbride
	G-BKUJ	Thunder Ax6-56 balloon	R. J. Bent
	G-BKUR	CP.301A Emeraude	R. Wells
	G-BKUS	Bensen B.8M	A. Charles
	G-BKUU	Thunder Ax7-77-1 balloon	D. A. Kozuba-Kozubska
	G-BKUY	BAe Jetstream 3102	Jetstream Aircraft Ltd/Prestwick
	G-BKVA	SOCATA Rallye 180T	Buckminster Gliding Club Syndicate
	G-BKVB	SOCATA Rallye 110ST	Air Touring Services Ltd/Biggin Hill
	G-BKVC	SOCATA TB.9 Tampico	H. P. Aubin-Parvu
	G-BKVE	Rutan Vari-Eze	R. M. Smith (G-EZLT)
	G-BKVF	FRED Srs 3	A. R. Hawes
	G-BKVG	Scheibe SF.25E Super Falke	G-BKVG Ltd
	G-BKVK	Auster AOP.9 (WZ662)	J. D. Butcher
	G-BKVL	Robin DR.400/160	The Cotswold Aero Club Ltd/Staverton
	G-BKVM	PA-18 Super Cub 150 (115684)	D. G. Caffrey
	G-BKVN	PA-23 Aztec 250F	R. K. Pugh
	G-BKVO	Pietenpol Air Camper	B. P. Waites
	G-BKVP	Pitts S-1D Special	P. J. Leggo
	G-BKVR	PA-28 Cherokee 140	D. P. Alexander
	G-BKVS	Bensen B.8M	A. J. Unwin & J. W. Holland
	G-BKVT	PA-23 Aztec 250E	R. E. Woolsey (G-HARV)
	G-BKVW	Airtour 56 balloon	L. D. & H. Vaughan
	G-BKVX	Airtour 56 balloon	E. G. Woolnough
	G-BKVY	Airtour 31 balloon	M. Davies
	G-BKWD	Taylor JT.2 Titch	E. H. Booker
	G-BKWE	Colt 17A balloon	Hot-Air Balloon Co Ltd
	G-BKWG	PZL-104 Wilga 35A	M. A. Johnston/Tayside
	G-BKWR	Cameron V-65 balloon	K. J. Foster
	G-BKWW	Cameron O-77 balloon	A. M. Marten
	G-BKWY	Cessna F.152	Cambridge Aero Club
	G-BKXA	Robin R.2100	G. J. Anderson & ptnrs
	G-BKXD	SA.365N Dauphin 2	Bond Helicopters Ltd
	G-BKXF	PA-28R Cherokee Arrow 200	P. L. Brunton/Caernarfon
	G-BKXG	Cessna T.303	W. M. Ewington & Co Ltd
	G-BKXM	Colt 17A balloon	R. G. Turnbull
	G-BKXN	ICA IS-28M2A	T. J. Mills/Shobdon
	G-BKXO	Rutan LongEz	D. F. P. Finan & Cambridge Perfusion Services Ltd
	G-BKXP	Auster AOP.6	B. J. & W. J. Ellis
	G-BKXR	D.31A Turbulent	M. B. Hill
	G-BKXX	Cameron V-65 balloon	T. Fonteyn
	G-BKYA	Boeing 737-236	British Airways Birmingham *Ariel*
	G-BKYB	Boeing 737-236	British Airways Birmingham *Portia*
	G-BKYC	Boeing 737-236	British Airways *River Wye*
	G-BKYE	Boeing 737-236	British Airways Birmingham *Hippolyta*
	G-BKYF	Boeing 737-236	British Airways Birmingham *Mistress Quickly*
	G-BKYG	Boeing 737-236	British Airways Birmingham *Prospero*
	G-BKYH	Boeing 737-236	British Airways Birmingham *Hotspur*
	G-BKYI	Boeing 737-236	British Airways *River Waveney*
	G-BKYJ	Boeing 737-236	British Airways Birmingham *Touchstone*
	G-BKYK	Boeing 737-236	British Airways *River Foyle*
	G-BKYL	Boeing 737-236	British Airways Birmingham *Titania*
	G-BKYM	Boeing 737-236	British Airways Birmingham *Moonshine*
	G-BKYN	Boeing 737-236	British Airways Birmingham *Prince Hal*
	G-BKYO	Boeing 737-236	British Airways Birmingham *Oberon*
	G-BKYP	Boeing 737-236	British Airways Manchester *River Ystwyth*
	G-BKZB	Cameron V-77 balloon	A. J. Montgomery
	G-BKZE	AS.332L Super Puma	British International Helicopters
	G-BKZF	Cameron V-56 balloon	C. D. Monk
	G-BKZG	AS.332L Super Puma	British International Helicopters
	G-BKZH	AS.332L Super Puma	British International Helicopters
	G-BKZI	Bell 206B JetRanger 2	Western Air Trading Ltd/Thruxton
	G-BKZJ	Bensen B.8MV	J. C. Birdsall
	G-BKZM	Isaacs Fury II	B. Jones
	G-BKZT	FRED Srs 2	M. G. Rusby
	G-BKZV	Bede BD-4A	G. I. J. Thomson
	G-BLAA	Fournier RF-5	A. D. Wren/Southend
	G-BLAC	Cessna FA.152	Ofteneasy Ltd
	G-BLAD	Thunder Ax7-77-1 balloon	P. J. Bish
	G-BLAF	Stolp SA.900 V-Star	P. R. Skeels
	G-BLAG	Pitts S-1D Special	G. Ferriman

Reg.	Type	Owner or Operator	Notes
G-BLAH	Thunder Ax7-77-1 balloon	T. M. Donnelly	
G-BLAI	Monnett Sonerai IIL	T. Simpon	
G-BLAM	Jodel DR.360	B. F. Baldock	
G-BLAT	Jodel 150	D. J. Dulborough & A. J. Court	
G-BLAX	Cessna FA.152	Shoreham Flight Simulation/Bournemouth	
G-BLAY	Robin HR.100/200B	B. A. Mills	
G-BLCA	Bell 206B JetRanger 3	R.M.H. Stainless Ltd	
G-BLCF	EAA Acro Sport 2	M. J. Watkins & ptnrs	
G-BLCG	SOCATA TB.10 Tobago	Charlie Golf Flying Group (G-BHES)/ Shoreham	
G-BLCH	Colt 65D balloon	Balloon Flights Club Ltd	
G-BLCI	EAA Acro Sport	M. R. Holden	
G-BLCK	V.S.361 Spitfire F.IX (TE566)	Historic Aircraft Collection Ltd	
G-BLCM	SOCATA TB.9 Tampico	Repclif Aviation Ltd/Liverpool	
G-BLCT	Jodel DR.220 2+2	D. Young	
G-BLCU	Scheibe SF.25B Falke	C. F. Sellers	
G-BLCV	Hoffmann H-36	Dimona	
G-BLCW	Evans VP-1	K. D. Pearce	
G-BLDB	Taylor JT.1 Monoplane	C. J. Bush	
G-BLDC	K&S Jungster 1	A. W. Brown	
G-BLDD	WAG-Aero CUBy AcroTrainer	C. A. Laycock	
G-BLDG	PA-25 Pawnee 260C	Ouse Gliding Club Ltd/Rufforth	
G-BLDK	Robinson R-22	Warrenform Ltd	
G-BLDN	Rand KR-2	M. T. Taylor	
G-BLDP	Slingsby T.67M Firefly	Sherburn Aero Club Ltd	
G-BLDV	BN-2A Islander	Loganair Ltd/British Airways	
G-BLEB	Colt 69A balloon	I. R. M. Jacobs	
G-BLEJ	PA-28-161 Warrior II	Eglinton Flying Club Ltd	
G-BLEP	Cameron V-65 balloon	D. Chapman	
G-BLES	Stolp SA.750 Acroduster Too	T. W. Harris	
G-BLET	Thunder Ax7-77-1 balloon	Servatruc Ltd	
G-BLEW	Cessna F.182Q	D. J. Cross	
G-BLEZ	SA.365N Dauphin 2	Bond Helicopters Ltd	
G-BLFI	PA-28-181 Archer II	Bonus Aviation Ltd	
G-BLFW	AA-5 Traveler	Grumman Club	
G-BLFY	Cameron V-77 balloon	A. N. F. Pertwee	
G-BLFZ	PA-31-310 Turbo Navajo C	London Executive Aviation Ltd	
G-BLGB	Short SD3-60 Variant 100	British Regional Airlines/BA Express	
G-BLGE	Short SD3-60 Variant 100	Gill Airways Ltd	
G-BLGH	Robin DR.300/180R	Booker Gliding Club Ltd	
G-BLGO	Bensen B.8MV	F. Vernon	
G-BLGR	Bell 47G-4A	Lowland Advertising Ltd	
G-BLGS	SOCATA Rallye 180T	Lasham Gliding Society Ltd	
G-BLGT	PA-18 Super Cub 95	T. A. Reed/Dunkeswell	
G-BLGV	Bell 206B JetRanger 3	Part Reward Ltd/Shobdon	
G-BLGX	Thunder Ax7-65 balloon	The 45	
G-BLHH	Jodel DR.315	G. G. Milton	
G-BLHI	Colt 17A balloon	J. A. Folkes	
G-BLHJ	Cessna F.172P	J. Easson/Edinburgh	
G-BLHK	Colt 105A balloon	Hale Hot-Air Balloon Club	
G-BLHM	PA-18 Super Cub 95	B. N. C. Mogg	
G-BLHN	Robin HR.100/285	Tarist Ltd	
G-BLHR	GA-7 Cougar	Falcon Flying Services/Biggin Hill	
G-BLHS	Bellanca 7ECA Citabria	N. J. F. Campbell	
G-BLHW	Varga 2150A Kachina	Kachina Hotel Whisky Group	
G-BLID	D.H.112 Venom FB.50 (J-1605) ★	P. G. Vallance Ltd/Charlwood	
G-BLIE	D.H.112 Venom FB.50 (J-1614)	R. J. Everett	
G-BLIG	Cameron V-65 balloon	W. Davison	
G-BLIH	PA-18 Super Cub 135	I. R. F. Hammond	
G-BLIK	Wallis WA-116/F/S	K. H. Wallis	
G-BLIP	Cameron N-77 balloon	L. A. Beardall & G. R. Hunt	
G-BLIT	Thorp T-18 CW	K. B. Hallam	
G-BLIW	P.56 Provost T.51 (177)	Provost Flying Group/Shoreham	
G-BLIX	Saro Skeeter Mk 12 (XL809)	A. P. Nowicki	
G-BLIY	M.S.892A Rallye Commodore	A. J. Brasher & K. R. Haynes	
G-BLJD	Glaser-Dirks DG.400	G. G. Hearne & M. I. Gee/Rufforth	
G-BLJF	Cameron O-65 balloon	M. D. Mitchell	
G-BLJH	Cameron N-77 balloon	Phillair	
G-BLJI	Colt 105A balloon	Tempowish Ltd	
G-BLJJ	Cessna 305 Bird Dog	P. Dawe	
G-BLJM	Beech 95-B55 Baron	Elstree Aircraft Hire Ltd	
G-BLJN	Nott-Cameron ULD-1 balloon	J. R. P. Nott	
G-BLJO	Cessna F.152	Redhill School of Flying Ltd	

Notes	Reg.	Type	Owner or Operator
	G-BLJP	Cessna F.150L	C. R. & S. Hardiman
	G-BLKA	D.H.112 Venom FB.54 (WR410)	De Havilland Aviation Ltd/Swansea
	G-BLKJ	Thunder Ax7-65 balloon	D. T. Watkins
	G-BLKK	Evans VP-1	S. R. Roberts
	G-BLKL	D.31 Turbulent	D. L. Ripley
	G-BLKM	Jodel DR.1051	T. C. Humphreys
	G-BLKP	BAe Jetstream 3102	British Aerospace (Operations) Ltd/Warton
	G-BLKY	Beech 95-58 Baron	P. R. Earp
	G-BLKZ	Pilatus P2-05	Cooper Aerial Surveys Ltd/Sandtoft
	G-BLLA	Bensen B.8M	K. T. Donaghey
	G-BLLB	Bensen B.8M	D. H. Moss
	G-BLLD	Cameron O-77 balloon	A. Bevis
	G-BLLH	Jodel DR.220A 2+2	P. Chamberlain & D. E. Starkey
	G-BLLM	PA-23 Aztec 250E	C. & M. Thomas (G-BBNM)/Cardiff
	G-BLLN	PA-18 Super Cub 95	A. L. Hall-Carpenter
	G-BLLO	PA-18 Super Cub 95	D. G. & M. G. Margetts
	G-BLLP	Slingsby T.67B	Cleveland Flying School Ltd/Teesside
	G-BLLR	Slingsby T.67B	Trent Air Services Ltd/Cranfield
	G-BLLS	Slingsby T.67B	Western Air Training Ltd/Thruxton
	G-BLLV	Slingsby T.67B	R. L. Brinklow
	G-BLLW	Colt 56B balloon	J. C. Stupples
	G-BLLZ	Rutan LongEz	R. S. Stoddart-Stones
	G-BLMA	Zlin 326 Trener Master	G. P. Northcott/Redhill
	G-BLMC	Avro 698 Vulcan B.2A (XM575) ★	Aeropark/E. Midlands
	G-BLME	Robinson R-22	Photractive
	G-BLMG	Grob G.109B	Mike Golf Syndicate
	G-BLMI	PA-18 Super Cub 95	B. J. Borsberry
	G-BLMN	Rutan LongEz	G-BLMN Flying Group
	G-BLMP	PA-17 Vagabond	M. Austin/Popham
	G-BLMR	PA-18 Super Cub 150	Bidford Gliding Centre Ltd
	G-BLMT	PA-18 Super Cub 135	I. S. Runnalls
	G-BLMW	T.66 Nipper 3	S. L. Millar
	G-BLMX	Cessna FR.172H	C. J. W. Littler/Felthorpe
	G-BLMZ	Colt 105A balloon	M. D. Dickinson
	G-BLNJ	BN-2B-26 Islander	British Regional Airlines/BA Express
	G-BLNO	FRED Srs 3	L. W. Smith
	G-BLNW	BN-2B-27 Islander	British Regional Airlines/ Scottish Air Ambulance Service
	G-BLOB	Colt 31A balloon	Jacques W. Soukup Enterprises Ltd/USA
	G-BLOR	PA-30 Twin Comanche 160	R. L. C. Appleton
	G-BLOS	Cessna 185A (also flown with floats)	E. Brun
	G-BLOT	Colt Ax6-56B balloon	H. J. Anderson
	G-BLOU	Rand KR-2	D. G. Cole
	G-BLPA	Piper J-3C-65 Cub	G. A. Card & C. G. Gray
	G-BLPB	Turner TSW Hot Two Wot	I. R. Hannah
	G-BLPE	PA-18 Super Cub 95	A. Haig-Thomas
	G-BLPF	Cessna FR.172G	W. A. F. Cuninghame
	G-BLPG	J/1N Alpha (16693)	Q. J. Ball (G-AZIH)
	G-BLPH	Cessna FRA.150L	New Aerobat Group/Shoreham
	G-BLPI	Slingsby T.67B	Keepcase Ltd
	G-BLPK	Cameron V-65 balloon	A. J. & C. P. Nicholls
	G-BLPP	Cameron V-77 balloon	L. P. Purfield
	G-BLRC	PA-18 Super Cub 135	A. J. McBurnie
	G-BLRD	MBB Bo.209 Monsun 150FV	M. D. Ward
	G-BLRF	Slingsby T.67C	Bristow Helicopters Ltd/Redhill
	G-BLRG	Slingsby T.67B	R. L. Brinklow
	G-BLRH	Rutan LongEz	G. L. Tompson
	G-BLRJ	Jodel DR.1051	M. P. Hallam
	G-BLRL	CP.301C-1 Emeraude	B. C. Davis
	G-BLRM	Glaser-Dirks DG.400	D. J. Barke/Tatenhill
	G-BLRN	D.H.104 Dove 8 (WB531) ★	Pionier Hangaar Collection/Lelystad
	G-BLRW	Cameron 77 Elephant SS balloon	Forbes Europe Inc/France
	G-BLRY	AS.332L Super Puma	Bristow Helicopters Ltd
	G-BLSF	AA-5A Cheetah	J. P. E. Walsh (G-BGCK)
	G-BLSH	Cameron V-77 balloon	C. N. Luffingham
	G-BLSK	Colt 77A balloon	Solarmoor Ltd
	G-BLSM	H.S.125 Srs 700B	Dravidian Air Services Ltd/Heathrow
	G-BLSN	Colt AS-56 airship	D. K. Fish
	G-BLSO	Colt AS-42 airship	Huntair Ltd/Germany
	G-BLST	Cessna 421C	Cecil Aviation Ltd/Cambridge
	G-BLSU	Cameron A-210 balloon	A. C. Elson
	G-BLSX	Cameron O-105 balloon	B. J. Petteford

Reg.	Type	Owner or Operator	Notes
G-BLTA	Thunder Ax7-77A	K. A. Schlussler	
G-BLTC	D.31A Turbulent	G. P. Smith & A. W. Burton	
G-BLTF	Robinson R-22A	Brian Seedle Helicopters/Blackpool	
G-BLTK	R. Commander 112TC	B. Rogalewski/Denham	
G-BLTM	Robin HR.200/100	B. D. Balcanquall	
G-BLTN	Thunder Ax7-65 balloon	J. A. Liddle	
G-BLTP	H.S.125 Srs 700B	Dravidian Air Services Ltd/Heathrow	
G-BLTR	Scheibe SF.25B Falke	V. Mallon/Germany	
G-BLTS	Rutan LongEz	R. W. Cutler	
G-BLTT	Slingsby T.67B	S. E. Marples	
G-BLTU	Slingsby T.67B	The Neiderhein Powered Flying Club/ Germany	
G-BLTV	Slingsby T.67B	R. L. Brinklow	
G-BLTW	Slingsby T.67B	Cheshire Air Training Services Ltd/ Liverpool	
G-BLTZ	SOCATA TB.10 Tobago	Martin Ltd/Biggin Hill	
G-BLUA	Robinson R-22	J. R. Budgen	
G-BLUE	Colt Ax7-77A balloon	D. P. Busby	
G-BLUI	Thunder Ax7-65 balloon	S. Johnson	
G-BLUJ	Cameron V-56 balloon	J. N. W. West	
G-BLUK	Bond Sky Dancer	J. Owen	
G-BLUL	Jodel DR.1051/M1	J. Owen	
G-BLUM	SA.365N Dauphin 2	Bond Helicopters Ltd	
G-BLUN	SA.365N Dauphin 2	Bond Helicopters Ltd	
G-BLUV	Grob G.109B	The 109 Fllying Group/North Weald	
G-BLUX	Slingsby T.67M	R. L. Brinklow	
G-BLUZ	D.H.82 Queen Bee (LF858)	The Bee Keepers Group	
G-BLVA	Airtour AH-56 balloon	A. Van Wyk	
G-BLVB	Airtour AH-56 balloon	T. C. Hinton	
G-BLVC	Airtour AH-31 balloon	Airtour Balloon Co Ltd	
G-BLVI	Slingsby T.67M	Slingsby Aviation Ltd/Kirkbymoorside	
G-BLVK	CAARP CAP-10B	E. K. Coventry/Earls Colne	
G-BLVL	PA-28-161 Warrior II	Marair (Jersey) Ltd	
G-BLVN	Cameron N-77 balloon	Servo & Electronic Sales Ltd	
G-BLVS	Cessna 150M	W. Lancs Aero Club Ltd/Woodvale	
G-BLVW	Cessna F.172H	R. & D. Holloway Ltd	
G-BLWB	Thunder Ax6-56 balloon	J. R. Tonkin/Norwich	
G-BLWD	PA-34-200T Seneca	Plane Talking Ltd/Kidlington	
G-BLWE	Colt 90A balloon	Huntair Ltd/Germany	
G-BLWF	Robin HR.100/210	Starguide Ltd	
G-BLWH	Fournier RF-6B-100	Gloster Aero Club Ltd/Staverton	
G-BLWM	Bristol M.1C (replica) (C4994) ★	RAF Museum/Hendon	
G-BLWP	PA-38-112 Tomahawk	A. Dodd/Booker	
G-BLWT	Evans VP-1	C. J. Bellworthy	
G-BLWV	Cessna F.152	Redhill Flying Club	
G-BLWW	Taylor Mini Imp Model C	M. K. Field	
G-BLWY	Robin 2161D	A. Spencer & D. A. Rolfe	
G-BLXA	SOCATA TB.20 Trinidad	Shropshire Aero Club Ltd/Sleap	
G-BLXF	Cameron V-77 balloon	G. McFarland	
G-BLXG	Colt 21A balloon	A. Walker	
G-BLXH	Fournier RF-3	A. Rawicz-Szczerbo	
G-BLXI	CP.1310-C3 Super Emeraude	R. Howard	
G-BLXO	Jodel 150	P. R. Powell	
G-BLXP	PA-28R Cherokee Arrow 200	M. B. Hamlett	
G-BLXR	AS.332L Super Puma	Bristow Helicopters Ltd	
G-BLXS	AS.332L Super Puma	Bristow Helicopters Ltd	
G-BLXT	RAF SE-5A (B4863) ★	Museum of Army Flying/Middle Wallop	
G-BLXX	PA-23 Aztec 250F	Falcon Flying Service (G-PIED)/Biggin Hill	
G-BLXY	Cameron V-65 balloon	Gone With The Wind Ltd/Tanzania	
G-BLYD	SOCATA TB.20 Trinidad	Gourmet Trotters	
G-BLYE	SOCATA TB.10 Tobago	G. Hatton	
G-BLYK	PA-34-220T Seneca III	Wellfield Developments Ltd	
G-BLYP	Robin 3000/120	Weald Air Services/Headcorn	
G-BLYT	Airtour AH-77 balloon	I. J. & B. A. Taylor	
G-BLYY	PA-28-181 Archer II	A. C. Clarke & ptnrs	
G-BLZA	Scheibe SF.25B Falke	M. J. Fogarty	
G-BLZB	Cameron N-65 balloon	D. Bareford	
G-BLZD	Robin R.1180T	Berkshire Aviation Services Ltd	
G-BLZE	Cessna F.152 II	Flairhire Ltd (G-CSSC)/Redhill	
G-BLZF	Thunder Ax7-77 balloon	H. M. Savage	
G-BLZH	Cessna F.152 II	Plane Talking Ltd/Elstree	
G-BLZM	Rutan LongEz	Zulu Mike Group/Shoreham	
G-BLZN	Bell 206B JetRanger	Helicopter Services	

Notes	Reg.	Type	Owner or Operator
	G-BLZP	Cessna F.152	E. Midlands Flying School Ltd
	G-BLZR	Cameron A-140 balloon	Clipper Worldwide Trading/Venezuela
	G-BLZS	Cameron O-77 balloon	M. M. Cobbold
	G-BLZT	Short SD3-60 Variant 100	Gill Airways Ltd/Newcastle
	G-BMAD	Cameron V-77 balloon	M. A. Stelling
	G-BMAF	Cessna 180F	P. Channon
	G-BMAL	Sikorsky S-76A	Bond Helicopters Ltd
	G-BMAO	Taylor JT.1 Monoplane	V. A. Wordsworth
	G-BMAR	Short SD3-60 Variant 100	British Regional Airlines/BA Express (G-BLCR)
	G-BMAV	AS.350B Ecureuil	RCR Aviation Ltd/Thruxton
	G-BMAX	FRED Srs 2	D. A. Arkley
	G-BMAY	PA-18 Super Cub 135	R. W. Davies
	G-BMBB	Cessna F.150L	Dacebow Aviation
	G-BMBC	PA-31-350 Navajo Chieftain	Air Navigation & Trading Ltd/Blackpool
	G-BMBE	PA-46-310P Malibu	Barfax Distributing Co Ltd & Glasdon Group Ltd/Blackpool
	G-BMBJ	Schempp-Hirth Janus CM	Cleveland Gliding Club
	G-BMBS	Colt 105A balloon	H. G. Davies
	G-BMBT	Thunder Ax8-90 balloon	Capital Balloon Club Ltd
	G-BMBW	Bensen B.8MR	M. E. Vahdat
	G-BMBZ	Scheibe SF.25E Super Falke	Cornish Gliding & Flying Club Ltd/Perranporth
	G-BMCC	Thunder Ax7-77 balloon	H. N. Harben Ltd
	G-BMCD	Cameron V-65 balloon	M. C. Drye
	G-BMCG	Grob G.109B	Lagerholm Finnimport Ltd/Booker
	G-BMCI	Cessna F.172H	A. B. Davis/Edinburgh
	G-BMCK	Cameron O-77 balloon	D. L. Smith
	G-BMCN	Cessna F.152	Lincoln Aero Club Ltd/Sturgate
	G-BMCO	Colomban MC.15 Cri-Cri	G. P. Clarke/Enstone
	G-BMCS	PA-22 Tri-Pacer 135	Rickard Lazenby & Co. Ltd & T. A. Hodges
	G-BMCV	Cessna F.152	Leicestershire Aero Club Ltd
	G-BMCW	AS.332L Super Puma	Bristow Helicopters Ltd
	G-BMCX	AS.332L Super Puma	Bristow Helicopters Ltd
	G-BMDB	SE-5A (replica) (F235)	D. Biggs
	G-BMDC	PA-32-301 Saratoga	MacLaren Aviation/Newcastle
	G-BMDD	Slingsby T.29	A. R. Worters
	G-BMDE	Pientenpol Air Camper	P. B. Childs
	G-BMDJ	Price Ax7-77S balloon	D. A. Kozuba-Kozubska
	G-BMDK	PA-34-220T Seneca III	A1 Air Ltd
	G-BMDO	ARV Super 2	J. L. & L. J. Eden
	G-BMDP	Partenavia P.64B Oscar 200	T. Gracey
	G-BMDS	Jodel D.120	J. V. Thompson
	G-BMDY	GA-7 Cougar	Eurowide Ltd/Elstree
	G-BMEA	PA-18 Super Cub 95	C. L. Towell
	G-BMEE	Cameron O-105 balloon	A. G. R. Calder/Los Angeles
	G-BMEG	SOCATA TB.10 Tobago	G. H. N. & R. V. Chamberlain
	G-BMEH	Jodel 150 Special Super Mascaret	Wm. Coupar Ltd
	G-BMEK	Mooney M.20K	Atlantic Film Investments Ltd/USA
	G-BMET	Taylor JT.1 Monoplane	M. K. A. Blyth
	G-BMEU	Isaacs Fury II	A. W. Austin
	G-BMEV	PA-32RT-300T Turbo Lance II	Arrow Aviation Ltd
	G-BMEX	Cessna A.150K	S. G. Eldred & N. A. M. Brain
	G-BMFD	PA-23 Aztec 250F	Rangemile Ltd (G-BGYY)/Coventry
	G-BMFG	Dornier Do.27A-4 (3460)	R. F. Warner
	G-BMFI	PZL SZD-45A Ogar	S. L. Morrey
	G-BMFL	Rand KR-2	E. W. B. Comber & M. F. Leusby
	G-BMFN	QAC Quickie Tri-Q.200	A. H. Hartog
	G-BMFP	PA-28-161 Warrior II	Bravo-Mike-Fox-Papa Group
	G-BMFT	H.S.748 Srs 2A	Euroair Transport Ltd/Singapore
	G-BMFU	Cameron N-90 balloon	J. J. Rudoni
	G-BMFY	Grob G.109B	P. J. Shearer
	G-BMFZ	Cessna F.152 II	Cornwall Flying Club Ltd/Bodmin
	G-BMGB	PA-28R Cherokee Arrow 200	Malmesbury Specialist Cars
	G-BMGC	Fairey Swordfish Mk II (W5856)	F.A.A. Museum/Yeovilton
	G-BMGG	Cessna 152 II	Falcon Flying Services/Biggin Hill
	G-BMGR	Grob G.109B	M. Clarke & D. S. Hawes
	G-BMGY	Lake LA-4-200 Buccaneer	RL Estates Ltd (G-BWKS/G-BDDI)
	G-BMHA	Rutan LongEz	S. F. Elvins
	G-BMHC	Cessna U.206F	Clacton Aero Club (1988) Ltd
	G-BMHJ	Thunder Ax7-65 balloon	M. G. Robinson
	G-BMHL	Wittman W.8 Tailwind	T. G. Hoult

Reg.	Type	Owner or Operator	Notes
G-BMHS	Cessna F.172M	Tango X-Ray Flying Group	
G-BMHT	PA-28RT-201T Turbo Arrow IV	Scalpay Ltd	
G-BMHZ	PA-28RT-201T Turbo Arrow IV	F. Kratky	
G-BMID	Jodel D.120	M. J. Ireland	
G-BMIG	Cessna 172N	J. R. Nicholls/Sibson	
G-BMIH	H.S.125 Srs 700B	Inflite Executive Charter Ltd	
G-BMIM	Rutan LongEz	R. M. Smith	
G-BMIO	Stoddard-Hamilton Glasair RG	P. V. Carrington	
G-BMIP	Jodel D.112	M. T. Kinch	
G-BMIR	Westland Wasp HAS.1 (XT788)	R. Windley	
G-BMIS	Monnett Sonerai II	B. A. Bower/Thruxton	
G-BMIV	PA-28R-201T Turbo Arrow III	Maurice Mason Ltd	
G-BMIW	PA-28-181 Archer II	Oldbus Ltd	
G-BMIY	Oldfield Baby Great Lakes	J. B. Scott (G-NOME)	
G-BMJA	PA-32R-301 Saratoga SP	J. A. Varndell	
G-BMJB	Cessna 152 II	Bobbington Air Training School Ltd/ Halfpenny Green	
G-BMJC	Cessna 152 II	Cambridge Aero Club Ltd	
G-BMJD	Cessna 152 II	Donair Flying Club l.td/E. Midlands	
G-BMJG	PA-28R Cherokee Arrow 200	Western Air Training Ltd	
G-BMJL	R. Commander 114	H. Snelson	
G-BMJM	Evans VP-1	C. A. Macleod	
G-BMJN	Cameron O-65 balloon	P. M. Traviss	
G-BMJO	PA-34-220T Seneca III	Petlon Polymers Ltd	
G-BMJR	Cessna T.337H	John Roberts Services Ltd (G-NOVA)	
G-BMJS	Thunder Ax7-77 balloon	Foulger Transport Ltd	
G-BMJT	Beech 76 Duchess	Mike Osborne Properties Ltd	
G-BMJX	Wallis WA-116X	K. H. Wallis	
G-BMJY	Yakovlev C18M (07)	R. J. Lamplough/North Weald	
G-BMJZ	Cameron N-90 balloon	Bristol University Hot Air Ballooning Soc	
G-BMKB	PA-18 Super Cub 135	Cubair Ltd/Redhill	
G-BMKC	Piper J-3C-65 Cub (329854)	R. J. H. Springall	
G-BMKD	Beech C90A King Air	A. E. Bristow	
G-BMKF	Jodel DR.221	L. Gilbert	
G-BMKG	PA-38-112 Tomahawk II	Bobbington Air Training School Ltd	
G-BMKH	Colt 105A balloon	Scotia Balloons Ltd	
G-BMKJ	Cameron V-77 balloon	R. C. Thursby	
G-BMKK	PA-28R Cherokee Arrow 200	J. H. Hutchinson	
G-BMKP	Cameron V-77 balloon	R. Bayly	
G-BMKR	PA-28-161 Warrior II	Field Flying Group (G-BGKR)/Goodwood	
G-BMKV	Thunder Ax7-77 balloon	A. Hornak & M. J. Nadel	
G-BMKW	Cameron V-77 balloon	A. C. Garnett	
G-BMKY	Cameron O-65 balloon	M. E. White	
G-BMLB	Jodel D.120A	W. O. Brown	
G-BMLJ	Cameron N-77 balloon	C. J. Dunkley	
G-BMLK	Grob G.109B	Brams Syndicate	
G-BMLL	Grob G.109B	A. H. R. Stansfield	
G-BMLS	PA-28R-201 Arrow III	R. M. Shorter	
G-BMLT	Pietenpol Air Camper	W. E. R. Jenkins	
G-BMLU	Colt 90A balloon	L. J. Goldsmith	
G-BMLW	Cameron O-77 balloon	M. L. & L. P. Willoughby	
G-BMLX	Cessna F.150L	C. J. Freeman	
G-BMLZ	Cessna 421C	Hadagain Investments Ltd (G-OTAD/ G-BEVL)	
G-BMMC	Cessna T310Q	Cooper Clegg Ltd	
G-BMMD	Rand KR-2	D. J. Howell	
G-BMMF	FRED Srs 2	J. M. Jones	
G-BMMG	Thunder Ax 7-77 balloon	G. V. Beckwith	
G-BMMI	Pazmany PL.4A	M. K. Field/Sleap	
G-BMMJ	Siren PIK-30	J. R. Greig	
G-BMMK	Cessna 182P	M. S. Knight/Goodwood	
G-BMML	PA-38-112 Tomahawk	Western Air Training Ltd/Thruxton	
G-BMMM	Cessna 152 II	Luton Flight Training Ltd	
G-BMMP	Grob G.109B	E. W. Reynolds	
G-BMMR	Dornier Do.228-200	Suckling Airways Ltd/Cambridge	
G-BMMU	Thunder Ax8-105 balloon	N. Metcalfe	
G-BMMV	ICA-Brasov IS-28M2A	T. Cust	
G-BMMW	Thunder Ax7-77 balloon	P. A. Georges	
G-BMMX	ICA-Brasov IS-28M2A	G-BMMX Syndicate	
G-BMMY	Thunder Ax7-77 balloon	D. A. Lawson	
G-BMNL	PA-28R Cherokee Arrow 200	I. H. Nettleton	
G-BMNP	PA-38-112 Tomahawk II	APB Leasing Ltd/Welshpool	
G-BMNT	PA-34-220T Seneca III	Channel Airways Ltd	

Notes	Reg.	Type	Owner or Operator
	G-BMNV	SNCAN Stampe SV-4D	Wessex Aviation & Transport Ltd
	G-BMNW	PA-31-350 Navajo Chieftain	Crosswind Consultants
	G-BMNX	Colt 56A balloon	J. H. Dryden
	G-BMOE	PA-28R Cherokee Arrow 200	B. J. Mason/Shoreham
	G-BMOF	Cessna U206G	Wild Geese Skydiving Centre
	G-BMOG	Thunder Ax7-77A balloon	P. J. Burn
	G-BMOH	Cameron N-77 balloon	P. J. Marshall & M. A. Clarke
	G-BMOI	Partenavia P.68B	Simmette Ltd
	G-BMOJ	Cameron V-56 balloon	S. R. Bridge
	G-BMOK	ARV Super 2	P. E. Barker
	G-BMOL	PA-23 Aztec 250D	LDL Enterprises (G-BBSR)/Elstree
	G-BMOM	ICA-Brasov IS-28M2A	Brasov Flying Group
	G-BMOO	FRED Srs 2	N. Purllant
	G-BMOP	PA-28R-201T Turbo Arrow III	P. Murer
	G-BMOT	Bensen B.8M	R. S. W. Jones
	G-BMOV	Cameron O-105 balloon	C. Gillott
	G-BMOX	Hovey Beta Bird	A. K. Jones
	G-BMPC	PA-28-181 Archer II	C. J. & R. J. Barnes
	G-BMPD	Cameron V-65 balloon	D. E. & J. M. Hartland
	G-BMPL	Optica Industries OA.7 Optica	FLS Aerospace (Lovaux) Ltd/Bournemouth
	G-BMPP	Cameron N-77 balloon	I. B. Lumsden
	G-BMPR	PA-28R-201 Arrow III	AH Flight Services Ltd
	G-BMPS	Strojnik S-2A	G. J. Green
	G-BMPY	D.H.82A Tiger Moth	S. M. F. Eisenstein
	G-BMRA	Boeing 757-236	British Airways *Beaumaris Castle*
	G-BMRB	Boeing 757-236	British Airways *Colchester Castle*
	G-BMRC	Boeing 757-236	British Airways *Rochester Castle*
	G-BMRD	Boeing 757-236	British Airways *Bothwell Castle*
	G-BMRE	Boeing 757-236	British Airways *Killyleagh Castle*
	G-BMRF	Boeing 757-236	British Airways *Hever Castle*
	G-BMRG	Boeing 757-236	British Airways *Caerphilly Castle*
	G-BMRH	Boeing 757-236	British Airways *Norwich Castle*
	G-BMRI	Boeing 757-236	British Airways *Tonbridge Castle*
	G-BMRJ	Boeing 757-236	British Airways *Old Wardour Castle*
	G-BMSA	Stinson HW.75 Voyager	M. A. Thomas (G-BCUM)/Barton
	G-BMSB	V.S.509 Spitfire IX (MJ627)	M. S. Bayliss (G-ASOZ)/Bruntingthorpe
	G-BMSC	Evans VP-2	T. C. Barron
	G-BMSD	PA-28-181 Archer II	General Airline Ltd
	G-BMSE	Valentin Taifun 17E	A. J. Nurse
	G-BMSF	PA-38-112 Tomahawk	B. Catlow
	G-BMSG	SAAB 32A Lansen ★	Aces High Ltd/Cranfield
	G-BMSI	Cameron N-105 balloon	Direction Air Conditioning Ltd
	G-BMSL	FRED Srs 3	A. C. Coombe
	G-BMSU	Cessna 152 II	G-BMSU Group
	G-BMTA	Cessna 152 II	Turnhouse Flying Club
	G-BMTB	Cessna 152 II	Southern Air Ltd/Shoreham
	G-BMTJ	Cessna 152 II	Creaton Aviation Services Ltd
	G-BMTL	Cessna F.152 II	Agricultural & General Aviation/Bournemouth
	G-BMTN	Cameron O-77 balloon	Industrial Services (MH) Ltd
	G-BMTO	PA-38-112 Tomahawk	Falcon Flying Services/Biggin Hill
	G-BMTP	PA-38-112 Tomahawk	R. A. Wakefield
	G-BMTR	PA-28-161 Warrior II	Aeroshow Ltd
	G-BMTS	Cessna 172N	Falcon Flying Services/Biggin Hill
	G-BMTU	Pitts S-1E Special	O. R. Howe
	G-BMTX	Cameron V-77 balloon	J. A. Langley
	G-BMUD	Cessna 182P	J. P. Edwards
	G-BMUG	Rutan LongEz	P. Richardson & J. Shanley
	G-BMUJ	Colt Drachenfisch balloon	Air 2 Air Ltd
	G-BMUK	Colt UFO balloon	Air 2 Air Ltd
	G-BMUL	Colt Kindermond balloon	Air 2 Air Ltd
	G-BMUN	Cameron 78 Harley SS balloon	Forbes Europe Inc/France
	G-BMUO	Cessna A.152	Redhill Flying Club
	G-BMUT	PA-34-200T Seneca II	Newcastle Aeroplane Co. Ltd
	G-BMUU	Thunder Ax7-77 balloon	G. Anorewartha
	G-BMUZ	PA-28-161 Warrior II	Newcastle-upon-Tyne Aero Club Ltd
	G-BMVA	Schiebe SF.25B Falke	C. A. Simmonds
	G-BMVB	Cessna 152	LAC (Enterprises) Ltd/Barton
	G-BMVE	PA-28RT-201 Arrow IV	F. E. Gooding/Biggin Hill
	G-BMVG	QAC Quickie Q.1	P. M. Wright
	G-BMVI	Cameron O-105 balloon	Heart of England Balloons
	G-RMVJ	Cessna 172N	Green Aviation Associates Ltd
	G-BMVL	PA-38-112 Tomahawk	Airways Aero Associations Ltd/Booker

Reg.	Type	Owner or Operator	Notes
G-BMVM	PA-38-112 Tomahawk	Airways Aero Associations Ltd/Booker	
G-BMVO	Cameron O-77 balloon	Warners Motors (Leasing) Ltd	
G-BMVT	Thunder Ax7-77A balloon	M. L. & L. P. Willoughby	
G-BMVU	Monnett Moni	F. S. Beckett	
G-BMVW	Cameron O-65 balloon	S. P. Richards	
G-BMWA	Hughes 269C	Fenlands Helicopter Centre	
G-BMWE	ARV Super 2	N. R. F. McNally	
G-BMWF	ARV Super 2	N. R. Beale	
G-BMWJ	ARV Super 2	Mid-West Engines Ltd	
G-BMWM	ARV Super 2	R. Scroby	
G-BMWN	Cameron 80 SS Temple balloon	Forbes Europe Inc/France	
G-BMWP	PA-34-200T Seneca II	R. Aarons	
G-BMWR	R. Commander 112A	M. & J. Edwards	
G-BMWU	Cameron N-42 balloon	The Hot Air Balloon Co Ltd	
G-BMWV	Putzer Elster B	E. A. J. Hibbard	
G-BMWX	Robinson R-22B	Lateq Aviation Ltd	
G-BMXA	Cessna 152 II	Chamberlain Leasing	
G-BMXC	Cessna 152 II	European Flyers/Blackbushe	
G-BMXD	F.27 Friendship Mk 500	Air UK Ltd *Victor Hugo*/Norwich	
G-BMXJ	Cessna F.150L	Arrow Aircraft Group	
G-BMXL	PA-38-112 Tomahawk	Airways Aero Associations Ltd/Booker	
G-BMXX	Cessna 152 II	Aerohire Ltd/Halfpenny Green	
G-BMYA	Colt 56A balloon	Flying Pictures (Balloons) Ltd	
G-BMYC	SOCATA TB.10 Tobago	E. A. Grady	
G-BMYD	Beech A36 Bonanza	Seabeam Partners Ltd	
G-BMYF	Bensen B.8M	T. H. G. Russell	
G-BMYG	Cessna FA.152	Rolim Ltd/Aberdeen	
G-BMYI	AA-5 Traveler	W. C. & S. C. Westran	
G-BMYJ	Cameron V-65 balloon	A. Lutz	
G-BMYN	Colt 77A balloon	J. D. Shapland & ptnrs	
G-BMYP	Fairey Gannet AEW.3 (XL502)	R. H. Cooper/Gamston	
G-BMYS	Thunder Ax7-77Z balloon	J. E. Weidema	
G-BMYU	Jodel D.120	P. M. Standen & A. J. Roxburgh	
G-BMYW	Hughes 269C	March Helicopters Ltd/Sywell	
G-BMZA	Air Command 503 Commander	R. W. Husband	
G-BMZB	Cameron N-77 balloon	D. C. Eager	
G-BMZC	Cessna 421C	Air Nova PLC/Liverpool	
G-BMZD	Beech C90 King Air	Colt Transport Ltd	
G-BMZE	SOCATA TB.9 Tampico	Air Touring Services Ltd/Biggin Hill	
G-BMZF	Mikoyan Gurevich MiG-15 (1420) ★	F.A.A. Museum/Yeovilton	
G-BMZG	QAC Quickie Q.2	T. D. Edmunds	
G-BMZJ	Colt 400A balloon	G. J. Bell	
G-BMZN	Everett gyroplane	A. Gault	
G-BMZP	Everett gyroplane	B. C. Norris	
G-BMZS	Everett gyroplane	L. W. Cload	
G-BMZW	Bensen B.8MR	P. D. Widdicombe	
G-BMZX	Wolf W-II Boredom Fighter (146-11042)	A. R. Meakin & S. W. Watkins	
G-BMZZ	Stephens Akro 2	F. Actis/Switzerland	
G-BNAD	Rand KR-2	P. J. Brookman	
G-BNAG	Colt 105A balloon	R. W. Batchelor	
G-BNAH	Colt Paper Bag SS balloon	Thrustell Ltd/USA	
G-BNAI	Wolf W-II Boredom Fighter (146-11083)	P. J. D. Gronow	
G-BNAJ	Cessna 152 II	Galair Ltd/Biggin Hill	
G-BNAN	Cameron V-65 balloon	A. M. Lindsay	
G-BNAO	Colt AS-105 airship	Heather Flight Ltd	
G-BNAP	Colt 240A balloon	Heather Flight Ltd	
G-BNAR	Taylor JT.1 Monoplane	C. J. Smith	
G-BNAU	Cameron V-65 balloon	C. L. E. Lewis	
G-BNAW	Cameron V-65 balloon	A. Walker	
G-BNBL	Thunder Ax7-77 balloon	E. Stivala	
G-BNBM	Colt 90A balloon	Huntair Ltd	
G-BNBR	Cameron N-90 balloon	Airborne Promotions Ltd	
G-BNBU	Bensen B.8MV	R. Retallick	
G-BNBV	Thunder Ax7-77 balloon	J. M. Robinson	
G-BNBW	Thunder Ax7-77 balloon	I. S. & S. W. Watthews	
G-BNBY	Beech 95-B55A Baron	Richard Hannon Ltd (G-AXXR)	
G-BNBZ	LET L-200D Morava	C. A. Suckling/Redhill	
G-BNCB	Cameron V-77 balloon	Tyred & Battered Balloon Group	
G-BNCC	Thunder Ax7-77 balloon	C. J. Burnhope	

Notes	Reg.	Type	Owner or Operator
	G-BNCE	G.159 Gulfstream 1★	(stored)/Aberdeen
	G-BNCG	QAC Quickie Q.2	T. F. Francis
	G-BNCH	Cameron V-77 balloon	Royal Engineers Balloon Club
	G-BNCJ	Cameron V-77 balloon	I. S. Bridge
	G-BNCK	Cameron V-77 balloon	G. Randall/Germany
	G-BNCL	WG.13 Lynx HAS.2 (XX469) ★	Lancashire Fire Brigade HQ/Lancaster
	G-BNCM	Cameron N-77 balloon	S. & A. Stone Ltd
	G-BNCN	Glaser-Dirks DG.400	M. C. Costin/Husbands Bosworth
	G-BNCO	PA-38-112 Tomahawk	Aerohire Ltd/Halfpenny Green
	G-BNCR	PA-28-161 Warrior II	Airways Aero Associations Ltd/Booker
	G-BNCS	Cessna 180	C. Elwell Transport Ltd
	G-BNCU	Thunder Ax7-77 balloon	P. Mann
	G-BNCV	Bensen B.8	J. M. Benton
	G-BNCX	Hunter T.7 ★	Lovaux Ltd (stored)/Bournemouth
	G-BNCY	F.27 Friendship Mk 500	Air UK Ltd Lillie Langtry/Norwich
	G-BNCZ	Rutan LongEz	R. M. Bainbridge/Sherburn
	G-BNDG	Wallis WA-201/R Srs1	K. H. Wallis
	G-BNDH	Colt 21A balloon	Hot-Air Balloon Co Ltd
	G-BNDN	Cameron V-77 balloon	J. A. Smith
	G-BNDO	Cessna 152 II	Simair Ltd
	G-BNDP	Brügger MB.2 Colibri	D. A. Peet
	G-BNDR	SOCATA TB.10 Tobago	A. N. Reardon/Woodvale
	G-BNDS	PA-31-350 Navajo Chieftain	Owen Air Ltd/Biggin Hill
	G-BNDT	Brügger MB.2 Colibri	Colibri Flying Group
	G-BNDV	Cameron N-77 balloon	R. E. Jones
	G-BNDW	D.H.82A Tiger Moth	N. D. Welch
	G-BNDY	Cessna 425-1	Standard Aviation Ltd/Newcastle
	G-BNED	PA-22 Tri-Pacer 135	P. Storey
	G-BNEE	PA-28R-201 Arrow III	Britannic Management (Aviation) Ltd
	G-BNEI	PA-34-200T Seneca II	A. Bucknole
	G-BNEJ	PA-38-112 Tomahawk II	V. C. & S. G. Swindell
	G-BNEK	PA-38-112 Tomahawk II	APB Leasing Ltd/Welshpool
	G-BNEL	PA-28-161 Warrior II	Southern Air Ltd/Shoreham
	G-BNEN	PA-34-200T Seneca II	Warwickshire Aerocentre Ltd
	G-BNEO	Cameron V-77 balloon	J. G. O'Connell
	G-BNER	PA-34-200T Seneca II	R. I. Sharpe
	G-BNES	Cameron V-77 balloon	G. Wells
	G-BNET	Cameron O-84 balloon	J. Bennett & Son (Insurance Brokers) Ltd
	G-BNEV	Viking Dragonfly	N. W. Eyre
	G-BNEX	Cameron O-120 balloon	The Balloon Club Ltd
	G-BNFG	Cameron O-77 balloon	Capital Balloon Club Ltd
	G-BNFI	Cessna 150J	T. D. Aitken
	G-BNFK	Cameron 89 Egg SS balloon	Forbes Europe Inc/France
	G-BNFL	WHE Airbuggy	Roger Savage (Photography) (G-AXXN)
	G-BNFM	Colt 21A balloon	M. E. Dworski
	G-BNFN	Cameron N-105 balloon	P. Glydon
	G-BNFO	Cameron V-77 balloon	D. C. Patrick-Brown
	G-BNFP	Cameron O-84 balloon	B. F. G. Ribbans
	G-BNFR	Cessna 152 II	London Flight Centre (Stansted) Ltd
	G-BNFS	Cessna 152 II	London Flight Centre (Stansted) Ltd
	G-BNFV	Robin DR.400/120	Exeter Flying Club Ltd
	G-BNFW	H.S.125 Srs 700B	Lynton Aviation Ltd
	G-BNFY	Cameron N-77 balloon	The New Holker Estates Co Ltd
	G-BNGD	Cessna 152 II	AV Aviation Ltd
	G-BNGE	Auster AOP.6 (TW536)	R. W. W. Eastman
	G-BNGJ	Cameron V-77 balloon	Latham Timber Centres (Holdings) Ltd
	G-BNGN	Cameron V-77 balloon	A. R. & L. J. McGregor
	G-BNGO	Thunder Ax7-77 balloon	J. S. Finlan
	G-BNGP	Colt 77A balloon	Headland Services Ltd
	G-BNGR	PA-38-112 Tomahawk	Teesside Flight Centre Ltd
	G-BNGS	PA-38-112 Tomahawk	Frontline Aviation Ltd/Teesside
	G-BNGT	PA-28-181 Archer II	Berry Air/Edinburgh
	G-BNGV	ARV Super 2	N. A. Onions
	G-BNGW	ARV Super 2	Southern Gas Turbines Ltd
	G-BNGX	ARV Super 2	Southern Gas Turbines Ltd
	G-BNGY	ARV Super 2	T. E. G. Buckett (G-BMWL)
	G-BNHB	ARV Super 2	Super Two Group
	G-BNHC	ARV Super 2	I. C. Whyte
	G-BNHD	ARV Super 2	Aviation (Scotland) Ltd
	G-BNHE	ARV Super 2	L. J. Joyce/Liverpool
	G-BNHG	PA-38-112 Tomahawk II	D. A. Whitmore
	G-BNHH	Thunder Ax7-77 balloon	Gee-Tee Signs Ltd
	G-BNHI	Cameron V-77 balloon	P. J. Feltham & C. J. Nicholls

Reg.	Type	Owner or Operator	Notes
G-BNHJ	Cessna 152 II	The Pilot Centre Ltd/Denham	
G-BNHK	Cessna 152 II	General Airline Ltd	
G-BNHL	Colt 90 Beer Glass SS balloon	G. V. Beckwith	
G-BNHN	Colt Ariel Bottle SS balloon ★	British Balloon Museum/Newbury	
G-BNHO	Thunder Ax7-77 balloon	M. J. Forster	
G-BNHP	Saffrey S.330 balloon	N. H. Ponsford *Alpha II*	
G-BNHR	Cameron V-77 balloon	P. C. Waterhouse	
G-BNHT	Fournier RF-3	G-BNHT Group	
G-BNIB	Cameron A-105 balloon	A. G. E. Faulkner	
G-BNID	Cessna 152 II	Mercia Aircraft Leasing & Sales Ltd/ Coventry	
G-BNIE	Cameron O-160 balloon	D. K. Fish	
G-BNIF	Cameron O-56 balloon	D. V. Fowler	
G-BNII	Cameron N-90 balloon	Continu-Forms Holdings PLC	
G-BNIJ	SOCATA TB.10 Tobago	Flying Start Aviation	
G-BNIK	Robin HR.200/120	A. J. McNeal/Popham	
G-BNIM	PA-38-112 Tomahawk	T. S. Kemp	
G-BNIN	Cameron V-77 balloon	Cloud Nine Balloon Group	
G-BNIO	Luscombe 8A Silvaire	G. G. Pugh	
G-BNIP	Luscombe 8A Silvaire	D. R. C. Hunter & S. Maric	
G-BNIU	Cameron O-77 balloon	Nottingham Hot Air Balloon Club & Mitchell Air Power Ltd	
G-BNIV	Cessna 152 II	Aerohire Ltd/Halfpenny Green	
G-BNIW	Boeing Stearman PT-17	Lintally Ltd/E. Midlands	
G-BNIX	EMB-110P1 Bandeirante	Air Tabernacle Ltd	
G-BNIZ	F.27 Friendship Mk.600	Channel Express (Air Services) Ltd/Bournemouth	
G-BNJA	WAG-Aero Wag-a-Bond	B. E. Maggs	
G-BNJB	Cessna 152 II	Klingair Ltd/Conington	
G-BNJC	Cessna 152 II	Stapleford Flying Club Ltd	
G-BNJD	Cessna 152 II	Southern Air Ltd/Shoreham	
G-BNJE	Cessna A.152	D. D. Delaney	
G-BNJF	PA-32RT-300 Lance II	Biggles Aviation Ltd	
G-BNJG	Cameron O-77 balloon	A. M. Figiel	
G-BNJH	Cessna 152 II	Turnhouse Flying Club	
G-BNJM	PA-28-161 Warrior II	Teesside Flight Centre Ltd	
G-BNJO	QAC Quickie Q.2	J. D. McKay	
G-BNJR	PA-28RT-201T Turbo Arrow IV	Intelligent Micro Software Ltd	
G-BNJT	PA-28-161 Warrior II	Hawarden Flying Group	
G-BNJU	Cameron 80 Bust SS balloon	Forbes Europe Inc/France	
G-BNJX	Cameron N-90 balloon	Mars UK Ltd	
G-BNJZ	Cassutt Racer IIIM	A. P. Meredith & J. R. Burry	
G-BNKC	Cessna 152 II	Herefordshire Aero Club Ltd/Shobdon	
G-BNKD	Cessna 172N	Bristol Flying Centre Ltd	
G-BNKE	Cessna 172N	Kilo Echo Flying Group	
G-BNKF	Colt AS-56 airship	Formtrack Ltd	
G-BNKH	PA-38-112 Tomahawk	Goodwood Terrena Ltd	
G-BNKI	Cessna 152 II	RAF Halton Aeroplane Club Ltd	
G-BNKP	Cessna 152 II	Clacton Aero Club (1988) Ltd	
G-BNKR	Cessna 152 II	Marnham Investments Ltd	
G-BNKS	Cessna 152 II	Shropshire Aero Club Ltd/Sleap	
G-BNKT	Cameron O-77 balloon	British Airways PLC	
G-BNKV	Cessna 152 II	Vectair Aviation 1995 Ltd	
G-BNKW	PA-38-112 Tomahawk	D. M. MacLean	
G-BNKX	Robinson R-22	Brian Seedle Helicopters/Blackpool	
G-BNLA	Boeing 747-436	British Airways *City of London*	
G-BNLB	Boeing 747-436	British Airways *City of Edinburgh*	
G-BNLC	Boeing 747-436	British Airways *City of Cardiff*	
G-BNLD	Boeing 747-436	British Airways *City of Belfast*	
G-BNLE	Boeing 747-436	British Airways *City of Newcastle*	
G-BNLF	Boeing 747-436	British Airways *City of Leeds*	
G-BNLG	Boeing 747-436	British Airways *City of Southampton*	
G-BNLH	Boeing 747-436	British Airways *City of Westminster*	
G-BNLI	Boeing 747-436	British Airways *City of Sheffield*	
G-BNLJ	Boeing 747-436	British Airways *City of Nottingham*	
G-BNLK	Boeing 747-436	British Airways *City of Bristol*	
G-BNLL	Boeing 747-436	British Airways *City of Leicester*	
G-BNLM	Boeing 747-436	British Airways *City of Durham*	
G-BNLN	Boeing 747-436	British Airways *City of Portsmouth*	
G-BNLO	Boeing 747-436	British Airways *City of Dundee*	
G-BNLP	Boeing 747-436	British Airways *City of Aberdeen*	
G-BNLR	Boeing 747-436	British Airways *City of Hull*	
G-BNLS	Boeing 747-436	British Airways *City of Chester*	

Notes	Reg.	Type	Owner or Operator
	G-BNLT	Boeing 747-436	British Airways *City of Lincoln*
	G-BNLU	Boeing 747-436	British Airways *City of Bangor*
	G-BNLV	Boeing 747-436	British Airways *City of Exeter*
	G-BNLW	Boeing 747-436	British Airways *City of Norwich*
	G-BNLX	Boeing 747-436	British Airways *City of Worcester*
	G-BNLY	Boeing 747-436	British Airways *City of Swansea*
	G-BNLZ	Boeing 747-436	British Airways *City of Perth*
	G-BNMA	Cameron O-77 balloon	T. A. Hains
	G-BNMB	PA-28-151 Warrior	Britannia Airways Ltd/Luton
	G-BNMC	Cessna 152 II	M. L. Jones/Egginton
	G-BNMD	Cessna 152 II	T. M. Jones/Egginton
	G-BNME	Cessna 152 II	L. V. Atkinson
	G-BNMF	Cessna 152 II	Aerohire Ltd
	G-BNMG	Cameron O-77 balloon	Windsor Life Assurance Co Ltd
	G-BNMH	Pietenpol Air Camper	N. M. Hitchman
	G-BNMI	Colt Flying Fantasy SS balloon	Air 2 Air Ltd
	G-BNMK	Dornier Do.27A-1	G. Mackie
	G-BNML	Rand KR-2	H. C. Walker
	G-BNMO	Cessna TR.182RG	R. R. Greaves
	G-BNMP	Cessna R.182RG	P. M. Breton
	G-BNMX	Thunder Ax7-77 balloon	S. A. D. Beard
	G-BNNA	Stolp SA.300 Starduster Too	D. F. Simpson
	G-BNNC	Cameron N-77 balloon	T. M. McCoy/Barrow
	G-BNNE	Cameron N-77 balloon	The Balloon Stable Ltd
	G-BNNG	Cessna T.337D	Somet Ltd (G-COLD)
	G-BNNI	Boeing 727-276	Sabre Airways Ltd/Gatwick
	G-BNNK	Boeing 737-4Q8	GB Airways Ltd
	G-BNNL	Boeing 737-4Q8	GB Airways Ltd
	G-BNNO	PA-28-161 Warrior II	W. Lancs Aero Club Ltd/Woodvale
	G-BNNR	Cessna 152	Sussex Flying Club Ltd/Shoreham
	G-BNNS	PA-28-161 Warrior II	M. J. Allen & B. E. Davies
	G-BNNT	PA-28-151 Warrior	S. T. Gilbert & D. J. Kirkwood
	G-BNNU	PA-38-112 Tomahawk	Edinburgh Flying Club Ltd
	G-BNNX	PA-28R-201T Turbo Arrow III	P. J. Lague
	G-BNNY	PA-28-161 Warrior II	Falcon Flying Services/Biggin Hill
	G-BNNZ	PA-28-161 Warrior II	D. Heater/Fairoaks
	G-BNOB	Wittman W.8 Tailwind	M. Robson-Robinson
	G-BNOE	PA-28-161 Warrior II	Sherburn Aero Club Ltd
	G-BNOF	PA-28-161 Warrior II	BAe Flying College/Prestwick
	G-BNOG	PA-28-161 Warrior II	BAe Flying College/Prestwick
	G-BNOH	PA-28-161 Warrior II	Sherburn Aero Club Ltd
	G-BNOI	PA-28-161 Warrior II	BAe Flying College/Prestwick
	G-BNOJ	PA-28-161 Warrior II	BAe (Warton) Flying Club
	G-BNOK	PA-28-161 Warrior II	BAe Flying College/Prestwick
	G-BNOL	PA-28-161 Warrior II	BAe Flying College/Prestwick
	G-BNOM	PA-28-161 Warrior II	Sherburn Aero Club Ltd
	G-BNON	PA-28-161 Warrior II	BAe Flying College/Prestwick
	G-BNOO	PA-28-161 Warrior II	BAe Flying College/Prestwick
	G-BNOP	PA-28-161 Warrior II	BAe Flying College/Prestwick
	G-BNOR	PA-28-161 Warrior II	BAe Flying College/Prestwick
	G-BNOS	PA-28-161 Warrior II	BAe Flying College/Prestwick
	G-BNOT	PA-28-161 Warrior II	BAe Flying College/Prestwick
	G-BNOU	PA-28-161 Warrior II	BAe Flying College/Prestwick
	G-BNOV	PA-28-161 Warrior II	BAe Flying College/Prestwick
	G-BNOW	PA-28-161 Warrior II	BAe Flying College/Prestwick
	G-BNOX	Cessna R.182RG II	Char Wallahs Ltd
	G-BNOY	Colt 90A balloon	Huntair Ltd
	G-BNOZ	Cessna 152 II	APB Leasing Ltd/Welshpool
	G-BNPD	PA-23 Aztec 250E	County Garage (Cheltenham) Ltd/ Staverton
	G-BNPE	Cameron N-77 balloon	Kent Garden Centres Ltd
	G-BNPF	Slingsby T.31M	S. Luck & ptnrs
	G-BNPH	P.66 Pembroke C.1 (WV740)	M. J. Willing/Jersey
	G-BNPI	Colt 21A balloon	Virgin Airship & Balloon Co Ltd
	G-BNPL	PA-38-112 Tomahawk	Modern Air (UK) Ltd/Fowlmere
	G-BNPM	PA-38-112 Tomahawk	Papa Mike Aviation Ltd
	G-BNPN	PA-28-181 Archer II	Sherani Aviation/Elstree
	G-BNPO	PA-28-181 Archer II	Bonus Aviation Ltd
	G-BNPV	Bowers Fly-Baby 1B	J. G. Day & R. Gauld-Galliers
	G-BNPY	Cessna 152 II	Traffic Management Services/Gamston
	G-BNPZ	Cessna 152 II	Bristol Flying Centre Ltd
	G-BNRA	SOCATA TB.10 Tobago	W. R. M. Beesley
	G-BNRG	PA-28-161 Warrior II	RAF Brize Norton Flying Club Ltd

Reg.	Type	Owner or Operator	Notes
G-BNRI	Cessna U.206G	Target Technology Ltd	
G-BNRK	Cessna 152 II	Redhill Flying Club	
G-BNRL	Cessna 152 II	J. R. Nicholls/Sibson	
G-BNRP	PA-28-181 Archer II	Bonua Aviation Ltd/Cranfield	
G-BNRR	Cessna 172P	Skyhawk Group	
G-BNRU	Cameron V-77 balloon	M. A. Mueller	
G-BNRW	Colt 69A balloon	Callers Pegasus Travel Service Ltd	
G-BNRX	PA-34-200T Seneca II	R. A. & K. M. Roberts	
G-BNRY	Cessna 182Q	Reefly Ltd	
G-BNRZ	Robinson R-22B	W. Jordan Millers Ltd	
G-BNSG	PA-28R-201 Arrow III	Armada Aviation Ltd/Redhill	
G-BNSI	Cessna 152 II	Sky Leisure Aviation Ltd/Shoreham	
G-BNSL	PA-38-112 Tomahawk II	M. H. Kleiser	
G-BNSM	Cessna 152 II	Cornwall Flying Club Ltd/Bodmin	
G-BNSN	Cessna 152 II	M. K. Barnes & G. N. Olson/Bristol	
G-BNSO	Slingsby T.67M Mk II	Trent Air Services Ltd/Cranfield	
G-BNSP	Slingsby T.67M Mk II	Trent Air Services Ltd/Cranfield	
G-BNSR	Slingsby T.67M Mk II	Trent Air Services Ltd/Cranfield	
G-BNST	Cessna 172N	Traffic Management Services/Gamston	
G-BNSU	Cessna 152 II	Channel Aviation Ltd	
G-BNSV	Cessna 152 II	Channel Aviation Ltd	
G-BNSW	Cessna 152 II	One Zero One Three Ltd	
G-BNSY	PA-28-161 Warrior II	Carill Aviation Ltd/Southampton	
G-BNSZ	PA-28-161 Warrior II	Carill Aviation Ltd/Southampton	
G-BNTC	PA-28RT-201T Turbo Arrow IV	Hollingworth & Co (Midlands) Ltd	
G-BNTD	PA-28-161 Warrior II	A. M. Patel & ptnrs	
G-BNTE	FFA AS.202/18A4 Bravo	BAe Flying College Ltd/Prestwick	
G-BNTF	FFA AS.202/18A4 Bravo	BAe Flying College Ltd/Prestwick	
G-BNTH	FFA AS.202/18A4 Bravo	BAe Flying College Ltd/Prestwick	
G-BNTI	FFA AS.202/18A4 Bravo	BAe Flying College Ltd/Prestwick	
G-BNTJ	FFA AS.202/18A4 Bravo	BAe Flying College Ltd/Prestwick	
G-BNTK	FFA AS.202/18A4 Bravo	BAe Flying College Ltd/Prestwick	
G-BNTL	FFA AS.202/18A4 Bravo	BAe Flying College Ltd/Prestwick	
G-BNTM	FFA AS.202/18A4 Bravo	BAe Flying College Ltd/Prestwick	
G-BNTN	FFA AS.202/18A4 Bravo	BAe Flying College Ltd/Prestwick	
G-BNTO	FFA AS.202/18A4 Bravo	BAe Flying College Ltd/Prestwick	
G-BNTP	Cessna 172N	Westnet Ltd	
G-BNTS	PA-28RT-201T Turbo Arrow IV	Nasaire Ltd/Liverpool	
G-BNTT	Beech 76 Duchess	L. & J. Donne	
G-BNTW	Cameron V-77 balloon	P. Goss	
G-BNTX	Short SD3-30 Variant 100	Shorts Aircraft Leasing Ltd (G-BKDN)	
G-BNTY	Short SD3-30 Variant 100	Shorts Aircraft Leasing Ltd (G-BKDO)	
G-BNTZ	Cameron N-77 balloon	Balloon Team	
G-BNUC	Cameron O-77 balloon	T. J. Bucknall	
G-BNUI	Rutan Vari-Eze	D. A. Paine	
G-BNUL	Cessna 152 II	Exeter Air Training School Ltd	
G-BNUN	Beech 95-58PA Baron	British Midland Airways Ltd/E. Midlands	
G-BNUO	Beech 76 Duchess	G. A. F. Tilley	
G-BNUR	Cessna 172E	Cardiff Aeronautical Services Ltd	
G-BNUS	Cessna 152 II	Stapleford Flying Club Ltd	
G-BNUT	Cessna 152 Turbo	Stapleford Flying Club Ltd	
G-BNUV	PA-23 Aztec 250F	L. J. Martin	
G-BNUX	Hoffmann H-36 Dimona	Buckminster Dimona Syndicate	
G-BNUY	PA-38-112 Tomahawk II	Aerohire Ltd	
G-BNUZ	Robinson R-22B	J. C. Reid	
G-BNVB	AA-5A Cheetah	W. J. Siertsema & A. M. Glazer	
G-BNVD	PA-38-112 Tomahawk	Channel Aviation Ltd	
G-BNVE	PA-28-181 Archer II	Steve Parrish Racing	
G-BNVI	ARV Super 2	Adrianair Ltd	
G-BNVT	PA-28RT-201T Turbo Arrow III	Victor Tango Group	
G-BNVZ	Beech 95-B55 Baron	W. J. Forrest & P. Schon	
G-BNWA	Boeing 767-336ER	British Airways *City of Brussels*	
G-BNWB	Boeing 767-336ER	British Airways *City of Paris*	
G-BNWC	Boeing 767-336ER	British Airways *City of Frankfurt*	
G-BNWD	Boeing 767-336ER	British Airways *City of Copenhagen*	
G-BNWE	Boeing 767-336ER	British Airways *City of Lisbon*	
G-BNWF	Boeing 767-336ER	British Airways *City of Milan*	
G-BNWG	Boeing 767-336ER	British Airways *City of Strasbourg*	
G-BNWH	Boeing 767-336ER	British Airways *City of Rome*	
G-BNWI	Boeing 767-336ER	British Airways *City of Madrid*	
G-BNWJ	Boeing 767-336ER	British Airways *City of Athens*	
G-BNWK	Boeing 767-336ER	British Airways *City of Amsterdam*	
G-BNWL	Boeing 767-336ER	British Airways *City of Luxembourg*	

Notes	Reg.	Type	Owner or Operator
	G-BNWM	Boeing 767-336ER	British Airways *City of Toulouse*
	G-BNWN	Boeing 767-336ER	British Airways *City of Berlin*
	G-BNWO	Boeing 767-336ER	British Airways *City of Barcelona*
	G-BNWP	Boeing 767-336ER	British Airways *City of Dublin*
	G-BNWR	Boeing 767-336ER	British Airways *City of Hamburg*
	G-BNWS	Boeing 767-336ER	British Airways *City of Oporto*
	G-BNWT	Boeing 767-336ER	British Airways *City of Cork*
	G-BNWU	Boeing 767-336ER	British Airways *Robert Burns*
	G-BNWV	Boeing 767-336ER	British Airways *City of Bonn*
	G-BNWW	Boeing 767-336ER	British Airways *City of Marseilles*
	G-BNWX	Boeing 767-336ER	British Airways *City of Bilbao*
	G-BNWY	Boeing 767-336ER	British Airways
	G-BNWZ	Boeing 767-336ER	British Airways
	G-BNXA	BN-2A-26 Islander	Atlantic Air Transport Ltd/Coventry
	G-BNXC	Cessna 152 II	Sir W. G. Armstrong-Whitworth Flying Group/Coventry
	G-BNXD	Cessna 172N	A. Jahanfar
	G-BNXE	PA-28-161 Warrior II	Rugby Autobody Repairs/Coventry
	G-BNXI	Robin DR.400/180R	London Gliding Club Pty Ltd/Dunstable
	G-BNXK	Nott-Cameron ULD-3 balloon	J. R. P. Nott
	G-BNXL	Glaser-Dirks DG.400	A. J. Chappell & J. McLaughlin
	G-BNXM	PA-18 Super Cub 95	G-BNXM Group
	G-BNXR	Cameron O-84 balloon	J. A. & N. J. Ballard Gray
	G-BNXT	PA-28-161 Warrior II	Falcon Flying Services/Manston
	G-BNXU	PA-28-161 Warrior II	Friendly Warrior Group
	G-BNXV	PA-38-112 Tomahawk	Falcon Flying Services/Manston
	G-BNXX	SOCATA TB.20 Trinidad	D. M. Carr
	G-BNXZ	Thunder Ax7-77 balloon	Hale Hot Air Balloon Group
	G-BNYB	PA-28-201T Turbo Dakota	A. G. E. Camisa & C. J. Freeman
	G-BNYD	Bell 206B JetRanger 3	Sterling Helicopters Ltd/Norwich
	G-BNYJ	Cessna 421B	Charles Robertson (Developments) Ltd
	G-BNYK	PA-38-112 Tomahawk	APB Leasing Ltd/Welshpool
	G-BNYL	Cessna 152 II	APB Leasing Ltd/Welshpool
	G-BNYM	Cessna 172N	N. B. Lindley
	G-BNYN	Cessna 152 II	Redhill Flying Club
	G-BNYO	Beech 76 Duchess	Skyhawk Ltd
	G-BNYP	PA-28-181 Archer II	R. D. Cooper/Cranfield
	G-BNYS	Boeing 767-204ER	Britannia Airways Ltd/Luton
	G-BNYU	Faithfull Ax7-61A balloon	M. L. Faithfull
	G-BNYV	PA-38-112 Tomahawk	Channel Aviation Ltd/Guernsey
	G-BNYX	Denney Kitfox Mk 1	R. W. Husband
	G-BNYY	PA-28RT-201T Turbo Arrow IV	Metafin Group Holdings
	G-BNYZ	SNCAN Stampe SV-4E	Tapestry Colour Ltd
	G-BNZB	PA-28-161 Warrior II	Falcon Flying Services/Biggin Hill
	G-BNZC	D.H.C.1 Chipmunk 22 (18671)	D. A. Horsley
	G-BNZG	PA-28RT-201T Turbo Arrow IV	Brightday Ltd
	G-BNZJ	Colt 21A balloon	N. Charbonnier
	G-BNZK	Thunder Ax7-77 balloon	T. D. Marsden
	G-BNZL	Rotorway Scorpion 133	J. R. Wraight
	G-BNZM	Cessna T.210N	A. J. M. Freeman
	G-BNZO	Rotorway Executive	M. G. Wiltshire
	G-BNZR	FRED Srs 2	R. M. Waugh
	G-BNZS	Mooney M.20K	D. G. Millington
	G-BNZV	PA-25 Pawnee 235	Northumbria Soaring Co Ltd
	G-BNZZ	PA-28-161 Warrior II	Zoom Photographic Ltd
	G-BOAA	Concorde 102	British Airways (G-N94AA)
	G-BOAB	Concorde 102	British Airways (G-N94AB)
	G-BOAC	Concorde 102	British Airways (G-N81AC)
	G-BOAD	Concorde 102	British Airways (G-N94AD)
	G-BOAE	Concorde 102	British Airways (G-N94AE)
	G-BOAF	Concorde 102	British Airways (G-N94AF/G-BFKX)
	G-BOAG	Concorde 102	British Airways (G-BFKW)
	G-BOAH	PA-28-161 Warrior II	Plane Talking Ltd/Elstree
	G-BOAI	Cessna 152 II	Galair Ltd/Biggin Hill
	G-BOAK	PA-22 Tri-Pacer 150	A. M. Noble
	G-BOAL	Cameron V-65 balloon	A. M. Lindsay
	G-BOAM	Robinson R-22B	Bristow Helicopters Ltd/Redhill
	G-BOAO	Thunder Ax7-77 balloon	D. V. Fowler
	G-BOAS	Air Command 503 Commander	R. Robinson
	G-BOAU	Cameron V-77 balloon	G. T. Barstow
	G-BOBA	PA-28R-201 Arrow III	Bobbington Air Training School Ltd/ Halfpenny Green

Reg.	Type	Owner or Operator	Notes
G-BOBB	Cameron O-120 balloon	J. M. Albury	
G-BOBC	BN-2T Turbine Islander	Pilatus BN Ltd (G-BJYZ)/Bembridge	
G-BOBD	Cameron O-160 balloon	A. C. K. Rawson & J. J. Rudoni	
G-BOBF	Brügger MB.2 Colibri	R. Bennett	
G-BOBG	Jodel 150	C. A. Laycock	
G-BOBH	Airtour AH-77 balloon	J. & K. Francis	
G-BOBJ	PA-38-112 Tomahawk	Air Touring Services Ltd/Biggin Hill	
G-BOBK	PA-38-112 Tomahawk	Air Touring Services Ltd/Biggin Hill	
G-BOBL	PA-38-112 Tomahawk	Aerohire Ltd/Halfpenny Green	
G-BOBN	Cessna 310R	Edinburgh Air Charter Ltd	
G-BOBR	Cameron N-77 balloon	C. Bradley	
G-BOBS	Quickie Q.2	M. A. Hales	
G-BOBT	Stolp SA.300 Starduster Too	G-BOBT Group	
G-BOBU	Colt 90A balloon	Prescott Hot Air Balloons Ltd	
G-BOBV	Cessna F.150M	Sheffield Aero Club Ltd/Netherthorpe	
G-BOBY	Monnett Sonerai II	R. G. Hallam *(stored)*/Sleap	
G-BOBZ	PA-28-181 Archer II	Trustcomms International Ltd	
G-BOCC	PA-38-112 Tomahawk	B. Gradidge & R. A. Sparshatt-Worley	
G-BOCF	Colt 77A balloon	Lindstrand Balloons Ltd	
G-BOCG	PA-34-200T Seneca II	Magenta Ltd/Kidlington	
G-BOCH	PA-32 Cherokee Six 300	J. W. Moss	
G-BOCI	Cessna 140A	G. J. Slater	
G-BOCK	Sopwith Triplane (replica) (N6290)	The Shuttleworth Collection/O. Warden	
G-BOCL	Slingsby T.67C	C.S.E. Aviation Ltd/Kidlington	
G-BOCM	Slingsby T.67C	C.S.E. Aviation Ltd/Kidlington	
G-BOCN	Robinson R-22B	Sloane Helicopters Ltd/Sywell	
G-BOCP	PA-34-220T Seneca III	BAe Flying College Ltd/Prestwick	
G-BOCR	PA-34-220T Seneca III	BAe Flying College Ltd/Prestwick	
G-BOCS	PA-34-220T Seneca III	BAe Flying College Ltd/Prestwick	
G-BOCT	PA-34-220T Seneca III	BAe Flying College Ltd/Prestwick	
G-BOCU	PA-34-220T Seneca III	BAe Flying College Ltd/Prestwick	
G-BOCV	PA-34-220T Seneca III	BAe Flying College Ltd/Prestwick	
G-BOCW	PA-34-220T Seneca III	BAe Flying College Ltd/Prestwick	
G-BOCX	PA-34-220T Seneca III	BAe Flying College Ltd/Prestwick	
G-BOCY	PA-34-220T Seneca III	BAe Flying College Ltd/Prestwick	
G-BODA	PA-28-161 Warrior II	C.S.E. Aviation Ltd/Kidlington	
G-BODB	PA-28-161 Warrior II	C.S.E. Aviation Ltd/Kidlington	
G-BODC	PA-28-161 Warrior II	C.S.E. Aviation Ltd/Kidlington	
G-BODD	PA-28-161 Warrior II	C.S.E. Aviation Ltd/Kidlington	
G-BODE	PA-28-161 Warrior II	C.S.E. Aviation Ltd/Kidlington	
G-BODF	PA-28-161 Warrior II	C.S.E. Aviation Ltd/Kidlington	
G-BODG	Slingsby T.31 Motor Cadet III	H. P. Vox	
G-BODH	Slingsby T.31 Motor Cadet III	H. P. Vox (G-ALNK)	
G-BODI	Stoddard-Hamilton Glasair III	Jackson Barr Ltd	
G-BODK	Rotorway Scorpion 133	J. Brannigan	
G-BODM	PA-28 Cherokee 180	W. B. Ware	
G-BODO	Cessna 152	A. R. Sarson	
G-BODP	PA-38÷-112 Tomahawk	D. A. Whitmore	
G-BODR	PA-28-161 Warrior II	Airways Aero Associations Ltd/Booker	
G-BODS	PA-38-112 Tomahawk	Ipswich School of Flying Ltd	
G-BODT	Jodel D.18	L. D. McPhillips	
G-BODU	Scheibe SF.25C	Monica English Memorial Trust	
G-BODX	Beech 76 Duchess	R. J. Dajczak/Welshpool	
G-BODY	Cessna 310R	Atlantic Air Transport Ltd/Coventry	
G-BODZ	Robinson R-22B	Langley Construction Ltd	
G-BOEC	PA-38-112 Tomahawk	R. A. Wakefield	
G-BOEE	PA-28-181 Archer II	T. B. Parmenter	
G-BOEH	Jodel DR.340	Piper Flyers Group	
G-BOEK	Cameron V-77 balloon	A. J. E. Jones	
G-BOEM	Aerotek-Pitts S-2A	Walsh Bros (Tunneling) Ltd	
G-BOEN	Cessna 172M	G-BOEN Group	
G-BOER	PA-28-161 Warrior II	M. & W. Fraser-Urquhart	
G-BOET	PA-28RT-201 Arrow IV	B. C. Chambers (G-IBEC)	
G-BOEW	Robinson R-22B	Bristow Helicopters Ltd/Redhill	
G-BOEX	Robinson R-22B	Bristow Helicopters Ltd/Redhill	
G-BOEY	Robinson R-22B	Bristow Helicopters Ltd/Redhill	
G-BOEZ	Robinson R-22B	Bristow Helicopters Ltd/Redhill	
G-BOFC	Beech 76 Duchess	Magenta Ltd/Kidlington	
G-BOFD	Cessna U.206G	D. M. Penny	
G-BOFE	PA-34-200T Seneca II	P. R. & J. S. Covell/Ipswich	
G-BOFF	Cameron N-77 balloon	Systems-80 Double Glazing Ltd & N. M. Gabriel	

Notes	Reg.	Type	Owner or Operator
	G-BOFL	Cessna 152	GEM Rewinds Ltd/Coventry
	G-BOFM	Cessna 152	GEM Rewinds Ltd/Coventry
	G-BOFO	Ultimate Aircraft 10-200	M. Werdmuller
	G-BOFW	Cessna A.150M	Vectair Aviation 1995 Ltd
	G-BOFX	Cessna A.150M	TDR Aviation Ltd
	G-BOFY	PA-28 Cherokee 140	BCT Aircraft Leasing Ltd
	G-BOFZ	PA-28-161 Warrior II	R. W. Harris
	G-BOGC	Cessna 152	Skyviews & General Ltd/Leeds
	G-BOGG	Cessna 152	The Royal Artillery Aero Club Ltd/ Middle Wallop
	G-BOGI	Robin DR.400/180	A. L. M. Shepherd
	G-BOGK	ARV Super 2	D. R. Trouse
	G-BOGM	PA-28RT-201T Turbo Arrow IV	RJP Aviation
	G-BOGO	PA-32R-301T Saratoga SP	G. W. Dimmer
	G-BOGP	Cameron V-77 balloon	The Wealden Balloon Group
	G-BOGR	Colt 180A balloon	The Balloon Club of Great Britain Ltd
	G-BOGT	Colt 77A balloon	The Hot Air Balloon Co Ltd
	G-BOGV	Air Command 532 Elite	G. M. Hobman
	G-BOGW	Air Command 532 Elite	K. Ashford
	G-BOGY	Cameron V-77 balloon	C. J. Royden
	G-BOHA	PA-28-161 Warrior II	London Flight Centre (Headcorn) Ltd
	G-BOHD	Colt 77A balloon	D. B. Court
	G-BOHF	Thunder Ax8-84 balloon	J. A. Harris
	G-BOHG	Air Command 532 Elite	T. E. McDonald
	G-BOHH	Cessna 172N	T. Scott
	G-BOHI	Cessna 152 II	Clacton Aero Club (1988) Ltd
	G-BOHJ	Cessna 152 II	Semloh Aviation Services/Andrewsfield
	G-BOHL	Cameron A-120 balloon	J. M. Holmes
	G-BOHM	PA-28 Cherokee 180	M. J. Anthony & B. Keogh
	G-BOHO	PA-28-161 Warrior II	Egressus Flying Group
	G BOHR	PA-28-151 Warrior	G. & J. A. Cockerton
	G-BOHS	PA-38-112 Tomahawk	Falcon Flying Services/Biggin Hill
	G-BOHT	PA-38-112 Tomahawk	Falcon Flying Services/Manston
	G-BOHU	PA-38-112 Tomahawk	Scottish Airways Flyers (Prestwick) Ltd
	G-BOHV	Wittman W.8 Tailwind	R. A. Povall
	G-BOHW	Vans RV-4	N. Woodworth
	G-BOHX	PA-44-180 Seminole	Airport Supply Ltd/Booker
	G-BOIA	Cessna 180K	R. E. Styles & ptnrs
	G-BOIB	Wittman W.10 Tailwind	M. G. E. Hutton
	G-BOIC	PA-28R-201T Turbo Arrow III	M. J. Pearson
	G-BOID	Bellanca 7ECA Citabria	D. Mallinson
	G-BOIG	PA-28-161 Warrior II	D. Vallence-Pell/Jersey
	G-BOIH	Pitts S-1E Special	C. R. A. Scrope
	G-BOIJ	Thunder Ax7-77 balloon	R. A. Hughes
	G-BOIK	Air Command 503 Commander	F. G. Shepherd
	G-BOIL	Cessna 172N	Upperstack Ltd
	G-BOIN	Bellanca 7ECA Citabria	LAC (Enterprises) Ltd/Barton
	G-BOIO	Cessna 152	AV Aviation Ltd
	G-BOIP	Cessna 152	Stapleford Flying Club Ltd
	G-BOIR	Cessna 152	Shropshire Aero Club Ltd/Sleap
	G-BOIS	PA-31 Turbo Navajo	Air Care (South West) Ltd (G-AYNB)/Plymouth
	G-BOIT	SOCATA TB.10 Tobago	Shoreham Flight Simulation/Bournemouth
	G-BOIU	SOCATA TB.10 Tobago	R & B Aviation Ltd
	G-BOIV	Cessna 150M	J. B. Green
	G-BOIW	Cessna 152	Falcon Flying Services/Biggin Hill
	G-BOIX	Cessna 172N	JR Flying Ltd
	G-BOIY	Cessna 172N	ABK Aviation Services Ltd
	G-BOIZ	PA-34-200T Seneca II	S. F. Tebby & Son
	G-BOJB	Cameron V-77 balloon	K. L. Heron & R. M. Trotter
	G-BOJD	Cameron V-77 balloon	L. H. Ellis
	G-BOJF	Air Command 532 Elite	C. Verlaan/Netherlands
	G-BOJH	PA-28R Cherokee Arrow 200	P. S. Kirby
	G-BOJI	PA-28RT-201 Arrow IV	B. A. Mintowt-Czyz & T. A. Stoate
	G-BOJK	PA-34-220T Seneca III	Redhill Flying Club (G-BRUF)
	G-BOJL	M.S.885 Super Rallye	J. A. Rees
	G-BOJM	PA-28-181 Archer II	Fernborough Ltd
	G-BOJO	Colt 120A balloon	J. G. Morwood
	G-BOJR	Cessna 172P	Exeter Flying Club Ltd
	G-BOJS	Cessna 172P	I. S. H. Paul
	G-BOJU	Cameron N-77 balloon	M. A. Scholes
	G-BOJW	PA-28-161 Warrior II	G-BOJW Flying Group
	G-BOJZ	PA-28-161 Warrior II	Southern Air Ltd/Shoreham

Reg.	Type	Owner or Operator	Notes
G-BOKA	PA-28-201T Turbo Dakota	CBG Aviation Ltd/Biggin Hill	
G-BOKB	PA-28-161 Warrior II	Southern Air Ltd/Shoreham	
G-BOKE	PA-34-200T Seneca II	Saint Associates Ltd	
G-BOKF	Air Command 532 Elite	D. Beevers	
G-BOKG	Slingsby T.31 Motor Cadet III	A. M. Witt	
G-BOKH	Whittaker MW.7	I. D. Evans	
G-BOKI	Whittaker MW.7	R. K. Willcox	
G-BOKJ	Whittaker MW.7	M. R. Payne	
G-BOKL	PA-28-161 Warrior II	BAe Flying College Ltd/Prestwick	
G-BOKM	PA-28-161 Warrior II	BAe Flying College Ltd/Prestwick	
G-BOKN	PA-28-161 Warrior II	BAe Flying College Ltd/Prestwick	
G-BOKO	PA-28-161 Warrior II	BAe Flying College Ltd/Prestwick	
G-BOKP	PA-28-161 Warrior II	BAe Flying College Ltd/Prestwick	
G-BOKR	PA-28-161 Warrior II	BAe Flying College Ltd/Prestwick	
G-BOKS	PA-28-161 Warrior II	BAe Flying College Ltd/Prestwick	
G-BOKT	PA-28-161 Warrior II	BAe Flying College Ltd/Prestwick	
G-BOKU	PA-28-161 Warrior II	BAe Flying College Ltd/Prestwick	
G-BOKX	PA-28-161 Warrior II	W. P. J. Jackson	
G-BOKY	Cessna 152 II	D. F. F. & J. E. Poore	
G-BOLB	Taylorcraft BC-12-65	G-BOLB Flying Group	
G-BOLC	Fournier RF-6B-100	W. H. Hendy/Dunkeswell	
G-BOLD	PA-38-112 Tomahawk	B. R. Pearson & B. F. Fraser-Smith/ Eaglescott	
G-BOLE	PA-38-112 Tomahawk	M. W. Kibble & E. A. Minard	
G-BOLF	PA-38-112 Tomahawk	Teesside Flight Centre Ltd	
G-BOLG	Bellanca 7KCAB Citabria	B. R. Pearson/Eaglescott	
G-BOLI	Cessna 172P	Boli Flying Club	
G-BOLL	Lake LA-4 Skimmer	S. D. Foster	
G-BOLN	Colt 21A balloon	Virgin Airship & Balloon Co Ltd	
G-BOLO	Bell 206B JetRanger	Hargreaves Construction Co Ltd/ Shoreham	
G-BOLP	Colt 21A balloon	Virgin Airship & Balloon Co Ltd	
G-BOLR	Colt 21A balloon	Virgin Airship & Balloon Co Ltd	
G-BOLS	FRED Srs 2	I. F. Vaughan	
G-BOLT	R. Commander 114	R. D. Rooke/Elstree	
G-BOLU	Robin R.3000/120	Classair/Biggin Hill	
G-BOLV	Cessna 152 II	Falcon Flying Services/Biggin Hill	
G-BOLW	Cessna 152 II	JRB Aviation Ltd/Southend	
G-BOLX	Cessna 172N	R. J. Burrough/Headcorn	
G-BOLY	Cessna 172N	London Flight Centre (Headcorn) Ltd	
G-BOLZ	Rand KR-2	B. Normington	
G-BOMB	Cassutt Racer IIIM	P. P. Chapman/Biggin Hill	
G-BOML	Hispano HA.1112MIL (—)	Classic Aviation Ltd/Duxford	
G-BOMN	Cessna 150F	D. G. Williams	
G-BOMO	PA-38-112 Tomahawk II	APB Leasing Ltd/Welshpool	
G-BOMP	PA-28-181 Archer II	Falcon Flying Services/Manston	
G-BOMS	Cessna 172N	Aerohire Ltd/Halfpenny Green	
G-BOMT	Cessna 172N	E. Alexander	
G-BOMU	PA-28-181 Archer II	RJ Aviation/Blackbushe	
G-BOMY	PA-28-161 Warrior II	Carill Aviation Ltd/Southampton	
G-BOMZ	PA-38-112 Tomahawk	BOMZ Aviation/White Waltham	
G-BONC	PA-28RT-201 Arrow IV	K. A. Hemming	
G-BOND	Sikorsky S-76A	Manchester Helicopter Centre/Barton	
G-BONE	Pilatus P2-06 (U-142)	P. S. Watts	
G-BONG	Enstrom F-28A-UK	TR Bitz	
G-BONK	Colt 180A balloon	Wye Valley Aviation Ltd	
G-BONO	Cessna 172N	C. R. Cox	
G-BONP	CFM Streak Shadow	T. J. Palmer	
G-BONR	Cessna 172N	Atlaslocal Ltd/Biggin Hill	
G-BONS	Cessna 172N	BONS Group/Elstree	
G-BONT	Slingsby T.67M Mk II	Slingsby Aviation Ltd/Kirkbymoorside	
G-BONU	Slingsby T.67B	R. L. Brinklow	
G-BONV	Colt 17A balloon	Bryant Group PLC	
G-BONW	Cessna 152 II	Lincoln Aero Club Ltd/Sturgate	
G-BONY	Denney Kitfox Mk 1	M. J. Walker	
G-BONZ	Beech V35B Bonanza	P. M. Coulten	
G-BOOB	Cameron N-65 balloon	C. V. Legate-Pearce	
G-BOOC	PA-18 Super Cub 150	R. R. & S. A. Marriott	
G-BOOD	Slingsby T.31M Motor Tutor	G. F. M. Garner	
G-BOOE	GA-7 Cougar	G. L. Cailes	
G-BOOF	PA-28-181 Archer II	European Flyers/Blackbushe	
G-BOOG	PA-28RT-201T Turbo Arrow IV	Simair Ltd	
G-BOOH	Jodel D.112	M. J. Hayman	

Notes	Reg.	Type	Owner or Operator
	G-BOOI	Cessna 152	Stapleford Flying Club Ltd
	G-BOOJ	Air Command 532 Elite	Roger Savage (Gyroplanes) Ltd
	G-BOOL	Cessna 172N	Hockstar Ltd/Biggin Hill
	G-BOOM	Hunter T.7 (800)	R. V. Aviation Ltd/Bournemouth
	G-BOON	PA-32RT-300 Lance II	G-BOON Ltd/Luton
	G-BOOO	Brügger MB .2 Colibri	D. G. Cole
	G-BOOP	Cameron N-90 balloon	Oxford University Hot Air Balloon Club (G-BOMX)
	G-BOOU	Cameron N-77 balloon	Aqualisa Products Ltd
	G-BOOV	AS.355F-2 Twin Squirrel	Merseyside Police Authority
	G-BOOW	Aerosport Scamp	Walavia
	G-BOOX	Rutan LongEz	I. R. Thomas & I. R. Wilde
	G-BOOZ	Cameron N-77 balloon	J. E. F. Kettlety
	G-BOPA	PA-28-181 Archer II	J. E. Strutt (London) Ltd
	G-BOPB	Boeing 767-204ER	Britannia Airways Ltd *Captain Sir Ross Smith*
	G-BOPC	PA-28-161 Warrior II	Channel Aviation Ltd
	G-BOPD	Bede BD-4	S. T. Dauncey
	G-BOPG	Cessna 182Q	G. Wimlett
	G-BOPH	Cessna TR.182RG	E. A. L. Sturmer
	G-BOPM	Brooklands OA.7 Optica	FLS Aerospace (Lovaux) Ltd/Bournemouth
	G-BOPN	FLS Aerospace OA.7 Optica	FLS Aerospace (Lovaux) Ltd/Bournemouth
	G-BOPR	FLS Aerospace OA.7 Optica	FLS Aerospace (Lovaux) Ltd/Bournemouth
	G-BOPT	Grob G.115	LAC (Enterprises) Ltd/Barton
	G-BOPU	Grob G.115	LAC (Enterprises) Ltd/Barton
	G-BOPV	PA-34-200T Seneca II	Tewin Aviation
	G-BOPW	Cessna A.152	Northamptonshire School of Flying Ltd/Sywell
	G-BOPX	Cessna A.152	Aerohire Ltd/Halfpenny Green
	G-BORA	Colt 77A balloon	Cala Homes (Southern) Ltd
	G-BORB	Cameron V-77 balloon	M. H. Wolff
	G-BORC	Colt 180A balloon	Virgin Balloon Flights Ltd
	G-BORD	Thunder Ax7-77 balloon	D. D. Owen
	G-BORE	Colt 77A balloon	Little Secret Hot-Air Balloon Group
	G-BORG	Campbell Cricket	N. G. Bailey
	G-BORH	PA-34-200T Seneca II	Airlong Charter Ltd
	G-BORI	Cessna 152 II	Staryear Ltd
	G-BORJ	Cessna 152 II	APB Leasing Ltd/Welshpool
	G-BORK	PA-28-161 Warrior II	A. W. Collett
	G-BORL	PA-28-161 Warrior II	Westair Flying Services Ltd/Blackpool
	G-BORM	H.S.748 Srs 2B ★	Airport Fire Service/Exeter
	G-BORN	Cameron N-77 balloon	I. Chadwick
	G-BORO	Cessna 152 II	East Midlands Flying School
	G-BORR	Thunder Ax8-90 balloon	W. J. Harris
	G-BORS	PA-28-181 Archer II	Neric Ltd
	G-BORT	Colt 77A balloon	I. E. A. Joslyn/Germany
	G-BORV	Bell 206B JetRanger 3	C. A. Rosenberg/Redhill
	G-BORW	Cessna 172P	Briter Aviation Ltd/Coventry
	G-BORY	Cessna 150L	Harrison Aviation Ltd
	G-BOSB	Thunder Ax7-77 balloon	M. Gallagher
	G-BOSD	PA-34-200T Seneca II	Barnes Olson Aeroleasing Ltd
	G-BOSE	PA-28-181 Archer II	G. Fleck
	G-BOSF	Colt 69A balloon	Virgin Airship & Balloon Co Ltd
	G-BOSG	Colt 17A balloon	Virgin Airship & Balloon Co Ltd
	G-BOSJ	Nord 3400 (124)	A. I. Milne
	G-BOSM	Jodel DR.253B	Sierra Mike (Ware) Group
	G-BOSO	Cessna A.152	Redhill Flying Club
	G-BOSP	PA-28-151 Warrior	M. E. Williams/Andrewsfield
	G-BOSR	PA-28 Cherokee 140	B. G. Bailey
	G-BOSU	PA-28 Cherokee 140	A. & R. Windley
	G-BOSV	Cameron V-77 balloon	K. H. Greenaway
	G-BOTB	Cessna 152	Stapleford Flying Club Ltd
	G-BOTD	Cameron O-105 balloon	P. J. Beglan
	G-BOTF	PA-28-151 Warrior	G-BOTF Group/Southend
	G-BOTG	Cessna 152	Donington Aviation Ltd/E. Midlands
	G-BOTH	Cessna 182Q	G-BOTH Group
	G-BOTI	PA-28-151 Warrior	Falcon Flying Services/Biggin Hill
	G-BOTK	Cameron O-105 balloon	F. R. & V. L. Higgins
	G-BOTM	Bell 206B JetRanger 3	David McLean Homes Ltd
	G-BOTN	PA-28-161 Warrior II	W. Lancs Aero Club Ltd/Woodvale
	G-BOTO	Bellanca 7ECA Citabria	G-BOTO Group
	G-BOTP	Cessna 150J	R. E. Thorne
	G-BOTS	Hughes 269C	Cloghran Helicopter Club Ltd

Reg.	Type	Owner or Operator	Notes
G-BOTU	Piper J-3C-65 Cub	T. L. Giles	
G-BOTV	PA-32RT-300 Lance II	Robin Lance Aviation Association Ltd	
G-BOTW	Cameron V-77 balloon	D. N. Malcolm	
G-BOTY	Cessna 150J	P. Thompson	
G-BOTZ	Bensen B.8MR	C. Jones	
G-BOUD	PA-38-112 Tomahawk	T. K. Gough	
G-BOUE	Cessna 172N	K. W. Johnson	
G-BOUF	Cessna 172N	Amber Valley Aviation	
G-BOUJ	Cessna 150M	J. B. Mills	
G-BOUK	PA-34-200T Seneca II	P. Sisson	
G-BOUL	PA-34-200T Seneca II	C.S.E. Aviation Ltd/Kidlington	
G-BOUM	PA-34-200T Seneca II	C.S.E. Aviation Ltd/Kidlington	
G-BOUN	Rand KR-2	W. J. Allan	
G-BOUP	PA-28-161 Warrior II	C.S.E. Aviation Ltd/Kidlington	
G-BOUR	PA-28-161 Warrior II	C.S.E. Aviation Ltd/Kidlington	
G-BOUS	PA-28RT-201 Arrow IV	Hamilton Compass Aviation Ltd	
G-BOUT	Colomban MC.12 Cri-Cri	C. K. Farley	
G-BOUV	Bensen B.8R	A. J. Dickson	
G-BOUZ	Cessna 150G	Atlantic Bridge Aviation Ltd/Lydd	
G-BOVB	PA-15 Vagabond	Oscar Flying Group/Shoreham	
G-BOVC	Everett gyroplane	J. W. Highton	
G-BOVH	PA-28-161 Warrior II	R. W. Tebby	
G-BOVK	PA-28-161 Warrior II	Air Nova/Liverpool	
G-BOVR	Robinson R-22	P. J. Homan	
G-BOVS	Cessna 150M	H. Daines Electronics Ltd	
G-BOVT	Cessna 150M	D. H. Jacobs	
G-BOVU	Stoddard-Hamilton Glasair III	P. Young	
G-BOVV	Cameron V-77 balloon	J. P. Clifford	
G-BOVW	Colt 69A balloon	V. Hyland	
G-BOVX	Hughes 269C	Elite Helicopters Ltd	
G-BOVY	Hughes 269C	Redhill Helicopter Centre	
G-BOWB	Cameron V-77 balloon	R. C. Stone	
G-BOWD	Cessna F.337G	Badgehurst Ltd (G-BLSB)	
G-BOWE	PA-34-200T Seneca II	C.S.E. Aviation Ltd/Kidlington	
G-BOWK	Cameron N-90 balloon	S. R. Bridge	
G-BOWL	Cameron V-77 balloon	P. G. & G. R. Hall	
G-BOWM	Cameron V-56 balloon	C. G. Caldecott & G. Pitt	
G-BOWN	PA-12 Super Cruiser	R. W. Bucknell	
G-BOWO	Cessna R.182	D. P. Bennett (G-BOTR)	
G-BOWP	Jodel D.120A	A. R. Gedney & ptnrs/Sibson	
G-BOWU	Cameron O-84 balloon	St Elmos Fire Syndicate	
G-BOWV	Cameron V-65 balloon	R. A. Harris	
G-BOWY	PA-28RT-201T Turbo Arrow IV	S. Chappell	
G-BOWZ	Bensen B.80V	W. M. Day	
G-BOXA	PA-28-161 Warrior II	Jersey Aero Club	
G-BOXB	PA-28-161 Warrior II	Jersey Aero Club	
G-BOXC	PA-28-161 Warrior II	Jersey Aero Club	
G-BOXG	Cameron O-77 balloon	C. M. Love	
G-BOXH	Pitts S-1S Special	D. Medrek	
G-BOXJ	Piper J-3C-65 Cub	J. L. Quick & A. J. P. Jackson/Biggin Hill	
G-BOXK	Slingsby T.67C	Slingsby Aviation Ltd/Kirkbymoorside	
G-BOXN	Robinson R-22B	Conguess Aviation Ltd	
G-BOXR	GA-7 Cougar	Plane Talking Ltd/Elstree	
G-BOXT	Hughes 269C	Goldenfly Ltd	
G-BOXU	AA-5B Tiger	Marcher Aviation Group	
G-BOXV	Pitts S-1S Special	G. R. Clark	
G-BOXW	Cassutt Racer Srs IIIM	D. I. Johnson	
G-BOXX	Robinson R-22B	BLS Aviation Ltd/Elstree	
G-BOXY	PA-28-181 Archer II	Sheffield Aero Club Ltd/Netherthorpe	
G-BOYB	Cessna A.152	Northamptonshire School of Flying Ltd/ Sywell	
G-BOYC	Robinson R-22B	Yorkshire Helicopters/Leeds	
G-BOYF	Sikorsky S-76B	Darley Stud Management Co Ltd	
G-BOYH	PA-28-151 Warrior	Superpause Ltd/Booker	
G-BOYI	PA-28-161 Warrior II	S. J. Harris	
G-BOYL	Cessna 152 II	Aerohire Ltd/Halfpenny Green	
G-BOYM	Cameron O-84 balloon	Frontline Distribution Ltd	
G-BOYO	Cameron V-20 balloon	J. M. Willard	
G-BOYP	Cessna 172N	Guildtons Ltd	
G-BOYR	Cessna F.337G	G. F. Morton	
G-BOYT	PA-38-112 Tomahawk II	APB Leasing Ltd/Welshpool	
G-BOYU	Cessna A.150L	Upperstack Ltd	
G-BOYV	PA-28R-201T Turbo Arrow III	A. W. Rorke	

Notes	Reg.	Type	Owner or Operator
	G-BOYX	Robinson R-22B	R. Towle
	G-BOYY	Cameron A-105 balloon	Hoyers (UK) Ltd
	G-BOZI	PA-28-161 Warrior II	Klingair Ltd/Conington
	G-BOZM	PA-38-112 Tomahawk	S. J. Green
	G-BOZN	Cameron N-77 balloon	Calarel Developments Ltd
	G-BOZO	AA-5B Tiger	Caslon Ltd
	G-BOZP	Beech 76 Duchess	Newcastle upon Tyne Aero Club Ltd
	G-BOZR	Cessna 152 II	Gem Rewinds Ltd
	G-BOZS	Pitts S-1C Special	R. J. & M. B. Trickey
	G-BOZU	Sparrow Hawk Mk II	R. V. Phillimore
	G-BOZV	CEA DR.340 Major	EH Group
	G-BOZW	Bensen B.8M	M. E. Wills
	G-BOZY	Cameron RTW-120 balloon	Oxford Promotions (UK) Ltd
	G-BOZZ	AA-5B Tiger	Solent Tiger Group/Southampton
	G-BPAA	Acro Advanced	Acro Engines & Airframes Ltd
	G-BPAB	Cessna 150M	D. J. French & ptnrs/Earls Colne
	G-BPAC	PA-28-161 Warrior II	G. G. Pratt
	G-BPAE	Cameron V-77 balloon	I. J. Jackson
	G-BPAF	PA-28-161 Warrior II	Hendafern Ltd
	G-BPAH	Colt 69A balloon	International Distillers & Vintners Ltd
	G-BPAI	Bell 47G-3B-1 (modified)	LRC Leisure Ltd
	G-BPAJ	D.H.82A Tiger Moth	P. A. Jackson (G-AOIX)
	G-BPAL	D.H.C.1 Chipmunk 22 (WG350)	K. F. & P. Tomsett (G-BCYE)
	G-BPAO	Air Command 503 Commander	D. J. Sagar
	G-BPAS	SOCATA TB.20 Trinidad	South East Aviation Ltd
	G-BPAU	PA-28-161 Warrior II	Lapwing Flying Group Ltd/Denham
	G-BPAV	FRED Srs 2	P. A. Valentine
	G-BPAW	Cessna 150M	A. Phillips
	G-BPAX	Cessna 150M	Barry Aviation Ltd/Shoreham
	G-BPAY	PA-28-181 Archer II	C. Rees/Rush Green
	G-BPBA	Bensen B.80MR	M. E. Green
	G-BPBB	Evans VP-2	J. S. & J. D. Penny
	G-BPBG	Cessna 152 II	Atlantic Air Transport Ltd/Coventry
	G-BPBI	Cessna 152 II	B. W. Wells & Burbage Farms Ltd
	G-BPBJ	Cessna 152 II	W. Shaw & P. G. Haines
	G-BPBK	Cessna 152 II	Burbage Farms Ltd
	G-BPBM	PA-28-161 Warrior II	Halfpenny Green Flight Centre Ltd
	G-BPBO	PA-28RT-201T Turbo Arrow IV	Music Connections Ltd
	G-BPBP	Brügger MB.2 Colibri	D. A. Preston
	G-BPBR	PA-38-112 Tomahawk	M. A. Boocock
	G-BPBU	Cameron V-77 balloon	G-BPBU Skymaid Balloon
	G-BPBV	Cameron V-77 balloon	W. E. & L. A. Newman
	G-BPBW	Cameron O-105 balloon	R. J. Mansfield
	G-BPBY	Cameron V-77 balloon	L. Hutley (G-BPCS)
	G-BPBZ	Thunder Ax7-77 balloon	A. W. J. Weston
	G-BPCA	BN-2B-26 Islander	British Regional Airlines/Scottish Air Ambulance Service (G-BLNX)
	G-BPCF	Piper J-3C-65 Cub	A. J. Cook
	G-BPCG	Colt AS-80 airship	N. Carbonnier
	G-BPCI	Cessna R.172K	B. E. Simpson
	G-BPCK	PA-28-161 Warrior II	W. G. Booth
	G-BPCL	SA Bulldog Srs 120/128	Isohigh Ltd/Denham
	G-BPCM	Rotorway Executive	Aircare Group
	G-BPCN	Cameron A-160 balloon	Golf Centres Balloons Ltd
	G-BPCR	Mooney M.20K	T. & R. Harris
	G-BPCV	Montgomerie-Bensen B.8MR	O. J. Blackbourn
	G-BPCX	PA-28-236 Dakota	Offshore Marine Consultants Ltd
	G-BPCY	PA-34-200T Seneca	Compton Abbas Airfield Ltd
	G-BPDA	H.S.748 Srs 2A	Emerald Airways Ltd *John J. Goodall* (G-GLAS)/Liverpool
	G-BPDD	Colt 240A balloon	Heather Flight Ltd
	G-BPDE	Colt 56A balloon	J. E. Weidema
	G-BPDF	Cameron V-77 balloon	The Ballooning Business Ltd
	G-BPDG	Cameron V-77 balloon	A. & M. A. Dunning
	G-BPDJ	Christena Mini Coupe	J. J. Morrissey/Popham
	G-BPDK	Sorrell SNS-7 Hyperbipe	A. J. Cable/Barton
	G-BPDM	C.A.S.A. 1.131E Jungmann 2000 (781-32)	Spanish Acquisition/Shoreham
	G-BPDT	PA-28-161 Warrior II	Channel islands Aero Holdings (Jersey) Ltd
	G-BPDU	PA-28-161 Warrior II	Sky Leisure Aviation Ltd
	G-BPDV	Pitts S-1S Special	J. Vize/Sywell
	G-BPDY	Westland-Bell 47G-3B1	Howden Helicopters/Spaldington

Reg.	Type	Owner or Operator	Notes
G-BPEA	Boeing 757-236	British Airways *Castell Cydweli*	
G-BPEB	Boeing 757-236	British Airways	
G-BPEC	Boeing 757-236	British Airways *Sir Simon Rattle*	
G-BPED	Boeing 757-236	British Airways *Blair Castle*	
G-BPEE	Boeing 757-236	British Airways *Robert Louis Stevenson*	
G-BPEF	Boeing 757-236	British Airways (G-BOHC)	
G-BPEI	Boeing 757-236	British Airways (G-BMRK) *Winchester Castle*	
G-BPEJ	Boeing 757-236	British Airways (G-BMRL) *Castell Dinas Bran*	
G-BPEK	Boeing 757-236	British Airways (G-BMRM) *Carew Castle*	
G-BPEL	PA-28-151 Warrior	R. W. Harris & A. J. Jahanfar	
G-BPEM	Cessna 150K	R. G. Lindsey & R. Strong	
G-BPEO	Cessna 152	Seawing Flying Club Ltd & Eastern Executive Air Charter Ltd/Southend	
G-BPER	PA-38-112 Tomahawk II	APB Leasing Ltd/Welshpool	
G-BPES	PA-38-112 Tomahawk II	Sherwood Flying Club Ltd/Tollerton	
G-BPEW	Robinson R-22B	Dann Antiques Ltd	
G-BPEZ	Colt 77A balloon	A. Stace	
G-BPFB	Colt 77A balloon	S. Ingram	
G-BPFC	Mooney M.20C	D. P. Tinsley	
G-BPFD	Jodel D.112	K. Manley	
G-BPFF	Cameron DP-70 airship	Cameron Balloons Ltd	
G-BPFG	SOCATA TB.20 Trinidad	F. T. Arnold	
G-BPFH	PA-28-161 Warrior II	M. H. Kleiser	
G-BPFI	PA-28-181 Archer II	G-BPFI Group	
G-BPFJ	Cameron 90 Can SS balloon	The Hot-Air Balloon Co Ltd	
G-BPFK	Montgomerie-Bensen B.8MR	J. W. Birkett	
G-BPFL	Davis DA-2	B. W. Griffiths	
G-BPFM	Aeronca 7AC Champion	L. A. Borrill	
G-BPFV	Boeing 767-204ER	Britannia Airways Ltd/*Bobby Moore OBE*	
G-BPFX	Colt 21A balloon	The Hot-Air Balloon Co Ltd	
G-BPFY	Consolidated PBY-6A Catalina	Bitteswell Ltd	
G-BPFZ	Cessna 152 II	C. J. Ward	
G-BPGA	Mooney M.20J	Medallionair Ltd	
G-BPGB	Cessna 150J	Magnificent Obsessions Ltd	
G-BPGC	Air Command 532 Elite	E. C. E. Brown	
G-BPGD	Cameron V-65 balloon	Gone With The Wind Ltd	
G-BPGE	Cessna U.206C	Scottish Parachute Club/Strathallan	
G-BPGF	Thunder Ax7-77 balloon	M. Schiavo	
G-BPGH	EAA Acro Sport II	G. M. Bradley	
G-BPGK	Aeronca 7AC Champion	T. M. Williams	
G-BPGL	PA-28 Cherokee 180	C. N. Ellerbrook	
G-BPGM	Cessna 152 II	J. Easson/Edinburgh	
G-BPGU	PA-28-181 Archer II	G. Underwood	
G-BPGV	Robinson R-22B	Polo Aviation Ltd	
G-BPGX	SOCATA TB.9 Tampico	M. Stock & M. J. Aitkin	
G-BPGY	Cessna 150H	Three Counties Aero Engineering Ltd/Lasham	
G-BPGZ	Cessna 150G	J. W. Halfpenny	
G-BPHB	PA-28-161 Warrior II	Channel Islands Aero Holdings (Jersey) Ltd	
G-BPHD	Cameron N-42 balloon	P. J. Marshall & M. A. Clarke	
G-BPHE	PA-28-161 Warrior II	Pool Aviation Ltd/Welshpool	
G-BPHG	Robin DR.400/180	K. J. & M. B. White/Redhill	
G-BPHH	Cameron V-77 balloon	C. D. Aindow	
G-BPHI	PA-38-112 Tomahawk	S. A. Boyall	
G-BPHJ	Cameron V-77 balloon	C. W. Brown	
G-BPHK	Whittaker MW.7	R. V. Hogg	
G-BPHL	PA-28-161 Warrior II	Teesside Flight Centre Ltd	
G-BPHO	Taylorcraft BC-12D	J. Roberts & J. K. Carr	
G-BPHP	Taylorcraft BC-12-65	D. C. Stephens	
G-BPHR	D.H.82A Tiger Moth (A17-48)	N. Parry	
G-BPHT	Cessna 152	Bobbington Air Training School Ltd/Halfpenny Green	
G-BPHU	Thunder Ax7-77 balloon	R. P. Waite	
G-BPHW	Cessna 140	J. A. Pothecary/Shoreham	
G-BPHX	Cessna 140	M. McChesney	
G-BPHZ	M.S.505 Criquet (TA+RC)	The Aircraft Restoration Co/Duxford	
G-BPID	PA-28-161 Warrior II	K. J. Newman	
G-BPIE	Bell 206B JetRanger 3	Frey Aviation Ltd	
G-BPIF	Bensen-Parsons 2 seat	A. P. Barden	
G-BPIH	Rand KR-2	J. R. Rowley	

Notes	Reg.	Type	Owner or Operator
	G-BPII	Denney Kitfox	J. K. Cross
	G-BPIJ	Brantly B.2B	R. B. Payne
	G-BPIK	PA-38-112 Tomahawk	Cormack (Aircraft Services) Ltd
	G-BPIL	Cessna 310B	A. L. Brown & R. A. Parsons
	G-BPIM	Cameron N-77 balloon	Thermalite Ltd
	G-BPIN	Glaser-Dirks DG.400	M. P. Seth-Smith & J. N. Stevenson
	G-BPIO	Cessna F.152 II	S. Harcourt/Biggin Hill
	G-BPIP	Slingsby T.31 Motor Cadet III	J. H. Beard
	G-BPIR	Scheibe SF.25E Super Falke	Coventry Gliding Club Ltd/ Husbands Bosworth
	G-BPIT	Robinson R-22B	NA Air Ltd
	G-BPIU	PA-28-161 Warrior II	G. D. Corbin
	G-BPIV	B.149 Bolingbroke Mk IVT (L8841))	The Aircraft Restoration Co/Duxford
	G-BPIY	Cessna 152 II	Rentair Ltd
	G-BPIZ	AA-5B Tiger	D. A. Horsley
	G-BPJA	Beech 95-58 Baron	J. F. Britten
	G-BPJB	Schweizer 269C	Elborne Holdings Ltd
	G-BPJD	SOCATA Rallye 110ST	D. Carr
	G-BPJE	Cameron A-105 balloon	J. S. Eckersley
	G-BPJF	PA-38-112 Tomahawk	Air Yorkshire Ltd
	G-BPJG	PA-18 Super Cub 150	M. W. Stein
	G-BPJH	PA-18 Super Cub 95	P. J. Heron
	G-BPJL	Cessna 152 II	London Flight Centre (Headcorn) Ltd
	G-BPJN	Jodel D.18	W. J. Evans
	G-BPJO	PA-28-161 Cadet	Plane Talking Ltd/Elstree
	G-BPJP	PA-28-161 Cadet	C.S.E. Aviation Ltd/Kidlington
	G-BPJR	PA-28-161 Cadet	Plane Talking Ltd/Elstree
	G-BPJS	PA-28-161 Cadet	C.S.E. Aviation Ltd/Kidlington
	G-BPJU	PA-28-161 Cadet	C.S.E. Aviation Ltd/Kidlington
	G-BPJV	Taylorcraft F-21	TC Flying Group
	G-BPJW	Cessna A.150K	G. & S. A. Jones
	G-BPJZ	Cameron O-160 balloon	M. L. Gabb
	G-BPKF	Grob G.115	Soaring (Oxford) Ltd
	G-BPKI	EAA Acro Sport 1	I. C. Underwood
	G-BPKK	Denney Kitfox Mk 1	R. J. Baron
	G-BPKL	Mooney M.20J	London Link Flying Ltd
	G-BPKM	PA-28-161 Warrior II	M. J. Greasby
	G-BPKO	Cessna 140	I. R. March
	G-BPKR	PA-28-151 Warrior	Aeroshow Ltd
	G-BPLE	Cameron A-160 balloon	A. Derbyshire
	G-BPLF	Cameron V-77 balloon	C. L. Luffingham
	G-BPLG	Morane-Saulnier M.S.317	R. A. Anderson
	G-BPLH	Jodel DR.1051	M. N. King
	G-BPLI	Colt 77A balloon	Yanin International Ltd
	G-BPLM	AIA Stampe SV-4C	C. J. Jesson/Redhill
	G-BPLV	Cameron V-77 balloon	Jessops (Tailors) Ltd
	G-BPLY	Pitts S-2B Special	M. Mountstephen
	G-BPLZ	Hughes 369HS	Pyramid Precision Engineering Ltd
	G-BPMB	Maule M5-235C Lunar Rocket	R. A. Fleming
	G-BPMC	Air Command 503 Commander	M. A. Cheshire
	G-BPME	Cessna 152 II	Eastern Executive Air Charter Ltd
	G-BPMF	PA-28-151 Warrior	L. & A. Hill
	G-BPMH	Schempp-Hirth Nimbus 3DM	Southern Sailplanes/Lasham
	G-BPML	Cessna 172M	J. Birnie/Sandown
	G-BPMM	Champion 7ECA Citabria	J. Murray
	G-BPMP	Douglas C-47A-50-DL (224211)	Air Atlantique Ltd/Coventry
	G-BPMR	PA-28-161 Warrior II	B. McIntyre
	G-BPMU	Nord 3202B	A. I. Milne (G-BIZJ)
	G-BPMV	PA-28-161 Warrior II	J. W. E. P. Donald
	G-BPMW	QAC Quickie Q.2	C. W. Tattersall (G-OICI/G-OGKN)
	G-BPMX	ARV Super 2	C. R. James
	G-BPNA	Cessna 150L	Griffin Marston Ltd
	G-BPNC	Rotorway Executive	S. J. Hanson
	G-BPND	Boeing 727-2D3	Sabre Airways Ltd/Gatwick
	G-BPNF	Robinson R-22B	R. J. Chilton
	G-BPNG	Bell 206B JetRanger 3	West Helicopters (G-ORTC)/Belgium
	G-BPNI	Robinson R-22B	S. T. Rabi
	G-BPNL	QAC Quickie Q.2	J. Catley
	G-BPNN	Montgomerie-Bensen B.8MR	M. E. Vahdat
	G-BPNO	Zlin Z.326 Trener Master	J. A. S. Bailey & S. T. Logan
	G-BPNT	BAe 146-300	Palmair Flightline/Bournemouth
	G-BPNU	Thunder Ax7-77 balloon	J. Fenton

Reg.	Type	Owner or Operator	Notes
G-BPOA	Gloster Meteor T.7 (WF877)	39 Restoration Group/North Weald	
G-BPOB	Sopwith Camel F.1 (replica) (B2458)	Bianchi Aviation Film Services Ltd/ Booker	
G-BPOE	Colt 77A balloon	Albatross Aviation Ltd	
G-BPOL	Pietenpol Air Camper	G. W. Postance	
G-BPOM	PA-28-161 Warrior II	Light Aircraft Leasing Ltd	
G-BPON	PA-34-200T Seneca II	Aeroshare Ltd/Staverton	
G-BPOO	Montgomerie-Bensen B.8MR	M. E. Vahdat	
G-BPOR	Bell 206B JetRanger 3	P. F. Copeland Ltd	
G-BPOS	Cessna 150M	G. Loxton	
G-BPOT	PA-28-181 Archer II	P. Fraser	
G-BPOU	Luscombe 8A Silvaire	M. J. Negus & R. Hardley	
G-BPOV	Cameron 90 Magazine SS balloon	Forbes Europe Inc/France	
G-BPOZ	Enstrom F-28A	PR Aviation	
G-BPPA	Cameron O-65 balloon	Rix Petroleum Ltd	
G-BPPD	PA-38-112 Tomahawk	AT Aviation Ltd/Cardiff	
G-BPPE	PA-38-112 Tomahawk	Norwich School of Flying	
G-BPPF	PA-38-112 Tomahawk	Bristol Strut Flying Group	
G-BPPG	PA-38-112 Tomahawk	AT Aviation Ltd/Cardiff	
G-BPPI	Colt 180A balloon	A. G. E. Faulkner	
G-BPPJ	Cameron A-180 balloon	H. R. Evans	
G-BPPK	PA-28-151 Warrior	Balgold Ltd	
G-BPPL	Enstrom F-28A	M. & P. Food Products Ltd	
G-BPPM	Beech B200 Super King Air	Gama Aviation Ltd/Fairoaks	
G-BPPO	Luscombe 8A Silvaire	I. K. Ratcliffe	
G-BPPP	Cameron V-77 balloon	Sarnia Balloon Group	
G-BPPR	Air Command 532 Elite	T. D. Inch	
G-BPPS	Mudry CAARP CAP.21	J. E. Davies	
G-BPPU	Air Command 532 Elite	J. Hough	
G-BPPW	Schweizer 269C	Aviation Bureau	
G-BPPY	Hughes 269B	N. J. Edmonds	
G-BPPZ	Taylorcraft BC-12D	Zulu Warriors Flying Group	
G-BPRA	Aeronca 11AC Chief	R. M. C. Hunter	
G-BPRC	Cameron Elephant SS balloon	Cameron Balloons Ltd	
G-BPRD	Pitts S-1C Special	S. M. Trickey	
G-BPRJ	AS.355F-1 Twin Squirrel	G. Greenall	
G-BPRL	AS.355F-1 Twin Squirrel	Gas & Air Ltd	
G-BPRM	Cessna F.172L	A. J. Moseley (G-AZKG)	
G-BPRN	PA-28-161 Warrior II	Air Navigation & Trading Co Ltd/Blackpool	
G-BPRO	Cessna A.150K	Armphase Ltd	
G-BPRP	Cessna 150E	P. A. Griffin	
G-BPRR	Rand KR-2	M. W. Albery	
G-BPRS	Air Command 532 Elite	B. K. Snoxall	
G-BPRT	Piel CP.328	N. Reddish	
G-BPRV	PA-28-161 Warrior II	Devon School of Flying/Dunkeswell	
G-BPRX	Aeronca 11AC Chief	R. D. Ward & J. M. Taylor	
G-BPRY	PA-28-161 Warrior II	White Wings Aviation	
G-BPSA	Luscombe 8A Silvaire	K. P. Gorman/Staverton	
G-BPSB	Air Command 532 Elite	D. K. Duckworth	
G-BPSH	Cameron V-77 balloon	P. G. Hossack	
G-BPSI	Thunder Ax10-160 balloon	Airborne Adventures Ltd	
G-BPSJ	Thunder Ax6-56 balloon	Capricorn Balloons Ltd	
G-BPSK	Montgomerie-Bensen B.8M	R. J. Mann	
G-BPSL	Cessna 177	G-BPSL Group	
G-BPSO	Cameron N-90 balloon	J. Oberprieler	
G-BPSP	Cameron 90 Ship SS balloon	Forbes Europe Inc/France	
G-BPSR	Cameron V-77 balloon	K. J. A. Maxwell	
G-BPSS	Cameron A-120 balloon	Anglian Countryside Balloons	
G-BPSZ	Cameron N-180 balloon	A. Bolger	
G-BPTA	Stinson 108-2	P. S. Dudderidge	
G-BPTB	Boeing Stearman A.75N1 (442)	Aero Vintage Ltd	
G-BPTC	Taylorcraft BC-12D	R. A. Horsman	
G-BPTD	Cameron V-77 balloon	J. Lippett	
G-BPTE	PA-28-181 Archer II	London Flight Centre (Stansted) Ltd/Lydd	
G-BPTF	Cessna 152 II	London Flight Centre (Stansted) Ltd/Lydd	
G-BPTG	R. Commander 112TC	M. A. Watteau	
G-BPTH	Air Command 532 Elite	R. Wheeler	
G-BPTI	SOCATA TB.20 Trinidad	N. Davis	
G-BPTL	Cessna 172N	Cleveland Flying School Ltd/Teesside	
G-BPTM	Pitts S-1T Special	RPM Aviation Ltd	
G-BPTO	Zenith CH.200-AA	B. Philips	
G-BPTP	Robinson R-22	East Air (UK) Ltd	
G-BPTS	C.A.S.A. 1.131E Jungmann 1000 (E3B-153)	Aerobatic Displays Ltd/Duxford	

Notes	Reg.	Type	Owner or Operator
	G-BPTT	Robin DR.400/120	The Cotswold Aero Club Ltd/Staverton
	G-BPTU	Cessna 152	A. M. Alam/Panshanger
	G-BPTV	Bensen B.8	L. Chiappi
	G-BPTX	Cameron O-120 balloon	Skybus Ballooning
	G-BPTZ	Robinson R-22B	J. Lucketti
	G-BPUA	EAA Sport Biplane	V. Millard
	G-BPUB	Cameron V-31 balloon	M. T. Evans
	G-BPUC	QAC Quickie Q.200	S. R. Harvey
	G-BPUD	Ryan PT-22 (I-492)	R. I. Warman
	G-BPUE	Air Command 532 Elite	A. H. Brent
	G-BPUF	Thunder Ax6-56Z balloon	R. C. & M. A. Trimble (G-BHRL)
	G-BPUG	Air Command 532 Elite	T. A. Holmes
	G-BPUH	Cameron A-180 balloon	Golf Centres Balloons Ltd
	G-BPUI	Air Command 532 Elite	M. A. Turner
	G-BPUJ	Cameron N-90 balloon	D. Grimshaw
	G-BPUL	PA-18 Super Cub 150	C. D. Duthy-James
	G-BPUM	Cessna R.182RG	R. C. Chapman
	G-BPUP	Whittaker MW-7	J. H. Beard
	G-BPUR	Piper J-3L-65 Cub	J3 Group
	G-BPUS	Rans S.9	T. A. Wright
	G-BPUU	Cessna 140	A. R. Lansdown/Swansea
	G-BPUW	Colt 90A balloon	Huntair Ltd
	G-BPUX	Cessna 150J	H. H. Goodman
	G-BPUY	Cessna 150K	M. Hewison/Luton
	G-BPVA	Cessna 172F	S. Lancashire Flyers Ltd
	G-BPVC	Cameron V-77 balloon	J. B. R. Elliot
	G-BPVE	Bleriot IX (replica) (1197) ★	Bianchi Aviation Film Services Ltd/Booker
	G-BPVH	Cub Aircraft J-3C-65 Prospector	D. E. Cooper-Maguire
	G-BPVI	PA-32R-301 Saratoga SP	M. T. Coppen/Booker
	G-BPVJ	Cessna 152 II	Knight Air/Leeds
	G-BPVK	Varga 2150A Kachina	H. W. Hall
	G-BPVM	Cameron V-77 balloon	Royal Engineers Balloon Club
	G-BPVN	PA-32R-301T Turbo Saratoga SP	Michael J. Sparshatt-Worley (Holdings) Ltd
	G-BPVO	Cassutt Racer IIIM	R. J. Adams & D. R. Puleston
	G-BPVU	Thunder Ax7-77 balloon	J. C. K. Robinson
	G-BPVW	C.A.S.A. 1.131E Jungmann 2000	S. A. W. Becker/Goodwood
	G-BPVX	Cassutt Racer IIIM	J. H. Tetley
	G-BPVY	Cessna 172D	Unitek Aviation Ltd/Eaton Bray
	G-BPVZ	Luscombe 8E Silvaire	W. E. Gillham & P. Ryman
	G-BPWA	PA-28-161 Warrior II	Leisure Park Management Ltd
	G-BPWC	Cameron V-77 balloon	H. B. Roberts
	G-BPWD	Cessna 120	Peregrine Flying Group
	G-BPWE	PA-28-161 Warrior II	AT Aircraft Leasing Ltd/Cardiff
	G-BPWF	PA-28 Cherokee 140 ★	(static display)/1244 Sqdn ATC/Swindon
	G-BPWG	Cessna 150M	W. R. Spicer
	G-BPWI	Bell 206B JetRanger 3	S. Taylor
	G-BPWK	Sportavia Fournier RF-5B	S. L. Reed
	G-BPWL	PA-25-235 Pawnee	Marchington Gliding Club Ltd/Tatenhill
	G-BPWM	Cessna 150L	M. E. Creasey
	G-BPWN	Cessna 150L	Scionet Ltd
	G-BPWP	Rutan LongEz	J. F. O'Hara & A. J. Voyle
	G-BPWR	Cessna R.172K	A. M. Skelton
	G-BPWS	Cessna 172P	Plane Talking Ltd/Elstree
	G-BPWT	Cameron DG-19 airship	Airspace Outdoor Advertising Ltd
	G-BPWV	Colt 56A balloon	W. D. Young
	G-BPWW	Piaggio FWP.149D	G-BPWW Group
	G-BPWY	Isaacs Fury II	R. J. Knights
	G-BPWZ	PA-28-161 Warrior II	Air Nova/Liverpool
	G-BPXA	PA-28-181 Archer II	Cherokee Flying Group/Netherthorpe
	G-BPXB	Glaser-Dirks DG.400	K. M. Fresson & G. C. Westgate
	G-BPXE	Enstrom 280C Shark	A. Healy
	G-BPXF	Cameron V-65 balloon	D. Pascall
	G-BPXG	Colt 42A balloon	Cooper Group Ltd
	G-BPXH	Colt 17A balloon	Sport Promotion SRL/Italy
	G-BPXJ	PA-28RT-201T Turbo Arrow IV	K. M. Hollamby/Biggin Hill
	G-BPXX	PA-34-200T Seneca II	HoÖckstar Ltd
	G-BPXY	Aeronca 11AC Chief	S. Hawksworth
	G-BPXZ	Cameron V-77 balloon	British School of Ballooning
	G-BPYC	Cessna 310R	P. Clements/Biggin Hill
	G-BPYI	Cameron O-77 balloon	Fly by Night Balloon Group
	G-BPYJ	Wittman W.8 Tailwind	J. Dixon
	G-BPYK	Thunder Ax7-77 balloon	A. R. Swinnerton
	G-BPYN	Piper J-3C-65 Cub	The Aquila Group/White Waltham

Reg.	Type	Owner or Operator	Notes
G-BPYO	PA-28-181 Archer II	Sherburn Aero Club Ltd	
G-BPYR	PA-31-310 Turbo Navajo	Multi Ltd (G-ECMA)	
G-BPYS	Cameron O-77 balloon	D. J. Goldsmith	
G-BPYT	Cameron V-77 balloon	C. M. Hodges	
G-BPYV	Cameron V-77 balloon	M. E. Weston	
G-BPYW	Air Command 532 Elite	W. V. Tatters	
G-BPYY	Cameron A-180 balloon	G. D. Fitzpatrick	
G-BPYZ	Thunder Ax7-77 balloon	J. E. Astall	
G-BPZA	Luscombe 8A Silvaire	T. P. W. Hyde	
G-BPZB	Cessna 120	C. & M. A. Grime	
G-BPZC	Luscombe 8A Silvaire	C. C. & J. M. Lovell	
G-BPZD	SNCAN NC.858S	G. Richards	
G-BPZE	Luscombe 8E Silvaire	WFG Luscombe Associates	
G-BPZI	Christen Eagle II	S. D. Quigley	
G-BPZK	Cameron O-120 balloon	D. L. Smith	
G-BPZM	PA-28RT-201 Arrow IV	J. H. Kimber (G-ROYW/G-CRTI)	
G-BPZO	Cameron N-90 balloon	Seaward PLC	
G-BPZP	Robin DR.400/180R	Lasham Gliding Soc. Ltd	
G-BPZS	Colt 105A balloon	L. V. Mastis	
G-BPZU	Scheibe SF.25C Falke	G-BPZU Group/Parham Park	
G-BPZX	Cessna 152 II	Traffic Management Services	
G-BPZY	Pitts S-1C Special	J. S. Mitchell	
G-BPZZ	Thunder Ax8-105 balloon	Capricorn Balloons Ltd	
G-BRAA	Pitts S-1C Special	C. Davidson	
G-BRAE	Colt 69A balloon	Jentime Ltd	
G-BRAJ	Cameron V-77 balloon	H. R. Evans	
G-BRAK	Cessna 172N	C. Docketty	
G-BRAM	Mikoyan MiG-21PF (503)	Universal Aviation Group/North Weald	
G-BRAP	Thermal Aircraft 104	Thermal Aircraft	
G-BRAR	Aeronca 7AC Champion	C. D. Ward	
G-BRAV	PA-23 Aztec 250E	D. D. Smith (G-BBCM)	
G-BRAW	Pitts S-1C Special	P. G. Bond & P. B. Hunter	
G-BRAX	Payne Knight Twister 85B	R. Earl	
G-BRBA	PA-28-161 Warrior II	Halfpenny Green Flight Centre Ltd	
G-BRBB	PA-28-161 Warrior II	D. P. Hughes	
G-BRBC	NA T-6G Texan	A. P. Murphy	
G-BRBD	PA-28-151 Warrior	B. E. Simpson & C. R. Hughes	
G-BRBE	PA-28-161 Warrior II	Solo Services Ltd/Shoreham	
G-BRBF	Cessna 152 II	Jackson's Tool & Plant Hire	
G-BRBG	PA-28 Cherokee 180	Ken Macdonald & Co	
G-BRBH	Cessna 150H	Professional Flight Management Ltd & S. J. Reeves	
G-BRBI	Cessna 172N	G-BRBI Flying Group	
G-BRBJ	Cessna 172M	I. R. March	
G-BRBK	Robin DR.400/180	R. Kemp	
G-BRBL	Robin DR.400/180	C. A. Merren	
G-BRBM	Robin DR.400/180	R. W. Davies/Headcorn	
G-BRBN	Pitts S-1S Special	D. R. Evans	
G-BRBO	Cameron V-77 balloon	M. B. Murby	
G-BRBP	Cessna 152	Staverton Flying Services Ltd	
G-BRBS	Bensen B.8M	J. Simpson	
G-BRBT	Trotter Ax3-20 balloon	R. M. Trotter	
G-BRBU	Colt 17A balloon	Virgin Airship & Balloon Co Ltd	
G-BRBV	Piper J-4A Cub Coupé	M. Yeo & J. Schonburg	
G-BRBW	PA-28 Cherokee 140	Cherokee Cruiser Aircraft Group/ Shoreham	
G-BRBX	PA-28-181 Archer II	M. J. Ireland	
G-BRBY	Robinson R-22B	BLS Aviation Ltd	
G-BRCA	Jodel D.112	G. R. Hill & R. C. Jordan	
G-BRCD	Cessna A.152	D. E. Simmons/Shoreham	
G-BRCE	Pitts S-1C Special	R. O. Rogers	
G-BRCF	Montgomerie-Bensen B.8MR	J. S. Walton	
G-BRCG	Grob G.109	Oxfordshire Sportflying Ltd/Enstone	
G-BRCI	Pitts S-1C Special	G. L. Carpenter	
G-BRCJ	Cameron NS-20 balloon	P. de Cock/Belgium	
G-BRCM	Cessna 172L	S. G. E. Plessis & D. C. C. Handley	
G-BRCO	Cameron NS-20 balloon	M. Davies	
G-BRCR	Cameron V-77 balloon	E. E. Clark	
G-BRCT	Denney Kitfox Mk 2	Wessex Aviation & Transport Ltd	
G-BRCV	Aeronca 7AC Champion	J. M. Gale	
G-BRCW	Aeronca 11AC Chief	R. B. McComish	
G-BRDB	Zenair CH.701 STOL	D. L. Bowtell	

101

Notes	Reg.	Type	Owner or Operator
	G-BRDC	Thunder Ax7-77 balloon	N. J. Morley & D. M. Levene
	G-BRDD	Avions Mudry CAP.10B	R. D. Dickson/Gamston
	G-BRDE	Thunder Ax7-77 balloon	C. C. Brash
	G-BRDF	PA-28-161 Warrior II	White Waltham Airfield Ltd
	G-BRDG	PA-28-161 Warrior II	White Waltham Airfield Ltd
	G-BRDJ	Luscombe 8A Silvaire	C. C. & J. M. Lovell
	G-BRDL	Bell 206B JetRanger 3	Bond Helicopters ltd
	G-BRDM	PA-28-161 Warrior II	White Waltham Airfield Ltd
	G-BRDN	M.S.880B Rallye Club	B. J. D. Peatfield
	G-BRDO	Cessna 177B	Cardinal Group
	G-BRDP	Colt Jumbo SS balloon	Virgin Airship & Balloon Co Ltd
	G-BRDT	Cameron DP-70 airship	M. M. Cobbold
	G-BRDV	Viking Wood Products Spitfire Prototype replica (K5054)	C. Du Cros
	G-BRDW	PA-24 Comanche 180	I. P. Gibson/Switzerland
	G-BREA	Bensen B.8MR	T. J. Deane
	G-BREB	Piper J-3C-65 Cub	L. J. A. Cordes/Sywell
	G-BREE	Whittaker MW.7	G. Hawkins
	G-BREH	Cameron V-65 balloon	S. E. & V. D. Hurst
	G-BREK	Piper J-3C-65 Cub	C. L. H. Parr & I. Watts
	G-BREL	Cameron O-77 balloon	A. J. Moore & D. J. Green
	G-BREM	Air Command 532 Elite	T. W. Freeman
	G-BREP	PA-28RT-201 Arrow IV	P. G. McQuaid
	G-BRER	Aeronca 7AC Champion	B. & S. Medley
	G-BREU	Montgomerie-Bensen B.8MR	M. A. Hayward
	G-BREX	Cameron O-84 balloon	Ovolo Ltd
	G-BREY	Taylorcraft BC-12D	BREY Group
	G-BRFA	PA-31-350 Navajo Chieftain	Comed Aviation Ltd (G-BREW)
	G-BRFB	Rutan LongEz	R. A. Gardiner
	G-BRFC	P.57 Sea Prince T.1 (WP321)	Aces High Ltd/North Weald
	G-BRFE	Cameron V-77 balloon	N. J. Appleton
	G-BRFF	Colt 90A balloon	Amber Valley Aviation
	G-BRFH	Colt 90A balloon	Polydron UK Ltd
	G-BRFI	Aeronca 7DC Champion	I. J. Boyd & D. J. McCooke
	G-BRFJ	Aeronca 11AC Chief	C. M. G. Ellis
	G-BRFL	PA-38-112 Tomahawk	Teesside Flight Centre Ltd
	G-BRFM	PA-28-161 Warrior II	G. C. J. Moffatt & Co Ltd
	G-BRFN	PA-38-112 Tomahawk	Technology & Marketing Ltd
	G-BRFO	Cameron V-77 balloon	Hedge Hoppers Balloon Group
	G-BRFP	Schweizer 269C	Daedalus Aviation Ltd
	G-BRFR	Cameron N-105 balloon	Flying Pictures (Balloons) Ltd
	G-BRFS	Cameron N-90 balloon	Flying Pictures (Balloons) Ltdê
	G-BRFW	Montgomerie-Bensen B.8 Two Seat	J. M. Montgomerie
	G-BRFX	Pazmany PL.4A	D. E. Hills
	G-BRGD	Cameron O-84 balloon	J. R. H. & M. A. Ashworth
	G-BRGE	Cameron N-90 balloon	Oakfield Farm Products Ltd
	G-BRGF	Luscombe 8E Silvaire	The Luscombe Flying Group
	G-BRGG	Luscombe 8A Silvaire	M. P. & V. H. Weatherby
	G-BRGI	PA-28 Cherokee 180	Golf India Aviation Ltd/Redhill
	G-BRGN	BAe Jetstream 3102	Jetstream Aircraft Ltd(G-BLHC)/Prestwick
	G-BRGO	Air Command 532 Elite	D. A. Wood
	G-BRGT	PA-32 Cherokee Six 260	P. Cowley
	G-BRGW	GY-201 Minicab	R. G. White
	G-BRGX	Rotorway Executive	D. W. J. Lee
	G-BRHA	PA-32RT-300 Lance II	Lance G-BRHA Group
	G-BRHB	Boeing Stearman B.75N1	D. Calabritto
	G-BRHC	Cameron V-77 balloon	Golf Centres Balloons Ltd
	G-BRHG	Colt 90A balloon	Bath University Students Union
	G-BRHJ	PA-34-200T Seneca II	Draycott Seneca Group
	G-BRHL	Montgomerie-Bensen B.8M	A. McCredie
	G-BRHM	Bensen B.8M	H. P. Latham
	G-BRHN	Robinson R-22B	Barhale Surveying Ltd
	G-BRHO	PA-34-200 Seneca	D. A. Lewis/Luton
	G-BRHP	Aeronca O-58B Grasshopper (31923)	J. G. Townsend
	G-BRHR	PA-38-112 Tomahawk	Air Nova/Liverpool
	G-BRHS	PA-38-112 Tomahawk	Air Nova/Liverpool
	G-BRHT	PA-38-112 Tomahawk	Air Nova/Liverpool
	G-BRHU	Montgomerie-Bensen B.8MR	G. L. & S. R. Moon
	G-BRHW	D.H.82A Tiger Moth	P. J. & A. J. Borsberry
	G-BRHX	Luscombe 8E Silvaire	J. Lakin
	G-BRHY	Luscombe 8E Silvaire	D. Lofts & A. R. W. Taylor/Sleap

Reg.	Type	Owner or Operator	Notes
G-BRHZ	Stephens Akro Astro 235	N. M. Bloom & ptnrs	
G-BRIA	Cessna 310L	R. C. Pugsley	
G-BRIB	Cameron N-77 balloon	D. Stitt	
G-BRIE	Cameron N-77 balloon	Vokins Estates Ltd	
G-BRIF	Boeing 767-204ER	Britannia Airways Ltd *Horatio Nelson*	
G-BRIG	Boeing 767-204ER	Britannia Airways Ltd *Eglantyne Jebb*	
G-BRIH	Taylorcraft BC-12D	G. J. Taylor	
G-BRII	Zenair CH.600 Zodiac	A. C. Bowdrey	
G-BRIJ	Taylorcraft F-19	M. Beamand & K. E. Ballington	
G-BRIK	T.66 Nipper 3	C. W. R. Piper	
G-BRIL	Piper J-5A Cub Cruiser	P. L. Jobes	
G-BRIM	Cameron O-160 balloon	Golf Centres Balloons Ltd	
G-BRIN	SOCATA TB.20 Trinidad	Halfpenny Green Flight Centre Ltd	
G-BRIO	Turner Super T-40A	D. McIntyre	
G-BRIR	Cameron V-56 balloon	H. G. Davies & C. Dowd	
G-BRIS	Steen Skybolt	P. D. Harrison	
G-BRIV	SOCATA TB.9 Tampico Club	M. Stock & M. J. Aitkin	
G-BRIY	Taylorcraft DF-65 (42-58678)	J. A. Rollason/North Weald	
G-BRIZ	D.31 Turbulent	M. C. Hunt	
G-BRJA	Luscombe 8A Silvaire	A. D. Keen	
G-BRJB	Zenair CH.600 Zodiac	E. G. Brown	
G-BRJC	Cessna 120	One Twenty Group	
G-BRJI	Boeing 757-236	Rednall Ltd	
G-BRJK	Luscombe 8A Silvaire	C. J. L. Peat	
G-BRJL	PA-15 Vagabond	C. P. Ware & C. R. Leech	
G-BRJM	Cameron A-210 balloon	T. M. Donnelly	
G-BRJN	Pitts S-1C Special	G-BRJN Group	
G-BRJR	PA-38-112 Tomahawk	Chester Aviation Ltd	
G-BRJT	Cessna 150H	J. Eagles	
G-BRJV	PA-28-161 Cadet	Newcastle-upon-Tyne Aero Club Ltd	
G-BRJW	Bellanca 7GCBC Citabria	H. W. Weston/Staverton	
G-BRJX	Rand KR-2	D. H. Evans	
G-BRJY	Rand KR-2	R. E. Taylor	
G-BRKA	Luscombe 8F Silvaire	T. I. Carlin	
G-BRKC	J/1 Autocrat	J. W. Conlon	
G-BRKD	Piaggio FWP.149D	Operation Ability Ltd	
G-BRKE	Hawker Sea Hurricane XIIA (BW853)	AJD Engineering Ltd	
G-BRKH	PA-28-236 Dakota	P. A. Wright & P. W. Lever	
G-BRKJ	Stoddard-Hamilton Glasair III	R. F. E. Simard	
G-BRKL	Cameron H-34 balloon	B. J. Newman	
G-BRKN	Robinson R-22 Mariner	P. M. Webber/Greece	
G-BRKO	Oldfield Baby Great Lakes	C. Wren	
G-BRKP	Colt 31A balloon	Bavarian Balloon Co Ltd	
G-BRKR	Cessna 182R	A. R. D. Brooker	
G-BRKS	Air Command 532 Elite	G. Sandercock	
G-BRKW	Cameron V-77 balloon	T. J. Parker	
G-BRKX	Air Command 532 Elite	K. Davis	
G-BRKY	Viking Dragonfly Mk II	G. D. Price	
G-BRKZ	Air Command 532 Elite	D. C. E. Streeter	
G-BRLB	Air Command 532 Elite	F. G. Shepherd	
G-BRLC	Thunder Ax7-77 balloon	Fuji Photo Film (UK) Ltd	
G-BRLF	Campbell Cricket (replica)	D. Wood	
G-BRLG	PA-28RT-201T Turbo Arrow IV	C. G. Westwood	
G-BRLH	Air Command 532 Elite	Childs Garages (Sherborne) Ltd	
G-BRLI	Piper J-5A Cub Cruiser	Little Bear Ltd	
G-BRLJ	Evans VP-2	R. L. Jones	
G-BRLK	Air Command 532 Elite	G. L. Hunt	
G-BRLL	Cameron A-105 balloon	Adventure Flights Ltd	
G-BRLO	PA-38-112 Tomahawk	Scotia Safari Ltd/Prestwick	
G-BRLP	PA-38-112 Tomahawk	Lightstrong Ltd	
G-BRLR	Cessna 150G	D. C. Maxwell	
G-BRLS	Thunder Ax7-77 balloon	E. C. Meek	
G-BRLT	Colt 77A balloon	D. Bareford	
G-BRLU	Cameron H-24 balloon	D. K. Fish	
G-BRLV	CCF Harvard IV (93542)	B. C. Abela	
G-BRLX	Cameron N-77 balloon	National Power	
G-BRLY	BAe ATP	Manx Airlines Ltd	
G-BRMA	W.S.51 Dragonfly HR.5 (WG718) ★	IHM/Weston-s-Mare	
G-BRMB	B.192 Belvedere HC.1 (XG452) ★	IHM/Weston-s-Mare	
G-BRME	PA-28-181 Archer II	S. Edgar	
G-BRMG	V.S.384 Seafire XVII (SX336)	P. J. Woods	

Notes	Reg.	Type	Owner or Operator
	G-BRMI	Cameron V-65 balloon	M. Davies
	G-BRMJ	PA-38-112 Tomahawk	Aerohire Ltd/Halfpenny Green
	G-BRML	PA-38-112 Tomahawk	P. H. Rogers/Coventry
	G-BRMM	Air Command 532 Elite	R. de Serville
	G-BRMN	Thunder Ax7-77 balloon	G. Restell & R. Higham
	G-BRMS	PA-28RT-201 Arrow IV	Fleetbridge Ltd
	G-BRMT	Cameron V-31 balloon	R. M. Trotter & K. L. Heron
	G-BRMU	Cameron V-77 balloon	K. J. & G. R. Ibbotson
	G-BRMV	Cameron O-77 balloon	P. D. Griffiths
	G-BRMW	Whittaker MW.7	N. Crisp
	G-BRNC	Cessna 150M	D. C. Bonsall
	G-BRND	Cessna 152 II	T. M. & M. L. Jones
	G-BRNE	Cessna 152 II	Aerohire Ltd/Halfpenny Green
	G-BRNJ	PA-38-112 Tomahawk	Aerohire Ltd/Halfpenny Green
	G-BRNK	Cessna 152 II	Sheffield Aero Club Ltd/Netherthorpe
	G-BRNM	Chichester-Miles Leopard	Chichester-Miles Consultants Ltd
	G-BRNN	Cessna 152 II	Sheffield Aero Club Ltd/Netherthorpe
	G-BRNP	Rotorway Executive	C. A. Laycock
	G-BRNR	Schweizer 269C	C.S.E. Aviation Ltd/Kidlington
	G-BRNT	Robin DR.400/180	M. J. Cowham
	G-BRNU	Robin DR.400/180	November Uniform Travel Syndicate Ltd/ Booker
	G-BRNV	PA-28-181 Archer II	B. S. Hobbs
	G-BRNW	Cameron V-77 balloon	N. Robertson & G. Smith
	G-BRNX	PA-22 Tri-Pacer 150	R. S. Tomlinson & B. Yager
	G-BRNY	Thunder Ax6-56A balloon	P. J. Beglan/France
	G-BRNZ	PA-32 Cherokee Six 300B	IML Aviation Ltd
	G-BROB	Cameron V-77 balloon	R. W. Richardson
	G-BROE	Cameron N-65 balloon	R. H. Sanderson
	G-BROF	Air Command 532 Elite	M. J. Hoskins
	G-BROG	Cameron V-65 balloon	R. Kunert
	G-BROH	Cameron O-90 balloon	P. A. Wenlock
	G-BROI	CFM Streak Shadow Srs SA	G. W. Rowbotham
	G-BROJ	Colt 31A balloon	Virgin Airship & Balloon Co Ltd
	G-BROL	Colt AS-80 Mk II airship	Wellfarrow Ltd
	G-BROO	Luscombe 8A Silvaire	Bedwell Hey Flying Group
	G-BROP	Vans RV-4	K. E. Armstrong
	G-BROR	Piper J-3C-65 Cub	White Hart Flying Group
	G-BROX	Robinson R-22B	Zeuros Ltd
	G-BROY	Cameron V-77 balloon	T. G. S. Dixon
	G-BROZ	PA-18 Super Cub 150	P. G. Kynsey
	G-BRPE	Cessna 120	M. A. N. Newall
	G-BRPF	Cessna 120	D. Sharp
	G-BRPG	Cessna 120	I. C. Lomax
	G-BRPH	Cessna 120	J. A. Cook
	G-BRPJ	Cameron N-90 balloon	Cloud Nine Balloon Co
	G-BRPK	PA-28 Cherokee 140	J. P. A. Gomes
	G-BRPL	PA-28 Cherokee 140	Comed Aviation Ltd/Blackpool
	G-BRPM	T.66 Nipper 3	T. C. Horner
	G-BRPO	Enstrom 280C	K. Payne & ptnrs
	G-BRPP	Brookland Hornet	D. E. Cox
	G-BRPR	Aeronca O-58B Grasshopper (31952)	C. S. Tolchard
	G-BRPS	Cessna 177B	N. W. Beresford
	G-BRPT	Rans S.10 Sakota	B. G. Morris
	G-BRPU	Beech 76 Duchess	Hamilton Compass Aviation Ltd
	G-BRPV	Cessna 152	GEM Rewinds Ltd/Coventry
	G-BRPX	Taylorcraft BC-12D	M. J. Brett
	G-BRPY	PA-15 Vagabond	J. P. Esson
	G-BRPZ	Luscombe 8A Silvaire	S. L. & J. P. Waring
	G-BRRA	V.S.361 Spitfire LF.IXe (MK912)	Historic Aircraft Collection Ltd
	G-BRRB	Luscombe 8E Silvaire	C. G. Ferguson & D. W. Gladwin
	G-BRRD	Scheibe SF.25B Falke	M. N. Martin
	G-BRRE	Colt 69A balloon	P. Patel
	G-BRRF	Cameron O-77 balloon	Mid-Bucks Farmers Balloon Group
	G-BRRG	Glaser-Dirks DG.500M	Glider Syndicate/Sutton Bank
	G-BRRJ	PA-28RT-201T Turbo Arrow IV	M. & E. Machinery Ltd
	G-BRRK	Cessna 182Q	M. Cligman & ptnrs
	G-BRRL	PA-18 Super Cub 95	Acebell G-BRRL Syndicate/Redhill
	G-BRRM	PA-28-161 Cadet	R. H. Sellier
	G-BRRN	PA-28-161 Warrior II	Spinseal Ltd
	G-BRRO	Cameron N-77 balloon	Newbury Building Soc
	G-BRRR	Cameron V-77 balloon	L. M. Heal & A. P. Wilcox

Reg.	Type	Owner or Operator	Notes
G-BRRS	Pitts S-1C Special	R. C. Atkinson	
G-BRRT	C.A.S.A. 1.131E Jungmann 2000	P. G. Kynsey	
G-BRRU	Colt 90A balloon	Reach For The Sky Ltd	
G-BRRW	Cameron O-77 balloon	D. V. Fowler	
G-BRRY	Robinson R-22B	Bristow Helicopters Ltd/Redhill	
G-BRSA	Cameron N-56 balloon	C. Wilkinson	
G-BRSC	Rans S.10 Sakota	M. A. C. Stephenson	
G-BRSD	Cameron V-77 balloon	T. J. Porter & J. E. Kelly	
G-BRSE	PA-28-161 Warrior II	Startown Ltd	
G-BRSG	PA-28-161 Cadet	Holmes Rentals/Denham	
G-BRSH	C.A.S.A. 1.131E Jungmann 2000 (781-25)	A. J. E. Smith/Breighton	
G-BRSI	PA-28-161 Cadet	Plane Talking Ltd/Denham	
G-BRSJ	PA-38-112 Tomahawk II	APB Leasing Ltd/Welshpool	
G-BRSK	Boeing Stearman N2S-3 (1180)	Wymondham Engineering	
G-BRSL	Cameron N-56 balloon	S. Budd	
G-BRSN	Rand-Robinson KR-2	K. W. Darby	
G-BRSO	CFM Streak Shadow Srs SA	D. J. Smith	
G-BRSP	Air Command 532 Elite	D. R. G. Griffith	
G-BRSW	Luscombe 8A Silvaire	Moravian Flying Group	
G-BRSX	PA-15 Vagabond	C. Milne-Fowler	
G-BRSY	Hatz CB-1	G. A. Barrett & Son	
G-BRTA	PA-38-112 Tomahawk	R. A. Wakefield	
G-BRTB	Bell 206B JetRanger 3	Harris Technology Ltd	
G-BRTC	Cessna 150G	Thorpe Air Ltd/Goodwood	
G-BRTD	Cessna 152 II	152 Group/Goodwood	
G-BRTH	Cameron A-180 balloon	The Ballooning Business Ltd	
G-BRTJ	Cessna 150F	Jersey ATC Flying Ltd	
G-BRTK	Boeing Stearman E.75 (217786)	Eastern Stearman Ltd/North Walsham	
G-BRTL	Hughes 369E	Crewhall Ltd	
G-BRTM	PA-28-161 Warrior II	C.S.E. Aviation Ltd/Kidlington	
G-BRTN	Beech 95-B58 Baron	Colneway Ltd/Guernsey	
G-BRTP	Cessna 152 II	CBS Aerohire Ltd/Earls Colne	
G-BRTT	Schweizer 269C	Fairthorpe Ltd/Denham	
G-BRTV	Cameron O-77 balloon	C. Vening	
G-BRTW	Glaser-Dirks DG.400	I. J. Carruthers	
G-BRTX	PA-28-151 Warrior	Spectrum Flying Group	
G-BRTZ	Slingsby T.31 Motor Cadet III	R. R. Walters	
G-BRUA	Cessna 152 II	Griffin Marston/Compton Abbas	
G-BRUB	PA-28-161 Warrior II	Flytrek Ltd/Bournemouth	
G-BRUD	PA-28-181 Archer II	Wilkins & Wilkins Special Auctions Ltd	
G-BRUE	Cameron V-77 balloon	B. J. Newman & P. L. Harrison	
G-BRUG	Luscombe 8E Silvaire	P. A. Cain & N. W. Barratt	
G-BRUH	Colt 105A balloon	D. C. Chipping	
G-BRUI	PA-44-180 Seminole	Tatenhill Aviation	
G-BRUJ	Boeing Stearman A.75N1 (16136)	M. Walker/Liverpool	
G-BRUM	Cessna A.152	Flychoice Ltd/Birmingham	
G-BRUN	Cessna 120	O. C. Brun (G-BRDH)	
G-BRUO	Taylor JT.1 Monoplane	G. Verity	
G-BRUT	Thunder Ax8-90 balloon	Moet & Chandon (London) Ltd	
G-BRUU	EAA Biplane Model P.1	R. D. Harper	
G-BRUV	Cameron V-77 balloon	T. W. & R. F. Benbrook	
G-BRUX	PA-44-180 Seminole	Hambrair Ltd/Tollerton	
G-BRUZ	Raven Europe FS-57A balloon	R. H. Etherington	
G-BRVB	Stolp SA.300 Starduster Too	M. N. Petchey & S. Turner	
G-BRVC	Cameron N-180 balloon	A. J. Street	
G-BRVE	Beech D.17S	Intrepid Aviation Co/North Weald	
G-BRVF	Colt 77A balloon	Airborne Adventures Ltd	
G-BRVG	NA SNJ-7 Texan (27)	Intrepid Aviation Co/North Weald	
G-BRVH	Smyth Model S Sidewinder	I. S. Bellamy	
G-BRVI	Robinson R-22B	Burnell Helicopters Ltd	
G-BRVJ	Slingsby T.31 Motor Cadet III	B. Outhwaite	
G-BRVK	Cameron A-210 Balloon	A. J. Street	
G-BRVL	Pitts S-1C Special	N. I. Gibson	
G-BRVN	Thunder Ax7-77 balloon	D. L. Beckwith	
G-BRVO	AS.350B Ecureuil	Malcolm Wilson (Motorsport) Ltd	
G-BRVR	Barnett J4B-2 rotorcraft	Ilkeston Contractors	
G-BRVS	Barnett J4B-2 rotorcraft	Ilkeston Contractors	
G-BRVT	Pitts S-2B Special	C. J. & M. D. Green	
G-BRVU	Colt 77A balloon	D. J. Harber	
G-BRVV	Colt 56B balloon	S. J. Hollingsworth	
G-BRVX	Cameron A-210 balloon	G. C. Ludlow	
G-BRVY	Thunder Ax8-90 balloon	G. E. Morris	

Notes	Reg.	Type	Owner or Operator
	G-BRVZ	Jodel D.117	J. G. Patton
	G-BRWA	Aeronca 7AC Champion	D. D. Smith & J. R. Edwards
	G-BRWB	NA T-6G Texan (51-14526)	Monafield Ltd
	G-BRWC	Cessna 152 II	T. Hayselden (Doncaster) Ltd
	G-BRWD	Robinson R22B	Matrix Aviation Ltd
	G-BRWF	Thunder Ax7-77	D. J. Greaves
	G-BRWH	Cameron N-77	D. J. Usher
	G-BRWO	PA-28 Cherokee 140	Spitfire Aviation Ltd/Bournemouth
	G-BRWP	CFM Streak Shadow Srs SA	J. M. Bain
	G-BRWR	Aeronca 11AC Chief	M. S. Moon & R. M. Lee
	G-BRWT	Scheibe SF.25C Falke	J. E. Steenson & Booker Gliding Club Ltd
	G-BRWU	Luton LA-4A Minor	R. B. Webber & P. K. Pike
	G-BRWV	Brügger MB.2 Colibri	S. J. McCollum
	G-BRWX	Cessna 172P	D. A. Abels
	G-BRWY	Cameron H-34 balloon	E. Kraft/Belgium
	G-BRWZ	Cameron 90 Macaw SS balloon	Forbes Europe Inc/France
	G-BRXA	Cameron O-120 balloon	Gone With The Wind Ltd & R. J. Mansfield
	G-BRXB	Thunder Ax7-77 balloon	H. Peel
	G-BRXC	PA-28-161 Warrior II	C.S.E. Aviation Ltd/Kidlington
	G-BRXD	PA-28-181 Archer II	D. D. Stone
	G-BRXE	Taylorcraft BC-12D	W. J. Durrad
	G-BRXF	Aeronca 11AC Chief	A. B. Newman
	G-BRXG	Aeronca 7AC Champion	X-Ray Golf Flying Group
	G-BRXH	Cessna 120	J. N. Pittock & A. P. Fox
	G-BRXL	Aeronca 11AC Chief (42-78044)	G-BRXL Group
	G-BRXN	Montgomerie-Bensen B.8MR	J. C. Aitken
	G-BRXO	PA-34-200T Seneca II	Aviation Services Ltd
	G-BRXP	SNCAN Stampe SV-4C (modified)	P. G. Kavanagh & D. T. Kaberry
	G-BRXS	Howard Special T Minus	A. Shuttleworth
	G-BRXU	AS.332L Super Puma	Bristow Helicopters Ltd
	G-BRXV	Robinson R-22B	Pearce Enterprise Ltd
	G-BRXW	PA-24 Comanche 260	The Oak Group
	G-BRXY	Pietenpol Air Camper	P. S. Ganczakowski
	G-BRXZ	Robinson R-22B	Helisport Ltd
	G-BRYA	D.H.C.7-110 Dash Seven	Brymon Off Shore Charter
	G-BRYD	D.H.C.7-110 Dash Seven	Brymon Off Shore Charter
	G-BRYI	D.H.C.8-311 Dash Eight	Brymon Airways Ltd/British Airways Northumberland
	G-BRYJ	D.H.C.8-311 Dash Eight	Brymon Airways Ltd/British Airways Somerset
	G-BRYK	D.H.C.8-311 Dash Eight	Brymon Airways Ltd/British Airways
	G-BRYM	D.H.C.8-311 Dash Eight	Brymon Airways Ltd/British Airways
	G-BRYN	SOCATA TB.20 Trinidad	Jones & Bradbourn (Guernsey) Ltd
	G-BRYO	D.H.C.8-311 Dash Eight	Brymon Airways Ltd/British Airways
	G-BRYP	D.H.C.8-311 Dash Eight	Brymon Airways Ltd/British Airways
	G-BRYR	D.H.C.8-311 Dash Eight	Brymon Airways Ltd/British Airways
	G-BRZA	Cameron O-77 balloon	L. & R. J. Mold
	G-BRZB	Cameron A-105 balloon	Headland Services Ltd
	G-BRZC	Cameron N-90 balloon	Flying Pictures (Balloons) Ltd
	G-BRZD	Hapi Cygnet SF-2A	L. G. Millen
	G-BRZE	Thunder Ax7-77 balloon	G. V. Beckwith
	G-BRZG	Enstrom F-28A	Chart Planes Inland Ltd
	G-BRZI	Cameron N-180 balloon	Eastern Balloon Rides
	G-BRZK	Stinson 108-2	J. A. Webb & G. F. Wheeler
	G-BRZL	Pitts S-1D Special	R. T. Cardwell/Elstree
	G-BRZO	Jodel D.18	J. D. Anson
	G-BRZP	PA-28-161 Warrior II	Air Service Training Ltd/Perth
	G-BRZS	Cessna 172P	YP Flying Group/Blackpool
	G-BRZT	Cameron V-77 balloon	B. Drawbridge
	G-BRZU	Colt Flying Cheese SS balloon	N. Carbonnier
	G-BRZV	Colt Flying Apple SS balloon	Thrust Drive Ltd
	G-BRZW	Rans S.10 Sakota	D. L. Davies
	G-BRZX	Pitts S-1S Special	G-BRZX Group
	G-BRZZ	CFM Streak Shadow	P. R. Oakes
	G-BSAB	PA-46-350P Malibu Mirage	D. O. Hooper
	G-BSAI	Stoddard-Hamilton Glasair III	K. J. & P. J. Whitehead
	G-BSAJ	C.A.S.A. 1.131E Jungmann 2000	P. G. Kynsey/Redhill
	G-BSAK	Colt 21A balloon	Northern Flights
	G-BSAR	Air Command 532 Elite	T. A. Holmes
	G-BSAS	Cameron V-65 balloon	J. R. Barber
	G-BSAT	PA-28-181 Archer II	A1 Aircraft Ltd/Biggin Hill

Reg.	Type	Owner or Operator	Notes
G-BSAV	Thunder Ax7-77 balloon	E. A. Evans & ptnrs	
G-BSAW	PA-28-161 Warrior II	Carill Aviation Ltd/Southampton	
G-BSAX	Piper J-3C-65 Cub	Crop Aviation (UK) Ltd	
G-BSAZ	Denney Kitfox Mk 2	L. A. James	
G-BSBA	PA-28-161 Warrior II	APB Leasing Ltd/Welshpool	
G-BSBG	CCF Harvard IV (20310)	A. P. St John/Liverpool	
G-BSBH	Short SD3-30 ★	Ulster Aviation Soc Museum (stored)	
G-BSBI	Cameron O-77 balloon	Calibre Motor Co Ltd	
G-BSBK	Colt 105A balloon	Zebra Ballooning Ltd	
G-BSBM	Cameron N-77 balloon	Nuclear Electric	
G-BSBN	Thunder Ax7-77 balloon	B. Pawson	
G-BSBP	J°odel D.18	R. T. Pratt	
G-BSBR	Cameron V-77 balloon	B. Bromiley	
G-BSBT	Piper J-3C-65 Cub	M. B. & L. J. Proudfoot	
G-BSBU	Firefly 8B balloon	A. R. Peart	
G-BSBV	Rans S.10 Sakota	Sportair UK Ltd	
G-BSBW	Bell 206B JetRanger 3	Leeds Central Helicopters Ltd	
G-BSBX	Montgomerie-Bensen B.8MR	B. Ibbott	
G-BSBZ	Cessna 150M	DTG Aviation	
G-BSCA	Cameron N-90 balloon	P. J. Marshall & M. A. Clarke	
G-BSCB	Air Command 532 Elite	P. H. Smith	
G-BSCC	Colt 105A balloon	A. F. Selby	
G-BSCD	Hughes 269C	Aviation Bureau/Redhill	
G-BSCE	Robinson R-22B	H. Sugden	
G-BSCF	Thunder Ax7-77 balloon	V. P. Gardiner	
G-BSCG	Denney Kitfox Mk 2	N. L. Beever	
G-BSCH	Denney Kitfox Mk 2	M. P. M. Read	
G-BSCI	Colt 77A balloon	J. L. & S. Wrigglesworth	
G-BSCK	Cameron H-24 balloon	J. D. Shapland	
G-BSCL	Robinson R-22B	Sandhill Ltd	
G-BSCM	Denney Kitfox Mk 2	W. T. Price & S. B. Churchill	
G-BSCN	SOCATA TB.20 Trinidad	B. W. Dye	
G-BSCO	Thunder Ax7-77 balloon	F. J. Whalley	
G-BSCP	Cessna 152 II	Moray Flying Club (1990) Ltd/Kinloss	
G-BSCR	Cessna 172M	London Link Flying Ltd	
G-BSCS	PA-28-181 Archer II	Wing Task Ltd	
G-BSCV	PA-28-161 Warrior II	Southwood Flying Group/Southend	
G-BSCW	Taylorcraft BC-65	S. Leach	
G-BSCX	Thunder Ax8-105 balloon	Balloon Flights Club Ltd	
G-BSCY	PA-28-151 Warrior	Falcon Flying Services/Biggin Hill	
G-BSCZ	Cessna 152 II	London Flight Centre (Stansted) Ltd/Lydd	
G-BSDA	Taylorcraft BC-12D	D. G. Edwards	
G-BSDB	Pitts S-1C Special	G. Gregg	
G-BSDD	Denney Kitfox Mk 2	J. Windmill	
G-BSDG	Robin DR.400/180	B. Hodge	
G-BSDH	Robin DR.40i0/180	R. L. Brucciani	
G-BSDI	Corben Junior Ace Model E	J. Pearson/Eaglescott	
G-BSDJ	Piper J-4E Cub Coupé	J. H. Tope & R. D. Furnivall	
G-BSDK	Piper J-5A Cub Cruiser	S. Haughton & I. S. Hodge	
G-BSDL	SOCATA TB.10 Tobago	Delta Lima Group	
G-BSDN	PA-34-200T Seneca II	Belso Aviation Ltd	
G-BSDO	Cessna 152 II	J. Vickers	
G-BSDP	Cessna 152 II	I. S. H. Paul	
G-BSDS	Boeing Stearman E.75 (118)	E. Hopper	
G-BSDU	Bell 206B JetRanger 3	Eaglecury Ltd	
G-BSDV	Colt 31A balloon	Virgin Airship & Balloon Co Ltd	
G-BSDW	Cessna 182P	Delta Whisky Ltd	
G-BSDY	Beech 58 Baron	Astra Ltd	
G-BSDZ	Enstrom 280FX	Southern Air Ltd (G-ODSC)/Shoreham	
G-BSED	PA-22 Tri-Pacer 160 (modified)	M. Henderson	
G-BSEE	Rans S.9	P. M. Semler	
G-BSEF	PA-28 Cherokee 180	Prestwick Pilots Group	
G-BSEG	Ken Brock KB-2 gyroplane	S. J. M. Ledingham	
G-BSEJ	Cessna 150M	Halfpenny Green Flight Centre Ltd	
G-BSEK	Robinson R-22	Heli Air Ltd/Booker	
G-BSEL	Slingsby T.61G Super Falke	RAFGSA/Hullavington	
G-BSEP	Cessna 172	A. Washington & A. P. Wall/Redhill	
G-BSER	PA-28 Cherokee 160	Yorkair Ltd	
G-BSES	Denney Kitfox	M. Albert-Recht & J. J. M. Donnelly	
G-BSET	B.206 Srs 1 Basset	Beagle Basset Ltd/Shoreham	
G-BSEU	PA-28-181 Archer II	Euro Aviation 91 Ltd	
G-BSEV	Cameron O-77 balloon	UK Transplant Co-ordinators Assoc	
G-BSEW	Sikorsky S-76A	Bond Helicopters Ltd	

Notes	Reg.	Type	Owner or Operator
	G-BSEX	Cameron A-180 balloon	Heart of England Balloons
	G-BSEY	Beech A36 Bonanza	K. Phillips Ltd
	G-BSEZ	Air Command 532 Elite	D. S. Robinson
	G-BSFA	Aero Designs Pulsar	S. A. Gill
	G-BSFB	C.A.S.A. 1.131E Jungmann 2000 (S5-B06)	J. A. Sykes
	G-BSFD	Piper J-3C-65 Cub	E. G. & N. S. C. English
	G-BSFE	PA-38-112 Tomahawk II	D. J. Campbell
	G-BSFF	Robin DR.400/180R	Lasham Gliding Soc Ltd
	G-BSFJ	Thunder Ax8-105 balloon	Airborne Adventures Ltd
	G-BSFK	PA-28-161 Warrior II	C.S.E. Aviation Ltd/Kidlington
	G-BSFN	SE.313B Alouette II	M & P Food Products Ltd
	G-BSFP	Cessna 152T	J. R. Nicholls/Sibson
	G-BSFR	Cessna 152 II	Galair Ltd/Biggin Hill
	G-BSFS	SE.313B Alouette II	M & P Food Products Ltd
	G-BSFV	Woods Woody Pusher	M. J. Wells
	G-BSFW	PA-15 Vagabond	J. R. Kimberley
	G-BSFX	Denney Kitfox Mk 2	D. A. McFadyean
	G-BSFY	Denney Kitfox Mk 2	J. R. Howard
	G-BSGB	Gaertner Ax4 Skyranger balloon	B. Gaertner
	G-BSGC	PA-18 Super Cub 95	G. Churchill
	G-BSGD	PA-28 Cherokee 180	R. J. Cleverley
	G-BSGF	Robinson R-22B	Direct Helicopters (Southend) Ltd
	G-BSGG	Denney Kitfox Mk 2	C. G. Richardson
	G-BSGH	Airtour AH-56B balloon	G. Luck
	G-BSGJ	Monnett Sonerai II	G. A. Brady
	G-BSGK	PA-34-200T Seneca II	R. Hope & M. J. Martin
	G-BSGL	PA-28-161 Warrior II	Keywest Air Charter Ltd/Liverpool
	G-BSGM	Cameron V-77 balloon	A. M. Dare
	G-BSGN	PA-28-151 Warrior	J. R. Whetlor & M. Gipps/Denham
	G-BSGP	Cameron N-65 balloon	Mid-Sussex Flying School
	G BSGR	Boeing Stearman E.75	A. G. Dunkerley
	G-BSGS	Rans S.10 Sakota	M. R. Parr
	G-BSGT	Cessna T.210N	B. J. Sharpe/Booker
	G-BSGY	Thunder Ax7-77 balloon	P. B. Kenington
	G-BSHA	PA-34-200T Seneca II	Shepherd Aviation Ltd
	G-BSHC	Colt 69A balloon	L. V. Mastis
	G-BSHD	Colt 69A balloon	D. K. Fish
	G-BSHE	Cessna 152 II	J. A. Pothecary/Shoreham
	G-BSHH	Luscombe 8E Silvaire	Golf Centres Balloons Ltd
	G-BSHI	Luscombe 8F Silvaire	W. H. J. Knowles
	G-BSHK	Denney Kitfox Mk 2	A. E. Cree & G. J. Cuzzocrea
	G-BSHM	Slingsby T.31 Motor Cadet III	D. Shrimpton
	G-BSHO	Cameron V-77 balloon	T. P. Barlass & D. J. Duckworth
	G-BSHP	PA-28-161 Warrior II	Air Service Training Ltd/Perth
	G-BSHR	Cessna F.172N	A. Simmers Ltd (G-BFGE)
	G-BSHS	Colt 105A balloon	I. Novosad
	G-BSHT	Cameron V-77 balloon	ECM Construction Ltd
	G-BSHV	PA-18 Super Cub 135	Fen Tigers Flying Group
	G-BSHW	Hawker Tempest II (MW800)	P. Y. C. Denis/France
	G-BSHX	Enstrom F-28A	Stephenson Aviation Ltd/Goodwood
	G-BSHY	EAA Acro Sport I	R. J. Hodder
	G-BSHZ	Enstrom F-28F	Flemming & Co Dublin Ltd
	G-BSIB	PA-28-161 Warrior II	Bobbington Air Training School Ltd Halfpenny Green
	G-BSIC	Cameron V-77 balloon	P. D. Worthy
	G-BSIF	Denney Kitfox Mk 2	R. M. Kimbell & M. H. Wylde
	G-BSIG	Colt 21A balloon	E. C. & A. J. Moore
	G-BSIH	Rutan LongEz	W. S. Allen
	G-BSII	PA-34-200T Seneca II	N. H. N. Gardner
	G-BSIJ	Cameron V-77 balloon	A. S. Jones
	G-BSIK	Denney Kitfox Mk 1	I. A. Davies & B. Barr
	G-BSIM	PA-28-181 Archer II	E. Midlands Aircraft Hire Ltd
	G-BSIN	Robinson R-22B	Actionbound Building Co Ltd
	G-BSIO	Cameron 80 Shed SS balloon	R. E. Jones
	G-BSIR	Cessna 340	Airmaster Aviation Ltd/Cardiff
	G-BSIT	Robinson R-22B	Controlled Demolition Group Ltd
	G-BSIU	Colt 90A balloon	S. Travaglia
	G-BSIW	BAe Jetstream 3100	Jetstream Aircraft Ltd (G-OEDL/G-OAKK)
	G-BSIY	Schleicher ASK.14	Winwick Flying Group
	G-BSIZ	PA-28-181 Archer II	Firmdane Ltd
	G-BSJA	Cameron N-77 balloon	N. Sanders (G-SPAR)
	G-BSJB	Bensen B.8	J. W. Limbrick

Reg.	Type	Owner or Operator	Notes
G-BSJU	Cessna 150M	A. C. Williamson	
G-BSJV	Cessna 172N	J. C. M. van Tilburg	
G-BSJW	Everett Srs 2 gyroplane	A. R. Willis	
G-BSJX	PA-28-161 Warrior II	Border Air Training Ltd/Ronaldsway	
G-BSJZ	Cessna 150J	Simair Ltd	
G-BSKA	Cessna 150M	Cubair Ltd/Redhill	
G-BSKC	PA-38-112 Tomahawk	J. Marioni/Panshanger	
G-BSKD	Cameron V-77 balloon	M. J. Gunston	
G-BSKE	Cameron O-84 balloon	The Blunt Arrows Balloon Team	
G-BSKG	Maule MX-7-180	J. R. Surbey	
G-BSKH	Cessna 421C	Widehawk Aviation Ltd/Ipswich	
G-BSKI	Thunder Ax8-90 balloon	G-BSKI Balloon Group	
G-BSKK	PA-38-112 Tomahawk	Falcon Flying Services/Biggin Hill	
G-BSKL	PA-38-112 Tomahawk	Falcon Flying Services/Biggin Hill	
G-BSKO	Maule MXT-7-180	M. A. Ashmole	
G-BSKP	V.S.379 Spitfire F.XIV (RN201)	Historic Aircraft Collection Ltd	
G-BSKR	Rand Robinson KR-2	I. L. Griffiths	
G-BSKT	Maule MX-7-180	D. D. Smith	
G-BSKU	Cameron O-84 balloon	Alfred Bagnall & Sons (West) Ltd	
G-BSKW	PA-28-181 Archer II	Shropshire Aero Club Ltd/Sleap	
G-BSLA	Robin DR.400/180	A. B. McCoig/Biggin Hill	
G-BSLD	PA-28RT-201 Arrow IV	E. D. Gawronek	
G-BSLE	PA-28-161 Warrior II	C.S.E. Aviation Ltd/Kidlington	
G-BSLG	Cameron A-180 balloon	B. J. Newman	
G-BSLH	C.A.S.A. 1.131E Jungmann 2000	P. Warden	
G-BSLI	Cameron V-77 balloon	J. D. C. & F. E. Bevan	
G-BSLJ	Denney Kitfox Mk 2	A. F. Reid	
G-BSLK	PA-28-161 Warrior II	R. A. Rose	
G-BSLM	PA-28 Cherokee 160	Old Sarum Cherokee Group	
G-BSLO	Cameron A-180 balloon	Adventure Balloon Co Ltd	
G-BSLT	PA-28-161 Warrior II	P. A. Lancaster	
G-BSLU	PA-28 Cherokee 140	D. J. Budden/Shobdon	
G-BSLW	Bellanca 7ECA Citabria	J. A. Killerby	
G-BSLX	WAR Focke-Wulf Fw.190 (replica) (4+)	B. F. L. & T. A. Hodges	
G-BSLY	Colt AS-80 GD airship	Huntair Ltd	
G-BSMB	Cessna U.206E	Army Parachute Association/Netheravon	
G-BSMD	Nord 1101 Noralpha (+114)	R. J. Lamplough	
G-BSME	Bo 208C1 Junior	D. J. Hampson	
G-BSMF	Avro 652A Anson C.19 (TX183)	G. M. K. Fraser	
G-BSMG	Montgomerie-Bensen B.8M	A. C. Timperley	
G-BSMH	Colt 240A balloon	Formtrack Ltd	
G-BSMK	Cameron O-84 balloon	J. C. Reavley	
G-BSML	Schweizer 269C	Handy Rise Ltd	
G-BSMM	Colt 31A balloon	D. V. Fowler	
G-BSMN	CFM Streak Shadow	K. Daniels	
G-BSMO	Denney Kitfox	G-BSMO Group	
G-BSMP	PA-34-220T Seneca III	Manor Developments Ltd	
G-BSMS	Cameron V-77 balloon	Sade Balloons Ltd	
G-BSMT	Rans S.10 Sakota	D. K. Webb	
G-BSMU	Rans S.6 Coyote II	W. D. Walker (G-MWJE)	
G-BSMV	PA-17 Vagabond (modified)	A. Cheriton	
G-BSMX	Bensen B.8MR	J. S. E. McGregor	
G-BSND	Air Command 532 Elite	K. Brogden & W. B. Lumb	
G-BSNE	Luscombe 8E Silvaire	Aerolite Luscombe Group	
G-BSNF	Piper J-3C-65 Cub	D. A. Hammant	
G-BSNG	Cessna 172N	A. J. & P. C. MacDonald/Edinburgh	
G-BSNI	Bensen B.8V	B. D. Gibbs	
G-BSNJ	Cameron N-90 balloon	D. P. H. Smith	
G-BSNL	Bensen B.8MR	A. C. Breane	
G-BSNN	Rans S.10 Sakota	O. & S. D. Barnard	
G-BSNO	Denney Kitfox	A. G. V. McClintock	
G-BSNP	PA-28-201T Turbo Arrow III	V. Dowd/Stapleford	
G-BSNR	BAe 146-300A	Air UK Ltd/Stansted	
G-BSNS	BAe 146-300A	Air UK Ltd/Stansted	
G-BSNT	Luscombe 8A Silvaire	G. J. Slater	
G-BSNU	Colt 105A balloon	Sun Life Assurance Soc PLC	
G-BSNV	Boeing 737-4Q8	British Airways	
G-BSNW	Boeing 737-4Q8	British Airways	
G-BSNX	PA-28-181 Archer II	G-WATS Aviation Ltd/Halfpenny Green	
G-BSNY	Bensen B.8M	A. S. Deakin	
G-BSNZ	Cameron O-105 balloon	Aire Valley Balloons	
G-BSOE	Luscombe 8A Silvaire	S. B. Marsden	

Notes	Reg.	Type	Owner or Operator
	G-BSOG	Cessna 172M	B. Chapman & A. R. Budden/Goodwood
	G-BSOI	AS.332L Super Puma	Brintel Helicopters Ltd
	G-BSOJ	Thunder Ax7-77 balloon	R. J. S. Jones
	G-BSOK	PA-28-161 Warrior II	Voyager Aviation Ltd
	G-BSOM	Glaser-Dirks DG.400	G-BSOM Group/Tibenham
	G-BSON	Green S.25 balloon	J. J. Green
	G-BSOO	Cessna 172F	Double Oscar Flying Group
	G-BSOR	CFM Streak Shadow Srs SA	J. P. Sorenson
	G-BSOT	PA-38-112 Tomahawk II	D. J. Campbell/Edinburgh
	G-BSOU	PA-38-112 Tomahawk II	D. J. Campbell/Prestwick
	G-BSOV	PA-38-112 Tomahawk II	A. Dodd/Panshanger
	G-BSOX	Luscombe 8AE Silvaire	D. Gill
	G-BSOY	PA-34-220T Seneca III	BAe Flying College Ltd/Prestwick
	G-BSOZ	PA-28-161 Warrior II	Moray Flying Club Ltd/Kinloss
	G-BSPA	QAC Quickie Q.2	M. Ward
	G-BSPB	Thunder Ax8-84 balloon	Nigs Pertwee Ltd
	G-BSPC	Jodel D.140C	*stored*/Headcorn
	G-BSPE	Cessna F.172P	A. M. J. Clark
	G-BSPF	Cessna T.303	G-BSPF Crusader Group
	G-BSPG	PA-34-200T Seneca II	C. M. Vlieland-Boddy/Compton Abbas
	G-BSPI	PA-28-161 Warrior II	Snapfleet Ltd/Wellesbourne
	G-BSPJ	Bensen B.8	P. Soanes
	G-BSPK	Cessna 195A	Walavia
	G-BSPL	CFM Streak Shadow Srs SA	MEL (Aviation Oxygen) Ltd
	G-BSPM	PA-28-161 Warrior II	White Waltham Airfield Ltd
	G-BSPN	PA-28R-201T Turbo Arrow III	R. G. & W. Allison
	G-BSPW	Light Aero Avid Flyer C	M. J. Sewell
	G-BSPX	Lancair 320	C. H. Skelt
	G-BSPY	BN-2A Islander	G-WATS Aviation Ltd (G-AXYM)/ Halfpenny Green
	G-BSRC	Cessna 150M	S. O'Ceallaigh
	G-BSRH	Pitts S-1C Special	M. R. Janney
	G-BSRI	Lancair 235	G. Lewis
	G-BSRK	ARV Super 2	J. K. Davies
	G-BSRL	Everett Srs 2 gyroplane	R. F. E. Burley
	G-BSRP	Rotorway Executive	R. J. Baker
	G-BSRR	Cessna 182Q	Select Management Services Ltd
	G-BSRT	Denney Kitfox Mk 2	A. J. Lloyd
	G-BSRX	CFM Streak Shadow	R. G. M. Proost & F-J. Luckhurst
	G-BSRZ	Air Command 532 Elite 2-seat	A. S. G. Crabb
	G-BSSA	Luscombe 8E Silvaire	Punters Promotions Ltd/Denham
	G-BSSB	Cessna 150L	D. T. A. Rees
	G-BSSC	PA-28-161 Warrior II	C.S.E. Aviation Ltd/Kidlington
	G-BSSE	PA-28 Cherokee 140	Comed Aviation Ltd/Blackpool
	G-BSSF	Denney Kitfox Mk 2	D. M. Orrock
	G-BSSI	Rans S.6 Coyote II	J. S. Yates & K. Handley (G-MWJA)
	G-BSSJ	FRED Srs 2	R. F. Jopling
	G-BSSK	QAC Quickie Q.2	D. G. Greatrex
	G-BSSN	Air Command 532 Elite 2-seat	R. C. Bettany
	G-BSSO	Cameron O-90 balloon	R. R. & J. E. Hatton
	G-BSSP	Robin DR.400/180R	Soaring (Oxford) Ltd
	G-BSSR	PA-28-151 Warrior	H. M. B. Lundgren/Tilstock
	G-BSST	Concorde 002 ★	F.A.A. Museum/Yeovilton
	G-BSSV	CFM Streak Shadow	R. W. Payne
	G-BSSW	PA-28-161 Warrior II	R. L. Hayward
	G-BSSX	PA-28-161 Warrior II	Airways Aero Associations Ltd/Booker
	G-BSTC	Aeronca 11AC Chief	B. Bridgman & N. J. Mortimore
	G-BSTE	AS.355F-2 Twin Squirrel	Hygrade Foods Ltd
	G-BSTH	PA-25 Pawnee 235	Scottish Gliding Union Ltd/Portmoak
	G-BSTI	Piper J-3C-65 Cub	I. Fraser & G. L. Nunn
	G-BSTJ	D.H.82A Tiger Moth (N9192)	C. A. Parker
	G-BSTK	Thunder Ax8-90 balloon	M. Williams
	G-BSTL	Rand Robinson KR-2	C. S. Hales
	G-BSTM	Cessna 172L	G-BSTM Group/Cambridge
	G-BSTO	Cessna 152 II	Plymouth School of Flying Ltd
	G-BSTP	Cessna 152 II	FR Aviation Ltd/Bournemouth
	G-BSTR	AA-5 Traveler	James Allan (Aviation & Engineering) Ltd/ Dundee
	G-BSTT	Rans S.6 Coyote II	D. G. Palmer
	G-BSTU	Cessna P.210N	Astec Electronic Maintenance Ltd
	G-BSTV	PA-32 Cherokee Six 300	B. C. Hudson
	G-BSTX	Luscombe 8A Silvaire	A. A. Alderdice
	G-BSTY	Thunder Ax8-90 balloon	J. W. Cato

Reg.	Type	Owner or Operator	Notes
G-BSTZ	PA-28 Cherokee 140	Air Navigation & Trading Co Ltd/Blackpool	
G-BSUA	Rans S.6 Coyote II	A. J. Todd	
G-BSUB	Colt 77A balloon	R. R. J. Wilson & M. P. Hill	
G-BSUD	Luscombe 8A Silvaire	I. G. Harrison/Egginton	
G-BSUE	Cessna U.206G	R. A. Robinson	
G-BSUF	PA-32RT-300 Lance II	M. J. Parker	
G-BSUJ	Brügger MB.2 Colibri	M. A. Farrelly	
G-BSUK	Colt 77A balloon	K. J. Foster	
G-BSUM	Scheibe SF.27MB	M Syndicate	
G-BSUO	Scheibe SF.25C Falke	British Gliding Association Ltd	
G-BSUR	Rotorway Executive 90	Coaching for Results Ltd	
G-BSUT	Rans S.6-ESA Coyote II	P. J. Clegg	
G-BSUU	Colt 180A balloon	British School of Ballooning	
G-BSUV	Cameron O-77 balloon	R. Moss	
G-BSUW	PA-34-200T Seneca II	TG Aviation Ltd/Manston	
G-BSUX	Carlson Sparrow II	J. Stephenson	
G-BSUZ	Denney Kitfox Mk 3	M. W. Oliver	
G-BSVB	PA-28-181 Archer II	Redhill Flying Club	
G-BSVC	Cameron A-210 balloon	British School of Ballooning	
G-BSVE	Binder CP.301S Smaragd	Smaragd Flying Group	
G-BSVF	PA-28-161 Warrior II	Airways Aero Associations Ltd/Booker	
G-BSVG	PA-28-161 Warrior II	Airways Aero Associations Ltd/Booker	
G-BSVH	Piper J-3C-65 Cub	A. R. Meakin	
G-BSVI	PA-16 Clipper	I. R. Blakemore	
G-BSVJ	Piper J-3C-65 Cub	V. S. E. Norman/Rendcomb	
G-BSVK	Denney Kitfox Mk 2	C. M. Looney	
G-BSVM	PA-28-161 Warrior II	Falcon Flying Services/Biggin Hill	
G-BSVN	Thorp T-18	J. H. Kirkham	
G-BSVP	PA-23 Aztec 250	Time Electronics Ltd/Biggin Hill	
G-BSVR	Schweizer 269C	Martinair Ltd	
G-BSVS	Robin DR.400/100	D. McK. Chalmers	
G-BSVV	PA-38-112 Tomahawk	J. Maffia & H. Merkado/Panshanger	
G-BSVW	PA-38-112 Tomahawk	Falcon Flying Services/Biggin Hill	
G-BSVX	PA-38-112 Tomahawk	D. J. Hockings/Biggin Hill	
G-BSVY	PA-38-112 Tomahawk	Cardiff-Wales Flying Club Ltd	
G-BSVZ	Pietenpol Air Camper	A. F. Cashin	
G-BSWA	Luscombe 8A Silvaire	Beeswax Flying Group	
G-BSWB	Rans S.10 Sakota	F. A. Hewitt	
G-BSWC	Boeing Stearman E.75 (112)	R. R. White	
G-BSWF	PA-16 Clipper	T. M. Storey	
G-BSWG	PA-17 Vagabond	K. S. Woodard	
G-BSWH	Cessna 152 II	Airspeed Aviation Ltd	
G-BSWI	Rans S.10 Sakota	A. Gault	
G-BSWJ	Cameron O-77 balloon	T. Charlwood	
G-BSWK	Robinson R-22B	Clarity Aviation Ltd	
G-BSWM	Slingsby T.61F	L. J. McKelvie/Bellarena	
G-BSWR	BN-2T-26 Turbine Islander	Police Authority for Northern Ireland	
G-BSWV	Cameron N-77 balloon	Leicester Mercury Ltd	
G-BSWX	Cameron V-90 balloon	Cameron Balloons Ltd	
G-BSWY	Cameron N-77 balloon	Nottingham Hot Air Balloon Club	
G-BSWZ	Cameron A-180 balloon	G. C. Ludlow	
G-BSXA	PA-28-161 Warrior II	Falcon Flying Services/Biggin Hill	
G-BSXB	PA-28-161 Warrior II	Aeroshow Ltd	
G-BSXC	PA-28-161 Warrior II	L. T. Halpin/Booker	
G-BSXD	Soko P-2 Kraguj (30146)	C. J. Pearce	
G-BSXE	Bell 206B JetRanger	Markoss Aviation Ltd/Biggin Hill	
G-BSXI	Mooney M.20E	Mooney Group	
G-BSXM	Cameron V-77 balloon	C. A. Oxby	
G-BSXN	Robinson R-22B	J. G. Gray	
G-BSXP	Air Command 532 Elite	B. J. West	
G-BSXR	Air Command 532 Elite	T. Wing	
G-BSXS	PA-28-181 Archer II	Pipe-Air Ltd	
G-BSXT	Piper J-5A Cub Cruiser	M. G. & K. J. Thompson	
G-BSXW	PA-28-161 Warrior II	Ryland Aviation Ltd/Wellesbourne	
G-BSXX	Whittaker MW.7	H. J. Stanley	
G-BSXY	Oldfield Baby Great Lakes	B. Freeman-Jones (G-JENY)	
G-BSYA	Jodel D.18	S. Harrison	
G-BSYB	Cameron N-120 balloon	M. Buono/Italy	
G-BSYC	PA-32R-300 Lance	Arrow Aviation	
G-BSYD	Cameron A-180 balloon	A. A. Brown	
G-BSYE	Cessna 140	R. Brown & W. Tank	
G-BSYF	Luscombe 8A Silvaire	Atlantic Aviation	
G-BSYG	PA-12 Super Cruiser	S. D. Rudkin & C. W. Udale	

Notes	Reg.	Type	Owner or Operator
	G-BSYH	Luscombe 8A Silvaire	N. R. Osborne
	G-BSYI	AS.355F-1 Twin Squirrel	Lynton Aviation Ltd/Denham
	G-BSYJ	Cameron N-77 balloon	Chubb Fire Ltd
	G-BSYK	PA-38-112 Tomahawk II	Flychoice Ltd/Halfpenny Green
	G-BSYL	PA-38-112 Tomahawk II	Flychoice Ltd/Halfpenny Green
	G-BSYM	PA-38-112 Tomahawk II	Flychoice Ltd/Coventry
	G-BSYO	Piper J-3C-90 Cub	C. R. Reynolds & J. D. Fuller (G-BSMJ/G-BRHE)
	G-BSYP	Bensen B.8MR	C. R. Gordon
	G-BSYU	Robin DR.400/180	P. A. Desoutter/France
	G-BSYV	Cessna 150M	Fenland Flying School
	G-BSYW	Cessna 150M	J. A. F. Waller
	G-BSYY	PA-28-161 Warrior II	C.S.E. Aviation Ltd/Kidlington
	G-BSYZ	PA-28-161 Warrior II	Air Service Training Ltd/Perth
	G-BSZB	Stolp SA.300 Starduster Too	D. T. Gethin/Swansea
	G-BSZC	Beech C-45H (51 11701A)	A. A. Hodgson
	G-BSZD	Robin DR.400/180	R. Hitchman & Son & P. J. Rowland & Sons (Farmers) Ltd
	G-BSZF	Jodel DR.250/160	J. B. Randle
	G-BSZG	Stolp SA.100 Starduster	S. W. Watkins & D. F. Chapman
	G-BSZH	Thunder Ax7-77 balloon	K. E. Viney & L. J. Weston
	G-BSZI	Cessna 152 II	Eglinton Flying Club Ltd
	G-BSZJ	PA-28-181 Archer II	R. D. Fuller
	G-BSZL	Colt 77A balloon	Staedtler Mars GmbH & Co/Germany
	G-BSZM	Bensen B.8MR	J. H. H. Turner
	G-BSZN	Bucker Bu133D-1 Jungmeister	V. Lindsay
	G-BSZO	Cessna 152	A. T. Hooper & T. E. Evans/Wellesbourne
	G-BSZS	Robinson R-22B	TDR Aviation Ltd
	G-BSZT	PA-28-161 Warrior II	Thornhill Aviation Ltd
	G-BSZU	Cessna 150F	L. A. Maynard
	G-BSZV	Cessna 150F	Midair Aviation Ltd/Bournemouth
	G-BSZW	Cessna 152	Haimoss Ltd
	G-BSZY	Cameron A-180 balloon	K. H. Benning
	G-BTAB	BAe 125 Srs 800B	Dean Finance Co Ltd (G-BOOA)
	G-BTAD	Macair Merlin	A. T. & M. R. Dowie
	G-BTAG	Cameron O-77 balloon	H. Phethean & R. A. Shapland
	G-BTAH	Bensen B.8M	T. B. Johnson
	G-BTAJ	PA-34-200T Seneca II	Ravenair Aircraft Engineering Ltd/ Manchester
	G-BTAK	EAA Acro Sport II	P. G. Harrison
	G-BTAL	Cessna F.152 II	Thanet Flying Club/Manston
	G-BTAM	PA-28-181 Archer II	Tri-Star Films Ltd
	G-BTAN	Thunder Ax7-65Z balloon	A. S. Newham
	G-BTAP	PA-38-112 Tomahawk	I. J. McGarrigle
	G-BTAR	PA-38-112 Tomahawk	Aerohire Ltd/Halfpenny Green
	G-BTAS	PA-38-112 Tomahawk	B. Brooks
	G-BTAT	Denney Kitfox Mk 2	O. W. Owen
	G-BTAU	Thunder Ax7-77 balloon	S. L. G. Williams
	G-BTAV	Colt 105A balloon	D. C. Chipping
	G-BTAW	PA-28-161 Warrior II	A. J. Wiggins
	G-BTAX	PA-31-350 Navajo Chieftain	Jet West Ltd/Exeter
	G-BTAZ	Evans VP-2	G. S. Poulter
	G-BTBA	Robinson R-22B	Forestdale Hotels Ltd
	G-BTBB	Thunder Ax8-90 balloon	Scotia Balloons Ltd
	G-BTBC	PA-28-161 Warrior II	M. J. L. MacDonald
	G-BTBE	PA-34-200T Seneca II	–
	G-BTBF	Super Koala	E. A. Taylor (G-MWOZ)
	G-BTBG	Denney Kitfox	J. Catley
	G-BTBH	Ryan ST3KR (854)	Ryan Group
	G-BTBI	WAR P-47 Thunderbolt (replica) (85)	S. W. Ballantyne
	G-BTBJ	Cessna 195B	P. G. Palumbo
	G-BTBL	Montgomerie-Bensen B.8MR	R. de H. Dobree-Carey
	G-BTBN	Denney Kitfox Mk 2	T. M. W. & S. A. Webster
	G-BTBO	Cameron N-77 balloon	Cameron Balloons Ltd
	G-BTBP	Cameron N-90 balloon	Chianti Balloon Club
	G-BTBR	Cameron DP-80 airship	Cameron Balloons Ltd
	G-BTBS	Cameron N-180 balloon	British School of Ballooning
	G-BTBU	PA-18 Super Cub 150	Acebell Aviation Ltd & H. J. Rose/Redhill
	G-BTBV	Cessna 140	A. Brinkley
	G-BTBW	Cessna 120	S. J. Brinkley
	G-BTBX	Piper J-3C-65 Cub	Henlow Taildraggers

Reg.	Type	Owner or Operator	Notes
G-BTBY	PA-17 Vagabond	G. J. Smith & J. A. Clark	
G-BTCA	PA-32R-300 Lance	P. Taylor	
G-BTCB	Air Command 582 Sport	G. Scurrah	
G-BTCC	Grumman F6F-5 Hellcat (19)	Patina Ltd/Duxford	
G BTCD	P-51D-25-NA Mustang (463221)	Patina Ltd/Duxford	
G-BTCE	Cessna 152	S. T. Gilbert	
G-BTCH	Luscombe 8E Silvaire	J. Grewcock & R. C. Carroll	
G-BTCI	PA-17 Vagabond	T. R. Whittome	
G-BTCJ	Luscombe 8AE Silvaire	C. C. & J. M. Lovell	
G-BTCK	Cameron A-210 balloon	H-O-T Air Balloons	
G-BTCM	Cameron N-90 balloon	J. D. & K. Griffiths (G-BMPW)	
G-BTCO	FRED Srs 2	I. P. Manley	
G-BTCR	Rans S.10 Sakota	S. H. Barr	
G-BTCS	Colt 90A balloon	D. N. Belton	
G-BTCT	AS.332L Super Puma	Bristow Helicopters Ltd	
G-BTCU	WSK PZL Antonov An-2T (77)	Wessex Aviation & Transport Ltd/ Henstridge	
G-BTCW	Cameron A-180 balloon	Bristol Balloons	
G-BTCZ	Cameron 84 Chateau SS balloon	Forbes Europe Inc/France	
G-BTDA	Slingsby T.61G Falke	RAFGSA/Bicester	
G-BTDC	Denney Kitfox Mk 2	D. Collinson	
G-BTDD	CFM Streak Shadow	S. J. Evans	
G-BTDE	Cessna C-165 Airmaster	G. S. Moss	
G-BTDF	Luscombe 8A Silvaire	M. Stow	
G-BTDH	P.56 Provost T.1 (WV666)	Flying Services	
G-BTDI	Robinson R-22B	R. L. Moody/Denham	
G-BTDK	Cessna 421C	RK Carbon Fibre Ltd/Manchester	
G-BTDN	Denney Kitfox Mk 2	Foxy Flyers Group	
G-BTDP	TBM-3R Avenger (53319)	A. Haig-Thomas/North Weald	
G-BTDR	Aero Designs Pulsar	R. M. Hughes	
G-BTDS	Colt 77A balloon	C. P. Witter Ltd	
G-BTDT	C.A.S.A. 1.131E Jungmann 2000	T. A. Reed	
G-BTDV	PA-28-161 Warrior II	R. E. Thorne	
G-BTDW	Cessna 152 II	J. A. Blenkharn/Carlisle	
G-BTDX	PA-18 Super Cub 150	Cubair Ltd/Redhill	
G-BTDY	PA-18 Super Cub 150	Rodger Aircraft Ltd	
G-BTDZ	C.A.S.A. 1.131E Jungmann 2000	R. J. Pickin & I. M. White	
G-BTEA	Cameron N-105 balloon	H.O.T. Air Balloons	
G-BTEE	Cameron O-120 balloon	W. H. & J. P. Morgan	
G-BTEF	Pitts S-1 Special	Northwest Aerobatics	
G-BTEI	Everett Srs 3 gyroplane	D. G. H. Oswald	
G-BTEK	SOCATA TB.20 Trinidad	D. F. Fagan/Booker	
G-BTEL	CFM Streak Shadow	J. E. Eatwell	
G-BTES	Cessna 150H	Takecare Aviation Ltd/Elstree	
G-BTET	Piper J-3C-65 Cub	R. M. Jones	
G-BTEU	SA.365N-2 Dauphin	Bond Helicopters Ltd	
G-BTEV	PA-38-112 Tomahawk	Cardiff Aeronautical Services Ltd	
G-BTEW	Cessna 120	D. J. Carter/Little Snoring	
G-BTEX	PA-28 Cherokee 140	McAully Flying Group Ltd/Little Snoring	
G-BTFA	Denney Kitfox Mk 2	K. R. Peek	
G-BTFC	Cessna F.152 II	Tayside Aviation Ltd/Dundee	
G-BTFD	Colt AS-105 airship Mk II	Media Fantasy Aviation UK Ltd	
G-BTFE	Bensen-Parsons 2-seat gyroplane	I. Brewster	
G-BTFF	Cessna T.310R II	Rajmech Ltd	
G-BTFG	Boeing Stearman A.75N1 (441)	S. J. Ellis	
G-BTFJ	PA-15 Vagabond	K. G. Day	
G-BTFK	Taylorcraft BC-12D	D. J. S. McLean	
G-BTFL	Aeronca 11AC Chief	BTFL Group	
G-BTFM	Cameron O-105 balloon	Edinburgh University Hot Air Balloon Club	
G-BTFN	Beech F33C Bonanza	Robert Hinton Design & Creative Communications Ltd	
G-BTFO	PA-28-161 Warrior II	Flyfar Ltd	
G-BTFP	PA-38-112 Tomahawk	Teesside Flight Centre Ltd	
G-BTFR	Colt AS-105 airship	Heather Flight Ltd	
G-BTFS	Cessna A.150M	S. J. & F. J. Bailey	
G-BTFT	Beech 58 Baron	Roseberry Management Ltd	
G-BTFU	Ciameron N-90 balloon	J. J. Rudoni & A. C. K. Rawson	
G-BTFV	Whittaker MW.7	S. J. Luck	
G-BTFW	Montgomerie-Bensen B.8MR	A. Mansfield	
G-BTFX	Bell 206B JetRanger 2	J. Selwyn Smith (Shepley) Ltd	
G-BTFY	Bell 206B JetRanger 2	Yorkshire Helicopters/Leeds	
G-BTGA	Boeing Stearman A.751N1	J. C. Lister	
G-BTGC	PA-38-112 Tomahawk	T. Hayselden	

Notes	Reg.	Type	Owner or Operator
	G-BTGD	Rand-Robinson KR-2	D. W. Mullin
	G-BTGG	Rans S.10 Sakota	A. R. Cameron
	G-BTGH	Cessna 152 II	R. S. Trayhurn & P. D. Myson
	G-BTGI	Rearwin 175 Skyranger	A. H. Hunt/St Just
	G-BTGJ	Smith DSA-1 Miniplane	G. J. Knowles
	G-BTGL	Light Aero Avid Flyer	A. F. Vizoso
	G-BTGM	Aeronca 7AC Champion	G. Gregg
	G-BTGN	Cessna 310R	Air Service Training Ltd/Perth
	G-BTGO	PA-28 Cherokee 140	Rankart Ltd
	G-BTGP	Cessna 150M	Billins Air Service Ltd
	G-BTGR	Cessna 152 II	A. J. Gomes/Shoreham
	G-BTGS	Stolp SA.300 Starduster Too	T. G. Solomon (G-AYMA)/Shoreham
	G-BTGT	CFM Streak Shadow	N. L. Howard (G-MWPY)
	G-BTGU	PA-34-220T Seneca III	Carill Aviation Ltd
	G-BTGV	PA-34-200T Seneca II	MS 124 Ltd/Shobdon
	G-BTGW	Cessna 152 II	Stapleford Flying Club Ltd
	G-BTGX	Cessna 152 II	Stapleford Flying Club Ltd
	G-BTGY	PA-28-161 Warrior II	Stapleford Flying Club Ltd
	G-BTGZ	PA-28-181 Archer II	Allzones Travel Ltd/Biggin Hill
	G-BTHA	Cessna 182P	N. J. Douglas
	G-BTHD	Yakovlev Yak-3U	Patina Ltd/Duxford
	G-BTHE	Cessna 150L	Humberside Police Flying Club
	G-BTHF	Cameron V-90 balloon	N. J. & S. J. Langley
	G-BTHH	Jodel DR.100A	H. R. Leefe
	G-BTHI	Robinson R-22B	R. Bean Commercial Vehicles
	G-BTHJ	Evans VP-2	C. J. Moseley
	G-BTHK	Thunder Ax7-77 balloon	M. J. Chandler
	G-BTHM	Thunder Ax8-105 balloon	Anglia Balloons
	G-BTHN	Murphy Renegade 912	F. A. Purvis
	G-BTHP	Thorp T.211	M. Gardner
	G-BTHR	SOCATA TB.10 Tobago	M. J. Newton
	G-BTHU	Light Aero Avid Flyer	R. C. Bowley
	G-BTHW	Beech F33C Bonanza	Robin Lance Aviation Associates Ltd
	G-BTHX	Colt 105A balloon	R. Ollier
	G-BTHY	Bell 206B JetRanger 3	J. W. Sandle
	G-BTHZ	Cameron V-56 balloon	C. N. Marshall
	G-BTIC	PA-22 Tri-Pacer 150	T. Richards & G. C. Winters
	G-BTID	PA-28-161 Warrior II	Plymouth School of Flying Ltd
	G-BTIE	SOCATA TB.10 Tobago	JGH Computer Services Ltd
	G-BTIF	Denney Kitfox Mk 3	C. R. Thompson
	G-BTIG	Montgomerie-Bensen B.8MR	P. Crawley
	G-BTIH	PA-28-151 Warrior	MPM Aviation
	G-BTII	AA-5B Tiger	B. D. Greenwood
	G-BTIJ	Luscombe 8E Silvaire	S. J. Hornsby
	G-BTIK	Cessna 152 II	P. R. Edwards & E. Alexander
	G-BTIL	PA-38-112 Tomahawk	B. R. Pearson/Eaglescott
	G-BTIM	PA-28-161 Cadet	Mid-Sussex Timber Co Ltd
	G-BTIN	Cessna 150C	Cormack (Aircraft Services) Ltd
	G-BTIO	SNCAN Stampe SV-4C	M. D. & C. F. Garratt
	G-BTIP	Denney Kitfox Mk 3	P. A. Hardy
	G-BTIR	Denney Kitfox Mk 2	M. Stevenson
	G-BTIS	AS.355F-1 Twin Squirrel	Walsh Aviation (G-TALI)/Elstree
	G-BTIU	M.S.892A Rallye Commodore 150	W. H. Cole
	G-BTIV	PA-28-161 Warrior II	Warrior Group/Eaglescott
	G-BTIX	Cameron V-77 balloon	S. A. Simington
	G-BTIZ	Cameron A-105 balloon	A. G. E. Faulkner
	G-BTJA	Luscombe 8E Silvaire	M. W. & L. M. Rudkin/Liverpool
	G-BTJB	Luscombe 8E Silvaire	M. Loxton
	G-BTJC	Luscombe 8F Silvaire	S. C. & M. Goddard
	G-BTJD	Thunder Ax8-90 balloon	S. J. Wardle
	G-BTJE	Hiller UH-12E4	T. J. Clark
	G-BTJF	Thunder Ax10-180 balloon	Airborne Adventures Ltd
	G-BTJH	Cameron O-77 balloon	H. Stringer
	G-BTJK	PA-38-112 Tomahawk	Western Air Training Ltd/Thruxton
	G-BTJL	PA-38-112 Tomahawk	W. C. Cowie
	G-BTJN	Montgomerie-Bensen B.8MR	A. Hamilton
	G-BTJO	Thunder Ax9-140 balloon	Abbey Plant Co Ltd
	G-BTJS	Montgomerie-Bensen B.8MR	T. C. & P. K. Jackson
	G-BTJU	Cameron V-90 balloon	C. W. Jones (Floorings) Ltd
	G-BTJV	PZL SZD-50-3 Puchacz	Kent Gliding Club Ltd/Challock
	G-BTJX	Rans S.10 Sakota	M. Goacher
	G-BTKA	Piper J-5A Cub Cruiser	J. M. Lister
	G-BTKB	Renegade Spirit 912	G. S. Blundell

Reg.	Type	Owner or Operator	Notes
G-BTKD	Denney Kitfox Mk 4	J. F. White	
G-BTKG	Light Aero Avid Flyer	Kilo Golf Group	
G-BTKI	NA T-6G Texan	P. S. & S. M. Warner	
G-BTKL	MBB Bo 105DB-4	Veritair Ltd/Halfpenny Green	
G-BTKN	Cameron O-120 balloon	The Ballooning Business Ltd	
G-BTKP	CFM Streak Shadow	G. D. Martin	
G-BTKS	Rans S.10 Sakota	J. R. I. Rolfe & ptnrs	
G-BTKT	PA-28-161 Warrior II	Eastern Executive Air Charter Ltd	
G-BTKU	Cameron A-105 balloon	S. Bedir	
G-BTKV	PA-22 Tri-Pacer 160	R. A. More	
G-BTKW	Cameron O-105 balloon	P. Spellward	
G-BTKX	PA-28-181 Archer II	Symtec Computers Ltd	
G-BTKZ	Cameron V-77 balloon	S. P. Richards	
G-BTLA	Sikorsky S-76B	Falcon of Friendship Ltd	
G-BTLB	Wassmer WA.52 Europa	M. D. O'Brien/Shoreham	
G-BTLE	PA-31-350 Navajo Chieftain	Boal Air Services (UK) Ltd	
G-BTLG	PA-28R Cherokee Arrow 200	A. P. Reilly	
G-BTLM	PA-22 Tri-Pacer 160	F & H (Aircraft)	
G-BTLP	AA-1C Lynx	Partlease Ltd	
G-BTMA	Cessna 172N	East of England Flying Group Ltd	
G-BTMF	Taylorcraft BC-12D	C. M. Churchill/Cambridge	
G-BTMH	Colt 90A balloon	Douwe Egberts UK Ltd	
G-BTMJ	Maule MX-7-180	C. M. McGill/Biggin Hill	
G-BTMK	Cessna R.172K XPII	S. P. & A. C. Barker	
G-BTML	Cameron 90 Rupert Bear SS balloon	Flying Pictures (Balloons) Ltd	
G-BTMM	Cameron N-105 balloon	M. F. Glue	
G-BTMN	Thunder Ax9-120 S2 balloon	Canterbury Balloons	
G-BTMO	Colt 69A balloon	Thunder & Colt	
G-BTMP	Campbell Cricket	P. W. McLaughlin	
G-BTMR	Cessna 172M	Cumbria Aero Club/Carlisle	
G-BTMS	Light Aero Avid Flyer	M. J. Schyns	
G-BTMT	Denney Kitfox Mk 1	Skulk Flying Group	
G-BTMV	Everett Srs 2 gyroplane	L. Armes	
G-BTMW	Zenair CH.701 STOL	L. Lewis	
G-BTMX	Denney Kitfox Mk 3	P. B. Lowry	
G-BTMY	Cameron 80 Train SS balloon	Cameron Balloons Ltd	
G-BTMZ	PA-38-112 Tomahawk	T. Drew	
G-BTNA	Robinson R-22B	MG Group Ltd	
G-BTNB	Robinson R-22B	Davron Aviation	
G-BTNC	AS.365N-2 Dauphin 2	Bond Helicopters Ltd	
G-BTND	PA-38-112 Tomahawk	R. B. Turner	
G-BTNE	PA-28-161 Warrior II	A. T. Hooper & T. E. Evans/Wellesbourne	
G-BTNH	PA-28-161 Warrior II	Falcon Flying Services/Biggin Hill	
G-BTNJ	Cameron V-90 balloon	P. L. Harrison & B. J. Newman	
G-BTNK	BAe ATP	Trident Aviation Leasing Services Ltd	
G-BTNL	Thunder Ax10-180 balloon	Adventure Balloon Co Ltd	
G-BTNN	Colt 21A balloon	Cameron Balloons Ltd	
G-BTNO	Aeronca 7AC Champion	November Oscar Group/Netherthorpe	
G-BTNP	Light Aero Avid Flyer Commuter	N. Evans	
G-BTNR	Denney Kitfox Mk 3	J. W. G. Ellis	
G-BTNS	PZL-104 Wilga 80	R. W. Husband	
G-BTNT	PA-28-151 Warrior	Britannia Airways Ltd/Luton	
G-BTNV	PA-28-161 Warrior II	D. K. Oakeley & A. M. Dawson	
G-BTNW	Rans S.6-ESA Coyote II	A. F. Stafford	
G-BTOA	Mong Sport MS-2	G. Gilding	
G-BTOC	Robinson R-22B	N. Parkhouse	
G-BTOD	PA-38-112 Tomahawk	V. F. & J. A. Shirley	
G-BTOG	D.H.82A Tiger Moth	P. T. Szluha	
G-BTOI	Cameron N-77 balloon	The Nestle Co Ltd	
G-BTOL	Denney Kitfox Mk 3	P. J. Gibbs	
G-BTON	PA-28 Cherokee 140	W. A. & K. C. Ryan	
G-BTOO	Pitts S-1C Special	G. H. Matthews	
G-BTOP	Cameron V-77 balloon	J. J. Winter	
G-BTOR	Lancair 320	R. W. Fairless	
G-BTOS	Cessna 140	J. L. Kaiser	
G-BTOT	PA-15 Vagabond	P. J. Rutter	
G-BTOU	Cameron O-120 balloon	R. St. J. Gillespie	
G-BTOW	SOCATA Rallye 180GT	Cambridge University Gliding Trust Ltd/ Gransden Lodge	
G-BTOZ	Thunder Ax9-120 S2 balloon	H. G. Davies	
G-BTPA	BAe ATP	British Airways *Strathallan*/Glasgow	
G-BTPB	Cameron N-105 balloon	Test Valley Balloon Group	

Notes	Reg.	Type	Owner or Operator
	G-BTPC	BAe ATP	British Airways *Strathblane*/Glasgow
	G-BTPD	BAe ATP	British Airways *Strathconon*/Glasgow
	G-BTPE	BAe ATP	British Airways *Strathdon*/Glasgow
	G-BTPF	BAe ATP	British Airways *Strathearn*/Glasgow
	G-BTPG	BAe ATP	British Airways *Strathfillan*/Glasgow
	G-BTPH	BAe ATP	British Airways *Strathnaver*/Glasgow
	G-BTPJ	BAe ATP	British Airways *Strathpeffer*/Glasgow
	G-BTPM	BAe ATP	British Airways/Glasgow
	G-BTPN	BAe ATP	British Airways/Glasgow
	G-BTPO	BAe ATP	British Airways/Glasgow
	G-BTPT	Cameron N-77 balloon	Derbyshire Building Soc
	G-BTPV	Colt 90A balloon	Virgin Airship & Balloon Co Ltd
	G-BTPX	Thunder Ax8-90 balloon	J. L. Guy
	G-BTPZ	Isaacs Fury II	M. A. Farrelly
	G-BTRC	Light Aero Avid Speedwing	Grangecote Ltd
	G-BTRE	Cessna F.172H	M. L. J. Warwick
	G-BTRF	Aero Designs Pulsar	C. Smith
	G-BTRG	Aeronca 65C Super Chief	H. J. Cox
	G-BTRH	Aeronca 7AC Champion	D. W. Leach
	G-BTRI	Aeronca 11CC Super Chief	J. R. Kimberley
	G-BTRK	PA-28-161 Warrior II	Stapleford Flying Club Ltd
	G-BTRL	Cameron N-105 balloon	J. Lippett
	G-BTRN	Thunder Ax9-120 S2 balloon	Solar Communications Ltd
	G-BTRO	Thunder Ax8-90 balloon	Capital Balloon Club Ltd
	G-BTRP	Hughes 369E	P. C. Shann
	G-BTRR	Thunder Ax7-77 balloon	S. M. Roberts
	G-BTRS	PA-28-161 Warrior II	Tyberry Aviation/Liverpool
	G-BTRT	PA-28R Cherokee Arrow 200-II	C. E. Yates/Barton
	G-BTRU	Robin DR.400/180	R. & M. Engineering Ltd
	G-BTRW	Slingsby T.61F Venture T.2	B. Kerby & G. Grainer
	G-BTRX	Cameron V-77 balloon	R. P. Jones & N. P.Hemsley
	G-BTRY	PA-28-161 Warrior II	C.S.E. Aviation Ltd/Kidlington
	G-BTRZ	Jodel D.18	R. M. Johnson & R. Collin
	G-BTSA	Cessna 150K	M. E. Bartlett
	G-BTSB	Corben Baby Ace D	D. G. Kelly
	G-BTSC	Evans VP-2	G. B. O'Neill
	G-BTSD	Midget Mustang	R. Fitzpatrick
	G-BTSI	BAe 125-1000	Shell Aircraft Ltd/Heathrow
	G-BTSJ	PA-28-161 Warrior II	Plymouth School of Flying Ltd
	G-BTSK	Beech F33C Bonanza	Jetwing Ltd/White Waltham
	G-BTSL	Cameron 70 Glass SS balloon	M. R. Humphrey & J. R .Clifton
	G-BTSM	Cessna 180A	C. Couston
	G-BTSN	Cessna 150G	N. A. Bilton/Norwich
	G-BTSP	Piper J-3C-65 Cub	J. A. Walshe & A. Corcoran
	G-BTSR	Aeronca 11AC Chief	P. A. Wensak
	G-BTST	Bensen B.9	V. Scott
	G-BTSU	Bensen B.8MR	B. T. Goggin
	G-BTSV	Denney Kitfox Mk 3	D. J. Sharland
	G-BTSW	Colt AS-80 Mk II airship	Huntair Ltd
	G-BTSX	Thunder Ax7-77 balloon	C. Moris-Gallimore
	G-BTSY	EE Lightning F.6 (XR724)	Lightning Association
	G-BTSZ	Cessna 177A	K. D. Harvey
	G-BTTA	Hawker Sea Fury FB.10 (243)	Classic Aviation Ltd/Duxford
	G-BTTB	Cameron V-90 balloon	Royal Engineers Balloon Club
	G-BTTD	Montgomerie-Bensen B.8MR	P. A. Howell
	G-BTTE	Cessna 150L	A. Watson
	G-BTTH	Beech F33C Bonanza	Bonanza Flying Group/Booker
	G-BTTI	Thunder Ax8-90 balloon	Capital Balloon Club Ltd
	G-BTTJ	Thunder Ax9-120 S2 balloon	G. D. & L. Fitzpatrick
	G-BTTK	Thunder Ax8-105 balloon	Tempowish Ltd
	G-BTTL	Cameron V-90 balloon	A. J. Baird
	G-BTTP	BAe 146-300	Air UK Ltd/Stansted
	G-BTTR	Aerotek Pitts S-2A Special	Ebork Ltd/Biggin Hill
	G-BTTS	Colt 77A balloon	Rutland Balloon Club
	G-BTTW	Thunder Ax7-77 balloon	J. Kenny
	G-BTTY	Denney Kitfox Mk 2	K. J. Fleming
	G-BTTZ	Slingsby T.61F Venture T.2	I. R. F. Hammond
	G-BTUA	Slingsby T.61F Venture T.2	M. W. Olliver
	G-BTUB	Yakovlev C.11	M. G. & J. R. Jefferies
	G-BTUD	CFM Image	D. G. Cook (G-MWPV)
	G-BTUG	SOCATA Rallye 180T	Herefordshire Gliding Club Ltd/Shobdon
	G-BTUH	Cameron N-65 balloon	B. J. Godding
	G-BTUJ	Thunder Ax9-120 balloon	ECM Construction Ltd

Reg.	Type	Owner or Operator	Notes
G-BTUK	Aerotek Pitts S-2A Special	Wickenby Aviation Ltd	
G-BTUL	Aerotek Pitts S-2A Special	C & S Aviation	
G-BTUM	Piper J-3C-65 Cub	G-BTUM Syndicate	
G-BTUN	Colt Flying Drinks Can SS balloon	BIAS UK Ltd	
G-BTUR	PA-18 Super Cub 95 (modified)	L-18 Syndicate	
G-BTUS	Whittaker MW.7	J. D. Webb	
G-BTUU	Cameron O-120 balloon	J. L. Guy	
G-BTUV	Aeronca A65TAC Defender	J. T. Ingrouille	
G-BTUW	PA-28-151 Warrior	F. Lennon	
G-BTUX	AS.365N-2 Dauphin 2	Bond Helicopters Ltd/Aberdeen	
G-BTUZ	American General AG-5B Tiger	Grocontinental Ltd/Tilstock	
G-BTVA	Thunder Ax7-77 balloon	C. E. Wood	
G-BTVB	Everett Srs 3 gyroplane	J. Pumford	
G-BTVC	Denney Kitfox Mk 2	P. Mitchell	
G-BTVE	Hawker Demon I (K8203)	Demon Displays Ltd	
G-BTVF	Rotorway Executive 90	E. P. Sadler	
G-BTVG	Cessna 140	V. C. Gover	
G-BTVH	Colt 77A balloon	D. N. & L. J. Close (G-ZADT/G-ZBCA)	
G-BTVR	PA-28 Cherokee 140	Full Sutton Flying Centre Ltd	
G-BTVU	Robinson R-22B	B. Enzo/Italy	
G-BTVV	Cessna FA.337G	B. Maddock	
G-BTVW	Cessna 152 II	A. T. Hooper & T. E. Evans/Wellesbourne	
G-BTVX	Cessna 152 II	A. T. Hooper & T. E. Evans/Wellesbourne	
G-BTWB	Denney Kitfox Mk 3	J. E. Tootell (G-BTTM)	
G-BTWC	Slingsby T.61F Venture T.2	RAFGSA/Bicester	
G-BTWD	Slingsby T.61F Venture T.2	York Gliding Centre/Rufforth	
G-BTWE	Slingsby T.61F Venture T.2	RAFGSA/Bicester	
G-BTWF	D.H.C.1 Chipmunk 22	J. A. & V. G. Sims	
G-BTWI	EAA Acro Sport I	WI Group	
G-BTWJ	Cameron V-77 balloon	S. J. & J. A. Bellaby	
G-BTWL	WAG-Aero Acro Sport Trainer	M. T. Lewis	
G-BTWM	Cameron V-77 balloon	D. I. Gray-Fisk	
G-BTWN	Maule MXT-7-180	C. T. Rolls/Redhill	
G-BTWP	Robinson R-22B	M. Kane	
G-BTWR	Bell P-63A-7-BE Kingcobra (269097)	Patina Ltd/Duxford	
G-BTWS	Thunder Ax7-77 balloon	Bavarian Balloon Co Ltd	
G-BTWU	PA-22 Tri-Pacer 135	Prestige Air (Engineers) Ltd	
G-BTWV	Cameron O-90 balloon	Bodkin House Hotel	
G-BTWW	AB-206B JetRanger 2	PLM Dollar Group Ltd	
G-BTWX	SOCATA TB.9 Tampico	Parkers Properties Ltd/Biggin Hill	
G-BTWY	Aero Designs Pulsar	J. J. Pridal	
G-BTWZ	Rans S.10 Sakota	D. G. Hey	
G-BTXB	Colt 77A balloon	Shellgas South West Area	
G-BTXD	Rans S.6-ESA Coyote II	M. Isterling	
G-BTXF	Cameron V-90 balloon	Gone With The Wind Ltd	
G-BTXH	Colt AS-56 airship	Huntair Ltd	
G-BTXI	Noorduyn AT-16 Harvard IIB (FE695)	Patina Ltd/Duxford	
G-BTXK	Thunder Ax7-65 balloon	T. M. Dawson	
G-BTXM	Colt 21A balloon	Virgin Airship & Balloon Co Ltd	
G-BTXR	Cassutt Racer	S. N. Lester	
G-BTXS	Cameron O-120 balloon	Southern Balloon Group	
G-BTXT	Maule MXT-7-180	R. G. Humphries	
G-BTXV	Cameron A-210 balloon	The Ballooning Business Ltd	
G-BTXW	Cameron V-77 balloon	P. C. Waterhouse	
G-BTXX	Bellanca 8KCAB Decathlon	Sherwood Flying Club Ltd/Tollerton	
G-BTXZ	Zenair CH.250	I. Parris & P. W. J. Bull	
G-BTYC	Cessna 150L	Polestar Aviation Ltd	
G-BTYD	Cameron N-90 balloon	Skybus Ballooning	
G-BTYE	Cameron A-180 balloon	K. J. A. Maxwell & D. S. Messmer	
G-BTYF	Thunder Ax10-180 S2 balloon	P. Glydon	
G-BTYH	Pottier P.80S	R. Pickett	
G-BTYI	PA-28-181 Archer II	C. A. Saville	
G-BTYK	Cessna 310R	E. H. J. Moody	
G-BTYT	Cessna 152 II	M. J. Green	
G-BTYW	Cessna 120	P. J. Singleton & C. J. Archer	
G-BTYX	Cessna 140	G-BTYX Group	
G-BTYY	Curtiss Robin C-2	R. R. L. Windus	
G-BTYZ	Colt 210A balloon	T. M. Donnelly	
G-BTZA	Beech F33A Bonanza	G-BTZA Group/Edinburgh	
G-BTZB	Yakovlev Yak-50 (69)	J. S. Allison	
G-BTZD	Yakovlev Yak-1	Historic Aircraft Collection Ltd/Audley End	

Notes	Reg.	Type	Owner or Operator
	G-BTZE	LET Yakovlev C.11	Bianchi Aviation Film Services Ltd/Booker
	G-BTZL	Oldfield Baby Lakes	J. M. Roach
	G-BTZN	BAe 146-300	British Aerospace PLC
	G-BTZO	SOCATA TB.20 Trinidad	Hydrodiesel Ltd
	G-BTZP	SOCATA TB.9 Tampico	Newcastle-upon-Tyne Aero Club Ltd
	G-BTZR	Colt 77B balloon	P. J. Fell
	G-BTZS	Colt 77A balloon	P. T. R. Ollivers
	G-BTZU	Cameron Concept SS balloon	Gone With The Wind Ltd
	G-BTZV	Cameron V-77 balloon	A. W. Sumner
	G-BTZX	Piper J-3C-65 Cub	D. A. Woodhams & J. T. Coulthard
	G-BTZY	Colt 56A balloon	T. M. Donnelly
	G-BTZZ	CFM Streak Shadow	D. R. Stennett
	G-BUAA	Corben Baby Ace D	B. F. Hill
	G-BUAB	Aeronca 11AC Chief	J. Reed
	G-BUAC	Slingsby T.31 Motor Cadet III	D. A. Wilson
	G-BUAF	Cameron N-77 balloon	S. J. Colin
	G-BUAG	Jodel D.18	A. L. Silcox
	G-BUAI	Everett Srs 3 gyroplane	C. J. Sullivan
	G-BUAJ	Cameron N-90 balloon	J. R. & S. J. Huggins
	G-BUAK	Thunder Ax8-105 S2 balloon	G. D. & L. Fitzpatrick
	G-BUAM	Cameron V-77 balloon	N. Florence
	G-BUAN	Cessna 172N	Bell Aviation
	G-BUAO	Luscombe 8A Silvaire	G. H. Matthews
	G-BUAR	V.S.358 Seafire LF.IIIc (PP972)	Wizzard Investments Ltd
	G-BUAT	Thunder Ax9-120 balloon	J. Fenton
	G-BUAU	Cameron A-180 balloon	Out Of This World Balloons
	G-BUAV	Cameron O-105 balloon	K. D. Johnson
	G-BUAW	Pitts S-1C Special	E. J. Hedges
	G-BUAX	Rans S.10 Sakota	S. P. Wakeham
	G-BUAY	Cameron A-210 balloon	Virgin Balloon Flights Ltd
	G-BUBA	PA-18S Super Cub 150 (floatplane)	B. Jackson
	G-BUBB	Light Aero Avid Flyer	D. Hookins
	G-BUBC	QAC Quickie Tri-Q.200	D. J. Clarke
	G-BUBL	Thunder Ax8-105 balloon ★	British Balloon Museum
	G-BUBN	BN-2B-26 Islander	Isles of Scilly Skybus Ltd/St Just
	G-BUBR	Cameron A-250 balloon	Bath Hot-Air Balloon Club
	G-BUBS	Lindstrand LBL-77B balloon	B. J. Bower
	G-BUBT	Stoddard-Hamilton Glasair IIRGS	M. D. Evans
	G-BUBU	PA-34-220T Seneca III	Brinor (Holdings) Ltd/Ipswich
	G-BUBW	Robinson R-22B	Forth Helicopters/Edinburgh
	G-BUBY	Thunder Ax8-105 S2 balloon	T. M. Donnelly
	G-BUCA	Cessna A.150K	T. R. Kingsley
	G-BUCB	Cameron H-34 balloon	Flying Pictures (Balloons) Ltd
	G-BUCC	C.A.S.A. 1.131E Jungmann 2000 (BU+CC)	R. A. Roberts (G-BUEM)/Shoreham
	G-BUCG	Schleicher ASW.20L (modified)	W. B. Andrews
	G-BUCH	Stinson V-77 Reliant	Pullmerit Ltd
	G-BUCI	Auster AOP.9 (XP242)	Historic Aircraft Flight Reserve Collection/ Middle Wallop
	G-BUCJ	D.H.C.2 Beaver 1 (XP772)	Historic Aircraft Flight Reserve Collection/ Middle Wallop
	G-BUCK	C.A.S.A. 1.131E Jungmann 1000 (BU+CK)	Jungmann Flying Group/White Waltham
	G-BUCM	Hawker Sea Fury FB.11 (VX653)	Patina Ltd/Duxford
	G-BUCO	Pietenpol Air Camper	A. James
	G-BUCS	Cessna 150F	Atlantic Bridge Aviation Ltd/Lydd
	G-BUCT	Cessna 150L	Atlantic Bridge Aviation Ltd/Lydd
	G-BUDA	Slingsby T.61F Venture T.2	RAF Germany Gliding Association
	G-BUDB	Slingsby T.61F Venture T.2	RAF Germany Gliding Association
	G-BUDC	Slingsby T.61F Venture T.2	R. A. Boddy
	G-BUDE	PA-22 Tri-Pacer 135 (tailwheel)	B. A. Bower/Thruxton
	G-BUDF	Rand-Robinson KR-2	J. B. McNab/Wellsbourne
	G-BUDH	Light Aero Avid Flyer	D. Cowen
	G-BUDI	Aero Designs Pulsar	R. W. L. Oliver
	G-BUDK	Thunder Ax7-77 balloon	W. Evans
	G-BUDL	Auster 3 (NX534)	M. Pocock
	G-BUDM	Colt Flying Hand SS balloon	BIAS (UK) Ltd
	G-BUDN	Cameron 90 Shoe SS balloon	L. Mastis
	G-BUDO	PZL-110 Koliber 150	A. S. Vine/Goodwood
	G-BUDR	Denney Kitfox Mk 3	N. J. P. Mayled
	G-BUDS	Rand-Robinson KR-2	D. W. Munday

Reg.	Type	Owner or Operator	Notes
G-BUDT	Slingsby T.61F Venture T.2	G-BUDT Group	
G-BUDU	Cameron V-77 balloon	T. M. G. Amery	
G-BUDV	Cameron A-210 balloon	Balloonair SA	
G-BUDW	Brügger MB.2 Colibri	J. M. Hoblyn (G-GODS)	
G-BUEA	Aérospatiale ATR-42-300	CityFlyer Express Ltd/BA Express	
G-BUEB	Aérospatiale ATR-42-300	CityFlyer Express Ltd/BA Express	
G-BUEC	Vans RV-6	D. W. Richardson & R. D. Harper	
G-BUED	Slingsby T.61F Venture T.2	SE Kent Civil Service Flying Club	
G-BUEE	Cameron A-210 balloon	Bristol Balloons	
G-BUEF	Cessna 152 II	Three Counties Aero Engineering Ltd/ Lasham	
G-BUEG	Cessna 152 II	Plymouth School of Flying Ltd	
G-BUEI	Thunder Ax8-105 balloon	Anglia Balloons	
G-BUEK	Slingsby T.61F Venture T.2	P. B. Duhig & W. Retzler	
G-BUEL	Colt Bottle 11 SS balloon	Jentime Ltd	
G-BUEN	VPM M.14 Scout	W. M. Day	
G-BUEO	Maule MX-7-180	K. & S. C. Knight	
G-BUEP	Maule MX-7-180	G. M. Bunn	
G-BUES	Cameron N-77 balloon	Bath City Council – Parks Section	
G-BUET	Colt Flying Drinks Can SS balloon	Flying Pictures (Balloons) Ltd	
G-BUEU	Colt 21A balloon	Flying Pictures (Balloons) Ltd	
G-BUEV	Cameron O-77 balloon	R. R. McCormack & R. J. Mercer	
G-BUEX	Schweizer 269C	Fenland Helicopter Centre (G-HFLR)	
G-BUEZ	Hunter F.6A (XF375)	Old Flying Machine Co Ltd/Duxford	
G-BUFA	Cameron R-77 gas balloon	Noble Adventures Ltd	
G-BUFC	Cameron R-77 gas balloon	Noble Adventures Ltd	
G-BUFE	Cameron R-77 gas balloon	Noble Adventures Ltd	
G-BUFG	Slingsby T.61F Venture T.2	T. W. Eagles	
G-BUFH	PA-28-161 Warrior II	The Tiger Leisure Group	
G-BUFJ	Cameron V-90 balloon	S. P. Richards	
G-BUFK	Cassutt Racer IIIM	D. I. H. Johnstone & W. T. Barnard	
G-BUFL	BAe Jetstream 3101	Jetstream Aircraft Ltd/Prestwick	
G-BUFN	Slingsby T.61F Venture T.2	BUFN Group	
G-BUFO	Cameron 70 UFO SS balloon	Virgin Airship & Balloon Co Ltd	
G-BUFP	Slingsby T.61F Venture T.2	Venture Group	
G-BUFR	Slingsby T.61F Venture T.2	R. F. Warren & P. A. Hazell	
G-BUFT	Cameron O-120 balloon	N. D. Hicks	
G-BUFU	Colt 105A balloon	Basemore Ltd	
G-BUFV	Light Aero Avid Flyer	S. C. Ord	
G-BUFX	Cameron N-90 balloon	Kerridge Computer Co Ltd	
G-BUFY	PA-28-161 Warrior II	Bickertons Aerodromes Ltd	
G-BUGB	Stolp SA.750 Acroduster Too	D. Burnham	
G-BUGC	Jurca MJ.5 Sirocco	A. Burani (G-BWDJ)	
G-BUGD	Cameron V-77 balloon	Cameron Balloons Ltd	
G-BUGE	Bellanca 7GCAA Citabria	Welsh Dragon Aviation Ltd	
G-BUGG	Cessna 150F	C. P. J. Taylor & D. M. Forshaw/ Panshanger	
G-BUGH	Rans S.10 Sakota	D. T. Smith	
G-BUGI	Evans VP-2	R. G. Boyes	
G-BUGJ	Robin DR.400/180	Alfred Graham Ltd	
G-BUGL	Slingsby T.61F Venture T.2	VMG Group	
G-BUGM	CFM Streak Shadow	The Shadow Group	
G-BUGN	Colt 210A balloon	Balloon Club of GB Ltd	
G-BUGO	Colt 56B balloon	D. W. Allum	
G-BUGP	Cameron V-77 balloon	G. J. & R. Plant	
G-BUGS	Cameron V-77 balloon	A Load of Hot Air	
G-BUGT	Slingsby T.61F Venture T.2	J. F. R. Jones	
G-BUGV	Slingsby T.61F Venture T.2	The Gliding Centre/Edgehill	
G-BUGW	Slingsby T.61F Venture T.2	Rankart Ltd	
G-BUGX	M.S.880B Rallye Club	The Rallye Group	
G-BUGY	Cameron V-90 balloon	Dante Balloon Group	
G-BUGZ	Slingsby T.61F Venture T.2	Dishforth Flying Club	
G-BUHA	Slingsby T.61F Venture T.2 (ZA634)	A. W. Swales/Rufforth	
G-BUHC	BAe 146-300	Air UK Ltd (G-BTMI)/Stansted	
G-BUHJ	Boeing 737-4Q8	British Airways/Gatwick	
G-BUHK	Boeing 737-4Q8	British Airways/Gatwick	
G-BUHL	Boeing 737-4S3	GB Airways Ltd/Gatwick	
G-BUHM	Cameron V-77 balloon	L. A. Watts	
G-BUHO	Cessna 140	CAW Corporation Ltd	
G-BUHP	Flyair 1100 balloon	R. White	
G-BUHR	Slingsby T.61F Venture T.2	Lleweni Parc Ltd	
G-BUHS	Stoddard-Hamilton Glasair SH-TD-1	S. J. Marsh	

Notes	Reg.	Type	Owner or Operator
	G-BUHT	Cameron A-210 balloon	British School of Ballooning
	G-BUHU	Cameron N-105 balloon	Flying Pictures (Balloons) Ltd
	G-BUHX	Robinson R-22B	Seiont Construction
	G-BUHY	Cameron A-210 balloon	Adventure Balloon Co Ltd
	G-BUHZ	Cessna 120	C. P. & C. J. Wilkes
	G-BUIB	MBB Bo 105DBS/4	Bond Helicopters Ltd (G-BDYZ)
	G-BUIC	Denney Kitfox Mk 2	C. R. Northrop & B. M. Chilvers
	G-BUIE	Cameron N-90 balloon	Flying Pictures (Balloons) Ltd
	G-BUIF	PA-28-161 Warrior II	Newcastle-upon-Tyne Aero Club Ltd
	G-BUIG	Campbell Cricket (replica)	T. A. Holmes
	G-BUIH	Slingsby T.61F Venture T.2	Yorkshire Gliding Club (Pty) Ltd
	G-BUII	Cameron A-210 balloon	Aire Valley Balloons
	G-BUIJ	PA-28-161 Warrior II	Tradecliff Ltd
	G-BUIK	PA-28-161 Warrior II	I. H. Webb/Luton
	G-BUIL	CFM Streak Shadow	P. N. Bevan & L. M. Poor
	G-BUIN	Thunder Ax7-77 balloon	Free Flight Aerostat Group
	G-BUIP	Denney Kitfox Mk 2	Avcomm Developments Ltd
	G-BUIR	Light Aero Avid Speedwing Mk 4	K. N. Pollard
	G-BUIU	Cameron V-90 balloon	H. Micketeit/Germany
	G-BUIW	Robinson R-22B	Findon Air Services/Shoreham
	G-BUIZ	Cameron N-90 balloon	Virgin Airship & Balloon Co Ltd
	G-BUJA	Slingsby T.61F Venture T.2	RAFGSA/Cosford
	G-BUJB	Slingsby T.61F Venture T.2	Falke Syndicate/Shobdon
	G-BUJE	Cessna 177B	FG93 Group
	G-BUJG	AS.350B-2 Ecureuil	R. J. & E. M. Frost (G-HEAR)
	G-BUJH	Colt 77B balloon	A. D. Watt & ptnrs
	G-BUJI	Slingsby T.61F Venture T.2	R. A. Boddy
	G-BUJJ	Light Aero Avid Flyer	A. C. Debrett
	G-BUJK	Montgomerie-Bensen B.8MR	J. M. Montgomerie
	G-BUJL	Aero Designs Pulsar	J. J. Lynch
	G-BUJM	Cessna 120	De Cadenet Engineering Ltd/Bickmarsh
	G-BUJN	Cessna 172N	De Cadenet Engineering Ltd/Coventry
	G-BUJO	PA-28-161 Warrior II	Channel Islands Aero Holdings Ltd
	G-BUJP	PA-28-161 Warrior II	De Cadenet Engineering Ltd/Coventry
	G-BUJR	Cameron A-180 balloon	W. I. Hooker & C. Parker
	G-BUJT	BAe Jetstream 3100	British Aerospace PLC/Prestwick
	G-BUJU	Cessna 150H	S. J. N. Robbie
	G-BUJV	Light Aero Avid Speedwing Mk 4	C. Thomas
	G-BUJW	Thunder Ax8-90 S2 balloon	R. T. Fagan
	G-BUJX	Slingsby T.61F Venture T.2	R. J. Chichester-Constable
	G-BUJY	D.H.82A Tiger Moth	Aero Vintage Ltd
	G-BUJZ	Rotorway Executive 90	T. W. Aisthorpe & R. J. D. Crick
	G-BUKA	Fairchild SA227AC Metro III	Air Corbière Ltd/Coventry
	G-BUKB	Rans S.10 Sakota	M. K. Blatch & M. P. Lee
	G-BUKC	Cameron A-180 balloon	Cloud Nine Balloon Co
	G-BUKE	Boeing Stearman A.75N1 (243)	R. G. Rance (G-BRIP)/Goodwood
	G-BUKF	Denney Kitfox Mk 4	M. R. Crosland
	G-BUKH	D.31 Turbulent	J. S. Smith
	G-BUKI	Thunder Ax7-77 balloon	Adventures Aloft
	G-BUKK	Bucker Bu133C Jungmeister (U-80)	E. J. F. McEntee/White Waltham
	G-BUKN	PA-15 Vagabond	M. A. & A. M. Watts
	G-BUKO	Cessna 120	N. G. Abbott
	G-BUKP	Denney Kitfox Mk 2	T. D. Reid
	G-BUKR	M.S.880B Rallye Club 100T	G-BUKR Flying Group
	G-BUKS	Colt 77B balloon	R. & M. Bairstow
	G-BUKT	Luscombe 8A Silvaire	M. G. Talbot & J. N. Willshaw
	G-BUKU	Luscombe 8E Silvaire	F. G. Miskelly
	G-BUKX	PA-28-161 Warrior II	LNP Ltd
	G-BUKY	CCF Harvard IVM (52-8543)	P. R. Monk & A. H. Soper/Rochester
	G-BUKZ	Evans VP-2	P. R. Farnell
	G-BULB	Thunder Ax7-77 balloon	Shiltons of Rothbury
	G-BULC	Light Aero Avid Flyer Mk 4	A. G. Batchelor
	G-BULD	Cameron N-105 balloon	S. J. Boxall
	G-BULE	Price TPB.2 balloon	A. G. R. Calder
	G-BULF	Colt 77A balloon	M. V. Farrant
	G-BULG	Vans RV-4	J. R. Ware
	G-BULH	Cessna 172N	B. R. Gaunt
	G-BULJ	CFM Steak Shadow	C. C. Brown
	G-BULK	Thunder Ax9-120 S2 balloon	Lindsay Marketing Associates
	G-BULL	SA Bulldog 120/128	C. D. Weiswall
	G-BULM	Aero Designs Pulsar	J. Webb
	G-BULN	Colt 210A balloon	H. G. Davies

Reg.	Type	Owner or Operator	Notes
G-BULO	Luscombe 8A Silvaire	G-BULO Flying Group/Andrewsfield	
G-BULR	PA-28 Cherokee 140	R. & W. Wale (General Woodworks) Ltd	
G-BULT	Campbell Cricket	A. T. Pocklington	
G-BULW	Rans S.10 Sakota	V. G. Gale	
G-BULY	Light Aero Avid Flyer	D. R. Piercy	
G-BULZ	Denney Kitfox Mk 2	T. G. F. Trenchard	
G-BUMP	PA-28-181 Archer II	M. Dunlop	
G-BUNB	Slingsby T.61F Venture T.2	RAFGSA Cranwell Gliding Club	
G-BUNC	PZL-104 Wilga 35	Paravia Group	
G-BUND	PA-28RT-201T Turbo Arrow IV	Jenrick Ltd & A. Somerville	
G-BUNE	Colt Flying Drinks Can SS balloon	Pepsi Cola Overseas Ltd	
G-BUNF	Colt Flying Drinks Can SS balloon	Pepsi Cola Overseas Ltd	
G-BUNG	Cameron N-77 balloon	The Balloon Squad	
G-BUNH	PA-28RT-201T Turbo Arrow IV	QA Communications Ltd	
G-BUNI	Cameron 90 Bunny SS balloon	Virgin Airship & Balloon Co Ltd	
G-BUNJ	Squarecraft SA.102-5 Cavalier	J. A. Smith	
G-BUNM	Denney Kitfox Mk 3	P. J. Carter	
G-BUNO	Lancair 320	J. Softley	
G-BUNS	Cessna F.150K	R. W. H. Cole	
G-BUNV	Thunder Ax7-77 balloon	J. A. Lister	
G-BUNZ	Thunder Ax10-180 S2 balloon	T. M. Donnelly	
G-BUOA	Whittaker MW.6-S Fat Boy Flyer	D. A. Izod	
G-BUOB	CFM Streak Shadow	A. M. Simmons	
G-BUOC	Cameron A-210 balloon	G. N. & K. A. Connolly	
G-BUOD	SE-5A (replica) (B595)	M. D. Waldron	
G-BUOE	Cameron V-90 balloon	Dusters & Co	
G-BUOF	D.62B Condor	K. Jones	
G-BUOI	PA-20 Pacer	Foley Farm Flying Group	
G-BUOJ	Cessna 172N	Falcon Flying Services/Biggin Hill	
G-BUOK	Rans S.6-ESA Coyote II	M. Morris	
G-BUOL	Denney Kitfox Mk 3	J. G. D. Barbour	
G-BUON	Light Aero Avid Aerobat	I. A. J. Lappin	
G-BUOO	QAC Quickie Tri-Q.200	P. Crossman	
G-BUOP	Skycycle D.2 airship	G. E. Dorrington	
G-BUOR	C.A.S.A. 1.131E Jungmann 2000	M. S. Voest/Lelystad	
G-BUOS	V.S.394 Spitfire FR.XVIII (SM845)	A. J. Reynard & Park Avenue Investments Ltd	
G-BUOW	Aero Designs Pulsar XP	DRA Bedford Flying Club	
G-BUOX	Cameron V-77 balloon	R. M. Pursey & C. M. Richardson	
G-BUOZ	Thunder Ax10-180 balloon	Ashleader Ltd	
G-BUPA	Rutan LongEz	G. J. Banfield	
G-BUPB	Stolp SA.300 Starduster Too	Summit Aviation Ltd/Shoreham	
G-BUPC	Rollason Beta B.2	C. A. Rolph	
G-BUPF	Bensen B.8R	G. M. Hobman	
G-BUPG	Cessna 180K	T. P. A. Norman/Rendcomb	
G-BUPH	Colt 25A balloon	Wellfarrow Ltd	
G-BUPI	Cameron V-77 balloon	S. A. Masey (G-BOUC)	
G-BUPJ	Fournier RF-4D	M. R. Shelton	
G-BUPM	VPM M.16 Tandem Trainer	J. G. Erskine	
G-BUPN	PA-46-350P Malibu	K. Fletcher/Coventry	
G-BUPO	Zlin Z.526F Trener Master	P. J. Behr & F. Mendelssohn/France	
G-BUPP	Cameron V-42 balloon	T. M. Gilchrist	
G-BUPR	Jodel D.18	R. W. Burrows	
G-BUPS	Aérospatiale ATR-42-300	Titan Airways Ltd/Stansted	
G-BUPT	Cameron O-105 balloon	Chiltern Balloons	
G-BUPU	Thunder Ax7-77 balloon	R. C. Barkworth & D. G. Maguire	
G-BUPV	Great Lakes 2T-1A	R. J. Fray	
G-BUPW	Denney Kitfox Mk 3	D. Sweet	
G-BURA	Thunder Ax8-105 S2 balloon	Airship Shop Ltd	
G-BURD	Cessna F.172N	L. M. Bateman & Co Ltd/Halfpenny Green	
G-BURE	Jodel D.9	L. J. Kingsford	
G-BURF	Rand-Robinson KR-2	P. J. H. Moorhouse & B. L. Hewart	
G-BURG	Colt 77A balloon	S. J. Humphreys/Popham	
G-BURH	Cessna 150E	BURH Flying Group	
G-BURI	Enstrom F-28C	F. B. Holben/Goodwood	
G-BURK	Luscombe 8A Silvaire	M. Stow	
G-BURL	Colt 105A balloon	Scotia Balloons Ltd	
G-BURM	EE Canberra TT.18 (WJ680)	Mitchell Aircraft Ltd/North Weald	
G-BURN	Cameron O-120 balloon	I. Bentley	
G-BURP	Rotorway Executive 90	N. K. Newman	
G-BURR	Auster AOP.9 (WZ706)	R. P. D. Folkes/Middle Wallop	
G-BURS	Sikorsky S-76A	Lynton Aviation Ltd (G-OHTL)	
G-BURT	PA-28-161 Warrior II	I. P. Stockwell	

Notes	Reg.	Type	Owner or Operator
	G-BURW	Light Aero Avid Speedwing	A. Charlton
	G-BURY	Cessna 152 II	M. L. Grunnill/White Waltham
	G-BURZ	Hawker Nimrod II (K3661)	Historic Aircraft Collection Ltd
	G-BUSB	Airbus A.320-111	British Airways *Island of Jersey*
	G-BUSC	Airbus A.320-111	British Airways
	G-BUSD	Airbus A.320-111	British Airways *Island of Mull*
	G-BUSE	Airbus A.320-111	British Airways *Isles of Scilly*
	G-BUSF	Airbus A.320-111	British Airways *Isle of Man*
	G-BUSG	Airbus A.320-211	British Airways *Isle of Wight*
	G-BUSH	Airbus A.320-211	British Airways *Isle of Jura*
	G-BUSI	Airbus A.320-211	British Airways *Isle of Anglesey*
	G-BUSJ	Airbus A.320-211	British Airways *Isle of Sark*
	G-BUSK	Airbus A.320-211	British Airways *Island of Guernsey*
	G-BUSN	Rotorway Executive 90	B. Seymour
	G-BUSR	Aero Designs Pulsar	S. S. Bateman & R. A. Watts
	G-BUSS	Cameron 90 Bus SS balloon	L. V. Mastis
	G-BUST	Lancair IV	C. C. Butt
	G-BUSV	Colt 105A balloon	M. N. J. Kirby
	G-BUSW	R. Commander 114	Costello Automotive Ltd/Biggin Hill
	G-BUSY	Thunder Ax6-56A balloon	M. E. Hooker
	G-BUSZ	Light Aero Avid Speedwing Mk 4	G. N. S. Farrant
	G-BUTA	C.A.S.A. 1.131E Jungmann 2000	K. D. Dunkerley
	G-BUTB	CFM Streak Shadow	F. A. H. Ashmead
	G-BUTC	Cyclone AX3/582	P. R. Berridge
	G-BUTD	Vans RV-6	N. W. Beadle
	G-BUTE	Anderson EA-1 Kingfisher	T. Crawford (G-BRCK)
	G-BUTF	Aeronca 11AC Chief	N. J. Mortimore
	G-BUTG	Zenair CH.601HD	J. M. Scott
	G-BUTH	CEA DR.220 2+2	A. R. Norman
	G-BUTJ	Cameron O-77 balloon	A. J. A. Bubb
	G-BUTK	Murphy Rebel	D. Webb/Shobdon
	G-BUTL	PA-24 Comanche 250	D. Buttle (G-ARLB)/Blackbushe
	G-BUTM	Rans S.6-116 Coyote II	M. Rudd
	G-BUTN	MBB Bo 105DBS/4	Bond Helicopters Ltd (G-AZTI)
	G-BUTO	Pitts S-1 Special	J. M. Alexander
	G-BUTP	Bede BD-5G	Heather Flight Ltd
	G-BUTT	Cessna FA.150K	C. R. Guggenheim (G-AXSJ)/ Bournemouth
	G-BUTU	OA.7 Optica Srs 300	FLS Aerospace (Lovaux) Ltd/Bournemouth
	G-BUTV	OA.7 Optica Srs 300	FLS Aerospace (Lovaux) Ltd/Bournemouth
	G-BUTX	C.A.S.A. 1.133C Jungmeister	A. J. E. Smith
	G-BUTY	Brügger MB.2 Colibri	R. M. Lawday
	G-BUTZ	PA-28 Cherokee 180C	A. J. & J. M. Davis (G-DARL)
	G-BUUA	Slingsby T.67M Mk II	Hunting Aircraft Ltd/Barkston Heath
	G-BUUB	Slingsby T.67M Mk II	Hunting Aircraft Ltd/Barkston Heath
	G-BUUC	Slingsby T.67M Mk II	Hunting Aircraft Ltd/Barkston Heath
	G-BUUD	Slingsby T.67M Mk II	Hunting Aircraft Ltd/Barkston Heath
	G-BUUE	Slingsby T.67M Mk II	Hunting Aircraft Ltd/Barkston Heath
	G-BUUF	Slingsby T.67M Mk II	Hunting Aircraft Ltd/Barkston Heath
	G-BUUG	Slingsby T.67M Mk II	Hunting Aircraft Ltd/Barkston Heath
	G-BUUI	Slingsby T.67M Mk II	Hunting Aircraft Ltd/Barkston Heath
	G-BUUJ	Slingsby T.67M Mk II	Hunting Aircraft Ltd/Barkston Heath
	G-BUUK	Slingsby T.67M Mk II	Hunting Aircraft Ltd/Barkston Heath
	G-BUUL	Slingsby T.67M Mk II	Hunting Aircraft Ltd/Barkston Heath
	G-BUUM	PA-28RT-201 Arrow IV	Bluebird Flying Group
	G-BUUN	Lindstrand LBL-105A balloon	Flying Pictures (Balloons) Ltd
	G-BUUO	Cameron N-90 balloon	Bryan Bros Ltd
	G-BUUP	BAe ATP	Manx Airlines Ltd
	G-BUUS	Skyraider gyroplane	Sycamore Aviation Ltd
	G-BUUT	Interavia 70TA	Aero Vintage Ltd
	G-BUUU	Cameron 77 Bottle SS balloon	United Distillers UK Ltd
	G-BUUV	Lindstrand LBL-77A balloon	Virgin Airship & Balloon Co Ltd
	G-BUUX	PA-28 Cherokee 180D	Aero Group 78/Netherthorpe
	G-BUVA	PA-22 Tri-Pacer 135	Oaksey VA Group
	G-BUVB	Colt 77A balloon	T. L. Regan
	G-BUVE	Colt 77B balloon	M. P. & M. Nicholson
	G-BUVF	D.H.C.2 Beaver 1	DSG (Guernsey) Ltd
	G-BUVG	Cameron N-56 balloon	Cameron Balloons Ltd
	G-BUVK	Cameron A-210 balloon	British School of Ballooning
	G-BUVL	Fisher Super Koala	A. D. Malcolm
	G-BUVM	CEA DR.250/160	G. G. Milton
	G-BUVN	C.A.S.A. 1.131E Jungmann 2000	W. Van Egmond/Netherlands
	G-BUVO	Cessna F.182P	BUVO Group (G-WTFA)/Southend

Reg.	Type	Owner or Operator	Notes
G-BUVP	C.A.S.A. 1.131E Jungmann 2000	M. I. M. S. Voest/Lelysted	
G-BUVR	Christen A.1 Husky	A. E. Poulson	
G-BUVS	Colt 77A balloon	Supergas Ltd	
G-BUVT	Colt 77A balloon	Supergas Ltd	
G-BUVW	Cameron N-90 balloon	Bristol Balloon Fiestas Ltd	
G-BUVX	CFM Streak Shadow	G. K. R. Linney	
G-BUVZ	Thunder Ax10-180 S2 balloon	Lakeside Lodge Balloon Rides (Cambridgeshire) Ltd	
G-BUWA	V.S.349 Spitfire Vc (AR614)	Classic Aviation Ltd/Duxford	
G-BUWE	SE-5A (replica) (C9533)	D. Biggs	
G-BUWF	Cameron N-105 balloon	R. E. Jones	
G-BUWH	Parsons 2-seat gyroplane	R. V. Brunskill	
G-BUWI	Lindstrand LBL-77A balloon	Capital Balloon Club Ltd	
G-BUWJ	Pitts S-1C Special	D. I. Cooke	
G-BUWK	Rans S.6-116 Coyote II	R. Warriner	
G-BUWL	Piper J-4A Cub Coupé	V. F. Kemp	
G-BUWM	BAe ATP	Jetstream Aircraft Ltd/Prestwick	
G-BUWN	Lindstrand LBL-180A balloon	Lindstrand Balloons Ltd	
G-BUWO	Lindstrand LBL-240A balloon	Lindstrand Balloons Ltd	
G-BUWP	BAe ATP	British Airways *Strathisla*	
G-BUWR	CFM Streak Shadow	T. Harvey	
G-BUWS	Denney Kitfox Mk 2	J. E. Brewis	
G-BUWT	Rand-Robinson KR-2	C. M. Coombe	
G-BUWU	Cameron V-77 balloon	M. J. Newman	
G-BUWV	CFM Streak Shadow	J. Morris	
G-BUWW	Cameron O-105 balloon	M. T. Evans	
G-BUWY	Cameron V-77 balloon	P. A. Sachs & A. G. Caley	
G-BUWZ	Robin HR.200/120B	A. Cox	
G-BUXA	Colt 210A balloon	R. S. Hunjan	
G-BUXB	Sikorsky S-76A	Air Hanson Ltd/Blackbushe	
G-BUXC	CFM Streak Shadow	J. Hosier	
G-BUXD	Maule MXT-7-160	A. R. Binnington	
G-BUXE	Cameron A-250 balloon	B. J. Petteford	
G-BUXG	Glaser-Dirks DG.400	J. J. Mason	
G-BUXI	Steen Skybolt	M. Frankland/Liverpool	
G-BUXJ	Slingsby T.61F Venture T.2	XIX Crawley Flying Club/Redhill	
G-BUXK	Pietenpol Air Camper	G. R. G. Smith/Shobdon	
G-BUXL	Taylor JT.1 Monoplane	M. W. Elliott	
G-BUXM	QAC Quickie Q.2	A. J. Ross & D. Ramwell	
G-BUXN	Beech C23 Sundowner	Private Pilots Syndicate	
G-BUXO	Pober P-9 Pixie	P-9 Flying Group	
G-BUXP	Falcon XPS	J. C. & B. E. Greenslade	
G-BUXR	Cameron A-250 balloon	Celebration Balloon Flights	
G-BUXS	MBB Bo 105DBS/4	Bond Helicopters Ltd (G-PASA/G-BGWP)	
G-BUXT	Dornier Do.228-202K	Suckling Airways Ltd/Cambridge	
G-BUXU	Beech D.17S	S. J. Ellis	
G-BUXV	PA-22 Tri-Pacer 160 (tailwheel)	Bogavia Two	
G-BUXW	Thunder Ax8-90 S2 balloon	C. W. Brown	
G-BUXX	PA-17 Vagabond	R. H. Hunt/Old Sarum	
G-BUXY	PA-25 Pawnee 235	Bath, Wilts & North Dorset Gliding Club Ltd	
G-BUXZ	Yakovlev Yak-3U	Old Flying Machine Co/Duxford	
G-BUYA	Lindstrand LBL-77A balloon	Lindstrand Balloons Ltd	
G-BUYB	Aero Designs Pulsar	A. P. Fenn/Shobdon	
G-BUYC	Cameron 80 Concept balloon	P. J. Dorward	
G-BUYD	Thunder Ax8-90 balloon	Anglia Balloons	
G-BUYE	Aeronca 7AC Champion	R. Mazey	
G-BUYF	Falcon XP	J. C. Greenslade	
G-BUYG	Colt 12 Flying Bottle SS balloon	United Distillers PLC	
G-BUYH	Cameron A-210 balloon	Newbury Ballooning Co & Land Securities Properties Ltd	
G-BUYI	Thunder Ax7-77 balloon	Chelmsford Management Ltd	
G-BUYJ	Lindstrand LBL-105A balloon	H. Vickerman	
G-BUYK	Denney Kitfox Mk 4	R. D. L. Mayes	
G-BUYL	RAF 2000GT gyroplane	Newtownair Gyroplanes Ltd	
G-BUYM	Thunder Ax8-105 balloon	Scotair Balloons	
G-BUYN	Cameron O-84 balloon	J. T. L. Challenger	
G-BUYO	Colt 77A balloon	R. J. W. Deans	
G-BUYR	Mooney M.20C	C. R. Weldon	
G-BUYS	Robin DR.400/180	F. A. Spear	
G-BUYT	Ken Brock KB-2 gyroplane	J. E. Harris	
G-BUYU	Bowers Fly-Baby 1A	J. A. Nugent	
G-BUYW	BAe ATP	Jetstream Aircraft Ltd/Prestwick	

Notes	Reg.	Type	Owner or Operator
	G-BUYY	PA-28 Cherokee 180	Global Trading Aviation Services Ltd
	G-BUZA	Denney Kitfox Mk 3	R. Hill
	G-BUZB	Aero Designs Pulsar XP	M. J. Whatley
	G-BUZC	Everett Srs 3A gyroplane	M. P. L'Hermette
	G-BUZD	AS.332L Super Puma	Brintel Helicopters Ltd
	G-BUZE	Light Aero Avid Speedwing	N. L. E. & R. A. Dupee
	G-BUZF	Colt 77B balloon	I. J. Jackson
	G-BUZG	Zenair CH.601HD	N. C. White
	G-BUZH	Aero Designs Star-Lite SL-1	R. J. W. Wood
	G-BUZI	AS.355F-1 Twin Squirrel	B. C. Seedle Helicopters/Blackpool
	G-BUZJ	Lindstrand LBL-105A balloon	Flying Pictures (Balloons) Ltd
	G-BUZK	Cameron V-77 balloon	J. T. Wilkinson & E. Evans
	G-BUZL	VPM M.16 Tandem Trainer	Roger Savage (Photography)
	G-BUZM	Light Aero Avid Flyer Mk 3	R. McLuckie & O. G. Jones
	G-BUZN	Cessna 172H	H. Jones
	G-BUZO	Pietenpol Air Camper	D. A. Jones
	G-BUZR	Lindstrand LBL-77A balloon	Lindstrand Balloons Ltd
	G-BUZS	Colt Flying Pig SS balloon	Banco Bilbao Vizcaya
	G-BUZT	Kölb Twinstar Mk 3	A. C. Goadby
	G-BUZV	Ken Brock KB-2 gyroplane	K. Hughes
	G-BUZY	Cameron A-250 balloon	P. J. D. Kerr
	G-BUZZ	AB-206B JetRanger 2	Autopilot Ltd
	G-BVAA	Light Aero Avid Aerobat Mk 4	R. W. Brown
	G-BVAB	Zenair CH.601HDS	A. R. Bender
	G-BVAC	Zenair CH.601HD	A. G. Cozens
	G-BVAF	Piper J-3C-65 Cub	N. M. Hitchman
	G-BVAG	Lindstrand LBL-90A balloon	T. Moult & ptnrs
	G-BVAH	Denney Kitfox Mk 3	V. A. Hutchinson
	G-BVAI	PZL-110 Koliber 150	N. J. & R. F. Morgan
	G-BVAJ	Rotorway Executive 90	Rotorbuild Helicopters Ltd
	G-BVAM	Evans VP-1	R. F. Selby
	G-BVAN	M.S.892E Rallye 150	D. R. Stringer/Elstree
	G-BVAO	Colt 25A balloon	J. M. Frazer
	G-BVAT	Murphy Renegade 912	J. Hatswell
	G-BVAU	Cameron A-210 balloon	Broadland Balloons Ltd
	G-BVAW	Staaken Z-1 Flitzer (D-692)	D. J. Evans & L. R. Williams
	G-BVAX	Colt 77A balloon	Vax Appliances Ltd
	G-BVAY	Rutan Vari-Eze	D. A. Young
	G-BVAZ	Montgomerie-Bensen B.8MR	R. Patrick
	G-BVBD	Sikorsky S-52-3	J. Windmill
	G-BVBE	P.84 Jet Provost T.3A (XN461)	R. E. Todd
	G-BVBF	PA-28-151 Warrior	R. K. Spence
	G-BVBG	PA-32R Cherokee Lance 300	R. K. Spence
	G-BVBJ	Colt Flying Jar 1 SS balloon	Flying Pictures (Balloons) Ltd
	G-BVBK	Colt Flying Jar 2 SS balloon	Flying Pictures (Balloons) Ltd
	G-BVBL	PA-38-112 Tomahawk	Aerohire Ltd/Halfpenny Green
	G-BVBM	Lindstrand LBL-180A balloon	A. M. Rocliffe & S. R. Wong
	G-BVBN	Cameron A-210 balloon	Heart of England Balloons
	G-BVBO	Sikorsky S-52-3	Ilkeston Contractors
	G-BVBP	Avro 683 Lancaster X	Aooc High Ltd/North Weald
	G-BVBR	Light Aero Avid Speedwing	H. R. Rowley
	G-BVBS	Cameron N-77 balloon	Marley Building Materials Ltd
	G-BVBT	D.H.C.1 Chipmunk T.10 (WK511)	T. J. Manna/Cranfield
	G-BVBU	Cameron V-77 balloon	S. van Havere/Belgium
	G-BVBV	Light Aero Avid Flyer	L. W. M. Summers
	G-BVBX	Cameron N-90M balloon	Virgin Airship & Balloon Co Ltd
	G-BVCA	Cameron N-105 balloon	Flying Pictures (Balloons) Ltd
	G-BVCB	Rans S.10 Sakota	M. D. T. Barley
	G-BVCC	Monnett Sonerai 2LT	J. Eggleston
	G-BVCF	Lindstrand Flying M SS balloon	International Balloons Ltd
	G-BVCG	Vans RV-6	C. A. Simmonds
	G-BVCI	Robinson R-22B	Ocean Shields Ltd
	G-BVCJ	Agusta A.109A-II	Castle Air Charters Ltd (G-CLRL/G-EJCB)
	G-BVCK	Lindstrand LBL-105A balloon	International Balloons Ltd
	G-BVCL	Rans S.6-116 Coyote II	S. R. A. Blackbourn & J. K. McFarlane
	G-BVCM	Cessna 525 CitationJet	Kwik Fit PLC/Edinburgh
	G-BVCN	Colt 56A balloon	N. R. Mason
	G-BVCO	FRED Srs 2	I. W. Bremner
	G-BVCP	Piper CP.1 Metisse	C. W. R. Piper
	G-BVCS	Aeronca 7BCM Champion	P. C. Isbell
	G-BVCT	Denney Kitfox Mk 4	A. F. Reid
	G-BVCV	Fairchild PT-19A Cornell (233752)	R. J. Fox

Reg.	Type	Owner or Operator	Notes
G-BVCX	Sikorsky S-76A	Brintel Helicopters Ltd	
G-BVCY	Cameron H-24 balloon	Bryant Group PLC	
G-BVCZ	Colt 240A balloon	Schemedraw Ltd	
G-BVDA	Lindstrand LBL-240A balloon	International Balloons Ltd	
G-BVDB	Thunder Ax7-77 balloon	M. J. Smith	
G-BVDC	Vans RV-3	D. Calabritto	
G-BVDD	Colt 69A balloon	R. M. Cambridge & D. Harrison-Morris	
G-BVDE	Taylor JT.1 Monoplane	C. R. J. Norman	
G-BVDF	Cameron 115 Doll SS balloon	Cameron Balloons Ltd	
G-BVDH	PA-28RT-201 Arrow IV	P. Heffron	
G-BVDI	Vans RV-4	J. P. Leigh	
G-BVDJ	Campbell Cricket (replica)	S. Jennings	
G-BVDM	Cameron C-60 balloon	M. P. Young	
G-BVDN	PA-34-220T Seneca III	W. S. Roberson (G-IGHA/G-IPUT)	
G-BVDO	Lindstrand LBL-105A balloon	J. Burlinson	
G-BVDP	Sequoia F.8L Falco	T. G. Painter	
G-BVDR	Cameron O-77 balloon	T. Duggan	
G-BVDS	Lindstrand LBL-69A balloon	I. Ollerenshaw	
G-BVDT	CFM Streak Shadow	H. J. Bennet	
G-BVDW	Thunder Ax8-90 balloon	R. P. Jones	
G-BVDY	Cameron 60 Concept balloon	K. A. & G. N. Connolly	
G-BVDZ	Taylorcraft BC-12D	P. N. W. England	
G-BVEA	Mosler Motors N.3 Pup	N. Lynch (G-MWEA)	
G-BVEB	PA-32R-301 Saratoga HP	Transea Trading Co. Ltd	
G-BVEC	Aérospatiale ATR-42-300	CityFlyer Express Ltd/BA Express	
G-BVED	Aérospatiale ATR-42-300	CityFlyer Express Ltd/BA Express	
G-BVEE	—	—	
G-BVEF	Aérospatiale ATR-42-300	CityFlyer Express Ltd/BA Express	
G-BVEG	P.84 Jet Provost T.3A (XN629)	Transair (UK) Ltd/North Weald	
G-BVEH	Jodel D.112	B. A. Ridgway	
G-BVEI	Colt 90A balloon	Thunder & Colt	
G-BVEJ	Cameron V-90 balloon	J. D. A. Snields & A. R. Craze	
G-BVEK	Cameron 80 Concept balloon	J. G. Andrews	
G-BVEL	Evans VP-1 Srs 2	M. J. & S. J. Quinn	
G-BVEN	Cameron 80 Concept balloon	Aire Valley Balloons	
G-BVEO	BAe ATP	Jetstream Aircraft Ltd/Prestwick	
G-BVEP	Luscombe 8A Silvaire	Mid-West Aviation Ltd	
G-BVER	D.H.C.2 Beaver 1 (XV268)	A. F. Allen (G-BTDM)	
G-BVES	Cessna 340A	Firfax Systems Ltd	
G-BVEU	Cameron O-105 balloon	H. C. Wright	
G-BVEV	PA-34-200 Seneca	R. W. Harris & ptnrs	
G-BVEW	Lindstrand LBL-150A balloon	P. A. & N. J. Foot	
G-BVEX	Lindstrand LBL-105A balloon	Lindstrand Balloons Ltd	
G-BVEY	Denney Kitfox Mk 4	Penny Hydraulics Ltd	
G-BVEZ	P.84 Jet Provost T.3A (XM479)	Newcastle Jet Provost Co Ltd	
G-BVFA	Rans S.10 Sakota	D. Parkinson & D. Allam/Redhill	
G-BVFB	Cameron N-31 balloon	Bath City Council	
G-BVFF	Cameron V-77 balloon	R. G. Barry	
G-BVFK	BN-2T Turbine Islander	Pilatus BN Ltd/Bembridge	
G-BVFL	Lindstrand LBL-21A balloon	International Balloons Ltd	
G-BVFM	Rans S.6-116 Coyote II	P. G. Walton	
G-BVFN	Pitts S-1E Special	N. W. Parkinson	
G-BVFO	Light Aero Avid Speedwing	P. Chisman	
G-BVFP	Cameron V-90 balloon	C. Duppa-Miller	
G-BVFR	CFM Streak Shadow	M. G. B. Stebbing	
G-BVFS	Slingsby T.31M Cadet	V. M. Crabb	
G-BVFT	Maule M5-235C	R. T. Love	
G-BVFU	Cameron 105 Sphere SS balloon	Lascar Investments Ltd	
G-BVFX	Nanchang CJ-6A (1532008)	Elmair Ltd	
G-BVFY	Colt 210A balloon	G. M. Houston	
G-BVFZ	Maule M5-180C	C. N. White	
G-BVGA	Bell 206B JetRanger 3	Findon Air Services/Shoreham	
G-BVGB	Thunder Ax8-105 S2 balloon	Flying Pictures (Balloons) Ltd	
G-BVGC	Cessna 411A	Taylor Aircraft Services Ltd (G-AVEK)	
G-BVGD	Aerotechnik L-13 SEH Vivat	Oxfordshire Sport Flying Ltd/Enstone	
G-BVGE	W.S.55 Whirlwind HAR.10 (XJ729)	Austen Associates Partnership	
G-BVGF	Shaw Europa	A. Graham & G. G. Beal	
G-BVGG	Lindstrand LBL-69A balloon	Lindstrand Balloons Ltd	
G-BVGH	Hunter T.7 (Xl.573)	B. J. Pover	
G-BVGI	Pereira Osprey II	B. Weare	
G-BVGJ	Cameron C-80 balloon	D. T. Watkins	
G-BVGK	Lindstrand LBL Flying Newspaper SS balloon	International Balloons Ltd	

Notes	Reg.	Type	Owner or Operator
	G-BVGL	Sikorsky S-76A	Bond Helicopters Ltd
	G-BVGM	Sikorsky S-76A	Bond Helicopters Ltd
	G-BVGO	Denney Kitfox Mk 4-1200	Willow Motors
	G-BVGP	Bücker Bü133C Jungmeister (U-95)	R. G. Jones
	G-BVGR	RAF BE-2e (A1325)	Aero Vintage Ltd
	G-BVGS	Robinson R-22B	Independent Car Auctions (UK) Ltd
	G-BVGT	Auster J/1 (modified)	L. A. Groves
	G-BVGW	Luscombe 8A Silvaire	L. A. Groves
	G-BVGX	Thunder Ax8-90 S2 balloon	G-BVGX Group
	G-BVGY	Luscombe 8E Silvaire	T. Groves
	G-BVGZ	Fokker Dr.1 (replica)	Museum of Army Flying/Middle Wallop
	G-BVHC	Grob G.115D-2	Short Bros PLC/Plymouth
	G-BVHD	Grob G.115D-2	Short Bros PLC/Plymouth
	G-BVHE	Grob G.115D-2	Short Bros PLC/Plymouth
	G-BVHF	Grob G.115D-2	Short Bros PLC/Plymouth
	G-BVHG	Grob G.115D-2	Short Bros PLC/Plymouth
	G-BVHI	Rans S.10 Sakota	P. D. Rowley
	G-BVHJ	Cameron A-180 balloon	Southern Flight Company Ltd
	G-BVHK	Cameron V-77 balloon	A. R. Rich
	G-BVHL	Nicollier HN.700 Menestrel II	I. H. R. Walker
	G-BVHM	PA-38-112 Tomahawk	A. J. Gomes (G-DCAN)
	G-BVHN	Lindstrand LBL G144 balloon	Lindstrand Balloons Ltd
	G-BVHO	Cameron V-90 balloon	N. W. B. Bews
	G-BVHP	Colt 42A balloon	Huntair Ltd
	G-BVHR	Cameron V-90 balloon	D. C. Boxall
	G-BVHS	Murphy Rebel	J. Brown & ptnrs
	G-BVHT	Light Aero Avid Speedwing Mk 4	R. S. Holt
	G-BVHU	Colt 13 Flying Bottle SS balloon	BIAS International Ltd
	G-BVHV	Cameron N-105 balloon	Flying Pictures (Balloons) Ltd
	G-BVHX	BN-2T-4R Defender 4000	Pilatus BN Ltd/Bembridge
	G-BVHY	BN-2T-4R Defender 4000	Pilatus BN Ltd/Bembridge
	G-BVIA	Rand-Robinson KR-2	K. Atkinson
	G-BVIC	EE Canberra B.6 (XH568)	Classic Aviation Projects Ltd
	G-BVID	Lindstrand Lozenge SS balloon	Respatex International Ltd
	G-BVIE	PA-18 Super Cub 95 (modified)	R. W. Sage (G-CLIK/G-BLMB))
	G-BVIF	Montgomerie-Bensen B.8MR	R. M. & D. Mann
	G-BVIG	Cameron A-250 balloon	Balloon Flights International Ltd
	G-BVIH	PA-28-161 Warrior II	Ocean Developments Ltd (G-GFCE/ G-BNJP)
	G-BVIK	Maule MXT-7-180	R. D. Masters
	G-BVIL	Maule MXT-7-180	K. & S. C. Knight
	G-BVIM	Cameron V-77 balloon	The Ballooning Business Ltd
	G-BVIN	Rans S.6-ESA Coyote II	K. J. Vincent
	G-BVIO	Colt Flying Drinks Can SS balloon	Flying Pictures (Balloons) Ltd
	G-BVIR	Lindstrand LBL-69A balloon	A. G. E. Faulkner
	G-BVIS	Brügger MB.2 Colibri	M. J. Sharp
	G-BVIT	Campbell Cricket	A. N. Nisbet
	G-BVIV	Light Aero Avid Aerobat	J. & V. Hobday
	G-BVIW	PA-18-Super Cub 150	Rodger Aircraft Ltd
	G-BVIX	Lindstrand LBL-180A balloon	Humbug Balloon Group
	G-BVIY	Cameron A-105 balloon	J. L. M. Van Hoesel
	G-BVIZ	Shaw Europa	T. J. Punter & P. G. Jeffers
	G-BVJA	Fokker 100	British Midland Airways Ltd/E. Midlands
	G-BVJB	Fokker 100	British Midland Airways Ltd/E. Midlands
	G-BVJC	Fokker 100	British Midland Airways Ltd/E. Midlands
	G-BVJD	Fokker 100	British Midland Airways Ltd/E. Midlands
	G-BVJE	AS.350B-1 Ecureuil	I. S. & G. Steel Stockholders Ltd
	G-BVJF	Montgomerie-Bensen B.8MR	D. M. F. Harvey
	G-BVJG	Cyclone AX3/K	T. D. Reid (G-MYOP)
	G-BVJH	Aero Designs Pulsar	J. A. C. Tweedle
	G-BVJJ	Cameron DP-90 airship	Cameron Balloons Ltd
	G-BVJK	Glaser-Dirks DG.400	B. A. Eastwell
	G-BVJL	Colt 240A balloon	Anglian Countryside Balloons
	G-BVJN	Shaw Europa	N. Adam
	G-BVJO	Cameron R-77 balloon	Bondbaste Ltd
	G-BVJP	Aérospatiale ATR-42-300	Gill Airways Ltd/Newcastle
	G-BVJS	Colt Piggy Bank SS balloon	Iduna-Bausparkasse AG
	G-BVJT	Cessna F.406	Nor Leasing
	G-BVJU	Evans VP-1	B. A. Schlussler
	G-BVJV	Airbus A.320-231	Airworld Aviation Ltd/Gatwick
	G-BVJW	Airbus A.320-231	Airworld Aviation Ltd Mallorca/Gatwick

Reg.	Type	Owner or Operator	Notes
G-BVJX	Marquart MA.5 Charger	M. L. Martin	
G-BVJY	H.S.125 Srs 700B	Aviamost Ltd	
G-BVJZ	PA-28-161 Warrior II	A. R. Fowkes	
G-BVKA	Boeing 737-59D	British Midland Airways Ltd/E. Midlands	
G-BVKB	Boeing 737-59D	British Midland Airways Ltd/E. Midlands	
G-BVKC	Boeing 737-59D	British Midland Airways Ltd/E. Midlands	
G-BVKD	Boeing 737-59D	British Midland Airways Ltd/E. Midlands	
G-BVKE	Team Minimax 88	A. M. Pepper	
G-BVKF	Shaw Europa	T. R. Sinclair	
G-BVKG	Colt Flying Hot Dog SS balloon	Longbreak Ltd	
G-BVKH	Thunder Ax8-90 balloon	R. G. Gruzelier	
G-BVKJ	Bensen B.8	J. Bagnall	
G-BVKK	Slingsby T.61F Venture T.2	The Gliding Centre/Edgehill	
G-BVKL	Cameron A-180 balloon	W. I. & C. Hooker	
G-BVKM	Rutan Vari-Eze	B. Bochatay	
G-BVKP	Sikorsky S-76A	Bristow Helicopters Ltd	
G-BVKR	Sikorsky S-76A	Bristow Helicopters Ltd	
G-BVKU	Slingsby T.61F Venture T.2	R. W. Curtis	
G-BVKV	Cameron N-90 balloon	Pringle of Scotland Ltd	
G-BVKW	Lindstrand LBL-240A balloon	Bridges Van Hire Ltd	
G-BVKX	Colt 14A balloon	H. C. J. Williams	
G-BVKZ	Thunder Ax9-120 balloon	D. J. Head	
G-BVLA	Lancair 320	A. R. Welstead	
G-BVLB	Cameron 77 Can SS balloon	Cameron Balloons Ltd	
G-BVLC	Cameron N-42 balloon	Cameron Balloons Ltd	
G-BVLD	Campbell Cricket (replica)	C. Berry	
G-BVLE	McCandless M.4 gyroplane	H. Walls	
G-BVLF	Starstreak Shadow SS-D	B. R. Johnson	
G-BVLG	AS.355F-1 Twin Squirrel	PLM Dollar Group PLC	
G-BVLH	Shaw Europa	D. Barraclough	
G-BVLI	Cameron V-77 balloon	Autographics Ltd	
G-BVLK	Rearwin 8125 Cloudster	M. C. Hiscock	
G-BVLL	Lindstrand LBL-210A balloon	A. G. E. Faulkner	
G-BVLM	D.H.115 Vampire T.55 (209)	R. J. Verrall/Bournemouth	
G-BVLN	Aero Designs Pulsar XP	D. A. Campbell	
G-BVLP	PA-38-112 Tomahawk	D. A. Whitmore	
G-BVLR	Vans RV-4	RV4 Group	
G-BVLS	Thunder Ax8-90 S2 balloon	J. R. Henderson	
G-BVLT	Bellanca 7GCBC Citabria	Rodger Aircraft Ltd	
G-BVLU	D.31 Turbulent	C. D. Bancroft	
G-BVLV	Shaw Europa	Euro 39 Group	
G-BVLW	Light Aero Avid Flyer Mk 4	D. M. Johnstone/Shobdon	
G-BVLX	Slingsby T.61F Venture T.2	RAFGSA/Bicester	
G-BVLZ	Lindstrand LBL-120A balloon	Balloon Flights Club Ltd	
G-BVMA	Beech 200 Super King Air	Manhattan Air Ltd (G-VPLC)/Blackbushe	
G-BVMB	Hunter T.7 (XL613)	Hunter Aviation Ltd	
G-BVMC	Robinson R-44 Astro	E. Wooton	
G-BVMD	Luscombe 8E Silvaire	G. M. Scott	
G-BVMF	Cameron V-77 balloon	P. A. Meecham	
G-BVMG	Bensen B.80V	D. Moffat	
G-BVMH	WAG-Aero Sport Trainer (39624)	D. M. Jagger	
G-BVMI	PA-18 Super Cub 150	T. P. & M. M. Spurge	
G-BVMJ	Cameron 95 Eagle SS balloon	Classic Event/Berlin	
G-BVML	Lindstrand LBL-210A balloon	Ballooning Adventures Ltd	
G-BVMN	Ken Brock KB-2 gyroplane	S. McCullagh	
G-BVMO	R. Commander 685	Flightpath Ltd	
G-BVMR	Cameron V-90 balloon	I. R. Comley	
G-BVMU	Yakovlev Yak-52	J. E. & A. Ashby	
G-BVMV	Lindstrand LBL-150A balloon	International Balloons Ltd	
G-BVMW	Lindstrand LBL-77A balloon	International Balloons Ltd	
G-BVMX	Short SD3-60 Variant 300	Gill Airways Ltd (G-BPFS/G-REGN/G-OCIA)/Newcastle	
G-BVMY	Short SD3-60 Variant 100	British Regional Airlines/BA Express (G-OEEC/G-BPKY)	
G-BVMZ	Robin HR.100/210	Chiltern Handbags (London) Ltd/Booker	
G-BVNA	Cuby II	P. Scott (G-MYMA)	
G-BVNG	D.H.60G-III Moth Major	J. A. Pothecary/Shoreham	
G-BVNH	Agusta A.109C	Brecqhou Development Ltd (G-LAXO)	
G-BVNI	Taylor JT-2 Titch	T. V. Adamson	
G-BVNL	R. Commander 114	W. J. Hemmings & ptnrs	
G-BVNM	Boeing 737-4S3	British Airways (G-BPKA)	
G-BVNN	Boeing 737-4S3	British Airways (G-BPKB)	
G-BVNO	Boeing 737-4S3	British Airways (G-BPKE)	

Notes	Reg.	Type	Owner or Operator
	G-BVNR	Cameron N-105 balloon	Novogas SpA
	G-BVNS	PA-28-181 Archer II	Sub Marine Services Ltd
	G-BVNU	FLS Aerospace Sprint Club	FLS Aerospace (Lovaux) Ltd/Bournemouth
	G-BVNY	Rans S.7 Courier	Sportair UK Ltd
	G-BVOA	PA-28-181 Archer II	Millen Aviation Services
	G-BVOB	F.27 Friendship Mk 500	Air UK Ltd/Stansted
	G-BVOC	Cameron V-90 balloon	S. A. Masey
	G-BVOD	Montgomerie-Parsons 2-seat gyroplane	J. M. Montgomerie
	G-BVOG	Cameron RN-9 balloon	Cameron Balloons Ltd
	G-BVOH	Campbell Cricket (replica)	B. F. Pearson
	G-BVOI	Rans S.6-116 Coyote II	A. P. Bacon
	G-BVOJ	Lindstrand LBL-31A balloon	Flying Pictures (Balloons) Ltd
	G-BVOK	Yakovlev Yak-52	D. J. Gilmour/North Weald
	G-BVOM	F.27 Friendship Mk 500	Air UK Ltd/Stansted
	G-BVON	Lindstrand LBL´-105A balloon	International Balloons Ltd
	G-BVOO	Lindstrand LBL-105A balloon	International Balloons Ltd
	G-BVOP	Cameron N-90 balloon	Cambury Ltd
	G-BVOR	CFM Streak Shadow	J. A. Lord
	G-BVOS	Shaw Europa	Durham Europa Group
	G-BVOT	Glaser-Dirks DG.800A	W. R. McNair
	G-BVOU	H.S.748 Srs 2A	Emerald Airways Ltd/Liverpool
	G-BVOV	H.S.748 Srs 2A	Emerald Airways Ltd/Liverpool
	G-BVOW	Shaw Europa	Europa Syndicate
	G-BVOX	Taylorcraft F-22	Cubair Ltd/Redhill
	G-BVOY	Rotorway Executive 90	E. Drinkwater
	G-BVOZ	Colt 56A balloon	British School of Ballooning
	G-BVPA	Thunder Ax8-105 S2 balloon	Firefly Balloon Promotions
	G-BVPD	C.A.S.A. 1.131E Jungmann 2000	M. C. Garland
	G-BVPF	Lindstrand LBL-69A balloon	International Balloons Ltd
	G-BVPG	Lindstrand LBL-180A balloon	International Balloons Ltd
	G-BVPH	Bensen-Parsons 2-seat gyroplane	I. A. Leedham
	G-BVPI	Evans VP-1	C. M. Gibson
	G-BVPK	Cameron O-90 balloon	Mobil Oil Co ¬Ltd
	G-BVPL	Zenair CH.601HD	D. Harker
	G-BVPM	Evans VP-2 Coupé	P. Marigold
	G-BVPN	Piper J-3C-65 Cub	R. W. Sage (G-TAFY)
	G-BVPO	D.H.100 Vampire FB.6 (109)	R. J. Verrall/Bournemouth
	G-BVPP	Folland Gnat T.1 (XR993)	T. J. Manna/Cranfield
	G-BVPR	Robinson R-22B	Datum Enterprises Ltd (G-KNIT)/Staverton
	G-BVPS	Jodel D.112	P. J. Sharp
	G-BVPT	Dornier Do.228-202K	Suckling Airways Ltd/Cambridge
	G-BVPU	Cameron A-140 balloon	Cameron Balloons Ltd
	G-BVPV	Lindstrand LBL-77B balloon	A. R. Greensides
	G-BVPW	Rans S.6-116 Coyote II	J. G. Beesley
	G-BVPX	Lovegrove Tyro Gyro Mk II	P. C. Lovegrove
	G-BVPY	CFM Streak Shadow	R. J. Mitchell
	G-BVPZ	Lindstrand LBL-210A balloon	International Balloons Ltd
	G-BVRA	Shaw Europa	E. J. J. & S. W. Pels
	G-BVRD	VPM M.16 Tandem Trainer	Whisky Mike (Aviation) Ltd
	G-BVRE	Vans RV-6A	J. J. Martin
	G-BVRH	Taylorcraft BL-65	Ebork Ltd
	G-BVRI	Thunder Ax6-56 balloon	Voyager Balloons
	G-BVRK	Rans S.6-ESA Coyote II	J. Secular (G-MYPK)
	G-BVRL	Lindstrand LBL-21A balloon	M. J. Green
	G-BVRM	Cameron A-210 balloon	Virgin Balloon Flights Ltd
	G-BVRN	F.27 Friendship Mk 500	Air UK Ltd/Stansted
	G-BVRP	Lindstrand LBL-90A balloon	Lindstrand Balloons Ltd
	G-BVRR	Lindstrand LBL-77A balloon	I. Ollerenshaw
	G-BVRS	Beech B90 King Air	Cook Aviation Services Ltd (G-KJET/G-AXFE)
	G-BVRU	Lindstrand LBL-105A balloon	Flying Pictures (Balloons) Ltd
	G-BVRV	Vans RV-4	A. Troughton
	G-BVRY	Cyclone AX3/582	J. Toone/Popham
	G-BVRZ	PA-18 Super Cub 95	R. G. Warwick
	G-BVSB	Team Minimax	C. Nice/Popham
	G-BVSD	SE.3130 Alouette II (V-54)	R. E. Dagless/Shoreham
	G-BVSF	Aero Designs Pulsar	S. N. & R. J. Freestone
	G-BVSJ	BN-2B-26 Islander	Pilatus BN Ltd/Bembridge
	G-BVSL	BN-2T Turbine Islander	Pilatus BN Ltd/Bembridge
	G-BVSM	RAF 2000 gyroplane	K. Quigley
	G-BVSN	Light Aero Avid Speedwing	D. J. & C. Park

Reg.	Type	Owner or Operator
G-BVSO	Cameron A-120 balloon	Heavens Above
G-BVSP	P.84 Jet Provost T.3A	Lorch Schilling UK Ltd
G-BVSR	Colt 210A balloon	Eagle Security Ltd
G-BVSS	Jodel D.150	A. P. Burns
G-BVST	Jodel D.150	A. Shipp
G-BVSV	Cameron C-80 balloon	Cameron Balloons Ltd
G-BVSW	Cameron C-80 balloon	Cameron Balloons Ltd
G-BVSX	Team Minimax 91	G. N. Smith
G-BVSY	Thunder Ax9-120 balloon	Candytwist Balloons
G-BVSZ	Pitts S-1E (S) Special	R. C. F. Bailey
G-BVTA	Tri-R Kis	P. J. Webb
G-BVTC	P.84 Jet Provost T.5A (XW333)	Global Aviation Ltd
G-BVTD	CFM Streak Shadow	M. Walton
G-BVTE	Fokker 70	British Midland Airways Ltd/E. Midlands
G-BVTF	Fokker 70	British Midland Airways Ltd/E. Midlands
G-BVTG	Fokker 70	British Midland Airways Ltd/E. Midlands
G-BVTH	Fokker 70	British Midland Airways Ltd/E. Midlands
G-BVTJ	Aérospatiale ATR-72-202	CityFlyer Express Ltd/BA Express
G-BVTK	Aérospatiale ATR-72-202	CityFlyer Express Ltd/BA Express
G-BVTL	Colt 31A balloon	A. Lindsay
G-BVTM	Cessna F.152 II	RAF Halton Aeroplane Club (G-WACS)
G-BVTN	Cameron N-90 balloon	P. Zulehner/Austria
G-BVTO	PA-28-151 Warrior	Falcon Flying Services (G-SEWL)/ Biggin Hill
G-BVTU	Lindstrand LBL-105A balloon	International Balloons Ltd
G-BVTV	Rotorway Executive 90	Southern Helicopters Ltd
G-BVTW	Aero Designs Pulsar	J. D. Webb
G-BVTX	D.H.C.1 Chipmunk 22A (WP809)	Airspares UK
G-BVUA	Cameron O-105 balloon	D. C. Eager
G-BVUC	Colt 56A balloon	Thunder & Colt
G-BVUD	Cameron A-250 balloon	British School of Ballooning
G-BVUE	Cameron C-80 balloon	British School of Ballooning
G-BVUF	Thunder Ax10-180 S2 balloon	A. J. Nunns
G-BVUG	Betts TB.1	T. A. Betts
G-BVUH	Thunder Ax6-65B balloon	N. C. A. Crawley
G-BVUI	Lindstrand LBL-25A balloon	Lindstrand Balloons Ltd
G-BVUJ	Ken Brock KB-2 gyroplane	R. J. Hutchinson
G-BVUK	Cameron V-77 balloon	H. G. Griffiths & W. A. Steel
G-BVUM	Rans S.6-116 Coyote II	G. L. Donaldson
G-BVUN	Vans RV-4	I. G. & M. Glenn
G-BVUO	Cameron R-150 balloon	M. Sevrin/Belgium
G-BVUP	Schleicher ASW-24E	E. & C. F. Sprecht/Husbands Bosworth
G-BVUT	Evans VP-1 Srs 2	P. J. Weston
G-BVUU	Cameron C-80 balloon	T. M. C. McCoy
G-BVUV	Shaw Europa	A. P. Marks
G-BVUW	BAe 146-100	British Aerospace PLC
G-BVUX	BAe 146-100	British Aerospace (Operations) Ltd
G-BVUZ	Cessna 120	N. O. Anderson
G-BVVA	Yakovlev Yak-52	T. W. Freeman
G-BVVB	Carlson Sparrow Mk II	L. M. McCullen
G-BVVC	Hunter F.6A (XF516)	P. Hellier
G-BVVE	Jodel D.112	D. Silsbury
G-BVVF	Nanchang CJ-6A	Yak China Ltd
G-BVVG	Nanchang CJ-6A	Yak China Ltd
G-BVVH	Shaw Europa	T. G. Hoult
G-BVVI	Hawker Audax I (K5600)	Aero Vintage Ltd
G-BVVJ	Cameron N-77 balloon	Cameron Balloons Ltd
G-BVVK	D.H.C.6 Twin Otter 310	British Regional Airlines/BA Express
G-BVVL	EAA Acro Sport II	D. Park
G-BVVM	Zenair CH.601HD	J. G. Small
G-BVVN	Brügger MB.2 Colibri	N. F. Andrews
G-BVVO	Yakovlev Yak-50	J. M. Roach
G-BVVP	Shaw Europa	J. S. Melville
G-BVVR	Stits SA-3A Playboy	A. D. Pearce
G-BVVS	Vans RV-4	E. G. & N. S. C. English
G-BVVT	Colt 240A balloon	R. W. Keron
G-BVVV	Bell 206L-1 LongRanger 2	Romany Aeronautical (CI) Ltd
G-BVVW	Yakovlev Yak-52	David Young Cars
G-BVVX	Yakovlev Yak-18A	J. M. & E. M. Wicks
G-BVVY	Air Command 532 Elite	T. A. Holmes (G-CORK)
G-BVVZ	Corby CJ-1 Starlet	A. E. Morris
G-BVWA	M. S. 880B Rallye Club	A. P. Evans
G-BVWB	Thunder Ax8-90 S2 balloon	S. C. Clayton

Notes	Reg.	Type	Owner or Operator
	G-BVWC	EE Canberra B.6 (WK163)	Classic Aviation Projects Ltd/ Bruntingthorpe
	G-BVWE	Cameron C-80 balloon	Mid-Bucks Farmers Balloon Group
	G-BVWH	Cameron N-90 Bulb SS balloon	Virgin Airship & Balloon Co Ltd
	G-BVWI	Cameron 65 Bulb SS balloon	Virgin Airship & Balloon Co Ltd
	G-BVWK	Air & Space 18A gyroplane	Whisky Mike (Aviation) Ltd
	G-BVWL	Air & Space 18A gyroplane	Whisky Mike (Aviation) Ltd
	G-BVWM	Shaw Europa	Europa Syndicate
	G-BVWO	Lindstrand LBL-90A balloon	International Balloons Ltd
	G-BVWP	D.H.C.1 Chipmunk 22 (WP856)	T. W. M. Beck
	G-BVWR	Bell 206B JetRanger 2	Ford Helicopters Ltd
	G-BVWW	Lindstrand LBL-90A balloon	R. B. Naylor
	G-BVWX	VPM M.16 Tandem Trainer	M. L. Smith
	G-BVWY	Porterfield CP.65	B. Morris
	G-BVWZ	PA-32-301 Saratoga	R. Howton/Biggin Hill
	G-BVXA	Cameron N-105 balloon	R. E. Jones
	G-BVXB	Cameron V-77 balloon	J. A. Lawton
	G-BVXC	EE Canberra B.6 (WT333)	Classic Aviation Projects Ltd/ Bruntingthorpe
	G-BVXD	Cameron O-84 balloon	N. J. Langley
	G-BVXE	Steen Skybolt	T. J. Reeve (G-LISA)
	G-BVXF	Cameron O-120 balloon	Gone With The Wind Ltd
	G-BVXG	Lindstrand LBL-90A balloon	G. C. Elson
	G-BVXH	Lindstrand LBL-77A balloon	International Balloons Ltd
	G-BVXI	Klemm Kl.35D	J. J. van Egmond/Netherlands
	G-BVXJ	C.A.S.A. 1.133 Jungmeister	J. D. Haslam
	G-BVXK	Yakovlev Yak-52	E. Gavazzi
	G-BVXM	AS.350B Ecureuil	The Berkeley Leisure Group Ltd
	G-BVXP	Cameron N-105 balloon	P. M. Gaines
	G-BVXR	D.H.104 Devon C.2 (XA880)	M. Whale & M. W. A. Lunn
	G-BVXS	Taylorcraft BC-12D	J. M. Allison
	G-BVXU	Zenair CH.601HD	P. J. Roy
	G-BVXV	—	
	G-BVXW	SC.7 Skyvan Srs 3a Variant 100	Hunting Aviation Ltd/Kidlington
	G-BVXZ	Lindstrand LBL-210A balloon	Aerial Promotions Ltd
	G-BVYA	Airbus A.320-231	Caledonian Airways Ltd *Loch Katrine*
	G-BVYB	Airbus A.320-231	Caledonian Airways Ltd *Loch Hourn*
	G-BVYC	Airbus A.320-231	Caledonian Airways Ltd *Loch Tay*
	G-BVYE	BN-2B-26 Islander	Pilatus BN Ltd/Bembridge
	G-BVYF	PA-31-350 Navajo Chieftain	Warwickshire Aerocentre Ltd (G-SAVE)
	G-BVYG	CEA DR.300/180	London Gliding Club (Pty) Ltd/Dunstable
	G-BVYJ	Cameron 90 SS balloon	Chubb Fire Ltd
	G-BVYK	Team Minimax	S. B. Churchill
	G-BVYL	Colt 56A balloon	Old St. Andrews Ltd
	G-BVYM	CEA DR. 300/180	London Gliding Club (Pty) Ltd/Dunstable
	G-BVYN	Agusta-Bell 412	RCR Aviation Ltd
	G-BVYO	Robin R.2160	The Cotswold Aero Club Ltd/Staverton
	G-BVYP	PA-25 Pawnee 235B ★	Bidford Gliding Centre Ltd
	G-BVYR	Cameron A-250 balloon	Voyager Balloons
	G-BVYT	QAC Quickie Q.2	Quickie Club
	G-BVYU	Cameron A-120 balloon	B. J. Petteford
	G-BVYX	Light Aero Avid Speedwing Mk 4	G. J. Keen
	G-BVYY	Pietenpol Air Camper	J. R. Orchard
	G-BVYZ	Stemme S.10V	L. Gubbay & S. Sagar
	G-BVZA	Lindstrand LBL-77A balloon	International Balloons Ltd
	G-BVZB	Lindstrand LBL-31A balloon	International Balloons Ltd
	G-BVZD	Tri Kis	R. T. Clegg
	G-BVZE	Boeing 737-59D	British Midland Airways Ltd/E. Midlands
	G-BVZF	Boeing 737-59D	British Midland Airways Ltd/E. Midlands
	G-BVZG	Boeing 737-5Q8	British Midland Airways Ltd/E. Midlands
	G-BVZH	Boeing 737-5Q8	British Midland Airways Ltd/E. Midlands
	G-BVZI	Boeing 737-5Q8	British Midland Airways Ltd/E. Midlands
	G-BVZJ	Rand-Robinson KR-2	J. P. McConnell-Wood
	G-BVZM	Cessna 210M	Zone Travel Ltd
	G-BVZN	Cameron C-80 balloon	Sky Fly Balloons
	G-BVZO	Rans S.6-116 Coyote II	P. Atkinson
	G-BVZP	Rotorway Executive 90	P. D. Logan
	G-BVZR	Zenair CH.601HD	J. D. White
	G-BVZS	H.S.748 Andover CC.2	Arch Aviation Ltd
	G-BVZT	Lindstrand LBL-90A balloon	Pork Farms Bowyers
	G-BVZU	Airbus A.320-231	Airworld Aviation Ltd (EC-GKM)/Gatwick
	G-BVZV	Rans S.6-116 Coyote II	A. G. Cameron & W. G. Dunn
	G-BVZW	F.27 Friendship Mk 500	Channel Express (Air Services) Ltd/ Bournemouth

Reg.	Type	Owner or Operator	Notes
G-BVZX	Cameron H-34 balloon	Chianti Balloon Club	
G-BVZY	Mooney M.20R	Shipping & Airlines Ltd/Biggin Hill	
G-BVZZ	D.H.C.1 Chipmunk 22	Portsmouth Naval Gliding Club	
G-BWAA	Cameron N-133 balloon	Brunel Ford	
G-BWAB	Jodel D.14	W. A. Braim	
G-BWAC	Waco YKS-7	D. N. & C. E. Peters	
G-BWAD	RAF 2000GT gyroplane	J. R. Legge	
G-BWAE	RAF 2000GT gyroplane	B. J. Crockett	
G-BWAF	Hunter F.6A	R. V. Aviation Ltd/Bournemouth	
G-BWAG	Cameron O-120 balloon	M. F. Glue	
G-BWAH	Montgomerie-Bensen B.8MR	S. J. O. Tinn	
G-BWAI	CFM Streak Shadow	J. M. Heath	
G-BWAJ	Cameron V-77 balloon	R. S. & S. H. Ham	
G-BWAK	Robinson R-22B	Caudwell Communications Ltd	
G-BWAM	Cameron C-60 balloon	C. Schabus GmbH & Co KEG	
G-BWAN	Cameron N-77 balloon	Virgin Airship & Balloon Co Ltd	
G-BWAO	Cameron C-80 balloon	Virgin Airship & Balloon Co Ltd	
G-BWAP	FRED Srs 3	R. J. Smyth	
G-BWAR	Denney Kitfox Mk 3	C. E. Brookes	
G-BWAT	Pietenpol Air Camper	D. R. Waters	
G-BWAU	Cameron V-90 balloon	K. M. & A. M. F. Hall	
G-BWAV	Schweizer 269C	C.S.E. Aviation Ltd/Kidlington	
G-BWAW	Lindstrand LBL-77A balloon	D. Bareford	
G-BWAZ	AS.350B-2 Ecureuil	Bellini Aviation (1993) Ltd	
G-BWBA	Cameron V-65 balloon	Dante Balloon Group	
G-BWBB	Lindstrand LBL-14A balloon	Oxford Promotions (UK) Ltd	
G-BWBC	Cameron N-90AS balloon	Radio/Tele FFH GmbH & Co	
G-BWBD	Lindstrand LBL-90A balloon	International Balloons Ltd	
G-BWBE	Colt Flying Ice Cream Cone SS balloon	Benedikt Haggeney GmbH	
G-BWBF	Colt Flying Ice Cream Cone SS balloon	Benedikt Haggeney GmbH	
G-BWBG	Cvjetkovic CA-65 Skyfly	T. White & M. C. Fawkes	
G-BWBH	Colt Fork Lift Truck SS balloon	Jungheinrich AG	
G-BWBI	Taylorcraft F-22A	P. J. Wallace	
G-BWBJ	Colt 21A balloon	U. Schneider	
G-BWBK	Lindstrand LBL-77B balloon	International Balloons Ltd	
G-BWBL	Lindstrand LBL-90A balloon	International Balloons Ltd	
G-BWBM	Lindstrand LBL-90A balloon	International Balloons Ltd	
G-BWBN	Cameron V-90 balloon	The Small School at Red House Ltd	
G-BWBO	Lindstrand LBL-77A balloon	Lindstrand Balloons Ltd	
G-BWBP	Bell 212	Bristow Helicopters Ltd	
G-BWBR	Cameron A-180 balloon	Virgin Balloon Flights Ltd	
G-BWBS	P.84 Jet Provost T.5A	Downbird UK	
G-BWBT	Lindstrand LBL-90A balloon	British Telecommunications PLC	
G-BWBV	Colt Piggy Bank SS balloon	Iduna-Bausparkasse AG	
G-BWBW	Cameron A-180 balloon	Virgin Balloon Flights Ltd	
G-BWBY	Schleicher ASH.26E	F. B. Jeynes	
G-BWBZ	ARV Super 2	J. N. C. Shields	
G-BWCA	CFM Streak Shadow	R. Thompson	
G-BWCC	Van Den Bemden Gas balloon	Piccard Balloon Group	
G-BWCE	Campbell Cricket	M. K. Hoban	
G-BWCG	Lindstrand LBL-42A balloon	Oxford Promotions (UK) Ltd	
G-BWCH	Lindstrand LBL-9S balloon	International Balloons Ltd	
G-BWCI	Light Aero Avid Hauler Mk 4	J. B. Seidel	
G-BWCJ	Lindstrand LBL-14M balloon	International Balloons Ltd	
G-BWCK	Everett Srs 2 gyroplane	A. C. S. M. Hart	
G-BWCL	Lindstrand LBL-180A balloon	G. McFarland	
G-BWCM	Lindstrand LBL-77A balloon	International Balloons Ltd	
G-BWCN	Dornier Do.28D-2	Wingglider Ltd	
G-BWCO	Dornier Do.28D-2	Wingglider Ltd	
G-BWCS	P.84 Jet Provost T.5	Downbird UK/Liverpool	
G-BWCT	Tipsy T.66 Nipper 1	J. S. Hemmings & C. R. Steer	
G-BWCU	Bell 206L-1 LongRanger	Aeromega Ltd	
G-BWCV	Shaw Europa	M. P. Chetwynd-Talbot	
G-BWCW	Barnett J4B rotorcraft	S. H. Kirkby	
G-BWCX	Lindstrand LBL-90A balloon	Virgin Airship & Balloon Co Ltd	
G-BWCY	Murphy Rebel	A. Konieczek	
G-BWCZ	Mini-500	D. Nieman	
G-BWDA	Aerospatiale ATR-72-202	Gill Airways Ltd/Newcastle	
G-BWDB	Aerospatiale ATR-72-202	Gill Airways Ltd/Newcastle	
G-BWDE	PA-31P Pressurised Navajo	Tomkat Aviation Ltd (G-HWKN)	

Notes	Reg.	Type	Owner or Operator
	G-BWDF	PZL-104 Wilga 35A	Shivair Ltd
	G-BWDG	Lindstrand LBL-240A balloon	International Balloons Ltd
	G-BWDH	Cameron N-105 balloon	Bridges Van Hire Ltd
	G-BWDI	Cessna 340	Planstable Enterprises Ltd
	G-BWDL	Cameron 80 Concept balloon	Pegasus Ballooning Ltd
	G-BWDM	Lindstrand LBL-120A balloon	G. D. & L. Fitzpatrick
	G-BWDN	CFM Streak Shadow SA	White Rabbit Ltd
	G-BWDO	Sikorsky S-76B	Air Hanson Ltd
	G-BWDP	Shaw Europa	J. S. J. Valentine
	G-BWDR	P.84 Jet Provost T.3A	Global Aviation Ltd
	G-BWDS	P.84 Jet Provost T.3A	Global Aviation Ltd
	G-BWDT	PA-34-220T Seneca II	A. C. Morgan (G-BKHS)/Biggin Hill
	G-BWDU	Cameron V-90 balloon	Bath & West Security
	G-BWDV	Schweizer 269C	C.S.E Aviation Ltd/Kidlington
	G-BWDX	Shaw Europa	J. B. Crane
	G-BWDY	Sky 65-24 balloon	Sky Balloons Ltd
	G-BWDZ	Sky 105-24 balloon	G. Andrewartha
	G-BWEA	Lindstrand LBL-120A balloon	S. R. Seager
	G-BWEB	P.84 Jet Provost T.5A	C. J. Thompson/North Weald
	G-BWEC	Cassutt-Colson Variant	N. R. Thomason & M. P. J. Hill
	G-BWED	Thunder Ax7-77 balloon	J. Tod
	G-BWEE	Cameron V-42 balloon	Aeromantics Ltd
	G-BWEF	SNCAN Stampe SV-4C	Acebell BWEF Syndicate (G-BOVL)
	G-BWEG	Shaw Europa	Wessex Europa Group
	G-BWEH	HOAC Katana DV.20	Tayside Aviation Ltd/Dundee
	G-BWEI	Cessna 172N	C. A. S. Atha
	G-BWEL	Sky 200-24 balloon	H-O-T Air Balloons
	G-BWEM	V.S.358 Seafire L.IIIC	C. J. Warrillow/Booker
	G-BWEN	Macair Merlin GT	B. W. Davies
	G-BWEO	Lindstrand AM400 balloon	Lindstrand Balloons Ltd
	G-BWEP	Lindstrand AM2200 balloon	Lindstrand Balloons Ltd
	G-BWER	Lindstrand AM400 balloon	Lindstrand Balloons Ltd
	G-BWEU	Cessna F.152 II	Sky Pro Ltd
	G-BWEV	Cessna 152 II	Haimoss Ltd
	G-BWEW	Cameron N-105 balloon	Flying Pictures (Balloons) Ltd
	G-BWEX	Dornier Do.228-202K	Suckling Airways (Luton) Ltd
	G-BWEY	Bensen B.8	F. G. Shepherd
	G-BWEZ	Piper J-3C-65 Cub	J. G. McTaggart
	G-BWFB	D.H.104 Devon C.2	ASB Colton Aviation Ltd
	G-BWFD	HOAC Katana DV.20	Tayside Aviation Ltd/Dundee
	G-BWFE	HOAC Katana DV.20	Tayside Aviation Ltd/Dundee
	G-BWFG	Robin HR.200/120B	Air Caernarfon Ltd
	G-BWFH	Shaw Europa	R. W. Baylie & B. L. Wratten
	G-BWFI	HOAC Katana DV.20	Tayside Aviation Ltd/Dundee
	G-BWFJ	Evans VP-1	P. A. West
	G-BWFK	Lindstrand LBL-77A balloon	Virgin Airship & Balloon Co. Ltd
	G-BWFM	Yakovlev Yak-50	Classic Aviation Ltd/Duxford
	G-BWFN	Hapi Cygnet SF-2A	T. Crawford
	G-BWFO	Colomban MC.15 Cri-Cri	O. G. Jones
	G-BWFP	Yakovlev Yak-52	M. C. Lee
	G-BWFR	Hunter F.58 (J-4031)	The Old Flying Machine Co. Ltd/Duxford
	G-BWFS	Hunter F.58 (XL741)	The Old Flying Machine Co. Ltd/Duxford
	G-BWFT	Hunter T.8M	B. J. Pover & B. R. Pearson
	G-BWFU	Yakovlev C.11	M. Rusche
	G-BWFV	HOAC Katana DV.20	HOAC Austria Flugzeugwerk Weiner Neustadt GmbH
	G-BWFW	HOAC Katana DV.20	HOAC Austria Flugzeugwerk Weiner Neustadt GmbH
	G-BWFX	Shaw Europa	A. D. Stewart
	G-BWFY	AS.350B-1 Ecureuil	P. Pilkington & K. M. Armitage
	G-BWFZ	Murphy Rebel	I. E. Spencer (G-SAVS)
	G-BWGA	Lindstrand LBL-105A balloon	Virgin Airship & Balloon Co Ltd
	G-BWGF	P.84 Jet Provost T.5A	Specialscope Jet Provost Group
	G-BWGG	MH.1521C-1 Broussard	R. H. Reeves
	G-BWGH	Shaw Europa	J. H. Frizell
	G-BWGJ	Chilton DW.1A	T. J. Harrison
	G-BWGK	Hunter GA.11	B. J. Pover & B. J. Pearson/Exeter
	G-BWGL	Hunter T.8C	B. J. Pover & B. J. Pearson/Exeter
	G-BWGM	Hunter T.8C	B. J. Pover & B. J. Pearson/Exeter
	G-BWGN	Hunter T.8C	B. J. Pover & B. J. Pearson/Exeter
	G-BWGO	Slingsby T.67M-200	R. Gray
	G-BWGP	Cameron C-80 balloon	P. J. & C. M. Gentle
	G-BWGR	TB-25N Mitchell (151632)	Aces High Ltd/North Weald

Reg.	Type	Owner or Operator	Notes
G-BWGS	P.84 Jet Provost T.5A	J. S. Everett	
G-BWGT	P.84 Jet Provost T.4	R. E. Todd/Sandtoft	
G-BWGU	Cessna 150F	W. Davies	
G-BWGX	Cameron N-42 balloon	Newbury Building Soc.	
G-BWGY	HOAC Katana DV.20	HOAC Austria Flugzeugwerk Weiner Neustadt GmbH	
G-BWGZ	HOAC Katana DV.20	HOAC Austria Flugzeugwerk Weiner Neustadt GmbH	
G-BWHA	Hawker Hurricane IIB	Historic Flying Ltd/Audley End	
G-BWHB	Cameron O-65 balloon	G. Aimo	
G-BWHC	Cameron N-77 balloon	Travelsphere Ltd	
G-BWHD	Lindstrand LBL-31A balloon	Army Air Corps Balloon Club	
G-BWHF	PA-31-325 Navajo	Awyr Cymru Cyf/Welshpool	
G-BWHG	Cameron N-65 balloon	Coffee Nannini SRL	
G-BWHH	PA-18 Super Cub 135 (44)	J. W. Macleod	
G-BWHI	D.H.C.1 Chipmunk 22A	J. Romain/Duxford	
G-BWHJ	Starstreak Shadow SA-II	N. Irwin	
G-BWHK	Rans S.6-116 Coyote II	N. D. White	
G-BWHM	Sky 140-24 balloon	Sky Balloons Ltd	
G-BWHN	AS.332L Super Puma	Brintel Helicopters Ltd	
G-BWHP	C.A.S.A. 1.131E Jungmann	J. F. Hopkins	
G-BWHR	Tipsy T.66 Nipper Srs 1	L. R. Marnef	
G-BWHS	RAF 2000 gyroplane	V. G. Freke	
G-BWHT	Everett Campbell Cricket	B. B. Woodman	
G-BWHU	Westland Scout AH.1	N. J. F. Boston	
G-BWHV	Denney Kitfox Mk 2	A. C. Dove	
G-BWHW	Cameron A-180 balloon	Societe Bombard SARL	
G-BWHX	Mil Mi-8	Orbit Resources Ltd	
G-BWHY	Robinson R-22	Helicentre Ltd/Blackpool	
G-BWHZ	Mil Mi-8	Orbit Resources Ltd	
G-BWIA	Rans S.10 Sakota	P. A. Beck	
G-BWIB	SA Bulldog Srs 120/122	L. Bax	
G-BWID	D.31 Turbulent	A. M. Turney	
G-BWIE	Hunter T.7A	Lansen Ltd/Bruntingthorpe	
G-BWII	Cessna 150G	J. D. G. Hicks (G-BSKB)	
G-BWIJ	Shaw Europa	R. Lloyd	
G-BWIK	D.H.82A Tiger Moth	G. H. Fullbrook & B. J. Ellis	
G-BWIL	Rans S.10 Sakota	J. C. Longmore (G-WIEN)	
G-BWIM	Sikorsky S-76A (modified)	Bristow Helicopters Ltd	
G-BWIO	HOAC Katana DV.20	HOAC Flugzeugwerk Wiener Neustadt GmbH	
G-BWIP	Cameron N-90 balloon	Noble Adventures Ltd	
G-BWIR	Dornier Do.328-100	Suckling Airways (Luton) Ltd	
G-BWIS	Mooney M.20M	Flemming Frandsen Aircraft Sales Ltd	
G-BWIT	QAC Quickie 1	D. E. Johnson & ptnrs	
G-BWIU	Hunter F.58	Historic Flying Ltd/Duxford	
G-BWIV	Shaw Europa	J. R. Lockwood-Goose	
G-BWIW	Sky 180-24 balloon	G. D. & L. Fitzpatrick	
G-BWIX	Sky 120-24 balloon	J. M. Percival	
G-BWIY	Lindstrand LBL-105A balloon	Lindstrand Balloons Ltd	
G-BWIZ	QAC Quickie Tri-Q	B. J. Cain	
G-BWJA	Boeing 737-3Y0	Monarch Airlines Ltd (G-TEAA)/Luton	
G-BWJB	Thunder Ax8-105 balloon	Justerini & Brooks Ltd	
G-BWJC	Cameron N-65 balloon	Cameron Balloons Ltd	
G-BWJD	Cameron R-200 balloon	Bondbaste Ltd	
G-BWJE	Sky 105-24 balloon	Sky Balloons Ltd	
G-BWJG	Mooney M.20J	Samic Ltd	
G-BWJH	Shaw Europa	A. R. R. & J. A. S. T. Hood	
G-BWJI	Cameron V-90 balloon	Calarel Developments Ltd	
G-BWJJ	Cameron N-105 balloon	Cameron Balloons Ltd	
G-BWJK	Rotorway Executive 152	N. Kirk (G-OKIT)	
G-BWJL	Cameron N-120 balloon	Cameron Balloons Ltd	
G-BWJM	Bristol M1C (replica)	The Shuttleworth Collection/O. Warden	
G-BWJN	Montgomerie-Bensen B.8	M. G. Mee	
G-BWJO	BN-2T Turbine Islander	Pilatus BN Ltd/Bembridge	
G-BWJP	Cessna 172C	Midair Aviation Ltd/Bournemouth	
G-BWJR	Sky 120-24 balloon	B. Brogan	
G-BWJT	Yakovlev Yak-50	Badsaddle Stables Ltd	
G-BWJU	D.H.C.1 Chipmunk 22 (WK639)	Bolsover Consultancy Ltd	
G-BWJW	Westland Scout AH.1	Austen Associates Partnership	
G-BWJY	D.H.C.1 Chipmunk 22 (WG469)	K. J. Thompson	
G-BWJZ	D.H.C.1 Chipmunk 22 (WK638)	J. Zemlik	
G-BWKA	Hunter F.58	R.V. Aviation Ltd/Bournemouth	

Notes	Reg.	Type	Owner or Operator
	G-BWKB	Hunter F.58	R.V. Aviation Ltd/Bournemouth
	G-BWKC	Hunter F.58	R.V. Aviation Ltd/Bournemouth
	G-BWKD	Cameron O-120 balloon	K.E. Viney
	G-BWKE	Cameron AS-105GD airship	Gefe-Flug GmbH/Germany
	G-BWKF	Cameron N-105 balloon	R. M. M. Botti/Italy
	G-BWKG	Shaw Europa	T. C. Jackson
	G-BWKJ	Rans S.7 Courier	J. P. Kovacs
	G-BWKK	Auster A.O.P.9 (XP279)	R. W. Fairless & D. R. White
	G-BWKL	H.S.125 Srs 700B	Kemekod Exports Ltd (G-BIHZ)
	G-BWKP	Sky 105-24 balloon	Sky Balloons Ltd
	G-BWKR	Sky 90-24 balloon	B. Drawbridge
	G-BWKT	Stephens Akro Laser	P. D. Begley
	G-BWKU	Cameron A-250 balloon	British School of Ballooning
	G-BWKV	Cameron V-77 balloon	Poppies (UK) Ltd
	G-BWKW	Thunder Ax8-90 balloon	Venice Simplon Orient Express Ltd
	G-BWKX	Cameron A-250 balloon	Hot Airlines
	G-BWKZ	Lindstrand LBL-77A balloon	Lambert Smith Hampton Group Ltd
	G-BWLA	Lindstrand LBL-69A balloon	Virgin Airship & Balloon Co Ltd
	G-BWLB	Lindstrand Dreher Bottle SS balloon	International Balloons Ltd
	G-BWLD	Cameron O-120 balloon	D. Pedri & ptnrs
	G-BWLE	Bell 212	Bristow Helicopters Ltd/Redhill
	G-BWLF	Cessna 404	Nor Leasing (G-BNXS)
	G-BWLH	Lindstrand LBL HS-110 airship	International Balloons Ltd
	G-BWLJ	Taylorcraft DCO-65	C. Evans
	G-BWLK	Lindstrand LBL-69A balloon	International Balloons Ltd
	G-BWLL	Murphy Rebel	F. W. Parker
	G-BWLM	Sky 65-24 balloon	Dachstein Tauern Balloons KG
	G-BWLN	Cameron O-84 balloon	Reggiana Riduttori SRL
	G-BWLO	Bell 206A JetRanger	RCR Aviation Ltd
	G-BWLP	HOAC Katana DV.20	HOAC Austria Weiner Neustadt GmbH
	G-BWLR	MH.1521M Broussard	Chicory Crops Ltd
	G-BWLS	HOAC Katana DV.20	HOAC Austria Weiner Neustadt GmbH
	G-BWLT	HOAC Katana DV.20	HOAC Austria Weiner Neustadt GmbH
	G-BWLV	HOAC Katana DV.20	HOAC Austria Weiner Neustadt GmbH
	G-BWLW	Light Aero Avid Speedwing Mk4	P. C. & S. A. Creswick
	G-BWLX	Westland Scout AH.1	R. E. Dagless
	G-BWLY	Rotorway Executive 90	P. W. & I. P. Bewley
	G-BWLZ	Wombat gyroplane	J. M. Shippen
	G-BWMA	Colt 105A balloon	C. C. Duppa-Miller
	G-BWMB	Jodel D.119	C. Hughes
	G-BWMC	Cessna 182P	Astra Associates
	G-BWMD	Enstrom 480	Southern Air Ltd/Shoreham
	G-BWME	Lindstrand LBL-150A balloon	International Balloons Ltd
	G-BWMF	Gloster Meteor T.7 (WA591)	Meteor Flight (Yatesbury)
	G-BWMG	AS.332L Super Puma	Bristow Helicopters Ltd
	G-BWMH	Lindstrand LBL-77B balloon	Lindstrand Balloons Ltd
	G-BWMI	PA-28RT-201T Turbo Arrow IV	C. H. R. Hewitt & D. H. Saunders
	G-BWMJ	Nieuport 17/2B (replica)	R. Gauld-Galliers & L. J. Day
	G-BWMK	D.H.82A Tiger Moth	Schneider Trophy Ltd
	G-BWML	Cameron A-275 balloon	A. J. Street
	G-BWMM	Lindstrand LBL-31A balloon	International Balloons Ltd
	G-BWMN	Rans S.7 Courier	T. M. Turnbull
	G-BWMO	Oldfield Baby Lakes	P. J. Tanulak (G-CIII)
	G-BWMS	D.H.82A Tiger Moth	Foundation Early Birds/Netherlands
	G-BWMU	Cameron 105 Monster Truck SS balloon	Cameron Balloons Ltd
	G-BWMV	Colt AS-105 Mk II airship	Aereo Grupo Arashi SL/Spain
	G-BWMX	D.H.C.1 Chipmunk 22	W. H. Sanaghan
	G-BWMY	Cameron 90 Bradford & Bingley SS balloon	Flying Pictures (Balloons) Ltd
	G-BWNB	Cessna 152	Galair International Ltd
	G-BWNC	Cessna 152	Galair International Ltd
	G-BWND	Cessna 152	Galair International Ltd
	G-BWNE	BN-2B-20 Islander	Pilatus BN Ltd/Bembridge
	G-BWNF	BN-2B-20 Islander	Pilatus BN Ltd/Bembridge
	G-BWNG	BN-2B-20 Islander	Pilatus BN Ltd/Bembridge
	G-BWNH	Cameron A-375 balloon	Noble Adventures Ltd
	G-BWNI	PA-24 Comanche 180	B. Walker & Co (Dursley) Ltd
	G-BWNJ	Hughes 269C	L. R. Fenwick
	G-BWNK	D,H,C,1 Chipmunk 22	B. A. Groves
	G-BWNL	Shaw Europa	H. Smith
	G-BWNM	PA-28R Cherokee Arrow 180	CRD Tool & Engineering Ltd

Reg.	Type	Owner or Operator
G-BWNN	Rand Robinson KR-2	C. Clark
G-BWNO	Cameron O-90 balloon	Action Research
G-BWNP	Cameron 90 Club SS balloon	T. G. Read & S. F. Arnold
G-BWNR	PA-38-112 Tomahawk	APB Leasing Ltd/Welshpool
G-BWNS	Cameron O-90 balloon	Inland Revenue Corporate Communications
G-BWNT	D.H.C.1 Chipmunk 22	Three Point Aviation
G-BWNU	PA-38-112 Tomahawk	G-BWNU Group
G-BWNV	PA-38-112 Tomahawk	CEA Aircraft Leasing
G-BWNW	Lindstrand LBL-25A balloon	International Balloons Ltd
G-BWNX	Thunder Ax10-180 S2 balloon (G-OWBC)	Gone With The Wind Ltd
G-BWNY	Aeromot AMT-200 Super Ximango	H. G. Nicklin
G-BWNZ	Agusta A.109C	Lynton Helicopter Charters Ltd
G-BWOA	Sky 105-24 balloon	Akhter Group Holdings PLC
G-BWOB	Luscombe 8F Silvaire	P. J. Tanulak & H. T. Law
G-BWOD	Yakovlev Yak-52	Inshurefast Ltd
G-BWOE	Yakovlev Yak-3U	R. G. Hanna/Duxford
G-BWOF	P.84 Jet Provost T.5	Transair (UK) Ltd/North Weald
G-BWOH	PA-28-161 Cadet	C.S.E. Aviation Ltd/Kidlington
G-BWOI	PA-28-161 Cadet	C.S.E. Aviation Ltd/Kidlington
G-BWOJ	PA-28-161 Cadet	C.S.E. Aviation Ltd/Kidlington
G-BWOK	Lindstrand LBL GB-1000 balloon	Lindstrand Balloons Ltd
G-BWOL	Hawker Sea Fury FB.11	Old Flying Machine Co Ltd/Duxford
G-BWOM	Cessna 550 Citation II	Ferron Trading Ltd
G-BWON	Shaw Europa	G. T. Birks
G-BWOO	Lindstrand LBL HS-110 balloon	International Balloons Ltd
G-BWOR	PA-18 Super Cub 135	S. F. Bancroft
G-BWOS	Bell 212	Heliwork Services Ltd/Thruxton
G-BWOT	P.84 Jet Provost T.3A	Transair (UK) Ltd/North Weald
G-BWOU	Hunter F.58A	Old Flying Machine Co. Ltd/Duxford
G-BWOV	Enstrom F-28A	Earthline Aviation Ltd
G-BWOW	Cameron N-105 balloon	S. J. Colin & A. S. Pinder
G-BWOX	D.H.C.1 Chipmunk 22	J. St. Clair-Quentin
G-BWOY	Sky 31-24 balloon	Virgin Airship & Balloon Co. Ltd
G-BWOZ	CFM Streak Shadow SA	H. Witt/Switzerland
G-BWPA	Cameron A-340 balloon	A. A. Brown
G-BWPB	Cameron V-77 balloon	Fair Weather Friends Ballooning Co
G-BWPC	Cameron V-77 balloon	H. Vaughan
G-BWPD	Cameron V-90 balloon	Flying Pictures (Balloons) Ltd
G-BWPE	Murphy Renegade Spirit UK	G. Wilson
G-BWPF	Sky 120-24 balloon	Humbug Balloon Group
G-BWPG	Robin HR.200/120	Air Alba Ltd
G-BWPH	PA-28-181 Archer II	J. Maffia
G-BWPI	Sky 120-24 balloon	Sky Balloons Ltd
G-BWPJ	Steen Skybolt	W. R. Penaluna
G-BWPK	BN-2T-4R MSSA	Pilatus BN Ltd/Bembridge
G-BWPL	Airtour AH-56 balloon	A. S. Newham
G-BWPM	BN-2T-4R MSSA	Pilatus BN Ltd/Bembridge
G-BWPN	BN-2T-4S Defender 4000	Pilatus BN Ltd/Bembridge
G-BWPO	BN-2T-4S Defender 4000	Pilatus BN Ltd/Bembridge
G-BWPP	Sky 105-24 balloon	The Sarnia Balloon Group
G-BWPR	BN-2T-4S Defender 4000	Pilatus BN Ltd/Bembridge
G-BWPS	CFM Streak Shadow SA	P. G. A. Sumner
G-BWPT	Cameron N-90 balloon	Workplace Technologies Ltd
G-BWPU	BN-2T-4S Defender 4000	Pilatus BN Ltd/Bembridge
G-BWPV	BN-2T-4S Defender 4000	Pilatus BN Ltd/Bembridge
G-BWPW	BN-2T-4S Defender 4000	Pilatus BN Ltd/Bembridge
G-BWPX	BN-2T-4S Defender 4000	Pilatus BN Ltd/Bembridge
G-BWPY	Diamond Katana DV.20	Tayside Aviation Ltd/Dundee
G-BWPZ	BN-2T-4S Defender 4000	Pilatus BN Ltd/Bembridge
G-BWRA	Sopwith Triplane (replica)	Triplane Trio (G-PENY)
G-BWRC	Light Aero Avid Speedwing	B. Williams
G-BWRD	Klemm Kl.35D	The Island Aeroplane Co/Sandown
G-BWRE	SNCAN Stampe SV4C	The Island Aeroplane Co/Sandown
G-BWRF	M.S.505 Criquet	The Island Aeroplane Co/Sandown
G-BWRG	Mraz M.1D Sokol	The Island Aeroplane Co/Sandown
G-BWRH	Bleriot XI (replica)	The Island Aeroplane Co/Sandown
G-BWRI	Mignet HM.19C Pou-du-Ciel	The Island Aeroplane Co/Sandown
G-BWRJ	Fokker Dr.1 (replica)	The Island Aeroplane Co/Sandown
G-BWRK	Lindstrand LBL Man SS balloon	International Balloons Ltd
G-BWRL	Sky 77-24 balloon	Sky Balloons Ltd
G-BWRM	Colt 105A balloon	N. Charbonnier/Italy
G-BWRO	Shaw Europa	E. C, Clark

Notes	Reg.	Type	Owner or Operator
	G-BWRP	Beech 58 Baron	Astra Aviation Ltd
	G-BWRR	Cessna 182Q	W. Rennie-Roberts
	G-BWRS	SNCAN Stampe SV-4C	G. P. J. M. Valvekens/Belgium
	G-BWRT	Cameron Concept 60 balloon	W. R. Teasdale
	G-BWRU	Lindstrand LBL Saloon Car SS balloon	Flying Pictures (Balloons) Ltd
	G-BWRV	Lindstrand LBL-90A balloon	Flying Pictures (Balloons) Ltd
	G-BWRW	Sky 220-24 balloon	Sky Trek Ballooning Ltd
	G-BWRY	Cameron N-105 balloon	G. Aimo/Italy
	G-BWRZ	Lindstrand LBL-105A balloon	Flying Pictures (Balloons) Ltd
	G-BWSB	Lindstrand LBL-105A balloon	Flying Pictures (Balloons) Ltd
	G-BWSC	PA-38-112 Tomahawk II	APB Leasing Ltd/Welshpool
	G-BWSD	Campbell Cricket	R. F. G. Moyle
	G-BWSF	Sky 180-24 balloon	A. Bolger
	G-BWSG	P.84 Jet Provost T.5 (XW324)	Adavia Ltd
	G-BWSH	P.84 Jet Provost T.3A	Global Aviation Ltd/Binbrook
	G-BWSI	K & S SA.102.5 Cavalier	B. W. Shaw
	G-BWSJ	Denney Kitfox Mk 3	J. M. Miller
	G-BWSK	Enstrom 280FX	Southern Air Ltd/Shoreham
	G-BWSL	Sky 77-24 balloon	The Balloon Co Ltd
	G-BWSM	Cameron 95 Maple Leaf SS balloon	Cameron Balloons Ltd
	G-BWSN	Denney Kitfox Mk 3	W. J. Forrest
	G-BWSO	Cameron 90 Apple SS balloon	Flying Pictures (Balloons) Ltd
	G-BWSP	Cameron 80 Carrots SS balloon	Flying Pictures (Balloons) Ltd
	G-BWSR	Cameron A-210 balloon	Gone With The Wind Ltd
	G-BWSS	Sky 200-24 balloon	Suneven Ltd
	G-BWST	Sky 200-24 balloon	S. A. Townley
	G-BWSU	Cameron N-105 balloon	A. M. Marten
	G-BWSV	Yakovlev Yak-52	Aeroanglia
	G-BWSW	Yakovlev Yak-52	Aeroanglia
	G-BWSX	PA-28-236 Dakota	C. & C. Bowie
	G-BWSY	BAe 125 Srs 800B	British Aerospace Airbus Ltd (G-OCCI)/Filton
	G-BWSZ	Montgomerie-Bensen B.8MR	D. Cawkwell
	G-BWTA	Diamond Katana DV.20	Tayside Aviation Ltd/Dundee
	G-BWTB	Lindstrand LBL-105A balloon	Servatruc Ltd
	G-BWTC	Zlin Z.242L	C.S.E. Aviation Ltd/Kidlington
	G-BWTD	Zlin Z.242L	C.S.E. Aviation Ltd/Kidlington
	G-BWTE	Cameron O-140 balloon	R. J. & A. J. Mansfield
	G-BWTF	Lindstrand LBL Bear SS balloon	International Balloons Ltd
	G-BWTG	D.H.C.1 Chipmunk 22	W, M, Van Doorne/Netherlands
	G-BWTH	Robinson R-22B	Sloane Helicopters Ltd/Sywell
	G-BWTJ	Cameron V-77 balloon	A. J. Montgomery
	G-BWTK	RAF 2000 GTX-SE gyroplane	Terrafirma Services Ltd
	G-BWTL	Aerospatiale ATR-72-202	CityFlyer Express Ltd/BA Express
	G-BWTM	Aerospatiale ATR-72-202	CityFlyer Express Ltd/BA Express
	G-BWTN	Lindstrand LBL-90A balloon	Clarks Drainage Ltd
	G-BWTO	D.H.C.1 Chipmunk 22	Skycraft Services Ltd
	G-BWTP	Montgomerie-Parsons 2-seat gyroplane	J. M. Montgomerie
	G-BWTR	Slingsby T.61F Venture T.2	P. R. Williams
	G-BWTS	Aero L-39ZO Albatros	Aces High Ltd/North Weald
	G-BWTT	Aero L-39ZO Albatros	Aces High Ltd/North Weald
	G-BWTU	Lindstrand LBL-77A balloon	Virgin Airship & Balloon Co Ltd
	G-BWTW	Mooney M.20C	R. W. Boote
	G-BWTY	Air Command 532 Elite	A. J. Unwin
	G-BWUA	Campbell Cricket	R. T. Lancaster
	G-BWUB	PA-18 Super Cub 135	Caledonian Seaplanes Ltd
	G-BWUC	PA-18 Super Cub 135	Caledonian Seaplanes Ltd
	G-BWUD	Lavochkin LA-9	Classic Aviation Ltd/Duxford
	G-BWUE	Hispano HA.1112MIL	Classic Aviation Ltd/Duxford
	G-BWUF	WSK Lim-5	Classic Aviation Ltd/Duxford
	G-BWUG	Piper J-5C Cub Cruiser	W. D. Lincoln
	G-BWUH	PA-28-181 Archer III	Technical Flight Services Ltd
	G-BWUI	BAe Jetstream 4102	Jetstream Aircraft Ltd/Prestwick
	G-BWUJ	Rotorway Executive 162F	Southern Helicopters Ltd
	G-BWUK	Sky 160-24 balloon	G. M. Houston
	G-BWUL	Noorduyn AT-16 Harvard IIB	Nucleo Aereo Aerobatico Parmense SRL/Italy
	G-BWUM	Sky 105-24 balloon	P. Stern & F. Kirchberger
	G-BWUN	D.H.C.1 Chipmunk 22	T. Henderson
	G-BWUO	PA-18 Super Cub 95	L. H. Marsh

Reg.	Type	Owner or Operator	Notes
G-BWUP	Shaw Europa	T. J. Harrison	
G-BWUR	Thunder Ax10-210 S2 balloon	T. J. Bucknall	
G-BWUS	Sky 65-24 balloon	Sky Balloons Ltd	
G-BWUT	D.H.C.1 Chipmunk 22	Aero Vintage Ltd	
G-BWUU	Cameron N-90 balloon	South Western Electricity Ltd	
G-BWUV	D.H.C.1 Chipmunk 22A	P. Ray	
G-BWUW	P.84 Jet Provost T.5A	R. E. Dagless	
G-BWUX	Lindstrand LBL-210A balloon	International Balloons Ltd	
G-BWUY	Thunder Ax10-180 balloon	D. C. Chipping	
G-BWUZ	Campbell Cricket	M. A. Concannon	
G-BWVB	Pietenpol Air Camper	M. J. Whatley	
G-BWVC	Jodel D.18	R. W. J. Cripps	
G-BWVD	Cameron R-210 gas balloon	Cameron Balloons Ltd	
G-BWVE	Bell 206B JetRanger 3	Willow Vale Electronics Ltd (G-BOSX)	
G-BWVF	Pietenpol Air Camper	R. M. Sharphouse	
G-BWVG	Robin HR.200/120	Mistral Aviation Ltd	
G-BWVH	Robinson R-44 Astro	Sefton Ltd	
G-BWVI	Stern ST.80	P. E. Barker	
G-BWVJ	Cameron R-450 gas balloon	Noble Adventures Ltd	
G-BWVK	Cameron 110 Calling Card SS balloon	Cameron Balloons Ltd	
G-BWVL	Cessna 150M	CEA Aircraft Leasing	
G-BWVM	Cameron AA-1050 balloon	D. A. Gleed	
G-BWVN	Whittaker MW.7	J. W. May	
G-BWVO	PA-32 Cherokee Six 300	Taylor Aircraft Services Ltd	
G-BWVP	Sky 160-24 balloon	Sky Balloons Ltd	
G-BWVR	Yakovlev Yak-52	J. H. Askew	
G-BWVS	Shaw Europa	D. R. Bishop	
G-BWVT	D.H.A.82A Tiger Moth	R. Jewitt	
G-BWVU	Cameron O-90 balloon	J. Atkinson	
G-BWVV	Jodel D.18	P. Cooper	
G-BWVW			
G-BWVX	Yakovlev Yak-52	C. J. M. Van Den Broek & R. V. De Vries	
G-BWVY	D.H.C.1 Chipmunk 22A	P. W. Portelli	
G-BWVZ	D.H.C.1 Chipmunk 22A	D. Campion/Belgium	
G-BWWA	Pelican Club GS	E. F. Clapham & N. R. Beale	
G-BWWB	Shaw Europa	M. G. Dolphin	
G-BWWC	D.H.104 Dove 7	Cormack (Aircraft Services) Ltd	
G-BWWE	Lindstrand LBL-90A balloon	B. J. Newman	
G-BWWF	Cessna 185	A. O. Hill	
G-BWWG	SOCATA Rallye 235E	C. G. Wheeler	
G-BWWH	Yakovlev Yak-50	De Cadenet Motor Racing Ltd	
G-BWWI	AS.332L Super Puma	Bristow Helicopters Ltd	
G-BWWJ	Hughes 269C	Dave Nieman Models Ltd (G-BMYZ)	
G-BWWK	Hawker Nimrod I	Historic Aircraft Collection Ltd	
G-BWWL	Colt Flying Egg SS balloon	L. V. Mastis	
G-BWWM	Diamond Katana DA.20-A1	Diamond Aircraft Industries GmbH	
G-BWWN	Isaacs Fury II	D. H. Pattison	
G-BWWP	Rans S.6-116 Coyote II	S. A. Beddus	
G-BWWR	Robinson R-44 Astro	Sloane Helicopters Ltd/Sywell	
G-BWWS	RAF 2000 GTX-SE gyroplane	G. R. Williams	
G-BWWT	Dornier Do.328-100	Suckling Airways (Norwich) Ltd	
G-BWWU	PA-22 Tri-Pacer 150	Aerocars Ltd	
G-BWWV	Bell 206B JetRanger 3	R & M International Engineering Ltd	
G-BWWW	BAe Jetstream 3102	British Aerospace PLC/Warton	
G-BWWX	Yakovlev Yak-50	J. L. Pfundt/Netherlands	
G-BWWY	Lindstrand LBL-105A balloon	M. J. Smith	
G-BWWZ	Denney Kitfox Mk 3	K. M. Allan	
G-BWXA	Slingsby T.67M-260	Hunting Aviation Ltd/Barkston Heath	
G-BWXB	Slingsby T.67M-260	Hunting Aviation Ltd/Barkston Heath	
G-BWXC	Slingsby T.67M-260	Hunting Aviation Ltd/Barkston Heath	
G-BWXD	Slingsby T.67M-260	Hunting Aviation Ltd/Barkston Heath	
G-BWXE	Slingsby T.67M-260	Hunting Aviation Ltd/Barkston Heath	
G-BWXF	Slingsby T.67M-260	Hunting Aviation Ltd/Barkston Heath	
G-BWXG	Slingsby T.67M-260	Hunting Aviation Ltd/Barkston Heath	
G-BWXH	Slingsby T.67M-260	Hunting Aviation Ltd/Barkston Heath	
G-BWXI	Slingsby T.67M-260	Hunting Aviation Ltd/Barkston Heath	
G-BWXJ	Slingsby T.67M-260	Hunting Aviation Ltd/Barkston Heath	
G-BWXK	Slingsby T.67M-260	Hunting Aviation Ltd/Barkston Heath	
G-BWXL	Slingsby T.67M-200	Hunting Aviation Ltd/Barkston Heath	
G-BWXM	Slingsby T.67M-260	Hunting Aviation Ltd/Barkston Heath	
G-BWXN	Slingsby T.67M-260	Hunting Aviation Ltd/Barkston Heath	
G-BWXO	Slingsby T.67M-260	Hunting Aviation Ltd/Barkston Heath	

Notes	Reg.	Type	Owner or Operator
	G-BWXP	Slingsby T.67M-260	Hunting Aviation Ltd/Barkston Heath
	G-BWXR	Slingsby T.67M-260	Hunting Aviation Ltd/Barkston Heath
	G-BWXS	Slingsby T.67M-260	Hunting Aviation Ltd/Barkston Heath
	G-BWXT	Slingsby T.67M-260	Hunting Aviation Ltd/Barkston Heath
	G-BWXU	Slingsby T.67M-260	Hunting Aviation Ltd/Barkston Heath
	G-BWXV	Slingsby T.67M-260	Hunting Aviation Ltd/Barkston Heath
	G-BWXW	Slingsby T.67M-260	Hunting Aviation Ltd/Barkston Heath
	G-BWXX	Slingsby T.67M-260	Hunting Aviation Ltd/Barkston Heath
	G-BWXY	Slingsby T.67M-260	Hunting Aviation Ltd/Barkston Heath
	G-BWXZ	Slingsby T.67M-260	Hunting Aviation Ltd/Barkston Heath
	G-BWYB	PA-28 Cherokee 160	R. Dispain
	G-BWYC	Cameron N-90 balloon	Cameron Balloons Ltd
	G-BWYD	Shaw Europa	H. J. Bendiksen
	G-BWYE	Cessna 310R II	Edinburgh Air Centre Ltd
	G-BWYF	Sky 90-24 balloon	Sky Balloons Ltd
	G-BWYG	Cessna 310R II	Edinburgh Air Centre Ltd
	G-BWYH	Cessna 310R II	Edinburgh Air Centre Ltd
	G-BWYI	Denney Kitfox Mk3	J. Adamson
	G-BWYJ	Bell 206L-1 LongRanger	R&M International Engineering Ltd
	G-BWYK	Yakovlev Yak-50	M. G. & J. R. Jefferies
	G-BWYL	Cameron A-200 balloon	Aire Valley Balloons
	G-BWYM	Diamond Katana DV.20	Diamond Aircraft Industries GmbH
	G-BWYN	Cameron O-77 balloon	W. H. Morgan (G-ODER)
	G-BWYO	Sequoia F.8L Falco	S. Harper
	G-BWYP	Sky 56-24 balloon	Sky High Leisure
	G-BWYR	Rans S.6-116 Coyote II	Stephen Palmer Ltd
	G-BWYS	Cameron O-120 balloon	Aire Valley Balloons
	G-BWYT	BAe ATP	Jetstream Aircraft Ltd/Prestwick
	G-BWYU	Sky 120-24 balloon	Bramley Park Garages
	G-BWYV	Lindstrand LBL-210A balloon	A. Derbyshire
	G-BWYW	BN-2B-20 Islander	Pilatus BN Ltd/Bembridge
	G-BWYX	BN-2B-20 Islander	Pilatus BN Ltd/Bembridge
	G-BWYY	BN-2B-20 Islander	Pilatus BN Ltd/Bembridge
	G-BWYZ	BN-2B-20 Islander	Pilatus BN Ltd/Bembridge
	G-BWZA	Shaw Europa	M. C. Costin
	G-BWZB	AB-206B JetRanger 3	RCR Engineering Ltd
	G-BWZC	AS.355F-1 Twin Squirrel	Castle Aviation (G-MOBZ)
	G-BWZD	Light Aero Avid Flyer Mk 4	B. Moore
	G-BWZE	P.84 Jet Provost T.3A	Global Aviation Ltd
	G-BWZF	BN-2B-20 Islander	Pilatus BN Ltd/Bembridge
	G-BWZG	Robin R.2160	Mistral Aviation Ltd
	G-BWZI	Agusta A. 109A II	Castle Air Charters Ltd
	G-BWZJ	Cameron A-250 balloon	Balloon Club of Great Britain
	G-BWZK	Cameron A-210 balloon	Balloon Club of Great Britain
	G-BWZL	Fokker 50	Airfinance Europe (767) Ltd
	G-BWZM	Fokker 50	Airfinance Europe (767) Ltd
	G-BWZN	Beech F33A Bonanza	M. R. Masters
	G-BWZO	Cameron 110 Spaceship SS balloon	Flying Pictures (Balloons) Ltd
	G-BWZP	Cameron 105 Home Special SS balloon	Flying Pictures (Balloons) Ltd
	G-BWZR	Bell 412EP	FBS Ltd
	G-BWZS	AS.350BB Ecureuil	FBS Ltd
	G-BWZT	Shaw Europa	GBWZT Group
	G-BWZU	Lindstrand LBL-90B balloon	K. D. Peirce
	G-BWZV	Robinson R-22B	Sloane Helicopters Ltd (G-LIAN)/Sywell
	G-BWZW	Bell 206B JetRanger 2	Yorkshire Helicopter Centre Ltd (G-CTEK)
	G-BWZX	AS.332L Super Puma	Bristow Helicopters Ltd
	G-BWZY	Hughes 269A	K. B. Elliott (G-FSDT)
	G-BWZZ	P.84 Jet Provost T.3A	Jet Aviation (Northwest) Ltd
	G-BXAA	—	—
	G-BXAB	PA-28-161 Warrior II	Tindon Ltd (G-BTGK)/Little Snoring
	G-BXAC	RAF 2000 GTX-SE gyroplane	D. C. Fairbrass
	G-BXAD	Thunder Ax11-225 S2 balloon	C. E. Wood
	G-BXAE	Sikorsky S-61N	Bond Helicopters Ltd
	G-BXAF	Pitts S-1D Special	F. Sharples
	G-BXAG	AS.350BB Ecureuil	Eurocopter France
	G-BXAH	CP.301A Emeraude	E. J. Horsfall/Blackpool
	G-BXAI	Colt 120A balloon	Cameron Balloons Ltd
	G-BXAJ	Lindstrand LBL-14A balloon	Oscair Project AB/Sweden
	G-BXAK	Yakovlev Yak-52	S. L. Flannigan

Reg.	Type	Owner or Operator	Notes
G-BXAL	Cameron 90 Bertie Bassett SS balloon	Trebor Bassett Ltd	
G-BXAM	Cameron N-90 balloon	Trebor Bassett Ltd	
G-BXAN	Scheibe SF-25C	Falke Syndicate	
G-BXAO	Jabiru SK	I. M. Donnelly	
G-BXAP	Cameron 90 Hard Hat SS balloon	Norwest Holst Ltd & C. S. Perceval	
G-BXAR	Avro RJ100	CityFlyer Express Ltd/BA Express	
G-BXAS	Avro RJ100	CityFlyer Express Ltd/BA Express	
G-BXAT	—	—	
G-BXAU	Pitts S-1 Special	D. Dobson	
G-BXAV	Yakovlev Yak-52	G. M. Sharp	
G-BXAW	—	—	
G-BXAX	Cameron N-77 balloon	Flying Pictures Balloons Ltd	
G-BXAY	Bell 206B JetRanger	R. & M. International Ltd	
G-BXBA	Cameron A-210 balloon	Reach For The Sky Ltd	
G-BXBB	PA-20 Pacer 150	M. E. R. Coghlan	
G-BXBC	EA.1 Kingfisher amphibian	S. Bichan	
G-BXBD	C.A.S.A 1-131E Jungmann	B. L. Robinson	
G-BXBE	Bell 412EP	FBS Ltd	
G-BXBF	Bell 412EP	FBS Ltd	
G-BXBG	Cameron A-275 balloon	M. L. Gabb	
G-BXBH	P.84 Jet Provost T.3A	Global Aviation Ltd	
G-BXBI	P.84 Jet Provost T.3A	Global Aviation Ltd	
G-BXBJ	P.84 Jet Provost T.3A	Global Aviation Ltd	
G-BXBK	Avions Mudry CAP-10E	R. W. H. Cole	
G-BXBL	Lindstrand LBL-240A balloon	Firefly Balloon Promotions	
G-BXBM	Cameron O-105 balloon	Bristol University Hot Air Ballooning	
G-BXBN	Rans S.6-116 Coyote II	W. S. Long	
G-BXBO	—	—	
G-BXBP	—	—	
G-BXBR	—	—	
G-BXBS	—	—	
G-BXBT	—	—	
G-BXBU	—	—	
G-BXBV	—	—	
G-BXBW	—	—	
G-BXBY	—	—	
G-BXBZ	—	—	
G-BXCA	Hapi Cygnet SF-2A	G. E. Collard	
G-BXCX	Robinson R-22B	Plane Talking Ltd (G-MFHL)/Elstree	
G-BXCY	AA-5A Cheetah	Plane Talking Ltd	
G-BXCZ	AA-5A Cheetah	Plane Talking Ltd	
G-BXDB	Cessna 206F	Tindon Ltd (G-BMNZ)/Little Snoring	
G-BXDD	RAF 2000 GTX-SE gyroplane	Roger Savage (Photography)	
G-BXDE	RAF 2000 GTX-SE gyroplane	A. McRedie	
G-BXEG	Aerospatiale ATR-42-300	CityFlyer Express Ltd/BA Express	
G-BXEH	Aerospatiale ATR-42-300	CityFlyer Express Ltd/BA Express	
G-BXPS	PA-23 Aztec 250C	W. A. Moore (G-AYLY)	
G-BXUK	Robinson R-44 Astro	Heli Air Ltd	
G-BXWT	Vans RV-6	R. C. Owen	

Out-of-Sequence Registrations

Notes	Reg.	Type	Owner or Operator
	G-BYAA	Boeing 767-204ER	Britannia Airways Ltd *Sir Matt Busby CBE*
	G-BYAB	Boeing 767-204ER	Britannia Airways Ltd *Brian Johnston CBE MC*
	G-BYAC	Boeing 757-204	Britannia Airways Ltd
	G-BYAD	Boeing 757-204	Britannia Airways Ltd
	G-BYAE	Boeing 757-204	Britannia Airways Ltd
	G-BYAF	Boeing 757-204	Britannia Airways Ltd
	G-BYAG	Boeing 757-204	Britannia Airways Ltd
	G-BYAH	Boeing 757-204	Britannia Airways Ltd
	G-BYAI	Boeing 757-204	Britannia Airways Ltd
	G-BYAJ	Boeing 757-204	Britannia Airways Ltd
	G-BYAK	Boeing 757-28A	Britannia Airways Ltd
	G-BYAL	Boeing 757-28A	Britannia Airways Ltd
	G-BYAM	Boeing 757-2T7	Britannia Airways Ltd (G-DRJC)
	G-BYAN	Boeing 757-204	Britannia Airways Ltd
	G-BYAO	Boeing 757-204	Britannia Airways Ltd
	G-BYAP	Boeing 757-204	Britannia Airways Ltd
	G-BYAR	Boeing 757-204	Britannia Airways Ltd
	G-BYAS	Boeing 757-204	Britannia Airways Ltd
	G-BYAT	Boeing 757-204	Britannia Airways Ltd
	G-BYAU	Boeing 757-204	Britannia Airways Ltd
	G-BYAW	Boeing 757-204	Britannia Airways Ltd *Eric Morecombe OBE*
	G-BYEE	Mooney M.20K	H. W. Robertson
	G-BYIJ	C.A.S.A. 1.131E Jungmann 2000	K. B. Palmer
	G-BYLL	F.8L Falco	N. J. Langrick/Breighton
	G-BYLS	Bede BD-4	G. H. Bayliss/Shobdon
	G-BYNG	Cessna T.303	J. M. E. Byng (G-PTWB)
	G-BYRE	Rans S.10 Sakota	R. J. & M. B. Trickey
	G-BYSE	AB-206B JetRanger 2	Bewise Ltd (G-BFND)
	G-BYSL	Cameron O-56 balloon	S. S. M. Askey
	G-BYTE	Robinson R-22B	Capital Helicopters Ltd
	G-BZBH	Thunder Ax6-65 balloon	R. B. & G. Clarke
	G-BZKK	Cameron V-56 balloon	P. J. Green & C. Bosley *Gemini II*
	G-CAFZ	PA-31-350 Navajo Chieftain	London Flight Centre (Stansted) Ltd (G-BPPT)
	G-CALL	PA-23 Aztec 250F	Woodgate Aviation (IOM) Ltd
	G-CALV	PA-39 Twin Comanche 160 C/R	M. & V. Rahmani (G-AZFO)
	G-CAMB	AS.355F-2 Twin Squirrel	Cambridgeshire & Essex Air Support
	G-CAMM	Hawker Cygnet (replica)	D. M. Cashmore
	G-CARS	Pitts S-2A Special (replica) (BAPC134) ★	Toyota Ltd
	G-CAXF	Cameron O-77 balloon	R. D. & S. J. Sarjeant
	G-CBAC	Short SD3-60 Variant 200	BAC Leasing Ltd (G-BLYH)
	G-CBAL	PA-28-161 Warrior 3	Britannia Airways Ltd
	G-CBEA	BAe Jetstream 3102-01	European Airways Ltd
	G-CBIL	Cessna 182K	G. H. Parsons
	G-CBJB	Sikorsky S-76A	Bond Helicopters Ltd
	G-CBKT	Cameron O-77 balloon	Caledonian Airways Ltd
	G-CBOR	Cessna F.172N	P. Seville
	G-CBRA	AS.365N-2 Dauphin 2	Lattice Ltd
	G-CCAO	AS.355F-1 Twin Squirrel	McAlpine Helicopters Ltd (G-SETA/G-NEAS/G-CMMM/G-BNBJ)/Kidlington
	G-CCAR	Cameron N-77 balloon	The Colt Car Co Ltd
	G-CCAT	AA-5A Cheetah	Plane Talking Ltd (G-OAJH/G-KILT/G-BJFA)/Elstree
	G-CCCC	Cessna 172H	K. E. Wilson
	G-CCCP	Yakovlev Yak-52	R. J. N. Howarth
	G-CCDI	Cameron N-77 balloon	Charles Church Developments PLC
	G-CCLY	Bell 206B JetRanger 3	Ciceley Ltd (G-TILT/G-BRJO)
	G-CCOA	SA Bulldog Srs 120/122	Cranfield University (G-BCUU)
	G-CCOL	AA-5A Cheetah	Lowlog Ltd (G-BIVU)/Elstree
	G-CCON	Beech F33C Bonanza	P. J. Withinshaw
	G-CCOZ	Monnett Sonerai II	P. R. Cozens
	G-CCUB	Piper J-3C-65 Cub	Cormack (Aircraft Services) Ltd
	G-CDBS	MBB Bo 105DBS	Bond Helicopters Ltd/Aberdeen
	G-CDET	Culver LCA Cadet	H. B. Fox/Booker
	G-CDGA	Taylor JT.1 Monoplane	R. M. Larimore

Reg.	Type	Owner or Operator	Notes
G-CDON	PA-28-161 Warrior II	East Midlands Flying Club PLC	
G-CDRU	C.A.S.A. 1.131E Jungmann 2000	P. Cunniff/White Waltham	
G-CEAP	L.1011-385 TriStar 50	Caledonian Airways Ltd/Gatwick	
G-CEAS	HPR-7 Herald 214	Channel Express (Air Services) Ltd (G-BEBB)/Bournemouth	
G-CEGA	PA-34-200T Seneca II	Mercia Aviation/Wellesbourne	
G-CEJA	Cameron V-77 balloon	L. & C. Gray (G-BTOF)	
G-CERT	Mooney M.20K	S. T. Newington	
G-CEXA	F.27 Friendship Mk 500	Channel Express (Air Services) Ltd/ Bournemouth	
G-CEXB	F.27 Friendship Mk 500	Channel Express (Air Services) Ltd/ Bournemouth	
G-CEXC	Airbus A.300F4-103	Channel Express (Air Services) Ltd/ Bournemouth	
G-CEXP	HPR-7 Herald 209 ★	*Spectators' Terrace*/Gatwick	
G-CEXS	L.188C Electra	Channel Express (Air Services) Ltd/ Bournemouth	
G-CFBI	Colt 56A balloon	G. A. Fisher	
G-CFLY	Cessna 172F	I. Hughes & B. T. Williams	
G-CGCG	Robinson R-22B	J .M. Henderson	
G-CGHM	PA-28 Cherokee 140	M. J. Flynn	
G-CGOD	Cameron N-77 balloon	Abbey Plant Co Ltd	
G-CHAA	Cameron O-90 balloon	The Balloon Club Ltd	
G-CHAL	Robinson R-22B	Plane Talking Ltd/Elstree	
G-CHAM	Cameron 90 Pot SS balloon	F. Horsfall & B. J. Reeves	
G-CHAR	Grob G.109B	RAFGSA/Bicester	
G-CHAS	PA-28-181 Archer II	C. H. Elliott	
G-CHAV	Shaw Europa	Chavenage Flying Group	
G-CHEB	Shaw Europa	C. H. P. Bell	
G-CHEM	PA-34-200T Seneca II	Channel Islands Air Charter Ltd	
G-CHES	BN-2A-26 Islander	The Cheshire Constabulary (G-PASY/ G-BPCB/G-BEXA/G-MALI/G-DIVE)/ Liverpool	
G-CHIK	Cessna F.152	Stapleford Flying Club Ltd (G-BHAZ)	
G-CHIP	PA-28-181 Archer II	C. M. Hough/Fairoaks	
G-CHIS	Robinson R-22B	Bradmore Helicopter Leasing	
G-CHKL	Cameron 120 Kookaburra SS balloon	Eagle Ltd	
G-CHLT	Stemme S.10	F. C. Y. Cheung/Hong Kong	
G-CHMP	Bellanca 7ACA Champ	I. J. Langley	
G-CHNL	F.27 Friendship Mk 600	Channel Express (Air Services) Ltd/ Bournemouth	
G-CHNX	L.188AF Electra	Channel Express (Air Services) Ltd/ Bournemouth	
G-CHOK	Cameron V-77 balloon	A. J. Moore	
G-CHOP	Westland-Bell 47G-3B1	Image Computer Systems Ltd	
G-CHRP	Colt Flying Book SS balloon	Chronicle Communications Ltd	
G-CHRR	Colt Flying Book SS balloon	Chronicle Communications Ltd	
G-CHTA	AA-5A Cheetah	Rapid Spin Ltd (G-BFRC)/Biggin Hill	
G-CHUB	Colt N-51 balloon	Chubb Fire Security Ltd	
G-CHUG	Shaw Europa	C. M. Washington	
G-CHUK	Cameron O-77 balloon	L. C. Taylor	
G-CHYL	Robinson R-22B	Pentech	
G-CIAS	BN-2B-21 Islander	Channel Island Air Search Ltd (G-BKJM)	
G-CICI	Cameron R-15 balloon	Ballooning Endeavours Ltd	
G-CINY	Stoddard-Hamilton Glasair IIRG	P. N. Haigh	
G-CIPI	AJEP Wittman W.8 Tailwind	N. R. Hurley (G-AYDU)/France	
G-CITY	PA-31-350 Navajo Chieftain	Woodgate Aviation (IOM) Ltd	
G-CIVA	Boeing 747-436	British Airways *City of St. Davids*	
G-CIVB	Boeing 747-436	British Airways *City of Lichfield*	
G-CIVC	Boeing 747-436	British Airways *City of St. Andrews*	
G-CIVD	Boeing 747-436	British Airways *City of Coventry*	
G-CIVE	Boeing 747-436	British Airways *City of Sunderland*	
G-CIVF	Boeing 747-436	British Airways *City of St Albans*	
G-CIVG	Boeing 747-436	British Airways *City of Wells*	
G-CIVH	Boeing 747-436	British Airways *City of Hereford*	
G-CIVI	Boeing 747-436	British Airways *City of Gloucester*	
G-CIVJ	Boeing 747-436	British Airways	
G-CIVK	Boeing 747-436	British Airways	
G-CIVL	Boeing 747-436	British Airways	
G-CIVM	Boeing 747-436	British Airways	
G-CJBC	PA-28 Cherokee 180	J. B. Cave/Halfpenny Green	
G-CJCI	Pilatus P2-06 (CC+43)	Pilatus P2 Flying Group	

Notes	Reg.	Type	Owner or Operator
	G-CJIM	Taylor JT.1 Monoplane	J. Crawford
	G-CJUD	Denney Kitfox Mk 3	C. W. Judge
	G-CKCK	Enstrom 280FX	G. H. Harding
	G-CKEN	Wombat gyroplane	K. H. Durran
	G-CLAC	PA-28-161 Warrior II	Clacton Light Aviation Co
	G-CLAS	Short SD3-60 Variant 100	BAC Express Ltd (G-BLED)
	G-CLEA	PA-28-161 Warrior II	Creative Logistics Enterprises & Aviation Ltd & R. J. Harrison
	G-CLEM	Bo 208A2 Junior	A. W. Webster (G-ASWE)
	G-CLIC	Cameron A-105 balloon	Matrix Computer Maintenance Ltd
	G-CLIP	AS.355N Twin Squirrel	Quantel Ltd/Biggin Hill
	G-CLOE	Sky 90-24 balloon	C. J. Sandell
	G-CLOS	PA-34-200 Seneca II	Greenclose Aviation Services Ltd/ Bournemouth
	G-CLUB	Cessna FRA.150N	Osprey Flying Club/Cranfield
	G-CLUE	PA-34-200T Seneca II	Bristol Office Machines Ltd
	G-CLUX	Cessna F.172N	J. & K. Aviation/Liverpool
	G-CLYV	Robinson R-22B	Helifly Ireland Ltd
	G-CMDR	R. Commander 114	J. N. Scott & G. C. Bishop
	G-CMGC	PA-25 Pawnee 235	Midland Gliding Club Ltd (G-BFEX)/ Long Mynd
	G-COCO	Cessna F.172M	P. C. Sheard & R. C. Larder
	G-CODE	Bell 206B JetRanger 3	Datel Direct Ltd
	G-COEZ	Airbus A.320-231	Airbus International Airways Ltd
	G-COIN	Bell 206B JetRanger 2	C. Sarno
	G-COKE	Cameron O-65 balloon	M. C. Bradley
	G-COLA	Beech F33C Bonanza	John Bradley & Barry Ltd and J. A. Kelman (G-BUAZ)
	G-COLL	Enstrom 280C-UK-2 Shark	SG Aviation Services Ltd
	G-COLR	Colt 69A balloon	British School of Ballooning
	G-COMB	PA-30 Twin Comanche 160B	J. T. Bateson (G-AVBL)/Ronaldsway
	G-COMM	PA-23 Aztec 250C	Airtime Aviation Ltd (G-AZMG)/ Bournemouth
	G-COMP	Cameron N-90 balloon	Computacenter Ltd
	G-CONB	Robin DR.400/180	Winchcombe Farm (G-BUPX)
	G-CONC	Cameron N-90 balloon	British Airways
	G-COOK	Cameron N-77 balloon	IAZ (International) Ltd
	G-COOP	Cameron N-31 balloon	Rango Balloon & Kite Co
	G-COOT	Taylor Coot A	P. M. Napp
	G-COPS	Piper J-3C-65 Cub	R. W. Sproat & C. E. Simpson
	G-COPY	AA-5A Cheetah	Emberden Ltd (G-BIEU)/Biggin Hill
	G-CORC	Bell 206B JetRanger 2	Air Corcoran Ltd (G-CJHI/G-BBFB)
	G-CORD	Slingsby T.66 Nipper 3	B. A. Wright & K. E. Wilson (G-AVTB)
	G-CORT	AB-206B JetRanger	Helicopter Training & Hire Ltd
	G-COSY	Lindstrand LBL-56A balloon	D. D. Owen
	G-COTT	Cameron 60 Cottage SS balloon	Nottingham Hot-Air Balloon Club
	G-COUP	Ercoupe 415C	S. M. Gerrard
	G-COUR	AB-206B JetRanger 3	Speed Helicopters Ltd (G-FSDG/G-ROOT/ G-JETR/G-BKBR)
	G-COWS	ARV Super 2	T. C. Harrold (G-BONB)
	G-COZI	Rutan Cozy III	D. G. Machin
	G-CPCD	CEA DR.221	P. G. Bumpus & R. Thwaites
	G-CPCH	PA-28-151 Warrior	P. C. Hancock (G-BRGJ)
	G-CPEL	Boeing 757-236	British Airways (G-BRJE) *Walmer Castle*
	G-CPEM	Boeing 757-236	British Airways
	G-CPEN	Boeing 757-236	British Airways
	G-CPEO	Boeing 757-236	British Airways
	G-CPFC	Cessna F.152	Falcon Flying Services/Biggin Hill
	G-CPMK	D.H.C.1 Chipmunk 22	Towerdrive Ltd
	G-CPOL	AS.355F-1 Twin Squirrel	Thames Valley Police Authority
	G-CPTM	PA-28-151 Warrior	T. J. Mackay & C. M. Pollett (G-BTOE)
	G-CPTS	AB-206B JetRanger 3	A. R. B. Aspinall
	G-CRAK	Cameron N-77 balloon	Mobile Windscreens Ltd
	G-CRAY	Robinson R-22B	W. H. Grimshaw
	G-CRES	Denney Kitfox Mk 3	K. M. James
	G-CRIC	Colomban MC.15 Cri-Cri	A. B. Cameron
	G-CRIL	R. Commander 112B	Rockwell Aviation Group/Cardiff
	G-CRIS	Taylor JT.1 Monoplane	C. R. Steer
	G-CRML	Cessna 414A	Anglo International Holdings Ltd
	G-CROL	Maule MXT-7-180	D. C. Croll & ptnrs
	G-CRPH	Airbus A.320-231	Airtours International Airways Ltd
	G-CRUS	Cessna T.303	B. A. Groves
	G-CRUZ	Cessna T.303	Bank Farm Ltd

Reg.	Type	Owner or Operator	Notes
G-CRZY	Thunder Ax8-105 balloon	R. Carr (G-BDLP)/France	
G-CSBM	Cessna F.150M	Motorglider Centre `Ltd	
G-CSCS	Cessna F.172N	Conegate Ltd	
G-CSFC	Cessna 150L	Shropshire Aero Club Ltd/Sleap	
G-CSFT	PA-23 Aztec 250D	Aces High Ltd (G-AYKU)/North Weald	
G-CSNA	Cessna 421C	William Loughran Ltd	
G-CSVS	Boeing 757-236	Airtours International Airways Ltd (G-IEAC)	
G-CSZB	V.807B Viscount	British World Airlines Ltd (G-AOXU)	
G-CTCL	SOCATA TB.10 Tobago	Merryfield Leasing Ltd (G-BSIV)	
G-CTEL	Cameron N-90 balloon	Cabletel Surrey & Hampshire Ltd	
G-CTKL	Noorduyn AT-16 Harvard IIB (54137)	Key Audio Systems Ltd	
G-CTOY	Denney Kitfox Mk 3	M. J. Wilkinson	
G-CTPW	Bell 206B JetRanger 3	C. T. Wheatley	
G-CTRN	Enstrom F-28C-UK	J. & S. Lewis Ltd	
G-CTWW	PA-34-200T Seneca II	Control Techniques Drives Ltd (G-ROYZ/G-GALE)/Welshpool	
G-CUBB	PA-18 Super Cub 180	Bidford Gliding Centre Ltd	
G-CUBI	PA-18 Super Cub 135 (51-15673)	T. Watson	
G-CUBP	PA-18 Super Cub 150	P. Grenet	
G-CUBY	Piper J-3C-65 Cub	C. A. Bloom (G-BTZW)	
G-CUCU	Colt 180A balloon	G. M. N. & S. Spencer	
G-CURE	Colt 77A balloon	Flying Pictures (Balloons) Ltd	
G-CUTY	Shaw Europa	D. J. & M. Watson	
G-CVBF	Cameron A-210 balloon	Virgin Balloon Flights Ltd	
G-CVIL	Piper J-3C-65 Cub	H. A. D. Munro	
G-CVIX	D.H.110 Sea Vixen D.3 (XP924)	de Havilland Aviation Ltd	
G-CWAG	Sequoia F. 8L Falco	C. C. Wagner	
G-CWBM	Currie Wot	B. V. Mayo (G-BTVP)	
G-CWIZ	AS.350B Ecureuil	HFI Engineering (G-DJEM/G-ZBAC/ G-SEBI/G-BMCU)	
G-CWOT	Currie Wot	T. E. G. Buckett	
G-CXCX	Cameron N-90 balloon	Cathay Pacific Airways (London) Ltd	
G-CYGI	Hapi Cygnet SF-2A	B. Brown	
G-CYLS	Cessna T.303	Gledhill Water Storage Ltd (G-BKXI)/Blackpool	
G-CYMA	GA-7 Cougar	Cyma Petroleum Ltd (G-BKOM)/Elstree	
G-CZAR	Cessna 560 Citation V	Stadium City Ltd	
G-CZCZ	Avions Mudry CAP.10B	P. R. Moorhead	
G-DAAH	PA-28RT-201T Turbo Arrow IV	R. Peplow/Halfpenny Green	
G-DAAL	Avro 748 Srs 1	Emerald Airways Ltd (G-BEKG/G-VAJK)/ Liverpool	
G-DAAM	Robinson R-22B	A. A. Macaskill	
G-DACA	P.57 Sea Prince T.1 ★	P. G. Vallance Ltd/Charlwood	
G-DACC	Cessna 401B	Niglon Ltd (G-AYOU)/Birmingham	
G-DADS	Hughes 369HS	Executive Aviation Services Ltd	
G-DADY	Lindstrand LBL-77A balloon	International Balloons Ltd	
G-DAFY	Beech 58 Baron	Ortac Air Ltd/Guernsey	
G-DAJB	Boeing 757-2T7	Monarch Airlines Ltd/Luton	
G-DAJC	Boeing 767-31KER	Airtours International Airways Ltd	
G-DAJR	Airbus A.320-231	Airtours International Airways Ltd	
G-DAKK	Douglas C-47A	South Coast Airways/Bournemouth	
G-DAKS	Douglas C-47A (TS423)	Aces High Ltd/North Weald	
G-DAMY	Shaw Europa	Panelite	
G-DAND	SOCATA TB.10 Tobago	Whitemoor Engineering Co Ltd	
G-DANS	AS.355F-2 Twin Squirrel	Frewton Ltd (G-BTNM)	
G-DANT	R. Commander 114	Keyplay Ltd	
G-DAPH	Cessna 180K	M. R. L. Astor	
G-DARA	PA-34-220T Seneca III	Pinta Investments Ltd	
G-DARR	Cessna 421C	Channon Asset Management Ltd (G-BNEZ)/Liverpool	
G-DASH	R. Commander 112A	Josef D. J. Jons & Co Ltd (G-BDAJ)	
G-DASI	Short SD3-60 Variant 100	Gill Airways Ltd (G-BKKW)/Newcastle	
G-DASU	Cameron V-77 balloon	D. & L. S. Litchfield	
G-DAVE	Jodel D.112	D. A. Porter/Sturgate	
G-DAVO	AA-5B Tiger	Kadala Aviation Ltd (G-GAGA/ G-BGPG)/Elstree	
G-DAVT	Schleicher ASH-26E	D. A. Triplett	
G-DAYI	Shaw Europa	A. F. Day	
G-DAYS	Shaw Europa	A. Hall & ptnrs	
G-DAYY	Lindstrand Fruit Bottle SS balloon	International Balloons Ltd	

Notes	Reg.	Type	Owner or Operator
	G-DBAL	H.S.125 Srs 3B ★	Southampton Airport Fire Section (G-BSAA)
	G-DBHH	AB-206B JetRanger	Helisport Ltd (G-AWVO)
	G-DBMW	Bell 206B JetRanger 4	Lind Ltd
	G-DCCH	MBB Bo 105D	Devon & Cornwall Police Authority
	G-DCEA	PA-34-200T Seneca II	M. J. Greasby/Booker
	G-DCFR	Cessna 550 Citation II	Chauffair (CI) Ltd (G-WYLX/G-JETD)
	G-DCIO	Douglas DC-10-30	British Airways *Epping Forest*/Gatwick
	G-DCKK	Cessna F.172N	M. Manston
	G-DCSW	PA-32R-301 Saratoga SP	A. W. Kendrick
	G-DCXL	Jodel D.140C	X-Ray Lima Group
	G-DDAY	PA-28R-201T Turbo Arrow III	G-DDAY Group (G-BPDO)
	G-DDCD	D.H.104 Dove 8	C. Daniel (G-ARUM)/Biggin Hill
	G-DDMV	NA T-6G Texan (41)	E. A. Morgan
	G-DEBA	BAe 146-200	Debonair Airways Ltd/Luton
	G-DEBB	Beech 35-B33 Debonair	Spitfire Aviation Ltd/Bournemouth
	G-DEBC	BAe 146-200	Debonair Airways Ltd/Luton
	G-DEBD	BAe 146-200	Debonair Airways Ltd/Luton
	G-DEBE	BAe 146-200	Debonair Airways Ltd/Luton
	G-DEBF	BAe 146-200	Debonair Airways Ltd/Luton
	G-DEBG	BAe 146-200	Debonair Airways Ltd/Luton
	G-DEBH	BAe 146-200	Debonair Airways Ltd/Luton
	G-DEJL	Robinson R-22B	D. E. J. Lomas
	G-DELI	Thunder Ax7-77 balloon	Heather Flight Ltd
	G-DELL	Robinson R-22B	Delaware Collective
	G-DELT	Robinson R-22B	D. P. Fiske
	G-DEMH	Cessna F.172M (modified)	M. Hammond (G-BFLO)
	G-DENA	Cessna F.150G	Aviators Flight Centre (G-AVEO)/Southend
	G-DENB	Cessna F.150G	Aviators Flight Centre (G-ATZZ)/Southend
	G-DENC	Cessna F.150G	Aviators Flight Centre (G-AVAP)/Southend
	G-DENI	PA-32 Cherokee Six 300	Aviators Flight Centre (G-BAIA)/Southend
	G-DENN	Bell 206B JetRanger 3	Abbey Flight Ltd
	G-DENS	Binder CP.301S Smaragd	J. K. Davies
	G-DENW	PA-44-180 Seminole	D. A. Woodhams
	G-DERB	Robinson R-22B	Derbyshire Helicopters (G-BPYH)
	G-DERV	Cameron Truck SS balloon	J. M. Percival
	G-DESI	Aero Designs Pulsar XP	D. F. Gaughan
	G-DESS	Mooney M.20J	W. E. Newnes
	G-DEVS	PA-28 Cherokee 180	180 Group (G-BGVJ)
	G-DEXP	ARV Super 2	Smedley Ltd
	G-DEXY	Beech E90 King Air	Tornado Ltd
	G-DEZC	H.S.125 Srs 700B	Frewton Ltd (G-BWCR)
	G-DFLT	Cessna F.406	Direct Flight Ltd/Norwich
	G-DFLY	PA-38-112 Tomahawk	Western Air Training Ltd/Thruxton
	G-DFVA	Cessna R.172K	R. A. Plowright
	G-DGDG	Glaser-Dirks DG.400/17	DG400 Flying Group/Lasham
	G-DGWW	Rand-Robinson KR-2	W. Wilson/Liverpool
	G-DHAV	D.H.115 Vampire T.11 (U-1234)	De Havilland Aviation Ltd
	G-DHCB	D.H.C.2 Beaver 1	Seaflite Ltd (G-BTDL)
	G-DHCI	D.H.C.1 Chipmunk 22	Felthorpe Flying Group Ltd (G-BBSE)
	G-DHGS	Robinson R-22B	Driver Hire Group Services Ltd
	G-DHLB	Cameron N-90 balloon	DHL International (UK) Ltd
	G-DHLI	Colt 90 World SS balloon	Virgin Airship & Balloon Co Ltd
	G-DHLZ	Colt 31A balloon	Virgin Airship & Balloon Co Ltd
	G-DHTM	D.H.82A Tiger Moth (replica)	E. G. Waite-Roberts
	G-DHTT	D.H.112 Venom FB.1	D. J. Lindsay Wood
	G-DHUU	D.H.112 Venom FB.1 (WR410)	D. J. Lindsay Wood
	G-DHVV	D.H.115 Vampire T.55 (U-1214)	Lindsay Wood Promotions Ltd
	G-DHWW	D.H.115 Vampire T.55 (XG775)	Lindsay Wood Promotions Ltd
	G-DHXX	D.H.100 Vampire FB.6 (LZ551/G)	Lindsay Wood Promotions Ltd
	G-DHYY	D.H.115 Vampire T.11	Lindsay Wood Promotions Ltd
	G-DHZZ	D.H.115 Vampire T.55 (U-1230)	Lindsay Wood Promotions Ltd
	G-DIAL	Cameron N-90 balloon	A. J. Street
	G-DIAT	PA-28 Cherokee 140	RAF Benevolent Fund's IAT/Bristol & Wessex Aeroplane Club (G-BCGK)/ Lulsgate
	G-DICE	Enstrom F-28F	Stephenson Marine Co Ltd
	G-DICK	Thunder Ax6-56Z balloon	R. D. Sargeant
	G-DIET	Lindstrand Drinks Can SS balloon	Pepsi Cola Overseas Ltd
	G-DIMB	Boeing 767-31KER	Airtours International Airways Ltd
	G-DIME	R. Commander 114	B. J. Ratcliffe & H. B. Richardson
	G-DINA	AA-5B Tiger	MRM of Fenton
	G-DING	Colt 77A balloon	G. J. Bell

Reg.	Type	Owner or Operator	Notes
G-DINT	B.156 Beaufighter IF	T. E. Moore	
G-DIPI	Cameron Tub SS balloon	M. Sevrin/Belgium	
G-DIPS	Taylor JT.1 Monoplane	B. J. Halls	
G-DIRE	Robinson R-22B	Techspan Aviation Ltd	
G-DIRK	Glaser-Dirks DG.400	C. J. Lowrie	
G-DIRT	Thunder Ax7-77Z balloon	R. J. Ngbaronye	
G-DISK	PA-24 Comanche 250	A. Johnston (G-APZG)	
G-DISO	Jodel 150	P. F. Craven & J. H. Shearer	
G-DIVA	Cessna R.172K XPII	M. Gardner	
G-DIWY	PA-32 Cherokee Six 300	Industrial Foam Systems Ltd	
G-DIZO	Jodel D.120A	D. Aldersea (G-EMKM)/Breighton	
G-DIZY	PA-28R-201T Turbo Arrow III	Medway Arrow Group	
G-DJCR	Varga 2150A Kachina	D. J. C. Robertson (G-BLWG)	
G-DJHB	Beech A23-19 Musketeer	Nayland Aiglet Group (G-AZZE)	
G-DJIM	MHCA-1	J. Crawford	
G-DJJA	PA-28-181 Archer II	Choice Aircraft/Fowlmere	
G-DJLW	H.S.125 Srs 3B/RA	Source Ltd (G-AVVB)	
G-DJNH	Denney Kitfox Mk 3	D. J. N. Hall	
G-DKDP	Grob G.109	D. W. & J. E. Page	
G-DKGF	Viking Dragonfly	P. C. Dowbor	
G-DLCB	Shaw Europa	D. J. Lockett	
G-DLDL	Robinson R-22B	A. J. Wagstaff	
G-DLOM	SOCATA TB.20 Trinidad	J. N. A. Adderley/Guernsey	
G-DLTR	PA-28 Cherokee 180E	D. A. Williams (G-AYAV)	
G-DMCA	Douglas DC-10-30	Monarch Airlines Ltd/Luton	
G-DMCD	Robinson R-22B	R. W. Pomphrett	
G-DMCS	PA-28R Cherokee Arrow 200-II	D. L. Johns & F. K. Parker (G-CPAC)	
G-DNCS	PA-28R-201T Turbo Arrow III	BRT Arrow Ltd/Barton	
G-DNLB	MBB Bo 105DBS/4	Bond Helicopters Ltd (G-BCDH/G-BTBD/G-BUDP)	
G-DNLD	Cameron 97 Donald SS balloon	The Walt Disney Co Ltd	
G-DNVT	G.1159C Gulfstream IV	Shell Aircraft Ltd/Heathrow	
G-DOBN	Cessna 402B	Edinburgh Air Charter Ltd	
G-DOCA	Boeing 737-436	British Airways *River Ballindery*	
G-DOCB	Boeing 737-436	British Airways *River Bush*	
G-DOCC	Boeing 737-436	British Airways *River Affric*	
G-DOCD	Boeing 737-436	British Airways *River Aire*	
G-DOCE	Boeing 737-436	British Airways *River Alness*	
G-DOCF	Boeing 737-436	British Airways *River Beauly*	
G-DOCG	Boeing 737-436	British Airways *River Blackwater*	
G-DOCH	Boeing 737-436	British Airways *River Bruna*	
G-DOCI	Boeing 737-436	British Airways *River Carron*	
G-DOCJ	Boeing 737-436	British Airways *River Glass*	
G-DOCK	Boeing 737-436	British Airways *River Lochay*	
G-DOCL	Boeing 737-436	British Airways *River Lune*	
G-DOCM	Boeing 737-436	British Airways *River Meon*	
G-DOCN	Boeing 737-436	British Airways *River Ottery*	
G-DOCO	Boeing 737-436	British Airways *River Parett*	
G-DOCP	Boeing 737-436	British Airways *River Swift*	
G-DOCR	Boeing 737-436	British Airways *River Tavy*	
G-DOCS	Boeing 737-436	British Airways *River Teifi*	
G-DOCT	Boeing 737-436	British Airways *River Tene*	
G-DOCU	Boeing 737-436	British Airways *River Teviot*	
G-DOCV	Boeing 737-436	British Airways *River Thurso*	
G-DOCW	Boeing 737-436	British Airways *River Till*	
G-DOCX	Boeing 737-436	British Airways *River Tirry*	
G-DOCY	Boeing 737-436	British Airways (G-BVBY)	
G-DOCZ	Boeing 737-436	British Airways (G-BVBZ) *River Wharfe*	
G-DODB	Robinson R-22B	Exmoor Helicopters Ltd	
G-DODD	Cessna F.172P-II	K. Watts/Elstree	
G-DODI	PA-46-350P Malibu	Sunseeker Sales (UK) Ltd	
G-DODR	Robinson R-22B	Exmoor Helicopters Ltd	
G-DOEA	AA-5A Cheetah	Plane Talking Ltd (G-RJMI)/Elstree	
G-DOFY	Bell 206B JetRanger 3	Cinnamond Ltd	
G-DOGS	Cessna R.182RG	J. R. Shawe	
G-DOLY	Cessna T.303	R. M. Jones (G-BJZK)	
G-DONI	AA-5B Tiger	D. M. Maclean (G-BLLT)	
G-DONS	PA-28RT-201T Turbo Arrow IV	D. J. Murphy	
G-DONZ	Shaw Europa	D. J. Smith & D. McNicholl	
G-DOOR	M.S.893E Rallye 180GT	Lynair Flying Group	
G-DOOZ	AS.355F-2 Twin Squirrel	Lynton Aviation Ltd (G-BNSX)	
G-DORB	Bell 206B JetRanger 3	Dorb Crest Homes Ltd	
G-DOVE	Cessna 182Q	P. J. Contracting	

Notes	Reg.	Type	Owner or Operator
	G-DOWN	Colt 31A balloon	M. Williams
	G-DPPS	AS.355N Twin Squirrel	Dyfed-Powys Police Authority
	G-DPST	Phillips ST.2	S. E. Phillips
	G-DRAC	Cameron Dracula Skull SS balloon	Shiplake Investments Ltd
	G-DRAG	Cessna 152 (tailwheel)	L. A. Maynard & M. E. Scouller (G-REME/G-BRNF)
	G-DRAI	Robinson R-22B	J. M. Hawkes
	G-DRAR	Hughes 369E	Readmans Ltd
	G-DRAW	Colt 77A balloon	Readers Digest Association Ltd
	G-DRBG	Cessna 172M	M. R. & K. E. Slack (G-MUIL)
	G-DRGN	Cameron N-105 balloon	W. I. Hooker & C. Parker
	G-DRNT	Sikorsky S-76A	Bond Helicopters Ltd/Aberdeen
	G-DROP	Cessna U.206C	Peterborough Parachute Centre Ltd (G-UKNO/G-BAMN)/Sibson
	G-DRSV	CEA DR.315 (modified)	R. S. Voice
	G-DRYI	Cameron N-77 balloon	J. Barbour & Sons Ltd
	G-DRYS	Cameron N-90 balloon	J. Barbour & Sons Ltd
	G-DRZF	CEA DR.360	C. A. Parker/Sywell
	G-DSGC	PA-25 Pawnee 235C	Devon & Somerset Gliding Club Ltd
	G-DSID	PA-34-220T Seneca III	D. Sidoli & Sons (Shrewsbury) Ltd/ Welshpool
	G-DTCP	PA-32R Cherokee Lance 300	Campbell Aviation Ltd (G-TEEM)
	G-DUDS	C.A.S.A. 1.131E Jungmann 2000	D. H. Pattison
	G-DUET	Wood Duet	C. Wood
	G-DUNN	Zenair CH.250	A. Dunn
	G-DURO	Shaw Europa	R. Swinden
	G-DURX	Thunder 77A balloon	V. Trimble
	G-DUST	Stolp SA.300 Starduster Too	J. V. George
	G-DUVL	Cessna F.172N	A. J. Simpson/Denham
	G-DVBF	Lindstrand LBL-210A balloon	Virgin Balloon Flights Ltd
	G-DVON	D.H.104 Devon C.2 (VP955)	C. I. Thatcher
	G-DWIA	Chilton D.W.1A	D. Elliott
	G-DWIB	Chilton D.W.1B (replica)	J. Jennings
	G-DWPH	Ultramagic M-77	Ultramagic UK
	G-DYNE	Cessna 414	Commair Aviation Ltd/E. Midlands
	G-DYOU	PA-38-112 Tomahawk	Airways Aero Associations Ltd/Booker
	G-DZEL	Shaw Europa	R. J. W. Wood
	G-EAGL	Cessna 421C	Moseley Group (PSV) Ltd & Clowes Estates Ltd/E. Midlands
	G-EBJI	Hawker Cygnet (replica)	C. J. Essex
	G-ECAS	Boeing 737-36N	British Midland Airways Ltd/E. Midlands
	G-ECAV	Beech 200 Super King Air	GEC Avionics Ltd/Rochester
	G-ECBH	Cessna F.150K	J. P. Hosford
	G-ECDX	D.H.71 Tiger Moth (replica)	M. D. Souch
	G-ECGC	Cessna F.172N-II	Leicestershire Aero Club Ltd
	G-ECGO	Bo 208C1 Junior	M. F. R. B. Collett
	G-ECHO	Enstrom 280C-UK-2 Shark	ALP Electrical (Maidenhead) Ltd (G-LONS/G-BDIB)/Booker
	G-ECJM	PA-28R-201T Turbo Arrow III	Regishire Ltd (G-FESL/G-BNRN)
	G-ECKE	Avro 504K (replica) (D8781)	N. Wright & C. M. Kettlewell
	G-ECOS	AS.355F-1 Twin Squirrel	Pace Micro Technology Ltd (G-DOLR/G-BPVB)
	G-ECOX	Grega GN.1 Air Camper	H. C. Cox
	G-EDEN	SOCATA TB.10 Tobago	N. G. Pistol & ptnrs
	G-EDGE	Jodel 150	A. D. Edge
	G-EDIE	Robinson R-44 Astro	Serve Offer Ltd
	G-EDNA	PA-38-112 Tomahawk	D. J. Clucas
	G-EDRY	Cessna T.303	Pat Eddery Ltd
	G-EEAC	PA-31 Turbo Navajo	E. Alexander (G-SKKA/G-FOAL/ G-RMAE/G-BAEG)
	G-EEGL	Christen Eagle II	A. J. Wilson
	G-EENY	GA-7 Cougar	Plane Talking Ltd/Elstree
	G-EESA	Shaw Europa	C. B. Stirling (G-HIIL)
	G-EEUP	SNCAN Stampe SV-4C	A. M. Wajih
	G-EEZE	Rutan LongEz	A. J. Nurse
	G-EFRY	Light Aero Avid Aerobat	J. J. Donely
	G-EFSM	Slingsby T.67M-260	Slingsby Aviation Ltd (G-BPLK)
	G-EFTE	Bolkow Bo 207	L. J. & A. A. Rice
	G-EGAL	Christen Eagle II	P. N. Davis
	G-EGEE	Cessna 310Q	D. J. Pursey & H. Kloosterboer (G-AZVY)
	G-EGEL	Christen Eagle II	D. J. Daly

Reg.	Type	Owner or Operator	Notes
G-EGGG	Lindstrand Humpty SS balloon	International Balloons Ltd	
G-EGGS	Robin DR.400/180	R. Foot	
G-EGHB	Ercoupe 415D	J. H. Spanton	
G-EGHH	Hunter F.58	Jet Heritage Charitable Foundation Ltd/ Bournemouth	
G-EGJA	SOCATA TB.20 Trinidad	D. A. Williamson/Alderney	
G-EGLD	PA-28-161 Cadet	J. Appleton/Denham	
G-EGLE	Christen Eagle II	R. L. Mitcham & ptnrs	
G-EGLT	Cessna 310R	Tilling Associates Ltd (G-BHTV)	
G-EGUL	Christen Eagle II	G-EGUL Flying Group (G-FRYS)	
G-EGVL	Cameron A-250 balloon	The Balloon Club Ltd	
G-EHAP	Sportavia-Pützer RF.7	R. G. Boyes	
G-EHBJ	C.A.S.A. 1.131E Jungmann 2000	E. P. Howard	
G-EHIL	Westland-Agusta EH.101 (ZH647)	Westland Helicopters Ltd/Yeovil	
G-EHJM	PA-31P Pressurised Navajo	Galunggung Ltd	
G-EHMM	Robin DR.400/180R	Booker Gliding Club Ltd	
G-EIBM	Robinson R-22B	Trustees of Bernard Hunter (G-BUCL)	
G-EIIR	Cameron N-77 balloon	D. V. Howard	
G-EIKY	Shaw Europa	J. D. Milbank	
G-EIWT	Cessna FR.182RG	P. P. D. Howard-Johnston/Edinburgh	
G-EJGO	Z.226HE Trener	N. J. Radford	
G-EJOC	AS.350B Ecureuil	Elmsdale (UK) Ltd (G-GEDS/G-HMAN/ G-SKIM/G-BIVP)	
G-ELBC	PA-34-200 Seneca II	Stapleford Flying Club Ltd (G-BANS)	
G-ELEC	Westland WG.30 Srs 200	Westland Helicopters Ltd (G-BKNV)/Yeovil	
G-ELFI	Robinson R-22B	Tiger Helicopters/Shobdon	
G-ELIZ	Denney Kitfox Mk 2	A. J. Ellis	
G-ELKA	Christen Eagle II	Activity Aviation Ltd & D. Aitken	
G-ELLA	PA-32R-301 Saratoga IIHP	South Yorkshire Air Services Ltd	
G-ELMH	NA AT-6D Harvard III (42-84555)	M. Hammond	
G-ELRA	BAe 125-1000	Raytheon Corporate Jets Inc	
G-EMAK	PA-28R-201 Arrow III	D. & G. Rathbone	
G-EMAN	AS.355F-1 Twin Squirrel	Heliking Ltd (G-WEKR/G-CHLA)	
G-EMAU	AS.355N Twin Squirrel	E. Midlands Air Support Unit	
G-EMAZ	PA-28-181 Archer II	E. J. Stanley	
G-EMER	PA-34-200 Seneca II	Haimoss Ltd & R. P. Thomas/Old Sarum	
G-EMIN	Shaw Europa	Gemini Group	
G-EMJA	C.A.S.A. 1.131E Jungmann 2000	P. J. Brand	
G-EMMA	Cessna F.182Q	Watkiss Group Aviation	
G-EMMS	PA-38-112 Tomahawk	Ravenair/Manchester	
G-EMMY	Rutan Vari-Eze	M. J. Tooze	
G-EMNI	Speedtwin Mk 2	A. J. Clarry	
G-EMRD	H.S.748 Srs 2B	Emerald Airways Ltd (G-HDBD)/Liverpool	
G-EMSI	Shaw Europa	P. W. L. Thomas	
G-EMSY	D.H.82A Tiger Moth	B. E. Micklewright (G-ASPZ)	
G-ENCE	Partenavia P.68B	P. Davies (G-OROY/G-BFSU)	
G-ENIE	Tipsy T.66 Nipper 3	E. J. Clarke	
G-ENII	Cessna F.172M	J. Howley	
G-ENNA	PA-28-161 Warrior II	G-ENNA Group	
G-ENNY	Cameron V-77 balloon	B. G. Jones	
G-ENOA	Cessna F.172F	M. K. Acors (G-ASZW)	
G-ENRI	Lindstrand LBL-105A balloon	P. G. Hall	
G-ENRY	Cameron N-105 balloon	P. G. & G. R. Hall	
G-ENSI	Beech F33A Bonanza	Special Analysis & Simulation Technology Ltd	
G-ENTT	Cessna F.152 II	Southern Flight Training Ltd (G-BHHI)	
G-ENTW	Cessna F.152 II	Southern Flight Training Ltd (G-BFLK)	
G-ENUS	Cameron N-90 balloon	Wye Valley Aviation Ltd	
G-EOFF	Taylor JT.2 Titch	G. H. Wylde	
G-EORG	PA-38-112 Tomahawk	Airways Aero Association/Booker	
G-EPDI	Cameron N-77 balloon	R. Moss	
G-EPED	PA-31-350 Navajo Chieftain	Pedley Furniture International Ltd (G-BMCJ)	
G-EPOX	Aero Designs Pulsar XP	K. F. Farey	
G-ERCO	Ercoupe 415D	A. R. & M. V. Tapp	
G-ERDS	D.H.82A Tiger Moth	W. A. Gerdes	
G-ERIC	R. Commander 112TC	Atomchoice Ltd	
G-ERIK	Cameron N-77 balloon	T. M. Donnelly	
G-ERIS	Hughes 369D	R. J. Howard (G-PJMD/G-BMJV)	
G-ERIX	Boeing Stearman A75N-1	P. P. Stanitzeck/Munich	
G-ERMO	ARV Super 2	P. R. Booth (G-BMWK)	
G-ERMS	Thunder Ax3 balloon	B. R. & M. Boyle	
G-ERNI	PA-28-181 Archer II	E. L. Collins (G-OSSY)	
G-EROS	Cameron H-34 balloon	Evening Standard Co Ltd	

Notes	Reg.	Type	Owner or Operator
	G-ERRY	AA-5B Tiger	Herefordshire Aero Club Ltd (G-BFMJ)/ Shobdon
	G-ERTY	D.H.82A Tiger Moth	M. Meuser (G-ANDC)/Germany
	G-ESKU	PA-23 Aztec 250C	A. J. Keen (G-AWIY)
	G-ESKY	PA-23 Aztec 250	Keen Leasing Ltd (G-BBNN)
	G-ESSX	PA-28-161 Warrior II	Courtenay Enterprises (G-BHYY)/ Biggin Hill
	G-ESTE	AA-5A Cheetah	Biblio International Ltd (G-GHNC)
	G-ESUS	Rotorway Executive 162F	J. Tickner
	G-ETBY	PA-32 Cherokee Six 260	G-ETBY Group (G-AWCY)
	G-ETCD	Colt 77A balloon	Philips Electronics Ltd
	G-ETDA	PA-28-161 Warrior II	T. Griffiths
	G-ETDC	Cessna 172P	Osprey Air Services Ltd
	G-ETFT	Colt Financial Times SS balloon	Financial Times Ltd (G-BSGZ)
	G-ETIN	Robinson R-22B	I. & E. Whitmore
	G-ETOM	BAe 125 Srs 800B	TWR Group Ltd (G-BVFC/G-TPHK/ G-FDSL)
	G-EURA	Agusta-Bell 47J-2	E. W. Schnedlitz (G-ASNV)
	G-EVAN	Taylor JT.2 Titch	E. Evans
	G-EVER	Robinson R-22B	Technology Sales Training Ltd
	G-EVET	Cameron 80 Concept balloon	K. J. Foster
	G-EVNT	Lindstrand LBL-180A balloon	Redmalt Ltd
	G-EWAN	Prostar PT-2C	C. G. Shaw
	G-EWEL	Sikorsky S-76A	Chase Montagu Ltd
	G-EWFN	SOCATA TB-20 Trinidad	Trinidair Ltd (G-BRTY)
	G-EWIZ	Pitts S-2E Special	S. J. Carver & D. Howdle
	G-EXEC	PA-34-200 Seneca	Sky Air Travel Ltd
	G-EXEX	Cessna 404	Atlantic Air Transport Ltd/Coventry
	G-EXIT	M.S.893E Rallye 180GT	K. J. Reynolds/Rochester
	G-EXLR	BAe 125-1000B	Raytheon Corporate Jets Inc
	G-EXPL	Champion 7GCBC Citabria	J. J. Young
	G-EXPR	Colt 90A balloon	Lakeside Lodge Golf Centre
	G-EXTR	Extra EA.260	D. M. Britten
	G-EYAS	Denney Kitfox Mk 2	E. J. Young
	G-EYCO	Robin DR.400/180	L. M. Gould
	G-EYES	Cessna 402C	Air Corbière Ltd (G-BLCE)/Coventry
	G-EYNL	MBB Bo 105DBS/5	Humberside Police Helicopter Support Project
	G-EYRE	Bell 206L-1 LongRanger	Hideroute Ltd (G-STVI)
	G-EZOS	Rutan Vari-Eze	O. Smith/Teesside
	G-EZYA	Boeing 737-3Y0	easyJet Airline Co Ltd (G-MONG)/Luton
	G-EZYB	Boeing 737-3M8	easyJet Airline Co Ltd/Luton
	G-EZYC	Boeing 737-3M8	easyJet Airline Co Ltd/Luton
	G-	Boeing 737-300	easyJet Airline Co Ltd/Luton
	G-	Boeing 737-300	easyJet Airline Co Ltd/Luton
	G-FABB	Cameron V-77 balloon	P. Trumper
	G-FABM	Beech 95-B55 Baron	F. B. Miles (G-JOND/G-BMVC)
	G-FAGN	Robinson R-22B	C. R. Weldon
	G-FAIR	SOCATA TB.10 Tobago	Sally Marine Ltd/Guernsey
	G-FALC	Aeromere F.8L Falco	P. W. Hunter (G-AROT)/Elstree
	G-FAME	Starstreak Shadow SA-II	T. J. Palmer
	G-FAMY	Maule M5-180C	R. J. & K. C. Grimstead
	G-FANC	Fairchild 24R-46 Argus III	A. T. Fines
	G-FANL	Cessna FR.172K XP-II	J. Eagles
	G-FARM	SOCATA Rallye 235GT	Bristol Cars Ltd
	G-FARO	Aero Designs Star-Lite SL.1	M. K. Faro
	G-FARR	Jodel 150	G. H. Farr
	G-FAST	Cessna 337G	Pelham Trust Co Ltd
	G-FATB	R. Commander 114B	J. W. McIllwraith
	G-FAYE	Cessna F.150M	Cheshire Air Training Services Ltd/ Liverpool
	G-FBHH	Hughes 369HS	Helisport Ltd
	G-FBIX	D.H.100 Vampire FB.9 (WL505)	D. G. Jones
	G-FBMW	Cameron N-90 balloon	Auto Braig GmbH/Germany
	G-FBWH	PA-28R Cherokee Arrow 180	F. A. Short
	G-FCAL	Cessna 441	FR Finances Ltd/Bournemouth
	G-FCSP	Robin DR.400/180	FCS Photochemicals
	G-FDAV	SA.341G Gazelle 1	Federal Aviation Ltd (G-RIFA/G-ORGE/ G-BBHU)
	G-FEBE	Cessna 340A	C. Dugard Ltd & E. C. Dugard
	G-FEFE	Scheibe SF.25B Falke	Aston Down Falke Syndicate
	G-FELT	Cameron N-77 balloon	Allan Industries Ltd

Reg.	Type	Owner or Operator	Notes
G-FERM	Cessna 425	Miton Ltd (G-DCFB/G-BMSH)	
G-FFBR	Thunder Ax8-105 balloon	Fuji Photo Film (UK) Ltd	
G-FFEN	Cessna F.150M	Suffolk Aero Club Ltd/Ipswich	
G-FFOR	Cessna 310R II	Air Service Training Ltd (G-BMGF)/Perth	
G-FFOX	Hunter T.7 (XL318)	Delta Engineering Aviation Ltd/Kemble	
G-FFRA	Dassault Falcon 20DC	FR Aviation Ltd/Bournemouth	
G-FFRB	Dassault Falcon 20DC	FR Aviation Ltd/Bournemouth	
G-FFRI	AS.355F-1 Twin Squirrel	Ford Farm Racing (G-GLOW/G-PAPA/ G-CNET/G-MCAH)	
G-FFTI	SOCATA TB.20 Trinidad	Romsure Ltd	
G-FFTN	Bell 206B JetRanger 3	Kensington Aviation Ltd	
G-FFWD	Cessna 310R	Keef & Co Ltd (G-TVKE/G-EURO)	
G-FGID	FG-1D Corsair (88297)	Patina Ltd/Duxford	
G-FHAS	Scheibe SF.25E Super Falke	Burn Gliding Club Ltd	
G-FIAT	PA-28 Cherokee 140	RAF Benevolent Fund's IAT/ Bristol & Wessex Aeroplane Club (G-BBYW)/Lulsgate	
G-FIBS	AS.350B Ecureuil	Irvine Aviation Ltd/Denham	
G-FIFE	Cessna FA.152	Tayside Aviation Ltd (G-BFYN)/Dundee	
G-FIFI	SOCATA TB.20 Trinidad	OLM Aviation Ltd (G-BMWS)/Denham	
G-FIGA	Cessna 152	Aerohire Ltd/Halfpenny Green	
G-FIGB	Cessna 152	Aerohire Ltd/Halfpenny Green	
G-FIJR	L.188PF Electra	Hunting Cargo Airlines Ltd/E. Midlands	
G-FIJV	L.188CF Electra	Hunting Cargo Airlines Ltd/E. Midlands	
G-FILE	PA-34-200T Seneca	S. D. Cole	
G-FILL	PA-31-310 Navajo	P. V. Naylor-Leyland	
G-FILO	Robin DR.400/180	Baron G. van der Elst	
G-FINA	Cessna F.150L	D. Norris (G-BIFT)	
G-FINS	AB-206B JetRanger 3	P. B. Ellis (G-FSCL)	
G-FISH	Cessna 310R-II	Warner Group	
G-FISK	Pazmany PL-4A	K. S. Woodard	
G-FITZ	Cessna 335	White Knuckle Airways Ltd (G-RIND)	
G-FIZU	L.188C Electra	Hunting Cargo Airlines Ltd/E. Midlands	
G-FIZZ	PA-28-161 Warrior II	Arrow Air Centre Ltd/Shipdham	
G-FJMS	Partenavia P.68B	F. J. M. Sanders (G-SVHA)	
G-FLAG	Colt 77A balloon	B. A. Williams	
G-FLAK	Beech 95-E55 Baron	Pinewood Aviation Ltd	
G-FLAV	PA-28-161 Warrior II	The Crew Flying Group/Tollerton	
G-FLCA	Fleet Model 80 Canuck	E. C. Taylor	
G-FLEN	PA-28-161 Warrior II	Winchfield Enterprises Ltd	
G-FLII	GA-7 Cougar	Plane Talking Ltd (G-GRAC)/Elstree	
G-FLIK	Pitts S-1S Special	R. P. Millinship/Leicester	
G-FLIP	Cessna FA.152	J. R. Nicholls (G-BOES)/Sibson	
G-FLOA	Cameron O-120 balloon	Floating Sensations Ltd	
G-FLOX	Shaw Europa	DPT Group	
G-FLPI	R. Commander 112A	L. Freeman & Son/Newcastle	
G-FLSI	FLS Aerospace Sprint 160	FLS Aerospace (Lovaux) Ltd/Bournemouth	
G-FLTI	Beech F90 King Air	Flightline Ltd/Southend	
G-FLTY	EMB-110P1 Bandeirante	Flightline Ltd (G-ZUSS/G-REGA)/ Southend	
G-FLTZ	Beech 58 Baron	Stesco Ltd (G-PSVS)	
G-FLUF	Lindstrand Bunny SS balloon	Lindstrand Balloons Ltd	
G-FLUG	Gyroflug SC.01B-160 Speed Canard	C. R. Mowle	
G-FLYA	Mooney M.20J	Flya Aviation Ltd	
G-FLYI	PA-34-200 Seneca	BLS Aviation Ltd (G-BHVO)/Elstree	
G-FLYR	AB-206B JetRanger 2	Kwik Fit Euro Ltd (G-BAKT)	
G-FLYT	Shaw Europa	D. W. Adams	
G-FLYU	Robinson R-22B	Clifton Helicopter Hire	
G-FMAM	PA-28-151 Warrior	Essex Radio PLC (G-BBXV)/Southend	
G-FMSG	Cessna FA.150K	G. Owen (G-POTS/G-AYUY)/Gamston	
G-FNLD	Cessna 172N	Papa Hotel Flying Group	
G-FNLY	Cessna F.172M	Plane Talking Ltd (G-WACX/G-BAEX)/ Elstree	
G-FOGG	Cameron N-90 balloon	J. P. E. Money-Kyrle	
G-FOKW	Focke Wulf Fw.190-AS	Wizzard Investments Ltd	
G-FOLD	Light Aero Avid Speedwing	R. H. Green	
G-FOLY	Aerotek Pitts S-2A Modified	A. A. Laing	
G-FOPP	Lancair 320	Airsport (UK) Ltd	
G-FORC	SNCAN Stampe SV-4C	I. A. Marsh/Elstree	
G-FORM	Lindstrand Newspaper SS balloon	International Balloons Ltd	

Notes	Reg.	Type	Owner or Operator
	G-FOTO	PA-E23 Aztec 250F	Aerofilms Ltd (G-BJDH/G-BDXV)
	G-FOWL	Colt 90A balloon	G-FOWL Ballooning Group
	G-FOWS	Cameron N-105 balloon	Fowlers of Bristol Ltd
	G-FOXA	PA-28-161 Cadet	Leicestershire Aero Club Ltd
	G-FOXC	Denney Kitfox Mk 3	L. A. James
	G-FOXD	Denney Kitfox	M. Hanley
	G-FOXE	Denney Kitfox Mk 2	K. M. Pinkard
	G-FOXG	Denney Kitfox Mk 2	Kitfox Group
	G-FOXI	Denney Kitfox	B. Johns
	G-FOXM	Bell 206B JetRanger 2	Tyringham Charter & Group Services (G-STAK/G-BNIS)
	G-FOXS	Denney Kitfox Mk 2	S. P. Watkins & C. C. Rea
	G-FOXX	Denney Kitfox	R. O. F. Harper
	G-FOXZ	Denney Kitfox	M. Smalley & ptnrs
	G-FPCL	GA-7 Cougar	Eurowide Ltd
	G-FRAD	Dassault Falcon 20E	FR Aviation Ltd (G-BCYF)/Bournemouth
	G-FRAE	Dassault Falcon 20E	FR Aviation Ltd/Bournemouth
	G-FRAF	Dassault Falcon 20E	FR Aviation Ltd/Bournemouth
	G-FRAG	PA-32 Cherokee Six 300E	G-FRAG Group
	G-FRAH	Dassault Falcon 20DC	FR Aviation Ltd/Bournemouth
	G-FRAI	Dassault Falcon 20E	FR Aviation Ltd/Bournemouth
	G-FRAJ	Dassault Falcon 20E	FR Aviation Ltd/Bournemouth
	G-FRAK	Dassault Falcon 20DC	FR Aviation Ltd/Bournemouth
	G-FRAL	Dassault Falcon 20DC	FR Aviation Ltd/Bournemouth
	G-FRAM	Dassault Falcon 20DC	FR Aviation Ltd/Bournemouth
	G-FRAN	Piper J-3C-90 Cub(480321)	Essex L-4 Group (G-BIXY)
	G-FRAO	Dassault Falcon 20DC	FR Aviation Ltd/Bournemouth
	G-FRAP	Dassault Falcon 20DC	FR Aviation Ltd/Bournemouth
	G-FRAR	Dassault Falcon 20DC	FR Aviation Ltd/Bournemouth
	G-FRAS	Dassault Falcon 20C	FR Aviation Ltd/Bournemouth
	G-FRAT	Dassault Falcon 20C	FR Aviation Ltd/Bournemouth
	G-FRAU	Dassault Falcon 20C	FR Aviation Ltd/Bournemouth
	G-FRAW	Dassault Falcon 20ECM	FR Aviation Ltd/Bournemouth
	G-FRAX	Cessna 441	FR Aviation Ltd (G-BMTZ)/Bournemouth
	G-FRAY	Cassutt IIIM (modified)	C. I. Fray
	G-FRAZ	Cessna 441	FR Aviation Ltd/Bournemouth
	G-FRBA	Dassault Falcon 20C	FR Finances Ltd/Bournemouth
	G-FRBY	Beech E55 Baron	FR Finances Ltd
	G-FRCE	H.S. Gnat T.1	Butane Buzzard Aviation Ltd/Cranfield
	G-FREE	Pitts S-2A Special	Pegasus Flying Group/Fairoaks
	G-FRGN	PA-28-236 Dakota	Fregon Aviation Ltd
	G-FRJB	Britten Sheriff SA-1 H	Aeropark/E. Midlands
	G-FRST	PA-44-180T Turbo Seminole	WAM (GB) Ltd
	G-FRYI	Beech 200 Super King Air	Pelham Aviation Ltd (G-OAVX/G-IBCA/ G-BMCA)
	G-FSII	Gregory Free Spirit Mk II balloon	M. J. Gregory & R. P. Hallam
	G-FSIX	EE Lightning F.6	Downderry Construction Group Ltd
	G-FSPL	PA-32R Cherokee Lance 300	G. de-W. W. Harries
	G-FTAX	Cessna 421C	CRV Leasing (G-BFFM)
	G-FTFT	Colt Financial Times SS balloon	Financial Times Ltd
	G-FTIL	Robin DR.400/180R	Niederrhein Powered Flying Club
	G-FTIM	Robin DR.400/100	W. C. Cowie
	G-FTIN	Robin DR.400/100	G. D. Clark & M. J. D. Theobold/ Blackpool
	G-FTWO	AS.355F-2 Twin Squirrel	McAlpine Helicopters Ltd (G-OJOR/ G-BMUS)/Hayes
	G-FUEL	Robin DR.400/180	R. Darch/Compton Abbas
	G-FUGA	Fouga CM.170R Magister	Royalair Services Ltd (G-BSCT)
	G-FULL	PA-28R Cherokee Arrow 200-II	Arrow Flight Services Ltd (G-HWAY/G-JULI)/Shoreham
	G-FUND	Thunder Ax7-65Z balloon	Soft Sell Ltd
	G-FUNN	Plumb BGP-1	J. D. Anson
	G-FUSI	Robinson R-22B	F. M. Usher-Smith
	G-FUZY	Cameron N-77 balloon	Allan Industries Ltd
	G-FUZZ	PA-18 Super Cub 95	G. W. Cline
	G-FVBF	Lindstrand LBL-210A balloon	Virgin Balloon Flights Ltd
	G-FWPW	PA-28-236 Dakota	P. A. & F. C. Winters
	G-FWRP	Cessna 421C	Adavia Ltd
	G-FXII	V.S.366 Spitfire F.XII (EN224)	P. R. Arnold
	G-FXIV	V.S.379 Spitfire FR.XIV (MV370)	R. Lamplough
	G-FZZI	Cameron H-34 balloon	Virgin Airship & Balloon Co Ltd
	G-FZZY	Colt 69A balloon	Hot-Air Balloon Co Ltd
	G-FZZZ	Colt 56A balloon	Hot-Air Balloon Co Ltd

Reg.	Type	Owner or Operator	Notes
G-GABD	GA-7 Cougar	Scotia Safari Ltd/Prestwick	
G-GACA	P.57 Sea Prince T.1 ★	P. G. Vallance Ltd/Charlwood	
G-GAII	Hunter GA.11 (XE685)	B. J. Pover	
G-GAJB	AA-5B Tiger	G. A. J. Bowles (G-BHZN)	
G-GALA	PA-28 Cherokee 180E	E. Alexander (G-AYAP)	
G-GAME	Cessna T.303	Twinflite Aviation Ltd	
G-GANE	Sequoia F.8L Falco	S. J. Gane	
G-GANJ	Fournier RF-6B-100	Soaring Equipment Ltd/Coventry	
G-GASC	Hughes 369HS	Crewhall Ltd (G-WELD/G-FROG)	
G-GASP	PA-28-181 Archer II	G-GASP Flying Group	
G-GASS	Thunder Ax7-77 balloon	Servowarm Balloon Syndicate	
G-GAUL	Cessna 550 Citation II	Chauffair Ltd	
G-GAWA	Cessna 140	R. A. Page (G-BRSM)/Coventry	
G-GAZA	SA.341G Gazelle 1	Stratton Motor Co (Norfolk) Ltd (G-RALE/G-SFTG)	
G-GAZI	SA.341G Gazelle 1	Stratton Motor Co (Norfolk) Ltd & UCC International Group Ltd (G-BKLU)	
G-GAZZ	SA.341G Gazelle 1	Stratton Motor Co (Norfolk) Ltd & UCC International Group Ltd	
G-GBAO	Robin R.1180TD	J. Kay-Movat	
G-GBHH	Hughes 269C	Helisport Ltd/Biggin Hill	
G-GBLP	Cessna F.172M	Edinburgh Air Centre Ltd (G-GWEN)	
G-GBLR	Cessna F.150L	Blue Max Flying Group	
G-GBSL	Beech 76 Duchess	M. H. Cundsy (G-BGVG)	
G-GBTA	Boeing 737-436	British Airways (G-BVHA) County of Middlesex	
G-GBTB	Boeing 737-436	British Airways (G-BVHB)	
G-GBUE	Robin DR.400/120A	G-GBUE Group (G-BPXD)	
G-GCAA	PA-28R Cherokee Arrow 200	Southern Air Ltd/Shoreham	
G-GCAB	PA-30 Twin Comanche 180	Southern Air Ltd/Shoreham	
G-GCAT	PA-28 Cherokee 140B	H. Skelton (G-BFRH)	
G-GCCL	Beech 76 Duchess	A. J. & S. B. Duckworth	
G-GCJL	BAe Jetstream 4100	Jetstream Aircraft Ltd/Prestwick	
G-GCKI	Mooney M.20K	A. L. Burton & A. J. Daly	
G-GCNZ	Cessna 150M	Firecrest Aviation Ltd/Elstree	
G-GDAM	PA-18 Super Cub 135	A. D. Martin	
G-GDAY	Robinson R-22B	C. J. H. & P. A. J. Richardson	
G-GDEZ	BAe 125-1000B	Frewton Ltd	
G-GDOG	PA-28R Cherokee Arrow 200-II	S. J. Rogers (G-BDXW)/Blackbushe	
G-GEAR	Cessna FR.182Q	Deeperton Ltd	
G-GEEE	Hughes 369HS	B. P. Stein (G-BDOY)	
G-GEEP	Robin R.1180T	Organic Concentrates Ltd/Booker	
G-GEES	Cameron N-77 balloon	N. A. Carr	
G-GEEZ	Cameron N-77 balloon	Charnwood Forest Turf Accountants Ltd	
G-GEMS	Thunder Ax8-90 S2 balloon	Alexander The Jewellers Ltd (G-BUNP)	
G-GENN	GA-7 Cougar	Chalrey Ltd (G-BNAB/G-BGYP)	
G-GEOF	Pereira Osprey 2	G. Crossley	
G-GEUP	Cameron N-77 balloon	D. P. & B. O. Turner	
G-GFAB	Cameron N-105 balloon	The Andrew Brownsword Collection Ltd	
G-GFCA	PA-28-161 Cadet	A. M. Norman & A. N. Cox	
G-GFCB	PA-28-161 Cadet	Applied Marketing & Technology Ltd	
G-GFCC	PA-28-161 Cadet	C. P. Scamp/Staverton	
G-GFCD	PA-34-220T Seneca III	Stonehurst Aviation Ltd (G-KIDS)	
G-GFCF	PA-28-161 Cadet	Aerohire Ltd (G-RHBH)	
G-GFKY	Zenair CH.250	K. Jarman & KM Services Ltd	
G-GFLY	Cessna F.150L	W. Lancs Aero Club Ltd/Woodvale	
G-GFRY	Bell 206L-3 LongRanger	Turbine Helicopters Ltd	
G-GGGG	Thunder Ax7-77A balloon	T. A. Gilmour	
G-GGLE	PA-22 Colt 108 (tailwheel)	J. R. Colthurst	
G-GGOW	Colt 77A balloon	City of Glasgow District Council	
G-GHCL	Bell 206B JetRanger 2	Grampian Helicopter Charter Ltd (G-SHVV)	
G-GHIA	Cameron N-120 balloon	J. R. & S. M. Christopher	
G-GHIN	Thunder Ax7-77 balloon	N. T. Parry	
G-GHRW	PA-28RT-201 Arrow IV	Leavesden Flight Centre Ltd (G-ONAB/ G-BHAK)	
G-GHSI	PA-44-180T Turbo Seminole	M. G. Roberts	
G-GHZM	Robinson R-22B	Grampian Helicopter Charter Ltd (G-FENI)	
G-GIGI	M.S.893A Rallye Commodore	D. J. Moore (G-AYVX)	
G-GIRO	Schweizer 269C	D. E. McDowell	
G-GJCD	Robinson R-22B	J. C. Lane	
G-GJET	Learjet 35A	Gama Aviation Ltd (G-CJET/G-SEBE/ G-ZIPS/G-ZONE)	

Notes	Reg.	Type	Owner or Operator
	G-GJKK	Mooney M.20K	Davey & Shaw
	G-GLAD	G.37 Gladiator II	Patina Ltd/Duxford
	G-GLAM	BAe Jetstream 3102-09	British Regional Airlines/BA Express (G-OEDG/G-IBLX)
	G-GLAW	Cameron N-90 balloon	George Law Ltd
	G-GLBL	Lindstrand AM-32000 balloon	Lindstrand Balloons Ltd
	G-GLED	Cessna 150M	Firecrest Aviation Ltd/Booker
	G-GLUE	Cameron N-65 balloon	L. J. M. Muir & G. D. Hallett
	G-GLUG	PA-31-350 Navajo Chieftain	Champagne-Air Ltd (G-BLOE/ G-NITE)/Newcastle
	G-GMAX	SNCAN Stampe SV-4C	Glidegold Ltd (G-BXNW)
	G-GMPA	AS.355F-2 Twin Squirrel	Greater Manchester Police Authority (G-BPOI)
	G-GMSI	SOCATA TB.9 Tampico	D. Ormrod
	G-GNAT	H.S. Gnat T.1 (XS101)	Ruanil Investments Ltd/Cranfield
	G-GNSY	HPR-7 Herald 209	Channel Express (Air Services) Ltd (G-BFRK)/Bournemouth
	G-GNTA	SAAB SF.340A	Business Air Ltd
	G-GNTB	SAAB SF.340A	Business Air Ltd/British Midland
	G-GNTC	SAAB SF.340A	Business Air Ltd/British Midland
	G-GNTD	SAAB SF.340A	Business Air Ltd
	G-GNTE	SAAB SF.340A	Business Air Ltd
	G-GNTF	SAAB SF.340A	Business Air Ltd/British Midland
	G-GNTG	SAAB SF.340A	Business Air Ltd
	G-GNTH	SAAB SF.340B	Business Air Ltd
	G-GNTI	SAAB SF.340B	Business Air Ltd
	G-GNTJ	SAAB SF.340B	Business Air Ltd
	G-GNTZ	BAe 146-200	Business Air Ltd/Frankfurt
	G-GOAL	Lindstrand LBL-105A balloon	Virgin Airship & Balloon Co Ltd
	G-GOBT	Colt 77A balloon	British Telecom PLC
	G-GOCC	AA-5A Cheetah	Lowlog Ltd (G-BPIX)/Elstree
	G-GOCX	Cameron N-90 balloon	Cathay Pacific Airways Ltd
	G-GOGW	Cameron N-90 balloon	Great Western Trains Ltd
	G-GOKT	Douglas DC-10-30	Caledonian Airways Ltd/Gatwick
	G-GOLD	Thunder Ax6-56A balloon	Joseph Terry & Sons Ltd
	G-GOLF	SOCATA TB.10 Tobago	E. H. Scamell & ptnrs
	G-GONE	D.H.112 Venom FB.50	J. E. Davies
	G-GOOD	SOCATA TB-20 Trinidad	Skyforce Charters Ltd
	G-GORE	CFM Streak Shadow	D. N. & E. M. Gore
	G-GOSS	Jodel DR.221	Avon Flying Group
	G-GOZO	Cessna R.182	Transmatic Fyllan Ltd (G-BJZO)/ Cranfield
	G-GPMW	PA-28RT-201T Turbo Arrow IV	M. Worrall & ptnrs
	G-GPST	Phillips ST.1 Speedtwin	P. J. C. Phillips
	G-GRAM	PA-31-350 Navajo Chieftain	BAC Leasing Ltd (G-BRHF)
	G-GRAY	Cessna 172N	Truman Aviation Ltd/Tollerton
	G-GREG	Jodel DR.220 2+2	J. T. Wilson
	G-GREN	Cessna T.310R	D. Hughes
	G-GRID	AS.355F-1 Twin Squirrel	National Grid Co PLC
	G-GRIF	R. Commander 112TCA	M. J. Chilton (G-BHXC)
	G-GROW	Cameron N-77 balloon	Derbyshire Building Society
	G-GSFC	Robinson R-22B	Weller Helicopters Ltd/Redhill
	G-GTAX	PA-31-350 Navajo Chieftain	Hadagain Investments Ltd (G-OIAS)
	G-GTHM	PA-38-112 Tomahawk	Truman Aviation Ltd/Tollerton
	G-GTPL	Mooney M.20K	W. R. Emberton/Spain
	G-GUCK	Beech C23 Sundowner 180	G-GUCK Group (G-BPYG)
	G-GULF	Lindstrand LBL-105A balloon	Virgin Balloon Flights Ltd
	G-GULL	Petrel Amphibian	Amphibians UK Ltd
	G-GUNN	Cessna F.172H	J. G. Gunn (G-AWGC)
	G-GUNS	Cameron V-77 balloon	Royal School of Artillery Hot Air Balloon Club
	G-GURL	Cameron A-210 balloon	British School of Ballooning
	G-GUSS	PA-28-151 Warrior	A. M. R. Dudley (G-BJRY)
	G-GUST	AB-206B JetRanger	Arena Aviation Ltd (G-CBHH/G-AYBE)
	G-GUYS	PA-34-200T Seneca	G. B. Faulkner (G-BMWT)
	G-GVBF	Lindstrand LBL-180A balloon	Virgin Balloon Flights Ltd
	G-GWIZ	Colt Clown SS balloon	Oxford Promotions (UK) Ltd
	G-GWYN	Cessna F.172M	Gwyn Aviation
	G-GYAV	Cessna 172N	Southport & Merseyside Aero Club (1979) Ltd/Liverpool
	G-GYMM	PA-28R Cherokee Arrow 200	GYMM Group (G-AYWW)
	G-GYRO	Campbell Cricket	J. W. Pavitt
	G-GZDO	Cessna 172N	Cambridge Hall Aviation

Reg.	Type	Owner or Operator	Notes
G-HADA	Enstrom 480	W. B. Steele	
G-HAEC	CAC-18 Mustang 23 (A68-192)	Classic Aviation Ltd/Duxford	
G-HAHA	PA-18 Super Cub 150	D. J. Hockings (G-BSWE)	
G-HAIG	Rutan LongEz	R. Carey & D. W. Parfrey	
G-HAJJ	Glaser-Dirks DG.400	P. W. Endean	
G-HALC	PA-28R Cherokee Arrow 200	Halcyon Aviation Ltd	
G-HALJ	Cessna 140	H. A. Lloyd-Jennings	
G-HALL	PA-22 Tri-Pacer 160	F. P. Hall (G-ARAH)	
G-HALO	Elisport CH-7 Angel	Taylor Woodhouse Ltd	
G-HALP	SOCATA TB.10 Tobago	D. H. Halpern (G-BITD)/Elstree	
G-HAMA	Beech 200 Super King Air	Gama Aviation Ltd/Fairoaks	
G-HAMI	Fuji FA.200-180	S. A. R. Rose & K. G. Cameron (G-OISF/G-BAPT)	
G-HAMP	Bellanca 7ACA Champ	K. MacDonald	
G-HAND	Cameron 105 Startac SS balloon	Redmalt Ltd	
G-HANS	Robin DR.400 2+2	Headcorn Flying School Ltd	
G-HAPR	B.171 Sycamore HR.14 (XG547) ★	IHM/Weston-s-Mare	
G-HAPY	D.H.C.1 Chipmunk 22A	G-HAPY Ltd	
G-HARD	AS.355F-2 Twin Squirrel	Air Harrods Ltd (G-DAFT/G-BNNN)	
G-HARE	Cameron N-77 balloon	C. E. & J. Falkingham	
G-HARF	G.1159C Gulfstream 4	Fayair (Jersey) 1984 Ltd	
G-HARH	Sikorsky S-76B	Fayair (Jersey) 1984 Ltd	
G-HART	Cessna 152	Atlantic Air Transport Ltd/Coventry	
G-HARY	Alon A-2 Aircoupe	I. Wilson (G-ATWP)/Newcastle	
G-HATZ	Hatz CB-1	J. Pearson	
G-HAUL	Westland WG.30 Srs 300 ★	IHM/Weston-super-Mare	
G-HAYN	Enstrom 280C-UK	Southern Air Ltd (G-BPOX)/Shoreham	
G-HAZE	Thunder Ax8-90 balloon	T. G. Church	
G-HBBC	D.H.104 Dove 8	BBC Air Ltd (G-ALFM)	
G-HBMW	Robinson R-22	Howarth Helicopter Services Ltd (G-BOFA)	
G-HBUG	Cameron N-90 balloon	R. T. & H. Revel (G-BRCN)	
G-HCSL	PA-34-220T Seneca III	Hollowbrook Properties Ltd	
G-HCTL	PA-31-350 Navajo Chieftain	Field Aircraft Services (Heathrow) Ltd (G-BGOY)	
G-HDEW	PA-32R-301 Saratoga SP	Lord Howard de Walden (G-BRGZ)	
G-HDOG	Colt Flying Hot Dog SS balloon	Longbreak Ltd	
G-HEAD	Colt 56 Flying Head SS balloon	Lindstrand Balloons Ltd	
G-HELE	Bell 206B JetRanger 3	B. E. E. Smith (G-OJFR)	
G-HELN	PA-18 Super Cub 95	J. J. Anziani (G-BKDG)/Booker	
G-HELP	Colt 17A balloon	Virgin Airship & Balloon Co Ltd	
G-HELV	D.H.115 Vampire T.55 (U-1215)	Hunter Wing Ltd/Bournemouth	
G-HEMS	SA.365N Dauphin 2	Express Newspapers PLC/Denham	
G-HENS	Cameron N-65 balloon	Harrells Dairies Ltd	
G-HENY	Cameron V-77 balloon	R. S. D'Alton	
G-HERA	Robinson R-22B	T. Pexton	
G-HERB	PA-28R-201 Arrow III	J. E. Shepherd	
G-HERO	PA-32RT-300 Lance II	Air Alize Communication (G-BOGN)/ Stapleford	
G-HERS	Jodel D.18	A. Usherwood	
G-HEWI	Piper J-3C-90 Cub	Denham Grasshopper Group (G-BLEN)	
G-HEWS	Hughes 369D ★	Spares' use/Sywell	
G-HEYY	Cameron 77 Bear SS balloon	Hot-Air Balloon Co Ltd George	
G-HFBM	Curtiss Robin C-2	D. M. Forshaw	
G-HFCA	Cessna A.150L	Horizon Flying Club Ltd/Ipswich	
G-HFCB	Cessna F.150L	Horizon Flying Club Ltd (G-AZVR)/Ipswich	
G-HFCI	Cessna F.150L	Horizon Flying Club Ltd/Ipswich	
G-HFCL	Cessna F.152	Horizon Flying Club Ltd (G-BGLR)/Ipswich	
G-HFCT	Cessna F.152	Stapleford Flying Club Ltd	
G-HFIX	V.S.361 Spitfire HF.IXe (MJ730)	D. W. Pennell (G-BLAS)	
G-HFLA	Schweizer 269C	Sterling Helicopters Ltd/Norwich	
G-HFTG	PA-23 Aztec 250E	Hawkair (G-BSOB/G-BCJR)	
G-HGAS	Cameron N-77 balloon	Handygas Ltd	
G-HGPI	SOCATA TB.20 Trinidad	M. J. Jackson/Bournemouth	
G-HHUN	Hunter F.4 (XE677)	Hunter Wing Ltd/Bournemouth	
G-HIAH	Mini-500	H. I. A. Hopkinson	
G-HIBM	Cameron N-145 balloon	IBM UK Ltd	
G-HIEL	Robinson R-22B	Hields Aviation	
G-HIHI	PA-32R-301 Saratoga SP	Longslow Dairy Ltd	
G-HIII	Extra EA.300	Firebird Aerobatics Ltd/Booker	
G-HILS	Cessna F.172H	Lowdon Aviation Group (G-AWCH)	
G-HILT	SOCATA TB.10 Tobago	B. A. Groves	

Notes	Reg.	Type	Owner or Operator
	G-HINT	Cameron N-90 balloon	Hinton Garage Bath Ltd
	G-HIPE	Sorrell SNS-7 Hiperbipe	T. A. S. Rayner/Glenrothes
	G-HIPO	Robinson R-22B	J. Clark (G-BTGB)
	G-HIRE	GA-7 Cougar	London Aerial Tours Ltd (G-BGSZ)/ Biggin Hill
	G-HISS	Aerotek Pitts S-2A Special	L. V. Adams & J. Maffia (G-BLVU)/ Panshanger
	G-HIVA	Cessna 337A	High Voltage Applications Ltd (G-BAES)
	G-HIVE	Cessna F.150M	M. P. Lynn (G-BCXT)/Sibson
	G-HJCB	BAe 125-1000B	J. C. Bamford Excavators Ltd (G-BUUY)
	G-HJSS	AIA Stampe SV-4C (modified)	H. J. Smith (G-AZNF)
	G-HLCF	Starstreak Shadow	S. M. E. Solomon
	G-HLEN	AS.350B Ecureuil	N. Edmonds (G-LOLY)
	G-HLFT	SC.5 Belfast 2	HeavyLift Cargo Airlines Ltd/Stansted
	G-HLIX	Cameron 80 Oil Can SS balloon	Hot-Air Balloon Co Ltd
	G-HMES	PA-28-161 Warrior II	Cleveland Flying School Ltd/Teesside
	G-HMJB	PA-34-220T Seneca III	Overview Europe Ltd
	G-HMPH	Bell 206B JetRanger 2	Mightycraft Ltd (G-BBUY)
	G-HMPT	AB-206B JetRanger 2	Kensington Aviation Ltd
	G-HNRY	Cessna 650 Citation VI	Quantel Ltd/Biggin Hill
	G-HNTR	Hunter T.7 (XL572) ★	Hunter Wing Ltd/Bournemouth
	G-HOBO	Denney Kitfox Mk 4	W. M. Hodgkins & C. A. Boswell
	G-HOCK	PA-28 Cherokee 180	Arabact Ltd (G-AVSH)
	G-HOFC	Shaw Europa	J. W. Lang
	G-HOFM	Cameron N-56 balloon	Hot-Air Balloon Co Ltd
	G-HOHO	Colt Santa Claus SS balloon	Oxford Promotions (UK) Ltd
	G-HOLY	ST.10 Diplomate	M. K. Barsham
	G-HOME	Colt 77A balloon	Anglia Balloon School Tardis
	G-HONG	Slingsby T.67M-200	Hunting Aviation Ltd
	G-HONK	Cameron O-105 balloon	T. F. W. Dixon & Son Ltd
	G-HOOP	PA-46-350P Malibu Mirage	D. O. Hooper/Italy
	G-HOOV	Cameron N-56 balloon	H. R. Evans
	G-HOPE	Beech F33A Bonanza	Hurn Aviation Ltd
	G-HOPI	Cameron N-42 balloon	Ballonwerbung Hamburg GmbH/Germany
	G-HOPS	Thunder Ax8-90 balloon	A. C. & B. Munn
	G-HOPY	Vans RV-6A	R. C. Hopkinson
	G-HORN	Cameron V-77 balloon	S. Herd
	G-HOST	Cameron N-77 balloon	D. Grimshaw
	G-HOTI	Colt 77A balloon	R. Ollier
	G-HOTT	Cameron O-120 balloon	D. L. Smith
	G-HOTZ	Colt 77B balloon	C. J. & S. M. Davies
	G-HOUS	Colt 31A balloon	Anglia Balloons Ltd
	G-HOWE	Thunder Ax7-77 balloon	M. F. Howe
	G-HPAA	BN-2B-26 Islander	Hampshire Police Authority (Air Support Unit) (G-BSWP)
	G-HRAY	AB-206B JetRanger 3	Hecray Co Ltd (G-VANG/G-BIZA)
	G-HRHI	B.206 Srs 1 Basset (XS770)	Haroldon Ltd
	G-HRIO	Robin HR.100/120	D. Peters
	G-HRIS	Cessna P210N	Birmingham Aerocentre Ltd
	G-HRLK	SAAB 91D/2 Safir	Sylmar Aviation & Services Ltd (G-BRZY)
	G-HRLM	Brügger MB.2 Colibri	S. J. Perkins & D. Dobson
	G-HROI	R. Commander 112A	Intereuropean Aviation Ltd
	G-HRON	D.H.114 Heron 2 (XR442)	M. E. R. Coghlan (G-AORH)
	G-HRVD	CCF Harvard IV	M. Slater (G-BSBC)
	G-HRZN	Colt 77A balloon	A. J. Spindler
	G-HSAA	Hughes 369HS	Heliwork Services Ltd/Thruxton
	G-HSDW	Bell 206B JetRanger	Winfield Shoe Co Ltd
	G-HSHS	Colt 105A balloon	H. & S. Aviation Ltd
	G-HSOO	Hughes 369HE	Edwards Aviation (G-BFYJ)
	G-HTAX	PA-31-350 Navajo Chieftain	Hadagain Inve\stments Ltd
	G-HTPS	SA. 341G Gazelle 1	J. Malcolm (G-BRNI)
	G-HTVI	Cameron N-90 balloon	HTV Group PLC (G-PRIT)
	G-HUBB	Partenavia P.68B	G-HUBB Ltd
	G-HUCH	Cameron 80 Carrots SS balloon	L. V. Mastis (G-BYPS)
	G-HUEY	Bell UH-1H	Butane Buzzard Aviation Corporation Ltd
	G-HUFF	Cessna 182P	A. E. G. Cousins
	G-HUGG	Learjet 35A	1427 Ltd
	G-HUGO	Colt 240A balloon	P. G. Hall
	G-HULL	Cessna F.150M	A. D. McLeod
	G-HUMF	Robinson R-22B	Plane Talking Ltd/Elstree
	G-HUNI	Bellanca 7GCBC Scout	T. I. M. Paul
	G-HURI	CCF Hawker Hurricane XIIA (Z7381)	Patina Ltd/Duxford

Reg.	Type	Owner or Operator	Notes
G-HURN	Robinson R-22B	Coventry Helicopter Centre Ltd	
G-HURR	Hawker Hurricane XIIB (BE417)	–	
G-HURY	Hawker Hurricane IV (KZ321)	Patina Ltd/Duxford	
G-HUTT	Denney Kitfox Mk 2	D. Watt	
G-HVBF	Lindstrand LBL-210A balloon	Virgin Balloon Flights Ltd	
G-HVDM	V.S.361 Spitfire F.IX (MK732)	Nostalgic Flying/Netherlands	
G-HVIP	Hunter T.68	Golden Europe Jet De Luxe Club Ltd/Bournemouth	
G-HVRD	PA-31-350 Navajo Chieftain	London Flight Centre (Stansted) Ltd (G-BEZU)	
G-HVRS	Robinson R-22B	Yorkshire Helicopters/Leeds	
G-HWKR	Colt 90A balloon	P. A. Henderson	
G-HYLT	PA-32R-301 Saratoga SP	Pump & Plant Services	
G-IABC	Tri-R Kis	A. & B. Caple/Biggin Hill	
G-IAFT	Cessna 152 II	Marnham Investments Ltd	
G-IAMP	Cameron H-34 balloon	Virgin Airship & Balloon Co Ltd	
G-IBBS	Shaw Europa	R. H. Gibbs	
G-IBED	Robinson R-22A	P. D. Spinks (G-BMHN)	
G-IBET	Cameron 70 Can SS balloon	M. R. Humphrey & J. R. Clifton	
G-IBFW	PA-28R-201 Arrow III	J. B. Roberts	
G-IBRO	Cessna F.152 II	E. Midlands Aircraft Hire Ltd	
G-ICAB	Robinson R-44 Astro	J. R. Clark Ltd	
G-ICCL	Robinson R-22B	Thorneygrove Ltd (G-ORZZ)	
G-ICES	Thunder Ax6-56 balloon	British Balloon Museum & Library Ltd	
G-ICEY	Lindstrand LBL-77A balloon	Iceland Frozen Foods PLC	
G-ICFR	BAe 125 Srs 800A	Chauffair (CI) Ltd (G-BUCR)/ Farnborough	
G-ICKY	Lindstrand LBL-77A balloon	M. J.. Green	
G-ICOM	Cessna F.172M	T. J. & P. S. Nicholson (G-BFXI)	
G-ICSG	AS.355F-1 Twin Squirrel	Industrial Control Services PLC (G-PAMI/G-BUSA)	
G-IDAY	Skyfox CA-25N Gazelle	The Anglo-Pacific Aircraft Co & G. Horne	
G-IDDI	Cameron N-77 balloon	Allen & Harris Ltd	
G-IDDY	D.H.C.1 Super Chipmunk	P. G. Kavanagh & D. T. Kaberry (G-BBMS)	
G-IDEA	AA-5A Cheetah	Lowlog Ltd (G-BGNO)	
G-IDUP	Enstrom 280C Shark	Antique Buildings Ltd (G-BRZF)	
G-IDWR	Hughes 369HS	Copley Electrical Contractors (G-AXEJ)	
G-IEJH	Jodel 150A	E. J. Horsfall (G-BPAM)/Blackpool	
G-IEYE	Robin DR. 400/180	J. S. Haslam	
G-IFIT	PA-31-350 Navajo Chieftain	Dart Group PLC (G-NABI/ G-MARG)/Bournemouth	
G-IFLI	AA-5A Cheetah	ABC Aviation Ltd	
G-IFLP	PA-34-200T Seneca II	Golf-Sala Ltd/Coventry	
G-IFOX	Robinson R-22B	Brillant PR/Booker	
G-IFTB	Beech 200C Super King Air	Albion Aviation Management Ltd	
G-IFTC	H.S.125 Srs F3B/RA	Albion Aviation Management Ltd (G-OPOL/G-BXPU/G-IBIS/G-AXPU)	
G-IFTE	H.S.125 Srs 700B	Albion Aviation Management Ltd (G-BFVI)	
G-IGEL	Cameron N-90 balloon	Computacenter Ltd	
G-IGLA	Colt 240A balloon	Heart of England Balloons	
G-IGLE	Cameron V-90 balloon	A. A. Laing	
G-IHSA	Robinson R-22B	R. J. Everett	
G-IHSB	Robinson R-22B	Advanced Business Solutions Ltd	
G-IIAC	Aeronca 11AC Chief	J. N. W. Moss & ptnrs (G-BTPY)	
G-IIAN	Aero Designs Pulsar	I. G. Harrison	
G-IIIG	Boeing Stearman A.75N1	Aerosuperbatics Ltd (G-BSDR)/Rendcomb	
G-IIII	Aerotek Pitts S-2B Special	B. K. Lecomber	
G-IIIR	Pitts S-1 Special	R. O. Rogers	
G-IIIT	Aerotek Pitts S-2A Special	Aerobatic Displays Ltd	
G-IIIX	Pitts S-1S Special	L. C. Seeger (G-LBAT/G-UCCI/G-BIYN)	
G-IIPM	AS.350B Ecureuil	CSR Ltd (G-GWIL)	
G-IIRB	Bell 206B JetRanger 3	Robard Consultants Ltd	
G-IIRG	Stoddard-Hamilton Glasair IIRGS	D. S. Watson	
G-IITI	Extra EA.300	Aerobatic Displays Ltd/Booker	
G-IIXX	Parsons 2-seat gyroplane	J. K. Padden	
G-IIZI	Pitts S-1D Special	11-21 Flying Group/Sandown	
G-IJAC	Light Aero Avid Speedwing Mk 4	I. J. A. Charlton	
G-IJCB	Sikorsky S-76C (modified)	Air Hanson Aircraft Sales Ltd	
G-IJJB	Beech B200 Super King Air	JJB Sports Ltd (G-BMVY)	
G-IJOE	PA-28RT-201T Turbo Arrow IV	R. P. Wilson	
G-IJRC	Robinson R-22B	J. R. Clark Ltd (G-BTJP)	

Notes	Reg.	Type	Owner or Operator
	G-IJYS	BAe Jetstream 3102	Jackie Stewart (G-BTZT)
	G-IKBP	PA-28-161 Warrior II	Hendafern Ltd/Shoreham
	G-IKIS	Cessna 210M	A. C. Davison
	G-IKPS	PA-31-325 Navajo C	Channel Aviation Ltd
	G-ILEE	Colt 56A balloon	Lindsay Marketing Associates
	G-ILES	Cameron O-90 balloon	G. N. Lantos
	G-ILLE	Boeing Stearman A.75L3 (379)	J. Griffin
	G-ILLY	PA-28-181 Archer II	A. G. & K. M. Spiers
	G-ILSE	Corby CJ-1 Starlet	S. Stride
	G-ILTS	PA-32 Cherokee Six 300	P. G. Teasdale (G-CVOK)
	G-ILYS	Robinson R-22B	BJ Aviation/Welshpool
	G-IMAG	Colt 77A balloon	Flying Pictures (Balloons) Ltd
	G-IMAN	Colt 31A balloon	Benedikt Haggeney GmbH
	G-IMBY	Pietenpol Air Camper	P. F. Bockh
	G-IMLI	Cessna 310Q	P. D. Carne (G-AZYK)
	G-IMPW	PA-32R-301 Saratoga SP	C. M. Juggins
	G-IMPX	R. Commander 112B	T. L. & S. Hull
	G-IMPY	Light Aero Avid Flyer C	T. R. C. Griffin
	G-INAV	Aviation Composites Mercury	Europa Aviation Ltd
	G-INCA	Glaser-Dirks DG.400	H. W. Ober
	G-INCH	Montgomerie-Bensen B.8MR	I. H. C. Branson (G-BRES)
	G-INDC	Cessna T.303	Howarth Timber (Aircharters) Ltd
	G-INDE	PA-44-180 Seminole	Le Patron Holdings Ltd (G-BHNM)
	G-INDY	Robinson R-44 Astro	Reynard Racing Cars Ltd
	G-INGA	Thunder Ax8-84 balloon	M. L. J. Ritchie
	G-INGB	Robinson R-22B	Ashton Helicopters Ltd
	G-INGR	Cessna F.150J	K. J. C. Bradmar Communications Ltd (G-AWXU)
	G-INNI	Jodel D.112	R. G. Andrews
	G-INNS	Robinson H-44 Astro	Everards Brewery Ltd
	G INNY	SE-5A (replica) (F5459)	K. S. Matcham
	G-INOW	Monnett Moni	T. W. Clark
	G-INTC	Robinson R-22B	J. C. Lane
	G-INTL	Short SD3-60 Variant 100	Interline Ltd
	G-INVU	AB-206B JetRanger 2	Burman Aviation Ltd (G-XXII/G-GGCC/ G-BEHG)
	G-IOCO	Beech 58 Baron	Sea & Air Charter Ltd
	G-IOCS	Short SD3-30 Variant 100	Air Tabernacle Ltd (G-BIFH)
	G-IOIO	Bell 206B JetRanger 3	Lynton Air Ltd/Denham
	G-IOOI	Robin DR.400/160	N. B. Mason & S. J. O'Rourke
	G-IOSI	Jodel DR.1051	A. Burbidge & R. Slater
	G-IPSI	Grob G.109B	G-IPSI Ltd (G-BMLO)
	G-IPSY	Rutan Vari-Eze	R. A. Fairclough/Biggin Hill
	G-IPUP	B.121 Pup 2	M. Sowerby/Elstree
	G-IRAF	RAF 2000 GTX-SE gyroplane	C. D. Julian
	G-IRIS	AA-5B Tiger	Carlisle Flight Centre (G-BIXU)
	G-IRLS	Cessna FR.172J	J. A. & G. M. Rees
	G-IRLY	Colt 90A balloon	S. A. Burnett & L. P. Purfield
	G-IRPC	Cessna 182Q	R. P. Carminke (G-BSKM)
	G-ISCA	PA-28RT-201 Arrow IV	D. J. & P. Pay
	G-ISDB	PA-28-161 Warrior II	Action Air Services Ltd (G-BWET)
	G-ISDN	Boeing Stearman A.75N1	D. R. L. Jones
	G-ISEE	BAe 146-200	British Aerospace PLC
	G-ISEH	Cessna 182R	HBC Group Ltd (G-BIWS)
	G-ISFC	PA-31-310 Turbo Navajo B	SFC (Air Taxis) Ltd (G-BNEF)/ Stapleford
	G-ISIS	D.H.82A Tiger Moth	D. R. & M. Wood (G-AODR)
	G-ISKY	Bell 206B JetRanger 3	RJS Aviation Ltd (G-PSCI/G-BOKD)
	G-ISLE	Short SD3-60 Variant 100	British Regional Airlines/BA Express (G-BLEG)
	G-ISMO	Robinson R-22B	Sloane Helicopters Ltd/Sywell
	G-ISTT	Thunder Ax8-84 balloon	RAF Halton Hot Air Balloon Club
	G-ITAL	Cameron N-77 balloon	P. Leith-Smith
	G-ITII	Aerotech Pitts S-2A Special	Aerobatic Displays Ltd
	G-ITON	Maule MX-7-235	J. R. S. Heaton
	G-ITTU	PA-23 Aztec 250E	D. Byrne & M. Cummings (G-BCSW)
	G-IVAC	Airtour AH-77B balloon	R. B. Webb
	G-IVAN	Shaw TwinEze	I. Shaw
	G-IVAR	Yakovlev Yak-50	I. G. Anderson
	G-IVEL	Fournier RF-4D	V. S. E. Norman (G-AVNY)/Rendcomb
	G-IVIV	Robinson R-44 Astro	Rahtol Ltd
	G-IVOR	Aeronca 11AC Chief	South Western Aeronca Group/Plymouth
	G-IWON	Cameron V-90 balloon	D. P. P. Jenkinson (G-BTCV)

Reg.	Type	Owner or Operator	Notes
G-IYAK	Yakovlev C-11	E. K. Coventry/Earls Colne	
G-IZEL	SA.341G Gazelle 1	Fairview Securities (Investments) Ltd (G-BBHW)	
G-IZIT	Rans S.6-ESD Coyote II	D. A. Crompton	
G-JACT	Partenavia P.68C	JCT 600 Ltd (G-NVIA)/Leeds	
G-JAKE	D.H.C.1 Chipmunk 22	K. Ritter (G-BBMY)	
G-JAKI	Mooney M.20R	A. D. Russell	
G-JALC	Boeing 757-225	Airtours International Airways Ltd	
G-JAMP	PA-28-151 Warrior	ANP Ltd (G-BRJU)/White Waltham	
G-JANA	PA-28-181 Archer II	Croaker Aviation/Stapleford	
G-JANB	Colt Flying Bottle SS balloon	Justerini & Brooks Ltd	
G-JANI	Robinson R-44 Astro	Heli Air Ltd	
G-JANK	PA-E23 Aztec 250C	Liverpool Flying School Ltd (G-ATCY)	
G-JANN	PA-34-220T Seneca III	TEL (IOM) Ltd	
G-JANS	Cessna FR.172J	I. G. Aizlewood/Luton	
G-JANT	PA-28-181 Archer II	Janair Aviation Ltd	
G-JARA	Robinson R-22B	J. A. R. Allwright	
G-JASE	PA-28-161 Warrior II	Ipswich School of Flying Ltd	
G-JASP	PA-23 Turbo Aztec 250E	Cooper Aerial Surveys Ltd/Sandtoft	
G-JAWZ	Pitts S-1S Special	S. Howes	
G-JAYI	J/1 Autocrat	Bravo Aviation Ltd	
G-JAZZ	AA-5A Cheetah	Jazz Club	
G-JBAC	EMB-110P1 Bandeirante	BAC Leasing (G-BGYV)	
G-JBDB	AB-206B JetRanger	Brad Helicopters Ltd (G-OOPS/G-BNRD)	
G-JBDH	Robin DR.400/180	P. R. Liddle	
G-JBJB	Colt 69A balloon	Justerini & Brooks Ltd	
G-JBPR	Wittman W.10 Tailwind	P. A. Rose & J. P. Broadhurst	
G-JBWI	Robinson R-22B	N. J. Wagstaff Leasing	
G-JCAS	PA-28-181 Archer II	Charlie Alpha Ltd	
G-JCBI	Dassault Falcon 2000	J. C. Bamford Excavators Ltd/E. Midlands	
G-JCFR	Cessna 550 Citation II	Chauffair Ltd (G-JETC)/Gatwick	
G-JCGR	Cessna T.207	Ingenieur Gesellschaft fur Interfaces GmbH	
G-JCJC	Colt Flying Jeans SS balloon	J. C. Balloon Co Ltd	
G-JCUB	PA-18 Super Cub 135	Piper Cub Consortium Ltd/Jersey	
G-JDEE	SOCATA TB.20 Trinidad	Melville Associates Ltd (G-BKLA)	
G-JDEL	Jodel 150	K. F. & R. Richardson (G-JDLI)	
G-JDIX	Mooney M.20B	ADH Ltd (G-ARTB)	
G-JDTI	Cessna 421C	MLP Aviation Ltd/Elstree	
G-JEAD	F.27 Friendship Mk 500	Jersey European Airways Ltd	
G-JEAE	F.27 Friendship Mk 500	Jersey European Airways Ltd	
G-JEAF	F.27 Friendship Mk 500	Jersey European Airways Ltd	
G-JEAG	F.27 Friendship Mk 500	Jersey European Airways Ltd	
G-JEAH	F.27 Friendship Mk 500	Jersey European Airways Ltd	
G-JEAI	F.27 Friendship Mk 500	Jersey European Airways Ltd	
G-JEAJ	BAe 146-200	Jersey European Airways (UK) Ltd (G-OLCA) *Pride of Guernsey*	
G-JEAK	BAe 146-200	Jersey European Airways (UK) Ltd (G-OLCB)	
G-JEAL	BAe 146-300	Jersey European Airways (UK) Ltd (G-BTXN) *Pride of Belfast*	
G-JEAM	BAe 146-300	Jersey European Airways (UK) Ltd (G-BTJT) *Pride of Jersey*	
G-JEAN	Cessna 500 Citation	Foster Associates Ltd	
G-JEAO	BAe 146-100	Jersey European Airways Ltd/ Air France Express (G-UKPC/G-BKXZ)	
G-JEAP	F.27 Friendship Mk 500	Jersey European Airways Ltd/ Channel Express (Air Services) Ltd	
G-JEAR	BAe 146-200	Jersey European Airways (UK) Ltd (G-HWPB/G-BSRU/G-OSKI)	
G-JEAS	BAe 146-200	Jersey European Airways (UK) Ltd (G-OLHB/G-BSRV/G-OSUN)	
G-JEAT	BAe 146-100	Jersey European Airways Ltd/ Air France Express (G-BVUY)	
G-JEAU	BAe 146-100	Jersey European Airways Ltd/ Air France Express (G-BVUW)	
G-JEET	Cessna FA.152	Luton Flight Training (G-BHMF)	
G-JEFF	PA-38-112 Tomahawk	R. J. Alford	
G-JENA	Mooney M.20K	P. Leverkuehn/Biggin Hill	
G-JENI	Cessna R.182	R. A. Bentley	
G-JENN	AA-5B Tiger	Plane Talking Ltd/Elstree	
G-JERS	Robinson R-22B	Ravenheat Manufacturing Ltd	

Notes	Reg.	Type	Owner or Operator
	G-JESS	PA-28R-201T Turbo Arrow III	N. E. & M. A. Bedggood (G-REIS)
	G-JETA	Cessna 550 Citation II	IDS Aircraft Ltd/Heathrow
	G-JETH	Hawker Sea Hawk FGA.6 (XE489) ★	P. G. Vallance Ltd/Charlwood
	G-JETI	BAe 125 Srs 800B	Alkharafi Aviation Ltd
	G-JETJ	Cessna 550 Citation II	Birmingham Aerocentre Ltd (G-EJET/ G-DJBE)
	G-JETM	Gloster Meteor T.7 (VZ638) ★	P. G. Vallance Ltd/Charlwood
	G-JETN	Learjet 35A	Heathrow Jet Charter Ltd (G-JJSG)
	G-JETP	P.84 Jet Provost T.52A (T.4)	Shadow Valley Investments Ltd
	G-JETU	AS.355F-2 Twin Squirrel	Debis Financial Services Ltd
	G-JETX	Bell 206B JetRanger 3	Tripgate Ltd
	G-JFOX	Denney Kitfox Mk 2	J. Fox (G-LANG)
	G-JFWI	Cessna F.172N	Staryear Ltd
	G-JGMN	C.A.S.A. 1.131E Jungmann 2000	P. D. Scandrett/Staverton
	G-JHAS	Schweizer 269C	Barton & Co (Farmers) Ltd
	G-JHEW	Robinson R-22B	Burbage Farms Ltd
	G-JIII	Stolp SA.300 Starduster Too	VTIO Co/Cumbernauld
	G-JILL	R. Commander 112TCA	Westcroft American Motorhomes Ltd
	G-JIMB	B.121 Pup 1	BLS Aviation Ltd (G-AWWF)/Elstree
	G-JIMW	AB-206B JetRanger 2	R. J. Watt (G-UNIK/G-TPPH/G-BCYP)
	G-JJAN	PA-28-181 Archer II	Redhill Flying Club
	G-JLEE	AB-206B JetRanger 3	Lee Aviation Ltd (G-JOKE/G-CSKY/ G-TALY)
	G-JLHS	Beech A36 Bonanza	I. G. Meredith
	G-JLMW	Cameron V-77 balloon	J. L. McK. Watkins
	G-JLRW	Beech 76 Duchess	Moorfield Developments Ltd/Elstree
	G-JLXI	BAe Jetstream 61	Jetstream Aircraft Ltd/Prestwick
	G JMAC	BAe Jetstream 4100	British Aerospace PLC (G-JAMD/G-JXLI)
	G-JMAT	Schweizer 269C	John Matchett Ltd
	G-JMDI	Schweizer 269C	Dunstan Hall Ltd (G-FLAT)
	G-JMTS	Robin DR.400/180	J. R. Whiting
	G-JMTT	PA-28R-201T Turbo Arrow III	C. E. Passmore (G-BMHM)
	G-JNNB	Colt 90A balloon	Justerini & Brooks Ltd
	G-JODL	Jodel DR.1050/M	M. J. Barton
	G-JODY	Bell 206B JetRanger 3	Bellini Aviation (1993) Ltd
	G-JOEY	BN-2A Mk III-2 Trislander	Aurigny Air Services (G-BDGG)/Guernsey
	G-JOIN	Cameron V-65 balloon	Derbyshire Building Society
	G-JOJO	Cameron A-210 balloon	Worcester Balloons
	G-JOLY	Cessna 120	J. D. Tarrant & B. V. Meade
	G-JONB	Robinson R-22B	J. Bignall
	G-JONE	Cessna 172M	A. Pierce
	G-JONH	Robinson R-22B	Scotia Helicopters Ltd
	G-JONI	Cessna FA.152	Barmoor Aviation (G-BFTU)
	G-JONO	Colt 77A balloon	The Sandcliffe Motor Group
	G-JONP	Mini-500	J. Pearson
	G-JONZ	Cessna 172P	Truman Aviation Ltd/Tollerton
	G-JOON	Cessna 182D	J. Maffia
	G-JOYS	Beech 58 Baron	Dunmhor Transport Ltd
	G-JOYT	PA-28-181 Archer II	Plane Talking Ltd (G-BOVO)/Elstree
	G-JOYZ	PA-28-181 Archer III	S. W. & J. E. Taylor
	G-JPAD	Robinson R-44 Astro	Selby Farms Ltd
	G-JPOT	PA-32R-301 Saratoga SP	S. W. Turley (G-BIYM)
	G-JPRO	P.84 Jet Provost T.5A XW433)	Ruddington Aviation Ltd
	G-JPTV	P.84 Jet provost T.5A	B. Johansson
	G-JPVA	P.84 Jet Provost T.5A (XW289)	T. J. Manna (G-BVXT)/Cranfield
	G-JSCL	Rans S.10 Sakota	D. L. Davies
	G-JSON	Cameron N-105 balloon	Up and Away Ballooning Ltd
	G-JSPC	BN-2T Turbine Islander	Rhine Army Parachute Association (G-BUBG)
	G-JSSD	H.P.137 Jetstream 3001★	Museum of Flight/E. Fortune
	G-JTCA	PA-23 Aztec 250E	J. D. Tighe (G-BBCU)/Sturgate
	G-JTWO	Piper J-2 Cub	A. T. Hooper & C. C. Silk (G-BPZR)
	G-JTYE	Aeronca 7AC Champion	G. D. Horn
	G-JUDE	CEA DR.400/180	R. G. Carrell
	G-JUDI	AT-6D Harvard III (FX301)	A. A. Hodgson
	G-JUDY	AA-5A Cheetah	Plane Talking Ltd/Elstree
	G-JUIN	Cessna 303	M. J. Newman/Denham
	G-JULU	Cameron V-90 balloon	Datacentre Ltd
	G-JULZ	Shaw Europa	M. Parkin
	G-JUNG	C.A.S.A. 1.131E Jungmann 1000 (E3B-143)	K. H. Wilson/White Waltham
	G-JURE	SOCATA TB.10 Tobago	P. M. Ireland

Reg.	Type	Owner or Operator	Notes
G-JURG	R. Commander 114A	P. J. Taylor	
G-JVBF	Lindstrand LBL-210A balloon	Virgin Balloon Flights Ltd	
G-JVMD	Cessna 172N	Brandon Aviation (G-BNTV)	
G-JWBB	Jodel DR.1050	D. J. Durell (G-LAKI)	
G-JWBI	AB-206B JetRanger 2	J. W. Bonser (Walsall) Ltd (G-RODS/ G-NOEL/G-BCWN)	
G-JWDG	AA-5A Cheetah	Plane Talking Ltd (G-OCML/G-JAVA)	
G-JWDS	Cessna F.150G	C. R. & S. A. Hardiman (G-AVNB)	
G-JWFT	Robinson R-22B	Tukair Aircraft Charter	
G-JWIV	Jodel DR.1051	C. M. Fitton	
G-KAFE	Cameron N-65 balloon	M. Sarti	
G-KAIR	PA-28-181 Archer II	Academy Lithoplates Ltd	
G-KAMM	Hawker Hurricane XIIA	M. Hammond	
G-KARA	Brugger MB.2 Colibri	C. L. Hill	
G-KARI	Fuji FA.200-160	I. Mansfield & F. M. Fiore (G-BBRE)	
G-KART	PA-28-161 Warrior II	Newcastle-upon-Tyne Aero Club Ltd	
G-KARY	Fuji FA.200-180AO	C. J. Zetter (G-BEYP)	
G-KATA	HOAC Katana DV.20	Aeromarine Ltd	
G-KATE	Westland WG.30 Srs 100	*(stored)*/Penzance	
G-KATI	Rans S.7 Courier	S. M. & K. E. Hall	
G-KATS	PA-28 Cherokee 140	P. S. Scott (G-BIRC)	
G-KATT	Cessna 152 II	Aerohire Ltd (G-BMTK)/Halfpenny Green	
G-KAUR	Colt 315A balloon	R. S. Hunjan	
G-KAWA	Denney Kitfox Mk 2	T. W. Maton	
G-KAXF	Hunter F.6A	T. J. Manna	
G-KAXL	Westland Scout AH.1	T. J. Manna	
G-KBKB	Thunder Ax8-90 S2 balloon	G. Boulden	
G-KBPI	PA-28-161 Warrior II	Goodwood Aerodrome & Motor Circuit Ltd (G-BFSZ)	
G-KCIG	Sportavia RF-5B	Exeter Sperber Syndicate	
G-KDET	PA-28-161 Cadet	Rapidspin Ltd/Biggin Hill	
G-KDFF	Scheibe SF.25E Super Falke	K. & S. C. A. Dudley	
G-KDIX	Jodel D.9 Bebe	D. J. Wells	
G-KDLN	Zlin Z.37A-2 Cmelak	J. Richardsz	
G-KEAB	Beech 65-B80 Queen Air ★	*Instructional airframe* (G-BSSL/ G-BFEP)/Shoreham	
G-KEAC	Beech 65-A80 Queen Air	G-KEAC Flying Group (G-REXY/G-AVNG)/ Elstree	
G-KEEN	Stolp SA.300 Starduster Too	Holland Aerobatics Ltd	
G-KELL	Vans RV-6	J. D. Kelsall	
G-KEMC	Grob G.109	Eye-Fly	
G-KENB	Air Command 503 Commander	K. Brogden	
G-KENI	Rotorway Executive	A. J. Wheatley	
G-KENM	Luscombe 8EF Silvaire	J. R. Malpass	
G-KERY	PA-28 Cherokee 180	Seawing Flying Club Ltd (G-ATWO)/ Southend	
G-KEST	Steen Skybolt	S. Thursfield & K. E. Eld	
G-KEVN	Robinson R-22B	Helicopter Training & Hire Ltd (G-BONX)	
G-KEYB	Cameron O-84 balloon	B. P. Key	
G-KEYS	PA-23 Aztec 250F	T. M. Tuke & W. T. McCarter/Eglinton	
G-KEYY	Cameron N-77 balloon	R. Astill & ptnrs (G-BORZ)	
G-KFAN	Scheibe SF.25B Falke	L. J. Trute	
G-KFZI	KFZ-1 Tigerfalck	L. R. Williams	
G-KHRE	M.S.893E Rallye 150SV	J. L. Clarke	
G-KILY	Robinson R-22A	Heli Air Ltd	
G-KIMB	Robin DR.340/1Q40	R. M. Kimbell	
G-KINE	AA-5A Cheetah	Walsh Aviation	
G-KINK	Cessna 340	Hulbert of Dudley (Holdings) Ltd (G-PLEV)	
G-KIRK	Piper J-3C-65 Cub	M. J. Kirk	
G-KISS	Rand KR-2	E. A. Rooney	
G-KITE	PA-28-181 Archer II	CAVOK Aviation	
G-KITF	Denney Kitfox	L. A. James	
G-KITI	Pitts S-2E Special	B. R. Cornes	
G-KITS	Shaw Europa	Europa Aviation Ltd	
G-KITY	Denney Kitfox Mk 2	Kitfox KFM Group	
G-KIWI	Cessna 404	Aviation Beauport Ltd (G-BHNI)	
G-KKDL	SOCATA TB.20 Trinidad	Egerton Hospital Equipment Ltd (G-BSHU)	
G-KKES	SOCATA TB.20 Trinidad	Kestrel Shipping Ltd (G-BTLH)	
G-KLEE	Bell 206B JetRanger 3	Taylor-Ryan Aviation (G-SIZL/G-BOSW)	
G-KLIK	Air Command 532 Elite	Roger Savage (Photography)	
G-KMCD	Beech B200 Super King Air	Gamston Aviation Ltd	
G-KNAP	PA-28-161 Warrior II	Newland Aeroleasing Ltd (G-BIUX)	

Notes	Reg.	Type	Owner or Operator
	G-KNOB	Lindstrand LBL-180A balloon	Wye Valley Aviation Ltd
	G-KNOW	PA-32 Cherokee Six 300	P. J. Fydelor
	G-KODA	Cameron O-77 balloon	United Photofinishers Ltd
	G-KOLB	Kölb Twinstar Mk 3	P. A. Akines
	G-KOLI	PZL-110 Koliber 150	D. Sadler
	G-KONG	Slingsby T.67M-200	Hunting Aviation Ltd
	G-KOOL	D.H.104 Devon C.2 ★	E. Surrey Technical College/nr Redhill
	G-KOTA	PA-28-236 Dakota	JF Packaging
	G-KRAY	Robinson R-22HP	Direct Helicopters (Southend) Ltd (G-BOBO)
	G-KRES	Stoddard-Hamilton Glasair IISRG	G. Kresfelder
	G-KRII	Rand KR-2	M. R. Cleveley
	G-KRIS	Maule M5-235C Lunar Rocket	M. Penny
	G-KSIR	Stoddard-Hamilton Glasair IIRGS	R. Cayzer
	G-KSVB	PA-24 Comanche 260	J. R. Pettit (G-ENIU/G-AVJU)
	G-KTEE	Cameron V-77 balloon	D. C. & N. P. Bull
	G-KUTU	Quickie Q.2	R. Nash & J. Parkinson
	G-KWAX	Cessna 182E Skylane	J. E. & V. T. Brewis
	G-KWIK	Partenavia P.68B	ACD Cidra BV/Belgium
	G-KWIP	Shaw Europa	D. Elliott
	G-KWKI	QAC Quickie Q.200	B. M. Jackson
	G-LABS	Shaw Europa	C. T. H. Pattinson
	G-LACA	PA-28-161 Warrior II	LAC (Enterprises) Ltd/Barton
	G-LACB	PA-28-161 Warrior II	LAC (Enterprises) Ltd/Barton
	G-LACE	Shaw Europa	J. H. Phillingham
	G-LACR	Denney Kitfox	C. M. Rose
	G-LADE	PA-32 Cherokee Six 300E	Telefax 2000 Ltd
	G-LADI	PA-30 Twin Comanche 160	E. C. Clark (G-ASOO)/Biggin Hill
	G-LADS	R. Commander 114	D. F. Soul
	G-LAGR	Cameron N-90 balloon	Bass & Tennent Sales Ltd
	G-LAIN	Robinson R-22B	R&R Developments Ltd
	G-LAIR	Stoddard-Hamilton Glasair IIS	D. L. Swallow
	G-LAKE	Lake LA-250 Renegade	Stanford Ltd
	G-LAMM	Shaw Europa	S. A Lamb
	G-LAMS	Cessna F.152 II	Rentair Ltd
	G-LANC	Avro 683 Lancaster X (KB889) ★	Imperial War Museum/Duxford
	G-LAND	Robinson R-22B	Helicopter Training & Hire Ltd/Belfast
	G-LANE	Cessna F.172N	G. C. Bantin
	G-LAPN	Light Aero Avid Aerobat	R. M. & A. P. Shorter
	G-LARA	Robin DR.400/180	K. D. & C. A. Brackwell
	G-LARE	PA-39 Twin Comanche 160 C/R	Glareways (Neasden) Ltd
	G-LARK	Helton Lark 95	J. Fox
	G-LASR	Stoddard-Hamilton Glasair II	G. Lewis
	G-LASS	Rutan Vari-Eze	S. Roberts/Liverpool
	G-LAST	Cessna 340 II	Last Engineering Ltd (G-UNDY/G-BBNR)
	G-LATK	Robinson R-44 Astro	Ardern Consultancy Ltd (G-BVMK)/Booker
	G-LAXY	Everett Srs 3 gyroplane	G. D. Western
	G-LAZA	Lazer Z.200	M. Hammond
	G-LAZR	Cameron O-77 balloon	Laser Civil Engineering Ltd
	G-LAZY	Lindstrand Armchair SS balloon	The Air Chair Co. Ltd
	G-LAZZ	Glastar	G. K. Brunwin
	G-LBCS	Colt 31A balloon	Virgin Airship & Balloon Co Ltd
	G-LBLB	Lindstrand LBL-105A balloon	Lindstrand Balloons Ltd
	G-LBLI	Lindstrand LBL-105A balloon	Lindstrand Balloons Ltd
	G-LBLZ	Lindstrand LBL-105A balloon	Lindstrand Balloons Ltd
	G-LBMM	PA-28-161 Warrior II	S. C. May
	G-LBNK	Cameron N-105 balloon	Virgin Airship & Balloon Co. Ltd
	G-LBRC	PA-28RT-201 Arrow IV	D. J. V. Morgan
	G-LCGL	CLA.7 Swift (replica)	J. M. Greenland
	G-LCOK	Colt 69A balloon	Hot-Air Balloon Co Ltd (G-BLWI)
	G-LCON	AS.355N Twin Squirrel	Lancashire Constabulary/Warton
	G-LCRC	Boeing 757-23A	Airtours International Airways Ltd (G-IEAB)
	G-LDYS	Colt 56A balloon	P. Glydon & J. Coote
	G-LEAF	Cessna F.406	Atlantic Air Transport Ltd/Coventry
	G-LEAM	PA-28-236 Dakota	South Yorkshire Caravans Ltd (G-BHLS)
	G-LEAP	BN-2T Turbine Islander	Army Parachute Association (G-BLND)/ Netheravon
	G-LEAR	Learjet 35A	Northern Executive Aviation Ltd/ Manchester
	G-LEAU	Cameron N-31 balloon	P. L. Mossman
	G-LECA	AS.355F-1 Twin Squirrel	S. W. Electricity Board (G-BNBK)/Bristol
	G-LEDN	Short SD3-30 Variant 100	Streamline Aviation (SW) Ltd (G-BIOF)/Exeter

Reg.	Type	Owner or Operator	Notes
G-LEED	Denney Kitfox Mk 2	G. T. Leedham	
G-LEES	Glaser-Dirks DG.400	G-LEES Group	
G-LEEZ	Bell 206L-1 LongRanger 2	Pennine Helicopters Ltd (G-BPCT)	
G-LEGG	Cessna T.182Q	P. J. Clegg (G-GOOS)	
G-LEGO	Cameron O-77 balloon	C. H. Pearce Construction PLC	
G-LEGS	Short SD3-60 Variant 100	British Regional Airlines/BA Express (G-BLEF)	
G-LEIC	Cessna FA.152	Leicestershire Aero Club Ltd	
G-LEND	Cameron N-77 balloon	Southern Flight Co Ltd	
G-LENI	AS.355F-1 Twin Squirrel	Mala Services (South West) Ltd (G-ZFDB/G-BLEV)	
G-LENN	Cameron V-56 balloon	Anglia Balloon School Ltd	
G-LENS	Thunder Ax7-77Z balloon	Big Yellow Balloon Group	
G-LEOS	Robin DR.400/120	P. G. Newens	
G-LEPF	Fairchild 24R-46A Argus III	J. M. Greenland	
G-LESJ	Denney Kitfox Mk 3	G-LESJ Flying Group	
G-LEVI	Aeronca 7AC Champion	G-LEVI Group	
G-LEZE	Rutan LongEz	K. G. M. Loyal & ptnrs	
G-LEZJ	Denney Kitfox Mk 4-1200 Speedster	L. J. James	
G-LFBA	MBB BK-117C-1C	McAlpine Helicopters Ltd/Kidlington	
G-LFIX	V.S.509 Spitfire T.IX (ML407)	C. S. Grace	
G-LFSA	PA-38-112 Tomahawk	Liverpool Flying School Ltd (G-BSFC)	
G-LFSB	PA-38-112 Tomahawk	Liverpool Flying School Ltd (G-BLYC)	
G-LFSC	PA-28 Cherokee 140	Liverpool Flying School Ltd (G-BGTR)	
G-LFSD	PA-38-112 Tomahawk II	Liverpool Flying School Ltd (G-BNPT)	
G-LFSI	PA-28 Cherokee 140	Soko Aviation Ltd (G-AYKV)/Liverpool	
G-LFVB	V.S.349 Spitfire LF.Vb (EP120)	Patina Ltd/Duxford	
G-LGAS	Lindstrand LBL-210S balloon	A. Derbyshire	
G-LIBB	Cameron V-77 balloon	R. R. McCormick & R. J. Mercer	
G-LIBS	Hughes 369HS	A. Harvey & R. White	
G-LICK	Cessna 172N	Dacebow Aviation (G-BNTR)	
G-LIDA	Hoffmann HK-36R Super Dimona	W. D. Inglis	
G-LIDE	PA-31-350 Navajo Chieftain	Keen Leasing Ltd	
G-LIDR	Hoffmann H-36 Dimona	J. MacGilvray	
G-LIFE	Thunder Ax6-56Z balloon	D. F. Maine	
G-LILI	Cessna 425	Ortac Air Ltd (G-YOTT/G-NORC/G-BICL)	
G-LILY	Bell 206B JetRanger 3	T. S. Brown (G-NTBI)	
G-LIMA	R. Commander 114	Tricolore Aeroclub Ltd	
G-LINC	Hughes 369HS	Hawkair Ltd	
G-LINE	AS.355N Twin Squirrel	National Grid PLC	
G-LIOA	Lockheed 10A Electra ★ (NC5171N)	Science Museum/Wroughton	
G-LION	PA-18 Super Cub 135 (R-167)	C. Moore	
G-LIOT	Cameron O-77 balloon	D. Eliot	
G-LIPE	Robinson R-22B	Westleigh Construction Ltd (G-BTXJ)	
G-LIPP	BN-2T Turbine Islander	Rhine Army Parachute Association (G-BKJG)	
G-LITE	R. Commander 112A	J. Males	
G-LITZ	Pitts S-1E Special	J. A. Hughes/Leicester	
G-LIVH	Piper J-3C-65 Cub (330238)	M. D. Cowburn/Barton	
G-LIZA	Cessna 340A	J. H. Fry & J. C. Merkens (G-BMDM)	
G-LIZI	PA-28 Cherokee 160	R. J. Walker & J. R. Lawson (G-ARRP)	
G-LIZY	Westland Lysander III (V9673) ★	G. A. Warner/Duxford	
G-LIZZ	PA-E23 Aztec 250E	T. D. Nathan & M. J. Barge (G-BBWM)	
G-LLYD	Cameron N-31 balloon	Virgin Airship & Balloon Co Ltd	
G-LNYS	Cessna F.177RG	J. W. Clarke (G-BDCM)	
G-LOAF	Schempp-Hirth Janus CM	G. W. Kirton	
G-LOAN	Cameron N-77 balloon	Newbury Building Soc	
G-LOBO	Cameron O-120 balloon	Solo Aerostatics	
G-LOCH	Piper J-3C-90 Cub	J. M. Greenland	
G-LOFA	L.188CF Electra	Air Atlantique Ltd/Coventry	
G-LOFB	L.188CF Electra	Air Atlantique Ltd/Coventry	
G-LOFC	L.188CF Electra	Air Atlantique Ltd/Coventry	
G-LOFM	Maule MX-7-180A	Atlantic Air Transport Ltd/Coventry	
G-LOFT	Cessna 500 Citation	Atlantic Air Transport Ltd/Coventry	
G-LOGO	Hughes 369E	R. M. Briggs (G-BWLC)	
G-LOGS	Robinson R-22B	M. Chantler & ptnrs	
G-LOGV	BAe Jetstream 3102	British Regional Airlines/BA Express (G-OEDA/G-BSZK)	
G-LOLL	Cameron V-77 balloon	Test Valley Balloon Group	
G-LOLO	Robinson R-22B	Taylor-Ryan Helicopters Ltd (G-NIKI)	
G-LONG	Bell 206L LongRanger	Walsh Aviation	

Notes	Reg.	Type	Owner or Operator
	G-LOOP	Pitts S-1C Special	G. M. Roberts & K. E. Wells
	G-LOOT	EMB-110P1 Bandeirante	*stored* (G-BNOC)/Southend
	G-LORA	Cameron A-250 balloon	Global Ballooning Ltd
	G-LORD	PA-34-200T Seneca II	Aerohire Ltd/Halfpenny Green
	G-LORI	H.S.125 Srs 403B	Re-Enforce Trading Co Ltd (G-AYOJ)
	G-LORR	PA-28-181 Archer III	J. A. Robson
	G-LORT	Light Aero Avid Speedwing 4	G. E. Laucht
	G-LORY	Thunder Ax4-31Z balloon	A. J. Moore
	G-LOSM	Gloster Meteor NF.11 (WM167)	Hunter Wing Ltd/Bournemouth
	G-LOSS	Cameron N-77 balloon	D. K. Fish
	G-LOST	Denney Kitfox Mk 3	H. Balfour-Paul
	G-LOTI	Bleriot XI (replica) ★	Brooklands Museum Trust Ltd
	G-LOTO	BN-2A-26 Islander	Scottish Parachute Club (Islander) Ltd (G-BDWG)
	G-LOWA	Colt 77A balloon	K. D. Pierce
	G-LOWE	Monnett Sonerai I	R. M. Kinch
	G-LOWS	Sky 77-24 balloon	A. J. Byrne & D. J. Bellinger
	G-LOYA	Cessna FR.172J	T. R. Scorer (G-BLVT)
	G-LOYD	SA.341G Gazelle 1	Apollo Manufacturing (Derby) Ltd (G-SFTC)
	G-LRBW	Lindstrand HS-110 balloon	International Balloons Ltd
	G-LSFI	AA-5A Cheetah	T. G. Dughan (G-BGSK)
	G-LSHI	Colt 77A balloon	Lambert Smith Hampton Ltd
	G-LSMI	Cessna F.152	Falcon Flying Services/Biggin Hill
	G-LTEK	Bell 206B JetRanger 2	Grid Aviation Ltd (G-BMIB)
	G-LTFC	PA-28 Cherokee 140B	London Transport Flying Club Ltd (G-AXTI)/Fairoaks
	G-LTNG	EE Lightning T.5 (XS451)	Lightning Flying Club
	G-LUAR	SOCATA TB.10 Tobago	M. E. Muldoon
	G-LUBE	Cameron N 77 balloon	A. C. K. Rawson
	G-LUCA	Thunder Ax7-77Z balloon	R. De-Leyser
	G-LUCK	Cessna F.150M	Aviators Ltd
	G-LUED	Aero Designs Pulsar	J. C. Anderson
	G-LUFT	Pützer Elster C	Bath Stone Co Ltd (G-BOPY)
	G-LUKE	Rutan LongEz	S. G. Busby
	G-LULU	Grob G.109	A. P. Bowden
	G-LUNA	PA-32RT-300T Turbo Lance II	R. J. H. Creese
	G-LUSC	Luscombe 8E Silvaire	M. Fowler
	G-LUSI	Luscombe 8F Silvaire	J. P. Hunt & D. M. Robinson
	G-LUST	Luscombe 8E Silvaire	M. Griffiths
	G-LUXE	BAe 146-300	British Aerospace PLC (G-SSSH)
	G-LYDA	Hoffmann H-36 Dimona	G-LYDA Flying Group/Booker
	G-LYND	PA-25 Pawnee 235	Glyndwr Soaring Group (G-BSFZ/G-ASFZ)/Lleweni Parc
	G-LYNE	P-51D-20-NA Mustang (44-72028)	E. N. Robinson & M. C. B. Anderson
	G-LYNX	Westland WG.13 Lynx (ZB500) ★	IHM/Weston-s-Mare
	G-LYTE	Thunder Ax7-77 balloon	G. M. Bulmer
	G-MAAC	Advanced Airship Corporation ANR-1	Advanced Airship Corporation Ltd
	G-MACH	SIAI-Marchetti SF.260	Cheyne Motors Ltd/Popham
	G-MACK	PA-28R Cherokee Arrow 200-II	Haimoss Ltd
	G-MADD	Robinson R-22B	Great Excitement Ltd (G-MEAT)
	G-MAFE	Dornier Do.228-202K	FR Aviation Ltd (G-OALF/G-MLDO)/Bournemouth
	G-MAFF	BN-2T Turbine Islander	FR Aviation Ltd (G-BJEO)/Bournemouth
	G-MAFI	Dornier Do.228-200	FR Aviation Ltd/Bournemouth
	G-MAGC	Cameron Grand Illusion SS balloon	L. V. Mastis
	G-MAGG	Pitts S-1SE Special	C. A. Boardman
	G-MAIR	PA-34-200T Seneca II	Barnes Olson Aeroleasing Ltd
	G-MAJA	BAe Jetstream 4102	Manx Airlines Ltd
	G-MAJB	BAe Jetstream 4102	British Regional Airlines/BA Express (G-BVKT)
	G-MAJC	BAe Jetstream 4102	British Regional Airlines/BA Express (G-LOGJ)
	G-MAJD	BAe Jetstream 4102	British Regional Airlines/BA Express (G-WAWR)
	G-MAJE	BAe Jetstream 4102	British Regional Airlines/BA Express (G-LOGK)
	G-MAJF	BAe Jetstream 4102	British Regional Airlines/BA Express (G-WAWL)

Reg.	Type	Owner or Operator	Notes
G-MAJG	BAe Jetstream 4102	British Regional Airlines/BA Express (G-LOGL)	
G-MAJH	BAe Jetstream 4102	British Regional Airlines/BA Express (G-WAYR)	
G-MAJI	BAe Jetstream 4102	British Regional Airlines/BA Express (G-WAND)	
G-MAJJ	BAe Jetstream 4102	British Regional Airlines/BA Express (G-WAFT)	
G-MAJK	BAe Jetstream 4102	British Regional Airlines/BA Express	
G-MAJL	BAe Jetstream 4102	British Regional Airlines/BA Express	
G-MAJM	BAe Jetstream 4102	British Regional Airlines/BA Express	
G-MAJR	D.H.C.1 Chipmunk 22	Deltair Engines Ltd	
G-MAJS	Airbus A.300-605R	Monarch Airlines Ltd/Luton	
G-MALA	PA-28-181 Archer II	M. & D. Aviation (G-BIIU)	
G-MALC	AA-5 Traveler	B. P. Hogan (G-BCPM)	
G-MALK	Cessna F.172N	J. Easson/Edinburgh	
G-MALS	Mooney M.20K-231	G-MALS Group/White Waltham	
G-MALT	Colt Flying Hop SS balloon	P. J. Stapley	
G-MAMC	Rotorway Executive 90	J. R. Carmichael	
G-MAMO	Cameron V-77 balloon	The Marble Mosaic Co Ltd	
G-MANA	BAe ATP	Manx Airlines Ltd (G-LOGH)	
G-MANB	BAe ATP	Manx Airlines Ltd (G-LOGG/G-JATP)	
G-MANC	BAe ATP	Manx Airlines Ltd (G-LOGF)	
G-MAND	PA-28-161 Warrior II	Halfpenny Green Flight Centre Ltd (G-BRKT)	
G-MANE	BAe ATP	British Regional Airlines/BA Express (G-LOGB)	
G-MANF	BAe ATP	British Regional Airlines/BA Express (G-LOGA)	
G-MANG	BAe ATP	British Regional Airlines/BA Express (G-LOGD/G-OLCD)	
G-MANH	BAe ATP	British Regional Airlines/BA Express (G-LOGC/G-OLCC)	
G-MANI	Cameron V-90 balloon	M. P. G. Papworth	
G-MANJ	BAe ATP	British Regional Airlines/BA Express (G-LOGE/G-BMYL)	
G-MANL	BAe ATP	Manx Airlines Ltd (G-ERIN/G-BMYK)	
G-MANM	BAe ATP	British Regional Airlines/BA Express (G-OATP/G-BZWW)	
G-MANN	SA.341G Gazelle 1	First City Air PLC (G-BKLW)	
G-MANO	BAe ATP	Manx Airlines Ltd (G-UIET)	
G-MANP	BAe ATP	British Regional Airines/BA Express (G-PEEL)	
G-MANS	BAe 146-200	British Regional Airlines/BA Express (G-CHSR)	
G-MANW	Tri-R Kis	M. T. Manwaring	
G-MANX	FRED Srs 2	S. Styles	
G-MAPR	Beech A36 Bonanza	Openair Ltd	
G-MARE	Schweizer 269C	The Earl of Caledon	
G-MART	Cessna 208B	Martini Airfreight Services Ltd	
G-MASC	Jodel 150A	K. F. & R. Richardson	
G-MASH	Westland-Bell 47G-4A	Defence Products Ltd (G-AXKU)	
G-MASK	AS.355F-1 Twin Squirrel	Medical Aviation Services Ltd (G-PASK)	
G-MASS	Cessna 152	MK Aero Support Ltd (G-BSHN)	
G-MATE	Moravan Zlin Z.50LX	D. T. Karberry	
G-MATS	Colt GA-42 airship	Lindstrand Balloons Ltd	
G-MATT	Robin R.2160	S. J. Lim (G-BKRC)	
G-MATZ	PA-28 Cherokee 140	Midland Air Training School (G-BASI)	
G-MAUD	BAe ATP	Manx Airlines Ltd (G-BMYM)	
G-MAUK	Colt 77A balloon	B. Meeson	
G-MAVE	Shaw Europa	D. A. & A. D. Field	
G-MAVI	Robinson R-22B	Yorkshire Helicopter Centre Ltd/Doncaster	
G-MAWL	Maule M4-210C Rocket	D. Wallace	
G-MAXI	PA-34-200T Seneca II	G. C. Rogers	
G-MAYO	PA-28-161 Warrior II	Jermyk Engineering/Fairoaks	
G-MAZY†	D.H.82A Tiger Moth ★	Newark Air Museum	
G-MCAR	PA-32 Cherokee Six 300D	B. M. Jordan (G-LADA/G-AYWK)	
G-MCEA	Boeing 757-225	Airtours International Airways Ltd	
G-MCMS	Aero Designs Pulsar	M. C. Manning	
G-MCOX	Fuji FA.200-180AO	W. Surrey Engineering (Shepperton) Ltd	
G-MCPI	Bell 206B JetRanger 3	D. A. C. Pipe (G-ONTB)	
G-MDAC	PA-28-181 Archer II	B. R. McKay/Bournemouth	
G-MDEW	Lindstrand Drinks Can SS balloon	Pepsi Cola Overseas Ltd	

Notes	Reg.	Type	Owner or Operator
	G-MDKD	Robinson R-22B	D. K. Duckworth
	G-MEAH	PA-28R Cherokee Arrow 200-II	Stapleford Flying Club Ltd (G-BSNM)
	G-MEDA	Airbus A.320-231	British Mediterranean Airways Ltd
	G-MEGA	PA-28R-201T Turbo Arrow III	Travelworth Ltd
	G-MELD	AA-5A Cheetah	Meld Ltd (G-BHCB)/Blackbushe
	G-MELT	Cessna F.172H	Vectair Aviation Ltd (G-AWTI)
	G-MELV	SOCATA Rallye 235E	Wallis & Sons Ltd (G-BIND)
	G-MEME	PA-28R-201 Arrow III	Henry J. Clare Ltd
	G-MEOW	CFM Streak Shadow	S. D. Hicks
	G-MERC	Colt 56A balloon	A. F. & C. D. Selby
	G-MERE	Lindstrand LBL-77A balloon	G. T. Restell
	G-MERF	Grob G.115A	W. Murphy (G-EGVV)
	G-MERI	PA-28-181 Archer II	Scotia Safari Ltd/Glasgow
	G-MERL	PA-28RT-201 Arrow IV	M. Giles
	G-METE	Gloster Meteor F.8 (VZ467)	Classic Jets Ltd
	G-MEUP	Cameron A-120 balloon	N. J. Tovey
	G-MEYO	Enstrom 280FX	I. G. Shrigley
	G-MFHL	Robinson R-22B	BLS Aviation Ltd/Elstree
	G-MFHT	Robinson R-22B	MFH Ltd
	G-MFLI	Cameron V-90 balloon	J. M. Percival
	G-MFMF	Bell 206B JetRanger 3	S.W. Electricity Board (G-BJNJ)/Bristol
	G-MFMM	Scheibe SF.25C Falke	S. Lancs Falke Syndicate/Liverpool
	G-MHBD	Cameron O-105 balloon	K. Hull
	G-MHCA	Enstrom F-28C-UK	A. G. Forshaw (G-SHWW/G-SMUJ/ G-BHTF)
	G-MHCB	Enstrom 280C	Manchester Helicopter Centre/Barton
	G-MHCD	Enstrom 280C-UK	Manchester Helicopter Centre (G-SHGG)/ Barton
	G-MHCE	Enstrom F-28A	K. Bickley (G-BBHD)/Barton
	G-MHCF	Enstrom 280C-UK	Manchester Helicopter Centre (G-GSML/ G-BNNV)/Barton
	G-MICH	Robinson R-22B	A. P. Codling (G-BNKY)/Shobdon
	G-MICK	Cessna F.172N	G-MICK Flying Group
	G-MICY	Everett Srs 1 gyroplane	D. M. Hughes
	G-MICZ	PA-46-310P Malibu	Mitchell Instruments Ltd
	G-MIDG	Midget Mustang	C. E. Bellhouse
	G-MIFF	Robin DR.400/180	G. E. Bickerton
	G-MIII	Extra EA.300/L	Firebird Aerobatics Ltd
	G-MIKE	Brookland Hornet	M. H. J. Goldring
	G-MIKY	Cameron 90 Mickey SS balloon	The Walt Disney Co Ltd
	G-MILE	Cameron N-77 balloon	Miles Air Ltd
	G-MILI	Bell 206B JetRanger 3	CK's Supermarket
	G-MILY	AA-5A Cheetah	Plane Talking Ltd (G-BFXY)/Elstree
	G-MIMA	BAe 146-200	Manx Airlines Ltd (G-CNMF)
	G-MIND	Cessna 404	Atlantic Air Transport Ltd (G-SKKC/G-OHUB)/Coventry
	G-MINI	Currie Wot	D. Collinson
	G-MINS	Nicollier HN.700 Menestrel II	R. Fenion
	G-MINT	Pitts S-1S Special	T. G. Sanderson/Tollerton
	G-MINX	Bell 47G-4A	R. F. Warner (G-FOOR)
	G-MIOO	M.100 Student	Aces High Ltd (G-APLK)/North Weald
	G-MISH	Cessna 182R	M. Konstantinovic (G-RFAB/G-BIXT)
	G-MISS	Taylor JT.2 Titch	P. L. A. Brenen
	G-MIST	Cessna T.210K	J. Summers (G-AYGM)
	G-MITS	Cameron N-77 balloon	Colt Car Co Ltd
	G-MITZ	Cameron N-77 balloon	Colt Car Co Ltd
	G-MIWS	Cessna 310R II	R. W. F. Warner (G-ODNP)
	G-MKAK	Colt 77A balloon	Virgin Airship & Balloon Co Ltd
	G-MKVB	V.S.349 Spitfire LF.VB (BM597)	Historic Aircraft Collection Ltd
	G-MKVI	D.H. Vampire FB.6 (VZ304)	De Havilland Aviation Ltd/Swansea
	G-MKXI	V.S.365 Spitfire PR.XI (PL965)	C. P. B. Horsley
	G-MLAS	Cessna 182E ★	Parachute jump trainer/St Merryn
	G-MLFF	PA-23 Aztec 250E	Channel Islands Aero Holdings (Jersey) Ltd (G-WEBB/G-BJBU)
	G-MLGL	Colt 21A balloon	Colt Balloons Ltd
	G-MLWI	Thunder Ax7-77 balloon	M. L. & L. P. Willoughby
	G-MOAC	Beech F33A Bonanza	Chalkfarm Productions Ltd/Elstree
	G-MOAK	Schempp-Hirth Nimbus 3DM	P. W. Lever/Portmoak
	G-MOBI	AS.355F-1 Twin Squirrel	M. J. O'Brien (G-MUFF/G-CORR)
	G-MOFF	Cameron O-77 balloon	D. M. Moffat
	G-MOFZ	Cameron O-90 balloon	D. M. Moffat
	G-MOGI	AA-5A Cheetah	TL Aviation Ltd (G-BFMU)
	G-MOGY	Robinson R-22B	Hireheli Ltd/Booker

Reg.	Type	Owner or Operator	Notes
G-MOHS	PA-31-350 Navajo Chieftain	Sky Air Travel Ltd (G-BWOC)	
G-MOKE	Cameron V-77 balloon	D. D. Owen	
G-MOLE	Taylor JT.2 Titch	S. R. Mowle	
G-MOLI	Cameron A-250 balloon	J. J. Rudoni	
G-MOLL	PA-32-301T Turbo Saratoga	Auto Recovery & Repair Services Ltd	
G-MOLY	PA-23 Apache 160	R. R. & M. T. Thorogood (G-APFV)/St Just	
G-MONB	Boeing 757-2T7	Monarch Airlines Ltd/Luton	
G-MONC	Boeing 757-2T7	Monarch Airlines Ltd/Luton	
G-MOND	Boeing 757-2T7	Monarch Airlines Ltd/Luton	
G-MONE	Boeing 757-2T7	Monarch Airlines Ltd/Luton	
G-MONI	Monnett Moni	B. S. Carpenter/Booker	
G-MONJ	Boeing 757-2T7	Monarch Airlines Ltd/Luton	
G-MONK	Boeing 757-2T7	Monarch Airlines Ltd/Luton	
G-MONR	Airbus A.300-605R	Monarch Airlines Ltd/Luton	
G-MONS	Airbus A.300-605R	Monarch Airlines Ltd/Luton	
G-MONW	Airbus A.320-212	Monarch Airlines Ltd/Luton	
G-MONX	Airbus A.320-212	Monarch Airlines Ltd/Luton	
G-MONY	Airbus A.320-212	Monarch Airlines Ltd/Canada 3000 (C-GVNY)	
G-MONZ	Airbus A.320-212	Monarch Airlines Ltd/Luton	
G-MOON	Mooney M.20K	M. A. Eccles	
G-MOOR	SOCATA TB.10 Tobago	J. R. Smith & ptnrs (G-MILK)	
G-MOOS	P.56 Provost T.1 (XF690)	T. J. Manna (G-BGKA)/Cranfield	
G-MORE	Schleicher ASH.26E	B. H. Owen	
G-MOSS	Beech D55 Baron	A. W. Moss & Son (Civil & Railway Engineering Ltd (G-AWAD)	
G-MOSY	Cameron O-84 balloon	P. L. Mossman	
G-MOTH	D.H.82A Tiger Moth (K2567)	M. C. Russell	
G-MOTO	PA-24 Comanche 160	C. C. Letchford & A. J. Redknapp (G-EDHE/G-ASFH)	
G-MOTT	Light Aero Avid Speedwing	J. B. Ott	
G-MOUL	Maule M6-235	E. L. Klinge	
G-MOUR	H.S. Gnat T.1 (XR991)	D. J. Gilmour/North Weald	
G-MOUS	Cameron 90 Mickey SS balloon	The Walt Disney Co Ltd	
G-MOVE	PA-60-601P Aerostar	A. Cazaz & A. Gillen	
G-MOVI	PA-32R-301 Saratoga SP	Rentair (G-MARI)	
G-MOZZ	Avions Mudry CAP.10B	M. B. Smith/Booker	
G-MPBH	Cessna FA.152	Metropolitan Police Flying Club (G-FLIC/ G-BILV)/Biggin Hill	
G-MPCD	Airbus A.320-212	Monarch Airlines Ltd/Canada 3000 (C-FTDU)	
G-MPWH	Rotorway Executive	Neric Ltd	
G-MPWI	Robin HR.100/210	Propwash Investments Ltd/Cardiff	
G-MPWT	PA-34-220T Seneca III	Neric Ltd	
G-MRED	Christavia Mk 1	E. Hewett	
G-MRKT	Lindstrand LBL-90A balloon	Marketplace Public Relations (London) Ltd	
G-MRPP	PA-34-220T Seneca III	Dagless Ltd	
G-MRSN	Robinson R-22B	Yorkshire Helicopters/Leeds	
G-MRST	PA-28 RT-201 Arrow IV	Winchfield Enterprises Ltd	
G-MRTI	Cameron 110 Eagle SS balloon	Eagle Airways Ltd	
G-MRTY	Cameron N-77 balloon	R. A. & P. G. Vale	
G-MSAL	MS.733 Alcyon (143)	D. R. C. Bell/Booker	
G-MSDJ	AS.350B-1 Ecureuil	Denis Ferranti Hoverknights Ltd G-BPOH)	
G-MSFC	PA-38-112 Tomahawk	Sherwood Flying Club Ltd/Tollerton	
G-MSKA	Boeing 737-5L9	Maersk Air Ltd/British Airways	
G-MSKB	Boeing 737-5L9	Maersk Air Ltd/British Airways	
G-MSKC	Boeing 737-5L9	Maersk Air Ltd/British Airways	
G-MSKJ	BAe Jetstream 4100	Maersk Air Ltd (G-BWIH)	
G-MSOO	Mini-500	R. H. Ryan	
G-MSTC	AA-5A Cheetah	Mid-Sussex Timber Co Ltd (G-BIJT)	
G-MUFY	Robinson R-22B	Rotormurf Ltd	
G-MUIR	Cameron V-65 balloon	L. C. M. Muir	
G-MULL	Douglas DC-10-30	British Airways *New Forest*/Gatwick	
G-MUMS	PA-28-161 Warrior II	A. J. Wood	
G-MUNI	Mooney M.20J	Sequoia Aviation Ltd	
G-MURY	Robinson R-44 Astro	Simlot Ltd	
G-MUSO	Rutan LongEz	M. Moran	
G-MUST	CA-18 Mustang 22	Fairoaks Aviation Services Ltd	
G-MUTE	Colt 31A balloon	Redmalt Ltd	
G-MUZO	Shaw Europa	J. T. Grant	
G-MXVI	V.S.361 Spitfire LF.XVIe (TE184)	De Cadenet Motor Racing Ltd	

Notes	Reg.	Type	Owner or Operator
	G-NAAS	AS.355F-1 Twin Squirrel	Northumbria Ambulance Service NHS Trust (G-BPRG/G-NWPA)
	G-NACA	Norman NAC.2 Freelance 180	NDN Aircraft Ltd/Sandown
	G-NACI	Norman NAC.1 Srs 100	L. J. Martin
	G-NACL	Norman NAC.6 Fieldmaster	EPA Aircraft Co Ltd (G-BNEG)
	G-NACM	Norman NAC.6 Fieldmaster	EPA Aircraft Co Ltd
	G-NACN	Norman NAC.6 Fieldmaster	EPA Aircraft Co Ltd
	G-NACO	Norman NAC.6 Fieldmaster	EPA Aircraft Co Ltd
	G-NACP	Norman NAC.6 Fieldmaster	EPA Aircraft Co Ltd
	G-NANA	VPM M.16 Tandem Trainer	J. W. P. Lewis
	G-NASA	Lockheed T-33A-5-LO (91007)	De Havilland Aviation Ltd (G-TJET)/ Swansea
	G-NASH	AA-5A Cheetah	F. P. Lund
	G-NATT	R. Commander 114A	Northgleam Ltd
	G-NATX	Cameron O-65 balloon	A. G. E. Faulkner
	G-NATY	H. S. Gnat T.1 (XR537)	F. C. Hackett-Jones
	G-NAVO	PA-31-325 Navajo C/R	Air Care (Southwest) Ltd (G-BMPV)
	G-NBDD	Robin DR.400/180	J. N. Binks
	G-NBSI	Cameron N-77 balloon	Nottingham Hot-Air Balloon Club
	G-NCUB	Piper J-3C-65 Cub	N. Thomson (G-BGXV)/Norwich
	G-NDGC	Grob G.109	R. G. Trute
	G-NDNI	NDN.1 Firecracker	N. W. G. Marsh
	G-NDOL	Shaw Europa	G. K. Brunwin
	G-NDRW	Colt AS-80 Mk II airship	Huntair Ltd
	G-NEAL	PA-32 Cherokee Six 260	VSD Group (G-BFPY)
	G-NEAT	Shaw Europa	M. Burton
	G-NEEL	Rotorway Executive 90	P. N. Haigh
	G-NEGS	Thunder Ax7-77 balloon	R. Holden
	G-NEIL	Thunder Ax3 balloon	Islington Motors (Trowbridge) Ltd
	G-NEPB	Cameron N-77 balloon	The Post Office
	G-NERC	PA-31-350 Navajo Chieftain	Natural Environment Research Council (G-BBXX)
	G-NERI	PA-28-181 Archer II	Moulin Ltd (G-BMKO)
	G-NESU	BN-2B-20 Islander	Northumbria Police Authority (G-BTVN)
	G-NETY	PA-18 Super Cub 150	N. B. Mason
	G-NEVS	Aero Designs Pulsar XP	N. Warrener
	G-NEWR	PA-31-350 Navajo Chieftain	Eastern Air Executive Ltd/Sturgate
	G-NEWS	Bell 206B JetRanger 3	David Reed Homes Ltd
	G-NEWT	Beech 35 Bonanza	J. A. West (G-APVW)
	G-NEXT	AS.355F-1 Twin Squirrel	Bristow Helicopters Ltd (G-WDKR/ G-OMAV)
	G-NFLC	H.P.137 Jetstream Mk1	Cranfield University (G-AXUI)
	G-NGRM	Spezio DAL.1	C. D. O'Malley
	G-NHRH	PA-28 Cherokee 140	J-E. & I. Parkinson
	G-NHVH	Maule M5-235C Lunar Rocket	Commercial Go-Karts Ltd/Exeter
	G-NICH	Robinson R-22B	Panair Ltd
	G-NIGE	Luscombe 8E Silvaire	Garden Party Ltd (G-BSHG)
	G-NIGL	Shaw Europa	N. M. Graham
	G-NIGS	Thunder Ax7-65 balloon	A. N. F. Pertwee
	G-NIKE	PA-28-181 Archer II	Key Properties Ltd/White Waltham
	G-NINA	PA-28-161 Warrior II	A. G. Bailey (G-BEUC)
	G-NINE	Murphy Renegade 912	R. F. Bond
	G-NIOS	PA-32R-301 Saratoga SP	E. L. Sasso de Terza
	G-NIPA	Slingsby T.66 Nipper 3	R. J. O. Walker (G-AWDD)
	G-NISR	R. Commander 690A	Z. I. Bilbeisi
	G-NITA	PA-28 Cherokee 180	T. Clifford (G-AVVG)
	G-NIUK	Douglas DC-10-30	Caledonian Airways Ltd Loch Loyal
	G-NJAG	Cessna 207	G. H. Nolan Ltd
	G-NJML	PA-34-220T Seneca III	Oxford Management Ltd
	G-NJSH	Robinson R-22B	T. F. Hawes
	G-NLEE	Cessna 182Q	J. S. Lee (G-TLTD)
	G-NNAC	PA-18 Super Cub 135	P. A. Wilde
	G-NOBI	Spezio HES-1 Tuholer Sport	R. Wheeler
	G-NOCK	Cessna FR.182RG II	D. J. Morris & R. A. D. Wilson
	G-NODE	AA-5B Tiger	Abraxas Aviation Ltd/Elstree
	G-NODY	American General AG-5B Tiger	Curd & Green Ltd/Elstree
	G-NOIR	Bell 222	Arlington Securities PLC (G-OJLC/ G-OSEB/G-BNDA)
	G-NONI	AA-5 Traveler	P. Nutley (G-BBDA)
	G-NORD	SNCAN NC.854	W. J. McCollum
	G-NOSE	Cessna 402B	Atlantic Air Transport Ltd (G-MPCU)/ Coventry
	G-NOTR	McD Douglas MD-520N Notar	Air Hanson Ltd/Blackbushe

Reg.	Type	Owner or Operator	Notes
G-NOTT	Nott ULD-2 balloon	J. R. P. Nott	
G-NOVO	Colt AS-56 airship	Astec Communications Ltd	
G-NPNP	Cameron N-105 balloon	Virgin Airship & Balloon Co Ltd (G-BURX)	
G-NPWR	Cameron RX-100 balloon	Nuclear Electric PLC	
G-NRDC	NDN-6 Fieldmaster	EPA Aircraft Co Ltd	
G-NROY	PA-32RT-300 Lance II	Roys Motor Co (G-LYNN/G-BGNY)	
G-NSFT	PA-28-161 Warrior II	SFT Aviation Ltd (G-BSMZ)/Bournemouth	
G-NSTG	Cessna F.150F	N. S. T. Griffin (G-ATNI)/Blackpool	
G-NTEE	Robinson R-44 Astro	Springfield Helicopters Ltd	
G-NTWO	SA.365N-2 Dauphin 2	Bond Helicopters Ltd	
G-NVBF	Lindstrand LBL-210A balloon	Virgin Balloon Flights Ltd	
G-NWAC	PA-31-310 Turbo Navajo	North West Air Charters Ltd (G-BDUJ)/ Liverpool	
G-NWNW	Cameron V-90 balloon	Royal Mail	
G-NWPI	AS.355F-2 Twin Squirrel	North Wales Police Authority	
G-NWPR	Cameron N-77 balloon	Post Office N.W. Postal Board	
G-NYTE	Cessna F.337G	Photoair (G-BATH)	
G-NZGL	Cameron O-105 balloon	P. G. & P. M. Vale	
G-NZSS	Boeing Stearman N2S-5 (27)	Ace Aviation Ltd	
G-OAAA	PA-28-161 Warrior II	Halfpenny Green Flight Centre Ltd	
G-OAAC	Airtour AH-77B balloon	Army Air Corps	
G-OAAL	PA-38-112 Tomahawk	Topcat Aviation Ltd	
G-OAAS	Short SD3-60 Variant 100	Aurigny Air Services Ltd (G-BLIL)/Guernsey	
G-OABC	Colt 69A balloon	P. A. C. Stuart-Kregor	
G-OACE	Valentin Taifun 17E	J. E. Dallison	
G-OACG	PA-34-200T Seneca II	ACG Building Contractors Ltd (G-BUNR)	
G-OACP	D.H.C.1 Chipmunk 20	Aeroclub de Portugal	
G-OADY	Beech 76 Duchess	Citation Leasing Ltd	
G-OAER	Lindstrand LBL-105A balloon	T. M. Donnelly	
G-OAFC	Airtour 56AH balloon	P. J. Donnellan & L. A. Watts	
G-OAFT	Cessna 152 II	Bobbington Air Training School Ltd (G-BNKM)/Halfpenny Green	
G-OAHC	Beech F33C Bonanza	Clacton Aero Club (1988) Ltd (G-BTTF)	
G-OAJS	PA-39 Twin Comanche 160 C/R	Go-AJS Ltd (G-BCIO)	
G-OAKA	BAe Jetstream 3102	Ai r Kilroe Ltd (G-BUFM/G-LAKH)/ Mancester	
G-OAKI	BAe Jetstream 3102	Air Kilroe Ltd/Manchester	
G-OAKJ	BAe Jetstream 3202	Air Kilroe Ltd (G-BOTJ)/Manchester	
G-OALA	Airbus A.320-231	All Leisure Airlines Ltd/Gatwick	
G-OALD	SOCATA TB.20 Trinidad	Gold Aviation/Biggin Hill	
G-OAMG	Bell 206B JetRanger 3	Alan Mann Helicopters Ltd/Fairoaks	
G-OAML	Cameron AML-105 balloon	Aston Martin Lagonda Ltd	
G-OAMP	Cessna F.177RG	Ampy Automation Digilog Ltd (G-AYPF)	
G-OAMY	Cessna 152 II	Warwickshire Flying Training Centre Ltd/ Birmingham	
G-OANC	PA-28-161 Warrior II	Millwood Ltd(G-BFAD)	
G-OANI	PA-28-161 Warrior II	J. A. Caliva	
G-OANN	Zenair CH.601HS	P. Noden	
G-OAPR	Brantly B.2B	Helicopter International Magazine/ Weston-s-Mare	
G-OAPW	Glaser-Dirks DG.400	S. W. Brown & D. T. S. Walsh	
G-OARG	Cameron C-80 balloon	G. & R. Madelin	
G-OART	PA-23 Aztec 250D	Levenmere Ltd (G-AXKD)	
G-OARV	ARV Super 2	P. R. Snowden	
G-OASH	Robinson R-22B	J. C. Lane	
G-OASP	AS.355F-1 Twin Squirrel	Avon & Somerset Constabulary & Gloucestershire Constabulary	
G-OATS	PA-38-112 Tomahawk	Truman Aviation Ltd/Tollerton	
G-OATV	Cameron V-77 balloon	W. G. Andrews	
G-OAUS	Sikorsky S-76A	Darley Stud Management Co Ltd	
G-OBAA	Beech B200 Super King Air	BAA PLC	
G-OBAL	Mooney M.20J	Britannia Airways Ltd/Luton	
G-OBAN	Jodel D.140B	S. R. Cameron (G-ATSU)/North Connel	
G-OBAT	Cessna F.152 II	M. & M. Entwistle (G-OENT)	
G-OBBC	Colt 90A balloon	R. A. & M. A. Riley	
G-OBEA	BAe Jetstream 3102-01	European Airways Ltd	
G-OBEN	Cessna 152 II	Astra Associates (G-NALI/G-BHVM)	
G-OBEY	PA-23 Aztec 250C	Creaton Aircraft Services (G-BAAJ)	
G-OBFC	PA-28-161 Warrior II	Shoreham Flight Simulation/Bournemouth	
G-OBHD	Short SD3-60 Variant 100	Jersey European Airways Ltd (G-BNDK)	
G-OBHH	Bell 206A JetRanger	Helisport Ltd (G-WLLY/G-RODY/ G-ROGR/G-AXMM)	

Notes	Reg.	Type	Owner or Operator
	G-OBHX	Cessna F.172H	BHX Flying Group (G-AWMU)
	G-OBIG	AS.355F-1 Twin Squirrel	Plane Talking Ltd (G-SVJM/G-BOPS)
	G-OBIL	Robinson R-22B	PAC Helicopters/Sandtoft
	G-OBJH	Colt 77A balloon	Eurogas & Corralgas
	G-OBLC	Beech 76 Duchess	Tatenhill Aviation
	G-OBLK	Short SD3-60 Variant 100	Jersey European Airways Ltd (G-BNDI)
	G-OBLN	D.H.115 Vampire T.11	de Havilland Aviation Ltd
	G-OBMD	Boeing 737-33A	British Midland Airways Ltd/E. Midlands
	G-OBMF	Boeing 737-4Y0	British Midland Airways Ltd/E. Midlands
	G-OBMG	Boeing 737-4Y0	British Midland Airways Ltd/E. Midlands
	G-OBMH	Boeing 737-33A	British Midland Airways Ltd/E. Midlands
	G-OBMJ	Boeing 737-33A	British Midland Airways Ltd/E. Midlands
	G-OBMK	Boeing 737-4S3	British Midland Airways Ltd/E. Midlands
	G-OBMM	Boeing 737-4Y0	British Midland Airways Ltd/E. Midlands
	G-OBMN	Boeing 737-46B	British Midland Airways Ltd (G-BOPJ)/ E. Midlands
	G-OBMO	Boeing 737-4Q8	British Midland Airways Ltd/E. Midlands
	G-OBMP	Boeing 737-3Q8	British Midland Airways Ltd/E. Midlands
	G-OBMR	Boeing 737-5Y0	British Midland Airways Ltd/E. Midlands
	G-OBMS	Cessna F.172N	D. Beverley & W. F. van Schoten
	G-OBMW	AA-5 Traveler	Fretcourt Ltd (G-BDFV)
	G-OBMX	Boeing 737-59D	British Midland Airways Ltd/E. Midlands
	G-OBMY	Boeing 737-59D	British Midland Airways Ltd/E. Midlands
	G-OBMZ	Boeing 737-53A	British Midland Airways Ltd/E. Midlands
	G-OBNF	Cessna 310K	Fadmoor Flying Group
	G-OBOH	Short SD3-60 Variant 100	BAC Express Ltd (G-BNDJ)
	G-OBOY	Aviat Pitts S-2B Special	G. L. Carpenter
	G-OBRU	Bell 206B JetRanger 2	Bond Helicopters Ltd (G-GOBP/G-BOUY)
	G-OBRY	Cameron N-180 balloon	Bryant Group PLC
	G-OBSF	AA-5A Cheetah	Lowlog Ltd (G-ODSF/G-BEUW)
	G-OBTS	Cameron C-80 balloon	Bedford Tyre Service (Chichester) Ltd
	G-OBTW	Bell 206B JetRanger	B. T. W. Allen
	G-OBUD	Colt 69A balloon	Hot-Air Balloon Co Ltd
	G-OBUY	Colt 69A balloon	Virgin Airship & Balloon Co Ltd
	G-OBWA	BAC One-Eleven 518FG	British World Airlines Ltd (G-BDAT/ G-AYOR)/Stansted
	G-OBWB	BAC One-Eleven 518FG	British World Airlines Ltd (G-BDAS/ G-AXMH)/Stansted
	G-OBWC	BAC One-Eleven 520FN	British World Airlines Ltd (G-BEKA)/ Stansted
	G-OBWD	BAC One-Eleven 518FG	British World Airlines Ltd (G-BDAE/ G-AXMI)/Stansted
	G-OBWE	BAC One-Eleven 531FS	British World Airlines Ltd (G-BJYM)/ Stansted
	G-OBYA	Boeing 767-304ER	Britannia Airways Ltd
	G-OBYB	Boeing 767-304ER	Britannia Airways Ltd
	G-OBYC	Boeing 767-304ER	Britannia Airways Ltd
	G-OBYD	Boeing 767-304ER	Britannia Airways Ltd
	G-OBYT	AB-206A JetRanger	Specialist Computer Holdings Ltd (G-BNRC)
	G-OCAA	H.S.125 Srs 700B	MAGEC Aviation Ltd (G-BHLF)/Luton
	G-OCAD	Sequoia F.8L Falco	Falco Flying Group
	G-OCAM	AA-5A Cheetah	Plane Talking Ltd (G-BLHO)/Elstree
	G-OCAR	Colt 77A balloon	Ridgeway Balloon Group
	G-OCAT	Eiri PIK-20E	P. D. Turner/Rufforth
	G-OCAW	Lindstrand LBL Bananas SS balloon	Flying Pictures (Balloons) Ltd
	G-OCBB	Bell 206B JetRanger 2	Helispeed Ltd (G-BASE)
	G-OCCA	PA-32R-301 Saratoga SP	LSS Ireland Ltd (G-BRIX)/Elstree
	G-OCCB	Robinson R-44 Astro	C. C. Blakey (G-STMM)
	G-OCDB	Cessna 550 Citation II	Paycourt Ltd (G-ELOT)
	G-OCDS	Aviamilano F.8L Falco II	C. O. P. Barth (G-VEGL)
	G-OCFR	Learjet 35A	Chauffair (CI) Ltd (G-VIPS/G-SOVN/ G-PJET)
	G-OCGJ	Robinson R-22B	Sloane Helicopters Ltd/Sywell
	G-OCJK	Schweizer 269C	Bradford Independent Helicopters
	G-OCJS	Cameron V-90 balloon	C. J. Sandell
	G-OCND	Cameron O-77 balloon	D. P. H. Smith & Dalby
	G-OCOP	Bell 206LT LongRanger 4	Veritair Ltd
	G-OCPC	Cessna FA.152	Westward Airways (Lands End) Ltd/St Just
	G-OCPI	Cessna 500 Citation	Stadium City Ltd (G-OXEC)
	G-OCPL	AA-5A Cheetah	BLS Aviation Ltd (G-RCPW/G-BERM)
	G-OCPS	Colt 120A balloon	CPS Fuels Ltd

Reg.	Type	Owner or Operator	Notes
G-OCRI	Colomban MC.15 Cri-Cri	M. J. J. Dunning	
G-OCSI	EMB-110P2 Bandeirante	Air Tabernacle Ltd(G-BHJZ)	
G-OCST	AB-206B JetRanger 3	Fieldgrove Trading (G-BMKM)	
G-OCSZ	EMB-110P1 Bandeirante	Air Tabernacle (G-DORK)	
G-OCTA	BN-2A Mk III-2 Trislander	Aurigny Air Services Ltd (G-BCXW)	
G-OCTI	PA-32 Cherokee Six 260	J. K. Sharkey (G-BGZX)/Elstree	
G-OCTU	PA-28-161 Cadet	Plane Talking Ltd/Denham	
G-OCUB	Piper J-3C-90 Cub	C. A. Foss & P. A. Brook/Shoreham	
G-OCWT	AS.350B-2 Ecureuil	Carter Wind Turbines (Aviation) Ltd	
G-ODAC	Cessna F.152 II	T. M. Jones (G-BITG)	
G-ODAD	Colt 77A balloon	K. Meehan	
G-ODAM	AA-5A Cheetah	Stop & Go Ltd (G-FOUX)	
G-ODBN	Lindstrand LBL Flowers SS balloon	Flying Pictures (Balloons) Ltd	
G-ODDY	Lindstrand LBL-105A balloon	V. Hyland	
G-ODEL	Falconar F-11-3	G. F. Brummell	
G-ODEN	PA-28-161 Cadet	J. Appleton/Denham	
G-ODHL	Cameron N-77 balloon	DHL International (UK) Ltd	
G-ODIG	Bell 206B JetRanger 2	Lothian Helicopter Services (G-NEEP)	
G-ODIL	Bell 206B JetRanger	Yorkshire Helicopter Centre Ltd	
G-ODIN	Avions Mudry CAP.10B	D. E. Hickson	
G-ODIS	Cameron Cabin SS balloon	Cameron Balloons Ltd	
G-ODIY	Colt 69A balloon	P. Glydon	
G-ODJG	Shaw Europa	D. J. Goldsmith	
G-ODJH	Mooney M.20C	J. W. E. de Frayssinet (G-BMLH)	
G-ODLY	Cessna 310J	R. J. Huband (G-TUBY/G-ASZZ)	
G-ODMC	AS.350B-1 Ecureuil	D. M. Coombs (G-BPVF)/Denham	
G-ODOG	PA-28R Cherokee Arrow 200-II	S. Brown (G-BAAR)	
G-ODTI	Shaw Europa	Europa Aviation Ltd	
G-ODTW	Shaw Europa	D. T. Walters	
G-OEAC	Mooney M.20J	N. R. Capon/Elstree	
G-OEBA	Robin DR.400/140B	EB Aviation (G-JMHB)	
G-OECH	AA-5A Cheetah	Plane Talking Ltd (G-BKBE)/Elstree	
G-OEDB	PA-38-112 Tomahawk	Air Delta Bravo Ltd (G-BGGJ)/Elstree	
G-OEDP	Cameron N-77 balloon	M. J. Betts	
G-OEGG	Cameron 65 Egg SS balloon	Virgin Airship & Balloon Co Ltd	
G-OEJA	Cessna 500 Citation	Eurojet Aviation Ltd (G-BWFL)	
G-OERS	Cessna 172N	E. R. Stevens (G-SSRS)	
G-OERX	Cameron O-65 balloon	R. Roehsler/Austria	
G-OEYE	Rans S.10 Sakota	P. Thompson	
G-OEZY	Shaw Europa	A. W. Wakefield	
G-OFBJ	Thunder Ax7-77 balloon	N. D. Hicks	
G-OFCM	Cessna F17 2L	F. C. M. Aviation Ltd (G-AZUN)/Guernsey	
G-OFER	PA-18 Super Cub 150	M. S. W. Meagher/Edgehill	
G-OFHJ	Cessna 441	Tilling Associates Ltd (G-HSON)	
G-OFHL	AS.350B Ecureuil	Ford Helicopters Ltd (G-BLSP)	
G-OFIT	SOCATA TB.10 Tobago	G. S.M. Brain (G-BRIU)	
G-OFIZ	Cameron 80 Can SS balloon	Virgin Airship & Balloon Co Ltd	
G-OFJC	Eiri PIK-20E	M. J. Aldridge	
G-OFJS	Robinson R-22B	Burman Aviation Ltd (G-BNXJ)/Cranfield	
G-OFLG	SOCATA TB.10 Tobago	Studley Pool Management Ltd (G-JMWT)	
G-OFLI	Colt 105A balloon	Virgin Airship & Balloon Co Ltd	
G-OFLT	EMB-110P1 Bandeirante	Flightline Ltd (G-MOBL/G-BGCS)/Southend	
G-OFLY	Cessna 210M	A. P. Mothew/Stapleford	
G-OFOR	Thunder Ax3 balloon	T. J. Ellenreider & ptnrs	
G-OFOX	Denney Kitfox	P. R. Skeels	
G-OFRB	Everett gyroplane	Roger Savage (Photography)	
G-OFRT	L.188C Electra	Channel Express (Air Services) Ltd/Bournemouth	
G-OFRY	Cessna 152 II	Devon School of Flying (G-BPHS)/Dunkeswell	
G-OFTI	PA-28 Cherokee 140	I. Chaplin (G-BRKU)	
G-OGAN	Shaw Europa	G-OGAN Group	
G-OGAR	PZL SZD-45A Ogar	N. C. Grayson	
G-OGAS	Westland WG.30 Srs 100	(stored) (G-BKNW)/Penzance	
G-OGAT	Beech 200 Super King Air	Branderman Ltd	
G-OGAV	Lindstrand LBL-240A balloon	Out Of This World	
G-OGAZ	SA.341G Gazelle 1	M. Wood Haulage (G-OCJR/G-BRGS)	
G-OGCA	PA-28-161 Warrior II	Aerohire Ltd/Halfpenny Green	
G-OGEE	Pitts S-2B Special	R. G. Gee	
G-OGEM	PA-28-181 Archer II	GEM Rewinds Ltd	
G-OGET	PA-39 Twin Comanche 160 C/R	P. G. Kitchingman (G-AYXY)	

Notes	Reg.	Type	Owner or Operator
	G-OGGS	Thunder Ax8-84 balloon	G. Gamble & Sons (Quorn) Ltd
	G-OGHH	Enstrom 480	G. H. Harding
	G-OGIL	Short SD3-30 Variant 100 ★	N.E. Aircraft Museum (G-BITV)/Usworth
	G-OGJS	Puffer Cozy	G. J. Stamper
	G-OGOA	AS.350B Ecureuil	Lomas Helicopters Ltd (G-PLMD/G-NIAL)
	G-OGOB	Schweizer 269C	Kingfisher Helicopters Ltd (G-GLEE/ G-BRUW)
	G-OGOC	Robinson R-22B	Avonline Group Ltd (G-HODG)
	G-OGTS	Air Command 532 Elite	GTS Engineering (Coventry) Ltd
	G-OHAL	Pietenpol Air Camper	H. C. Danby
	G-OHCP	AS.355F-1 Twin Squirrel	Cabair Helicopters Ltd (G-BTVS/ G-STVE/G-TOFF/G-BKJX)
	G-OHDC	Colt Agfa Film Cassette SS balloon	Flying Pictures (Balloons) Ltd
	G-OHEA	H.S.125 Srs 3B/RA	B. L. Schroder (G-AVRG)
	G-OHHL	Robinson R-22B	Helicopter Training & Hire Ltd
	G-OHIG	EMB-110P1 Bandeirante	Air Tabernacle Ltd (G-OPPP)
	G-OHMS	AS.355F-1 Twin Squirrel	S.W. Electricity PLC
	G-OHOG	PA-28 Cherokee 140	C. R. Guggenheim (G-AVFY)
	G-OHOP	PA-31 Turbo Navajo	Channel Islands Air Charter Ltd (G-BEYY)
	G-OIBM	R. Commander 114	Airys Communications Technology Ltd (G-BLVZ)
	G-OIBO	PA-28 Cherokee 180	Britannia Airways Ltd (G-AVAZ)
	G-OICE	Cessna 525 Citationjet	Iceland Frozen Foods PLC/Hawarden
	G-OICV	Robinson R-22B	ICV Ltd (G-BPWH)
	G-OIDW	Cessna F.150G	I. D. Wakeling
	G-OIEA	PA-31P Pressurised Navajo	Skyrock Aviation Ltd (G-BBTW)/Cyprus
	G-OIFM	Cameron 90 Dude SS balloon	L. V. Mastis
	G-OIGS	Enstrom F-28C	M. Thompson (G-BGSN)
	G-OILA	Aérospatiale ATR-72-210	British World Airlines Ltd/Aberdeen
	G-OILB	Aérospatiale ATR-72-210	British World Airlines Ltd/Aberdeen
	G-OILX	AS.355F-1 Twin Squirrel	Firstearl Ltd (G-RMGN/G-BMCY)
	G-OIMC	Cessna 152 II	E. Midlands Flying School Ltd
	G-OING	AA-5A Cheetah ★	Abraxas Aviation Ltd (G-BFPD)/Denham
	G-OINK	Piper J-3C-65 Cub	A. R. Harding (G-BILD/G-KERK)
	G-OISK	Cameron N-90 balloon	First County Finance (UK) Ltd
	G-OISO	Cessna FRA.150L	Les Oiseaux (G-BBJW)
	G-OITA	Boeing 767-33AER	Alitalia
	G-OITB	Boeing 767-33AER	Alitalia
	G-OITG	Boeing 767-33AER	Alitalia
	G-OITL	Boeing 767-33AER	Alitalia
	G-OITN	AS.355F-1 Twin Squirrel	Lynton Aviation Ltd/Denham
	G-OITV	Enstrom 280C	Arena Aviation Ltd (G-HRVY/G-DUGY/ G-BEEL)
	G-OJAB	Jabiru SK	ST Aviation Ltd
	G-OJAC	Mooney M.20J	Hornet Engineering Ltd
	G-OJAE	Hughes 269C	J. A. & C. M. Wilson
	G-OJAV	BN-2A Mk III-2 Trislander	Willowjet Ltd (G-BDOS)
	G-OJBM	Cameron N-90 balloon	JBM Communications Ltd
	G-OJCB	AB-206B JetRanger 2	Yorkshire Helicopter Centre Ltd
	G-OJCW	PA-32RT-300 Lance II	CW Group
	G-OJDC	Thunder Ax7-77 balloon	J. Crosby
	G-OJEM	H.S.748 Srs 2B	Emerald Airways Ltd (G-BKAL)/Liverpool
	G-OJEN	Cameron V-77 balloon	Jensport Ltd
	G-OJFC	Beech A36 Bonanza	J. Cross
	G-OJHB	Colt Flying Ice Cream Cone SS balloon	Benedikt Haggeney GmbH
	G-OJIM	PA-28R-201T Turbo Arrow III	Motomecca Spares Ltd
	G-OJJB	Mooney M.20K	Fly Over Ltd
	G-OJMR	Airbus A.300-605R	Monarch Airlines Ltd/Luton
	G-OJNB	Linsdstrand LBL-21A balloon	Justerini & Brooks Ltd
	G-OJON	Taylor JT.2 Titch	J. H. Fell
	G-OJSY	Short SD3-60 Variant 100	BAC Express Ltd (G-BKKT)
	G-OJTA	Stemme S-10V	OJT Associates
	G-OJVA	Vans RV-6	J. A. Village
	G-OJVH	Cessna F.150H	Yorkshire Light Aircraft Ltd (G-AWJZ)/ Leeds
	G-OJVI	Robinson R-22B	Defence Products Ltd (G-OJVJ)
	G-OJWS	PA-28-161 Warrior II	L. E. Guernieri
	G-OKAG	PA-28R Cherokee Arrow 180	N. F. & B. R. Green/Stapleford
	G-OKAY	Pitts S-1E Special	J. S. Mortimore & R. J. Allan
	G-OKBT	Colt 25A Mk II balloon	British Telecommunications PLC
	G-OKCC	Cameron N-90 balloon	D. J. Head

Reg.	Type	Owner or Operator	Notes
G-OKED	Cessna 150L	Haimoss Ltd/Old Sarum	
G-OKEN	PA-28R-201T Turbo Arrow III	W. B. Bateson/Blackpool	
G-OKES	Robinson R-44 Astro	Kestrel Shipping Ltd	
G-OKEY	Robinson R-22B	Key Properties Ltd/Booker	
G-OKIS	Tri-R Kis	B. W. Davies	
G-OKMA	Tri-R Kis	K. Miller	
G-OKPW	Tri-R Kis	K. P. Wordsworth	
G-OKYA	Cameron V-77 balloon	Army Balloon Club	
G-OKYM	PA-28 Cherokee 140	D. Hotham (G-AVLS)	
G-OLAH	Short SD3-60 Variant 100	Gill Airways Ltd (G-BPCO/G-RMSS/ G-BKKU)/Newcastle	
G-OLAU	Robinson R-22B	MPW Aviation Ltd	
G-OLAW	Lindstrand LBL-25A balloon	George Law Plant	
G-OLDE	Cessna 421C	Richard Nash Cars Ltd (G-BBSV)	
G-OLDN	Bell 206L LongRanger	Gulfstream Air Services (UK) Ltd (G-TBCA/G-BFAL)	
G-OLDV	Colt 90A balloon	Virgin Airship & Balloon Co Ltd	
G-OLDY	Luton LA-5 Major	M. P. & A. P. Sargent	
G-OLDZ	Beech 200 Super King Air	Gold Group International Ltd (G-MCEO/ G-SWFT/G-SIBE/G-BILY)	
G-OLEE	Cessna F.152	Aerohire Ltd/Halfpenny Green	
G-OLFC	PA-38-112 Tomahawk	M. W. Glencross (G-BGZG)	
G-OLFT	R. Commander 114	B. C. Richens (G-WJMN)/Redhill	
G-OLIZ	Robinson R-22B	Randall Photographic	
G-OLLE	Cameron O-84 balloon	N. A. Robertson	
G-OLLI	Cameron O-31 SS balloon	N. A. Robertson	
G-OLLY	PA-31-350 Navajo Chieftain	Barnes Olsen Aeroleasing Ltd (G-BCES)	
G-OLMA	Partenavia P.68B	C. M. Evans (G-BGBT)	
G-OLOW	Robinson R-44 Astro	Rotaspot Ltd	
G-OLPG	Colt 77A balloon	Eurogas & Corralgas	
G-OLRT	Robinson R-22B	Universal Rides Ltd	
G-OLSC	Cessna 182A	Factultra (G-ATNU)	
G-OLVR	FRED Srs 2	A. R. Oliver	
G-OMAC	Cessna FR.172E	RK Consultants	
G-OMAF	Dornier Do.228-200	FR Aviation Ltd/Bournemouth	
G-OMAP	R. Commander 685	Cooper Aerial Surveys Ltd/Sandtoft	
G-OMAR	PA-34-220T Seneca III	Redhill Flying Club	
G-OMAT	PA-28 Cherokee 140	Midland Air Training School (G-JIMY/ G-AYUG)/Coventry	
G-OMAX	Brantly B.2B	P. D. Benmax (G-AVJN)	
G-OMDH	Hughes 369E	Stilgate Ltd/Booker	
G-OMEC	AB-206B JetRanger 3	Kallas Ltd (G-OBLD)	
G-OMEL	Robinson R-44 Astro	Moffett Engineering Ltd (G-BVPB)	
G-OMGD	H.S.125 Srs 700B	MAGEC Aviation Ltd/Luton	
G-OMGE	BAe 125 Srs 800B	GEC Marconi Ltd (G-BTMG)/Luton	
G-OMGG	BAe 125 Srs 800B	MAGEC Aviation Ltd/Luton	
G-OMHC	PA-28RT-201 Arrow IV	Tatenhill Aviation	
G-OMIG	Aero-Vodochody MiG-15UTI (6247)	Classic Aviation Ltd/Duxford	
G-OMJB	Bell 206B JetRanger 2	Coventry Helicopter Centre Ltd	
G-OMJT	Rutan LongEz	M. J. Timmons	
G-OMKF	Aero Designs Pulsar	M. K. Faro	
G-OMMG	Robinson R-22B	BLS Aviation Ltd (G-BPYX)/Elstree	
G-OMMM	Colt 90A balloon	3M Health Care Ltd	
G-OMNI	PA-28R Cherokee Arrow 200D	R. J. Fray (G-BAWA)	
G-OMOG	AA-5A Cheetah	Popham Flight (G-BHWR)	
G-OMRB	Cameron V-77 balloon	M. R. Bayne	
G-OMRG	Hoffmann H-36 Dimona	M. R. Grimwood (G-BLHG)	
G-OMXS	Lindstrand LBL-105A balloon	Virgin Airship & Balloon Co Ltd	
G-ONAF	Naval Aircraft Factory N3N-3	R. P. W. Steel & J. E. Hutchinson	
G-ONAV	PA-31-310 Turbo Navajo C	Panther Aviation Ltd (G-IGAR)	
G-ONCB	Lindstrand LBL-31A balloon	Flying Pictures (Balloons) Ltd	
G-ONCL	Colt 77A balloon	N. C. Lindsay	
G-ONHH	Forney F-1A Aircoupe	H. Dodd (G-ARHA)/Newcastle	
G-ONKA	Aeronca K	N. J. R. Minchin	
G-ONOW	Bell 206A JetRanger 2	J. Luckett (G-AYMX)	
G-ONUN	Vans RV-6A	R. E. Nunn	
G-ONZO	Cameron N-77 balloon	K. Temple	
G-OOAA	Airbus A.320-231	Air 2000 Ltd/Manchester	
G-OOAB	Airbus A.320-231	Air 2000 Ltd/Manchester	
G-OOAC	Airbus A.320-231	Air 2000 Ltd/Manchester	
G-OOAD	Airbus A.320-231	Air 2000 Ltd/Manchester	
G-OODE	SNCAN Stampe SV-4C (G)	Chocks Away Ltd (G-AZNN)	

Notes	Reg.	Type	Owner or Operator
	G-OODI	Pitts S-1D Special	M. J. Walden (G-BBBU)
	G-OODW	PA-28-181 Archer II	Goodwood Terrena Ltd
	G-OOER	Lindstrand LBL-25A balloon	Airborne Adventures Ltd
	G-OOGA	GA-7 Cougar	Plane Talking Ltd/Elstree
	G-OOGI	GA-7 Cougar	Plane Talking Ltd (G-PLAS/G-BGHL)
	G-OOJB	Cessna 421C	Melman Investments Ltd (G-BKSO)
	G-OOLE	Cessna 172M	P. S. Eccersley (G-BOSI)
	G-OONE	Mooney M.20J	J. H. Donald & K. B. Moore
	G-OONI	Thunder Ax7-77 balloon	Fivedata Ltd
	G-OONS	AB-206B JetRanger 3	Helicopter Training & Hire Ltd (G-LIND)
	G-OONY	PA-28-161 Warrior II	D. A. Field & P. B. Jenkins
	G-OOOA	Boeing 757-28A	Air 2000/Canada 3000 (C-FOOA)
	G-OOOB	Boeing 757-28A	Air 2000/Canada 3000 (C-FOOB)
	G-OOOC	Boeing 757-28A	Air 2000/Canada 3000 (C-FXOC)
	G-OOOD	Boeing 757-28A	Air 2000/Canada 3000 (C-FXOD)
	G-OOOG	Boeing 757-23A	Air 2000/Canada 3000 (C-FOOG)
	G-OOOI	Boeing 757-23A	Air 2000 Ltd/Manchester
	G-OOOJ	Boeing 757-23A	Air 2000 Ltd/Manchester
	G-OOOO	Mooney M.20J	Pergola Ltd
	G-OOOS	Boeing 757-236	Air 2000 Ltd (G-BRJD)/Manchester
	G-OOOT	Boeing 757-236	Air 2000 Ltd (G-BRJJ)/Manchester
	G-OOOU	Boeing 757-2Y0	Air 2000 Ltd/Manchester
	G-OOOV	Boeing 757-225	Air 2000 Ltd/Manchester
	G-OOOW	Boeing 757-225	Air 2000 Ltd/Manchester
	G-OOOX	Boeing 757-2Y0	Air 2000 Ltd/Manchester
	G-OOSE	Rutan Vari-Eze	J. A. Towers
	G-OOSY	D.H.82A Tiger Moth	M. Goosey
	G-OOTC	PA-28R-201T Turbo Arrow III	T. J. Caton (G-CLIV)
	G-OOUT	Colt Flying Shuttlecock SS balloon	Shiplake Investments Ltd
	G-OOXP	Aero Designs Pulsar XP	T. D. Baker
	G-OPAG	PA-34-200 Seneca II	A. H. Lavender (G-BNGB)/Biggin Hill
	G-OPAL	Robinson R-22B	Pebblestar Ltd
	G-OPAM	Cessna F.152	PJC Leasing Ltd (G-BFZS)/Stapleford
	G-OPAS	V.806 Viscount	British World Airlines Ltd (G-AOYN)
	G-OPAT	Beech 76 Duchess	Ray Holt (Land Drainage) Ltd/(G-BHAO)
	G-OPBH	Aero Designs Pulsar	P. B. Hutchinson
	G-OPDS	Denney Kitfox Mk 4	P. D. Sparling
	G-OPFI	V.802 Viscount	British World Airlines Ltd (G-BLNB/ G-AOHV)
	G-OPIB	EE Lightning F.6	Downderry Construction Group Ltd
	G-OPIC	Cessna FRA.150L	Air Survey (G-BGNZ)
	G-OPIK	Eiri PIK-20E	A. J. McWilliam/Newtownards
	G-OPIT	CFM Streak Shadow Srs SA	W. M. Kilner
	G-OPJC	Cessna 152 II	PJC Leasing Ltd/Stapleford
	G-OPJD	PA-28RT-201T Turbo Arrow IV	F. T. Ahmed
	G-OPJK	Shaw Europa	P. J. Kember
	G-OPKF	Cameron 90 Bowler SS balloon	Flying Pictures (Balloons) Ltd
	G-OPLB	Cessna 340A II	Ridgewood Ltd (G-FCHJ/G-BJLS)
	G-OPLC	D.H.104 Dove 8	W. G. T. Pritchard & I. Darcy-Bean (G-BLRB)
	G-OPME	PA-23 Aztec 250D	P. H. Zeitsman & J. C. Macartney (G-ODIR/G-AZGB)
	G-OPMT	Lindstrand LBL-105A balloon	Pace Micro Technology Ltd
	G-OPNI	Bell 206B JetRanger	P & I Data Services Ltd (G-BXAA)
	G-OPPL	AA-5A Cheetah	London School of Flying Ltd (G-BGNN)/ Elstree
	G-OPPS	Mudry CAP.231	Bianchi Aviation Film Services Ltd/Booker
	G-OPRA	PA-31 Turbo Navajo	Lakeland Airways (G-VICK/G-AWED)
	G-OPSF	PA-38-112 Tomahawk	Panshanger School of Flying (G-BGZI)
	G-OPST	Cessna 182R	Lota Ltd/Shoreham
	G-OPUB	Slingsby T.67M Firefly 160	P. M. Barker (G-DLTA/G-SFTX)
	G-OPUP	B.121 Pup 2	Brinkley Light Aircraft Services (G-AXEU)
	G-OPWH	Dassault Falcon 900B	Aviation Partnership/Kidlington
	G-OPWK	AA-5A Cheetah	A. H. McVicar (G-OAEL)/Prestwick
	G-OPWS	Mooney M.20K	A. C. Clarke
	G-ORAF	CFM Streak Shadow	G. A. Taylor
	G-ORAR	PA-28-181 Archer III	Pesqueras Gran Sol SL/Spain
	G-ORAY	Cessna F.182Q II	G. A. Barrett (G-BHDN)
	G-ORBY	Sukhoi Su-26MX	N. J. Wakefield & ptnrs/White Waltham
	G-ORCL	Cessna 421C	G. W. Squire
	G-ORDN	PA-28R Cherokee Arrow 200-II	M. Pugh (G-BAJT)
	G-ORDO	PA-30 Twin Comanche B	A. C. & A. M. Gordon

Reg.	Type	Owner or Operator	Notes
G-ORED	BN-2T Turbine Islander	The Red Devils (G-BJYW)/Farnborough	
G-OREV	Mini -500	R. H. Everett	
G-OREY	Cameron O-90 balloon	P. McCallum	
G-ORFC	Jurca MJ.5 Sirocco	D. J. Phillips	
G-ORFE	Cameron 76 Golf SS balloon	British School of Ballooning	
G-ORFH	Aérospatiale ATR-42-300	Gill Airways Ltd/Newcastle	
G-ORIG	Glaser-Dirks DG.800A	I. Godfrey	
G-ORHE	Cessna 500 Citation	Earthline Aviation (G-OBEL/G-BOGA)	
G-ORIX	ARV K1 Super 2	P. M. Harrison (G-BUXH/G-BNVK)	
G-ORJB	Cessna 500 Citation	L'Equipe Air Ltd (G-OKSP)	
G-ORJW	Laverda F.8L Falco Srs 4	W. R. M. Sutton	
G-ORMB	Robinson R-22B	R. M. Bailey	
G-OROB	Robinson R-22B	Corniche Helicopters (G-TBFC)	
G-OROD	PA-18 Super Cub 150	R. J. O. Walker	
G-OROM	AS.355N Twin Squirrel	McAlpine Helicopters Ltd/Kidlington	
G-ORON	Cameron 77A balloon	A. M. Rocliffe	
G-OROZ	AS.350B-2 Ecureuil	Flightpaths Ltd	
G-ORPR	Cameron O-77 balloon	T. Strauss & A. Sheehan	
G-ORSP	Beech A36 Bonanza	Select Plant Hire Co Ltd	
G-ORTM	Glaser-Dirks DG.400	J. P. C. Fuchs	
G-ORTW	Lindstrand AM-25000 balloon	Lindstrand Balloons Ltd	
G-ORVB	McCulloch J-2	R. V. Bowles (G-BLGI/G-BKKL)	
G-ORVR	Partenavia P.68B	Ravenair (G-BFBD)/Manchester	
G-OSAB	Enstrom 280FX	S. Atherton	
G-OSAL	Cessna 421C	Yorkshire Helicopters/Leeds	
G-OSCA	Cessna 500 Citation	Oscar Aviation Ltd (G-SWET)	
G-OSCB	Colt 90A balloon	J. Willis	
G-OSCC	PA-32 Cherokee Six 300	Plant Aviation Ltd (G-BGFD)/Elstree	
G-OSCH	Cessna 421C	Sureflight Aviation Ltd (G-SALI)	
G-OSCO	Team Minimax	P. J. Schofield	
G-OSDI	Beech 95-58 Baron	K. L. Hawes (G-BHFY)	
G-OSEA	BN-2B-26 Islander	W. T. Johnson & Sons (Huddersfield) Ltd (G-BKOL)	
G-OSEE	Robinson R-22B	J. P. Dennison	
G-OSFC	Cessna F.152	Stapleford Flying Club Ltd (G-BIVJ)	
G-OSFT	PA-31-310 Turbo Navajo C	Glidair (G-MDAS/G-BCJZ)	
G-OSII	Cessna 172N	Propwash Aviation Ltd (G-BIVY)	
G-OSIS	Pitts S-1S Special	M. C. Boddington & I. M. Castle	
G-OSIX	PA-32 Cherokee Six 260	A. E. Whittle (G-AZMO)	
G-OSKY	Cessna 172M	Gosky Aviation Ltd	
G-OSLO	Schweizer 269C	Hanover Aviation Leasing Ltd	
G-OSMR	Lake LA-4-200 Buccaneer	J. P. Billingham	
G-OSMT	Shaw Europa	S. M. Thomas	
G-OSNB	Cessna 550 Citation II	Scottish & Newcastle Breweries PLC (G-JFRS)	
G-OSND	Cessna FRA.150M	Wilkins & Wilkins Special Auctions Ltd (G-BDOU)	
G-OSOO	Hughes 369E	Tyrone Fabrication Ltd	
G-OSOW	PA-28 Cherokee 140	Go-Hog Flying Ltd (G-AVWH)/Bournemouth	
G-OSPS	PA-18 Super Cub 95	J. W. Macleod	
G-OSST	Colt 77A balloon	British Airways PLC	
G-OSTC	AA-5A Cheetah	C. B. Dew	
G-OSTU	AA-5A Cheetah	Plane Talking Ltd (G-BGCL)/Elstree	
G-OSUP	Lindstrand LBL-90A balloon	British Airways Balloon Club	
G-OSUS	Mooney M.20K	J. B. King/Goodwood	
G-OSVO	Cameron 30 Hopper Servo SS balloon	Servo & Electronic Sales Ltd	
G-OSWA	Enstrom F-28C-UK-2	S. Atherton (G-BZZZ/G-BBBZ)	
G-OTAF	Aero L-39ZO Albatros	A. J. E. Smith & R. A. Fleming/Breighton	
G-OTAL	ARV Super 2	N. R. Beale (G-BNGZ)	
G-OTAM	Cessna 172M	T. W. Woods	
G-OTAN	PA-18 Super Cub 135	E. Alexander	
G-OTBY	PA-32 Cherokee Six 300	GOTBY Ltd	
G-OTCH	CFM Streak Shadow	H. E. Gotch	
G-OTED	Robinson R-22HP	Andrews Heli-Lease Ltd (G-BMYR)	
G-OTEL	Thunder Ax8-90 balloon	D. N. Belton	
G-OTHE	Enstrom 280C-UK Shark	GTS Engineering (Coventry) Ltd (G-OPJT/G-BKCO)	
G-OTHL	Robinson R-22B	TWS Helicopters Ltd (G-DSGN)	
G-OTIM	Bensen B.8MV	T. J. Deane	
G-OTNT	Cameron Cider Bottle SS balloon	A. J. Round	
G-OTOE	Aeronca 7AC Champion	J. M. Gale (G-BRWW)	
G-OTOW	Cessna 175BX	C. P. & C. J. Wilkes	

Notes	Reg.	Type	Owner or Operator
	G-OTRG	Cessna TR.182RG	Thermodata Components
	G-OTTI	Cameron 34 Otti SS balloon	Ballonwerbung Hamburg GmbH/Germany
	G-OTTO	Cameron 82 Katalog SS balloon	Ballonwerbung Hamburg GmbH/Germany
	G-OTUG	PA-18 Super Cub 150	B. Walker & Co (Dursley) Ltd
	G-OTUP	Lindstrand LBL-180A balloon	Airborne Adventures Ltd
	G-OTVS	BN-2T Turbine Islander	Headcorn Parachute Club Ltd (G-BPBN/ G-BCMY) *(stored)*
	G-OTWO	Rutan Defiant	D. G. Foreman
	G-OTYJ	PA-28-161 Cadet	Holmes Rentals (G-OLSF)
	G-OULD	Gould Mk I balloon	C. A. Gould
	G-OURO	Shaw Europa	D. Dufton
	G-OUSA	Colt 105A balloon	Continental Airlines Inc
	G-OUVI	Cameron O-105 balloon	Bristol University Hot Air Ballooning Soc
	G-OUZO	Airbus A.320-231	Virgin Atlantic Airways Ltd
	G-OVAA	Colt Jumbo SS balloon	Virgin Airship & Balloon Co Ltd
	G-OVAX	Colt AS-80 Mk II airship	Vax Appliances Ltd
	G-OVBF	Cameron A-250 balloon	Virgin Balloon Flights Ltd
	G-OVET	Cameron O-56 balloon	E. J. A. Macholc
	G-OVFM	Cessna 120	Commair Group
	G-OVFR	Cessna F.172N	Western Air Training Ltd
	G-OVID	Light Aero Avid Flyer	J. M. Walsh & D. F. Chamberlain
	G-OVMC	Cessna F.152 II	Staverton Flying Services Ltd
	G-OVNE	Cessna 401A	M. A. Billings/Ipswich
	G-OVNR	Robinson R-22B	Heli-Fun Ltd
	G-OVVB	Beech A36 Bonanza	Air Hanson Aircraft Sales Ltd
	G-OWAC	Cessna F.152	Barnes Olson Aeroleasing Ltd (G-BHEB)
	G-OWAK	Cessna F.152	Falcon Flying Services (G-BHEA)/ Biggin Hill
	G-OWAR	PA-28-161 Warrior II	Bickertons Aerodromes Ltd
	G-OWAZ	Pitts S-1C Special	P. E. S. Latham (G-BRPI)
	G-OWCG	Bell 222	Winchester Commodities Group Ltd (G-VERT/G-JLBZ/G-BNDB)
	G-OWEL	Colt 105A balloon	S. R. Seager
	G-OWEN	K & S Jungster	R. C. Owen
	G-OWET	Thurston TSC-1A2 Teal	D. Nieman
	G-OWGC	Slingsby T.61F Venture T.2	Wolds Gliding Club Ltd/Pocklington
	G-OWIN	BN-2A-8 Islander	UK Parachute Services Ltd (G-AYXE)
	G-OWIZ	Luscombe 8A Silvaire	J. Wilson & J. V. George
	G-OWLC	PA-31 Turbo Navajo	Top Nosh Ltd (G-AYFZ)
	G-OWLD	BAe 146-200	CityJet Ltd
	G-OWOW	Cessna 152 II	Falcon Flying Services (G-BMSZ)/ Biggin Hill
	G-OWVA	PA-28 Cherokee 140	Woodvale Aviation Co Ltd
	G-OWWF	Colt 2500A balloon	Virgin Atlantic Airways Ltd
	G-OWWW	Shaw Europa	J. F. & W. R. C. Williams-Wynne
	G-OWYN	Aviamilano F.14 Nibbio	J. R. Wynn
	G-OXBY	Cameron N-90 balloon	C. A. Oxby
	G-OXKB	Cameron 110 Sports Car SS balloon	Flying Pictures (Balloons) Ltd
	G-OXLI	BAe Jetstream 4100	British Aerospace PLC/Prestwick
	G-OXRG	Colt Film Can SS balloon	Flying Pictures (Balloons) Ltd
	G-OXTC	PA-23 Aztec 250D	Falcon Flying Services (G-AZOD)/ Biggin Hill
	G-OXVI	V.S.361 Spitfire LF.XVIe (TD248)	Silver Victory BVBA/Belgium
	G-OYAK	Yakovlev C-11 (27)	E. K. Coventry/Earls Colne
	G-OZAR	Enstrom 480	Heliway Aviation (G-BWFF)
	G-OZBA	Airbus A.320-212	Monarch Airlines Ltd (G-MALE)/Luton
	G-OZBB	Airbus A.320-212	Monarch Airlines Ltd (C-FTDW)/Luton
	G-OZEE	Light Aero Avid Speedwing Mk 4	S. C. Goozee
	G-OZLN	Zlin Z.242L	G. G. L. Thomas/Swansea
	G-OZOI	Cessna R.182	J. R. G. & F. L. G. Fleming (G-ROBK)
	G-OZRH	BAe 146-200	Flightline Ltd/Stansted
	G-OZUP	Colt 77A balloon	Yanin International Ltd
	G-PACE	Robin R.1180T	Millicron Instruments Ltd/Coventry
	G-PACL	Robinson R-22B	D. K. Griffiths
	G-PADI	Cameron V-77 balloon	T. R. Duffell
	G-PAGS	SA.341G Gazelle 1	P. A. G. Seers (G-OAFY/G-SFTH/ G-BLAP)
	G-PAIZ	PA-12 Super Cruiser	B. R. Pearson/Eaglescott
	G-PALS	Enstrom 280C-UK-2 Shark	G. Firbank
	G-PAMS	PA-60 Aerostar 601P	Wyndley Nurseries Ltd (G-GAIR)
	G-PAPU	Beech 58PA Baron	Jetmore Ltd (G-NIPU)

Reg.	Type	Owner or Operator
G-PARA	Cessna 207	Activity Aviation Ltd
G-PARI	Cessna 172RG Cutlass	Applied Signs Ltd
G-PARR	Cameron 90 Bottle SS balloon	Virgin Airship & Balloon Co Ltd
G-PASC	MBB Bo 105DBS/4	Police Aviation Services Ltd (G-BNPS)
G-PASD	MBB Bo 105DBS/4	Police Aviation Services Ltd (G-BNRS)
G-PASE	AS.355F-1 Twin Squirrel	Police Aviation Services Ltd
G-PASF	AS.355F-1 Twin Squirrel	Police Aviation Services Ltd (G-SCHU)
G-PASG	MBB Bo 105DBS/4	Police Aviation Services Ltd (G-MHSL)
G-PASH	AS.355F-1 Twin Squirrel	Police Aviation Services Ltd
G-PASU	BN-2T Turbine Islander	Police Aviation Services Ltd (G-BJYY)
G-PASV	BN-2B-21 Islander	Police Aviation Services Ltd (G-BKJH)
G-PASX	MBB Bo 105DBS/4	Police Aviation Services Ltd
G-PATG	Cameron O-90 balloon	P. A. & A. J. A. Bubb
G-PATS	Shaw Europa	N. Surman
G-PATY	Colt Flying Sausage balloon	Colt Balloons Ltd
G-PAVL	Robin R.3000/120	Newcharter (UK) Ltd
G-PAWL	PA-28 Cherokee 140	M. Y. Choudhury (G-AWEU)
G-PAWS	AA-5A Cheetah	Plane Talking Ltd/Elstree
G-PAXX	PA-20 Pacer 135	D. W. & M. R. Grace
G-PAZY	Pazmany PL.4A	C. R. Nash (G-BLAJ)
G-PBAC	EMB-110P1 Bandeirante	Air South West Ltd/Exeter
G-PBBT	Cameron N-56 balloon	Test Valley Balloon Club
G-PBES	Robinson R-22B	P. B. Ellis (G-EXOR/G-CMCM)
G-PCAF	Pietenpol Air Camper	C. C. & F. M. Barley
G-PCDP	Zlin Z.526F Trener Master	Zlin Group
G-PCUB	PA-18 Super Cub 135	M. J. Wilson/Redhill
G-PDHJ	Cessna T.182R	P. G. Vallance Ltd
G-PDOC	PA-44-180 Seminole	Medicare (G-PVAF)/Newcastle
G-PDON	WMB.2 Windtracker balloon	P. J. Donnellan
G-PDSI	Cessna 172N	DA Flying Group
G-PEAK	AB-206B JetRanger 2	Peak Air Charter (G-BLJE)
G-PEAL	Aerotek Pitts S-2A	Plymouth Executive Aviation Ltd
G-PEAT	Cessna 421B	Golden Airways Ltd (G-BBIJ)
G-PEGG	Colt 90A balloon	Michael Pegg Partnership Ltd
G-PEGI	PA-34-200T Seneca II	Tayflite Ltd
G-PEKT	SOCATA TB.20 Trinidad	Gamebore Cartridge Co. Ltd
G-PENN	AA-5B Tiger	L. F. Banks
G-PENY	Sopwith LC-1T Triplane (5492)	J. S. Penny
G-PERR	Cameron 60 Bottle SS balloon ★	British Balloon Museum/Newbury
G-PERS	Colt Soapbox SS balloon	G. V. Beckwith
G-PEST	Hawker Tempest II	–/Sandtoft
G-PETR	PA-28 Cherokee 140	L. C. Barham & R. T. Muir (G-BCJL)
G-PFAA	EAA Biplane Model P	E. W. B. Comber
G-PFAC	FRED Srs 2	G. R. Yates
G-PFAD	Wittman W.8 Tailwind	M. R. Stamp
G-PFAF	FRED Srs 2	M. S. Perkins
G-PFAG	Evans VP-1	P. A. Evans
G-PFAH	Evans VP-1	J. A. Scott
G-PFAI	Clutton EC.2 Easy Too	G. W. Cartledge
G-PFAL	FRED Srs 2	J. McD. Robinson/Bann Foot
G-PFAO	Evans VP-1	P. W. Price
G-PFAP	Currie Wot/SE-5A (C1904)	J. H. Seed
G-PFAR	Isaacs Fury II (K2059)	C. J. Repik
G-PFAT	Monnett Sonerai II	H. B. Carter
G-PFAU	Rand KR-2	D. E. Peace
G-PFAW	Evans VP-1	R. F. Shingler
G-PFAY	EAA Biplane	A. K. Lang & A. L. Young
G-PFBT	V.806 Viscount	British World Airways Ltd (G-AOYP)/ Southend
G-PFML	Robinson R-44 Astro	D. A. Walker & Co
G-PHEL	Robinson R-22B	Focal Point Communications Ltd (G-RUMP)
G-PHIL	Brookland Hornet	A. J. Philpotts
G-PHON	Cameron Phone SS balloon	Redmalt Ltd (G-BTEY)
G-PHSI	Colt 90A balloon	P. H. Strickland & Simpson (Piccadilly) Ltd
G-PHTG	SOCATA TB.10 Tobago	A. R. Murray
G-PIAF	Thunder Ax7-65 balloon	L. Battersley
G-PICT	Colt 180A balloon	J. L. Guy
G-PIDS	Boeing 757-225	Airtours International Airways Ltd
G-PIEL	CP.301A Emeraude	P. R. Thorne (G-BARY)
G-PIES	Thunder Ax7-77Z balloon	Pork Farms Ltd
G-PIET	Pietenpol Air Camper	N. D. Marshall
G-PIGS	SOCATA Rallye 150ST	Boonhill Flying Group (G-BDWB)

Notes	Reg.	Type	Owner or Operator
	G-PIGY	SC.7 Skyvan Srs 3A Variant 100	Hunting Aviaton Ltd
	G-PIIX	Cessna P.210N	D. E. Glass (G-KATH)
	G-PIKE	Robinson R-22 Mariner	Sloane Helicopters Ltd/Sywell
	G-PIKK	PA-28 Cherokee 140	L. P. & I. Keegan (G-AVLA)
	G-PILE	Rotorway Executive 90	J. B. Russell
	G-PINE	Thunder Ax8-90 balloon	J. A. Pine
	G-PING	AA-5A Cheetah	Plane Talking Ltd (G-OCWC/G-WULL)/ Elstree
	G-PINT	Cameron 65 Barrel SS balloon	D. K. Fish
	G-PINX	Lindstrand Pink Panther SS balloon	Virgin Airship & Balloon Co Ltd
	G-PIPA	PA-28-181 Archer III	N. J. & P. D. Fuller
	G-PIPR	PA-18 Super Cub 95	R. G. Trute (G-BCDC)
	G-PIPS	Vans RV-4	C. J. Marsh
	G-PIPY	Cameron 105 Pipe SS balloon	Cameron Balloons Ltd
	G-PITS	Pitts S-2AE Special	The Eitlean Group
	G-PITZ	Pitts S-2A Special	A. K. Halvorsen
	G-PIXS	Cessna 336	Atlantic Bridge Aviation Ltd/Biggin Hill
	G-PJRT	BAe Jetstream 4100	British Aerospace PLC/Prestwick
	G-PKPK	Schweizer 269C	G. B. Parsons
	G-PLAN	Cessna F.150L	G-PLAN Flying Group
	G-PLAX	AS.355F-1 Twin Squirrel	PLM Dollar Group Ltd (G-BPMT)
	G-PLAY	Robin R.2100A	D. R. Austin
	G-PLEE	Cessna 182Q	W. J. & M. Barnes
	G-PLGI	H.S.125 Srs 700B	Polygram Record Operations Ltd (G-BFXT)
	G-PLIV	Pa zmany PL.4	B. P. North
	G-PLMB	AS.350B Ecureuil	PLM Dollar Group Ltd (G-BMMB)
	G-PLMC	AS.350B Ecureuil	PLM Dollar Group Ltd (G-BKUM)
	G-PLMF	AS.350B-1 Ecureuil	PLM Helicopters Ltd
	G-PLMH	AS.350B-2 Ecureuil	PLM Dollar Group Ltd
	G-PLMI	SA.365C-1 Dauphin	PLM Helicopters Ltd
	G-PLOW	Hughes 269B	Sulby Aerial Surveys Ltd (G-AVUM)
	G-PLUS	PA-34-200T Seneca II	C. G. Strasser/Jersey
	G-PLXI	BAe ATP/Jetstream 61	Jetstream Aircraft Ltd (G-MATP)/Prestwick
	G-PLYD	SOCATA TB.20 Trinidad	Bath Stone Co. Ltd
	G-PMAM	Cameron V-65 balloon	P. A. Meecham
	G-PMNF	V.S.361 Spitfire HF.IX	P. R. Monk
	G-POAH	Sikorsky S-76B	P&O Aviation Ltd
	G-POLY	Cameron N-77 balloon	Empty Wallets Balloon Group
	G-POND	Oldfield Baby Lakes	H. Hillenbrand/Germany
	G-PONY	Colt 31A balloon	Ace Balloons (Bath) Ltd
	G-POOH	Piper J-3C-65 Cub	P. & H. Robinson
	G-POOL	ARV Super 2	P. A. Dawson (G-BNHA)
	G-POPA	Beech A36 Bonanza	R. G. Jones
	G-POPE	Eiri PIK-20E-1	C. J. Hadley
	G-POPI	SOCATA TB.10 Tobago	I. S. Hacon & C. J. Earle (G-BKEN)
	G-POPP	Colt 105A balloon	Flying Pictures (Balloons) Ltd
	G-POPS	PA-34-220T Seneca III	Alpine Ltd
	G-PORK	AA-5B Tiger	J. W. & B. A. Flint (G-BFHS)
	G-PORT	Bell 206B JetRanger 3	Image Computer System Ltd
	G-POSA	VPM M.16 Tandem Trainer	P. Crawley (G-BVJM)
	G-POSH	Colt 56A balloon	B. K. Rippon (G-BMPT)
	G-POWE	Robinson R-44 Astro	Heli Air Ltd
	G-POWL	Cessna 182R	Hillhouse Estates Ltd
	G-PPLH	Robinson R-22B	Henderson Financial Management Ltd
	G-PPPP	Denney Kitfox Mk 3	W. J. Dale
	G-PRAG	Brügger MB.2 Colibri	Colibri Flying Group
	G-PRIM	PA-38-112 Tomahawk	Braddock Ltd
	G-PRNT	Cameron V-90 balloon	GS Print (West Midlands) Ltd
	G-PROD	AS.350B-2 Ecureuil	Prodrive Ltd
	G-PROM	AS.350B Ecureuil	JPM Ltd (G-MAGY/G-BIYC)
	G-PROP	AA-5A Cheetah	Photonic Science Ld (G-BHKU)
	G-PROV	P.84 Jet Provost T.52A (T.4)	Bushfire Investments Ltd
	G-PRTT	Cameron N-31 balloon	J. M. Albury
	G-PRUE	Cameron O-84 balloon	Lalondes Residential Ltd
	G-PRXI	V.S.365 Spitfire PR.XI (PL983)	Old Flying Machine Co/Duxford
	G-PSFT	PA-28-161 Warrior II	SFT Aviation Ltd (G-BPDS)/Bournemouth
	G-PSON	Colt Cylinder One SS balloon	M. E. White
	G-PTER	Beech C90 King Air	Moseley Group (PSV) Ltd (G-BIEE)
	G-PTRE	SOCATA TB.20 Trinidad	Trantshore Ltd (G-BNKU)
	G-PTWO	Pilatus P2-05 (U-110)	C. M. Lee
	G-PTYE	Shaw Europa	J. Tye
	G-PUBS	Colt 56 Glass SS balloon	The Balloonatics

Reg.	Type	Owner or Operator	Notes
G-PUFF	Thunder Ax7-77A balloon	Intervarsity Balloon Club	
G-PUFN	Cessna 340A	The Puffin Club	
G-PUMA	AS.332L Super Puma	Bond Helicopters Ltd	
G-PUMB	AS.332L Super Puma	Bond Helicopters Ltd	
G-PUMD	AS.332L Super Puma	Bond Helicopters Ltd	
G-PUME	AS.332L Super Puma	Bond Helicopters Ltd	
G-PUMG	AS.332L Super Puma	Bond Helicopters Ltd	
G-PUMH	AS.332L Super Puma	Bond Helicopters Ltd	
G-PUMI	AS.332L Super Puma	Bond Helicopters Ltd	
G-PUMK	AS.332L Super Puma	Bond Helicopters Ltd	
G-PUML	AS.332L Super Puma	Bond Helicopters Ltd	
G-PUNK	Thunder Ax8-105 balloon	D. J. Farrar	
G-PUPP	B.121 Pup 2	P. A. Teichman (G-BASD)/Elstree	
G-PURE	Cameron 70 Can SS balloon	The Hot-Air Balloon Co Ltd	
G-PURR	AA-5A Cheetah	Plane Talking Ltd (G-BJDN)	
G-PURS	Rotorway Executive	J. E. Houseman	
G-PUSH	Rutan LongEz	E. G. Peterson	
G-PUSI	Cessna T.303	W. R. Swinburn Ltd	
G-PUSS	Cameron N-77 balloon	Bristol Balloons	
G-PUTT	Cameron 76 Golf SS balloon	Lakeside Lodge Golf Centre	
G-PYLN	Cameron Pylon SS balloon	Virgin Airship & Balloon Co Ltd (G-BUSO)	
G-PYOB	SA.341G Gazelle 1	Starbuc Ltd (G-WELA/G-SFTD/G-RIFC)	
G-PYRO	Cameron N-65 balloon	A. C. Booth	
G-PZAZ	PA-31-350 Navajo Chieftain	ML Associates (G-VTAX/G-UTAX)	
G-RAAD	Mooney M.20L	As-Al Ltd	
G-RAAR	BAe 125 Srs 800B	Osprey Executive Aviation Ltd/Southend	
G-RACH	Robinson R-22B	Heli Air Ltd	
G-RACO	PA-28R Cherokee Arrow 200-II	Graco Group Ltd	
G-RADA	Soko P-2 Kraguj	Steerworld Ltd	
G-RAEM	Rutan LongEz	G. F. H. Singleton	
G-RAFA	Grob G.115	RAF College Flying Club Ltd/Cranwell	
G-RAFB	Grob G.115	RAF College Flying Club Ltd/Cranwell	
G-RAFC	Robin R.2112	Group Alpha	
G-RAFE	Thunder Ax7-77 balloon	N. A. Fishlock	
G-RAFF	Learjet 35A	Graff Aviation Ltd/Heathrow	
G-RAFG	Slingsby T.67C	BBC Club/Denham	
G-RAFI	P.84 Jet Provost T.4 (XP672)	R. M. Muir/Jurby	
G-RAFT	Rutan LongEz	H. C. Mackinnon	
G-RAFW	Mooney M.20E	Lukegate Ltd (G-ATHW)	
G-RAGG	Maule M5-235C Lunar Rocket	P. Ragg	
G-RAGS	Pietenpol Air Camper	R. F. Billington	
G-RAHL	Beech 400A Beechjet	Air Hanson Aircraft Sales Ltd	
G-RAID	AD-4NA Skyraider (126922)	Patina Ltd/Duxford	
G-RAIL	Colt 105A balloon	Ballooning World Ltd	
G-RAIN	Maule M5-235C Lunar Rocket	D. S. McKay & J. A. Rayment/ Hinton-in-the-Hedges	
G-RALD	Robinson R-22HP	Heli Air Ltd (G-CHIL)	
G-RAMI	Bell 206B JetRanger 3	Yorkshire Helicopters/Leeds	
G-RAMM	Hughes 369HM	R. A. Kingson	
G-RAMP	Piper J-3C-65 Cub	K. N. Whittall	
G-RAMS	PA-32R-301 Saratoga SP	Air Tobago Ltd/Netherthorpe	
G-RAMY	Bell 206B JetRanger 2	Eastman Aviation Ltd	
G-RANA	Cameron 82 Cheese SS balloon	Consorizio per la Tutela del Formaggio	
G-RAND	Rand KR-2	R. L. Wharmby	
G-RANG	Cameron A-340 balloon	Champagne Balloon Flights Ltd	
G-RANS	Rans S.10 Sakota	J. D. Weller	
G-RANZ	Rans S-10 Sakota	B. A. Phillips	
G-RAPA	BN-2T-4R Defender 4000	Pilatus BN Ltd (G-BJBH)/Bembridge	
G-RAPE	Colt 300A balloon	Adventure Balloon Co Ltd	
G-RAPH	Cameron O-77 balloon	P. B. D. Bird	
G-RAPP	Cameron H-34 balloon	Cameron Balloons Ltd	
G-RARB	Cessna 172N	Richlyn Aviation Ltd (G-BOII)	
G-RARE	Thunder Ax5-42 SS balloon	International Distillers & Vintners Ltd	
G-RASC	Evans VP-2	K. A. Stewart & G. Oldfield	
G-RATE	AA-5A Cheetah	Holmes Rentals (G-BIFF)	
G-RATZ	Shaw Europa	R. Muller	
G-RAVI	Colt 300A balloon	R. S. Hunjan	
G-RAVL	H.P.137 Jetstream Srs 200	Cranfield University (G-AWVK)	
G-RAYA	Denney Kitfox Mk 4	A. K. Ray	
G-RAYE	PA-32 Cherokee Six 260	F. J. Wadia (G-ATTY)	
G-RAYS	Zenair CH.250	B. O. & F. A. Smith	
G-RBBB	Shaw Europa	W. M. Goodburn & I. H. MacLeod	

Notes	Reg.	Type	Owner or Operator
	G-RBOS	Colt AS-105 airship ★	Science Museum/Wroughton
	G-RBOW	Thunder Ax-7-65 balloon	P. G. & S. D. Viney
	G-RBSI	BN-2A Mk III-2 Trislander	Aurigny Air Services Ltd (G-OTSB/ G-BDTO)
	G-RCDI	H.S.125 Srs 700B	Aravco Ltd (G-BJDJ)/Heathrow
	G-RCED	R. Commander 114	Echo Delta Ltd
	G-RCEJ	BAe 125 Srs 800B	Aravco Ltd (G-GEIL)/Farnborough
	G-RCMC	Murphy Renegade 912	R. C. M. Collisson
	G-RCMF	Cameron V-77 balloon	Mouldform Ltd
	G-RDCI	R. Commander 112A	A. C. Hendriksen (G-BFWG)
	G-RDON	WMB.2 Windtracker balloon	P. J. Donnellan (G-BICH)
	G-RDVE	Airbus A.320-231	Airtours International Airways Ltd
	G-READ	Colt 77A balloon	J. Keena
	G-REAH	PA-32R-301 Saratoga SP	T. & S. Y. Reah (G-CELL)/Elstree
	G-REAP	Pitts S-1S Special	R. Dixon
	G-REAS	Vans RV-6A	D. W. Reast
	G-REAT	GA-7 Cougar	Plane Talking Ltd/Elstree
	G-REBI	Colt 90A balloon	Capricorn Balloons Ltd (G-BOYD)
	G-REBL	Hughes 269B	GTS Engineering (Coventry) Ltd
	G-RECK	PA-28 Cherokee 140B	R. J. Grantham & D. Boatswain (G-AXJW)
	G-RECO	Jurca MJ-5L Sirocco	J. D. Tseliki
	G-REDB	Cessna 310Q	Leisure Park Management Ltd (G-BBIC)
	G-REDD	Cessna 310R II	G. Wightman (G-BMGT)
	G-REDX	Experimental Aviation Berkut	G. V. Waters
	G-REEC	Sequoia F.8L Falco	J. D. Tseliki
	G-REEK	AA-5A Cheetah	MPB Flying Group
	G-REEN	Cessna 340	E. & M. Green (G-AZYR)/Guernsey
	G-REES	Jodel D.140C	W. H. Greenwood
	G-REGS	Thunder Ax7-77 balloon	M. E. Gregory
	G-REID	Rotorway Scorpion 133	G. F. Burridge & S. B. Evans (G-BGAW)
	G-RENE	Murphy Renegade 912	J. A. Cuthbertson
	G-RENO	SOCATA TB.10 Tobago	Lamond Ltd
	G-RENT	Robinson R-22B	Rentatruck Self Drive Ltd
	G-REPM	PA-38-112 Tomahawk	Nultree Ltd
	G-REST	Beech P35 Bonanza	C. R. Taylor (G-ASFJ)
	G-RETA	C.A.S.A. 1.131 Jungmann 2000	R. I. Warman (G-BGZC)
	G-REXS	PA-28-181 Archer II	Tatenhill Aviation
	G-REZE	Rutan Vari-Eze	S. D. Brown & S. P. Evans
	G-RFIL	Colt 77A balloon	The Aerial Display Co Ltd
	G-RFIO	Aeromot AMT-200 Super Ximango	G. McLean & R. B. Beck
	G-RFSB	Sportavia RF-5B	S. W. Brown
	G-RGEN	Cessna T.337D	R. J. Willies (G-EDOT/G-BJIY)
	G-RGUS	Fairchild 24R-46A Argus 3 (44-83184)	R. C. Handgraff
	G-RHHT	PA-32RT-300 Lance II	R. W. & M. Struth
	G-RHYS	Rotorway Executive 90	G. Todd
	G-RICC	AS.350B-2 Ecureuil	McAlpine Helicopters Ltd & Gabriel Enterprises Ltd (G-BTXA)
	G-RICH	Cessna F.152	Cloudshire Ltd/Wellesbourne
	G-RICK	Beech 95-B55 Baron	James Jack (Invergordon) Ltd (G-BAAG)
	G-RICS	Shaw Europa	The Flying Property Doctor
	G-RIDE	Stephens Akro	R. Mitchell/Coventry
	G-RIFB	Hughes 269C	R. F. Rhodes & J. C. McHugh
	G-RIFN	Avion Mudry CAP.10B	S. A. W. Becker
	G-RIGB	Thunder Ax7-77 balloon	Antrum & Andrews Ltd
	G-RIGS	PA-60 Aerostar 601P	Techno Engineering
	G-RILY	Monnett Sonerai II	R. Wheeler
	G-RINO	Thunder Ax7-77 balloon	D. J. Head
	G-RINT	CFM Streak Shadow	D. Grint
	G-RISE	Cameron V-77 balloon	D. L. Smith
	G-RIST	Cessna 310R II	GT Aviation (G-DATS)/Bournemouth
	G-RIVT	Vans RV-6	N. Reddish
	G-RIZE	Cameron O-90 balloon	S. F. Burden/Netherlands
	G-RIZI	Cameron N-90 balloon	R. Wiles
	G-RJAH	Boeing Stearman A.75N1	R. J. Horne
	G-RJCP	R. Commander 114B	R. J. Jackson
	G-RJGR	Boeing 757-225	Airtours International Airways Ltd
	G-RJMS	PA-28R-201 Arrow III	M. G. Hill
	G-RJWW	Maule M5-235C Lunar Rocket	Paw Flying Services Ltd (G-BRWG)
	G-RLFI	Cessna FA.152	Tayside Aviation Ltd (G-DFTS)/Aberdeen
	G-RLMC	Cessna 421C	R. D. Lygo
	G-RMCT	Short SD3-60 Variant 100	Gill Airways Ltd (G-BLPU)/Newcastle

Reg.	Type	Owner or Operator	Notes
G-RMIT	Vans RV-4	J. P. Kloos	
G-RMUG	Cameron 90 Mug SS balloon	Nestle UK Ltd	
G-RNAS	D.H.104 Sea Devon C.20 (XK896)	D. W. Hermiston-Hooper/Staverton	
G-RNIE	Cameron 70 Ball SS balloon	Virgin Airship & Balloon Co Ltd	
G-RNLD	Agusta A.109A	Direct Worktops Ltd	
G-RNLI	V.S.236 Walrus I	R. E. Melton	
G-RNRM	Cessna A.185F	RN & R. Marines Sport Parachute Association/Dunkeswell	
G-ROAM	Schempp-Hirth Nimbus 4DM	B. A. Eastwell	
G-ROAR	Cessna 401	Special Scope Ltd (G-BZFL/G-AWSF)	
G-ROBB	Grob G.109B	A. P. Mayne	
G-ROBD	Shaw Europa	R. D. Davies	
G-ROBI	Grob G.109B	A. W. McGarrigle/Cardiff	
G-ROBN	Robin R.1180T	J. G. Beaumont	
G-ROBT	Hawker Hurricane I	R. A. Roberts	
G-ROBY	Colt 17A balloon	Virgin Airship & Balloon Co Ltd	
G-ROCH	Cessna T.303	R. S. Bentley	
G-ROCK	Thunder Ax7-77 balloon	M. A. Green	
G-ROCR	Schweizer 269C	C.S.E. Aviation Ltd/Kidlington	
G-RODD	Cessna 310R II	R. J. Herbert Engineering Ltd (G-TEDD/G-MADI)	
G-RODI	Isaacs Fury (K3731)	M. R. Baker/Shoreham	
G-ROGG	Robinson R-22B	Burman Aviation Ltd/Cranfield	
G-ROGY	Cameron 60 Concept balloon	A. A. Laing	
G-ROKI	R. Commander 114	N. G. P. Evans (G-BFKD)	
G-ROLA	PA-34-200T Seneca	Mala Services Ltd	
G-ROLF	PA-32R-301 Saratoga SP	P. F. Larkins	
G-ROLL	Pitts S-2A Special	Aerial & Aerobatic Services	
G-ROLO	Robinson R-22B	BLS Aviation Ltd	
G-ROMA	Hughes 369HS	Helicopters (Northern) Ltd (G-ROPI/G-ONPP)/Blackpool	
G-ROMS	Lindstrand LBL-105G balloon	International Balloons Ltd	
G-RONA	Shaw Europa	C. M. Noakes	
G-RONC	Aeronca 11AC Chief	I. A. Scott (G-BULV)	
G-RONG	PA-28R Cherokee Arrow 200-II	W. R. Griffiths	
G-RONI	Cameron V-77 balloon	R. E. Simpson	
G-RONS	Robin DR.400/180	R. & K. Baker	
G-RONW	FRED Srs 2	K. Atkinson	
G-ROOK	Cessna F.172P	R. B. & J. E. Kempster	
G-ROPA	Shaw Europa	R. G. Gray	
G-RORI	Folland Gnat T.1	R. C. McCarthy	
G-RORO	Cessna 337B	C. Keane (G-AVIX)	
G-RORY	Piaggio FWP.149D	R. McCarthy (G-TOWN)/Booker	
G-ROSE	Evans VP-1	W. K. Rose	
G-ROSI	Thunder Ax7-77 balloon	J. E. Rose	
G-ROSS	Practavia Pilot Sprite	F. M. T. Ross	
G-ROTI	Luscombe 8A Silvaire	A. L. Chapman & ptnrs	
G-ROTO	Rotorway Executive 90	S. R. Porter	
G-ROTR	Brantly B.2B	GP Services	
G-ROTS	CFM Streak Shadow Srs SA	P. White	
G-ROUP	Cessna F.172M	Stapleford Flying Club Ltd (G-BDPH)	
G-ROUS	PA-34-200T Seneca II	C.S.E. Aviation Ltd/Kidlington	
G-ROUT	Robinson R-22B	R. C. Hields	
G-ROVE	PA-18 Super Cub 135	Caledonian Seaplanes Ltd/Cumbernauld	
G-ROWE	Cessna F.182P	D. Rowe	
G-ROWL	AA-5B Tiger	Aviation Simulation/Biggin Hill	
G-ROWN	Beech 200 Super King Air	Holiday Chemical Holdings Ltd (G-BHLC)	
G-ROWS	PA-28-151 Warrior	Mustarrow Ltd/Liverpool	
G-ROZI	Robinson R-44 Astro	Aquaprint Ltd	
G-ROZY	Cameron R.36 balloon	Jacques W. Soukup Enterprises Ltd	
G-RPEZ	Rutan LongEz	B. A. Fairston & D. Richardson	
G-RRGN	V.S.390 Spitfire PR.XIX (PS853)	Rolls-Royce PLC	
G-RRSG	Thunder Ax7-77 balloon	M. T. Stevens	
G-RSFT	PA-28-181 Warrior II	SFT Aviation Ltd (G-WARI)/Bournemouth	
G-RSKR	PA-28-161 Warrior II	Southern Air Ltd (G-BOJY)/Shoreham	
G-RSMA	Bell 206B JetRanger 3	Gama Leasing Ltd (G-SHZZ/G-BNUW)	
G-RSSF	Denney Kitfox Mk 2	R. W. Somerville	
G-RSWW	Robinson R-22B	Woodstock Enterprises	
G-RTBI	Thunder Ax6-56 balloon	P. J. Waller	
G-RUBB	AA-5B Tiger	R. Bessant	
G-RUBI	Thunder Ax7-77 balloon	Warren & Johnson	
G-RUBY	PA-28RT-201T Turbo Arrow IV	Arrow Aircraft Group (G-BROU)	
G-RUDD	Cameron V-65 balloon	N. A. Apsey	

Notes	Reg.	Type	Owner or Operator
	G-RUDI	QAC Quickie Q.2	R. Brandenberger
	G-RUGB	Cameron 89 Egg SS balloon	D. N. Belton
	G-RUIA	Cessna F.172M	F. Daly
	G-RUMN	AA-1A Trainer	D. A. Whitmore & A. Ward
	G-RUNT	Cassutt Racer IIIM	The Cassutt Flying Group
	G-RUSO	Robinson R-22B	N. P. Graham
	G-RUSS	Cessna 172N	Leisure Lease/Southend
	G-RVEE	Vans RV-6	J. C. A. Wheeler
	G-RVIT	Vans RV-6	P. J. Shotbolt
	G-RVVI	Vans RV-6	J. E. Alsford & J. N. Parr
	G-RWHC	Cameron A-180 balloon	Hourds Ltd
	G-RWIN	Rearwin 175	G. Kay
	G-RWSS	Denney Kitfox Mk 2	R. W. Somerville
	G-RWWW	W.S.55 Whirlwind HCC.12 (XR486)	Whirlwind Helicopters Ltd/Redhill
	G-RXUK	Lindstrand LBL-105A balloon	Flying Pictures (Balloons) Ltd
	G-SAAB	R. Commander 112TC	SAAB Group (G-BEFS)
	G-SAAM	Cessna T.182R	H. C. Danby & M. D. Harvey (G-TAGL)
	G-SABA	PA-28R-201T Turbo Arrow III	C. Geravelis (G-BFEN)
	G-SABR	NA F-86A Sabre (8178)	Golden Apple Operations Ltd/Bournemouth
	G-SACB	Cessna F.152 II	Sky Pro Ltd (G-BFRB)
	G-SACD	Cessna F.172H	Northbrook College of Design & Technology (G-AVCD)/Shoreham
	G-SACE	Cessna F.150L	Arrow Aircraft Ltd (G-AZLK)
	G-SACF	Cessna 152 II	T. M. & M. L. Jones
	G-SACI	PA-28-161 Warrior II	PJC (Leasing) Ltd
	G-SACO	PA-28-161 Warrior II	The Barn Gallery
	G-SACR	PA-28-161 Cadet	Sherburn Aero Club Ltd
	G-SACS	PA-28-161 Cadet	Sherburn Aero Club Ltd
	G-SACT	PA-28-161 Cadet	Sherburn Aero Club Ltd
	G-SACU	PA-28-161 Cadet	Sherburn Aero Club Ltd
	G-SACZ	PA-28-161 Warrior II	Cee-Zed Aviation Ltd
	G-SADE	Cessna F.150L	N. E. Sams (G-AZJW)
	G-SAEW	AS.355F-2 Twin Squirrel	Veritair Ltd
	G-SAFE	Cameron N-77 balloon	P. J. Waller
	G-SAFR	SAAB 91D Safir	B. Johansson
	G-SAGA	Grob G.109B	G-GROB Ltd/Booker
	G-SAGE	Luscombe 8A Silvaire	R. D. Masters (G-AKTL)
	G-SAHI	Trago Mills SAH-1	Lovaux Ltd/Bournemouth
	G-SAIR	Cessna 421C	Air Support Aviation Services Ltd (G-OBCA)
	G-SALA	PA-32 Cherokee Six 300E	Stonebold Ltd
	G-SALL	Cessna F.150L (Tailwheel)	D. D. Smith
	G-SAMG	Grob G.109B	RAFGSA/Bicester
	G-SAMI	Cameron N-90 balloon	Flying Pictures (Balloons) Ltd (G-BWSE)
	G-SAMM	Cessna 340A	M. R. Cross
	G-SAMY	Shaw Europa	N. Starling
	G-SAMZ	Cessna 150D	N. E. Sams (G-ASSO)/Cranfield
	G-SANB	Beech E90 King Air	Maynard & Harris Holdings Ltd (G-BGNU)
	G-SAND	Schweizer 269C	Aerocroft Ltd
	G-SARA	PA-28-181 Archer II	R. P. Lewis
	G-SARH	PA-28-161 Warrior II	Sussex Flying Club Ltd/Shoreham
	G-SARK	BAC.167 Strikemaster Mk 84	Sark International Airways Ltd
	G-SARO	Saro Skeeter Mk 12 (XL812)	F. F. Chamberlain
	G-SASU	AS.355F-1 Twin Squirrel	Aeromega Ltd (G-BSSM/G-BMTC/G-BKUK)
	G-SATL	Cameron 105 Sphere SS balloon	Ballonwerbung Hamburg GmbH/Germany
	G-SAUF	Colt 90A balloon	K. H. Medau
	G-SAXO	Cameron N-105 balloon	Flying Pictures (Balloons) Ltd
	G-SBAS	Beech B200 Super King Air	Bond Helicopters Ltd (G-BJJV)/Aberdeen
	G-SBEA	Boeing 737-204ADV	Sabre Airways Ltd (G-BFVB)/Peach Air
	G-SBEB	Boeing 737-204ADV	Sabre Airways Ltd (G-BAZH)/Peach Air
	G-SBLT	Steen Skybolt	M. A. McCallum & H. Lees
	G-SBUS	BN-2A-26 Islander	Isles of Scilly Skybus Ltd (G-BMMH)/St Just
	G-SCAN	Vinten-Wallis WA-116/100	K. H. Wallis
	G-SCAT	Cessna F.150F (tailwheel)	Broxburn & Wallis Ltd (G-ATRN)
	G-SCFO	Cameron O-77 balloon	M. K. Grigson
	G-SCLX	FLS Aerospace Sprint 160	FLS Aerospace (Lovaux) Ltd (G-PLYM)/Bournemouth
	G-SCPL	PA-28 Cherokee 140	R. D. Coombes (G-BPVL)/Staverton

Reg.	Type	Owner or Operator	Notes
G-SCRU	Cameron A-250 balloon	Societe Bombard SARL/France	
G-SCTA	Westland Scout AH.1	H. Butcher Technology Realisation Ltd	
G-SCTT	HPR-7 Herald 210	Channel Express (Air Services) Ltd (G-ASPJ)/Bournemouth	
G-SCUB	PA-18 Super Cub 135 (542447)	N. D. Needham Farms	
G-SDEV	D.H.104 Sea Devon C.20 (XK895)	De Havilland Aviation Ltd/Swansea	
G-SDLW	Cameron O-105 balloon	P. J. Smart	
G-SEAB	Republic RC-3 Seabee	B. A. Farries	
G-SEAI	Cessna U.206G (amphibian)	Aerofloat Ltd	
G-SEAT	Colt 42 balloon	Virgin Airship & Balloon Co Ltd	
G-SEED	Piper J-3C-65 Cub	J. H. Seed	
G-SEEK	Cessna T.210N	Verikeen Ltd	
G-SEGA	Cameron 90 Sonic SS balloon	Virgin Airship & Balloon Co Ltd	
G-SEGO	Robinson R-22B	Burman Aviation Ltd/Cranfield	
G-SEJW	PA-28-161 Warrior II	Truman Aviation Ltd/Tollerton	
G-SELL	Robin DR.400/180	G-SELL Flying Group	
G-SELY	AB-206B JetRanger 3	Greencraft Ltd	
G-SENA	Rutan LongEz	G. Bennett	
G-SEND	Colt 90A balloon	Redmalt Ltd	
G-SENX	PA-34-200T Seneca II	Senair Charter Ltd (G-DARE/G-WOTS/ G-SEVL)	
G-SEPA	AS.355N Twin Squirrel	Receiver for the Metroplitan Police (G-METD/G-BUJF)	
G-SEPB	AS.355N Twin Squirrel	Metropolitan Police (G-BVSE)	
G-SEPC	AS.355N Twin Squirrel	Receiver for Metropolitan Police (G-BWGV)	
G-SEPT	Cameron N-105 balloon	Deproco UK Ltd	
G-SERA	Enstrom F-28A-UK	W. R. Pitcher (G-BAHU)	
G-SERL	SOCATA TB.10 Tobago	R. J. & G. Searle (G-LANA)/Rochester	
G-SEUK	Cameron 80 TV SS balloon	Flying Pictures (Balloons) Ltd	
G-SEVA	SE-5A (replica) (F141)	I. D. Gregory	
G-SEVE	Cessna 172N	M. Connolly	
G-SEXI	Cessna 172M	S. J. Ellis	
G-SEXY	AA-1 Yankee	*stored*/Liverpool (G-AYLM)	
G-SFBH	Boeing 737-46N	British Midland Airways Ltd/E. Midlands	
G-SFHR	PA-23 Aztec 250F	Comed Aviation Ltd (G-BHSO)	
G-SFOX	Rotorway Executive 90	Magpie Computer Services Ltd (G-BUAH)	
G-SFPA	Cessna F.406	Scottish Fisheries Protection Agency	
G-SFPB	Cessna F.406	Scottish Fisheries Protection Agency	
G-SFRY	Thunder Ax7-77 balloon	R. J. Fry	
G-SFTZ	Slingsby T.67M Firefly	Airborne Services Ltd	
G-SGAS	Colt 77A balloon	Avongas Ltd	
G-SGSE	PA-28-181 Archer II	G. E. J. Spooner (G-BOJX)	
G-SHAA	Enstrom 280-UK Shark	Ribble Aviation Ltd	
G-SHAW	PA-30 Twin Comanche 160B	E. R. Meredith & M. D. Faiers	
G-SHCB	Schweizer 269C-1	C.S.E. Aviation Ltd/Kidlington	
G-SHCC	AB-206B JetRanger 2	Yorkshire Helicopter Centre Ltd	
G-SHEA	BAe 125 Srs 800B	Shell Aircraft Ltd (G-BUWC)/Heathrow	
G-SHEC	BAe 125-1000B	Shell Aircraft Ltd (G-SCCC)	
G-SHED	PA-28-181 Archer II	P. T. Crouch & R. M. Gingell (G-BRAU)	
G-SHEL	Cameron O-56 balloon	The Shell Company of Hong Kong Ltd	
G-SHFL	Cameron N-77 balloon	M. C. Bradley/Hong Kong	
G-SHIM	CFM Streak Shadow	E. S. Shimmin/Shobdon	
G-SHIP	PA-23 Aztec 250F ★	Midland Air Museum/Coventry	
G-SHIV	GA-7 Cougar	Westley Aviation Services	
G-SHNN	Enstrom 280C	CJ Services	
G-SHOG	Colomban MC.15 Cri-Cri	V. S. E. Norman (G-PFAB)/Rendcomb	
G-SHOO	Hughes TH-55A	Starline Helicopters Ltd	
G-SHOT	Cameron V-77 balloon	E. C. Moore	
G-SHOW	M.S.733 Alycon	Vintage Aircraft Team/Cranfield	
G-SHPP	Hughes TH-55A	R. P. Bateman & A. C. Braithwaite	
G-SHRL	Jodel D.18	M. W. Kilvert & G. Trevor	
G-SHRR	AB-206B JetRanger 2	Frank Owen Commercial Vehicle Spares (G-FSDA/G-AWJW)	
G-SHSS	Enstrom 280C-UK Shark	PR Aviation (G-BENO)	
G-SHUG	PA-28R-201T Turbo Arrow III	N. E. Rennie	
G-SHUU	Enstrom 280C-UK-2 Shark	D. Ellis (G-OMCP/G-KENY/G-BJFG)	
G-SIAL	Hunter F.58	Sark International Airways Ltd	
G-SIAN	Cameron V-77 balloon	S. M. Jones	
G-SIGN	PA-39 Twin Comanche 160 C/R	M. P. Bolshaw & P. Karl/Elstree	
G-SIIB	Pitts S-2B Special	G. P. Clemans-Gibbon (G-BUVY)	
G-SIII	Extra EA.300	Firebird Aerobatics Ltd/Booker	
G-SIMI	Cameron A-315 balloon	R. S. Hunjan	

Notes	Reg.	Type	Owner or Operator
	G-SING	Beech B60 Duke	T & G Engineering Co Ltd
	G-SION	PA-38-112 Tomahawk II	Naiad Air Services
	G-SIPA	SIPA 903	T. J. McRae (G-BGBM)
	G-SITE	AS.355F-1 Twin Squirrel	Bridge Street Nominees Ltd (G-BPHC)
	G-SIVA	MDH Hughes 369E	C. J. Siva-Jothy (G-TBIX)/Redhill
	G-SIXC	Douglas DC-6A	Atlantic Air Transport Ltd/Coventry
	G-SIXX	Colt 77A balloon	G. E. Harris & S. C. Kinsey
	G-SIZE	Lindstrand LBL-310A balloon	Adventure Balloon Co Ltd
	G-SJAB	PA-39 Twin Comanche 160 C/R	Foyle Flyers Ltd
	G-SJGM	Cessna 182R	S. J. G. Mole/Halfpenny Green
	G-SJMC	Boeing 767-31KER	Airtours International Airways Ltd
	G-SKAN	Cessna F.172M	Bustard Flying Club Ltd (G-BFKT)
	G-SKIL	Cameron N-77 balloon	M. C. & W. A. Swift
	G-SKIP	Cameron N-77 balloon	Skipton Building Soc
	G-SKIS	Tri-R Kis	S. D. Barnard
	G-SKKB	PA-31 Turbo Navajo	Rentair Ltd (G-BBDS)
	G-SKYD	Pitts S-2B Special	Skydancer Aviation Ltd
	G-SKYE	Cessna TU.206G	RAF Sport Parachute Association
	G-SKYH	Cessna 172N	Elgor Hire Purchase & Credit Ltd/ Southend
	G-SKYI	Air Command 532 Elite	P. J. Troy-Davies
	G-SKYM	Cessna F.337E	Bencray Ltd (G-AYHW) *(stored)*/Blackpool
	G-SKYP	Cameron A-120 balloon	Esthwaite Holidays Ltd
	G-SKYR	Cameron A-180 balloon	PSH Skypower Ltd
	G-SKYS	Cameron O-84 balloon	J. R. Christopher
	G-SKYT	Sky Arrow 650TC	C. L. Farrell
	G-SKYY	Cameron A-250 balloon	PSH Skypower Ltd
	G-SKYZ	PA-34-200T Seneca II	Park Aeroleasing Ltd
	G-SLAC	Cameron N-77 balloon	The Scottish Life Assurance Co
	G-SLCI	Thunder Ax8-90 balloon	S. L. Cuhat
	G-SLEA	Mudry/CAARP CAP.10B	P. D. Southerington/Sturgate
	G-SLII	Cameron O-90 balloon	R. B. & A. M. Harris
	G-SLIM	Colt 56A balloon	Hot-Air Balloon Co Ltd
	G-SLNE	Agusta A.109A-II	Sloane Helicopters Ltd (G-EEVS/ G-OTSL/Sywell
	G-SLYN	PA-28-161 Warrior II	G. E. Layton
	G-SMAF	Sikorsky S-76A	Fayair (Jersey) 1984 Ltd
	G-SMAX	Cameron O-105 balloon	Cameron Balloons Ltd
	G-SMDB	Boeing 737-36N	British Midland Airways Ltd/E. Midlands
	G-SMIG	Cameron O-65 balloon	Hong Kong Balloon & Airship Club
	G-SMIT	Messerschmitt Bf.109G-6	Fairoaks Aviation Services Ltd
	G-SMJJ	Cessna 414A	Gull Air Ltd/Guernsey
	G-SMTC	Colt Flying Hut SS balloon	Shiplake Investments Ltd
	G-SMTH	PA-28 Cherokee 140	D. M. Banner (G-AYJS)/Liverpool
	G-SNAK	Lindstrand LBL-105A balloon	Ballooning Adventures Ltd
	G-SNAP	Cameron V-77 balloon	C. J. S. Limon
	G-SNAX	Colt 69A balloon	Derwent Valley Foods Ltd
	G-SNAZ	Enstrom F-28F	Thornhill Music Ltd (G-BRCP)
	G-SNDY	Piper J-3C-65 Cub	R. R. K. Mayall
	G-SNEV	CFM Streak Shadow SA	N. G. Smart
	G-SNOW	Cameron V-77 balloon	M. J. Snow
	G-SOAR	Eiri PIK-20E	F. W. Fay
	G-SOFA	Cameron N-65 balloon	M. J. Axtell
	G-SOFT	Thunder Ax7-77 balloon	A. J. Bowen
	G-SOKO	Soko P-2 Kraguj (30149)	Soko Aviation (G-BRXK)/Liverpool
	G-SOLA	Aero Designs Star-Lite SL.1	J. P. Lethaby
	G-SOLD	Robinson R-22A	Travel Management Ltd
	G-SOLO	Pitts S-2S Special	Landitfast Ltd
	G-SONA	SOCATA TB.10 Tobago	J. Greenwood (G-BIBI)
	G-SONY	Aero Commander 200D	General Airline Ltd (G-BGPS)
	G-SOOC	Hughes 369HS	Colour Library Books (G-BRRX)
	G-SOOE	Hughes 369E	R. W. Nash
	G-SOOK	Sukhoi Su-26M	S. Jones
	G-SOOM	Glaser-Dirks DG.500M	Glaser-Dirks UK/Rufforth
	G-SOOR	AB-206A JetRanger	Thorneygrove Ltd (G-FMAL/G-RIAN/ G-BHSG)
	G-SOOS	Colt 21A balloon	P. J. Stapley
	G-SOOT	PA-28 Cherokee 180	Thornton Browne Ltd (G-AVNM)/Exeter
	G-SORT	Cameron N-90 balloon	A. Brown
	G-SOUL	Cessna 310R	Atlantic Air Transport Ltd/Coventry
	G-SOUP	Cameron C-80 balloon	M. G. Barlow
	G-SPAM	Light Aero Avid Aerobat	R. W. Fair
	G-SPEE	Robinson R-22B	Speed Helicopters Ltd (G-BPJC)/Redhill

Reg.	Type	Owner or Operator	Notes
G-SPEL	Sky 220-24 balloon	Pendle Balloon Co	
G-SPEY	AB-206B JetRanger 3	Castle Air Charters Ltd (G-BIGO)	
G-SPIN	Pitts S-2A Special	R. P. Grace & P. L. Goldberg	
G-SPIT	V.S.379 Spitfire FR.XIV (MV293)	Patina Ltd (G-BGHB)/Duxford	
G-SPOG	Jodel DR.1050	A. C. Frost (G-AXVS)	
G-SPOL	MBB Bo 105CBS/4	Bond Helicopters Ltd	
G-SPYI	Bell 206B JetRanger 3	A. J. Sinclair (G-BVRC/G-BSJC)	
G-SROE	Westland Scout AH.1	Bolenda Engineering Ltd	
G-SRVO	Cameron N-90 balloon	Servo & Electronic Sales Ltd	
G-SSBS	Colting Ax77 balloon	K. J. & M. E. Gregory	
G-SSFC	PA-34-200 Seneca II	SFC (Air Taxis) Ltd (G-BBXG)/ Stapleford	
G-SSFT	PA-28-161 Warrior II	SFT Aviation Ltd (G-BHIL)/Bournemouth	
G-SSGS	Shaw Europa	SGS Partnership	
G-SSIX	Rans S.6-116 Coyote II	J. V. Squires	
G-SSKY	BN-2B-26 Islander	Isles of Scilly Skybus Ltd (G-BSWT)	
G-SSSC	Sikorsky S-76C	Bond Helicopters Ltd/Aberdeen	
G-SSSD	Sikorsky S-76C	Bond Helicopters Ltd/Aberdeen	
G-SSSE	Sikorsky S-76C	Bond Helicopters Ltd/Aberdeen	
G-SSTI	Cameron N-105 balloon	British Airways	
G-SSWV	Sportavia Fournier RF-5B	Skylark Flying Group	
G-STAG	Cameron O-65 balloon	The New Holker Estates Co Ltd	
G-STAT	Cessna U.206F	Wingglider Ltd	
G-STAV	Cameron O-84 balloon	F. Horsfall & B. J. Reeves	
G-STEF	Hughes 369HS	Source Ltd (G-BKTK)/Thruxton	
G-STEN	Stemme S.10	W. A. H. Kahn	
G-STEP	Schweizer 269C	Geraint Hill Car Sales Ltd	
G-STER	Bell 206B JetRanger 3	Albany Helicopters Ltd	
G-STEV	Jodel DR.221	S. W. Talbot/Long Marston	
G-STMP	SNCAN Stampe SV-4A	W. R. Partridge	
G-STOX	Bell 206B JetRanger 2	Burman Aviation Ltd (G-BNIR)/Cranfield	
G-STOY	Robinson R-22B	Tickstop Ltd	
G-STRK	CFM Streak Shadow Srs SA	E. J. Hadley	
G-STRM	Cameron N-90 balloon	Royal Mail Streamline	
G-STUA	Aerotek Pitts S-2A Special (modified)	Aero-Balance Aviation/White Waltham	
G-STUB	Christen Pitts S-2B Special	R. N. Goode & T. L. P. Delaney/ White Waltham	
G-STVN	HPR-7 Herald 210	Channel Express (Air Services) Ltd/ Bournemouth	
G-STWF	Boeing 737-36N	British Midland Airways Ltd/E. Midlands	
G-STWO	ARV Super 2	G. E. Morris	
G-STYL	Pitts S-1S Special	A. Stanford/Crosland Moor	
G-SUEE	Airbus A.320-231	Airtours International Airways Ltd (G-IEAG)	
G-SUFC	H.S.125 Srs 600B	Chase Montagu Ltd (G-BETV)	
G-SUIT	Cessna 210N	Edinburgh Air Centre Ltd	
G-SUKI	PA-38-112 Tomahawk	Western Air Training Ltd (G-BPNV)/ Thruxton	
G-SULY	Monnett Moni	M. J. Sullivan	
G-SUMT	Robinson R-22B	Frankham Bros Ltd (G-BUKD)	
G-SUPA	PA-18 Super Cub 150	Crop Aviation (UK) Ltd	
G-SURG	PA-30 Twin Comanche 160B	A. R. Taylor (G-VIST/G-AVHZ)	
G-SURV	BN-2T-4R Defender 4000	Pilatus BN Ltd (G-BVHZ)	
G-SUSI	Cameron V-77 baloon	H. S. & C. J. Dryden	
G-SUSY	P-51D-25-NA Mustang (472773)	P. J. Morgan	
G-SUZI	Beech 95-B55 Baron	Bebecar (UK) Ltd (G-BAXR)	
G-SUZN	PA-28-161 Warrior II	The St. George Flying Club/Teesside	
G-SUZY	Taylor JT.1 Monoplane	D. I. Law	
G-SVBF	Cameron A-180 balloon	Virgin Balloon Flights Ltd	
G-SVIV	SNCAN Stampe SV-4C	A. J. Clarry & S. F. Bancroft	
G-SVLB	H.S.125 Srs 700B	Solvalub Trading Ltd (G-BNBO)	
G-SWEB	Cameron N-90 balloon	Air 2 Air Ltd	
G-SWEL	Hughes 369HS	I. C. & L. E. Stigwell (G-RBUT)	
G-SWIF	V.S.541 Swift F.7	Jet Heritage Ltd/Bournemouth	
G-SWIM	Taylor Coot Amphibian (modified)	R. J. Hopkins	
G-SWIS	D.H.100 Vampire FB.6 (J-1149)	Hunter Wing Ltd/Bournemouth	
G-SWIV	Lindstrand LBL-240A balloon	Airborne Adventures Ltd	
G-SWOT	Currie Super Wot (C3011)	J. D. Haslam/Breighton	
G-SWPR	Cameron N-56 balloon	A. Brown	
G-SWSH	Mini-500	Aerial Enterprises Ltd	
G-SWUN	Pitts S-1M Special (modified)	T. G. Lloyd (G-BSXH)	
G-SYCO	Shaw Europa	J. T. Fillingham	

Notes	Reg.	Type	Owner or Operator
	G-SYFW	Focke-Wulf Fw.190 replica (2+1)	M. R. Parr
	G-SYPA	AS.355F-2 Twin Squirrel	South Yorkshire Police Authority (G-BPRE)
	G-TACK	Grob G.109B	Oval (275) Ltd/Bristol
	G-TAFF	C.A.S.A. 1.131E Jungmann 1000	A. Horsfall (G-BFNE)Breighton
	G-TAFI	Bücker Bu133 Jungmeister	R. J. Lamplough
	G-TAGS	PA-28-161 Warrior II	C.S.E. Aviation Ltd/Kidlington
	G-TAIL	Cessna 150J	Aviators Flight Centre/Southend
	G-TAIR	PA-34-200T Seneca II	Branksome Dene Garage/Bournemouth
	G-TAMY	Cessna 421B	Malcolm Enamellers (Midlands) Ltd
	G-TANI	GA-7 Cougar	S. Spier (G-VJAI/G-OCAB/G-BICF)/Elstree
	G-TANK	Cameron N-90 balloon	Hoyers (UK) Ltd
	G-TAPE	PA-23 Aztec 250D	D. J. Hare (G-AWVW)
	G-TART	PA-28-236 Dakota	C. A. Herbert
	G-TARV	ARV Super 2	B. & P. B. Childs
	G-TASK	Cessna 404	Bravo Aviation Ltd
	G-TATE	Cameron A-180 balloon	Freetime (UK) Ltd
	G-TATT	GY-20 Minicab	L. Tattershall
	G-TAXI	PA-23 Aztec 250E	Yorkair Ltd/Leeds
	G-TAYI	Grob G.115	Soaring (Oxford) Ltd (G-DODO)
	G-TAYS	Cessna F.152 II	Tayside Aviation Ltd (G-LFCA)/Aberdeen
	G-TBAG	Murphy Renegade II	M. R. Tetley
	G-TBIC	BAe 146-200	Flightline Ltd/Stansted
	G-TBIO	SOCATA TB.10 Tobago	R. A. Perrot
	G-TBRD	Lockheed T-33A (54-21261)	Classic Aviation Ltd (G-JETT/G-OAHB)
	G-TBXX	SOCATA TB.20 Trinidad	D. A. Phillips & Co
	G-TBZI	SOCATA TB.21 Trinidad	W. R. M. Beesley
	G-TBZO	SOCATA TB.20 Trinidad	D. L. Clarke & M. J. M. Hopper/Shoreham
	G-TCAN	Colt 69A balloon	H. C. J. Williams
	G-TCAP	BAe 125 Srs 800B	British Aerospace PLC
	G-TCDI	H.S.125 Srs 403B	Aravco Ltd (G-SHOP/G-BTUF)
	G-TCMP	Robinson R-22B	Thornhill Aviation Ltd
	G-TCOM	PA-30 Twin Comanche 160B	Mega Yield Ltd
	G-TCTC	PA-28RT-201 Arrow IV	Terry Coleman (UK) Ltd
	G-TCUB	Piper J-3C-65 Cub	C. Kirk
	G-TDFS	IMCO Callair A.9	Dollarhigh Ltd (G-AVZA)
	G-TDTW	Hawker Hurricane XIIB (5450)	Hawker Restorations Ltd
	G-TEAL	Thurston TSC-1A1 Teal	K. Heeley/Crosland Moor
	G-TECC	Aeronca 7AC Champion	T. E. C. Cushing/Little Snoring
	G-TECH	R. Commander 114	P. A. Reed (G-BEDH)/Denham
	G-TECK	Cameron V-77 balloon	G. M. N. Spencer
	G-TEDF	Cameron N-90 balloon	Fort Vale Engineering Ltd
	G-TEDS	SOCATA TB.10 Tobago	E. W. Lyon (G-BHCO)
	G-TEDY	Evans VP-1	N. K. Marston (G-BHGN)
	G-TEDZ	Tipsy T.66 Nipper Srs 3	C. J. D. Edwards
	G-TEEZ	Cameron N-90 balloon	Fresh Air Ltd
	G-TEFC	PA-28 Cherokee 140	A. R. Knight
	G-TELY	Agusta A.109A-II	Castle Air Charters Ltd
	G-TEMP	PA-28 Cherokee 180	BEV Piper Group (G-AYBK)/Andrewsfield
	G-TEMT	Hawker Tempest II	–/Sandtoft
	G-TENT	J/1N Alpha	R. Callaway-Lewis (G-AKJU)
	G-TERY	PA-28-181 Archer II	T. Barlow (G-BOXZ)/Barton
	G-TEST	PA-34-200 Seneca	Stapleford Flying Club Ltd (G-BLCD)
	G-TEWS	PA-28 Cherokee 140	G-TEWS Flying Group (G-KEAN/ G-AWTM)
	G-TFCI	Cessna FA.152	Tayside Aviation Ltd/Dundee
	G-TFOX	Denney Kitfox Mk 2	F. A. Roberts
	G-TFRB	Air Command 532 Elite	F. R. Blennerhassett
	G-TFUN	Valentin Taifun 17E	NW Taifun Group
	G-TGAS	Cameron O-160 balloon	Zebedee Balloon Service
	G-TGER	AA-5B Tiger	Plane Talking Ltd (G-BFZP)/Elstree
	G-THCL	Cessna 550 Citation II	Tower House Consultants Ltd
	G-THEA	Boeing Stearman E.75	L. M. Walton
	G-THLS	MBB Bo 105DBS/4	Bond Helicopters Ltd (G-BCXO)
	G-THOM	Thunder Ax6-56 balloon	T. H. Wilson
	G-THOR	Thunder Ax8-105 balloon	N. C. Faithfull/Holland
	G-THOS	Thunder Ax7-77 balloon	M. J. Wilson-Whitaker & S. Walwin
	G-THSL	PA-28R-201 Arrow III	D. M. Markscheffe
	G-THUR	Beech 200 Super King Air	Bilina Consultants Ltd
	G-THZL	SOCATA TB.20 Trinidad	Thistle Aviation Ltd
	G-TICK	Cameron V-77 balloon	T. J. Tickler
	G-TICL	Airbus A.320-231	Airtours International Airways Ltd

Reg.	Type	Owner or Operator	Notes
G-TIDS	Jodel 150	J. B. Dovey/Ipswich	
G-TIGA	D.H.82A Tiger Moth	D. E. Leatherland (G-AOEG)	
G-TIGB	AS.332L Super Puma	Bristow Helicopters Ltd (G-BJXC)	
G-TIGC	AS.332L Super Puma	Bristow Helicopters Ltd (G-BJYH)	
G-TIGE	AS.332L Super Puma	Bristow Helicopters Ltd (G-BJYJ)	
G-TIGF	AS.332L Super Puma	Bristow Helicopters Ltd	
G-TIGG	AS.332L Super Puma	Bristow Helicopters Ltd	
G-TIGI	AS.332L Super Puma	Bristow Helicopters Ltd	
G-TIGL	AS.332L Super Puma	Bristow Helicopters Ltd	
G-TIGM	AS.332L Super Puma	Bristow Helicopters Ltd	
G-TIGO	AS.332L Super Puma	Bristow Helicopters Ltd	
G-TIGP	AS.332L Super Puma	Bristow Helicopters Ltd	
G-TIGR	AS.332L Super Puma	Bristow Helicopters Ltd	
G-TIGS	AS.332L Super Puma	Bristow Helicopters Ltd	
G-TIGT	AS.332L Super Puma	Bristow Helicopters Ltd	
G-TIGU	AS.332L Super Puma	Bristow Helicopters Ltd	
G-TIGW	AS.332L Super Puma	Bristow Helicopters Ltd	
G-TIGZ	AS.332L Super Puma	British International Helicopters	
G-TIII	Aerotek Pitts S-2A	M. R. Jones (G-BGSE)	
G-TILE	Robinson R-22B	M. J. Webb & C. R. Woodwise	
G-TILI	Bell 206B JetRanger	CIM Helicopters	
G-TILL	Robinson R-22B	P. A. Till	
G-TIMB	Rutan Vari-Eze	T. M. Bailey (G-BKXJ)	
G-TIME	Ted Smith Aerostar 601P	Business Aircraft Rental Service Ltd	
G-TIMJ	Rand KR-2	N. Seaton	
G-TIMK	PA-28-181 Archer II	T. Baker	
G-TIMM	Folland Gnat T.1 (XM693)	T. J. Manna/Cranfield	
G-TIMP	Aeronca 7BCM Champion	T. E. Phillips	
G-TIMS	Falconar F-12A	T. Sheridan	
G-TIMW	PA-28 Cherokee 140C	W. H. Sanders (G-AXSH)	
G-TINA	SOCATA TB.10 Tobago	A. Lister	
G-TING	Cameron O-120 balloon	Floating Sensations Ltd	
G-TINS	Cameron N-90 balloon	Bass & Tennent Sales Ltd	
G-TINY	Z.526F Trener Master	Air V8 Ltd	
G-TIPS	Tipsy T.66 Nipper Srs 5	R. F. L. Cuypers	
G-TJAY	PA-22 Tri-Pacer 135	D. D. Saint	
G-TJHI	Cessna 500 Citation	Trustair Ltd (G-CCCL/G-BEIZ)/Blackpool	
G-TJPM	BAe 146-300QT	TNT Express Worldwide (UK) Ltd (G-BRGK)	
G-TKGR	Lindstrand Racing Car SS balloon	International Balloons Ltd	
G-TKIS	Tri-R Kis	T. J. Bone	
G-TKPZ	Cessna 310R	Ace Aviation Consultancy & Edinburgh Air Charter Ltd (G-BRAH)	
G-TLME	Robinson R-44 Astro	TJB Associates Ltd	
G-TMDP	Airbus A.320-231	Airtours International Airways Ltd	
G-TMKI	P.56 Provost T.1	T. J. Manna/Cranfield	
G-TMMC	AS.355F-1 Twin Squirrel	McAlpine Helicopters Ltd (G-JLCO)	
G-TNTA	BAe 146-200QT	TNT Express Worldwide Ltd	
G-TNTB	BAe 146-200QT	TNT Express Worldwide Ltd	
G-TNTE	BAe 146-300QT	TNT Express Worldwide Ltd (G-BRPW)	
G-TNTG	BAe 146-300QT	TNT European Airlines Ltd (G-BSUY)	
G-TNTK	BAe 146-300QT	TNT European Airlines Ltd (G-BSXL)	
G-TNTL	BAe 146-300QT	TNT European Airlines Ltd (G-BSGI)	
G-TNTM	BAe 146-300QT	TNT European Airlines Ltd (G-BSLZ)	
G-TNTN	Thunder Ax6-56 balloon	D. P. & A. Dickinson	
G-TNTR	BAe 146-300QT	TNT Express Worldwide (UK) Ltd (G-BRGM)	
G-TOAD	Jodel D.140B	J. H. Stevens	
G-TOAK	SOCATA TB.20 Trinidad	R. Chown/Newcastle	
G-TOBA	SOCATA TB.10 Tobago	E. Downing	
G-TOBE	PA-28R Cherokee Arrow 200	J. Bradley & Barry Ltd (G-BNRO)	
G-TOBI	Cessna F.172K	G. Hall (G-AYVB)	
G-TODD	ICA IS-28M2A	C. I. Roberts & C. D. King/Shobdon	
G-TODE	Ruschmeyer R.90-230RG	Tode Ltd	
G-TOFT	Colt 90A balloon	C. S. Perceval	
G-TOMG	P.84 Jet Provost T.4 (XW428)	Gosh That's Aviation Ltd	
G-TOMS	PA-38-112 Tomahawk	R. J. Alford	
G-TOOL	Thunder Ax8-105 balloon	W. J. Honey	
G-TOPS	AS.355F-1 Twin Squirrel	Sterling Helicopters (G-BPRH)	
G-TORE	P.84 Jet Provost T.3A (XM405)	Butane Buzzard Aviation Ltd/Cranfield	
G-TOTO	Cessna F.177RG	C. R. & J. Cox (G-OADE/G-AZKH)	
G-TOUR	Robin R.2112	Barnes Martin Ltd	
G-TOWS	PA-25 Pawnee 260	Lasham Gliding Soc Ltd	

Notes	Reg.	Type	Owner or Operator
	G-TOYS	Enstrom 280C-UK-2 Shark	Stephenson Aviation Ltd (G-BISE)
	G-TOYZ	Bell 206B JetRanger 3	P. B. Ellis (G-RGER)
	G-TPTT	Airbus A.320-212	Airtours International Airways Ltd
	G-TRAK	Optica Industries OA.7 Optica	FLS Aerospace (Lovaux) Ltd (G-BLFC)/Bournemouth
	G-TRAN	Beech 76 Duchess	Astle Aviation Ltd (G-NIFR)
	G-TRAV	Cameron A-210 balloon	Bakers World Travel Ltd
	G-TREC	Cessna 421C	C. P. Lockyer (G-TLOL)
	G-TREE	Bell 206B JetRanger 3	LGH Aviation Ltd
	G-TREK	Jodel D.18	R. H. Mole/Leicester
	G-TREN	Boeing 737-4S3	GB Airways Ltd (G-BRKG)/Gatwick
	G-TRIB	Lindstrand HS-110 balloon	International Balloons Ltd
	G-TRIC	D.H.C.1 Chipmunk 22A (18013)	D. M. Barnett (G-AOSZ)
	G-TRIM	Monnett Moni	J. E. Bennell
	G-TRIN	SOCATA TB.20 Trinidad	Isnet Ltd
	G-TRIO	Cessna 172M	Plane Talking Ltd (G-BNXY)/Elstree
	G-TRIP	PA-32R-301 Saratoga SP	K. L. Burnett (G-HOSK)
	G-TRIX	V.S.509 Spitfire T.IX (PV202)	R. A. Roberts/Goodwood
	G-TROP	Cessna 310R	Southern Air Ltd/Shoreham
	G-TRUC	Cassutt Speed One	J. A. H. Chadwick
	G-TRUE	MDH Hughes 369E	Horizon Helicopter Hire
	G-TRUK	Stoddard-Hamilton Glasair RG	M. P. Jackson
	G-TRUX	Colt 77A balloon	Highway Truck Rental Ltd
	G-TSAM	BAe 125 Srs 800B	British Aerospace PLC/Warton
	G-TSAR	Beech 58 Baron	Czar Aviation Ltd
	G-TSFT	PA-28-161 Warrior II	SFT Aviation Ltd (G-BLDJ)/Bournemouth
	G-TSGJ	PA-28-181 Archer II	Golf Juliet Flying Club
	G-TSIX	AT-6C Harvard IIA (111836)	J. Zemlik/Breighton
	G-TSMI	R. Commander 114	J. J. J. C. Herbaux
	G-TTAM	Taylor JT.2 Titch	C. H. Morris
	G-TTEL	PA-E23 Aztec 250D	Target Technology Electronics Ltd (G-BBXE)
	G-TTHC	Robinson R-22B	North West Auto Engineering
	G-TTOY	CFM Streak Shadow	D. A. Payne
	G-TUBS	Beech 65-80 Queen Air	A. H. Bowers (G-ASKM)
	G-TUDR	Cameron V-77 balloon	Jacques W. Soukup Enterprises Ltd
	G-TUGG	PA-18 Super Cub 150	Ulster Gliding Club Ltd/Bellarena
	G-TUKE	Robin DR.400/160	Tukair/Headcorn
	G-TURF	Cessna F.406	Air Alba Ltd
	G-TURK	Cameron 80 Sultan SS balloon	Forbes Europe Inc/France
	G-TURN	Steen Skybolt	M. Hammond
	G-TVIJ	CCF Harvard IV (T-6J) (28521)	R. W. Davies (G-BSBE)
	G-TVMM	Cessna 310Q	Carroll Aviation (Hurn) Ltd (G-CETA/ G-BBIM)
	G-TVPA	AS.355F-1 Twin Squirrel	Thames Valley Police Authority (G-BPRI)
	G-TVSI	Campbell Cricket	C. Smith (G-AYHH)
	G-TVTV	Cameron 90 TV SS balloon	Cameron Balloons Ltd
	G-TWEL	PA-28-181 Archer II	Universal Salvage (Holdings) Ltd
	G-TWEY	Colt 69A balloon	British Telecom Thameswey
	G-TWIN	PA-44-180 Seminole	Bonus Aviation Ltd/Cranfield
	G-TWIZ	R. Commander 114	B. C. Cox & K. E. Kirkland
	G-TWTD	Hawker Sea Hurricane X (AE977)	Hawker Restorations Ltd
	G-TXSE	RAF 2000 gyroplane	Software Development International Ltd
	G-TYGA	AA-5B Tiger	G. J. Wilshurst (G-BHNZ)
	G-TYRE	Cessna F.172M	Staverton Flying Services Ltd
	G-UAPA	Robin DR.400/140B	Aeromarine Ltd
	G-UAPO	Ruschmeyer R.90-230RG	Iberian Investments Ltd
	G-UBAC	Short SD3-60 Variant 100	BAC Leasing Ltd (G-BMLD)
	G-UCCC	Cameron 90 Sign SS balloon	Flying Pictures (Balloons) Ltd
	G-UDAY	Robinson R-22B	Burman Aviation Ltd
	G-UEST	Bell 206B JetRanger 2	Leisure & Retail Consultants Ltd (G-RYOB/G-BLWU)
	G-UFLY	Cessna F.150H	Westair Flying Services Ltd (G-AVVY)/ Blackpool
	G-UIDA	Aero Designs Star-Lite SL.1	I. J. Widger (G-BRKK)
	G-UIDE	Jodel D.120	S. T. Gilbert/Popham
	G-UILD	Grob G.109B	Runnymede Consultants Ltd
	G-UILE	Lancair 320	R. J. Martin
	G-UKAC	BAe 146-300	Air UK Ltd/Stansted
	G-UKAG	BAe 146-300	Air UK Ltd/Stansted
	G-UKFA	Fokker 100	Air UK Ltd/Stansted

Reg.	Type	Owner or Operator	Notes
G-UKFB	Fokker 100	Air UK Ltd/Stansted	
G-UKFC	Fokker 100	Air UK Ltd/Stansted	
G-UKFD	Fokker 100	Air UK Ltd/Stansted	
G-UKFE	Fokker 100	Air UK Ltd/Stansted	
G-UKFF	Fokker 100	Air UK Ltd/Stansted	
G-UKFG	Fokker 100	Air UK Ltd/Stansted	
G-UKFH	Fokker 100	Air UK Ltd/Stansted	
G-UKFI	Fokker 100	Air UK Ltd/Stansted	
G-UKFJ	Fokker 100	Air UK Ltd/Stansted	
G-UKFK	Fokker 100	Air UK Ltd/Stansted	
G-UK	Fokker 100	Air UK Ltd/Stansted	
G-UK	Fokker 100	Air UK Ltd/Stansted	
G-UK	Fokker 100	Air UK Ltd/Stansted	
G-UK	Fokker 100	Air UK Ltd/Stansted	
G-UK	Fokker 100	Air UK Ltd/Stansted	
G-UK	Fokker 100	Air UK Ltd/Stansted	
G-UKHP	BAe 146-300	Air UK Ltd/Stansted	
G-UKID	BAe 146-300	Air UK Ltd/Stansted	
G-UKJF	BAe 146-100	Air UK Ltd/Stansted	
G-UKLA	Boeing 737-4Y0	K.L.M.	
G-UKLB	Boeing 737-4Y0	K.L.M.	
G-UKLC	Boeing 737-42C	K.L.M.	
G-UKLD	Boeing 737-42C	K.L.M.	
G-UKLE	Boeing 737-4Y0	K.L.M.	
G-UKLF	Boeing 737-42C	K.L.M.	
G-UKLG	Boeing 737-42C	K.L.M.	
G-UKLH	Boeing 767-39HER	Leisure International Airways Ltd *Caribbean Star*	
G-UKLI	Boeing 767-39HER	Leisure International Airways Ltd *Atlantic Star*	
G-UKLJ	Airbus A.320-212	Leisure International Airways Ltd (G-BWKN)	
G-UKLK	Airbus A.320-212	Leisure International Airways Ltd (G-BWKO)	
G-UKLL	Airbus A.320-212	Leisure International Airways Ltd (G-BWCP)	
G-UKLM	Sikorsky S-76B	KLM ERA Helicopters BV/Norwich	
G-UKLS	Sikorsky S-76B	KLM ERA Helicopters BV/Norwich	
G-UKLT	Sikorsky S-76B	KLM ERA Helicopters BV/Norwich	
G-UKLU	Sikorsky S-76B	KLM ERA Helicopters BV/Norwich	
G-UKRB	Colt 105A balloon	Virgin Airship & Balloon Co Ltd	
G-UKRC	BAe 146-300	Air UK Ltd (G-BSMR)/Stansted	
G-UKSC	BAe 146-300	Air UK Ltd/Stansted	
G-UKTA	Fokker 50	Air UK Ltd *City of Norwich*/Stansted	
G-UKTB	Fokker 50	Air UK Ltd *City of Aberdeen*/Stansted	
G-UKTC	Fokker 50	Air UK Ltd *City of Bradford*/Stansted	
G-UKTD	Fokker 50	Air UK Ltd *City of Leeds*/Stansted	
G-UKTE	Fokker 50	Air UK Ltd *City of Hull*/Stansted	
G-UKTF	Fokker 50	Air UK Ltd *City of York*/Stansted	
G-UKTG	Fokker 50	Air UK Ltd *City of Durham*/Stansted	
G-UKTH	Fokker 50	Air UK Ltd *City of Amsterdam*/Stansted	
G-UKTI	Fokker 50	Air UK Ltd *City of Stavanger*/Stansted	
G-ULAB	Robinson R-22B	Bradmore Helicopter Leasing	
G-ULAS	D.H.C.1 Chipmunk 22	Search & Management Services Ltd	
G-ULIA	Cameron V-77 balloon	J. & R. Bayly	
G-ULPS	Everett Srs 1 gyroplane	The Aziz Corporation Ltd (G-BMNY)	
G-UMBO	Thunder Ax7-77A balloon	Virgin Airship & Balloon Co Ltd	
G-UMMI	PA-31-310 Turbo Navajo	Greystones Aviation Holdings Ltd (G-BGSO)	
G-UNGE	Lindstrand LBL-90A balloon	I. Chadwick (G-BVPJ)	
G-UNIP	Cameron Oil Container SS balloon	Flying Pictures (Balloons) Ltd	
G-UNIT	Partenavia P.68B	Phlight Aviation Ltd (G-BCNT)/Coventry	
G-UNRL	Lindstrand LBL-21A balloon	Virgin Balloon & Airship Co. Ltd	
G-UORO	Shaw Europa	D. Dufton	
G-UPCC	Robinson R-22B	Deltair Ltd (G-MUSS)/Liverpool	
G-UPDN	Cameron V-65 balloon	R. J. O. Evans	
G-UPHL	Cameron 80 Concept SS balloon	Uphill Motor Co Ltd	
G-UPMW	Robinson R-22B	Burman Aviation Ltd/Cranfield	
G-UPPP	Colt 77A balloon	M. Williams	
G-UPPY	Cameron DP-80 airship	Jacques W. Soukup Enterprises Ltd	
G-UPUP	Cameron V-77 balloon	S. F. Burden	
G-UROP	Beech 95-B55 Baron	Pooler International Ltd/Sleap	

Notes	Reg.	Type	Owner or Operator
	G-URRR	Air Command 582 Sport	L. Armes
	G-USAM	Cameron Uncle Sam SS balloon	Jacques W. Soukup Enterprises Ltd
	G-USGB	Colt 105A balloon	Virgin Airship & Balloon Co. Ltd
	G-USIL	Thunder Ax7-77 balloon	Window On The World Ltd
	G-USMC	Cameron 90 Chestie SS balloon	Jacques W. Soukup Enterprises Ltd
	G-USSR	Cameron 90 Doll SS balloon	Jacques W. Soukup Enterprises Ltd
	G-USSY	PA-28-181 Archer II	Western Air Training Ltd/Thruxton
	G-USTA	Agusta A.109A	Castle Air Charters Ltd (G-MEAN/ G-BRYL/G-ROPE/G-OAMH)
	G-USTV	Messerschmitt Bf.109G-2 (6)	Imperial War Museum/Duxford
	G-USTY	FRED Srs 2	K. Jones
	G-UTSI	Rand KR-2	K. B. Gutridge/Thruxton
	G-UTSY	PA-28R-201 Arrow III	Arrow Aviation Ltd
	G-UTZY	SA.341G Gazelle 1	MW Helicopters Ltd (G-BKLV)
	G-UZEL	SA.341G Gazelle 1	S. E. Hobbs (UK) Ltd (G-BRNH)
	G-UZLE	Colt 77A balloon	Flying Pictures (Balloons) Ltd
	G-VAEL	Airbus A.340-311	Virgin Atlantic Airways Ltd *Maiden Toulouse*
	G-VAGA	PA-15 Vagabond	P. A. Howell
	G-VAJT	M.S.894E Rallye 220GT	R. W. B. Rolfe
	G-VANS	Vans RV-4	T. R. Grief
	G-VANZ	Vans RV-6A	S. J. Baxter
	G-VARG	Varga 2150A Kachina	D. Orford
	G-VASA	PA-34-200 Seneca	V. Babic (G-BNNB)
	G-VAUN	Cessna 340	H. E. Peacock
	G-VBIG	Boeing 747-4Q8	Virgin Atlantic Airways Ltd
	G-VBUS	Airbus A.340-311	Virgin Atlantic Airways Ltd *Lady in Red*
	G-VCED	Airbus A.320-231	Airtours International Airways Ltd
	G-VCJH	Robinson R-22B	Great Northern Helicopters Ltd
	G-VCSI	Rotorway Executive	Qual-Rect Ltd
	G-VDIR	Cessna T.310R	Thornhill Music Ltd
	G-VEGA	Slingsby T.65A Vega (BGA2729)	C. H. Griffiths
	G-VELA	SIAI-Marchetti S.205-22R	D. P. & P. A. Dawson
	G-VENI	D.H.112 Venom FB.50 (WE402)	Lindsay Wood Promotions Ltd/ Bournemouth
	G-VERA	GY-201 Minicab	D. K. Shipton
	G-VETA	Hunter T.7	Jet Heritage Ltd (G-BVWN)/Bournemouth
	G-VETS	Enstrom 280C-UK Shark	D. I. Rees (G-FSDC/G-BKTG)
	G-VEZE	Rutan Vari-Eze	S. D. Brown & ptnrs
	G-VFAB	Boeing 747-4Q8	Virgin Atlantic Airways Ltd *Lady Penelope*
	G-VFLY	Airbus A.340-311	Virgin Atlantic Airways Ltd *Dragon Lady*
	G-VFSI	Robinson R-22B	Sloane Helicopters Ltd/Sywell
	G-VGIN	Boeing 747-243B	Virgin Atlantic Airways Ltd *Scarlet Lady*
	G-VHFA	PA-23 Aztec 250	Martini Airport Services (G-BZFE/G-AZFE)
	G-VHOT	Boeing 747-4Q8	Virgin Atlantic Airways Ltd *Tubular Belle*
	G-VIBA	Cameron DP-80 airship	Jacques W. Soukup Enterprises Ltd
	G-VICC	PA-28-161 Warrior II	Design Publications Ltd (G-JFHL)
	G-VICE	MDH Hughes 369E	Controlled Demolition Group Ltd
	G-VICI	D.H.112 Venom FB.50	Lindsay Wood Promotions Ltd (G-BMOB)/ Bournemouth
	G-VICM	Beech F33C Bonanza	Charles W. Michie Ltd
	G-VIDI	D.H.112 Venom FB.50 (WE275)	Lindsay Wood Promotions Ltd/Bournemouth
	G-VIEW	Vinten-Wallis WA-116/100	K. H. Wallis
	G-VIIA	Boeing 777-236	British Airways
	G-VIIB	Boeing 777-236	British Airways
	G-VIIC	Boeing 777-236	British Airways
	G-VIID	Boeing 777-236	British Airways
	G-VIIE	Boeing 777-236	British Airways
	G-VIIF	Boeing 777-236	British Airways
	G-VIIG	Boeing 777-236	British Airways
	G-VIIH	Boeing 777-236	British Airways
	G-VIKE	Bellanca 1730A Viking	Peter Dolan & Co Ltd
	G-VIKY	Cameron A-120 balloon	D. W. Pennell
	G-VILL	Lazer Z.200 (modified)	M. G. Jefferies (G-BOYZ)
	G-VIPI	BAe 125 Srs 800B	Yeates of Leicester Ltd
	G-VIPP	PA-31-350 Navajo Chieftain	Capital Trading Aviation Ltd (G-OGRV/ G-BMPX)
	G-VIRG	Boeing 747-287B	Virgin Atlantic Airways Ltd *Maiden Voyager*
	G-VITE	Robin R.1180T	G-VITE Flying Group
	G-VIVA	Thunder Ax7-65 balloon	G. C. Ludlow

Reg.	Type	Owner or Operator	Notes
G-VIVI	Taylor JT.2 Titch	D. G. Tucker	
G-VIVM	P.84 Jet Provost T.5	Gone Flying Ltd (G-BVWF)/North Weald	
G-VIXN	D.H.110 Sea Vixen FAW.2 (XS587) ★	P. G. Vallance Ltd/Charlwood	
G-VIZZ	Sportavia RS.180 Sportsman	Exeter Fournier Group	
G-VJCB	Agusta A.109A-II	J. C. Bamford Excavators Ltd (G-BOUA)	
G-VJET	Avro 698 Vulcan B.2 (XL426)	Vulcan Restoration Trust/Southend	
G-VJFK	Boeing 747-238B	Virgin Atlantic Airways Ltd *Boston Belle*	
G-VJIM	Colt 77 Jumbo Jim SS balloon	L. V. Mastis	
G-VLAD	Yakovlev Yak-50	W. J. J. Kamper	
G-VLAX	Boeing 747-238B	Virgin Atlantic Airways Ltd *California Girl*	
G-VLCN	Avro 698 Vulcan B.2 (XH558)	C. Walton Ltd/Bruntingthorpe	
G-VMAX	Mooney M.20K	Glidegold Ltd	
G-VMDE	Cessna P.210N	Royton Express Deliveries (Welwyn) Ltd	
G-VMIA	Boeing 747-123	Virgin Atlantic Airways Ltd (G-HIHO) *Spirit of Sir Freddie*	
G-VMJM	SOCATA TB.10 Tobago	J. H. Michaels (G-BTOK)/Denham	
G-VMPR	D.H.115 Vampire T.11 (XE920)	J. N. Kerr & J. Jones	
G-VNOM	D.H.112 Venom FB.50 (J-1632)	De Havilland Aviation Ltd/Swansea	
G-VOAR	PA-28-181 Archer III	Aeronaval Ltd	
G-VODA	Cameron N-77 balloon	Racal Telecom PLC	
G-VOID	PA-28RT-201 Arrow IV	Newbus Aviation Ltd	
G-VOLT	Cameron N-77 balloon	National Power	
G-VOYG	Boeing 747-283B	Virgin Atlantic Airways Ltd (G-BMGS) *Shady Lady*	
G-VPII	Evans VP-2	V. D. J. Hitchings (G-EDIF)	
G-VPSJ	Shaw Europa	J. D. Bean	
G-VRVI	Cameron O-90 balloon	Cooling Services Ltd	
G-VSBC	Beech B200 Super King Air	Vickers Shipbuilding & Engineering Ltd/Walney Island	
G-VSFT	PA-23 Aztec 250F	SFT Aviation Ltd (G-TOMK/G-BFEC)/Bournemouth	
G-VSKY	Airbus A.340-311	Virgin Atlantic Airways Ltd *China Girl*	
G-VSOP	Cameron 60 Bottle SS balloon	J. R. Parkington & Co Ltd	
G-VSUN	Airbus A.340-313	Virgin Atlantic Airways Ltd	
G-VTII	D.H.115 Vampire T.11 (WZ507)	De Havilland Aviation Ltd/Swansea	
G-VTOL	H.S. Harrier T.52 ★	Brooklands Museum of Aviation/Weybridge	
G-VTOP	Boeing 747-4Q8	Virgin Atlantic Airways Ltd	
G-VULC	Avro 698 Vulcan B.2A (XM655) ★	Radarmoor Ltd/Wellesbourne	
G-VVBK	PA-34-200T Seneca II	Computaplane Ltd (G-BSBS/G-BDRI)	
G-VVIP	Cessna 421C	Capital Trading Aviation Ltd (G-BMWB)	
G-VYGR	Colt 120A balloon	The Ballooning Experience Ltd	
G-WAAC	Cameron N-56 balloon	N. P. Hemsley	
G-WACA	Cessna F.152 II	Wycombe Air Centre Ltd	
G-WACB	Cessna F.152 II	Wycombe Air Centre Ltd	
G-WACE	Cessna F.152 II	Wycombe Air Centre Ltd	
G-WACF	Cessna 152 II	Wycombe Air Centre Ltd	
G-WACG	Cessna 152 II	Wycombe Air Centre Ltd	
G-WACH	Cessna FA.152 II	Wycombe Air Centre Ltd	
G-WACI	Beech 76 Duchess	Wycombe Air Centre Ltd	
G-WACJ	Beech 76 Duchess	Wycombe Air Centre Ltd	
G-WACK	Short SD3-60 Variant 100	British Regional Airlines/BA Express (G-BMAJ)	
G-WACL	Cessna F.172N	Wycombe Air Centre Ltd (G-BHGG)	
G-WACO	Waco UPF-7	RGV (Aircraft Services) & Co/Staverton	
G-WACP	PA-28 Cherokee 180	Wycombe Air Centre Ltd (G-BBPP)	
G-WACR	PA-28 Cherokee 180	Wycombe Air Centre Ltd (G-BCZF)	
G-WACT	Cessna F.152 II	Plymouth School of Flying Ltd (G-BKFT)	
G-WACU	Cessna FA.152	Wycombe Air Centre Ltd (G-BJZU)	
G-WACW	Cessna 172P	Wycombe Air Centre Ltd	
G-WACY	Cessna F.172P	Wycombe Air Centre Ltd	
G-WACZ	Cessna F.172M	Wycombe Air Centre Ltd (G-BCUK)	
G-WADS	Robinson R-22B	R. K. Hallam & S. E. Watts (G-NICO)	
G-WAFC	Cessna F.150M	Aviators Flight Centre (G-BDFI)/Southend	
G-WAGI	Robinson R-22B	J. Wagstaff	
G-WAIR	PA-32-301 Saratoga	Thorne Aviation	
G-WAIT	Cameron V-77 balloon	C. P. Brown	
G-WALS	Cessna A.152	Redhill Flying Club	
G-WALT	Cameron Flying Castle SS balloon	Cameron Balloons Ltd	
G-WARD	Taylor JT.1 Monoplane	R. P. J. Hunter	
G-WARE	PA-28-161 Warrior II	W. J. Ware	

Notes	Reg.	Type	Owner or Operator
	G-WARK	Schweizer 269C	J. & J. Havakin
	G-WARP	Cessna 182F	L. Rawson (G-ASHB)
	G-WARR	PA-28-161 Warrior II	T. J. & G. M. Laundy
	G-WASH	Noble 1250 balloon	Noble Adventures Ltd
	G-WASP	Brantly B.2B	N. J. R. Minchin (G-ASXE)
	G-WATH	Colt 77A balloon	Ballooning Adventures Ltd
	G-WATS	PA-34-220T Seneca III	G-WATS Aviation Ltd (G-BOVJ)
	G-WATT	Cameron Cooling Tower SS balloon	National Power
	G-WATZ	PA-28-151 Warrior	Air Nova/Liverpool
	G-WAVE	Grob G.109B	M. L. Murdoch/Cranfield
	G-WAZZ	Pitts S-1S Special	T. A. Shears (G-BRRP)/White Waltham
	G-WBAT	Wombat gyroplane	C. D. Julian (G-BSID)
	G-WBMG	Cameron N Ele-90 SS balloon	M. Sevrin (G-BUYV)/Belgium
	G-WBPR	BAe 125 Srs 800B	Trusthouse Forte PLC/Heathrow
	G-WBTS	Falconar F-11	W. C. Brown (G-BDPL)
	G-WCAT	Colt Flying Mitt SS balloon	Interline Develoments Ltd
	G-WCEI	M.S.894E Rallye 220GT	R. A. L. Lucas (G-BAOC)
	G-WDEB	Thunder Ax-7-77 balloon	W. de Bock
	G-WEAC	BN-2A Mk III-2 Trislander	Keen Leasing Ltd (G-BEFP)
	G-WEEZ	Mooney M.20J	Weyland Ltd
	G-WELI	Cameron N-77 balloon	M. A. Shannon
	G-WELL	Beech E90 King Air	CEGA Aviation Ltd/Goodwood
	G-WELS	Cameron N-65 balloon	K. J. Vickery
	G-WEND	PA-28RT-201 Arrow IV	G-WEND Group
	G-WERY	SOCATA TB.20 Trinidad	WERY Flying Group/Sherburn
	G-WEST	Agusta A.109A	Westland Helicopters Ltd/Yeovil
	G-WESX	CFM Streak Shadow	D. J. Sagar
	G-WETI	Cameron N-31 balloon	C. A. Butter & J. J. T. Cooke
	G-WFFW	PA-28-161 Warrior II	N. F. Duke
	G-WFRD	Bell 206L-4 LongRanger	Wickford Development Co Ltd
	G-WGAL	Bell 206B JetRanger 3	Watkiss Group Aviation Ltd (G-OICS)
	G-WGCL	Aero Commander 685	Cooper Aeiral Surveys Ltd/Sandtoft
	G-WGCS	PA-18 Super Cub 95	S. C. Thompson
	G-WGSC	Pilatus PC-6/B2-H4 Turbo Porter	D. M. Penny
	G-WHAT	Colt 77A balloon	M. A. Scholes
	G-WHIM	Colt 77A balloon	D. L. Morgan
	G-WHIR	Montgomerie-Bensen B.8MR	A. P. Barden (G-BROT)
	G-WHIZ	Pitts S-1 Special	K. M. McLeod
	G-WHOG	CFM Streak Shadow	B. R. Cannell
	G-WHST	AS.350B2 Ecureuil	Hawkrise Ltd (G-BWYA)
	G-WIBB	Jodel D.18	J. & D. Wibberley
	G-WILD	Pitts S-1T Special	J. D. Haslam/Breighton
	G-WILS	PA-28RT-201T Turbo Arrow IV	T. W. Stanley & V. F. A. Dimock
	G-WILY	Rutan LongEz	B. Wronski & W. S. Allen
	G-WIMP	Colt 56A balloon	C. Wolstenholme
	G-WINE	Thunder Ax7-77Z balloon	R. Brooker
	G-WINK	AA-5B Tiger	B. St J. Cooke
	G-WINS	PA-32 Cherokee Six 300	Cheyenne Ltd
	G-WIRE	AS.355F-1 Twin Squirrel	National Grid Co PLC (G-CEGB/G-BLJL)
	G-WIRL	Robinson R-22B	C. A. Rosenberg
	G-WISH	Lindstrand LBL Cake SS balloon	Oxford Promotions (UK) Ltd
	G-WIZA	Robinson R-22B	Burman Aviation Ltd (G-PERL)/Cranfield
	G-WIZD	Lindstrand LBL-180A balloon	T. H. Wilson
	G-WIZO	PA-34-220T Seneca III	Focusfar Ltd
	G-WIZZ	AB-206B JetRanger 2	Rotor Wing Aviation Ltd
	G-WJAN	Boeing 757-21K	Airtours International Airways Ltd
	G-WLCY	BAe 146-200	—
	G-WLGA	PZL-104 Wilga 80	RCR Aviation Ltd/Thruxton
	G-WMAA	MBB Bo 105DBS/4	Bond Helicopters Ltd (G-PASB/G-BDMC)
	G-WMCC	BAe Jetstream 3102	Maersk Air/British Airways (G-TALL)/ Birmingham
	G-WMPA	AS.355F-2 Twin Squirrel	W. Midlands Police Authority/Birmingham
	G-WMTM	AA-5B Tiger	T. & W. E. Menham/Biggin Hill
	G-WOLF	PA-28 Cherokee 140	Werewolf Aviation Ltd
	G-WOOD	Beech 95-B55A Baron	T. D. Broadhurst (G-AYID)/Sleap
	G-WOOL	Colt 77A balloon	A. P. Woolhouse
	G-WORK	Thunder Ax10-180 S2 balloon	T. J. Bucknall
	G-WOTG	BN-2T Turbine Islander	RAF Sport Parachute Association (G-BJYT)
	G-WOZA	PA-32RT-300 Lance II	O. C. Kruppa (G-BYBB)/Germany
	G-WRCF	Beech 200 Super King Air	Air Foyle Ltd/Luton
	G-WREN	Pitts S-2A Special	Northamptonshire School of Flying Ltd/ Sywell

Reg.	Type	Owner or Operator	Notes
G-WRFM	Enstrom 280C-UK Shark	Skywalker Enterprises (G-CTSI/ G-BKIO)/Shoreham	
G-WRIT	Thunder Ax7-77A balloon	G. Pusey	
G-WSEC	Enstrom F-28C	M. J. Easy (G-BONF)	
G-WSFT	PA-23 Aztec 250F	SFT Aviation Ltd (G-BTHS)/Bournemouth	
G-WSKY	Enstrom 280C-UK-2 Shark	M. I. Edwards Engineers (G-BEEK)	
G-WULF	WAR Focke-Wulf Fw.190 (8)	B. Brown/Breighton	
G-WVBF	Lindstrand LBL-210A balloon	Virgin Balloon Flights Ltd	
G-WWAS	PA-34-220T Seneca III	A. Smith (G-BPPB)	
G-WWII	V.S.379 Spitfire XIV (SM832)	Patina Ltd/Duxford	
G-WWIZ	Beech 95-58 Baron	Chase Aviation Ltd (G-GAMA/G-BBSD)	
G-WWWG	Shaw Europa	C. F. Williams-Wynne	
G-WYCH	Cameron 90 Witch SS balloon	Jacques W. Soukup Enterprises Ltd	
G-WYMP	Cessna F.150J	L. Scattergood & R. Hall (G-BAGW)	
G-WYNN	Rand KR-2	W. Thomas	
G-WYNS	Aero Designs Pulsar XP	H. E. Perkins	
G-WYNT	Cameron N-56 balloon	Jacques W. Soukup Enterprises Ltd	
G-WYPA	MBB Bo 105DBS/4	W. Yorkshire Police Authority	
G-WYZZ	Air Command 532 Elite	C. H. Gem (G-BPAK)	
G-WZZZ	Colt AS-56 airship	Lindstrand Balloons Ltd	
G-XALP	Schweizer 269C	Heli Air Ltd	
G-XANT	Cameron N-105 balloon	Flying Pictures (Balloons) Ltd	
G-XARV	ARV Super 2	P. R. Snowden (G-OPIG/G-BMSJ)	
G-XCEL	AS.355F-1 Twin Squirrel	Tri-Ventures Group Ltd (G-HBAC/G-HJET)	
G-XCUB	PA-18 Super Cub 150	M. C. Barraclough	
G-XIIX	Robinson R-22B	Helitech (Luton) Ltd	
G-XLXL	Robin DR.400/160	40 - 40 Aero Group (G-BAUD)/Biggin Hill	
G-XPOL	AS.355F-1 Twin Squirrel	Aeromega Ltd (G-BPRF)	
G-XPXP	Aero Designs Pulsar XP	B. J. Edwards	
G-XRAY	Rand KR-2	R. S. Smith	
G-XRMC	BAe 125 Srs 800B	RMC Group Services Ltd	
G-XSFT	PA-23 Aztec 250F	SFT Aviation Ltd (G-CPPC/G-BGBH)/ Bournemouth	
G-XSKY	Cameron N-77 balloon	Ballooning World Ltd	
G-XTOR	BN-2A Mk III-2 Trislander	Aurigny Air Services Ltd (G-BAXD)	
G-XTRA	Extra EA.230	Firebird Aerobatics Ltd/Booker	
G-XVIE	V.S.361 Spitfire LF.XVIe (TB252)	Historic Flying Ltd	
G-XXIV	AB-206B JetRanger 3	Hampton Printing (Bristol) Ltd	
G-XXVI	Sukhoi Su-26M	A. N. Onn & T. R. G. Barnaby	
G-YAKA	Yakovlev Yak-50	J. Griffen	
G-YAKI	Yakovlev Yak-52	Yak One Ltd/White Waltham	
G-YAKS	Yakovlev Yak-52	Two Bees Associates Ltd	
G-YAKX	Yakovlev Yak-52	M. Gardner	
G-YAKY	Yakovlev Yak-52	Kilo Yankee Group	
G-YANK	PA-28-181 Archer II	G-YANK Flying Group	
G-YAWW	PA-28RT-201T Turbo Arrow IV	Barton Aviation Ltd	
G-YBAA	Cessna FR.172J	H. Norman	
G-YCUB	PA-18 Super Cub 150	F. W. Rogers Garage (Saltash) Ltd	
G-YEAR	Mini-500	D. J. Waddington	
G-YELL	Murphy Rebel	A. D. Keen	
G-YEOM	PA-31-350 Navajo Chieftain	Foster Yeoman Ltd/Exeter	
G-YEWS	Rotorway Executive 152	D. G. Pollard	
G-YFLY	VPM M.16 Tandem Trainer	A. J. Unwin (G-BWGI)	
G-YIII	Cessna F.150L	Skyviews & General Ltd/Sherburn	
G-YJBM	Airbus A.320-231	Airtours International Airways Ltd (G-IEAF)	
G-YJET	Montgomerie-Bensen B.8MR	A. Shuttleworth (G-BMUH)	
G-YKSZ	Yakovlev Yak-52	J. N. & C. J. Carter	
G-YMBO	Robinson R-22M Mariner	Coax Connectors Ltd	
G-YMYM	Lindstrand LBL Ice Cream SS balloon	Lindstrand Balloons Ltd	
G-YNOT	D.62B Condor	T. Littlefair (G-AYFH)	
G-YOGI	Robin DR.400/140B	R. M. & A. M. Gosling (G-BDME)	
G-YORK	Cessna F.172M	P. J. Smith	
G-YOYO	Pitts S-1E Special	J. D. L. Richardson (G-OTSW/G-BLHE)	
G-YPSY	Andreasson BA-4B	C. W. N. Huke & A-L. N. M. Cox	
G-YRIL	Luscombe 8E Silvaire	C. Potter	
G-YROI	Air Command Commander 532	W. B. Lumb	
G-YROS	Montgomerie-Bensen B.8M	N. B. Gray	
G-YROY	Montgomerie-Bensen B.8MR	R. D. Armishaw	
G-YSFT	PA-23 Aztec 250F	SFT Aviation Ltd (G-BEJT)/Bournemouth	
G-YSKY	PA-31-350 Navajo Chieftain	Hawkair	

Notes	Reg.	Type	Owner or Operator
	G-YTWO	Cessna F.172M	Sherburn Aero Club Ltd
	G-YUGO	H.S.125 Srs 1B/R-522	RCR Aviation Ltd (G-ATWH)
	G-YULL	PA-28 Cherokee 180E	Fortescue Investments Ltd (G-BEAJ)
	G-YUMM	Cameron N-90 balloon	Wunderbar Ltd
	G-YUPI	Cameron N-90 balloon	H. C. Wright
	G-YURO	Shaw Europa	Europa Aviation Ltd
	G-YVET	Cameron V-90 balloon	K. J. Foster
	G-ZACH	Robin DR.400/100	A. P. Wellings/Sandown (G-FTIO)
	G-ZAIR	Zenair CH 601HD	C. B. Shaw
	G-ZAPC	Short SD3-30 Variant 100	Titan Airways Ltd (G-RNMO/G-BFZW)/ Stansted
	G-ZAPD	Short SD3-60 Variant 100	Titan Airways Ltd (G-OLGW/ G-BOFK)/Stansted
	G-ZAPG	Short SD3-60 Variant 100	Titan Airways Ltd (G-CPTL/ G-BOFI)/Stansted
	G-ZAPI	Cessna 500 Citation	Titan Airways Ltd (G-BHTT)/Stansted
	G-ZAPJ	Aerospatiale ATR-42-300	Titan Airways Ltd/Stansted
	G-ZAPK	BAe 146-200QC	Titan Airways Ltd (G-BTIA/G-PRIN)/ Stansted
	G-ZARA	Nord 3400	D. E. Bain & ptnrs
	G-ZARI	AA-5B Tiger	C. A. Ringrose (G-BHVY)
	G-ZAZA	PA-18 Super Cub 95	Airbourne Taxi Services Ltd
	G-ZBRA	Thunder Ax10-160 balloon	Zebra Ballooning Ltd
	G-ZEBO	Thunder Ax8-105 S2 balloon	E. Herndon
	G-ZEBR	Colt 210A balloon	Zebra Ballooning Ltd
	G-ZEIN	Slingsby T.67M-260	R.V. Aviation Ltd/Bournemouth
	G-ZEPI	Colt GA-42 gas airship	Lindstrand Balloons Ltd (G-ISPY/G-BPRB)
	G-ZENO	Learjet 35A	Northern Executive Aviation Ltd (G-GAYL/ G-ZING)
	G-ZEPY	Colt GA-42 gas airship	Keelex 195 Ltd
	G-ZERO	AA-5B Tiger	G-ZERO Syndicate
	G-ZGBE	Beech 95-58PA Baron	GB Express Ltd (G-BNKL)/Bournemouth
	G-ZIGG	Robinson R-22B	Uriah Woodhead & Son Ltd
	G-ZIGI	Robin DR.400/180	Golf India Flying Group
	G-ZIPI	Robin DR.400/180	Stahl Engineering Co Ltd/Headcorn
	G-ZIPY	Wittman W.8 Tailwind	M. J. Butler
	G-ZLIN	Z.526 Trener Master	N. J. Arthur
	G-ZLYN	Z.526F Trener	Air V8 Ltd
	G-ZOOI	Lindstrand LBL-105A balloon	Flying Pictures (Balloons) Ltd
	G-ZOOL	Cessna FA.152	Falcon Flying Services (G-BGXZ)/ Biggin Hill
	G-ZORO	Shaw Europa	N. T. Read
	G-ZSFT	PA-23 Aztec 250F	SFT Aviation Ltd (G-SALT/G-BGTH)/ Bournemouth
	G-ZSOL	Zlin Z.50L	T. W. Cassells
	G-ZTED	Shaw Europa	J. J. Kennedy & E. W. Gladstone
	G-ZULU	PA-28-161 Warrior II	S. F. Tebby & Son
	G-ZUMP	Cameron N-77 balloon	Allen & Harris Ltd
	G-ZUMY	Task Silhouette	P. J. Wells
	G-ZZIP	Mooney M.20J	D. A. H. Dixon
	G-ZZZA	Boeing 777-236	British Airways
	G-ZZZB	Boeing 777-236	British Airways
	G-ZZZC	Boeing 777-236	British Airways *Sir Charles Edward Kingsford-Smith*
	G-ZZZD	Boeing 777-236	British Airways *Wilbur/Orville Wright*
	G-ZZZE	Boeing 777-236	British Airways

Serial carried	Civil identity	Serial carried	Civil identity
07 (Fr AF)	G-BKPT	16136 (205 USN)	G-BRUJ
3 (Luftwaffe)	G-BAYV	16693 (693 RCAF)	G-BLPG
6 (Luftwaffe)	G-USTV	18013 (RCAF)	G-TRIC
19 (USN)	G-BTCC	18263 (822 USAAF)	N38940
23 (USAAC)	N49272	18393 (RCAF)	G-BCYK
26 (US)	G-BAVO	18671 (671 RCAF)	G-BNZC
27 (USN)	G-BRVG	20310 (310 RCAF)	G-BSBG
27 (CIS)	G-OYAK	20385 (385 RCAF)	G-BGPB
27 (USAAC)	G-AGYY	28521 (TA-521 USAF)	G-TVIJ
27 (USAAC)	G-NZSS	30146 (Yugoslav Army)	G-BSXD
28 (USAAC)	N8162G	30149 (Yugoslav Army)	G-SOKO
41/BA (USN)	G-DDMV	31145 (G-26 USAAF)	G-BBLH
44 (USAAF)	G-BWHH	31923 (USAAC)	G-BRHP
44 (K-33 USAAF)	G-BJLH	31952 (USAAC)	G-BRPR
45 (Aeronavale)	G-BHFG	34037 (USAAF)	N9115Z
69 (CIS)	G-BTZB	39624 (D-39 USAAF)	G-BVMH
75	G-AFDX	53319 (319/RB USN)	G-BTDP
77 (Soviet AF)	G-BTCU	54137 (69 USN)	G-CTKL
85 (USAAC)	G-BTBI	56321 (U-AB RNorAF)	G-BKPY
109 (RJordanAF)	G-BVPO	80425 (USN)	N7235C
112 (USAAC)	G-BSWC	86711 (USN)	N4845V
118 (USAAC)	G-BSDS	88439 (USN)	N55JP
120 (Fr AF)	G-AZGC	91007 (USAF)	G-NASA
143 (Fr AF)	G-MSAL	93542 (LTA-542 USAF)	G-BRLV
152/17	G-ATJM	111836 (JZ-6 USN)	G-TSIX
168	G-BFDE	115042 (TA-042 USAF)	G-BGHU
177 (Irish AC)	G-BLIW	115302 (TP USAAF)	G-BJTP
177 (USAAF)	G-BRTK	115684 (D-C USAAF)	G-BKVM
208 (USN)	N75664	121714	NX700HL
209 (RJordanAF)	G-BVLM	121752 (USN)	N800H
243 (Iraq A F)	G-BTTA	124485 (DF-A USAAF)	G-BEDF
243 (USAAC)	G-BUKE	126922 (JS/937 USN)	G-RAID
320 (USAAC)	G-BPMD	151632 (USAAF)	G-BWGR
379 (USAAC)	G-ILLE	1532008 (08 China AAF)	G-BVFX
385 (RCAF)	G-BGPB	18-2001 (USAAF)	G-BIZV
390 (USAAC)	G-BTRJ	219993 (USAAF)	N139DP
422-15	G-AVJO	224211 (M2-Z USAF)	G-BPMP
441 (USN)	G-BTFG	226671 (MX-X USAAF)	N47DD
442 (USN)	G-BPTB	231983 (USAAF)	F-BDRS
503 (Hungarian AF)	G-BRAM	233752 (52 USAAC)	G-BVCV
781-25 (Span AF)	G-BRSH	236800 (A-44 USAAF)	G-BHPK
781-32 (Span AF)	G-BPDM	269097 (USAF)	G-BTWR
800 (RJordan AF)	G-BOOM	314887 (USAAF)	G-AJPI
854 (USAAC)	G-BTBH	315509 (W7 USAAF)	G-BHUB
855 (USAAC)	N56421	329405 (A-23 USAAF)	G-BCOB
897 (USN)	G-BJEV	329417 (USAAF)	G-BDHK
1164 (USAAC)	G-BKGL	329471 (F-44 USAAF)	G-BGXA
1180 (USN)	G-BRSK	329601 (D-44 USAAF)	G-AXHR
1197	G-BPVE	329854 (R-44 USAAF)	G-BMKC
1377 (Portuguese AF)	G-BARS	329934 (B-72 USAAF)	G-BCPH
1411 (US Coast Guard)	N444M	330238 (A-24 USAAF)	G-LIVH
1420 (Polish AF)	G-BMZF	330485 (C-44 USAAF)	G-AJES
2345	G-ATVP	40-1766	N50755
2807 (VE-103 USN)	G-BHTH	408133 (B-44 USAAF)	G-BDCD
3066	G-AETA	413573 (B6-K USAF)	N6526D
3398 (Fr AF)	G-BFYO	454467 (J-44 USAAF)	G-BILI
3460	G-BMFG	454537 (J-04 USAAF)	G-BFDL
4253/18	G-BFPL	461748	G-BHDK
5450 (RCAF)	G-TDTW)	463221 (G4-S USAAF)	G-BTCD
5492	G-PENY	472216 (AJ-L USAAF)	G-BIXL
5894	G-BFVH	472773 (AJ-C USAF)	G-SUSY
6247 (Polish AF)	G-OMIG	474008 (VF-R USAF)	N51RR
7198/18	G-AANJ	474425 (OC-G USAF)	N11T
7797 (USAAF)	G-BFAF	479744 (M-49 USAAF)	G-BGPD
8178 (FU-178 USAF)	G-SABR	479766 (D-63 USAAF)	G-BKHG
8449M	G-ASWJ	480015 (M-44 USAAF)	G-AKIB
14863 (USAAC)	G-BGOR	480133 (B-44 USAAF)	G-BDCD

Serial carried	Civil identity	Serial carried	Civil identity
480321 (H-44 USAAF)	G-FRAN	K2059	G-PFAR
480480 (E-44 USAAF)	G-BECN	K2075	G-BEER
480636 (A-58 USAAF)	G-AXHP	K2567	G-MOTH
480752 (E-39 USAAF)	G-BCXJ	K2572	G-AOZH
41-33275 (CE USAAC)	G-BICE	K2587	G-BJAP
42-58678 (IY USAAC)	G-BRIY	K3215	G-AHSA
42-78044 (USAAC)	G-BRXL	K3661	G-BURZ
42-84555 (EP-H)	G-ELMH	K3731	G-RODI
44-30861	N9089Z	K4235 (KX-H)	G-AHMJ
44-72028	G-LYNE	K5054	G-BRDV
44-79609 (PR USAAF)	G-BHXY	K5414 (XV)	G-AENP
44-80594 (USAAF)	G-BEDJ	K5600	G-BVVI
44-83184	G-RGUS	K8203	G-BTVE
45-49192	N47DD	L2301	G-AIZG
51-1371 (VF-S USAAF)	NL1051S	L8841 (QY-C)	G-BPIV
542447	G-SCUB	N1854	G-AIBE
542474 (R-184)	G-PCUB	N2308 (HP-B)	G-AMRK
51 11701A (AF258 USAF)	G-BSZC	N4877 (VX-F)	G-AMDA
51-14526 (USAF)	G-BRWB	N5182	G-APUP
51-15227 (USN)	G-BKRA	N5195	G-ABOX
51-15673 (USAF)	G-CUBI	N6181	G-EBKY
52-8543 (16 USAF)	G-BUKY	N6290	G-BOCK
54-21261 (USAF)	N33VC	N6452	G-BIAU
607327 (09-L USAAF)	G-ARAO	N6466	G-ANKZ
A16-199 (SF-R RAAF)	G-BEOX	N6532	G-ANTS
A17-48 (RAAF)	G-BPHR	N6797	G-ANEH
A-57 (Swiss AF)	G-BECT	N6847	G-APAL
A68-192 (RAAF)	G-HAEC	N6848	G-BALX
A-806 (Swiss AF)	G-BTLL	N6965 (FL-J)	G-AJTW
A1325	G-BVGR	N6985	G-AHMN
A8226	G-BIDW	N9191	G-ALND
B595	G-BUOD	N9192 (RCO-N)	G-BSTJ
B1807	G-EAVX	N9389	G-ANJA
B2458	G-BPOB	P5865 (LE-W)	G-BKCK
B4863 (G)	G-BLXT	P6382	G-AJRS
B6401	G-AWYY	R-163 (RNethAF)	G-BIRH
B7270	G-BFCZ	R-167 (RNethAF)	G-LION
C1904 (Z)	G-PFAP	R1914	G-AHUJ
C3011 (S)	G-SWOT	R5250	G-AODT
C4994	G-BLWM	S1287	G-BEYB
C9533 (M)	G-BUWE	S1579	G-BBVO
D5397/17	G-BFXL	T5424	G-AJOA
D7889	G-AANM	T5672	G-ALRI
D8084	G-ACAA	T5854	G-ANKK
D8096 (D)	G-AEPH	T5879	G-AXBW
D8781	G-ECKE	T6099	G-AOGR
E-15 (RNethAF)	G-BIYU	T6313	G-AHVU
E3B-143 (Span AF)	G-JUNG	T6818 (44)	G-ANKT
E3B-153 (781-75 Span AF)	G-BPTS	T6991	G-ANOR
E449	G-EBJE	T7230	G-AFVE
EM-01 (Spanish AF)	G-AAOR	T7281	G-ARTL
F141 (G)	G-SEVA	T7404 (04)	G-ANMV
F235 (B)	G-BMDB	T7471	G-AJHU
F904	G-EBIA	T7793	G-ANKV
F938	G-EBIC	T7842	G-AMTF
F943	G-BIHF	T7909	G-ANON
F943	G-BKDT	T7997	G-AHUF
F5447 (N)	G-BKER	T9707	G-AKKR
F5459 (Y)	G-INNY	T9738	G-AKAT
F8010 (Z)	G-BDWJ	U-0247 (Class B identity)	G-AGOY
F8614	G-AWAU	U-80 (Swiss AF)	G-BUKK
G-48-1 (Class B)	G-ALSX	U-95 (Swiss AF)	G-BVGP
H5199	G-ADEV	U-108 (Swiss AF)	G-BJAX
— (I-492 USAAC)	G-BPUD	U-110 (Swiss AF)	G-PTWO
J-1149 (Swiss AF)	G-SWIS	U-142 (Swiss AF)	G-BONE
J-1605 (Swiss AF)	G-BLID	U-1214	G-DHVV
J-1614 (Swiss AF)	G-BLIE	U-1215 (215)	G-HELV
J-1632 (Swiss AF)	G-VNOM	U-1230 (Swiss AF)	G-DHZZ
J7326	G-EBQP	U-1234 (Swiss AF)	G-DHAV
J9941 (57)	G-ABMR	V-54 (Swiss AF)	G-BVSD
K1786	G-AFTA	V1075	G-AKPF
K2050	G-ASCM	V3388	G-AHTW

194

Serial carried	Civil identity	Serial carried	Civil identity
V9441 (AR-A)	G-AZWT	MW800 (HF-V)	G-BSHW
V9545 (BA-C)	G-BCWL	NJ673	G-AOCR
V9673 (MA-J)	G-LIZY	NJ695	G-AJXV
W7 (Italian AF)	G-AGFT	NJ703	G-AKPI
W5856 (A2A)	G-BMGC	NJ719	G-ANFU
W9385 (YG-L)	G-ADND	NL750	G-AOBH
Z7015 (7-L)	G-BKTH	NM181	G-AZGZ
Z7197	G-AKZN	NP181	G-AOAR
Z7381 (XR-T)	G-HURI	NP184	G-ANYP
AE977	G-TWTD	NP303	G-ANZJ
AP506	G-ACWM	NX534	G-BUDL
AP507 (KX-P)	G-ACWP	NX611 (YF-C)	G-ASXX
AR213 (PR-D)	G-AIST	NZ5648	NX55JP
AR501 (NN-D)	G-AWII	PL965	G-MKXI
AR614 (DU-Z)	G-BUWA	PL983	G-PRXI
BB807	G-ADWO	PP972 (6M-D)	G-BUAR
BE417 (AE-K)	G-HURR	PV202 (VZ-M)	G-TRIX
BM597 (JH-B)	G-MKVB	RG333	G-AIEK
BW853	G-BRKE	RG333	G-AKEZ
DE208	G-AGYU	RH377	G-ALAH
DE470	G-ANMY	RL962	G-AHED
DE623	G-ANFI	RM221	G-ANXR
DE673	G-ADNZ	RN201	G-BKSP
DE970	G-AOBJ	RN218 (N)	G-BBJI
DE992	G-AXXV	RT486	G-AJGJ
DF128 (RCO-U)	G-AOJJ	RT520	G-ALYB
DF155	G-ANFV	RX168	G-BWEM
DF198	G-BBRB	SM832 (YB-A)	G-WWII
DE470	G-ANMY	SM845	G-BUOS
DG590	G-ADMW	SX336	G-BRMG
DK431	G-ASTL	TA634 (8K-K)	G-AWJV
DR613	G-AFJB	TA719	G-ASKC
EM720	G-AXAN	TB252 (GW-H)	G-XVIE
EM903	G-APBI	TD248 (D)	G-OXVI
EN224	G-FXII	TE184	G-MXVI
EP120 (AE-A)	G-LFVB	TE566 (DU-A)	G-BLCK
FB226 (MT-A)	G-BDWM	TJ569	G-AKOW
FE695	G-BTXI	TJ672	G-ANIJ
FE992 (K-T)	G-BDAM	TJ704 (JA)	G-ASCD
FH153	G-BBHK	TS423	G-DAKS
FR870 (GA-S)	N1009N	TS798	G-AGNV
FR886	G-BDMS	TW439	G-ANRP
FT239	G-BIWX	TW467 (ROD-F)	G-ANIE
FT391	G-AZBN	TW511	G-APAF
FX301 (FD-NQ)	G-JUDI	TW517	G-BDFX
HB275	G-BKGM	TW536 (TS-V)	G-BNGE
HB751	G-BCBL	TW591	G-ARIH
HH982	G-AHXE	TW641	G-ATDN
HM580	G-ACUU	TX183	G-BSMF
KB889 (NA-I)	G-LANC	VF512 (PF-M)	G-ARRX
KD572	G-FGID	VF516	G-ASMZ
KL161 (VO-B)	N88972	VF526	G-ARXU
KZ321	G-HURY	VF548	G-ASEG
LB294	G-AHWJ	VL348	G-AVVO
LB375	G-AHGW	VL349	G-AWSA
LF858	G-BLUZ	VM360	G-APHV
LZ551/G	G-DHXX	VP955	G-DVON
LZ766	G-ALCK	VR192	G-APIT
MD497	G-ANLW	VR249 (FA-EY)	G-APIY
MH434 (MN-B)	G-ASJV	VR259 (M)	G-APJB
MJ627 (9G-P)	G-BMSB	VS356	G-AOLU
MJ730 (GN-?)	G-HFIX	VS610 (K-L)	G-AOKL
MK732 (OU-U)	G-HVDM	VS623	G-AOKZ
MK912 (MN-P)	G-BRRA	VX118	G-ASNB
ML407 (OU-V)	G-LFIX	VX147	G-AVIL
ML417 (2I-T)	G-BJSG	VX653	G-BUCM
MP425	G-AITB	VX926	G-ASKJ
MS824 (Fr AF)	G-AWBU	VZ304 (A-T)	G-MKVI
MT438	G-AREI	VZ467	G-METE
MT928 (ZX-M)	G-BKMI	VZ638	G-JETM
MV293 (OI-C)	G-SPIT	VZ728	G-AGOS
MV370 (EB-Q)	G-FXIV	WA576	G-ALSS

Serial carried	Civil identity	Serial carried	Civil identity
WA577	G-ALST	XE677	G-HHUN
WA591	G-BWMF	XE685	G-GAII
WB531	G-BLRN	XE920	G-VMPR
WB571 (34)	G-AOSF	XF375	G-BUEZ
WB585 (RCU-X)	G-AOSY	XF516 (66.F)	G-BVVC
WB588 (D)	G-AOTD	XF597 (AH)	G-BKFW
WB660	G-ARMB	XF690	G-MOOS
WB702	G-AOFE	XF785	G-ALBN
WB703	G-ARMC	XF836 (J-G)	G-AWRY
WB763 (14)	G-BBMR	XF877 (JX)	G-AWVF
WD286 (J)	G-BBND	XG452	G-BRMB
WD292	G-BCRX	XG496	G-ANDX
WD305	G-ARGG	XG547	G-HAPR
WD363 (5)	G-BCIH	XG775	G-DHWW
WD379 (K)	G-APLO	XH558	G-VLCN
WD413	G-BFIR	XH568	G-BVIC
WE275	G-VIDI	XJ389	G-AJJP
WE402	G-VENI	XJ729	G-BVGE
WE569	G-ASAJ	XJ763	G-BKHA
WF877	G-BPOA	XK416	G-AYUA
WG307	G-BCYJ	XK417	G-AVXY
WG316	G-BCAH	XK482	G-BJWC
WG348	G-BBMV	XK895 (19/CU)	G-SDEV
WG350	G-BPAL	XK896	G-RNAS
WG422 (16)	G-BFAX	XK940	G-AYXT
WG469	G-BWJY	XL318	G-FFOX
WG472	G-AOTY	XL426	G-VJET
WG718	G-BRMA	XL502	G-BMYP
WJ358	G-ARYD	XL572	G-HNTR
WJ680 (C-T)	G-BURM	XL573	G-BVGH
WJ945	G-BEDV	XL600	G-BVWN
WK163	G-BVWC	XL613	G-BVMB
WK511 (905 RN)	G-BVBT	XL809	G-BLIX
WK522	G-BCOU	XL812	G-SARO
WK611	G-ARWB	XL954	N4232C
WK622	G-BCZH	XM405 (42)	G-TORE
WK628	G-BBMW	XM470	G-BWZZ
WK638	G-BWJZ	XM479 (54)	G-BVEZ
WK639 (L)	G-BWJU	XM553	G-AWSV
WL505	G-FBIX	XM575	G-BLMC
WL626	G-BHDD	XM655	G-VULC
WM167	G-LOSM	XM685 (513/PO)	G-AYZJ
WP321 (750/CU)	G-BRFC	XM693	G-TIMM
WP788	G-BCHL	XM819	G-APXW
WP790	G-BBNC	XN351	G-BKSC
WP800 (2)	G-BCXN	XN435	G-BGBU
WP808	G-BDEU	XN437	G-AXWA
WP809 (778)	G-BVTX	XN441	G-BGKT
WP835	G-BDCB	XN461 (28)	G-BVBE
WP843 (F)	G-BDBP	XN629 (49)	G-BVEG
WP851	G-BDET	XN637	G-BKOU
WP856 (904 RN)	G-BVWP	XP772	G-BUCJ
WP857 (24)	G-BDRJ	XP254	G-ASCC
WP903	G-BCGC	XP279	G-BWKK
WP971	G-ATHD	XP282	G-BGTC
WP977	G-BHRD	XP355	G-BEBC
WR410 (N)	G-BLKA	XP924	G-CVIX
WT333	G-BVXC	XR240	G-BDFH
WT933	G-ALSW	XR241	G-AXRR
WV198	G-BJWY	XR246	G-AZBU
WV493 (A-P)	G-BDYG	XR267	G-BJXR
WV666 (O-D)	G-BTDH	XR442	G-HRON
WV686	G-BLFT	XR486	G-RWWW
WV740	G-BNPH	XR537	G-NATY
WV783	G-ALSP	XR724	G-BTSY
WZ507	G-VTII	XR944	G-ATTB
WZ662	G-BKVK	XR991	G-MOUR
WZ706	G-BURR	XR993	G-BVPP
WZ711	G-AVHT	XS101	G-GNAT
WZ868 (H CUAS)	G-ARMF	XS165 (37)	G-ASAZ
XA880	G-BVXR	XS451	G-LTNG
XE489	G-JETH	XS587 (252/V)	G-VIXN

MILITARY/CIVIL CROSS REFERENCE

Serial carried	Civil identity	Serial carried	Civil identity
XS770	G-HRHI	F+IS (Luftwaffe)	G-BIRW
XT788 (442)	G-BMIR	BU+CC (Luftwaffe)	G-BUCC
XV268	G-BVER	BU+CK (Luftwaffe)	G-BUCK
XW289 (73)	G-JPVA	CC+43 (Luftwaffe)	G-CJCI
XW293 (2)	G-BWCS	LG+01 (Luftwaffe)	G-AYSJ
XW324	G-BWSG	LG+03 (Luftwaffe)	G-AEZX
XW333 (79)	G-BVTC	NJ+C11 (Luftwaffe)	G-ATBG
XW428	G-TOMG	RF+16 (Luftwaffe)	G-PTWO
XW433	G-JPRO	S5-B06 (Luftwaffe)	G-BSFB
XW635	G-AWSW	TA+RC (Luftwaffe)	G-BPHZ
XW784	G-BBRN	6J+PR (Luftwaffe)	G-AWHB
XX469	G-BNCL	7A+WN (Luftwaffe)	G-AZMH
ZA634	G-BUHA	57-H (USAAC)	G-AKAZ
ZA647	G-EHIL	97+04 (Luftwaffe)	G-APVF
2+1 (Luftwaffe)	G-SYFW	+114 (Luftwaffe)	G-BSMD
4+ (Luftwaffe)	G-BSLX	— (Luftwaffe)	G-BOML
6+ (Luftwaffe)	G-USTV	— (HL-67/8 USAAF)	G-AKAZ
07 (Russian AF)	G-BMJY	146-11042 (7)	G-BMZX
8+ (Luftwaffe)	G-WULF	146-11083 (5)	G-BNAI
14+ (Luftwaffe)	G-BBII		

Toy Balloons

Notes	Reg.	Type	Owner or Operator
	G-FYAN	Williams	M. D. Williams
	G-FYAO	Williams	M. D. Williams
	G-FYAU	Williams MK 2	M. D. Williams
	G-FYAV	Osprey Mk 4E2	C. D. Egan & C. Stiles
	G-FYAZ	Osprey Mk 4D2	M. A. Roblett
	G-FYBP	European E.84PW	D. Eaves
	G-FYBR	Osprey Mk 4G2	A. J. Pugh
	G-FYBU	Portswood Mk XVI	M. A. Roblett
	G-FYBX	Portswood Mk XVI	I. Chadwick
	G-FYCC	Osprey Mk 4G2	A. Russell
	G-FYCL	Osprey Mk 4G	P. J. Rogers
	G-FYCV	Osprey Mk 4D	M. Thomson
	G-FYCZ	Osprey Mk 4D2	P. Middleton
	G-FYDC	European EDH-1	D. Eaves & H. Goddard
	G-FYDF	Osprey Mk 4D	K. A. Jones
	G-FYDI	Williams Westwind Two	M. D. Williams
	G-FYDN	European 8C	P. D. Ridout
	G-FYDO	Osprey Mk 4D	N. L. Scallan
	G-FYDP	Williams Westwind Three	M. D. Williams
	G-FYDS	Osprey Mk 4D	N. L. Scallan
	G-FYDW	Osprey Mk 4B	R. A. Balfre
	G-FYEB	Rango Rega	N. H. Ponsford
	G-FYEI	Portswood Mk XVI	A. Russell
	G-FYEJ	Rango NA.24	N. H. Ponsford
	G-FYEK	Unicorn UE.1C	D. & D. Eaves
	G-FYEL	European E.84Z	D. Eaves
	G-FYEO	Eagle Mk 1	M. E. Scallan
	G-FYEV	Osprey Mk 1C	M. E. Scallan
	G-FYEZ	Firefly Mk 1	M. E. & N. L. Scallan
	G-FYFA	European E.84LD	D. Goddard & D. Eaves
	G-FYFG	European E.84DE	D. Eaves
	G-FYFH	European E.84DS	D. Eaves
	G-FYFI	European E.84DS	M. Stelling
	G-FYFJ	Williams Westland 2	M. D. Williams
	G-FYFN	Osprey Saturn 2	J. & M. Woods
	G-FYFT	Rango NA-32BC	Rango Kite & Balloon Co
	G-FYFV	Saffrey Grand Edinburgh	I. G. & G. M. McIntosh
	G-FYFW	Rango NA-55	Rango Kite & Balloon Co
	G-FYFY	Rango NA-55RC	A. M. Lindsay
	G-FYGA	Rango NA-50RC	Rango Kite & Balloon Co
	G-FYGB	Rango NA-105RC	Rango Kite & Balloon Co
	G-FYGC	Rango NA-42B	L. J. Wardle
	G-FYGI	Rango NA-55RC	Advertair Ltd
	G-FYGJ	Airspeed 300	N. Wells
	G-FYGK	Rango NA-42POC	Rango Balloon & Kite Co
	G-FYGL	Glowball	J. J. Noble

Microlights

Reg.	Type	Notes	Reg.	Type	Notes
G-MBAA	Hiway Skytrike Mk 2		G-MBHP	American Aerolights Eagle II	
G-MBAB	Hovey Whing-Ding II		G-MBHT	Chargus T.250	
G-MBAD	Weedhopper JC-24A		G-MBHX	Pterodactyl Ptraveller	
G-MBAF	R. J. Swift 3		G-MBHZ	Pterodactyl Ptraveller	
G-MBAL	Hiway Demon		G-MBIA	Flexiform Sealander Skytrike	
G-MBAN	American Aerolights Eagle				
G-MBAR	Skycraft Scout		G-MBIO	American Aerolights Eagle Z Drive	
G-MBAS	Typhoon Tripacer 250				
G-MBAU	Hiway Skytrike		G-MBIT	Hiway Demon Skytrike	
G-MBAW	Pterodactyl Ptraveller		G-MBIV	Flexiform Skytrike	
G-MBAZ	Rotec Rally 2B		G-MBIW	Hiway Demon Tri-Flyer Skytrike	
G-MBBB	Skycraft Scout 2				
G-MBBG	Weedhopper JC-24B		G-MBIY	Ultra Sports	
G-MBBM	Eipper Quicksilver MX		G-MBIZ	Mainair Tri-Flyer	
G-MBBT	Ultrasports Tripacer 330		G-MBJA	Eurowing Goldwing	
G-MBBY	Flexiform Sealander		G-MBJD	American Aerolights Eagle	
G-MBCA	Chargus Cyclone T.250		G-MBJE	Airwave Nimrod	
G-MBCI	Hiway Skytrike		G-MBJF	Hiway Skytrike Mk II	
G-MBCJ	Mainair Sports Tri-Flyer		G-MBJG	Airwave Nimrod	
G-MBCK	Eipper Quicksilver MX		G-MBJI	Southern Aerosports Scorpion	
G-MBCL	Hiway Demon Triflyer				
G-MBCM	Hiway Demon 175		G-MBJK	American Aerolights Eagle	
G-MBCO	Flexiform Sealander Buggy		G-MBJL	Airwave Nimrod	
			G-MBJM	Striplin Lone Ranger	
G-MBCU	American Aerolights Eagle		G-MBJN	Electraflyer Eagle	
G-MBCX	Airwave Nimrod 165		G-MBJO	Birdman Cherokee	
G-MBCZ	Chargus Skytrike 160		G-MBJP	Hiway Skytrike	
G-MBDD	Skyhook Skytrike		G-MBJR	American Aerolights Eagle	
G-MBDE	Flexiform Skytrike		G-MBJT	Hiway Skytrike II	
G-MBDF	Rotec Rally 2B		G-MBJU	American Eagle 215B	
G-MBDG	Eurowing Goldwing		G-MBJZ	Eurowing Catto CP.16	
G-MBDI	Flexiform Sealander		G-MBKC	Southdown Lightning	
G-MBDJ	Flexiform Sealander Triflyer		G-MBKS	Hiway Skytrike 160	
			G-MBKT	Mitchell Wing B.10	
G-MBDM	Southdown Sigma Trike		G-MBKU	Hiway Demon Skytrike	
G-MBDZ	Eipper Quicksilver MX		G-MBKW	Pterodactyl Ptraveller	
G-MBEA	Hornet Nimrod		G-MBKY	American Aerolight Eagle	
G-MBED	Chargus Titan 38		G-MBKZ	Hiway Skytrike	
G-MBEG	Eipper Quicksilver MX		G-MBLB	Eipper Quicksilver MX	
G-MBEJ	Electraflyer Eagle		G-MBLF	Hiway Demon 195 Tri Pacer	
G-MBEN	Eipper Quicksilver MX				
G-MBEP	American Aerolights Eagle		G-MBLJ	Eipper Quicksilver MX	
G-MBES	Skyhook Cutlass		G-MBLK	Southdown Puma	
G-MBET	MEA Mistral Trainer		G-MBLM	Hiway Skytrike	
G-MBEU	Hiway Demon T.250		G-MBLN	Pterodactyl Ptraveller	
G-MBEV	Chargus Titan 38		G-MBLO	Sealander Skytrike	
G-MBFA	Hiway Skytrike 250		G-MBLR	Ultrasports Tripacer	
G-MBFE	American Aerolights Eagle		G-MBLU	Southdown Lightning L.195	
G-MBFF	Southern Aerosports Scorpion				
			G-MBLV	Ultrasports Hybrid	
G-MBFK	Hiway Demon		G-MBLY	Flexiform Sealander Trike	
G-MBFM	Hiway Hang Glider		G-MBLZ	Southern Aerosports Scorpion	
G-MBFU	Ultrasports Tripacer				
G-MBFX	Hiway Skytrike 250		G-MBME	American Aerolights Eagle Z Drive	
G-MBFY	Mirage II				
G-MBFZ	M. S. S. Goldwing		G-MBMG	Rotec Rally 2B	
G-MBGA	Solar Wings Typhoon		G-MBMJ	Mainair Tri-Flyer	
G-MBGB	American Aerolights Eagle		G-MBMO	Hiway Skytrike 160	
G-MBGF	Twamley Trike		G-MBMR	Ultrasports Tripacer Typhoon	
G-MBGJ	Hiway Skytrike Mk 2				
G-MBGK	Electra Flyer Eagle		G-MBMS	Hornet	
G-MBGP	Solar Wings Typhoon		G-MBMT	Mainair Tri-Flyer	
G-MBGS	Rotec Rally 2B		G-MBMU	Eurowing Goldwing	
G-MBGX	Southdown Lightning		G-MBMW	Solar Wings Typhoon	
G-MBGY	Hiway Demon Skytrike		G-MBMZ	Sealander Tripacer	
G-MBHA	Trident Trike		G-MBNA	American Aerolights Eagle	
G-MBHE	American Aerolights Eagle		G-MBNG	Hiway Demon Skytrike	
G-MBHK	Flexiform Skytrike				

Reg.	Type	Notes	Reg.	Type	Notes
G-MBNH	Southern Airsports Scorpion		G-MBVV	Hiway Skytrike	
			G-MBVW	Skyhook TR.2	
G-MBNJ	Eipper Quicksilver MX		G-MBWA	American Aerolights Eagle	
G-MBNK	American Aerolights Eagle		G-MBWB	Hiway Skytrike	
G-MBNN	Southern Microlight Gazelle P.160N		G-MBWE	American Aerolights Eagle	
			G-MBWF	Mainair Triflyer Striker	
G-MBNT	American Aerolights Eagle		G-MBWG	Huntair Pathfinder	
G-MBNY	Steer Terror Fledge II		G-MBWH	Designability Duet I	
G-MBOA	Flexiform Hilander		G-MBWL	Huntair Pathfinder	
G-MBOD	American Aerolights Eagle		G-MBWP	Ultrasports Trike	
G-MBOE	Solar Wing Typhoon Trike		G-MBWT	Huntair Pathfinder	
G-MBOF	Pakes Jackdaw		G-MBWW	Southern Aerosports Scorpion	
G-MBOH	Microlight Engineering Mistral		G-MBWX	Southern Aerosports Scorpion	
G-MBOK	Dunstable Microlight		G-MBWY	American Aerolights Eagle	
G-MBOM	Hiway Hilander		G-MBXE	Hiway Skytrike	
G-MBON	Eurowing Goldwing Canard		G-MBXJ	Hiway Demon Skytrike	
G-MBOR	Chotia 460B Weedhopper		G-MBXK	Ultrasports Puma	
G-MBOT	Hiway 250 Skytrike		G-MBXO	Sheffield Trident	
G-MBOU	Wheeler Scout		G-MBXR	Hiway Skytrike 150	
G-MBOX	American Aerolights Eagle		G-MBXT	Eipper Quicksilver MX2	
G-MBPA	Weedhopper Srs 2		G-MBXW	Hiway Skytrike	
G-MBPD	American Aerolights Eagle		G-MBXX	Ultraflight Mirage II	
G-MBPG	Hunt Skytrike		G-MBYD	American Aerolights Eagle	
G-MBPJ	Moto-Delta		G-MBYH	Maxair Hummer	
G-MBPM	Eurowing Goldwing		G-MBYI	Ultraflight Lazair	
G-MBPN	American Aerolights Eagle		G-MBYK	Huntair Pathfinder Mk 1	
G-MBPO	Volnik Arrow		G-MBYL	Huntair Pathfinder 330	
G-MBPU	Hiway Demon		G-MBYM	Eipper Quicksilver MX	
G-MBPW	Weedhopper		G-MBYO	American Aerolights Eagle	
G-MBPX	Eurowing Goldwing		G-MBYR	American Aerolights Eagle	
G-MBPY	Ultrasports Tripacer 330		G-MBYS	Ultraflight Mirage II	
G-MBRB	Electraflyer Eagle 1		G-MBYX	American Aerolights Eagle	
G-MBRD	American Aerolights Eagle		G-MBYY	Southern Aerosports Scorpion	
G-MBRE	Wheeler Scout				
G-MBRH	Ultraflight Mirage Mk II		G-MBZB	Hiway Skytrike	
G-MBRM	Hiway Demon		G-MBZF	American Aerolights Eagle	
G-MBRS	American Aerolights Eagle		G-MBZG	Twinfield Scorpion 2 seat	
G-MBRV	Eurowing Goldwing		G-MBZH	Eurowing Goldwing	
G-MBSD	Southdown Puma DS		G-MBZJ	Southdown Puma	
G-MBSF	Ultraflight Mirage II		G-MBZL	Weedhopper	
G-MBSG	Ultraflight Mirage II		G-MBZM	UAS Storm Buggy	
G-MBSN	American Aerolights Eagle		G-MBZN	Ultrasports Puma	
G-MBSS	Ultrasports Puma 2		G-MBZP	Skyhook TR2	
G-MBST	Mainair Gemini Sprint		G-MBZV	American Aerolights Eagle	
G-MBSX	Ultraflight Mirage II		G-MBZZ	Southern Aerosports Scorpion	
G-MBTA	UAS Storm Buggy 5 Mk 2				
G-MBTC	Weedhopper JC-24B				
G-MBTE	Hiway Demon		G-MGAG	Aviasud Mistral	
G-MBTF	Mainair Tri-Flyer Skytrike		G-MGCB	Cycl Pegasus XL-Q	
G-MBTG	Mainair Gemini		G-MGEF	Cycl Pegasus Quantum 15	
G-MBTH	Whittaker MW.4		G-MGGT	CFM Streak Shadow SAM	
G-MBTI	Hovey Whing Ding		G-MGMT	Cycl Pegasus Quantum 15	
G-MBTJ	Solar Wings Microlight		G-MGOD	Medway Raven	
G-MBTO	Mainair Tri-Flyer 250		G-MGOM	Medway Hybred 44XLR	
G-MBTW	Raven Vector 600		G-MGOO	Renegade Spirit UK Ltd	
G-MBUA	Hiway Demon		G-MGPD	Cycl Pegasus XL-R	
G-MBUB	Horne Sigma Skytrike		G-MGRW	Cyclone AX3/503	
G-MBUC	Huntair Pathfinder		G-MGUN	Cyclone AX2000	
G-MBUH	Hiway Skytrike		G-MGUY	CFM Shadow Srs BD	
G-MBUI	Wheeler Scout Mk I		G-MGWH	Thruster T.300	
G-MBUK	Mainair 330 Tri Pacer				
G-MBUO	Southern Aerosports Scorpion		G-MJAB	Ultrasports Skytrike	
			G-MJAD	Eipper Quicksilver MX	
G-MBUP	Hiway Skytrike		G-MJAE	American Aerolights Eagle	
G-MBUZ	Wheeler Scout Mk II		G-MJAF	Ultrasports Puma 440	
G-MBVA	Volmer Jensen VJ-23E		G-MJAG	Skyhook TR1	
G-MBVC	American Aerolights Eagle		G-MJAH	American Aerolights Eagle	
G-MBVK	Ultraflight Mirage II		G-MJAI	American Aerolights Eagle	
G-MBVL	Southern Aerosports Scorpion		G-MJAJ	Eurowing Goldwing	
			G-MJAL	Wheeler Scout 3	
G-MBVS	Hiway Skytrike		G-MJAM	Eipper Quicklsilver MX	

Reg.	Type	Notes	Reg.	Type	Notes
G-MJAN	Hiway Skytrike		G-MJHU	Eipper Quicksilver MX	
G-MJAP	Hiway 160		G-MJHV	Hiway Demon 250	
G-MJAZ	Aerodyne Vector 610		G-MJHW	Ultrasports Puma 1	
G-MJBI	Eipper Quicksilver MX		G-MJHX	Eipper Quicksilver MX	
G-MJBK	Swallow AeroPlane		G-MJHZ	Southdown Sailwings	
	Swallow B		G-MJIA	Flexiform Striker	
G-MJBL	American Aerolights Eagle		G-MJIB	Hornet 250	
G-MJBS	Ultralight Stormbuggy		G-MJIC	Ultrasports Puma 330	
G-MJBV	American Aerolights Eagle		G-MJIE	Hornet 330	
G-MJBX	Pterodactyl Ptraveller		G-MJIF	Mainair Triflyer	
G-MJBZ	Huntair Pathfinder		G-MJIJ	Ultrasports Tripacer 250	
G-MJCB	Hornet 330		G-MJIK	Southdown Sailwings	
G-MJCD	Sigma Tetley Skytrike			Lightning	
G-MJCE	Ultrasports Tripacer		G-MJIN	Hiway Skytrike	
G-MJCI	Kruchek Firefly 440		G-MJIO	American Aerolights Eagle	
G-MJCJ	Hiway Spectrum		G-MJIR	Eipper Quicksilver MX	
G-MJCK	Southern Aerosports		G-MJIZ	Southdown Lightning	
	Scorpion		G-MJJA	Huntair Pathfinder	
G-MJCL	Eipper Quicksilver MX		G-MJJB	Eipper Quicksilver MX	
G-MJCN	S.M.C. Flyer Mk 1		G-MJJF	Solar Wings Typhoon	
G-MJCU	Tarjani		G-MJJJ	Moyes Knight	
G-MJCW	Hiway Super Scorpion		G-MJJK	Eipper Quicksilver MX2	
G-MJCX	American Aerolights Eagle		G-MJJM	Birdman Cherokee Mk 1	
G-MJCZ	Southern Aerosports		G-MJJN	Ultrasports Puma	
	Scorpion 2		G-MJJO	Flexiform Skytrike Dual	
G-MJDA	Hornet Trike Executive		G-MJJV	Wheeler Scoutá	
G-MJDE	Huntair Pathfinder		G-MJJX	Hiway Skytrike	
G-MJDG	Hornet Supertrike		G-MJJY	Tirith Firefly	
G-MJDH	Huntair Pathfinder		G-MJKB	Striplin Skyranger	
G-MJDJ	Hiway Skytrike Demon		G-MJKE	Mainair Triflyer 330	
G-MJDK	American Aerolights Eagle		G-MJKF	Hiway Demon	
G-MJDO	Southdown Puma 440		G-MJKG	John Ivor Skytrike	
G-MJDP	Eurowing Goldwing		G-MJKH	Eipper Quicksilver MX II	
G-MJDR	Hiway Demon Skytrike		G-MJKI	Eipper Quicksilver MX	
G-MJDU	Eipper Quicksilver àMX2		G-MJKJ	Eipper Quicksilver MX	
G-MJDW	Eipper Quicksilver MX		G-MJKO	Goldmarque 250 Skytrike	
G-MJEE	Mainair Triflyer Trike		G-MJKS	Mainair Triflyer	
G-MJEF	Gryphon 180		G-MJKV	Hornet	
G-MJEG	Eurowing Goldwing		G-MJKX	Ultralight Skyrider Phantom	
G-MJEH	Rotec Rally 2B		G-MJLA	Ultrasports Puma 2	
G-MJEJ	American Aerolights Eagle		G-MJLB	Ultrasports Puma 2	
G-MJEL	GMD-01 Trike		G-MJLH	American Aerolights	
G-MJEO	American Aerolights Eagle			Eagle 2	
G-MJER	Flexiform Striker		G-MJLI	Hiway Demon Skytrike	
G-MJET	Stratos Prototype 3 Axis 1		G-MJLL	Hiway Demon Skytrike	
G-MJEX	Eipper Quicksilver MX		G-MJLR	Skyhook SK-1	
G-MJEY	Southdown Lightning		G-MJLS	Rotec Rally 2B	
G-MJFB	Flexiform Striker		G-MJLT	American Aerolights Eagle	
G-MJFD	Ultrasports Tripacer		G-MJLY	American Aerolights Eagle	
G-MJFH	Eipper Quicksilver MX		G-MJMA	Hiway Demon	
G-MJFI	Flexiform Striker		G-MJME	Ultrasports Tripacer	
G-MJFJ	Hiway Skytrike 250			Mega II	
G-MJFK	Flexiform Skytrike Dual		G-MJMM	Chargus Vortex	
G-MJFM	Huntair Pathfinder		G-MJMP	Eipper Quicksilver MX	
G-MJFO	Eipper Quicksilver MX		G-MJMR	Solar Wings Typhoon	
G-MJFP	American Aerolights Eagle		G-MJMS	Hiway Skytrike	
G-MJFS	American Aerolights Eagle		G-MJMT	Hiway Demon Skytrike	
G-MJFV	Ultrasports Tripacer		G-MJMW	Eipper Quicksilver MX2	
G-MJFX	Skyhook TR-1		G-MJMX	Ultrasports Tripacer	
G-MJGE	Eipper Quicksilver MX		G-MJNB	Hiway Skytrike	
G-MJGG	Skyhook TR-1		G-MJNE	Hornet Supreme Dual	
G-MJGI	Eipper Quicksilver MX			Trike	
G-MJGN	Greenslade Monotrike		G-MJNH	Skyhook Cutlass Trike	
G-MJGO	Barnes Avon Skytrike		G-MJNK	Hiway Skytrike	
G-MJGT	Skyhook Cutlass Trike		G-MJNL	American Aerolights Eagle	
G-MJGV	Eipper Quicksilver MX2		G-MJNM	American Aerolights	
G-MJGW	Solar Wings TrikeB			Double Eagle	
G-MJHC	Ultrasports Tripacer 330		G-MJNN	Ultraflight Mirage II	
G-MJHF	Skyhook Sailwing Trike		G-MJNO	American Aerolights	
G-MJHK	Hiway Demon 195			Double Eagle	
G-MJHM	Ultrasports Trike		G-MJNR	Ultralight Solar Buggy	
G-MJHN	American Aerolights Eagle		G-MJNS	Swallow AeroPlane	
G-MJHR	Southdown Lightning			Swallow B	

Reg.	Type	Notes	Reg.	Type	Notes
G-MJNT	Hiway Skytrike		G-MJUV	Huntair Pathfinder 1	
G-MJNU	Skyhook Cutlass		G-MJUW	MBA Tiger Cub 440	
G-MJNV	Eipper Quicksilver MX		G-MJUX	Skyrider Airsports Phantom	
G-MJNY	Skyhook Sabre Trike		G-MJUZ	Dragon Srs 150	
G-MJOC	Huntair Pathfinder		G-MJVA	Skyrider Airsports Phantom	
G-MJOD	Rotec Rally 2B		G-MJVE	Hybred Skytrike	
G-MJOE	Eurowing Goldwing		G-MJVF	CFM Shadow	
G-MJOG	American Aerolights Eagle		G-MJVG	Hiway Skytrike	
G-MJOI	Hiway Demon		G-MJVJ	Flexiform Striker Dual	
G-MJOJ	Flexiform Skytrike		G-MJVL	Flexiform Striker	
G-MJOL	Skyhook Cutla00ss		G-MJVM	Dragon 150	
G-MJOM	Southdown Puma 40F		G-MJVN	Ultrasports Puma 440	
G-MJOU	Hiway Demon 175		G-MJVP	Eipper Quicksilver MX II	
G-MJOW	Eipper Quicksilver MX		G-MJVR	Flexiforn Striker	
G-MJPA	Rotec Rally 2B		G-MJVT	Eipper Quicksilver MX	
G-MJPC	American Aerolights Double Eagle		G-MJVU	Eipper Quicksilver MX II	
			G-MJVW	Airwave Nimrod	
G-MJPD	Hiway Demon Skytrike		G-MJVX	Skyrider Phantom	
G-MJPE	Hiway Demon Skytrike		G-MJVY	Dragon Srs 150	
G-MJPG	American Aerolights Eagle 430R		G-MJVZ	Hiway Demon Tripacer	
			G-MJWB	Eurowing Goldwing	
G-MJPI	Flexiform Striker		G-MJWD	Solar Wings Typhoon XL	
G-MJPK	Hiway Vulcan		G-MJWF	Tiger Cub 440	
G-MJPO	Eurowing Goldwing		G-MJWG	MBA Tiger Cub	
G-MJPT	Dragon		G-MJWI	Flexiform Striker	
G-MJPU	Solar Wings Typhoon		G-MJWJ	MBA Tiger Cub 440	
G-MJPV	Eipper Quicksilver MX		G-MJWK	Huntair Pathfinder	
G-MJRD	Hiway Super Scorpion		G-MJWN	Flexiform Striker	
G-MJRE	Hiway Demon		G-MJWR	MBA Tiger Cub 440	
G-MJRI	American Aerolights Eagle		G-MJWS	Eurowing Goldwing	
G-MJRK	Flexiform Striker		G-MJWU	Maxair Hummer TX	
G-MJRL	Eurowing Goldwing		G-MJWW	MBA Super Tiger Cub 440	
G-MJRN	Flexiform Striker		G-MJWZ	Ultrasports Panther XL	
G-MJRO	Eurowing Goldwing		G-MJXD	MBA Tiger Cub 440	
G-MJRP	Mainair Triflyer 330		G-MJXE	Hiway Demon	
G-MJRR	Striplin Skyranger Srs 1		G-MJXF	MBA Tiger Cub 440	
G-MJRS	Eurowing Goldwing		G-MJXJ	MBA Tiger Cub 440	
G-MJRT	Southdown Lightning DS		G-MJXM	Hiway Skytrike	
G-MJRU	MBA Tiger Cub 440		G-MJXR	Huntair Pathfinder II	
G-MJRV	Eurowing Goldwing		G-MJXS	Huntair Pathfinder II	
G-MJRX	Ultrasports Puma II		G-MJXV	Flexiform Striker	
G-MJSA	Mainair 2-Seat Trike		G-MJXX	Flexiform Striker Dual	
G-MJSE	Skyrider Airsports Phantom		G-MJXY	Hiway Demon Skytrike	
G-MJSF	Skyrider Airsports Phantom		G-MJXZ	Hiway Demon	
G-MJSL	Dragon 200		G-MJYA	Huntair Pathfinder	
G-MJSO	Hiway Skytrike		G-MJYC	Ultrasports Panther XL Dual 440	
G-MJSP	MBA Super Tiger Cub 440				
G-MJSS	American Aerolights Eagle		G-MJYD	MBA Tiger Cub 440	
G-MJST	Pterodactyl Ptraveler		G-MJYF	Mainair Gemini Flash	
G-MJSV	MBA Tiger Cub		G-MJYG	Skyhook Orion Canard	
G-MJSY	Eurowing Goldwing		G-MJYM	Southdown Puma Sprint	
G-MJSZ	DH Wasp		G-·MJYP	Mainair Triflyer 440	
G-MJTC	Solar Wings Typhoon		G-MJYR	Catto CP.16	
G-MJTD	Gardner T-M Scout		G-MJYS	Southdown Puma Sprint	
G-MJTE	Skyrider Airsports Phantom		G-MJYT	Southdown Puma Sprint	
G-MJTF	Gryphon Wing		G-MJYV	Mainair Triflyer 2 Seat	
G-MJTM	Aerostructure Pipistrelle 2B		G-MJYW	Wasp Gryphon III	
G-MJTN	Eipper Quicksilver MX		G-MJYX	Mainair Triflyer	
G-MJTO	Jordan Duet Srs 1		G-MJYY	Hiway Demon	
G-MJTP	Flexiform Striker		G-MJZA	MBA Tiger Cub	
G-MJTR	Southdown Puma DS Mk 1		G-MJZB	Flexiform Striker Dual	
G-MJTW	Eurowing Trike		G-MJZC	MBA Tiger Cub 440	
G-MJTX	Skyrider Phantom		G-MJZD	Mainair Gemini Flash	
G-MJTZ	Skyrider Airsports Phantom		G-MJZH	Southdown Lightning 195	
G-MJUC	MBA Tiger Cub 440		G-MJZJ	Hiway Cutlass Skytrike	
G-MJUE	Southdown Lightning II		G-MJZK	Southdown Puma Sprint 440	
G-MJUI	Flexiform Striker				
G-MJUJ	Eipper Quicksilver Mk II		G-MJZL	Eipper Quicksilver MX II	
G-MJUM	Flexiform Striker		G-MJZO	Flexiform Striker	
G-MJUR	Skyrider Airsports Phantom		G-MJZP	MBA Tiger Cub 440	
G-MJUS	MBA Tiger Cub 440		G-MJZT	Flexiform Striker	
G-MJUT	Eurowing Goldwing		G-MJZU	Flexiform Striker	
G-MJUU	Eurowing Goldwing		G-MJZW	Eipper Quicksilver MX II	

Reg.	Type	Notes	Reg.	Type	Notes
G-MJZX	Maxair Hummer TX		G-MMEY	MBA Tiger Cub 440	
			G-MMFC	Flexiform Striker	
G-MMAC	Dragon Srs 150		G-MMFD	Flexiform Striker	
G-MMAE	Dragon Srs 150		G-MMFE	Flexiform Striker	
G-MMAG	MBA Tiger Cub 440		G-MMFG	Flexiform Striker	
G-MMAH	Eipper Quicksilver MX II		G-MMFI	Flexiform Striker	
G-MMAI	Dragon Srs 150		G-MMFK	Flexiform Striker	
G-MMAJ	Mainair Tri-Flyer 440		G-MMFL	Flexiform Striker	
G-MMAK	MBA Tiger Cub 440		G-MMFM	Piranha Srs 200	
G-MMAL	Flexiform Striker Dual		G-MMFN	MBA Tiger Cub 440	
G-MMAM	MBA Tiger Cub 440		G-MMFS	MBA Tiger Cub 440	
G-MMAN	Flexiform Striker		G-MMFT	MBA Tiger Cub 440	
G-MMAO	Southdown Puma Sprint		G-MMFV	Tri-Flyer 440	
G-MMAP	Hummer TX		G-MMFZ	AES Sky Ranger	
G-MMAR	Southdown Puma Sprint		G-MMGA	Bass Gosling	
G-MMAT	Southdown Puma Sprint		G-MMGB	Southdown Puma Sprint	
G-MMAU	Flexiform Rapier		G-MMGC	Southdown Puma Sprint	
G-MMAW	Mainair Rapier		G-MMGD	Southdown Puma Sprint	
G-MMAX	Flexiform Striker		G-MMGE	Hiway Super Scorpion	
G-MMAZ	Southdown Puma Sprint		G-MMGF	MBA Tiger Cub 440	
G-MMBD	Spectrum 330		G-MMGL	MBA Tiger Cub 440	
G-MMBE	MBA Tiger Cub 440		G-MMGN	Southdown Puma Sprint	
G-MMBH	MBA Super Tiger Cub 440		G-MMGT	Solar Wings Typhoon	
G-MMBJ	Solar Wings Typhoon		G-MMGU	Flexiform Sealander	
G-MMBL	Southdown Puma		G-MMGX	Southdown Puma	
G-MMBN	Eurowing Goldwing		G-MMHB	Skyhook TR-1 Pixie	
G-MMBS	Flexiform Striker		G-MMHE	Southdown Puma Sprint	
G-MMBT	MBA Tiger Cub 440		G-MMHF	Southdown Puma Sprint	
G-MMBU	Eipper Quicksilver MX II		G-MMHK	Hiway Super Scorpion	
G-MMBV	Huntair Pathfinder		G-MMHL	Hiway Super Scorpion	
G-MMBX	MBA Tiger Cub 440		G-MMHM	Goldmarque Gyr	
G-MMBY	Solar Wings Panther XL		G-MMHN	MBA Tiger Cub 440	
G-MMBZ	Solar Wings Typhoon P		G-MMHP	Hiway Demon	
G-MMCD	Southdown Lightning DS		G-MMHR	Southdown Puma Sprint	
G-MMCE	MBA Tiger Cub 440		G-MMHS	SMD Viper	
G-MMCF	Solar Wings Panther 330		G-MMHX	Hornet Invader 440	
G-MMCG	Eipper Quicksilver MX I		G-MMHY	Hornet Invader 440	
G-MMCI	Southdown Puma Sprint		G-MMHZ	Solar Wings Typhoon XL	
G-MMCJ	Flexiform Striker		G-MMIC	Luscombe Vitality	
G-MMCM	Southdown Puma Sprint		G-MMIE	MBA Tiger Cub 440	
G-MMCO	Southdown Sprint		G-MMIF	Wasp Gryphon	
G-MMCS	Southdown Puma Sprint		G-MMIH	MBA Tiger Cub 440	
G-MMCV	Solar Wings Typhoon III		G-MMII	Southdown Puma Sprint 440	
G-MMCW	Southdown Puma Sprint				
G-MMCX	MBA Super Tiger Cub 440		G-MMIJ	Ultrasports Tripacer	
G-MMCY	Flexiform Striker		G-MMIL	Eipper Quicksilver MX II	
G-MMCZ	Flexiform Striker		G-MMIM	MBA Tiger Cub 440	
G-MMDC	Eipper Quicksilver MXII		G-MMIR	Mainair Tri-Flyer 440	
G-MMDE	Solar Wings Typhoon		G-MMIV	Southdown Puma Sprint	
G-MMDF	Southdown Lightning II		G-MMIW	Southdown Puma Sprint	
G-MMDJ	Solar Wings Typhoon		G-MMIY	Eurowing Goldwing	
G-MMDK	Flexiform Striker		G-MMJD	Southdown Puma Sprint	
G-MMDN	Flexiform Striker		G-MMJE	Southdown Puma Sprint	
G-MMDO	Southdown Sprint		G-MMJF	Ultrasports Panther Dual 440	
G-MMDP	Southdown Sprint				
G-MMDR	Huntair Pathfinder II		G-MMJG	Mainair Tri-Flyer 440	
G-MMDS	Ultrasports Panther XLS		G-MMJJ	Solar Wings Typhoon	
G-MMDU	MBA Tiger Cub 440		G-MMJM	Southdown Puma Sprint	
G-MMDV	Ultrasports Panther		G-MMJN	Eipper Quicksilver MX II	
G-MMDW	Pterodactyl Pfledgling		G-MMJT	Southdown Puma Sprint	
G-MMDX	Solar Wings Typhoon		G-MMJU	Hiway Demon	
G-MMDZ	Flexiform Dual Strike		G-MMJV	MBA Tiger Cub 440	
G-MMEE	American Aerolights Eagle		G-MMJX	Teman Mono-Fly	
G-MMEF	Hiway Super Scorpion		G-MMJY	MBA Tiger Cub 440	
G-MMEG	Eipper Quicksilver MX		G-MMJZ	Skyhook Pixie	
G-MMEI	Hiway Demon		G-MMKA	Ultrasports Panther Dual	
G-MMEJ	Flexiform Striker		G-MMKD	Southdown Puma Sprint	
G-MMEK	Solar Wings Typhoon XL2		G-MMKE	Birdman Chinook WT-11	
G-MMEN	Solar Wings Typhoon XL2		G-MMKG	Solar Wings Typhoon XL	
G-MMEP	MBA Tiger Cub 440		G-MMKH	Solar Wings Typhoon XL	
G-MMES	Southdown Puma Sprint		G-MMKI	Ultrasports Panther 330	
G-MMET	Skyhook Sabre TR-1 Mk II		G-MMKJ	Ultrasports Panther 330	
G-MMEW	MBA Tiger Cub 440		G-MMKK	Mainair Flash	
G-MMEX	Solar Wings Sprint				

G-MMKL – G-MMWF

Reg.	Type	Notes	Reg.	Type	Notes
G-MMKL	Mainair Flash		G-MMRP	Mainair Gemini	
G-MMKM	Flexiform Dual Striker		G-MMRT	Southdown Puma Sprint	
G-MMKP	MBA Tiger Cub 440		G-MMRU	Tirith Firebird FB-2	
G-MMKR	Southdown Lightning DS		G-MMRV	MBA Tiger Cub 440	
G-MMKU	Southdown Puma Sprint		G-MMRW	Flexiform Dual Striker	
G-MMKV	Southdown Puma Sprint		G-MMRY	Chargus T.250	
G-MMKW	Solar Wings Storm		G-MMRZ	Ultrasports Panther Dual	
G-MMKZ	Ultrasports Puma 440			440	
G-MMLB	MBA Tiger Cub 440		G-MMSA	Ultrasports Panther XL	
G-MMLE	Eurowing Goldwing SP		G-MMSC	Mainair Gemini	
G-MMLF	MBA Tiger Cub 440		G-MMSE	Eipper Quicksilver MX	
G-MMLH	Hiway Demon		G-MMSG	Solar Wings Panther XL-S	
G-MMLK	MBA Tiger Cub 440		G-MMSH	Solar Wings Panther XL	
G-MMLM	MBA Tiger Cub 440		G-MMSO	Mainair Tri-Flyer 440	
G-MMLO	Skyhook Pixie		G-MMSP	Mainair Gemini Flash	
G-MMLP	Southdown Sprint		G-MMSR	MBA Tiger Cub 440	
G-MMLV	Southdown Puma 330		G-MMSS	Solar Wings Panther 330	
G-MMLX	Solar Wings Panther XL-S		G-MMST	Southdown Puma Sprint	
G-MMMB	Mainair Tri-Flyer		G-MMSV	Southdown Puma Sprint	
G-MMMD	Flexiform Dual Striker		G-MMSW	MBA Tiger Cub 440	
G-MMMG	Eipper Quicksilver MXL		G-MMSZ	Medway Half Pint	
G-MMMH	Hadland Willow		G-MMTA	Ultrasports Panther XL	
G-MMMI	Southdown Lightning		G-MMTC	Ultrasports Panther Dual	
G-MMMJ	Southdown Sprint		G-MMTD	Mainair Tri-Flyer 330	
G-MMMK	Hornet Invader		G-MMTG	Mainair Gemini	
G-MMML	Dragon 150		G-MMTH	Southdown Puma Sprint	
G-MMMN	Ultrasports Panther Dual		G-MMTI	Southdown Puma Sprint	
	440		G-MMTK	Medway Hybred	
G-MMMP	Flexiform Dual Striker		G-MMTL	Mainair Gemini	
G-MMMR	Flexiform Striker		G-MMTM	Mainair Tri-Flyer 440	
G-MMMS	MBA Tiger Cub 440		G-MMTO	Mainair Tri-Flyer	
G-MMMW	Flexiform Striker		G-MMTR	Ultrasports Panther	
G-MMNA	Eipper Quicksilver MX II		G-MMTS	Solar Wings Panther XL	
G-MMNB	Eipper Quicksilver MX		G-MMTT	Solar Wings Panther XL	
G-MMNC	Eipper Quicksilver MX		G-MMTV	American Aerolights Eagle	
G-MMND	Eipper Quicksilver MX II-Q2		G-MMTX	Mainair Gemini 440	
G-MMNF	Hornet		G-MMTY	Fisher FP.202U	
G-MMNG	Solar Wings Typhoon XL		G-MMTZ	Eurowing Goldwing	
G-MMNN	Buzzard		G-MMUA	Southdown Puma Sprint	
G-MMNS	Mitchell U-2 Super Wing		G-MMUC	Mainair Gemini 440	
G-MMNT	Flexiform Striker		G-MMUE	Mainair Gemini Flash	
G-MMNW	Mainair Tri-Flyer 330		G-MMUG	Mainair Tri-Flyer	
G-MMNX	Solar Wings Panther XL		G-MMUH	Mainair Tri-Flyer	
G-MMOB	Southdown Sprint		G-MMUJ	Southdown Puma Sprint	
G-MMOF	MBA Tiger Cub 440			440	
G-MMOH	Solar Wings Typhoon XL		G-MMUK	Mainair Tri-Flyer	
G-MMOI	MBA Tiger Cub 440		G-MMUL	Ward Elf E.47	
G-MMOK	Solar Wings Panther XL		G-MMUN	Ultrasports Panther Dual XL	
G-MMOL	Skycraft Scout R3		G-MMUO	Mainair Gemini Flash	
G-MMOO	Southdown Storm		G-MMUP	Airwave Nimrod 140	
G-MMOW	Mainair Gemini Flash		G-MMUS	Mainair Gemini	
G-MMOY	Mainair Gemini Sprint		G-MMUU	ParaPlane PM-1	
G-MMPG	Southdown Puma		G-MMUV	Southdown Puma Sprint	
G-MMPH	Southdown Puma Sprint		G-MMUW	Mainair Gemini Flash	
G-MMPI	Pterodactyl Ptraveller		G-MMUX	Mainair Gemini	
G-MMPJ	Mainair Tri-Flyer 440		G-MMVA	Southdown Puma Sprint	
G-MMPL	Flexiform Dual Striker		G-MMVC	Ultrasports Panther XL	
G-MMPN	Chargus T250		G-MMVG	MBA Tiger Cub 440	
G-MMPO	Mainair Gemini Flash		G-MMVH	Southdown Raven	
G-MMPT	SMD Gazelle		G-MMVI	Southdown Puma Sprint	
G-MMPU	Ultrasports Tripacer 250		G-MMVL	Ultrasports Panther XL-S	
G-MMPW	Airwave Nimrod		G-MMVM	Whiteley Orion 1	
G-MMPX	Ultrasports Panther Dual		G-MMVN	Solar Wings Typhoon	
	440		G-MMVO	Southdown Puma Sprint	
G-MMPZ	Teman Mono-Fly		G-MMVP	Mainair Gemini Flash	
G-MMRA	Mainair Tri-Flyer 250		G-MMVR	Hiway Skytrike 1	
G-MMRF	MBA Tiger Cub 440		G-MMVS	Skyhook Pixie	
G-MMRH	Hiway Demon		G-MMVX	Southdown Puma Sprint	
G-MMRJ	Solar Wings Panther XL		G-MMVZ	Southdown Puma Sprint	
G-MMRK	Ultrasports Panther XL		G-MMWA	Mainair Gemini Flash	
G-MMRL	Solar Wings Panther XL		G-MMWB	Huntair Pathfinder II	
G-MMRN	Southdown Puma Sprint		G-MMWC	Eipper Quicksilver MXII	
G-MMRO	Mainair Gemini 440		G-MMWF	Hiway Skytrike 250	

Reg.	Type	Notes	Reg.	Type	Notes
G-MMWG	Greenslade Mono-Trike		G-MNAK	Solar Wings Panther XL-S	
G-MMWH	Southdown Puma Sprint 440		G-MNAL	MBA Tiger Cub 440	
			G-MNAM	Solar Wings Panther XL-S	
G-MMWI	Southdown Lightning		G-MNAN	Solar Wings Panther XL-S	
G-MMWJ	Pterodactyl Ptraveler		G-MNAO	Solar Wings Panther XL-S	
G-MMWL	Eurowing Goldwing		G-MNAT	Solar Wings Pegasus XL-R	
G-MMWN	Ultrasports Tripacer		G-MNAU	Solar Wings Pegasus XL-R	
G-MMWO	Ultrasports Panther XL		G-MNAV	Southdown Puma Sprint	
G-MMWS	Mainair Tri-Flyer		G-MNAW	Solar Wings Pegasus XL-R	
G-MMWT	CFM Shadow		G-MNAX	Solar Wings Pegasus XL-R	
G-MMWX	Southdown Puma Sprint		G-MNAY	Ultrasports Panther XL-S	
G-MMXC	Mainair Gemini Flash		G-MNAZ	Solar Wings Pegasus XL-R	
G-MMXD	Mainair Gemini Flash		G-MNBA	Solar Wings Pegasus XL-R	
G-MMXE	Mainair Gemini Flash		G-MNBB	Solar Wings Pegasus XL-R	
G-MMXG	Mainair Gemini Flash		G-MNBC	Solar Wings Pegasus XL-R	
G-MMXH	Mainair Gemini Flash		G-MNBD	Mainair Gemini Flash	
G-MMXI	Horizon Prototype		G-MNBE	Southdown Puma Sprint	
G-MMXJ	Mainair Gemini Flash		G-MNBF	Mainair Gemini Flash	
G-MMXK	Mainair Gemini Flash		G-MNBG	Mainair Gemini Flash	
G-MMXL	Mainair Gemini Flash		G-MNBH	Southdown Puma Sprint	
G-MMXM	Mainair Gemini Flash		G-MNBI	Ultrasports Panther XL	
G-MMXN	Southdown Puma Sprint		G-MNBJ	Skyhook Pixie	
G-MMXO	Southdown Puma Sprint		G-MNBM	Southdown Puma Sprint	
G-MMXP	Southdown Puma Sprint		G-MNBN	Mainair Gemini Flash	
G-MMXT	Mainair Gemini Flash		G-MNBP	Mainair Gemini Flash	
G-MMXU	Mainair Gemini Flash		G-MNBR	Mainair Gemini Flash	
G-MMXV	Mainair Gemini Flash		G-MNBS	Mainair Gemini Flash	
G-MMXW	Mainair Gemini		G-MNBT	Mainair Gemini Flash	
G-MMXX	Mainair Gemini		G-MNBU	Mainair Gemini Flash	
G-MMYA	Solar Wings Pegasus XL		G-MNBV	Mainair Gemini Flash	
G-MMYB	Solar Wings Pegasus XL		G-MNBW	Mainair Gemini Flash	
G-MMYD	CFM Shadow Srs B		G-MNCA	Hiway Demon 175	
G-MMYF	Southdown Puma Sprint		G-MNCF	Mainair Gemini Flash	
G-MMYI	Southdown Puma Sprint		G-MNCG	Mainair Gemini Flash	
G-MMYJ	Southdown Puma Sprint		G-MNCH	Lancashire Micro Trike 330	
G-MMYL	Cyclone 70		G-MNCI	Southdown Puma Sprint	
G-MMYN	Ultrasports Panther XL		G-MNCJ	Mainair Gemini Flash	
G-MMYO	Southdown Puma Sprint		G-MNCK	Southdown Puma Sprint	
G-MMYR	Eipper Quicksilver MXII		G-MNCL	Southdown Puma Sprint	
G-MMYS	Southdown Puma Sprint		G-MNCM	CFM Shadow Srs B	
G-MMYT	Southdown Puma Sprint		G-MNCO	Eipper Quicksilver MXII	
G-MMYU	Southdown Puma Sprint		G-MNCP	Southdown Puma Sprint	
G-MMYV	Webb Trike		G-MNCR	Flexiform Striker	
G-MMYY	Southdown Puma Sprint		G-MNCS	Skyrider Airsports Phantom	
G-MMYZ	Southdown Puma Sprint		G-MNCU	Medway Hybred	
G-MMZA	Mainair Gemini Flash		G-MNCV	Medway Typhoon XL	
G-MMZB	Mainair Gemini Flash		G-MNCZ	Solar Wings Pegasus XL	
G-MMZE	Mainair Gemini Flash		G-MNDA	Thruster TST	
G-MMZF	Mainair Gemini Flash		G-MNDC	Mainair Gemini Flash	
G-MMZG	Ultrasports Panther XL-S		G-MNDD	Mainair Scorcher Solo	
G-MMZI	Medway 130SX		G-MNDE	Medway Half Pint	
G-MMZJ	Mainair Gemini Flash		G-MNDF	Mainair Gemini Flash	
G-MMZK	Mainair Gemini Flash		G-MNDG	Southdown Puma Sprint	
G-MMZL	Mainair Gemini Flash		G-MNDH	Hiway Skytrike	
G-MMZM	Mainair Gemini Flash		G-MNDI	MBA Tiger Cub 440	
G-MMZN	Mainair Gemini Flash		G-MNDM	Mainair Gemini Flash	
G-MMZO	Microflight Spectrum		G-MNDO	Mainair Flash	
G-MMZP	Ultrasports Panther XL		G-MNDP	Southdown Puma Sprint	
G-MMZR	Southdown Puma Sprint		G-MNDU	Midland Sirocco 377GB	
G-MMZS	Eipper Quicksilver MX1		G-MNDV	Midland Sirocco 377GB	
G-MMZU	Southdown Puma DS		G-MNDW	Midland Sirocco 377GB	
G-MMZV	Mainair Gemini Flash		G-MNDY	Southdown Puma Sprint	
G-MMZW	Southdown Puma Sprint		G-MNEF	Mainair Gemini Flash	
G-MMZX	Southdown Puma Sprint		G-MNEG	Mainair Gemini Flash	
G-MMZY	Ultrasports Tripacer 330		G-MNEH	Mainair Gemini Flash	
G-MMZZ	Maxair Hummer		G-MNEI	Medway Hybred 440	
			G-MNEK	Medway Half Pint	
G-MNAA	Striplin Sky Ranger		G-MNEL	Medway Half Pint	
G-MNAE	Mainair Gemini Flash		G-MNEM	Solar Wings Pegasus Dual	
G-MNAF	Solar Wings Panther XL		G-MNEP	Aerostructure Pipstrelle P.2B	
G-MNAH	Solar Wings Panther XL				
G-MNAI	Ultrasports Panther XL-S		G-MNER	CFM Shadow Srs B	
G-MNAJ	Solar Wings Panther XL-S		G-MNET	Mainair Gemini Flash	

Reg.	Type	Notes	Reg.	Type	Notes
G-MNEV	Mainair Gemini Flash		G-MNIU	Solar Wings Pegasus	
G-MNEY	Mainair Gemini Flash			Photon	
G-MNEZ	Skyhook TR1 Mk 2		G-MNIV	Solar Wings Typhoon	
G-MNFA	Solar Wings Typhoon		G-MNIW	Airwave Nimrod 165	
G-MNFB	Southdown Puma Sprint		G-MNIX	Mainair Gemini Flash	
G-MNFE	Mainair Gemini Flash		G-MNIY	Skyhook Pixie Zipper	
G-MNFF	Mainair Gemini Flash		G-MNIZ	Mainair Gemini Flash	
G-MNFG	Southdown Puma Sprint		G-MNJB	Southdown Raven	
G-MNFH	Mainair Gemini Flash		G-MNJC	MBA Tiger Cub 440	
G-MNFI	Medway Half Pint		G-MNJD	Southdown Puma Sprint	
G-MNFJ	Mainair Gemini Flash		G-MNJF	Dragon 150	
G-MNFK	Mainair Gemini Flash		G-MNJG	Mainair Tri-Flyer	
G-MNFL	AMF Chevvron		G-MNJH	SW Pegasus Flash	
G-MNFM	Mainair Gemini Flash		G-MNJI	SW Pegasus Flash	
G-MNFN	Mainair Gemini Flash		G-MNJJ	SW Pegasus Flash	
G-MNFP	Mainair Gemini Flash		G-MNJK	SW Pegasus Flash	
G-MNFR	Wright Tri-Flyer		G-MNJL	SW Pegasus Flash	
G-MNFV	Ultrasports Trike		G-MNJM	SW Pegasus Flash	
G-MNFW	Medway Hybred 44XL		G-MNJN	SW Pegasus Flash	
G-MNFX	Southdown Puma Sprint		G-MNJO	SW Pegasus Flash	
G-MNFY	Hornet 250		G-MNJP	SW Pegasus Flash	
G-MNFZ	Southdown Puma Sprint		G-MNJR	SW Pegasus Flash	
G-MNGA	Aerial Arts Chaser 110SX		G-MNJS	Southdown Puma Sprint	
G-MNGB	Mainair Gemini Flash		G-MNJT	Southdown Raven	
G-MNGD	Quest Air Services		G-MNJU	Mainair Gemini Flash	
G-MNGF	Solar Wings Pegasus		G-MNJV	Medway Half Pint	
G-MNGG	Solar Wings Pegasus XL-R		G-MNJW	Mitchell Wing B10	
G-MNGH	Skyhook Pixie		G-MNJX	Medway Hybred 44XL	
G-MNGJ	Skyhook Zipper		G-MNKB	SW Pegasus Photon	
G-MNGK	Mainair Gemini Flash		G-MNKC	SW Pegasus Photon	
G-MNGL	Mainair Gemini Flash		G-MNKD	SW Pegasus Photon	
G-MNGM	Mainair Gemini Flash		G-MNKE	SW Pegasus Photon	
G-MNGN	Mainair Gemini Flash		G-MNKG	SW Pegasus Photon	
G-MNGO	Solar Wings Storm		G-MNKH	SW Pegasus Photon	
G-MNGR	Southdown Puma Sprint		G-MNKI	SW Pegasus Photon	
G-MNGS	Southdown Puma 330		G-MNKK	SW Pegasus Photon	
G-MNGT	Mainair Gemini Flash		G-MNKL	Mainair Gemini Flash	
G-MNGU	Mainair Gemini Flash		G-MNKM	MBA Tiger Cub 440	
G-MNGW	Mainair Gemini Flash		G-MNKN	Skycraft Scout Mk III	
G-MNGX	Southdown Puma Sprint		G-MNKO	SW Pegasus Flash	
G-MNGZ	Mainair Gemini Flash		G-MNKP	SW Pegasus Flash	
G-MNHB	Solar Wings Pegasus XL-R		G-MNKR	SW Pegasus Flash	
G-MNHC	Solar Wings Pegasus XL-R		G-MNKS	SW Pegasus Flash	
G-MNHD	Solar Wings Pegasus XL-R		G-MNKT	Solar Wings Typhoon S4	
G-MNHE	Solar Wings Pegasus XL-R		G-MNKU	Southdown Puma Sprint	
G-MNHF	Solar Wings Pegasus XL-R		G-MNKV	SW Pegasus Flash	
G-MNHH	Solar Wings Panther XL-S		G-MNKW	SW Pegasus Flash	
G-MNHI	Solar Wings Pegasus XL-R		G-MNKX	SW Pegasus Flash	
G-MNHJ	Solar Wings Pegasus XL-R		G-MNKZ	Southdown Raven	
G-MNHK	Solar Wings Pegasus XL-R		G-MNLB	Southdown Raven X	
G-MNHL	Solar Wings Pegasus XL-R		G-MNLH	Romain Cobra Biplane	
G-MNHM	Solar Wings Pegasus XL-R		G-MNLI	Mainair Gemini Flash	
G-MNHN	Solar Wings Pegasus XL-R		G-MNLK	Southdown Raven	
G-MNHP	Solar Wings Pegasus XL-R		G-MNLL	Southdown Raven	
G-MNHR	Solar Wings Pegasus XL-R		G-MNLM	Southdown Raven	
G-MNHS	Solar Wings Pegasus XL-R		G-MNLN	Southdown Raven	
G-MNHT	Solar Wings Pegasus XL-R		G-MNLO	Southdown Raven	
G-MNHU	Solar Wings Pegasus XL-R		G-MNLP	Southdown Raven	
G-MNHV	Solar Wings Pegasus XL-R		G-MNLT	Southdown Raven	
G-MNHX	Solar Wings Typhoon S4		G-MNLU	Southdown Raven	
G-MNHZ	Mainair Gemini Flash		G-MNLV	Southdown Raven	
G-MNID	Mainair Gemini Flash		G-MNLW	Medway Half Pint	
G-MNIE	Mainair Gemini Flash		G-MNLX	Mainair Gemini Flash	
G-MNIF	Mainair Gemini Flash		G-MNLY	Mainair Gemini Flash	
G-MNIG	Mainair Gemini Flash		G-MNLZ	Southdown Raven	
G-MNIH	Mainair Gemini Flash		G-MNMC	Southdown Puma MS	
G-MNII	Mainair Gemini Flash		G-MNMD	Southdown Raven	
G-MNIL	Southdown Puma Sprint		G-MNME	Hiway Skytrike	
G-MNIM	Maxair Hummer		G-MNMG	Mainair Gemini Flash	
G-MNIO	Mainair Gemini Flash		G-MNMH	Mainair Gemini Flash	
G-MNIP	Mainair Gemini Flash		G-MNMI	Mainair Gemini Flash	
G-MNIS	CFM Shadow Srs B		G-MNMJ	Mainair Gemini Flash	
G-MNIT	Aerial Arts 130SX		G-MNMK	Solar Wings Pegasus XL-R	

Reg.	Type	Notes	Reg.	Type	Notes
G-MNML	Southdown Puma Sprint		G-MNSR	Mainair Gemini Flash	
G-MNMM	Aerotech MW.5 Sorcerer		G-MNSS	American Aerolights Eagle	
G-MNMN	Medway Hybred 44XLR		G-MNSV	CFM Shadow Srs B	
G-MNMO	Mainair Gemini Flash		G-MNSW	Southdown Raven X	
G-MNMR	Solar Wings Typhoon 180		G-MNSX	Southdown Raven X	
G-MNMS	Wheeler Scout		G-MNSY	Southdown Raven X	
G-MNMT	Southdown Raven		G-MNTC	Southdown Raven X	
G-MNMU	Southdown Raven		G-MNTD	Aerial Arts Chaser 110SX	
G-MNMV	Mainair Gemini Flash		G-MNTF	Southdown Raven X	
G-MNMW	Aerotech MW.6 Merlin		G-MNTG	Southdown Raven X	
G-MNMY	Cyclone 70		G-MNTH	Mainair Gemini Flash	
G-MNNA	Southdown Raven		G-MNTI	Mainair Gemini Flash	
G-MNNB	Southdown Raven		G-MNTK	CFM Shadow Srs B	
G-MNNC	Southdown Raven		G-MNTM	Southdown Raven X	
G-MNND	SW Pegasus Flash		G-MNTN	Southdown Raven X	
G-MNNE	Mainair Gemini Flash		G-MNTO	Southdown Raven X	
G-MNNF	Mainair Gemini Flash		G-MNTP	CFM Shadow Srs B	
G-MNNG	Solar Wings Photon		G-MNTS	Mainair Gemini Flash II	
G-MNNI	Mainair Gemini Flash		G-MNTT	Medway Half Pint	
G-MNNJ	Mainair Gemini Flash		G-MNTU	Mainair Gemini Flash II	
G-MNNK	Mainair Gemini Flash		G-MNTV	Mainair Gemini Flash II	
G-MNNL	Mainair Gemini Flash		G-MNTW	Mainair Gemini Flash II	
G-MNNM	Mainair Scorcher Solo		G-MNTX	Mainair Gemini Flash II	
G-MNNN	Southdown Raven		G-MNTY	Southdown Raven X	
G-MNNO	Southdown Raven		G-MNTZ	Mainair Gemini Flash II	
G-MNNP	Mainair Gemini Flash		G-MNUA	Mainair Gemini Flash II	
G-MNNR	Mainair Gemini Flash		G-MNUB	Mainair Gemini Flash II	
G-MNNS	Eurowing Goldwing		G-MNUD	SW Pegasus Flash II	
G-MNNU	Mainair Gemini Flash		G-MNUE	SW Pegasus Flash II	
G-MNNV	Mainair Gemini Flash		G-MNUF	Mainair Gemini Flash II	
G-MNNY	SW Pegasus Flash		G-MNUG	Mainair Gemini Flash II	
G-MNNZ	SW Pegasus Flash		G-MNUH	Southdown Raven X	
G-MNPA	SW Pegasus Flash		G-MNUI	Skyhook Cutlass Dual	
G-MNPB	SW Pegasus Flash		G-MNUJ	SW Pegasus Photon	
G-MNPC	Mainair Gemini Flash		G-MNUM	Southdown Puma Sprint	
G-MNPF	Mainair Gemini Flash		G-MNUO	Mainair Gemini Flash II	
G-MNPG	Mainair Gemini Flash		G-MNUP	Mainair Gemini Flash II	
G-MNPH	Flexiform Dual Striker		G-MNUR	Mainair Gemini Flash II	
G-MNPI	Southdown Pipistrelle 2C		G-MNUS	Mainair Gemini Flash II	
G-MNPL	Ultrasports Panther 330		G-MNUT	Southdown Raven X	
G-MNPV	Mainair Scorcher Solo		G-MNUU	Southdown Raven X	
G-MNPW	AMF Chevvron		G-MNUW	Southdown Raven X	
G-MNPX	Mainair Gemini Flash		G-MNUX	Solar Wings Pegasus XL-R	
G-MNPY	Mainair Scorcher Solo		G-MNUY	Mainair Gemini Flash II	
G-MNPZ	Mainair Scorcher Solo		G-MNVA	Solar Wings Pegasus XL-R	
G-MNRA	CFM Shadow Srs B		G-MNVB	Solar Wings Pegasus XL-R	
G-MNRD	Ultraflight Lazair		G-MNVC	Solar Wings Pegasus XL-R	
G-MNRE	Mainair Scorcher Solo		G-MNVE	Solar Wings Pegasus XL-R	
G-MNRF	Mainair Scorcher Solo		G-MNVF	SW Pegasus Flash II	
G-MNRG	Mainair Scorcher Solo		G-MNVG	SW Pegasus Flash II	
G-MNRI	Hornet Dual Trainer		G-MNVH	SW Pegasus Flash II	
G-MNRJ	Hornet Dual Trainer		G-MNVI	CFM Shadow Srs B	
G-MNRK	Hornet Dual Trainer		G-MNVJ	CFM Shadow Srs B	
G-MNRL	Hornet Dual Trainer		G-MNVK	CFM Shadow Srs B	
G-MNRM	Hornet Dual Trainer		G-MNVL	Medway Half Pint	
G-MNRN	Hornet Dual Trainer		G-MNVN	Southdown Raven X	
G-MNRP	Southdown Raven		G-MNVO	Hovey Whing-Ding II	
G-MNRS	Southdown Raven		G-MNVP	Southdown Raven X	
G-MNRT	Midland Ultralights Sirocco		G-MNVR	Mainair Gemini Flash II	
G-MNRW	Mainair Gemini Flash II		G-MNVS	Mainair Gemini Flash II	
G-MNRX	Mainair Gemini Flash II		G-MNVT	Mainair Gemini Flash II	
G-MNRY	Mainair Gemini Flash		G-MNVU	Mainair Gemini Flash II	
G-MNRZ	Mainair Scorcher Solo		G-MNVV	Mainair Gemini Flash II	
G-MNSA	Mainair Gemini Flash		G-MNVW	Mainair Gemini Flash II	
G-MNSB	Southdown Puma Sprint		G-MNVZ	SW Pegasus Photon	
G-MNSE	Mainair Gemini Flash		G-MNWA	Southdown Raven X	
G-MNSF	Hornet Dual Trainer		G-MNWB	Thruster TST	
G-MNSI	Mainair Gemini Flash		G-MNWC	Mainair Gemini Flash II	
G-MNSJ	Mainair Gemini Flash		G-MNWD	Mainair Gemini Flash	
G-MNSL	Southdown Raven X		G-MNWF	Southdown Raven X	
G-MNSM	Hornet Demon		G-MNWG	Southdown Raven X	
G-MNSN	SW Pegasus Flash II		G-MNWH	Aerial Arts Alpha	
G-MNSP	Aerial Arts 130SX		G-MNWI	Mainair Gemini Flash II	

Reg.	Type	Notes	Reg.	Type	Notes
G-MNWJ	Mainair Gemini Flash II		G-MTAA	Solar Wings Pegasus XL-R	
G-MNWK	CFM Shadow Srs B		G-MTAB	Mainair Gemini Flash II	
G-MNWL	Aerial Arts 130SX		G-MTAC	Mainair Gemini Flash II	
G-MNWN	Mainair Gemini Flash II		G-MTAE	Mainair Gemini Flash II	
G-MNWO	Mainair Gemini Flash II		G-MTAF	Mainair Gemini Flash II	
G-MNWP	SW Pegasus Flash II		G-MTAG	Mainair Gemini Flash II	
G-MNWR	Medway Hybred 44LR		G-MTAH	Mainair Gemini Flash II	
G-MNWU	SW Pegasus Flash II		G-MTAI	Solar Wings Pegasus XL-R	
G-MNWV	SW Pegasus Flash II		G-MTAJ	Solar Wings Pegasus XL-R	
G-MNWW	Solar Wings Pegasus XL-R		G-MTAK	Solar Wings Pegasus XL-R	
G-MNWX	Solar Wings Pegasus XL-R		G-MTAL	Solar Wings Photon	
G-MNWY	CFM Shadow Srs B		G-MTAM	SW Pegasus Flash	
G-MNWZ	Mainair Gemini Flash II		G-MTAO	Solar Wings Pegasus XL-R	
G-MNXA	Southdown Raven X		G-MTAP	Southdown Raven X	
G-MNXB	Solar Wings Photon		G-MTAR	Mainair Gemini Flash II	
G-MNXC	Aerial Arts 110SX		G-MTAS	Whittaker MW.5 Sorcerer	
G-MNXD	Southdown Raven		G-MTAT	Solar Wings Pegasus XL-R	
G-MNXE	Southdown Raven X		G-MTAV	Solar Wings Pegasus XL-R	
G-MNXF	Southdown Raven		G-MTAW	Solar Wings Pegasus XL-R	
G-MNXG	Southdown Raven X		G-MTAX	Solar Wings Pegasus XL-R	
G-MNXI	Southdown Raven X		G-MTAY	Solar Wings Pegasus XL-R	
G-MNXM	Medway Hybred 44XLR		G-MTAZ	Solar Wings Pegasus XL-R	
G-MNXN	Medway Hybred 44XLR		G-MTBA	Solar Wings Pegasus XL-R	
G-MNXO	Medway Hybred 44XLR		G-MTBB	Southdown Raven X	
G-MNXR	Mainair Gemini Flash II		G-MTBD	Mainair Gemini Flash II	
G-MNXS	Mainair Gemini Flash II		G-MTBE	CFM Shadow Srs BD	
G-MNXT	Mainair Gemini Flash II		G-MTBF	Mirage Mk II	
G-MNXU	Mainair Gemini Flash II		G-MTBG	Mainair Gemini Flash II	
G-MNXX	CFM Shadow Srs BD		G-MTBH	Mainair Gemini Flash II	
G-MNXZ	Whittaker MW.5 Sorcerer		G-MTBI	Mainair Gemini Flash II	
G-MNYA	SW Pegasus Flash II		G-MTBJ	Mainair Gemini Flash II	
G-MNYB	Solar Wings Pegasus XL-R		G-MTBK	Southdown Raven X	
G-MNYC	Solar Wings Pegasus XL-R		G-MTBL	Solar Wings Pegasus XL-R	
G-MNYD	Aerial Arts 110SX Chaser		G-MTBN	Southdown Raven X	
G-MNYE	Aerial Arts 110SX Chaser		G-MTBO	Southdown Raven X	
G-MNYF	Aerial Arts 110SX Chaser		G-MTBP	Aerotech MW.5 Sorcerer	
G-MNYG	Southdown Raven		G-MTBR	Aerotech MW.5 Sorcerer	
G-MNYH	Southdown Puma Sprint		G-MTBS	Aerotech MW.5 Sorcerer	
G-MNYI	Southdown Raven X		G-MTBV	Solar Wings Pegasus XL-R	
G-MNYJ	Mainair Gemini Flash II		G-MTBW	Mainair Gemini Flash II	
G-MNYK	Mainair Gemini Flash II		G-MTBX	Mainair Gemini Flash II	
G-MNYL	Southdown Raven X		G-MTBY	Mainair Gemini Flash II	
G-MNYM	Southdown Raven X		G-MTBZ	Southdown Raven X	
G-MNYO	Southdown Raven X		G-MTCA	CFM Shadow Srs B	
G-MNYP	Southdown Raven X		G-MTCB	Snowbird Mk III	
G-MNYS	Southdown Raven X		G-MTCC	Mainair Gemini Flash II	
G-MNYT	Solar Wings Pegasus XL-R		G-MTCD	Southdown Raven X	
G-MNYU	Solar Wings Pegasus XL-R		G-MTCE	Mainair Gemini Flash II	
G-MNYV	Solar Wings Pegasus XL-R		G-MTCG	Solar Wings Pegasus XL-R	
G-MNYW	Solar Wings Pegasus XL-R		G-MTCH	Solar Wings Pegasus XL-R	
G-MNYX	Solar Wings Pegasus XL-R		G-MTCK	SW Pegasus Flash	
G-MNYZ	SW Pegasus Flash		G-MTCL	Southdown Raven X	
G-MNZB	Mainair Gemini Flash II		G-MTCM	Southdown Raven X	
G-MNZC	Mainair Gemini Flash II		G-MTCN	Solar Wings Pegasus XL-R	
G-MNZD	Mainair Gemini Flash II		G-MTCO	Solar Wings Pegasus XL-R	
G-MNZE	Mainair Gemini Flash II		G-MTCP	Aerial Arts Chaser 110SX	
G-MNZF	Mainair Gemini Flash II		G-MTCR	Solar Wings Pegasus XL-R	
G-MNZG	Aerial Arts 110SX		G-MTCT	CFM Shadow Srs BD	
G-MNZI	Prone Power Typhoon 2		G-MTCU	Mainair Gemini Flash II	
G-MNZJ	CFM Shadow Srs BD		G-MTCV	Microflight Spectrum	
G-MNZK	Solar Wings Pegasus XL-R		G-MTCW	Mainair Gemini Flash II	
G-MNZL	Solar Wings Pegasus XL-R		G-MTCX	Solar Wings Pegasus XL-R	
G-MNZM	Solar Wings Pegasus XL-R		G-MTCZ	Ultrasports Tripacer 250	
G-MNZN	SW Pegasus Flash II		G-MTDA	Hornet Dual Trainer	
G-MNZO	SW Pegasus Flash II		G-MTDB	Owen Pola Mk 1	
G-MNZP	CFM Shadow Srs B		G-MTDC	Owen Pola Mk 1	
G-MNZR	CFM Shadown Srs BD		G-MTDD	Aerial Arts Chaser 110SX	
G-MNZS	Aerial Arts 130SX		G-MTDE	American Aerolights 110SX	
G-MNZU	Eurowing Goldwing		G-MTDF	Mainair Gemini Flash II	
G-MNZW	Southdown Raven X		G-MTDG	Solar Wings Pegasus XL-R	
G-MNZY	Striker Tri-Flyer 330		G-MTDH	Solar Wings Pegasus XL-R	
G-MNZZ	CFM Shadow Srs B		G-MTDI	Solar Wings Pegasus XL-R	
			G-MTDJ	Medway Hybred 44XL	

Reg.	Type	Notes	Reg.	Type	Notes
G-MTDK	Aerotech MW.5 Sorcerer		G-MTGX	Hornet Dual Trainer	
G-MTDL	Solar Wings Pegasus XL-R		G-MTGY	Southdown Lightning	
G-MTDM	Mainair Gemini Flash II		G-MTHB	Aerotech MW.5B Sorcerer	
G-MTDN	Ultraflight Lazair IIIE		G-MTHC	Raven X	
G-MTDO	Eipper Quicksilver MXII		G-MTHD	Hiway Demon 195	
G-MTDP	Solar Wings Pegasus XL-R		G-MTHG	Solar Wings Pegasus XL-R	
G-MTDR	Mainair Gemini Flash II		G-MTHH	Solar Wings Pegasus XL-R	
G-MTDS	Solar Wings Photon		G-MTHI	Solar Wings Pegasus XL-R	
G-MTDT	Solar Wings Pegasus XL-R		G-MTHJ	Solar Wings Pegasus XL-R	
G-MTDU	CFM Shadow Srs BD		G-MTHK	Solar Wings Pegasus XL-R	
G-MTDV	Solar Wings Pegasus XL-R		G-MTHN	Solar Wings Pegasus XL-R	
G-MTDW	Mainair Gemini Flash II		G-MTHO	Solar Wings Pegasus XL-R	
G-MTDX	CFM Shadow Srs BD		G-MTHS	CFM Shadow Srs BD	
G-MTDY	Mainair Gemini Flash II		G-MTHT	CFM Shadow Srs BD	
G-MTDZ	Eipper Quicksilver MXII		G-MTHU	Hornet Dual Trainer	
G-MTEA	Solar Wings Pegasus XL-R		G-MTHV	CFM Shadow Srs BD	
G-MTEB	Solar Wings Pegasus XL-R		G-MTHW	Mainair Gemini Flash II	
G-MTEC	Solar Wings Pegasus XL-R		G-MTHY	Mainair Gemini Flash IIA	
G-MTED	Solar Wings Pegasus XL-R		G-MTHZ	Mainair Gemini Flash IIA	
G-MTEE	Solar Wings Pegasus XL-R		G-MTIA	Mainair Gemini Flash IIA	
G-MTEG	Mainair Gemini Flash II		G-MTIB	Mainair Gemini Flash IIA	
G-MTEH	Mainair Gemini Flash II		G-MTIC	Mainair Gemini Flash IIA	
G-MTEJ	Mainair Gemini Flash II		G-MTID	Southdown Raven X	
G-MTEK	Mainair Gemini Flash II		G-MTIE	Solar Wings Pegasus XL-R	
G-MTEN	Mainair Gemini Flash II		G-MTIF	Solar Wings Pegasus XL-R	
G-MTEO	Midland Ultralight Sirocco 337		G-MTIH	Solar Wings Pegasus XL-R	
			G-MTII	Solar Wings Pegasus XL-R	
G-MTER	Solar Wings Pegasus XL-R		G-MTIJ	Solar Wings Pegasus XL-R	
G-MTES	Solar Wings Pegasus XL-R		G-MTIK	Southdown Raven X	
G-MTET	Solar Wings Pegasus XL-R		G-MTIL	Mainair Gemini Flash IIA	
G-MTEU	Solar Wings Pegasus XL-R		G-MTIM	Mainair Gemini Flash IIA	
G-MTEV	Solar Wings Pegasus XL-R		G-MTIN	Mainair Gemini Flash IIA	
G-MTEW	Solar Wings Pegasus XL-R		G-MTIO	Solar Wings Pegasus XL-R	
G-MTEX	Solar Wings Pegasus XL-R		G-MTIP	Solar Wings Pegasus XL-R	
G-MTEY	Mainair Gemini Flash II		G-MTIR	Solar Wings Pegasus XL-R	
G-MTFA	Solar Wings Pegasus XL-R		G-MTIS	Solar Wings Pegasus XL-R	
G-MTFB	Solar Wings Pegasus XL-R		G-MTIT	Solar Wings Pegasus XL-R	
G-MTFC	Medway Hybred 44XLR		G-MTIU	Solar Wings Pegasus XL-R	
G-MTFE	Solar Wings Pegasus XL-R		G-MTIV	Solar Wings Pegasus XL-R	
G-MTFF	Mainair Gemini Flash II		G-MTIW	Solar Wings Pegasus XL-R	
G-MTFG	AMF Chevvron 232		G-MTIX	Solar Wings Pegasus XL-R	
G-MTFH	Aerotech MW.5B Sorcerer		G-MTIY	Solar Wings Pegasus XL-R	
G-MTFI	Mainair Gemini Flash II		G-MTIZ	Solar Wings Pegasus XL-R	
G-MTFJ	Mainair Gemini Flash II		G-MTJA	Mainair Gemini Flash IIA	
G-MTFL	AMF Lazair IIIE		G-MTJC	Mainair Gemini Flash IIA	
G-MTFM	Solar Wings Pegasus XL-R		G-MTJD	Mainair Gemini Flash IIA	
G-MTFN	Aerotech MW.5 Sorcerer		G-MTJE	Mainair Gemini Flash IIA	
G-MTFO	Solar Wings Pegasus XL-R		G-MTJG	Medway Hybred 44XLR	
G-MTFP	Solar Wings Pegasus XL-R		G-MTJH	SW Pegasus Flash	
G-MTFR	Solar Wings Pegasus XL-R		G-MTJI	Raven X	
G-MTFS	Solar Wings Pegasus XL-R		G-MTJK	Mainair Gemini Flash IIA	
G-MTFT	Solar Wings Pegasus XL-R		G-MTJL	Mainair Gemini Flash IIA	
G-MTFU	CFM Shadow Series BD		G-MTJM	Mainair Gemini Flash IIA	
G-MTFX	Mainair Gemini Flash		G-MTJN	Midland Ultralights Sirocco 377GB	
G-MTFZ	CFM Shadow Srs BD				
G-MTGA	Mainair Gemini Flash		G-MTJP	Medway Hybred 44XLR	
G-MTGB	Thruster TST Mk 1		G-MTJR	Solar Wings Pegasus XL-R	
G-MTGC	Thruster TST Mk 1		G-MTJS	Solar Wings Pegasus XL-Q	
G-MTGD	Thruster TST Mk 1		G-MTJT	Mainair Gemini Flash IIA	
G-MTGE	Thruster TST Mk 1		G-MTJV	Mainair Gemini Flash IIA	
G-MTGF	Thruster TST Mk 1		G-MTJW	Mainair Gemini Flash IIA	
G-MTGH	Mainair Gemini Flash IIA		G-MTJX	Hornet Dual Trainer	
G-MTGJ	Solar Wings Pegasus XL-R		G-MTJY	Mainair Gemini Flash IIA	
G-MTGK	Solar Wings Pegasus XL-R		G-MTJZ	Mainair Gemini Flash IIA	
G-MTGL	Solar Wings Pegasus XL-R		G-MTKA	Thruster TST Mk 1	
G-MTGM	Solar Wings Pegasus XL-R		G-MTKB	Thruster TST Mk 1	
G-MTGO	Mainair Gemini Flash		G-MTKD	Thruster TST Mk 1	
G-MTGP	Thruster TST Mk 1		G-MTKE	Thruster TST Mk 1	
G-MTGR	Thruster TST Mk 1		G-MTKG	Solar Wings Pegasus XL-R	
G-MTGS	Thruster TST Mk 1		G-MTKH	Solar Wings Pegasus XL-R	
G-MTGT	Thruster TST Mk 1		G-MTKI	Solar Wings Pegasus XL-R	
G-MTGU	Thruster TST Mk 1		G-MTKJ	Solar Wings Pegasus XL-R	
G-MTGV	CFM Shadow Srs BD		G-MTKM	Gardner T-M Scout S.2	

Reg.	Type	Notes	Reg.	Type	Notes
G-MTKN	Mainair Gemini Flash IIA		G-MTNV	Thruster TST Mk 1	
G-MTKO	Mainair Gemini Flash IIA		G-MTNW	Thruster TST Mk 1	
G-MTKP	Solar Wings Pegasus XL-R		G-MTNX	Mainair Gemini Flash II	
G-MTKR	CFM Shadow Srs BD		G-MTNY	Mainair Gemini Flash IIA	
G-MTKS	CFM Shadow Srs BD		G-MTOA	Solar Wings Pegasus XL-R	
G-MTKU	CFM Shadow Srs BD		G-MTOB	Solar Wings Pegasus XL-R	
G-MTKV	Mainair Gemini Flash		G-MTOC	Solar Wings Pegasus XL-R	
G-MTKW	Mainair Gemini Flash IIA		G-MTOD	Solar Wings Pegasus XL-R	
G-MTKX	Mainair Gemini Flash IIA		G-MTOE	Solar Wings Pegasus XL-R	
G-MTKY	Mainair Gemini Flash IIA		G-MTOF	Solar Wings Pegasus XL-R	
G-MTKZ	Mainair Gemini Flash IIA		G-MTOG	Solar Wings Pegasus XL-R	
G-MTLA	Mainair Gemini Flash IIA		G-MTOH	Solar Wings Pegasus XL-R	
G-MTLB	Mainair Gemini Flash IIA		G-MTOI	Solar Wings Pegasus XL-R	
G-MTLC	Mainair Gemini Flash IIA		G-MTOJ	Solar Wings Pegasus XL-R	
G-MTLD	Mainair Gemini Flash IIA		G-MTOK	Solar Wings Pegasus XL-R	
G-MTLE	See main Register		G-MTOL	Solar Wings Pegasus XL-R	
G-MTLG	Solar Wings Pegasus XL-R		G-MTOM	Solar Wings Pegasus XL-R	
G-MTLH	Solar Wings Pegasus XL-R		G-MTON	Solar Wings Pegasus XL-R	
G-MTLI	Solar Wings Pegasus XL-R		G-MTOO	Solar Wings Pegasus XL-R	
G-MTLJ	Solar Wings Pegasus XL-R		G-MTOP	Solar Wings Pegasus XL-R	
G-MTLK	Raven X		G-MTOR	Solar Wings Pegasus XL-R	
G-MTLL	Mainair Gemini Flash IIA		G-MTOS	Solar Wings Pegasus XL-R	
G-MTLM	Thruster TST Mk 1		G-MTOT	Solar Wings Pegasus XL-R	
G-MTLN	Thruster TST Mk 1		G-MTOU	Solar Wings Pegasus XL-R	
G-MTLO	Thruster TST Mk 1		G-MTOV	Solar Wings Pegasus XL-R	
G-MTLR	Thruster TST Mk 1		G-MTOW	Solar Wings Pegasus XL-R	
G-MTLS	Solar Wings Pegasus XL-R		G-MTOX	Solar Wings Pegasus XL-R	
G-MTLT	Solar Wings Pegasus XL-R		G-MTOY	Solar Wings Pegasus XL-R	
G-MTLU	Solar Wings Pegasus XL-R		G-MTOZ	Solar Wings Pegasus XL-R	
G-MTLV	Solar Wings Pegasus XL-R		G-MTPA	Mainair Gemini Flash IIA	
G-MTLW	Solar Wings Pegasus XL-R		G-MTPB	Mainair Gemini Flash IIA	
G-MTLX	Medway Hybred 44XLR		G-MTPE	Solar Wings Pegasus XL-R	
G-MTLY	Solar Wings Pegasus XL-R		G-MTPF	Solar Wings Pegasus XL-R	
G-MTLZ	Whittaker MW.5 Sorceror		G-MTPG	Solar Wings Pegasus XL-R	
G-MTMA	Mainair Gemini Flash IIA		G-MTPH	Solar Wings Pegasus XL-R	
G-MTMB	Mainair Gemini Flash IIA		G-MTPI	Solar Wings Pegasus XL-R	
G-MTMC	Mainair Gemini Flash IIA		G-MTPJ	Solar Wings Pegasus XL-R	
G-MTMD	Whittaker MW.6 Merlin		G-MTPK	Solar Wings Pegasus XL-R	
G-MTME	Solar Wings Pegasus XL-R		G-MTPL	Solar Wings Pegasus XL-R	
G-MTMF	Solar Wings Pegasus XL-R		G-MTPM	Solar Wings Pegasus XL-R	
G-MTMG	Solar Wings Pegasus XL-R		G-MTPN	Solar Wings Pegasus XL-Q	
G-MTMH	Solar Wings Pegasus XL-R		G-MTPO	Solar Wings Pegasus XL-Q	
G-MTMI	Solar Wings Pegasus XL-R		G-MTPP	Solar Wings Pegasus XL-R	
G-MTMJ	Maxair Hummer		G-MTPR	Solar Wings Pegasus XL-R	
G-MTMK	Raven X		G-MTPS	Solar Wings Pegasus XL-Q	
G-MTML	Mainair Gemini Flash IIA		G-MTPT	Thruster TST Mk 1	
G-MTMO	Raven X		G-MTPU	Thruster TST Mk 1	
G-MTMP	Hornet Dual Trainer/Raven		G-MTPV	Thruster TST Mk 1	
G-MTMR	Hornet Dual Trainer/Raven		G-MTPW	Thruster TST Mk 1	
G-MTMT	Mainair Gemini Flash IIA		G-MTPX	Thruster TST Mk 1	
G-MTMV	Mainair Gemini Flash IIA		G-MTPY	Thruster TST Mk 1	
G-MTMW	Mainair Gemini Flash IIA		G-MTRA	Mainair Gemini Flash IIA	
G-MTMX	CFM Shadow Srs BD		G-MTRB	Mainair Gemini Flash IIA	
G-MTMY	CFM Shadow Srs BD		G-MTRC	Midlands Ultralights	
G-MTMZ	CFM Shadow Srs BD			Sirocco 377GB	
G-MTNB	Raven X		G-MTRD	Midlands Ultralights	
G-MTNC	Mainair Gemini Flash IIA			Sirocco 377GB	
G-MTND	Medway Hybred 44XLR		G-MTRE	Whittaker MW.6 Merlin	
G-MTNE	Medway Hybred 44XLR		G-MTRF	Mainair Gemini Flash IIA	
G-MTNF	Medway Hybred 44XLR		G-MTRJ	AMF Chevvron 232	
G-MTNG	Mainair Gemini Flash IIA		G-MTRK	Hornet Dual Trainer	
G-MTNH	Mainair Gemini Flash IIA		G-MTRL	Hornet Dual Trainer	
G-MTNI	Mainair Gemini Flash IIA		G-MTRM	Solar Wings Pegasus XL-R	
G-MTNJ	Mainair Gemini Flash IIA		G-MTRN	Solar Wings Pegasus XL-R	
G-MTNK	Weedhopper JC-24B		G-MTRO	Solar Wings Pegasus XL-R	
G-MTNL	Mainair Gemini Flash IIA		G-MTRP	Solar Wings Pegasus XL-R	
G-MTNM	Mainair Gemini Flash IIA		G-MTRR	Solar Wings Pegasus XL-R	
G-MTNO	Solar Wings Pegasus XL-Q		G-MTRS	Solar Wings Pegasus XL-R	
G-MTNP	Solar Wings Pegasus XL-Q		G-MTRT	Raven X	
G-MTNR	Thruster TST Mk 1		G-MTRU	Solar Wings Pegasus XL-Q	
G-MTNS	Thruster TST Mk 1		G-MTRV	Solar Wings Pegasus XL-Q	
G-MTNT	Thruster TST Mk 1		G-MTRW	Raven X	
G-MTNU	Thruster TST Mk 1		G-MTRX	Whittaker MW.5 Sorceror	

Reg.	Type	Notes	Reg.	Type	Notes
G-MTRZ	Mainair Gemini Flash IIA		G-MTVN	Solar Wings Pegasus XL-R	
G-MTSB	Mainair Gemini Flash IIA		G-MTVO	Solar Wings Pegasus XL-R	
G-MTSC	Mainair Gemini Flash IIA		G-MTVP	Thruster TST Mk 1	
G-MTSD	Raven X		G-MTVR	Thruster TST Mk 1	
G-MTSG	CFM Shadow Srs BD		G-MTVS	Thruster TST Mk 1	
G-MTSH	Thruster TST Mk 1		G-MTVT	Thruster TST Mk 1	
G-MTSI	Thruster TST Mk 1		G-MTVV	Thruster TST Mk 1	
G-MTSJ	Thruster TST Mk 1		G-MTVX	Solar Wings Pegasus XL-Q	
G-MTSK	Thruster TST Mk 1		G-MTVZ	Powerchute Raider	
G-MTSL	Thruster TST Mk 1		G-MTWA	Solar Wings Pegasus XL-R	
G-MTSM	Thruster TST Mk 1		G-MTWB	Solar Wings Pegasus XL-R	
G-MTSN	Solar Wings Pegasus XL-R		G-MTWD	Solar Wings Pegasus XL-R	
G-MTSO	Solar Wings Pegasus XL-R		G-MTWE	Solar Wings Pegasus XL-R	
G-MTSP	Solar Wings Pegasus XL-R		G-MTWF	Mainair Gemini Flash IIA	
G-MTSR	Solar Wings Pegasus XL-R		G-MTWG	Mainair Gemini Flash IIA	
G-MTSS	Solar Wings Pegasus XL-R		G-MTWH	CFM Shadow Srs BD	
G-MTST	Thruster TST Mk 1		G-MTWK	CFM Shadow Srs BD	
G-MTSU	Solar Wings Pegasus XL-R		G-MTWL	CFM Shadow Srs BD	
G-MTSV	Solar Wings Pegasus XL-R		G-MTWM	CFM Shadow Srs BD	
G-MTSX	Solar Wings Pegasus XL-R		G-MTWN	CFM Shadow Srs BD	
G-MTSY	Solar Wings Pegasus XL-R		G-MTWP	CFM Shadow Srs BD	
G-MTSZ	Solar Wings Pegasus XL-R		G-MTWR	Mainair Gemini Flash IIA	
G-MTTA	Solar Wings Pegasus XL-R		G-MTWS	Mainair Gemini Flash IIA	
G-MTTB	Solar Wings Pegasus XL-R		G-MTWW	Solar Wings Typhoon	
G-MTTD	Solar Wings Pegasus XL-R		G-MTWX	Mainair Gemini Flash IIA	
G-MTTE	Solar Wings Pegasus XL-R		G-MTWY	Thruster TST Mk 1	
G-MTTF	Aerotech MW.6 Merlin		G-MTWZ	Thruster TST Mk 1	
G-MTTH	CFM Shadow Srs BD		G-MTXA	Thruster TST Mk 1	
G-MTTI	Mainair Gemini Flash IIA		G-MTXB	Thruster TST Mk 1	
G-MTTK	Southdown Lightning DS		G-MTXC	Thruster TST Mk 1	
G-MTTL	Hiway Sky-Trike		G-MTXD	Thruster TST Mk 1	
G-MTTM	Mainair Gemini Flash IIA		G-MTXE	Hornet Dual Trainer	
G-MTTN	Ultralight Flight Phantom		G-MTXH	Solar Wings Pegasus XL-Q	
G-MTTO	Mainair Gemini Flash IIA		G-MTXI	Solar Wings Pegasus XL-Q	
G-MTTP	Mainair Gemini Flash IIA		G-MTXJ	Solar Wings Pegasus XL-Q	
G-MTTR	Mainair Gemini Flash IIA		G-MTXK	Solar Wings Pegasus XL-Q	
G-MTTS	Mainair Gemini Flash IIA		G-MTXL	Noble Hardman Snowbird Mk IV	
G-MTTW	Mainair Gemini Flash IIA				
G-MTTX	Solar Wings Pegasus XL-Q		G-MTXM	Mainair Gemini Flash IIA	
G-MTTZ	Solar Wings Pegasus XL-Q		G-MTXO	Whittaker MW.6	
G-MTUA	Solar Wings Pegasus XL-R		G-MTXP	Mainair Gemini Flash IIA	
G-MTUB	Thruster TST Mk 1		G-MTXR	CFM Shadow Srs BD	
G-MTUC	Thruster TST Mk 1		G-MTXS	Mainair Gemini Flash IIA	
G-MTUD	Thruster TST Mk 1		G-MTXT	MBA Tiger Cub 440	
G-MTUE	Thruster TST Mk 1		G-MTXW	Noble Hardman Snowbird Mk IV	
G-MTUF	Thruster TST Mk 1				
G-MTUG	Thruster TST Mk 1		G-MTXY	Hornet Dual Trainer	
G-MTUH	Solar Wings Pegasus XL-R		G-MTXZ	Mainair Gemini Flash IIA	
G-MTUI	Solar Wings Pegasus XL-R		G-MTYA	Solar Wings Pegasus XL-Q	
G-MTUJ	Solar Wings Pegasus XL-R		G-MTYC	Solar Wings Pegasus XL-Q	
G-MTUK	Solar Wings Pegasus XL-R		G-MTYD	Solar Wings Pegasus XL-Q	
G-MTUL	Solar Wings Pegasus XL-R		G-MTYE	Solar Wings Pegasus XL-Q	
G-MTUN	Solar Wings Pegasus XL-Q		G-MTYF	Solar Wings Pegasus XL-Q	
G-MTUP	Solar Wings Pegasus XL-Q		G-MTYG	Solar Wings Pegasus XL-Q	
G-MTUR	Solar Wings Pegasus XL-Q		G-MTYH	Solar Wings Pegasus XL-Q	
G-MTUS	Solar Wings Pegasus XL-Q		G-MTYI	Solar Wings Pegasus XL-Q	
G-MTUT	Solar Wings Pegasus XL-Q		G-MTYL	Solar Wings Pegasus XL-Q	
G-MTUU	Mainair Gemini Flash IIA		G-MTYM	Solar Wings Pegasus XL-Q	
G-MTUV	Mainair Gemini Flash IIA		G-MTYN	Solar Wings Pegasus XL-Q	
G-MTUX	Medway Hybred 44XLR		G-MTYP	Solar Wings Pegasus XL-Q	
G-MTUY	Solar Wings Pegasus XL-Q		G-MTYR	Solar Wings Pegasus XL-Q	
G-MTVA	Solar Wings Pegasus XL-R		G-MTYS	Solar Wings Pegasus XL-Q	
G-MTVB	Solar Wings Pegasus XL-R		G-MTYT	Solar Wings Pegasus XL-Q	
G-MTVC	Solar Wings Pegasus XL-R		G-MTYU	Solar Wings Pegasus XL-Q	
G-MTVE	Solar Wings Pegasus XL-R		G-MTYV	Raven X	
G-MTVF	Solar Wings Pegasus XL-R		G-MTYX	Raven X	
G-MTVG	Mainair Gemini Flash IIA		G-MTYY	Solar Wings Pegasus XL-R	
G-MTVH	Mainair Gemini Flash IIA		G-MTZA	Thruster TST Mk 1	
G-MTVI	Mainair Gemini Flash IIA		G-MTZB	Thruster TST Mk 1	
G-MTVJ	Mainair Gemini Flash IIA		G-MTZC	Thruster TST Mk 1	
G-MTVK	Solar Wings Pegasus XL-R		G-MTZD	Thruster TST Mk 1	
G-MTVL	Solar Wings Pegasus XL-R		G-MTZE	Thruster TST Mk 1	
G-MTVM	Solar Wings Pegasus XL-R		G-MTZF	Thruster TST Mk 1	

Reg.	Type	Notes	Reg.	Type	Notes
G-MTZG	Mainair Gemini Flash IIA		G-MVCI	Noble Hardman Snowbird Mk IV	
G-MTZH	Mainair Gemini Flash IIA				
G-MTZI	Solar Wings Pegasus XL-R		G-MVCJ	Noble Hardman Snowbird Mk IV	
G-MTZJ	Solar Wings Pegasus XL-R				
G-MTZK	Solar Wings Pegasus XL-R		G-MVCL	Solar Wings Pegasus XL-Q	
G-MTZL	Mainair Gemini Flash IIA		G-MVCM	Solar Wings Pegasus XL-Q	
G-MTZK	Solar Wings Pegasus XL-R		G-MVCN	Solar Wings Pegasus XL-Q	
G-MTZM	Mainair Gemini Flash IIA		G-MVCO	Solar Wings Pegasus XL-Q	
G-MTZN	Mainair Gemini Flash IIA		G-MVCP	Solar Wings Pegasus XL-Q	
G-MTZO	Mainair Gemini Flash IIA		G-MVCR	Solar Wings Pegasus XL-Q	
G-MTZR	Solar Wings Pegasus XL-Q		G-MVCS	Solar Wings Pegasus XL-Q	
G-MTZS	Solar Wings Pegasus XL-Q		G-MVCT	Solar Wings Pegasus XL-Q	
G-MTZT	Solar Wings Pegasus XL-Q		G-MVCV	Solar Wings Pegasus XL-Q	
G-MTZV	Mainair Gemini Flash IIA		G-MVCW	CFM Shadow Srs BD	
G-MTZW	Mainair Gemini Flash IIA		G-MVCY	Mainair Gemini Flash IIA	
G-MTZX	Mainair Gemini Flash IIA		G-MVDA	Mainair Gemini Flash IIA	
G-MTZY	Mainair Gemini Flash IIA		G-MVDB	Medway Hybred 44XLR	
G-MTZZ	Mainair Gemini Flash IIA		G-MVDC	Medway Hybred 44XLR	
			G-MVDD	Thruster TST Mk 1	
G-MVAA	Mainair Gemini Flash IIA		G-MVDE	Thruster TST Mk 1	
G-MVAB	Mainair Gemini Flash IIA		G-MVDF	Thruster TST Mk 1	
G-MVAC	CFM Shadow Srs BD		G-MVDG	Thruster TST Mk 1	
G-MVAD	Mainair Gemini Flash IIA		G-MVDH	Thruster TST Mk 1	
G-MVAF	Southdown Puma Sprint		G-MVDJ	Medway Hybred 44XLR	
G-MVAG	Thruster TST Mk 1		G-MVDK	Aerial Arts Chaser S	
G-MVAH	Thruster TST Mk 1		G-MVDL	Aerial Arts Chaser S	
G-MVAI	Thruster TST Mk 1		G-MVDN	Aerial Arts Chaser S	
G-MVAJ	Thruster TST Mk 1		G-MVDO	Aerial Arts Chaser S	
G-MVAK	Thruster TST Mk 1		G-MVDP	Aerial Arts Chaser S	
G-MVAL	Thruster TST Mk 1		G-MVDR	Aerial Arts Chaser S	
G-MVAM	CFM Shadow Srs BD		G-MVDT	Mainair Gemini Flash IIA	
G-MVAN	CFM Shadow Srs BD		G-MVDU	Solar Wings Pegasus XL-R	
G-MVAO	Mainair Gemini Flash IIA		G-MVDV	Solar Wings Pegasus XL-R	
G-MVAP	Mainair Gemini Flash IIA		G-MVDW	Solar Wings Pegasus XL-R	
G-MVAR	Solar Wings Pegasus XL-R		G-MVDX	Solar Wings Pegasus XL-R	
G-MVAS	Solar Wings Pegasus XL-R		G-MVDZ	Solar Wings Pegasus XL-R	
G-MVAT	Solar Wings Pegasus XL-R		G-MVEA	Solar Wings Pegasus XL-R	
G-MVAU	Solar Wings Pegasus XL-R		G-MVEC	Solar Wings Pegasus XL-R	
G-MVAV	Solar Wings Pegasus XL-R		G-MVED	Solar Wings Pegasus XL-R	
G-MVAW	Solar Wings Pegasus XL-Q		G-MVEE	Medway Hybred 44XLR	
G-MVAX	Solar Wings Pegasus XL-Q		G-MVEF	Solar Wings Pegasus XL-R	
G-MVAY	Solar Wings Pegasus XL-Q		G-MVEG	Solar Wings Pegasus XL-R	
G-MVAZ	Solar Wings Pegasus XL-Q		G-MVEH	Mainair Gemini Flash IIA	
G-MVBA	Solar Wings Pegasus XL-Q		G-MVEI	CFM Shadow Srs BD	
G-MVBB	CFM Shadow Srs BD		G-MVEJ	Mainair Gemini Flash IIA	
G-MVBC	Aerial Arts Tri-Flyer 130SX		G-MVEK	Mainair Gemini Flash IIA	
G-MVBD	Mainair Gemini Flash IIA		G-MVEL	Mainair Gemini Flash IIA	
G-MVBE	Mainair Scorcher		G-MVEN	CFM Shadow Srs BD	
G-MVBF	Mainair Gemini Flash IIA		G-MVEO	Mainair Gemini Flash IIA	
G-MVBG	Mainair Gemini Flash IIA		G-MVEP	Mainair Gemini Flash IIA	
G-MVBH	Mainair Gemini Flash IIA		G-MVER	Mainair Gemini Flash IIA	
G-MVBI	Mainair Gemini Flash IIA		G-MVES	Mainair Gemini Flash IIA	
G-MVBJ	Solar Wings Pegasus XL-R		G-MVET	Mainair Gemini Flash IIA	
G-MVBK	Mainair Gemini Flash IIA		G-MVEV	Mainair Gemini Flash IIA	
G-MVBL	Mainair Gemini Flash IIA		G-MVEW	Mainair Gemini Flash IIA	
G-MVBM	Mainair Gemini Flash IIA		G-MVEX	Solar Wings Pegasus XL-Q	
G-MVBN	Mainair Gemini Flash IIA		G-MVEZ	Solar Wings Pegasus XL-Q	
G-MVBO	Mainair Gemini Flash IIA		G-MVFA	Solar Wings Pegasus XL-Q	
G-MVBP	Thruster TST Mk 1		G-MVFB	Solar Wings Pegasus XL-Q	
G-MVBR	Thruster TST Mk 1		G-MVFC	Solar Wings Pegasus XL-Q	
G-MVBS	Thruster TST Mk 1		G-MVFD	Solar Wings Pegasus XL-Q	
G-MVBT	Thruster TST Mk 1		G-MVFE	Solar Wings Pegasus XL-Q	
G-MVBU	Thruster TST Mk 1		G-MVFF	Solar Wings Pegasus XL-Q	
G-MVBY	Solar Wings Pegasus XL-R		G-MVFG	Solar Wings Pegasus XL-Q	
G-MVBZ	Solar Wings Pegasus XL-R		G-MVFH	CFM Shadow Srs BD	
G-MVCA	Solar Wings Pegasus XL-R		G-MVFJ	Thruster TST Mk 1	
G-MVCB	Solar Wings Pegasus XL-R		G-MVFK	Thruster TST Mk 1	
G-MVCC	CFM Shadow Srs BD		G-MVFL	Thruster TST Mk 1	
G-MVCD	Medway Hybred 44XLR		G-MVFM	Thruster TST Mk 1	
G-MVCE	Mainair Gemini Flash IIA		G-MVFN	Thruster TST Mk 1	
G-MVCF	Mainair Gemini Flash IIA		G-MVFO	Thruster TST Mk 1	
G-MVCH	Noble Hardman Snowbird Mk IV		G-MVFP	Solar Wings Pegasus XL-R	
			G-MVFR	Solar Wings Pegasus XL-R	

Reg.	Type	Notes	Reg.	Type	Notes
G-MVFS	Solar Wings Pegasus XL-R		G-MVIU	Thruster TST Mk 1	
G-MVFT	Solar Wings Pegasus XL-R		G-MVIV	Thruster TST Mk 1	
G-MVFV	Solar Wings Pegasus XL-R		G-MVIW	Thruster TST Mk 1	
G-MVFW	Solar Wings Pegasus XL-R		G-MVIX	Mainair Gemini Flash IIA	
G-MVFX	Solar Wings Pegasus XL-R		G-MVIY	Mainair Gemini Flash IIA	
G-MVFY	Solar Wings Pegasus XL-R		G-MVIZ	Mainair Gemini Flash IIA	
G-MVFZ	Solar Wings Pegasus XL-R		G-MVJA	Mainair Gemini Flash IIA	
G-MVGA	Aerial Arts Chaser S		G-MVJB	Mainair Gemini Flash IIA	
G-MVGB	Medway Hybred 44XLR		G-MVJC	Mainair Gemini Flash IIA	
G-MVGC	AMF Chevvron 2-32		G-MVJD	Solar Wings Pegasus XL-R	
G-MVGD	AMF Chevvron 2-32		G-MVJE	Mainair Gemini Flash IIA	
G-MVGE	AMF Chevvron 2-32		G-MVJF	Aerial Arts Chaser S	
G-MVGF	Aerial Arts Chaser S		G-MVJG	Aerial Arts Chaser S	
G-MVGG	Aerial Arts Chaser S		G-MVJH	Aerial Arts Chaser S	
G-MVGH	Aerial Arts Chaser S		G-MVJI	Aerial Arts Chaser S	
G-MVGI	Aerial Arts Chaser S		G-MVJJ	Aerial Arts Chaser S	
G-MVGJ	Aerial Arts Chaser S		G-MVJK	Aerial Arts Chaser S	
G-MVGK	Aerial Arts Chaser S		G-MVJL	Mainair Gemini Flash IIA	
G-MVGL	Medway Hybred 44XLR		G-MVJM	Microflight Spectrum	
G-MVGM	Mainair Gemini Flash IIA		G-MVJN	Solar Wings Pegasus XL-Q	
G-MVGN	Solar Wings Pegasus XL-R		G-MVJO	Solar Wings Pegasus XL-Q	
G-MVGO	Solar Wings Pegasus XL-R		G-MVJP	Solar Wings Pegasus XL-Q	
G-MVGR	Solar Wings Pegasus XL-R		G-MVJR	Solar Wings Pegasus XL-Q	
G-MVGS	Solar Wings Pegasus XL-R		G-MVJS	Solar Wings Pegasus XL-Q	
G-MVGT	Solar Wings Pegasus XL-Q		G-MVJT	Solar Wings Pegasus XL-Q	
G-MVGU	Solar Wings Pegasus XL-Q		G-MVJU	Solar Wings Pegasus XL-Q	
G-MVGV	Solar Wings Pegasus XL-Q		G-MVJV	Solar Wings Pegasus XL-Q	
G-MVGX	Solar Wings Pegasus XL-Q		G-MVJW	Solar Wings Pegasus XL-Q	
G-MVGY	Medway Hybred 44XL		G-MVJZ	Birdman Cherokee	
G-MVGZ	Ultraflight Lazair IIIE		G-MVKA	Medway Hybred 44XLR	
G-MVHA	Aerial Arts Chaser S		G-MVKB	Medway Hybred 44XLR	
G-MVHB	Powerchute Raider		G-MVKC	Mainair Gemini Flash IIA	
G-MVHC	Powerchute Raider		G-MVKE	Solar Wings Pegasus XL-R	
G-MVHD	CFM Shadow Srs BD		G-MVKF	Solar Wings Pegasus XL-R	
G-MVHE	Mainair Gemini Flash IIA		G-MVKG	Solar Wings Pegasus XL-R	
G-MVHF	Mainair Gemini Flash IIA		G-MVKH	Solar Wings Pegasus XL-R	
G-MVHG	Mainair Gemini Flash IIA		G-MVKJ	Solar Wings Pegasus XL-R	
G-MVHH	Mainair Gemini Flash IIA		G-MVKK	Solar Wings Pegasus XL-R	
G-MVHI	Thruster TST Mk 1		G-MVKL	Solar Wings Pegasus XL-R	
G-MVHJ	Thruster TST Mk 1		G-MVKM	Solar Wings Pegasus XL-R	
G-MVHK	Thruster TST Mk 1		G-MVKN	Solar Wings Pegasus XL-R	
G-MVHL	Thruster TST Mk 1		G-MVKO	Solar Wings Pegasus XL-R	
G-MVHM	Whittaker MW.5 Sorcerer		G-MVKP	Solar Wings Pegasus XL-R	
G-MVHN	Aerial Arts Chaser S		G-MVKR	Solar Wings Pegasus XL-R	
G-MVHO	Solar Wings Pegasus XL-Q		G-MVKS	Solar Wings Pegasus XL-R	
G-MVHP	Solar Wings Pegasus XL-Q		G-MVKT	Solar Wings Pegasus XL-Q	
G-MVHR	Solar Wings Pegasus XL-Q		G-MVKU	Solar Wings Pegasus XL-Q	
G-MVHS	Solar Wings Pegasus XL-Q		G-MVKV	Solar Wings Pegasus XL-Q	
G-MVHT	Solar Wings Pegasus XL-Q		G-MVKW	Solar Wings Pegasus XL-Q	
G-MVHU	Solar Wings Pegasus XL-Q		G-MVKX	Solar Wings Pegasus XL-Q	
G-MVHV	Solar Wings Pegasus XL-Q		G-MVKY	Aerial Arts Chaser S	
G-MVHW	Solar Wings Pegasus XL-Q		G-MVKZ	Aerial Arts Chaser S	
G-MVHX	Solar Wings Pegasus XL-Q		G-MVLA	Aerial Arts Chaser S	
G-MVHY	Solar Wings Pegasus XL-Q		G-MVLB	Aerial Arts Chaser S	
G-MVHZ	Hornet Dual Trainer		G-MVLC	Aerial Arts Chaser S	
G-MVIA	Solar Wings Pegasus XL-R		G-MVLD	Aerial Arts Chaser S	
G-MVIB	Mainair Gemini Flash IIA		G-MVLE	Aerial Arts Chaser S	
G-MVIC	Mainair Gemini Flash IIA		G-MVLF	Aerial Arts Chaser S	
G-MVIE	Aerial Arts Chaser S		G-MVLG	Aerial Arts Chaser S	
G-MVIF	Medway Hybred 44XLR		G-MVLH	Aerial Arts Chaser S	
G-MVIG	CFM Shadow Srs B		G-MVLJ	CFM Shadow Srs B	
G-MVIH	Mainair Gemini Flash IIA		G-MVLL	Mainair Gemini Flash IIA	
G-MVIL	Noble Hardman Snowbird Mk IV		G-MVLP	CFM Shadow Srs BD	
			G-MVLR	Mainair Gemini Flash IIA	
G-MVIM	Noble Hardman Snowbird Mk IV		G-MVLS	Aerial Arts Chaser S	
			G-MVLT	Aerial Arts Chaser S	
G-MVIN	Noble Hardman Snowbird Mk IV		G-MVLU	Aerial Arts Chaser S	
			G-MVLW	Aerial Arts Chaser S	
G-MVIO	Noble Hardman Snowbird Mk IV		G-MVLX	Solar Wings Pegasus XL-Q	
			G-MVLY	Solar Wings Pegasus XL-Q	
G-MVIP	AMF Chevvron 232		G-MVMA	Solar Wings Pegasus XL-Q	
G-MVIR	Thruster TST Mk 1		G-MVMB	Solar Wings Pegasus XL-Q	
G-MVIS	Thruster TST Mk 1		G-MVMC	Solar Wings Pegasus XL-Q	

Reg.	Type	Notes	Reg.	Type	Notes
G-MVME	Thruster TST Mk 1		G-MVPE	Mainair Gemini Flash IIA	
G-MVMG	Thruster TST Mk 1		G-MVPF	Medway Hybred 44XLR	
G-MVMI	Thruster TST Mk 1		G-MVPG	Medway Hybred 44XLR	
G-MVMK	Medway Hybred 44XLR		G-MVPH	Whittaker MW.6 Merlin	
G-MVML	Aerial Arts Chaser S		G-MVPI	Mainair Gemini Flash IIA	
G-MVMM	Aerial Arts Chaser S		G-MVPJ	Rans S.5	
G-MVMN	Mainair Gemini Flash IIA		G-MVPK	CFM Shadow Srs B	
G-MVMO	Mainair Gemini Flash IIA		G-MVPL	Medway Hybred 44XLR	
G-MVMR	Mainair Gemini Flash IIA		G-MVPM	Whittaker MW.6 Merlin	
G-MVMT	Mainair Gemini Flash IIA		G-MVPN	Whittaker MW.6 Merlin	
G-MVMU	Mainair Gemini Flash IIA		G-MVPO	Mainair Gemini Flash IIA	
G-MVMV	Aerotech MW.5 (K) Sorcerer		G-MVPR	Solar Wings Pegasus XL-Q	
			G-MVPS	Solar Wings Pegasus XL-Q	
G-MVMW	Mainair Gemini Flash IIA		G-MVPT	Solar Wings Pegasus XL-Q	
G-MVMX	Mainair Gemini Flash IIA		G-MVPU	Solar Wings Pegasus XL-Q	
G-MVMY	Mainair Gemini Flash IIA		G-MVPW	Solar Wings Pegasus XL-R	
G-MVMZ	Mainair Gemini Flash IIA		G-MVPX	Solar Wings Pegasus XL-Q	
G-MVNA	Powerchute Raider		G-MVPY	Solar Wings Pegasus XL-Q	
G-MVNB	Powerchute Raider		G-MVPZ	Rans S.5	
G-MVNC	Powerchute Raider		G-MVRA	Mainair Gemini Flash IIA	
G-MVNE	Powerchute Raider		G-MVRB	Mainair Gemini Flash IIA	
G-MVNF	Powerchute Raider		G-MVRC	Mainair Gemini Flash IIA	
G-MVNI	Powerchute Raider		G-MVRD	Mainair Gemini Flash IIA	
G-MVNK	Powerchute Raider		G-MVRE	CFM Shadow Srs BD	
G-MVNL	Powerchute Raider		G-MVRF	Rotec Rally 2B	
G-MVNM	Mainair Gemini Flash IIA		G-MVRG	Aerial Arts Chaser S	
G-MVNN	Whittaker MW.5 (K) Sorcerer		G-MVRH	Solar Wings Pegasus XL-Q	
			G-MVRI	Solar Wings Pegasus XL-Q	
G-MVNO	Aerotech MW.5 (K) Sorcerer		G-MVRJ	Solar Wings Pegasus XL-Q	
			G-MVRK	Solar Wings Pegasus XL-Q	
G-MVNP	Aerotech MW.5 (K) Sorcerer		G-MVRL	Aerial Arts Chaser S	
			G-MVRM	Mainair Gemini Flash IIA	
G-MVNR	Aerotech MW.5 (K) Sorcerer		G-MVRN	Rans S.4 Coyote	
			G-MVRO	CFM Shadow Srs BD	
G-MVNS	Aerotech MW.5 (K) Sorcerer		G-MVRP	CFM Shadow Srs BD	
			G-MVRR	CFM Shadow Srs BD	
G-MVNT	Whittaker MW.5 (K) Sorcerer		G-MVRT	CFM Shadow Srs BD	
			G-MVRU	Solar Wings Pegasus XL-Q	
G-MVNU	Aerotech MW.5 Sorcerer		G-MVRV	Powerchute Kestrel	
G-MVNV	Aerotech MW.5 Sorcerer		G-MVRW	Solar Wings Pegasus XL-Q	
G-MVNW	Mainair Gemini Flash IIA		G-MVRX	Solar Wings Pegasus XL-Q	
G-MVNX	Mainair Gemini Flash IIA		G-MVRY	Medway Hybred 44XLR	
G-MVNY	Mainair Gemini Flash IIA		G-MVRZ	Medway Hybred 44XLR	
G-MVNZ	Mainair Gemini Flash IIA		G-MVSA	Solar Wings Pegasus XL-Q	
G-MVOA	Aerial Arts Alligator		G-MVSB	Solar Wings Pegasus XL-Q	
G-MVOB	Mainair Gemini Flash IIA		G-MVSD	Solar Wings Pegasus XL-Q	
G-MVOD	Aerial Arts Chaser 110SX		G-MVSG	Aerial Arts Chaser S	
G-MVOE	Solar Wings Pegasus XL-R		G-MVSI	Medway Hybred 44XLR	
G-MVOF	Mainair Gemini Flash IIA		G-MVSJ	Aviasud Mistral 532	
G-MVOH	CFM Shadow Srs B		G-MVSK	Aerial Arts Chaser S	
G-MVOI	Noble Hardman Snowbird Mk IV		G-MVSL	Aerial Arts Chaser S	
			G-MVSM	Midland Ultralights Sirocco	
G-MVOJ	Noble Hardman Snowbird Mk IV		G-MVSN	Mainair Gemini Flash IIA	
			G-MVSO	Mainair Gemini Flash IIA	
G-MVOK	Noble Hardman Snowbird Mk IV		G-MVSP	Mainair Gemini Flash IIA	
			G-MVSR	Medway Hybred 44XLR	
G-MVOL	Noble Hardman Snowbird Mk IV		G-MVSS	Hornet RS-ZA	
			G-MVST	Mainair Gemini Flash IIA	
G-MVON	Mainair Gemini Flash IIA		G-MVSU	Microflight Spectrum	
G-MVOO	AMF Chevvron 2-32		G-MVSV	Mainair Gemini Flash IIA	
G-MVOP	Aerial Arts Chaser S		G-MVSW	Solar Wings Pegasus XL-Q	
G-MVOR	Mainair Gemini Flash IIA		G-MVSX	Solar Wings Pegasus XL-Q	
G-MVOS	Southdown Raven		G-MVSY	Solar Wings Pegasus XL-Q	
G-MVOT	Thruster TST Mk 1		G-MVSZ	Solar Wings Pegasus XL-Q	
G-MVOU	Thruster TST Mk 1		G-MVTA	Solar Wings Pegasus XL-Q	
G-MVOV	Thruster TST Mk 1		G-MVTC	Mainair Gemini Flash IIA	
G-MVOW	Thruster TST Mk 1		G-MVTD	Whittaker MW.6 Merlin	
G-MVOX	Thruster TST Mk 1		G-MVTE	Whittaker MW.6 Merlin	
G-MVOY	Thruster TST Mk 1		G-MVTF	Aerial Arts Chaser S	
G-MVPA	Mainair Gemini Flash IIA		G-MVTG	Solar Wings Pegasus XL-Q	
G-MVPB	Mainair Gemini Flash IIA		G-MVTI	Solar Wings Pegasus XL-Q	
G-MVPC	Mainair Gemini Flash IIA		G-MVTJ	Solar Wings Pegasus XL-Q	
G-MVPD	Mainair Gemini Flash IIA		G-MVTK	Solar Wings Pegasus XL-Q	

Reg.	Type	Notes	Reg.	Type	Notes
G-MVTL	Aerial Arts Chaser S		G-MVXZ	Minimax	
G-MVTM	Aerial Arts Chaser S		G-MVYA	Aerial Arts Chaser S	
G-MVUA	Mainair Gemini Flash IIA		G-MVYB	Solar Wings Pegasus XL-Q	
G-MVUB	Thruster T.300		G-MVYC	Solar Wings Pegasus XL-Q	
G-MVUC	Medway Hybred 44XLR		G-MVYD	Solar Wings Pegasus XL-Q	
G-MVUD	Medway Hybred 44XLR		G-MVYE	Thruster TST Mk 1	
G-MVUE	Solar Wings Pegasus XL-Q		G-MVYG	Hornet R-ZA	
G-MVUF	Solar Wings Pegasus XL-Q		G-MVYH	Hornet R-ZA	
G-MVUG	Solar Wings Pegasus XL-Q		G-MVYI	Hornet R-ZA	
G-MVUH	Solar Wings Pegasus XL-Q		G-MVYJ	Hornet R-ZA	
G-MVUI	Solar Wings Pegasus XL-Q		G-MVYK	Hornet R-ZA	
G-MVUJ	Solar Wings Pegasus XL-Q		G-MVYM	Hornet R-ZA	
G-MVUK	Solar Wings Pegasus XL-Q		G-MVYN	Hornet R-ZA	
G-MVUL	Solar Wings Pegasus XL-Q		G-MVYO	Hornet R-ZA	
G-MVUM	Solar Wings Pegasus XL-Q		G-MVYP	Medway Hybred 44XLR	
G-MVUN	Solar Wings Pegasus XL-Q		G-MVYR	Medway Hybred 44XLR	
G-MVUO	AMF Chevvron 2-32		G-MVYS	Mainair Gemini Flash IIA	
G-MVUP	Aviasud Mistral		G-MVYT	Noble Hardman Snowbird Mk IV	
G-MVUR	Hornet ZA				
G-MVUS	Aerial Arts Chaser S		G-MVYU	Noble Hardman Snowbird Mk IV	
G-MVUT	Aerial Arts Chaser S				
G-MVUU	Hornet R-ZA		G-MVYV	Noble Hardman Snowbird Mk IV	
G-MVVF	Medway Hybred 44XLR				
G-MVVG	Medway Hybred 44XLR		G-MVYW	Noble Hardman Snowbird Mk IV	
G-MVVH	Medway Hybred 44XLR				
G-MVVI	Medway Hybred 44XLR		G-MVYX	Noble Hardman Snowbird Mk IV	
G-MVVJ	Medway Hybred 44XLR				
G-MVVK	Solar Wings Pegasus XL-R		G-MVYY	Aerial Arts Chaser S508	
G-MVVM	Solar Wings Pegasus XL-R		G-MVYZ	CFM Shadow Srs BD	
G-MVVN	Solar Wings Pegasus XL-Q		G-MVZA	Thruster T.300	
G-MVVP	Solar Wings Pegasus XL-Q		G-MVZB	Thruster T.300	
G-MVVR	Medway Hybred 44XLR		G-MVZC	Thruster T.300	
G-MVVT	CFM Shadow Srs BD		G-MVZD	Thruster T.300	
G-MVVU	Aerial Arts Chaser S		G-MVZE	Thruster T.300	
G-MVVV	AMF Chevvron 2-32		G-MVZG	Thruster T.300	
G-MVVW	Aerial Arts Chaser S		G-MVZH	Thruster T.300	
G-MVVZ	Powerchute Raider		G-MVZI	Thruster T.300	
G-MVWB	Powerchute Raider		G-MVZJ	Solar Wings Pegasus XL-Q	
G-MVWD	Powerchute Raider		G-MVZK	Challenger II	
G-MVWE	Powerchute Raider		G-MVZL	Solar Wings Pegasus XL-Q	
G-MVWF	Powerchute Raider		G-MVZM	Aerial Arts Chaser S	
G-MVWH	Powerchute Raider		G-MVZN	Aerial Arts Chaser S	
G-MVWN	Thruster T.300		G-MVZO	Medway Hybred 44XLR	
G-MVWO	Thruster T.300		G-MVZP	Renegade Spirit UK	
G-MVWP	Thruster T.300		G-MVZR	Aviasud Mistral	
G-MVWR	Thruster T.300		G-MVZS	Mainair Gemini Flash IIA	
G-MVWS	Thruster T.300		G-MVZT	Solar Wings Pegasus XL-Q	
G-MVWU	Medway Hybred 44XLR		G-MVZU	Solar Wings Pegasus XL-Q	
G-MVWV	Medway Hybred 44XLR		G-MVZV	Solar Wings Pegasus XL-Q	
G-MVWW	Aviasud Mistral		G-MVZW	Hornet R-ZA	
G-MVWX	Microflight Spectrum		G-MVZX	Renegade Spirit UK	
G-MVWZ	Aviasud Mistral		G-MVZY	Aerial Arts Chaser S	
G-MVXA	Whittaker MW.6 Merlin		G-MVZZ	AMF Chevvron 232	
G-MVXB	Mainair Gemini Flash IIA				
G-MVXC	Mainair Gemini Flash IIA		G-MWAB	Mainair Gemini Flash IIA	
G-MVXD	Medway Hybred 44XLR		G-MWAC	Solar Wings Pegasus XL-Q	
G-MVXE	Medway Hybred 44XLR		G-MWAD	Solar Wings Pegasus XL-Q	
G-MVXF	Weedhopper JC-31A		G-MWAE	CFM Shadow Srs BD	
G-MVXG	Aerial Arts Chaser S		G-MWAF	Solar Wings Pegasus XL-R	
G-MVXH	Microflight Spectrum		G-MWAG	Solar Wings Pegasus XL-R	
G-MVXI	Medway Hybred 44XLR		G-MWAI	Solar Wings Pegasus XL-R	
G-MVXJ	Medway Hybred 44XLR		G-MWAJ	Renegade Spirit UK	
G-MVXL	Thruster TST Mk 1		G-MWAL	Solar Wings Pegasus XL-Q	
G-MVXM	Medway Hybred 44XLR		G-MWAM	Thruster T.300	
G-MVXN	Aviasud Mistral		G-MWAN	Thruster T.300	
G-MVXP	Aerial Arts Chaser S		G-MWAP	Thruster T.300	
G-MVXR	Mainair Gemini Flash IIA		G-MWAR	Thruster T.300	
G-MVXS	Mainair Gemini Flash IIA		G-MWAS	Thruster T.300	
G-MVXT	Mainair Gemini Flash IIA		G-MWAT	Solar Wings Pegasus XL-Q	
G-MVXU	Aviasud Mistral		G-MWAU	Mainair Gemini Flash IIA	
G-MVXV	Aviasud Mistral		G-MWAV	Solar Wings Pegasus XL-R	
G-MVXW	Rans S.4 Coyote		G-MWAW	Whittaker MW.6 Merlin	
G-MVXX	AMF Chevvron 232		G-MWBH	Hornet RS-ZA	

Reg.	Type	Notes	Reg.	Type	Notes
G-MWBI	Medway Hybred 44XLR		G-MWFG	Powerchute Kestrel	
G-MWBJ	Medway Sprint		G-MWFH	Powerchute Kestrel	
G-MWBK	Solar Wings Pegasus XL-Q		G-MWFI	Powerchute Kestrel	
G-MWBL	Solar Wings Pegasus XL-Q		G-MWFK	Powerchute Kestrel	
G-MWBM	Hornet RS-ZA		G-MWFL	Powerchute Kestrel	
G-MWBN	Hornet RS-ZA		G-MWFN	Powerchute Kestrel	
G-MWBO	Rans S.4 Coyote		G-MWFO	Solar Wings Pegasus XL-R	
G-MWBP	Hornet RS-ZA		G-MWFP	Solar Wings Pegasus XL-R	
G-MWBR	Hornet RS-ZA		G-MWFS	Solar Wings Pegasus XL-Q	
G-MWBS	Hornet RS-ZA		G-MWFT	MBA Tiger Cub 440	
G-MWBU	Hornet RS-ZA		G-MWFU	Quad City Challenger II UK	
G-MWBW	Hornet RS-ZA		G-MWFV	Quad City Challenger II UK	
G-MWBX	Hornet RS-ZA		G-MWFW	Rans S.4 Coyote	
G-MWBY	Hornet RS-ZA		G-MWFX	Quad City Challenger II UK	
G-MWBZ	Hornet RS-ZA		G-MWFY	Quad City Challenger II UK	
G-MWCA	Hornet RS-ZA		G-MWFZ	Quad City Challenger II UK	
G-MWCB	Solar Wings Pegasus XL-Q		G-MWGA	Rans S.5 Coyote	
G-MWCE	Mainair Gemini Flash IIA		G-MWGC	Medway Hybred 44XLR	
G-MWCF	Solar Wings Pegasus XL-R		G-MWGD	Medway Hybred 44XLR	
G-MWCG	Microflight Spectrum		G-MWGE	Medway Hybred 44XLR	
G-MWCH	Rans S.6 Coyote		G-MWGF	Renegade Spirit UK	
G-MWCI	Powerchute Kestrel		G-MWGG	Mainair Gemini Flash IIA	
G-MWCJ	Powerchute Kestrel		G-MWGI	Whittaker MW.5 (K)	
G-MWCK	Powerchute Kestrel			Sorcerer	
G-MWCL	Powerchute Kestrel		G-MWGJ	Whittaker MW.5 (K)	
G-MWCM	Powerchute Kestrel			Sorcerer	
G-MWCN	Powerchute Kestrel		G-MWGK	Whittaker MW.5 (K)	
G-MWCO	Powerchute Kestrel			Sorcerer	
G-MWCP	Powerchute Kestrel		G-MWGL	Solar Wings Pegasus XL-Q	
G-MWCR	Southdown Puma Sprint		G-MWGM	Solar Wings Pegasus XL-Q	
G-MWCS	Powerchute Kestrel		G-MWGN	Rans S.4 Coyote	
G-MWCU	Solar Wings Pegasus XL-R		G-MWGO	Aerial Arts Chaser 110SX	
G-MWCV	Solar Wings Pegasus XL-Q		G-MWGR	Solar Wings Pegasus XL-Q	
G-MWCW	Mainair Gemini Flash IIA		G-MWGT	Powerchute Kestrel	
G-MWCX	Medway Hybred 44XLR		G-MWGU	Powerchute Kestrel	
G-MWCY	Medway Hybred 44XLR		G-MWGV	Powerchute Kestrel	
G-MWCZ	Medway Hybred 44XLR		G-MWGW	Powerchute Kestrel	
G-MWDB	CFM Shadow Srs BD		G-MWGY	Powerchute Kestrel	
G-MWDC	Solar Wings Pegasus XL-R		G-MWGZ	Powerchute Kestrel	
G-MWDD	Solar Wings Pegasus XL-Q		G-MWHC	Solar Wings Pegasus XL-Q	
G-MWDE	Hornet RS-ZA		G-MWHD	Microflight Spectrum	
G-MWDF	Hornet RS-ZA		G-MWHE	Microflight Spectrum	
G-MWDG	Hornet RS-ZA		G-MWHF	Solar Wings Pegasus XL-Q	
G-MWDH	Hornet RS-ZA		G-MWHG	Solar Wings Pegasus XL-Q	
G-MWDI	Hornet RS-ZA		G-MWHH	Team Minimax	
G-MWDJ	Mainair Gemini Flash IIA		G-MWHI	Mainair Gemini Flash IIA	
G-MWDK	Solar Wings Pegasus XL-R		G-MWHJ	Solar Wings Pegasus XL-Q	
G-MWDL	Solar Wings Pegasus XL-R		G-MWHL	Solar Wings Pegasus XL-Q	
G-MWDM	Renegade Spirit UK		G-MWHM	Whittaker MW.6 Merlin	
G-MWDN	CFM Shadow Srs BD		G-MWHO	Mainair Gemini Flash IIA	
G-MWDP	Thruster TST Mk 1		G-MWHP	Rans S.6-ESD Coyote	
G-MWDS	Thruster T.300		G-MWHR	Mainair Gemini Flash IIA	
G-MWDZ	Eipper Quicksilver MXL II		G-MWHT	SW Pegasus Quasar	
G-MWEE	Solar Wings Pegasus XL-Q		G-MWHU	SW Pegasus Quasar	
G-MWEF	Solar Wings Pegasus XL-Q		G-MWHV	SW Pegasus Quasar	
G-MWEG	Solar Wings Pegasus XL-Q		G-MWHW	Solar Wings Pegasus XL-Q	
G-MWEH	Solar Wings Pegasus XL-Q		G-MWHX	Solar Wings Pegasus XL-Q	
G-MWEK	Whittaker MW.5 Sorcerer		G-MWHY	Mainair Gemini Flash IIA	
G-MWEL	Mainair Gemini Flash IIA		G-MWHZ	Trion J-1	
G-MWEN	CFM Shadow Srs BD		G-MWIA	Mainair Gemini Flash IIA	
G-MWEO	Whittaker MW.5 Sorcerer		G-MWIB	Aviasud Mistral	
G-MWEP	Rans S.4 Coyote		G-MWIC	Whittaker MW.5 Sorcerer	
G-MWER	Solar Wings Pegasus XL-Q		G-MWID	Solar Wings Pegasus XL-Q	
G-MWES	Rans S.4 Coyote		G-MWIE	Solar Wings Pegasus XL-Q	
G-MWEU	Hornet RS-ZA		G-MWIF	Rans S.6-ESD Coyote II	
G-MWEV	Hornet RS-ZA		G-MWIG	Mainair Gemini Flash IIA	
G-MWEZ	CFM Shadow Srs CD		G-MWIH	Mainair Gemini Flash IIA	
G-MWFA	Solar Wings Pegasus XL-R		G-MWIK	Medway Hybred 44XLR	
G-MWFB	CFM Shadow Srs BD		G-MWIL	Medway Hybred 44XLR	
G-MWFC	Team Minimax (G-BTXC)		G-MWIM	SW Pegasus Quasar	
G-MWFD	Team Minimax		G-MWIN	Mainair Gemini Flash IIA	
G-MWFE	Robin 330/Lightning 195		G-MWIO	Rans S.4 Coyote	
G-MWFF	Rans S.4 Coyote		G-MWIP	Whittaker MW.6 Merlin	

Reg.	Type	Notes	Reg.	Type	Notes
G-MWIR	Solar Wings Pegasus XL-Q		G-MWML	SW Pegasus Quasar	
G-MWIS	Solar Wings Pegasus XL-Q		G-MWMM	Mainair Gemini Flash IIA	
G-MWIT	Solar Wings Pegasus XL-Q		G-MWMN	Solar Wings Pegasus XL-Q	
G-MWIU	Solar Wings Pegasus XL-Q		G-MWMO	Solar Wings Pegasus XL-Q	
G-MWIV	Mainair Gemini Flash IIA		G-MWMP	Solar Wings Pegasus XL-Q	
G-MWIW	SW Pegasus Quasar		G-MWMR	Solar Wings Pegasus XL-R	
G-MWIX	SW Pegasus Quasar		G-MWMS	Mainair Gemini Flash	
G-MWIY	SW Pegasus Quasar		G-MWMT	Mainair Gemini Flash IIA	
G-MWIZ	CFM Shadow Srs BD		G-MWMU	CFM Shadow Srs CD	
G-MWJD	SW Pegasus Quasar		G-MWMV	Solar Wings Pegasus XL-R	
G-MWJF	CFM Shadow Srs BD		G-MWMW	Renegade Spirit UK	
G-MWJG	Solar Wings Pegasus XL-R		G-MWMX	Mainair Gemini Flash IIA	
G-MWJH	SW Pegasus Quasar		G-MWMY	Mainair Gemini Flash IIA	
G-MWJI	SW Pegasus Quasar		G-MWMZ	Solar Wings Pegasus XL-Q	
G-MWJJ	SW Pegasus Quasar		G-MWNA	Solar Wings Pegasus XL-Q	
G-MWJK	SW Pegasus Quasar		G-MWNB	Solar Wings Pegasus XL-Q	
G-MWJL	AMF Chevvron 232		G-MWNC	Solar Wings Pegasus XL-Q	
G-MWJM	AMF Chevvron 232		G-MWND	Tiger Cub Developments	
G-MWJN	Solar Wings Pegasus XL-Q			RL.5A	
G-MWJO	Solar Wings Pegasus XL-Q		G-MWNE	Mainair Gemini Flash IIA	
G-MWJP	Medway Hybred 44XLR		G-MWNF	Renegade Spirit UK	
G-MWJR	Medway Hybred 44XLR		G-MWNG	Solar Wings Pegasus XL-Q	
G-MWJS	SW Pegasus Quasar		G-MWNK	SW Pegasus Quasar	
G-MWJT	SW Pegasus Quasar		G-MWNL	SW Pegasus Quasar	
G-MWJU	SW Pegasus Quasar		G-MWNM	SW Pegasus Quasar	
G-MWJV	SW Pegasus Quasar		G-MWNN	SW Pegasus Quasar	
G-MWJW	Whittaker MW.5 Sorcerer		G-MWNO	AMF Chevvron 232	
G-MWJX	Medway Puma Sprint		G-MWNP	AMF Chevvron 232	
G-MWJY	Mainair Gemini Flash IIA		G-MWNR	Renegade Spirit UK	
G-MWJZ	CFM Shadow Srs CD		G-MWNS	Mainair Gemini Flash IIA	
G-MWKA	Renegade Spirit UK		G-MWNT	Mainair Gemini Flash IIA	
G-MWKE	Hornet R-ZA		G-MWNU	Mainair Gemini Flash IIA	
G-MWKO	Solar Wings Pegasus XL-Q		G-MWNV	Powerchute Kestrel	
G-MWKP	Solar Wings Pegasus XL-Q		G-MWNW	Powerchute Kestrel	
G-MWKW	Microflight Spectrum		G-MWNX	Powerchute Kestrel	
G-MWKX	Microflight Spectrum		G-MWNY	Powerchute Kestrel	
G-MWKY	Solar Wings Pegasus XL-Q		G-MWNZ	Powerchute Kestrel	
G-MWKZ	Solar Wings Pegasus XL-Q		G-MWOB	Powerchute Kestrel	
G-MWLA	Rans S.4 Coyote		G-MWOC	Powerchute Kestrel	
G-MWLB	Medway Hybred 44XLR		G-MWOD	Powerchute Kestrel	
G-MWLC	Medway Hybred 44XLR		G-MWOE	Powerchute Kestrel	
G-MWLD	CFM Shadow Srs BD		G-MWOH	Solar Wings Pegasus XL-R	
G-MWLE	Solar Wings Pegasus XL-R		G-MWOI	Solar Wings Pegasus XL-R	
G-MWLF	Solar Wings Pegasus XL-R		G-MWOJ	Mainair Gemini Flash IIA	
G-MWLG	Solar Wings Pegasus XL-R		G-MWOK	Mainair Gemini Flash IIA	
G-MWLH	Solar Wings Pegasus XL-R		G-MWOL	Mainair Gemini Flash IIA	
G-MWLI	SW Pegasus Quasar		G-MWOM	SW Pegasus Quasar TC	
G-MWLJ	SW Pegasus Quasar		G-MWON	CFM Shadow Srs CD	
G-MWLK	SW Pegasus Quasar		G-MWOO	Renegade Spirit UK	
G-MWLL	Solar Wings Pegasus XL-Q		G-MWOP	SW Pegasus Quasar	
G-MWLM	Solar Wings Pegasus XL-Q		G-MWOR	Solar Wings Pegasus XL-Q	
G-MWLN	Whittaker MW.6-S Fatboy		G-MWOS	Cosmos Chronos	
	Flyer		G-MWOV	Whittaker MW.6 Merlin	
G-MWLO	Whittaker MW.6 Merlin		G-MWOW	CFM Shadow Srs B	
G-MWLP	Mainair Gemini Flash IIA		G-MWOX	Solar Wings Pegasus XL-Q	
G-MWLR	Mainair Gemini Flash IIA		G-MWOY	Solar Wings Pegasus XL-Q	
G-MWLS	Medway Hybred 44XLR		G-MWPA	Mainair Gemini Flash IIA	
G-MWLT	Mainair Gemini Flash IIA		G-MWPB	Mainair Gemini Flash IIA	
G-MWLU	Solar Wings Pegasus XL-R		G-MWPC	Mainair Gemini Flash IIA	
G-MWLW	Team Minimax		G-MWPD	Mainair Gemini Flash IIA	
G-MWLX	Mainair Gemini Flash IIA		G-MWPE	Solar Wings Pegasus XL-Q	
G-MWLY	Rans S.4 Coyote		G-MWPF	Mainair Gemini Flash IIA	
G-MWLZ	Rans S.4 Coyote		G-MWPG	Microflight Spectrum	
G-MWMA	Powerchute Kestrel		G-MWPH	Microflight Spectrum	
G-MWMB	Powerchute Kestrel		G-MWPI	Microflight Spectrum	
G-MWMC	Powerchute Kestrel		G-MWPJ	Solar Wings Pegasus XL-Q	
G-MWMD	Powerchute Kestrel		G-MWPK	Solar Wings Pegasus XL-Q	
G-MWMF	Powerchute Kestrel		G-MWPL	MBA Tiger Cub 440	
G-MWMG	Powerchute Kestrel		G-MWPN	CFM Shadow Srs CD	
G-MWMH	Powerchute Kestrel		G-MWPO	Mainair Gemini Flash IIA	
G-MWMI	SW Pegasus Quasar		G-MWPP	CFM Streak Shadow	
G-MWMJ	SW Pegasus Quasar			(G-BTEM)	
G-MWMK	SW Pegasus Quasar		G-MWPR	Whittaker MW.6 Merlin	

G-MWPS – G-MWXB

Reg.	Type	Notes	Reg.	Type	Notes
G-MWPS	Renegade Spirit UK		G-MWTT	Rans S.6-ESD Coyote II	
G-MWPT	Hunt Wing		G-MWTU	Solar Wings Pegasus XL-R	
G-MWPU	SW Pegasus Quasar TC		G-MWTY	Mainair Gemini Flash IIA	
G-MWPX	Solar Wings Pegasus XL-R		G-MWTZ	Mainair Gemini Flash IIA	
G-MWPZ	Renegade Spirit UK		G-MWUA	CFM Shadow Srs CD	
G-MWRA	Mainair Gemini Flash IIA		G-MWUB	Solar Wings Pegasus XL-R	
G-MWRB	Mainair Gemini Flash IIA		G-MWUC	Solar Wings Pegasus XL-R	
G-MWRC	Mainair Gemini Flash IIA		G-MWUD	Solar Wings Pegasus XL-R	
G-MWRD	Mainair Gemini Flash IIA		G-MWUF	Solar Wings Pegasus XL-R	
G-MWRE	Mainair Gemini Flash IIA		G-MWUG	Solar Wings Pegasus XL-R	
G-MWRF	Mainair Gemini Flash IIA		G-MWUH	Renegade Spirit UK	
G-MWRG	Mainair Gemini Flash IIA		G-MWUI	AMF Chevvron 2-32C	
G-MWRH	Mainair Gemini Flash IIA		G-MWUJ	Medway Hybred 44XLR	
G-MWRI	Mainair Gemini Flash IIA		G-MWUK	Rans S.6-ESD Coyote II	
G-MWRJ	Mainair Gemini Flash IIA		G-MWUL	Rans S.6-ESD Coyote II	
G-MWRK	Rans S.6 Coyote II		G-MWUO	Solar Wings Pegasus XL-Q	
G-MWRL	CFM Shadow Srs CD		G-MWUP	Solar Wings Pegasus XL-R	
G-MWRM	Medway Hybred 44XLR		G-MWUR	Solar Wings Pegasus XL-R	
G-MWRN	Solar Wings Pegasus XL-R		G-MWUS	Solar Wings Pegasus XL-R	
G-MWRO	Solar Wings Pegasus XL-R		G-MWUU	Solar Wings Pegasus XL-R	
G-MWRP	Solar Wings Pegasus XL-R		G-MWUV	Solar Wings Pegasus XL-R	
G-MWRR	Mainair Gemini Flash IIA		G-MWUW	Solar Wings Pegasus XL-R	
G-MWRS	Ultravia Super Pelican		G-MWUX	Solar Wings Pegasus XL-Q	
G-MWRT	Solar Wings Pegasus XL-R		G-MWUY	Solar Wings Pegasus XL-Q	
G-MWRU	Solar Wings Pegasus XL-R		G-MWUZ	Solar Wings Pegasus XL-Q	
G-MWRV	Solar Wings Pegasus XL-R		G-MWVA	Solar Wings Pegasus XL-Q	
G-MWRW	Solar Wings Pegasus XL-Q		G-MWVB	Solar Wings Pegasus XL-R	
G-MWRX	Solar Wings Pegasus XL-Q		G-MWVE	Solar Wings Pegasus XL-R	
G-MWRY	CFM Shadow Srs CD		G-MWVF	Solar Wings Pegasus XL-R	
G-MWRZ	AMF Chevvron 232		G-MWVG	CFM Shadow Srs CD	
G-MWSA	Team Minimax		G-MWVH	CFM Shadow Srs CD	
G-MWSB	Mainair Gemini Flash IIA		G-MWVI	Whittaker MW.6 Merlin	
G-MWSC	Rans S.6-ESD Coyote II		G-MWVK	Mainair Mercury	
G-MWSD	Solar Wings Pegasus XL-Q		G-MWVL	Rans S.6-ESD Coyote II	
G-MWSE	Solar Wings Pegasus XL-R		G-MWVM	SW Pegasus Quasar II	
G-MWSF	Solar Wings Pegasus XL-R		G-MWVN	Mainair Gemini Flash IIA	
G-MWSG	Solar Wings Pegasus XL-R		G-MWVO	Mainair Gemini Flash IIA	
G-MWSH	SW Pegasus Quasar TC		G-MWVP	Renegade Spirit UK	
G-MWSI	SW Pegasus Quasar TC		G-MWVS	Mainair Gemini Flash IIA	
G-MWSJ	Solar Wings Pegasus XL-Q		G-MWVT	Mainair Gemini Flash IIA	
G-MWSK	Solar Wings Pegasus XL-Q		G-MWVU	Medway Hybred 44XLR	
G-MWSL	Mainair Gemini Flash IIA		G-MWVW	Mainair Gemini Flash IIA	
G-MWSM	Mainair Gemini Flash IIA		G-MWVY	Mainair Gemini Flash IIA	
G-MWSN	SW Pegasus Quasar TC		G-MWVZ	Mainair Gemini Flash IIA	
G-MWSO	Solar Wings Pegasus XL-R		G-MWWA	SW Pegasus Quasar II	
G-MWSP	Solar Wings Pegasus XL-R		G-MWWB	Mainair Gemini Flash IIA	
G-MWSR	Solar Wings Pegasus XL-R		G-MWWC	Mainair Gemini Flash IIA	
G-MWSS	Medway Hybred 44XLR		G-MWWD	Mainair Gemini Flash IIA	
G-MWST	Medway Hybred 44XLR		G-MWWE	Team Minimax	
G-MWSU	Medway Hybred 44XLR		G-MWWF	Kolb Twinstar Mk 3	
G-MWSV	SW Pegasus Quasar TC		G-MWWG	Solar Wings Pegasus XL-Q	
G-MWSW	Whittaker MW.6 Merlin		G-MWWH	Solar Wings Pegasus XL-Q	
G-MWSX	Whittaker MW.5 Sorcerer		G-MWWI	Mainair Gemini Flash IIA	
G-MWSY	Whittaker MW.5 Sorcerer		G-MWWJ	Mainair Gemini Flash IIA	
G-MWSZ	CFM Shadow Srs CD		G-MWWK	Mainair Gemini Flash IIA	
G-MWTA	Solar Wings Pegasus XL-Q		G-MWWL	Rans S.6-ESD Coyote II	
G-MWTB	Solar Wings Pegasus XL-Q		G-MWWM	Kolb Twinstar Mk 2	
G-MWTC	Solar Wings Pegasus XL-Q		G-MWWN	Mainair Gemini Flash IIA	
G-MWTD	Microflight Spectrum		G-MWWO	Solar Wings Pegasus XL-R	
G-MWTE	Microflight Spectrum		G-MWWP	Rans S.4 Coyote	
G-MWTF	Mainair Gemini		G-MWWR	Mainair Gemini Flash IIA	
G-MWTG	Mainair Gemini Flash IIA		G-MWWR	Microflight Spectrum	
G-MWTH	Mainair Gemini Flash IIA		G-MWWS	Thruster T.300	
G-MWTI	Solar Wings Pegasus XL-Q		G-MWWT	Thruster Super T.300	
G-MWTJ	CFM Shadow Srs CD		G-MWWU	Air Creation Fun 18 GTBI	
G-MWTK	Solar Wings Pegasus XL-R		G-MWWV	Solar Wings Pegasus XL-Q	
G-MWTL	Solar Wings Pegasus XL-R		G-MWWW	Whittaker MW.6-S Fatboy Flyer	
G-MWTM	Solar Wings Pegasus XL-R		G-MWWX	Microflight Spectrum	
G-MWTN	CFM Shadow Srs CD		G-MWWY	Microflight Spectrum	
G-MWTO	Mainair Gemini Flash IIA		G-MWWZ	Cyclone Chaser S	
G-MWTP	CFM Shadow Srs CD		G-MWXA	Mainair Gemini Flash IIA	
G-MWTR	Mainair Gemini Flash IIA		G-MWXB	Mainair Gemini Flash IIA	
G-MWTS	Whittaker MW.6-S Fatboy Flyer				

Reg.	Type	Notes	Reg.	Type	Notes
G-MWXC	Mainair Gemini Flash IIA		G-MYAG	Quad City Challenger II	
G-MWXD	Mainair Gemini Flash IIA		G-MYAH	Whittaker MW.5 Sorcerer	
G-MWXE	Flexiform Skytrike		G-MYAI	Mainair Mercury	
G-MWXF	Mainair Mercury		G-MYAJ	Rans S.6-ESD Coyote II	
G-MWXG	SW Pegasus Quasar IITC		G-MYAK	SW Pegasus Quasar IITC	
G-MWXH	SW Pegasus Quasar IITC		G-MYAL	Rotec Rally 2B	
G-MWXI	SW Pegasus Quasar IITC		G-MYAM	Renegade Spirit UK	
G-MWXJ	Mainair Mercury		G-MYAN	Whittaker MW.5 (K)	
G-MWXK	Mainair Mercury			Sorcerer	
G-MWXL	Mainair Gemini Flash IIA		G-MYAO	Mainair Gemini Flash IIA	
G-MWXN	Mainair Gemini Flash IIA		G-MYAP	Thruster T.300	
G-MWXO	Mainair Gemini Flash IIA		G-MYAR	Thruster T.300	
G-MWXP	Solar Wings Pegasus XL-Q		G-MYAS	Mainair Gemini Flash IIA	
G-MWXR	Solar Wings Pegasus XL-Q		G-MYAT	Team Minimax	
G-MWXS	Mainair Gemini Flash IIA		G-MYAV	Mainair Mercury	
G-MWXU	Mainair Gemini Flash IIA		G-MYAW	Team Minimax	
G-MWXV	Mainair Gemini Flash IIA		G-MYAY	Microflight Spectrum	
G-MWXW	Cyclone Chaser S		G-MYAZ	Renegade Spirit UK	
G-MWXX	Cyclone Chaser S 447		G-MYBA	Rans S.6-ESD Coyote II	
G-MWXY	Cyclone Chaser S 447		G-MYBB	Maxair Drifter	
G-MWXZ	Cyclone Chaser S 508		G-MYBC	CFM Shadow Srs CD	
G-MWYA	Mainair Gemini Flash IIA		G-MYBD	SW Pegasus Quaser IITC	
G-MWYB	Solar Wings Pegasus XL-Q		G-MYBE	SW Pegasus Quaser IITC	
G-MWYC	Solar Wings Pegasus XL-Q		G-MYBF	Solar Wings Pegasus XL-Q	
G-MWYD	CFM Shadow Srs C		G-MYBG	Solar Wings Pegasus XL-Q	
G-MWYE	Rans S.6-ESD Coyote II		G-MYBH	Quicksilver GT500	
G-MWYF	Rans S.6 Coyote II		G-MYBI	Rans S.6-ESD Coyote II	
G-MWYG	Mainair Gemini Flash IIA		G-MYBJ	Mainair Gemini Flash IIA	
G-MWYH	Mainair Gemini Flash IIA		G-MYBK	SW Pegasus Quasar IITC	
G-MWYI	SW Pegasus Quasar II		G-MYBL	CFM Shadow Srs C	
G-MWYJ	SW Pegasus Quasar IITC		G-MYBM	Team Minimax	
G-MWYL	Mainair Gemini Flash IIA		G-MYBN	Hiway Demon 175	
G-MWYM	Cyclone Chaser S 1000		G-MYBO	Solar Wings Pegasus XL-R	
G-MWYN	Rans S.6-ESD Coyote II		G-MYBP	Solar Wings Pegasus XL-R	
G-MWYS	CGS Hawk 1 Arrow		G-MYBR	Solar Wings Pegasus XL-Q	
G-MWYT	Mainair Gemini Flash IIA		G-MYBS	Solar Wings Pegasus XL-Q	
G-MWYU	Solar Wings Pegasus XL-Q		G-MYBT	SW Pegasus Quasar IITC	
G-MWYV	Mainair Gemini Flash IIA		G-MYBU	Cyclone Chaser S447	
G-MWYX	Mainair Gemini Flash IIA		G-MYBV	Solar Wings Pegasus XL-Q	
G-MWYY	Mainair Gemini Flash IIA		G-MYBW	Solar Wings Pegasus XL-Q	
G-MWYZ	Solar Wings Pegasus XL-Q		G-MYBX	Solar Wings Pegasus XL-Q	
G-MWZA	Mainair Mercury		G-MYBY	Solar Wings Pegasus XL-Q	
G-MWZB	AMF Chevvron 2-32C		G-MYBZ	Solar Wings Pegasus XL-Q	
G-MWZC	Mainair Mercury		G-MYCA	Whittaker MW.6 Merlin	
G-MWZD	SW Pegasus Quasar IITC		G-MYCB	Cyclone Chaser S 447	
G-MWZE	SW Pegasus Quasar IITC		G-MYCD	CFM Shadow Srs CD	
G-MWZF	SW Pegasus Quasar IITC		G-MYCE	SW Pegasus Quasar IITC	
G-MWZG	Mainair Gemini Flash IIA		G-MYCF	SW Pegasus Quasar IITC	
G-MWZH	Solar Wings Pegasus XL-R		G-MYCJ	Mainair Mercury	
G-MWZI	Solar Wings Pegasus XL-R		G-MYCK	Mainair Gemini Flash IIA	
G-MWZJ	Solar Wings Pegasus XL-R		G-MYCL	Mainair Mercury	
G-MWZK	Solar Wings Pegasus XL-R		G-MYCM	CFM Shadow Srs CD	
G-MWZL	Mainair Gemini Flash IIA		G-MYCN	Mainair Mercury	
G-MWZM	Team Minimax 91		G-MYCO	Whittaker MW.6 Merlin	
G-MWZN	Mainair Gemini Flash IIA		G-MYCP	Whittaker MW.6 Merlin	
G-MWZO	SW Pegasus Quasar IITC		G-MYCR	Mainair Gemini Flash IIA	
G-MWZP	SW Pegasus Quasar IITC		G-MYCS	Mainair Gemini Flash IIA	
G-MWZR	SW Pegasus Quasar IITC		G-MYCT	Team Minimax	
G-MWZS	SW Pegasus Quasar IITC		G-MYCV	Mainair Mercury	
G-MWZT	Solar Wings Pegasus XL-R		G-MYCW	Powerchute Kestrel	
G-MWZU	Solar Wings Pegasus XL-R		G-MYCX	Powerchute Kestrel	
G-MWZV	Solar Wings Pegasus XL-R		G-MYCY	Powerchute Kestrel	
G-MWZW	Solar Wings Pegasus XL-R		G-MYCZ	Powerchute Kestrel	
G-MWZX	Solar Wings Pegasus XL-R		G-MYDA	Powerchute Kestrel	
G-MWZY	Solar Wings Pegasus XL-R		G-MYDB	Powerchute Kestrel	
G-MWZZ	Solar Wings Pegasus XL-R		G-MYDC	Mainair Mercury	
			G-MYDD	CFM Shadow Srs CD	
G-MYAA	CFM Shadow Srs CD		G-MYDE	CFM Shadow Srs CD	
G-MYAB	Solar Wings Pegasus XL-R		G-MYDF	Team Minimax	
G-MYAC	Solar Wings Pegasus XL-Q		G-MYDG	Solar Wings Pegasus XL-R	
G-MYAD	Solar Wings Pegasus XL-Q		G-MYDI	Solar Wings Pegasus XL-R	
G-MYAE	Solar Wings Pegasus XL-Q		G-MYDJ	Solar Wings Pegasus XL-R	
G-MYAF	Solar Wings Pegasus XL-Q		G-MYDK	Rans S.6-ESD Coyote II	

Reg.	Type	Notes
G-MYDL	Whittaker MW.5 (K) Sorcerer	
G-MYDM	Whittaker MW.6-S Fatboy Flyer	
G-MYDN	Quad City Challenger II	
G-MYDO	Rans S.5 Coyote	
G-MYDP	Kolb Twinstar Mk 3	
G-MYDR	Thruster Tn.300	
G-MYDS	Quad City Challenger II	
G-MYDT	Thruster T.300	
G-MYDU	Thruster T.300	
G-MYDV	Thruster T.300	
G-MYDW	Whittaker MW.6 Merlin	
G-MYDX	Rans S.6-ESD Coyote II	
G-MYDZ	Mignet HM.1000 Balerit	
G-MYEA	Solar Wings Pegasus XL-Q	
G-MYEC	Solar Wings Pegasus XL-Q	
G-MYED	Solar Wings Pegasus XL-R	
G-MYEE	Thruster TST Mk 1	
G-MYEF	–	
G-MYEG	Solar Wings Pegasus XL-R	
G-MYEH	Solar Wings Pegasus XL-R	
G-MYEI	Cyclone Chaser S447	
G-MYEJ	Cyclone Chaser S447	
G-MYEK	SW Pegasus Quasar IITC	
G-MYEL	SW Pegasus Quasar IITC	
G-MYEM	SW Pegasus Quasar IITC	
G-MYEN	SW Pegasus Quasar IITC	
G-MYEO	SW Pegasus Quasar IITC	
G-MYEP	CFM Shadow Srs CD	
G-MYER	Cyclone AX3/503	
G-MYES	Rans S.6-ESD Coyote II	
G-MYET	Whittaker MW.6 Merlin	
G-MYEU	Mainair Gemini Flash IIA	
G-MYEV	Whittaker MW.6 Merlin	
G-MYEX	Powerchute Kestrel	
G-MYFA	Powerchute Kestrel	
G-MYFE	Rans S.6-ESD Coyote II	
G-MYFF	–	
G-MYFG	Hunt Avon Skytrike	
G-MYFH	Quad City Challenger II	
G-MYFI	Cyclone AX3/503	
G-MYFJ	SW Pegasus Quasar IITC	
G-MYFK	SW Pegasus Quasar IITC	
G-MYFL	SW Pegasus Quasar IITC	
G-MYFM	Renegade Spirit UK	
G-MYFN	Rans S.5 Coyote	
G-MYFO	Cyclone Chaser S	
G-MYFP	Mainair Gemini Flash IIA	
G-MYFR	Mainair Gemini Flash IIA	
G-MYFS	Solar Wings Pegasus XL-R	
G-MYFT	Mainair Scorcher	
G-MYFU	Mainair Gemini Flash IIA	
G-MYFV	Cyclone AX3/503	
G-MYFW	Cyclone AX3/503	
G-MYFX	Solar Wings Pegasus XL-Q	
G-MYFY	Cyclone AX3/503	
G-MYFZ	Cyclone AX3/503	
G-MYGD	Cyclone AX3/503	
G-MYGE	Whittaker MW.6 Merlin	
G-MYGF	Team Minimax	
G-MYGG	Mainair Mercury	
G-MYGH	Rans S.6-ESD Coyote II	
G-MYGI	Cyclone Chaser S 447	
G-MYGJ	Mainair Mercury	
G-MYGK	Cyclone Chaser S 508	
G-MYGL	Team Minimax	
G-MYGM	Quad City Challenger II	
G-MYGN	AMF Chevvron 2-32C	
G-MYGO	CFM Shadow Srs CD	
G-MYGP	Rans S.6-ESD Coyote II	
G-MYGR	Rans S.6-ESD Coyote II	
G-MYGS	Whittaker MW.5 (K) Sorcerer	
G-MYGT	Solar Wings Pegasus XL-R	
G-MYGU	Solar Wings Pegasus XL-R	
G-MYGV	Solar Wings Pegasus XL-R	
G-MYGZ	Mainair Gemini Flash IIA	
G-MYHF	Mainair Gemini Flash IIA	
G-MYHG	Cyclone AX/503	
G-MYHH	Cyclone AX/503	
G-MYHI	Rans S.6-ESD Coyote II	
G-MYHJ	Cyclone AX3/503	
G-MYHK	Rans S.6-ESD Coyote II	
G-MYHL	Mainair Gemini Flash IIA	
G-MYHM	Cyclone AX3/503	
G-MYHN	Mainair Gemini Flash IIA	
G-MYHP	Rans S.6-ESD Coyote II	
G-MYHR	Cyclone AX3/503	
G-MYHS	Powerchute Kestrel	
G-MYHX	Mainair Gemini Flash IIA	
G-MYIA	Quad City Challenger II	
G-MYIE	Whittaker MW.6 Merlin	
G-MYIF	CFM Shadow Srs CD	
G-MYIG	Renegade Spirit	
G-MYIH	Mainair Gemini Flash IIA	
G-MYII	Team Minimax	
G-MYIJ	Cyclone AX3/503	
G-MYIK	Kolb Twinstar Mk 3	
G-MYIL	Cyclone Chaser S 508	
G-MYIN	SW Pegasus Quasar IITC	
G-MYIO	SW Pegasus Quasar IITC	
G-MYIP	CFM Shadow Srs CD	
G-MYIR	Rans S.6-ESD Coyote II	
G-MYIS	Hans S.6-ESD Coyote II	
G-MYIT	Cyclone Chaser S 508	
G-MYIU	Cyclone AX3/503	
G-MYIV	Mainair Gemini Flash IIA	
G-MYIW	Mainair Mercury	
G-MYIX	Quad City Challenger II	
G-MYIY	Mainair Gemini Flash IIA	
G-MYIZ	Team Minimax 2	
G-MYJA	–	
G-MYJB	Mainair Gemini Flash IIA	
G-MYJC	Mainair Gemini Flash IIA	
G-MYJD	Rans S.6-ESD Coyote II	
G-MYJE	CFM Shadow Srs CD	
G-MYJF	Thruster T.300	
G-MYJG	Thruster Super T.300	
G-MYJH	Thruster Super T.300	
G-MYJJ	SW Pegasus Quasar IITC	
G-MYJK	SW Pegasus Quasar IITC	
G-MYJL	Rans S.6-ESD Coyote II	
G-MYJM	Mainair Gemini Flash IIA	
G-MYJN	Mainair Mercury	
G-MYJO	Cyclone Chaser S 508	
G-MYJP	Renegade Spirit UK	
G-MYJR	Mainair Mercury	
G-MYJS	SW Pegasus Quasar IITC	
G-MYJT	SW Pegasus Quasar IITC	
G-MYJU	SW Pegasus Quasar IITC	
G-MYJW	Cyclone Chaser S 508	
G-MYJX	Whittaker MW.8	
G-MYJY	Rans S.6-ESD Coyote II	
G-MYJZ	Whittaker MW.5D Sorcerer	
G-MYKA	Cyclone AX3/503	
G-MYKB	Kölb Twinstar Mk 3	
G-MYKC	Mainair Gemini Flash IIA	
G-MYKD	Cyclone Chaser S 447	
G-MYKE	CFM Shadow Srs BD	
G-MYKF	Cyclone AX3/503	
G-MYKG	Mainair Gemini Flash IIA	
G-MYKH	Mainair Gemini Flash IIA	
G-MYKI	Mainair Mercury	
G-MYKJ	Team Minimax	
G-MYKK	–	
G-MYKL	Medway Raven	

Reg.	Type	Notes	Reg.	Type	Notes
G-MYKM	Medway Raven		G-MYNK	SW Pegasus Quantum 15	
G-MYKN	Rans S.6-ESD Coyote II		G-MYNL	SW Pegasus Quantum 15	
G-MYKO	Whittaker MW.6-S Fat Boy		G-MYNN	SW Pegasus Quantum 15	
	Flyer		G-MYNO	SW Pegasus Quantum 15	
G-MYKP	SW Pegasus Quasar IITC		G-MYNP	SW Pegasus Quantum 15	
G-MYKR	SW Pegasus Quasar IITC		G-MYNR	SW Pegasus Quantum 15	
G-MYKS	SW Pegasus Quasar IITC		G-MYNS	SW Pegasus Quantum 15	
G-MYKT	Cyclone AX3/503		G-MYNT	SW Pegasus Quantum 15	
G-MYKU	Medway Raven		G-MYNU	SW Pegasus Quantum 15	
G-MYKV	Mainair Gemini Flash IIA		G-MYNV	SW Pegasus Quantum 15	
G-MYKW	Mainair Mercury		G-MYNW	Cyclone Chaser S 447	
G-MYKX	Mainair Mercury		G-MYNX	CFM Streak Shadow	
G-MYKY	Mainair Mercury			Srs S-A1	
G-MYKZ	Team Minimax (G-BVAX)		G-MYNY	Kölb Twinstar Mk 3	
G-MYLA	Rans S.6-ESD Coyote II		G-MYNZ	SW Pegasus Quantum 15	
G-MYLB	Team Minimax		G-MYOA	Rans S.6-ESD Coyote II	
G-MYLC	SW Pegasus Quantum 15		G-MYOB	Mainair Mercury	
G-MYLD	Rans S.6-ESD Coyote II		G-MYOE	SW Pegasus Quantum 15	
G-MYLE	SW Pegasus Quantum 15		G-MYOF	Mainair Mercury	
G-MYLF	Rans S.6-ESD Coyote II		G-MYOG	Kölb Twinstar Mk 3	
G-MYLG	Mainair Gemini Flash IIA		G-MYOH	CFM Shadow Srs CD	
G-MYLH	SW Pegasus Quantum 15		G-MYOI	Rans S.6-ESD Coyote II	
G-MYLI	SW Pegasus Quantum 15		G-MYOL	Air Creation Fun 18S	
G-MYLJ	Cyclone Chaser S 447			GTBIS	
G-MYLK	SW Pegasus Quantum 15		G-MYOM	Mainair Gemini Flash IIA	
G-MYLL	SW Pegasus Quantum 15		G-MYON	CFM Shadow Srs CD	
G-MYLM	SW Pegasus Quasar IITC		G-MYOO	Kölb Twinstar Mk 3	
G-MYLN	Kölb Twinstar Mk 3		G-MYOR	Kölb Twinstar Mk 3	
G-MYLO	Rans S.6-ESD Coyote II		G-MYOT	Rans S.6-ESD Coyote II	
G-MYLP	Kölb Twinstar Mk 3		G-MYOU	SW Pegasus Quantum 15	
	(G-BVCR)		G-MYOV	Mainair Mercury	
G-MYLR	Mainair Gemini Flash IIA		G-MYOW	Mainair Gemini Flash IIA	
G-MYLS	Mainair Mercury		G-MYOX	Mainair Mercury	
G-MYLT	Mainair Blade		G-MYOY	Cyclone AX3/503	
G-MYLU	Experience/Hunt Wing		G-MYOZ	Quad City Challenger II UK	
G-MYLV	CFM Shadow Srs CD		G-MYPA	Rans S.6-ESD Coyote II	
G-MYLW	Rans S.6-ESD Coyote II		G-MYPB	Cyclone Chaser S 447	
G-MYLX	Medway Raven		G-MYPC	Kölb Twinstar Mk 3	
G-MYLY	Medway Raven		G-MYPD	Mainair Mercury	
G-MYLZ	SW Pegasus Quantum 15		G-MYPE	Mainair Gemini Flash IIA	
G-MYMB	SW Pegasus Quantum 15		G-MYPF	SW Pegasus Quasar IITC	
G-MYMC	SW Pegasus Quantum 15		G-MYPG	SW Pegasus XL-Q	
G-MYMD	SW Pegasus Quantum 15		G-MYPH	SW Pegasus Quantum 15	
G-MYME	Cyclone AX3/503		G-MYPI	SW Pegasus Quantum 15	
G-MYMF	Cyclone AX3/503		G-MYPJ	Rans S.6-ESD Coyote II	
G-MYMG	Team Minimax		G-MYPK	Rans S.6-ESD Coyote II	
G-MYMH	Rans S.6-ESD Coyote II		G-MYPL	CFM Shadow Srs CD	
G-MYMI	Kölb Twinstar Mk 3		G-MYPM	Cyclone AX3/503	
G-MYMJ	Medway Raven		G-MYPN	SW Pegasus Quantum 15	
G-MYMK	Mainair Gemini Flash IIA		G-MYPO	Hunt Wing/Experience	
G-MYML	Mainair Mercury		G-MYPP	Whittaker MW.6-S Fatboy	
G-MYMM	Ultraflight Fun 18S			Flyer	
G-MYMN	Whittaker MW.6 Merlin		G-MYPR	Cyclone AX3/503	
G-MYMO	Mainair Gemini Flash IIA		G-MYPS	Whittaker MW.6 Merlin	
G-MYMP	Rans S.6-ESD Coyote II		G-MYPT	CFM Shadow Srs CD	
	(G-CHAZ)		G-MYPU	Microchute UQ	
G-MYMR	Rans S.6-ESD Coyote II		G-MYPV	Mainair Mercury	
G-MYMS	Rans S.6-ESD Coyote II		G-MYPW	Mainair Gemini Flash IIA	
G-MYMT	Mainair Mercury		G-MYPX	SW Pegasus Quantum 15	
G-MYMV	Mainair Gemini Flash IIA		G-MYPY	SW Pegasus Quantum 15	
G-MYMW	Cyclone AX3/503		G-MYPZ	Quad City Challenger II	
G-MYMX	SW Pegasus Quantum 15		G-MYRA	Kölb Twinstar Mk 3	
G-MYMY	Cyclone Chaser S 508		G-MYRB	Whittaker MW.5 Sorcerer	
G-MYMZ	Cyclone AX3/503		G-MYRC	Mainair Blade	
G-MYNA	CFM Shadow Srs BD		G-MYRD	Mainair Blade	
G-MYNB	SW Pegasus Quantum 15		G-MYRE	Cyclone Chaser S	
G-MYNC	Mainair Mercury		G-MYRF	SW Pegasus Quantum 15	
G-MYND	Mainair Gemini Flash IIA		G-MYRG	Team Minimax	
G-MYNE	Rans S.6-ESD Coyote II		G-MYRH	Quad City Challenger II	
G-MYNF	Mainair Mercury		G-MYRI	Medway 44XLR	
G-MYNH	Rans S.6-ESD Coyote II		G-MYRJ	Quad City Challenger II	
G-MYNI	Team Minimax		G-MYRK	Renegade Spirit UK	
G-MYNJ	Mainair Mercury		G-MYRL	Team Minimax	

Reg.	Type	Notes	Reg.	Type	Notes
G-MYRM	SW Pegasus Quantum 15		G-MYUN	Mainair Blade	
G-MYRN	SW Pegasus Quantum 15		G-MYUO	Cycl Pegasus Quantum 15	
G-MYRO	Cyclone AX3/503		G-MYUP	Letov LK-2M Sluka	
G-MYRP	Letov LK-2M Sluka		G-MYUR	Hunt Wing	
G-MYRR	Letov LK-2M Sluka		G-MYUS	CFM Shadow Srs CD	
G-MYRS	SW Pegasus Quantum 15		G-MYUT	Hunt Wing	
G-MYRT	SW Pegasus Quantum 15		G-MYUU	Cycl Pegasus Quantum 15	
G-MYRU	Cyclone AX3/503		G-MYUV	Cycl Pegasus Quantum 15	
G-MYRV	Cyclone AX3/503		G-MYUW	Mainair Mercury	
G-MYRW	Mainair Mercury		G-MYUY	Microchute UQ	
G-MYRX	Mainair Gemini Flash IIA		G-MYUZ	Rans S.6-ESD Coyote II	
G-MYRY	SW Pegasus Quantum 15		G-MYVA	Kolb Twinstar Mk 3	
G-MYRZ	SW Pegasus Quantum 15		G-MYVB	Mainair Blade	
G-MYSA	Cyclone Chaser S 508		G-MYVC	Cycl Pegasus Quantum 15	
G-MYSB	SW Pegasus Quantum 15		G-MYVE	Mainair Blade	
G-MYSC	SW Pegasus Quantum 15		G-MYVF	Cycl Pegasus Quantum 15	
G-MYSD	Quad City Challenger II		G-MYVG	Letov LK-2M Sluka	
G-MYSG	Mainair Mercury		G-MYVH	Mainair Mercury	
G-MYSH	Mainair Blade		G-MYVI	Air Creation Fun 18S	
G-MYSI	HM14/93			GTBIS	
G-MYSJ	Mainair Gemini Flash IIA		G-MYVJ	Cycl Pegasus Quantum 15	
G-MYSK	Team Minimax		G-MYVK	Cycl Pegasus Quantum 15	
G-MYSL	Aviasud Mistral		G-MYVL	Mainair Mercury	
G-MYSM	CFM Shadow Srs CD		G-MYVM	Cycl Pegasus Quantum 15	
G-MYSN	Whittaker MW.6 Merlin		G-MYVN	Cyclone AX3/503	
G-MYSO	Cyclone AX3/503		G-MYVO	Mainair Blade	
G-MYSP	Rans S.6-ESD Coyote II		G-MYVP	Rans S.6-ESD Coyote II	
G-MYSR	SW Pegasus Quatum 15		G-MYVR	Cycl Pegasus Quantum 15	
G-MYST	Aviasud Mistral		G-MYVS	Mainair Mercury	
G-MYSU	Rans S.6-ESD Coyote II		G-MYVT	Letov LK-2M Sluka	
G-MYSV	Aerial Arts Chaser		G-MYVU	Medway Raven	
G-MYSW	SW Pegasus Quantum 15		G-MYVV	Medway Hybred 44XLR	
G-MYSX	SW Pegasus Quantum 15		G-MYVW	Medway Raven	
G-MYSY	SW Pegasus Quantum 15		G-MYVX	Medway Hybred 44XLR	
G-MYSZ	Mainair Mercury		G-MYVY	Mainair Blade	
G-MYTA	Team Minimax		G-MYVZ	Maianir Blade	
G-MYTB	Mainair Mercury		G-MYWA	Mainair Mercury	
G-MYTC	SW Pegasus XL-Q		G-MVWB	Corniche/Scorpion	
G-MYTD	Mainair Blade		G-MYWC	Hunt Wing	
G-MYTE	Rans S.6-ESD Coyote II		G-MYWD	Thruster T.600	
G-MYTG	Mainair Blade		G-MYWE	Thruster T.600	
G-MYTH	CFM Shadow Srs CD		G-MYWF	CFM Shadow Srs CD	
G-MYTI	Cycl Pegasus Quantum 15		G-MYWG	Cycl Pegasus Quantum 15	
G-MYTJ	SW Pegasus Quantum 15		G-MYWH	Hunt Wing/Experience	
G-MYTK	Mainair Mercury		G-MYWI	Cycl Pegasus Quantum 15	
G-MYTL	Mainair Blade		G-MYWJ	Cycl Pegasus Quantum 15	
G-MYTM	Cyclone AX3/503		G-MYWK	Cycl Pegasus Quantum 15	
G-MYTN	SW Pegasus Quantum 15		G-MYWL	Cycl Pegasus Quantum 15	
G-MYTO	Quad City Challenger II		G-MYWM	CFM Shadow Srs CD	
G-MYTP	Arrowflight Hawk II		G-MYWN	Cyclone Chaser S 508	
G-MYTR	Cycl Pegasus Quantum 15		G-MYWO	Cycl Pegasus Quantum 15	
G-MYTS	Hunt Avon Trike		G-MYWP	Kolb Twinstar Mk 3	
G-MYTT	Quad City Challenger II		G-MYWR	Cycl Pegasus Quantum 15	
G-MYTU	Mainair Blade		G-MYWS	Cyclone Chaser S 447	
G-MYTV	Hunt Avon Skytrike		G-MYWT	Cycl Pegasus Quantum 15	
G-MYTW	Mainair Blade		G-MYWU	Cycl Pegasus Quantum 15	
G-MYTX	Mainair Mercury		G-MYWV	Rans S.4 Coyote	
G-MYTY	CFM Streak Shadow Srs M		G-MYWW	Cycl Pegasus Quantum 15	
G-MYTZ	Air Creation Fun 18S		G-MYWX	Cycl Pegasus Quantum 15	
	GTBIS		G-MYWY	Cycl Pegasus Quantum 15	
G-MYUA	Air Creation Fun 18S		G-MYWZ	Thruster TST Mk 1	
	GTBIS		G-MYXA	Team Minimax 91	
G-MYUB	Mainair Mercury		G-MYXB	Rans S.6-ESD Coyote II	
G-MYUC	Mainair Blade		G-MYXC	Quad City Challenger II	
G-MYUD	Mainair Mercury		G-MYXD	Cycl Pegasus Quasar IITC	
G-MYUE	Mainair Mercury		G-MYXE	Cycl Pegasus Quantum 15	
G-MYUF	Renegade Spirit		G-MYXF	Air Creation Fun GT503	
G-MYUG	Hunt Avon Skytrike		G-MYXG	Rans S.6-ESD Coyote II	
G-MYUH	SW Pegasus XL-Q		G-MYXH	Cyclone AX3/503	
G-MYUJ	Maverick		G-MYXI	Aries 1	
G-MYUK	Mainair Mercury		G-MYXJ	Mainair Blade	
G-MYUL	Quad City Challenger II		G-MYXK	Quad City Challenger II	
G-MYUM	Mainair Blade		G-MYXL	Mignet HM.1000 Balerit	

Reg.	Type	Notes	Reg.	Type	Notes
G-MYXM	Mainair Blade		G-MZAH	Rans S.6-ESD Coyote II	
G-MYXN	Mainair Blade		G-MZAI	Mainair Blade	
G-MYXO	Letov LK-2M Sluka		G-MZAJ	Mainair Blade	
G-MYXP	Rans S.6-ESD Coyote II		G-MZAK	Mainair Mercury	
G-MYXR	Renegade Spirit UK		G-MZAL	Mainair Blade	
G-MYXS	Kolb Twinstar Mk 3		G-MZAM	Mainair Blade	
G-MYXT	Cycl Pegasus Quantum 15		G-MZAN	Cycl Pegasus Quantum 15	
G-MYXU	Thruster T.300		G-MZAO	Mainair Blade 912	
G-MYXV	Quad City Challenger II		G-MZAP	Mainair Blade	
G-MYXW	Cycl Pegasus Quantum 15		G-MZAR	Mainair Blade	
G-MYXX	Cycl Pegasus Quantum 15		G-MZAS	Mainair Blade	
G-MYXY	CFM Shadow Srs CD		G-MZAT	Mainair Blade	
G-MYXZ	Cycl Pegasus Quantum 15		G-MZAU	Mainair Blade	
G-MYYA	Mainair Blade		G-MZAV	Mainair Blade	
G-MYYB	Cycl Pegasus Quantum 15		G-MZAW	Cycl Pegasus Quantum 15	
G-MYYC	Cycl Pegasus Quantum 15		G-MZAX	Cycl Pegasus Quantum 15	
G-MYYD	Cyclone Chaser S 447		G-MZAY	Mainair Blade	
G-MYYE	Hunt Wing		G-MZAZ	Mainair Blade	
G-MYYF	Quad City Challenger II		G-MZBA	Mainair Blade 912	
G-MYYG	Mainair Blade		G-MZBB	Cycl Pegasus Quantum 15	
G-MYYH	Mainair Blade		G-MZBC	Cycl Pegasus Quantum 15	
G-MYYI	Cycl Pegasus Quantum 15		G-MZBD	Rans S.6-ESD Coyote II	
G-MYYJ	Hunt Wing		G-MZBE	CFM Streak Shadow Srs SA-M	
G-MYYK	Cycl Pegasus Quantum 15				
G-MYYL	Cyclone AX3/503		G-MZBF	Letov LK-2M Sluka	
G-MYYM	Microchute Motor 27		G-MZBG	Whittaker MW.6-S Fatboy Flyer	
G-MYYN	Cycl Pegasus Quantum 15				
G-MYYO	Medway Raven X		G-MZBH	Rans S.6-ESD Coyote II	
G-MYYP	AMF Chevvron 2-45CS		G-MZBI	Cycl Pegasus Quantum 15	
G-MYYR	Team Minimax 91		G-MZBJ	Cyclone Chaser S 508	
G-MYYS	Team Minimax		G-MZBK	Letov LK-2M Sluka	
G-MYYT	Hunt Wing		G-MZBL	Mainair Blade	
G-MYYU	Mainair Mercury		G-MZBM	Cycl Pegasus Quantum 15	
G-MYYV	Rans S.6-ESD Coyote IIXL		G-MZBN	CFM Shadow Srs BD	
G-MYYW	Mainair Blade		G-MZBO	Cycl Pegasus Quantum 15	
G-MYYX	Cycl Pegasus Quantum 15		G-MZBP	Microchute UQ/Motor 27	
G-MYYY	Mainair Blade		G-MZBR	Southdown Raven	
G-MYYZ	Medway Raven X		G-MZBS	CFM Shadow Srs D	
G-MYZA	Whittaker MW.6 Merlin		G-MZBT	Cycl Pegasus Quantum 15	
G-MYZB	Cycl Pegasus Quantum 15		G-MZBU	Rans S.6-ESD Coyote II	
G-MYZC	Cyclone AX3/503		G-MZBV	Rans S.6-ESD Coyote II	
G-MYZD	Cycl Pegasus Quantum 15		G-MZBW	Quad City Challenger II UK	
G-MYZE	Team Minimax		G-MZBX	Whittaker MW.6-S Fatboy Flyer	
G-MYZF	Cyclone AX3/503				
G-MYZG	Cyclone AX3/503		G-MZBY	Cycl Pegasus Quantum 15	
G-MYZH	Chargus Titan 38		G-MZBZ	Quad City Challenger II UK	
G-MYZI	RL-5A LW Sherwood Ranger		G-MZCA	Rans S.6-ESD Coyote II	
			G-MZCB	Cyclone Chaser S 447	
G-MYZJ	Cycl Pegasus Quantum 15		G-MZCC	Mainair Blade 912	
G-MYZK	Cycl Pegasus Quantum 15		G-MZCD	Mainair Blade	
G-MYZL	Cycl Pegasus Quantum 15		G-MZCE	Mainair Blade	
G-MYZM	Cycl Pegasus Quantum 15		G-MZCF	Mainair Blade	
G-MYZN	Whittaker MW.6-S Fatboy Flyer		G-MZCG	Mainair Blade	
			G-MZCH	Whittaker MW.6-S Fatboy Flyer	
G-MYZO	Medway Ravem X				
G-MYZP	CFM Shadow Srs DD		G-MZCI	Cycl Pegasus Quantum 15	
G-MYZR	Rans S.6-ESD Coyote II		G-MZCJ	Cycl Pegasus Quantum 15	
G-MYZS	Airware Rave		G-MZCK	AMF Chevvron 2-32C	
G-MYZT	Airware Rave		G-MZCL	Ultrasports Tri-Pacer	
G-MYZU	Airware Rave		G-MZCM	Cycl Pegasus Quantum 15	
G-MYZV	Rans S.6-ESD Coyote II		G-MZCN	Mainair Blade	
G-MYZW	Cyclone Chaser S 508		G-MZCO	Mainair Mercury	
G-MYZX	Cyclone Chaser S 508		G-MZCP	SW Pegasus XL-Q	
G-MYZY	Cycl Pegasus Quantum 15		G-MZCR	Cycl Pegasus Quantum 15	
G-MYZZ	Cycl Pegasus Quantum 15		G-MZCS	Team Minimax	
			G-MZCT	CFM Shadow Srs CD	
G-MZAA	Mainair Blade		G-MZCU	Mainair Blade	
G-MZAB	Mainair Blade		G-MZCV	Cycl Pegasus Quantum 15	
G-MZAC	Quad City Challenger II		G-MZCW	Cycl Pegasus Quantum 15	
G-MZAD	Mainair Blade 912		G-MZCX	Hunt Wing	
G-MZAE	Mainair Blade		G-MZCY	Cycl Pegasus Quantum 15	
G-MZAF	Mainair Blade		G-MZCZ	Hunt Wing	
G-MZAG	Mainair Blade		G-MZDA	Rans S.6-ESD Coyote IIXL	

Reg.	Type	Notes	Reg.	Type	Notes
G-MZDB	Cycl Pegasus Quantum 15		G-MZFF	Hunt Wing	
G-MZDC			G-MZFG	Cycl Pegasus Quantum 15	
G-MZDD	Cycl Pegasus Quantum 15		G-MZFH	—	
G-MZDE	Cycl Pegasus Quantum 15		G-MZFI	Iolaire	
G-MZDF	Mainair Blade		G-MZFJ	—	
G-MZDG	Rans S.6-ESD Coyote IIXL		G-MZFK	—	
G-MZDH	Cycl Pegasus Quantum 15		G-MZFL	—	
G-MZDI	Whittaker MW.6-S Fatboy		G-MZFM	—	
	Flyer		G-MZFN	—	
G-MZDJ	Medway Raven X		G-MZFO	—	
G-MZDK	Mainair Blade		G-MZFP	—	
G-MZDL	Whittaker MW.6-S Fatboy		G-MZFR	—	
	Flyer		G-MZFS	Mainair Blade	
G-MZDM	Rans S.6-ESD Coyote II		G-MZFT	Cycl Pegasus Quantum 15	
G-MZDN	Cycl Pegasus Quantum 15		G-MZFU	—	
G-MZDO	Cyclone AX3/503		G-MZFV	—	
G-MZDP	AMF Chevvron 2-32		G-MZFW	Mainair Rapier	
G-MZDR	Rans S.6-ESD Coyote IIXL		G-MZFX	—	
G-MZDS	Cyclone AX3/503		G-MZFY	—	
G-MZDT	Mainair Blade		G-MZFZ	—	
G-MZDU	Cycl Pegasus Quantum 15		G-MZGA	Cyclone AX2000	
G-MZDV	Cycl Pegasus Quantum 15		G-MZGB	Cyclone AX2000	
G-MZDW	Microchute UQ		G-MZGC	Cyclone AX2000	
G-MZDX	Letov LK-2M Sluka		G-MZGD	—	
G-MZDY	Cycl Pegasus Quantum 15		G-MZGE	—	
G-MZDZ	Hunt Wing		G-MZGF	—	
G-MZEA	Quad City Challenger II UK		G-MZGG	—	
G-MZEB	Mainair Blade		G-MZGH	Hunt Wing	
G-MZEC	Cycl Pegasus Quantum 15		G-MZGI	—	
G-MZED	Mainair Blade		G-MZGJ	—	
G-MZEE	Cycl Pegasus Quantum 15		G-MZGK	—	
G-MZEF	Mainair Blade		G-MZGL	Mainair Rapier	
G-MZEG	Mainair Blade		G-MZHM	Team Himax 1700R	
G-MZEH	Cycl Pegasus Quantum 15		G-MZIP	Renegade Spirit UK	
G-MZEI	Whittaker MW.5-D Sorcerer		G-MZIZ	Renegade Spirit UK	
G-MZEJ	Mainair Blade			(G-MWGP)	
G-MZEK	Mainair Mercury		G-MZJK	Mainair Blade	
G-MZEL	Cyclone AX3/503		G-MZKJ	Mainair Blade	
G-MZEM	Cycl Pegasus Quantum 15		G-MZKW	Quad City Challenger II	
G-MZEN	Rans S.6-ESD Coyote II		G-MZMA	SW Pegasus Quasar IITC	
G-MZEO	Rans S.6-ESD Coyote IIXL		G-MZMC	Cycl Pegasus Quatum 15	
G-MZEP	Mainair Rapier		G-MZMW	Mignet HM.1000 Balerit	
G-MZER	Cyclone AX2000		G-MZMZ	Mainair Blade	
G-MZES	Letov LK-2N Sluka		G-MZPB	Mignet HM.1000 Balerit	
G-MZET	Cycl Pegasus Quantum 15		G-MZPD	Cycl Pegasus Quantum 15	
G-MZEU	Rans S.6-ESD Coyote IIXL		G-MZPJ	Team Minimax	
G-MZEV	Mainair Rapier		G-MZPW	Cycl Pegasus Quantum 15	
G-MZEW	Mainair Blade		G-MZRH	Cycl Pegasus Quantum 15	
G-MZEX	Cycl Pegasus Quantum 15		G-MZRS	CFM Shadow Srs CD	
G-MZEY	Micro Bantam B.22		G-MZSM	Mainair Blade	
G-MZEZ	Cycl Pegasus Quantum 15		G-MZTA	Mignet HM.1000 Balerit	
G-MZFA	Cyclone AX2000		G-MZTS	Aerial Arts Chaser S	
G-MZFB	Mainair Blade			(G-MVDM)	
G-MZFC	Letov LK-2M Sluka		G-MZZY	Mainair Blade 912	
G-MZFD	Mainair Rapier		G-MZZZ	Whittakers MW.6-S Fatboy	
G-MZFE	Hunt Wing			Flyer	

G-ARHW, D.H.104 Dove 8.

G-BWIR, Dornier Do.328-100 of Suckling Airways.

G-DAKK, Douglas DC-3 of South Coast Airways.

G-OTAF, Aero L-39ZO Albatross.

G-RMCT, Short SD3-60 Variant 100.

G-UKLI, Boeing 767-39HER of Leisure International.

Overseas Airliner Registrations

(Aircraft included in this section are those most likely to be seen at UK
and major European airports on scheduled or charter services.)

Reg.	Type	Owner or Operator	Notes

A4O (Oman)

A4O-GH	Boeing 767-3P6ER (603)	Gulf Air	
A4O-GI	Boeing 767-3P6ER (604)	Gulf Air	
A4O-GJ	Boeing 767-3P6ER (605)	Gulf Air *Al Muharraq*	
A4O-GK	Boeing 767-3P6ER (606)	Gulf Air	
A4O-GL	Boeing 767-3P6ER (607)	Gulf Air *Musandam*	
A4O-GM	Boeing 767-3P6ER (608)	Gulf Air	
A4O-GN	Boeing 767-3P6ER (609)	Gulf Air	
A4O-GO	Boeing 767-3P6ER (610)	Gulf Air	
A4O-GP	Boeing 767-3P6ER (611)	Gulf Air	
A4O-GR	Boeing 767-3P6ER (612)	Gulf Air *A'Rostaq*	
A4O-GS	Boeing 767-3P6ER (613)	Gulf Air	
A4O-GT	Boeing 767-3P6ER (614)	Gulf Air *Auwakrah*	
A4O-GU	Boeing 767-3P6ER (615)	Gulf Air	
A4O-GV	Boeing 767-3P6ER (616)	Gulf Air *Doha*	
A4O-GW	Boeing 767-3P6ER (617)	Gulf Air *Muscat*	
A4O-GY	Boeing 767-3P6ER (619)	Gulf Air	
A4O-GZ	Boeing 767-3P6ER (620)	Gulf Air	
A4O-LA	Airbus A.340-312	Gulf Air *Dhofar*	
A4O-LB	Airbus A.340-312	Gulf Air *Al Fateh*	
A4O-LC	Airbus A.340-312	Gulf Air *Doha*	
A4O-LD	Airbus A.340-312	Gulf Air/Philippine Airlines	
A4O-LE	Airbus A.340-312	Gulf Air/EgyptAir	
A4O-LF	Airbus A.340-312	Gulf Air	
A4O-SO	Boeing 747SP-27	Oman Royal Flight	
A4O-SP	Boeing 747SP-27	Oman Government	
A4O-TA	L.1011-385 TriStar 200 (105)	Gulf Air	
A4O-TB	L.1011-385 TriStar 200 (106)	Gulf Air	
A4O-TT	L.1011-385 TriStar 200 (107)	Gulf Air	
A4O-TV	L.1011-385 TriStar 200 (108)	Gulf Air	
A4O-TZ	L.1011-385 TriStar 200 (104)	Gulf Air	

A6 (United Arab Emirates)

A6-EKA	Airbus A.310-304	Emirate Airlines	
A6-EKB	Airbus A.310-304	Emirate Airlines	
A6-EKC	Airbus A.300-605R	Emirate Airlines	
A6-EKD	Airbus A.300-605R	Emirate Airlines	
A6-EKE	Airbus A.300-605R	Emirate Airlines	
A6-EKF	Airbus A.300-605R	Emirate Airlines	
A6-EKG	Airbus A.310-308	Emirate Airlines	
A6-EKH	Airbus A.310-308	Emirate Airlines	
A6-EKI	Airbus A.310-308	Emirate Airlines	
A6-EKJ	Airbus A.310-308	Emirate Airlines	
A6-EKK	Airbus A.310-308	Emirate Airlines	
A6-EKL	Airbus A.310-308	Emirate Airlines	
A6-EKM	Airbus A.300-605R	Emirate Airlines	
A6-EKN	Airbus A.310-308	Emirate Airlines	
A6-EKO	Airbus A.300-605R	Emirate Airlines	
A6-EKP	Airbus A.310-308	Emirate Airlines	
A6-EMD	Boeing 777-21H	Emirate Airlines	
A6-EME	Boeing 777-21H	Emirate Airlines	
A6-EMF	Boeing 777-21H	Emirate Airlines	
A6-EMG	Boeing 777-21H	Emirate Airlines	
A6-EMH	Boeing 777-21H	Emirate Airlines	
A6-EMI	Boeing 777-21H	Emirate Airlines	
A6-EMJ	Boeing 777-21H	Emirate Airlines	

Notes	Reg.	Type	Owner or Operator

A7 (Qatar)

A7-AAA	Boeing 707-3P1C	Qatar Government
A7-ABK	Boeing 747SR-81	Qatar Airways
A7-ABL	Boeing 747SR-81	Qatar Airways
A7-AHM	Boeing 747SP-27	Qatar Government
A7-HHK	Airbus A.340-211	Qatar Government

AP (Pakistan)

AP-AXG	Boeing 707-340C	Pakistan International Airlines
AP-AYV	Boeing 747-282B	Pakistan International Airlines
AP-AYW	Boeing 747-282B	Pakistan International Airlines
AP-BAK	Boeing 747-240B (SCD)	Pakistan International Airlines
AP-BAT	Boeing 747-240B (SCD)	Pakistan International Airlines
AP-BBK	Boeing 707-323C	Pakistan International Airlines
AP-BCL	Boeing 747-217B	Pakistan International Airlines
AP-BCM	Boeing 747-217B	Pakistan International Airlines
AP-BCN	Boeing 747-217B	Pakistan International Airlines
AP-BCO	Boeing 747-217B	Pakistan International Airlines
AP-BDZ	Airbus A.310-308	Pakistan International Airlines
AP-BEB	Airbus A.310-308	Pakistan International Airlines
AP-BEC	Airbus A.310-308	Pakistan International Airlines
AP-BEG	Airbus A.310-308	Pakistan International Airlines
AP-BEQ	Airbus A.310-308	Pakistan International Airlines
AP-BEU	Airbus A.310-308	Pakistan International Airlines

B (China/Taiwan)

B-150	McD Douglas MD-11	China Airlines
B-151	McD Douglas MD-11	China Airlines
B-152	McD Douglas MD-11	China Airlines
B-153	McD Douglas MD-11	China Airlines
B-160	Boeing 747-209F (SCD)	China Airlines
B-161	Boeing 747-409	China Airlines
B-162	Boeing 747-409	China Airlines
B-163	Boeing 747-409	China Airlines
B-164	Boeing 747-409	China Airlines
B-1862	Boeing 747SP-09	China Airlines
B-1864	Boeing 747-209B (SCD)	China Airlines
B-1866	Boeing 747-209B	China Airlines
B-1880	Boeing 747SP-09	China Airlines
B-1886	Boeing 747-209B	China Airlines
B-1888	Boeing 747-209B	China Airlines
B-1894	Boeing 747-209F (SCD)	China Airlines
B-2438	Boeing 747SP-J6	Air China
B-2442	Boeing 747SP-J6	Air China
B-2443	Boeing 747-4J6	Air China
B-2445	Boeing 747-4J6	Air China
B-2446	Boeing 747-2J6B (SCD)	Air China
B-2447	Boeing 747-4J6	Air China
B-2448	Boeing 747-2J6B (SCD)	Air China
B-2450	Boeing 747-2J6B (SCD)	Air China
B-2452	Boeing 747SP-J6	Air China
B-2454	Boeing 747SP-27	Air China
B-2456	Boeing 747-4J6 (SCD)	Air China
B-2458	Boeing 747-4J6 (SCD)	Air China
B-2460	Boeing 747-4J6 (SCD)	Air China
B-2462	Boeing 747-2J6F (SCD)	Air China
B-2464	Boeing 747-4J6	Air China
B-2466	Boeing 747-4J6	Air China
B-16401	Boeing 747-45E	EVA Airways
B-16402	Boeing 747-45E	EVA Airways
B-16461	Boeing 747-45E (SCD)	EVA Airways
B-16462	Boeing 747-45E (SCD)	EVA Airways
B-16463	Boeing 747-45E (SCD)	EVA Airways
B-16465	Boeing 747-45E (SCD)	EVA Airways

Note: China Airlines also operates N4508H and N4522V, both Boeing 747SP-09s. EVA Airways operates Boeing 747-45Es which retain the US registrations N403EV, N405EV, N406EV, N407EV, N408EV and N409EV.

Reg.	Type	Owner or Operator	Notes

C-F and C-G (Canada)

C-FBCA	Boeing 747-475 (884)	Canadian Airlines International Grant McConachie	
C-FBEF	Boeing 767-233ER (617)	Air Canada	
C-FBEG	Boeing 767-233ER (618)	Air Canada	
C-FBEM	Boeing 767-233ER (619)	Air Canada	
C-FCAB	Boeing 767-375ER (631)	Canadian Airlines International	
C-FCAE	Boeing 767-375ER (632)	Canadian Airlines International	
C-FCAF	Boeing 767-375ER (633)	Canadian Airlines International	
C-FCAG	Boeing 767-375ER (634)	Canadian Airlines International	
C-FCAJ	Boeing 767-375ER (635)	Canadian Airlines International	
C-FCAU	Boeing 767-375ER (636)	Canadian Airlines International	
C-FCRA	Boeing 747-475 (882)	Canadian Airlines International T. Russ Baker	
C-FCRD	Douglas DC-10-30 (912)	Canadian Airlines International Pride of Canadian	
C-FCRE	Douglas DC-10-30 (911)	Canadian Airlines International	
C-FGHZ	Boeing 747-4F6 (885)	Canadian Airlines International	
C-FMWP	Boeing 767-333ER (631)	Air Canada	
C-FMWQ	Boeing 767-333ER (632)	Air Canada	
C-FMWU	Boeing 767-333ER (633)	Air Canada	
C-FMWV	Boeing 767-333ER (634)	Air Canada	
C-FMWY	Boeing 767-333ER (635)	Air Canada	
C-FMXC	Boeing 767-333ER (636)	Air Canada	
C-FOCA	Boeing 767-375ER (640)	Canadian Airlines International	
C-FOOA	Boeing 757-28A	Canada 3000/Air 2000 (G-OOOA)	
C-FOOB	Boeing 757-28A	Canada 3000/Air 2000 (G-OOOB)	
C-FOOE	Boeing 757-28A	Canada 3000 Airlines	
C-FOOG	Boeing 757-23A	Canada 3000/Air 2000 (G-OOOG)	
C-FOOH	Boeing 757-23A	Canada 3000 Airlines	
C-FOON	Boeing 757-28A	Canada 3000 Airlines	
C-FPCA	Boeing 767-375ER (637)	Canadian Airlines International	
C-FTCA	Boeing 767-375ER (638)	Canadian Airlines International	
C-FTNA	L.1011-385 TriStar 150 (501)	Air Transat	
C-FTNB	L.1011-385 TriStar 150 (549)	Air Transat	
C-FTNC	L.1011-385 TriStar 150 (503)	Air Transat	
C-FTNH	L.1011-385 TriStar 150 (508)	Air Transat	
C-FTNI	L.1011-385 TriStar 100	Royal Airlines	
C-FTNK	L.1011-385 TriStar 100	Royal Airlines	
C-FTNL	L.1011-385 TriStar 100	Air Transat	
C-FTNP	Airbus A.340-313 (982)	Air Canada	
C-FTNQ	Airbus A.340-313 (981)	Air Canada	
C-FTOC	Boeing 747-133 (303)	Air Canada	
C-FTOD	Boeing 747-133 (304)	Air Canada	
C-FTOE	Boeing 747-133 (305)	Air Canada	
C-FUCL	Boeing 767-209ER (622)	Air Canada	
C-FVNM	Boeing 767-209ER (621)	Air Canada	
C-FWCR	L.1011-385 TriStar 1	Air Transat	
C-FXCA	Boeing 767-375ER (639)	Canadian Airlines International	
C-FXOC	Boeing 757-28A	Canada 3000/Air 2000 (G-OOOC)	
C-FXOF	Boeing 757-28A	Canada 3000 Airlines	
C-FXOK	Boeing 757-23A	Canada 3000 Airlines	
C-FXOO	Boeing 757-2Q8	Canada 3000 Airlines	
C-FYKX	Airbus A.340-313X	Air Canada	
C-FYKZ	Airbus A.340-313X	Air Canada	
C-FYLC	Airbus A.340-313X	Air Canada	
C-FYLD	Airbus A.340-313X	Air Canada	
C-FYLG	Airbus A.340-313X	Air Canada	
C-FYLU	Airbus A.340-313X	Air Canada	
C-GAGA	Boeing 747-233B (SCD) (306)	Air Canada	
C-GAGB	Boeing 747-233B (SCD) (307)	Air Canada	
C-GAGC	Boeing 747-238B (SCD) (308)	Air Canada	
C-GAGL	Boeing 747-433 (SCD) (341)	Air Canada	
C-GAGM	Boeing 747-433 (SCD) (342)	Air Canada	
C-GAGN	Boeing 747-433 (SCD) (343)	Air Canada	
C-GAUY	Boeing 767-233ER (609)	Air Canada	
C-GAVA	Boeing 767-233ER (610)	Air Canada	
C-GAVC	Boeing 767-233ER (611)	Air Canada	
C-GAVF	Boeing 767-233ER (612)	Air Canada	
C-GCIL	Airbus A.310-324	Air Club International	
C-GCIO	Airbus A.310-324	Air Club International	
C-GCIT	Airbus A.310-324	Air Club International	

Notes	Reg.	Type	Owner or Operator
	C-GCIV	Airbus A.310-324	Air Club International
	C-GCPC	Douglas DC-10-30 (901)	Canadian Airlines International
	C-GCPD	Douglas DC-10-30 (902)	Canadian Airlines International
	C-GCPE	Douglas DC-10-30ER (903)	Canadian Airlines International
	C-GCPF	Douglas DC-10-30ER (904)	Canadian Airlines International
	C-GCPG	Douglas DC-10-30ER (905)	Canadian Airlines International
	C-GCPH	Douglas DC-10-30ER (906)	Canadian Airlines International
	C-GCPI	Douglas DC-10-30ER (907)	Canadian Airlines International
	C-GCPJ	Douglas DC-10-30 (908)	Canadian Airlines International
	C-GDSP	Boeing 767-233ER (613)	Air Canada
	C-GDSS	Boeing 767-233ER (614)	Air Canada
	C-GDSU	Boeing 767-233ER (615)	Air Canada
	C-GDSY	Boeing 767-233ER (616)	Air Canada
	C-GLCA	Boeing 767-375ER (641)	Canadian Airlines International
	C-GMWW	Boeing 747-475 (881)	Canadian Airlines International
			Maxwell W. Ward
	C-GTSE	Boeing 757-23A	Air Transat
	C-GTSF	Boeing 757-23A	Air Transat
	C-GTSJ	Boeing 757-28A	Air Transat
	C-GTSK	L.1011-385 TriStar 1	Air Transat
	C-G	L.1011-385 TriStar 500	Air Transat
	C-G	L.1011-385 TriStar 500	Air Transat
	C-GTSN	Boeing 757-28A	Air Transat
	C-GTSX	L.1011-385 TriStar 1 (547)	Air Transat
	C-GTSY	L.1011-385 TriStar 1	Air Transat
	C-GTSZ	L.1011-385 TriStar 100 (548)	Air Transat

Note: Airline fleet number carried on aircraft is shown in parenthesis.

CN (Morocco)

	CN-RGA	Boeing 747-428	Royal Air Maroc
	CN-RME	Boeing 747-2B6B (SCD)	Royal Air Maroc
	CN-RMF	Boeing 737-4B6	Royal Air Maroc
	CN-RMG	Boeing 737-4B6	Royal Air Maroc
	CN-RMI	Boeing 737-2B6	Royal Air Maroc *El Ayounne*
	CN-RMJ	Boeing 737-2B6	Royal Air Maroc *Oujda*
	CN-RMK	Boeing 737-2B6	Royal Air Maroc *Smara*
	CN-RML	Boeing 737-2B6	Royal Air Maroc
	CN-RMM	Boeing 737-2B6C	Royal Air Maroc
	CN-RMN	Boeing 737-2B6C	Royal Air Maroc
	CN-RMP	Boeing 727-2B6	Royal Air Maroc
	CN-RMQ	Boeing 727-2B6	Royal Air Maroc
	CN-RMR	Boeing 727-2B6	Royal Air Maroc
	CN-RMT	Boeing 757-2B6	Royal Air Maroc
	CN-RMV	Boeing 737-5B6	Royal Air Maroc
	CN-RMW	Boeing 737-5B6	Royal Air Maroc
	CN-RMX	Boeing 737-4B6	Royal Air Maroc
	CN-RMY	Boeing 737-5B6	Royal Air Maroc
	CN-RMZ	Boeing 757-2B6	Royal Air Maroc
	CN-RNA	Boeing 737-4B6	Royal Air Maroc
	CN-RNB	Boeing 737-5B6	Royal Air Maroc
	CN-RNC	Boeing 737-4B6	Royal Air Maroc
	CN-RND	Boeing 737-4B6	Royal Air Maroc
	CN-RNF	Boeing 737-4B6	Royal Air Maroc
	CN-RNG	Boeing 737-5B6	Royal Air Maroc
	CN-RNH	Boeing 737-5B6	Royal Air Maroc

CS (Portugal)

	CS-TEA	L.1011-385 TriStar 500	B.W.I.A.
	CS-TEC	L.1011-385 TriStar 500	TAP — Air Portugal *Gago Coutinho*
	CS-TEH	Airbus A.310-304	TAP — Air Portugal *Bartolomeu Dias*
	CS-TEI	Airbus A.310-304	TAP — Air Portugal *Fernao de Magalhaes*
	CS-TEJ	Airbus A.310-304	TAP — Air Portugal *Pedro Nunes*
	CS-TEM	Boeing 737-282	TAP — Air Portugal *Setubal*
	CS-TEN	Boeing 737-282	TAP — Air Portugal *Braga*
	CS-TEO	Boeing 737-282	TAP — Air Portugal *Evora*
	CS-TEP	Boeing 737-282	TAP — Air Portugal *Porto*
	CS-TEQ	Boeing 737-282C	TAP — Air Portugal *Vila Real*

Reg.	Type	Owner or Operator	Notes
CS-TES	Boeing 737-230	TAP — Air Portugal *Viana do Castelo*	
CS-TEW	Airbus A.310-304	TAP — Air Portugal *Vasco da Gama*	
CS-TEX	Airbus A.310-304	TAP — Air Portugal *Joao XXI*	
CS-TGP	Boeing 737-3Q8	SATA Air Acores	
CS-TIB	Boeing 737-382	TAP — Air Portugal *Acores*	
CS-TIC	Boeing 737-382	TAP — Air Portugal *Algarve*	
CS-TID	Boeing 737-382	TAP — Air Portugal *Alto Minho*	
CS-TIE	Boeing 737-382	TAP — Air Portugal *Costa Azul*	
CS-TIF	Boeing 737-3K9	TAP — Air Portugal *Costa Verde*	
CS-TIG	Boeing 737-3K9	TAP — Air Portugal	
CS-TIH	Boeing 737-3K9	TAP — Air Portugal	
CS-TIK	Boeing 737-382	TAP — Air Portugal *Costa do Estoril*	
CS-TIL	Boeing 737-382	TAP — Air Portugal *Lisboa*	
CS-TIN	Boeing 737-33A	TAP — Air Portugal	
CS-TIO	Boeing 737-33A	TAP — Air Portugal	
CS-TNA	Airbus A.320-211	TAP — Air Portugal *Grao Vasco*	
CS-TNB	Airbus A.320-211	TAP — Air Portugal *Gil Vicente*	
CS-TNC	Airbus A.320-211	TAP — Air Portugal *Pero da Covilha*	
CS-TND	Airbus A.320-211	TAP — Air Portugal *Garcia de Orta*	
CS-TNE	Airbus A.320-211	TAP — Air Portugal *Sa de Miranda*	
CS-TNF	Airbus A.320-211	TAP — Air Portugal *Fernao Lopes*	
CS-TOA	Airbus A.340-312	TAP — Air Portugal *Ferrei Mendes Pinto*	
CS-TOB	Airbus A.340-312	TAP — Air Portugal *D. Joao de Castro*	
CS-TOC	Airbus A.340-312	TAP — Air Portugal *Wenceslau de Moraes*	
CS-TOD	Airbus A.340-312	TAP — Air Portugal *D. Francisco de Almeida*	
CS-TPA	Fokker 100	Portugalia *Albatroz*	
CS-TPB	Fokker 100	Portugalia *Pelican*	
CS-TPC	Fokker 100	Portugalia *Flamingo*	
CS-TPD	Fokker 100	Portugalia *Condor*	
CS-TPE	Fokker 100	Portugalia *Gaviao*	
CS-TPF	Fokker 100	Portugalia *Grifo*	

CU (Cuba)

CU-T1208	Ilyushin IL-62M	Cubana *Capt Wifredo Perez*	
CU-T1209	Ilyushin IL-62M	Cubana	
CU-T1215	Ilyushin IL-62M	Cubana	
CU-T1216	Ilyushin IL-62M	Cubana	
CU-T1217	Ilyushin IL-62M	Cubana	
CU-T1218	Ilyushin IL-62M	Cubana	
CU-T1225	Ilyushin IL-62M	Cubana	
CU-T1259	Ilyushin IL-62M	Cubana	
CU-T1280	Ilyushin IL-62M	Cubana	
CU-T1282	Ilyushin IL-62M	Cubana	
CU-T1283	Ilyushin IL-62M	Cubana	
CU-T1284	Iluushin IL-62M	Cubana	

Note: AOM French Airlines operate European flights for Cubana using DC-10-30s.

D2 (Angola)

D2-THZ	L.100-30 Hercules	HeavyLift Cargo Airlines	
D2-TOJ	Boeing 707-349C	TAAG Angola Airlines	
D2-TOK	Boeing 707-324C	Angola Air Charter	
D2-TOL	Boeing 707-347C	Angola Air Charter	
D2-TON	Boeing 707-324C	Angola Air Charter	
D2-TOP	Boeing 707-382B	TAAG Angola Airlines	
D2-TOR	Boeing 707-351C	Angola Air Charter	
D2-TPR	Boeing 707-3J6B	TAAG Angola Airlines	

D (Germany)

D-AARS	F.27 Friendship Mk 600	Alkair Express Cargo Services	
D-ABAB	Boeing 737-4K5	Air Berlin	
D-ABAD	Boeing 737-4Y0	Air Berlin	
D-ABAE	Boeing 737-46J	Air Berlin	
D-ABAG	Boeing 737-46J	Air Berlin	

Notes	Reg.	Type	Owner or Operator
	D-ABAH	Boeing 737-46J	Air Berlin
	D-ABAI	Boeing 737-46J	Air Berlin
	D-ABAK	Boeing 737-46J	Air Berlin
	D-ABAL	Boeing 737-46J	Air Berlin
	D-ABEA	Boeing 737-330	Lufthansa *Saarbrücken*
	D-ABEB	Boeing 737-330	Lufthansa *Xanten*
	D-ABEC	Boeing 737-330	Lufthansa *Karlsrühe*
	D-ABED	Boeing 737-330	Lufthansa *Hagen*
	D-ABEE	Boeing 737-330	Lufthansa *Ulm*
	D-ABEF	Boeing 737-330	Lufthansa *Weiden i.d. Opf*
	D-ABEH	Boeing 737-330	Lufthansa *Bad Kissingen*
	D-ABEI	Boeing 737-330	Lufthansa *Bamberg*
	D-ABEK	Boeing 737-330	Lufthansa *Wuppertal*
	D-ABEL	Boeing 737-330	Lufthansa *Pforzheim*
	D-ABEM	Boeing 737-330	Lufthansa *Eberswalde*
	D-ABEN	Boeing 737-330	Lufthansa *Neubrandenburg*
	D-ABEO	Boeing 737-330	Lufthansa *Plauen*
	D-ABEP	Boeing 737-330	Lufthansa *Naumburg (Saale)*
	D-ABER	Boeing 737-330	Lufthansa *Merseburg*
	D-ABES	Boeing 737-330	Lufthansa *Koethen/Anhalt*
	D-ABET	Boeing 737-330	Lufthansa *Gelsenkirchen*
	D-ABEU	Boeing 737-330	Lufthansa *Goslar*
	D-ABEW	Boeing 737-330	Lufthansa *Detmold*
	D-ABFP	Boeing 737-230	Lufthansa *Offenbach*
	D-ABFR	Boeing 737-230	Lufthansa *Solingen*
	D-ABIA	Boeing 737-530	Lufthansa *Greifswald*
	D-ABIB	Boeing 737-530	Lufthansa *Esslingen*
	D-ABIC	Boeing 737-530	Lufthansa *Krefeld*
	D-ABID	Boeing 737-530	Lufthansa *Aachen*
	D-ABIE	Boeing 737-530	Lufthansa *Hildesheim*
	D-ABIF	Boeing 737-530	Lufthansa *Landau*
	D-ABIH	Boeing 737-530	Lufthansa *Bruchsal*
	D-ABII	Boeing 737-530	Lufthansa *Lörrach*
	D-ABIK	Boeing 737-530	Lufthansa *Rastatt*
	D-ABIL	Boeing 737-530	Lufthansa *Memmingen*
	D-ABIM	Boeing 737-530	Lufthansa *Salzgitter*
	D-ABIN	Boeing 737-530	Lufthansa *Langenhagen*
	D-ABIO	Boeing 737-530	Lufthansa *Wesel*
	D-ABIP	Boeing 737-530	Lufthansa *Oberhausen*
	D-ABIR	Boeing 737-530	Lufthansa *Anklam*
	D-ABIS	Boeing 737-530	Lufthansa *Rendsburg*
	D-ABIT	Boeing 737-530	Lufthansa *Neumünster*
	D-ABIU	Boeing 737-530	Lufthansa *Limburg a.d. Lahn*
	D-ABIW	Boeing 737-530	Lufthansa *Bad Nauheim*
	D-ABIX	Boeing 737-530	Lufthansa *Iserlohn*
	D-ABIY	Boeing 737-530	Lufthansa *Lingen*
	D-ABIZ	Boeing 737-530	Lufthansa *Kirchheim unter Teck*
	D-ABJA	Boeing 737-530	Lufthansa *Bad Segeberg*
	D-ABJB	Boeing 737-530	Lufthansa *Rheine*
	D-ABJC	Boeing 737-530	Lufthansa *Erding*
	D-ABJD	Boeing 737-530	Lufthansa *Freising*
	D-ABJE	Boeing 737-530	Lufthansa *Ingelheim am Rhein*
	D-ABJF	Boeing 737-530	Lufthansa *Aalen*
	D-ABJH	Boeing 737-530	Lufthansa *Heppenheim/Bergstr*
	D-ABJI	Boeing 737-530	Lufthansa *Siegburg*
	D-ABMA	Boeing 737-230	Lufthansa *Idar-Oberstein*
	D-ABMB	Boeing 737-230	Lufthansa *Ingolstadt*
	D-ABMD	Boeing 737-230	Lufthansa *Paderborn*
	D-ABME	Boeing 737-230	Lufthansa *Schweinfurt*
	D-ABMF	Boeing 737-230	Lufthansa *Verden*
	D-ABNA	Boeing 757-230	Condor Flugdienst
	D-ABNB	Boeing 757-230	Condor Flugdienst
	D-ABNC	Boeing 757-230	Condor Flugdienst
	D-ABND	Boeing 757-230	Condor Flugdienst
	D-ABNE	Boeing 757-230	Condor Flugdienst
	D-ABNF	Boeing 757-230	Condor Flugdienst
	D-ABNH	Boeing 757-230	Condor Flugdienst
	D-ABNI	Boeing 757-230	Condor Flugdienst
	D-ABNK	Boeing 757-230	Condor Flugdienst
	D-ABNL	Boeing 757-230	Condor Flugdienst
	D-ABNM	Boeing 757-230	Condor Flugdienst
	D-ABNN	Boeing 757-230	Condor Flugdienst
	D-ABNO	Boeing 757-230	Condor Flugdienst
	D-ABNP	Boeing 757-230	Condor Flugdienst

Reg.	Type	Owner or Operator	Notes
D-ABNR	Boeing 757-230	Condor Flugdienst	
D-ABNS	Boeing 757-230	Condor Flugdienst	
D-ABNT	Boeing 757-230	Condor Flugdienst	
D-ABNX	Boeing 757-230	Condor Flugdienst	
D-ABTA	Boeing 747-430 (SCD)	Lufthansa *Sachsen*	
D-ABTB	Boeing 747-430 (SCD)	Lufthansa *Brandenburg*	
D-ABTC	Boeing 747-430 (SCD)	Lufthansa *Mecklenburg-Verpommern*	
D-ABTD	Boeing 747-430 (SCD)	Lufthansa/Condor Flugdienst *Hamburg*	
D-ABTE	Boeing 747-430 (SCD)	Lufthansa *Sachsen-Anhalt*	
D-ABTF	Boeing 747-430 (SCD)	Lufthansa *Thüringen*	
D-ABTH	Boeing 747-430 (SCD)	Lufthansa *Duisburg*	
D-ABUA	Boeing 767-330ER	Condor Flugdienst	
D-ABUB	Boeing 767-330ER	Condor Flugdienst	
D-ABUC	Boeing 767-330ER	Condor Flugdienst/Lufthansa	
D-ABUD	Boeing 767-330ER	Condor Flugdienst	
D-ABUE	Boeing 767-330ER	Condor Flugdienst	
D-ABUF	Boeing 767-330ER	Condor Flugdienst	
D-ABUH	Boeing 767-330ER	Condor Flugdienst	
D-ABUI	Boeing 767-330ER	Condor Flugdienst	
D-ABUZ	Boeing 767-330ER	Condor Flugdienst	
D-ABVA	Boeing 747-430	Lufthansa *Berlin*	
D-ABVB	Boeing 747-430	Lufthansa *Bonn*	
D-ABVC	Boeing 747-430	Lufthansa *Baden-Württemberg*	
D-ABVD	Boeing 747-430	Lufthansa *Bochum*	
D-ABVE	Boeing 747-430	Lufthansa *Potsdam*	
D-ABVF	Boeing 747-430	Lufthansa *Frankfurt am Main*	
D-ABVH	Boeing 747-430	Lufthansa *Düsseldorf*	
D-ABVK	Boeing 747-430	Lufthansa *Hannover*	
D-ABVL	Boeing 747-430	Lufthansa *Muenchen*	
D-ABVN	Boeing 747-430	Lufthansa *Dortmund*	
D-ABVO	Boeing 747-430	Lufthansa	
D-ABVP	Boeing 747-430	Lufthansa	
D-ABVR	Boeing 747-430	Lufthansa	
D-ABVS	Boeing 747-430	Lufthansa	
D-ABVT	Boeing 747-430	Lufthansa	
D-ABWA	Boeing 737-330	Germania	
D-ABWB	Boeing 737-330	Germania	
D-ABWC	Boeing 737-330QC	Lufthansa	
D-ABWD	Boeing 737-330QC	Lufthansa *Westerland/Sylt*	
D-ABWE	Boeing 737-330QC	Lufthansa *Goerlitz*	
D-ABWF	Boeing 737-330QC	Lufthansa *Ruedesheim am Rhein*	
D-ABWH	Boeing 737-330	Lufthansa *Rothenburg*	
D-ABWS	Boeing 737-3S3F	Lufthansa *Cargo*	
D-ABXA	Boeing 737-330QC	Lufthansa *Giessen*	
D-ABXB	Boeing 737-330QC	Lufthansa *Passau*	
D-ABXC	Boeing 737-330QC	Lufthansa *Delmenhorst*	
D-ABXD	Boeing 737-330	Lufthansa *Siegen*	
D-ABXE	Boeing 737-330	Lufthansa *Hamm*	
D-ABXF	Boeing 737-330	Lufthansa *Minden*	
D-ABXH	Boeing 737-330	Lufthansa *Cuxhaven*	
D-ABXI	Boeing 737-330	Lufthansa *Berchtesgaden*	
D-ABXK	Boeing 737-330	Lufthansa *Ludwigsburg*	
D-ABXL	Boeing 737-330	Lufthansa *Neuss*	
D-ABXM	Boeing 737-330	Lufthansa *Herford*	
D-ABXN	Boeing 737-330	Lufthansa *Böblingen*	
D-ABXO	Boeing 737-330	Lufthansa *Schwäbisch-Gmünd*	
D-ABXP	Boeing 737-330	Lufthansa *Fulda*	
D-ABXR	Boeing 737-330	Lufthansa *Celle*	
D-ABXS	Boeing 737-330	Lufthansa *Sindelfingen*	
D-ABXT	Boeing 737-330	Lufthansa *Reutlingen*	
D-ABXU	Boeing 737-330	Lufthansa *Seeheim-Jugenheim*	
D-ABXW	Boeing 737-330	Lufthansa *Hanau*	
D-ABXX	Boeing 737-330	Lufthansa *Bad Homburg v.d. Höhe*	
D-ABXY	Boeing 737-330	Lufthansa *Hof*	
D-ABXZ	Boeing 737-330	Lufthansa *Bad Mergentheim*	
D-ABYM	Boeing 747-230B (SCD)	Lufthansa *Schleswig-Holstein*	
D-ABYO	Boeing 747-230F (SCD)	Lufthansa *Cargo America*	
D-ABYP	Boeing 747-230B	Lufthansa *Niedersachen*	
D-ABYQ	Boeing 747-230B	Lufthansa *Bremen*	
D-ABYR	Boeing 747-230B (SCD)	Lufthansa *Nordrhein-Westfalen*	
D-ABYT	Boeing 747-230F (SCD)	Lufthansa Cargo	
D-ABYU	Boeing 747-230F (SCD)	Lufthansa Cargo Asia	
D-ABYW	Boeing 747-230F (SCD)	Lufthansa Cargo	
D-ABYX	Boeing 747-230B (SCD)	Lufthansa *Köln*	

Notes	Reg.	Type	Owner or Operator
	D-ABYY	Boeing 747-230F (SCD)	Lufthansa Cargo
	D-ABYZ	Boeing 747-230F (SCD)	Lufthansa Cargo
	D-ABZA	Boeing 747-230F (SCD)	Lufthansa Cargo *Düsseldorf*
	D-ABZB	Boeing 747-230F (SCD)	Lufthansa Cargo *Europa*
	D-ABZC	Boeing 747-230F (SCD)	Lufthansa Cargo
	D-ABZD	Boeing 747-230B	Lufthansa *Kiel*
	D-ABZE	Boeing 747-230B (SCD)	Lufthansa *Stuttgart*
	D-ABZF	Boeing 747-230F (SCD)	Lufthansa *Cargo Africa*
	D-ABZH	Boeing 747-230B	Lufthansa *Bonn*
	D-ABZI	Boeing 747-230F (SCD)	Lufthansa Cargo *Australia*
	D-ACFA	BAe 146-200	Eurowings
	D-ACJA	Canadair Regional Jet 100ER	Lufthansa CityLine
	D-ACJB	Canadair Regional Jet 100ER	Lufthansa CityLine
	D-ACJC	Canadair Regional Jet 100ER	Lufthansa CityLine
	D-ACJD	Canadair Regional Jet 100ER	Lufthansa CityLine
	D-ACLA	Canadair Regional Jet 100ER	Lufthansa CityLine
	D-ACLB	Canadair Regional Jet 100ER	Lufthansa CityLine
	D-ACLC	Canadair Regional Jet 100ER	Lufthansa CityLine
	D-ACLD	Canadair Regional Jet 100ER	Lufthansa CityLine
	D-ACLE	Canadair Regional Jet 100ER	Lufthansa CityLine
	D-ACLF	Canadair Regional Jet 100ER	Lufthansa CityLine
	D-ACLG	Canadair Regional Jet 100ER	Lufthansa CityLine
	D-ACLH	Canadair Regional Jet 100ER	Lufthansa CityLine
	D-ACLI	Canadair Regional Jet 100ER	Lufthansa CityLine
	D-ACLJ	Canadair Regional Jet 100ER	Lufthansa CityLine
	D-ACLK	Canadair Regional Jet 100ER	Lufthansa CityLine
	D-ACLL	Canadair Regional Jet 100ER	Lufthansa CityLine
	D-ACLM	Canadair Regional Jet 100ER	Lufthansa CityLine
	D-ACLN	Canadair Regional Jet 100ER	Lufthansa CityLine/Tyrolean Airways (OE-LRQ)
	D-ACLO	Canadair Regional Jet 100ER	Lufthansa CityLine
	D-ACLP	Canadair Regional Jet 100ER	Lufthansa CityLine
	D-ACLQ	Canadair Regional Jet 100ER	Lufthansa CityLine
	D-ACLR	Canadair Regional Jet 100ER	Lufthansa CityLine
	D-ACLS	Canadair Regional Jet 100ER	Lufthansa CityLine
	D-ACLT	Canadair Regional Jet 100ER	Lufthansa CityLine
	D-ACLU	Canadair Regional Jet 100ER	Lufthansa CityLine
	D-ACLV	Canadair Regional Jet 100ER	Lufthansa CityLine
	D-ACLW	Canadair Regional Jet 100ER	Lufthansa CityLine
	D-ACLX	Canadair Regional Jet 100ER	Lufthansa CityLine
	D-ACLY	Canadair Regional Jet 100ER	Lufthansa CityLine
	D-ACLZ	Canadair Regional Jet 100ER	Lufthansa CityLine
	D-ADBA	Boeing 737-3L9	Deutsche BA
	D-ADBB	Boeing 737-3L9	Deutsche BA
	D-ADBC	Boeing 737-3L9	Deutsche BA
	D-ADBD	Boeing 737-3L9	Deutsche BA
	D-ADBE	Boeing 737-3L9	Deutsche BA
	D-ADBF	Boeing 737-3L9	Deutsche BA
	D-ADBG	Boeing 737-3L9	Deutsche BA
	D-ADBH	Boeing 737-3L9	Deutsche BA
	D-ADBJ	Boeing 737-3L9	Deutsche BA
	D-ADEI	BAe 146-200QT	Eurowings/TNT Express Europe
	D-ADEP	F.27 Friendship Mk 600	Ratioflug
	D-ADFA	Fokker 100	Deutsche BA
	D-ADFB	Fokker 100	Deutsche BA
	D-ADFC	Fokker 100	Deutsche BA
	D-ADFD	Fokker 100	Deutsche BA
	D-ADFE	Fokker 100	Deutsche BA
	D-ADJO	Douglas DC-10-30	Condor Flugdienst
	D-ADLO	Douglas DC-10-30	Condor Flugdienst
	D-ADOP	F.27 Friendship Mk 600	WDL
	D-ADPO	Douglas DC-10-30	Condor Flugdienst
	D-ADQO	Douglas DC-10-30	Condor Flugdienst
	D-ADSA	SAAB 2000	Deutsche BA
	D-ADSB	SAAB 2000	Deutsche BA
	D-ADSC	SAAB 2000	Deutsche BA
	D-ADSD	SAAB 2000	Deutsche BA
	D-ADSE	SAAB 2000	Deutsche BA
	D-ADSO	Douglas DC-10-30	Condor Flugdienst
	D-ADUP	F.27 Friendship Mk 500	Ratioflug
	D-AELC	F.27 Friendship Mk 600	WDL
	D-AELD	F.27 Friendship Mk 600	WDL
	D-AELE	F.27 Friendship Mk 600	WDL
	D-AELF	F.27 Friendship Mk 600	WDL

Reg.	Type	Owner or Operator	Notes
D-AELG	F.27 Friendship Mk 600	WDL	
D-AELH	F.27 Friendship Mk 600	WDL	
D-AELI	F.27 Friendship Mk 600	WDL	
D-AELJ	F.27 Friendship Mk 600	WDL	
D-AELK	F.27 Friendship Mk 600	WDL	
D-AELL	F.27 Friendship Mk 200	WDL	
D-AERB	McD Douglas MD-11	LTU	
D-AERF	Airbus A.330-322	LTU	
D-AERH	Airbus A.330-322	LTU	
D-AERJ	Airbus A.330-322	LTU	
D-AERK	Airbus A.330-322	LTU	
D-AERQ	Airbus A.330-322	LTU	
D-AERS	Airbus A.330-322	LTU	
D-AERW	McD Douglas MD-11	LTU	
D-AERX	McD Douglas MD-11	LTU	
D-AERZ	McD Douglas MD-11	LTU	
D-AEWA	BAe 146-300	Eurowings	
D-AEWB	BAe 146-300	Eurowings	
D-AEWG	Aérospatiale ATR-72-212	Eurowings	
D-AEWH	Aérospatiale ATR-72-212	Eurowings	
D-AEWI	Aérospatiale ATR-72-212	Eurowings	
D-AEWK	Aérospatiale ATR-72-212	Eurowings	
D-AEWL	Aérospatiale ATR-72-212	Eurowings	
D-AFKK	Fokker 50	Contactair/Team Lufthansa	
D-AFKL	Fokker 50	Contactair/Team Lufthansa	
D-AFKM	Fokker 50	Contactair/Team Lufthansa	
D-AFKN	Fokker 50	Contactair/Team Lufthansa	
D-AFKO	Fokker 50	Lufthansa CityLine	
D-AFKP	Fokker 50	Lufthansa CityLine	
D-AFKU	Fokker 50	Contactair/Team Lufthansa	
D-AGEA	Boeing 737-35B	Germania	
D-AGEB	Boeing 737-35B	Germania	
D-AGEC	Boeing 737-35B	Germania/Condor Flugdienst	
D-AGED	Boeing 737-35B	Germania/Condor Flugdienst	
D-AGEE	Boeing 737-35B	Germania	
D-AGEF	Boeing 737-35B	Germania	
D-AGEG	Boeing 737-35B	Germania	
D-AGEH	Boeing 737-3L9	Germania	
D-AGEI	Boeing 737-3L9	Germania	
D-AGEJ	Boeing 737-3L9	Germania	
D-AGEK	Boeing 737-3M8	Germania	
D-	Boeing 737-75B	Germania	
D-	Boeing 737-75B	Germania	
D-	Boeing 737-75B	Germania	
D-AGWB	McD Douglas MD-83	Aero Lloyd	
D-AGWC	McD Douglas MD-83	Aero Lloyd	
D-AHLA	Airbus A.310-304	Hapag-Lloyd	
D-AHLB	Airbus A.310-304	Hapag-Lloyd	
D-AHLC	Airbus A.310-308	Hapag-Lloyd	
D-AHLD	Boeing 737-5K5	Hapag-Lloyd	
D-AHLE	Boeing 737-5K5	Hapag-Lloyd	
D-AHLF	Boeing 737-5K5	Hapag-Lloyd	
D-AHLG	Boeing 737-4K5	Hapag-Lloyd	
D-AHLI	Boeing 737-5K5	Hapag-Lloyd	
D-AHLJ	Boeing 737-4K5	Hapag-Lloyd	
D-AHLK	Boeing 737-4K5	Hapag-Lloyd	
D-AHLL	Boeing 737-4K5	Hapag-Lloyd	
D-AHLM	Boeing 737-4K5	Hapag-Lloyd	
D-AHLN	Boeing 737-5K5	Hapag-Lloyd	
D-AHLO	Boeing 737-4K5	Hapag-Lloyd	
D-AHLP	Boeing 737-4K5	Hapag-Lloyd	
D-AHLQ	Boeing 737-4K5	Hapag-Lloyd	
D-AHLR	Boeing 737-4K5	Hapag-Lloyd	
D-AHLS	Boeing 737-4K5	Hapag-Lloyd	
D-AHLT	Boeing 737-4K5	Hapag-Lloyd	
D-AHLU	Boeing 737-4K5	Hapag-Lloyd	
D-AHLV	Airbus A.310-204	Hapag-Lloyd	
D-AHLW	Airbus A.310-204	Hapag-Lloyd	
D-AHLX	Airbus A.310-204	Hapag-Lloyd	
D-AHLZ	Airbus A.310-204	Hapag-Lloyd	
D-AHOI	BAe 146-300	Hamburg Airlines	
D-AIAH	Airbus A.300-603	Lufthansa *Lindau/Bodensee*	
D-AIAI	Airbus A.300-603	Lufthansa *Erbach/Odenwald*	
D-AIAK	Airbus A.300-603	Lufthansa *Kronberg/Taunus*	

Notes	Reg.	Type	Owner or Operator
	D-AIAL	Airbus A.300-603	Lufthansa *Stade*
	D-AIAM	Airbus A.300-603	Lufthansa *Rosenheim*
	D-AIAN	Airbus A.300-603	Lufthansa *Nördlingen*
	D-AIAP	Airbus A.300-603	Lufthansa *Donauwörth*
	D-AIAR	Airbus A.300-603	Lufthansa *Bingen am Rhein*
	D-AIAS	Airbus A.300-603	Lufthansa *Monchengladbach*
	D-AIAT	Airbus A.300-603	Lufthansa *Bottrop*
	D-AIAU	Airbus A.300-603	Lufthansa *Bocholt*
	D-AIAW	Airbus A.300-605R	Lufthansa *Witten*
	D-AIAX	Airbus A.300-605R	Lufthansa
	D-AIBA	Airbus A.340-211	Lufthansa *Neurnberg*
	D-AIBC	Airbus A.340-211	Lufthansa *Leverkusen*
	D-AIBD	Airbus A.340-211	Lufthansa *Essen*
	D-AIBE	Airbus A.340-211	Lufthansa *Stuttgart*
	D-AIBF	Airbus A.340-211	Lufthansa *Luebeck*
	D-AIBH	Airbus A.340-211	Lufthansa *Bremerhaven*
	D-AIDC	Airbus A.310-304	Lufthansa *Neustadt a.d. Weinstrasse*
	D-AIDD	Airbus A.310-304	Lufthansa *Emden*
	D-AIDE	Airbus A.310-304	Lufthansa *Speyer*
	D-AIDF	Airbus A.310-304	Lufthansa *Aschaffenburg*
	D-AIDH	Airbus A.310-304	Lufthansa *Wetzlar*
	D-AIDI	Airbus A.310-304	Lufthansa *Fellbach*
	D-AIDK	Airbus A.310-304	Lufthansa *Donaueschingen*
	D-AIDL	Airbus A.310-304	Lufthansa *Obersdorf*
	D-AIDM	Airbus A.310-304	Lufthansa *Chemnitz*
	D-AIDN	Airbus A.310-304	Lufthansa *Gütersloh*
	D-AIGA	Airbus A.340-311	Lufthansa *Oldenburg*
	D-AIGB	Airbus A.340-311	Lufthansa *Recklinghausen*
	D-AIGC	Airbus A.340-311	Lufthansa *Wilhelmshaven*
	D-AIGD	Airbus A.340-311	Lufthansa *Remscheid*
	D-AIGF	Airbus A.340-311	Lufthansa *Gottingen*
	D-AIGH	Airbus A.340-311	Lufthansa *Koblenz*
	D-AIGI	Airbus A.340-311	Lufthansa *Worms*
	D-AIGK	Airbus A.340-311	Lufthansa *Bayreuth*
	D-AIGL	Airbus A.340-313X	Lufthansa *Herne*
	D-AIGM	Airbus A.340-313X	Lufthansa
	D-AILA	Airbus A.319-114	Lufthansa *Frankfurt (Oder)*
	D-AILB	Airbus A.319-114	Lufthansa *Lutherstadt Wittenburg*
	D-AILC	Airbus A.319-114	Lufthansa
	D-AILD	Airbus A.319-114	Lufthansa *Dinkelsbühl*
	D-AILE	Airbus A.319-114	Lufthansa
	D-AILF	Airbus A.319-114	Lufthansa
	D-AILH	Airbus A.319-114	Lufthansa
	D-AILI	Airbus A.319-114	Lufthansa
	D-AILK	Airbus A.319-114	Lufthansa
	D-AILL	Airbus A.319-114	Lufthansa
	D-AILM	Airbus A.319-114	Lufthansa
	D-AILN	Airbus A.319-114	Lufthansa
	D-AILP	Airbus A.319-114	Lufthansa
	D-AILR	Airbus A.319-114	Lufthansa
	D-AILS	Airbus A.319-114	Lufthansa
	D-AIPA	Airbus A.320-211	Lufthansa *Buxtehude*
	D-AIPB	Airbus A.320-211	Lufthansa *Heidelberg*
	D-AIPC	Airbus A.320-211	Lufthansa *Braunschweig*
	D-AIPD	Airbus A.320-211	Lufthansa *Freiburg*
	D-AIPE	Airbus A.320-211	Lufthansa *Kassel*
	D-AIPF	Airbus A.320-211	Lufthansa *Leipzig*
	D-AIPH	Airbus A.320-211	Lufthansa *Münster*
	D-AIPK	Airbus A.320-211	Lufthansa *Wiesbaden*
	D-AIPL	Airbus A.320-211	Lufthansa *Ludwigshafen am Rhein*
	D-AIPM	Airbus A.320-211	Lufthansa *Troisdorf*
	D-AIPP	Airbus A.320-211	Lufthansa *Starnberg*
	D-AIPR	Airbus A.320-211	Lufthansa *Kaufbeuren*
	D-AIPS	Airbus A.320-211	Lufthansa *Augsburg*
	D-AIPT	Airbus A.320-211	Lufthansa *Cottbus*
	D-AIPU	Airbus A.320-211	Lufthansa *Dresden*
	D-AIPW	Airbus A.320-211	Lufthansa *Schwerin*
	D-AIPX	Airbus A.320-211	Lufthansa *Mannheim*
	D-AIPY	Airbus A.320-211	Lufthansa *Magdeburg*
	D-AIPZ	Airbus A.320-211	Lufthansa *Erfurt*
	D-AIQA	Airbus A.320-211	Lufthansa *Mainz*
	D-AIQB	Airbus A.320-211	Lufthansa *Bielefeld*
	D-AIQC	Airbus A.320-211	Lufthansa *Zwickau*
	D-AIQD	Airbus A.320-211	Lufthansa *Jena*

Reg.	Type	Owner or Operator	Notes
D-AIQE	Airbus A.320-211	Lufthansa *Gera*	
D-AIQF	Airbus A.320-211	Lufthansa *Halle a.d. Saale*	
D-AIQH	Airbus A.320-211	Lufthansa *Dessau*	
D-AIQK	Airbus A.320-211	Lufthansa *Rostock*	
D-AIQL	Airbus A.320-211	Lufthansa *Stralsund*	
D-AIQM	Airbus A.320-211	Lufthansa *Nordenham*	
D-AIQN	Airbus A.320-211	Lufthansa *Laupheim*	
D-AIQP	Airbus A.320-211	Lufthansa *Suhl*	
D-AIQR	Airbus A.320-211	Lufthansa *Lahr/Schwarzwald*	
D-AIQS	Airbus A.320-211	Lufthansa *Eisenach*	
D-AIRA	Airbus A.321-131	Lufthansa *Finkenwerder*	
D-AIRB	Airbus A.321-131	Lufthansa *Baden-Baden*	
D-AIRC	Airbus A.321-131	Lufthansa *Erlangen*	
D-AIRD	Airbus A.321-131	Lufthansa *Coburg*	
D-AIRE	Airbus A.321-131	Lufthansa *Osnabrueck*	
D-AIRF	Airbus A.321-131	Lufthansa *Kempen*	
D-AIRH	Airbus A.321-131	Lufthansa *Garmisch-Partenkirchen*	
D-AIRK	Airbus A.321-131	Lufthansa *Freudenstadt/Schwarzwald*	
D-AIRL	Airbus A.321-131	Lufthansa *Kulmbach*	
D-AIRM	Airbus A.321-131	Lufthansa *Darmstadt*	
D-AIRN	Airbus A.321-131	Lufthansa *Kaiserslautern*	
D-AIRO	Airbus A.321-131	Lufthansa *Konstanz*	
D-AIRP	Airbus A.321-131	Lufthansa	
D-AIRR	Airbus A.321-131	Lufthansa *Wismar*	
D-AIRS	Airbus A.321-131	Lufthansa *Husum*	
D-AIRT	Airbus A.321-131	Lufthansa	
D-AIRU	Airbus A.321-131	Lufthansa	
D-AIRW	Airbus A.321-131	Lufthansa	
D-AIRX	Airbus A.321-131	Lufthansa	
D-AIRY	Airbus A.321-131	Lufthansa	
D-AISY	F.27 Friendship Mk 600	Ratioflug	
D-AJET	BAe 146-200	Eurowings	
D-ALAA	Airbus A.320-232	Aero Lloyd	
D-ALAB	Airbus A.320-232	Aero Lloyd	
D-ALAC	Airbus A.320-232	Aero Lloyd	
D-A	Airbus A.320-232	Aero Lloyd	
D-A	Airbus A.320-232	Aero Lloyd	
D-A	Airbus A.321-200	Aero Lloyd	
D-A	Airbus A.321-200	Aero Lloyd	
D-A	Airbus A.321-200	Aero Lloyd	
D-ALLD	McD Douglas MD-83	Aero Lloyd	
D-ALLE	McD Douglas MD-83	Aero Lloyd	
D-ALLF	McD Douglas MD-83	Aero Lloyd	
D-ALLG	McD Douglas MD-87	Aero Lloyd	
D-ALLJ	McD Douglas MD-87	Aero Lloyd	
D-ALLK	McD Douglas MD-83	Aero Lloyd *Oberursel Taunus*	
D-ALLL	McD Douglas MD-83	Aero Lloyd	
D-ALLM	McD Douglas MD-83	Aero Lloyd	
D-ALLN	McD Douglas MD-83	Aero Lloyd	
D-ALLO	McD Douglas MD-83	Aero Lloyd	
D-ALLP	McD Douglas MD-83	Aero Lloyd *Kassel*	
D-ALLQ	McD Douglas MD-83	Aero Lloyd	
D-ALLR	McD Douglas MD-83	Aero Lloyd	
D-ALLS	McD Douglas MD-82	Aero Lloyd	
D-ALLT	McD Douglas MD-82	Aero Lloyd	
D-ALLU	McD Douglas MD-83	Aero Lloyd	
D-ALLV	McD Douglas MD-83	Aero Lloyd	
D-ALOA	BAe 146-200	Hamburg Airlines	
D-AMUI	Boeing 757-2G5	LTU-Sud	
D-AMUJ	Boeing 767-3G5ER	LTU-Sud	
D-AMUK	Boeing 757-225	LTU-Sud	
D-AMUM	Boeing 757-2G5	LTU-Sud	
D-AMUN	Boeing 767-3G5ER	LTU-Sud	
D-AMUP	Boeing 767-33AER	LTU-Sud	
D-AMUQ	Boeing 757-2G5	LTU-Sud	
D-AMUR	Boeing 767-3G5ER	LTU-Sud	
D-AMUS	Boeing 767-3G5ER	LTU-Sud	
D-AMUU	Boeing 757-225	LTU-Sud	
D-AMUV	Boeing 757-2G5	LTU-Sud	
D-AMUW	Boeing 757-2G5	LTU-Sud	
D-AMUX	Boeing 757-2G5	LTU-Sud	
D-AMUY	Boeing 757-2G5	LTU-Sud	
D-AMUZ	Boeing 757-2G5	LTU-Sud	
D-ANFA	Aérospatiale ATR-72-202	Eurowings	

Notes	Reg.	Type	Owner or Operator
	D-ANFB	Aérospatiale ATR-72-202	Eurowings
	D-ANFC	Aérospatiale ATR-72-202	Eurowings
	D-ANFD	Aérospatiale ATR-72-202	Eurowings
	D-ANFE	Aérospatiale ATR-72-202	Eurowings
	D-ANFF	Aérospatiale ATR-72-202	Eurowings
	D-ANTJ	BAe 146-200QT	Eurowings/TNT Express Europe
	D-APOM	Airbus A.310-304	Hapag-Lloyd/Eurowings
	D-AQUA	BAe 146-300	Hamburg Airlines
	D-AQUI	Junkers Ju.52/3m	Lufthansa Traditionsflug
	D-AVRA	Avro RJ85	Lufthansa CityLine
	D-AVRB	Avro RJ85	Lufthansa CityLine
	D-AVRC	Avro RJ85	Lufthansa CityLine
	D-AVRD	Avro RJ85	Lufthansa CityLine
	D-AVRE	Avro RJ85	Lufthansa CityLine
	D-AVRF	Avro RJ85	Lufthansa CityLine
	D-AVRG	Avro RJ85	Lufthansa CityLine
	D-AVRH	Avro RJ85	Lufthansa CityLine
	D-AVRI	Avro RJ85	Lufthansa CityLine
	D-AVRJ	Avro RJ85	Lufthansa CityLine
	D-AVRK	Avro RJ85	Lufthansa CityLine
	D-AVRL	Avro RJ85	Lufthansa CityLine
	D-AVRM	Avro RJ85	Lufthansa CityLine
	D-AVRN	Avro RJ85	Lufthansa CityLine
	D-AVRO	Avro RJ85	Lufthansa CityLine
	D-AVRP	Avro RJ85	Lufthansa CityLine
	D-AVRQ	Avro RJ85	Lufthansa CityLine
	D-AVRR	Avro RJ85	Lufthansa CityLine
	D-AZUR	BAe 146-200	Hamburg Airlines
	D-BAAA	Aérospatiale ATR-42-300	Eurowings
	D-BACH	D.H.C.8-311 Dash Eight	Augsburg Airways
	D-BAGB	D.H.C.8-103 Dash Eight	Augsburg Airways/Team Lufthansa
	D-BAKA	F.27 Friendship Mk 100	WDL
	D-BAKB	F.27 Friendship Mk 600	WDL
	D-BAKC	F.27 Friendship Mk 600	WDL
	D-BAKD	F.27 Friendship Mk 600	WDL
	D-BAKE	F.27 Friendship Mk 200	WDL
	D-BBBB	Aérospatiale ATR-42-300	Eurowings
	D-BCCC	Aérospatiale ATR-42-300	Eurowings
	D-BCRM	Aérospatiale ATR-42-300	Eurowings
	D-BCRN	Aérospatiale ATR-42-300	Eurowings
	D-BCRO	Aérospatiale ATR-42-300QC	Eurowings
	D-BCRP	Aérospatiale ATR-42-300QC	Eurowings
	D-BCRQ	Aérospatiale ATR-42-300	Eurowings
	D-BCRR	Aérospatiale ATR-42-300	Eurowings
	D-BCRS	Aérospatiale ATR-42-300	Eurowings
	D-BCRT	Aérospatiale ATR-42-300	Eurowings
	D-BDDD	Aérospatiale ATR-42-300	Eurowings
	D-BEEE	Aérospatiale ATR-42-300	Eurowings
	D-BELT	D.H.C.8-311 Dash Eight	Contactair/Lufthansa CityLine
	D-BFFF	Aérospatiale ATR-42-300	Eurowings
	D-BGGG	Aérospatiale ATR-42-300	Eurowings
	D-BHHH	Aérospatiale ATR-42-300	Eurowings
	D-BIER	D.H.C.8-102 Dash Eight	Augsburg Airways
	D-BIRT	D.H.C.8-103 Dash Eight	Augsburg Airways
	D-BJJJ	Aérospatiale ATR-42-300	Eurowings
	D-BKIM	D.H.C.8-311 Dash Eight	Augsburg Airways/Team Lufthansa
	D-BKIR	D.H.C.8-311 Dash Eight	Contactair/Lufthansa CityLine
	D-BKIS	D.H.C.8-311 Dash Eight	Contactair/Lufthansa CityLine
	D-BMUC	D.H.C.8-314 Dash Eight	Augsburg Airways
	D-BOBA	D.H.C.8-311 Dash Eight	Hamburg Airlines
	D-BOBL	D.H.C.8-102 Dash Eight	Hamburg Airlines
	D-BOBO	D.H.C.8-102 Dash Eight	Hamburg Airlines
	D-BOBU	D.H.C.8-311 Dash Eight	Hamburg Airlines
	D-BOBY	D.H.C.8-102 Dash Eight	Hamburg Airlines
	D-CABE	Swearingen SA227AC Metro III	Saxonia Airlines
	D-COLC	Swearingen SA227AC Metro III	OLT/Roland Air
	D-COLT	Swearingen SA226AC Metro III	OLT/Roland Air
	D-ICRJ	Swearingen SA226TC Metro II	OLT/Roland Air
	D-ICRL	Swearingen SA226TC Metro II	OLT/Roland Air
	D-IHCW	Swearingen SA226TC Metro II	OLT/Roland Air

EC (Spain)

Reg.	Type	Owner or Operator
EC-BIH	Douglas DC-9-32	Aviaco *Roncesvalles*
EC-BIK	Douglas DC-9-32	Aviaco *Castillo de Guanapay*
EC-BIM	Douglas DC-9-32	Binter Canarias
EC-BIP	Douglas DC-9-32	Aviaco *Castillo de Monteagudo*
EC-BIT	Douglas DC-9-32	Binter Canarias
EC-BQY	Douglas DC-9-32	Aviaco *Mar Menor*
EC-BQZ	Douglas DC-9-32	Binter Canarias
EC-BYE	Douglas DC-9-32	Aviaco *Cala Galdana*
EC-BYF	Douglas DC-9-32	Aviaco *Hernan Cortes*
EC-BYI	Douglas DC-9-32	Aviaco *Pedro de Valdivia*
EC-BYJ	Douglas DC-9-32	Aviaco
EC-CBA	Boeing 727-256	Iberia *Vascongadas*
EC-CBF	Boeing 727-256	Iberia *Gran Canaria*
EC-CBM	Boeing 727-256	Iberia *Castilla La Vieja*
EC-CBP	Douglas DC-10-30	Iberia *Costa Dorada*
EC-CEZ	Douglas DC-10-30	Iberia *Costa del Azahar*
EC-CFA	Boeing 727-256	Iberia *Jerez Xeres Sherry*
EC-CFB	Boeing 727-256	Iberia *Rioja*
EC-CFC	Boeing 727-256	Iberia *Tarragona*
EC-CFD	Boeing 727-256	Iberia *Montilla-Moriles*
EC-CFE	Boeing 727-256	Iberia *Penedes*
EC-CFF	Boeing 727-256	Iberia *Valdepenas*
EC-CFG	Boeing 727-256	Iberia *La Mancha*
EC-CFH	Boeing 727-256	Iberia *Priorato*
EC-CFI	Boeing 727-256	Iberia *Carinena*
EC-CFK	Boeing 727-256	Iberia *Rivero*
EC-CGN	Douglas DC-9-32	Aviaco *Martin Alonso Pinzon*
EC-CGO	Douglas DC-9-32	Aviaco *Pedro Alonso Nino*
EC-CGP	Douglas DC-9-32	Aviaco *Juan Sebastian Elcano*
EC-CGQ	Douglas DC-9-32	Aviaco *Alonso de Ojeda*
EC-CGR	Douglas DC-9-32	Aviaco *Francisco de Orellana*
EC-CID	Boeing 727-256	Iberia *Malaga*
EC-CIE	Boeing 727-256	Iberia *Esparragosa*
EC-CLB	Douglas DC-10-30	Iberia *Costa Blanca*
EC-CLD	Douglas DC-9-32	Aviaco *Hernando de Soto*
EC-CTR	Douglas DC-9-34CF	Iberia *Hernan Cortes*
EC-CTS	Douglas DC-9-34CF	Aviaco *Francisco de Pizarro*
EC-CTT	Douglas DC-9-34CF	Iberia *Pedro de Valladolid*
EC-CTU	Douglas DC-9-34CF	Aviaco *Pedro de Alvarado*
EC-DCC	Boeing 727-256	Iberia *Albarino*
EC-DCD	Boeing 727-256	Iberia *Chacoli*
EC-DCE	Boeing 727-256	Iberia *Mentrida*
EC-DDV	Boeing 727-256	Iberia *Acueducto de Segovia*
EC-DDX	Boeing 727-256	Iberia *Monasterio de Poblet*
EC-DDY	Boeing 727-256	Iberia *Cuevas de Altamira*
EC-DDZ	Boeing 727-256	Iberia *Murallas de Avila*
EC-DEA	Douglas DC-10-30	Iberia *Rias Gallegas*
EC-DGB	Douglas DC-9-34	Iberia *Castillo de Javier*
EC-DGC	Douglas DC-9-34	Aviaco *Castillo de Sotomayor*
EC-DGD	Douglas DC-9-34	Aviaco *Castillo de Arcos*
EC-DGE	Douglas DC-9-34	Aviaco *Castillo de Bellver*
EC-DHZ	Douglas DC-10-30	Iberia *Costas Canarias*
EC-DIA	Boeing 747-256B	Iberia *Tirso de Molina*
EC-DIB	Boeing 747-256B	Iberia *Cervantes*
EC-DLC	Boeing 747-256B (SCD)	Iberia *Francisco de Quevedo*
EC-DLD	Boeing 747-256B (SCD)	Iberia *Lupe de Vega*
EC-DLE	Airbus A.300B4-120	Iberia *Donana*
EC-DLF	Airbus A.300B4-120	Iberia *Canadas del Teide*
EC-DLG	Airbus A.300B4-120	Iberia *Las Tablas de Daimiel*
EC-DLH	Airbus A.300B4-120	Iberia *Aigues Tortes*
EC-DNP	Boeing 747-256B	Iberia *Juan Ramon Jimenez*
EC-DNQ	Airbus A.300B4-120	Iberia *Islas Cies*
EC-DNR	Airbus A.300B4-120	Iberia *Ordesa*
EC-EEK	Boeing 747-256B (SCD)	Iberia *Garcia Lorca*
EC-EFX	Boeing 757-2G5	LTE International Airways *Bluebird I*
EC-EGH	Boeing 757-2G5	LTE International Airways *Bluebird II*
EC-EIG	McD Douglas MD-83	Spanair *Sunlight*
EC-ELT	BAe 146-200QT	Pan Air Lineas Aéreas/TNT
EC-ELY	Boeing 737-3K9	Viva Air
EC-EMX	Douglas DC-8-62F	Iberia Cargo
EC-ENQ	Boeing 757-2G5	LTE International Airways *Bluebird III*
EC-EON	Airbus A.300B4-203	Iberia *Penalara*

Notes	Reg.	Type	Owner or Operator
	EC-EOO	Airbus A.300B4-203	Iberia *Covadouga*
	EC-EPA	BAe 146-200QT	Pan Air Lineas Aéreas/TNT
	EC-ETB	Boeing 737-4Y0	Futura International Airways
	EC-EUC	McD Douglas MD-87	Iberia *Ciudad de Burgos*
	EC-EUD	McD Douglas MD-87	Iberia *Ciudad de Toledo*
	EC-EUE	McD Douglas MD-87	Iberia *Ciudad de Sevilla*
	EC-EUL	McD Douglas MD-87	Iberia *Ciudad de Cadiz*
	EC-EVB	McD Douglas MD-87	Iberia *Arrecife de Lanzarote*
	EC-EVE	Boeing 737-4Y0	Futura International Airways
	EC-EXF	McD Douglas MD-87	Iberia *Ciudad de Pamplona*
	EC-EXG	McD Douglas MD-87	Iberia *Ciudad de Almeria*
	EC-EXM	McD Douglas MD-87	Iberia *Ciudad de Zaragoza*
	EC-EXN	McD Douglas MD-87	Iberia *Ciudad de Badajoz*
	EC-EXR	McD Douglas MD-87	Iberia *Ciudad de Oviedo*
	EC-EXT	McD Douglas MD-87	Iberia *Ciudad de Albacete*
	EC-EXY	Boeing 737-4Y0	Futura International Airways
	EC-EYB	McD Douglas MD-87	Iberia *Cangas de Onis*
	EC-EYX	McD Douglas MD-87	Iberia *Ciudad de Caceres*
	EC-EYY	McD Douglas MD-87	Iberia *Ciudad de Barcelona*
	EC-EYZ	McD Douglas MD-87	Iberia *Ciudad de Las Palmas*
	EC-EZA	McD Douglas MD-87	Iberia *Ciudad de Segovia*
	EC-EZS	McD Douglas MD-87	Iberia *Ciudad de Mahon*
	EC-FAS	Airbus A.320-211	Iberia *Sierra de Cazorla*
	EC-FBQ	Airbus A.320-211	Iberia *Montseny*
	EC-FBR	Airbus A.320-211	Iberia *Sierra de Segura*
	EC-FBS	Airbus A.320-211	Iberia *Timanfaya*
	EC-FCB	Airbus A.320-211	Iberia *Montana de Covadonga*
	EC-FCU	Boeing 767-3Y0ER	Spanair *Baleares*
	EC-FDA	Airbus A.320-211	Iberia *Lagunas de Ruidera*
	EC-FDB	Airbus A.320-211	Iberia *Lago de Sanabria*
	EC-FEF	Boeing 757-236	Air Europa *Catalunya*
	EC-FEF	Boeing 757-236	Air Europa
	EC-FEO	Airbus A.320-211	Iberia *Delta del Ebro*
	EC-FEY	McD Douglas MD-87	Iberia *Ciudad de Jaen*
	EC-FEZ	McD Douglas MD-87	Iberia *Ciudad de Malaga*
	EC-FFA	McD Douglas MD-87	Iberia *Ciudad de Avila*
	EC-FFH	McD Douglas MD-87	Iberia *Ciudad de Logrono*
	EC-FFI	McD Douglas MD-87	Iberia *Ciudad de Cuenca*
	EC-FFK	Boeing 757-236	Air Europa *Galicia*
	EC-FFN	Boeing 737-36E	Viva Air
	EC-FFY	BAe 146-300QT	Pan Air Lineas Aéreas/TNT
	EC-FGH	Airbus A.320-211	Iberia *Caldera de Taburiente*
	EC-FGM	McD Douglas MD-88	Aviaco *Torre de Hercules*
	EC-FGR	Airbus A.320-211	Iberia *Dehesa de Moncayo*
	EC-FGU	Airbus A.320-211	Iberia *Sierra Espuna*
	EC-FGV	Airbus A.320-211	Iberia *Monfrague*
	EC-FHA	Boeing 767-3Y0ER	Spanair *Canarias*
	EC-FHD	McD Douglas MD-87	Iberia *Ciudad de Leon*
	EC-FHG	McD Douglas MD-88	Aviaco *La Almudiana*
	EC-FHK	McD Douglas MD-87	Iberia *Ciudad de Tarragona*
	EC-FHR	Boeing 737-36E	Viva Air
	EC-FIA	Airbus A.320-211	Iberia *Isla de la Cartuja*
	EC-FIC	Airbus A.320-211	Iberia *Sierra de Grazalema*
	EC-FIG	McD Douglas MD-88	Aviaco *Penon de Ifach*
	EC-FIH	McD Douglas MD-88	Aviaco *Albaicin*
	EC-FIX	McD Douglas MD-83	Centennial Airlines
	EC-FJE	McD Douglas MD-88	Aviaco *Gibralfaro*
	EC-FJZ	Boeing 737-3Y0	Air Europa
	EC-FKD	Airbus A.320-211	Iberia *Monte Alhoya*
	EC-FKH	Airbus A.320-211	Iberia *Canon del Rio Lobos*
	EC-FKI	Boeing 737-375	Air Europa *Virgen de la Vega*
	EC-FKJ	Boeing 737-3Y0	Air Europa
	EC-FLF	Boeing 737-36E	Viva Air
	EC-FLG	Boeing 737-36E	Viva Air
	EC-FLK	McD Douglas MD-88	Aviaco *Palacio de la Magdalena*
	EC-FLN	McD Douglas MD-88	Aviaco *Puerta de Tierra*
	EC-FLP	Airbus A.320-211	Iberia *Torcal de Antequera*
	EC-FLQ	Airbus A.320-211	Iberia *Dunas de Liencres*
	EC-FML	Airbus A.320-211	Iberia *Hayedo de Tejera Negra*
	EC-FMN	Airbus A.320-211	Iberia *Cadi Moixero*
	EC-FND	McD Douglas MD-88	Aviaco *Playa de la Concha*
	EC-FNR	Airbus A.320-211	Iberia *Monte el Valle*
	EC-FOF	McD Douglas MD-88	Aviaco *Cesar Manrique Lanzarote*
	EC-FOG	McD Douglas MD-88	Aviaco *La Giralda*

Reg.	Type	Owner or Operator	Notes
EC-FOZ	McD Douglas MD-88	Aviaco *Montjuic*	
EC-FPD	McD Douglas MD-88	Aviaco *Lagos de Coradonga*	
EC-FPJ	McD Douglas MD-88	Aviaco *Rio de Vigo*	
EC-FQY	Airbus A.320-211	Iberia *Joan Miro*	
EC-FSY	McD Douglas MD-83	Spanair *Sunrise*	
EC-FTL	Boeing 757-236	Air Europa *Castilla y Leon*	
EC-FTR	Boeing 757-256	Iberia *Sierra de Guadarrama*	
EC-FTS	McD Douglas MD-83	Spanair *Sunbird*	
EC-FTT	McD Douglas MD-83	Spanair *Sunray*	
EC-FTU	McD Douglas MD-83	Spanair *Sunshine*	
EC-FUT	Boeing 737-3Q8	Air Europa	
EC-FVA	Douglas DC-8-71F	Iberia cargo	
EC-FVB	McD Douglas MD-83	Oasis International Airlines	
EC-FVC	McD Douglas MD-83	Oasis International Airlines	
EC-FVJ	Boeing 737-3Y0	Air Europa	
EC-FVR	McD Douglas MD-83	Spanair *Sundance*	
EC-FVY	BAe 146-200QT	Pan Air Lineas Aéreas/TNT	
EC-FXA	McD Douglas MD-83	Spanair *Sunstar*	
EC-FXB	Airbus A.310-324	Oasis International Airlines	
EC-FXC	Boeing 737-3Q8	Air Europa	
EC-FXI	McD Douglas MD-83	Spanair *Sunseeker*	
EC-FXP	Boeing 737-4Q8	Air Europa *Villanueva del Conde*	
EC-FXQ	Boeing 737-4Q8	Air Europa *Salamanca*	
EC-FXU	Boeing 757-256	Iberia *Xacobeo 93*	
EC-FXV	Boeing 757-256	Iberia *Argentina*	
EC-FXX	McD Douglas MD-87	Oasis International Airlines	
EC-FXY	McD Douglas MD-83	Spanair *Sunbeam*	
EC-FYF	Boeing 737-3Y0	Air Europa *Canarias*	
EC-FYJ	Boeing 757-256	Iberia *Venezuela*	
EC-FYK	Boeing 757-256	Iberia *Chile*	
EC-FYL	Boeing 757-256	Iberia *Cuba*	
EC-FYM	Boeing 757-256	Iberia *Mexico*	
EC-FYN	Boeing 757-256	Iberia *Costa Rica*	
EC-FZC	McD Douglas MD-83	Spanair *Sunflower*	
EC-FZE	BAe 146-200QT	Pan Air Lineas Aéreas/TNT	
EC-FZT	Boeing 737-4Y0	Futura International Airways	
EC-FZZ	Boeing 737-4Y0	Air Europa *Baleares*	
EC-GAG	Boeing 747-256B	Iberia *Calderon de la Barca*	
EC-GAP	Boeing 737-36E	Viva Air	
EC-GAT	McD Douglas MD-83	Spanair *Sunmyth*	
EC-GAZ	Boeing 737-4Y0	Air Europa	
EC-GBA	McD Douglas MD-83	Spanair *Sungod*	
EC-GBN	Boeing 737-4Y0	Air Europa	
EC-GBU	Boeing 737-36E	Viva Air	
EC-GBX	Boeing 757-236	Air Europa	
EC-GBY	McD Douglas MD-83	Oasis International Airlines	
EC-GCA	Boeing 757-236	Air Europa	
EC-GCB	Boeing 757-236	Air Europa *Formentara*	
EC-GCI	Boeing 727-256	Iberia *Murcia*	
EC-GCJ	Boeing 727-256	Iberia *Galicia*	
EC-GCK	Boeing 727-256	Iberia *Asturias*	
EC-GCL	Boeing 727-256	Iberia *Andalucia*	
EC-GCM	Boeing 727-256	Iberia *Tenerife*	
EC-GCV	McD Douglas MD-82	Spanair	
EC-GEO	BAe 146-100	Paukn Air/Pan Air Lineas Aereas	
EC-GEP	BAe 146-100	Paukn Air/Pan Air Lineas Aereas	
EC-GEQ	Boeing 737-3Y0	Air Europa	
EC-GEU	Boeing 737-375	Air Europa	
EC-GFE	Boeing 737-4Y0	Futura International Airways	
EC-GFU	Boeing 737-3Y0	Air Europa	
EC-GGE	Boeing 737-36E	Viva Air	
EC-GGO	Boeing 737-3M8	Air Europa	
EC-GGS	Airbus A.340-313	Iberia	
EC-GGV	McD Douglas MD-83	Spanair *Sunbow*	
EC-GGZ	Boeing 737-36E	Viva Air	
EC-GHD	Boeing 737-3M8	Air Europa	
EC-GHE	McD Douglas MD-83	Spanair *Sunset*	
EC-GHF	Boeing 737-4Y0	Futura International Airways	
EC-GHH	McD Douglas MD-83	Spanair	
EC-GHM	Boeing 767-204	Air Europa	
EC-GHT	Boeing 737-4Y0	Futura International Airways	
EC-GHX	Airbus A.340-313	Iberia	
EC-GJT	Airbus A.340-313	Iberia	
EC-GKG	McD Douglas MD-83	Spanair	
EC-GKM	Airbus A.320-231	BCM Airlines (G-BVZU)	

EI (Republic of Ireland)

Including complete current Irish Civil Register

Reg.	Type	Owner or Operator
EI-ABI	D.H.84 Dragon	Aer Lingus Teo Iolar (EI-AFK)
EI-ADV	PA-12 Super Cruiser	R. E. Levis
EI-AFE	Piper J3C-65 Cub	J. Conlon
EI-AFF	B.A. Swallow 2	J. J. Sullivan & ptnrs
EI-AFN	B.A. Swallow 2 ★	J. McCarthy
EI-AGB	Miles M.38 Messenger 4 ★	J. McLoughlin
EI-AGD	Taylorcraft Plus D	B. & K. O'Sullivan
EI-AGJ	J/1 Autocrat	W. G. Rafter
EI-AHA	D.H.82A Tiger Moth ★	J. H. Maher
EI-AHI	D.H.82A Tiger Moth	High Fidelity Flyers
EI-AHR	D.H.C.1 Chipmunk 22 ★	C. Lane
EI-AKM	Piper J-3C-65 Cub	Setanta Flying Group
EI-ALH	Taylorcraft Plus D	N. Reilly
EI-ALP	Avro 643 Cadet	J. C. O'Loughlin
EI-ALU	Avro 631 Cadet	M. P. Cahill (stored)
EI-AMK	J/1 Autocrat	Irish Aero Club
EI-ANT	Champion 7ECA Citabria	S. Donohoe
EI-ANY	PA-18 Super Cub 95	Bogavia Group
EI-AOB	PA-28 Cherokee 140	J. Surdival & ptnrs
EI-AOK	Cessna F.172G	O. Bruton
EI-AOP	D.H.82A Tiger Moth ★	Institute of Technology/Dublin
EI-AOS	Cessna 310B	Joyce Aviation Ltd
EI-APF	Cessna F.150F	L. O. Kennedy
EI-APS	Schleicher ASK.14	SLG Group
EI-ARH	Currie Wot/S.E.5 Replica	L. Garrison
EI-ARM	Currie Wot/S.E.5 Replica	L. Garrison
EI-ARW	Jodel D.R.1050	P. Walsh & P. Ryan
EI-AST	Cessna F.150H	P. McKenna
EI-ATJ	B.121 Pup 1	L. O'Leary
EI-ATK	PA-28 Cherokee 140	Mayo Flying Club Ltd
EI-ATS	M.S.880B Rallye Club	ATS Group
EI-AUC	Cessna FA.150K	O. Bruton
EI-AUE	M.S.880B Rallye Club	Kilkenny Flying Club Ltd
EI-AUG	M.S.894 Rallye Minerva 220	K. O'Leary
EI-AUJ	M.S.880B Rallye Club	Ormond Flying Club Ltd
EI-AUM	J/1 Autocrat	J. G. Rafter
EI-AUO	Cessna FA.150K Aerobat	Kerry Aero Club
EI-AUS	J/5F Aiglet Trainer	T. Stephens & T. Lennon
EI-AUT	Forney F-1A Aircoupe	Joyce Aviation Ltd
EI-AUV	PA-23 Aztec 250C	Shannon Executive Aviation
EI-AUY	Morane-Saulnier M.S.502	G. Warner/Duxford
EI-AVB	Aeronca 7AC Champion	T. Brett
EI-AVC	Cessna F.337F	Christy Keane (Saggart) Ltd
EI-AVM	Cessna F.150L	J. Cowell
EI-AWE	Cessna F.150M	Third Flight Group
EI-AWH	Cessna 210J	Rathcode Flying Club Ltd
EI-AWP	D.H.82A Tiger Moth	O. Bruton
EI-AWR	Malmo MFI-9 Junior	M. R. Nesbitt & S. Duignan
EI-AWU	M.S.880B Rallye Club	Longford Aviation Ltd
EI-AYA	M.S.880B Rallye Club	Limerick Flying Club Ltd
EI-AYB	GY-80 Horizon 180	Westwing Flying Group
EI-AYD	AA-5 Traveler	P. Howick & ptnrs
EI-AYF	Cessna FRA.150L	K. A. O'Connor
EI-AYI	M.S.880B Rallye Club	J. McNamara
EI-AYK	Cessna F.172M	S. T. Scully
EI-AYN	BN-2A-8 Islander	Gallway Aviation Services Ltd
EI-AYO	Douglas DC-3A ★	Science Museum, Wroughton
EI-AYR	Schleicher ASK-16	Kilkenny Airport Ltd
EI-AYS	PA-22 Colt 108	M. F. Skelly
EI-AYV	M.S.892A Rallye Commodore 150	P. Murtagh
EI-AYY	Evans VP-1	M. Donoghue
EI-BAF	Thunder Ax6-56 balloon	W. G. Woollett
EI-BAJ	SNCAN Stampe SV-4C	Dublin Tiger Group
EI-BAO	Cessna F.172G	O. Bruton
EI-BAR	Thunder Ax8-105 balloon	J. Burke & V. Hourihane
EI-BAS	Cessna F.172M	Falcon Aviation Ltd
EI-BAT	Cessna F.150M	Donegal Aero Club Ltd
EI-BAV	PA-22 Colt 108	J. Davy
EI-BBC	PA-28 Cherokee 180C	Piper Aero Club Ltd
EI-BBD	Evans VP-1	Volksplane Group

Reg.	Type	Owner or Operator	Notes
EI-BBE	Champion 7FC Tri-Traveler (tailwheel)	P. Forde & D. Connaire	
EI-BBG	M.S.880B Rallye Club	Weston Ltd	
EI-BBI	M.S.892 Rallye Commodore	Kilkenny Airport Ltd	
EI-BBJ	M.S.880B Rallye Club	Weston Ltd	
EI-BBM	Cameron O-65 balloon	Dublin Ballooning Club	
EI-BBN	Cessna F.150M	Sligo N.W. Aero Club	
EI-BBO	M.S.893E Rallye 180GT	G. P. Moorhead	
EI-BBV	Piper J-3C-65 Cub	F. Cronin	
EI-BCE	BN-2A-26 Islander	Galway Aviation Services Ltd	
EI-BCF	Bensen B.8M	T. A. Brennan	
EI-BCH	M.S.892A Rallye Commodore 150	The Condor Group	
EI-BCJ	F.8L Falco 1 Srs 3	D. Kelly	
EI-BCK	Cessna F.172K	H. Caulfield	
EI-BCL	Cessna 182P	F. Doherty	
EI-BCM	Piper J-3C-65 Cub	Kilmoon Flying Group	
EI-BCN	Piper J-3C-65 Cub	Snowflake Flying Group	
EI-BCO	Piper J-3C-65 Cub	J. Molloy	
EI-BCP	D.628 Condor	A. Delaney	
EI-BCS	M.S.880B Rallye Club	Organic Fruit & Vegetables of Ireland Ltd	
EI-BCU	M.S.880B Rallye Club	Weston Ltd	
EI-BCW	M.S.880B Rallye Club	Kilkenny Flying Club	
EI-BDH	M.S.880B Rallye Club	Munster Wings Ltd	
EI-BDK	M.S.880B Rallye Club	Limerick Flying Club Ltd	
EI-BDL	Evans VP-2	M. Blake	
EI-BDM	PA-23 Aztec 250D ★	Industrial Training School	
EI-BDP	Cessna 182P	S. Bruton	
EI-BDR	PA-28 Cherokee 180	Cherokee Group	
EI-BEA	M.S.880B Rallye 100ST	Weston Ltd	
EI-BEN	Piper J-3C-65 Cub	J. J. Sullivan	
EI-BEO	Cessna 310Q	C. Keane	
EI-BEP	M.S.892A Rallye Commodore 150	H. Lynch & J. O'Leary	
EI-BEY	Naval N3N-3 ★	Huntley & Huntley Ltd	
EI-BFF	Beech A.23 Musketeer	E. Hopkins	
EI-BFH	Bell 212	Irish Helicopters Ltd	
EI-BFI	M.S.880B Rallye 100ST	J. O'Neill	
EI-BFM	M.S.893E Rallye 235GT	Limerick Flying Group	
EI-BFO	Piper J-3C-90 Cub	D. Gordon	
EI-BFP	M.S.800B Rallye 100ST	Weston Ltd	
EI-BFR	M.S.880B Rallye 100ST	J. Power	
EI-BFV	M.S.880B Rallye 100T	Ormond Flying Club	
EI-BGA	SOCATA Rallye 100ST	J. J. Frew	
EI-BGB	M.S.880B Rallye Club	Limerick Flying Club Ltd	
EI-BGD	M.S.880B Rallye Club	N. Kavanagh	
EI-BGG	M.S.892E Rallye 150GT	M. J. Hanlon	
EI-BGH	Cessna F.172N	Golf Hotel Group	
EI-BGJ	Cessna F.152	K. Higgins	
EI-BGT	Colt 77A balloon	K. Haugh	
EI-BGU	M.S.880B Rallye Club	M. F. Neary	
EI-BHB	M.S.887 Rallye 125	Hotel Bravo Flying Club	
EI-BHC	Cessna F.177RG	P. V. Maguire	
EI-BHF	M.S.892A Rallye Commodore 150	B. Mullen	
EI-BHI	Bell 206B JetRanger 2	J. Mansfield	
EI-BHK	M.S.880B Rallye Club	J. Lawlor & B. Lyons	
EI-BHL	Beech E90 King Air	Stewart Singlam Fabrics Ltd	
EI-BHM	Cessna F.337E ★	Dublin Institute of Technology	
EI-BHN	M.S.893A Rallye Commodore 180	T. Garvan	
EI-BHO	Sikorsky S-61N	Irish Helicopters Ltd	
EI-BHP	M.S.893A Rallye Commodore 180	Spanish Point Flying Club	
EI-BHT	Beech 77 Skipper	Waterford Aero Club	
EI-BHV	Champion 7EC Traveler	Condor Group	
EI-BHW	Cessna F.150F	R. Sharpe	
EI-BHY	SOCATA Rallye 150ST	Liberty Flying Group	
EI-BIB	Cessna F.152	Galway Flying Club	
EI-BIC	Cessna F.172N	Oriel Flying Group Ltd	
EI-BID	PA-18 Super Cub 95	D. MacCarthy	
EI-BIG	Zlin 526	P. von Lonkhuyzen	
EI-BIJ	AB-206B JetRanger 2	Medavia Properties Ltd	
EI-BIK	PA-18 Super Cub 180	Dublin Gliding Club	
EI-BIM	M.S.880B Rallye Club	D. Millar	
EI-BIO	Piper J-3C-65 Cub	Monasterevin Flying Club	
EI-BIR	Cessna F.172M	B. Harrison & ptnrs	
EI-BIS	Robin R.1180TD	Robin Aiglon Group	
EI-BIT	M.S.887 Rallye 125	Spanish Point Flying Club	

Notes	Reg.	Type	Owner or Operator
	EI-BIU	Robin R.2112A	Wicklow Flying Group
	EI-BIV	Bellanca 8KCAB Citabria	Aerocrats Flying Group
	EI-BIW	M.S.880B Rallye Club	E. J. Barr
	EI-BJA	Cessna FRA.150L	Blackwater Flying Group
	EI-BJC	Aeronca 7AC Champion	E. Griffin
	EI-BJG	Robin R.1180	N. Hanley
	EI-BJJ	Aeronca 15AC Sedan	O. Bruton
	EI-BJK	M.S.880B Rallye 110ST	Jordan Larkin Flying Group
	EI-BJM	Cessna A.152	Leinster Aero Club
	EI-BJO	Cessna R.172K	P. Hogan & G. Ryder
	EI-BJS	AA-5B Tiger	P. Morrisey
	EI-BJT	PA-38-112 Tomahawk	O. Bruton
	EI-BKC	Aeronca 15AC Sedan	J. Lynch
	EI-BKF	Cessna F.172H	M. & M. C. Veale
	EI-BKK	Taylor JT.1 Monoplane	Waterford Aero Club
	EI-BKN	M.S.880B Rallye 100ST	Weston Ltd
	EI-BKS	Eipper Quicksilver	Irish Microlight Ltd
	EI-BKT	AB-206B JetRanger 3	Irish Helicopters Ltd
	EI-BKU	M.S.892A Rallye Commodore 150	Limerick Flying Club Ltd
	EI-BLB	SNCAN Stampe SV-4C	J. E. Hutchinson & R. A. Stafford
	EI-BLD	Bolkow Bo 105C	Irish Helicopters Ltd
	EI-BLE	Eipper Microlight	R. P. St George-Smith
	EI-BLG	AB-206B JetRanger 3	Monarch Property Services Ltd
	EI-BLN	Eipper Quicksilver MX	O. J. Conway & B. Daffy
	EI-BLO	Catto CP.16	R. W. Hall
	EI-BLU	Evans VP-1	S. Pallister
	EI-BLW	PA-23 Aztec 250C	— (stored)
	EI-BLY	Sikorsky S-61N	Irish Helicopters Ltd
	EI-BMA	M.S.880B Rallye Club	W. Rankin & M. Kelleher
	EI-BMB	M.S.880B Rallye 100T	Clyde Court Development Ltd
	EI-BMC	Hiway Demon Skytrike	S. Pallister
	EI-BMF	Laverda F.8L Falco	M. Slazenger & H. McCann
	EI-BMH	M.S.880B Rallye Club	N. J. Bracken
	EI-BMI	SOCATA TB.9 Tampico	Ashford Flying Group
	EI-BMJ	M.S.880B Rallye 100T	Weston Ltd
	EI-BML	PA-23 Aztec 250	Bruton Aircraft Engineering Ltd
	EI-BMM	Cessna F.152 II	P. Redmond
	EI-BMN	Cessna F.152 II	Iona National Airways Ltd
	EI-BMO	Robin R.2160	L. Gavin & ptnrs
	EI-BMU	Monnett Sonerai II	P. Forde & D. Connaire
	EI-BMV	AA-5 Traveler	E. Tierney & K. Harold
	EI-BMW	Vulcan Air Trike	L. Maddock
	EI-BNA	Douglas DC-8-63CF	Aer Turas Teo
	EI-BNF	Goldwing Canard	T. Morelli
	EI-BNG	M.S.892A Rallye Commodore 150	Shannon Executive Aviation
	EI-BNH	Hiway Skytrike	M. Martin
	EI-BNJ	Evans VP-2	G. A. Cashman
	EI-BNK	Cessna U.206F	Irish Parachute Club Ltd
	EI-BNL	Rand KR-2	K. Hayes
	EI-BNP	Rotorway 133	R. L. Renfroe
	EI-BNT	Cvjetkovic CA-65	B. Tobin & P. G. Ryan
	EI-BNU	M.S.880B Rallye Club	P. A. Doyle
	EI-BOA	Pterodactyl Ptraveller	A. Murphy
	EI-BOE	SOCATA TB.10 Tobago	P. Byron & ptnrs
	EI-BOH	Eipper Quicksilver	J. Leech
	EI-BOR	Bell 222	Westair Ltd
	EI-BOV	Rand KR-2	G. O'Hara & G. Callan
	EI-BOX	Duet	K. Riccius
	EI-BPE	Viking Dragonfly	G. Bracken
	EI-BPJ	Cessna 182A	Falcon Parachute Club Ltd
	EI-BPL	Cessna F.172K	Phoenix Flying
	EI-BPO	Southdown Sailwings	A. Channing
	EI-BPP	Quicksilver MX	J. A. Smith
	EI-BPT	Skyhook Sabre	T. McGrath
	EI-BPU	Hiway Demon	A. Channing
	EI-BRH	Mainair Gemini Flash	J. Deeney
	EI-BRK	Flexiform Trike	L. Maddock
	EI-BRS	Cessna P.172D	D. & M. Hillery
	EI-BRU	Evans VP-1	R. Smith & T. Coughlan
	EI-BRV	Hiway Demon	M. Garvey & C. Tully
	EI-BRW	Ultralight Deltabird	A. & E. Aerosports
	EI-BRX	Cessna FRA.150L	Trim Flying Club Ltd
	EI-BSB	Jodel D.112	J. M. Finnan & M. O'Reilly
	EI-BSC	Cessna F.172N	S. Phelan

Reg.	Type	Owner or Operator	Notes
EI-BSD	Enstrom F-28A	Clark Aviation	
EI-BSF	Avro 748 Srs 1 ★	Ryanair *cabin trainer*/Dublin	
EI-BSG	Bensen B.80	J. Todd	
EI-BSK	SOCATA TB.9 Tampico	Weston Ltd	
EI-BSL	PA-34-220T Seneca	E. L. Symmons	
EI-BSN	Cameron O-65 balloon	W. Woollett	
EI-BSO	PA-28 Cherokee 140B	H. M. Hanley	
EI-BST	Bell 206B JetRanger	Celtic Helicopters Ltd	
EI-BSU	Champion 7KCAB	R. Bentley	
EI-BSV	SOCATA TB.20 Trinidad	J. Condron	
EI-BSW	Solar Wings Pegasus XL-R	E. Fitzgerald	
EI-BSX	Piper J-3C-65 Cub	J. & T. O'Dwyer	
EI-BTS	Boeing 747-283B (SCD)	Air Tara Ltd *(leased to Philippine A/L)*	
EI-BTX	McD Douglas MD-82	Air Tara Ltd *(leased to AeroMexico)*	
EI-BTY	McD Douglas MD-82	Air Tara Ltd	
EI-BUA	Cessna 172M	Skyhawks Flying Club	
EI-BUC	Jodel D.9 Bebe	D. Lyons	
EI-BUF	Cessna 210N	210 Group	
EI-BUG	SOCATA ST.10 Diplomate	J. Cooke	
EI-BUH	Lake LA.4-200 Buccaneer	Derg Aviation (Group) Ltd	
EI-BUJ	M.S.892A Rallye Commodore 150	T. Cunniffe	
EI-BUL	MW-5 Sorcerer	J. Conlon	
EI-BUN	Beech 76 Duchess	K. A. O'Connor & ptnrs	
EI-BUO	Quickkit Glass S.005E	C. Lavery & C. Donaldson	
EI-BUR	PA-38-112 Tomahawk	Westair Aviation Ltd	
EI-BUS	PA-38-112 Tomahawk	Westair Aviation Ltd	
EI-BUT	M.S.893A Commodore 180	T. Keating	
EI-BUU	Solar Wings Pegasus XL-R	R. L. T. Hudson	
EI-BUV	Cessna 172RG	J. J. Spollen	
EI-BUW	Noble Hardman Snowbird IIIA	T.I.F.C. & I.S. Ltd	
EI-BUX	Agusta A.109A	Orring Ltd	
EI-BVB	Whittaker MW.6 Merlin	R. England	
EI-BVC	Cameron N-65 balloon	E. Shepherd	
EI-BVF	Cessna F.172N	First Phantom Group	
EI-BVJ	AMF Chevvron 232	S. J. Dunn	
EI-BVK	PA-38-112 Tomahawk	Pegasus Flying Group Ltd	
EI-BVN	Bell 206B Jet Ranger 3	Helicopter Hire (Ireland) Ltd	
EI-BVS	Cessna 172RG	P. Bruno	
EI-BVT	Evans VP-2	P. Morrison	
EI-BVY	Zenith 200AA-RW	J. Matthews & ptnrs	
EI-BWD	McD Douglas MD-83	Airplanes IAL Ltd *(leased to TWA)*	
EI-BWH	Partenavia P.68C	K. Buckley	
EI-BXA	Boeing 737-448	Aer Lingus Teo *St Conleth*	
EI-BXB	Boeing 737-448	Aer Lingus Teo *St Gall*	
EI-BXC	Boeing 737-448	Aer Lingus Teo *St Brendan*	
EI-BXD	Boeing 737-448	Aer Lingus Teo *St Colman*	
EI-BXI	Boeing 737-448	Aer Lingus Teo *St Finnian*	
EI-BXK	Boeing 737-448	Aer Lingus Teo *St Caimin*	
EI-BXL	Polaris F1B-OK350	M. McKeon	
EI-BXM	Boeing 737-2T4	Air Tara Ltd	
EI-BXN	Boeing 737-448	Aer Lingus Teo	
EI-BXO	Fouga CM.170 Magister	G. W. Connolly	
EI-BXT	D.62B Condor	J. Sweeney	
EI-BXU	PA-28-161 Warrior II	W. T. King	
EI-BXX	AB-206B JetRanger 3	Westair Aviation Ltd	
EI-BYA	Thruster TST Mk 1	E. Fagan	
EI-BYD	Cessna 150J	Kestrel Flying Group	
EI-BYE	PA-31-350 Navajo Chieftain	EI-Air Exports Ltd	
EI-BYF	Cessna 150M	Twentieth Air Training Group	
EI-BYG	SOCATA TB.9 Tampico	Weston Ltd	
EI-BYJ	Bell 206B JetRanger	Celtic Helicopters Ltd	
EI-BYK	PA-23 Aztec 250E	Aztec Holdings Ltd	
EI-BYL	Zenith CH.250	M. Guckian	
EI-BYR	Bell 206L-3 LongRanger 3	Ven Air Ltd	
EI-BYV	Hughes 369D	Irish Helicopters Ltd	
EI-BYX	Champion 7GCAA	P. J. Gallagher	
EI-BYY	Piper J-3C-85 Cub	A. J. Haines	
EI-BYZ	PA-44-180 Seminole	O. Bruton	
EI-BZA	Boeing 747-283B	Air Tara Ltd *(leased to Philippine A/L)*	
EI-BZB	Airbus A.300C4-203	Airplanes Finance Ltd *(leased to Philippine A/L)*	
EI-BZE	Boeing 737-3Y0	GPA Group Ltd *(leased to Philippine A/L)*	
EI-BZF	Boeing 737-3Y0	Pergola Ltd *(leased to Philippine A/L)*	
EI-BZH	Boeing 737-3Y0	Dormacken Ltd *(leased to Philippine A/L)*	

Notes	Reg.	Type	Owner or Operator
	EI-BZI	Boeing 737-3Y0	Dormacken Ltd (leased to Philippine A/L)
	EI-BZJ	Boeing 737-3Y0	Pergola Ltd (leased to Philippine A/L)
	EI-BZK	Boeing 737-3Y0	Dormacken Ltd (leased to Philippine A/L)
	EI-BZL	Boeing 737-3Y0	Dormacken Ltd (leased to Philippine A/L)
	EI-BZM	Boeing 737-3Y0	Dormacken Ltd (leased to Philippine A/L)
	EI-BZN	Boeing 737-3Y0	Airplanes Finance Ltd (leased to Philippine A/L)
	EI-CAA	Cessna FR.172J	O. Bruton
	EI-CAC	Grob G.115	European College of Aeronautics
	EI-CAD	Grob G.115	I. Valentine
	EI-CAE	Grob G.115	D. Kehoe
	EI-CAM	Boeing 767-3Y0ER	Aer Lingus Teo (leased to TWA)
	EI-CAN	Aerotech MW.5 Sorcerer	V. Vaughan
	EI-CAP	Cessna R.182RG	M. J. Hanlon
	EI-CAU	AMF Chevvron 232	J. Farrant
	EI-CAW	Bell 206B JetRanger	Celtic Helicopters Ltd
	EI-CAX	Cessna P.210N	J. J. Dunne
	EI-CAY	Mooney M.20C	Ranger Flights Ltd
	EI-CBB	Douglas DC-9-15	GPA Finance Ltd (stored)
	EI-CBC	Aérospatiale ATR-72-201	Air Tara Ltd (leased to American Eagle)
	EI-CBD	Aérospatiale ATR-72-201	Air Tara Ltd (leased to American Eagle)
	EI-CBF	Aérospatiale ATR-42-300	Air Tara Ltd (leased to Trans World Express)
	EI-CBG	Douglas DC-9-51	GPA Finance Ltd (leased to Hawaiian)
	EI-CBH	Douglas DC-9-51	GPA Finance Ltd (leased to Hawaiian)
	EI-CBI	Douglas DC-9-51	Air Tara Ltd (leased to Hawaiian)
	EI-CBJ	D.H.C. 8-102 Dash Eight	GPA Group Ltd (leased in Alaska)
	EI-CBK	Aérospatiale ATR-42-300	Air Tara Ltd
	EI-CBO	McD Douglas MD-83	Irish Aerospace Ltd (leased to Nouvelair Tunisie)
	EI-CBR	McD Douglas MD-83	Airplanes 111 Ltd (leased to Avianca)
	EI-CBS	McD Douglas MD-83	Dormacken Ltd (leased to Avianca)
	EI-CBU	McD Douglas MD-87	Air Tara Ltd (leased to AeroMexico)
	EI-CBY	McD Douglas MD-83	Dormacken Ltd (leased to Avianca)
	EI-CBZ	McD Douglas MD-83	Dormacken Ltd (leased to Avianca)
	EI-CCA	Beech 19A Musketeer	P. F. McCooke
	EI-CCB	PA-44-180 Seminole	S. Bruton
	EI-CCC	McD Douglas MD-83	Airplanes 111 Ltd (leased to Avianca)
	EI-CCD	Grob G.115A	M.O.D. Aviation Ltd
	EI-CCE	McD Douglas MD-83	Dormacken Ltd (leased to Avianca)
	EI-CCF	Aeronca 11AC Chief	O. Bruton
	EI-CCH	Piper J-3C-65 Cub	M. Slattery
	EI-CCJ	Cessna 152 II	Irish Aero Club
	EI-CCK	Cessna 152 II	Irish Aero Club
	EI-CCM	Cessna 152 II	Irish Aero Club
	EI-CCN	Grob G.115A	European College of Aeronautics
	EI-CCO	PA-44-180 Seminole	S. Bruton
	EI-CCQ	Slingsby T.61F Venture T.2	Kerry Aero Club Ltd
	EI-CCT	Robinson R-22B	Air Investments Ltd
	EI-CCV	Cessna R.172K-XP	Kerry Aero Club
	EI-CCY	AA-1B Trainer	N. & C. Whisler
	EI-CDA	Boeing 737-548	Aer Lingus Teo St Columba
	EI-CDB	Boeing 737-548	Aer Lingus Teo St Albert
	EI-CDC	Boeing 737-548	Aer Lingus Teo St Munchin
	EI-CDD	Boeing 737-548	Aer Lingus Teo St Macartan
	EI-CDE	Boeing 737-548	Aer Lingus Teo St Jarlath
	EI-CDF	Boeing 737-548	Aer Lingus Teo St Cronan
	EI-CDG	Boeing 737-548	Aer Lingus Teo St Moling
	EI-CDH	Boeing 737-548	Aer Lingus Teo St Ronan
	EI-CDI	McD Douglas MD-11	GPA Finance Ltd (leased to Garuda)
	EI-CDJ	McD Douglas MD-11	GPA Finance Ltd (leased to Garuda)
	EI-CDK	McD Douglas MD-11	GPA Finance Ltd (leased to Garuda)
	EI-CDQ	SA.300 Starduster Too	A. O'Rourke
	EI-CDS	Boeing 737-548	Aer Lingus Teo St Malachy
	EI-CDV	Cessna 150F	Blue Heron Aircraft Services Ltd
	EI-CDX	Cessna 210K	Falcon Aviation Ltd
	EI-CDY	McD Douglas MD-83	Dormacken Ltd (leased to Avianca)
	EI-CEB	Airbus A.300B4-203	Pergola Ltd (leased to Philippine A/L)
	EI-CEG	M.S.893A Rallye 180GT	M. Farrelly
	EI-CEK	McD Douglas MD-83	Airplanes IAL Ltd (leased to Eurofly)
	EI-CEL	Rans S.6 Coyote	D. O'Gorman
	EI-CEN	Thruster T.300	P. J. Murphy
	EI-CEO	Boeing 747-259B (SCD)	Airplanes Hldings Lte (leased to Tower Air)
	EI-CEP	McD Douglas MD-83	Dormacken Ltd (leased to Avianca)

Reg.	Type	Owner or Operator	Notes
EI-CEQ	McD Douglas MD-83	Dormacken Ltd (leased to Avianca)	
EI-CER	McD Douglas MD-83	Airplanes 111 Ltd (leased to Avianca)	
EI-CES	Taylorcraft BC-65	N. O'Brien	
EI-CET	L.188CF Electra	Hunting Cargo Airlines (Ireland) Ltd	
EI-CEX	Lake LA-4-200	Derg Developments Ltd	
EI-CEY	Boeing 757-2Y0	Pergola Ltd (leased to Avianca)	
EI-CEZ	Boeing 757-2Y0	GPA 11 Ltd (leased to Avianca)	
EI-CFE	Robinson R-22B	Windsor Motors Ltd	
EI-CFF	PA-12 Super Cruiser	J. O'Dwyer & J. Molloy	
EI-CFG	CP.301B Emeraude	Southlink Ltd	
EI-CFH	PA-12 Super Cruiser	G. Treacy	
EI-CFL	Airbus A.300B4	Air Tara Ltd	
EI-CFM	Cessna 172P	Hibernian Flying Club	
EI-CFN	Cessna 172P	L. Kane & B. Fitzmaurice	
EI-CFO	Piper J-3C-65 Cub	D. O'Connor & ptnrs	
EI-CFP	Cessna 172P	S. Bruton	
EI-CFV	M.S.880B Rallye Club	Kilkenny Flying Club	
EI-CFX	Robinson R-22B	Glenwood Transport	
EI-CFY	Cessna 172N	K. A. O'Conner	
EI-CFZ	McD Douglas MD-83	Airplanes 111 Ltd (leased to Avianca)	
EI-CGB	Team Minimax	M. Garvey	
EI-CGC	Stinson 108-3	S. Bruton	
EI-CGD	Cessna 172M	W. Phelan & M. Casey	
EI-CGE	Hiway Demon	T. E. Carr	
EI-CGF	Luton LA-5 Major	F. Doyle & J. Duggan	
EI-CGG	Ercoupe 415C	Irish Ercoupe Group	
EI-CGH	Cessna 210N	J. J. Spollen	
EI-CGI	McD Douglas MD-83	Irish Aerospace Ltd (leased to Air Liberte Tunisia)	
EI-CGJ	Solar Wings Pegasus XL-R	P. Heraty	
EI-CGK	Robinson R-22B	Skyfare Ltd	
EI-CGM	Solar Wings Pegasus XL-R	Microflight Ltd	
EI-CGN	Solar Wings Pegasus XL-R	M. French	
EI-CGO	Douglas DC-8-63AF	Aer Turas Teo	
EI-CGP	PA-28 Cherokee 140C	A. Barlow	
EI-CGQ	AS.350B Ecureuil	Caulstown Air Ltd	
EI-CGT	Cessna 152 II	J. J. Dunne	
EI-CGU	Robinson R-22HP	Santail Ltd	
EI-CGV	Piper J-5A Cub Cruiser	J5 Group	
EI-CGW	Powerchute Kestrel	C. Kiernan	
EI-CHF	PA-44-180 Seminole	A. Barlow	
EI-CHH	Boeing 737-317	Airplanes Finance Ltd (leased to Frontier A/L)	
EI-CHJ	Cessna FR.172K	Westpoint Flying Group Ltd	
EI-CHK	Piper J-3C-65 Cub	N. Higgins	
EI-CHL	Bell 206L-3 Long Ranger 3	Celtic Helicopters Ltd	
EI-CHM	Cessna 150M	K. A. O'Connor	
EI-CHN	M.S.880B Rallye Club	P. & O. Furlong	
EI-CHP	D.H.C.8-103 Dash Eight	GPA Propjet Ltd (leased to USAir Express)	
EI-CHR	CFM Shadow Srs BD	J. Smith	
EI-CHS	Cessna 172M	Kerry Aero Club Ltd	
EI-CHT	Solar Wings Pegasus XL-R	G. W. Maher	
EI-CHV	Agusta A.109A	Celtic Helicopters Ltd	
EI-CHW	L.188CF Electra	Hunting Cargo Airlines (Ireland) Ltd	
EI-CHX	L.188CF Electra	Hunting Cargo Airlines (Ireland) Ltd	
EI-CHY	—	—	
EI-CHZ	L.188CF Electra	Hunting Cargo Airlines (Ireland) Ltd	
EI-CIA	M.S.880B Rallye Club	M. Maher	
EI-CIF	PA-28 Cherokee 180C	AA Flying Group	
EI-CIG	PA-18 Super Cub 150	K. A. O'Connor	
EI-CIH	Ercoupe 415CD	J. T. Haycock	
EI-CIJ	Cessna 340	Airlink Airways Ltd	
EI-CIK	Mooney M.20C	A. & P. Aviation Ltd	
EI-CIM	Light Aero Avid Speedwing Mk IV	P. Swan	
EI-CIN	Cessna 150K	F. McGovern	
EI-CIO	Bell 206L-3 LongRanger	Sean Quinn Properties Ltd	
EI-CIR	Cessna 551 Citation II	Air Group Finance Ltd	
EI-CIV	PA-28 Cherokee 140	G. Cashman & E. Callanan	
EI-CIW	McD Douglas MD-83	Carotene Ltd (leased to TWA)	
EI-CIY	Boeing 767-330ER	ILFC Ireland (leased to Air Europe SpA)	
EI-CIZ	Steen Skybolt	J. Keane	
EI-CJA	Boeing 767-35HER	Hikone Ltd (leased to Air Europe SpA)	
EI-CJB	Boeing 767-35HER	Hikone Ltd (leased to Air Europe SpA)	
EI-CJC	Boeing 737-204ADV	Ryanair Ltd	

Notes	Reg.	Type	Owner or Operator
	EI-CJD	Boeing 737-204ADV	Ryanair Ltd
	EI-CJE	Boeing 737-204ADV	Ryanair Ltd (Jaguar)
	EI-CJF	Boeing 737-204ADV	Ryanair Ltd
	EI-CJG	Boeing 737-204ADV	Ryanair Ltd
	EI-CJH	Boeing 737-204ADV	Ryanair Ltd
	EI-CJI	Boeing 737-2E7ADV	Ryanair Ltd
	EI-CJK	Airbus A.300B4-103	TransAer Ltd
	EI-CJR	SNCAN Stampe SV-4A	C. Scully & P. Ryan
	EI-CJS	Jodel D.120A	L. Maddock
	EI-CJT	Slingsby Motor Cadet III	J. Tarrant
	EI-CJV	Moskito 2	M. Peril & ptnrs
	EI-CJW	Boeing 737-2P6	Dormacken Ltd (leased to Air Tran)
	EI-CJX	Boeing 757-2Y0	Dormacken Ltd (leased to Transaero)
	EI-CJY	Boeing 757-2Y0	Dormacken Ltd (leased to Transaero)
	EI-CJZ	Whittaker MW.6 Merlin	M. McCarthy
	EI-CKA	Jodel DR.400/180R	D. & B. Lodge
	EI-CKD	Boeing 767-3Y0ER	GPA Group Ltd (leased to Aeroflot)
	EI-CKE	Boeing 767-3Y0ER	GPA Group Ltd (leased to Aeroflot)
	EI-CKG	Avon Hunt Weightlift	B. Kelly
	EI-CKH	PA-18 Super Cub 95	G. Brady & C. Keenan
	EI-CKI	Thruster TST Mk 1	S. Pallister
	EI-CKJ	Cameron N-77 balloon	F. Meldon
	EI-CKK	Boeing 737-2P6	Dormacken Ltd (leased to Air South)
	EI-CKL	Boeing 737-2P6	Dormacken Ltd (leased to Air South)
	EI-CKN	Whittaker MW.6-S Fatboy Flyer	B. Audoire
	EI-CKP	Boeing 737-2K2	Ryanair Ltd
	EI-CKQ	Boeing 737-2K2	Ryanair Ltd
	EI-CKR	Boeing 737-2K2	Ryanair Ltd
	EI-CKS	Boeing 737-2T5	Ryanair Ltd
	EI-CKT	Mainair Gemini Flash	C. Burke
	EI-CKU	Solar Wings Pegasus SLR	M. O'Regan
	EI-CKV	Boeing 737-3Y0	Wedgeling Ltd (leased to America West)
	EI-CKW	Boeing 737-2P6	Dormacken Ltd (leased to Air South)
	EI-CKX	Jodel D.112	J. Greene
	EI-CKZ	Jodel D.18	J. O'Brien
	EI-CLA	HOAC Katana DV.20	Weston Ltd
	EI-CLB	Aerospatiale ATR-72-212	Tarquin Ltd (leased to Avianova)
	EI-CLC	Aerospatiale ATR-72-212	Tarquin Ltd (leased to Avianova)
	EI-CLD	Aerospatiale ATR-72-212	Tarquin Ltd (leased to Avianova)
	EI-CLE	Quad City Challenger II	M. Tormey
	EI-CLF	FH.227E Friendship	Ireland Airways
	EI-CLG	BAe 146-300	Aer Lingus Commuter St Finbarr
	EI-CLH	BAe 146-300	Aer Lingus Commuter St Aoife
	EI-CLI	BAe 146-300	Aer Lingus Commuter St Eithne
	EI-CLJ	BAe 146-300	Aer Lingus Commuter
	EI-CLK	Boeing 737-2P6	Dormacken Ltd
	EI-CLL	Whittaker MW.6-S Fat Boy Flyer	S. Curtin
	EI-CLM	Boeing 757-28A	ILFC Ireland Ltd (leased to Transaero)
	EI-CLN	Boeing 737-2C9	Airlease (103) Ltd (leased to Transaero)
	EI-CLO	Boeing 737-2C9	Airlease (103) Ltd (leased to Transaero)
	EI-CLQ	Cessna F.172N	A. H. Soper
	EI-CLS	Boeing 767-352ER	ILFC Ireland (leased to Air Europe SpA) Spa)
	EI-CLT	Bell 206B JetRanger	Mistwood Ltd
	EI-CLU	Boeing 757-28A	ILFC (Ireland) Ltd (leased to Transaero)
	EI-CLV	Boeing 757-28A	ILFC (Ireland) Ltd (leased to Transaero)
	EI-CLW	Boeing 737-3Y0	Airplanes Finance Ltd (leased to Air One)
	EI-CLX	Cessna 310Q	Cork Aviation Centre
	EI-CLZ	Boeing 737-3Y0	Airplanes Finance Ltd (leased to Air One)
	EI-CMB	PA-28 Cherokee 140	Kestrel Flying Group Ltd
	EI-CMC	—	
	EI-CMF	CFM Streak Shadow	O. Williams
	EI-CMG	Short SD3-60 Variant 100	Irish Air Transport
	EI-CMI	Robinson R-22B	Toriamos Ltd
	EI-CMJ	Aérospatiale ATR-72-212	Tarquin Ltd (leased to Avianova)
	EI-CMK	Goldwing ST	M. Gavigan
	EI-CML	Cessna 150M	K. A. O'Connor
	EI-CMM	McD Douglas MD-83	Irish Aerospace Ltd (leased to Eurofly)
	EI-CMN	PA-12 Super Cruiser	O. Bruton
	EI-CMQ	Boeing 767-3Q8ER	ILFC Ireland (leased to Air Europe SpA)
	EI-CMR	Rutan LongEz	F. & C. O'Caoimh
	EI-CMS	BAe 146-200	CityJet Ltd
	EI-CMT	PA-34-200T Seneca II	Atlantic Air Ltd
	EI-CMU	Mainair Mercury	J. Deeney

Reg.	Type	Owner or Operator	Notes
EI-CMV	Cessna 150L	Santail Ltd	
EI-CMW	Rotorway Executive	B. McNamee	
EI-CMX	Beech 76 Duchess	F. Doherty	
EI-CMY	BAe 146-200	CityJet Ltd	
EI-CMZ	McD Douglas MD-83	Airplane Finances Ltd (leased to Eurofly)	
EI-CNA	Letov LK-2M Sluka	G-Doody	
EI-CNB	BAe 146-200	CityJet Ltd	
EI-CNC	Team Minimax	A. M. S. Allen	
EI-CNE	Boeing 737-4S3	Aer Lingus Teo (leased to Ryan International)	
EI-CNF	Boeing 737-4Y0	Aer Lingus Teo (leased to Ryan International)	
EI-CNG	Air & Space 18A gyroplane	P. Joyce	
EI-CNH	—	—	
EI-CNI	Avro RJ85	Azzurra Air	
EI-CNJ	Avro RJ85	Azzurra Air	
EI-CNK	—	—	
EI-CNL	Sikorsky S-61N	Bond Helicopters (Ireland) Ltd	
EI-CNM	PA-31-350 Navajo Chieftain	M. Goss	
EI-CNN	—	—	
EI-CNO	—	—	
EI-CNP	—	—	
EI-CNR	—	—	
EI-CNS	—	—	
EI-CNT	Boeing 737-230	Ryanair Ltd	
EI-CNU	—	—	
EI-CNV	—	—	
EI-CNW	—	—	
EI-CNX	—	—	
EI-CNY	—	—	
EI-CNZ	—	—	
EI-CRI	Beech 350 Super King Air	Westair Aviation Ltd	
EI-CRK	Airbus A.330-301	Aer Lingus Teo St Brigid	
EI-CUB	Piper J-3C-65 Cub	J. Conneely & ptnrs	
EI-DLA	Douglas DC-10-30	Dormacken Ltd (leased to Continental)	
EI-DMI	PA-31-325 Turbo Navajo C	Dawn Meats	
EI-DUB	Airbus A.330-301	Aer Lingus Teo St Patrick	
EI-DWN	Cessna 421C	Dawn Meats (Waterford) Ltd	
EI-EDR	PA-28R Cherokee Arrow 200	Victor Mike Flying Group Ltd	
EI-EEC	PA-23 Aztec 250	Westair Ltd	
EI-EIO	PA-34-200T Seneca II	K. A. O'Connor	
EI-ETC	Aeronca 15AC Sedan	H. Moreau	
EI-EWW	Boeing 727-243	Hunting Cargo Airlines/TNT	
EI-EXP	Short SD3-30 Variant 100	Ireland Airways	
EI-FKA	Fokker 50	Aer Lingus Commuter St Fintan	
EI-FKB	Fokker 50	Aer Lingus Commuter St Fergal	
EI-FKC	Fokker 50	Aer Lingus Commuter St Fidelma	
EI-FKD	Fokker 50	Aer Lingus Commuter St Flannan	
EI-FKE	Fokker 50	Aer Lingus Commuter St Pappin	
EI-FKF	Fokker 50	Aer Lingus Commuter St Ultan	
EI-FLY	SOCATA TB.9 Tampico	Hotel Bravo Flying Group Ltd	
EI-GER	Maule MX7-180A	P. Costigan	
EI-GFC	SOCATA TB.9 Tampico	Galway Flying Club Ltd	
EI-HAM	Light Aero Avid Flyer	H. Goulding	
EI-HCA	Boeing 727-225F	Hunting Cargo Airlines (Ireland) Ltd	
EI-HCB	Boeing 727-223F	Hunting Cargo Airlines (Ireland) Ltd	
EI-HCC	Boeing 727-223F	Hunting Cargo Airlines (Ireland) Ltd	
EI-HCD	Boeing 727-223F	Hunting Cargo Airlines (Ireland) Ltd	
EI-HCI	Boeing 727-225F	Hunting Cargo Airlines (Ireland) Ltd/TNT	
EI-HCS	Grob G.109B	H. Sydner	
EI-HER	Bell 206B JetRanger 3	Irish Helicopters Ltd	
EI-IRV	AS.350B Ecureuil	Santail Ltd	
EI-JFK	Airbus A.330-301	Aer Lingus Teo Colmcille	
EI-JTC	PA-31-350 Navajo Chieftain	T. Brennan	
EI-JWM	Robinson R-22B	Jair Aviation Co Ltd	
EI-LCH	Boeing 727-281	Hunting Cargo Airlines (Ireland) Ltd	
EI-LIT	MBB Bo 105S	Irish Helicopters Ltd	
EI-LRS	Hughes 269C	Lynch Roofing Systems Ltd	
EI-MAS	Canadair CL.600 Challenger	—	
EI-MIP	SA.365N Dauphin 2	Bond Helicopters (Ireland) Ltd	
EI-ONE	Bell 206B JetRanger	E. M. Corcoran	
EI-PAK	Boeing 727-227	TNT Express Worldwide	
EI-POD	Cessna 177B	Trim Flying Club Ltd	
EI-SHN	Airbus A.330-301	Aer Lingus Teo St Flannan	

Notes	Reg.	Type	Owner or Operator
	EI-SKY	Boeing 727-281	Hunting Cargo Airlines (Ireland) Ltd/TNT
	EI-SXT	Canadair CL.600 Challenger	Sextant Ireland Ltd
	EI-TBG	L.1011-385 TriStar1	Aer Turas Teo
	EI-TCK	Cessna 421A	T. C. Killeen
	EI-TKI	Robinson R-22B	G.T.Investigations (International) Ltd
	EI-TLB	Airbus A.300B4-103	Airplanes Holdings Ltd *(leased to TransAer Ltd)*
	EI-TLE	Airbus A.320-231	TransAer Ltd
	EI-TLF	Airbus A.320-231	TransAer Ltd
	EI-TLG	Airbus A.320-231	TransAer Ltd
	EI-TLH	Airbus A.320-231	TransAer Ltd
	EI-TLI	Airbus A.320-231	TransAer Ltd
	EI-TLJ	Airbus A.320-231	TransAer Ltd
	EI-TNT	Boeing 727-281	TNT Express Worldwide Ltd
	EI-UFO	PA-22 Tri-Pacer 150	W. Treacy
	EI-WAC	PA-23 Aztec 250E	Westair Aviation Ltd
	EI-WCC	Robinson R-22B	Westair Aviation Ltd
	EI-WDC	H.S.125 Srs 3B	Westair Aviation Ltd
	EI-XMA	Robinson R-22B	Westair Aviation Ltd
	EI-XMC	Robinson R-22B	McAuliffe Photographic Laboratories

Notes	Reg.	Type	Notes	Reg.	Type

EK (Armenia)

The following are operated by Armenian Airlines with the registrations prefixed by EK.

Reg.	Type		Reg.	Type
65044	Tu-134A		85196	Tu-154B
65072	Tu-134A		85200	Tu-154B
65650	Tu-134A		85210	Tu-154B
65731	Tu-134A-3		85279	Tu-154B-1
65822	Tu-134A		85403	Tu-154B 2
65831	Tu-134A3		85442	Tu-154B-2
65848	Tu-134A-3		85536	Tu-154B-2
65884	Tu-134A		85566	Tu-154B-2
65975	Tu-134A3		86117	IL-86
85162	Tu-154B		86118	IL-86
85166	Tu-154B			

Notes	Reg.	Type	Owner or Operator

EL (Liberia)

Reg.	Type	Owner or Operator
EL-AJO	Douglas DC-8-55F	Liberia World Airlines
EL-AJQ	Douglas DC-8-54F	Liberia World Airlines
EL-AKJ	Boeing 707-321C	Occidental Airlines
EL-AKK	Boeing 707-323B	Omega Air
EL-AKL	Boeing 707-351C	Liberia World Airlines
EL-AKU	Boeing 707-347C	Occidental Airlines
EL-ALG	Boeing 707-369C	Shuttle Air Cargo
EL-JNS	Boeing 707-323C	Transway Air International33
EL-RDS	Boeing 707-323C	Air Cess (Liberia) Amino

EP (Iran)

Reg.	Type	Owner or Operator
EP-IAA	Boeing 747SP-86	Iran Air *Kurdistan*
EP-IAB	Boeing 747SP-86	Iran Air
EP-IAC	Boeing 747SP-86	Iran Air *Fars*
EP-IAD	Boeing 747SP-86	Iran Air
EP-IAG	Boeing 747-286B (SCD)	Iran Air *Azarabadegan*
EP-IAH	Boeing 747-286B (SCD)	Iran Air *Khuzestan*
EP-IAM	Boeing 747-186B	Iran Air
EP-IBA	Airbus A.300-605R	Iran Air
EP-IBB	Airbus A.300-605R	Iran Air
EP-ICA	Boeing 747-2J9F	Iran Air
EP-ICC	Boeing 747-2J9F	Iran Air

Reg.	Type	Notes	Reg.	Type	Notes

ER (Moldova)

The following are operated by Air Moldova with the registrations prefixed by ER.

Reg.	Type		Reg.	Type
65036	Tu-134A-3		65791	Tu-134A-3
65050	Tu-134A-3		65897	Tu-134A-3
65051	Tu-134A-3		85090	Tu-154B
65071	Tu-134A-3		85285	Tu-154B-1
65094	Tu-134A-3		85324	Tu-154B-2
65140	Tu-134A-3		85332	Tu-154B-2
65707	Tu-134A-3		85384	Tu-154B-2
65736	Tu-134A-3		85405	Tu-154B-2
65741	Tu-134A-3		85565	Tu-154B-2

Reg.	Type	Owner or Operator	Notes

ES (Estonia)

Reg.	Type	Owner or Operator
ES-ABC	Boeing 737-5Q8	Estonian Air
ES-ABD	Boeing 737-5Q8	Estonian Air *Hamarik*
ES-AFK	Fokker 50	Estonian Air
ES-AFL	Fokker 50	Estonian Air
ES-LTP	Tupolev Tu-154M	ELK Airways
ES-LTR	Tupolev Tu-154M	ELK Airways

ET (Ethiopia)

Reg.	Type	Owner or Operator
ET-AIE	Boeing 767-260ER	Ethiopian Airlines
ET-AIF	Boeing 767-260ER	Ethiopian Airlines
ET-AIV	Boeing 707-327C	Ethiopian Airlines
ET-AJS	Boeing 757-260PF	Ethiopian Airlines
ET-AJX	Boeing 757-260	Ethiopian Airlines
ET-AKC	Boeing 757-260	Ethiopian Airlines
ET-AKE	Boeing 757-260	Ethiopian Airlines
ET-AKF	Boeing 757-260	Ethiopian Airlines

Reg.	Type	Notes	Reg.	Type	Notes

EW (Belarus)

The following are operated by Belavia with the registrations prefixed by EW.

Reg.	Type		Reg.	Type
65049	Tu-134A		85465	Tu-154B-2
65082	Tu-134A		85509	Tu-154B-2
65085	Tu-134A		85538	Tu-154B-2
65106	Tu-134A		85545	Tu-154B-2
65108	Tu-134A		85580	Tu-154B-2
65133	Tu-134A-3		85581	Tu-154B-2
65145	Tu-134A		85583	Tu-154B-2
65149	Tu-134A		85591	Tu-154B-2
65676	Tu-134A		85593	Tu-154B-2
65754	Tu-134A		85703	Tu-154M
65772	Tu-134A		85706	Tu-154M
65803	Tu-134A		85724	Tu-154M
65821	Tu-134A		75725	Tu-154M
65832	Tu-134A		85748	Tu-154M
65861	Tu-134A-3		85815	Tu-154M
65892	Tu-134A		86062	IL-86
65957	Tu-134A			
65974	Tu-134A		The following are operated by Belair:	
85260	Tu-154B-1		65565	Tu-134A
85352	Tu-154B-2		65605	Tu-134A
85411	Tu-154B-2		76836	IL-76TD
85419	Tu-154B-2		78849	IL-76MD

Notes	Reg.	Type	Notes	Reg.	Type

EX (Kyrgyzstan)

The following are operated by Kyrgyzstan Airlines with the registrations prefixed by EX.

Reg.	Type	Reg.	Type
65111	Tu-134A-3	85294	Tu-154B-1
65119	Tu-134A-3	85313	Tu-154B-2
65125	Tu-134A-3	85369	Tu-154B-2
65778	Tu-134A-3	85444	Tu-154B-2
65779	Tu-134A-3	85491	Tu-154B-2
65789	Tu-134A-3	85497	Tu-154B-2
76815	IL-76TD	85519	Tu-154B-2
85021	Tu-154B-1	85590	Tu-154B-2
85252	Tu-154B-1	85718	Tu-154M
85257	Tu-154B-1	85762	Tu-154M
85259	Tu-154B-1		

EY (Tajikistan)

The following are operated by Tajik Air with the registrations prefixed by EY.

Reg.	Type	Reg.	Type
65003	Tu-134A-3	85385	Tu-154B-2
65763	Tu-134A-3	85406	Tu-154B-2
65788	Tu-134A-3	85440	Tu-154B-2
65814	Tu-134A-3	85466	Tu-154B-2
65820	Tu-134A-3	85469	Tu-154B-2
65835	Tu-134A-3	85475	Tu-154B-2
65875	Tu-134A-3	85487	Tu-154B-2
65876	Tu-134A-3	85511	Tu-154B-2
65895	Tu-134A-3	85691	Tu-154M
85247	Tu-154B-1	85692	Tu-154M
85251	Tu-154B-1	85717	Tu-154M
85281	Tu-154B-1		

EZ (Turkmenistan)

Turkmenistan Airlines operates the following with the registrations prefixed by EZ.

Reg.	Type	Reg.	Type
A001	Boeing 737-341	F428	IL-76TD
A002	Boeing 737-332	85241	Tu-154B-1
A003	Boeing 737-332	85246	Tu-154B-1
A010	Boeing 757-23A	85250	Tu-154B-1
A011	Boeing 757-22K	85345	Tu-154B-2
A012	Boeing 757-22K	85383	Tu-154B-2
F421	IL-76TD	85394	Tu-154B-2
F422	IL-76TD	85410	Tu-154B-2
F423	IL-76TD	85492	Tu-154B-2
F424	IL-76TD	85507	Tu-154B-2
F425	IL-76TD	85532	Tu-154B-2
F426	IL-76TD	85549	Tu-154B-2
F427	IL-76TD	85560	Tu-154B-2

Notes	Reg.	Type	Owner or Operator

F (France)

Reg.	Type	Owner or Operator
F-BGNR	V.708 Viscount ★	—/Perth
F-BMKS	S.E.210 Caravelle 10B	Air Toulouse International
F-BPPA	Aero Spacelines Super Guppy-201	Airbus Inter Transport Airbus Skylink 2
F-BPUA	F.27 Friendship Mk 500	Air France
F-BPUC	F.27 Friendship Mk 500	Air France
F-BPUD	F.27 Friendship Mk 500	Air France
F-BPUE	F.27 Friendship Mk 500	Air France
F-BPUF	F.27 Friendship Mk 500	Air France
F-BPUG	F.27 Friendship Mk 500	Air France
F-BPUH	F.27 Friendship Mk 500	Air France
F-BPUJ	F.27 Friendship Mk 500	Air France
F-BPVE	Boeing 747-128 ★	British Aviation Heritage/Bruntingthorpe
F-BPVF	Boeing 747-128	Air France
F-BPVG	Boeing 747-128	Corsair
F-BPVJ	Boeing 747-128	Air France
F-BPVM	Boeing 747-128	Air France

Reg.	Type	Owner or Operator	Notes
F-BPVP	Boeing 747-128	Air France	
F-BPVR	Boeing 747-228F (SCD)	Air France	
F-BPVS	Boeing 747-228B (SCD)	Air France	
F-BPVT	Boeing 747-228B (SCD)	Air France	
F-BPVU	Boeing 747-228B (SCD)	Air France	
F-BPVV	Boeing 747-228F (SCD)	Air France	
F-BPVX	Boeing 747-228B (SCD)	Air France	
F-BPVY	Boeing 747-228B	Air France	
F-BPVZ	Boeing 747-228F (SCD)	Air France	
F-BSUN	F.27 Friendship Mk 500	Air France	
F-BSUO	F.27 Friendship Mk 500	Air France	
F-BTDD	Douglas DC-10-30	AOM French Airlines	
F-BTDE	Douglas DC-10-30	AOM French Airlines	
F-BTDG	Boeing 747-2B3B (SCD)	Air France	
F-BTDH	Boeing 747-2B3B (SCD)	Air France	
F-BTGV	Aero Spacelines Super Guppy 201 ★	British Aviation Heritage/Bruntingthorpe	
F-BTSC	Concorde 101	Air France	
F-BTSD	Concorde 101	Air France	
F-BUAF	Airbus A.300B2-1C	Air France Europe	
F-BUAG	Airbus A.300B2-1C	Air France Europe	
F-BUAH	Airbus A.300B2-1C	Air France Europe	
F-BUAI	Airbus A.300B2-1C	Air France Europe	
F-BUAJ	Airbus A.300B2-1C	Air France Europe	
F-BUAK	Airbus A.300B2K-3C	Air France Europe	
F-BUAN	Airbus A.300B2-1C	Air France Europe	
F-BUAO	Airbus A.300B2-1C	Air France	
F-BUAP	Airbus A.300B2-1C	Air France	
F-BUAQ	Airbus A.300B4-2C	Air France Europe	
F-BUTI	F.28 Fellowship 1000	T.A.T. European	
F-BVFA	Concorde 101	Air France	
F-BVFB	Concorde 101	Air France	
F-BVFC	Concorde 101	Air France	
F-BVFF	Concorde 101	Air France	
F-BVGA	Airbus A.300B2-101	Air France	
F-BVGB	Airbus A.300B2-101	Air France	
F-BVGI	Airbus A.300B4-203	Air France/Air Charter	
F-BVGL	Airbus A.300B4-203	Air France	
F-BVGM	Airbus A.300B4-203	Air France	
F-BVGN	Airbus A.300B4-203	Air France	
F-BVGO	Airbus A.300B4-203	Air France	
F-BVGT	Airbus A.300B4-203	Air France/Air Charter	
F-BVJL	Beech 99A	T.A.T. European	
F-GBBR	F.28 Fellowship 1000	T.A.T. European	
F-GBBS	F.28 Fellowship 1000	T.A.T. European	
F-GBBT	F.28 Fellowship 1000	T.A.T. European	
F-GBBX	F.28 Fellowship 1000	T.A.T. European	
F-GBEA	Airbus A.300B2-1C	Air France Europe	
F-GBGA	EMB-110P2 Bandeirante	Aigle Azur	
F-GBLE	EMB-110P2 Bandeirante	Air Atlantique	
F-GBME	EMB-110P2 Bandeirante	Air Atlantique	
F-GBOX	Boeing 747-2B3F (SCD)	Air France Cargo	
F-GBRM	EMB-110P2 Bandeirante	Air Atlantique	
F-GBRQ	FH.227B Friendship	Air Provence	
F-GBRU	F.27J Friendship	T.A.T. European	
F-GBYA	Boeing 737-228	Air France	
F-GBYB	Boeing 737-228	Air France	
F-GBYC	Boeing 737-228	Air France	
F-GBYD	Boeing 737-228	Air France	
F-GBYE	Boeing 737-228	Air France	
F-GBYF	Boeing 737-228	Air France	
F-GBYG	Boeing 737-228	Air France	
F-GBYH	Boeing 737-228	Air France	
F-GBYI	Boeing 737-228	Air France	
F-GBYJ	Boeing 737-228	Air France	
F-GBYK	Boeing 737-228	Air France	
F-GBYL	Boeing 737-228	Air France	
F-GBYM	Boeing 737-228	Air France	
F-GBYN	Boeing 737-228	Air France	
F-GBYO	Boeing 737-228	Air France	
F-GBYP	Boeing 737-228	Air France	
F-GBYQ	Boeing 737-228	Air France	
F-GCBA	Boeing 747-228B	Air France	
F-GCBB	Boeing 747-228B (SCD)	Air France/SABENA	

Notes	Reg.	Type	Owner or Operator
	F-GCBD	Boeing 747-228B (SCD)	Air France
	F-GCBE	Boeing 747-228F (SCD)	Air France
	F-GCBF	Boeing 747-228B (SCD)	Air France
	F-GCBG	Boeing 747-228F (SCD)	Air France Cargo
	F-GCBH	Boeing 747-228F (SCD)	Air France Cargo
	F-GCBI	Boeing 747-228B (SCD)	Air France
	F-GCBJ	Boeing 747-228B (SCD)	Air France
	F-GCBK	Boeing 747-228F (SCD)	Air France Cargo
	F-GCBL	Boeing 747-228F (SCD)	Air France Cargo
	F-GCBM	Boeing 747-228F	Air France Asia Cargo
	F-GCFC	FH.227B Friendship	T.A.T. European
	F-GCGQ	Boeing 727-227	EAS Europe Airlines
	F-GCJL	Boeing 737-222	Air Liberte
	F-GCLL	Boeing 737-222	Air Liberte
	F-GCPT	FH.227B Friendship	T.A.T. European
	F-GCPU	FH.227B Friendship	T.A.T. European
	F-GCPX	FH.227B Friendship	T.A.T. European
	F-GCPY	FH.227B Friendship	T.A.T. European
	F-GCSL	Boeing 737-222	Air Liberte
	F-GCVL	S.E.210 Caravelle 12	Air Provence International
	F-GCVM	S.E.210 Caravelle 12	Air Provence International
	F-GDAQ	L.100-30 Hercules	Jet Fret
	F-GDFC	F.28 Fellowship 4000	T.A.T. European
	F-GDFD	F.28 Fellowship 4000	T.A.T. European
	F-GDPP	Douglas DC-3C	France DC-3/L'Envolée Air Inter
	F-GDSG	UTA Super Guppy	Airbus Inter Transport Airbus *Skylink 3*
	F-GDSK	F.28 Fellowship 4000	T.A.T. European
	F-GDUS	F.28 Fellowship 2000	T.A.T. European
	F-GDUT	F.28 Fellowship 2000	T.A.T. European
	F-GDUU	F.28 Fellowship 2000	T.A.T. European/British Airways
	F-GDUV	F.28 Fellowship 2000	T.A.T. European
	F-GDUY	F.28 Fellowship 4000	T.A.T. European
	F-GDUZ	F.28 Fellowship 4000	T.A.T. European
	F-GDXL	Aérospatiale ATR-42-300	Brit Air/Air France
	F-GEAI	UTA Super Guppy	Airbus Inter Transport Airbus *Skylink 4*
	F-GECK	F.28 Fellowship 1000	T.A.T. European
	F-GEGD	Aérospatiale ATR-42-300	Air Littoral
	F-GEGE	Aérospatiale ATR-42-300	Air Littoral
	F-GELG	SAAB SF.340A	Brit Air/Air France
	F-GELP	S.E.210 Caravelle	Air Toulouse International
	F-GEMA	Airbus A.310-203	Air France
	F-GEMB	Airbus A.310-203	Air France
	F-GEMC	Airbus A.310-203	Air France
	F-GEMD	Airbus A.310-203	Air France
	F-GEME	Airbus A.310-203	Air France
	F-GEMG	Airbus A.310-203	Air France
	F-GEMN	Airbus A.310-304	Air France
	F-GEMO	Airbus A.310-304	Air France
	F-GEMP	Airbus A.310-304	Air France
	F-GEMQ	Airbus A.310-304	Air France
	F-GEQJ	Aérospatiale ATR-42-300	Regional Airlines/T.A.T. European
	F-GETA	Boeing 747-3B3 (SCD)	Air France
	F-GETB	Boeing 747-3B3 (SCD)	Air France
	F-GEXA	Boeing 747-4B3	Air France
	F-GEXB	Boeing 747-4B3	Air France
	F-GEXI	Boeing 737-2L9	Air Toulouse
	F-GEXJ	Boeing 737-2Q8	Euralair
	F-GFBZ	SAAB SF.340A	Brit Air
	F-GFEN	EMB-120 Brasilia	Air Littoral
	F-GFEO	EMB-120 Brasilia	Air Littoral
	F-GFEP	EMB-120 Brasilia	Air Littoral
	F-GFEQ	EMB-120 Brasilia	Air Littoral
	F-GFER	EMB-120 Brasilia	Air Littoral
	F-GFIN	EMB-120 Brasilia	Air Littoral
	F-GFJP	Aérospatiale ATR-42-300	Brit Air/Air France
	F-GFKA	Airbus A.320-111	Air France *Ville de Paris*
	F-GFKB	Airbus A.320-111	Air France *Ville de Rome*
	F-GFKD	Airbus A.320-111	Air France *Ville de Londres*
	F-GFKE	Airbus A.320-111	Air France *Ville de Bonn*
	F-GFKF	Airbus A.320-111	Air France *Ville de Madrid*
	F-GFKG	Airbus A.320-111	Air France *Ville d'Amsterdam*
	F-GFKH	Airbus A.320-211	Air France *Ville de Bruxelles*
	F-GFKI	Airbus A.320-211	Air France *Ville de Lisbonne*
	F-GFKJ	Airbus A.320-211	Air France *Ville de Copenhague*

Reg.	Type	Owner or Operator	Notes
F-GFKK	Airbus A.320-211	Air France *Ville d'Athenes*	
F-GFKL	Airbus A.320-211	Air France/Air Charter *Ville de Dublin*	
F-GFKM	Airbus A.320-211	Air France *Ville de Luxembourg*	
F-GFKN	Airbus A.320-211	Air France	
F-GFKO	Airbus A.320-211	Air France	
F-GFKP	Airbus A.320-211	Air France *Ville de Nice*	
F-GFKQ	Airbus A.320-111	Air France *Ville de Berlin*	
F-GFKR	Airbus A.320-211	Air France *Ville de Barcelona*	
F-GFKS	Airbus A.320-211	Air France	
F-GFKT	Airbus A.320-211	Air France	
F-GFKU	Airbus A.320-211	Air France	
F-GFKV	Airbus A.320-211	Air France *Ville de Bordeaux*	
F-GFKX	Airbus A.320-211	Air France/Air Charter *Ville de Francfurt*	
F-GFKY	Airbus A.320-211	Air France *Ville de Toulouse*	
F-GFKZ	Airbus A.320-211	Air France *Ville de Turin*	
F-GFLV	Boeing 737-2K5	Air France/Air Charter	
F-GFLX	Boeing 737-2K5	Air France/Air Charter	
F-GFPR	Swearingen SA226AT Merlin IVA	Regional Airlines	
F-GFUA	Boeing 737-33A	Air France	
F-GFUD	Boeing 737-33A	Air France	
F-GFUE	Boeing 737-3B3QC	L'Aeropostale	
F-GFUF	Boeing 737-3B3QC	L'Aeropostale	
F-GFUG	Boeing 737-4B3	Corsair	
F-GFUH	Boeing 737-4B3	Corsair	
F-GFUJ	Boeing 737-33A	Air France	
F-GFVI	Boeing 737-230C	L'Aeropostale	
F-GFYL	Boeing 737-2A9C	Air Liberte	
F-GFYN	Aérospatiale ATR-42-300	Air Littoral	
F-GFZB	McD Douglas MD-83	Air Liberte	
F-GGBV	SAAB SF.340A	Aigle Azur	
F-GGEA	Airbus A.320-111	Air France Europe	
F-GGEB	Airbus A.320-111	Air France Europe	
F-GGEC	Airbus A.320-111	Air France Europe	
F-GGEE	Airbus A.320-111	Air France Europe	
F-GGEF	Airbus A.320-111	Air France Europe	
F-GGEG	Airbus A.320-111	Air France Europe	
F-GGGR	Boeing 727-2H3	Belair *Villa Squeville*	
F-GGLK	Aérospatiale ATR-42-300	T.A.T. European	
F-GGLR	Aérospatiale ATR-42-300	Brit Air/Air France	
F-GGMA	McD Douglas MD-83	AOM French Airlines	
F-GGMB	McD Douglas MD-83	AOM French Airlines	
F-GGMD	McD Douglas MD-83	AOM French Airlines	
F-GGME	McD Douglas MD-83	AOM French Airlines	
F-GGMF	McD Douglas MD-83	AOM French Airlines	
F-GGTD	EMB-120ER Brasilia	Flandre Air/T.A.T European	
F-GGVP	Boeing 737-2K2C	L'Aéropostale	
F-GGVQ	Boeing 737-2K2C	L'Aéropostale	
F-GHDB	SAAB SF.340A	Brit Air/Air France	
F-GHEB	McD Douglas MD-83	Air Liberte	
F-GHEC	McD Douglas MD-83	Air Liberte	
F-GHED	McD Douglas MD-83	Air Liberte	
F-GHEI	McD Douglas MD-83	Air Liberte	
F-GHEJ	Airbus A.310-324	Air Liberte	
F-GHEK	McD Douglas MD-83	Air Liberte	
F-GHEX	EMB-120ER Brasilia	Flandre Air/T.A.T. European	
F-GHEY	EMB-120ER Brasilia	Flandre Air/T.A.T. European	
F-GHGD	Boeing 767-27EER	Air France/Balkan *Pliska*	
F-GHGE	Boeing 767-27EER	Air France/Balkan *Preslav*	
F-GHGF	Boeing 767-3Q8ER	Air France	
F-GHGG	Boeing 767-3Q8ER	Air France	
F-GHGH	Boeing 767-37EER	Air France	
F-GHGI	Boeing 767-328ER	Air France	
F-GHGJ	Boeing 767-328ER	Air France	
F-GHHO	McD Douglas MD-83	Air Liberte	
F-GHHP	McD Douglas MD-83	Air Liberte	
F-GHIA	EMB-120RT Brasilia	Air Littoral	
F-GHIB	EMB-120RT Brasilia	Air Littoral	
F-GHJE	Aérospatiale ATR-42-300	Brit Air	
F-GHMI	SAAB SF.340A	Brit Air/Air France	
F-GHMJ	SAAB SF.340A	Brit Air	
F-GHMK	SAAB SF.340A	Brit Air	
F-GHMU	S.E.210 Caravelle 10B3	Air Toulouse International	
F-GHOI	Douglas DC-10-30	AOM French Airlines	
F-GHOL	Boeing 737-53C	Euralair International/Air France	

Notes	Reg.	Type	Owner or Operator
	F-GHPI	Aérospatiale ATR-42-300	Brit Air
	F-GHPK	Aérospatiale ATR-42-300	Brit Air
	F-GHPS	Aérospatiale ATR-42-300	Brit Air/Air France
	F-GHPU	Aérospatiale ATR-72-101	Brit Air
	F-GHPV	Aérospatiale ATR-72-101	Brit Air
	F-GHPY	Aérospatiale ATR-42-300	Brit Air/Air France
	F-GHPZ	Aérospatiale ATR-42-300	Brit Air/Air France
	F-GHQA	Airbus A.320-211	Air France Europe
	F-GHQB	Airbus A.320-211	Air France Europe
	F-GHQC	Airbus A.320-211	Air France Europe
	F-GHQD	Airbus A.320-211	Air France Europe
	F-GHQE	Airbus A.320-211	Air France Europe
	F-GHQF	Airbus A.320-211	Air France Europe
	F-GHQG	Airbus A.320-211	Air France Europe
	F-GHQH	Airbus A.320-211	Air France Europe
	F-GHQI	Airbus A.320-211	Air France Europe
	F-GHQJ	Airbus A.320-211	Air France Europe
	F-GHQK	Airbus A.320-211	Air France Europe
	F-GHQL	Airbus A.320-211	Air France Europe
	F-GHQM	Airbus A.320-211	Air France Europe
	F-GHQO	Airbus A.320-211	Air France Europe
	F-GHQP	Airbus A.320-211	Air France Europe
	F-GHQQ	Airbus A.320-211	Air France Europe
	F-GHQR	Airbus A.320-211	Air France Europe
	F-GHSE	Beech 1900C-1	Flandre Air
	F-GHSI	Beech 1900C-1	Flandre Air
	F-GHUL	Boeing 737-53C	Euralair International/Air France
	F-GHVA	Swearingen SA227AC Metro III	Regional Airlines
	F-GHVG	Swearingen SA227AC Metro III	Regional Airlines
	F-GHVM	Boeing 737-33A	Air France
	F-GHVN	Boeing 737-33A	Air France
	F-GHVO	Boeing 737-33A	Air France
	F-GHVS	SAAB SF.340B	Regional Airlines
	F-GHVT	SAAB SF.340B	Regional Airlines
	F-GHVU	SAAB SF.340B	Regional Airlines
	F-GHXK	Boeing 737-2A1	Corsair
	F-GHXL	Boeing 737-2S3	Air Toulouse International
	F-GHXM	Boeing 737-53A	Air France/Air Charter
	F-GIAH	F.28 Fellowship 1000	T.A.T. European
	F-GIAI	F.28 Fellowship 1000	T.A.T. European
	F-GIDK	Douglas DC-3C	Dakota Air
	F-GIIA	Aérospatiale ATR-42-300	Air Atlantique
	F-GIJS	Airbus A.300B4-203	Air France Europe
	F-GILN	Swearingen SA227AC Metro III	Regional Airlines
	F-GIMH	F.28 Fellowship 1000	T.A.T. European
	F-GIMJ	Boeing 747-121	Corsair
	F-GINL	Boeing 737-53C	Euralair International/Air France
	F-GIOA	Fokker 100	T.A.T. European/British Airways
	F-GIOG	Fokker 100	T.A.T European
	F-GIOH	Fokker 100	T.A.T. European
	F-GIOI	Fokker 100	T.A.T. European
	F-GIOJ	Fokker 100	T.A.T. European/British Airways
	F-GIOK	Fokker 100	T.A.T. European
	F-GIRC	Aérospatiale ATR-42-300	T.A.T. European
	F-GISA	Boeing 747-428 (SCD)	Air France
	F-GISB	Boeing 747-428 (SCD)	Air France
	F-GISC	Boeing 747-428 (SCD)	Air France
	F-GISD	Boeing 747-428 (SCD)	Air France
	F-GISE	Boeing 747-428 (SCD)	Air France
	F-GITA	Boeing 747-428	Air France
	F-GITB	Boeing 747-428	Air France
	F-GITC	Boeing 747-428	Air France
	F-GITD	Boeing 747-428	Air France
	F-GITE	Boeing 747-428	Air France
	F-GITF	Boeing 747-428	Air France
	F-GITH	Boeing 747-428	Air France
	F-GIUB	Boeing 747-428F (SCD)	Air France Cargo
	F-GIVG	Aérospatiale ATR-42-300	Regional Airlines
	F-GIVK	EMB-120ER Brasilia	Flandre Air/T.A.T. European
	F-GIXA	Boeing 737-2K2C	L'Aéropostale
	F-GIXB	Boeing 737-33AQC	L'Aéropostale
	F-GIXC	Boeing 737-38BQC	L'Aéropostale
	F-GIXD	Boeing 737-33AQC	L'Aéropostale
	F-GIXE	Boeing 737-3B3QC	L'Aéropostale

Reg.	Type	Owner or Operator	Notes
F-GIXF	Boeing 737-3B3QC	L'Aéropostale	
F-GIXG	Boeing 737-382QC	L'Aéropostale	
F-GIXH	Boeing 737-3S3QC	L'Aéropostale	
F-GIXI	Boeing 737-348QC	L'Aéropostale	
F-GIXJ	Boeing 737-3Y0QC	L'Aéropostale	
F-GIXK	Boeing 737-33AQC	L'Aéropostale	
F-GIXL	Boeing 737-348QC	L'Aéropostale	
F-GIXO	Boeing 737-3Q8QC	L'Aéropostale	
F-GIXP	Boeing 737-3M8F	L'Aéropostale	
F-GJAK	EMB-120RT Brasilia	Air Littoral	
F-GJDL	Boeing 737-210C	Air Liberte	
F-GJEG	Beech 1900-1	T.A.T. European	
F-GJNA	Boeing 737-528	Air France	
F-GJNB	Boeing 737-528	Air France	
F-GJNC	Boeing 737-528	Air France	
F-GJND	Boeing 737-528	Air France	
F-GJNE	Boeing 737-528	Air France	
F-GJNF	Boeing 737-528	Air France	
F-GJNG	Boeing 737-528	Air France	
F-GJNH	Boeing 737-528	Air France	
F-GJNI	Boeing 737-528	Air France	
F-GJNJ	Boeing 737-528	Air France	
F-GJNK	Boeing 737-528	Air France	
F-GJNM	Boeing 737-528	Air France	
F-GJNN	Boeing 737-528	Air France	
F-GJNO	Boeing 737-528	Air France	
F-GJTP	Beech 1900C-1	Flandre Air	
F-GJVA	Airbus A.320-211	Air France Europe	
F-GJVB	Airbus A.320-211	Air France Europe	
F-GJVC	Airbus A.320-211	Air France Europe	
F-GJVD	Airbus A.320-211	Air France Europe	
F-GJVE	Airbus A.320-211	Air France Europe	
F-GJVF	Airbus A.320-211	Air France Europe	
F-GJVG	Airbus A.320-211	Air France Europe	
F-GJVV	Airbus A.320-211	Air France Europe	
F-GJVW	Airbus A.320-211	Air France Europe	
F-GJVX	Airbus A.320-211	Air France Europe	
F-GJVY	Airbus A.320-211	Air France Europe	
F-GJVZ	Airbus A.320-211	Air France Europe	
F-GKDY	Boeing 727-225F	L'Aéropostale	
F-GKDZ	Boeing 727-225F	L'Aéropostale	
F-GKHD	Fokker 100	Compagnie Corse Meditteranee	
F-GKHE	Fokker 100	Compagnie Corse Meditteranee	
F-GKLJ	Boeing 747-121	Corsair	
F-GKMY	Douglas DC-10-30	AOM French Airlines	
F-GKNA	Aérospatiale ATR-42-300	T.A.T. European	
F-GKNB	Aérospatiale ATR-42-300	T.A.T. European	
F-GKNC	Aérospatiale ATR-42-300	T.A.T. European	
F-GKND	Aérospatiale ATR-42-300	T.A.T. European	
F-GKNG	Aérospatiale ATR-42-300	T.A.T. European	
F-GKNH	Aérospatiale ATR-42-300	T.A.T. European/Brit Air	
F-GKOA	Aérospatiale ATR-72-202	T.A.T. European	
F-GKOB	Aérospatiale ATR-72-202	T.A.T. European	
F-GKOC	Aérospatiale ATR-72-202	T.A.T. European	
F-GKOD	Aérospatiale ATR-72-202	T.A.T. European	
F-GKPC	Aérospatiale ATR-72-102	Compagnie Corse Mediterranée	
F-GKPD	Aéropsatiale ATR-72-102	Compagnie Corse Mediterranée	
F-GKPE	Aérospatiale ATR-72-102	Compagnie Corse Mediterranée	
F-GKPF	Aérospatiale ATR-72-102	Compagnie Corse Mediterranée	
F-GKPH	Aérospatiale ATR-72-202	Compagnie Corse Mediterranée	
F-GKST	Beech 1900-1	Proteus Airlines	
F-GKTA	Boeing 737-3M8	TEA Europe/Air One	
F-GKTB	Boeing 737-3M8	TEA Europe/Air One	
F-GKTD	Airbus A.310-304	Sudan Airways	
F-GKXA	Airbus A.320-211	Air France Ville de Nantes	
F-GLGH	Airbus A.320-212	Air Charter	
F-GLGM	Airbus A.320-211	Air France/Air Charter	
F-GLGN	Airbus A.320-211	Air France/Air Charter	
F-GLIA	Aerospatiale ATR-42-300	Brit Air/Air France Express	
F-GLIB	Aérospatiale ATR-42-300	Brit Air/Air France Express	
F-GLIJ	Canadair Regional Jet 100ER	Air Littoral	
F-GLIK	Canadair Regional Jet 100ER	Air Littoral	
F-GLIR	Fokker 100	Air Littoral/Air France Europe	
F-GLIS	Fokker 70	Air Littoral/Air France Express	

Notes	Reg.	Type	Owner or Operator
	F-GLIT	Fokker 70	Air Littoral/Air France Express
	F-GLIU	Fokker 70	Air Littoral/Air France Express
	F-GLIV	Fokker 70	Air Littoral/Air France Express
	F-GLIX	Fokker 70	Air Littoral/Air France Express
	F-GLIY	Canadair Regional Jet 100ER	Air Littoral
	F-GLIZ	Canadair Regional Jet 100ER	Air Littoral
	F-GLLD	Boeing 737-3Y0	T.A.T. European/British Airways
	F-GLLE	Boeing 737-3Y0	T.A.T. European/British Airways
	F-GLMX	Douglas DC-10-30	AOM French Airlines
	F-GLNA	Boeing 747-206B	Corsair
	F-GLND	Beech 1900D	Flandre Air
	F-GLNE	Beech 1900D	Flandre Air
	F-GLNH	Beech 1900D	Flandre Air
	F-GLNI	BAe 146-200QC	Air Jet
	F-GLPJ	Beech 1900C-1	Flandre Air
	F-GLPK	Beech 1900C-1	Flandre Air
	F-GLPL	Beech 1900C-1	Flandre Air
	F-GLXF	Boeing 737-219	Air Toulouse International
	F-GLXG	Boeing 737-2M8	Air Toulouse International
	F-GLXH	Boeing 737-2D6	Air Toulouse International
	F-GLZA	Airbus A.340-311	Air France
	F-GLZB	Airbus A.340-311	Air France
	F-GLZC	Airbus A.340-311	Air France
	F-GLZD	Airbus A.340-211	Air France
	F-GLZE	Airbus A.340-211	Air France
	F-GLZF	Airbus A.340-211	Air France
	F-GLZG	Airbus A.340-311	Air France
	F-GLZH	Airbus A.340-311	Air France
	F-GLZI	Airbus A.340-311	Air France
	F-GMJD	Boeing 737-2K5	Aigle Azur
	F-GMMP	BAe 146-200QC	Air Jet
	F-GMPG	Fokker 100	T.A.T. European
	F-GMPP	McD Douglas MD-83	—
	F-GMVB	SAAB 2000	Regional Airlines
	F-GMVC	SAAB 2000	Regional Airlines
	F-GMVD	SAAB 2000	Regional Airlines
	F-GMVE	SAAB 2000	Regional Airlines
	F-GMVF	SAAB 2000	Regional Airlines
	F-GMVG	SAAB 2000	Regional Airlines
	F-GMVH	BAe Jetstream 3206	Regional Airlines
	F-GMVI	BAe Jetstream 3206	Regional Airlines
	F-GMVJ	BAe Jetstream 3206	Regional Airlines
	F-GMVK	BAe Jetstream 3206	Regional Airlines
	F-GMVL	BAe Jetstream 3206	Regional Airlines
	F-GMVM	BAe Jetstream 3206	Regional Airlines
	F-GMVN	BAe Jetstream 3206	Regional Airlines
	F-GMVO	BAe Jetstream 3206	Regional Airlines
	F-GMVP	BAe Jetstream 3206	Regional Airlines
	F-GMVQ	SAAB SF.340B	Regional Airlines
	F-GMVV	SAAB SF.340B	Regional Airlines
	F-GMVX	SAAB SF.340B	Regional Airlines
	F-GMVY	SAAB SF.340B	Regional Airlines
	F-GMVZ	SAAB SF.340B	Regional Airlines
	F-GMZA	Airbus A.321-111	Air France Europe
	F-GMZB	Airbus A.321-111	Air France Europe
	F-GMZC	Airbus A.321-111	Air France Europe
	F-GMZD	Airbus A.321-111	Air France Europe
	F-GMZE	Airbus A.321-111	Air France Europe
	F-GMZF	Airbus A.321-111	Air France Europe
	F-GMZG	Airbus A.321-111	Air France Europe
	F-GNBS	Dornier Do.328-110	Proteus Airlines
	F-GNDC	Douglas DC-10-30	AOM French Airlines
	F-GNEM	Douglas DC-10-30	AOM French Airlines
	F-GNME	Canadair Regional Jet 100ER	Air Littoral/Air France
	F-GNMN	Canadair Regional Jet 100ER	Air Littoral/Air France
	F-GNPA	Dornier Do.328-110	Proteus Airlines
	F-GNZB	F.28 Fellowship 1000	T.A.T European/Delta Air Transport
	F-GOMA	BAe 146-200QC	Air Jet
	F-GPAN	Boeing 747-2B3F (SCD)	Air France Cargo
	F-GPJM	Boeing 747-206B	Corsair
	F-GPMA	Airbus A.319-113	Air France Europe
	F-GPMB	Airbus A.319-113	Air France Europe
	F-GPMC	Airbus A.319-113	Air France Europe
	F-GPMD	Airbus A.319-113	Air France Europe

Reg.	Type	Owner or Operator	Notes
F-GPME	Airbus A.319-113	Air France Europe	
F-GPMF	Airbus A.319-113	Air France Europe	
F-GPMG	Airbus A.319-113	Air France Europe	
F-GPMH	Airbus A.319-113	Air France Europe	
F-GPMI	Airbus A.319-113	Air France Europe	
F-GPVA	Douglas DC-10-30	Air Liberte	
F-GPVB	Douglas DC-10-30	Air Liberte	
F-GPVD	Douglas DC-10-30	Air Liberte	
F-GPXA	Fokker 100	Air France Europe	
F-GPXB	Fokker 100	Air France Europe	
F-GPXC	Fokker 100	Air France Europe	
F-GPXD	Fokker 100	Air France Europe	
F-GPXE	Fokker 100	Air France Europe	
F-GPYA	Aérospatiale ATR-42-512	Air Littoral	
F-GPYB	Aérospatiale ATR-42-512	Air Littoral	
F-GPYC	Aérospatiale ATR-42-512	Air Littoral	
F-GPYD	Aérospatiale ATR-42-512	Air Littoral	
F-GPYE	Aérospatiale ATR-42-512	Air Littoral	
F-GPYF	Aérospatiale ATR 42-512	Air Littoral	
F-GPYG	Aérospatiale ATR-42-512	Air Littoral	
F-GPYH	Aérospatiale ATR-42-512	Air Littoral	
F-GPYI	Aérospatiale ATR-42-512	Air Littoral	
F-GPYJ	Aérospatiale ATR-42-512	Air Littoral	
F-GPYP	Canadair Regional Jet 100LR	Air Littoral/Air France Express	
F-GPYS	Beech 1900C-1	Air Littoral/UPS	
F-GPYT	Beech 1900C-1	Air Littoral/UPS	
F-GPYU	Beech 1900C-1	Air Littoral/UPS	
F-GPYV	Beech 1900C-1	Air Littoral/UPS	
F-GPYX	Beech 1900C-1	Air Littoral/UPS	
F-GPYY	Beech 1900C-1	Air Littoral/UPS	
F-GREG	Aerospatiale ATR-42-320	Regional Airlines	
F-GRJA	Canadair Regional Jet 100ER	Brit Air/Air France Express	
F-GRJB	Canadair Regional Jet 100ER	Brit Air/Air France Express	
F-GRJC	Canadair Regional Jet 100ER	Brit Air/Air France Express	
F-GRJD	Canadair Regional Jet 100ER	Brit Air/Air France Express	
F-GRJE	Canadair Regional Jet 100ER	Brit Air/Air France Express	
F-GRJF	Canadair Regional Jet 100ER	Brit Air/Air France Express	
F-GRJG	Canadair Regional Jet 100ER	Brit Air	
F-GRJH	Canadair Regional Jet 100ER	Brit Air	
F-GRJI	Canadair Regional Jet 100ER	Brit Air	
F-GRMC	McD Douglas MD-83	AOM French Airlines	
F-GRMG	McD Douglas MD-83	AOM French Airlines	
F-GRMH	McD Douglas MD-83	AOM French Airlines	
F-GRMI	McD Douglas MD-83	AOM French Airlines	
F-GRMJ	McD Douglas MD-83	AOM French Airlines	
F-GRSA	Boeing 737-33A	Star Europe	
F-GRSB	Boeing 737-497	Star Europe	
F-GRSC	Boeing 737-497	Star Europe	
F-GSTA	Airbus A.300-608ST	Airbus Inter Transport	
F-GSTB	Airbus A.300-608ST	Airbus Inter Transport	
F-GSTC	Airbus A.300-608ST	Airbus Inter Transport	
F-GSTD	Airbus A.300-608ST	Airbus Inter Transport	
F-GSUN	Boeing 747-312	Corsair	
F-GTDF	Douglas DC-10-30	AOM French Airlines	
F-GTDG	Douglas DC-10-30	AOM French Airlines	
F-GTDH	Douglas DC-10-30	AOM French Airlines	
F-GTDI	Douglas DC-10-30	AOM French Airlines	
F-GTOM	Boeing 747SP-44	Corsair	
F-ODJG	Boeing 747-2Q2B	Air Gabon	
F-ODLX	Douglas DC-10-30	AOM French Airlines *Diamant*	
F-ODLY	Douglas DC-10-30	AOM French Airlines *Turquoise*	
F-ODLZ	Douglas DC-10-30	AOM French Airlines *Saphir*	
F-ODVF	Airbus A.310-304	Royal Jordanian	
F-ODVG	Airbus A.310-304	Royal Jordanian *Prince Faisal*	
F-ODVH	Airbus A.310-304	Royal Jordanian *Prince Hamzeh*	
F-ODVI	Airbus A.310-304	Royal Jordanian *Princess Haya*	
F-OGQQ	Airbus A.310-308	Aeroflot *Tchaikovsky*	
F-OGQR	Airbus A.310-308	Aeroflot *Rachmaninov*	
F-OGQT	Airbus A.310-308	Aeroflot *Moussorgski*	
F-OGQU	Airbus A.310-308	Aeroflot *Skriabin*	
F-OGQY	Airbus A.310-324	Uzbekistan Airways	
F-OGQZ	Airbus A.310-324	Uzbekistan Airways	
F-OGYA	Airbus A.320-211	Royal Jordanian *Cairo*	
F-OGYB	Airbus A.320-211	Royal Jordanian *Baghdad*	

Notes	Reg.	Type	Owner or Operator
	F-OGYC	Airbus A.320-212	Royal Jordanian
	F-OGYM	Airbus A.310-324	Aeroflot
	F-OGYN	Airbus A.310-324	Aeroflot
	F-OGYP	Airbus A.310-324	Aeroflot *Rymsky Korsakov*
	F-OGYT	Airbus A/.310-324	Aeroflot
	F-OGYU	Airbus A.310-324	Aeroflot
	F-OGYV	Airbus A.310-324	Aeroflot *Igor Stravinsky*
	F-OHLH	Airbus A.310-304	Middle East Airlines
	F-OHLI	Airbus A.310-304	Middle East Airlines
	F-OKAI	Airbus A.320-212	Sudan Airways

Note: After the merger of Air France and Air Inter Europe in April 1997, aircraft may still be seen carrying the previous titles.

HA (Hungary)

HA-LBN	Tupolev Tu-134A-3	Malev
HA-LBO	Tupolev Tu-134A-3	Malev
HA-LBP	Tupolev Tu-134A-3	Malev
HA-LBR	Tupolev Tu-134A-3	Malev
HA-LCM	Tupolev Tu-154B-2	Malev
HA-LCN	Tupolev Tu-154B-2	Malev
HA-LCO	Tupolev Tu-154B-2	Malev
HA-LCP	Tupolev Tu-154B-2	Malev
HA-LCR	Tupolev Tu-154B-2	Malev
HA-LCU	Tupolev Tu-154B-2	Malev
HA-LCV	Tupolev Tu-154B-2	Malev
HA-LEA	Boeing 737-2QB	Malev
HA-LEB	Boeing 737-2M8	Malev
HA-LEC	Boeing 737-2T5	Malev
HA-LED	Boeing 737-3Y0	Malev
HA-LEF	Boeing 737-3Y0	Malev
HA-LEG	Boeing 737-3Y0	Malev *Szent Istvan-Sanctus Stephanus*
HA-LEI	Boeing 737-2T4	Malev
HA-LEJ	Boeing 737-3Q8	Malev
HA-LEK	Boeing 737-2K9	Malev
HA-LEM	Boeing 737-2T4	Malev
HA-LEN	Boeing 737-4Y0	Malev
HA-LEO	Boeing 737-4Y0	Malev
HA-LHA	Boeing 767-27GER	Malev
HA-LHB	Boeing 767-27GER	Malev
HA-LMA	Fokker 70	Malev
HA-LMB	Fokker 70	Malev
HA-LMC	Fokker 70	Malev
HA-LMD	Fokker 70	Malev
HA-	Fokker 70	Malev

HB (Switzerland)

HB-AEE	Dornier Do.328-110	Air Engiadina
HB-AEF	Dornier Do.328-110	Air Engiadina
HB-AEG	Dornier Do.328-110	Air Engiadina
HB-AEH	Dornier Do.328-110	Air Engiadina
HB-AEI	Dornier Do.328-110	Air Engiadina
HB-AHB	SAAB SF.340A	Crossair
HB-AKA	SAAB SF.340B	Crossair
HB-AKB	SAAB SF.340B	Crossair
HB-AKC	SAAB SF.340B	Crossair
HB-AKD	SAAB SF.340B	Crossair
HB-AKE	SAAB SF.340B	Crossair
HB-AKF	SAAB SF.340B	Crossair
HB-AKG	SAAB SF.340B	Crossair
HB-AKH	SAAB SF.340B	Crossair
HB-AKI	SAAB SF.340B	Crossair
HB-AKK	SAAB SF.340B	Crossair
HB-AKL	SAAB SF.340B	Crossair
HB-AKM	SAAB SF.340B	Crossair
HB-AKN	SAAB SF.340B	Crossair
HB-AKO	SAAB SF.340B	Crossair

Reg.	Type	Owner or Operator	Notes
HB-AKP	SAAB SF.340B	Crossair	
HB-IEE	Boeing 757-23A	Petrolair	
HB-IEH	Boeing 737-2V6	Petrolair	
HB-IGC	Boeing 747-357 (SCD)	Swissair *Bern*	
HB-IGD	Boeing 747-357 (SCD)	Swissair *Basel*	
HB-IGE	Boeing 747-357	Swissair *Genéve*	
HB-IGF	Boeing 747-357	Swissair *Zürich*	
HB-IGG	Boeing 747-357 (SCD)	Swissair *Ticino*	
HB-IIA	Boeing 737-3M8	TEA Switzerland *City of Akureyri*	
HB-IIB	Boeing 737-3M8	TEA Switzerland *Isle of Avalon*	
HB-IIC	Boeing 737-3M8	TEA Switzerland *Emmental*	
HB-IID	Boeing 737-3Y0	TEA Switzerland *City of Hanoi*	
HB-IIE	Boeing 737-3Q8	TEA Switzerland *Isle of Kos*	
HB-IIF	Boeing 737-3Q8	TEA Switzerland *Spirit of Sabine*	
HB-IIG	Boeing 737-3Q8	TEA Switzerland	
HB-IIH	Boeing 737-7Q8	TEA Switzerland	
HB-III	Boeing 737-7Q8	TEA Switzerland	
HB-IJA	Airbus A.320-214	Swissair *Opfikon*	
HB-IJB	Airbus A.320-214	Swissair *Embrach*	
HB-IJC	Airbus A.320-214	Swissair *Winkle*	
HB-IJD	Airbus A.320-214	Swissair *Regensdorf*	
HB-IJE	Airbus A.320-214	Swissair *Dubendorf*	
HB-IJF	Airbus A.320-214	Swissair *Bellevue*	
HB-IJG	Airbus A.320-214	Swissair *Illnau-Effretikon*	
HB-IJH	Airbus A.320-214	Swissair *Wangen-Bruttisellen*	
HB-IJI	Airbus A.320-214	Swissair *Binningen*	
HB-IJJ	Airbus A.320-214	Swissair *Dietlikon*	
HB-IJK	Airbus A.320-214	Swissair *Hockfelden*	
HB-IJL	Airbus A.320-214	Swissair *Bassersdorf*	
HB-IJM	Airbus A.320-214	Swissair *Wallisellen*	
HB-IJN	Airbus A.320-214	Swissair *Meyrin*	
HB-IJO	Airbus A.320-214	Swissair *Grand-Saconnex*	
HB-IJP	Airbus A.320-214	Swissair *Vernier*	
HB-IJQ	Airbus A.320-214	Swissair	
HB-IJR	Airbus A.320-214	Swissair	
HB-IKM	McD Douglas MD-83	Edelweiss Air	
HB-IKN	McD Douglas MD-83	Edelweiss Air *Arosa*	
HB-INA	McD Douglas MD-81	Swissair *Höri*	
HB-INN	McD Douglas MD-81	Swissair *Bülach*	
HB-INP	McD Douglas MD-81	Swissair *Oberglatt*	
HB-INR	McD Douglas MD-82	Crossair	
HB-INS	McD Douglas MD-81	Swissair *Meyrin*	
HB-INT	McD Douglas MD-81	Swissair *Grand-Saconnex*	
HB-INU	McD Douglas MD-81	Swissair *Vernier*	
HB-INV	McD Douglas MD-82	Crossair	
HB-INW	McD Douglas MD-82	Crossair	
HB-INX	McD Douglas MD-81	Swissair *Wallisellen*	
HB-INY	McD Douglas MD-81	Swissair *Bassersdorf*	
HB-INZ	McD Douglas MD-82	Crossair	
HB-IOA	Airbus A.321-111	Swissair *Neuchâtel*	
HB-IOB	Airbus A.321-111	Swissair *Aargau*	
HB-IOC	Airbus A.321-111	Swissair *Lausanne*	
HB-IOD	Airbus A.321-111	Swissair *Kloten*	
HB-IOE	Airbus A.321-111	Swissair *Solothurn*	
HB-IOF	Airbus A.321-111	Swissair *Winterthur*	
HB-IOG	Airbus A.321-111	Swissair *Bulach*	
HB-IOH	Airbus A.321-111	Swissair	
HB-IPF	Airbus A.310-322	Swissair *Glarus*	
HB-IPG	Airbus A.310-322	Swissair *Zug*	
HB-IPH	Airbus A.310-322	Swissair *Appenzell i. Rh*	
HB-IPI	Airbus A.310-322	Swissair *Luzern*	
HB-IPK	Airbus A.310-322	Swissair	
HB-IPL	Airbus A.310-325	Swissair	
HB-IPM	Airbus A.310-325	Swissair	
HB-IPN	Airbus A.310-325	Swissair	
HB-IPS	Airbus A.319-112	Swissair	
HB-IPT	Airbus A.319-112	Swissair	
HB-IPU	Airbus A.319-112	Swissair	
HB-IPV	Airbus A.319-112	Swissair *Rumlang*	
HB-IPW	Airbus A.319-112	Swissair *Bachenbulach*	
HB-IPX	Airbus A.319-112	Swissair *Steinmaur*	
HB-IPY	Airbus A.319-112	Swissair *Hori*	
HB-IPZ	Airbus A.319-112	Swissair *Oberglatt*	

Notes	Reg.	Type	Owner or Operator
	HB-ISB	Douglas DC-3C	Classic Air
	HB-ISC	Douglas DC-3C	Classic Air
	HB-ISX	McD Douglas MD-83	Crossair
	HB-ISZ	McD Douglas MD-83	Crossair
	HB-IUG	McD Douglas MD-83	Crossair
	HB-IUH	McD Douglas MD-83	Crossair/McDonalds
	HB-IVC	Fokker 100	Swissair *Chur*
	HB-IVD	Fokker 100	Swissair *Dietlikon*
	HB-IVE	Fokker 100	Swissair *Baden*
	HB-IVF	Fokker 100	Swissair *Sion*
	HB-IVG	Fokker 100	Swissair *Genthod*
	HB-IVH	Fokker 100	Swissair *Stadel*
	HB-IVI	Fokker 100	Swissair *Bellevue*
	HB-IVK	Fokker 100	Swissair *Hochfelden*
	HB-IWA	McD Douglas MD-11	Swissair *Obwalden*
	HB-IWB	McD Douglas MD-11	Swissair *Graubünden*
	HB-IWC	McD Douglas MD-11	Swissair *Schaffhausen*
	HB-IWD	McD Douglas MD-11	Swissair *Thurgau*
	HB-IWE	McD Douglas MD-11	Swissair *Nidwalden*
	HB-IWF	McD Douglas MD-11	Swissair *Vaud*
	HB-IWG	McD Douglas MD-11	Swissair *Asia Valais/Wallis*
	HB-IWH	McD Douglas MD-11	Swissair *St Gallen*
	HB-IWI	McD Douglas MD-11	Swissair *Uri*
	HB-IWK	McD Douglas MD-11	Swissair *Fribourg*
	HB-IWL	McD Douglas MD-11	Swissair *Appenzell a.Rh*
	HB-IWM	McD Douglas MD-11	Swissair *Jura*
	HB-IWN	McD Douglas MD-11	Swissair *Basel-Land*
	HB-IWO	McD Douglas MD-11	Swissair
	HB-IWP	McD Douglas MD-11	Swissair
	HB-IWQ	McD Douglas MD-11	Swissair
	HB-IXF	Avro RJ85	Crossair
	HB-IXG	Avro RJ85	Crossair
	HB-IXH	Avro RJ85	Crossair
	HB-IXK	Avro RJ85	Crossair
	HB-IXM	Avro RJ100	Crossair
	HB-IXN	Avro RJ100	Crossair
	HB-IXO	Avro RJ100	Crossair
	HB-IXP	Avro RJ100	Crossair
	HB-IXQ	Avro RJ100	Crossair
	HB-IXR	Avro RJ100	Crossair
	HB-IXS	Avro RJ100	Crossair
	HB-IXT	Avro RJ100	Crossair
	HB-IXU	Avro RJ100	Crossair
	HB-IXV	Avro RJ100	Crossair
	HB-IXW	Avro RJ100	Crossair
	HB-IXX	Avro RJ100	Crossair
	HB-IZA	SAAB 2000	Crossair
	HB-IZB	SAAB 2000	Crossair
	HB-IZC	SAAB 2000	Crossair
	HB-IZD	SAAB 2000	Crossair
	HB-IZE	SAAB 2000	Crossair
	HB-IZF	SAAB 2000	Crossair
	HB-IZG	SAAB 2000	Crossair
	HB-IZH	SAAB 2000	Crossair
	HB-IZI	SAAB 2000	Crossair
	HB-IZK	SAAB 2000	Crossair
	HB-IZL	SAAB 2000	Crossair
	HB-IZM	SAAB 2000	Crossair
	HB-IZN	SAAB 2000	Crossair
	HB-IZO	SAAB 2000	Crossair
	HB-IZP	SAAB 2000	Crossair
	HB-IZQ	SAAB 2000	Crossair
	HB-IZR	SAAB 2000	Crossair
	HB-IZS	SAAB 2000	Crossair
	HB-IZT	SAAB 2000	Crossair
	HB-IZU	SAAB 2000	Crossair
	HB-IZV	SAAB 2000	Crossair
	HB-IZW	SAAB 2000	Crossair
	HB-IZX	SAAB 2000	Crossair
	HB-IZY	SAAB 2000	Crossair
	HB-IZZ	SAAB 2000	Crossair

Reg.	Type	Owner or Operator	Notes

HL (Korea)

HL7371	McD Douglas MD-11	Korean Air	
HL7372	McD Douglas MD-11F	Korean Air	
HL7373	McD Douglas MD-11F	Korean Air	
HL7374	McD Douglas MD-11	Korean Air	
HL7375	McD Douglas MD-11	Korean Air	
HL7401	Boeing 747-249F	Korean Air Cargo	
HL7441	Boeing 747-230F	Korean Air Cargo	
HL7443	Boeing 747-2B5B	Korean Air	
HL7451	Boeing 747-2B5F (SCD)	Korean Air Cargo	
HL7452	Boeing 747-2B5F (SCD)	Korean Air Cargo	
HL7453	Boeing 747-212B	Korean Air	
HL7454	Boeing 747-2B5F (SCD)	Korean Air Cargo	
HL7458	Boeing 747-2B5F (SCD)	Korean Air Cargo	
HL7459	Boeing 747-2B5F (SCD)	Korean Air Cargo	
HL7460	Boeing 747-4B5	Korean Air	
HL7461	Boeing 747-4B5	Korean Air	
HL7462	Boeing 747-4B5	Korean Air	
HL7463	Boeing 747-2B5B	Korean Air	
HL7464	Boeing 747-2B5B	Korean Air	
HL7468	Boeing 747-3B5	Korean Air	
HL7469	Boeing 747-3B5	Korean Air	
HL7470	Boeing 747-3B5 (SCD)	Korean Air	
HL7471	Boeing 747-273C	Korean Air Cargo	
HL7472	Boeing 747-4B5	Korean Air	
HL7473	Boeing 747-4B5	Korean Air	
HL7474	Boeing 747-2S4F (SCD)	Korean Air Cargo	
HL7475	Boeing 747-2B5F (SCD)	Korean Air Cargo	
HL7476	Boeing 747-2B5F (SCD)	Korean Air Cargo	
HL7477	Boeing 747-4B5	Korean Air	
HL7478	Boeing 747-4B5	Korean Air	
HL7479	Boeing 747-4B5	Korean Air	
HL7480	Boeing 747-4B5 (SCD)	Korean Air	
HL7481	Boeing 747-4B5	Korean Air	
HL7482	Boeing 747-4B5	Korean Air	
HL7483	Boeing 747-4B5	Korean Air	
HL7484	Boeing 747-4B5	Korean Air	
HL7485	Boeing 747-4B5	Korean Air	
HL7486	Boeing 747-4B5	Korean Air	
HL7487	Boeing 747-4B5	Korean Air	
HL7488	Boeing 747-4B5	Korean Air	
HL7489	Boeing 747-4B5	Korean Air	
HL7490	Boeing 747-4B5	Korean Air	
HL7491	Boeing 747-4B5	Korean Air	
HL7492	Boeing 747-4B5	Korean Air	
HL7493	Boeing 747-4B5	Korean Air	
HL7494	Boeing 747-4B5	Korean Air	
HL7495	Boeing 747-4B5	Korean Air	
HL7496	Boeing 747-4B5	Korean Air	
HL7497	Boeing 747-4B5	Korean Air	
HL7498	Boeing 747-4B5	Korean Air	

HS (Thailand)

HS-TGD	Boeing 747-3D7	Thai Airways International *Suchada*	
HS-TGE	Boeing 747-3D7	Thai Airways International *Chutamat*	
HS-TGH	Boeing 747-4D7	Thai Airways International *Chaiprakarn*	
HS-TGJ	Boeing 747-4D7	Thai Airways International *Hariphunchai*	
HS-TGK	Boeing 747-4D7	Thai Airways International *Alongkorn*	
HS-TGL	Boeing 747-4D7	Thai Airways International *Theparat*	
HS-TGM	Boeing 747-4D7	Thai Airways International *Chao Phraya*	
HS-TGN	Boeing 747-4D7	Thai Airways International *Simongkhon*	
HS-TGO	Boeing 747-4D7	Thai Airways International *Bowonrangsi*	
HS-TGP	Boeing 747-4D7	Thai Airways International *Thepprasit*	
HS-TGR	Boeing 747-4D7	Thai Airways International *Siriwatthana*	
HS-TGT	Boeing 747-4D7	Thai Airways International	
HS-TMA	Douglas DC-10-30ER	Thai Airways International *Kwanmuang*	
HS-TMB	Douglas DC-10-30ER	Thai Airways International *Thepalai*	
HS-TMC	Douglas DC-10-30ER	Thai Airways International *Sri Ubon*	

Notes	Reg.	Type	Owner or Operator
	HS-TMD	McD Douglas MD-11	Thai Airways International *Phra Nakhon*
	HS-TME	McD Douglas MD-11	Thai Airways International *Pathumwan*
	HS-TMF	McD Douglas MD-11	Thai Airways International *Phichit*
	HS-TMG	McD Douglas MD-11	Thai Airways International *Nakhon Sawan*

HZ (Saudi Arabia)

HZ-AHA	L.1011-385 TriStar 200	Saudia — Saudi Arabian Airlines
HZ-AHB	L.1011-385 TriStar 200	Saudia — Saudi Arabian Airlines
HZ-AHC	L.1011-385 TriStar 200	Saudia — Saudi Arabian Airlines
HZ-AHD	L.1011-385 TriStar 200	Saudia — Saudi Arabian Airlines
HZ-AHE	L.1011-385 TriStar 200	Saudia — Saudi Arabian Airlines
HZ-AHF	L.1011-385 TriStar 200	Saudia — Saudi Arabian Airlines
HZ-AHG	L.1011-385 TriStar 200	Saudia — Saudi Arabian Airlines
HZ-AHH	L.1011-385 TriStar 200	Saudia — Saudi Arabian Airlines
HZ-AHI	L.1011-385 TriStar 200	Saudia — Saudi Arabian Airlines
HZ-AHJ	L.1011-385 TriStar 200	Saudia — Saudi Arabian Airlines
HZ-AHL	L.1011-385 TriStar 200	Saudia — Saudi Arabian Airlines
HZ-AHM	L.1011-385 TriStar 200	Saudia — Saudi Arabian Airlines
HZ-AHN	L.1011-385 TriStar 200	Saudia — Saudi Arabian Airlines
HZ-AHO	L.1011-385 TriStar 200	Saudia — Saudi Arabian Airlines
HZ-AHP	L.1011-385 TriStar 200	Saudia — Saudi Arabian Airlines
HZ-AHQ	L.1011-385 TriStar 200	Saudia — Saudi Arabian Airlines
HZ-AHR	L.1011-385 TriStar 200	Saudia — Saudi Arabian Airlines
HZ-AIA	Boeing 747-168B	Saudia — Saudi Arabian Airlines
HZ-AIB	Boeing 747-168B	Saudia — Saudi Arabian Airlines
HZ-AIC	Boeing 747-168B	Saudia — Saudi Arabian Airlines
HZ-AID	Boeing 747-168B	Saudia — Saudi Arabian Airlines
HZ-AIE	Boeing 747-168B	Saudia — Saudi Arabian Airlines
HZ-AIF	Boeing 747SP-68	Saudia — Saudi Arabian Airlines
HZ-AIG	Boeing 747-168B	Saudia — Saudi Arabian Airlines
HZ-AII	Boeing 747-168B	Saudia — Saudi Arabian Airlines
HZ-AIJ	Boeing 747SP-68	Saudi Royal Flight
HZ-AIK	Boeing 747-368	Saudia — Saudi Arabian Airlines
HZ-AIL	Boeing 747-368	Saudia — Saudi Arabian Airlines
HZ-AIM	Boeing 747-368	Saudia — Saudi Arabian Airlines
HZ-AIN	Boeing 747-368	Saudia — Saudi Arabian Airlines
HZ-AIO	Boeing 747-368	Saudia — Saudi Arabian Airlines
HZ-AIP	Boeing 747-368	Saudia — Saudi Arabian Airlines
HZ-AIQ	Boeing 747-368	Saudia — Saudi Arabian Airlines
HZ-AIR	Boeing 747-368	Saudia — Saudi Arabian Airlines
HZ-AIS	Boeing 747-368	Saudia — Saudi Arabian Airlines
HZ-AIT	Boeing 747-368	Saudia — Saudi Arabian Airlines
HZ-AIU	Boeing 747-268F (SCD)	Saudia — Saudi Arabian Airlines
HZ-AIV	Boeing 747-468	Saudia — Saudi Arabian Airlines
HZ-HM5	L.1011-385 TriStar 500	Saudia VIP
HZ-HM6	L.1011-385 TriStar 500	Saudia VIP

Note: Saudia also operates other aircraft on lease.

I (Italy)

I-ALPK	Fokker 100	Alpi Eagles *San Antonio*
I-ALPL	Fokker 100	Alpi Eagles
I-ALPS	Fokker 100	Alpi Eagles *San Zeno*
I-ALPZ	Fokker 100	Alpi Eagles
I-BIXA	Airbus A.321-112	Alitalia *Piazza del Duomo Milano*
I-BIXB	Airbus A.321-112	Alitalia *Piazza Compostella Torino*
I-BIXC	Airbus A.321-112	Alitalia *Piazza del Campo Siena*
I-BIXD	Airbus A.321-112	Alitalia *Piazza Pretoria Palermo*
I-BIXE	Airbus A.321-112	Alitalia *Piazza di Spagna*
I-BIXF	Airbus A.321-112	Alitalia *Piazza Maggoire Bologna*
I-BIXG	Airbus A.321-112	Alitalia *Piazza del Miracoli Pisa*
I-BIXI	Airbus A.321-112	Alitalia *Piazza San Marco Venezia*
I-BIXL	Airbus A.321-112	Alitalia *Piazza del Duomo Lecce*
I-BIXM	Airbus A.321-112	Alitalia *Piazza di San Franceso Assisi*
I-BIXN	Airbus A.321-112	Alitalia *Piazza del Duomo Catania*
I-BIXO	Airbus A.321-112	Alitalia *Piazza Plebiscito Napoli*
I-BIXP	Airbus A.321-112	Alitalia *Carlo Morelli*

Reg.	Type	Owner or Operator	Notes
I-BIXQ	Airbus A.321-112	Alitalia	
I-BIXR	Airbus A.321-112	Alitalia	
I-BIXS	Airbus A.321-112	Alitalia	
I-BIXT	Airbus A.321-112	Alitalia	
I-BIXU	Airbus A.321-112	Alitalia *Piazza della Signoria Firenze*	
I-BIXV	Airbus A.321-112	Alitalia	
I-BIXZ	Airbus A.321-112	Alitalia	
I-BUSB	Airbus A.300B4-203	Alitalia *Tiziano*	
I-BUSC	Airbus A.300B4-203	Alitalia *Botticelli*	
I-BUSD	Airbus A.300B4-203	Alitalia *Caravaggio*	
I-BUSF	Airbus A.300B4-203	Alitalia *Tintoretto*	
I-BUSG	Airbus A.300B4-203	Alitalia *Canaletto*	
I-BUSH	Airbus A.300B4-203	Alitalia *Mantegna*	
I-BUSJ	Airbus A.300B4-203	Alitalia *Tiepolo*	
I-BUSL	Airbus A.300B4-203	Alitalia *Pinturicchio*	
I-BUSM	Airbus A.300B2-203	Alitalia *Raffaello*	
I-BUSN	Airbus A.300B2-203	Alitalia *Giotto*	
I-BUSP	Airbus A.300B4-103	Alitalia *Masaccio*	
I-BUSQ	Airbus A.300B4-103	Alitalia *Michelangelo*	
I-BUSR	Airbus A.300B4-103	Alitalia *Cimabue*	
I-BUST	Airbus A.300B4-103	Alitalia *Piero della Francesca*	
I-DACM	McD Douglas MD-82	Alitalia *La Spezia*	
I-DACN	McD Douglas MD-82	Alitalia *Rieti*	
I-DACP	McD Douglas MD-82	Alitalia *Padova*	
I-DACQ	McD Douglas MD-82	Alitalia *Taranto*	
I-DACR	McD Douglas MD-82	Alitalia *Carrara*	
I-DACS	McD Douglas MD-82	Alitalia *Maratea*	
I-DACT	McD Douglas MD-82	Alitalia *Valtellina*	
I-DACU	McD Douglas MD-82	Alitalia *Fabriano*	
I-DACV	McD Douglas MD-82	Alitalia *Riccione*	
I-DACW	McD Douglas MD-82	Alitalia *Vieste*	
I-DACX	McD Douglas MD-82	Alitalia *Piacenza*	
I-DACY	McD Douglas MD-82	Alitalia *Novara*	
I-DACZ	McD Douglas MD-82	Alitalia *Castelfidardo*	
I-DAND	McD Douglas MD-82	Alitalia *Bolzano*	
I-DANF	McD Douglas MD-82	Alitalia *Vicenza*	
I-DANG	McD Douglas MD-82	Alitalia *Benevento*	
I-DANH	McD Douglas MD-82	Alitalia *Messina*	
I-DANL	McD Douglas MD-82	Alitalia *Cosenza*	
I-DANM	McD Douglas MD-82	Alitalia *Vicenza*	
I-DANP	McD Douglas MD-82	Alitalia *Fabriano*	
I-DANQ	McD Douglas MD-82	Alitalia *Lecce*	
I-DANR	McD Douglas MD-82	Alitalia *Matera*	
I-DANU	McD Douglas MD-82	Alitalia *Trapani*	
I-DANV	McD Douglas MD-82	Alitalia *Forte dei Marmi*	
I-DANW	McD Douglas MD-82	Alitalia *Siena*	
I-DATA	McD Douglas MD-82	Alitalia *Gubbio*	
I-DATB	McD Douglas MD-82	Alitalia *Bergamo*	
I-DATC	McD Douglas MD-82	Alitalia *Foggia*	
I-DATD	McD Douglas MD-82	Alitalia *Savona*	
I-DATE	McD Douglas MD-82	Alitalia *Grosseto*	
I-DATF	McD Douglas MD-82	Alitalia *Vittorio Veneto*	
I-DATG	McD Douglas MD-82	Alitalia *Arezzo*	
I-DATH	McD Douglas MD-82	Alitalia *Pescara*	
I-DATI	McD Douglas MD-82	Alitalia *Siracusa*	
I-DATJ	McD Douglas MD-82	Alitalia *Lunigiana*	
I-DATK	McD Douglas MD-82	Alitalia *Ravenna*	
I-DATL	McD Douglas MD-82	Alitalia	
I-DATM	McD Douglas MD-82	Alitalia	
I-DATN	McD Douglas MD-82	Alitalia	
I-DATO	McD Douglas MD-82	Alitalia *Reggio Emilia*	
I-DATP	McD Douglas MD-82	Alitalia	
I-DATQ	McD Douglas MD-82	Alitalia *Modena*	
I-DATR	McD Douglas MD-82	Alitalia *Livorno*	
I-DATS	McD Douglas MD-82	Alitalia	
I-DATU	McD Douglas MD-82	Alitalia *Verona*	
I-DAVA	McD Douglas MD-82	Alitalia *Cuneo*	
I-DAVB	McD Douglas MD-82	Alitalia *Ferrara*	
I-DAVC	McD Douglas MD-82	Alitalia *Lucca*	
I-DAVD	McD Douglas MD-82	Alitalia *Mantova*	
I-DAVF	McD Douglas MD-82	Alitalia *Oristano*	
I-DAVG	McD Douglas MD-82	Alitalia *Pesaro*	
I-DAVH	McD Douglas MD-82	Alitalia *Salerno*	

Notes	Reg.	Type	Owner or Operator
	I-DAVI	McD Douglas MD-82	Alitalia *Assisi*
	I-DAVJ	McD Douglas MD-82	Alitalia *Parma*
	I-DAVK	McD Douglas MD-82	Alitalia *Pompei*
	I-DAVL	McD Douglas MD-82	Alitalia *Reggio Calabria*
	I-DAVM	McD Douglas MD-82	Alitalia *Caserta*
	I-DAVN	McD Douglas MD-82	Alitalia *Volterra*
	I-DAVP	McD Douglas MD-82	Alitalia *Gorizia*
	I-DAVR	McD Douglas MD-82	Alitalia *Pisa*
	I-DAVS	McD Douglas MD-82	Alitalia *Catania*
	I-DAVT	McD Douglas MD-82	Alitalia *Como*
	I-DAVU	McD Douglas MD-82	Alitalia *Udine*
	I-DAVV	McD Douglas MD-82	Alitalia *Pavia*
	I-DAVW	McD Douglas MD-82	Alitalia *Camerino*
	I-DAVX	McD Douglas MD-82	Alitalia *Asti*
	I-DAVZ	McD Douglas MD-82	Alitalia *Brescia*
	I-DAWA	McD Douglas MD-82	Alitalia *Roma*
	I-DAWB	McD Douglas MD-82	Alitalia *Cagliari*
	I-DAWC	McD Douglas MD-82	Alitalia *Campobasso*
	I-DAWD	McD Douglas MD-82	Alitalia *Catanzaro*
	I-DAWE	McD Douglas MD-82	Alitalia *Milano*
	I-DAWF	McD Douglas MD-82	Alitalia *Firenze*
	I-DAWG	McD Douglas MD-82	Alitalia *L'Aquila*
	I-DAWH	McD Douglas MD-82	Alitalia *Palermo*
	I-DAWI	McD Douglas MD-82	Alitalia *Ancona*
	I-DAWJ	McD Douglas MD-82	Alitalia *Genova*
	I-DAWL	McD Douglas MD-82	Alitalia *Perugia*
	I-DAWM	McD Douglas MD-82	Alitalia *Potenza*
	I-DAWO	McD Douglas MD-82	Alitalia *Bari*
	I-DAWP	McD Douglas MD-82	Alitalia *Torino*
	I-DAWQ	McD Douglas MD-82	Alitalia *Trieste*
	I-DAWR	McD Douglas MD-82	Alitalia *Venezia*
	I-DAWS	McD Douglas MD-82	Alitalia *Aosta*
	I-DAWT	McD Douglas MD-82	Alitalia *Napoli*
	I-DAWU	McD Douglas MD-82	Alitalia *Bologna*
	I-DAWV	McD Douglas MD-82	Alitalia *Trento*
	I-DAWW	McD Douglas MD-82	Alitalia *Riace*
	I-DAWY	McD Douglas MD-82	Alitalia *Agrigento*
	I-DAWZ	McD Douglas MD-82	Alitalia *Avellino*
	I-DEID	Boeing 767-33AER	Alitalia
	I-DEIF	Boeing 767-33AER	Alitalia
	I-DEMC	Boeing 747-243B (SCD)	Alitalia *Taormina*
	I-DEMF	Boeing 747-243B (SCD)	Alitalia *Portofino*
	I-DEMG	Boeing 747-243B	Alitalia *Cervinia*
	I-DEML	Boeing 747-243B	Alitalia *Sorrento*
	I-DEMN	Boeing 747-243B	Alitalia *Portocervo*
	I-DEMP	Boeing 747-243B	Alitalia *Capri*
	I-DEMR	Boeing 747-243F (SCD)	Alitalia *Titano*
	I-DEMS	Boeing 747-243B	Alitalia *Monte Argentario*
	I-DEMV	Boeing 747-243B	Alitalia *Sestriere*
	I-DEMY	Boeing 747-230B	Alitalia *Asolo*
	I-DIKM	Douglas DC-9-32	Alitalia *Positano*
	I-DIKP	Douglas DC-9-32	Alitalia *Isola di Marettimo*
	I-DIKR	Douglas DC-9-32	Alitalia *Piemonte*
	I-DIZE	Douglas DC-9-32	Alitalia *Isola della Meloria*
	I-DUPA	McD Douglas MD-11C	Alitalia *Gioacchino Rossini*
	I-DUPB	McD Douglas MD-11	Alitalia *Pietro Mascagni*
	I-DUPC	McD Douglas MD-11	Alitalia *V. Bellini*
	I-DUPD	McD Douglas MD-11	Alitalia *G. Donizetti*
	I-DUPE	McD Douglas MD-11C	Alitalia *Giuseppe Verdi*
	I-DUPI	McD Douglas MD-11C	Alitalia *Gioacomo Puccini*
	I-DUPO	McD Douglas MD-11C	Alitalia *Nicolo Paganini*
	I-DUPU	McD Douglas MD-11C	Alitalia *Antonio Vivaldi*
	I-FLRE	BAe 146-200	Meridiana
	I-FLRI	BAe 146-200	Meridiana
	I-FLRO	BAe 146-200	Meridiana
	I-FLRU	BAe 146-200	Meridiana
	I-FLYY	Douglas DC-9-51	Eurofly
	I-FLYZ	Douglas DC-9-51	Eurofly
	I-JETA	Boeing 737-229	Air One
	I-REJA	Fokker 70	Avianova *Scipione l'Africano*
	I-REJB	Fokker 70	Avianova *Cincinnato*

Reg.	Type	Owner or Operator	Notes
I-REJE	Fokker 70	Avianova *Cicerone*	
I-REJI	Fokker 70	Avianova *Lunigiana*	
I-REJO	Fokker 70	Avianova *Romolo*	
I-REJU	Fokker 70	Avianova *Tiberio Gracco*	
I-RIFJ	Douglas DC-9-32	Alitalia *Isola della Caprai*	
I-RIFS	Douglas DC-9-32	Alitalia *Basilicata*	
I-RIFT	Douglas DC-9-32	Alitalia *Friuli Venezia Giulia*	
I-RIFV	Douglas DC-9-32	Alitalia *Lazio*	
I-RIFW	Douglas DC-9-32	Alitalia *Lombardia*	
I-SMEA	Douglas DC-9-51	Meridiana	
I-SMEE	Douglas DC-9-51	Meridiana	
I-SMEI	Douglas DC-9-51	Meridiana	
I-SMEJ	Douglas DC-9-51	Meridiana	
I-SMEL	McD Douglas MD-82	Meridiana	
I-SMEM	McD Douglas MD-82	Meridiana	
I-SMEO	Douglas DC-9-51	Meridiana	
I-SMEP	McD Douglas MD-82	Meridiana	
I-SMER	McD Douglas MD-82	Meridiana	
I-SMES	McD Douglas MD-82	Meridiana	
I-SMET	McD Douglas MD-82	Meridiana	
I-SMEU	Douglas DC-9-51	Meridiana	
I-SMEV	McD Douglas MD-82	Meridiana	
I-TNTC	BAe 146-200QT	Mistral Air/TNT	

Note: Meridiana also operates an MD-82 which retains the registration PH-SEZ. while Air Europe SpA operates Boeing 767s registered EI-CIY, EI-CJA, EI-CJB, EI-CLS and EI-CMQ. Air One also operates Boeing 737s EI-CLW, EI-CLZ, F-GKTA and F-GKTB, while Eurofly leases the MD-83s EI-CEK and EI-CMM.

JA (Japan)

JA8071	Boeing 747-446	Japan Airlines	
JA8072	Boeing 747-446	Japan Airlines	
JA8073	Boeing 747-446	Japan Airlines	
JA8074	Boeing 747-446	Japan Airlines	
JA8075	Boeing 747-446	Japan Airlines	
JA8076	Boeing 747-446	Japan Airlines	
JA8077	Boeing 747-446	Japan Airlines	
JA8078	Boeing 747-446	Japan Airlines	
JA8079	Boeing 747-446	Japan Airlines	
JA8080	Boeing 747-446	Japan Airlines	
JA8081	Boeing 747-446	Japan Airlines	
JA8082	Boeing 747-446	Japan Airlines	
JA8085	Boeing 747-446	Japan Airlines	
JA8086	Boeing 747-446	Japan Airlines	
JA8087	Boeing 747-446	Japan Airlines	
JA8088	Boeing 747-446	Japan Airlines	
JA8089	Boeing 747-446	Japan Airlines	
JA8094	Boeing 747-481	All Nippon Airways	
JA8095	Boeing 747-481	All Nippon Airways	
JA8096	Boeing 747-481	All Nippon Airways	
JA8097	Boeing 747-481	All Nippon Airways	
JA8098	Boeing 747-481	All Nippon Airways	
JA8104	Boeing 747-246B	Japan Airlines	
JA8105	Boeing 747-246B	Japan Airlines	
JA8108	Boeing 747-246B	Japan Airlines	
JA8113	Boeing 747-246B	Japan Airlines	
JA8115	Boeing 747-146A	Japan Airlines	
JA8122	Boeing 747-246B	Japan Airlines	
JA8123	Boeing 747-246F (SCD)	Japan Airlines	
JA8125	Boeing 747-246B	Japan Airlines	
JA8130	Boeing 747-246B	Japan Airlines	
JA8131	Boeing 747-246B	Japan Airlines	
JA8132	Boeing 747-246F	Japan Airlines	
JA8140	Boeing 747-246B	Japan Airlines	
JA8141	Boeing 747-246B	Japan Airlines	
JA8154	Boeing 747-246B	Japan Airlines	
JA8160	Boeing 747-221F (SCD)	Japan Airlines	
JA8161	Boeing 747-246B	Japan Airlines	
JA8162	Boeing 747-246B	Japan Airlines	

Notes	Reg.	Type	Owner or Operator
	JA8163	Boeing 747-346	Japan Airlines
	JA8165	Boeing 747-221F (SCD)	Japan Airlines
	JA8166	Boeing 747-346	Japan Airlines
	JA8169	Boeing 747-246B	Japan Airlines
	JA8171	Boeing 747-246F (SCD)	Japan Airlines
	JA8173	Boeing 747-346	Japan Airlines
	JA8174	Boeing 747-281B	All Nippon Airways
	JA8175	Boeing 747-281B	All Nippon Airways
	JA8177	Boeing 747-346	Japan Airlines
	JA8178	Boeing 747-346	Japan Airlines
	JA8179	Boeing 747-346	Japan Airlines
	JA8180	Boeing 747-246F (SCD)	Japan Airlines
	JA8181	Boeing 747-281B	All Nippon Airways
	JA8182	Boeing 747-281B	All Nippon Airways
	JA8185	Boeing 747-346	Japan Airlines
	JA8190	Boeing 747-281B	All Nippon Airways
	JA8193	Boeing 747-212F (SCD)	Japan Airlines
	JA8901	Boeing 747-446	Japan Airlines
	JA8902	Boeing 747-446	Japan Airlines
	JA8906	Boeing 747-446	Japan Airlines
	JA8909	Boeing 747-446	Japan Airlines
	JA8910	Boeing 747-446	Japan Airlines
	JA8911	Boeing 747-446	Japan Airlines
	JA8912	Boeing 747-446	Japan Airlines
	JA8958	Boeing 747-481	All Nippon Airways
	JA8962	Boeing 747-481	All Nippon Airways

Note: Japan Airlines also operates a Boeing 747-246F which retains its US registration N211JL and two 747-346s N212JL and N213JL.

JY (Jordan)

	JY-AGA	L.1011-385 TriStar 500	Royal Jordanian *Amman*
	JY-AGB	L.1011-385 TriStar 500	Royal Jordanian *Princess Alia*
	JY-AGC	L.1011-385 TriStar 500	Royal Jordanian *Princess Zein*
	JY-AGD	L.1011-385 TriStar 500	Royal Jordanian *Prince Ali*
	JY-AGE	L.1011-385 TriStar 500	Royal Jordanian *Princess Aysha*
	JY-AGF	L.1011-385 TriStar 500	Royal Jordanian
	JY-AJM	Boeing 707-365C	Royal Jordanian Cargo
	JY-AJN	Boeing 707-3J6C	Royal Jordanian Cargo
	JY-AJO	Boeing 707-3J6C	Royal Jordanian Cargo
	JY-HKJ	L.1011-385 TriStar 500	Jordan Government

Note: Royal Jordanian also operates four A.310-304s registered F-ODVF, F-ODVG, F-ODVH and F-ODVI. Similarly three A.320s retain the registrations F-OGYA, F-OGYB and F-OGYC.

LN (Norway)

	LN-ASK	Dornier Do.328-100	Air Stord
	LN-ASL	Dornier Do.328-100	Air Stord
	LN-BRA	Boeing 737-405	Braathens SAFE *Eirik Blodoeks*
	LN-BRB	Boeing 737-405	Braathens SAFE *Inge Bardson*
	LN-BRC	Boeing 737-505	Braathens SAFE *Haakon IV Haakonsson*
	LN-BRD	Boeing 737-505	Braathens SAFE *Harald Gille*
	LN-BRE	Boeing 737-405	Braathens SAFE *Haakon V Magnusson*
	LN-BRF	Boeing 737-505	Braathens SAFE *Magnus Lagaboeter*
	LN-BRG	Boeing 737-505	Braathens SAFE *Oystein Magnusson*
	LN-BRH	Boeing 737-505	Braathens SAFE *Haakon den Gode*
	LN-BRI	Boeing 737-405	Braathens SAFE *Harald Haarfagre*
	LN-BRJ	Boeing 737-505	Braathens SAFE *Magnus Barfot*
	LN-BRK	Boeing 737-505	Braathens SAFE *Olav Tryggvason*
	LN-BRM	Boeing 737-505	Braathens SAFE *Olav den Hellige*
	LN-BRN	Boeing 737-505	Braathens SAFE *Haakon Herdebrei*
	LN-BRO	Boeing 737-505	Braathens SAFE *Magnus Haraldsson*
	LN-BRP	Boeing 737-405	Braathens SAFE *Harald Hardraade*
	LN-BRQ	Boeing 737-405	Braathens SAFE *Harald Graafell*
	LN-BRR	Boeing 737-505	Braathens SAFE *Halvdan Svarte*
	LN-BRS	Boeing 737-505	Braathens SAFE *Ovav Kyrre*
	LN-BRT	Boeing 737-505	Braathens SAFE *Sigurd Jorsalfar*
	LN-BRU	Boeing 737-505	Braathens SAFE *Eirik Magnusson*

Reg.	Type	Owner or Operator	Notes
LN-BRV	Boeing 737-505	Braathens SAFE *Haakon Sverresson*	
LN-BRX	Boeing 737-505	Braathens SAFE *Sigurd Munn*	
LN-BUC	Boeing 737-505	Braathens SAFE *Magnus Erlingsson*	
LN-BUD	Boeing 737-505	Braathens SAFE	
LN-BUE	Boeing 737-505	Braathens SAFE	
LN-BUF	Boeing 737-405	Braathens SAFE	
LN-BUG	Boeing 737-505	Braathens SAFE	
LN-FOG	L.188AF Electra	Fred Olsen Airtransport	
LN-FOH	L.188AF Electra	Fred Olsen Airtransport/DHL	
LN-FOI	L.188CF Electra	Fred Olsen Airtransport	
LN-FOL	L.188AF Electra	Fred Olsen Airtransport/DHL	
LN-FON	L.188PF Electra	Fred Olsen Airtransport/DHL	
LN-FOO	L.188AF Electra	Fred Olsen Airtransport/DHL	
LN-RCD	Boeing 767-383ER	Scandinavian Airlines System (S.A.S.) *Gyda Viking*	
LN-RCE	Boeing 767-383ER	S.A.S. *Aase Viking*	
LN-RCG	Boeing 767-383ER	S.A.S. *Yrsa Viking*	
LN-RCH	Boeing 767-383ER	S.A.S. *Ingegerd Viking*	
LN-RCI	Boeing 767-383ER	S.A.S. *Helga Viking*	
LN-RCK	Boeing 767-383ER	S.A.S. *Tor Viking*	
LN-RCL	Boeing 767-383ER	S.A.S. *Sven Viking*	
LN-RLA	Douglas DC-9-41	S.A.S. *Are Viking*	
LN-RLE	McD Douglas MD-82	S.A.S. *Ketiil Viking*	
LN-RLF	McD Douglas MD-82	S.A.S. *Finn Viking*	
LN-RLG	McD Douglas MD-82	S.A.S. *Trond Viking*	
LN-RLH	Douglas DC-9-41	S.A.S. *Einar Viking*	
LN-RLN	Douglas DC-9-41	S.A.S. *Halldor Viking*	
LN-RLP	Douglas DC-9-41	S.A.S. *Froste Viking*	
LN-RLR	McD Douglas MD-82	S.A.S. *Vegard Viking*	
LN-RLS	Douglas DC-9-41	S.A.S. *Asmund Viking*	
LN-RLT	Douglas DC-9-41	S.A.S. *Audun Viking*	
LN-RLZ	Douglas DC-9-41	S.A.S. *Bodvar Viking*	
LN-RMA	McD Douglas MD-81	S.A.S. *Hasting Viking*	
LN-RMD	McD Douglas MD-82	S.A.S. *Fenge Viking*	
LN-RMF	McD Douglas MD-83	S.A.S. *Torgny Viking*	
LN-RMG	McD Douglas MD-87	S.A.S. *Snorre Viking*	
LN-RMH	McD Douglas MD-87	S.A.S. *Solmund Viking*	
LN-RMJ	McD Douglas MD-81	S.A.S. *Rand Viking*	
LN-RMK	McD Douglas MD-87	S.A.S. *Ragnhild Viking*	
LN-RML	McD Douglas MD-81	S.A.S. *Aud Viking*	
LN-RMM	McD Douglas MD-81	S.A.S. *Blenda Viking*	
LN-RMN	McD Douglas MD-82	S.A.S. *Ivar Viking*	
LN-RMO	McD Douglas MD-81	S.A.S. *Bergljot Viking*	
LN-RMP	McD Douglas MD-87	S.A.S. *Reidun Viking*	
LN-RMR	McD Douglas MD-81	S.A.S. *Olav Viking*	
LN-RMS	McD Douglas MD-81	S.A.S. *Nial Viking*	
LN-RMT	McD Douglas MD-81	S.A.S. *Jarl Viking*	
LN-RMU	McD Douglas MD-87	S.A.S. *Grim Viking*	
LN-RMX	McD Douglas MD-87	S.A.S. *Vidar Viking*	
LN-RMY	McD Douglas MD-87	S.A.S. *Ingolf Viking*	
LN-RNB	Fokker 50	S.A.S. Commuter *Brae Viking*	
LN-RNC	Fokker 50	S.A.S. Commuter *Elvink Viking*	
LN-RND	Fokker 50	S.A.S. Commuter *Inge Viking*	
LN-RNE	Fokker 50	S.A.S. Commuter *Ebbe Viking*	
LN-RNF	Fokker 50	S.A.S. Commuter *Leif Viking*	
LN-RNG	Fokker 50	S.A.S. Commuter *Gudrid Viking*	
LN-RNH	Fokker 50	S.A.S. Commuter *Harald Viking*	
LN-ROA	McD Douglas MD-90-30	S.A.S. *Sigurd Viking*	
LN-ROB	McD Douglas MD-90-30	S.A.S. *Isrid Viking*	
LN-WND	Douglas DC-3C	Dakota Norway	

LV (Argentina)

LV-JNT	BAC One-Eleven 521FH	European Aviation Ltd	
LV-MEX	BAC One-Eleven 518FG	European Aviation Ltd (G-AXMF)	
LV-MLO	Boeing 747-287B	Aerolineas Argentinas	
LV-MLP	Boeing 747-287B	Aerolineas Argentinas	
LV-MLR	Boeing 747-287B	Aerolineas Argentinas	
LV-OEP	Boeing 747-287B	Aerolineas Argentinas	
LV-OOZ	Boeing 747-287B	Aerolineas Argentinas	
LV-OPA	Boeing 747-287B	Aerolineas Argentinas	

Notes	Reg.	Type	Owner or Operator

LX (Luxembourg)

LX-ACV	Boeing 747-271C (SCD)	Cargolux *City of Echternach*
LX-BCV	Boeing 747-271C (SCD)	Cargolux
LX-ECV	Boeing 747-271C (SCD)	Cargolux
LX-FCV	Boeing 747-4R7F (SCD)	Cargolux *City of Luxembourg*
LX-GCV	Boeing 747-4R7F (SCD)	Cargolux *City of Esch/Alzette*
LX-ICV	Boeing 747-428F (SCD)	Cargolux *City of Ettelbruck*
LX-LGB	Fokker 50	Luxair
LX-LGC	Fokker 50	Luxair *Prince Guillaume*
LX-LGD	Fokker 50	Luxair *Prince Felix*
LX-LGE	Fokker 50	Luxair *Prince Louis*
LX-LGF	Boeing 737-4C9	Sobelair
LX-LGG	Boeing 737-4C9	Luxair *Château de Bourscheid*
LX-LGK	EMB-120ER Brasilia	Luxair
LX-LGL	EMB-120ER Brasilia	Luxair
LX-LGM	EMB-120ER Brasilia	Luxair
LX-LGO	Boeing 737-5C9	Luxair *Château de Clervaux*
LX-LGP	Boeing 737-5C9	Luxair *Château de Bourglinster*
LX-LGR	Boeing 737-528	Luxair
LX-LGS	Boeing 737-528	Luxair *Château de Schengen*
LX-SKS	EMB-110P1 Bandeirante	Sky Service
LX-TLA	Douglas DC-8-62F	Cargo Lion
LX-TLB	Douglas DC-8-62F	Cargo Lion

LY (Lithuania)

LY-AAM	Yakovlev Yak-42	Lithuanian Airlines
LY-AAO	Yakovlev Yak-42	Lithuanian Airlines
LY-AAQ	Yakovlev Yak-42	Lithuanian Airlines
LY-AAR	Yakovlev Yak-42	Lithuanian Airlines
LY-AAS	Yakovlev Yak-42D	Lithuanian Airlines
LY-AAT	Yakovlev Yak-42	Lithuanian Airlines
LY-AAU	Yakovlev Yak-42D	Lithuanian Airlines
LY-AAW	Yakovlev Yak-42D	Lithuanian Airlines
LY-ABF	Tupolev Tu-134A-3	Lithuanian Airlines
LY-BSD	Boeing 737-2T4	Lithuanian Airlines *Steponas Darius*
LY-BSG	Boeing 737-2T2	Lithuanian Airlines
LY-GPA	Boeing 737-2Q8	Lithuanian Airlines

LZ (Bulgaria)

LZ-AZC	Ilyushin IL-18V	Air Zory
LZ-BAC	Antonov An-12	Balkan Bulgarian Airlines/HeavyLift
LZ-BAE	Antonov An-12	Balkan Bulgarian Airlines
LZ-BAF	Antonov An-12	Balkan Bulgarian Airlines
LZ-BEA	Ilyushin IL-18D	Balkan Bulgarian Airlines
LZ-BEH	Ilyushin IL-18V	Balkan Bulgarian Airlines
LZ-BEI	Ilyushin IL-18V	Balkan Bulgarian Airlines
LZ-BEU	Ilyushin IL-18V	Balkan Bulgarian Airlines
LZ-BOA	Boeing 737-53A	Balkan Bulgarian Airlines *City of Sofia*
LZ-BOB	Boeing 737-53A	Balkan Bulgarian Airlines *City of Plovdiv*
LZ-BOC	Boeing 737-53A	Balkan Bulgarian Airlines *City of Varna*
LZ-BTA	Tupolev Tu-154B	Balkan Bulgarian Airlines
LZ-BTC	Tupolev Tu-154B	Balkan Bulgarian Airlines
LZ-BTE	Tupolev Tu-154B	Balkan Bulgarian Airlines
LZ-BTF	Tupolev Tu-154B	Balkan Bulgarian Airlines
LZ-BTG	Tupolev Tu-154B	Balkan Bulgarian Airlines
LZ-BTH	Tupolev Tu-154M	Balkan Bulgarian Airlines
LZ-BTI	Tupolev Tu-154M	Balkan Bulgarian Airlines
LZ-BTJ	Tupolev Tu-154B-1	Balkan Bulgarian Airlines
LZ-BTK	Tupolev Tu-154B	Balkan Bulgarian Airlines
LZ-BTL	Tupolev Tu-154B	Balkan Bulgarian Airlines
LZ-BTM	Tupolev Tu-154B	Balkan Bulgarian Airlines
LZ-BTN	Tupolev Tu-154M	Balkan Bulgarian Airlines
LZ-BTO	Tupolev Tu-154B-1	Balkan Bulgarian Airlines
LZ-BTP	Tupolev Tu-154B-1	Balkan Bulgarian Airlines
LZ-BTQ	Tupolev Tu-154M	Balkan Bulgarian Airlines
LZ-BTR	Tupolev Tu-154M	Balkan Bulgarian Airlines

Reg.	Type	Owner or Operator	Notes
LZ-BTS	Tupolev Tu-154B-2	Balkan Bulgarian Airlines	
LZ-BTT	Tupolev Tu-154B-2	Balkan Bulgarian Airlines	
LZ-BTU	Tupolev Tu-154B-2	Balkan Bulgarian Airlines	
LZ-BTV	Tupolev Tu-154B-2	Balkan Bulgarian Airlines	
LZ-BTW	Tupolev Tu-154M	Balkan Bulgarian Airlines	
LZ-BTX	Tupolev Tu-154M	Balkan Bulgarian Airlines	
LZ-BTY	Tupolev Tu-154M	Balkan Bulgarian Airlines	
LZ-BTZ	Tupolev Tu-154M	Balkan Bulgarian Airlines	
LZ-MIG	Tupolev Tu-154M	Air VIA Bulgarian Airways	
LZ-MIK	Tupolev Tu-154M	Air VIA Bulgarian Airways	
LZ-MIL	Tupolev Tu-154M	Air VIA Bulgarian Airways	
LZ-MIR	Tupolev Tu-154M	Air VIA Bulgarian Airways	
LZ-MIS	Tupolev Tu-154M	Air VIA Bulgarian Airways	
LZ-MIV	Tupolev Tu-154M	Air VIA Bulgarian Airways	
LZ-SFA	Antonov An-12B	Air Sofia	
LZ-SFG	Antonov An-12	Air Sofia	
LZ-SFK	Antonov An-12	Air Sofia	
LZ-SFL	Antonov An-12	Air Sofia	
LZ-SFM	Antonov An-12	Air Sofia	
LZ-SFS	Antonov An-12	Air Sofia	
LZ-TUG	Tupolev Tu-134A-3	Bulgarian Government	
LZ-TUL	Tupolev Tu-134A-3	Hemus Air	
LZ-TUN	Tupolev Tu-134A-3	Albanian Airlines	

Note: Balkan also operates two Boeing 767-27EERs F-GHGD and F-GHGE on lease
from Air France.

N (USA)

N14AZ	Boeing 707-336C	Seagreen Air Transport	
N21AZ	Boeing 707-351C	Seagreen Air Transport	
N29AZ	Boeing 707-323C	Seagreen Air Transport	
N24UA	Douglas DC-8-61F	American International Airways	
N102CK	L.1011-385 TriStar 200	American International Airways	
N103CK	L.1011-385 TriStar 200	American International Airways	
N104CK	L.1011-385 TriStar 200	American International Airways	
N105CK	L.1011-385 TriStar 200	American International Airways	
N105UA	Boeing 747-451	United Airlines	
N106CK	L.1011-385 TriStar 200	American International Airways	
N106UA	Boeing 747-451	United Airlines	
N107CK	L.1011-385 TriStar200	American International Airways	
N107WA	Douglas DC-10-30CF	World Airways/Federal Express	
N110CK	L.1011-385 TriStar 50	American International Airways	
N112CK	L.1011-385 TriStar 50	American International Airways	
N114FE	Boeing 727-24C	Federal Express	
N115FE	Boeing 727-116C	Federal Express	
N117FE	Boeing 727-25C	Federal Express	
N117KC	Boeing 747-312	Singapore Airlines	
N117WA	Douglas DC-10-30	World Airways	
N121KG	Boeing 747-312	Singapore Airlines	
N122KH	Boeing 747-312	Singapore Airlines	
N123KJ	Boeing 747-312	Singapore Airlines	
N124KK	Boeing 747-312	Singapore Airlines	
N125KL	Boeing 747-312	Singapore Airlines	
N128TW	Boeing 747-143	Trans World Airlines	
N133JC	Douglas DC-10-40	Northwest Airlines	
N133TW	Boeing 747-156	Trans World Airlines	
N134TW	Boeing 747-156	Trans World Airlines	
N137AA	Douglas DC-10-30	American Airlines	
N140AA	Douglas DC-10-30	Transaero	
N140UA	Boeing 747SP-21	United Airlines	
N141AA	Douglas DC-10-30	Transaero	
N141UA	Boeing 747SP-21	United Airlines	
N141US	Douglas DC-10-40	Northwest Airlines	
N142AA	Douglas DC-10-30	Transaero	
N142UA	Boeing 747SP-21	United Airlines	
N143AA	Douglas DC-10-30	American Airlines	
N143FE	Boeing 727-21C	Federal Express	
N143UA	Boeing 747SP-21	United Airlines	
N144AA	Douglas DC-10-30	American Airlines	
N144FE	Boeing 727-21C	Federal Express	
N144JC	Douglas DC-10-40	Northwest Airlines	

Reg.	Type	Owner or Operator
N144UA	Boeing 747SP-21	United Airlines
N145SP	Boeing 707-323B	Seagreen Air Transport
N145UA	Boeing 747SP-21	United Airlines
N145US	Douglas DC-10-40	Northwest Airlines
N146UA	Boeing 747SP-21	United Airlines
N146US	Douglas DC-10-40	Northwest Airlines
N147UA	Boeing 747SP-21	United Airlines
N147US	Douglas DC-10-40	Northwest Airlines
N148UA	Boeing 747SP-21	United Airlines
N148US	Douglas DC-10-40	Northwest Airlines
N149US	Douglas DC-10-40	Northwest Airlines
N150US	Douglas DC-10-40	Northwest Airlines
N151UA	Boeing 747-222B	United Airlines
N151US	Douglas DC-10-40	Northwest Airlines
N152UA	Boeing 747-222B	United Airlines
N152US	Douglas DC-10-40	Northwest Airlines
N153UA	Boeing 747-123	United Airlines
N153US	Douglas DC-10-40	Northwest Airlines
N154US	Douglas DC-10-40	Northwest Airlines
N155UA	Boeing 747-123	United Airlines
N155US	Douglas DC-10-40	Northwest Airlines
N156UA	Boeing 747-123	United Airlines
N156US	Douglas DC-10-40	Northwest Airlines
N157UA	Boeing 747-123	United Airlines
N157US	Douglas DC-10-40	Northwest Airlines
N158UA	Boeing 747-238B	United Airlines
N158US	Douglas DC-10-40	Northwest Airlines
N159UA	Boeing 747-238B	United Airlines
N159US	Douglas DC-10-40	Northwest Airlines
N160UA	Boeing 747-238B	United Airlines
N160US	Douglas DC-10-40	Northwest Airlines
N161UA	Boeing 747-238B	United Airlines
N161US	Douglas DC-10-40	Northwest Airlines
N162US	Douglas DC-10-40	Northwest Airlines
N163AA	Douglas DC-10-30	American Airlines
N163UA	Boeing 747-238B	United Airlines
N164AA	Douglas DC-10-30	American Airlines
N164UA	Boeing 747-238B	United Airlines
N165UA	Boeing 747-238B	United Airlines
N166AA	Douglas DC-10-10ER	American Airlines
N171DN	Boeing 767-332ER	Delta Air Lines
N171UA	Boeing 747-422	United Airlines *Spirit of Seattle II*
N172DN	Boeing 767-332ER	Delta Air Lines
N172UA	Boeing 747-422	United Airlines
N173DN	Boeing 767-332ER	Delta Air Lines
N173UA	Boeing 747-422	United Airlines
N174DN	Boeing 767-332ER	Delta Air Lines
N174UA	Boeing 747-422	United Airlines
N175DN	Boeing 767-332ER	Delta Air Lines
N175UA	Boeing 747-422	United Airlines
N176DN	Boeing 767-332ER	Delta Air Lines
N176UA	Boeing 747-422	United Airlines
N177DN	Boeing 767-332ER	Delta Air Lines
N177UA	Boeing 747-422	United Airlines
N178DN	Boeing 767-332ER	Delta Air Lines
N178UA	Boeing 747-422	United Airlines
N179DN	Boeing 767-332ER	Delta Air Lines
N179UA	Boeing 747-422	United Airlines
N180DN	Boeing 767-332ER	Delta Air Lines
N180UA	Boeing 747-422	United Airlines
N181AT	L.1011-385 TriStar 100	American Trans Air
N181DN	Boeing 767-332ER	Delta Air Lines
N181UA	Boeing 747-422	United Airlines
N182DN	Boeing 767´-332ER	Delta Air Lines
N182UA	Boeing 747-422	United Airlines
N183AT	L.1011-385 TriStar 1	American Trans Air
N183DN	Boeing 767-332ER	Delta Air Lines
N183UA	Boeing 747-422	United Airlines
N184AT	L.1011-385 TriStar 1	American Trans Air
N184DN	Boeing 767-332ER	Delta Air Lines
N184UA	Boeing 747-422	United Airlines
N185AT	L.1011-385 TriStar 50	American Trans Air
N185DN	Boeing 767-332ER	Delta Air Lines
N185UA	Boeing 747-422	United Airlines
N186AT	L.1011-385 TriStar 50	American Trans Air

Reg.	Type	Owner or Operator	Notes
N186DN	Boeing 767-332ER	Delta Air Lines	
N186UA	Boeing 747-422	United Airlines	
N187AT	L.1011-385 TriStar 50	American Trans Air	
N187DN	Boeing 767-332ER	Delta Air Lines	
N187UA	Boeing 747-422	United Airlines	
N188AT	L.1011-385 TriStar 50	American Trans Air	
N188DN	Boeing 767-332ER	Delta Air Lines	
N188UA	Boeing 747-422	United Airlines	
N189AT	L.1011-385 TriStar 50	American Trans Air	
N189DN	Boeing 767-332ER	Delta Air Lines	
N189UA	Boeing 747-422	United Airlines	
N190AT	L.1011-385 TriStar 50	American Trans Air	
N190DN	Boeing 767-332ER	Delta Air Lines	
N190UA	Boeing 747-422	United Airlines	
N191AT	L.1011-385 TriStar 50	American Trans Air	
N191DN	Boeing 767-332ER	Delta Air Lines	
N191UA	Boeing 747-422	United Airlines	
N192AT	L.1011-385 TriStar 50	American Trans Air	
N192DN	Boeing 767-332ER	Delta Air Lines	
N192UA	Boeing 747-422	United Airlines	
N193AT	L.1011-385 TriStar 50	American Trans Air	
N193UA	Boeing 747-422	United Airlines	
N194AT	L.1011-385 TriStar 100	American Trans Air	
N194UA	Boeing 747-422	United Airlines	
N195AT	L.1011-385 TriStar 150	American Trans Air	
N195UA	Boeing 747-422	United Airlines	
N196AT	L.1011-385 TriStar 50	American Trans Air	
N196UA	Boeing 747-422	United Airlines	
N197AT	L.1011-385 TriStar 50	American Trans Air	
N197UA	Boeing 747-422	United Airlines	
N198UA	Boeing 747-422	United Airlines	
N199UA	Boeing 747-422	United Airlines	
N202AE	Boeing 747-2B4B (SCD)	Middle East Airlines	
N202PH	Boeing 747-121	Tower Air	
N203AE	Boeing 747-2B4B (SCD)	Middle East Airlines	
N204AE	Boeing 747-2B4B (SCD)	Middle East Airlines	
N207AE	Boeing 747-211B	Philippine Airlines	
N208AE	Boeing 747-211B	Philippine Airlines	
N211JL	Boeing 747-246F	Japan Airlines	
N211NW	Douglas DC-10-30	Northwest Airlines	
N212JL	Boeing 747-346	Japan Airlines	
N213JL	Boeing 747-346	Japan Airlines	
N220AU	Douglas DC-10-10	Orbis	
N220NW	Douglas DC-10-30	Northwest Airlines	
N221NW	Douglas DC-10-30	Northwest Airlines	
N223NW	Douglas DC-10-30	Northwest Airlines	
N224NW	Douglas DC-10-30	Northwest Airlines	
N225NW	Douglas DC-10-30	Northwest Airlines	
N226NW	Douglas DC-10-30	Northwest Airlines	
N227NW	Douglas DC-10-30	Northwest Airlines	
N228NW	Douglas DC-10-30	Northwest Airlines	
N229NW	Douglas DC-10-30	Northwest Airlines	
N230NW	Douglas DC-10-30	Northwest Airlines	
N232NW	Douglas DC-10-30	Northwest Airlines	
N234NW	Douglas DC-10-30	Northwest Airlines	
N235NW	Douglas DC-10-30	Northwest Airlines	
N236NW	Douglas DC-10-30	Northwest Airlines	
N275WA	McD Douglas MD-11CF	World Airways/Philippine Airlines	
N276WA	McD Douglas MD-11CF	World Airways/Philippine Airlines	
N278WA	McD Douglas MD-11	World Airways/Philippine Airlines	
N280WA	McD Douglas MD-11	World Airways/Ghana Airways	
N301FE	Douglas DC-10-30AF	Federal Express	
N301UP	Boeing 767-34AFER	United Parcel Service	
N302FE	Douglas DC-10-30AF	Federal Express	
N302UP	Boeing 767-34AFER	United Parcel Service	
N303EA	L.1011-385 TriStar 1	Rich International Airways	
N303FE	Douglas DC-10-30AF	Federal Express	
N303TW	Boeing 747-257B	Trans World Airlines	
N303UP	Boeing 767-34AFER	United Parcel Service	
N304FE	Douglas DC-10-30AF	Federal Express	
N304UP	Boeing 767-34AFER	United Parcel Service	
N305FE	Douglas DC-10-30AF	Federal Express *John David*	
N305TW	Boeing 747-284B	Trans World Airlines	
N305UP	Boeing 767-34AFER	United Parcel Service	
N306FE	Douglas DC-10-30AF	Federal Express *John Peter Jr*	

Notes	Reg.	Type	Owner or Operator
	N306GB	L.1011-385 TriStar 200	Arrow Air
	N306TW	Boeing 747-206B	Trans World Airlines
	N306UP	Boeing 767-34AFER	United Parcel Service
	N307FE	Douglas DC-10-30AF	Federal Express *Erin Lee*
	N307TW	Boeing 747-238B	Trans World Airlines
	N307UP	Boeing 767-34AFER	United Parcel Service
	N308FE	Douglas DC-10-30AF	Federal Express *Ann*
	N308UP	Boeing 767-34AFER	United Parcel Service
	N309FE	Douglas DC-10-30AF	Federal Express *Stacey*
	N309UP	Boeing 767-34AFER	United Parcel Service
	N310FE	Douglas DC-10-30AF	Federal Express *John Shelby*
	N310UP	Boeing 767-34AFER	United Parcel Service
	N311FE	Douglas DC-10-30AF	Federal Express *Abe*
	N311UP	Boeing 767-34AFER	United Parcel Service
	N312AA	Boeing 767-223ER	American Airlines
	N312FE	Douglas DC-10-30AF	Federal Express *Angela*
	N312UP	Boeing 767-34AFER	United Parcel Service
	N313AA	Boeing 767-223ER	American Airlines
	N313FE	Douglas DC-10-30AF	Federal Express *Brandon Parks*
	N313UP	Boeing 767-34AFER	United Parcel Service
	N314FE	Douglas DC-10-30AF	Federal Express *Caitlin-Ann*
	N314UP	Boeing 767-34AFER	United Parcel Service
	N315AA	Boeing 767-223ER	American Airlines
	N315FE	Douglas DC-10-30AF	Federal Express *Kevin*
	N315UP	Boeing 767-34AFER	United Parcel Service
	N316AA	Boeing 767-223ER	American Airlines
	N316FE	Douglas DC-10-30AF	Federal Express *Brandon*
	N316UP	Boeing 767-34AFER	United Parcel Service
	N317AA	Boeing 767-223ER	American Airlines
	N317FE	Douglas DC-10-30CF	Federal Express
	N317UP	Boeing 767-34AFER	United Parcel Service
	N318FE	Douglas DC-10-30CF	Federal Express
	N318UP	Boeing 767-34AFER	United Parcel Service
	N319AA	Boeing 767-223ER	American Airlines
	N319FE	Douglas DC-10-30CF	Federal Express
	N319UP	Boeing 767-34AFER	United Parcel Service
	N320AA	Boeing 767-223ER	American Airlines
	N320FE	Douglas DC-10-30CF	Federal Express
	N320UP	Boeing 767-34AFER	United Parcel Service
	N321AA	Boeing 767-223ER	American Airlines
	N321FE	Douglas DC-10-30CF	Federal Express
	N321UP	Boeing 767-34AFER	United Parcel Service
	N322AA	Boeing 767-223ER	American Airlines
	N322FE	Douglas DC-10-30CF	Federal Express *King Frank*
	N323AA	Boeing 767-223ER	American Airlines
	N323MC	Boeing 747-2D7B	Atlas Air
	N324AA	Boeing 767-223ER	American Airlines
	N325AA	Boeing 767-223ER	American Airlines
	N327AA	Boeing 767-223ER	American Airlines
	N328AA	Boeing 767-223ER	American Airlines
	N329AA	Boeing 767-223ER	American Airlines
	N330AA	Boeing 767-223ER	American Airlines
	N332AA	Boeing 767-223ER	American Airlines
	N334AA	Boeing 767-223ER	American Airlines
	N335AA	Boeing 767-223ER	American Airlines
	N336AA	Boeing 767-223ER	American Airlines
	N338AA	Boeing 767-223ER	American Airlines
	N339AA	Boeing 767-223ER	American Airlines
	N341AA	Boeing 767-323ER	American Airlines
	N341HA	L.188F Electra	Channel Express (Air Services) Ltd
	N343HA	L.188AF Electra	Channel Express (Air Services) Ltd
	N344HA	L.188AF Electra	Channel Express (Air Services) Ltd
	N345JW	Douglas DC-8-63AF	Arrow Air
	N351AA	Boeing 767-323ER	American Airlines
	N352AA	Boeing 767-323ER	American Airlines
	N353AA	Boeing 767-323ER	American Airlines
	N354AA	Boeing 767-323ER	American Airlines
	N355AA	Boeing 767-323ER	American Airlines
	N357AA	Boeing 767-323ER	American Airlines
	N358AA	Boeing 767-323ER	American Airlines
	N359AA	Boeing 767-323ER	American Airlines
	N360AA	Boeing 767-323ER	American Airlines
	N361AA	Boeing 767-323ER	American Airlines
	N362AA	Boeing 767-323ER	American Airlines
	N363AA	Boeing 767-323ER	American Airlines

Reg.	Type	Owner or Operator	Notes
N366AA	Boeing 767-323ER	American Airlines	
N368AA	Boeing 767-323ER	American Airlines	
N369AA	Boeing 767-323ER	American Airlines	
N370AA	Boeing 767-323ER	American Airlines	
N371AA	Boeing 767-323ER	American Airlines	
N372AA	Boeing 767-323ER	American Airlines	
N373AA	Boeing 767-323ER	American Airlines	
N374AA	Boeing 767-323ER	Am#erican Airlines	
N376AN	Boeing 767-323ER	American Airlines	
N377AN	Boeing 767-323ER	American Airlines	
N378AN	Boeing 767-323ER	American Airlines	
N379AA	Boeing 767-323ER	American Airlines	
N380AN	Boeing 767-323ER	American Airlines	
N381AN	Boeing 767-323ER	American Airlines	
N382AN	Boeing 767-323ER	American Airlines	
N383AN	Boeing 767-323ER	American Airlines	
N384AA	Boeing 767-323ER	American Airlines	
N385AM	Boeing 767-323ER	American Airlines	
N386AA	Boeing 767-323ER	American Airlines	
N387AM	Boeing 767-323ER	American Airlines	
N388AA	Boeing 767-323ER	American Airlines	
N389AA	Boeing 767-323ER	American Airlines	
N390AA	Boeing 767-323ER	American Airlines	
N391AA	Boeing 767-323ER	American Airlines	
N403EV	Boeing 747-45E	EVA Airways	
N405EV	Boeing 747-45E	EVA Airways	
N406EV	Boeing 747-45E	EVA Airways	
N407EV	Boeing 747-45E	EVA Airways	
N408EV	Boeing 747-45E	EVA Airways	
N409EV	Boeing 747-45E	EVA Airways	
N441J	Douglas DC-8-63CF	Arrow Air	
N470EV	Boeing 747-273C	Evergreen International Airlines	
N471EV	Boeing 747-273C	Evergreen International Airlines	
N472EV	Boeing 747-131	Evergreen International Airlines	
N473EV	Boeing 747-121F (SCD)	Evergreen International Airlines	
N474EV	Boeing 747-121	Evergreen International Airlines	
N479EV	Boeing 747-132 (SCD)	Evergreen International Airlines	
N480EV	Boeing 747-121F	Evergreen International Airlines	
N481EV	Boeing 747-132 (SCD)	Evergreen International Airlines	
N482EV	Boeing 747-212B (SCD)	Evergreen International Airlines	
N485EV	Boeing 747-212B (SCD)	Evergreen International Airlines	
N505MC	Boeing 747-2D3B (SCD)	Atlas Air	
N506MC	Boeing 747-2D3B (SCD)	Atlas Air	
N507MC	Boeing 747-230B (SCD)	Atlas Air	
N508MC	Boeing 747-230B (SCD)	Atlas Air	
N509MC	Boeing 747-230B (SCD)	Atlas Air	
N512AT	Boeing 757-225	American Trans Air Spirit of ATA	
N512MC	Boeing 747-230B (SCD)	Atlas Air	
N514AT	Boeing 757-23N	American Trans Air	
N515AT	Boeing 757-23N	American Trans Air	
N516AT	Boeing 757-23N	American Trans Air	
N516MC	Boeing 747-243B (SCD)	Atlas Air	
N517AT	Boeing 757-23N	American Trans Air	
N517MC	Boeing 747-243B (SCD)	Atlas Air/S.A.S.	
N518MC	Boeing 747-243B (SCD)	Atlas Air	
N520UP	Boeing 747-212B	United Parcel Service	
N521UP	Boeing 747-212B	United Parcel Service	
N522MC	Boeing 747-2D7B (SCD)	Atlas Air	
N522SJ	L.100-20 Hercules	Southern Air Transport	
N524MC	Boeing 747-2D7B	Atlas Air	
N524MD	Douglas DC-10-30	Aeroflot	
N582FE	McD Douglas MD-11F	Federal Express	
N586FE	McD Douglas MD-11F	Federal Express	
N587FE	McD Douglas MD-11F	Federal Express	
N601EV	Boeing 767-3T7ER	EVA Airways	
N601FE	McD Douglas MD-11F	Federal Express Christy	
N601TW	Boeing 767-231ER	Trans World Airlines	
N602AA	Boeing 747SP-31	American Airlines	
N602EV	Boeing 767-3T7ER	EVA Airways	
N602FE	McDouglas MD-11F	Federal Express Malcolm Baldrige	
N602FF	Boeing 747-124	Tower Air	
N602GC	Douglas DC-10-30	Gemini Air Cargo	
N602TW	Boeing 767-231ER	Trans World Airlines	
N602UA	Boeing 767-222ER	United Airlines	
N603FE	McD Douglas MD-11F	Federal Express Elizabeth	

Notes	Reg.	Type	Owner or Operator
	N603FF	Boeing 747-130	Tower Air
	N603GC	Douglas DC-10-30	Gemini Air Cargo
	N603TW	Boeing 767-231ER	Trans World Airlines
	N604FE	McD Douglas MD-11F	Federal Express *Hollis*
	N604FF	Boeing 747-121	Tower Air
	N604GC	Douglas DC-10-30	Gemini Air Cargo
	N605FE	McD Douglas MD-11F	Federal Express *April Star*
	N605GC	Douglas DC-10-30	Gemini Air Cargo
	N605TW	Boesing 767-231ER	Trans World Airlines
	N605UA	Boeing 767-222ER	United Airlines
	N606FE	McD Douglas MD-11F	Federal Express *Louis III*
	N606FF	Boeing 747-136	Tower Air
	N606TW	Boeing 767-231ER	Trans World Airlines
	N606UA	Boeing 767-222ER	United Airlines *City of Chicago*
	N607FE	McD Douglas MD-11F	Federal Express *Dana Elena*
	N607PE	Boeing 747-238B	Tower Air
	N607TW	Boeing 767-231ER	Trans World Airlines
	N607UA	Boeing 767-222ER	United Airlines *City of Denver*
	N608FE	McD Douglas MD-11F	Federal Express *Scott*
	N608FF	Boeing 747-131	Tower Air
	N608TW	Boeing 767-231ER	Trans World Airlines
	N608UA	Boeing 767-222ER	United Airlines
	N609FE	McD Douglas MD-11F	Federal Express
	N609FF	Boeing 747-121	Tower Air
	N609TW	Boeing 767-231ER	Trans World Airlines
	N609UA	Boeing 767-222ER	United Airlines
	N610FE	McD Douglas MD-11F	Federal Express
	N610FF	Boeing 747-282B	Tower Air
	N610TW	Boeing 767-231ER	Trans World Airlines
	N610UA	Boeing 767-222ER	United Airlines
	N611FE	McD Douglas MD-11F	Federal Express
	N611FF	Boeing 747-282B	Tower Air
	N611UA	Boeing 767-222ER	United Airlines
	N612FE	McD Douglas MD-11F	Federal Express
	N612US	Boeing 747-251B	Northwest Airlines
	N613FE	McD Douglas MD-11F	Federal Express
	N613FF	Boeing 747-121F (SCD)	Tower Air
	N613US	Boeing 747-251B	Northwest Airlines
	N614FE	McD Douglas MD-11F	Federal Express
	N614FF	Boeing 747-238B	Tower Air
	N614US	Boeing 747-251B	Northwest Airlines
	N615FE	McD Douglas MD-11F	Federal Express *Max*
	N615US	Boeing 747-251B	Northwest Airlines
	N616FE	McD Douglas MD-11F	Federal Express
	N616FF	Boeing 747-212B	Tower Air
	N616US	Boeing 747-251F (SCD)	Northwest Airlines
	N617FE	McD Douglas MD-11F	Federal Express
	N617FF	Boeing 747-121F (SCD)	Tower Air
	N617US	Boeing 747-251F (SCD)	Northwest Airlines
	N618FE	McD Douglas MD-11F	Federal Express
	N618FF	Boeing 747-212B	Tower Air
	N618US	Boeing 747-251F (SCD)	Northwest Airlines
	N619FE	McD Douglas MD-11F	Federal Express
	N619FF	Boeing 747-212B	Tower Air
	N619US	Boeing 747-251F (SCD)	Northwest Airlines
	N620FE	Boeing 747-133	Federal Express
	N620FF	Boeing 747-212B	Tower Air
	N621FF	Boeing 747-143	Tower Air
	N622US	Boeing 747-251B	Northwest Airlines
	N623US	Boeing 747-251B	Northwest Airlines
	N624US	Boeing 747-251B	Northwest Airlines
	N625US	Boeing 747-251B	Northwest Airlines
	N626US	Boeing 747-251B	Northwest Airlines
	N627US	Boeing 747-251B	Northwest Airlines
	N628US	Boeing 747-251B	Northwest Airlines
	N629US	Boeing 747-251F (SCD)	Northwest Airlines
	N630SJ	Boeing 747-124	Polar Air Cargo
	N630US	Boeing 747-2J9F	Northwest Airlines
	N631US	Boeing 747-251B	Northwest Airlines
	N632US	Boeing 747-251B	Northwest Airlines
	N633US	Boeing 747-227B	Northwest Airlines
	N634US	Boeing 747-227B	Northwest Airlines
	N635US	Boeing 747-227B	Northwest Airlines
	N636FE	Boeing 747-245F (SCD)	Federal Express
	N636US	Boeing 747-251B	Northwest Airlines

Reg.	Type	Owner or Operator	Notes
N637US	Boeing 747-251B	Northwest Airlines	
N638FE	Boeing 747-245F (SCD)	Federal Express	
N638US	Boeing 747-251B	Northwest Airlines	
N639FE	Boeing 747-2R7F (SCD)	Federal Express	
N639US	Boeing 747-251F (SCD)	Northwest Airlines	
N640FE	Boeing 747-245F (SCD)	Federal Express	
N640US	Boeing 747-251F (SCD)	Northwest Airlines	
N641FE	Boeing 747-245F (SCD)	Federal Express	
N641NW	Boeing 747-212B	Northwest Airlines	
N641UA	Boeing 767-322ER	United Airlines	
N642NW	Boeing 747-212B	Northwest Airlines	
N642UA	Boeing 767-322ER	United Airlines	
N643UA	Boeing 767-322ER	United Airlines	
N644UA	Boeing 767-322ER	United Airlines	
N645UA	Boeing 767-322ER	United Airlines	
N646UA	Boeing 767-322ER	United Airlines	
N647UA	Boeing 767-322ER	United Airlines	
N648UA	Boeing 767-322ER	United Airlines	
N649UA	Boeing 767-322ER	United Airlines	
N650TW	Boeing 767-205ER	Trans World Airlines	
N650UA	Boeing 767-322ER	United Airlines	
N651TW	Boeing 767-205ER	Trans World Airlines	
N651UA	Boeing 767-322ER	United Airlines	
N652UA	Boeing 767-322ER	United Airlines	
N653UA	Boeing 767-322ER	United Airlines	
N653US	Boeing 767-2B7ER	USAir/British Airways	
N654UA	Boeing 767-322ER	United Airlines	
N654US	Boeing 767-2B7ER	USAir/British Airways	
N655UA	Boeing 767-322ER	United Airlines	
N655US	Boeing 767-2B7ER	USAir/British Airways	
N656UA	Boeing 767-322ER	United Airlines	
N657UA	Boeing 767-322ER	United Airlines	
N658UA	Boeing 767-322ER	United Airlines	
N659UA	Boeing 767-322ER	United Airlines	
N660UA	Boeing 767-322ER	United Airlines	
N661AV	Douglas DC-8-63AF	Arrow Air	
N661UA	Boeing 767-322ER	United Airlines	
N661US	Boeing 747-451	Northwest Airlines	
N662UA	Boeing 767-322ER	United Airlines	
N662US	Boeing 747-451	Northwest Airlines	
N663UA	Boeing 767-322ER	United Airlines	
N663US	Boeing 747-451	Northwest Airlines	
N664US	Boeing 747-451	Northwest Airlines	
N665US	Boeing 747-451	Northwest Airlines	
N666US	Boeing 747-451	Northwest Airlines	
N667US	Boeing 747-451	Northwest Airlines	
N668US	Boeing 747-451	Northwest Airlines	
N669US	Boeing 747-451	Northwest Airlines	
N670US	Boeing 747-451	Northwest Airlines	
N671US	Boeing 747-451	Northwest Airlines	
N672UP	Boeing 747-123F (SCD)	United Parcel Service	
N672US	Boeing 747-451	Northwest Airlines	
N673UP	Boeing 747-123F (SCD)	United Parcel Service	
N674UP	Boeing 747-123F (SCD)	United Parcel Service	
N675UP	Boeing 747-123F (SCD)	United Parcel Service	
N676UP	Boeing 747-123F (SCD)	United Parcel Service	
N677UP	Boeing 747-123F (SCD)	United Parcel Service	
N681UP	Boeing 747-121F (SCD)	United Parcel Service	
N682UP	Boeing 747-121F (SCD)	United Parcel Service	
N683UP	Boeing 747-121F (SCD)	United Parcel Service	
N687AA	Boeing 757-223ET	American Airlines	
N688AA	Boeing 757-223ET	American Airlines	
N689AA	Boeing 757-223ET	American Airlines	
N690AA	Boeing 757-223ET	American Airlines	
N691AA	Boeing 757-223ET	American Airlines	
N692AA	Boeing 757-223ET	American Airlines	
N701CK	Boeing 747-146F (SCD)	American International Airways	
N702CK	Boeing 747-146F (SCD)	American International Airways	
N703CK	Boeing 747-146F (SCD)	American International Airways	
N704CK	Boeing 747-146F (SCD)	American International Airways	
N706CK	Boeing 747-238B	American International Airways	
N707CK	Boeing 747-269B (SCD)	American International Airways	
N708CK	Boeing 747-269B (SCD)	American International Airways	
N724DA	L.1011-385 TriStar 200	Delta Air Lines	
N735PL	Douglas DC-8-62AF	Air Transport International	

Notes	Reg.	Type	Owner or Operator
	N735SJ	Boeing 747-121F (SCD)	Polar Air Cargo
	N736DY	L.1011-385 TriStar 250	Delta Air Lines
	N737D	L.1011-385 TriStar 250	Delta Air Lines
	N740DA	L.1011-385 TriStar 250	Delta Air Lines
	N740SJ	Boeing 747-246F	Southern Air Transport
	N741DA	L.1011-385 TriStar 250	Delta Air Lines
	N741PR	Boeing 747-2F6B	Philippine Airlines
	N741SJ	Boeing 747-246F	Southern Air Transport
	N742PR	Boeing 747-2F6B	Philippine Airlines
	N742SJ	Boeing 747-249F (SCD)	Southern Air Transport
	N743PR	Boeing 747-2F6B	Philippine Airlines
	N744PR	Boeing 747-2F6B	Philippine Airlines
	N747MC	Boeing 747-230F (SCD)	Atlas Air
	N751DA	L.1011-385 TriStar 500	Delta Air Lines
	N751PR	Boeing 747-4F6	Philippine Airlines
	N752DA	L.1011-385 TriStar 500	Delta Air Lines
	N752PR	Boeing 747-4F6	Philippine Airlines
	N753DA	L.1011-385 TriStar 500	Delta Air Lines
	N753PR	Boeing 747-4F6	Philippine Airlines
	N754AT	Boeing 757-2Q8	American Trans Air
	N754DL	L.1011-385 TriStar 500	Delta Air Lines
	N754PR	Boeing 747-469 (SCD)	Philippine Airlines
	N755AT	Boeing 757-2Q8	American Trans Air
	N755DL	L.1011-385 TriStar 500	Delta Air Lines
	N756DR	L.1011-385 TriStar 500	Delta Air Lines
	N759DA	L.1011-385 TriStar 500	Delta Air Lines
	N760DH	L.1011-385 TriStar 500	Delta Air Lines
	N761DA	L.1011-385 TriStar 500	Delta Air Lines
	N762DA	L.1011-385 TriStar 500	Delta Air Lines
	N763DL	L.1011-385 TriStar 500	Delta Air Lines
	N764DA	L.1011-385 TriStar 500	Delta Air Lines
	N765DA	L.1011-385 TriStar 500	Delta Air Lines
	N766DA	L.1011-385 TriStar 500	Delta Air Lines
	N766UA	Boeing 777-222	United Airlines
	N767DA	L.1011-385 TriStar 500	Delta Air Lines
	N767UA	Boeing 777-222	United Airlines
	N768DL	L.1011-385 TriStar 500	Delta Air Lines
	N768UA	Boeing 777-222	United Airlines
	N769DL	L.1011-385 TriStar 500	Delta Air Lines
	N769UA	Boeing 777-222	United Airlines
	N770UA	Boeing 777-222	United Airlines
	N771UA	Boeing 777-222	United Airlines
	N772UA	Boeing 777-222	United Airlines
	N773UA	Boeing 777-222	United Airlines
	N774UA	Boeing 777-222	United Airlines
	N775UA	Boeing 777-222	United Airlines
	N776UA	Boeing 777-222	United Airlines
	N777UA	Boeing 777-222	United Airlines
	N778UA	Boeing 777-222	United Airlines
	N779UA	Boeing 777-222	United Airlines
	N780UA	Boeing 777-222	United Airlines
	N781UA	Boeing 777-222	United Airlines
	N782UA	Boeing 777-222B	United Airlines
	N783UA	Boeing 777-222B	United Airlines
	N784AL	Douglas DC-8-63CF	Arrow Air
	N784UA	Boeing 777-222B	United Airlines
	N785UA	Boeing 777-222B	United Airlines
	N786UA	Boeing 777-222B	United Airlines
	N787UA	Boeing 777-222B	United Airlines
	N788UA	Boeing 777-222B	United Airlines
	N789UA	Boeing 777-222B	United Airlines
	N790UA	Boeing 777-222B	United Airlines
	N791AL	Douglas DC-8-62AF	Arrow Air
	N791FT	Douglas DC-8-73AF	Emery Worldwide
	N791UA	Boeing 777-222B	United Airlines
	N792FT	Douglas DC-8-73AF	Emery Worldwide
	N792UA	Boeing 777-222B	United Airlines
	N793UA	Boeing 777-222B	United Airlines
	N795FT	Douglas DC-8-73AF	Emery Worldwide
	N796AL	Douglas DC-8-63AF	Emery Worldwide
	N796FT	Douglas DC-8-73AF	Emery Worldwide
	N797AL	Douglas DC-8-63AF	Emery Worldwide
	N801CK	Douglas DC-8-55F	American International Airways
	N801DE	McD Douglas MD-11	Delta Air Lines
	N801DH	Douglas DC-8-73AF	DHL Worldwide

Reg.	Type	Owner or Operator	Notes
N801UP	Douglas DC-8-73AF	United Parcel Service	
N802BN	Douglas DC-8-62AF	Arrow Air	
N802CK	Douglas DC-8-54F	American International Airways	
N802DE	McD Douglas MD-11	Delta Air Lines	
N802DH	Douglas DC-8-73AF	DHL Worldwide	
N802UP	Douglas DC-8-73AF	United Parcel Service	
N803DE	McD Douglas MD-11	Delta Air Lines	
N803DH	Douglas DC-8-73AF	DHL Worldwide	
N803UP	Douglas DC-8-63AF	United Parcel Service	
N804CK	Douglas DC-8-51F	American International Airways	
N804DE	McD Douglas MD-11	Delta Air Lines	
N804DH	Douglas DC-8-73AF	DHL Worldwide	
N804UP	Douglas DC-8-51	United Parcel Service	
N805CK	Douglas DC-8-51F	American International Airways	
N805DE	McD Douglas MD-11	Delta Air Lines	
N805DH	Douglas DC-8-73AF	DHL Worldwide	
N805UP	Douglas DC-8-73CF	United Parcel Service	
N806CK	Douglas DC-8-54F	American International Airways	
N806DE	McD Douglas MD-11	Delta Air Lines	
N806DH	Douglas DC-8-73CF	DHL Worldwide	
N806UP	Douglas DC-8-73AF	United Parcel Service	
N807CK	Douglas DC-8-55F	American International Airways	
N807DE	McD Douglas MD-11	Delta Air Lines	
N807DH	Douglas DC-8-73CF	DHL Worldwide	
N807UP	Douglas DC-8-73AF	United Parcel Service	
N808DE	McD Douglas MD-11	Delta Air Lines	
N808MC	Boeing 747-212B (SCD)	Atlas Air	
N808UP	Douglas DC-8-73AF	United Parcel Service	
N809CK	Douglas DC-8-55F	American International Airways	
N809DE	McD Douglas MD-11	Delta Air Lines	
N809MC	Boeing 747-228F (SCD)	Atlas Air/Cargolux	
N809UP	Douglas DC-8-73AF	United Parcel Service	
N810CK	Douglas DC-8-52F	American International Airways	
N810DE	McD Douglas MD-11	Delta Air Lines	
N810UP	Douglas DC-8-71AF	United Parcel Service	
N811CK	Douglas DC-8-63AF	American International Airways	
N811DE	McD Douglas MD-11	Delta Air Lines	
N811UP	Douglas DC-8-73AF	United Parcel Service	
N812CK	Douglas DC-8-61AF	American International Airways	
N812DE	McD Douglas MD-11	Delta Air Lines	
N812UP	Douglas DC-8-73AF	United Parcel Service	
N813CK	Douglas DC-8-61AF	American International Airways	
N813DE	McD Douglas MD-11	Delta Air Lines	
N813UP	Douglas DC-8-73AF	United Parcel Service	
N814DE	McD Douglas MD-11	Delta Air Lines	
N814UP	Douglas DC-8-73AF	United Parcel Service	
N815CK	Douglas DC-8-63F	American International Airways	
N815DE	McD Douglas MD-11	Delta Air Lines	
N815EV	Douglas DC-8-73CF	Evergreen International Airlines	
N816CK	Douglas DC-8-61F	American International Airways	
N817CK	Douglas DC-8-61F	American International Airways	
N817EV	Douglas DC-8-62AF	Evergreen International Airlines	
N818CK	Douglas DC-8-62F	American International Airways	
N818UP	Douglas DC-8-73AF	United Parcel Service	
N819UP	Douglas DC-8-73AF	United Parcel Service	
N820BX	Douglas DC-8-71AF	Burlington Express	
N821BX	Douglas DC-8-71AF	Burlington Express	
N822BX	Douglas DC-8-71AF	Burlington Express	
N824BX	Douglas DC-8-71AF	Burlington Express	
N831FT	Boeing 747-121F (SCD)	Polar Air Cargo	
N831LA	Douglas DC-10-30	Laker Airways	
N832FT	Boeing 747-121F (SCD)	Polar Air Cargo	
N832LA	Douglas DC-10-30	Laker Airways	
N833LA	Douglas DC-10-30	Laker Airways	
N835AB	Airbus A.310-324	Air Jamaica *Spirit of May Pen*	
N836UP	Douglas DC-8-73AF	United Parcel Service	
N837AB	Airbus A.310-324	Air Jamaica	
N838AB	Airbus A.310-324	Air Jamaica *Spirit of Spanish Town*	
N839AD	Airbus A.310-324	Air Jamaica *Spirit of Negril*	
N840AB	Airbus A.310-324	Air Jamaica *Spirit of Mandeville*	
N840SJ	Boeing 747-246F (SCD)	Southern Air Transport	
N840UP	Douglas DC-8-73AF	United Parcel Service	
N841AB	Airbus A.310-324	Air Jamaica	
N845FT	Boeing 747-122F	Polar Air Cargo	
N850FT	Boeing 747-122F	Polar Air Cargo	

Notes	Reg.	Type	Owner or Operator
	N851FT	Boeing 747-122F	Polar Air Cargo
	N851UP	Douglas DC-8-73AF	United Parcel Service
	N852FT	Boeing 747-122	Polar Air Cargo
	N852UP	Douglas DC-8-73AF	United Parcel Service
	N853FT	Boeing 747-122F	Polar Air Cargo
	N854FT	Boeing 747-122F	Polar Air Cargo
	N855FT	Boeing 747-124F	Polar Air Cargo
	N856FT	Boeing 747-132F (SCD)	Polar Air Cargo
	N857FT	Boeing 747-132F	Polar Air Cargo
	N858FT	Boeing 747-123F	Polar Air cargo
	N859FT	Boeing 747-123F	Polar Air Cargo
	N863BX	Boeing 707-321C	Burlington Express
	N865F	Douglas DC-8-63AF	Emery Worldwide
	N866UP	Douglas DC-8-73AF	United Parcel Service
	N867BX	Douglas DC-8-63AF	Burlington Express
	N867UP	Douglas DC-8-73AF	United Parcel Service
	N868BX	Douglas DC-8-63AF	Burlington Express
	N868UP	Douglas DC-8-73AF	United Parcel Service
	N869BX	Douglas DC-8-63AF	Burlington Express
	N870BX	Doulgas DC-8-63AF	Burlington Express
	N870SJ	Douglas DC-8-71AF	Southern Air Transport
	N870TV	Douglas DC-8-73AF	Emery Worldwide
	N872SJ	Douglas DC-8-71AF	Southern Air Transport
	N873SJ	Douglas DC-8-73AF	Southern Air Transport
	N874SJ	Douglas DC-8-73AF	Southern Air Transport
	N874UP	Douglas DC-8-73AF	United Parcel Service
	N875SJ	Douglas DC-8-71AF	Southern Air Transport
	N880UP	Douglas DC-8-73AF	United Parcel Service
	N894UP	Douglas DC-8-73AF	United Parcel Service
	N901SJ	L.100-30 Hercules	Southern Air Transport
	N905SJ	L.100-30 Hercules	Southern Air Transport
	N906R	Douglas DC-8-63CF	Air Transport International
	N906SJ	L.100-30 Hercules	Southern Air Transport
	N907SJ	L.100-30 Hercules	Southern Air Transport
	N908SJ	L.100-30 Hercules	Southern Air Transport
	N909SJ	L.100-30 Hercules	Southern Air Transport
	N910SJ	L.100-30 Hercules	Southern Air Transport
	N912SJ	L.100-30 Hercules	Southern Air Transport
	N916SJ	L.100-30 Hercules	Southern Air Transport
	N918SJ	L.100-30 Hercules	Southern Air Transport
	N919SJ	L.100-30 Hercules	Southern Air Transport
	N920FT	Boeing 747-249F	Polar Air Cargo
	N920SJ	L.100-30 Hercules	Southern Air Transport
	N921R	Douglas DC-8-63AF	Emery Worldwide
	N921SJ	L.100-30 Hercules	Southern Air Transport
	N923SJ	L.100-30 Hercules	Southern Air Transport
	N950R	Douglas DC-8-63AF	Emery Worldwide
	N951R	Douglas DC-8-63AF	Emery Worldwide
	N952R	Douglas DC-8-63AF	Emery Worldwide
	N957R	Douglas DC-8-63AF	Emery Worldwide
	N959R	Douglas DC-8-63AF	Emery Worldwide
	N961R	Douglas DC-8-73AF	Emery Worldwide
	N964R	Douglas DC-8-63AF	Emery Worldwide
	N990CF	Douglas DC-8-62AF	Emery Worldwide
	N993CF	Douglas DC-8-62AF	Emery Worldwide
	N994CF	Douglas DC-8-62AF	Emery Worldwide
	N995CF	Douglas DC-8-62AF	Emery Worldwide
	N996CF	Douglas DC-8-62AF	Emery Worldwide
	N997CF	Douglas DC-8-62AF	Emery Worldwide
	N998CF	Douglas DC-8-62AF	Emery Worldwide
	N1738D	L.1011-385 TriStar 250	Delta Air Lines
	N1739D	L.1011-385 TriStar 250	Delta Air Lines
	N1750B	McD Douglas MD-11 (1AA)	American Airlines
	N1752K	McD Douglas MD-11 (1AC)	American Airlines
	N1755	McD Douglas MD-11 (1AF)	American Airlines
	N1756	McD Douglas MD-11 (1AG)	American Airlines
	N1757A	McD Douglas MD-11 (1AH)	American Airlines
	N1758B	McD Douglas MD-11 (1AJ)	American Airlines
	N1759	McD Douglas MD-11 (1AK)	American Airlines
	N1760A	McD Douglas MD-11 (1AM)	American Airlines
	N1761R	McD Douglas MD-11 (1AN)	American Airlines
	N1762B	McD Douglas MD-11 (1AP)	American Airlines
	N1763	McD Douglas MD-11 (1AR)	American Airlines
	N1764B	McD Douglas MD-11 (1AS)	American Airlines

Reg.	Type	Owner or Operator	Notes
N1765B	McD Douglas MD-11 (1AT)	American Airlines	
N1766A	McD Douglas MD-11 (1AU)	American Airlines	
N1767A	McD Douglas MD-11 (1AV)	American Airlines	
N1768D	McD Douglas MD-11 (1AL)	American Airlines	
N1803	Douglas DC-8-62AF	Arrow Air	
N1804	Douglas DC-8-62AF	Arrow Air	
N1808E	Douglas DC-8-62AF	Arrow Air	
N2674U	Douglas DC-8-73AF	Emery Worldwide	
N3140D	L.1011-385 TriStar 500 (598)	B.W.I.A. Sunjet St. Lucia	
N4508H	Boeing 747SP-09	China Airlines	
N4522V	Boeing 747SP-09	China Airlines	
N4703U	Boeing 747-122F	Polar Air Cargo	
N4714U	Boeing 747-122	United Airlines	
N4716U	Boeing 747-122	United Airlines	
N4717U	Boeing 747-122	United Airlines Edward E. Carlson	
N4718U	Boeing 747-122	United Airlines Thomas F. Gleed	
N4719U	Boeing 747-122	United Airlines Friendship Japan	
N4720U	Boeing 747-122	United Airlines	
N4723U	Boeing 747-122	United Airlines William A. Patterson	
N4724U	Boeing 747-122	United Airlines	
N4727U	Boeing 747-122	United Airlines Robert E. Johnson	
N4728U	Boeing 747-122	United Airlines Gardner Cowles	
N4729U	Boeing 747-122	United Airlines	
N4732U	Boeing 747-122	United Airlines	
N4735U	Boeing 747-122	United Airlines	
N6186	Boeing 747-212B	Tower Air	
N7036U	L.1011-385 TriStar 100	Trans World Airlines	
N7375A	Boeing 767-323ER	American Airlines	
N8076U	Douglas DC-8-71AF	Emery Worldwide	
N8084U	Douglas DC-8-71AF	Emery Worldwide	
N8085U	Douglas DC-8-71AF	Emery Worldwide	
N8086U	Douglas DC-8-71AF	Emery Worldwide	
N8087U	Douglas DC-8-71AF	Emery Worldwide	
N8089U	Douglas DC-8-71AF	Southern Air Transport	
N8097U	Douglas DC-8-71AF	Southern Air Transport	
N8228P	Douglas DC-10-30	Aeromexico Castillo de Chapultepec	
N8968U	Douglas DC-8-62AF	Arrow Air	
N12061	Douglas DC-10-30	Continental Airlines Richard M. Adams	
N12064	Douglas DC-10-30	Continental Airlines	
N12114	Boeing 757-224	Continental Airlines	
N13066	Douglas DC-10-30	Continental Airlines	
N13067	Douglas DC-10-30	Continental Airlines	
N13110	Boeing 757-224	Continental Airlines	
N14062	Douglas DC-10-30	Continental Airlines	
N14063	Douglas DC-10-30	Continental Airlines	
N14074	Douglas DC-10-30	Continental Airlines	
N14075	Douglas DC-10-30	Continental Airlines	
N14115	Boeing 757-224	Continental Airlines	
N15069	Douglas DC-10-30	Continental Airlines	
N17011	Boeing 747-143	Continental Airlines	
N17025	Boeing 747-238B	Continental Airlines	
N17104	Boeing 757-224	Continental Airlines	
N17105	Boeing 757-224	Continental Airlines	
N19072	Douglas DC-10-30	Continental Airlines	
N31019	L.1011-385 TriStar 50	Trans World Airlines	
N31023	L.1011-385 TriStar 50	Trans World Airlines	
N31029	L.1011-385 TriStar 100	Trans World Airlines	
N31031	L.1011-385 TriStar 100	Trans World Airlines	
N33021	Boeing 747-243B	Continental Airlines	
N33103	Boeing 757-224	Continental Airlines	
N37077	Douglas DC-10-30	Continental Airlines	
N37078	Douglas DC-10-30	Continental Airlines	
N39356	Boeing 767-323ER	American Airlines	
N39364	Boeing 767-323ER	American Airlines	
N39365	Boeing 767-323ER	American Airlines	
N39367	Boeing 767-323ER	American Airlines	
N41068	Douglas DC-10-30	Continental Airlines	
N42086	Douglas DC-8-62AF	Arrow Air	
N49082	Douglas DC-10-30	Continental Airlines	
N53110	Boeing 747-131	Trans World Airlines	
N53116	Boeing 747-131	Trans World Airlines	
N68060	Douglas DC-10-30	Continental Airlines Robert F. Six	
N68065	Douglas DC-10-30	Continental Airlines Robert P. Gallaway	
N76073	Douglas DC-10-30	Continental Airlines	

Notes	Reg.	Type	Owner or Operator
	N78019	Boeing 747-230B	Continental Airlines
	N83071	Douglas DC-10-30ER	Continental Airlines
	N87070	Douglas DC-10-30ER	Continental Airlines
	N93104	Boeing 747-131	Trans World Airlines
	N93105	Boeing 747-131	Trans World Airlines
	N93107	Boeing 747-131	Trans World Airlines
	N93108	Boeing 747-131	Trans World Airlines
	N93109	Boeing 747-131	Trans World Airlines
	N93117	Boeing 747-131	Trans World Airlines

OD (Lebanon)

OD-AFD	Boeing 707-3B4C	Middle East Airlines
OD-AFE	Boeing 707-3B4C	Middle East Airlines
OD-AGD	Boeing 707-323C	TMA of Lebanon
OD-AGH	Boeing 747-2B4B (SCD)	Middle East Airlines
OD-AGO	Boeing 707-321C	TMA of Lebanon
OD-AGP	Boeing 707-321C	TMA of Lebanon
OD-AGS	Boeing 707-331C	TMA of Lebanon
OD-AGU	Boeing 707-347C	Middle East Airlines
OD-AGV	Boeing 707-347C	Middle East Airlines
OD-AGX	Boeing 707-327C	TMA of Lebanon
OD-AGY	Boeing 707-327C	TMA of Lebanon
OD-AHC	Boeing 707-323C	Middle East Airlines
OD-AHD	Boeing 707-323C	Middle East Airlines
OD-AHE	Boeing 707-323C	Middle East Airlines
OD-AHF	Boeing 707-323B	Middle East Airlines
OD-	Airbus A.320-231	Middle East Airlines
OD-	Airbus A.320-231	Middle East Airlines
OD-	Airbus A.321-131	Middle East Airlines
OD-	Airbus A.321-131	Middle East Airlines

Note: MEA also uses the 747s N203AE and N204AE when not on lease and two
A.310-304s registered F-OHLH and F-OHLI.

OE (Austria)

OE-ILF	Boeing 737-3Z9	Lauda Air *Bob Marley*
OE-ILG	Boeing 737-3Z9	Lauda Air *John Lennon*
OE-LAA	Airbus A.310-324	Austrian Airlines *New York*
OE-LAB	Airbus A.310-324	Austrian Airlines *Tokyo*
OE-LAC	Airbus A.310-324	Austrian Airlines *Paris*
OE-LAD	Airbus A.310-325	Austrian Airlines *Chicago*
OE-LAG	Airbus A.340-212	Austrian Airlines *Europe*
OE-LAH	Airbus A.340-212	Austrian Airlines *Asia*
OE-LAS	Boeing 767-33AER	Lauda Air *Ayrton Senna*
OE-LAT	Boeing 767-31AER	Lauda Air *Enzo Ferrari*
OE-LAU	Boeing 767-3Z9ER	Lauda Air *Johann Strauss*
OE-LAW	Boeing 767-3Z9ER	Lauda Air *Franz Schubert*
OE-LAX	Boeing 767-3Z9ER	Lauda Air *James Dean*
OE-LBA	Airbus A.321-111	Austrian Airlines *Salzkammergut*
OE-LBB	Airbus A.321-111	Austrian Airlines *Pinzgau*
OE-LBC	Airbus A.321-111	Austrian Airlines *Sudtirol*
OE-LBD	Airbus A.321-111	Austrian Airlines
OE-LBE	Airbus A.321-111	Austrian Airlines
OE-LBF	Airbus A.321-111	Austrian Airlines
OE-LCF	Canadair Regional Jet 200LR	Tyrolean Airways *St.Dusseldorf*
OE-LCG	Canadair Regional Jet 200LR	Tyrolean Airways *St.Koln*
OE-LCH	Canadair Regional Jet 200LR	Tyrolean Airways *Stadt Amsterdam*
OE-LCI	Canadair Regional Jet 200LR	Tyrolean Airways
OE-LCJ	Canadair Regional Jet 200LR	Tyrolean Airways
OE-LDP	McD Douglas MD-81	Austrian Airlines *Niederösterreich*
OE-LDR	McD Douglas MD-81	Austrian Airlines *Wien*
OE-LDS	McD Douglas MD-81	Austrian Airlines *Burgenland*
OE-LDT	McD Douglas MD-81	Austrian Airlines *Kärnten*
OE-LDU	McD Douglas MD-81	Austrian Airlines *Steiermark*
OE-LDV	McD Douglas MD-81	Austrian Airlines *Oberösterreich*
OE-LDW	McD Douglas MD-81	Austrian Airlines *Salzburg*

Reg.	Type	Owner or Operator	Notes
OE-LDX	McD Douglas MD-82	Austrian Airlines *Tirol*	
OE-LDY	McD Douglas MD-82	Austrian Airlines *Vorarlberg*	
OE-LDZ	McD Douglas MD-82	Austrian Airlines *Graz*	
OE-LEC	D.H.C.8-311 Dash Eight	Tyrolean Airways	
OE-LFG	Fokker 70	Tyrolean Airways *Stadt Innsbruck*	
OE-LFH	Fokker 70	Tyrolean Airways *Stadt Salzburg*	
OE-LFK	Fokker 70	Tyrolean Airways *Stadt Wien*	
OE-LFL	Fokker 70	Tyrolean Airways *Stadt Linz*	
OE-LFO	Fokker 70	Austrian Airlines *Wiener Neustadt*	
OE-LFP	Fokker 70	Austrian Airlines *Wels*	
OE-LFQ	Fokker 70	Austrian Airlines *Dornbirn*	
OE-LFR	Fokker 70	Austrian Airlines *Steyr*	
OE-LLE	D.H.C.8-106 Dash Eight	Tyrolean Airways *Zillertal*	
OE-LLF	D.H.C.8-106 Dash Eight	Tyrolean Airways *Seefeld*	
OE-LLG	D.H.C.8-106 Dash Eight	Tyrolean Airways *Kufstein*	
OE-LLH	D.H.C.8-106 Dash Eight	Tyrolean Airways *Stadt Kitzbühel*	
OE-LLI	D.H.C.8-102 Dash Eight	Tyrolean Airways	
OE-LLJ	D.H.C.8-103 Dash Eight	Tyrolean Airways	
OE-LLL	D.H.C.8-106 Dash Eight	Augsburg Airways	
OE-LLU	D.H.C.7-102 Dash Seven	Tyrolean Airways	
OE-LLV	D.H.C.8-314 Dash Eight	Tyrolean Airways *Land Tirol*	
OE-LLW	D.H.C.8-314 Dash Eight	Tyrolean Airways *Land Steiermark*	
OE-LLX	D.H.C.8-314 Dash Eight	Tyrolean Airways *Land Salzburg*	
OE-LLY	D.H.C.8-314 Dash Eight	Tyrolean Airways *Land Vorariberg*	
OE-LLZ	D.H.C.8-314 Dash Eight	Tyrolean Airways *Land Burgenland*	
OE-LMA	McD Douglas MD-82	Austrian Airlines *Linz*	
OE-LMB	McD Douglas MD-82	Austrian Airlines *Eisenstadt*	
OE-LMC	McD Douglas MD-82	Austrian Airlines *Baden*	
OE-LMD	McD Douglas MD-83	Austrian Airlines *Villach*	
OE-LME	McD Douglas MD-83	Austrian Airlines *Krems*	
OE-LMK	McD Douglas MD-87	Austrian Airlines *St Pölten*	
OE-LML	McD Douglas MD-87	Austrian Airlines *Salzburg*	
OE-LMM	McD Douglas MD-87	Austrian Airlines *Innsbruck*	
OE-LMN	McD Douglas MD-87	Austrian Airlines *Klagenfurt*	
OE-LMO	McD Douglas MD-87	Austrian Airlines *Bregenz*	
OE-LNH	Boeing 737-4Z9	Lauda Air *Elvis Presley*	
OE-LNI	Boeing 737-4Z9	Lauda Air *Janise Joplin*	
OE-LRA	Canadair Regional Jet 100LR	Lauda Air	
OE-LRB	Canadair Regional Jet 100LR	Lauda Air	
OE-LRC	Canadair Regional Jet 100LR	Lauda Air	
OE-LRD	Canadair Regional Jet 100LR	Lauda Air	
OE-LRE	Canadair Regional Jet 100LR	Lauda Air	
OE-LRF	Canadair Regional Jet 100LR	Lauda Air	
OE-LRG	Canadair Regional Jet 100LR	Lauda Air	
OE-LRH	Canadair Regional Jet 100LR	Lauda Air	
OE-LRQ	Canadair Regional Jet 100LR	Tyrolean Airways/Lufthansa CityLine (D-ACLN)	
OE-LTA	D.H.C.8-314 Dash Eight	Tyrolean Airways *Stadt Linz*	
OE-LTB	D.H.C.8-314 Dash Eight	Tyrolean Airways *Stadt Graz*	
OE-LTC	D.H.C.8-314 Dash Eight	Tyrolean Airways *Stadt Klagenfurt*	
OE-LTD	D.H.C.8-314 Dash Eight	Tyrolean Airways *Land Oberosterreich*	
OE-LTE	D.H.C.8-314 Dash Eight	Tyrolean Airways *Land Karnten*	
OE-LTF	D.H.C.8-314 Dash Eight	Tyrolean Airways *Land Niederosterreich*	
OE-LTG	D.H.C.8-314 Dash Eight	Tyrolean Airways	

OH (Finland)

OH-LAA	Airbus A.300B4-203	Finnair	
OH-LAB	Airbus A.300B4-203	Finnair	
OH-LGA	McD Douglas MD-11	Finnair	
OH-LGB	McD Douglas MD-11	Finnair	
OH-LGC	McD Douglas MD-11	Finnair	
OH-LGD	McD Douglas MD-11	Finnair	
OH-LMA	McD Douglas MD-87	Finnair	
OH-LMB	McD Douglas MD-87	Finnair	
OH-LMC	McD Douglas MD-87	Finnair	
OH-LMG	McD Douglas MD-83	Finnair	
OH-LMH	McD Douglas MD-82	Finnair	
OH-LMN	McD Douglas MD-82	Finnair	
OH-LMO	McD Douglas MD-82	Finnair	
OH-LMP	McD Douglas MD-82	Finnair	

Notes	Reg.	Type	Owner or Operator
	OH-LMR	McD Douglas MD-83	Finnair
	OH-LMS	McD Douglas MD-83	Finnair
	OH-LMT	McD Douglas MD-82	Finnair
	OH-LMU	McD Douglas MD-83	Finnair
	OH-LMV	McD Douglas MD-83	Finnair
	OH-LMW	McD Douglas MD-82	Finnair
	OH-LMX	McD Douglas MD-82	Finnair
	OH-LMY	McD Douglas MD-82	Finnair
	OH-LMZ	McD Douglas MD-82	Finnair
	OH-LPA	McD Douglas MD-82	Finnair
	OH-LPB	McD Douglas MD-83	Finnair
	OH-LPC	McD Douglas MD-83	Finnair
	OH-LPE	McD Douglas MD-83	Finnair
	OH-LPH	McD Douglas MD-83	Finnair
	OH-LYN	Douglas DC-9-51	Finnair
	OH-LYO	Douglas DC-9-51	Finnair
	OH-LYP	Douglas DC-9-51	Finnair
	OH-LYR	Douglas DC-9-51	Finnair
	OH-LYS	Douglas DC-9-51	Finnair
	OH-LYT	Douglas DC-9-51	Finnair
	OH-LYU	Douglas DC-9-51	Finnair
	OH-LYV	Douglas DC-9-51	Finnair
	OH-LYW	Douglas DC-9-51	Finnair
	OH-LYX	Douglas DC-9-51	Finnair
	OH-LYY	Douglas DC-9-51	Finnair
	OH-LYZ	Douglas DC-9-51	Finnair

OK (Czech Republic)

	OK-BYV	Ilyushin IL-62M	Georgia Air Prague
	OK-CGH	Boeing 737-55S	Ceskoslovenske Aerolinie (CSA)
	OK-CGJ	Boeing 737-55S	CSA
	OK-CGK	Boeing 737-55S	CSA
	OK-FBF	Ilyushin IL-62	Georgia Air Prague
	OK-GBH	Ilyushin IL-62	Georgia Air Prague
	OK-HFL	Tupolev Tu-134A	CSA
	OK-HFM	Tupolev Tu-134A	CSA
	OK-IFN	Tupolev Tu-134A	CSA
	OK-JBJ	Ilyushin IL-62M	Bemoair Praha
	OK-JEN	F.28 Fellowship 4000	Air Ostrava
	OK-JGT	Boeing 727-287	Air Ostrava
	OK-LGZ	Boeing 737-2P5	Bemoair Praha
	OK-MGS	Boeing 727-287	Air Ostrava
	OK-OBL	Ilyushin IL-62M	Bemoair Praha
	OK-TCD	Tupolev Tu-154M	CSA *Trencianske Teplice*
	OK-UCE	Tupolev Tu-154M	CSA *Marianske Lazne*
	OK-UCF	Tupolev Tu-154M	CSA *Smokovec*
	OK-VCG	Tupolev Tu-154M	CSA *Luhacovice*
	OK-VCP	Tupolev Tu-154M	Statni Letecky Utvar
	OK-WAA	Airbus A.310-304	CSA *Praha*
	OK-WAB	Airbus A.310-304	CSA *Bratislava*
	OK-WGF	Boeing 737-4Y0	CSA *Jihlava*
	OK-WGG	Boeing 737-4Y0	CSA *Liberec*
	OK-XGA	Boeing 737-55S	CSA *Pizen*
	OK-XGB	Boeing 737-55S	CSA *Olomouc*
	OK-XGC	Boeing 737-55S	CSA *Ceske Budejovice*
	OK-XGD	Boeing 737-55S	CSA *Poprad*
	OK-XGE	Boeing 737-55S	CSA *Kosice*
	OK-	Boeing 737-55S	CSA
	OK-	Boeing 737-55S	CSA
	OK-	Boeing 737-55S	CSA

OM (Slovakia)

	OM-AHK	Boeing 727-230	Air Slovakia *Krivan*
	OM-CHD	Boeing 727-230	Air Slovakia
	OM-GAT	Tupolev Tu-134A-3	Air Transport Europe
	OM-UFB	Boeing 707-321B	Slovtrans Air
	OM-UGT	SAAB SF.340B	Tatra Air
	OM-UGU	SAAB SF.340B	Tatra Air

OO (Belgium)

Reg.	Type	Owner or Operator	Notes
OO-CTB	McD Douglas MD-11	City Bird	
OO-DHC	Convair Cv.580	European Air Transport (DHL)	
OO-DHD	Convair Cv.580	European Air Transport (DHL)	
OO-DHE	Convair Cv.580	European Air Transport (DHL)	
OO-DHF	Convair Cv.580	European Air Transport (DHL)	
OO-DHJ	Convair Cv.580	European Air Transport (DHL)	
OO-DHL	Convair Cv.580	European Air Transport (DHL)	
OO-DHM	Boeing 727-31F	European Air Transport (DHL)	
OO-DHN	Boeing 727-31F	European Air Transport (DHL)	
OO-DHO	Boeing 727-31F	European Air Transport (DHL)	
OO-DHP	Boeing 727-35F	European Air Transport (DHL)	
OO-DHQ	Boeing 727-35F	European Air Transport (DHL)	
OO-DHR	Boeing 727-23F	European Air Transport (DHL)	
OO-DHS	Boeing 727-223F	European Air Transport (DHL)	
OO-DHT	Boeing 727-223F	European Air Transport (DHL)	
OO-DHU	Boeing 727-223F	European Air Transport (DHL)	
OO-DHV	Boeing 727-223F	European Air Transport (DHL)	
OO-DHW	Boeing 727-223F	European Air Transport (DHL)	
OO-DHX	Boeing 727-223F	European Air Transport (DHL)	
OO-DJE	BAe 146-200	Delta Air Transport/SABENA	
OO-DJF	BAe 146-200	Delta Air Transport/SABENA	
OO-DJG	BAe 146-200	Delta Air Transport/SABENA	
OO-DJH	BAe 146-200	Delta Air Transport/SABENA	
OO-DJJ	BAe 146-200	Delta Air Transport/SABENA	
OO-DJK	Avro RJ85	Delta Air Transport/SABENA	
OO-DJL	Avro RJ85	Delta Air Transport/SABENA	
OO-DJN	Avro RJ85	Delta Air Transport/SABENA	
OO-DJO	Avro RJ85	Delta Air Transport/SABENA	
OO-DJP	Avro RJ85	Delta Air Transport/SABENA	
OO-DJQ	Avro RJ85	Delta Air Transport/SABENA	
OO-DJR	Avro RJ85	Delta Air Transport/SABENA	
OO-DJS	Avro RJ85	Delta Air Transport/SABENA	
OO-DJT	Avro RJ85	Delta Air Transport/SABENA	
OO-DJV	Avro RJ85	Delta Air Transport/SABENA	
OO-DJW	Avro RJ85	Delta Air Transport/SABENA	
OO-DJX	Avro RJ85	Delta Air Transport/SABENA	
OO-DTF	EMB-120ER Brasilia	Delta Air Transport	
OO-DTG	EMB-120ER Brasilia	Delta Air Transport	
OO-DTH	EMB-120ER Brasilia	Delta Air Transport	
OO-DTI	EMB-120ER Brasilia	Delta Air Transport	
OO-DTJ	EMB-120RT Brasilia	Delta Air Transport	
OO-DTL	EMB-120ER Brasilia	Delta Air Transport	
OO-DTN	EMB-120ER Brasilia	Delta Air Transport	
OO-DTO	EMB-120ER Brasilia	Delta Air Transport	
OO-HPN	Douglas DC-10-15	Skyjet	
OO-HUB	Convair Cv.580	European Air Transport (DHL)	
OO-ILJ	Boeing 737-46B	Air Belgium	
OO-ILK	Boeing 737-3Q8QC	Air Belgium	
OO-JOT	Douglas DC-10-30	ChallengAir	
OO-LRM	Douglas DC-10-30	ChallengAir/Corsair	
OO-LTL	Boeing 737-3M8	Virgin European Express	
OO-LTM	Boeing 737-3M8	Virgin European Express	
OO-LTP	Boeing 737-33A	Virgin European Express	
OO-LTU	Boeing 737-33A	Virgin European Express	
OO-LTV	Boeing 737-3Y0	Virgin European Express	
OO-LTW	Boeing 737-33A	Virgin European Express	
OO-LTY	Boeing 737-3Q8	Virgin European Express	
OO-MJE	BAe 146-200	Delta Air Transport/SABENA	
OO-MTD	EMB-120ER Brasilia	Delta Air Transport	
OO-PHN	Douglas DC-10-30	Skyjet	
OO-SBJ	Boeing 737-46B	Sobelair *Juliette*	
OO-SBM	Boeing 737-429	Sobelair	
OO-SBN	Boeing 737-4Y0	EBA EuroBelgian Airlines	
OO-SBQ	Boeing 737-229	Sobelair	
OO-SBT	Boeing 737-229	Sobelair	
OO-SBX	Boeing 737-3M8	Sobelair	
OO-SBY	Boeing 767-33AER	Sobelair	
OO-SBZ	Boeing 737-329	Sobelair	
OO-SCA	Airbus A.310-222	SABENA	
OO-SCB	Airbus A.310-222	SABENA	

Notes	Reg.	Type	Owner or Operator
	OO-SCC	Airbus A.310-322	SABENA
	OO-SCW	Airbus A.340-211	SABENA
	OO-SCX	Airbus A.340-211	SABENA
	OO-SCY	Airbus A.340-311	SABENA
	OO-SCZ	Airbus A.340-311	SABENA
	OO-SDA	Boeing 737-229	SABENA
	OO-SDD	Boeing 737-229	SABENA
	OO-SDE	Boeing 737-229	SABENA
	OO-SDF	Boeing 737-229	SABENA
	OO-SDG	Boeing 737-229	SABENA
	OO-SDJ	Boeing 737-229C	SABENA
	OO-SDK	Boeing 737-229C	SABENA
	OO-SDL	Boeing 737-229	SABENA
	OO-SDM	Boeing 737-229	SABENA
	OO-SDN	Boeing 737-229	SABENA
	OO-SDO	Boeing 737-229	SABENA
	OO-SDP	Boeing 737-229C	SABENA
	OO-SDR	Boeing 737-229C	SABENA
	OO-SDV	Boeing 737-329	SABENA
	OO-SDW	Boeing 737-329	SABENA
	OO-SDX	Boeing 737-329	SABENA
	OO-SDY	Boeing 737-329	SABENA
	OO-SGC	Boeing 747-329 (SCD)	SABENA
	OO-SGD	Boeing 747-329 (SCD)	SABENA
	OO-STF	Boeing 767-328ER	Sobelair *Spirit of Brussels*
	OO-SYA	Boeing 737-329	SABENA
	OO-SYB	Boeing 737-329	SABENA
	OO-SYC	Boeing 737-429	SABENA
	OO-SYD	Boeing 737-429	SABENA
	OO-SYE	Boeing 737-529	SABENA
	OO-SYF	Boeing 737-429	SABENA
	OO-SYG	Boeing 737-529	SABENA
	OO-SYH	Boeing 737-529	SABENA
	OO-SYI	Boeing 737-529	SABENA
	OO-SYJ	Boeing 737-529	SABENA
	OO-SYK	Boeing 737-529	SABENA
	OO-VEA	Boeing 737-36M	Virgin Express
	OO-VEB	Boeing 737-36M	Virgin Express
	OO-VEC	Boeing 737-46M	Virgin Express
	OO-VED	Boeing 737-46M	Virgin Express
	OO-VLE	Fokker 50	V.L.M.
	OO-VLJ	Fokker 50	V.L.M.
	OO-VLK	Fokker 50	V.L.M. *City of Munchengladbach*
	OO-VLM	Fokker 50	V.L.M. *Rotterdam*
	OO-VLN	Fokker 50	V.L.M. *Royal Antwerp F.C.*

Note: SABENA also operates Dash Eights, PH-SDG, PH-SDI, PH-SDJ, PH-SDM, PH-SDP, PH-SDR and PH-SDT on lease from Schreiner Airways.

OY (Denmark)

	OY-APA	Boeing 737-5L9	Maersk Air
	OY-APB	Boeing 737-5L9	Maersk Air
	OY-APC	Boeing 737-5L9	Maersk Air
	OY-APD	Boeing 737-5L9	Maersk Air
	OY-APG	Boeing 737-5L9	Maersk Air
	OY-APH	Boeing 737-5L9	Maersk Air
	OY-API	Boeing 737-5L9	Maersk Air
	OY-ASY	EMB-110P1 Bandeirante	Muk Air
	OY-AUO	Swearingen SA226TC Metro II	Jetair
	OY-BHT	EMB-110P2 Bandeirante	Muk Air
	OY-BJT	Swearingen SA226TC Metro II	Jetair
	OY-BNM	EMB-110P2 Bandeirante	Muk Air
	OY-BPB	Douglas DC-3C	Flyvende MuseumsFly S.A.S. *Arv Viking*
	OY-CHA	Swearingen SA226AT Merlin IV	Jetair
	OY-CIB	Aérospatiale ATR-42-300	Cimber Air
	OY-CIC	Aérospatiale ATR-42-300	Cimber Air
	OY-CID	Aérospatiale ATR-42-300	Cimber Air
	OY-CIE	Aérospatiale ATR-42-300	Cimber Air
	OY-CIF	Aérospatiale ATR-42-300	Cimber Air
	OY-CIG	Aérospatiale ATR-42-300	Cimber Air

Reg.	Type	Owner or Operator	Notes
OY-CIH	Aérospatiale ATR-42-300	Cimber Air	
OY-CIJ	Aérospatiale ATR-42-512	Cimber Air	
OY-CIK	Aérospatiale ATR-42-512	Cimber Air	
OY-CIL	Aérospatiale ATR-42-512	Cimber Air	
OY-CIS	Aérospatiale ATR-42-310	Cimber Air	
OY-CLB	BAe Jetstream 3102	Newair Airservice	
OY-CLC	BAe Jetstream 3102	Newair Airservice	
OY-CNA	Airbus A.300B4-120	Premiair	
OY-CNB	Airbus A.320-212	Premiair	
OY-CNC	Airbus A.320-212	Premiair	
OY-CNK	Airbus A.300B4-120	Premiair	
OY-CNL	Airbus A.300B4-120	Premiair	
OY-CNM	Airbus A.320-212	Premiair	
OY-CNP	Airbus A.320-212	Premiair	
OY-CNR	Airbus A.320-212	Premiair	
OY-CNT	Douglas DC-10-10	Premiair *Dumbo*	
OY-CNU	Douglas DC-10-10	Premiair *Bamse*	
OY-CNW	Airbus A.320-212	Premiair	
OY-CNY	Douglas DC-10-10	Premiair *Snoopy*	
OY-EBA	FH.227B Friendship	Newair Airservice	
OY-EBB	FH.227B Friendship	Newair Airservice	
OY-EDA	BAe Jetstream 3103	Sun-Air/British Airways	
OY-EDB	BAe Jetstream 3103	Sun-Air/British Airways	
OY-FCM	F.27 Friendship Mk 600	Eastern Trade	
OY-JEO	Swearingen SA226TC Metro II	Jetair	
OY-JER	Swearingen SA226TC Metro II	Jetair	
OY-KAE	Fokker 50	S.A.S. Commuter *Hans Viking*	
OY-KAF	Fokker 50	S.A.S. Commuter *SigvatV Viking*	
OY-KAG	Fokker 50	S.A.S. Commuter *Odensis Viking*	
OY-KAH	Fokker 50	S.A.S. Commuter *Bjorn Viking*	
OY-KAI	Fokker 50	S.A.S. Commuter *Skjold VIking*	
OY-KAK	Fokker 50	S.A.S. Commuter *Turid Viking*	
OY-KDH	Boeing 767-383ER	S.A.S. *Tyra Viking*	
OY-KDL	Boeing 767-383ER	S.A.S. *Tjodhild Viking*	
OY-KDM	Boeing 767-383ER	S.A.S. *Ingvar Viking*	
OY-KDN	Boeing 767-383ER	S.A.S. *Ulf Viking*	
OY-KDO	Boeing 767-383ER	S.A.S. *Svea Viking*	
OY-KGF	Douglas DC-9-21	S.A.S. *Rolf Viking*	
OY-KGL	Douglas DC-9-41	S.A.S. *Angantyr Viking*	
OY-KGM	Douglas DC-9-41	S.A.S. *Arnfinn Viking*	
OY-KGN	Douglas DC-9-41	S.A.S. *Gram Viking*	
OY-KGO	Douglas DC-9-41	S.A.S. *Holte Viking*	
OY-KGP	Douglas DC-9-41	S.A.S. *Torbern Viking*	
OY-KGR	Douglas DC-9-41	S.A.S. *Holger Viking*	
OY-KGS	Douglas DC-9-41	S.A.S. *Hall Viking*	
OY-KGT	McD Douglas MD-82	S.A.S. *Hake Viking*	
OY-KGY	McD Douglas MD-81	S.A.S. *Rollo Viking*	
OY-KGZ	McD Douglas MD-81	S.A.S. *Hagbard Viking*	
OY-KHC	McD Douglas MD-81	S.A.S. *Faste Viking*	
OY-KHF	McD Douglas MD-87	S.A.S. *Ragnar Viking*	
OY-KHG	McD Douglas MD-81	S.A.S. *Alle Viking*	
OY-KHI	McD Douglas MD-87	S.A.S. *Torkel Viking*	
OY-KHK	McD Douglas MD-81	S.A.S. *Roald Viking*	
OY-KHL	McD Douglas MD-81	S.A.S. *Knud Viking*	
OY-KHM	McD Douglas MD-81	S.A.S. *Mette Viking*	
OY-KHN	McD Douglas MD-81	S.A.S. *Dan Viking*	
OY-KHP	McD Douglas MD-81	S.A.S. *Arild Viking*	
OY-KHR	McD Douglas MD-81	S.A.S. *Torkild Viking*	
OY-KHT	McD Douglas MD-82	S.A.S. *Gorm Viking*	
OY-KHU	McD Douglas MD-87	S.A.S. *Ravn Viking*	
OY-KHW	McD Douglas MD-87	S.A.S. *Ingemund Viking*	
OY-KIA	Douglas DC-9-21	S.A.S. *Guttorm Viking*	
OY-KID	Douglas DC-9-21	S.A.S. *Rane Viking*	
OY-KIE	Douglas DC-9-21	S.A.S. *Skate Viking*	
OY-KIG	McD Douglas MD-81	S.A.S. *Igor Viking*	
OY-KIH	McD Douglas MD-81	S.A.S. *Oleg Viking*	
OY-KII	McD Douglas MD-81	S.A.S. *Ellisiv Viking*	
OY-KIK	McD Douglas MD-81	S.A.S. *Ole Viking*	
OY-KIL	McD Douglas MD-90-30	S.A.S. *Kaare Viking*	
OY-KIM	McD Douglas MD-90-30	S.A.S. *Jon Viking*	
OY-KIN	McD Douglas MD-90-30	S.A.S. *Tormod Viking*	
OY-MAF	Boeing 737-5L9	Maersk Air	
OY-MAS	Boeing 737-3L9	Maersk Air	

Notes	Reg.	Type	Owner or Operator
	OY-MAT	Boeing 737-3L9	Maersk Air
	OY-MAU	Boeing 737-3L9	Maersk Air
	OY-MMA	Short SD3-60 Variant 200	Muk Air
	OY-MMG	Fokker 50	Maersk Air
	OY-MMH	Fokker 50	Maersk Air
	OY-MMS	Fokker 50	Maersk Air
	OY-MMT	Fokker 50	Maersk Air
	OY-MMU	Fokker 50	Maersk Air
	OY-MMV	Fokker 50	Maersk Air
	OY-MUA	EMB-110P1 Bandeirante	Muk Air
	OY-MUB	Short SD3-30 Variant 200	Muk Air
	OY-MUD	Short SD3-60 Variant 200	Muk Air
	OY-MUE	BAe Jetstream 3100	Muk Air
	OY-MUF	F.27 Friendship	Newair Airservice
	OY-SAU	Boeing 727-2J4	Sterling European Airlines
	OY-SBI	Boeing 727-270	Sterling European Airlines
	OY-SBN	Boeing 727-2B7	Sterling European Airlines
	OY-SBO	Boeing 727-2K3	Sterling European Airlines
	OY-SCC	Boeing 727-212	Sterling European Airlines
	OY-SEZ	Boeing 727-2M7	Sterling European Airlines
	OY-SVF	BAe Jetstream 3102	Sun-Air/British Airways
	OY-SVJ	BAe Jetstream 3102	Sun-Air/British Airways
	OY-SVK	BAe Jetstream 3102	Sun-Air/British Airways
	OY-SVO	BAe Jetstream 3102	Sun-Air/British Airways
	OY-SVP	BAe Jetstream 3102	Sun-Air/British Airways
	OY-SVR	BAe Jetstream 3103	Sun-Air/British Airways
	OY-SVS	BAe Jetstream 4102	Sun-Air/British Airways
	OY-SVW	BAe Jetstream 4102	Sun-Air/British Airways
	OY-SVY	BAe Jetstream 3102	Sun-Air/British Airways
	OY-SVZ	BAe Jetstream 3102	Sun-Air/British Airways
	OY-UPA	Boeing 727-31C	Starair/UPS
	OY-UPB	Boeing 727-180C	Starair/UPS
	OY-UPD	Boeing 727-22C	Starair/UPS
	OY-UPJ	Boeing 727-22C	Starair/UPS
	OY-UPM	Boeing 727-31C	Starair/UPS
	OY-UPS	Boeing 727-31C	Starair/UPS
	OY-UPT	Boeing 727-22C	Starair/UPS

Note: Atlas Air operates Boeing 747-243F (SCD) N517MC on behalf of S.A.S.

PH (Netherlands)

	PH-AHE	Boeing 757-27B	Air Holland
	PH-AHI	Boeing 757-27B	Air Holland
	PH-AJU	Douglas DC-2	Dutch Dakota Association
	PH-BDA	Boeing 737-306	Koninklijke Luchtvaart Maatschappij (K.L.M.) Willem Barentsz
	PH-BDB	Boeing 737-306	K.L.M. Olivier van Noort
	PH-BDC	Boeing 737-306	K.L.M. Cornelis De Houteman
	PH-BDD	Boeing 737-306	K.L.M. Anthony van Diemen
	PH-BDE	Boeing 737-306	K.L.M. Abel J. Tasman
	PH-BDG	Boeing 737-306	K.L.M. Michiel A. de Ruyter
	PH-BDH	Boeing 737-306	K.L.M. Petrus Plancius
	PH-BDI	Boeing 737-306	K.L.M. Maarten H. Tromp
	PH-BDK	Boeing 737-306	K.L.M. Jan H. van Linschoten
	PH-BDL	Boeing 737-306	K.L.M. Piet Heyn
	PH-BDN	Boeing 737-306	K.L.M. Willem van Ruysbroeck
	PH-BDO	Boeing 737-306	K.L.M. Jacob van Heemskerck
	PH-BDP	Boeing 737-306	K.L.M. Jacob Roggeveen
	PH-BDR	Boeing 737-406	K.L.M. Willem C. Schouten
	PH-BDS	Boeing 737-406	K.L.M. Jorris van Spilbergen
	PH-BDT	Boeing 737-406	K.L.M. Gerrit de Veer
	PH-BDU	Boeing 737-406	K.L.M. Marco Polo
	PH-BDW	Boeing 737-406	K.L.M. Leifur Eiriksson
	PH-BDY	Boeing 737-406	K.L.M. Vasco da Gama
	PH-BDZ	Boeing 737-406	K.L.M. Christophorus Columbus
	PH-BFA	Boeing 747-406	K.L.M. City of Atlanta
	PH-BFB	Boeing 747-406	K.L.M. City of Bangkok
	PH-BFC	Boeing 747-406 (SCD)	K.L.M. Asia City of Calgary
	PH-BFD	Boeing 747-406 (SCD)	K.L.M. Asia City of Dubai
	PH-BFE	Boeing 747-406 (SCD)	K.L.M. City of Melbourne
	PH-BFF	Boeing 747-406 (SCD)	K.L.M. City of Freetown

Reg.	Type	Owner or Operator	Notes
PH-BFG	Boeing 747-406	K.L.M. *City of Guayaquil*	
PH-BFH	Boeing 747-406 (SCD)	K.L.M. *City of Hong Kong*	
PH-BFI	Boeing 747-406 (SCD)	K.L.M. *City of Jakarta*	
PH-BFK	Boeing 747-406 (SCD)	K.L.M. *City of Karachi*	
PH-BFL	Boeing 747-406	K.L.M. *City of Lima*	
PH-BFM	Boeing 747-406 (SCD)	K.L.M. Asia *City of Mexico*	
PH-BFN	Boeing 747-406	K.L.M. *City of Nairobi*	
PH-BFO	Boeing 747-406 (SCD)	K.L.M. *City of Orlando*	
PH-BFP	Boeing 747-406 (SCD)	K.L.M. *City of Paramaribo*	
PH-BFR	Boeing 747-406 (SCD)	K.L.M. *City of Rio de Janiero*	
PH-BFS	Boeing 747-406	K.L.M. *City of Seoul*	
PH-BTA	Boeing 737-406	K.L.M. *Fernao de Magalhaes*	
PH-BTB	Boeing 737-406	K.L.M. *Henry Hudson*	
PH-BTC	Boeing 737-406	K.L.M. *David Livingstone*	
PH-BTD	Boeing 737-306	K.L.M. *James Cook*	
PH-BTE	Boeing 737-306	K.L.M. *Roald Amundsen*	
PH-BTF	Boeing 737-406	K.L.M. *Alexander von Humboldt*	
PH-BTG	Boeing 737-406	K.L.M. *Sir Henry Morton Stanley*	
PH-BUH	Boeing 747-306 (SCD)	K.L.M. *Dr Albert Plesman*	
PH-BUI	Boeing 747-306 (SCD)	K.L.M. *Wilbur Wright*	
PH-BUK	Boeing 747-306 (SCD)	K.L.M. *Louis Blériot*	
PH-BUL	Boeing 747-306 (SCD)	K.L.M. *Charles A. Lindbergh*	
PH-BUM	Boeing 747-306 (SCD)	K.L.M. *Charles E. Kingsford-Smith*	
PH-BUN	Boeing 747-306 (SCD)	K.L.M. *Anthony H. G. Fokker*	
PH-BUO	Boeing 747-306	K.L.M. *Missouri*	
PH-BUP	Boeing 747-306	K.L.M. *The Ganges*	
PH-BUR	Boeing 747-306	K.L.M. *The Indus*	
PH-BUT	Boeing 747-306	K.L.M. *Admiral Richard E. Byrd*	
PH-BUU	Boeing 747-306 (SCD)	K.L.M. *Sir Frank Whittle*	
PH-BUV	Boeing 747-306 (SCD)	K.L.M. *Sir Geoffrey de Havilland*	
PH-BUW	Boeing 747-306 (SCD)	K.L.M. *Leonardo da Vinci*	
PH-BZA	Boeing 767-306ER	K.L.M. *Blue Bridge*	
PH-BZB	Boeing 767-306ER	K.L.M. *Pont Neuf*	
PH-BZC	Boeing 767-306ER	K.L.M. *Brooklyn Bridge*	
PH-BZD	Boeing 767-306ER	K.L.M. *King Hussain Bridge*	
PH-BZE	Boeing 767-306ER	K.L.M. *Ponte Rialto*	
PH-BZF	Boeing 767-306ER	K.L.M. *Golden Gate Bridge*	
PH-BZG	Boeing 767-306ER	K.L.M. *Erasmus Bridge*	
PH-BZH	Boeing 767-306ER	K.L.M. *Tower Bridge*	
PH-BZI	Boeing 767-306ER	K.L.M. *Bosporus Bridge*	
PH-BZK	Boeing 767-306ER	K.L.M. *Zeeland Bridge*	
PH-DDS	Douglas DC-4	Dutch Dakota Association	
PH-DDZ	Douglas DC-3	Dutch Dakota Association	
PH-DMB	Fokker 50	Denim Air	
PH-DMC	Fokker 50	Denim Air	
PH-DMI	Fokker 50	Denim Air	
PH-DMO	Fokker 50	Denim Air	
PH-DTL	Douglas DC-10-30	African Safari Airways	
PH-FNV	F.27 Friendship Mk 500	Tulip Air	
PH-FNW	F.27 Friendship Mk 500	Tulip Air	
PH-FVA	EMB-110P2 Bandeirante	Fairlines	
PH-FVB	EMB-110P1 Bandeirante	Fairlines	
PH-HVF	Boeing 737-3K2	Transavia *Johan Cruijff*	
PH-HVG	Boeing 737-3K2	Transavia *Wubbo Ockels*	
PH-HVI	Boeing 737-33A	Transavia	
PH-HVJ	Boeing 737-3K2	Transavia *Nelli Cooman*	
PH-HVK	Boeing 737-3K2	Transavia	
PH-HVM	Boeing 737-3K2	Transavia	
PH-HVN	Boeing 737-3K2	Transavia	
PH-HVT	Boeing 737-3K2	Transavia	
PH-HVV	Boeing 737-3K2	Transavia	
PH-KCA	McD Douglas MD-11	K.L.M. *Amy Johnson*	
PH-KCB	McD Douglas MD-11	K.L.M. *Maria Montessori*	
PH-KCC	McD Douglas MD-11	K.L.M. *Marie Curie*	
PH-KCD	McD Douglas MD-11	K.L.M. *Florence Nightingale*	
PH-KCE	McD Douglas MD-11	K.L.M. *Audrey Hepburn*	
PH-KCF	McD Douglas MD-11	K.L.M. *Annie Romein*	
PH-KCG	McD Douglas MD-11	K.L.M. *Maria Callas*	
PH-KCH	McD Douglas MD-11	K.L.M. *Anna Pavlova*	
PH-KCI	McD Douglas MD-11	K.L.M. *Ingrid Bergman*	
PH-KCK	McD Douglas MD-11	K.L.M. *Marie Servaes*	
PH-KFG	F.27 Friendship Mk 200	F.27 Friendship Flight Association	
PH-KJA	BAe Jetstream 3108	BASE Airlines	
PH-KJB	BAe Jetstream 3108	BASE Airlines	

Notes	Reg.	Type	Owner or Operator
	PH-KJG	BAe Jetstream 3108	BASE Airlines
	PH-KSA	SAAB SF.340B	K.L.M. CityHopper *Straatsburg*
	PH-KSB	SAAB SF.340B	K.L.M. CityHopper *Bristol*
	PH-KSC	SAAB SF.340B	K.L.M. CityHopper *Cardiff*
	PH-KSD	SAAB SF.340B	K.L.M. CityHopper *Neurenberg*
	PH-KSE	SAAB SF.340B	K.L.M. CityHopper *Southampton*
	PH-KSF	SAAB SF.340B	K.L.M. CityHopper *Basel*
	PH-KSG	SAAB SF.340B	K.L.M. CityHopper *Mulhouse*
	PH-KSI	SAAB SF.340B	K.L.M. CityHopper *Eindhoven*
	PH-KSK	SAAB SF.340B	K.L.M. CityHopper *Rotterdam*
	PH-KSL	SAAB SF.340B	K.L.M. CityHopper *Luxembourg*
	PH-KSM	SAAB SF.340B	K.L.M. CityHopper *Malmoe*
	PH-KVA	Fokker 50	K.L.M. CityHopper *Bremen*
	PH-KVB	Fokker 50	K.L.M. CityHopper *Brussels*
	PH-KVC	Fokker 50	K.L.M. CityHopper *Stavanger*
	PH-KVD	Fokker 50	K.L.M. CityHopper *Dusseldorf*
	PH-KVE	Fokker 50	K.L.M. CityHopper *Amsterdam*
	PH-KVF	Fokker 50	K.L.M. CityHopper *Paris/Paris*
	PH-KVG	Fokker 50	K.L.M. CityHopper *Stuttgart*
	PH-KVH	Fokker 50	K.L.M. CityHopper *Hannover*
	PH-KVI	Fokker 50	K.L.M. CityHopper *Bordeaux*
	PH-KVK	Fokker 50	K.L.M. CityHopper *London*
	PH-KZA	Fokker 70	K.L.M. CityHopper
	PH-KZB	Fokker 70	K.L.M. CityHopper
	PH-KZC	Fokker 70	K.L.M. CityHopper
	PH-KZD	Fokker 70	K.L.M. CityHopper
	PH-KZE	Fokker 70	K.L.M. CityHopper
	PH-KZF	Fokker 70	K.L.M. CityHopper
	PH-KZH	Fokker 70	K.L.M. CityHopper
	PH-KZI	Fokker 70	K.L.M. CityHopper
	PH-KZK	Fokker 70	K.L.M. CityHopper
	PH-MCE	Boeing 747-21AC (SCD)	Martinair *Prins van Oranje*
	PH-MCF	Boeing 747-21AC (SCD)	Martinair *Prins Claus*
	PH-MCG	Boeing 767-31AER	Martinair *Prins Johan Friso*
	PH-MCH	Boeing 767-31AER	Martinair *Prins Constantijn*
	PH-MCI	Boeing 767-31AER	Martinair *Prins Pieter-Christiaan*
	PH-MCL	Boeing 767-31AER	Martinair *Koningin Beatrix*
	PH-MCM	Boeing 767-31AER	Martinair *Prins Floris*
	PH-MCN	Boeing 747-228F	Martinair *Prins Bernhard*
	PH-MCP	McD Douglas MD-11CF	Martinair
	PH-MCR	McD Douglas MD-11CF	Martinair
	PH-MCS	McD Douglas MD-11CF	Martinair
	PH-MCT	McD Douglas MD-11CF	Martinair
	PH-MCU	McD Douglas MD-11F	Martinair
	PH-MCV	Boeing 767-31AER	Martinair
	PH-NVF	F.27 Friendship Mk100	F.27 Friendship Flight Association
	PH-OZA	Boeing 737-3L9	Air Holland
	PH-OZB	Boeing 737-3Y0	Air Holland
	PH-PBA	Douglas DC-3C	Dutch Dakota Association
	PH-RAZ	Swearingen SA226TC Metro II	Rijnmond Air Services
	PH-SDG	D.H.C.8-311 Dash Eight	Schreiner Airways/SABENA
	PH-SDI	D.H.C.8-311A Dash Eight	Schreiner Airways/SABENA
	PH-SDJ	D.H.C.8-311A Dash Eight	Schreiner Airways/SABENA
	PH-SDM	D.H.C.8-311 Dash Eight	Schreiner Airways/SABENA
	PH-SDP	D.H.C.8-311 Dash Eight	Schreiner Airways/SABENA
	PH-SDR	D.H.C.8-311 Dash Eight	Schreiner Airways/SABENA
	PH-SDT	D.H.C.8-311 Dash Eight	Schreiner Airways/SABENA
	PH-SEZ	McD Douglas MD-82	Meridiana
	PH-TKA	Boeing 757-2K2	Transavia
	PH-TKB	Boeing 757-2K2	Transavia
	PH-TKC	Boeing 757-2K2	Transavia
	PH-TKD	Boeing 757-2K2	Transavia
	PH-TSU	Boeing 737-3Y0	Transavia
	PH-TSW	Boeing 737-3L9	Transavia
	PH-TSX	Boeing 737-3K2	Transavia
	PH-TSY	Boeing 737-3K2	Transavia
	PH-TSZ	Boeing 737-3K2	Transavia
	PH-TTA	D.H.C. 8-102 Dash Eight	Transtravel Airlines
	PH-XLA	EMB-120RT Brasilia	Air Exel Commuter
	PH-XLB	EMB-120RT Brasilia	Air Exel Commuter

Note: Air Holland also operates the Boeing 757 G-MONC on lease from Monarch. KLM operates seven Boeing 737-400s which retain the UK registrations G-UKLA to G-UKLG inclusive.

Reg.	Type	Owner or Operator	Notes

PK (Indonesia)

PK-GIG	McD Douglas MD-11	Garuda Indonesian Airways
PK-GII	McD Douglas MD-11	Garuda Indonesian Airways
PK-GIJ	McD Douglas MD-11	Garuda Indonesian Airways
PK-GIK	McD Douglas MD-11	Garuda Indonesian Airways
PK-GIL	McD Douglas MD-11	Garuda Indonesian Airways
PK-GIM	McD Douglas MD-11	Garuda Indonesian Airways
PK-GSA	Boeing 747-2U3B	Garuda Indonesian Airways
PK-GSB	Boeing 747-2U3B	Garuda Indonesian Airways
PK-GSC	Boeing 747-2U3B	Garuda Indonesian Airways
PK-GSD	Boeing 747-2U3B	Garuda Indonesian Airways
PK-GSE	Boeing 747-2U3B	Garuda Indonesian Airways
PK-GSF	Boeing 747-2U3B	Garuda Indonesian Airways

Note: MD-11s EI-CDI, EI-CDJ and EI-CDK are also operated by Garuda.

PP (Brazil)

PP-VMA	Douglas DC-10-30	Viacao Aerea Rio Grandense (VARIG)
PP-VMB	Douglas DC-10-30	VARIG
PP-VMD	Douglas DC-10-30	VARIG
PP-VMQ	Douglas DC-10-30	VARIG
PP-VMT	Douglas DC-10-30F	VARIG Cargo
PP-VMU	Douglas DC-10-30F	VARIG Cargo
PP-VMV	Douglas DC-10-30	VARIG
PP-VMW	Douglas DC-10-30	VARIG
PP-VMX	Douglas DC-10-30	VARIG
PP-VMY	Douglas DC-10-30	VARIG
PP-VOA	Boeing 747-341	VARIG
PP-VOB	Boeing 747-341	VARIG
PP-VOC	Boeing 747-341	VARIG
PP-VOP	McD Douglas MD-11	VARIG
PP-VOQ	McD Douglas MD-11	VARIG
PP-VPJ	McD Douglas MD-11	VARIG
PP-VPK	McD Douglas MD-11	VARIG
PP-VPL	McD Douglas MD-11	VARIG
PP-VPM	McD Douglas MD-11	VARIG

Reg.	Type	Notes	Reg.	Type	Notes

RA (Russia)

Although many of the aircraft previously operated by Aeroflot have been transferred to one of the numerous new CIS carriers, in many cases the livery and visible titles remain unchanged at present. Those known to be used by Russia International/Aeroflot are shown with the code AFL in parenthesis after the type. Other identities used are AIS (AIS Airlines), DCA (Dacono Air), EFR (Elf Air), HLA (HeavyLift), IKT (Sakhaavia), LSV (Alak Airlines), MSC (Moscow Airways), ORT (Orient Avia), PAR (Spair), PVV (Continental Airways), SDM (Russia State Transport), SVR (Ural Airlines), TRJ (AJT Air), TSO (Transaero), TUP (Tupolev Aerotrans), TYM (Tyumen Airlines), UPA (Air Foyle), URA (Uralinteravia), VDA (Volga Dnepr) and VKO (Vnukovo Airlines).

Reg.	Type	Reg.	Type
11003	An-12 (PAR)	65557	Tu-134A-3 (SDM)
11049	An-12 (PAR)	65559	Tu-134A-3 (AFL)
11338	An-12 (AFL)	65566	Tu-134A (AFL)
11356	An-12 (PAR)	65567	Tu-134A-3 (AFL)
11415	An-12 (PAR)	65568	Tu-134A (AFL)
13321	An-12 (EFR)	65604	Tu-134A (EFR)
		65607	Tu-134A (URA)
42441	Yak-42 (DCA)	65623	Tu-134A (AFL)
		65667	Tu-134A-3 (TUP)
65017	Tu-134A-3 (TYM)	65697	Tu-134A-3 (AFL)
65097	Tu-134A (EFR)	65717	Tu-134A-3 (AFL)
65099	Tu-134A (EFR)	65720	Tu-134B-3 (TUP)
65552	Tu-134A-3 (SDM)	65769	Tu-134A-3 (AFL)
65553	Tu-134A-3 (SDM)	65770	Tu-134A-3 (AFL)
65554	Tu-134A-3 (SDM)	65781	Tu-134A-3 (AFL)
65555	Tu-134A-3 (SDM)	65783	Tu-134A-3 (AFL)

Notes	Reg.	Type	Notes	Reg.	Type
	65784	Tu-134A-3 (AFL)		85075	Tu-154B (AIS)
	65785	Tu-134A-3 (AFL)		85084	Tu-154S (VKO)
	65855	Tu-134A-3 (AIS)		85099	Tu-154B (VKO)
	65904	Tu-134A-3 (SDM)		85140	Tu-154B (VKO)
	65905	Tu-134A-3 (SDM)		85141	Tu-154B-1 (SVR)
	65908	Tu-134A (EFR)		85156	Tu-154B-1 (VKO)
	65911	Tu-134A-3 (SDM)		85182	Tu-154B-1 (VKO)
	65912	Tu-134A-3 (SDM)		85193	Tu-154B (SVR)
	65914	Tu-134A-3 (SDM)		85215	Tu-154B-1 (VKO)
	65915	Tu-134A-3 (SDM)		85219	Tu-143B-1 (SVR)
	65916	Tu-134A-3 (SDM)		85255	Tu-154B-1 (TYM)
	65917	Tu-134A (TUP)		85299	Tu-154B-2 (VKO)
	65919	Tu-134A-3 (SDM)		85301	Tu-154B-2 (VKO)
	65921	Tu-134A-3 (SDM)		85304	Tu-154B-2 (VKO)
	65939	Tu-134A-3 (TUP)		85310	Tu-154B-2 (SVR)
	65940	Tu-134A-3 (TUP)		85312	Tu-154B-2 (TYM)
	65941	Tu-134A (TUP)		85314	Tu-154B-2 (TYM)
	65960	Tu-134A (TYM)		85319	Tu-154B-2 (SVR)
	65966	Tu-134A-3 (TUP)		85328	Tu-154B-2 (PAR)
	65978	Tu-134A-3 (SDM)		85335	Tu-154B-2 (TYM)
	65994	Tu-134A-3 (SDM)		85337	Tu-154B-2 (SVR)
	65995	Tu-134A-3 (SDM)		85348	Tu-154B-2 (IKT)
				85354	Tu-154B-2 (IKT)
	76360	IL-76TD (AFL)		85357	Tu-154B-2 (SVR)
	76352	IL-76TD (URA)		85361	Tu-154B-2 (TYM)
	76386	IL-76TD (URA)		85363	Tu-154B-2 (AFL)
	76401	IL-76TD (HLA)		85364	Tu-154B-2 (AFL)
	76421	IL-76TD (DCA)		85366	Tu-154B-2 (TYM)
	76467	IL-76TD (AFL)		85374	Tu-154B-2 (SVR)
	76468	IL-76TD (AFL)		85375	Tu-154B-2 (SVR)
	76469	IL-76TD (AFL)		85376	Tu-154B-2 (IKT)
	76470	IL-76TD (AFL)		85378	Tu-154B-2 (TYM)
	76476	IL-76TD (AFL)		85427	Tu-154B-2 (TYM)
	76478	IL-76TD (AFL)		85432	Tu-154B-2 (SVR)
	76479	IL-76TD (PVV)		85434	Tu-154B-2 (TYM)
	76482	IL-76TD (AFL)		85439	Tu-154B-2 (SVR)
	76485	IL-76TD (IKT)		85450	Tu-154B-2 (TYM)
	76486	IL-76TD (IKT)		85451	Tu-154B-2 (TYM)
	76487	IL-76TD (IKT)		85459	Tu-154B-2 (SVR)
	76488	IL-76TD (AFL)		85481	Tu-154B-2 (TYM)
	76498	IL-76TD (MSC)		85498	Tu-154B-2 (TYM)
	76506	IL-76T (URA)		85502	Tu-154B-2 (TYM)
	76513	IL-76T (PAR)		85508	Tu-154B-2 (SVR)
	76519	IL-76T (AFL)		85520	Tu-154B-2 (IKT)
	76527	IL-76T (PAR)		85522	Tu-154B-2 (TYM)
	76750	IL-76TD (AFL)		85523	Tu-154B-2 (TUP)
	76751	IL-76TD (AFL)		85550	Tu-154B-2 (TYM)
	76756	IL-76T (EFR)		85564	Tu-154B-2 (AFL)
	76758	IL-76TD (VDA)		85568	Tu-154B-2 (IKT)
	76785	IL-76TD (AFL)		85570	Tu-154B-2 (AFL)
	76787	IL-76TD (VDA)		85572	Tu-154B-2 (AFL)
	76790	IL-76TD (PAR)		85577	Tu-154B-2 (IKT)
	76795	IL-76TD (AFL)		85592	Tu-154B-2 (AFL)
	76796	IL-76TD (LSV)		85597	Tu-154B-2 (IKT)
	76797	IL-76TD (IKT)		85606	Tu-154M (TUP)
	76798	IL-76TD (VDA)		85607	Tu-154M (TUP)
	76814	IL-76TD (LSV)		85610	Tu-154M (VKO)
	76823	IL-76TD (EFR)		85611	Tu-154M (VKO)
				85612	Tu-154M (VKO)
	82042	An-124 (VDA/HLA)		85615	Tu-154M (VKO)
	82043	An-124 (VDA/HLA)		85618	Tu-154M (VKO)
	82044	An-124 (VDA/HLA)		85619	Tu-154M (VKO)
	82045	An-124 (VDA/HLA)		85620	Tu-154M (VKO)
	82046	An-124 (VDA/HLA)		85621	Tu-154M (VKO)
	82047	An-124 (VDA/HLA)		85622	Tu-154M (VKO)
	82069	An-124 (AFL)		85623	Tu-154M (VKO)
	82070	An-124 (AFL)		85624	Tu-154M (VKO)
	82072	An-124 (AFL)		85625	Tu-154M (AFL)
				85626	Tu-154M (AFL)
	85019	Tu-154S (TSO)		85627	Tu-154M (TUP)
	85028	Tu-154B (VKO)		85628	Tu-154M (VKO)
	85033	Tu-154B (VKO)		85629	Tu-154M (SDM)
	85057	Tu-154 (VKO)		85630	Tu-154M (SDM)

Reg.	Type	Notes	Reg.	Type	Notes
85632	Tu-154M (VKO)		86058	IL-86 (AFL)	
85633	Tu-154M (VKO)		86059	IL-86 (AFL)	
85634	Tu-154M (AFL)		86066	IL-86 (AFL)	
85635	Tu-154M (VKO)		86067	IL-86 (AFL)	
85637	Tu-154M (AFL)		86073	IL-86 (AFL)	
85638	Tu-154M (AFL)		86074	IL-86 (AFL)	
85639	Tu-154M (AFL)		86075	IL-86 (AFL)	
85640	Tu-154M (AFL)		86076	IL-86 (AFL)	
85641	Tu-154M (AFL)		86078	IL-86 (SVR)	
85642	Tu-154M (AFL)		86079	IL-86 (AFL)	
85643	Tu-154M (AFL)		86080	IL-86 (AFL)	
85644	Tu-154M (AFL)		86081	IL-86 (VKO)	
85645	Tu-154M (SDM)		86082	IL-86 (VKO)	
85646	Tu-154M (AFL)		86084	IL-86 (VKO)	
85647	Tu-154M (AFL)		86085	IL-86 (VKO)	
85648	Tu-154M (AFL)		86087	IL-86 (AFL)	
85649	Tu-154M (AFL)		86088	IL-86 (AFL)	
85650	Tu-154M (AFL)		86089	IL-86 (VKO)	
85651	Tu-154M (SDM)		86091	IL-86 (VKO)	
85653	Tu-154M (SDM)		86093	IL-86 (SVR)	
85658	Tu-154M (SDM)		86095	IL-86 (AFL)	
85659	Tu-154M (SDM)		86096	IL-86 (AFL)	
85661	Tu-154M (AFL)		86097	IL-86 (VKO)	
85662	Tu-154M (AFL)		86103	IL-86 (AFL)	
85663	Tu-154M (AFL)		86104	IL-86 (VKO)	
85665	Tu-154M (AFL)		86110	IL-86 (AFL)	
85666	Tu-154M (SDM)		86111	IL-86 (VKO)	
85668	Tu-154M (AFL)		86113	IL-86 (AFL)	
85669	Tu-154M (AFL)		86114	IL-86 (SVR)	
85670	Tu-154M (AFL)		86123	IL-86 (TSO)	
85673	Tu-154M (VKO)		86124	IL-86 (AFL)	
85674	Tu-154M (VKO)		86126	IL-62MK (ORT)	
85675	Tu-154M (SDM)		86136	IL-86 (PVV)	
85674	Tu-154M (VKO)		86138	IL-86 (PVV)	
85681	Tu-154M (MSV)		86140	IL-86 (TRJ)	
85686	Tu-154M (SDM)				
85704	Tu-154M (TRJ)		86466	IL-62M (SDM)	
85710	Tu-154M (AFL)		86467	IL-62M (SDM)	
85712	Tu-154M (LSV)		86468	IL-62M (SDM)	
85713	Tu-154M (LSV)		86474	IL-62M (AFL)	
85714	Tu-154M (LSV)		86483	IL-62M (AFL)	
85736	Tu-154M (VKO)		86485	IL-62M (AFL)	
85743	Tu-154M (VKO)		86488	IL-62M (AFL)	
85745	Tu-154M (VKO)		86489	IL-62M (AFL)	
85754	Tu-154M (AFL)		86492	IL-62M (AFL)	
85779	Tu-154M (TRJ)		86497	IL-62M (AFL)	
85790	Tu-154M (IKT)		86502	IL-62M (AFL)	
85791	Tu-154M (IKT)		86506	IL-62M (AFL)	
85793	Tu-154M (IKT)		86507	IL-62M (AFL)	
85794	Tu154M (IKT)		86510	IL-62M (AFL)	
85807	Tu-154M (SVR)		86512	IL-62M (AFL)	
85810	Tu-154M (AFL)		86514	IL-62M (AFL)	
85811	Tu-154M (AFL)		86515	IL-62M (MSC)	
85812	Tu-154M (IKT)		86517	IL-62MK (AFL)	
85814	Tu-154M (SVR)		86518	IL-62M (AFL)	
			86520	IL-62M (AFL)	
86002	IL-86 (AFL)		86522	IL-62M (AFL)	
86004	IL-86 (TRJ)		86523	IL-62M (AFL)	
86005	IL-86 (VKO)		86524	IL-62M (AFL)	
86006	IL-86 (VKO)		86531	IL-62M (AFL)	
86007	IL-86 (VKO)		86532	IL-62M (AFL)	
86008	IL-86 (VKO)		86533	IL-62M (AFL)	
86009	IL-86 (VKO)		86534	IL-62M (AFL)	
86010	IL-86 (VKO)		86536	IL-62M (SDM)	
86011	IL-86 (VKO)		86537	IL-62M (SDM)	
86013	IL-86 (VKO)		86540	IL-62M (SDM)	
86014	IL-86 (VKO)		86553	IL-62M (SDM)	
86015	IL-86 (AFL)		86554	IL-62M (SDM)	
86018	IL-86 (VKO)		86558	IL-62M (SDM)	
86051	IL-86 (SVR)		86559	IL-62M (SDM)	
86054	IL-86 (AFL)		86561	IL-61M (SDM)	
86055	IL-86 (VKO)		86562	IL-62M (AFL)	

Notes	Reg.	Type	Notes	Reg.	Type
	86564	IL-62M (AFL)		86712	IL-62M (SDM)
	86565	IL-62M (AFL)		86720	IL-76T (URA)
	86566	IL-62M (AFL)		86747	IL-76T (URA)
	86567	IL-62M (ORT)		96005	IL-96-300 (AFL)
	86568	IL-62M (ORT)		96007	IL-96-300 (AFL)
	86590	IL-62M (ORT)		96008	IL-96-300 (AFL)
	86627	IL-76T (URA)		96010	IL-96-300 (AFL)
	86710	IL-62M (SDM)		96011	IL-96-300 (AFL)
	86711	IL-62M (SDM)		96012	IL-96-300 (SDM)

Note: Aeroflot also operates Airbus A.310s registered F-OGQQ, F-OGQR, F-OQGT, F-OGQU, F-OGYM, F-OGYN, F-OGYP, F-OGYT, F-OGYU and F-OGYV, Boeing 767s EI-CKD and EI-CKE plus the DC-10-30 N524MD. Transaero operates Boeing 757s EI-CJX, EI-CJY, EI-CLM, EI-CLU and EI-CLV, DC-10-30s N140AA, N141AA and N142AA plus 737s EI-CLN and EI-CLO. The airline also has three Boeing 737-236s which are flown with the Latvian registrations YL-BAA, YL-BAB and YL-BAC

Notes	Reg.	Type	Owner or Operator

RP (Philippines)

Note: Philippine Airlines operates four Boeing 747-2F6Bs which retain their U.S. identities N741PR, N742PR, N743PR and N744PR, two 747-283Bs registered EI-BTS and EI-BZA and two 747-211Bs registered N207AE and N208AE. Similarly three 747-4F6 carry N751PR, N752PR and N753PR, while a 747-469 (SCD) remains N754PR. The MD-11s N275WA, N276WA and N278WA are leased from World Airways.

S2 (Bangladesh)

S2-ACO	Douglas DC-10-30	Bangladesh Biman *The City of Hazrat-Shah Makhdoom (R.A.)*
S2-ACP	Douglas DC-10-30	Bangladesh Biman *The City of Dhaka*
S2-ACQ	Douglas DC-10-30	Bangladesh Biman *The City of Hazrat-Shah Jalal (R.A.)*
S2-ACR	Douglas DC-10-30	Bangladesh Biman *The New Era*
S2-ADE	Airbus A.310-325	Bangladesh Biman
S2-ADF	Airbus A.310-325	Bangladesh Biman *City of Cittagong*

S5 (Slovenia)

S5-AAA	Airbus A.320-231	Adria Airways
S5-AAB	Airbus A.320-231	Adria Airways
S5-AAC	Airbus A.320-231	Adria Airways
S5-ABF	Douglas DC-9-32	Adria Airways *Ljubljana*
S5-ABH	Douglas DC-9-32	Adria Airways

S7 (Seychelles)

S7-AAS	Boeing 767-2Q8ER	Air Seychelles *Isle of Aldabra*
S7-AHM	Boeing 767-37DER	Air Seychelles

SE (Sweden)

SE-CFP	Douglas DC-3	Flygande Veteraner *Fridtjof Viking*
SE-DAR	Douglas DC-9-41	S.A.S. *Agnar Viking*
SE-DAS	Douglas DC-9-41	S.A.S. *Garder Viking*
SE-DAU	Douglas DC-9-41	S.A.S. *Hadding Viking*
SE-DAW	Douglas DC-9-41	S.A.S. *Gotrik Viking*
SE-DAX	Douglas DC-9-41	S.A.S. *Helsing Viking*
SE-DBM	Douglas DC-9-41	S.A.S. *Ossur Viking*
SE-DDP	Douglas DC-9-41	S.A.S. *Brun Viking*

Reg.	Type	Owner or Operator	Notes
SE-DDR	Douglas DC-9-41	S.A.S. *Atle Viking*	
SE-DDS	Douglas DC-9-41	S.A.S. *Alrik Viking*	
SE-DDT	Douglas DC-9-41	S.A.S. *Amund Viking*	
SE-DFR	McD Douglas MD-81	S.A.S. *Ingjald Viking*	
SE-DFS	McD Douglas MD-82	S.A.S. *Gaut Viking*	
SE-DFT	McD Douglas MD-82	S.A.S. *Assur Viking*	
SE-DFY	McD Douglas MD-81	S.A.S. *Ottar Viking*	
SE-DGA	F.28 Fellowship 1000	S.A.S. *Alf Viking*	
SE-DGB	F.28 Fellowship 1000	S.A.S. *Brage Viking*	
SE-DGC	F.28 Fellowship 1000	S.A.S. *Dag Viking*	
SE-DGE	F.28 Fellowship 4000	S.A.S. *Erik Viking*	
SE-DGF	F.28 Fellowship 4000	S.A.S. *Egil Viking*	
SE-DGG	F.28 Fellowship 4000	S.A.S. *Gunnhild Viking*	
SE-DGH	F.28 Fellowship 4000	S.A.S. *Hjalmar Viking*	
SE-DGI	F.28 Fellowship 4000	S.A.S. *Ingeborg Viking*	
SE-DGK	F.28 Fellowship 4000	S.A.S. *Knut Viking*	
SE-DGL	F.28 Fellowship 4000	S.A.S. *Loke Viking*	
SE-DGM	F.28 Fellowship 4000	S.A.S. *Hild Viking*	
SE-DGN	F.28 Fellowship 4000	S.A.S. *Gunnar Viking*	
SE-DGO	F.28 Fellowship 4000	S.A.S. *Odd Viking*	
SE-DGP	F.28 Fellowship 4000	S.A.S. *Steinar Viking*	
SE-DGR	F.28 Fellowship 4000	S.A.S. *Randver Viking*	
SE-DGS	F.28 Fellowship 4000	S.A.S. *Sigrun Viking*	
SE-DGT	F.28 Fellowship 4000	S.A.S. *Tola Viking*	
SE-DGU	F.28 Fellowship 4000	S.A.S. *Ulfljot Viking*	
SE-DGX	F.28 Fellowship 4000	S.A.S. *Vemund Viking*	
SE-DHB	McD Douglas MD-83	Blue Scandinavia	
SE-DHG	McD Douglas MD-87	Blue Scandinavia	
SE-DHI	McD Douglas MD-87	Blue Scandinavia	
SE-DHS	Douglas DC-10-10	Premiair Baloo	
SE-DIA	McD Douglas MD-81	S.A.S. *Ulvrik Viking*	
SE-DIB	McD Douglas MD-87	S.A.S. *Varin Viking*	
SE-DIC	McD Douglas MD-87	S.A.S. *Grane Viking*	
SE-DIF	McD Douglas MD-87	S.A.S. *Hjorulv Viking*	
SE-DIH	McD Douglas MD-87	S.A.S. *Slagfinn Viking*	
SE-DII	McD Douglas MD-81	S.A.S. *Sigtrygg Viking*	
SE-DIK	McD Douglas MD-82	S.A.S. *Stenkil Viking*	
SE-DIL	McD Douglas MD-81	S.A.S. *Tord Viking*	
SE-DIN	McD Douglas MD-81	S.A.S. *Eskil Viking*	
SE-DIP	McD Douglas MD-87	S.A.S. *Jarl Viking*	
SE-DIR	McD Douglas MD-81	S.A.S. *Nora Viking*	
SE-DIS	McD Douglas MD-81	S.A.S. *Sigmund Viking*	
SE-DIU	McD Douglas MD-87	S.A.S. *Torsten Viking*	
SE-DIX	McD Douglas MD-81	S.A.S. *Adils Viking*	
SE-DIY	McD Douglas MD-81	S.A.S. *Albin Viking*	
SE-DIZ	McD Douglas MD-82	S.A.S. *Sigyn Viking*	
SE-DKY	Boeing 767-3Y0ER	S.A.S. *Indun Viking*	
SE-DKZ	Boeing 767-3Y0ER	S.A.S. *Bjarke Viking*	
SE-DLS	McD Douglas MD-83	Blue Scandinavia *Piraten*	
SE-DLU	McD Douglas MD-83	Blue Scandinavia *Norrsken*	
SE-DMA	McD Douglas MD-87	S.A.S. *Lage Viking*	
SE-DMB	McD Douglas MD-81	S.A.S. *Bjarne Viking*	
SE-DMD	McD Douglas MD-81	S.A.S. *Holmfrid Viking*	
SE-DME	McD Douglas MD-81	S.A.S. *Kristen Viking*	
SE-DMF	McD Douglas MD-90-30	S.A.S. *Heidrek Viking*	
SE-DMG	McD Douglas MD-90-30	S.A.S. *Hervor Viking*	
SE-DMH	McD Douglas MD-90-30	S.A.S. *Torolf Viking*	
SE-DMU	McD Douglas MD-81	S.A.S. *Siv Viking*	
SE-DMX	McD Douglas MD-81	S.A.S. *Sigvard Viking*	
SE-DMY	McD Douglas MD-81	S.A.S. *Sten Viking*	
SE-DMZ	McD Douglas MD-81	S.A.S. *Maria Viking*	
SE-DOC	Boeing 767-383ER	S.A.S. *Gudrun Viking*	
SE-DPA	Boeing 737-33AQC	Falcon Aviation *Aftonfalken*	
SE-DPB	Boeing 737-33AQC	Falcon Aviation *Pilgrimsfalken*	
SE-DPC	Boeing 737-33AQC	Falcon Aviation *Tornfalken*	
SE-DPI	McD Douglas MD-83	S.A.S. *Erik Viking*	
SE-DPX	L.1011-385 Tristar 50	Nordic European Airlines	
SE-DRA	BAe 146-200	Malmö Aviation	
SE-DRB	BAe 146-200	Malmö Aviation	
SE-DRC	BAe 146-200	Malmö Aviation	
SE-DRD	BAe 146-200	Malmö Aviation	
SE-DRE	BAe 146-200	Malmö Aviation	

Notes	Reg.	Type	Owner or Operator
	SE-DRF	BAe 146-200	Malmö Aviation
	SE-DRG	BAe 146-200	Malmö Aviation
	SE-DRI	BAe 146-200	Malmö Aviation
	SE-DRK	BAe 146-200	Malmo Aviation
	SE-DSK	Boeing 757-236	Sunways Airlines
	SE-DSL	Boeing 757-236	Sunways Airlines
	SE-DSM	Boeing 757-23A	Sunways Airlines *Lennart Johansson*
	SE-DSN	Boeing 757-236	Sunways Airlines
	SE-DTA	Boeing 737-3Q8	Nordic European Airlines
	SE-DTB	Boeing 737-4Y0	Nordic European Airlines
	SE-DTC	L.1011-385 TriStar 1	Blue Scandinavia
	SE-DUC	Fokker 100	Transwede *Cornelis*
	SE-DUD	Fokker 100	Transwede *Tyst*
	SE-DUE	Fokker 100	Transwede *Emil*
	SE-DUH	Fokker 100	Transwede
	SE-DUI	Fokker 100	Transwede
	SE-DUK	Boeing 757-236	Blue Scandinavia
	SE-DUL	Boeing 757-2Y0	Blue Scandinavia
	SE-DUN	Boeing 757-225	Blue Scandinavia
	SE-KZD	F.27 Friendship Mk 100	Air Nordic
	SE-KZE	F.27 Friendship Mk 100	Air Nordic
	SE-KZF	F.27 Friendship Mk 100	Air Nordic
	SE-KZG	F.27 Friendship Mk 100	Air Nordic
	SE-KZH	F.27 Friendship Mk 100	Air Nordic
	SE-LFA	Fokker 50	S.A.S. Commuter *Jorund Viking*
	SE-LFB	Fokker 50	S.A.S. Commuter *Sture Viking*
	SE-LFC	Fokker 50	S.A.S. Commuter *Ylva Viking*
	SE-LFK	Fokker 50	S.A.S. Commuter *Alvar Viking*
	SE-LFN	Fokker 50	S.A.S. Commuter *Edmund Viking*
	SE-LFO	Fokker 50	S.A.S. Commuter *Folke Viking*
	SE-LFP	Fokker 50	S.A.S. Commuter *Ingemar Viking*
	SE-LFR	Fokker 50	S.A.S. Commuter *Vagn Viking*
	SE-LFS	Fokker 50	S.A.S. Commuter *Vigge Viking*

SP (Poland)

	SP-LKA	Boeing 737-55D	LOT *Polskie Linie Lotnicze (LOT)*
	SP-LKB	Boeing 737-55D	LOT
	SP-LKC	Boeing 737-55D	LOT
	SP-LKD	Boeing 737-55D	LOT
	SP-LKE	Boeing 737-55D	LOT
	SP-LKF	Boeing 737-55D	LOT
	SP-LLA	Boeing 737-45D	LOT
	SP-LLB	Boeing 737-45D	LOT
	SP-LLC	Boeing 737-45D	LOT
	SP-LLD	Boeing 737-45D	LOT
	SP-LLE	Boeing 737-45D	LOT
	SP-	Boeing 737-45D	LOT
	SP-	Boeing 737-45D	LOT
	SP-LMB	Boeing 737-3Q8	LOT
	SP-LOA	Boeing 767-25DER	LOT *Gneizao*
	SP-LOB	Boeing 767-25DER	LOT *Kracow*
	SP-LPA	Boeing 767-35DER	LOT *Warszawa*
	SP-LPB	Boeing 767-35DER	LOT *Gdansk*

ST (Sudan)

	ST-AFA	Boeing 707-3J8C	Sudan Airways
	ST-AFB	Boeing 707-3J8C	Sudan Airways
	ST-AIX	Boeing 707-369C	Sudan Airways
	ST-AKW	Boeing 707-330C	Azza Transport
	ST-AMF	Boeing 707-321C	Transarabian Air Transport
	ST-ANP	Boeing 707-351C	Transarabian Air Transport
	ST-DRS	Boeing 707-368C	Azza Transport

Note: Sudan Airways also operates the A.310-304 F-GKTD and A.320-212 F-OKAI.

Reg.	Type	Owner or Operator	Notes

SU (Egypt)

SU-BCB	Airbus A.300B4-203	EgyptAir *Osiris*	
SU-BCC	Airbus A.300B4-203	EgyptAir *Nout*	
SU-BDF	Airbus A.300B4-203	EgyptAir *Sharm El Sheikh*	
SU-BDG	Airbus A.300B4-203	EgyptAir *Aton*	
SU-GAC	Airbus A.300B4-203	EgyptAir	
SU-GAH	Boeing 767-266ER	EgyptAir *Nefertiti*	
SU-GAI	Boeing 767-266ER	EgyptAir *Nefertari*	
SU-GAJ	Boeing 767-266ER	EgyptAir *Tiye*	
SU-GAL	Boeing 747-366 (SCD)	EgyptAir *Hatshepsut*	
SU-GAM	Boeing 747-366 (SCD)	EgyptAir *Cleopatra*	
SU-GAO	Boeing 767-366ER	EgyptAir *Ramses II*	
SU-GAP	Boeing 767-366ER	EgyptAir *Thutmosis III*	
SU-GAR	Airbus A.300-622R	EgyptAir *Zoser*	
SU-GAS	Airbus A.300-622R	EgyptAir *Cheops*	
SU-GAT	Airbus A.300-622R	EgyptAir *Chephren*	
SU-GAU	Airbus A.300-622R	EgyptAir *Mycerinus*	
SU-GAV	Airbus A.300-622R	EgyptAir *Menes*	
SU-GAW	Airbus A.300-622R	EgyptAir *Ahmuse*	
SU-GAX	Airbus A.300-622R	EgyptAir *Tut-Ankh-Amun*	
SU-GAY	Airbus A.300-622R	EgyptAir *Seti I*	
SU-GAZ	Airbus A.300-622R	EgyptAir	
SU-GBA	Airbus A.320-231	EgyptAir *Aswan*	
SU-GBB	Airbus A.320-231	EgyptAir *Luxor*	
SU-GBC	Airbus A.320 231	EgyptAir *Hurghada*	
SU-GBD	Airbus A.320-231	EgyptAir *Taba*	
SU-GBE	Airbus A.320-231	EgyptAir *El Alamein*	
SU-GBF	Airbus A.320-231	EgyptAir *Sharm El Sheikh*	
SU-GBG	Airbus A.320-231	EgyptAir *Saint Catherine*	
SU-GBM	Airbus A.340-212	EygptAir *Osirus Express*	
SU-GBN	Airbus A.340-212	EygptAir	
SU-GBO	Airbus A.340-212	EygptAir	
SU-GBP	Boeing 777-266	EgyptAir	
SU-GBR	Boeing 777-266	EgyptAir	
SU-GBS	Boeing 777-266	EgyptAir	
SU-GBT	Airbus A.321-211	EgyptAir	
SU-PBA	Boeing 707-336C	Memphis Air	
SU-RAA	Airbus A.320-231	Shorouk Air	
SU-RAB	Airbus A.320-231	Shorouk Air	
SU-ZCA	McD Douglas MD-83	Heliopolis Airlines	
SU-	McD Douglas MD-90-30	Heliopolis Airlines	

Note: EgyptAir operates the A.340-312 A4O-LE on lease from Gulf Air.

SX (Greece)

SX-BAY	Airbus A.300B4-203	Apollo Airlines	
SX-BAZ	Airbus A.300B4-203	Apollo Airlines *City of Thessaloniki*	
SX-BBU	Boeing 737-33A	Cronus Airlines	
SX-BBZ	Boeing 757-236	Venus Airlines	
SX-BCA	Boeing 737-284	Olympic Airways *Apollo*	
SX-BCB	Boeing 737-284	Olympic Airways *Hermes*	
SX-BCC	Boeing 737-284	Olympic Airways *Hercules*	
SX-BCD	Boeing 737-284	Olympic Airways *Hephaestus*	
SX-BCE	Boeing 737-284	Olympic Airways *Dionysus*	
SX-BCF	Boeing 737-284	Olympic Airways *Poseidon*	
SX-BCG	Boeing 737-284	Olympic Airways *Phoebus*	
SX-BCH	Boeing 737-284	Olympic Airways *Triton*	
SX-BCI	Boeing 737-284	Olympic Airways *Proteus*	
SX-BCK	Boeing 737-284	Olympic Airways *Nereus*	
SX-BCL	Boeing 737-284	Olympic Airways *Isle of Thassos*	
SX-BED	Airbus A.300B4-103	Olympic Airways *Telemachus*	
SX-BEE	Airbus A.300B4-103	Olympic Airways *Nestor*	
SX-BEF	Airbus A.300B4-103	Olympic Airways *Ajax*	
SX-BEG	Airbus A.300B4-103	Olympic Airways *Diomedes*	
SX-BEH	Airbus A.300B4-103	Olympic Airways *Pileus*	
SX-BEI	Airbus A.300B4-103	Olympic Airways *Neoptolemos*	
SX-BEK	Airbus A.300-605R	Olympic Airways *Macedonia*	
SX-BEL	Airbus A.300-605R	Olympic Airways *Athena*	
SX-BFI	Airbus A.300B4-203	Apollo Airlines	

Notes	Reg.	Type	Owner or Operator
	SX-BKA	Boeing 737-484	Olympic Airways *Vergina*
	SX-BKB	Boeing 737-484	Olympic Airways *Olynthos*
	SX-BKC	Boeing 737-484	Olympic Airways *Philipoli*
	SX-BKD	Boeing 737-484	Olympic Airways *Amphipoli*
	SX-BKE	Boeing 737-484	Olympic Airways *Stagira*
	SX-BKF	Boeing 737-484	Olympic Airways *Dion*
	SX-BKG	Boeing 737-484	Olympic Airways
	SX-CBA	Boeing 727-284	Olympic Airways *Mount Olympus*
	SX-CBB	Boeing 727-284	Olympic Airways *Mount Pindos*
	SX-CBC	Boeing 727-284	Olympic Airways *Mount Parnassus*
	SX-CBD	Boeing 727-284	Olympic Airways *Mount Helicon*
	SX-CBE	Boeing 727-284	Olympic Airways *Mount Athos*
	SX-CBF	Boeing 727-284	Olympic Airways *Mount Taygetus*
	SX-CBG	Boeing 727-230	Olympic Airways *Mount Menalon*
	SX-CBH	Boeing 727-230	Olympic Airways *Mount Vermio*
	SX-CBI	Boeing 727-230	Greek Government (VIP) *Alexander The Great*
	SX-OAB	Boeing 747-284B	Olympic Airways *Olympic Eagle*
	SX-OAC	Boeing 747-212B	Olympic Airways *Olympic Spirit*
	SX-OAD	Boeing 747-212B	Olympic Airways *Olympic Flame*
	SX-OAE	Boeing 747-212B	Olympic Airways *Olympic Peace*

TC (Turkey)

Reg.	Type	Owner or Operator
TC-ACA	Boeing 737-4Y0	Istanbul Airlines
TC-AFA	Boeing 737-4Q8	Pegasus Airlines
TC-AFB	Boeing 727-228	Istanbul Airlines
TC-AFC	Boeing 727-228	Istanbul Airlines
TC-AFK	Boeing 737-4Y0	Pegasus Airlines
TC-AFM	Boeing 737-4Q8	Pegasus Airlines
TC-AFN	Boeing 727-230	Istanbul Airlines
TC-AFO	Boeing 727-230	Istanbul Airlines
TC-AFP	Boeing 727-230	Istanbul Airlines
TC-AFR	Boeing 727-230	Istanbul Airlines
TC-AFT	Boeing 727-230	Istanbul Airlines
TC-AFV	Boeing 727-230F	Istanbul Cargo
TC-AFZ	Boeing 737-4Y0	Pegasus Airlines
TC-AGA	Boeing 737-4Y0	Istanbul Airlines
TC-AHA	Boeing 757-236	Istanbul Airlines
TC-AJA	Boeing 757-236	Istanbul Airlines
TC-ALG	Airbus A.300B4-203	Air Alfa
TC-ALM	Boeing 727-230	Air Alfa
TC-ALN	Airbus A.300B4-103	Air Alfa *Umay-Ural*
TC-ALR	Airbus A.300B4-203	Air Alfa *Mert*
TC-ALS	Airbus A.300B4K-103	Air Alfa
TC-APA	Boeing 737-4S3	Istanbul Airlines
TC-AVA	Boeing 737-4S3	Istanbul Airlines
TC-AYA	Boeing 737-4Y0	Istanbul Airlines
TC-AZA	Boeing 737-4Y0	Istanbul Airlines
TC-DEL	Boeing 727-225F	Tayfunair
TC-GTA	Airbus A.300B4-203	GTI Airlines
TC-INA	McD Douglas MD-83	Sunway *Mesut Sen*
TC-INB	McD Douglas MD-83	Sunway
TC-INC	McD Douglas MD-83	Sunway *Fatin Terin*
TC-IND	McD Douglas MD-83	Sunway
TC-IYA	Boeing 727-2F2	Top Air *Hezarfen*
TC-IYB	Boeing 727-243	Top Air
TC-IYC	Boeing 727-2F2	Top Air
TC-JBF	Boeing 727-2F2	Turkish Airlines *Adana*
TC-JBG	Boeing 727-2F2	Kibris Turkish Airlines *Yavruvatan*
TC-JBJ	Boeing 727-2F2	Kibris Turkish Airlines *Besparmak*
TC-JCA	Boeing 727-2F2F	Turkish Airlines Cargo *Edirne*
TC-JCB	Boeing 727-2F2F	Turkish Airlines Cargo *Kars*
TC-JCD	Boeing 727-2F2F	Turkish Airlines Cargo *Sinop*
TC-JCL	Airbus A.310-203	Turkish Airlines *Seyhan*
TC-JCM	Airbus A.310-203	Turkish Airlines *Ceyhan*
TC-JCN	Airbus A.310-203	Turkish Airlines *Dicle*
TC-JCO	Airbus A.310-203	Turkish Airlines *Firat*
TC-JCR	Airbus A.310-203	Turkish Airlines *Kizilirmak*
TC-JCS	Airbus A.310-203	Turkish Airlines *Yesilirmak*
TC-JCU	Airbus A.310-203	Turkish Airlines *Sakarya*
TC-JCV	Airbus A.310-304	Turkish Airlines *Aras*

Reg.	Type	Owner or Operator	Notes
TC-JCY	Airbus A.310-304	Turkish Airlines *Coruh*	
TC-JCZ	Airbus A.310-304	Turkish Airlines *Ergene*	
TC-JDA	Airbus A.310-304	Turkish Airlines *Aksu*	
TC-JDB	Airbus A.310-304ET	Turkish Airlines *Göksu*	
TC-JDC	Airbus A.310-304ET	Turkish Airlines *Meric*	
TC-JDD	Airbus A.310-304ET	Turkish Airlines *Dalaman*	
TC-JDE	Boeing 737-4Y0	Turkish Airlines *Kemer*	
TC-JDF	Boeing 737-4Y0	Turkish Airlines *Ayvalik*	
TC-JDG	Boeing 737-4Y0	Turkish Airlines *Marmaris*	
TC-JDH	Boeing 737-4Y0	Turkish Airlines *Amasra*	
TC-JDI	Boeing 737-4Q8	Turkish Airlines *Urgup*	
TC-JDJ	Airbus A.340-311	Turkish Airlines *Istanbul*	
TC-JDK	Airbus A.340-311	Turkish Airlines *Isparta*	
TC-JDL	Airbus A.340-311	Turkish Airlines *Ankara*	
TC-JDM	Airbus A.340-311	Turkish Airlines	
TC-JDN	Airbus A.340-311	Turkish Airlines	
TC-JDT	Boeing 737-4Y0	Turkish Airlines *Istanbul*	
TC-JDU	Boeing 737-5Y0	Turkish Airlines *Trabzon*	
TC-JDV	Boeing 737-5Y0	Turkish Airlines *Bursa*	
TC-JDY	Boeing 737-4Y0	Turkish Airlines *Antalya*	
TC-JDZ	Boeing 737-4Y0	Turkish Airlines *Izmir*	
TC-JEA	Boeing 737-42J	Turkish Airlines *Kusadasi*	
TC-JEC	Boeing 727-228	Kibris Turkish Airlines *Yesilada*	
TC-JED	Boeing 737-4Q8	Turkish Airlines *Bodrum*	
TC-JEE	Boeing 737-4Q8	Turkish Airlines *Cesme*	
TC-JEF	Boeing 737-4Q8	Turkish Airlines *Goereme*	
TC-JEG	Boeing 737-4Q8	Turkish Airlines	
TC-JEH	Boeing 737-4Q8	Turkish Airlines	
TC-JEI	Boeing 737-4Q8	Turkish Airlines *Artvin*	
TC-JEJ	Boeing 737-4Q8	Turkish Airlines	
TC-JEK	Boeing 737-4Q8	Turkish Airlines	
TC-JEL	Boeing 737-4Q8	Turkish Airlines *Eskisehir*	
TC-JEM	Boeing 737-4Q8	Turkish Airlines *Malatya*	
TC-JEN	Boeing 737-4Q8	Turkish Airlines *Gelibolu*	
TC-JEO	Boeing 737-4Q8	Turkish Airlines *Anadolu*	
TC-JEP	Boeing 737-4Q8	Turkish Airlines *Trakya*	
TC-JER	Boeing 737-4Y0	Turkish Airlines *Mugla*	
TC-JET	Boeing 737-4Y0	Turkish Airlines *Canakkale*	
TC-JEU	Boeing 737-4Y0	Turkish Airlines *Kayseri*	
TC-JEV	Boeing 737-4Y0	Turkish Airlines *Efes*	
TC-JEY	Boeing 737-4Y0	Turkish Airlines *Side*	
TC-JEZ	Boeing 737-4Y0	Turkish Airlines *Bergama*	
TC-JYK	Airbus A.310-203	Kibris Turkish Airlines *Erenkoy*	
TC-ONC	Airbus A.320-211	Onur Air *Bosphorus*	
TC-OND	Airbus A.320-211	Onur Air *Yeditepe*	
TC-ONE	Airbus A.320-212	Onur Air *Marmara*	
TC-ONF	Airbus A.320-231	Onur Air *Nurce*	
TC-ONG	Airbus A.320-231	Onur Air *Gulnur*	
TC-ONH	Airbus A.321-131	Onur Air	
TC-ONI	Airbus A.321-131	Onur Air *Icli*	
TC-ONJ	Airbus A.321-131	Onur Air *Kaptan Soray Kahin*	
TC-ONK	Airbus A.300B4-103	Onur Air	
TC-ONL	Airbus A.300B4-103	Onur Air	
TC-	Airbus A.321-131	Onur Air	
TC-RAC	Boeing 727-230	Holiday Air *Igdis*	
TC-RAF	Boeing 737-217	Holiday Air *Berk*	
TC-SUN	Boeing 737-3Y0	Sun Express	
TC-SUP	Boeing 737-3Y0	Sun Express	
TC-SUR	Boeing 737-3Y0	Sun Express	
TC-SUS	Boeing 737-430	Sun Express	
TC-SUT	Boeing 737-4Y0	Sun Express	
TC-TMT	Airbus A.310-304	Kibris Turkish Airlines	

TF (Iceland)

TF-ABD	L.1011-385 TriStar 1	Air Atlanta Iceland	
TF-ABE	L.1011-385 TriStar 1	Air Atlanta Iceland	
TF-ABF	Boeing 737-230C	Air Atlanta Iceland	
TF-ABG	Boeing 737-266	Air Atlanta Iceland	
TF-ABH	L.1011-385 TriStar 1	Air Atlanta Iceland	
TF-ABI	Boeing 747-246B	Air Atlanta Iceland	
TF-ABK	Boeing 737-3Y0	Air Atlanta Iceland	

Notes	Reg.	Type	Owner or Operator
	TF-ABP	L.1011-385 TriStar 1 ★	British Aviation Heritage/Bruntingthorpe
	TF-ABU	L.1011-385 TriStar 1	Air Atlanta Iceland
	TF-ABW	Boeing 747-128	Air Atlanta Iceland
	TF-ABX	Boeing 737-230C	Air Atlanta Iceland
	TF-FIA	Boeing 737-408	Icelandair *Aldis*
	TF-FIB	Boeing 737-408	Icelandair *Eydis*
	TF-FIC	Boeing 737-408	Icelandair *Vedis*
	TF-FID	Boeing 737-408	Icelandair *Heiddis*
	TF-FIH	Boeing 757-208	Icelandair *Hafdis*
	TF-FII	Boeing 757-208	Icelandair *Fanndis*
	TF-FIJ	Boeing 757-208	Icelandair *Svandis*
	TF-FIK	Boeing 757-28A	Icelandair *Soldis*
	TF-FIR	Fokker 50	Icelandair *Asdis*
	TF-FIS	Fokker 50	Icelandair *Sigdis*
	TF-FIT	Fokker 50	Icelandair *Freydis*
	TF-FIU	Fokker 50	Icelandair *Valdis*

TJ (Cameroon)

	TJ-CAB	Boeing 747-2H7B (SCD)	Cameroon Airlines *Mont Cameroun*

TR (Gabon)

Note: Air Gabon operates Boeing 747-2Q2B F-ODJG President Leon Mba

TS (Tunisia)

	TS-IMA	Airbus A.300B4-203	Tunis-Air *Amilcar*
	TS-IMB	Airbus A.320-211	Tunis-Air *Farhat Hached*
	TS-IMC	Airbus A.320-211	Tunis-Air *7 Novembre*
	TS-IMD	Airbus A.320-211	Tunis-Air *Khereddine*
	TS-IME	Airbus A.320-211	Tunis-Air *Tabarka*
	TS-IMF	Airbus A.320-211	Tunis-Air *Jerba*
	TS-IMG	Airbus A.320-211	Tunis-Air *Abóu el Kacem Chebbi*
	TS-IMH	Airbus A.320-211	Tunis-Air *Ali Belhaouane*
	TS-IMI	Airbus A.320-211	Tunis-Air
	TS-IOC	Boeing 737-2H3	Tunis-Air *Salammbo*
	TS-IOD	Boeing 737-2H3C	Tunis-Air *Bulla Regia*
	TS-IOE	Boeing 737-2H3	Tunis-Air *Zarzis*
	TS-IOF	Boeing 737-2H3	Tunis-Air *Sousse*
	TS-IOG	Boeing 737-5H3	Tunis-Air *Sfax*
	TS-IOH	Boeing 737-5H3	Tunis-Air *Hammamet*
	TS-IOI	Boeing 737-5H3	Tunis-Air *Mahida*
	TS-IOJ	Boeing 737-5H3	Tunis-Air *Monastir*
	TS-JHN	Boeing 727-2H3	Tunis-Air *Carthago*
	TS-JHQ	Boeing 727-2H3	Tunis-Air *Tozeur-Nefta*
	TS-JHR	Boeing 727-2H3	Tunis-Air *Bizerte*
	TS-JHS	Boeing 727-2H3	Tunis-Air *Kairouan*
	TS-JHT	Boeing 727-2H3	Tunis-Air *Sidi Bousaid*
	TS-JHU	Boeing 727-2H3	Tunis-Air *Hannibal*
	TS-JHW	Boeing 727-2H3	Tunis-Air *Ibn Khaldoun*

TU (Ivory Coast)

	TU-TAC	Airbus A.310-304	Air Afrique
	TU-TAD	Airbus A.310-304	Air Afrique
	TU-TAE	Airbus A.310-304	Air Afrique
	TU-TAF	Airbus A.310-304	Air Afrique
	TU-TAG	Airbus A.310-304	Air Afrique
	TU-TAH	Airbus A.300-605R	Air Afrique
	TU-TAI	Airbus A.300-605R	Air Afrique
	TU-TAO	Airbus A.300B4-203	Air Afrique *Nouackchott*
	TU-TAS	Airbus A.300B4-203	Air Afrique *Bangui*
	TU-TAT	Airbus A.300B4-203	Air Afrique
	TU-TAU	Airbus A.310-308	Air Afrique

Reg.	Type	Notes	Reg.	Type	Notes

UK (Uzbekistan)

The following are operated by Uzbekistan Airways with registrations prefixed by UK.

Reg.	Type	Reg.	Type
75700	Boeing 757-23P	85449	Tu-154B-2
76351	IL-76TD	85575	Tu-154B-2
76353	IL-76TD	85578	Tu-154B-2
76358	IL-76TD	85600	Tu-154B-2
76359	IL-76TD	85711	Tu-154M
76419	IL-76TD	85764	Tu-154M
76448	IL-76TD	85776	Tu-154M
76449	IL-76TD	86012	IL-86
76782	IL-76TD	86016	IL-86
76793	IL-76TD	86017	IL-86
76794	IL-76TD	86052	IL-86
76805	IL-76TD	86053	IL-86
76811	IL-76TD	86056	IL-86
76813	IL-76TD	86057	IL-86
76824	IL-76TD	86063	IL-86
85189	Tu-154B	86064	IL-86
85245	Tu-154B-1	86065	IL-86
85248	Tu-154B-1	86072	IL-86
85249	Tu-154B-1	86083	IL-86
85272	Tu-154B-1	86090	IL-86
85286	Tu-154B-1	86148	IL-86
85322	Tu-154B-2	86569	IL-62M
85344	Tu-154B-2	86573	IL-62M
85356	Tu-154B-2	86574	IL-62M
85370	Tu-154B-2	86575	IL-62M
85397	Tu-154B-2	86576	IL-62M
85398	Tu-154B-2	86577	IL-62M
85401	Tu-154B-2	86578	IL-62M
85416	Tu-154B-2	86579	IL-62M
85423	Tu-154B-2	86659	IL-62
85433	Tu-154B-2	86694	IL-62
85438	Tu-154B-2		

Note: Uzbekistan Airways also operates two Airbus A.310-324s registered F-OGQY and F-OGQZ plus Boeing 767-33PERs VR-BUA and VR-BUB.

UN (Kazakhstan)

The following are operated by Air Kazakhstan with registrations prefixed by UN.

Reg.	Type	Reg.	Type
001	Boeing 747SP-31	85231	Tu-154B-1
002	Boeing 757-2M8	85240	Tu-154B-1
65115	Tu-134A-3	85271	Tu-154B-1
65121	Tu-134A-3	85276	Tu-154B-1
65130	Tu-134A-3	85290	Tu-154B-1
65138	Tu-134A	85387	Tu-154B-2
65147	Tu-134A-3	85396	Tu-154B-2
65551	Tu-134A-3	85431	Tu-154B-2
65683	Tu-134A	85455	Tu-154B-2
65767	Tu-134A-3	85464	Tu-154B-2
65776	Tu-134A	85478	Tu-154B-2
65787	Tu-134A	85521	Tu-154B-2
65900	Tu-134A-3	85537	Tu-154B-2
76371	IL-76TD	85589	Tu-154B-2
76374	IL-76TD	85719	Tu-154M
76810	IL-76TD	85775	Tu-154M
85066	Tu-154B	85780	Tu-154M
85076	Tu-154B-1	85781	Tu-154M
85111	Tu-154B	86068	IL-86
85113	Tu-154B	86069	IL-86
85151	Tu-154B-1	86071	IL-86
85173	Tu-154B	86077	IL-86
85194	Tu-154B	86086	IL-86
85221	Tu-154B	86101	IL-86
85230	Tu-154B-1	86116	IL-86

Notes	Reg.	Type		Owner or Operator

UR (Ukraine)

Reg.	Type	Owner or Operator
UR-BFA	Boeing 737-2L9	Aerosweet Airlines
UR-	Boeing 737-4Y0	Ukraine International
UR-GAC	Boeing 737-247	Ukraine International
UR-GAD	Boeing 737-2T4	Ukraine International

The following are prefixed with UR. Airline codes AKO – Trasago, BSL – BSL Airlines, KHO – Khors Air, UKC – Air Ukraine Cargo, UKR – Air Ukraine, UPA – Air Foyle, VPB – Veteran Airlines.

Notes	Reg.	Type	Notes	Reg.	Type
	65037	Tu-134A-3 (UKR)		76717	IL-76MD (VPB)
	65048	Tu-134A-3 (UKR)		76721	IL-76MD (BSL)
	65073	Tu-134A (UKR)		76728	IL-76MD (VPB)
	65076	Tu-134A-3 (UKR)		76729	IL-76MD (VPB)
	65077	Tu-134A (AKO)		76730	IL-76MD (BSL)
	65081	Tu-134A-3 (AKO)		76742	IL-76MD (BSL)
	65089	Tu-134A (UKR)		76744	IL-76MD (BSL)
	65093	Tu-134A-3 (UKR)		76748	IL-76MD (UKC)
	65107	Tu-134A (UKR)		76759	IL-76MD (BSL)
	65109	Tu-134A (UKR)		76760	IL-76MD (BSL)
	65114	Tu-134A-3 (UKR)		76775	IL-76MD (KHO)
	65134	Tu-134A-3 (UKR)		76778	IL-76MD (UKC)
	65135	Tu-134A-3 (UKR)		76755	IL-76MD (KHO/UPA)
	65556	Tu-134A-3 (UKR)		78758	IL-76MD (UKC)
	65718	Tu-134A-3 (UKR)		78772	IL-76MD (UKC)
	65746	Tu-134A (UKR)		85068	Tu-154B (UKR)
	65752	Tu-134A-3 (UKR)		85116	Tu-154B-1 (UKR)
	65757	Tu-134A-3 (UKR)		85118	Tu-154B (UKR)
	65761	Tu-134A (UKR)		85132	Tu-154B (UKR))
	65764	Tu-134A-3 (UKR)		85269	Tu-154B-1 (UKR)
	65765	Tu-134A (UKR)		85316	Tu-154B-2 (UKR)
	65773	Tu-134A-3 (UKR)		85350	Tu-154B-2 (UKR)
	65782	Tu-134A (UKR)		85362	Tu-154B-2 (UKR)
	65790	Tu-134A-3 (UKR)		85368	Tu-154B-2 (UKR)
	65826	Tu-134A-3 (UKR)		85379	Tu-154B-2 (UKR)
	65841	Tu-134A (UKR)		85395	Tu-154B-2 (UKR)
	65852	Tu-134A (UKR)		85399	Tu-154B-2 (UKR)
	65864	Tu-134A (UKR)		85407	Tu-154B-2 (UKR)
	65877	Tu-134A-3 (UKR)		85424	Tu-154B-2 (UKR)
	65888	Tu-134A-3 (UKR)		85445	Tu-154B-2 (UKR)
	76395	IL-76MD (KHO)		85460	Tu-154B-2 (UKR)
	76396	IL-76MD (KHO)		85476	Tu-154B-2 (UKR)
	76397	IL-76MD (KHO)		85482	Tu-154B-2 (UKR)
	76398	IL-76MD (KHO)		85490	Tu-154B-2 (UKR)
	76399	IL-76MD (KHO)		85499	Tu-154B-2 (UKR)
	76555	IL-76MD (UKC)		85513	Tu-154B-2 (UKR)
	76563	IL-76MD (UKC)		85526	Tu-154B-2 (UKR)
	76610	IL-76MD (BSL)		85535	Tu-154B-2 (UKR)
	76647	IL-76MD (VPB)		85561	Tu-154B-2 (BSL)
	76670	IL-76MD (BSL)		85700	Tu-154M (UKR)
	76671	IL-76MD (VPB)		85701	Tu-154M (UKR)
	76676	IL-76MD (VPB)		85707	Tu-154M (UKR)
	76677	IL-76MD (VPB)		86132	IL-62M (UKR)
	76689	IL-76MD (BSL)		86133	IL-62M (UKR)
	76690	IL-76MD (BSL)		86134	IL-62M (UKR)
	76694	IL-76MD (VPB)		86135	IL-62M (UKR)
	76698	IL-76MD (VPB)		86580	IL-62M (UKR)
	76705	IL-76MD (UKC)		86581	IL-62M (UKR)
	76707	IL-76MD (VPB)		86582	IL-62M (UKR)

Notes	Reg.	Type		Owner or Operator

V2 (Antigua)

Reg.	Type	Owner or Operator
V2-LEC	Airbus A.310-324	Air-India
V2-LEJ	L.1011-385 TriStar 500	stored
V2-LEK	L.1011-385 TriStar 500	stored
V2-LEO	L.1011-385 TriStar 500	stored

Note: Seagreen Air Transport operates Boeing 707s registered N14AZ, N21AZ and N29AZ.

Reg.	Type	Owner or Operator	Notes

V5 (Namibia)

V5-SPF	Boeing 747SP-44	Air Namibia	

Note: Air Namibia also leases the Boeing 747SP ZS-SPB from South African Airways.

V8 (Brunei)

V8-DPD	Airbus A.310-304	Brunei Royal Flight (Government/VIP)
V8-JBB	Airbus A.340-213	Brunei Government
V8-JP1	Airbus A.340-212	Royal Brunei Airlines (Government/VIP)
V8-MJB	Boeing 767-27GER	Royal Brunei Airlines (Government/VIP)
V8-RBA	Boeing 757-2M6	Royal Brunei Airlines
V8-RBB	Boeing 757-2M6	Royal Brunei Airlines
V8-RBE	Boeing 767-33AER	Royal Brunei Airlines
V8-RBF	Boeing 767-33AER	Royal Brunei Airlines
V8-RBG	Boeing 767-33AER	Royal Brunei Airlines
V8-RBH	Boeing 767-33AER	Royal Brunei Airlines
V8-RBJ	Boeing 767-33AER	Royal Brunei Airlines
V8-RBK	Boeing 767-33AER	Royal Brunei Airlines
V8-RBL	Boeing 767-33AER	Royal Brunei Airlines
V8-RBM	Boeing 767-328ER	Royal Brunei Airlines
V8-RBN	Boeing 767-328ER	Royal Brunei Airlines

VH (Australia)

VH-EBQ	Boeing 747-238B	Queensland and Northern Territory Aerial Service (QANTAS) *City of Bunbury*
VH-EBR	Boeing 747-238B	QANTAS *City of Mt Gambier*
VH-EBS	Boeing 747-238B	QANTAS *City of Broken Hill*
VH-EBT	Boeing 747-338	QANTAS *City of Wagga Wagga*
VH-EBU	Boeing 747-338	QANTAS *City of Warrnambool*
VH-EBV	Boeing 747-338	QANTAS *Geraldton*
VH-EBW	Boeing 747-338	QANTAS *City of Tamworth*
VH-EBX	Boeing 747-338	QANTAS *City of Wodonga*
VH-EBY	Boeing 747-338	QANTAS *City of Mildura*
VH-OJA	Boeing 747-438	QANTAS *City of Canberra*
VH-OJB	Boeing 747-438	QANTAS *City of Sydney*
VH-OJC	Boeing 747-438	QANTAS *City of Melbourne*
VH-OJD	Boeing 747-438	QANTAS *City of Brisbane*
VH-OJE	Boeing 747-438	QANTAS *City of Adelaide*
VH-OJF	Boeing 747-438	QANTAS *City of Perth*
VH-OJG	Boeing 747-438	QANTAS *City of Hobart*
VH-OJH	Boeing 747-438	QANTAS *City of Darwin*
VH-OJI	Boeing 747-438	QANTAS *Longreach*
VH-OJJ	Boeing 747-438	QANTAS *Winton*
VH-OJK	Boeing 747-438	QANTAS *City of Newcastle*
VH-OJL	Boeing 747-438	QANTAS *City of Ballaarat*
VH-OJM	Boeing 747-438	QANTAS *City of Gosford*
VH-OJN	Boeing 747-438	QANTAS *City of Dubbo*
VH-OJO	Boeing 747-438	QANTAS *City of Toowoomba*
VH-OJP	Boeing 747-438	QANTAS *City of Albury*
VH-OJQ	Boeing 747-438	QANTAS *City of Mandurah*
VH-OJR	Boeing 747-438	QANTAS *City of Bathurst*

VR-B (Bermuda)

VR-BUA	Boeing 767-33PER	Uzbekistan Airlines
VR-BUB	Boeing 767-33PER	Uzbekistan Airlines

VR-H (Hong Kong)

VR-HIA	Boeing 747-267B	Cathay Pacific Airways
VR-HIB	Boeing 747-267B	Cathay Pacific Airways
VR-HIC	Boeing 747-267B	Cathay Pacific Airways
VR-HID	Boeing 747-267B	Cathay Pacific Airways
VR-HIE	Boeing 747-267B	Cathay Pacific Airways

Notes	Reg.	Type	Owner or Operator
	VR-HIF	Boeing 747-267B	Cathay Pacific Airways
	VR-HIH	Boeing 747-267F (SCD)	Cathay Pacific Cargo
	VR-HII	Boeing 747-367	Cathay Pacific Airways
	VR-HIJ	Boeing 747-367	Cathay Pacific Airways
	VR-HIK	Boeing 747-367	Cathay Pacific Airways
	VR-HKG	Boeing 747-267B	Cathay Pacific Airways
	VR-HKM	Boeing 747-132F (SCD)	Air Hong Kong
	VR-HMD	Boeing 747-2L5F	Air Hong Kong
	VR-HME	Boeing 747-2L5F	Air Hong Kong
	VR-HMF	Boeing 747-2L5F	Air Hong Kong
	VR-HOL	Boeing 747-367	Cathay Pacific Airways
	VR-HOM	Boeing 747-367	Cathay Pacific Airways
	VR-HON	Boeing 747-367	Cathay Pacific Airways
	VR-HOO	Boeing 747-467	Cathay Pacific Airways
	VR-HOP	Boeing 747-467	Cathay Pacific Airways
	VR-HOR	Boeing 747-467	Cathay Pacific Airways
	VR-HOS	Boeing 747-467	Cathay Pacific Airways
	VR-HOT	Boeing 747-467	Cathay Pacific Airways
	VR-HOU	Boeing 747-467	Cathay Pacific Airways
	VR-HOV	Boeing 747-467	Cathay Pacific Airways
	VR-HOW	Boeing 747-467	Cathay Pacific Airways
	VR-HOX	Boeing 747-467	Cathay Pacific Airways
	VR-HOY	Boeing 747-467	Cathay Pacific Airways
	VR-HOZ	Boeing 747-467	Cathay Pacific Airways
	VR-HUA	Boeing 747-467	Cathay Pacific Airways
	VR-HUB	Boeing 747-467	Cathay Pacific Airways
	VR-HUD	Boeing 747-467	Cathay Pacific Airways
	VR-HUE	Boeing 747-467	Cathay Pacific Airways
	VR-HUF	Boeing 747-467	Cathay Pacific Airways
	VR-HUG	Boeing 747-467	Cathay Pacific Airways
	VR-HUH	Boeing 747-467F	Cathay Pacific Airways
	VR-HUI	Boeing 747-467	Cathay Pacific Airways
	VR-HUJ	Boeing 747-467	Cathay Pacific Airways
	VR-HUK	Boeing 747-467F	Cathay Pacific Airways
	VR-HVX	Boeing 747-267F (SCD)	Cathay Pacific Airways
	VR-HVY	Boeing 747-236F (SCD)	Cathay Pacific Airways
	VR-HVZ	Boeing 747-267F (SCD)	Cathay Pacific Airways

VT (India)

	VT-EBE	Boeing 747-237B	Air-India *Shahjehan*
	VT-EBN	Boeing 747-237B	Air-India *Rajendra Chola*
	VT-EDU	Boeing 747-237B	Air-India *Akbar*
	VT-EFJ	Boeing 747-237B	Air-India *Chandragupta*
	VT-EFU	Boeing 747-237B	Air-India *Krishna Deva Raya*
	VT-EGA	Boeing 747-237B	Air-India *Samudra Gupta*
	VT-EGB	Boeing 747-237B	Air-India *Mahendra Varman*
	VT-EGC	Boeing 747-237B	Air-India *Harsha Vardhana*
	VT-EJG	Airbus A.310-304	Air-India *Vamuna*
	VT-EJH	Airbus A.310-304	Air-India *Tista*
	VT-EJI	Airbus A.310-304	Air-India *Saraswati*
	VT-EJJ	Airbus A.310-304	Air-India *Beas*
	VT-EJK	Airbus A.310-304	Air-India *Gomti*
	VT-EJL	Airbus A.310-304	Air-India *Sabarmati*
	VT-ENQ	Boeing 747-212B	Air-India *Himalaya*
	VT-EPW	Boeing 747-337 (SCD)	Air-India *Shivaji*
	VT-EPX	Boeing 747-337 (SCD)	Air-India *Narasimha Varman*
	VT-EQS	Airbus A.310-304	Air-India *Krishna*
	VT-EQT	Airbus A.310-304	Air-India *Narmada*
	VT-ESM	Boeing 747-437	Air-India *Konark*
	VT-ESN	Boeing 747-437	Air-India *Tanjore*
	VT-ESO	Boeing 747-437	Air-India *Khajuraho*
	VT-ESP	Boeing 747-437	Air-India *Ajanta*
	VT-EVA	Boeing 747-437	Air-India *Agra*
	VT-EVB	Boeing 747-437	Air India

Note: Airbus A310-324 V2-LEC is also used by Air India and Air-India Cargo operates
Douglas DC-8s and Boeing 747s on lease from various airlines.

YA (Afghanistan)

YA-FAX	Boeing 727-228	Ariana Afghan Airlines
YA-FAY	Boeing 727-228	Ariana Afghan Airlines
YA-FAZ	Boeing 727-228	Ariana Afghan Airlines
YA-GAA	Boeing 727-51	Balkh Air
YA-PAM	Boeing 707-324C	Pamir Air

YI (Iraq)

All aircraft have remained inactive since the Gulf conflict in the early 1990s. Commercial flights have therefore been suspended as a result of UN sanctions, with little prospect of an early resumption.

YK (Syria)

YK-AGA	Boeing 727-294	Syrianair *October 6*
YK-AGB	Boeing 727-294	Syrianair *Damascus*
YK-AGC	Boeing 727-294	Syrianair *Palmyra*
YK-AGD	Boeing 727-269	Syrianair
YK-AGE	Boeing 727-269	Syrianair
YK-AGF	Boeing 727-269	Syrianair
YK-AHA	Boeing 747SP-94	Syrianair *16 Novembre*
YK-AHB	Boeing 747SP-94	Syrianair *Arab Solidarity*
YK-AIA	Tupolev Tu-154M	Syrianair
YK-AIB	Tupolev Tu-154M	Syrianair
YK-AIC	Tupolev Tu-154M	Syrianair
YK-ATA	Ilyushin IL-76M	Syrianair
YK-ATB	Ilyushin IL-76M	Syrianair
YK-ATC	Ilyushin IL-76M	Syrianair
YK-ATD	Ilyushin IL-76M	Syrianair
YK-AYA	Tupolev Tu-134B-3	Syrianair
YK-AYB	Tupolev Tu-134B-3	Syrianair
YK-AYC	Tupolev Tu-134B-3	Syrianair
YK-AYD	Tupolev Tu-134B-3	Syrianair
YK-AYE	Tupolev Tu-134B-3	Syrianair
YK-AYF	Tupolev Tu-134B-3	Syrianair

YL (Latvia)

YL-BAA	Boeing 737-236	Transaero
YL-BAB	Boeing 737-236	Transaero
YL-BAC	Boeing 737-236	Transaero
YL-BAG	SAAB SF.340A	Air Baltic
YL-BAK	Avro RJ70	Air Baltic
YL-BAL	Avro RJ70	Air Baltic
YL-BAN	Avro RJ70	Air Baltic
YL-LAI	Tupolev Tu-154M	BEL Baltic Express Line
YL-LAJ	Ilyushin IL-76T	Inversia
YL-LAK	Ilyushin IL-76T	Inversia
YL-LAL	Ilyushin IL-76T	Inversia
YL-LBE	Tupolev Tu-134B-3	Lat Charter
YL-LBF	Tupolev Tu-134B-3	Lat Charter
YL-LBH	Tupolev Tu-134B-3	Lat Charter
YL-LBJ	Tupolev Tu-134B-3	Lat Charter
YL-LBM	Tupolev Tu-134B-3	Lat Charter
YL-RAA	Antonov An-26	RAF-Avia
YL-RAB	Antonov An-26	RAF-Avia
YL-RAC	Antonov An-26	RAF-Avia

YR (Romania)

YR-ABA	Boeing 707-3K1C	Tarom
YR-ABC	Boeing 707-3K1C	Tarom
YR-BCI	BAC One-Eleven 525FT	Tarom
YR-BCJ	BAC One-Eleven 525FT	Tarom
YR-BCK	BAC One-Eleven 525FT	Tarom
YR-BCL	BAC One-Eleven 525FT	Tarom

Notes	Reg.	Type	Owner or Operator
	YR-BCM	BAC One-Eleven 525FT	Tarom
	YR-BCN	BAC One-Eleven 525FT	Tarom
	YR-BGA	Boeing 737-38J	Tarom *Alba Iulia*
	YR-BGB	Boeing 737-38J	Tarom *Bucuresti*
	YR-BGC	Boeing 737-38J	Tarom *Constanta*
	YR-BGD	Boeing 737-38J	Tarom *Deva*
	YR-BGE	Boeing 737-38J	Tarom *Timisoara*
	YR-BRB	RomBac One-Eleven 561RC	Tarom
	YR-BRC	RomBac One-Eleven 561RC	Tarom
	YR-IMF	Ilyushin IL-18V	Tarom
	YR-IMG	Ilyushin IL-18V	Tarom
	YR-IMJ	Ilyushin IL-18D	Tarom
	YR-IML	Ilyushin IL-18D	Tarom
	YR-IRD	Ilyushin IL-62M	Tarom
	YR-IRE	Ilyushin IL-62M	Tarom
	YR-JBA	BAC One-Eleven 528FL	Jaro International
	YR-JBB	BAC One-Eleven 528FL	Jaro International
	YR-JCA	Boeing 707-327C	Jaro International
	YR-JCB	Boeing 707-321B	Jaro International
	YR-JCC	Boeing 707-384C	Jaro International
	YR-LCA	Airbus A.310-325	Tarom *Transilvania*
	YR-LCB	Airbus A.310-325	Tarom *Moldova*
	YR-MDJ	Boeing 707-3L6C	Jaro International
	YR-TPB	Tupolev Tu-154B	Tarom
	YR-TPE	Tupolev Tu-154B-1	Tarom
	YR-TPF	Tupolev Tu-154B-1	Tarom
	YR-TPG	Tupolev Tu-154B-1	Tarom
	YR-TPK	Tupolev Tu-154B-2	Tarom
	YR-TPL	Tupolev Tu-154B-2	Tarom

YU (Yugoslavia)

YU-AHN	Douglas DC-9-32	Jugoslovenski Aerotransport (JAT)
YU-AHU	Douglas DC-9-32	JAT
YU-AHV	Douglas DC-9-32	JAT
YU-AJH	Douglas DC-9-32	JAT
YU-AJI	Douglas DC-9-32	JAT
YU-AJJ	Douglas DC-9-32	JAT
YU-AJK	Douglas DC-9-32	JAT
YU-AJL	Douglas DC-9-32	JAT
YU-AJM	Douglas DC-9-32	JAT
YU-AKB	Boeing 727-2H9	JAT
YU-AKD	Boeing 727-2L8	Aviogenex *Split*
YU-AKE	Boeing 727-2H9	JAT
YU-AKF	Boeing 727-2H9	JAT
YU-AKG	Boeing 727-2H9	JAT
YU-AKH	Boeing 727-2L8	Aviogenex *Dubrovnik*
YU-AKI	Boeing 727-2H9	JAT
YU-AKJ	Boeing 727-2H9	JAT
YU-AKM	Boeing 727-243	Aviogenex *Pula*
YU-AMB	Douglas DC-10-30	JAT *Edvard Rusijan*
YU-AND	Boeing 737-3H9	JAT
YU-ANF	Boeing 737-3H9	JAT
YU-ANI	Boeing 737-3H9	JAT
YU-ANK	Boeing 737-3H9	JAT
YU-ANP	Boeing 737-2K3	Aviogenex *Zadar*
YU-ANU	Boeing 737-2K3	Aviogenex *Tivat*
YU-ANV	Boeing 737-3H9	JAT
YU-AOH	F.28 Fellowship 4000	Montenegro Airlines
YU-	F.28 Fellowship 4000	Montenegro Airlines

Note: Both JAT and Aviogenex were affected by the war in Yugoslavia with aircraft grounded or leased out. Operations restarted in late 1994.

YV (Venezuela)

YV-134C	Douglas DC-10-30	Venezolana Internacional de Aviacion SA (VIASA)
YV-135C	Douglas DC-10-30	VIASA
YV-136C	Douglas DC-10-30	VIASA
YV-137C	Douglas DC-10-30	VIASA
YV-138C	Douglas DC-10-30	VIASA
YV-139C	Douglas DC-10-30	VIASA

Z3 (Macedonia)

Note: Palair Macedonia ceased operations in October 1996.

Z (Zimbabwe)

Z-WKS	Boeing 707-330B	Air Zimbabwe
Z-WKU	Boeing 707-330B	Air Zimbabwe
Z-WMJ	Douglas DC-8-55F	Affretair *Captain Jack Malloch*
Z-WPE	Boeing 767-2N0ER	Air Zimbabwe *Victoria Falls*
Z-WPF	Boeing 767-2N0ER	Air Zimbabwe *Chimanimani*
Z-WSB	Douglas DC-8-55F	Affretair

ZK (New Zealand)

ZK-NBS	Boeing 747-419	Air New Zealand *Mataatua*
ZK-NBT	Boeing 747-419	Air New Zealand
ZK-NBU	Boeing 747-419	Air New Zealand
ZK-NBV	Boeing 747-419	Air New Zealand
ZK-NZV	Boeing 747-219B	Air New Zealand *Aotea*
ZK-NZW	Boeing 747-219B	Air New Zealand *Tainui*
ZK-NZX	Boeing 747-219B	Air New Zealand *Takitimu*
ZK-NZY	Boeing 747-219B	Air New Zealand *Te Arawa*
ZK-NZZ	Boeing 747-219B	Air New Zealand *Tokomaru*
ZK-SUH	Boeing 747-475	Air New Zealand
ZK-SUI	Boeing 747-441	Air New Zealand

ZS (South Africa)

ZS-SAC	Boeing 747-312	South African Airways *Shosholoza*
ZS-SAJ	Boeing 747-312	South African Airways
ZS-SAK	Boeing 747-444	South African Airways
ZS-SAL	Boeing 747-244B	South African Airways *Tafelberg*
ZS-SAM	Boeing 747-244B	South African Airways *Drakensberg*
ZS-SAN	Boeing 747-244B	South African Airways *Lebombo*
ZS-SAO	Boeing 747-244B	South African Airways *Magaliesberg*
ZS-SAP	Boeing 747-244B	South African Airways *Swartberg*
ZS-SAR	Boeing 747-244F (SCD)	South African Airways *Waterberg*
ZS-SAT	Boeing 747-344	South African Airways *Johannesburg*
ZS-SAU	Boeing 747-344	South African Airways *Cape Town*
ZS-SAV	Boeing 747-444	South African Airways *Durban*
ZS-SAW	Boeing 747-444	South African Airways *Bloemfontein*
ZS-SAX	Boeing 747-444	South African Airways
ZS-SAY	Boeing 747-444	South African Airways *Vulindlela*
ZS-SAZ	Boeing 747-444	South African Airways
ZS-SPA	Boeing 747SP-44	South African Airways
ZS-SPB	Boeing 747SP-44	South African Airways/Air Namibia
ZS-SPC	Boeing 747SP-44	South African Airways
ZS-SPE	Boeing 747SP-44	South African Airways *Hantarn*

3B (Mauritius)

3B-NAK	Boeing 767-23BER	Air Mauritius *City of Curepipe*
3B-NAL	Boeing 767-23BER	Air Mauritius *City of Port Louis*
3B-NAT	Airbus A.340-312	Air Mauritius *Paille-en-Queue*
3B-NAU	Airbus A.340-312	Air Mauritius *Pink Pigeon*
3B-NAV	Airbus A.340-312	Air Mauritius *Kestrel*
3B-NAY	Airbus A.340-313	Air Mauritius *Cardinal*
3B-NAZ	Boeing 767-328ER	Air Mauritius *Parakeet*
3B-	Airbus A.340-313	Air Mauritius

Note: Air Mauitius also operates TriStar 500 V2-LEO.

Notes	Reg.	Type		Owner or Operator

3D (Swaziland)

Reg.	Type	Owner or Operator
3D-ADV	Douglas DC-8-54F	African International Airways
3D-AFR	Douglas DC-8-54F	African International Airways
3D-AFX	Douglas DC-8-54F	African International Airways

Notes	Reg.	Type	Notes	Reg.	Type

4K (Azerbaijan)

The following are operated by Azerbaijan Airlines with the registrations prefixed by 4K.

Reg.	Type	Reg.	Type
AZ1	Boeing 727-235	85177	Tu-154B-1
AZ2	Boeing 727-235	85192	Tu-154B-1
AZ3	Boeing 707-341C	85199	Tu-154B-1
AZ4	Boeing 707-399C	85211	Tu-154B-1
65702	Tu-134B-3	85214	Tu-154B-1
65705	Tu-134B-3	85274	Tu-154B-1
65708	Tu-134B-3	85329	Tu-154B-2
65709	Tu-134B-3	85364	Tu-154B-2
65710	Tu-134B-3	85391	Tu-154B-2
65711	Tu-134B-3	85548	Tu-154B-2
65713	Tu-134B-3	85698	Tu-154M
65714	Tu-134B-3	85729	Tu-154M
85147	Tu-154B-1	85734	Tu-154M
85158	Tu-154B-1		

Notes	Reg.	Type		Owner or Operator

4L (Georgia)

Reg.	Type	Owner or Operator
4L-AAA	Boeing 737-375	Orbi Georgian Airways

The following are operated by Orbi with the registrations prefixed by 4L. Airline codes
DVU – Orbi Georgian Airways, GEO – Air Georgia

Notes	Reg.	Type	Notes	Reg.	Type
	65750	Tu-134A-3 (DVU)		85197	Tu-154B (DVU)
	65774	Tu-134A-3 (DVU)		85359	Tu-154B-2 (DVU)
	65798	Tu-134A-3 (DVU)		85430	Tu-154B-2 (DVU)
	65810	Tu-134A-3 (DVU)		85496	Tu-154B-2 (DVU)
	65857	Tu-134A-3 (DVU)		85518	Tu-154B-2 (DVU)
	65865	Tu-134A-3 (DVU)		85547	Tu-154B-2 (GEO)
	85168	Tu-154B (DVU)		85558	Tu-154B-2 (GEO)

Notes	Reg.	Type		Owner or Operator

4R (Sri Lanka)

Reg.	Type	Owner or Operator
4R-ADA	Airbus A.340-311	Air Lanka
4R-ADB	Airbus A.340-311	Air Lanka
4R-ADC	Airbus A.340-311	Air Lanka
4R-ULA	L.1011-385 TriStar 500	Air Lanka City of Jayewardenepura
4R-ULB	L.1011-385 TriStar 500	Air Lanka City of Kandy
4R-ULC	L.1011-385 TriStar 100	Air Lanka City of Anuradhapura
4R-ULE	L.1011-385 TriStar 50	Air Lanka City of Ratnapura

4X (Israel)

Reg.	Type	Owner or Operator
4X-ABN	Boeing 737-258	El Al/Arkia
4X-ABO	Boeing 737-258	El Al/Arkia
4X-AXA	Boeing 747-258B	El Al
4X-AXB	Boeing 747-258B	El Al
4X-AXC	Boeing 747-258B	El Al
4X-AXD	Boeing 747-258C	El Al
4X-AXF	Boeing 747-258C	El Al
4X-AXH	Boeing 747-258B (SCD)	El Al

Reg.	Type	Owner or Operator	Notes
4X-AXK	Boeing 747-245F (SCD)	El Al	
4X-AXL	Boeing 747-245F (SCD)	El Al	
4X-AXQ	Boeing 747-238B	El Al	
4X-AXZ	Boeing 747-124F (SCD)	El Al	
4X-BAF	Boeing 737-281	Arkia	
4X-BAG	Boeing 737-281	Arkia	
4X-BAK	Boeing 737-281	Arkia	
4X-EAA	Boeing 767-258	El Al	
4X-EAB	Boeing 767-258	El Al	
4X-EAC	Boeing 767-258ER	El Al	
4X-EAD	Boeing 767-258ER	El Al	
4X-EBF	Boeing 757-27B	El Al	
4X-EBL	Boeing 757-258	El Al/Arkia	
4X-EBM	Boeing 757-258	El Al/Arkia	
4X-EBR	Boeing 757-258	El Al/Arkia	
4X-EBS	Boeing 757-258	El Al	
4X-EBT	Boeing 757-258	El Al	
4X-EBU	Boeing 757-258	El Al	
4X-EBV	Boeing 757-258	El Al	
4X-ELA	Boeing 747-458	El Al	
4X-ELB	Boeing 747-458	El Al	
4X-ELC	Boeing 747-458	El Al	

5A (Libya)

5A-DAI	Boeing 727-224	Libyan Arab Airlines	
5A-DAK	Boeing 707-3L5C	Libyan Arab Airlines	
5A-DIB	Boeing 727-2L5	Libyan Arab Airlines	
5A-DIC	Boeing 727-2L5	Libyan Arab Airlines	
5A-DID	Boeing 727-2L5	Libyan Arab Airlines	
5A-DIE	Boeing 727-2L5	Libyan Arab Airlines	
5A-DIF	Boeing 727-2L5	Libyan Arab Airlines	
5A-DIG	Boeing 727-2L5	Libyan Arab Airlines	
5A-DIH	Boeing 727-2L5	Libyan Arab Airlines	
5A-DII	Boeing 727-2L5	Libyan Arab Airlines	
5A-DJU	Boeing 707-351C	Libyan Arab Airlines	

Note: All international services were suspended in 1992 following UN sanctions. Domestic schedules are still operated.

5B (Cyprus)

5B-DAQ	Airbus A.310-203	Cyprus Airways *Soli*	
5B-DAR	Airbus A.310-203	Cyprus Airways *Aepia*	
5B-DAS	Airbus A.310-203	Cyprus Airways *Salamis*	
5B-DAT	Airbus A.320-231	Cyprus Airways *Praxandros*	
5B-DAU	Airbus A.320-231	Cyprus Airways *Evelthon*	
5B-DAV	Airbus A.320-231	Cyprus Airways *Kinyras*	
5B-DAW	Airbus A.320-231	Cyprus Airways *Agapinor*	
5B-DAX	Airbus A.310-204	Cyprus Airways *Engomi*	
5B-DAZ	Boeing 707-328C	Avistar	
5B-DBA	Airbus A.320-231	Cyprus Airways *Evagoras*	
5B-DBB	Airbus A.320-231	Eurocypria Airways *Akamas*	
5B-DBC	Airbus A.320-231	Eurocypria Airways *Tefkros*	
5B-DBD	Airbus A.320-231	Eurocypria Airways *Onosilos*	

5N (Nigeria)

5N-ANN	Douglas DC-10-30	Nigeria Airways *Yunkari*	
5N-ARQ	Boeing 707-338C	DAS Air Cargo	
5N-AUE	Airbus A.310-222	Nigeria Airways *River Yobe*	
5N-AUF	Airbus A.310-222	Nigeria Airways *River Ethiope*	
5N-AUG	Airbus A.310-222	Nigeria Airways *Lekki Peninsula*	
5N-AUH	Airbus A.310-222	Nigeria Airways *Rima River*	
5N-BBD	Boeing 707-338C	ADC Airlines	
5N-BBF	Boeing 727-231	ADC Airlines	
5N-BBH	Boeing 727-231	ADC Airlines	
5N-ECI	Boeing 707-321C	Air Atlantic Cargo	

Notes	Reg.	Type	Owner or Operator
	5N-EDO	Boeing 747-146	Okada Air *Lady Cherry*
	5N-EEO	Boeing 707-321C	Air Atlantic Cargo
	5N-MKE	Douglas DC-8-55F	MK Airlines
	5N-MXX	Boeing 707-323C	Merchant Express
	5N-TKE	Boeing 727-82	Triax Airlines *Eze-Ukpo*
	5N-TKT	Boeing 727-22	Triax Airlines
	5N-TTK	Boeing 727-264	Triax Airlines *Chinweze*
	5N-VRG	Boeing 707-355C	International Air Tours

5R (Madagascar)

	5R-MFT	Boeing 747-2B2B (SCD)	Air Madagascar *Ankoay*

5X (Uganda)

	5X-AMM	Boeing 727-76	Skyline International
	5X-JEF	Boeing 707-379C	DAS Air Cargo
	5X-JET	Boeing 707-351C	DAS Air Cargo
	5X-JOE	Douglas DC-10-30	DAS Air Cargo
	5X-UCF	L.100-30 Hercules	Uganda Air Cargo *The Silver Lady*

5Y (Kenya)

	5Y-AXI	Boeing 707-330B	African Airlines International
	5Y-BBI	Boeing 707-351B	African Airlines International
	5Y-BEL	Airbus A.310-304	Kenya Airways *Nyayo Star*
	5Y-BEN	Airbus A.310-304	Kenya Airways *Harambee Star*
	5Y-BFT	Airbus A.310-304	Kenya Airways *Uhuru Star*
	5Y-SIM	Boeing 707-336C	Simba Air Cargo

Note: ASA African Safari Airways operates a DC-10-30 which carries the registration PH-DTL.

6Y (Jamaica)

Note: Air Jamaica operates Airbus A.310-324s which retain the US registrations N835AB, N837AB, N838AB, N839AD, N840AB and N841AB.

7O (Yemen)

	7O-ACO	Boeing 707-336C	Yemen Government/VIP
	7O-ACV	Boeing 727-2N8	Yemenia
	7O-ACW	Boeing 727-2N8	Yemenia
	7O-ACX	Boeing 727-2N8	Yemenia
	7O-ACY	Boeing 727-2N8	Yemenia
	7O-ADA	Boeing 727-2N8	Yemenia
	7O-ADG	Iluyshin IL-76TD	Yemenia
	7O-	Airbus A.310-325	Yemenia
	7O-	Airbus A.310-325	Yemenia

7T (Algeria)

	7T-VEA	Boeing 727-2D6	Air Algerie *Tassili*
	7T-VEB	Boeing 727-2D6	Air Algerie *Hoggar*
	7T-VED	Boeing 737-2D6C	Air Algerie *Atlas Saharien*
	7T-VEF	Boeing 737-2D6	Air Algerie *Saoura*
	7T-VEG	Boeing 737-2D6	Air Algerie *Monts des Ouleds Neils*
	7T-VEH	Boeing 727-2D6	Air Algerie *Lalla Khadidja*
	7T-VEI	Boeing 727-2D6	Air Algerie *Djebel Amour*
	7T-VEJ	Boeing 737-2D6	Air Algerie *Chrea*
	7T-VEK	Boeing 737-2D6	Air Algerie *Edough*
	7T-VEL	Boeing 737-2D6	Air Algerie *Akfadou*

Reg.	Type	Owner or Operator	Notes
7T-VEM	Boeing 727-2D6	Air Algerie *Mont du Ksall*	
7T-VEN	Boeing 737-2D6	Air Algerie *La Soummam*	
7T-VEO	Boeing 737-2D6	Air Algerie *La Titteri*	
7T-VEP	Boeing 727-2D6	Air Algerie *Mont du Tessala*	
7T-VEQ	Boeing 737-2D6	Air Algerie *Le Zaccar*	
7T-VER	Boeing 737-2D6	Air Algerie *Le Souf*	
7T-VES	Boeing 737-2D6C	Air Algerie *Le Tadmaït*	
7T-VET	Boeing 727-2D6	Air Algerie *Georges du Rhumel*	
7T-VEU	Boeing 727-2D6	Air Algerie *Djurdjura*	
7T-VEV	Boeing 727-2D6	Air Algerie	
7T-VEW	Boeing 727-2D6	Air Algerie *Monts de Tlemcen*	
7T-VEX	Boeing 727-2D6	Air Algerie *Djemila*	
7T-VEY	Boeing 737-2D6	Air Algerie *Rhoufi*	
7T-VEZ	Boeing 737-2T4	Air Algerie *Monts du Daia*	
7T-VJA	Boeing 737-2T4	Air Algerie *Monts des Babors*	
7T-VJB	Boeing 737-2T4	Air Algerie *Monts des Bibons*	
7T-VJC	Airbus A.310-203	Air Algerie	
7T-VJD	Airbus A.310-203	Air Algerie	
7T-VJE	Airbus A.310-203	Air Algerie/Royal Jordanian	
7T-VJF	Airbus A.310-203	Air Algerie/Royal Jordanian	
7T-VJG	Boeing 767-3D6	Air Algerie	
7T-VJH	Boeing 767-3D6	Air Algerie	
7T-VJI	Boeing 767-3D6	Air Algerie	

9A (Croatia)

9A-CTA	Boeing 737-230	Croatia Airlines	
9A-CTB	Boeing 737-230	Croatia Airlines	
9A-CTC	Boeing 737-230	Croatia Airlines	
9A-CTD	Boeing 737-230	Croatia Airlines	
9A-CTE	Boeing 737-230	Croatia Airlines	

9G (Ghana)

9G-ADM	Boeing 707-321C	Continental Cargo Airlines	
9G-ADS	Boeing 707-323C	Continental Cargo Airlines	
9G-ANA	Douglas DC-10-30	Ghana Airways	
9G-EBK	Boeing 707-321C	Alpine Air	
9G-MKA	Douglas DC-8-55F	MK Airlines	
9G-MKC	Douglas DC-8-55F	MK Airlines	
9G-MKD	Douglas DC-8-55F	MK Airlines	
9G-MKF	Douglas DC-8-55F	MK Airlines	

9H (Malta)

9H-ABE	Boeing 737-2Y5	Air Malta *Alof de Wignacourt*	
9H-ABF	Boeing 737-2Y5	Air Malta *Manuel Pinto*	
9H-ABP	Airbus A.320-211	Air Malta *Nicholas de Cottoner*	
9H-ABQ	Airbus A.320-211	Air Malta *Hughes Loubenx de Verdelle*	
9H-ABR	Boeing 737-3Y5	Air Malta *Juan de Homedes*	
9H-ABS	Boeing 737-3Y5	Air Malta *Antoines de Paule*	
9H-ABT	Boeing 737-3Y5	Air Malta *Ferdinand von Hompesch*	
9H-ACM	Avro RJ70	Air Malta *Luqa*	
9H-ACN	Avro RJ70	Air Malta *San Lawrenz*	
9H-ACO	Avro RJ70	Air Malta *Dingli*	
9H-ACP	Avro RJ70	Air Malta *Pieta*	

Note: Air Malta Usually leases in one or two aircraft for the summer season.

9K (Kuwait)

9K-ADB	Boeing 747-269B (SCD)	Kuwait Airways	
9K-ADD	Boeing 747-269B (SCD)	Kuwait Airways *Al-Salmiya*	
9K-ADE	Boeing 747-469 (SCD)	Kuwait Airways *Al-Jabariya*	
9K-ADF	Boeing 747-469 (SCD)	Kuwait Airways *Al-Grain*	
9K-AHI	Airbus A300C-620	Kuwait Airways	

Notes	Reg.	Type	Owner or Operator
	9K-ALA	Airbus A.310-308	Kuwait Airways *Al-Jahra*
	9K-ALB	Airbus A.310-308	Kuwait Airways *Gharnada*
	9K-ALC	Airbus A.310-308	Kuwait Airways *Kadhma*
	9K-ALD	Airbus A.310-308	Kuwait Government *Al-Salmiya*
	9K-AMA	Airbus A.300-605R	Kuwait Airways *Failaka*
	9K-AMB	Airbus A.300-605R	Kuwait Airways *Burghan*
	9K-AMC	Airbus A.300-605R	Kuwait Airways *Wafra*
	9K-AMD	Airbus A.300-605R	Kuwait Airways *Wara*
	9K-AME	Airbus A.300-605R	Kuwait Airways *Al-Rawdhatain*
	9K-ANA	Airbus A.340-313	Kuwait Airways *Warba*
	9K-ANB	Airbus A.340-313	Kuwait Airways *Al-Sabahiya*
	9K-ANC	Airbus A.340-313	Kuwait Airways *Al-Mobarakia*
	9K-AND	Airbus A.340-313	Kuwait Airways *Al-Riggah*

9M (Malaysia)

9M-MHI	Boeing 747-236F (SCD)	Malaysian Airlines *Cargo Kuching*
9M-MHJ	Boeing 747-236F (SCD)	Malaysian Airlines *Cargo Johor Bahru*
9M-MHL	Boeing 747-4H6 (SCD)	Malaysian Airlines *Kuala Lumpur*
9M-MHM	Boeing 747-4H6 (SCD)	Malaysian Airlines *Penang*
9M-MHN	Boeing 747-4H6	Malaysian Airlines *Malacca*
9M-MHO	Boeing 747-4H6	Malaysian Airlines *Alor Setar*
9M-MPA	Boeing 747-4H6	Malaysian Airlines *Ipoh*
9M-MPB	Boeing 747-4H6	Malaysian Airlines *Shah Alam*
9M-MPC	Boeing 747-4H6	Malaysian Airlines *Kuantan*
9M-MPD	Boeing 747-4H6	Malaysian Airlines *Serembam*
9M-MPE	Boeing 747-4H6	Malaysian Airlines *Kangar*
9M-MPF	Boeing 747-4H6	Malaysian Airlines *Kota Bharu*
9M-MPG	Boeing 747-4H6	Malaysian Airlines *KualaTerengganu*
9M-MPH	Boeing 747-4H6	Malaysian Airlines *Langkawi*
9M-MPI	Boeing 747-4H6	Malaysian Airlines
9M-MPJ	Boeing 747-4H6	Malaysian Airlines

9N (Nepal)

9N-ACA	Boeing 757-2F8	Royal Nepal Airlines
9N-ACB	Boeing 757-2F8C	Royal Nepal Airlines

Note: Royal Nepal also operates Airbus A.310-304 registered D-APON.

9Q (Zaïre)

9Q-CBW	Boeing 707-329C	Scibe Airlift Zaïre
9Q-CJT	Boeing 707-123B	Transair Cargo
9Q-CJW	Boeing 707-321C	New ACS
9Q-CKG	Boeing 707-366C	Zaire Express
9Q-CKK	Boeing 707-366C	Zaire Express
9Q-CSB	Boeing 707-373C	Sky Deck Cargo
9Q-CSZ	Boeing 707-323C	Shabair
9Q-CVG	Boeing 707-358C	Zaire Express

9V (Singapore)

9V-SFA	Boeing 747-412F (SCD)	Singapore Airlines
9V-SFB	Boeing 747-412F (SCD)	Singapore Airlines
9V-SFC	Boeing 747-412F (SCD)	Singapore Airlines
9V-SFD	Boeing 747-412F (SCD)	Singapore Airlines
9V-SFE	Boeing 747-412F (SCD)	Singapore Airlines
9V-SFF	Boeing 747-412F (SCD)	Singapore Airlines
9V-SKM	Boeing 747-312 (SCD)	Singapore Airlines
9V-SKN	Boeing 747-312 (SCD)	Singapore Airlines
9V-SKP	Boeing 747-312 (SCD)	Singapore Airlines
9V-SKQ	Boeing 747-212F (SCD)	Singapore Airlines
9V-SMA	Boeing 747-412	Singapore Airlines
9V-SMB	Boeing 747-412	Singapore Airlines
9V-SMD	Boeing 747-412	Singapore Airlines

Reg.	Type	Owner or Operator	Notes
9V-SME	Boeing 747-412	Singapore Airlines	
9V-SMF	Boeing 747-412	Singapore Airlines	
9V-SMG	Boeing 747-412	Singapore Airlines	
9V-SMH	Boeing 747-412	Singapore Airlines	
9V-SMI	Boeing 747-412	Singapore Airlines	
9V-SMJ	Boeing 747-412	Singapore Airlines	
9V-SMK	Boeing 747-412	Singapore Airlines	
9V-SML	Boeing 747-412	Singapore Airlines	
9V-SMM	Boeing 747-412	Singapore Airlines	
9V-SMN	Boeing 747-412	Singapore Airlines	
9V-SMO	Boeing 747-412	Singapore Airlines	
9V-SMP	Boeing 747-412	Singapore Airlines	
9V-SMQ	Boeing 747-412	Singapore Airlines	
9V-SMR	Boeing 747-412	Singapore Airlines	
9V-SMS	Boeing 747-412	Singapore Airlines	
9V-SMT	Boeing 747-412	Singapore Airlines	
9V-SMU	Boeing 747-412	Singapore Airlines	
9V-SMV	Boeing 747-412	Singapore Airlines	
9V-SMW	Boeing 747-412	Singapore Airlines	
9V-SMY	Boeing 747-412	Singapore Airlines	
9V-SMZ	Boeing 747-412	Singapore Airlines	
9V-SPA	Boeing 747-412	Singapore Airlines	
9V-SPB	Boeing 747-412	Singapore Airlines	
9V-SPC	Boeing 747-412	Singapore Airlines	
9V-SPD	Boeing 747-412	Singapore Airlines	
9V-SPE	Boeing 747-412	Singapore Airlines	
9V-SPF	Boeing 747-412	Singapore Airlines	
9V-SPG	Boeing 747-412	Singapore Airlines	
9V-SPH	Boeing 747-412	Singapore Airlines	
9V-SPI	Boeing 747-412	Singapore Airlines	
9V-SPJ	Boeing 747-412	Singapore Airlines	
9V-SPK	Boeing 747-412	Singapore Airlines	
9V-SPL	Boeing 747-412	Singapore Airlines	
9V-SPM	Boeing 747-412	Singapore Airlines	

Note: Singapore Airlines also operates Boeing 747-312 N121KG, N122KH, N123KJ, N124KK and N125KL.

9XR (Rwanda)

9XR-VO	Boeing 707-328C	Rwandair Cargo	

9Y (Trinidad and Tobago)

9Y-TGJ	L.1011-385 TriStar 500 (595)	B.W.I.A. *Sunjet Trinidad*	
9Y-TGN	L.1011-385 TriStar 500 (596)	B.W.I.A. *Sunjet Barbados*	
9Y-THA	L.1011-385 TriStar 500 (597)	B.W.I.A. *Sunjet Antigua*	

Note: B.W.I.A. also operates a TriStar 500 which retains the registration N3140D (598) and named *Sunjet St Lucia*. Similarly CS-TEA is leased from Air Portugal.

EC-FVY, BA 146-200QT of Pan Air Líneas Aereas/TNT.

F-GRSB, Boeing 737-497 of Star Europe.

Aircraft included in this section are those based in the UK but which retain their non-British identities.

Notes	Reg.	Type	Owner or Operator
	A40-AB	V.1103 VC10 ★	Brooklands Museum of Aviation (G-ASIX)
	CF-EQS	Boeing-Stearman PT-17 ★	Imperial War Museum/Duxford
	CF-KCG	Grumman TBM-3E Avenger AS.3 ★	Imperial War Museum/Duxford
	D-692	Staaken Z-1 Flitzer	D. J. Evans & L. R. Williams (G-BVAW)
	D-FABE	CCF Harvard IVM	Island Aeroplane Co/Sandown
	D-FOFM	Antonov An-2	Island Aeroplane Co/Sandown
	D-HMQV	Bolkow Bo 102 ★	IHM)/Weston-s-Mare
	D-IFSB	D.H.104 Dove 6 ★	Mosquito Aircraft Museum
	F-BDRS	Boeing B-17G (231983) ★	Imperial War Museum/Duxford
	F-BMCY	Potez 840 ★	Sumburgh Fire Service
	HA-MEP	Antonov An-2	AeroSuperBatics Ltd
	HA-MKE	Antonov An-2	Air Foyle/White Waltham
	HA-MKF	Antonov An-2	–/White Waltham
	LY-AFA	Yakovlev Yak-52	Termikas Co Ltd
	LY-AFB	Yakovlev Yak-52	Termikas Co Ltd
	LY-AKQ	Yakovlev Yak-52	—
	LY-AKW	Yakovlev Yak-52	A. Harris
	LY-ALG	Yakovlev Yak-52	Warwick Aero Services Ltd
	LY-ALJ	Yakovlev Yak-52	—
	LY-ALN	Yakovlev Yak-52	G. G. L. James
	LY-ALO	Yakovlev Yak-52	Sky Associates (UK) Ltd
	LY-ALS	Yakovlev Yak-52	M. Jefferies
	LY-ALT	Yakovlev Yak-52	Titan Airways Ltd/Stansted
	LY-ALU	Yakovlev Yak-52	—
	LY-ALY	Yakovlev Yak-52	M. Jefferies
	LY-AMI	Yakovlev Yak-18T	—
	LY-AMP	Yakovlev Yak-52	—
	LY-AMS	Yakovlev Yak-52	Willow Air Ltd
	LY-AMU	Yakovlev Yak-52	G. Sharpe
	LY-ANI	Yakovlev Yak-52	—
	LY-AOB	Yakovlev Yak-52	M. Schwarz
	LY-AOC	Yakovlev Yak-52	—
	N2FU	Learjet 31A	Motor Racing Development Corpn
	N12FU	Dassault Falcon 20C	Motor Racing Development Corpn
	N14TV	Cessna 501 Citation	Helios Ltd
	N18E	Boeing 247D ★	Science Museum/Wroughton
	N18V	Beech D.17S Traveler (DR628)	R. Lamplough
	N27TS	Cessna 501 Citation	Eagle SP 147 Inc
	N30XX	Cessna 550 Citation II	Freshair Inc
	N36SF	Hawker Sea Fury FB.10 (361)	J. Bradshaw
	N43SV	Boeing Stearman E.75N-1 (796)	V. S. E. Norman
	N47AZ	Douglas C-47A	MLP Aviation Ltd/Elstree
	N47DD	Republic P-47D Thunderbolt (45-49192) ★	Imperial War Museum/Duxford
	N47FK	Douglas C-47A	MLP Aviation Ltd/Elstree
	N47FL	Douglas C-47A	MLP Aviation Ltd/Elstree
	N49AG	Douglas DC-3 (OT-CWG)	Dakota Air/Brussels
	N51PR	P-51B Mustang	The Fighter Collection/Duxford
	N51RR	P-51D Mustang (474008)	D. Gilmour/North Weald
	N55JP	FG-1D Corsair (NZ5648)	Old Flying Machine Co/Duxford
	N93GS	Grumman G.21C Goose	—
	N139DP	Bell P-39Q-5-BE Airacobra (219993)	The Fighter Collection/Duxford
	N200CX	Cessna 550 Citation II	Heron 550 Inc
	N260QB	Pitts S-2S Special	D. Baker
	N300GX	G.1159A Gulfstream 4	Glaxo PLC
	N339BB	Sikorsky S-76A	Air Hanson Ltd/Blackbushe
	N444M	Grumman G.44 Widgeon (1411)	M. Dunkerley/Biggin Hill
	N500LN	Howard 500	D. Baker
	N707KS	Boeing 707-321B	Kalair Corpn/Stansted
	N707TJ	Boeing Stearman A.75N1	V. S. E. Norman (Crunchie)/Rendcomb
	N736GX	Cessna R.172K (tailwheel)	Mission Aviation Fellowship/Headcorn
	N800H	F8F-2 Bearcat (121752)	The Fighter Collection/Duxford

Reg.	Type	Owner or Operator	Notes
N809P	Dassault Falcon 20C	FR Aviation Ltd	
N999PJ	M.S.760 Paris 2	Aces High Ltd/North Weald	
N1344	Ryan PT-22	H. Mitchell	
N2929W	PA-28-151 Warrior	R. Lobell	
N3922B	Boeing Stearman E.75N1	Eastern Stearman Ltd/Swanton Morley	
N3929B	Boeing Stearman E.75N1	Eastern Stearman Ltd/Swanton Morley	
N4234C	P.66 Pembroke (XL954)	Air Antique/Coventry	
N4565L	Douglas DC-3 ★	USAF Museum/Framlingham	
N4596N	Boeing Stearman PT-13D	Intrepid Aviation Co/North Weald	
N4712V	Boeing Stearman PT-13D	Wessex Aviation & Transport Ltd	
N4727V	Spad S.VII (S4523)	Imperial War Museum/Duxford	
N4806E	Douglas A-26C Invader ★	R. & R. Cadman (stored)/Manston	
N4845V	FM-2 Wildcat	Fighter Collection/Duxford	
N5057V	Boeing Stearman PT-13D	V. S. E. Norman/Rendcomb	
N5237V	Boeing B-17G (483868) ★	RAF Museum/Hendon	
N5345N	Boeing Stearman PT-13D	Eastern Stearman Ltd/Swanton Morley	
N5419	Bristol Scout D (replica) ★	Bristol Aero Collection	
N5824H	PA-38-112 Tomahawk	Lakenheath Aero Club	
N6268	Travel Air Model 2000 (626/18) ★	Personal Plane Services Ltd	
N6526D	P-51D Mustang (413573) ★	RAF Museum/Hendon	
N6690Z	PA-25 Pawnee 235	Marchington Gliding Club/Tatenhill	
N7253C	F7F-3 Tigercat (80425)	The Fighter Collection/Duxford	
N7614C	B-25J Mitchell ★	Imperial War Museum/Duxford	
N7777G	L.749A Constellation ★	Science Museum (G-CONI)/Wroughton	
N8162G	Boeing Stearman PT-17	Eastern Stearman Ltd	
N9050T	Douglas C-47A (parts only) ★	Dakota's American Bistro/Fleet	
N9089Z	TB-25J Mitchell (44-30861) ★	Aces High Ltd (G-BKXW)/North Weald	
N9115Z	TB-25N Mitchell (34037) ★	RAF Museum/Hendon	
N9606H	Fairchild M.62A Cornell ★	Rebel Air Museum/Earls Colne	
N26634	PA-24 Comanche 250	P. Biggs (G-BFKR)	
N33600	Cessna L-19A Bird Dog (111989) ★	Museum of Army Flying/Middle Wallop	
N38940	Boeing Stearman PT-17 (18263)	—	
N43069	PA-28-161 Warrior II	D. Wards	
N49272	Fairchild PT-23 (23)	PT Flight/Cosford	
N50755	Boeing Stearman PT-27	Eastern Stearman Ltd/Swanton Morely	
N53091	Boeing Stearman PT-17	Eastern Stearman Ltd/Swanton Morley	
N54922	Boeing Stearman N2S-4	V. S. E. Norman (Crunchie)/Rencomb	
N56421	Ryan PT-22 (855)	PT Flight/Cosford	
N58566	BT-13 Valiant	PT Flight/Cosford	
N63590	Boeing Stearman N2S-3 ★	Blackbarn Aviation/Tibenham	
N65200	Boeing Stearman D75N1	Eastern Stearman Ltd/Swanton Morley	
N68427	Boeing Stearman N2S-4 ★	Blackbarn Aviation/Tibenham	
N73410	Boeing Stearman N2S-3 ★	Blackbarn Aviation/Tibenham	
N75664	Boeing Stearman E.75N1 (208)	—	
N88972	B-25D-30-ND Mitchell (KL161)	Fighter Collection/Duxford	
N91342	PA-28-112 Tomahawk	Lakenheath Aero Club	
N91457	PA-38-112 Tomahawk	Lakenheath Aero Club	
N91590	PA-38-112 Tomahawk	Lakenheath Aero Club	
N96240	Beech D.18S ★	Visionair Ltd (G-AYAH) (derelict)/Rochester	
N99153	T-28C Trojan ★	Norfolk & Suffolk Aviation Museum/Flixton	
NC5171N	Lockheed 10A Electra ★	Science Museum (G-LIOA)/Wroughton	
NC16403	Cessna C.34 Airmaster	Sylmar Aviation (G-BSEB)	
NC18028	Beech D.17S	P. H. McConnell/Popham	
NX47DD	Republic P-47D Thunderbolt (226671)	The Fighter Collection/Duxford	
NX71MY	Vickers Vimy (replica)(G-EAOU)	Greenco (UK) Ltd	
NX700HL	F8F-2B Bearcat (121714)	B. J. S. Grey/Duxford	
OM-UIN	Antonov An-2	Avia Special/White Waltham	
RA-01325	Yakovlev Yak-52	Bar Belle Aviation/White Waltham	
RA-01378	Yakovlev Yak-52	T. Evans	
RA-01386	Yakovlev Yak-52 (51)	R. Warman	
RA-7503	Sukhoi Su-29	R. N. Goode/White Waltham	
RA-7604	Sukhoi Su-29	R. N. Goode/White Waltham	
RA-7702	Sukhoi Su-29	—	
RA-7802	Sukhoi Su-29	P. Williams/White Waltham	
RA-7803	Sukhoi Su-29	R. N. Goode/White Waltham	
RA-22521	Yakovlev Yak-52 (04)	D. Squires/Wellsbourne	
RA-44467	Yakovlev Yak-18T	—	
RA-44470	Yakovlev Yak-18T	B. Austen	
RA-44480	Yakovlev Yak-18T	R. N. Goode/White Waltham	
RA-44481	Yakovlev Yak-18T	R. N. Goode/White Waltham	

Notes	Reg.	Type	Owner or Operator
	RA-44483	Yakovlev Yak-18T	R. N. Goode/White Waltham
	RA-44500	Yakovlev Yak-55M	B. MacMillan
	RA-44508	Yakovlev Yak-52	—
	UR-67199	LET L-410UVP	—/Langar
	UR-67477	LET L-410UVP	—/Sibson
	UR-67519	LET L-410UVP	East West Aviation Ltd/Wymeswold
	VH-BRC	S.24 Sandringham ★	Southampton Hall of Aviation
	VH-SNB	D.H.84 Dragon ★	Museum of Flight/E. Fortune
	VH-UTH	GAL Monospar ST-12 ★	Newark Air Museum (stored)
	VP-FAZ	D.H.C.6-310 Twin Otter	British Antarctic Survey/Fairoaks
	VP-FBB	D.H.C.6-310 Twin Otter	British Antarctic Survey/Fairoaks
	VP-FBC	D.H.C.6-310 Twin Otter	British Antarctic Survey/Fairoaks
	VP-FBL	D.H.C.6-310 Twin Otter	British Antarctic Survey/Fairoaks
	VR-BAT	Boeing 747SP-21	Worldwide Aircraft Holding Co
	VR-BEP	WS.55 Whirlwind 3 ★	East Midlands Aeropark (G-BAMH)
	VR-BET	WS.55 Whirlwind 3 ★	IHM (G-ANJV)/Weston-s-Mare
	VR-BEU	WS.55 Whirlwind 3 ★	IHM (G-ATKV)/Weston-s-Mare
	VR-BKC	Boeing 727-1H2	USAL Inc
	VR-BKG	Dassault Falcon 50	Sioux Co Ltd/Luton
	VR-BKQ	Agusta A.109A-II	USAL Ltd/Fairoaks
	VR-BKY	H.S.125 Srs F.3B	Corporate Jet Services Inc
	VR-BMF	Dassault Falcon 50	Glaxo (Bermuda) Ltd/Heathrow
	VR-BMZ	Gulfstream Commander 690D	Marlborough Fine Art (London) Ltd
	VR-BNB	H.S.125 Srs 700A	Speedflight Ltd/Guernsey
	VR-BNZ	G.1159A Gulfstream 3	Dennis Vanguard International Ltd
	VR-BOO	McD Douglas MD-87	Ford Motor Co Ltd/Stansted
	VR-BOP	McD Douglas MD-87	Ford Motor Co Ltd/Stansted
	VR-BOR	Boeing 707-351B	Al Wisar Trading Ltd
	VR-BPS	Consolidated PBY-5A Catalina	Plane Sailing Ltd (G-BLSC)/Duxford
	VR-BUB	Cessna 500 Cltation	Starway Co Ltd
	VR-BUL	Cessna 560 Citation V	Fegotila Ltd/Staverton
	VR-BVI	H.S.125 Srs F400A	Group 4 Ltd/Staverton
	VR-CBQ	Boeing 727-212	Aravco Ltd
	VR-CBW	G.1159C Gulfstream 4	Rolls-Royce PLC
	VR-CCK	Agusta A.109A-II	Tarmac PLC/E. Midlands
	VR-CCO	Agusta A.109A	Aerospace Finance Ltd/Fairoaks
	VR-CCQ	Dassault Falcon 50	Frank Williams Racing/Kidlington
	VR-CCS	BAC One-Eleven 401AK	AMC Aviation
	VR-CCT	Beech C90-1 King Air	Corgi Investments Ltd
	VR-CDM	Cessna 501 Citation	Duke of Westminster
	VR-CEZ	Dassault Falcon 50	IIR Aviation/Biggin Hill
	VR-CGP	Dassault Falcon 900	Frank Williams Motor Racing Ltd/Kidlington
	VR-CIC	Canadair CL.601 Challenger	TGC Aviation Ltd/Stansted
	VR-CIT	Cessna 550 Citation II	TAG Aviation/Kidlington
	VR-CJB	Cessna 501 Citation	Brown Prestell Ltd/Biggin Hill
	VR-CJR	Cessna 550 Citation II	Broome & Wellington Aviation Ltd
	VR-CLA	Agusta A.109A II	Laura Ashley Holdings Ltd
	VR-CLL	Cessna 421C	Channel Aviation Ltd
	VR-CMF	G.1159C Gulfstream 4	Aravco Ltd/Heathrow
	VR-CMM	Boeing 727-30	MME Farms Maintenance
	VR-COM	Cessna 500 Citation	Robinson Publications Ltd/Leeds
	VR-CPR	Cessna 421C	Fifty North Ltd
	VR-CPT	BAe 125-1000B	Reno Investments Inc/Biggin Hill
	VR-CQZ	Dassault Falcon 50	Frank Willams Motor Racing Ltd/Kidlington
	VR-CSP	Cessna 500 Citation	SP Metal Ltd/Biggin Hill
	VR-CTA	Dassault Falcon 900	Aravco Ltd
	VR-CUB	G.1159B Gulfstream 2B	United Breweries Ltd
	VR-CYM	G.1159C Gulfstream 4	Jet Fly Aviation Ltd
	5N-ABW	Westland Widgeon 2 ★	IHM (G-AOZE)/Weston-s-Mare

Radio Frequencies

The frequencies used by the larger airfields/airports are listed below. Abbreviations used: TWR — Tower, APP — Approach, A/G — Air-ground advisory. It is possible for changes to be made from time to time with the frequencies allocated which are all quoted in Megahertz (MHz).

Airfield	TWR	APP	A/G
Aberdeen	118.1	120.4	
Alderney	125.35		
Andrewsfield			130.55
Audley End			122.35
Barton			122.7
Barrow			123.2
Belfast Intl	118.3	120.0	
Belfast City	130.75	130.85	
Bembridge			123.25
Biggin Hill	134.8	129.4	
Birmingham	118.3	118.05	
Blackbushe			122.3
Blackpool	118.4	119.95	
Bodmin			122.7
Booker			126.55
Bourn			129.8
Bournemouth	125.6	119.625	
Bristol/Filton	132.35	122.72	
Bristol/Lulsgate	133.85	128.55	
Cambridge	122.2	123.6	
Cardiff	125.0	125.85	
Carlisle		123.6	
Compton Abbas			122.7
Conington			129.725
Coventry	124.8	119.25	
Cranfield	123.2	122.85	
Denham			130.725
Dundee	122.9		
Dunkeswell			123.475
Dunsfold	124.325	135.17	
Duxford			122.075
Earls Colne			122.425
East Midlands	124.0	119.65	
Edinburgh	118.7	121.2	
Elstree			122.4
Exeter	119.8	128.15	
Fairoaks			123.425
Fenland			122.925
Fowlmere			120.925
Gamston			130.475
Gatwick	124.225	126.825	
Glasgow	118.8	119.1	
Gloucester/Staverton	122.9	125.65	
Goodwood	122.45		
Guernsey	119.95	128.65	
Halfpenny Green			123.0
Haverfordwest			122.2
Hawarden	124.95	123.35	
Headcorn			122.0
Heathrow	118.7	119.725	
	118.5	134.975	
Hethel			122.35
Hucknall			130.8
Humberside	118.55	124.675	
Inverness	122.6		
Jersey	119.45	120.3	
Kidlington	118.875	125.325	
Land's End	130.7		
Leeds Bradford	120.3	123.75	
Leicester	122.125		
Liverpool	118.1	119.85	
London City	118.075	132.7	
Luton	132.55	129.55	
Lydd	120.7	129.4	
Manchester	118.625	119.4	
Manston	119.27	126.35	
Netherthorpe			123.275
Newcastle	119.7	124.375	
Newquay	123.4	125.55	
North Denes	123.4		
North Weald			123.525
Norwich	124.25	119.35	
Old Warden			123.05
Perth	119.8	122.3	
Plymouth	122.6	133.55	
Popham			129.8
Prestwick	118.15	120.55	
Redhill	120.275		
Rochester			122.25
Ronaldsway	118.9	120.85	
Sandown			123.5
Sandtoft			130.425
Scilly Isles			123.15
Seething			122.6
Sherburn			122.6
Shipdham			119.55
Shobdon			123.5
Shoreham	125.4	123.15	
Sibson			122.3
Sleap			122.45
Southampton	118.2	122.2	
Southend	127.725	128.95	
Stansted	123.8	120.65	
Stapleford			122.8
Sumburgh	118.25	123.15	
Swansea	119.7		
Swanton Morley			123.5
Sywell			122.7
Teesside	119.8	118.85	
Thruxton			130.45
Tollerton			122.8
Wellesbourne			124.02
White Waltham			122.6
Wick	119.7		
Wickenby			122.45
Woodford	126.925	130.75	
Woodvale	119.75	121.0	

Airline Flight Codes

Those listed below identify both UK and overseas carriers appearing in the book.

Code	Airline	
AAF	Aigle Azur	F
AAG	Air Atlantique	G
AAL	American A/L	N
AAN	Oasis	EC
ABB	Air Belgium	OO
ABD	Air Atlanta Iceland	TF
ABK	Albatros A/L	TC
ABR	Hunting	G
ACA	Air Canada	C
ACF	Air Charter Intl	F
ADR	Adria A/W	S5
AEA	Air Europa	EC
AEF	Aero Lloyd	D
AEL	Air Europe Spa	I
AFG	Ariana	YA
AFL	Aeroflot	RA
AFM	Affretair	Z
AFR	Air France	F
AGX	Aviogenex	YU
AHK	Air Hong Kong	VR-H
AHR	Air Holland	PH
AIC	Air-India	VT
AIH	Airtours (European)	G
AIJ	Air Jet	F
AJM	Air Jamaica	6Y
AKL	Air Kilroe	G
AKV	Active Air	TC
ALK	Air Lanka	4R
ALT	All Leisure	G
AMC	Air Malta	9H
AMM	Air 2000	G
AMT	American Trans Air	N
ANA	All Nippon A/W	JA
ANZ	Air New Zealand	ZK
AOM	AOM French A/L	F
APW	Arrow Air	N
ARG	Argentine A/W	LV
ATT	Aer Turas	EI
AUA	Austrian A/L	OE
AUB	Augsburg A/W	D
AUI	Ukraine Intl	UR
AUR	Aurigny A/S	G
AVA	Avianca	HK
AWC	Titan A/W	G
AWD	Airworld	G
AXL	Air Exel	PH
AYC	Aviaco	EC
AZA	Alitalia	I
AZR	Air Zaire	9Q
AZW	Air Zimbabwe	Z
AZX	Air Bristol	G
BAG	Deutsche BA	D
BAL	Britannia A/L	G
BAW	British Airways	G
BBC	Bangladesh Biman	S2
BCS	European A/T	OO
BCY	CityJet	EI
BER	Air Berlin	N
BIH	British Intl Heli	G
BMA	British Midland	G
BRA	Braathens	LN
BRU	Belavia	EW
BTI	Air Baltic	YL
BWA	BWIA	9Y
BWL	British World	G
BZH	Brit Air	F
CCA	Air China	B
CDN	Canadian A/L Intl	C
CFE	CityFlyer	G
CFG	Condor	D
CIM	Cimber Air	OY
CKT	Caledonian	D
CLH	Lufthansa CityLine	D
CLX	Cargolux	LX
CMM	Canada 3000 A/L	C
COA	Continental A/L	N
CPA	Cathay Pacific	VR-H
CRL	Corse Air	F
CRX	Crossair	HB
CSA	Czech A/L	OK
CTN	Croatia A/L	9A
CUB	Cubana	CU
CYP	Cyprus A/W	5B
CYR	Ryanair UK	EI
DAH	Air Algerie	7T
DAL	Delta A/L	N
DAN	Maersk Air	OY
DAT	Delta Air Transport	OO
DHL	DHL Express	N/OO
DLH	Lufthansa	D
DNM	Denim Air	PH
DSR	DAS Air Cargo	5X
EAF	European A/Ch	G
EAW	European A/W	G
EDW	Edelweiss Air	HB
EIA	Evergreen Intl	N
EIN	Aer Lingus	EI
ELY	El Al	4X
ETH	Ethiopian A/L	ET
EUL	Euralair	F
EWW	Emery	N
EXS	Channel Express	G
EZY	easyJet	G
FDX	Federal Express	N
FIN	Finnair	OH
FLT	Flightline	G
FOB	Ford	G
FOF	Fred Olsen	LN
FRO	European A/L	OO
FUA	Futura	EC
GBL	GB Airways	G
GFA	Gulf Air	A40
GHA	Ghana A/W	9G
GIA	Garuda	PK
GIL	Gill A/W	G
GMI	Germania	G
GNT	Business Air	G
HAS	Hamburg A/L	D
HLA	HeavyLift	G
HLD	Holiday A/L	TC
HLF	Hapag-Lloyd	D
IBE	Iberia	EC
ICE	Icelandair	TF
INS	Instone A/L	G
IRA	Iran Air	EP
IOS	Skybus	G
ISS	Meridiana	I
IST	Istanbul A/L	TC
ITF	Air Inter Europe	F
JAL	Japan A/L	JA
JAT	JAT	YU
JEA	Jersey European A/W	G
JEM	Emerald A/W	G
KAC	Kuwait A/W	9K
KAL	Korean Air	HL
KAR	Kar-Air	OH
KIS	Contactair	D
KLM	KLM	PH
KQA	Kenya A/W	5Y
KYV	Kibris Turkish	TC
LAJ	British Meditrn	G
LAZ	Bulgarian A/L	LZ
LDA	Lauda Air	OE
LEI	Leisure Intl	G
LFA	Air Alfa	TC
LGL	Luxair	LX
LIB	Air Liberte	F
LIT	Air Littoral	F
LKA	Alkair	OY
LOG	Loganair	G
LOT	Polish A/L (LOT)	SP
LTE	LTE	EC
LTS	LTU Sud	D
LTU	LTU	D
MAH	Malev	HA
MAS	Malaysian A/L	9M
MAU	Air Mauritius	3B
MEA	Middle East A/L	OD
MNX	Manx A/L	G
MON	Monarch A/L	G
MPH	Martinair	PH
MSK	Maersk Air Ltd	G
MSR	Egyptair	SU
NAW	Newair	OY
NEX	Northern Executive	G
NGA	Nigeria A/W	5N
NWA	Northwest A/L	N
OAL	Olympic A/L	SX
OHY	Onur Air	TC
PAL	Philippine A/L	RP
PGA	Portugalia	CS
PGT	Pegasus	TC
PIA	Pakistan Intl	AP
PIE	Air South West	G
PRB	Proteus A/L	F
QFA	Qantas	VH
QSC	African Safaris	5Y
RAM	Royal Air Maroc	CN
RBA	Royal Brunei	V8
RJA	Royal Jordanian	JY
RNA	Royal Nepal A/L	9N
ROT	Tarom	YR
RPX	BAC Express A/L	G
RWD	Air Rwanda	9XR
RYR	Ryanair	EI
SAA	South African A/W	ZS
SAB	Sabena	OO
SAS	SAS	SE OY LN
SAY	Suckling A/W	G
SBE	Sabre A/W	G
SCW	Malmo Avn	SE
SEU	Star Europe	F
SEY	Air Seychelles	S7
SIA	Singapore A/L	9V
SJM	Southern A/T	N
SLR	Sobelair	OO
SNB	Sterling European	OY
SPP	Spanair	EC

SQA	Transwede	SE	TIH	Airtours (US)	G	UKR	Air Ukraine	UR
SSW	Streamline Avn	G	TLA	TransLift	EI	ULE	Leisure Intl	G
SUD	Sudan A/W	ST	TLE	Air Toulouse	F	UPA	Air Foyle	G
SVA	Saudia	HZ	TOP	Top Air	TC	UPS	United Parcels	N
SWE	Swedair	SE	TOW	Tower Air	N	UYC	Cameroon A/L	TJ
SWR	Swissair	HB	TRA	Transavia	PH	UZB	Uzbekistan A/W	UK
SWW	Sunway	TC	TSC	Air Transat	C	VIA	Viasa	YV
SWY	Sunways A/L	SE	TSW	TEA Switzerland	HB	VIR	Virgin Atlantic	G
SXS	Sun Express	TC	TWA	TWA	N	VIV	Viva Air	EC
SYR	Syrian Arab	YK	TWE	Blue Scandinavia	SE	VKG	Premiair	OY
TAP	Air Portugal	CS	TYR	Tyrolean	OE	VLM	VLM	OO
TAR	Tunis Air	TS	UAE	Emirates A/L	A6	VRG	Varig	PP
TAT	TAT	F	UAL	United A/L	N	WDL	WDL	D
THA	Thai A/W Intl	HS	UGA	Uganda A/L	5X	WOA	World A/W	N
THY	Turkish A/L	TC	UKA	Air UK	G			

N1768D, McD Douglas MD-11 of American Airlines.

RA-76401, Ilyshin IL-76TD of HeavyLift Cargo Airlines.

The British Aircraft Preservation Council was formed in 1967 to co-ordinate the works of all bodies involved in the preservation, restoration and display of historical aircraft. Membership covers the whole spectrum of national, Service, commercial and voluntary groups, and meetings are held regularly at the bases of member organisations. The Council is able to provide a means of communication, helping to resolve any misunderstandings or duplication of effort. Every effort is taken to encourage the raising of standards of both organisation and technical capacity amongst the member groups to the benefit of everyone interested in aviation. To assist historians, the B.A.P.C. register has been set up and provides an identity for those aircraft which do not qualify for a Service serial or inclusion in the UK Civil Register.

Aircraft on the current B.A.P.C. Register are as follows:

Notes	Reg.	Type	Owner or Operator
	6	Roe Triplane Type IV (replica)	Manchester Museum of Science & Industry
	7	Southampton University MPA	Southampton Hall of Aviation
	8	Dixon ornithopter	The Shuttleworth Collection
	9	Humber Monoplane (replica)	Midland Air Museum/Coventry
	10	Hafner R.II Revoplane	Museum of Army Flying/Middle Wallop
	12	Mignet HM.14	Museum of Flight/E. Fortune
	13	Mignet HM.14	Brimpex Metal Treatments
	14	Addyman standard training glider	N. H. Ponsford
	15	Addyman standard training glider	The Aeroplane Collection
	16	Addyman ultra-light aircraft	N. H. Ponsford
	17	Woodhams Sprite	The Aeroplane Collection
	18	Killick MP Gyroplane	N. H. Ponsford
	20	Lee-Richards annular biplane (replica)	Newark Air Musem
	21	Thruxton Jackaroo	M. J. Brett
	22	Mignet HM.14 (G-AEOF)	Aviodome/Schiphol
	25	Nyborg TGN-III glider	Midland Air Museum
	27	Mignet HM.14	M. J. Abbey
	28	Wright Flyer (replica)	Corn Exchange/Leeds
	29	Mignet HM.14 (replica) (G-ADRY)	Brooklands Museum of Aviation/ Weybridge
	32	Crossley Tom Thumb	Midland Air Museum
	33	DFS.108-49 Grunau Baby IIb	Russavia Collection
	34	DFS.108-49 Grunau Baby IIb	D. Elsdon
	35	EoN primary glider	Russavia Collection
	36	Fieseler Fi.103 (V-1) (replica)	Kent Battle of Britain Museum/Hawkinge
	37	Blake Bluetit	The Shuttleworth Collection
	38	Bristol Scout replica (A1742)	Stored/Wroughton
	40	Bristol Boxkite (replica)	Bristol City Museum
	41	B.E.2C (replica) (6232)	Historical Aircraft Museum/RAF St Athan
	42	Avro 504 (replica) (H1968)	Historical Aircraft Museum/RAF St Athan
	43	Mignet HM.14	Lincolnshire Aviation Museum
	44	Miles Magister (L6906)	Museum of Berkshire Aviation (G-AKKY)/ Woodley
	45	Pilcher Hawk (replica)	Stanford Hall Museum
	46	Mignet HM.14	Alan McKechnie Racing Ltd
	47	Watkins Monoplane	Historical Aircraft Museum/RAF St Athan
	48	Pilcher Hawk (replica)	Glasgow Museum of Transport
	49	Pilcher Hawk	Royal Scottish Museum/Edinburgh
	50	Roe Triplane Type 1	Science Museum/S. Kensington
	51	Vickers Vimy IV	Science Museum/S. Kensington
	52	Lilienthal glider	Science Museum Store/Hayes
	53	Wright Flyer (replica)	Science Museum/S. Kensington
	54	JAP-Harding monoplane	Science Museum/S. Kensington
	55	Levavasseur Antoinette VII	Science Museum/S. Kensington
	56	Fokker E.III (210/16)	Science Museum/S. Kensington
	57	Pilcher Hawk (replica)	Science Museum/S. Kensington
	58	Yokosuka MXY7 Ohka II (15-1585)	F.A.A. Museum/Yeovilton
	59	Sopwith Camel (replica) (D3419)	Historical Aircraft Museum/RAF St Athan
	60	Murray M.1 helicopter	The Aeroplane Collection Ltd
	61	Stewart man-powered ornithopter	Lincolnshire Aviation Museum
	62	Cody Biplane (304)	Science Museum/S. Kensington
	63	Hurricane (replica) (L1592)	Kent Battle of Britain Museum/Hawkinge
	64	Hurricane (replica) (P3059)	Kent Battle of Britain Museum/Hawkinge

Reg.	Type	Owner or Operator	Notes
65	Spitfire (replica) (N3289)	Kent Battle of Britain Museum/Hawkinge	
66	Bf 109 (replica) (1480)	Kent Battle of Britain Museum/Hawkinge	
67	Bf 109 (replica) (14)	Kent Battle of Britain Museum/Hawkinge	
68	Hurricane (replica) (H3426)	Midland Air Museum	
69	Spitfire (replica) (N3313)	Kent Battle of Britain Museum/Hawkinge	
70	Auster AOP.5 (TJ398)	Museum of Flight/E. Fortune	
71	Spitfire (replica) (P8140)	Norfolk & Suffolk Aviation Museum	
72	Hurricane (replica) (V7767)	N. Weald Aircraft Restoration Flight	
73	Hurricane (replica)	—	
74	Bf 109 (replica) (6357/6)	Kent Battle of Britain Museum/Hawkinge	
75	Mignet HM.14 (G-AEFG)	N. H. Ponsford	
76	Mignet HM.14 (G-AFFI)	Yorkshire Air Museum/Elvington	
77	Mignet HM.14 (replica) (G-ADRG)	Stratford Aircraft Collection	
79	Fiat G.46-4 (MM53211)	British Air Reserve/Lympne	
80	Airspeed Horsa (KJ351)	Museum of Army Flying/Middle Wallop	
81	Hawkridge Dagling	Russavia Collection	
82	Hawker Hind (Afghan)	RAF Museum/Hendon	
83	Kawasaki Ki-100-1b	Aerospace Museum/Cosford	
84	Nakajima Ki-46 (Dinah III)	Historical Aircraft Museum/RAF St Athan	
85	Weir W-2 autogyro	Museum of Flight/E. Fortune	
86	de Havilland Tiger Moth (replica)	Yorkshire Aircraft Preservation Soc	
87	Bristol Babe (replica) (G-EASQ)	Bomber County Museum/Hemswell	
88	Fokker Dr 1 (replica) (102/18)	F.A.A. Museum/Yeovilton	
89	Cayley glider (replica)	Manchester Museum of Science & Industry	
90	Colditz Cock (replica)	Imperial War Museum/Duxford	
91	Fieseler Fi 103 (V.1)	Lashenden Air Warfare Museum	
92	Fieseler Fi 103 (V.1)	Historical Aircraft Museum/RAF St Athan	
93	Fieseler Fi 103 (V.1)	Imperial War Museum/Duxford	
94	Fieseler Fi 103 (V.1)	Aerospace Museum/Cosford	
95	Gizmer autogyro	F. Fewsdale	
96	Brown helicopter	N.E. Aircraft Museum/Usworth	
97	Luton L.A.4A Minor	N.E. Aircraft Museum/Usworth	
98	Yokosuka MXY7 Ohka II	Manchester Museum of Science & Industry	
99	Yokosuka MXY7 Ohka II	Aerospace Museum/Cosford	
100	Clarke glider	RAF Museum/Hendon	
101	Mignet HM.14	Lincolnshire Aviation Museum	
103	Pilcher glider (replica)	Personal Plane Services Ltd	
105	Blériot XI (replica)	Aviodome/Schiphol	
106	Blériot XI	RAF Museum/Hendon	
107	Blériot XXVII	RAF Museum/Hendon	
108	Fairey Swordfish IV (HS503)	Cosford Aerospace Museum	
109	Slingsby Kirby Cadet TX.1	RAF Museum/Henlow store	
110	Fokker D.VII replica (static) (5125)	—	
111	Sopwith Triplane replica (static) (N5492)	F.A.A. Museum/Yeovilton	
112	D.H.2 replica (static) (5964)	Museum of Army Flying/Middle Wallop	
113	S.E.5A replica (static) (B4863)	—	
114	Vickers Type 60 Viking (static) (G-EBED)	Brooklands Museum of Aviation/Weybridge	
115	Mignet HM.14	Essex Aviation Group/Andrewsfield	
116	Santos-Dumont Demoiselle (replica)	Cornwall Aero Park/Helston	
117	B.E.2C (replica)	N. Weald Aircraft Restoration Flight	
118	Albatros D.V (replica) (C19/18)	S. Yorks Aviation Soc/Firbeck	
119	Bensen B.7	N.E. Aircraft Museum/Usworth	
120	Mignet HM.14 (G-AEJZ)	Bomber County Museum/Hemswell	
121	Mignet HM.14 (G-AEKR)	S. Yorks Aviation Soc/Firbeck	
122	Avro 504 (replica)	British Broadcasting Corp	
123	Vickers FB.5 Gunbus (replica)	A. Topen (stored)/Cranfield	
124	Lilienthal Glider Type XI (replica)	Science Museum/S. Kensington	
125	Clay Cherub (G-BDGP)	B. R. Clay	
126	D.31 Turbulent (static)	Midland Air Museum store	
127	Halton Jupiter MPA	The Shuttleworth Collection	
128	Watkinson Cyclogyroplane Mk IV	IHM/Weston-s-Mare	
129	Blackburn 1911 Monoplane (replica)	Cornwall Aero Park/Helston store	
130	Blackburn 1912 Monoplane (replica)	Cornwall Aero Park/Helston store	
131	Pilcher Hawk (replica)	C. Paton	
132	Blériot XI (G-BLXI)	Musée de L'Automobile/France	
133	Fokker Dr 1 (replica) (425/17)	Newark Air Museum	

Notes	Reg.	Type	Owner or Operator
	134	Pitts S-2A static (G-CARS)	Toyota Ltd/Sywell
	135	Bristol M.1C (replica) (C4912)	—
	136	Deperdussin Seaplane (replica)	Reno/Nevada
	137	Sopwith Baby Floatplane (replica) (8151)	—
	138	Hansa Brandenburg W.29 Floatplane (replica) (2292)	—
	139	Fokker Dr 1 (replica) 150/17	—
	142	SE-5A (replica) (F5459)	Cornwall Aero Park/Helston
	143	Paxton MPA	R. A. Paxton/Staverton
	144	Weybridge Mercury MPA	Cranwell Gliding Club
	145	Oliver MPA	D. Oliver (stored)/Warton
	146	Pedal Aeronauts Toucan MPA	The Shuttleworth Collection
	147	Bensen B.7	Norfolk & Suffolk Aviation Museum
	148	Hawker Fury II (replica) (K7271)	Aerospace Museum/Cosford
	149	Short S.27 (replica)	F.A.A. Museum (stored)/Yeovilton
	150	SEPECAT Jaguar GR.1 (replica) (XX725)	RAF Exhibition Flight
	151	SEPECAT Jaguar GR.1 (replica) (XZ363)	RAF Exhibition Flight
	152	BAe Hawk T.1 (replica) (XX263)	RAF Exhibition Flight
	153	Westland WG.33	IHM/Weston-s-Mare
	154	D.31 Turbulent	Lincolnshire Aviation Museum
	155	Panavia Tornado GR.1 (replica) (ZA446)	RAF Exhibition Flight
	157	Waco CG-4A	Pennine Aviation Museum
	158	Fieseler Fi 103 (V.1)	Defence Ordnance Disposal School/ Chattenden
	159	Yokosuka MXY7 Ohka II	Defence Ordnance Disposal School/ Chattenden
	160	Chargus 108 hang glider	Museum of Flight/E. Fortune
	161	Stewart Ornithopter Coppelia	Bomber County Museum
	162	Goodhart Newbury Manflier MPA	Science Museum/Wroughton
	163	AFEE 10/42 Rotabuggy (replica)	Museum of Army Flying/Middle Wallop
	164	Wight Quadruplane Type 1 (replica)	Wessex Aviation Soc/Wimborne
	165	Bristol F.2b (E2466)	RAF Museum/Hendon
	167	S.E.5A replica	Newark Air Museum
	168	D.H.60G Moth (static replica) (G-AAAH)	Hilton Hotel/Gatwick
	169	SEPECAT Jaguar GR.1 (static replica) (XX110)	No 1 S. of T.T. RAF Halton
	170	Pilcher Hawk (replica)	A. Gourlay/Strathallan
	171	BAe Hawk T.1 (replica) (XX297)	RAF Exhibition Flight/Abingdon
	172	Chargus Midas Super 8 hang glider	Science Museum/Wroughton
	173	Birdman Promotions Grasshopper	Science Museum/Wroughton
	174	Bensen B.7	Science Museum/Wroughton
	175	Volmer VJ-23 Swingwing	Manchester Museum of Science & Industry
	176	SE-5A (replica) (A4850)	S. Yorks Aviation Soc/Firbeck
	177	Avro 504K (replica) (G-AACA)	Brooklands Museum of Aviation/ Weybridge
	178	Avro 504K (replica) (E373)	Bygone Times Antique Warehouse/ Eccleston, Lancs
	179	Sopwith Pup (replica) (A7317)	Midland Air Museum/Coventry
	181	RAF B.E.2b (replica) (687)	RAF Museum/Hendon
	182	Wood Ornithopter	Manchester Museum of Science & Industry
	183	Zurowski ZP.1	Newark Air Museum
	184	Spitfire IX (replica) (EN398)	Aces High Ltd/North Weald
	185	Waco CG-4A (243809)	Museum of Army Flying/Middle Wallop
	186	D.H.82B Queen Bee (K3584)	Mosquito Aircraft Museum
	187	Roe Type 1 biplane (replica)	Brooklands Museum of Aviation/ Weybridge
	188	McBroom Cobra 88	Science Museum/Wroughton
	189	Blériot XI (replica)	—
	190	Spitfire (replica) (EN398)	Macclesfield Historical Aviation Soc
	191	BAe Harrier GR.5 (replica) (ZD472)	RAF Exhibition Flight
	192	Weedhopper JC-24	The Aeroplane Collection
	193	Hovey WD-11 Whing Ding	The Aeroplane Collection
	194	Santos Dumont Demoiselle	Brooklands Museum of Aviation/

BRITISH AIRCRAFT PRESERVATION

Reg.	Type	Owner or Operator	Notes
	(replica)	Weybridge	
195	Moonraker 77 hang glider	Museum of Flight/E. Fortune	
196	Sigma 2M hang glider	Museum of Flight/E. Fortune	
197	Cirrus III hang glider	Museum of Flight/E. Fortune	
198	Fieseler Fi.103 (V-1)	Imperial War Museum/Lambeth	
199	Fieseler Fi.103 (V-1)	Science Museum/S. Kensington	
200	Bensen B.7	K. Fern Collection/Stoke	
201	Mignet HM.14	Caernarfon Air Museum	
202	Spitfire V (replica) (MW467)	Maes Artro Craft Centre	
203	Chrislea LC.1 Airguard (G-AFIN)	The Aeroplane Collection	
204	McBroom hang glider	The Aeroplane Collection	
205	Hurricane (replica) (BE421)	RAF Museum/Hendon	
206	Spitfire (replica) (MH486)	RAF Museum/Hendon	
207	Austin Whippet (replica) (K.158)	N.E. Aircraft Museum/Usworth	
208	SE-5A (replica) (D2700)	Prince's Mead Shopping Precinct/ Farnborough	
209	Spitfire IX (replica) (MJ751)	Museum of D-Day Aviation/Shoreham	
210	Avro 504J (replica) (C4451)	Southampton Hall of Aviation	
211	Mignet HM.14 (replica) (G-ADVU)	N.E. Aircraft Museum/Usworth	
212	Bensen B.8	IHM/Weston-s-Mare	
213	Vertigo MPA	IHM/Weston-s-Mare	
214	Spitfire prototype (replica) (K5054)	The Spitfire Soc	
215	Airwave hang-glider	Southampton Hall of Aviation	
216	D.H.88 Comet (replica) (G-ACSS)	Trout Lake Air Force	
217	Spitfire (replica) (N9926)	RAF Museum/Bentley Priory	
218	Hurricane (replica) (P3386)	HAF Museum/Bentley Priory	
219	Hurricane (replica) (L1710)	RAF Memorial Chapel/Biggin Hill	
220	Spitfire (replica) (N3194)	RAF Memorial Chapel/Biggin Hill	
221	Spitfire (replica) (MH777)	RAF Museum/Northolt	
222	Spitfire (replica) (BR600)	RAF Museum/Uxbridge	
223	Hurricane (replica) (V7467)	RAF Museum/Coltishall	
224	Spitfire V (replica)	Ambassador Hotel/Norwich	
225	Spitfire (replica) (P8448)	RAF Museum/Swanton Morley	
226	Spitfire (replica) (EN343)	RAF Museum/Benson	
227	Spitfire (replica) (L1070)	RAF Museum/Turnhouse	
228	Olympus hang-glider	N.E. Aircraft Museum/Usworth	
229	Spitfire (replica) (MJ832)	RAF Museum/Digby	
230	Spitfire (replica) (AA908)	Eden Camp/Malton	
231	Mignet HM.14	South Copeland Aviation Group	
232	AS.58 Horsa I/II	Mosquito Aircraft Museum	
233	Broburn Wanderlust sailplane	Museum of Berkshire Aviation/Woodley	
234	Vickers FB.5 Gunbus (replica)	Macclesfield Historical Aviation Soc	
235	Fieseler Fi.103 (V-1) (replica)	Eden Camp Wartime Museum	
236	Hurricane (replica) (P2793)	Eden Camp Wartime Museum	
237	Fieseler Fi.103 (V-1)	RAF Museum/Cardington	
238	Waxflatter ornithopter	Personal Plane Services Ltd	
239	Fokker D.VIII 5/8 scale replica	Norfolk & Suffolk Aviation Museum	
251	Hiway Spectrum	Manchester Museum of Science & Industry	
252	Flexiform Sky Sails	Manchester Museum of Science & Industry	
253	Mignet HM.14 (G-ADZW)	The Island Aeroplane Collecton/Sandown	

Note: Registrations/Serials carried are mostly false identities. MPA = Man Powered Aircraft, IHM = International Helicopter Museum.

Future Allocations Log (In-Sequence)

The grid provides the facility to record future in-sequence registrations as they are issued or seen. To trace a particular code, refer to the left hand column which contains the three letters following the G prefix. The final letter can be found by reading across the columns headed A to Z. For example, the box for G-BXED is located five rows down (BXE) and then four across to the D column.

G-	A	B	C	D	E	F	G	H	I	J	K	L	M	N	O	P	R	S	T	U	V	W	X	Y	Z
BXA																									
BXB																									
BXC																									
BXD																									
BXE																									
BXF																									
BXG																									
BXH																									
BXI																									
BXJ																									
BXK																									
BXL																									
BXM																									
BXN																									
BXO																									
BXP																									
BXR																									
BXS																									
BXT																									
BXU																									
BXV																									
BXW																									
BXX																									
BXY																									
BXZ																									
BYA																									
BYB																									
BYC																									
BYD																									
BYE																									
BYF																									
BYG																									
BYH																									
BYI																									
	A	B	C	D	E	F	G	H	I	J	K	L	M	N	O	P	R	S	T	U	V	W	X	Y	Z

Credit: *Wal Gandy*

Future Allocations Log (Out-of-Sequence)

This grid can be used to record out-of-sequence registrations as they are issued or seen. The first column is provided for the ranges prefixed with G-B, ie from G-BXxx to G-BZxx. The remaining columns cover the sequences from G-Cxxx to G-Zxxx and in this case it is necessary to insert the last three letters in the appropriate section.

G-B	G-C	G-E	G-G	G-J	G-L	G-N	G-O	G-P	G-S	G-U
											G-V
	G-D	G-F	G-H		G-M	G-O				
			G-K							
										G-W
								G-R		
									G-T	
										G-X
G-C	G-E	G-G	G-I	G-L	G-N					
										G-Y
										G-Z

Overseas Airliners Registration Log

This grid may be used to record airliner registrations not included in the main section

Reg.	Type	Operator

Hot Spots
at
Manchester

Addenda

New or restored in-sequence registrations

Reg.	Type	Owner or Operator	Notes
G-AAHW	Klemm L.25-1A	The Island Aeroplane Co/Sandown	
G-AVLM	B.121 Pup 3	T. M. Jones	
G-BARN	Taylor JT.2 Titch	R. G. W. Newton	
G-BJDJ	H.S.125 Srs 700B	Falcon Jet centre Ltd (GRCDI/G-BJDJ)	

The following in-sequence registrations in the main section have been cancelled: G-AVBP, G-AXSV, G-AYMG, G-AYMT, G-BBDD, G-BCJF, G-BEWJ, G-BGMX, G-BNDS, G-BRNY, G-BSEW, G-BSIW, G-BTWP, G-BVEI, G-BWDL, G-BWFW, G-BWRL, G-BWZN

New or restored out-of-sequence registrations

Reg.	Type	Owner or Operator	Notes
G-CEXD	F.27 Friendship Mk 600	Channel Express (Air Services) Ltd	
G-DIRE	Robinson R-22B	Heli Air Ltd	
G-FCLA	Boeing 757-28A	Flying Colours Airlines Ltd	
G-FCLB	Boeing 757-28A	Flying Colours Airlines Ltd	
G-FCLC	Boeing 757-28A	Flying Colours Airlines Ltd	
G FCLD	Boeing 757-28F	Flying Colours Airlines Ltd	
G-HRHE	Robinson R-22B	R. H. Everett (G-BTWP)	
G-IBLW	BAe Jetstream 3109-09	Jetstream Aircraft Ltd (G-WENT)/ Prestwick	
G-LLTT	PA-32R-301 Saratoga SP	J. A. Robson	
G-LOUN	AS.355N Twin Squirrel	McAlpine Helicopters Ltd/Kidlington	
G-MEDB	Airbus A.320-231	British Mediteranean Airways Ltd	
G-MEDC	Airbus A.320-231	British Mediteranean Airways Ltd	
G-MENI	AS.355 F-2 Twin Squirrel	Castle Aviation	
G-MIDD	PA-28 Cherokee 140	Midland Air Training School (G-BBDD)	
G-MUVG	Cessna 421C	AJ Air Services	
G-OABB	Jodel D.150	A. B. Bailey	
G-OJJF	D.31 Turbulent	J. J. Ferguson	
G-OLDA	PA-31-350 Navajo Chieftain	Owen Air Ltd (G-BNDS)	
G-OLEO	Thunder Ax10-210 balloon	P. J. Waller	
G-OMUM	R. Commander 114	Armadafleet Ltd	
G-PERZ	Bell 206B Jet Ranger	Intrepid Aviation Co	
G-RMST	PA-46-350P Malibu	Winchfield Enterprises Ltd	
G-RVRA	PA-28 Cherokee 140	Ravenair (G-OWVA)	
G-SHRK	Enstrom 280C-UK	Aviation Bureau (G-BGMX/G-SHXX)	
G-TLDK	PA-22 Tri-Pacer 150	A. M. Thomson	
G-TUSK	Bell 206B JetRanger 3	First Flight (G-BWZH)	
G-VAIR	Airbus A.340-313X	Virgin Atlantic Airways Ltd	
G-VAST	Boeing 747-41R	Virgin Atlantic Airways Ltd	

The following out-of-sequence registrations in the main section have been cancelled: G-CAXF, G-ISEE, G-MFHL, G-OWVA, G-PLAX, G-RCDI, G-ZSOL.

New overseas airliner registrations

Reg.	Type	Owner or Operator	Notes
C-GTSB	L.1011-385 TriStar 1	Air Transat	
C-GTSU	Boeing 757-2Y0	Air Transat	
C-GTSV	Boeing 757-28A	Air Transat	
EC-GLE	Airbus A.340-313	Iberia	
F-GRSE	Airbus A.320-214	Star Europe	
F-GRSG	Airbus A.320-214	Star Europe	
N129TW	Boeing 747-128	Trans World Airlines	
N518AT	Boeing 757-23N	American Trans Air	
N521AT	Boeing 757-28A	American Trans Air	
N3075A	Airbus A.300-605R	American Airlines	
N7055A	Airbus A.300-605R	American Airlines	
N7062A	Airbus A.300-605R	American Airlines	
N7076A	Airbus A.300-605R	American Airlines	
N7082A	Airbus A.300-605R	American Airlines	

New overseas airliner registrations

Notes	Reg.	Type	Owner or Operator
	N7083A	Airbus A.300-605R	American Airlines
	N8067A	Airbus A.300-605R	American Airlines
	N11060	Airbus A.300-605R	American Airlines
	N12080	Douglas DC-10-30	Continental Airlines (EC-CLB)
	N14053	Airbus A.300-605R	American Airlines
	N14056	Airbus A.300-605R	American Airlines
	N14061	Airbus A.300-605R	American Airlines
	N14065	Airbus A.300-605R	American Airlines
	N14068	Airbus A.300-605R	American Airlines
	N14077	Airbus A.300-605R	American Airlines
	N17010	Boeing 747-143	Trans World Airlines (N128TW)
	N18066	Airbus A.300-605R	American Airlines
	N19059	Airbus A.300-605R	American Airlines
	N25071	Airbus A.300-605R	American Airlines
	N33096	Airbus A.300-605R	American Airlines
	N34078	Airbus A.300-605R	American Airlines
	N44064	Airbus A.300-605R	American Airlines
	N41063	Airbus A.300-605R	American Airlines
	N50051	Airbus A.300-605R	American Airlines
	N59081	Airbus A.300-605R	American Airlines
	N70054	Airbus A.300-605R	American Airlines
	N70072	Airbus A.300-605R	American Airlines
	N70073	Airbus A.300-605R	American Airlines
	N70074	Airbus A.300-605R	American Airlines
	N70079	Airbus A.300-605R	American Airlines
	N77080	Airbus A.300-605R	American Airlines
	N80052	Airbus A.300-605R	American Airlines
	N80057	Airbus A.300-605R	American Airlines
	N80058	Airbus A.300-605R	American Airlines
	N80084	Airbus A.300-605R	American Airlines
	N90070	Airbus A.300-605R	American Airlines
	N91050	Airbus A.300-605R	American Airlines
	OO-	Airbus A.320-212	Constellation International Airways
	OO-	Airbus A.320-212	Constellation International Airways
	OY-CNS	Douglac DC-10-10	Premiair (SE-DHS)
	TR-LEJ	Boeing 767-269	Air Gabon
	9G-JNR	Boeing 707-324C	Omega Air